BASIC CRIMINAL PROCEDURE

CASES, COMMENTS AND QUESTIONS

Eleventh Edition

By

Yale Kamisar
Professor of Law
University of San Diego
Clarence Darrow Distinguished University Professor Emeritus of Law,
University of Michigan

Wayne R. LaFave
David C. Baum Professor Emeritus of Law
and Center for Advanced Study Professor Emeritus,
University of Illinois

Jerold H. Israel
Ed Rood Eminent Scholar in Trial Advocacy and Procedure
University of Florida, Levin College of Law
Alene and Allan F. Smith Professor Emeritus of Law
University of Michigan

Nancy J. King
Lee S. & Charles A. Spier Professor of Law
Vanderbilt University Law School

AMERICAN CASEBOOK SERIES®

THOMSON
WEST

Mat #40346568

610 Opperman Drive
P.O. Box 64526
St. Paul, MN 55164–0526
1–800–328–9352

Printed in the United States of America

ISBN 0–314–15960–6

TEXT IS PRINTED ON 10% POST CONSUMER RECYCLED PAPER

Preface to the Eleventh Edition

Aside from two introductory chapters on the right to, and the role of, counsel, this volume – based on our much larger *Modern Criminal Procedure* (11th ed. 2005) – deals almost exclusively with "police practices" and other investigative alternatives (see Ch. 11, dealing with grand jury investigations). The success of the previous editions of "*Basic*" confirms our belief that when allocated 30 (or even 45) class hours for criminal procedure (or a third or half of the crowded first-year criminal law course for procedural problems), many teachers will find it more useful and meaningful to explore in depth a few fundamental and closely related areas (e.g., search and seizure, right to counsel, confessions and lineups) than to make a whirlwind tour through the investigatory process, joinder and severance, speedy trial, "trial by newspaper" (and TV), criminal discovery, sentencing appeals, post-conviction review and all of the other topics treated in the 29 chapters of our larger book. In preparing this shorter volume, therefore, rather than shrinking down each chapter in the larger book, we have kept the first twelve chapters intact and omitted all others.

Previous editions of "*Basic*" contained only one right to counsel chapter (the one dealing with such cases as *Gideon, Douglas* and *Ross v. Moffitt*). Treatment of the other counsel chapter, "the role of counsel" (dealing with such matters as the right to "effective" assistance of counsel, the division of authority over defense decisions, multiple representation and conflicts of interest), used to be postponed until the student dealt with the adversary system. However, a number of criminal procedure teachers have persuaded us to move the latter chapter up to the front, so there are now two introductory counsel chapters. This change provides a teacher with a much wider choice of materials on the right to, and the role of, counsel.

One of the special features of chapters 6 (search and seizure) and 7 (wiretapping and electronic surveillance) is material underscoring the threat to privacy posed by various kinds of new technology, such as secret video surveillance, cellular phone tracking, enclosed space detection devices, interception of computer communications (originally known as "Carnivore"), decryption, facial character recognition, and gas chromatography. Also discussed are closely related matters such as "national security" surveillance and the Foreign Intelligence Surveillance Act (FISA) and the USA Patriot Act's expansion of FISA's applicability.

One of the many issues discussed in Chapter 3 (some general reflections), and it is discussed at considerable length, is ethnic/racial profiling in light of the 9/11 attack on the World Trade Center. In addition to the material usually found in a chapter on police interrogation and confessions, Chapter 9 sets forth various positions on another controversial issue: when, if ever, torture should be permitted in order to obtain information from suspected terrorists.

Some instructors will welcome Ch. 11 (grand jury investigations) for providing an opportunity to compare and contrast police work with other investigative alternatives. However, we suspect other instructors, pressed for time, will pass quickly through Ch. 11 or even skip it entirely. But particular attention should be paid to the last section of this chapter: Fifth Amendment history and values. This section is designed to facilitate exploration of the general policies underlying the privilege against compelled self-incrimination. There is much to be said for taking up this material with the confessions chapter.

A final point about the organization of these materials. Although we have a separate chapter on the scope of the exclusionary rules (Ch. 12), which includes a section on the "fruit of the poisonous tree," we believe the recent *Miranda* "poisoned fruit" cases, *Patane* and *Seibert* shed so much light on the significance of *Dickerson*, the case that reaffirmed *Miranda*'s constitutional status (or perhaps one should say shed so much light on the lack of significance of *Dickerson*) that we decided to place *Patane* and *Seibert* in the confessions chapter, a few pages after *Dickerson*.

This volume includes significant developments up to January 31, 2005. Important developments thereafter will appear in annual supplements, which will also contain relevant federal court rules and statutory materials. The first annual supplement to this book, which will be published about two months after this volume appears, will contain all notable cases handed down by the U.S. Supreme Court during the 2004–05 Term. It will also include various extracts from the new criminal procedure literature.

Case citations to the text and the footnotes of judicial opinions and in the writings of commentators have been omitted without so specifying. Numbered footnotes are from the original materials; lettered footnotes are ours.[1] Omissions from the text of the original are indicated by asterisks and brackets.

If there are cross-references to cases beyond page 944 (the end of *Basic Criminal Procedure*), the citations to these cases can be found in the Table of Cases.

One or more of the authors has been fortunate enough to participate actively in four major criminal procedure projects: The American Bar Association's *Standards for Criminal Justice*; The American Law Institute's *Model Code of Pre-Arraignment Procedure*; The National Conference of Commissioners on Uniform State Laws' *Uniform Rules of Criminal Procedure*; and the ongoing revision of the *Federal Rules of Criminal Procedure*. We are indebted to the members of the various committees with whom we have worked for providing us with many leads and insights. We are also indebted to the many users of this book who have offered helpful suggestions on content as to this edition and previous editions. That list, like the list of our student research assistants over the years, has now grown far too long to mention each person individually.

---

1. Standard abbreviations are used throughout. On occasion, a book or article is used so frequently in a chapter as to call for a shorter citation form. Here we have given the full citation to the book or article in the first footnote of the chapter and indicated there the shorter citation form. For our own books, we simply have used the shorter citation form throughout the book. These are:

La Fave, *Search and Seizure: A Treatise on the Fourth Amendment* (4th ed. 2004), available on Westlaw under the database SEARCHSZR and cited as SEARCHSZR § ___.

LaFave, Israel, and King, *Criminal Procedure Treatise* (2d ed. 1999), available on Westlaw under the database CRIMPROC and cited as CRIMPROC § ___.

Articles collected in Kamisar, *Police Interrogation and Confessions: Essays in Law and Policy* (1980) are usually cited as Kamisar Essays.

We are especially appreciative of the able secretarial assistance provided on the eleventh edition, too often under great stress, by Rosemary Getty, Joyce Kenney, Mary Lebert, Carol Robison, and Tori Stamps.

YALE KAMISAR
WAYNE R. LAFAVE
JEROLD H. ISRAEL
NANCY J. KING

May, 2005

*

Acknowledgments

Excerpts from the following books and articles appear with the kind permission of the copyright holders.

Arenella, Peter, Foreword: O.J. Lessons, 69 S.Cal. 1233 (1996). Copyright © 1996 by the University of Southern California. Reprinted by permission.

Beale, Sara Sun, Reconsidering Supervisory Power in Criminal Cases: Constitutional and Statutory Limits on the Authority of the Federal Courts, 84 Colum.L.Rev. 1433 (1984). Copyright © 1984 by the Columbia Law Review Association. Reprinted by permission.

Berman, Mitchell, Constitutional Decision Rules, 90 Va. L.Rev. 1 (2004). Copyright © 2004 by the University of Virginia Law Review. Reprinted by permission.

Bloom, Robert M., Inevitable Discovery: An Exception beyond the Fruits, 20 Am.J.Crim.law 79 (1992). Copyright © 1992 by the American Journal of Criminal Law. Reprinted by permission.

Bradley, Craig M., On Custody, Trial Magazine, Feb. 2005, p. 58. Copyright © 2005 by Trial. Reprinted by permission.

Caplan, Gerald M., Questioning *Miranda*, 38 Vand.L.Rev. 1417 (1985). Copyright © 1985 by the Vanderbilt Law Review. Reprinted by permission.

Cassell, Paul G., *Miranda*'s Social Costs: An Empirical Assessment, 90 Nw.U.L.Rev. 387 (1996). Copyright © 1996 by the Northwestern University Law Review. Reprinted by special permission of Northwestern University School of Law, *Law Review*, vol. 90, issue 2, 1996.

______, The Paths Not Taken: The Supreme Court's Failures in *Dickerson*, 99 Mich.L.Rev. 898 (2001). Copyright © 2001 by the Michigan Law Review Association. Reprinted by permission.

Cloud, Morgan; Shepherd, George B.; Barkoff, Alison Nodwin; and Shur, Justin V., Words Without Meaning: The Constitution, Confessions, and Mentally Retarded Suspects, 69 U.Chi.L.Rev. 495 (2002). Copyright © 2002 by the University of Chicago Law Review. Reprinted by permission.

Colb, Sherry F., Why the Supreme Court Should Overrule the *Massiah* Doctrine and Permit *Miranda* Alone to Govern Interrogations, Findlaw's Writ at <http://writ.news.findlaw.com/colb/20010509.html (May 9, 2001). Copyright © 2001 by Findlaw's Writ. Reprinted by permission.

Davies, Sharon, Profiling Terror, 1 Ohio St. J. Crim. L. 45 (2003). Copyright © by the Ohio State Journal of Criminal Law. Reprinted with permission.

Dershowitz, Alan M., Torture Without Visibility and Accountability Is Worse than with It, 6 U.Pa.J.Const.L. 326 (2003). Copyright © 2003 by the University of Pennsylvania Journal of Constitutional Law. Reprinted by permission.

Dershowitz, Alan M., The Torture Warrant: A Response to Professor Strauss, 48 N.Y. Law Sch.Rev. 275 (2004). Copyright © 2004 by the New York Law School Review. Reprinted by permission.

Dressler, Joshua, Understanding Criminal Procedure (3d ed. 2002). Copyright © 1997 by Matthew Bender & Co. Inc. Reprinted by permission.

Dripps, Donald A., Constitutional Theory for Criminal Procedure: *Miranda, Dickerson*, and the Continuing Quest for Broad-But-Shallow, 43 Wm. & Mary L. Rev. 1 (2001). Copyright © 2001 by the William and Mary Law Review. Reprinted by permission.

Goldsmith, Michael, The Supreme Court and Title III: Rewriting the Law of Electronic Surveillance, 74 J.Crim.L. & Criminology 1 (1983). Copyright © 1983 by the Northwestern University School of Law. Reprinted by permission.

Goldwasser, Katherine, After Abscam: An Examination of Congressional Proposals to Limit Targeting Discretion in Federal Undercover Investigations, 36 Emory L.J. 75 (1987). Copyright © 1987 by the Emory University School of Law. Reprinted by permission.

Grano, Joseph D., Confessions, Truth and the Law (1993). Copyright © 1993 by the University of Michigan. Reprinted by permission.

Inbau, Fred E., Police Interrogation—A Practical Necessity, 52 J. Criminology & P.S. 16 (1961). Copyright © 1962 by the Northwestern University School of Law. Reprinted by permission.

Israel, Jerold, LaFave, Wayne, and King, Nancy, Criminal Procedure (2d ed. 1999). Copyright © 1999 by West Publishing Co. Reprinted by permission.

Kainen, James, The Impeachment Exception to the Exclusionary Rules: Policies, Principles, and Politics, 44 Stan.L.Rev. 1301 (1992). Copyright © 1992 by the Board of Trustees of the Leland Stanford Junior University. Reprinted by permission of the Stanford Law Review and Fred B. Rothman & Co.

Kamisar, Yale, Another Look at Patane and Seibert, the 2004 *Miranda* "Poisoned Fruit" Cases, 2 Ohio St. J. Crim. L. 97 (2004). Copyright © 2004 by the Ohio State Journal of Criminal Law. Reprinted with permission.

______, The Warren Court and Criminal Justice, in the Warren Court: A Retrospective 116, 140–43 (B. Schwartz ed. 1996). Copyright © 1996 by the Oxford University Press. Reprinted with permission.

______, Equal Justice in the Gatehouse and Mansions of American Criminal Procedure, in Kamisar, Inbau & Arnold, Criminal Justice in Our Time (Howard ed. 1965). Copyright © 1965 by the Rector and Visitors of the University of Virginia. Reprinted by permission.

______, Killing *Miranda* in Baltimore: Reflections on David Simon's Homicide, Jurist: Books-on-Law, Feb. 1999, vol. 2, no. 2. Copyright © 1999 by Jurist: Books-on-Law. Reprinted by permission.

______, *Miranda* Thirty-Five Years Later: A Close Look at the Majority and Dissenting Opinions in *Dickerson*, 33 Ariz. St. L. J. 387 (2001). Copyright © 2001 by the Arizona State Law Journal. Reprinted by permission.

Kennedy, Randall L., Race, Crime, and the Law (1997). Copyright © 1997 by Randall L. Kennedy. Reprinted by permission.

Kerr, Orin S., The Fourth Amendment and New Technologies; Constitutional Myths and the Case For Caution 102 Mich. L. Rev. 801 (2004). Copyright © 2004 by the Michigan Law Review. Reprinted by permission.

King, Nancy, LaFave, Wayne, and Israel, Jerold, Criminal Procedure (2d ed. 1999). Copyright © 1999 by West Publishing Co. Reprinted by permission.

Klarman, Michael J., The Racial Origins of Modern Criminal Procedure, 99 Mich.L. Rev. 48 (2000). Copyright © 2000 by the Michigan Law Review Association. Reprinted by permission.

Kreimer, Seth F., Too Close to the Rack and the Screw: Constitutional Constraints on Torture in the War on Terror, 6 U.Pa.J.Const.L. 278 (2003).

Copyright © 2003 by the University of Pennsylvania Journal of Constitutional Law. Reprinted by permission.

LaFave, Wayne, Israel, Jerold, and King, Nancy, Criminal Procedure (2d ed. 1999). Copyright © 1999 by West Publishing Co. Reprinted by permission.

LaFave, Wayne, Search and Seizure: A Treatise on the Fourth Amendment (3d ed. 1996). Copyright © 1996 by West Publishing Co. Reprinted by permission.

Loewy, Arnold, Police-Obtained Evidence and the Constitution: Distinguishing Unconstitutionally Obtained Evidence from Unconstitutionally Used Evidence, 87 Mich.L.Rev. 907 (1989). Copyright © 1989 by the Michigan Law Review. Reprinted by permission.

Maclin, Tracey, "Black and Blue Encounters"—Some Preliminary Thoughts about Fourth Amendment Seizures: Should Race Matter?, 26 Val.U.L.Rev. 243 (1991). Copyright © by the Valparaiso Law Review. Reprinted by permission.

Orfield, Myron, Deterrence, Perjury and the Heater Factor: An Exclusionary Rule in the Chicago Criminal Courts, 63 U.Colo.L.Rev. 75 (1992). Copyright © 1992 by the University of Colorado Law Review. Reprinted by permission.

Parry, John T., and White, Welsh S., Interrogating Suspected Terrorists: Should Torture Be An Option?, 63 U.Pitt.L.Rev. 743 (2002). Copyright © 2002 by the University of Pittsburgh Law Review. Reprinted by permission.

Schulhofer, Stephen J., Check and Balances in Wartime: American, British and Israeli Experiences, 103 Mich. L. Rev. 1907 (2004). Copyright © 2004 by the Michigan Law Review. Reprinted by permission.

______, *Miranda*'s Practical Effect: Substantial Benefits and Vanishingly Small Social Costs, 90 Nw.U.L.Rev. 500 (1996). Copyright © 1996 by the Northwestern University Law Review. Reprinted by permission.

______, The Enemy Within (2002). Copyright © 2002 by The Century Foundation. Reprinted by permission.

Simon, David, Homicide—A Year on the Killing Streets (1991). Copyright © 1991 by Houghton Mifflin Co. Reprinted by permission.

Slobogin, Christopher, Toward Taping, 1 Ohio St.J.Crim.L. 309 (2003). Copyright © 2003 by the Ohio State Journal of Criminal Law. Reprinted by permission.

Slobogin, Christopher & Whitebread, Charles, Criminal Procedure (4th ed. 2000). Copyright © 2000 by The Foundation Press, Inc. Reprinted by permission.

Smith, Stephen F., Activism as Restraint: Lessons from Criminal Procedure, 80 Texas L.Rev. 1056 (2002). Copyright © 2002 by the Texas Law Review. Reprinted by permission.

Strauss, Marcy, Torture, 48 N.Y. Law Sch.Rev. 203 (2004). Copyright © 2004 by the New York Law School Review.. Reprinted by permission.

Stuntz, William J., The Uneasy Relationship Between Criminal Procedure and Criminal Justice, 107 Yale L.J. (1997). Copyright © 1997 by the Yale Law Journal Co., Inc. Reprinted by permission of the Yale Law Journal Company and William S. Hein Company from *The Yale Law Journal*, Vol. 107, pages 1-76.

______, Waiving Rights in Criminal Procedure, 75 Va.L.Rev. 761 (1989). Copyright © 1989 by the Virginia Law Review. Reprinted by permission.

______, Warrants, and Fourth Amendment Remedies, 77 Va.L.Rev. 881 (1991). Copyright © 1991 by the Virginia Law Review. Reprinted by permission.

______, *Miranda*'s Mistake, 99 Mich.L.Rev. 975 (2001). Copyright © 2001 by the Michigan Law Review Association. Reprinted by permission.

Taylor, Stuart, Jr., Politically Incorrect Profiling: A Matter of Life or Death, Nov. 3, 2001, p. 3406. Copyright © 2001 by the National Journal. Reprinted by permission.

Thomas, George C. III, Plain Talk about the *Miranda* Empirical Debate: A "Steady-State" Theory of Confessions, 43 U.C.L.A.L.Rev. 933 (1966). Copyright © 1996 by the U.C.L.A. Law Review. Reprinted by permission.

______, Stories about *Miranda*, 102 Mich. L. Rev. 1959 (2004) Copyright © 2004 by the Michigan Law Review. Reprinted by permission

White, Welsh S., *Miranda*'s Waning Protections (2001). Copyright © 2001 by the University of Michigan. Reprinted by permission.

White, Welsh S., and Parry, John T., Interrogating Suspected Terrorists: Should Torture Be An Option?, 63 U.Pitt.L.Rev. 743 (2002). Copyright © 2002 by the University of Pittsburgh Law Review. Reprinted by permission.

Whitebread, Charles, and Slobogin, Christopher, Criminal Procedure (4th ed. 2000). Copyright © 2000 by The Foundation Press, Inc. Reprinted by permission.

Summary of Contents

*

Table of Contents

Table of Cases

The principal cases are in bold type. Cases cited or discussed in the text are in roman type. References are to pages. For Commonwealth v. ______, People v. ______, State v. ______, United States v. ______, see the name of the other party. For Ex Parte ______, In State ex rel. ______, United States ex rel. ______, see the name of the first party. Where a case is discussed in another case, reference is made only to the first page at which it is cited. No reference is made to discussion of a principal case in the Notes and Questions that follow that case.

Table of Authorities

Bold type indicates major extracts

Guide to Amending It, 72 Geo.Wash.L.rev. 1208 (2004), 838
Kerr, Orin S., The Fourth Amendment and New Technologies: Constitutional Myths and the Case for Caution, 482
Kerr, Orin S., Internet Surveillance Law After the USA Patriot Act: The Big Brother that Isn't, 97 Nw.U.L.Rev. 607 (2003), 470, 471, 472, 474, 475, 480
Kerr, Orin S., Technology, Privacy, and the Courts: A Reply to Colb and Swire, 102 Mich.L.Rev. 933 (2004), 484
Kerr, Orin S., The Fourth Amendment in Cyberspace: Can Encryption Create A "Reasonable Expectation of Privacy?," 33 Conn. L.Rev. 503 (2001), 482, 483
King, Nancy J., LaFave, Wayne R. & Israel, Jerold H., Criminal Procedure Treatise (2nd ed. 1999), *(passim)*
Kitch, Edmund W., Katz v. United States: The Limits of the Fourth Amendment, 1968 Supreme Court Rev. 133, p. 490, 493
Klarman, Michael J., The Racial Origins of Modern Criminal Procedure, 99 Mich. L.Rev. 48 (2000), 59, 729
Klein, Richard, The Constitutionalization of Ineffective Assistance of Counsel, 58 Md. L.Rev. 1433 (1999), 168
Klein, Richard, The Eleventh Commandment: Thou Shalt Not be Compelled to Render the Ineffective Assistance of Counsel, 68 Indiana L.J. 363 (1993), 188
Klein, Susan R., Identifying and (Re)Formulating Prophylactic Rules, Safe Harbors, and Incidental Rights in Constitutional Criminal Procedure, 99 Mich.L.Rev. 1030 (2001), 690, 691
Klinefelter, Ann, The Role of Librarians in Challenges to the USA Patriot Act, 5 N.C.J. L. & Tech. 219 (2004), 831
Knowlton, Robert, Schwartz, Richard & Dash, Samuel, The Eavesdroppers 339–79 (1959), 466
Koosed, Margaret Malkin, The Proposed Innocence Protection Act Won't—Unless It Also Curbs Mistaken Eyewitness Identifications, 63 Ohio St.L.J. 263 (2002), 756, 784
Krash, Abe, Lewis, Anthony, Podgor, Ellen & Kamisar, Yale, Gideon at 40: Facing the Crisis, Fulfilling the Promise, 41 Am.Crim. L.Rev. 131 (2004), 87
Krauss, Stanton D., The Life and Times of Boyd v. United States (1886–1976), 76 Mich.L.Rev. 184 (1977), 808, 809
Kreeger, Anne, Allen, Ronald J. & Luttrell, Melissa, Clarifying Entrapment, 89 J.Crim.L. & Criminology 407 (1999), 505, 534
Kreimer, Seth F., Too Close to the Rack and the Screw: Constitutional Constraints on Torture in the War on Terror, 6 U.Pa.J.Const.L. 278 (2003), 636
Ku, Raymond Shih Ray, The Founder's Privacy: The Fourth Amendment and the Power of Technological Surveillance, 86 Minn. L.Rev. 1325 (2002), 269
Kuckes, Niki, The Useful Dangerous Fiction of Grand Jury Independence, 41 Amer.Crim. L.Rev. 1 (2004), 800, 801
Kuhns, Richard B., The Concept of Personal Aggrievement in Fourth Amendment Standing Cases, 65 Iowa L.Rev. 493 (1980), 892

LaFave, Wayne R., Arrest: The Decision to Take a Suspect into Custody (1965), 595
LaFave, Wayne R., Controlling Discretion by Administrative Regulations: The Use, Misuse, and Nonuse of Police Rules and Policies in Fourth Amendment Adjudication, 89 Mich.L.Rev. 442 (1990), 401
LaFave, Wayne R., Pinguitudinous Police, Pachydermatous Prey: Whence Fourth Amendment "Seizures"?, 1991 U.Ill.L.Rev. 729, p. 414
LaFave, Wayne R., Search and Seizure: A Treatise on the Fourth Amendment (3d ed.1996), 217, 321, 429, 433, 894, 897, **898,** 904, 920, 939, 940
LaFave, Wayne R., "Street Encounters" and the Constitution: Terry, Sibron, Peters and Beyond, 67 Mich.L.Rev. 40 (1968), 416
LaFave, Wayne R., The "Routine Traffic Stop" From Start to Finish: Too Much "Routine," Not Enough Fourth Amendment, 102 Mich. L.Rev. 1843 (2004), 418, 427
LaFave, Wayne R., Israel, Jerold H. & King, Nancy J., Criminal Procedure Treatise (2nd ed. 1999), *(passim)*
Lagarias, P., Effective Closing Argument §§ 2.05–2.06 (1989), 175
Langan, Patrick A., et al., Contacts between Police and the Public (U.S. Dep't of Justice, 2001), 344
Larson, Mark R., DiTraglia, Caterina M. & Doyle, James M., The Eyes Have It–Or Do They?, Criminal Justice (ABA Criminal Justice Section), p. 12 (Fall, 2001), 756, 786
Latzer, Barry, State Constitutional Criminal Procedure (1995), 49
Lefcourt, Gerald, The Blank Lineup: An Aid to the Defense, 14 Crim.L.Bull. 428 (1978), 785
Leiken, Lawrence S., Police Interrogation in Colorado: The Implementation of Miranda, 47 Denver L.J. 1 (1970), 643
Leo, Richard A. & Drizin, Steven A., The Problem of False Confessions in the Post–DNA World, 82 N.C.L.Rev. 891 (2004), 639
Leo, Richard A., Inside the Interrogation Room, 86 J. Crim.L. & Criminology 266 (1996), 637
Leo, Richard A., Miranda's Revenge: Police Interrogation as a Confidence Game, 30 Law & Society Rev. 259 (1996), 677
Leo, Richard A., Questioning the Relevance of Miranda in the Twenty–First Century, 99 Mich.L.Rev. 975 (2001), 690
Leo, Richard A. & Ofshe, Richard J., The Consequences of False Confessions, 88 J.Crim.L. & C. 429 (1998), 724
Leo, Richard A. & Ofshe, Richard J., The Social Psychology of Police Interrogation, 16

Mosteller, Robert, Cowboy Prosecutors and Subpoenas for Incriminating Evidence: The Consequences and Corrections of Excess, 58 Wash. & Lee L.Rev. 487 (2001), 878

Mosteller, Robert P., Simplifying Subpoena Law: Taking the Fifth Amendment Seriously, 73 Va.L.Rev. 1 (1987), 866

Mulligan, Deidre, Reasonable Expectations in Electronic Communications: A Critical Perspective in the Electronics Communications Privacy Act, 72 Geo.Wash.L.Rev. 1557 (2004), 816

Murphy, James, An Evaluation of the Arguments Against the Use of Expert Testimony on Eyewitness Identification, 8 U.Bridgeport L.Rev. 21 (1987), 768

Murray, Daniel E., The Criminal Lineup at Home and Abroad, 1966 Utah L.Rev. 610, p. 760

Nagareta, Richard A., Compulsion "To Be a Witness" and the Resurrection of Boyd, 74 N.Y.U.L.Rev. 1575 (1999), 853, 877, 880

National Institute of Justice: A Guide for Law Enforcement (1999), 785

Nowak, John E., Due Process Methodology in the Postincorporation World, 70 J.Crim.L. & C. 397 (1979), 33

Ofshe, Richard J. & Leo, Richard A., The Consequences of False Confessions, 88 J.Crim.L. & C. 429 (1998), 724

Ofshe, Richard J. & Leo, Richard A., The Social Psychology of Police Interrogation, 16 Studies in Law, Politics & Society 189 (1997), 724

O'Hara, Charles, Fundamentals of Criminal Investigation, (1959), p. 576

O'Neill, Michael Edmund, Undoing Miranda, 2000 BYU L.Rev. 185, p. 679

O'Reilly, Gregory W., England Limits the Right to Silence and Moves Toward an Inquisitional System of Justice, 85 J.Crim.L. & C. 402 (1994), 587

Orfield, Myron W., Deterrence, Perjury, and the Heater Factor: An Exclusionary Rule in the Chicago Criminal Courts, 63 U.Colo.L.Rev. 75 (1992), 234

Packer, Herbert L., The Courts, the Police and the Rest of Us, 57 J.Crim.L.C. & P.S. (1966), 59

Park, Roger, The Entrapment Controversy, 60 Minn.L.Rev. 163 (1976), 512, 515, 525

Parry, John T. & White, Welsh S., Interrogating Suspected Terrorists: Should Torture Be An Option?, 63 U.Pitt.L.Rev. 743 (2002), 637

Paulsen, Monrad, The Fourteenth Amendment and the Third Degree, 6 Stan.L.Rev. 411 (1954), 554

Piccaretta, Michael L. & Keenan, Jefferson, Entrapment Targets and Tactics: Jacobson v. United States, 29 Crim.L.Bull. 241 (1993), 512, 536

Pitler, Robert, "The Fruit of the Poisonous Tree" Revisited and Shepardized, 56 Calif.L.Rev. 579 (1968), 765, 906, 907

Pizzi, William, Punishment and Procedure: A Different View of the American Criminal Justice System, 13 Const.Comm. 55 (1996), 59

Pizzi, William, The Privilege Against Self–Incrimination in a Rescue Situation, 76 J.Crim.L. & C. (1985), 634

Podgor, Ellen S. & Hall, John Wesley, Government Surveillance of Attorney–Client Communications: Invoked in the Name of Fighting Terrorism, 17 Geo.J.Legal Ethics 145 (2003), 495

Podgor, Ellen, Kamisar, Yale, Krash, Abe & Lewis, Anthony, Gideon at 40: Facing the Crisis, Fulfilling the Promise, 41 Am.Crim. L.Rev. 131 (2004), 87

Porsch, Cassandra & Cassidy, Charlie, Government Monitoring of Attorney–Client Communications in Terrorism–Related Cases: Ethical Implications for Defense Attorneys, 17 Geo.J.Legal Ethics 681 (2004), 495

Posner, Richard A., Excessive Sanctions for Governmental Misconduct in Criminal Cases, 57 Wash.L.Rev. 635 (1982), 238

Poulin, Anne Bowen, The Role of Standby Counsel in Criminal Cases: In the Twilight Zone of The Criminal Justice System, 76 N.Y.U.L.Rev. 676 (2000), 128

Priar & Martin, Searching and Disarming Criminals, 45 J.Crim.L.C. & P.S. 481, p. 403

Pulaski, Charles, Jr., Neil v. Biggers: The Supreme Court Dismantles the Wade Trilogy's Due Process Protection, 26 Stan.L.Rev. 1097 (1974), 779

Radack, Jesselyn, The Big Chill: Negative Effects of the McDade Amendment and Conflict Between Federal Statutes, 14 Geo.J. Legal Ethics 707 (2001), 832

Reid, John & Inbau, Fred E., Criminal Interrogation and Confessions (1962), 545, 576

Reid, John, Buckley & Inbau, Fred E., Criminal Interrogation and Confessions 216 (3d ed. 1986), 545

Rhodes, Deborah L., Simpson Sound Bites: What Is and Isn't News About Domestic Violence, in Postmortem: The O.J. Simpson Case 83 (Jeffrey Abramson ed. 1996), 64

Richman, Daniel C., Grand Jury Secrecy: Plugging the Leaks in an Empty Bucket, 36 Am.Crim.L.Rev. 399 (1999), 795

Rigg, Robert, The Constitution, Compensation, and Competence: A Case Study, 27 Am. J.Crim.L. 1 (1999), 466

Rogers, William P., The Case for Wire Tapping, 63 Yale L.J. 792 (1954), 351

Rosenberg, Irene & Rosenberg, Yale, A Modest Proposal for the Abolition of Custodial Confessions, 68 N.C.L.Rev. 69 (1989), 552

Rosenberg, Irene & Rosenberg, Yale, In the Beginning: The Talmudic Rule Against Self–Incrimination, 63 N.Y.U.L.Rev. 955 (1988), 579

*

BASIC CRIMINAL PROCEDURE

CASES, COMMENTS AND QUESTIONS

Eleventh Edition

Part One
INTRODUCTION

Chapter 1
AN OVERVIEW OF THE CRIMINAL JUSTICE PROCESS

SECTION 1. THE OVERVIEW'S OBJECTIVES

This chapter provides the introduction for three different books—*Modern Criminal Procedure*, *Basic Criminal Procedure* (containing chapters 1–12 of *Modern*), and *Advanced Criminal Procedure* (containing chapters 1 and 12–29 of *Modern*). All three books are designed for use in courses on the "criminal justice process"—that is, the process through which the substantive criminal law is enforced. That process starts with the investigation of possible criminality and the apprehension of the suspected criminal, the primary subjects considered in *Basic Criminal Procedure* and in the first half of *Modern Criminal Procedure*. The process then proceeds through the charging decision, a variety of pre-adjudication proceedings, the adjudication of the charge, the imposition of sentence upon persons found guilty, and any subsequent challenges to the conviction and sentence. These subjects are considered in *Advanced Criminal Procedure* and in the second half of *Modern Criminal Procedure*.

Single courses on the criminal justice process typically concentrate on only a portion of the process. Thus, a course may cover the investigative stages (as in a "police practices" course) or concentrate on the post-investigative stages of the process (as in the course commonly described as "the adversary process" or the "bail to jail" course), or it may treat selective parts of both the investigative and post-investigative stages of the process (as in the courses that concentrate on the various constitutional provisions regulating the process). A single semester simply is too short to explore *all* of the stages of the process. Yet, a general understanding of the totality of the process is critical to placing in context any particular portion of the process. The primary objective of this chapter is to provide that understanding through the overview of the process set forth in section two of the chapter. Hopefully, this overview will provide the student with a useful backdrop for considering the selected aspects of the process that are explored in greater detail in later chapters.

As noted in section two, there is no single American criminal justice process, as the steps in the process vary from jurisdiction to jurisdiction and even within a single jurisdiction, depending upon a variety of factors. Similarly, the legal standards regulating a particular step in the process are likely to vary from one jurisdiction to another (and sometimes even within the jurisdiction, depending upon such factors as the level of the offense). Even greater diversity is found in the administration of a particular step within the restrictions imposed by legal regulations. Section three of this chapter provides a brief introduction to the diversity in legal regulation and section four considers diversity in the administration of the process. As discussed there, the depth of that diversity significantly limits our descriptions in subsequent chapters of the governing legal standards and of administrative practice.

In common with the chapters that follow, the topics considered in Chapter One are treated in far more detail in Wayne R. LaFave, Jerold H. Israel & Nancy J. King, *Criminal Procedure* (6 vols., 2d ed.1999). That treatise is available in Westlaw under the database "CRIMPROC" (and is hereafter cited as CRIMPROC). Students seeking further documentation as to the general descriptions provided throughout this book should look at the corresponding chapter in CRIMPROC.[a]

SECTION 2. THE STEPS IN THE PROCESS

This section presents an overview of the procedural steps that carry the process from start to finish in an individual case. The basic objectives of the overview are to position each step within a "typical" progression of the process, to introduce the relevant terminology, and to briefly describe what occurs at each step. This information should provide a useful backdrop for the discussion in later chapters of the legal standards that govern the various steps in process. That discussion concentrates on those steps that commonly are the focus of litigation. This overview, in contrast, also takes note of many steps that are rarely, if ever, seen as raising legal difficulties. Their operation, however, contributes to the overall structure of the process, and often plays a role in shaping the law that governs those steps which frequently are a source of litigation.

There is, of course, no "standard" process applicable to all cases. Indeed, major limitations must be acknowledged even in providing an overview of a progression characterized as being no more than "typical." Initially, as discussed in Note 1 of Section 3, the procedural steps available to the participants in the process vary from one jurisdiction to another. Our overview concentrates on a description of the basic process found in a substantial majority (but not necessarily all) of our fifty-two basic lawmaking jurisdictions (i.e., the fifty states, the District of Columbia, and the federal system). Where the jurisdictions generally are divided, with a substantial group not utilizing a procedure (or utilizing an alternative procedure), that division will also be noted. Our overview will ignore,

a. The following sections in CRIMPROC correspond in subject coverage to the chapters of *Modern*, *Basic*, and *Advanced*; For Ch.1 (*Modern*, *Basic*, and *Advanced*), see CRIMPROC §§ 1.1–1.3, 1.6–1.8; for Ch. 2 (in *Modern, Basic* and *Advanced*), see §§ 2.1–2.7 and 2.10–2.11; for Ch. 3 (in *Modern, Basic*, and *Advanced*), see §§ 1.9, 2.8–2.9; for Ch. 4 (in *Modern*, *Basic* and *Advanced*), see §§ 11.1–11.5; for Ch. 5 (in *Modern*, *Basic*, and *Advanced*), see §§ 11.6–11.10; for Ch. 6 (in *Modern* and *Basic*), see §§ 3.1–3.10; for Ch. 7 (in *Modern* and *Basic*), see §§ 4.1–4.6; for Ch. 8 (in *Modern* and *Basic*), see §§ 5.1–5.4; for Ch. 9 (in *Modern* and *Basic*), see §§ 6.1–6.10; for Ch. 10 (in *Modern* and *Basic*), see § 7.1–7.5; for Ch. 11 (in *Modern* and *Basic*), see §§ 8.1–8.15; for Ch. 12 (in *Modern* and *Basic*), see §§ 9.1–9.6, 10.1–10.6; for Ch. 13 (in *Modern* and *Advanced*), see §§ 12.1–12.5; for Ch. 14 (in *Modern* and *Advanced*), see §§ 13.1–13.7; for Ch. 15 (in *Modern* and *Advanced*), see §§ 14.1–14.4; for Ch. 16 (in *Modern* and *Advanced*), see 15.1–15.7; for Ch. 17 (in *Modern* and *Advanced*), see §§ 19.1–19.6; for Ch. 18 (in *Modern* and *Advanced*), see §§ 16.1–16.3; for Ch. 19 (in *Modern* and *Advanced*), see §§ 17.1–17.4; for Ch. 20 (in *Modern* and *Advanced*), see §§ 18.1–18.5; for Ch. 21 (in *Modern* and *Advanced*), see §§ 20.1–20.6, 24.3; for Ch. 22 (in *Modern* and *Advanced*), see §§ 21.1–21.6; for Ch. 23 (in *Modern* and *Advanced*), see §§ 22.1–22.4; for Ch. 24 (in *Modern* and *Advanced*), see §§ 23.1–23.3; for Ch. 25 (in *Modern* and *Advanced*), see §§ 24.1–24.2, 24.5–24.11; for Ch. 26 (in *Modern* and *Advanced*), see §§ 25.1–25.5; for Ch. 27 (in *Modern* and *Advanced*), see §§ 26.1–26.7; for Ch. 28 (in *Modern* and *Advanced*), see §§ 26.8, 27.1–27.6; for Ch. 29 (in *Modern* and *Advanced*), see §§ 28.1–28.9.

however, minor variations found in numerous states and even major variations found in only a small group of states.

As discussed in Note 6 of Section 3, jurisdictions commonly draw distinctions as to available procedures based on the level of the offense involved (distinguishing in particular between felonies and misdemeanors).[b] Our overview is limited to the processes applicable to non-capital, felony offenses. It thus encompasses almost all proceedings relating to serious crimes (capital offenses being relatively few in number), but ignores the far larger number of proceedings relating to minor crimes.

As discussed in Section 4, the exercise of discretion determines in large part those procedures applied in a particular case. A procedure may be available under the law of the particular jurisdiction, but not utilized because an enforcement official (prosecutor or police officer),[c] a judicial official (magistrate court judge or trial court judge),[d] or a defendant chooses not to invoke the procedure. Our overview will discuss the full range of potential procedural steps in the processing of non-capital felony offenses, even though in a particular jurisdiction (or community within a jurisdiction), that step may not in fact be "typical" because of the exercise of discretion not to utilize it. Where reliable statistics are available, we will note the frequency of the use of a particular procedure, but in large part, these statistics are not based on national patterns.[e]

b. American jurisdictions commonly use one of two different standards in distinguishing between felonies and misdemeanors. Some classify as felonies all offenses punishable by a maximum term of imprisonment of more than one year; offenses punishable by imprisonment for one year or less are then misdemeanors. Others look to the location of the possible imprisonment. If the offense is punishable by imprisonment in a penitentiary, it is a felony; if punishable only by a jail term, it is a misdemeanor. This line in practice also tends to produce a one-year dividing line since state correction codes commonly provide for imprisonment in the penitentiary if a sentence exceeds one year and for imprisonment in jail if the sentence is for one year or less.

c. In describing the different participants in the process, the overview will not distinguish between different types of actors performing the same basic role in administering the process. Thus, the term "police" encompasses all government employees assigned to the task of enforcing the criminal law and given the authority (e.g., to carry weapons and to make arrests) that accompanies that responsibility. This includes officers employed by a wide variety of agencies (including for example, the country sheriff, the city police department, the state highway patrol and a park security force). Similarly "prosecutors" encompasses all government officials charged with presenting prosecutions on behalf of the state (officials typically known as "district attorneys," "state's attorneys," or "prosecuting attorneys").

d. The term "magistrate court" refers to the court (or branch of a court) which has jurisdiction over the preliminary stages in felony cases and both the preliminary stages and trial of misdemeanor cases (courts commonly known in the state systems as "municipal courts," "county courts," "justice of the peace courts," or "district courts"). The term "general trial court" refers to the court which has trial jurisdiction in felony cases (commonly carrying the titles in state systems of "circuit courts," "superior courts," or "district courts," where that title is not assigned to the magistrate court).

e. For a discussion of available statistical data, see CRIMPROC § 1.3. As noted there, as to many aspects of the process, the best statistical source is a series of Department of Justice tracking studies reviewing the administration of state criminal justice procedures in a select group of large urban counties. Statistics on the outcomes of various procedural steps are reported on a statewide basis in the reports of state criminal justice agencies and state judicial administrators, but fairly comprehensive reports are available only for a small group of states (typically, among the more populous states). The statistics cited in our overview come largely from these sources, and thus, while they may reflect the practice applicable to a significant portion of the population (the study of the 75 largest counties accounts for roughly 37% of the population and nearly 50% of all reported crimes), they may or may not reflect the practice typical of the nation as a whole.

One aspect of the statistical picture, clearly accurate on a national level, is the so-called "funnel" or "sieve" effect: at each of the basic stages of the process, fewer persons are subjected to the process than at the previous stage. More people are investigated than arrested; more are arrested than charged; more are charged than convicted; and more are convicted than subjected to incarceration.

Finally, our overview will not take account of variations in chronology. It will assume the chronology that occurs in the majority of felony cases, although many felony cases do not follow that chronology. Also, the overview discusses each step as occupying a specific place in the progression of a case, but that is not true of all procedures. While some steps have a definite starting and ending point, others are continuing and overlap other steps in the process. Investigative procedures, for example, do not always stop with the filing of charges, but may continue through to the initiation (and sometimes the end) of the trial. So too, the decision on pretrial release, though it comes initially at the first appearance, is subject to possible reconsideration as the case progresses.

Step 1: Prearrest Investigation. Various distinctions are used in grouping prearrest investigatory procedures. Lawyers tend to group procedures according to the governing legal standards. In this overview, however, we follow the lead of criminal justice analysts, stressing two dividing lines: (1) the agency involved (distinguishing primarily between the investigative activities of the police and the prosecutor) and (2) the focus of the procedure (distinguishing primarily between activities aimed at solving past reported crimes and activities aimed at unknown but anticipated crimes). These distinctions create three basic groups of prearrest investigative procedures: (1) police procedures that are aimed at solving specific past crimes known to the police (commonly described as "reactive" investigative procedures), (2) police procedures that are aimed at unknown but anticipated ongoing and future criminal activity (commonly described as "proactive" investigative procedures), and (3) prosecutorial and other non-police investigations conducted primarily through the use of subpoena authority. Each of these groups is discussed below, but initially we take note of the large number of cases in which arrests are made by police with little or no prearrest investigation.

"On–Scene" Arrests. A substantial percentage of arrests for a wide variety of crimes are of the "on-scene" variety. These are arrests made during the course of the crime or immediately thereafter either at the place where the crime occurred or in its immediate vicinity. Ordinarily, on-scene arrests will be based on the officer's own observations (leading to the alternative description of such arrests as "on-view"), although they will sometimes be based on the directive of a witness who has just viewed the crime. For some offenses, on-scene arrests typically are the product of proactive prearrest investigative activities designed to place the police in a position where they will be able to view the crime as it is committed. That often is the case, for example, with so-called "victimless" crimes (i.e., crimes which do not involve an interaction with another person, such as possession of a weapon, and crimes which ordinarily involve willing participants, such as vice crimes or narcotics-transfer offenses). For many other offenses, however, most on-scene arrests occur with basically no investigative activity. This typically involves a police officer on patrol responding to an event that calls the crime to his attention (e.g., a victim's call for assistance, a burglar alarm, or an observation) and immediately arresting the offender (who remains at the location or is promptly found nearby). Thus, one study concluded that 42% of all arrests for nonviolent property crimes (basically theft and burglary) were such on-scene arrests, made within 5 minutes of the commission of the offense.

Reactive Investigations. General purpose police agencies (e.g., local police departments), who employ over 85% of the police officers in this country, traditionally have devoted the vast majority of their investigative efforts to reactive investigations. This is an "incident driven" or "complaint-responsive" style of policing, flowing from various aspects of local policing, including the neighborhood patrol and the 911 emergency telephone link. The police receive a citizen report of a crime (typically from the victim or an eyewitness), or they discover physical evidence indicating that a crime has been committed, and they then proceed to initiate an investigation responsive to that "known crime."[f] This involves (1) determining initially whether there actually was a crime committed, (2) if so, then determining who committed the crime, (3) collecting evidence of that person's guilt, and (4) locating the offender so that he can be taken into custody. A wide variety of investigative activities may be utilized to achieve these objectives. Those activities include: (1) the interviewing of victims; (2) the interviewing of other witnesses present when the officer arrives at the crime scene; (3) canvassing the neighborhood for (and interviewing) still other persons with relevant information; (4) the interviewing of suspects, which may require a physical stopping of the suspect on the street and a frisking of the suspect (i.e., pat-down of the outer clothing) for possible weapons; (5) the examination of the crime scene and the collection of physical evidence found there; (6) checking departmental records and computer files; (7) seeking information from informants; (8) searching for physical evidence of the crime (e.g., stolen property or weapons) in places accessible to the suspect (e.g., his home or automobile) and seizing any evidence found there; (9) surveillance of a suspect (including electronic surveillance) aimed at obtaining leads to evidence or accomplices; and (10) using undercover operatives to gain information from the suspect.

A variety of factors will determine which of the investigative practices noted above will be used in a particular investigation. One key factor is the investigative direction suggested by those "traces" of the crime that are immediately available to the police. In some instances, the limitations of available traces foreclose the use of a particular investigative practice. Any attempt to interview suspects depends upon the presence of some trace (e.g., a witness who can describe the criminal or a unique modus operandi) that allows for the designation of a manageable group of persons who might be considered possible suspects. A search for physical evidence only makes sense if the traces indicate that the criminal activity was of a type that might produce such evidence. In other instances, though the available traces will not absolutely rule out the use of a particular investigative practice, they suggest that the likelihood of gaining useful information will be so remote that the time, energy, and financial costs involved simply do not make use of that practice worthwhile. There is almost always some possibility, for example, that canvassing the neighborhood will produce a witness who saw the offender, but police frequently will not canvass for witnesses unless there is a fairly substantial likelihood that such a witness might be found.

In general, the strength and nature of the available leads will determine the scope of the investigation, but other factors may alter that natural correlation. A more serious offense may lead police to utilize a technique that would be rejected as to a less serious crime because it is not sufficiently likely to be successful. A technique less likely to be successful may be chosen over one more likely to be successful because the latter simply is not available under the law without stronger leads (as in the case of a search requiring probable cause). In such a

f. Official reports also include in the "known crime" category (sometimes described as "reported crimes") those crimes witnessed by the police which result in an on-scene arrest. Thus, as to offenses that commonly are reported by victims (e.g., burglary), the reported number of known crimes will often far exceed the number of arrests for those crimes (e.g., only one in 5 reported crimes will lead to an arrest), but as to crimes that come to the attention of the police primarily through the officer's own observation, the percentage of reported "known crimes" leading to arrest will be much higher (e.g., almost 90% for drug abuse offenses). Where an arrest is made for a particular crime, that crime is further identified by police as "cleared" (although crimes also can be listed as cleared where the police conclude that the crime has been "solved," but an arrest is not practicable, e.g., the offender is dead or already in prison for another offense). The clearance designation is based strictly on the police department's own evaluation, so a crime may be listed as cleared even though the prosecution decided not to charge the arrestee, or a charge brought subsequently was dismissed or resulted in an acquittal.

situation, the second-choice procedure hopefully will produce additional information that will enable the police legally to use their first choice, but that strategy may not be successful and the investigation may end without the police ever using the preferred procedure. In some instances, a second-choice may be forced on the police by leads that are not useable in court. Where, for example, a witness insists on anonymity, the police may be forced to attempt to build their case through other means that rely upon that information, but mask its source (e.g., a wiretap or an undercover agent "plant").

While the variation among investigations is far too great to characterize any single combination of investigative procedures as "typical," even for a particular type of offense, it is clear that prearrest investigations rarely take on the characteristics of popular depictions of the crime solving process. In general, investigations do not involve the use of scientific methods of investigation, confrontations with crafty criminals, or reliance upon informants. A study of robbery and burglary investigations found, for example, that the interviewing of the victim and the examination of the crime scene were by far the most common steps in the investigative process. Aside from the canvassing for and the interviewing of additional witnesses, no other procedure was used in as many as a third of all cases. The frequency of interviews of suspects varied considerably, but even as to robberies (where victims were more likely to identify a specific suspect), such interviews occurred in less than 25% of all cases. Interviews of informants occurred in less than 5% of all investigations. Most of the other prearrest investigative procedures listed above are used even less frequently. Perhaps the most extreme example is the use of electronic surveillance through wiretaps and "bugs," a common feature of television dramas, but actually utilized in less than two thousand of the millions of felony investigations conducted annually throughout the United States.

Proactive Investigations. Although general purpose police agencies traditionally have concentrated their investigative efforts on solving known crimes, those agencies also have regularly used, in a limited fashion, proactive investigations. Indeed, in recent years, many local police departments in large communities have sharply increased their utilization of proactive investigative procedures. Also, many special-function police agencies (such as the federal Drug Enforcement Administration) traditionally have devoted a quite substantial portion of their resources to proactive investigations.

Proactive investigations are aimed at uncovering criminal activity that is not specifically known to the police. The investigation may be aimed at placing the police in a position where they can observe ongoing criminal activity that otherwise would both be hidden from public view and not reported (as typically is the case with offenses that prohibit the possession of contraband or proscribe transactions between willing participants). It may be aimed at inducing persons who have committed crimes of a certain type, including many unknown to the police, to reveal themselves (as in a "fencing sting"). Proactive investigations also often are aimed at anticipating future criminality and placing police in a position to intercept when the crime is attempted. Here, the investigative technique may be designed simply to gain information that will permit the police to predict when and where a crime is likely to be committed, or it may be designed to "induce" the criminal attempt at a particular time and place by creating a setting likely to spur into action those prone to criminality.

A variety of different procedures may be used in a proactive investigation, with the choice of procedure largely tied to the specific objective of the investigation. Deception is a common element of many proactive procedures. In traditional undercover operations, the police assume a false identity and present themselves as willing to participate in criminal activities (as where undercover agents "set up'' fencing operations or narcotics transactions). So too, deception is the key to a ''decoy tactic'' of providing what appears to be an easy target for victimization (e.g., a drunk with an exposed wallet or a business of the type that is readily subject to extortion). Deception commonly also is critical to the effective use of informants. Where police utilize as informants persons whose activities expose them to a criminal milieu, they are counting on the criminals associating with those persons being deceived by a belief that those persons will not take what they have learned to the police (usually because the persons are themselves engaged in criminal activity, gain their livelihood in part from criminals, or have social ties to the criminals). Surveillance through stakeouts, covert patrols, and electronic monitoring also rests on deception by hiding the surveillance.

Other proactive techniques rely on intrusive confrontations designed to place police in a position where they can observe what otherwise would be hidden or to elicit nervous or unthinking incriminatory responses that will provide a legal grounding for taking further investigative action (e.g., an arrest or stop). Thus, police following an aggressive motorized patrol strategy will fully utilize traffic laws to maximize stops of motorists, thereby gaining greater opportunity to peer into car windows, to ask questions, and to request consent to a search of the vehicle. Similarly, under a practice of heavy field interrogation, police will frequently approach pedestrians and initiate questions to determine who they are and what they are doing. Such intrusive confrontations are most often used on a selective basis, with police concentrating their efforts on those characteristics of the social environment that suggest to them possible criminality (e.g., high-crime neighborhood, suspicious class of persons, unusual behavior). In general, proactive investigative procedures are more resource intensive, more intrusive, arguably more likely to foster community opposition, and clearly pose more legal problems than typical reactive investigative procedures.

Prosecutorial Investigations. Not all prearrest investigations are conducted by police. For certain types of crimes, the best investigatory tool is the subpoena—a court order directing a person to appear in a particular proceeding for the purpose of testifying and presenting specified physical evidence (e.g., documents) within his possession. The subpoena authority typically is available for the general investigation of crime only through the grand jury, although many jurisdictions also grant a limited subpoena authority to enforcement agencies charged with regulating particular types of potentially criminal activities. The grand jury, although it tends to be known more for its screening function in reviewing the prosecution's decision to charge, also has authority to conduct investigations into the possible commission of crimes within the judicial district in which it sits. In carrying out this function, the grand jurors, being a group of laypersons with no special expertise in investigation, quite naturally rely heavily on the direction provided by their legal advisor, who is the prosecutor. Thus, grand jury investigations become, for all practical purposes, investigations by the prosecutor.

Grand jury investigations tend to be used (1) where witnesses will not cooperate with the police (they can be compelled by subpoena to testify before the grand jury and given immunity to replace their self-incrimination privilege should they refuse to testify on that ground); (2) where the critical evidence of the crime is likely to be a ''paper trail'' buried in voluminous records of business dealings (as the subpoena can be used to require production of such records where the police lack the necessary probable cause predicate for obtaining those documents through a search); and (3) where the area of investigation is especially sensitive, reflecting a strong need to keep the ongoing investigation from the public gaze (an objective facilitated by grand jury secrecy requirements) or to ensure public confidence in the integrity of the investigation (an objective facilitated by the participation of the lay grand jurors). Criminal investigations presenting such special needs tend to deal with crimes of public corruption (e.g., bribery), misuse of economic power (e.g., price-fixing), or widespread distribution of illegal services or goods (e.g., organized crime operations). The investigation of such offenses through the grand jury often has both reactive and proactive qualities. The investigation starts with some information (typically coming from informants or investigators) suggesting that a specific offense has been committed, but once that offense is established, the investigation often will branch out to determine whether there also exists similar or related criminal activity, not previously identified, by the same or other parties (a portion of the grand jury investigation often characterized as a "fishing expedition").

Step 2: Arrest. Once a police officer has obtained sufficient information to justify arresting a suspect (i.e., probable cause to believe the person has committed a crime), the arrest ordinarily becomes the next step in the criminal justice process. The term "arrest" is defined differently for different purposes. We refer here only to the act of taking a person into custody for the purpose of charging him with a crime (the standard commonly used in the reporting of arrest statistics). This involves the detention of the suspect (by force if necessary) for the purpose of first transporting him to a police facility and then requesting that charges be filed against him. As an alternative to such a "full custody" arrest, many jurisdictions authorize the officer in certain situations to briefly detain the suspect and then release him upon issuance of an official document (commonly titled a "citation," "summons" or "appearance ticket") which directs the suspect to appear in court on a set date to respond to the charge specified in the document. In most communities, this release-on-citation alternative is only infrequently used (if at all) for felonies (in contrast to misdemeanors, where its use is fairly common).

Where there is no immediate need to arrest a suspect, an officer may seek to obtain an arrest warrant (a court order authorizing the arrest) prior to taking the person into custody.[g] Arrest warrants in most jurisdictions are issued by magistrates. To obtain a warrant, the police must establish, to the satisfaction of the magistrate, that there exists probable cause to believe that the prospective arrestee committed the crime for which he will be arrested. The showing of probable cause may be made by affidavits or live testimony of either the investigating officer or a witness (usually the victim). Where a warrant is issued, it ordinarily will authorize the arrest to be made by any police officer in the state, not simply the officer seeking the warrant.

Step 3: Booking. Immediately after making an arrest, the arresting officer usually will search the arrestee's person and remove any weapons, contraband, or

g. Arresting without first obtaining a warrant is the predominant practice for felony arrests throughout the nation. In a large percentage of felony arrests (including, for example, "on scene" arrests), the police officer will make the arrest immediately after obtaining probable cause for believing the person committed a crime. However, even where the investigating officer, after establishing probable cause, expects a lapse of a day or more before making an arrest, the common practice in most jurisdictions is not to use that opportunity to obtain an arrest warrant. Officers here will obtain a warrant, rather than rely on a warrantless arrest, only where the special setting makes a warrant legally necessary or otherwise advantageous. The most common of those settings are: (1) cases in which the offender is located in another jurisdiction (as a warrant is needed to utilize procedures for having the person arrested by officers of another state and later extradited); (2) cases in which the person cannot be found and the police therefore want to add the person to the computerized state or local law enforcement information network's listing of persons subject to an arrest on the basis of an outstanding warrant; (3) cases in which there will probably be a need to enter into a dwelling without consent in order to make the arrest (a situation that requires a warrant); and (4) cases in which the police have sought the advice of the prosecutor before deciding to proceed (where the prosecutor responds affirmatively, a complaint typically will be filed immediately, with a warrant then obtained prior to the arrest).

evidence relating to a crime. If the arrested person was driving a vehicle, the officer may also search the passenger compartment of the vehicle for the same items. The arrestee will then be taken, either by the arresting officer or other officers called to the scene, to the police station, a centrally located jail, or some similar "holding" facility. It is at this facility that the arrestee will be taken through a process known as "booking." Initially, the arrestee's name, the time of his arrival, and the offense for which he was arrested are noted in the police "blotter" or "log."[h] This is strictly a clerical procedure, and it does not control whether the arrestee will be charged or what charge might be brought. As part of the booking process, the arrestee also will be photographed and fingerprinted.

Once the booking process is completed, the arrestee ordinarily will be allowed to make at least one telephone call. Some jurisdictions allow person's arrested on lower-level felonies to gain their release at this point on posting "stationhouse bail" (i.e., posting a specified amount of cash, as prescribed in a judicially approved bail schedule, and agreeing to appear in court on a specified date). Most jurisdictions, however, limit the stationhouse-bail option to misdemeanor defendants, and even where the option is available for lesser felonies, many arrestees will not have access to the needed cash. Thus, all felony arrestees in some jurisdictions, and almost all in others, will be placed following booking in a "lockup," which usually is some kind of cell. Before entering the lockup, they will be subjected to another search, more thorough than that conducted at the point of arrest. This search is designed primarily to inventory the arrestee's personal belongings and to prevent the introduction of contraband into the lockup.

Step 4: Post–Arrest Investigation. The initial post-arrest investigation by the police consists of the search of the person (and where the arrestee was stopped while driving, possibly searching also the interior of the automobile) as discussed above. The extent of any further post-arrest investigation will vary with the fact situation. In some cases, such as where the arrestee was caught "red-handed," there will be little left to be done. In others, police will utilize many of the same kinds of investigative procedures as are used before arrest (e.g., interviewing witnesses, searching the arrestee's home, and viewing the scene of the crime). Post-arrest investigation does offer one important investigative source, however, that ordinarily is not available prior to the arrest—the person of the arrestee. Thus, the police may seek to obtain an eyewitness identification of the arrestee by placing him in a lineup, having the witness view him individually (a "showup"), or taking his picture and showing it to the witness (usually with the photographs of several other persons in a "photographic lineup"). They may also require the arrestee to provide handwriting or hair samples that can be compared with evidence the police have found at the scene of the crime. The arrest similarly facilitates questioning the arrestee at length about either the crime for which he was arrested or other crimes thought to be related (although the police may not interrogate the arrestee unless he has been advised of his rights and consents to the interrogation). Studies of investigations conducted by local police departments suggest that such additional procedures made available through the custodial control of the person of the arrestee are not utilized in the majority of felony investigations.

Step 5: The Decision to Charge. *Police Screening*. The initial decision to charge a suspect with the commission of a crime ordinarily comes with the decision of a police officer to arrest the suspect. That decision will subsequently be reviewed at the point of booking by a superior officer. If that officer concludes that

h. The arrestee's age also will be noted, and if the arrestee is subject to juvenile court jurisdiction, the arrestee will be separated from the adult arrestees, and separately processed through the juvenile justice process. The discussion that follows assumes the arrestee is subject to the criminal justice process.

the evidence clearly does not justify a charge, or that the offense can more appropriately handled through a "stationhouse adjustment" (e.g., the reconciliation of victim and assailant in the case of an intra-family assault), the arrestee will be released. Studies tracking the disposition of felony arrestees in urban communities commonly report a release rate of 4–10% at this point.

Where the arrestee is not released (the police having decided to charge), the arrestee must be brought before the magistrate within a 24 or 48 hours (see step 8), and prior to that point, the charges against the arrestee must be filed with the magistrate. It is during this period that the ongoing process of prosecutorial review of the charging decision is likely to be initiated. The character and scope of the prosecutorial screening prior to the filing of charges bears heavily on the character and scope of prosecutorial screening at subsequent stages of the process, and therefore both pre-filing screening and post-filing screening (though it occurs at later stages) are described at this point.

Pre-Filing Prosecutor Screening. Prosecutors' offices vary substantially in their approach to pre-filing review of the decision to charge. In many jurisdictions, all arrests, both for misdemeanors and felonies, will be screened, and no charges will be filed except upon approval of the prosecutor. In many others, however, particularly in urban districts, police often file charges on their own initiative for at least lower-level felonies (as well as all misdemeanors). In these districts, the initial prosecutorial screening of many felony charges occurs sometime between the first appearance and the preliminary hearing or grand jury review.

A screening prosecutor may accept the charge recommended by the police, raise or reduce that charge, request that the police obtain further evidence (which may require releasing the arrestee at this point and then rearresting him when and if that evidence is obtained), decide not to prosecute if the arrestee will participate in a diversion program,[i] or simply decide against prosecution. A prosecutorial decision not to proceed commonly is described as a "rejection," "declination" or "no-paper" decision. That decision most often is based on anticipated difficulties of proof (e.g., the evidence is insufficient, the victim is reluctance to testify, or key evidence was obtained illegally and therefore will not be admissible). However, the prosecutor may decide against proceeding, even though the evidence clearly is sufficient, because other alternatives (e.g., diversion, probation revocation as to an arrestee on probation, or prosecution in another jurisdiction) are preferable, or special circumstances render prosecution not "in the interest of justice." As might be expected from the differences among prosecutors' offices in the proportion of arrests reviewed pre-filing, and the subjective nature of many of the grounds for declining prosecution, studies reveal considerable variation from one community to another in the impact of pre-filing prosecutorial screening. Thus, a study of 13 urban prosecutorial districts found that the percentage of felony arrests that did not result in charges ranged from a low of 0% (in a jurisdiction which apparently did no pre-filing screening) to a high of 38%.

i. A diversion program offers the arrestee the opportunity to avoid conviction if he or she is willing to perform prescribed "rehabilitative steps" (e.g., making restitution to the victim, undertaking a treatment program). The diversion agreement operates, in effect, to place the arrestee on a probationary status without conviction. In many jurisdictions, this is achieved by the prosecutor promising not to file charges if the arrestee complies with the prescribed conditions. In others, charges initially are filed with the court, then held in abeyance for the period during which the arrestee is to meet the prescribed conditions, and dismissed with prejudice once the arrestee meets those conditions. If the arrestee fails to meet the prescribed conditions, the prosecution against the arrestee proceeds (with the charges filed, if that had not been done previously). Diversion tends to be used primarily with non-violent misdemeanor arrestees, but many prosecutors' offices also utilize diversion regularly for first-offense felony arrestees involved in certain types of property offenses, and some extend that use to other felony offenders under special circumstances relating to the offender or the offense.

Assuming the prosecutor decides to charge, the screening prosecutor also must assess whether the charge is set at the correct level. The prosecutor may reduce or raise the level of charge recommended by the police. In some instances, the prosecutor must also consider the potential for charging multiple separate offenses (as where the arrested person allegedly committed several separate crimes in a single criminal transaction or engaged in more than one criminal transaction). Here the prosecutor must determine whether the charging instrument should allege all offenses or simply some of the offenses (e.g., only the most serious, or only those easiest to prove). Where the prosecutor chooses to proceed on more than one charge, the law may give to the prosecutor another choice—whether to bring the charges in a single prosecution or in multiple separate prosecutions. A similar choice must be made where several people have been arrested for their participation in same crime, as each can be proceeded against separately or the group can be prosecuted jointly through a single charging instrument naming multiple defendants.

Post-Filing Prosecutorial Screening. Post-filing prosecutorial review of the charging decision is inherent in the many post-filing procedures (e.g., the preliminary hearing) that require the prosecutor to review the facts of the case. If the prosecutor should determine that the charge is not justified, a dismissal will be obtained through a *nolle prosequi* motion (noting the prosecutor's desire to relinquish prosecution), which ordinarily will be granted in a perfunctory fashion by the court. Similarly, if the prosecutor considers the charge to be too high, a motion can be entered to reduce the charges. In deciding whether to make such motions, the prosecutor will look to basically the same grounds that might justify a pre-filing rejection or reduction of the charge. Even where a charge was carefully screened and approved prior to filing, post-filing review can readily lead to a contrary conclusion as circumstances change (e.g., evidence becomes unavailable) or the prosecutor learns more about the facts of the case. Of course, where the charge was not previously screened or was screened only on a skimpy arrest report, post-filing review is even more likely to lead to a decision to drop or reduce the charges.

What is the end product of the combined pre-filing screening by police and prosecutor and post-filing screening by the prosecutor? The best source on that question is a series of studies on the attrition of felony arrests. One leading study, using a dozen urban prosecutorial districts, found that those districts screened out of the criminal justice system from 31% to 46% of all felony arrests, with a jurisdictional mean of 39%. A later study, drawing information from 11 states, indicated that screening terminations (including diversions) fell in the range of 31–36% for those states as a group.

Step 6: Filing the Complaint. Assuming that the pre-charge screening results in a decision to prosecute, the next step is the filing of charges with the magistrate court. Typically, the initial charging instrument will be called a "complaint." For most offenses, the complaint will be a fairly brief document. Its basic function is to set forth concisely the allegation that the accused, at a particular time and place, committed specified acts constituting a violation of a particular criminal statute. The complaint will be signed by a "complainant," a person who swears under oath that he or she believes the factual allegations of the complaint to be true. The complainant usually will be either the victim or the investigating officer. When an officer-complainant did not observe the offense being committed, but relies on information received from the victim or other witnesses, the officer ordinarily will note that the allegations in the complaint are based on "information and belief."

With the filing of the complaint, the person accused in the complaint will have become a "defendant" in a criminal proceeding. The formal charge initiates a judicial record keeping procedure that puts the case on the docket and follows it through to its termination. Ordinarily that termination will come in a dismissal, a conviction, or an acquittal. However, some cases will either be transferred to an "inactive" docket, or dismissed with the prosecution specifically given authority to later reinstate the charge. These are the cases in which the defendant is "unavailable"—usually because he has absconded, but occasionally because he is incarcerated outside the jurisdiction. The portion of the docket handled in this fashion depends in part on how long a state is willing to wait for the apprehension of a defendant before the charge against him will be "written off" as a disposition. In some jurisdictions, this portion will exceed 10% of the annual dispositions, while in others, it may not even amount to 1%.

Step 7: Magistrate Review of the Arrest. Following the filing of the complaint and prior to or at the start of the first appearance (see step 8), the magistrate must undertake what is often described as the "*Gerstein* review." As prescribed by the Supreme Court's decision in *Gerstein v. Pugh*,[j] if the accused was arrested without a warrant and remains in custody (or is subject to restraints on his liberty as a condition of stationhouse bail), the magistrate must determine that there exists probable cause for the offense charged in the complaint. This ordinarily is an *ex parte* determination, similar to that made in the issuance of an arrest warrant and relying on the same sources of information (see step 2). If the magistrate finds that probable cause has not been established, she will direct the prosecution to promptly produce more information or release the arrested person. Such instances are exceedingly rare, however. Since a judicial probable cause determination already has been made where an arrest warrant was issued, a *Gerstein* review is not required in such cases (or in case in which the arrestee was indicted by a grand jury prior to his arrest).

Step 8: The First Appearance. Once the complaint is filed, the case is before the magistrate court, and the accused must appear before the court within a specified period. This appearance of the accused is usually described as the "first appearance," although the terminology varies, with jurisdictions also using "preliminary appearance," "initial presentment," "preliminary arraignment," "arraignment on the warrant," and "arraignment on the complaint." The timing of the first appearance varies with the custodial status of the accused. Where the accused was not taken into custody, but was released on issuance of a citation (see step 2) or stationhouse bail (see step 3), there is likely to be a gap of at least several days between that release and the first appearance date. Where the arrestee has been held in police custody (the usual situation for a felony arrestee), he must be brought before the magistrate for a first appearance in a fairly prompt fashion. Ordinarily, the time consumed in booking, transportation, limited post-arrest investigation, reviewing the decision to charge, and preparing and filing the complaint makes it unlikely that the arrestee will be presented before the magistrate court until at least several hours after his arrest. Thus, if the magistrate court does not have an evening session, a person arrested in the afternoon or evening will not be presented before the magistrate court until the next day. Many jurisdictions do not allow much longer detention than this, as they impose a 24 hour limit on pre-appearance detention, requiring both the filing of the complaint and the presentation of the detained arrestee within that period. Others, desiring to limit weekend sessions of the court, allow up to 48 hours of pre-appearance detention.

The first appearance often is a quite brief proceeding. Initially, the magistrate will make certain that the person before her is the person named in the complaint. The magistrate then will inform the defendant of the charge in the complaint and

j. Discussed at p. 326 of *Modern* and *Basic*, and Note 1, p. 1034 of *Modern* and *Advanced*.

will note various rights that the defendant may have in further proceedings. The range of rights mentioned will vary from one jurisdiction to another. Commonly, the magistrate will inform the defendant of his right to remain silent and warn him that anything he says in court or to the police may be used against him at trial. The defendant also will be informed of the next stage in the proceeding, but that varies with the jurisdiction and the level of the offense. In most jurisdictions, as to felony offenses, the next stage is the preliminary hearing, and the magistrate will so inform the defendant and set a date for the hearing unless the defendant desires to waive it.

Where the felony defendant is not represented by counsel at the first appearance, the magistrate will inform defendant of his right to be represented by retained counsel, and, if indigent, his right to court appointed counsel. Typically, the magistrate will also ask the defendant if he is indigent and desires the appointment of counsel, and if the defendant responds affirmatively, the magistrate (or the magistrate's staff) will subsequently determine whether the defendant is actually unable to afford retained counsel, and initiate the appointment process for defendants found to be indigent.

Appointed counsel will be required for a substantial percentage of all felony defendants. A sampling of felony defendants in the nation's 75 largest counties indicated that approximately 80% received court appointed counsel. Three basic systems are used to provide counsel for indigent defendants. In counties containing roughly 70% of the country's population, counsel is provided primarily through a state or county public defender service. In counties containing roughly 25% of the population, reliance is placed primarily upon an assigned counsel system. Here, appointed attorneys are selected from a list of available private attorneys, either on an ad hoc basis (with individual judges choosing attorneys as they please) or through a coordinated selection system (with selection by a single administrator according to established guidelines). A smaller group of counties, containing less than 10% of the population, rely primarily upon contract systems under which a private law firm, a group of private practitioners, or a nonprofit organization (such as a bar association) contracts to provide annually representation for the bulk of all indigent defendants.

One of the most important first-appearance functions of the magistrate is to set bail (i.e., the conditions under which the defendant can obtain his release from custody pending the final disposition of the charges against him). At one time, bail was limited almost entirely to the posting of cash or a secured bond purchased from a professional bondsman. Today, those are only two of several alternatives available to the magistrate. Others are: (1) release upon a promise to appear (release on "personal recognizance"); (2) release on making a personal promise to forfeit a specified dollar amount upon a failure to appear (an "unsecured" personal bond); (3) release upon the imposition of one or more nonfinancial conditions (e.g., restrictions on defendant's associations or travel); and (4) the posting with the court of a percentage of the bail forfeiture amount (commonly 10%), which will be returned to the defendant if he appears as scheduled. In a few states, the 10% alternative has basically replaced the secured bond, resulting in the elimination of professional bondsmen.

If the accused is unable to meet the conditions deemed needed to assure his appearance (e.g., unable to post the required bond), he will remain in custody (in a jail) pending final disposition of the charges against him. Also, roughly half of the fifty-two jurisdictions allow for preventive detention—a procedure under which the magistrate orders that the accused be detained, without setting bail conditions, upon a determination that the accused, if released, will pose a significant danger to the community (e.g., though the commission of a crime or violence) or is highly likely to flee. The combination of unmet bail conditions and preventive detention may result in a significant portion of all felony defendants remaining in custody. Thus, a study of the nation's 75 largest counties found that 37% of all felony defendants were detained until the final disposition of their charges, and that percentage rose to 50% or above for those charged with rape and robbery. As for the defendants who were released, more were released on non-financial conditions than on financial conditions. The group released did not necessarily remain free on bail pending trial; a non-appearance rate of 25% and a rearrest rate of 14% for new offenses led to revocation of bail for a significant number. Also, at the end of a year, 8% of those released were unapprehended fugitives.

Step 9: Preliminary Hearing. Following the first appearance, the next scheduled step in a felony case ordinarily is the preliminary hearing (sometimes called a preliminary "examination"). All but a few of our fifty-two jurisdictions grant the felony defendant a right to a preliminary hearing, to be held within a specified period (typically, within a week or two if the defendant does not gain pretrial release and within a few weeks if released). This hardly means, however, that the preliminary hearing will be held in almost all or even most cases. Initially, the critical stage for post-arrest prosecutorial screening of charges (see step 5) is in the period prior to the scheduled preliminary hearing, and a prosecution can readily dismiss 15–30% of the felony cases before the scheduled hearing (the higher percentage coming in those jurisdictions in which there is little or no pre-filing screening). Where the charges are not dismissed, two additional decisions—one by the prosecutor and one by the defense—can sharply reduce the number of preliminary hearings.

First, in almost all jurisdictions, if the prosecutor obtains a grand jury indictment prior to the scheduled preliminary hearing, the preliminary hearing will not be held, as the grand jury's finding of probable cause has rendered irrelevant any contrary finding that the magistrate might make at the preliminary hearing. Prosecutorial bypassing of the preliminary hearing by immediately obtaining a grand jury indictment occurs with great frequency in many prosecutorial districts, particularly those that regularly prosecute by grand jury indictment (see step 10 infra). Second, even where the preliminary hearing is made available to the defendant, there nonetheless may not be a preliminary hearing because the defendant prefers to waive the hearing and move directly to the trial court. That is often the strategy employed where the defendant intends to plead guilty.

Where the preliminary hearing is held, it will provide, like grand jury review, a screening of the decision to charge by a neutral body. In the preliminary hearing, that neutral body is the magistrate, who must determine whether, on the evidence presented, there is probable cause to believe that defendant committed the crime charged. Ordinarily, the magistrate will already have determined that probable cause exists as part of the *ex parte* screening of the complaint (see step 7). The preliminary hearing, however, provides screening in an adversary proceeding in which both sides are represented by counsel. Jurisdictions vary in the evidentiary rules applicable to the preliminary hearing, but most require that the parties rely primarily on live witnesses rather than affidavits. Typically, the prosecution will present its key witnesses and the defense will limit its response to the cross-examination of those witnesses. The defendant has the right to present his own evidence at the hearing, but traditional defense strategy advises against subjecting defense witnesses to prosecution cross-examination in any pretrial proceeding.

If the magistrate concludes that the evidence presented establishes probable cause, she will "bind the case over" to the next stage in the proceedings. In an indictment jurisdiction (see step 10), the case is bound over to the grand jury, and in a jurisdiction that permits the direct filing of an information (see step 11), the case is bound over directly to the general trial court. If the magistrate finds that the probable cause supports only a misdemeanor charge, she will reject the felony charge and allow the prosecutor to substitute the lower charge, which will then be set for trial in the magistrate court. If the magistrate finds that the prosecution's evidence does not support any charge, she will order that the defendant be released. The rate of dismissals at the preliminary hearing quite naturally varies with the degree of previous screening exercised by the prosecutor. In a jurisdiction with fairly extensive screening, the percentage of dismissals is likely to fall in the range of 5–10% of the cases heard. However, other jurisdictions (usually those in which hearings are more sparingly utilized) report a much higher dismissal rate. In either type of jurisdiction, the preliminary hearing dismissal is likely to account for the disposition of less than 5% of all felony complaints.

Step 10: Grand Jury Review. Although almost all American jurisdictions still have provisions authorizing grand jury screening of felony charges, such screening is mandatory only in those jurisdictions requiring felony prosecutions to be instituted by an indictment, a charging instrument issued by the grand jury. In a majority of the states, the prosecution is now allowed to proceed either by grand jury indictment or by information at its option. Because prosecutors in these states most often choose to prosecute by information, the states providing this option commonly are referred to as "information" states. Eighteen states, the federal system, and the District of Columbia currently require grand jury indictments for all felony prosecutions. These jurisdictions commonly are described as "indictment" jurisdictions. Four additional states are "limited indictment" jurisdictions, requiring prosecution by indictment only for their most severely punished offenses (capital, life imprisonment, or both). Apart possibly from capital offenses, the defendant may waive the right to be proceeded against by indictment, thereby allowing the prosecution to proceed by information. Waiver rates vary from one jurisdiction to another but waivers are likely to be made by at least 10% of all felony defendants.

The grand jury typically is selected randomly from the same pool of prospective jurors (the venire) as to the trial jury, but it sits not for a single case, but for a term that may range from one to several months. As in the case of the magistrate at the preliminary hearing, the primary function of the grand jury is to determine whether there is sufficient evidence to justify a trial on the charge sought by the prosecution. The grand jury, however, participates in a screening process quite different from the preliminary hearing. It meets in a closed session and hears only the evidence presented by the prosecution. The defendant has no right to offer his own evidence or to be present during grand jury proceedings. If there was a prior preliminary hearing, the grand jury is in no way bound by the ruling on probable cause at that hearing. The grand jury may indict even though the magistrate dismissed the charge at the preliminary hearing, and may refuse to indict even though the magistrate bound over to the grand jury.

If a majority of the grand jurors conclude that the prosecution's evidence is sufficient, the grand jury will issue the indictment requested by the prosecutor. The indictment will set forth a brief description of the offense charged, and the grand jury's approval of that charge will be indicated by its designation of the indictment as a "true bill." If the grand jury majority refuses to approve a proposed indictment, the charges against the defendant will be dismissed. Indictment jurisdictions vary in the percentage of cases in which grand jurors do not indict, although typically that percentage is quite low (e.g., 2–5%).

Step 11: The Filing of the Indictment or Information. If an indictment is issued, it will be filed with the general trial court and will replace the complaint as the accusatory instrument in the case. Where grand jury review either is not required or has been waived, an information will be filed with the trial court. Like the indictment, the information is a charging instrument which replaces the complaint, but it is issued by the prosecutor rather than the grand jury. In most information states, the charge in the information must be supported by a preliminary hearing bindover (unless the preliminary hearing was waived).

Step 12: Arraignment on the Information or Indictment. After the indictment or information has been filed, the defendant is arraigned—i.e., he is brought before the trial court, informed of the charges against him, and asked to enter a plea of guilty, not guilty, or, as is permitted under some circumstances, *nolo contendere*. In the end, most of those felony defendants whose cases reach the trial court will plead guilty. At the arraignment, however, they are likely to enter a plea of not guilty. Where there has not been a preliminary hearing, defense counsel probably will not be fully apprized of the strength of the prosecution's case at this point in the proceedings. Also, in most jurisdictions, guilty pleas in felony cases are the product of plea negotiations with the prosecution, and in many places, that process does not start until after the arraignment. When the defendant enters a plea of not guilty at the arraignment, the judge will set a trial date, but the expectation generally is that the trial will not be held.

Between the arraignment and the scheduled trial date, three possible dispositions can result in the termination of the case without trial. Although there will have been extensive prosecutorial screening by this point, changed circumstances and new information typically will lead to dismissals on a prosecutor's *nolle prosequi* motion in roughly 5–15% of the cases. A smaller percentage of the informations or indictments will be dismissed on motion of the defense, as discussed in step 13. The vast majority of the dispositions without trial will be the product of guilty pleas. General trial courts (particularly in urban judicial districts) regularly report a guilty plea rate within the range of 60–85% for felony defendants.

Step 13: Pretrial Motions. In most jurisdictions, a broad range of objections must be raised by a pretrial motion. Those motions commonly present challenges to the institution of the prosecution (e.g., claims regarding the grand jury indictment process), attacks upon the sufficiency of the charging instrument, challenges to the scope, location, and timing of the prosecution (claiming improper joinder of charges or parties, improper venue, or violation of speedy trial requirements), requests for discovery when there is a dispute over what is discoverable,[k] and requests for the suppression of evidence allegedly obtained through a constitutional violation. While some pretrial motions are made only by defendants who intend to go to trial, other motions (e.g., for discovery) may benefit as well defendants who expect in the end to plead guilty. Nevertheless, pretrial motions are likely to be made in only a small portion of the felony cases that reach the trial court. Their use does vary considerably, however, with the nature of the case. In narcotics cases, for example, motions to suppress are quite common. In the typical forgery case, on the other, pretrial motions of any type are quite rare. As a group, pretrial motions are highly unlikely to produce the dismissal of more than 5% of the cases before the general trial court, and commonly will not even reach a 2% dismissal rate.

Step 14: Plea Negotiation and Acceptance. As previously noted, a substantial majority of the felony prosecutions reaching the general trial court will end in a plea of guilty. Those guilty pleas commonly will be the product of a plea agreement under which the prosecution offers certain concessions in return for the defendant's entry of the plea. The concession is likely to take the form of a

k. Discovery is a process whereby the prosecution discloses to the defense some or all of the evidence it intends to use at trial and certain other evidence within its possession or control that may be useful to the defense. Jurisdictions vary considerable as to the range of discovery that the prosecution must provide. They generally require the defense to reciprocate by providing somewhat narrower discovery to the prosecution.

reduction of the charges (sometimes to a misdemeanor and sometimes to a lesser felony charge), a dismissal of related charges where the defendant faces multiple charges, a recommendation on sentence, or a specific reduced sentence (when also agreed to by the trial court). Prosecutors' offices vary in the concessions they offer and their willingness to bargain over concessions (as opposed to presenting a take-it-or-leave-it offer). Prosecutors also vary as to the types of cases in which they will offer concessions, with some generally refusing to do so where the defendant faces serious charges or has a lengthy record of prior convictions. Indeed, there are jurisdictions in which prosecutors will not plea bargain, although defendants here may still find an inducement to plead guilty in a general policy of trial judges to give favorable weight in sentencing to the defendant's willingness to plead guilty.

Guilty pleas must be reviewed by the trial court prior to their acceptance. The focus here is on ensuring that the defendant is aware of the consequence of entering a guilty plea and understands the terms of the plea bargain. In some instances, the defendant may enter a *nolo contendre* plea, which states that the defendant does not desire to contest his guilty (though not admitting that guilt). Here too, the court must determine that the plea is made voluntarily and intelligently, but even then, it may refuse to accept the plea if it concludes that such a plea is not in the interest of justice. Following the acceptance of a guilty plea or a nolo contendre plea, the court sets a date for sentencing.

Step 15: The Trial. Assuming that there has not been a dismissal and the defendant has not entered a guilty plea (or a *nolo contendere* plea), the next step in the criminal process is the trial. In most respects, the criminal trial resembles the civil trial. There are, however, several distinguishing features that are either unique to criminal trials or of special importance in such trials. These include (1) the presumption of defendant's innocence, (2) the requirement of proof beyond a reasonable doubt, (3) the right of the defendant not to take the stand, (4) the exclusion of evidence obtained by the state in an illegal manner, and (5) the more frequent use (by the prosecution) of incriminating statements previously made by the defendant (often to police).

As noted previously, most felony cases are likely to be disposed of either by a guilty plea or by a dismissal. Typically, no more than 15% of the felony prosecutions reaching the general trial court will be resolved by a trial—although there are some exceptional jurisdictions in which the percentage is over 30%. Setting aside dismissals, and looking only to guilty pleas and trials, the ratio of guilty pleas to trials in the general trial court typically will exceed ten to one.

The median time frame from the arrest of the defendant to the start of the felony trial can exceed a year in judicial districts with slow moving dockets, but for most judicial districts, it is likely to fall within the range of 5–8 months. The median will be influenced, in particular, by the mix of jury and bench trials, as the time frame tends to be considerably longer for jury trials. While most jurisdictions have speedy trial requirements that impose time limits of 6 months or less, there are various excludable time periods (for factors such as witness unavailability and the processing of motions) which commonly extend the time limit by at least a few months.

In all fifty-two jurisdictions, the defendant will have a right to a jury trial for all felony offenses (in contrast to misdemeanor trials, where some jurisdictions do not provide juries for those misdemeanors punishable by incarceration for no more than six months). Juries traditionally were composed of twelve persons, but several states use smaller juries (e.g., six persons) in non-capital felony cases. Prospective jurors are selected randomly from a pool of persons typically based on the voter registration list (and often some other list, such as the licensed driver list) for the geographical area constituting the judicial district. The prospective jurors called to jury service from this pool (the venire) are then randomly divided into panels for service on particular juries and seated on that jury only after being questioned by counsel as to their attitudes and background (*voir dire* questioning). Counsel may exclude particular panel members on a challenge for cause (showing the prospective juror is biased or otherwise not eligible for service) or on a peremptory challenge (limited in number and requiring automatic disqualification without a statement of reasons).

Of course, the right to a jury trial can be waived, and in most jurisdictions, a significant number of defendants will waive the jury in favor of a bench trial. Over the country as a whole, roughly 70% of all felony trials are tried to a jury, but in various individual judicial districts, as well as several states, bench trials actually outnumber jury trials. In all but a few jurisdictions, the jury verdict, whether for acquittal or conviction, must be unanimous. Where the jurors cannot agree, no verdict is entered and the case may be retried. For most communities, such "hung juries" occur in only a very small percentage of all jury trials (e.g., 3–6%), but there are large urban districts in which juries cannot reach a verdict in as many as 10–15% of all felony jury trials.

In state courts, most jury trials will be completed within 2–3 days. A key variable in setting the length of the trial is the type case, as certain types of offenses (e.g., white collar offenses and capital homicide cases) produce trials substantially longer than the typical felony. This explains in part why trials lasting a week or more are so common in the federal courts. In general, trials to the bench are considerably shorter, and in state courts, unlikely to last more than a day.

Whether a criminal case is tried to the bench or the jury, the odds favor conviction over acquittal. A fairly typical ratio for felony charges will be 3 convictions for every acquittal. That ratio may vary significantly, however, with the nature of the offense. In some jurisdictions, the rate of conviction at trial tends to be substantially lower (though still well above 50%) for some crimes (e.g., rape) than for others (e.g., drug trafficking).

With the end of the trial stage, the criminal justice process will have produced a disposition as to all persons who originally entered the process through an arrest or the issuance of citation. Studies of large urban districts suggest the following pattern of outcomes for felony arrestees. Only one out of a hundred will have had the case against him carried through to a trial that resulted in an acquittal. A much larger portion of the felony arrestees, anywhere from 30–50%, also will not have been convicted, but the dispositions in their favor will have come before the filing of the complaint, through pre-charge police and prosecutor screening, or after filing through *nolle prosequi* motions or judicial and grand jury screening procedures. Of the 50–70% of the felony arrestees who will have been convicted, many will not have been convicted of felonies. Depending upon the plea negotiation practices followed in the particular jurisdiction, anywhere from 10–30% of those felony arrestees convicted are likely to be convicted of misdemeanors.

Step 16: Sentencing. Following conviction, the next step in the process is the determination of the sentence. In all but a handful of jurisdictions (which allow for jury sentencing, even apart from capital punishment), the sentence determination is the function of the court. Basically three different types of sentences may be used: financial sanctions (e.g., fines, restitution orders); some form of release into the community (e.g., probation, unsupervised release, house arrest); and incarceration in a jail (for lesser sentences) or prison (for longer sentences). The process applied in determining the sentence is shaped in considerable part by the sentencing options made available to the court by the legislature.

For a particular offense, the court may have no choice. The legislature may have prescribed that conviction automatically carries with it a certain sentence and there is nothing left for the court to do except impose that sentence. Most frequently, however, legislative narrowing of options on a particular offense does not go beyond eliminating the community release option (by requiring incarceration) and setting maximums (and sometimes mandatory minimums) for incarceration and fines. However, states vary considerably in shaping the court's authority to choose within available options, particularly as to the length of incarceration. Their approaches include: allowing the sentencing judge considerable discretion within a broad range set by the legislature; narrowing the range and the discretion by imposing certain mandated minimums based on specified factual findings, and channeling discretion through the use of sentencing guidelines that also depend upon factual determinations.

The process utilized in felony sentencing varies to some extent according to whether judicial discretion is broad or is channeled or limited by guideline or legislative reference to specific sentencing circumstances. In all jurisdictions, the process is designed to obtain for the court information beyond that which will have come to its attention in the course of trial or in the acceptance of a guilty plea. The primary vehicle here is the presentence report prepared by the probation department, although the prosecution and defense commonly will be allowed to present additional information and to challenge the information contained in the presentence report. The presentation of this information is not subject to the rules governing the presentation of information at trial. The rules of evidence do not apply, and neither the prosecution nor the defense has a right to call witnesses or to cross-examine the sources of adverse information presented in the presentence report or in any additional documentation presented by the opposing side. However, where the sentencing authority of the judge is restricted or channeled by reference to specific factors, a judge commonly is required to make findings of fact as to those factors. Here, if relevant facts are in dispute, the court commonly will find it necessary to hold an evidentiary hearing and to utilize trial-type procedures to resolve that dispute.

***Step 17*: *Appeals*.**[a] For criminal convictions imposed by the general trial court, the initial appeal is to the intermediate appellate court. If the state has no intermediate appellate court, then the initial and final appeal within the state system is to the state's court of last resort. Although all convicted defendants are entitled to appeal their convictions, appeals are taken predominantly by convicted defendants who were sentenced to imprisonment. Imprisoned defendants convicted pursuant to a guilty plea are included in this group, but their portion of all appeals depends in large part on the jurisdiction's sentencing law. Though the trial court's acceptance of a guilty plea may be challenged on appeal, such appellate challenges are limited to exceptional cases, so that appeals by guilty plea defendants tend to be sentencing challenges. In jurisdictions permitting such challenges, challenges to the sentence alone can constitute a substantial portion (e.g., 15–30%) of all felony conviction appeals, and many of those are by guilty plea defendants.

Appeals challenging the conviction itself come primarily from imprisoned defendants who are seeking review of a trial conviction. Indeed, in some jurisdictions, as many as 90% of the defendants who were convicted after trial and sentenced to prison will appeal their convictions. Even with almost automatic

a. The focus here is on defense appeals from a conviction. The prosecution may appeal from certain types of dismissals, but may not appeal from an acquittal. Since the percentage of dismissals over the objection of the prosecution is low, and prosecutors do not regularly appeal such rulings (even when they could do so), prosecution appeals are infrequent as compared to defense appeals.

appeal by this group, however, because of the heavy rate of guilty pleas, the total number of appeals to the intermediate appeals court may readily amount to less than 10% of all felony convictions. State intermediate appellate courts commonly have a reversal rate on defense appeals of right in the 5–10% range, although those rates will be somewhat higher when reversals in part are included. Courts of last resort, with discretionary jurisdiction, tend to have a substantially higher rate of reversals than the intermediate appellate courts, as they grant review in cases presenting close questions.

Step 18*: *Collateral Remedies. After the appellate process is exhausted, imprisoned defendants may be able to use postconviction remedies to challenge their convictions on limited grounds. In particular, federal postconviction remedies are available to state as well as federal prisoners to challenge their convictions in the federal courts on most constitutional grounds. In the year 2000, the federal district courts received roughly 21,000 state-prisoner postconviction applications. Relief is granted on less than three percent of these petitions, however, and the relief often is limited to requiring a further hearing. In the state system, annual postconviction challenges typically fall below 5% of all felony filings.

SECTION 3. DIVERSITY IN LEGAL REGULATION

1. *Fifty-two lawmaking jurisdictions*. Under the American version of federalism, each of the fifty state governments retains the authority to enact its own criminal code, applicable within the territorial reach of its legislative powers. Each state also retains the power to provide for the enforcement of that criminal code through agencies and procedures that it creates. That authority has been used in each state to establish what is basically a single, general criminal justice process applicable throughout the state (with some variations, as discussed in note 7 infra). Congress has added to these fifty state criminal justice processes its two distinct federal criminal justice processes. First, it has created a separate criminal justice process for the District of Columbia, used to enforce a separate criminal code that applies only in the District. Second, it has created a criminal justice process for the enforcement of the general federal criminal code, which applies throughout the country. This process utilizes the national law enforcement agencies and relies on prosecutions brought in the federal district courts.

In many fields in which both state and federal governments exercise regulatory authority, the enforcement of federal law by federal officials so clearly dominates the field that law school courses focus almost exclusively on the federal enforcement system. A similar focus would be most inappropriate in the field of criminal procedure. While the federal criminal justice system may be the most prominent of the nation's fifty-two criminal justice systems, the traditional statistical measures of criminal justice systems rank it simply as one of the larger, but hardly the largest, of our fifty-two systems. Moreover, when the federal system is compared to the state systems as a group, the combined state systems clearly dominate, as they account for a much larger portion of the nation's criminal justice workload (e.g., roughly 97% of all felony prosecutions and over 99% of all misdemeanor prosecutions). Thus, the study of the law governing the criminal justice process must take account of the laws regulating the 50 state criminal justice processes as well as the two federal processes.

2. *The unifying role of federal constitutional regulation*. Taking account of fifty-two different criminal justice systems would be a less daunting task if the fifty-two jurisdictions were subject to a single source of law that mandated an exclusive, comprehensive regulation of the process in all fifty-two jurisdictions. There is, however, no such law. The regulation provided by the federal constitution (as interpreted by the Supreme Court) does, however, provide a common foundation that significantly shapes major portions of the process in all fifty-two jurisdictions.

The Bill of Rights of the Federal Constitution includes a large number of guarantees dealing specifically with the criminal justice process—all the guarantees of the Fourth, Sixth, and Eighth Amendments, and with the inclusion of the Fifth Amendment's due process clause (which clearly applies to criminal proceedings, although extending also to certain non-criminal proceedings), all but one of the guarantees (the just compensation guarantee) of the Fifth Amendment. As discussed in Chapter Two, these provisions bear upon the state criminal justice processes as well as the federal. Applying a "selective incorporation" reading of the Fourteenth Amendment's due process clause (which explicitly governs state governmental activities), the Court has concluded that almost all of these criminal-process Bill of Rights guarantees are fully applicable to the state criminal justice processes (the one notable exception being the grand jury clause of the Fifth Amendment, see fn. c, p. 29. The Supreme Court also has held that the due process clauses of the Fifth and Fourteenth Amendment have an independent content, extending beyond the guarantees specifically directed at the criminal process, and imposing further regulatory limits upon the state and federal criminal justice processes.

In light of their scope and their applicability to all fifty-two jurisdictions, the incorporated constitutional guarantees constitute the traditional starting point for describing the law regulating the criminal justice processes of the United States. All fifty-two jurisdictions must, at a minimum, meet the requirements of these guarantees (as interpreted by the Supreme Court). Constitutional regulation, however, is neither comprehensive nor exclusive. Initially, constitutional regulation does not govern all aspects of the criminal justice process. As to many steps in the process, constitutional regulation is limited to only a few aspects of the applicable procedures. Secondly, even where the constitutional regulation is comprehensive, the states remain free to go beyond the constitutionally mandated minimum and impose more rigorous safeguards.

The significance of federal constitutional regulation varies with the different stages of the criminal justice process. Three models provide a rough picture of that variation. First, as to some procedures (e.g., the preliminary hearing), the Constitution says very little. Here, legal regulation comes primarily from the laws of the individual jurisdiction. Second, as to other procedures, such as searches, the constitutional regulation is so comprehensive as to rival the Internal Revenue Code in its detail and complexity. Here, constitutional standards tend to dominate. Some jurisdictions may add more rigorous standards, and many may add their own requirements as to minor aspects of administration, but the constitutional standards constitute the critical legal standards for most of the country as to the basic regulation of the particular procedure. Finally, for still other elements of the process, such as the jury trial, the federal constitution provides a substantial, though not comprehensive, set of regulations. Here, it is not uncommon for a fairly large group of states to impose more rigorous standards under state law, and almost all will look to state law to cover important features that are not treated by the constitutional standards.

Our discussion of a particular step in the process will always start by considering applicable federal constitutional requirements (if any). When our coverage concentrates entirely on the constitutional standards, as set forth by the Supreme Court, it can be assumed that the first model prevails, i.e., the number of jurisdictions that add substantial requirements of their own is fairly small, and for the vast majority of the fifty-two jurisdictions, the federal constitutional standards provide the basic legal regulation. Where the constitution provides very little direction, or many jurisdictions establish standards more rigorous than the constitutional standard, our discussion will go beyond the constitutional standards and consider the general patterns of regulation under the laws of the fifty-two jurisdictions (as discussed in Note 4 infra).[a]

3. ***Natural divergence.*** With each jurisdiction regulating through its own laws, some degree of diversity is almost inevitable. The English common law provided a common starting point for the criminal justice systems of the original states and the federal system, and continues to provide an element of commonality even to this day. However, as the common law concepts have been adjusted to accommodate new developments in the administrative structure of the process (such as the creation of police departments), and as the process has been reshaped to accommodate new concerns, various factors have led the different jurisdictions to take diverse approaches on common issues. Four factors, in particular, point toward different states adopting somewhat different legal regulations: (1) criminal procedure is not one of those areas of lawmaking in which a need for reciprocity or the interaction of transactions forces the states to seek uniformity; a lack of uniformity in the criminal justice processes of adjoining states is not likely to be a deterrent to the free flow of goods, services, or persons between the states or to restrain economic development within the state; (2) the criminal justice process must be shaped in light of the state's administrative environment, including the demography of the population, the resources available to the process, and the structure of the institutions responsible for the administration of the process (particularly police, prosecutor, and judiciary); states vary considerably as to that administrative environment, particularly as to states that are largely urban and largely rural and as to different regions of the country; (3) criminal process issues tend to be issues of high visibility and, often, high emotional content, leading to lawmaking decisions (at least legislative lawmaking decisions[b]) that are influenced more by symbolic politics (which tend to vary with the ideological assumptions of the local constituency) than the views of those with presumed technical expertise; and (4) the integrated character of the criminal justice means that a divergence between states in their laws governing one part of the process most likely will necessitate further differences at other stages of the process.

4. ***Describing common patterns.*** The laws of the fifty-two jurisdictions are most likely to vary where (1) federal constitutional regulation is not comprehensive and detailed, and (2) the particular procedure was either unknown at common law or was substantially modified as a result of institutional, and process changes not anticipated by the common law. Even here, however, if the focus is on the basic structure of the regulation, and not upon administrative refinements, the legal regulations applicable in the vast majority of the fifty-two jurisdictions

a. While federal statutes regulating criminal procedure generally apply only to the federal system, Congress in a few instances has utilized its regulatory authority (e.g., its authority over interstate commerce) to prescribe criminal process standards that govern in both the federal and state systems. The prime example is the federal law governing wiretapping and other forms of electronic surveillance. Where such a statute is applicable, our discussion focuses on that federal statute rather than the laws of the states.

b. Legislative lawmaking plays a critical role in the field of criminal procedure as many states have detailed statutory codes of criminal procedure. Judicial lawmaking through the common law development of procedural requirements, once the most common form of criminal process lawmaking, is now fairly rare. See CRIMPROC § 1.6(h). Judicial lawmaking occurs primarily in the adoption of court rules, although in several states (as in the federal system), court rules go into effect only if accepted by the legislature. Id. at § 1.6(f). Courts also may be viewed as engaged in lawmaking in their interpretations of constitutions, statutes, and court rules.

While commentators generally agree that symbolic politics drives legislative lawmaking in the criminal justice field, most would not extend that characterization to judicial lawmaking. Many would, however, point to the value judgments of the judges as driving judicial lawmaking and that factor would similarly produce divergence in shaping the law.

usually can be characterized as following one or the other of two or three alternative approaches. We will not attempt in this single volume to go beyond describing these basic patterns that differentiate one major grouping from another. It should be kept in mind, however, that there will almost always be a few jurisdictions that take an entirely different approach. So too, jurisdictions described as following the same general approach commonly will present some variation in their implementation of that approach; a description of that approach as applied in a particular jurisdiction cannot be carried over in its entirety to all other jurisdictions adopting the same basic approach.

5. ***Models.*** Very often a basic pattern followed by a substantial grouping of jurisdiction is the product of states emulating reforms adopted in a particular jurisdiction. The federal law of criminal procedure is undoubtedly the most important model in this regard. Not withstanding the significant distinction in the role and institutions of the federal systems,[c] as to almost every aspect of the criminal justice process, a grouping of states, ranging from a handful to a majority, have adopted the basic features of the nonconstitutional law of the federal system. Thus, the discussion of that federal law in later chapters is presented not only to describe the law of the federal system, but also the law of a fair number of states.

The Federal Rules of Criminal Procedure provide the most prominent illustration of the influence of the "federal model." Roughly half of the states have court rules or statutory codes that borrow heavily from the Federal Rules (set forth in Appendix C of the Supplement to this book). Similarly, prominent federal legislative reforms, such as the Bail Reform Acts of 1966 and 1984 and the Speedy Trial Act of 1968 (set forth in Appendix B) have served as models for various states (although the state versions typically will depart from one or more of the provisions of such federal statutes).

The American Bar Association's *Standards for Criminal Justice* provide another important model. Now in their third edition, the *A.B.A. Standards* have been cited thousands of times by appellate courts and have been followed by numerous states in formulating their court rules and statutes. Unlike the Federal Rules, however, the *A.B.A. Standards* have been incorporated into state law on a piecemeal basis, with the state reforms typically looking either to an individual standard or a grouping of standards dealing with a particular aspect of the process (e.g., pretrial discovery). Accordingly, the Standards are not included in Appendix B, but are cited (and quoted) in the text discussion of those topics on which they have been especially influential.

6. ***Procedural subsets.*** Even within a single jurisdiction the law governing the criminal justice process will not be the same for each and every case. All fifty-two jurisdictions utilize at least a few lines of division that produce procedural subsets (i.e., different classes of cases governed by different procedural standards). The most common is the line drawn between felonies and misdemeanors (see fn.b, p. 3). All jurisdictions distinguish between felonies and misdemeanor as to some procedure. Indeed, some states add an additional subset for certain procedures by drawing a distinction between lower level misdemeanors (e.g., punishable by 90 days in jail or less) and higher level misdemeanors (which then may or may not be

c. These distinctions include: (1) the federal criminal justice process is applied to a narrower range of offenses than the state systems (concentrating on felony offenses, with an emphasis on regulatory offenses and white collar crimes far beyond that found any state system); (2) federal enforcement agencies are far less fragmented and generally do not carry the broad range of responsibilities borne by local police agencies (which are responsible for various social service and order maintenance functions as well as investigative functions); and (3) federal prosecutors and courts generally carry far lighter caseloads than their state counterparts. See also CRIMPROC § 1.2 (f) (noting further distinctions).

treated in the same manner as felonies). We will always take note of federal constitutional distinctions drawn between misdemeanors and felonies (or certain types of misdemeanors and more serious charges). As to distinctions drawn by state law, however, only the most significant differences in the treatment of misdemeanors will be cited. Our focus primarily is on describing the law applicable to felony prosecutions.

A similar approach will be taken as to state laws creating another procedural subset based on penalty—the distinction drawn, as to various procedures, between felonies subject to capital punishment (limited to certain types of murder) and all other felonies. Our focus will be on the processing of the non-capital case, although here again, distinctions drawn in constitutional regulation between capital and non-capital felonies will always be noted.

Within a single state, a variety of different agencies may provide the personnel who exercise the authority of the primary actors in the administration of the criminal justice process. Here again state law may draw procedural subsets tied to the type of official performing the particular role. Prosecutors, for example, typically are local officials (e.g., the county prosecutor), but some states also vest prosecutorial authority in the Attorney General, and in doing so, provide authority or restrictions on authority that do not apply to local prosecutors. Since such differences tend to be relatively minor, they will be ignored in our commentary (as well distinctions drawn in state law as to the authority of different types of police officers). The distinctions are not so minor as to magistrate courts (see § 2, fn. c), and here we will take account of certain major distinctions (e.g., for some types of magistrate courts, appellate review of a misdemeanor conviction will be by a trial de novo in the general trial court rather than the traditional appellate review in the trial record).

SECTION 4. DIVERSITY IN ADMINISTRATION

1. ***Significance of discretion***. Commentators commonly speak of the immense gap existing between the law of criminal procedure "on the books" and the law of criminal procedure "in action." Part of that gap is attributable to administrative deviance—that is, the failure of public administrators (particularly police, but also prosecutors, magistrates, and trial court judges) to adhere to the law in administering the process. The larger part of the gap, however, is a product of a narrow view of the "governing law," which fails to take account of discretion. As commonly defined, discretion flows from the authorization, explicit or implicit, of the law. Discretion exists where the law fails to prescribe standards and thereby either explicitly or implicitly leaves the administrator to his or her own standards. When commentators, in describing "the law," refer only to the various procedures recognized in constitutional provisions, statutes, court rules, and legal decisions, disregarding the options that are given to administrators as to the use of those procedures, they tend to characterize every failure to utilize a procedure as a departure from the "law on the books." What they are describing, however, is only a departure from the expectation that the law will mandate procedures, rather than simply authorize procedures to be used at the discretion of different participants in the process. The law of criminal procedure frequently departs from that expectation.

Discretion is a common component of almost all aspects of the criminal justice process. The law grants enforcement officials (police and prosecutor) the authority to institute certain procedures under specified conditions, but typically also grants those officials the discretion not to exercise that authority even when these conditions exist. The law authorizes, for example, the search of the arrested person incident to his arrest, but the police officer has discretion not to exercise that authority if he so chooses. On occasion, the law even grants to the enforcement official the discretion to control the procedural rights made available to a suspect or defendant (as where the prosecutor may determine whether the charges against the defendant are screened by a magistrate at a preliminary hearing or by a grand jury, see § 2, step 9).

The defendant's rights are also subject to the defendant's authority to relinquish those rights. Thus, there is no true gap between the "law" and the "practice" when most prosecutions are resolved without a trial. The law gives the defendant not only a right to a trial, but a right also to waive the trial and plead guilty. Also, the law does not prohibit the government from offering incentives to encourage such waivers.

2. ***Discretion and diversity***. When there exists a legal, normlessness or a legal norm so broad as to allow reference to personal values,[a] diversity in the exercise of authority is inevitable, as it can hardly be expected that all actors performing the same function will look to the same values exercising their discretion. Numerous studies suggest, however, that to considerable extent, the values of the individual administrator are shaped and confined by a combination of institutional influences, producing what is commonly described as the "dominant administrative culture," and it is this culture that more often than not guides the exercise of discretion. In the state systems, that culture tends to vary from one local community to another since the primary administrative units (police agencies, prosecutors' offices, and magistrate and trial courts) are either a part of local government or organized as local units of a statewide agency. A variety of factors will shape the local administrative culture, including: (1) the structure, management, and basic approach to task (the "organizational ethos") of police departments, and prosecutors' offices (and, to a lesser extent, of multi-judge courts and public defender offices); (2) the interactions of administrators (particularly the recurring interactions of prosecutor, public defender, and judge where assigned to the same courtroom); (3) the character and values of the local community, particularly as it bears upon agencies headed by (or responsive to) elected officials; and (4) the extent to which the local administration of the criminal justice process is subject to "caseload pressures" (i.e., quantitative demands that exceed the resources of the local administrative units).

With the administrative culture varying from one community to another (and where more than one agency performs the same role, variation as well within the community, depending on which agency is involved), it is not surprising that the criminal justice process, as applied, will differ in many respects even where the same legal standards govern. For example, in five different communities in a single state, the standard police response to otherwise similarly situated first offenders caught shoplifting, may be quite different: (1) in one community, the shoplifter may be sent on his way with a "warning"; (2) in another the shoplifter will be proceeded against, but released on a summons; (3) in another, the

a. Discretionary decisions are not necessarily decisions totally unregulated by the law, but decisions to which the law grants the actor sufficient leeway to look to personal value judgments. The leeway granted to the administrator tends to be broadest where the decision is not to exercise governmental power adversely to the individual (sometimes described as "ameliorative discretion"). Yet, even here, there usually are some legal limits. A prosecutor has great latitude, for example, in deciding not to prosecute, but that decision cannot be based on a bribe. Where the official exercises governmental power and the choice is between alternative procedures (e.g., the police officer's choice between taking a detained misdemeanant into custody or releasing him on issuance of a summons), the governing law tends to offer somewhat less discretionary latitude. Here the law typically will specify some general prerequisites for taking action, but then give the administrator a choice, based upon an open-ended standard, between different alternatives. Open-ended standards, such as that requiring that an action be consistent with "the interests of justice," commonly are seen as allowing for basically "discretionary" decisionmaking, though subject to judicial review.

shoplifter will be taken into custody and transported to the police station, but without being frisked or searched; (4) in another, the shoplifter will be frisked when taken into custody; and (5) in another, the shoplifter taken into custody will be searched. Moreover, the differences in approach are not likely to be limited to this initial police reaction. Where the shoplifter is proceeded against, further variations are likely to be found as to such matters as the availability of diversion, the use of plea bargains, the defense waiver of jury trial in cases that go to trial, and the exercise of sentencing discretion. In addition, while certain approaches on these issues may be "standard" for the particular community, the potential always exists for individual participants to exercise their discretion in a manner that deviates from that "standard."

Where the exercise of discretion plays a major rule in the application of a particular step in the criminal justice process, our commentary usually will offer illustrations of some alternative modes of exercising that discretion. Those illustrations come from studies which focus on the exercise of discretion in particular localities. Ordinarily, it can be assumed that something close to the same administrative environment can be found in certain other communities and the same style of discretionary decisionmaking probably prevails there as well. But it also must be kept in mind that the illustrations hardly cover the full range of possibilities, and that there are many communities in which a quite different environment and quite different use of discretion will be found.

Chapter 2

THE NATURE AND SCOPE OF FOURTEENTH AMENDMENT DUE PROCESS; RETROACTIVITY; THE FEDERAL "SUPERVISORY POWER"; STATE RIGHTS PROTECTIONS

SECTION 1. THE "ORDERED LIBERTY"—"FUNDAMENTAL FAIRNESS," "TOTAL INCORPORATION" AND "SELECTIVE INCORPORATION" THEORIES

In *Twining v. New Jersey,* 211 U.S. 78 (1908); *Palko v. Connecticut,* 302 U.S. 319 (1937); and *Adamson v. California,* 332 U.S. 46 (1947), the Court rejected the "total incorporation" view of the history of the Fourteenth Amendment, the view—which has never commanded a majority—that the Fourteenth Amendment made all of the provisions of the federal Bill of Rights fully applicable to the states.[a] But *Twining* recognized that "it is possible that some of the personal rights safeguarded by the first eight Amendments against National action may also be safeguarded against state action, because a denial of them would be a denial of due process of law." And the Court early found among the procedural

a. *Palko,* which held that the Fourteenth Amendment did not encompass at least certain aspects of double jeopardy prohibition of the Fifth Amendment, was later overruled in *Benton v. Maryland,* 395 U.S. 784 (1969). The position taken in *Twining* and *Adamson*—that the Fifth Amendment privilege against self-incrimination was not incorporated in the Fourteenth—was rejected in *Malloy v. Hogan* (1964), discussed below. *Griffin v. California,* p. 1453, subsequently applied *Malloy* to overrule the specific holdings of *Twining* and *Adamson,* which had permitted comment on a state defendant's failure to take the stand. These later decisions, while overruling *Palko, Twining* and *Adamson,* were still consistent with the rejection of the "total incorporation" interpretation.

The total incorporation position had received its strongest support in the *Adamson* dissents. In the principal dissent, Justice Black, joined by Douglas, J., maintained that the history of the Fourteenth Amendment suggested its purpose was to totally incorporate the federal Bill of Rights. Dissenting separately in *Adamson,* Justice Murphy, joined by Rutledge, J., "agree[d] that the specific guarantees of the Bill of Rights should be carried over intact into [the Fourteenth but was] not prepared to say that the latter is entirely and necessarily limited by the Bill of Rights. Occasions may arise where a proceeding falls so far short of conforming to fundamental standards of procedure as to warrant constitutional condemnation in terms of a lack of due process despite the absence of a specific provision of the Bill of Rights."

Responding to the dissents, Justice Frankfurter's concurring opinion in *Adamson* stressed the "independent potency" of the Fourteenth Amendment Due Process Clause, maintaining that that Amendment "neither comprehends the specific provisions by which the founders deemed it appropriate to restrict the federal government nor is confined to them."

requirements of Fourteenth Amendment due process certain rules paralleling provisions of the first eight amendments. For example, it held in *Powell v. Alabama* (1932) (discussed at pp. 82, 86) that defendants in a capital case were denied due process when a state refused them the aid of counsel. "The logically critical thing, however," pointed out Justice Harlan years later, "was not that the rights had been found in the Bill of Rights, but that they were deemed [to] be fundamental." *Duncan v. Louisiana,* p. 1379 (dissenting opinion joined by Stewart, J.).

Particular procedural safeguards included in the Bill of Rights were said to be applicable to the states if they were "implicit in the concept of ordered liberty," Cardozo J., in *Palko;* "of the very essence of a scheme of ordered liberty," ibid.; "a fair and enlightened system of justice would be impossible without them," ibid.; required by "the 'immutable principles of justice' as conceived by a civilized society," Frankfurter, J., concurring in *Adamson;* or "fundamental to the American scheme of justice," White, J., in *Duncan v. Louisiana.*

As Justice WHITE noted (fn. 14) for the Court in DUNCAN v. LOUISIANA, 391 U.S. 145 (1968) (holding the Sixth Amendment right to jury trial applicable to the states via the Fourteenth), the different phraseology is not without significance:

"Earlier the Court can be seen as having asked, when inquiring into whether some particular procedural safeguard was required of a State, if a civilized system could be imagined that would not accord the particular protection [quoting from *Palko*]. The recent cases, on the other hand, have proceeded upon the valid assumption that state criminal processes are not imaginary and theoretical schemes but actual systems bearing virtually every characteristic of the common-law system that has been developing contemporaneously in England and this country. The question thus is whether given this kind of system a particular procedure is fundamental—whether, that is, a procedure is necessary to an Anglo–American regime of ordered liberty. It is this sort of inquiry that can justify the conclusions that state courts must exclude evidence seized in violation of the Fourth Amendment, *Mapp v. Ohio* [p. 219] [and] that state prosecutors may not comment on a defendant's failure to testify, *Griffin v. California* [p. 1453]. [Of] each of these determinations that a constitutional provision originally written to bind the Federal Government should bind the States as well it might be said that the limitation in question is not necessarily fundamental to fairness in every criminal system that might be imagined but is fundamental in the context of the criminal processes maintained by the American States.

"When the inquiry is approached in this way the question whether the States can impose criminal punishment without granting a jury trial appears quite different from the way it appeared in the older cases opining that States might abolish jury trial. A criminal process which was fair and equitable but used no juries is easy to imagine. It would make use of alternative guarantees and protections which would serve the purposes that the jury serves in the English and American systems. Yet no American State has undertaken to construct such a system. Instead, every American State, including Louisiana, uses the jury extensively, and imposes very serious punishments only after a trial at which the defendant has a right to a jury's verdict. In every State, including Louisiana, the structure and style of the criminal process—the supporting framework and the subsidiary procedures—are of the sort that naturally complement jury trial, and have developed in connection with and in reliance upon jury trial."[b]

b. See also Justice Powell, concurring in the companion 1972 "jury unanimity" cases of *Johnson v. Louisiana* and *Apodaca v. Oregon* (discussed below) (fn. 9):

Although the Court has remained unwilling to accept the total incorporationists' reading of the Fourteenth Amendment, in the 1960's it "selectively" "incorporated" or "absorbed" more and more of the specifics of the Bill of Rights into the Fourteenth Amendment. As Justice White observed in *Duncan:*

"In resolving conflicting claims concerning the meaning of this spacious [Fourteenth Amendment] language, the Court has looked increasingly to the Bill of Rights for guidance; many of the rights guaranteed by the first eight Amendments to the Constitution have been held to be protected against state action by the Due Process Clause of the Fourteenth Amendment. That clause now protects [the] Fourth Amendment rights to be free from unreasonable searches and seizures and to have excluded from criminal trials any evidence illegally seized; the right guaranteed by the Fifth Amendment to be free of compelled self-incrimination; and the Sixth Amendment rights to counsel, to a speedy and public trial, to confrontation of opposing witnesses and to compulsory process for obtaining witnesses."[c]

Moreover, the Court seemed to be "incorporating" not only the basic notion or general concept of the "selected" provision of the Bill of Rights, but applying the provision to the states *to the same extent* it applied to the federal government. As some Justices, especially Harlan, protested, the federal guarantees were being incorporated into the Fourteenth "freighted with their entire accompanying body of federal doctrine" (Harlan, J., joined by Clark, J., dissenting in *Malloy v. Hogan,* discussed below); "jot-for-jot and case-for-case" (Harlan, J., joined by Stewart, J., dissenting in *Duncan*); "bag and baggage, however securely or insecurely affixed

"I agree with Mr. Justice White's analysis in *Duncan* that the departure from earlier decisions was, in large measure, a product of a change in focus in the Court's approach to due process. No longer are questions regarding the constitutionality of particular criminal procedures resolved by focusing alone on the element in question and ascertaining whether a system of criminal justice might be imagined in which a fair trial could be afforded in the absence of that particular element. Rather, the focus is, as it should be, on the fundamentality of that element viewed in the context of the basic Anglo–American jurisprudential system common to the States. That approach to due process readily accounts both for the conclusion that jury trial *is* fundamental and that unanimity *is not.*"

c. See also Justice Black, joined by Douglas, J., concurring in *Duncan:* "[I] believe as strongly as ever that the Fourteenth Amendment was intended to make the Bill of Rights applicable to the States. I have been willing to support the selective incorporation doctrine, however, as an alternative, although perhaps less historically supportable than complete incorporation [because it] keeps judges from roaming at will in their own notions of what policies outside the Bill of Rights are desirable and what are not. And, most importantly for me, the selective incorporation process has the virtue of having already worked to make most of the Bill of Rights' protections applicable to the States."

In the area of criminal procedure, the Court has indeed come very close to incorporation of all of the relevant Bill of Rights guarantees. Over a brief span of the "Warren Court era," the Court utilized the selective incorporation doctrine to make applicable to the states all but four of the guarantees dealing directly with criminal procedure. As for one of the four, the Fifth Amendment requirement of prosecution by indictment, the Court reaffirmed earlier rulings holding that guarantee not fundamental (and therefore not applicable to the states). See p. 1061. As for the other three (the Eighth Amendment prohibition of excessive bail, the Eighth Amendment prohibition against excessive fines, and the Sixth Amendment guarantee that the jury be selected "from the state and district where the crime shall have been committed, which district shall have been ascertained by law"), the Warren Court simply was not presented with cases requiring a ruling on their incorporation. Indeed, the Court has yet to rule on these three guarantees (although lower courts have done so, unanimously assuming that the Eighth Amendment guarantees are fundamental and dividing on the Sixth Amendment guarantee). See CRIMPROC § 2.6 (listing the Warren Court rulings making particular guarantees applicable to the states, and noting the current Court's complete acceptance of these rulings, as opposed to other aspects of the Warren Court's "criminal procedure revolution").

they may be by law and precedent to federal proceedings" (Fortas, J., concurring in *Duncan*).

Thus, Justice Brennan observed for a majority of the Court in *Malloy v. Hogan,* 378 U.S. 1 (1964):

"We hold that the Fourteenth Amendment guaranteed the petitioner the protection of the Fifth Amendment's privilege against self-incrimination, and that *under the applicable federal standard,* the [state court] erred in holding that the privilege was not properly invoked. [The State urges] that the availability of the federal privilege to a witness in a state inquiry is to be determined according to a less stringent safeguard than is applicable in a federal proceeding. We disagree. We have held that the guarantees of the First Amendment, the prohibition of unreasonable searches and seizures of the Fourth Amendment, and the right to counsel guaranteed by the Sixth Amendment, *Gideon v. Wainwright* [p. 85], are all to be enforced against the States under the Fourteenth Amendment *according to the same standards that protect those personal rights against federal encroachment.* [The] Court thus has rejected the notion that the Fourteenth Amendment applies to the States only a 'watered-down, subjective version of the individual guarantees of the Bill of Rights.'" (Emphasis added.)

And Justice White put it for a majority of the Court in *Duncan:* "Because we believe that trial by jury in criminal cases is fundamental to the American scheme of justice, we hold that the Fourteenth Amendment guarantees a right of jury trial in all criminal cases which—*were they to be tried in a federal court*—would come within the Sixth Amendment's guarantee." (Emphasis added.)

Justice Harlan repeatedly voiced his opposition to the *Malloy-Duncan* approach to Fourteenth Amendment Due Process. "The consequence," he protested in his *Malloy* dissent, "is inevitably disregard of all relevant differences which may exist between state and federal criminal law and its enforcement. The ultimate result is compelled uniformity, which is inconsistent with the purpose of our federal system and which is achieved either by encroachment on the State's sovereign powers or by dilution in federal law enforcement of the specific protections found in the Bill of Rights." See also Justice Harlan's concurring opinion in *Pointer v. Texas*, 380 U.S. 400 (1965) (holding that an accused's Sixth Amendment right to confront the witnesses against him applies in its entirety to the states via the Fourteenth Amendment) and his dissenting opinion in *Benton v. Maryland*, fn. a supra.

In the 1970's matters were brought to a head by the "right to jury trial" cases:[d] BALDWIN v. NEW YORK, 399 U.S. 117 (1970) (no offense can be deemed "petty," thus dispensing with the Fourteenth and Sixth Amendment rights to jury trial, where more than six months incarceration is authorized); WILLIAMS v. FLORIDA, 399 U.S. 78 (1970) ("that jury at common law was composed of precisely 12 is an historical accident, unnecessary to effect the purposes of the jury system"; thus 6–person jury in criminal cases does not violate Sixth Amendment, as applied to the states via Fourteenth);[e] and the 1972 *Apodaca* and *Johnson* cases, discussed below, dealing with whether unanimous jury verdicts are required in criminal cases.

Dissenting in *Baldwin* and concurring in *Williams,* Justice HARLAN maintained:

d. For a fuller discussion of these cases, see p. 1382.

e. But the Court subsequently held, in *Ballew v. Georgia*, 435 U.S. 223 (1978), that a state trial in a non-petty criminal case to a jury of only five persons did deprive a defendant of the right to trial by jury guaranteed him by the Sixth and Fourteenth Amendments.

"[*Williams*] evinces [a] recognition that the 'incorporationist' view of the Due Process Clause of the Fourteenth Amendment, which underlay *Duncan* and is now carried forward into *Baldwin,* must be tempered to allow the States more elbow room in ordering their own criminal systems. With that much I agree. But to accomplish this by diluting constitutional protections within the federal system itself is something to which I cannot possibly subscribe. Tempering the rigor of *Duncan* should be done forthrightly, by facing up to the fact that at least in this area the 'incorporation' doctrine does not fit well with our federal structure, and by the same token that *Duncan* was wrongly decided.

"[Rather] than bind the States by the hitherto undeviating and unquestioned federal practice of 12–member juries, the Court holds, based on a poll of state practice, that a six-man jury satisfies the guarantee of a trial by jury in a federal criminal system and consequently carries over to the States. This is a constitutional *renvoi.* With all respect, I consider that before today it would have been unthinkable to suggest that the Sixth Amendment's right to a trial by jury is satisfied by a jury of six, or less, as is left open by the Court's opinion in *Williams,* or by less than a unanimous verdict, a question also reserved in today's decision.[f]

"[These] decisions demonstrate that the difference between a 'due process' approach, that considers each particular case on its own bottom to see whether the right alleged is one 'implicit in the concept of ordered liberty,' and 'selective incorporation' is not an abstract one whereby different verbal formulae achieve the same results. The internal logic of the selective incorporation doctrine cannot be respected if the Court is both committed to interpreting faithfully the meaning of the federal Bill of Rights and recognizing the governmental diversity that exists in this country. The 'backlash' in *Williams* exposes the malaise, for there the Court dilutes a federal guarantee in order to reconcile the logic of 'incorporation,' the 'jot-for-jot and case-for-case' application of the federal right to the States, with the reality of federalism. Can one doubt that had Congress tried to undermine the common law right to trial by jury before *Duncan* came on the books the history today recited would have barred such action? Can we expect repeat performances when this Court is called upon to give definition and meaning to other federal guarantees that have been 'incorporated'? * * *

" 'Incorporation' in *Duncan* closed the door on debate, irrespective of local circumstances, such as the backlogs in urban courts like those of New York City, and has, without justification, clouded with uncertainty the constitutionality of these differing states modes of proceeding pending approval by this Court; it now promises to dilute in other ways the settled meaning of the federal right to a trial by jury. Flexibility for experimentation in the administration of justice should be returned to the States here and in other areas that now have swept into the rigid mold of 'incorporation.'

"[It] is time, I submit, for this Court to face up to the reality implicit in today's holdings and reconsider the 'incorporation' doctrine before its leveling tendencies further retard development in the field of criminal procedure by stifling flexibility in the States and by discarding the possibility of federal leadership by example."

In the companion cases of *Apodaca v. Oregon,* 406 U.S. 404 (1972) and *Johnson v. Louisiana,* 406 U.S. 356 (1972), upholding the constitutionality of less-than-unanimous jury verdicts in state criminal cases, eight Justices adhered to the

f. Cf. Frankfurter, J., for the Court in *Rochin v. California* (1952) (discussed in the next section): "Words being symbols do not speak without a gloss. [T]he gloss may be the deposit of history, whereby a term gains technical content. Thus the requirements of the Sixth and Seventh Amendments for trial by jury in the federal courts have a rigid meaning. No changes or chances can alter the content of the verbal symbol of 'jury'—a body of twelve men who must reach a unanimous conclusion if the verdict is to go against the defendant."

Duncan position that each element of the Sixth Amendment right to jury trial applies to the states to the same extent it applies to the federal government, but split 4–4 over whether the federal guarantee *did require* jury unanimity in criminal cases. State convictions by less than unanimous votes were sustained only because the ninth member of the Court, newly appointed Justice Powell read the Sixth Amendment as requiring jury unanimity, but—taking a Harlan-type approach—concluded that *this feature* of the federal right is not "so fundamental to the essentials of jury trial" as to require unanimity in state criminal cases as a matter of Fourteenth Amendment Due Process.[g]

Observed Powell: "[I]n holding that the Fourteenth Amendment has incorporated 'jot-for-jot and case-for-case' every element of the Sixth Amendment, the Court derogates principles of federalism that are basic to our system. In the name of uniform application of high standards of due process, the Court has embarked upon a course of constitutional interpretation that deprives the States of freedom to experiment with adjudicatory processes different from the federal model. At the same time, the Court's understandable unwillingness to impose requirements that it finds unnecessarily rigid (e.g., *Williams*), has culminated in the dilution of federal rights that were, until these decisions, never seriously questioned. The doubly undesirable consequence of this reasoning process, labeled by Mr. Justice Harlan as 'constitutional schizophrenia,' may well be detrimental both to the state and federal criminal justice systems. Although it is perhaps late in the day for an expression of my views, I [believe] that, at least in defining the elements of the right to jury trial, there is no sound basis for interpreting the Fourteenth Amendment to require blind adherence by the States to all details of the federal Sixth Amendment standards."[h]

Dissenting Justice Brennan, joined by Marshall, J., observed: "Readers of today's opinions may be understandably puzzled why convictions by 11–1 and 10–2 jury votes are affirmed [when] a majority of the Court agrees that the Sixth Amendment requires a unanimous verdict in federal criminal jury trials, and a majority also agrees that the right to jury trial guaranteed by the Sixth Amendment is to be enforced against the States according to the same standards that protect that right against federal encroachment. The reason is that while my Brother Powell agrees that a unanimous verdict is required in federal criminal trials, he does not agree that the Sixth Amendment right to a jury trial is to be applied in the same way to State and Federal Governments. In that circumstance, it is arguable that the affirmance of the convictions * * * is not inconsistent with a view that today's decision is a holding that only a unanimous verdict will afford the accused in a state criminal prosecution the jury trial guaranteed him by the Sixth Amendment. In any event, the affirmance must not obscure that the majority of the Court remains of the view that, as in the case of every specific of the Bill of Rights that extends to the States, the Sixth Amendment's jury trial guarantee, however it is to be construed, has identical application against both State and Federal Governments."[i]

g. But the Court subsequently held, in *Burch v. Louisiana*, p. 1385, per Rehnquist, J. (without a dissent on this issue), that conviction by a nonunanimous *six-person* jury in a state criminal trial for a non-petty offense did violate the Sixth and Fourteenth Amendment rights to trial by jury.

h. In his continued resistance to "jot-for-jot" or "bag and baggage" incorporation of a "selected" provision of the Bill of Rights, Justice Powell soon gained two allies. See Powell, J., joined by the Chief Justice and Rehnquist, J., dissenting in *Crist v. Bretz*, p. 1488. In *Ballew*, fn. e supra, although he concurred in the judgment, Justice Powell, again joined by the Chief Justice and Rehnquist, J., did not join Justice Blackmun's opinion because it "assumes full incorporation of the Sixth Amendment, contrary to my view in *Apodaca*."

i. In a separate dissent, Stewart, J., joined by Brennan Marshall, J.J., protested that "unless *Duncan* is to be overruled," "the only relevant question here is whether the Sixth Amendment [guarantees] that the verdict of

SECTION 2. THE PROBLEM OF BODILY EXTRACTIONS: ANOTHER LOOK AT THE "DUE PROCESS" AND "SELECTIVE INCORPORATION" APPROACHES

As noted in the previous section, dissenting in *Baldwin* and concurring in *Williams,* Justice Harlan maintained that "the difference between a 'due process' approach [and] 'selective incorporation' is not an abstract one whereby different formulae achieve the same results." But he made this observation in the context of the applicability to the states of the Sixth Amendment right to trial by jury, which had, or was thought to have, a relatively rigid meaning. Most language in the Bill of Rights, however, is rather vague and general, at least when specific problems arise under a particular phrase. In such cases, does dwelling on the literal language simply *shift the focus of broad judicial inquiry* from "due process" to, e.g., "freedom of speech," "establishment of religion," "unreasonable searches and seizures," "excessive bail," "cruel and unusual punishments," and "the assistance of counsel"? See Donald A. Dripps, *At the Borders of the Fourth Amendment: Why A Real Due Process Test Should Replace the Outrageous Government Conduct Defense*, 1993 U.Ill.L.Rev. 261 (defending, "as both more faithful to conventional sources of constitutional law and more consonant with the political values of a free society, a revitalized due process test"); John E. Nowak, *Due Process Methodology in the Postincorporation World*, 70 J. Crim. L. & C. 397, 400–01 (1979) (arguing that decisions based on specific guarantees tend to rely on definitional analysis and fail to explore the interest at stake). Consider too, Note 1, p.39. See also Henry J. Friendly, *The Bill of Rights as a Code of Criminal Procedure,* 53 Calif.L.Rev. 929, 937 (1965); Sanford H. Kadish, *Methodology and Criteria in Due Process Adjudication—A Survey and Criticism,* 66 Yale L.J. 319, (1957).

In considering whether the right to counsel "begins" at the time of arrest, preliminary hearing, arraignment, or not until the trial itself, or includes probation and parole revocation hearings or applies to juvenile delinquency proceedings, deportation hearings or civil commitments, or, where the defendant is indigent, includes the right to *assigned* counsel or an assigned psychiatrist at state expense, how helpful is the Sixth Amendment language entitling an accused to "the assistance of counsel for his defense"? Is the specificity or direction of this language significantly greater than the "due process" clause?

To turn to another cluster of problems—which form the basis for this section—in considering whether, and under what conditions, the police may direct the "pumping" of a person's stomach to uncover incriminating evidence, or the taking of a blood sample from him, without his consent, do the "specific guarantees" in the Bill of Rights against "unreasonable searches and seizures" and against compelling a person to be "a witness against himself" free the Court from the demands of appraising and judging involved in answering these questions by interpreting the "due process" clause?

ROCHIN v. CALIFORNIA, 342 U.S. 165 (1952), arose as follows: Having "some information" that Rochin was selling narcotics, three deputy sheriffs "forced open the door of [his] room and found him sitting partly dressed on the side of the bed, upon which his wife was lying. On a 'night stand' beside the bed

the jury must be unanimous. The answer to that question is clearly 'yes,' as my Brother Powell has cogently demonstrated * * *."

the deputies spied two capsules. When asked 'Whose stuff is this?' Rochin seized the capsules and put them in his mouth. A struggle ensued in the course of which the three officers 'jumped upon him' and [unsuccessfully] attempted to extract the capsules. [Rochin] was handcuffed and taken to a hospital. At the direction of one of the officers, a doctor forced an emetic solution through a tube into Rochin's stomach against his will. This 'stomach pumping' produced vomiting. In the vomited matter were found two capsules which proved to contain morphine. [Rochin was convicted of possessing morphine] and sentenced to sixty days' imprisonment. The chief evidence against him was the two capsules."

The Court, per FRANKFURTER, J., concluded that the police conduct violated fourteenth amendment due process: "This is conduct that shocks the conscience. Illegally breaking into the privacy of the petitioner, the struggle to open his mouth and remove what was there, the forcible extraction of his stomach's contents—this course of proceeding by agents of government to obtain evidence is bound to offend even hardened sensibilities. They are methods too close to the rack and the screw to permit of constitutional differentiation.

"It has long since ceased to be true that due process of law is heedless of the means by which otherwise relevant and credible evidence is obtained. [The confession] decisions [are] only instances of the general requirement that States in their prosecutions respect certain decencies of civilized conduct. Due process of law, as a historic and generative principle, precludes defining, and thereby confining, these standards of conduct more precisely than to say that convictions cannot be brought about by methods that offend 'a sense of justice.' It would be a stultification of the responsibility which the course of constitutional history has cast upon this Court to hold that in order to convict a man the police cannot extract by force what is in his mind but can extract what is in his stomach.

"[E]ven though statements contained in them may be independently established as true, [c]oerced confessions offend the community's sense of fair play and decency. So here, to sanction the brutal conduct which naturally enough was condemned by the court whose judgment is before us, would be to afford brutality the cloak of law. Nothing would be more calculated to discredit law and thereby to brutalize the temper of a society."

Concurring Justice BLACK reasoned that the Fifth Amendment's protection against compelled self-incrimination applied to the states and that "a person is compelled to be a witness against himself not only when he is compelled to testify, but also when as here, incriminating evidence is forcibly taken from him by a contrivance of modern science." He maintained that "faithful adherence to the specific guarantees in the Bill of Rights insures a more permanent protection of individual liberty than that which can be afforded by the nebulous [Fourteenth Amendment due process] standards stated by the majority."

In a separate concurring opinion, Justice DOUGLAS also criticized the majority's approach. He contended that the privilege against self-incrimination applied to the states as well as the federal government and because of the privilege "words taken from [an accused's] lips, capsules taken from his stomach, blood taken from his veins are all inadmissible provided they are taken from him without his consent. [This] is an unequivocal, definite and workable rule of evidence for state and federal courts. But we cannot in fairness free the state courts from the [restraints of the Fifth Amendment privilege against self-incrimination] and yet excoriate them for flouting the 'decencies of civilized conduct' when they admit the evidence. This is to make the rule turn not on the Constitution but on the idiosyncracies of the judges who sit here."

Irvine v. California, 347 U.S. 128 (1954), limited *Rochin* to situations involving coercion, violence or brutality to the person.[a] BREITHAUPT v. ABRAM, 352 U.S. 432 (1957), illustrated that under the *Rochin* test state police had considerable leeway even when the body of the accused was "invaded." In *Breithaupt,* the police took a blood sample from an unconscious person who had been involved in a fatal automobile collision. A majority, per CLARK, J., affirmed a manslaughter conviction based on the blood sample (which showed intoxication), stressing that the sample was "taken under the protective eye of a physician" and that "the blood test procedure has become routine in our everyday life." "[T]he interests of society in the scientific determination of intoxication, one of the great causes of the mortal hazards of the road," outweighed "so slight an intrusion" of a person's body.

Dissenting Chief Justice WARREN, joined by Black and Douglas, JJ., deemed *Rochin* controlling and argued that police efforts to curb the narcotics traffic, involved in *Rochin,* "is surely a state interest of at least as great magnitude as the interest in highway law enforcement. * * * Only personal reaction to the stomach pump and the blood test can distinguish the [two cases]."

Justice DOUGLAS, joined by Black, J., also wrote a separate dissent, maintaining that "if the decencies of a civilized state are the test, it is repulsive to me for the police to insert needles into an unconscious person in order to get the evidence necessary to convict him, whether they find the person unconscious, give him a pill which puts him to sleep, or use force to subdue him."

Nine years later, even though in the meantime the Court had held in *Mapp* that the federal exclusionary rule in search and seizure cases was binding on the states and in *Malloy v. Hogan,* supra, that the Fifth Amendment's protection against compelled self-incrimination was likewise applicable to the states, the Court still upheld the taking by a physician, at police direction, of a blood sample from an injured person, over his objection. SCHMERBER v. CALIFORNIA, 384 U.S. 757 (1966).[b] In affirming the conviction for operating a vehicle while under the influence of intoxicating liquor, a 5–4 majority, per BRENNAN, J., ruled: (1) that the extraction of blood from petitioner under the aforementioned circum-

a. In *Irvine* the police made repeated illegal entries into petitioner's home, first to install a secret microphone and then to move it to the bedroom, in order to listen to the conversations of the occupants—for over a month.

Jackson, J., who announced the judgment of the Court and wrote the principal opinion, recognized that "few police measures have come to our attention that more flagrantly, deliberately, and persistently violated the fundamental principle declared by the Fourth Amendment as a restriction on the Federal Government," but adhered to the holding in *Wolf v. Colorado* (1949), p. 217, that the exclusionary rule in federal search and seizure cases is not binding on the states. (*Wolf* was overruled in *Mapp v. Ohio* (1961), p. 219.) Nor did Justice Jackson deem *Rochin* applicable: "However obnoxious are the facts in the case before us, they do not involve coercion, violence or brutality to the person [as did *Rochin*], but rather a trespass to property, plus eavesdropping."

Because of the "aggravating" and "repulsive" police misconduct in *Irvine,* Frankfurter, J., joined by Burton, J., dissented, maintaining that *Rochin* was controlling, not *Wolf.* (He had written the majority opinions in both cases.) Black, J., joined by Douglas, J., dissented separately, arguing that petitioner had been convicted on the basis of evidence "extorted" from him in violation of the Fifth Amendment's privilege against compelled self-incrimination, which he considered applicable to the states. Douglas, J., dissenting separately, protested against the use in state prosecutions of evidence seized in violation of the Fourth Amendment.

Speaking for himself and Chief Justice Warren, Justice Jackson suggested that copies of the Court's opinion and the record in the case be sent to the U.S. Attorney General for possible federal prosecution. The FBI did conduct an investigation which revealed that the officers who placed the microphone in Irvine's home were acting under orders of the Chief of Police and with the full knowledge of the local prosecutor. Thus, concluded the Department of Justice, "it would be both useless and inadvisable to present [the] matter to the Federal grand jury." See Comment, 7 Stan.L.Rev. 76, 94, fn. 75 (1954).

b. For other aspects of *Schmerber,* see p. 348.

stances "did not offend 'that "sense of justice" ' of which we spoke in *Rochin,*" thus reaffirming *Breithaupt;* (2) that the privilege against self-incrimination, now binding on the states, "protects an accused only from being compelled to testify against himself, or otherwise provide the State with evidence of a testimonial or communicative nature and that the withdrawal of blood and use of the analysis in question did not involve compulsion to these ends";[c] and (3) that the protection against unreasonable search and seizure, now binding on the states, was satisfied because (a) "there was plainly probable cause" to arrest and charge petitioner and to suggest "the required relevance and likely success of a test of petitioner's blood for alcohol"; (b) the officer "might reasonably have believed that he was confronted with an emergency, in which the delay necessary to obtain a warrant, under the circumstances, threatened 'the destruction of evidence' "; and (c) "the test chosen to measure petitioner's blood-alcohol level was a reasonable one * * * performed in a reasonable manner."

Dissenting Justice BLACK, joined by Justice Douglas, expressed amazement at the majority's "conclusion that compelling a person to give his blood to help the State to convict him is not equivalent to compelling him to be a witness against himself." "It is a strange hierarchy of values that allows the State to extract a human being's blood to convict him of a crime because of the blood's content but proscribes compelled production of his lifeless papers."[d]

Notes and Questions

1. In light of *Rochin*, *Breithaupt* and *Schmerber,* when courts decide constitutional questions by "looking to" the Bill of Rights, to what extent do they proceed, as Justice Black expressed it in *Adamson,* "within clearly marked constitutional boundaries"? To what extent does resort to these "particular standards" enable courts to avoid substituting their "own concepts of decency and fundamental justice" for the language of the Constitution?

2. Did *Mapp* and *Malloy,* decided in the interim between *Breithaupt* and *Schmerber,* affect any Justice's vote? Did the applicability of the "particular standards" of the Fourth and Fifth Amendments inhibit Justices Black, Douglas or Brennan from employing their own concepts of "decency" and "justice" in *Schmerber?* After *Schmerber,* how much force is there in Justice Black's view, concurring in *Rochin,* that "faithful adherence to the specific guarantees in the Bill of Rights assures a more permanent protection of individual liberty than that which can be afforded by the nebulous standards stated by the majority"?

3. Applying the "shocks-the-conscience" test first articulated in the *Rochin* case, COUNTY OF SACRAMENTO v. LEWIS, 523 U.S. 833 (1998), held, per SOUTER, J., that a police officer did not violate substantive due process by causing death through "reckless indifference" to, or "reckless disregard" for, a person's life in a high-speed automobile chase of a speeding motorcyclist. (The chase resulted in the death of the motorcyclist's passenger when the police car

c. In fn. 7 to its opinion, the Court compared "Wigmore's view, 'that the privilege is limited to testimonial disclosure. It was directed at the employment of legal process *to extract from the person's own lips* an admission of guilt, which would thus take the place of other evidence.' 8 Wigmore, *Evidence* § 2263 (McNaughton rev. 1961)." "Our holding today," noted the Court, "is not to be understood as adopting the Wigmore formulation." But see *United States v. Wade,* p. 757.

d. Warren, C.J., and Douglas, J., dissented in separate opinions, each adhering to his dissenting views in *Breithaupt.* In a third dissenting opinion, Fortas, J., maintained that "petitioner's privilege against self-incrimination applies" and, moreover, "under the Due Process Clause, the State, in its role as prosecutor, has no right to extract blood from an accused or anyone else, over his protest."

skidded into the passenger after the cycle had tipped over). In such circumstances, concluded the Court, "only a purpose to cause harm unrelated to the legitimate object of arrest will satisfy the element of arbitrary conduct shocking to the conscience, necessary for a due process violation [and for police liability under 42 U.S.C. § 1983]." Regardless of whether the officer's behavior "offended the reasonableness held up by tort law on the balance struck in law enforcement's own codes of practice, it does not shock the conscience."

The Court recalled that it had held in *Graham v. Connor*, 490 U.S. 386 (1989), that "where a particular amendment provides an explicit textual source of constitutional protection against a particular sort of government behavior, that Amendment, not the more generalized notion of substantive due process, must be the guide for analyzing [claims of substantive due process violations]." But the "more-specific-provision" rule of *Graham* did not bar respondents' lawsuit because neither the high-speed chase of the motorcycle nor the accidental killing of the motorcycle passenger constituted a Fourth Amendment "seizure."[a]

4. *Continued application of "free-standing" due process.* As indicated in *County of Sacramento*, the Court in the "post-incorporation era" has continued to apply the independent content of due process that exists apart from the selectively incorporated guarantees (also described as "free-standing" due process). The applicable standard for cases presenting issues of procedural due process (in contrast to substantive due process) has been whether the state practice "offends some principle of justice so rooted in the traditions and conscience of our people to be ranked as fundamental." *Medina v. California*, 505 U.S. 437 (1992). Jerold Israel, *Free-Standing Due Process and Criminal Procedure: The Supreme Court's Search for Interpretive Guidelines*, 45 St. Louis U.L.J. 303 (2001), reviews the Court's application of that standard in the post-incorporation decades. The article concludes that while the Court has set forth various guidelines for determining the independent content of due process, it has not been consistent in applying those guidelines. The Court has noted that "beyond the specific guarantees enumerated in the Bill of Rights, the Due Process Clause has limited operation" and will be "construed very narrowly." *Dowling v. United States*, 493 U.S. 342 (1990). This position rests on the ground that, since the "Bill of Rights speaks in explicit terms to many aspects of criminal procedure," the expansion of constitutional regulation under the "open-ended rubric of the Due Process Clause * * * invite[s] undue interference with both considered legislative judgments and the careful balance that the constitution strikes between liberty and order." *Medina v. California*, supra. Notwithstanding such statements, free-standing due process has emerged as: (1) the dominant source of constitutional regulation of the pre-trial and post-trial stages of the process (most notable as to guilty pleas and sentencing); (2) a major source of constitutional regulation of the trial; (3) a lesser, but still significant source of regulation of police practices (see e.g., ch. 10, § 3). So too, while the Court has repeatedly stressed that the historical acceptance of a practice is a strong indicator that the practice does not offend fundamental fairness, it has on various occasions relied on deductive

a. Concurring in the judgment, Scalia, J., joined by Thomas, J., would not have decided the case by applying the "shocks-the-conscience" test but "on the ground that respondents offer no textual or historical support for their alleged due process right." The concurring Justices maintained that in *Washington v. Glucksberg*, 521 U.S. 702 (1997) (upholding a criminal prohibition against physician-assisted suicide), "the Court specifically rejected the method of substantive-due-process analysis employed by Justice Souter in that case, which is the very same method employed by Justice Souter in his opinion for the Court today."

Justice Kennedy, joined by O'Connor, J., joined the opinion of the Court, but also wrote separately. They "share[d] Justice Scalia's concerns about using the phrase 'shocks the conscience' in a manner suggesting that it is a self-defining test." The phrase, they observed, "has the unfortunate connotation of a standard laden with subjective assessments. In that respect, it must be viewed with considerable skepticism."

reasoning (often tied to the character of a "fair hearing") to hold unconstitutional practices that were entirely consistent with the common law (typically without discussing historical acceptance). Most often, the Court has described free-standing due process as looking to the circumstances of the particular case and resting, at least in part, on fact-sensitive determinations (particularly as to a likelihood of prejudicial impact), but in several areas, the Court has relied on free-standing due process to formulate per se prohibitions and automatically presume prejudice. The Court at times has advance a procedural due process counterpart of *Graham v. Connor*, but at other times has turned to free-standing due process without first considering the possible application of a specific guarantee (indeed, even announcing a preference for relying on free-standing due process in *Pennsylvania v. Ritchie*, p. 1288).

SECTION 3. THE RETROACTIVE EFFECT OF A HOLDING OF UNCONSTITUTIONALITY[a]

Rejecting what it called the Blackstonian theory that a new ruling merely sets forth the law as it always existed, *Linkletter v. Walker*, 381 U.S. 618 (1965), declined to apply *Mapp v. Ohio* (p. 219) (overruling *Wolf v. Colorado*, and imposing the Fourth Amendment exclusionary rule on the states as a matter of Fourteenth Amendment Due Process) to cases which had become final (i.e., direct appellate review had been exhausted) prior to the overturning of *Wolf*. The *Linkletter* Court maintained that the retroactivity of *Mapp* should be determined by examining the purpose of the exclusionary rule, the reliance of the states on prior law, and the effect on the administration of justice of a retroactive application of the exclusionary rule.

The prime purpose of *Mapp*, emphasized the Court, was to deter future police misconduct and the purpose would not be advanced by applying the rule to "finalized" cases. The Court recognized that it had given full retroactive effect to some recent law-changing decisions—*Gideon* (p. 85), *Griffin v. Illinois* (p. 97), and the coerced confession cases—but, unlike *Mapp*, the principles established in those cases "went to the fairness of the trial—the very integrity of the fact-finding process. [Here] the fairness of the trial is not under attack."

Relying upon the *Linkletter* analysis, *Stovall v. Denno*, 388 U.S. 293 (1967), set forth a framework for determining whether a new ruling should be given retroactive effect. The "criteria guiding the resolution of the question," observed *Stovall*, "implicate (a) the purpose to be served by the new standards, (b) the extent of the reliance by law enforcement authorities on the old standards, (c) the effect on the administration of justice of a retroactive application of the new standards." These three criteria were later described as the "*Linkletter* standard," "the *Stovall* standard," or the "*Linkletter–Stovall*" standard.

Prior to *Linkletter*, the *Mapp* case had already been applied to cases still pending on direct appeal, so the only issue considered by the *Linkletter* Court was whether *Mapp* should be applied to a collateral attack upon a conviction (there, habeas corpus challenge). In applying the *Linkletter* standard, however, *Stovall* and subsequent cases did not draw a distinction between final convictions attacked collaterally and convictions challenged at various stages of trial and direct review.

Moreover, in limiting the retroactive effect of new rulings, cases applying the *Linkletter* standard selected different "starting points." Because *Escobedo* (p. 563)

a. This cluster of problems has generated a vast literature, starting in the 1960's. For a helpful discussion, see Richard H. Fallon & Daniel J. Meltzer, *New Law, Non-Retroactivity, and Constitutional Remedies*, 104 Harv. L.Rev. 1733 (1991).

and *Miranda* (p. 575) were not primarily designed to protect the innocent from wrongful conviction, *Johnson v. New Jersey*, 384 U.S. 719 (1966) held that those landmark confession rulings affected only cases in which *the trial began* after the date of those decisions. Because the use of unfair lineups could still be challenged on due process grounds even if the law-changing decisions on lineups were not applied retroactively, *Stovall v. Denno*, supra, declined to give retroactive effect to *Wade* and *Gilbert* (p. 757), the 1967 cases establishing the right to counsel at certain pretrial lineups. But this time the Court selected a different starting point for application of the nonretroactive rulings: *Wade* and *Gilbert* "affect only those cases [involving] *confrontations for identification purposes* conducted in the absence of counsel *after* [the date of these decisions]." (Emphasis added).[b]

Selection of the date of the challenged *police conduct* as the starting point, rather than the date of the trial or some other point in the criminal process, indicated that *police reliance* on the overturned rule was a major factor in retroactivity disputes. In this respect, *Desist v. United States*, 394 U.S. 244 (1969), followed *Johnson v. New Jersey*. The *Desist* Court held that *Katz v. United States* (p. 247) (overruling *Olmstead*, p. 463, and holding that electronic surveillance is subject to Fourth Amendment restraints) should be given what the Court called "wholly prospective application," i.e., applied only to *police activity* occurring *after* the date of the *Katz* decision.[c]

The *Desist* Court saw no significant distinction for retroactivity purposes between direct review and collateral attack: All of the reasons for making *Katz* prospective only "also undercut any distinction between final convictions and those still pending on review. Both the deterrent purpose of the exclusionary rule and the reliance of law enforcement officers focus upon *the time of the search*, not any subsequent point in the prosecution as the relevant date." (Emphasis added.)

Twenty years later, Justice Harlan's dissent in *Desist* seems a good deal more significant than the opinion of the Court in that case. Unable to accept a rationale that "permits this Court to apply a 'new' constitutional rule entirely prospectively, while making an exception only for the particular litigant whose case was chosen as the vehicle for establishing that rule," dissenting Justice Harlan maintained:

"[A]ll 'new' rules of constitutional law must, at a minimum, be applied to all those cases which are still subject to direct review by this Court at the time the 'new' decision is handed down.

"[We release a prisoner] only because the Government has offended constitutional principle in the conduct of his case. And when another similarly situated defendant comes before us, we must grant the same relief or give a principled reason for acting differently. We depart from this basic judicial tradition when we

b. Although "at first glance the prospectivity rule appears to be an act of judicial self-abnegation," "in reality," observes Francis Allen, *The Judicial Quest for Penal Justice: The Warren Court and the Criminal Cases*, 1975 U.Ill.L.F. 518, 530, such a rule "encourages the making of new law by reducing some of the social costs." See also James Haddad, *Retroactivity Should be Rethought: A Call for the End of the Linkletter Doctrine*, 60 J.Crim.L.C. & P.S. 417, 439 (1969): "The alternative to the prospective-only technique is a more conservative approach to constitutional criminal procedure. * * * Detailed federal standards such as those laid down in *Miranda* would no longer be possible. Adoption of safeguards, such as the right to counsel at lineups, which not a single state anticipated, would also be impossible."

c. The Court recognized that "[o]f course, Katz himself benefitted from the new principle announced on [the date of the *Katz* decision], and [to] that extent the decision has not technically been given wholly prospective application. But [this] is an 'unavoidable consequence of the necessity that constitutional adjudications not stand as mere dictum.' Whatever inequity may arguably result from applying the new rule to those 'chance beneficiaries' is 'an insignificant cost for adherence to sound principles of decision-making.' "

simply pick and choose from among similarly situated defendants those who alone will receive the benefit of a 'new' rule of constitutional law.

"* * * If a 'new' constitutional doctrine is truly right, we should not reverse lower courts which have accepted it; nor should we affirm those which have rejected the very arguments we have embraced. Anything else would belie the truism that it is the task of this Court, like that of any other, to do justice to each litigant on the merits of his own case. It is only if each of our decisions can be justified in terms of this fundamental premise that they may properly be considered the legitimate products of a court of law, rather than the commands of a super-legislature."

RETHINKING RETROACTIVITY: HARLAN'S VIEWS COME TO THE FORE

More than a decade after the *Desist* Court had found no valid distinction for retroactivity purposes between final convictions and those still pending on direct review, the Court, relying heavily on Harlan, J.'s, dissent in *Desist,* deemed such a distinction persuasive and applied it in *United States v. Johnson,* 457 U.S. 537 (1982) (per Blackmun, J.). *Johnson* applied *Payton v. New York* (1980) (p. 364) (holding that police must obtain an arrest warrant when entering a suspect's home to make a routine felony arrest) to cases still pending on direct appeal at the time *Payton* was handed down. The Court pointed out that "*Payton* overturned no long-standing practice approved by a near-unanimous body of lower court authority [and thus] does not fall into that narrow class of decisions whose nonretroactivity is effectively preordained because they unmistakably signal 'a clean break with the past.' "

The *Johnson* Court "express[ed] no view on the retroactive application of decisions construing any constitutional provision other than the Fourth Amendment," but as *Shea v. Louisiana,* immediately below, soon made clear, the *Johnson* approach was not to be confined to the Fourth Amendment setting.

SHEA v. LOUISIANA, 470 U.S. 51 (1985) arose as follows: Upon being read his *Miranda* rights, petitioner asserted his right to counsel and the interview was then terminated. But the next day, before petitioner had communicated with a lawyer and without any indication from him that he was willing to be questioned, the police again read petitioner the *Miranda* warnings. Petitioner agreed to talk and confessed. The confession was admitted into evidence and petitioner was convicted. While his appeal was pending, the U.S. Supreme Court ruled in *Edwards v. Arizona,* p. 647, that a suspect's rights were violated by the use of his confession obtained by police-instigated interrogation—without counsel present—after he had requested a lawyer. The state supreme court held *Edwards* inapplicable to a case pending on direct appeal at the time *Edwards* was decided. The Court, per BLACKMUN, J., disagreed:

"The primary difference between *United States v. Johnson,* on the one hand, and *Solem v. Stumes,* 465 U.S. 638 (1984) [holding that *Edwards* does not apply retroactively to a state-court conviction finally affirmed by the state supreme court *before Edwards* was decided], on the other, is the difference between a pending and undecided direct review of a judgment of conviction and a federal collateral attack upon a state conviction which has become final. We must acknowledge [that] *Johnson* does not directly control the disposition of the present case.[a] [But] [w]e now conclude [that there] is nothing about a Fourth Amendment

a. The Court noted that *Johnson* specifically declined to address the implications of its approach to non-Fourth Amendment cases and "also declined to address situations clearly con-

rule that suggests that in this context it should be given greater retroactive effect than a Fifth Amendment rule. Indeed, a Fifth Amendment violation may be more likely to affect the truthfinding process than a Fourth Amendment violation. And Justice Harlan's reasoning—that principled decisionmaking and fairness to similarly situated petitioners requires application of a new rule to all cases pending on direct review—is applicable with equal force to the situation presently before us.

"[It is argued] that drawing a distinction between a case pending on direct review and a case on collateral attack produces inequities and injustices that are not any different from those that *Johnson* purported to cure. The argument is that the litigant whose *Edwards* claim will not be considered because it is presented on collateral review will be just as unfairly treated as the direct-review litigant whose claim would be by-passed were *Edwards* not the law. The distinction, however, properly rests on considerations of finality in the judicial process. The one litigant already has taken his case through the primary system. The other has not. For the latter, the curtain of finality has not been drawn. Somewhere, the closing must come."

WHITE, J., joined by the Chief Justice, and Rehnquist and O'Connor, JJ., dissented:

"[The] futility of this latest attempt to use retroactivity doctrine to avoid the super-legislature difficulty is highlighted by the majority's unwillingness to commit itself to the logic of its position. For even as it maintains that retroactivity is essential to the judicial function, today's majority, like the majority in *Johnson,* continues to hold out the possibility that a 'really' new rule—one that marks a clear break with the past—may not have to be applied retroactively even to cases pending on direct review at the time the new decision is handed down. Of course, if the majority were truly concerned with the super-legislature problem it would be 'clear break' decisions that would trouble it the most. Indeed, one might expect that a Court as disturbed about the problem as the majority purports to be would swear off such decisions altogether, not reserve the power both to issue them and to decline to apply them retroactively. In leaving open the possibility of an exception for 'clear break' decisions, the majority demonstrates the emptiness of its proposed solution to the super-legislature problem.

"[The] majority recognizes that the distinction between direct review and habeas is problematic, but justifies its differential treatment by appealing to the need to draw 'the curtain of finality' on those who were unfortunate enough to have exhausted their last direct appeal at the time *Edwards* was decided. Yet the majority offers no reasons for its conclusion that finality should be the decisive factor. When a conviction is overturned on direct appeal on the basis of an *Edwards* violation, the remedy offered the defendant is a new trial at which any inculpatory statements obtained in violation of *Edwards* will be excluded. It is not clear to me why the majority finds such a burdensome remedy more acceptable when it is imposed on the state on direct review than when it is the result of a collateral attack."

Notes and Questions

1. ***Rejection of the "clear break" exception.*** Answering a question left open in the *Johnson* and *Shea* cases, *Griffith v. Kentucky,* 479 U.S. 314 (1987),

trolled by existing retroactivity precedents, such as where the new rule of law is so clean a break with the past that it has been considered nonretroactive almost automatically. Whatever the merits of a different retroactivity rule for cases of that kind may be, [*Stumes*] recognized that *Edwards* was 'not the kind of clean break with the past that is automatically nonretroactive.' "

applied *Batson v. Kentucky* (p. 1403) (defendant may establish prima facie case of racial discrimination in selection of petit jury on basis of prosecution's use of peremptory challenges at defendant's trial) to all convictions not final at the time of the ruling even though *Batson* was "an explicit and substantial break with prior precedent." Observed a 6–3 majority, per Blackmun, J.: "[T]he 'clear break' exception * * * reintroduces precisely the type of case-specific analysis that Justice Harlan rejected as inappropriate for cases pending on direct review [and] creates the same problem of not treating similarly situated defendants the same. [The] fact that the new rule may constitute a clear break with the past has no bearing on the 'actual inequity that results' when only one of many similarly situated defendants receives the benefit of the new rule."

2. ***Adoption of the other part of Harlan's approach to retroactivity.*** Justice Harlan believed that new rulings should always be applied retroactively to cases on *direct* review (a view adopted in *Shea*), but that generally new rulings should not be applied retroactively to cases on *collateral* review. In TEAGUE v. LANE, 489 U.S. 288 (1989) (set forth in Ch. 29, § 4), seven Justices adopted Harlan's basic position with respect to retroactivity on collateral review. There was, however, no clear majority as to what the exceptions to this general approach should be.

A four-Justice plurality, per O'CONNOR, J. (joined by Rehnquist, C.J., and Scalia and Kennedy, JJ.), identified two exceptions: A new ruling should be applied retroactively to cases on collateral review only (1) if it "places 'certain kinds of primary, private individual conduct beyond the power of the criminal law-making authority to proscribe' " or (2) if it mandates "new procedures without which the likelihood of an accurate conviction is seriously diminished." The latter exception is " 'best illustrated by recalling the classic grounds for the issuance of a writ of habeas corpus—that the proceeding was dominated by mob violence; that the prosecutor knowingly made use of perjured testimony; or that the conviction was based on a confession extorted from the defendant by brutal methods.' "

A fifth member of the Court, concurring Justice White, characterized the plurality's view as "an acceptable application in collateral proceedings of the theories embraced by the Court in dealing with direct review." Two other members of the Court, concurring Justice STEVENS, joined by Blackmun, J., agreed that "the Court should adopt Justice Harlan's analysis of retroactivity for habeas corpus cases as well as for cases still on direct review," but disagreed with the plurality about the exceptions to such a general approach.

3. ***What constitutes a "new rule"?*** The *Teague* plurality, per O'Connor, J., observed that "a case announces a new rule when it breaks new ground or imposes a new obligation" on government or "if the result was not *dictated* by precedent existing at the time the defendant's conviction became final."

Consider *Butler v. McKellar*, 494 U.S. 407 (1990). At issue in *Butler* was the retroactive application on habeas of *Arizona v. Roberson* (1988) (p. 647). *Roberson* held that *Edwards v. Arizona* (1981), which prohibits the police from initiating further interrogation once a suspect has asserted his right to counsel, applies even when (unlike the facts in *Edwards*) the further interrogation relates to a different crime. Although the *Roberson* Court had characterized its ruling as "controlled" by *Edwards*, the *Butler* Court held that *Roberson* had announced a "new rule" under the *Teague* standard: Although the *Roberson* Court had said that its decision was within the "logical compass" of *Edwards*, "the outcome in *Roberson* was susceptible to debate among reasonable minds"—"it would not have been an illogical or even a grudging application of *Edwards* to decide that it did not extend to the facts of *Roberson.*"

Is *Teague*'s definition of the claims that will be deemed to rest on new law—and thus barred from relitigation on habeas, unless they fall within an exception—far too expansive? Don't most cases, as Justice Brennan argued in his *Teague* dissent, "involve a question of law that is at least debatable, permitting a rational judge to resolve the case in more than one way"? By disabling federal habeas corpus from granting relief whenever reasonable disagreement is possible about the scope or application of an existing rule, does *Teague* "reduce the incentives for state courts, and state law enforcement officials, to take account of the evolving direction of the law"? Should a "new rule" be defined more narrowly, "to exclude rules and decisions that are clearly foreshadowed, not just those that are 'dictated by precedents' "? See Richard H. Fallon & Daniel J. Meltzer, *New Law, Non-Retroactivity, and Constitutional Remedies,* 104 Harv.L.Rev. 1731, 1816–17 (1991).

4. ***Retroactivity in the context of the death sentence.*** Consider SCHRIRO v. SUMMERLIN, 124 S.Ct. 2519 (2004), which arose as follows: Respondent was convicted of murder and sentenced to death under Arizona's capital sentencing scheme then in effect, which authorized the trial judge, rather than the jury, to determine the presence of aggravating circumstances making the defendant eligible for the death sentence. (The aggravating circumstances included whether the offense was committed in an "especially heinous," "cruel," or "depraved" manner.) The state supreme court affirmed. While respondent was seeking federal habeas review, the Supreme Court decided *Apprendi v. New Jersey*, p. 1550, and *Ring v. Arizona*, p. 1555. *Apprendi* required that facts increasing the penalty for a crime beyond the prescribed statutory maximum be submitted to a jury and proved beyond a reasonable doubt. Applying the *Apprendi* principle to the Arizona death sentencing scheme, *Ring* held that because Arizona law authorized the death penalty only if an aggravating factor was present; the existence of such a factor had to be proved to a jury rather than to a judge.

The Ninth Circuit invalidated respondent's death sentence, inter alia, on the ground that the new rule announced in *Ring* was a "watershed" procedural rule entitled to retroactive effect. A 5–4 majority per SCALIA, J., reversed:

"[As for the argument] that *Ring* falls under the retroactivity exception for 'watershed rules of criminal procedure' implicating the fundamental fairness and accuracy of the criminal proceeding' [quoting *Teague*], [the] question here is not [whether] the Framers believed that juries are more accurate factfinders than judges [or] whether juries actually *are* more accurate factfinders than judges * * *. Rather, the questions is whether judicial factfinding so 'seriously diminishe[s]' accuracy that there is an 'impermissibly large risk' of punishing conduct the law does not reach. [*Teague*]. The evidence is simply too equivocal to support that conclusion.

"[The] dissent contends that juries are more accurate because they better reflect community standards in deciding whether, for example, a murder is heinous, cruel, or depraved *as determined by community standards*. It is easy to find enhanced accuracy in jury determination when one redefines the statute's substantive scope in such manner as to ensure that result.

"[The] right to jury trial is fundamental to our system of criminal procedure, and States are bound to enforce the Sixth Amendment's guarantees as we interpret them. But it does not follow that, when a criminal defendant has had a full trial and one round of appeals in which the State faithfully applied the Constitution as we understood it at the time, he may nevertheless continue to litigate his claims indefinitely in hopes that we will one day have a change of heart. *Ring* announce a new procedural rule that does not apply retroactively to cases already final on direct review."

BREYER, J., joined by Stevens, Souter and Ginsberg, JJ., dissented:

"[*Ring*] held that a jury, not a judge, must make the findings necessary to qualify a person for punishment by death. In my view, that holding amounts to a 'watershed' procedural ruling that a federal habeas court must apply when considering a constitutional challenge to a 'final' death sentence—i.e., a sentence that was already final on direct review when *Ring* was decided.

"[*Teague*] recognizes that important interests argue against, and indeed generally forbid, retroactive application of new procedural rules. These interests include the 'interest in insuring that there will at some point be the certainty that comes with an end to litigation'; the desirability of assuring that 'attention will ultimately be focused not on whether a conviction was free from error but rather on whether the prisoner can be restored to a useful place in the community'; and the fact that society does not have endless resources to spend upon retrials, which (where witnesses have become unavailable and other evidence stale) may well produce unreliable results.

"Certain of these interests are unusually weak where capital sentencing proceedings are at issue. Retroactivity here, for example, would not require inordinate expenditure of state resources. A decision making *Ring* retroactive would affect approximately 110 individuals on death row. This number, however large in absolute terms, is small compared with the approximately 1.2 million individuals presently confined in state prisons. Consequently, the impact on resources is likely to be much less than if a rule affecting the ordinary criminal process were made retroactive.

"[Finally,] I believe we should discount ordinary finality interests in a death case, for those interests are comparative in nature and death-related collateral proceedings, in any event, may stretch on for many years regardless.

"[The] majority does not deny that *Ring*'s rule makes *some* contribution to greater accuracy. It simply is unable to say 'confidently' that the absence of *Ring*'s rule creates an 'impermissibly large risk' that the death penalty was improperly imposed. For the reasons stated, I believe that the risk is one that the law need not and should not tolerate. Judged in light of *Teague's* basic purpose, *Ring*'s requirement that a jury, and not a judge, must apply the death sentence aggravators announces a watershed rule of criminal procedure that should be applied retroactively in habeas proceedings."[a]

SECTION 4. THE FEDERAL COURTS' "SUPERVISORY POWER" OVER THE ADMINISTRATION OF FEDERAL CRIMINAL JUSTICE

As the Court, per FRANKFURTER, J., observed in McNABB v. UNITED STATES (1943) (more extensively discussed at p. 558), "while the power of this Court to undo convictions in *state* courts is limited to the enforcement of those 'fundamental principles of liberty and justice' secured by [fourteenth amendment due process]" (emphasis added), the standards of *federal* criminal justice "are not satisfied merely by observance of those minimal historic safeguards." Rather, "[i]n the exercise of its supervisory authority over the administration of criminal justice in the federal courts, [this Court has] formulated rules of evidence to be applied in federal criminal prosecutions." Thus, in *McNabb,* the Court held incriminating statements obtained during prolonged and hence unlawful detention (i.e., while the suspect was held in violation of federal statutory requirements that he be promptly taken before a committing magistrate) inadmissible in federal courts "[q]uite apart from the Constitution."

a. See also *Beard v. Banks*, p. 1659.

For a long, hard look at *McNabb* itself and the federal "supervisory power" generally, see Sara Sun Beale, *Reconsidering Supervisory Power in Criminal Cases: Constitutional and Statutory Limits on the Authority of the Federal Courts,* 84 Colum.L.Rev. 1433 (1984). Professor Beale maintains, inter alia, that "the supervisory power has blurred the constitutional and statutory limitations on the authority of the federal courts [and] fostered the erroneous view that the federal courts exercise general supervision over federal prosecutors and investigators"; and that "there is no statutory or constitutional source of authority broad enough to encompass all of the supervisory power decisions." Id. at 1434–35.

"In cases not involving questions of judicial procedure or a statutory violation," concludes Beale, id. at 1521–22, the federal courts lack the authority "to exclude evidence or to dismiss a prosecution unless the government's conduct violated the Constitution. This analysis requires the federal courts to decide some constitutional issues they are now able to avoid—or at least defer—by grounding their rulings on supervisory power. [Requiring the federal courts to ground decisions on a constitutional basis] would be likely to result in eliminating some restrictions on federal investigators and prosecutors that have been grounded solely on supervisory power. This is as it should be.

"But this approach need not straitjacket the courts. Where there has been a legislative grant of authority, such as the rules enabling legislation, the power of the courts is extensive. Amendments to the Federal Rules of Criminal Procedure may properly regulate some matters that have been the subject of highly questionable supervisory power rulings. * * * But the concept of separation of powers dictates that federal prosecutors and investigators, like their state counterparts, should perform their duties subject only to the requirements imposed by the federal Constitution and statutes, not subject to the federal judiciary's preference for particular policies and practices."

In *United States v. Russell* (1973) (discussed at p. 505), in the course of rejecting respondent's argument that he had been "entrapped" because there had been an intolerable degree of government involvement in the criminal enterprise, the Court, per Rehnquist, J., observed:

"[Several lower federal court decisions] have undoubtedly gone beyond this Court's [precedents] in order to bar prosecutions because of what they [considered] 'overzealous law enforcement.' But the [entrapment defense] was not intended to give the federal judiciary a 'chancellor's foot' veto over law enforcement practices of which it does not disapprove. The execution of the federal laws under our Constitution is confined primarily to the Executive Branch of the Government, subject to applicable constitutional and statutory limitations and to judicially fashioned rules to enforce those limitations."

When a three-justice plurality (Rehnquist, J., joined by the Chief Justice and White, J.,) quoted the "chancellor's foot" passage with approval in *Hampton v. United States* (1976) (discussed at p. 516), concurring Justice Powell, joined by Blackmun, J., observed:

"The plurality's use of the 'chancellor's foot' passage from *Russell* may suggest that it also would foreclose reliance on our supervisory power to bar conviction of [a defendant predisposed to commit the crime] because of outrageous police conduct. * * * I do not understand *Russell* to have gone so far. There we indicated only that we should be extremely reluctant to invoke the supervisory power in cases of this kind because that power does not give the 'federal judiciary a 'chancellor's foot' veto over law enforcement practices of which it [does] not approve.' * * * I therefore am unwilling to join the plurality in concluding that, no matter what the circumstances, neither due process principles nor our supervisory power could support a bar to conviction in any case where the Government is able to prove predisposition [to commit the crime].''[a]

Whatever the implications of the ''chancellor's foot'' passage, both in *Payner,* infra, and in *Hasting,* infra, the Court left no doubt that it took a dim view of the federal courts' exercise of their ''supervisory power.''

UNITED STATES v. PAYNER, 447 U.S. 727 (1980), arose as follows: An IRS investigation into the financial activities of American citizens in the Bahamas focused on a certain Bahamian bank. When an official of that bank visited the United States, IRS agents stole his briefcase for a time, removed hundreds of documents from the briefcase and photographed them. As a result of this ''briefcase caper,'' defendant Payner was convicted of federal income tax violations. Because Payner lacked ''standing'' to challenge the ''briefcase caper'' under the Court's Fourth Amendment precedents (see Ch. 11, § 1), the federal district court invoked its supervisory power to exclude the tainted evidence. The district court found, and these findings were undisturbed by the higher courts, that ''the Government counsels its agents that the Fourth Amendment standing limitation permits them to purposefully conduct an unconstitutional search and seizure of one individual in order to obtain evidence against third parties who are the real targets of the government intrusion'' and that IRS agents ''transacted the 'briefcase caper' with a purposeful, bad faith hostility toward the Fourth Amendment rights of [the bank official] in order to obtain evidence against persons like Payner.'' But a 6–3 majority, per POWELL, J., held that the supervisory power ''does not authorize a federal court'' to exclude evidence that did not violate the defendant's Fourth Amendment rights:

''[T]he interest in deterring illegal searches does not justify the exclusion of tainted evidence at the instance of a party who was not the victim of the challenged practices. The values assigned to the competing interests do not change because a court has elected to analyze the question under the supervisory power instead of the Fourth Amendment. In either case, the need to deter the underlying conduct and the detrimental impact of excluding the evidence remain precisely the same. [The] district court's reasoning, which the [Sixth Circuit] affirmed, amounts to a substitution of individual judgment for the controlling decisions of this Court. Were we to accept this use of the supervisory power, we would confer on the judiciary discretionary power to disregard the considered limitations of the law it is charged with enforcing.''

Dissenting Justice MARSHALL, joined by Brennan and Blackmun, JJ., maintained that the Court's holding ''effectively turns the standing rules created by this Court for assertions of Fourth Amendment violations into a sword to be used by the Government to permit it deliberately to invade one person's Fourth Amendment rights in order to obtain evidence against another person. Unlike the Court, I do not believe that the federal courts are unable to protect the integrity of the judicial system from such gross government misconduct.'' Continued the dissent:

''The Court's decision to engraft the standing limitations of the Fourth Amendment onto the exercise of supervisory powers is puzzling not only because it runs contrary to the major purpose behind the exercise of the supervisory powers—to protect the integrity of the court—but also because it appears to render the supervisory powers superfluous. In order to establish that suppression

a. Dissenting Justice Brennan, joined by Stewart and Marshall, JJ., agreed with Justices Powell and Blackmun that ''*Russell* does not foreclose imposition of a bar to conviction—based upon our supervisory power or due process principles—where the conduct of law enforcement authorities is sufficiently offensive, even though the individuals entitled to invoke such a defense might be 'predisposed.' ''

of evidence under the supervisory powers would be proper, the Court would also require Payner to establish a violation of his Fourth or Fifth Amendment rights, in which case suppression would flow directly from the Constitution. This approach is totally unfaithful to our prior supervisory power cases, which, contrary to the Court's suggestion, are not constitutional cases in disguise."

UNITED STATES v. HASTING, 461 U.S. 499 (1983), arose as follows: Five defendants were convicted of kidnapping and transporting women across state lines for immoral purposes. Concluding that the prosecutor had violated *Griffin v. California* (p. 1453, fn. a) by, in effect, commenting on the failure of any defendant to take the stand in his own defense, the U.S. Court of Appeals for the Seventh Circuit reversed. The Seventh Circuit was motivated at least in part by what it perceived to be continuing violations of *Griffin* by the prosecutors within its jurisdiction. Although impermissible comment on a defendant's failure to take the stand is subject to a "harmless error" doctrine (See p. 1615), the Seventh Circuit declined to apply that doctrine, stating that its application "would impermissibly compromise the clear constitutional violation of the defendants' Fifth Amendment rights." The Court, per BURGER, C.J., reversed:

"[W]e proceed on the assumption that, without so stating, the court was exercising its supervisory powers to discipline the prosecutors of its jurisdiction. * * * We hold that the [harmless error doctrine] may not be avoided by an assertion of supervisory power, simply to justify a reversal of these criminal convictions.

"[I]n the exercise of supervisory powers, federal courts may, within limits, formulate procedural rules not specifically required by the Constitution or the Congress. The purposes underlying use of the supervisory powers are threefold: to implement a remedy for violation of recognized rights; to preserve judicial integrity by ensuring that a conviction rests on appropriate considerations validly before the jury; and finally, as a remedy designed to deter illegal conduct.

"[These goals] are not, however, significant in the context of this case if, as the Court of Appeals plainly implied, the errors alleged are harmless. Supervisory power to reverse a conviction is not needed as a remedy when the error to which it is addressed is harmless since by definition, the conviction would have been obtained notwithstanding the asserted error. Further, in this context, the integrity of the process carries less weight, for it is the essence of the harmless error doctrine that a judgment may stand only when there is no 'reasonable possibility that the [practice] complained of might have contributed to the conviction.' Finally, deterrence is an inappropriate basis for reversal where, as here, the prosecutor's remark is at most an attenuated violation of *Griffin* and where means more narrowly tailored to deter objectionable prosecutorial conduct are available."[5]

Justice BRENNAN, joined by Marshall, J., concurred in part and dissented in part, observing:

"[Various cases] indicate that the policy considerations supporting the harmless error rule and those supporting the existence of an appellate court's supervisory powers are not in irreconcilable conflict. Both the harmless error rule and the

5. Here, for example, the court could have dealt with the offending argument by directing the District Court to order the prosecutor to show cause why he should not be disciplined, or by asking the Department of Justice to initiate a disciplinary proceeding against him. The Government informs us that in the last three years, the Department of Justice's Office of Professional Responsibility has investigated 28 complaints of unethical conduct and that one assistant United States attorney resigned in the face of an investigation that he made improper arguments to a grand jury. The Court also could have publicly chastised the prosecutor by identifying him in its opinion.

exercise of supervisory powers advance the important judicial and public interest in the orderly and efficient administration of justice. [If] Government prosecutors have engaged in a pattern and practice of intentionally violating defendants' constitutional rights, a court of appeals certainly might be justified in reversing a conviction, even if the error at issue is harmless, in an effort to deter future violations. If effective as a deterrent, the reversal could avert further damage to judicial integrity. * * * Convictions are important, but they should not be protected at any cost."

Notes and Questions

1. Under the *Massiah* doctrine (p. 56), an indicted defendant has a Sixth Amendment right to counsel as well as his *Miranda* safeguards. Stressing that the "strict standard" governing waiver of counsel at trial should apply to an alleged waiver of the *Massiah* right to counsel as well, in *United States v. Mohabir*, 624 F.2d 1140 (2d Cir.1980), the court invoked its federal supervisory power to hold that a "valid waiver of the Sixth Amendment right to have counsel present during post-indictment interrogation must be preceded by a federal judicial officer's explanation of the content and significance of this right." However, in *Patterson v. Illinois* (1988) (p. 740), the Supreme Court specifically rejected *Mohabir*'s holding that warnings in addition to the *Miranda* warnings are required to effectuate a waiver of the *Massiah* right (see fn. 8 in *Patterson*), without mentioning that *Mohabir* was an exercise of the Second Circuit's federal supervisory power.

2. The *Hasting* Court noted that, within limits, federal courts may exercise their "supervisory power [to] formulate procedural rules not specifically required by the Constitution or the Congress." After *Payner* and *Hasting, what* procedural rules? Consider Note 2, p. 1100 (exercise of federal supervisory power over grand juries). After *Payner* and *Hasting,* may the federal courts still *exclude evidence* or reverse a conviction based in part on inadmissible evidence if such exclusion or reversal is not required by the Constitution or the Congress? Cf. *Bank of Nova Scotia v. United States*, 487 U.S. 250 (1988) (set forth at p. 1100).

3. Why has the effort to impose "extraconstitutional" standards on federal law enforcement officials, best illustrated by *McNabb* and its progeny, fared so badly in recent decades? Consider Bennett Gershman, *The New Prosecutors,* 53 U.Pitt.L.Rev. 393, 432 (1992): "First, [the supervisory power] required judges to impose on government officials their own notions of 'good policy.' The judiciary has resisted this invitation. Second, supervisory power increasingly has been viewed as an unwarranted judicial intrusion into the exclusive domain of a coordinate branch of the government. Finally, once supervisory power became subservient to the harmless error rule, it became largely irrelevant."

SECTION 5. TRENDS AND COUNTERTRENDS: THE "NEW FEDERALISM IN CRIMINAL PROCEDURE" AND NEW LIMITATIONS ON STATE RIGHTS PROTECTIONS[a]

When the Warren Court's "criminal procedure revolution" came to a halt, a number of state courts "greeted the Burger Court's retreat from activism not with submission, but with a stubborn independence that displays a determination to

a. The phrase "new federalism in criminal procedure" was coined by Professor Donald E. Wilkes, Jr., in his 1974 article, *The New Federalism in Criminal Procedure: State Court Evasion of the Burger Court*, 62 Ky.L.J. 421.

keep alive the Warren Court's philosophical commitment to protection of the criminal suspect." Donald E. Wilkes, *More on the New Federalism in Criminal Procedure,* 63 Ky.L.J. 873 (1975). The most influential article on the subject of state constitutional rights is Justice William Brennan's *State Constitutions and the Protection of Individual Rights,* 90 Harv.L.Rev. 489 (1977), one of the most frequently cited law review articles of modern times. See, too, Justice Brennan's updated views in *The Bill of Rights and the States: The Revival of State Constitutions as Guardians of Individual Rights,* 61 N.Y.U.L.Rev. 535 (1986). See also e.g., Barry Latzer, *State Constitutional Criminal Procedure* (1995); Robert F. Williams, *State Constitutional Law: Cases & Materials* (2d ed. 1993) (especially Ch.3); Ronald Collins, Foreword: *The Once "New Judicial Federalism" and Its Critics,* 64 Wash.L.Rev. 5 (1989); Hans Linde, *First Things First: Rediscovering the States' Bill of Rights,* 9 U.Balt.L.Rev. 379 (1980).

A state supreme court bent on providing the accused with greater protection than that said to be required by the federal constitution may insulate its decision from U.S. Supreme Court review if, to quote the High Court in *Michigan v. Long* (p. 435), the state court "indicates clearly and expressly" that its decision rests on "adequate and independent state grounds." Typically, the state court construes a state constitutional provision more expansively than the U.S. Supreme Court has interpreted a *textually identical* or *parallel* provision of the Federal Bill of Rights. But sometimes, as in *People v. Jackson,* 391 Mich. 323, 217 N.W.2d 22 (1974) (rejecting the position taken by the U.S. Supreme Court in two pretrial identification cases, *Kirby v. Illinois* (p. 769), and *United States v. Ash* (p. 772), the state court may rest its decision on its authority to establish rules of evidence for its own courts.

Justice Brennan and Marshall, who often found themselves in a dissenting role in the 1970's, frequently pointed to—and approved and encouraged—the practice of some state courts (a distinct minority) to interpret state procedural rights more expansively than does the current U.S. Supreme Court. See especially Justice Brennan's dissenting opinion in *Michigan v. Mosley* (p. 646). Justice Brennan also forcefully stated his views on this matter in his 1977 law review article, supra, emphasizing that "the decisions of the [U.S. Supreme] Court are not, and should not be, dispositive of questions regarding rights guaranteed by counterpart provisions of state law. [A]lthough in the past it might have been safe for counsel to raise only federal constitutional issues in state courts, plainly it would be most unwise these days not also to raise the state constitutional questions."

Justice Brennan's advice has not gone unheeded. A dozen years after Brennan wrote his first article on state constitutional rights, Washington Supreme Court Justice Robert Utter, *State Constitutional Law, the United States Supreme Court, and Democratic Accountability,* 64 Wash.L.Rev. 19, 27 (1989), reported that "more than 450 published state court opinions [had interpreted] state constitutions as going beyond federal constitutional guarantees."

For example, a number of state courts have declined to adopt the U.S. Supreme Court's position in *United States v. Leon,* p. 224 (establishing a so-called "good faith" exception to the fourth amendment exclusionary rule at least in search warrant cases); *Illinois v. Gates* (p. 280) (establishing a new approach to "probable cause"); *Harris v. New York* (permitting use of statements obtained in violation of *Miranda* for impeachment purposes); and *Moran v. Burbine* (p. 661) (police need not inform a suspect that a lawyer retained by relatives or friends is trying to reach him). See generally Charles H. Whitebread & Christopher Slogbogin, *Criminal Procedure* § 34.02 (c) (4th ed. 2000).

The New Federalism has not escaped strong criticism. Some judges and commentators, for example, have charged that it generates uncertainty and confusion among state officials and that "state activism" not based on local factors is a result-oriented response to U.S. Supreme Court decisions and therefore unprincipled. See Whitebread & Slobogin, supra, at 1035–42 and cases and authorities discussed therein.

Although the "new federalism in criminal procedure" became apparent in the early 1970's, "recent constitutional and statutory changes in state law * * * have imposed new restrictions on the new federalism." Donald E. Wilkes, *The New Federalism in Criminal Procedure in 1984: Death of the Phoenix?,* in Developments in State Constitutional Law 166, 169 (B. McGraw ed. 1985) (hereinafter referred to as "Wilkes").

"Many of the best and brightest of the new federalism decisions have come from the California Supreme Court," Wilkes at 171, but The California Victims' Bill of Rights, often called Proposition 8, an initiative approved by the voters in 1982, "represents a major victory for the opponents of the new federalism in California, who have become increasingly vocal in their attacks since the early 1970s." Id. Proposition 8 added a new Section 28 to Article I of the California Bill of Rights. A so-called "right to truth-in-evidence" provision of the new section reads: "Except as provided by statute hereafter enacted by a two thirds vote of the membership in each house of the Legislature, relevant evidence shall not be excluded in any criminal proceeding * * *." *In re Lance W.,* 694 P.2d 744 (Cal.1985), held that this provision abrogated the vicarious exclusionary rule that was established in *People v. Martin* (1955) (p. 851) and applied to both Fourth Amendment and state constitutional violations.

The New Federalism also suffered a setback in Florida. When the state supreme court held that the state guarantee against unreasonable search and seizure, Art. 1, § 12 of the Florida Constitution, furnished more protection against governmental intrusion than did the Fourth Amendment to the U.S. Constitution, Florida voters amended the state guarantee so that it now provides that "[t]his right shall be construed in conformity with the 4th Amendment to the United States Constitution, as interpreted by the United States Supreme Court." Unlike the California Amendment, which only affects the exclusionary remedy, the Florida amendment eliminates the power of its state courts to develop their own substantive law of search and seizure. See generally Christopher Slobogin, *State Adoption of Federal Law: Exploring the Limits of Florida's "Forced Linkage" Amendment*, 39 U.Fla.L.Rev. 653 (1987).

As might be expected, the state courts' interpretation of state constitutional provisions so that they provide greater protection than that required by the present Supreme Court's interpretation of analogous provisions of the Bill of Rights has received a chilly reception in some U.S. Supreme Court Justices' chambers. Thus, concurring in the dismissal of the writ of certiorari as improvidently granted in *Florida v. Casal,* 462 U.S. 637 (1983), Chief Justice Burger expressed satisfaction with the 1982 amendment to the Florida Constitution. "As amended," he noted, Art. 1, § 12 "ensures that Florida courts will no longer be able to rely on the State Constitution to suppress evidence that would be admissible under the decisions of the Supreme Court of the United States. [W]hen state courts interpret state law to require *more* than the Federal Constitution requires, the citizens of the state must be aware that they have the power to amend state law to ensure rational law enforcement."

In MICHIGAN v. LONG, 463 U.S. 1032 (1983) (also discussed at p. 435), rejecting the argument that "the Michigan courts have provided greater protection from searches and seizures under the state constitution than is afforded under the Fourth Amendment, and the [state supreme court's] references to the state constitution therefore establishes an adequate and independent ground for the decision below," the Court, per O'CONNOR, J., took the occasion to "reexamine our treatment of [the] jurisdictional issue in order to achieve the consistency that is necessary" when various forms of references to state law are said to constitute adequate and independent state grounds:

"[W]hen, as in this case, a state court decision fairly appears to rest primarily on federal law, or to be interwoven with the federal law, and when the adequacy and independence of any possible state law ground is not clear from the face of the opinion, we will accept as the most reasonable explanation that the state court decided the case the way it did because it believed that federal law required it to do so. If a state court chooses merely to rely on federal precedents as it would on the precedents of all other jurisdictions, then it need only make clear by a plain statement [that] the federal cases are being used only for the purpose of guidance, and do not themselves compel the result that the court has reached. In this way, both justice and judicial administration will be greatly improved. If the state court decision indicates clearly and expressly that it is alternatively based on bona fide separate, adequate, and independent grounds, we, of course, will not undertake to review the decision.

"The principle that we will not review judgments of state courts that rest on adequate and independent state grounds is based, in part, on 'the limitations of our own jurisdiction.' The jurisdictional concern is that we not 'render an advisory opinion, and if the same judgment would be rendered by the state court after we corrected its views of federal laws, our review could amount to nothing more than an advisory opinion.' "[a]

Dissenting Justice STEVENS could not accept the Court's decision "to presume that adequate state grounds are intended to be dependent on federal law unless the record plainly shows otherwise." He continued:

"I am confident that all members of this Court agree that there is a vital interest in the sound management of scarce federal judicial resources. All of those policies counsel against the exercise of federal jurisdiction. They are fortified by my belief that a policy of judicial restraint—one that allows other decisional bodies to have the last word in legal interpretation until it is truly necessary for this Court to intervene—enables this Court to make its most effective contribution to our federal system of government.

"The nature of the case before us hardly compels a departure from tradition. These are not cases in which an American citizen has been deprived of a right secured by the United States Constitution or a federal statute. Rather, they are cases in which a state court has upheld a citizen's assertion of a right, finding the citizen to be protected under both federal and state law. The complaining party is an officer of the state itself, who asks us to rule that the state court interpreted federal rights too broadly and 'over-protected' the citizen. Such cases should not be of inherent concern to this Court."[b]

---

a. The Court then reviewed the decision below under this framework and came away "unconvinced that it rests upon an independent state ground."

b. Although he was satisfied that the Court had jurisdiction in this particular case, concurring Justice Blackmun did not join the part of the Court's opinion "fashioning a new presumption of jurisdiction over cases coming here from state courts." Brennan, J., joined by Marshall, J., agreed that the Court had jurisdiction to decide the case, but dissented on the merits of the search and seizure issue. (See p. 435).

See also *Florida v. Meyers,* 466 U.S. 380 (1984) (per curiam), summarily reversing a state intermediate appellate court because it "either misunderstood or ignored our prior rulings with respect to the constitutionality of the warrantless search of an impounded automobile." (The state supreme court had denied discretionary review.) Respondent argued that the Court should not review the search and seizure issue because the state court had reversed the conviction on two independent grounds, one of which (restricted cross-examination) the state did not contest. But the Court found no "clear indication that the cross-examination ruling provided an independent and adequate basis for reversal of the conviction. See *Michigan v. Long.*"

SECTION 6. DUE PROCESS, INDIVIDUAL RIGHTS AND THE WAR ON TERRORISM: WHAT PROCESS IS CONSTITUTIONALLY DUE A CITIZEN WHO DISPUTES HIS ENEMY–COMBATANT DESIGNATION?

Consider HAMDI v. RUMSFELD, ___ U.S. ___, 124 S.Ct. 2633 (2004), which arose as follows: Petitioner Yasar Hamdi is an American citizen, born in Louisiana, who by 2001 resided in Afghanistan. In the immediate aftermath of the al Qaeda terrorist attacks of September 11, 2001, Congress passed a resolution authorizing the President to "use all necessary and appropriate force" against "nations, organizations or persons" that he determines "planned, authorized, committed or aided" in the September 11 attacks. Authorization for Use of Military Force (AUMF). A short time later, the President ordered the Armed Forces to subdue al Qaeda and oust the ruling Taliban regime. At a time when American forces were engaged in active combat, Hamdi was seized late in 2001 by the Northern Alliance, a military group opposed to the Taliban government, and turned over to the U.S. military as a Taliban fighter who had been captured on the battlefield. He was initially taken to the American naval base at Guantanamo Bay, Cuba, but when it was learned that he was an American citizen, he was transferred to a naval brig in the United States. In detaining Hamdi, the government took the position that he was an "enemy combatant," who had fought against the United States and its allies, and that his enemy combatant status justifies the U.S. in holding him indefinitely without bringing any formal charges against him.

Hamdi's father filed this habeas petition, alleging, inter alia, that the Government was holding his son in violation of the fifth and fourteenth amendments. He also claimed that his son's detention was prohibited by the Non–Detention Act, 18 U.S.C. § 4001(a), which forbids any imprisonment or detention of an American citizen "except pursuant to an Act of Congress." According to Hamdi's father, less than two months before the September 11 attacks his son went to Afghanistan to do "relief work" and could not have received any military training. The Government responded with a declaration from a Defense Department official (the Mobbs declaration) asserting in conclusory terms that Hamdi was affiliated with a Taliban army unit during a time when the Taliban was fighting U.S. allies. The Government maintained that Hamdi's habeas corpus petition should be dimissed on the basis of the Dobbs declaration.

There was no opinion of the Court. The principal opinion was written by Justice **O'Connor**, joined by Chief Justice Rehnquist and Justices Kennedy and Breyer. Although she concluded that the initial detention of Hamdi was authorized by the AUMF, and that the Non–Detention Act was satisfied because Hamdi's detention was "pursuant to an Act of Congress"—the AUMF—Justice O'Connor rejected the government's argument that Hamdi could be held indefinitely, without formal charges or proceedings. Justice **Souter**, joined by Ginsburg, J., disagreed with the O'Connor plurality that if Hamdi's designation as an enemy combatant were correct, his detention, at least for some period of time, was authorized by the AUMF. According to Souter, not only was the detention of a citizen like Hamdi unauthorized by the AUMF, but it was forbidden by the Non–Detention Act. Therefore, maintained Justice Souter, Hamdi was entitled to immediate release. However, in order to "give practical effect" to the conclusions of eight Justices rejecting the government's position, he "join[ed] with the plurality in ordering remand on terms closest to those I would impose."

According to dissenting Justice **Scalia**, joined by Stevens, J., absent suspension of the writ of habeas corpus by Congress, an American citizen accused of waging war against his country could not be imprisoned indefinitely; he had to be prosecuted for treason or some other crime. The AUMF did not suspend the writ and, noted Justice Scalia, nobody claims that it did. Absent suspension of the writ by Congress, the Executive's assertion of military exigency is not sufficient to permit detention without charge. Dissenting Justice **Thomas** was the only member of the Court who believed Hamdi's habeas challenge should fail. He maintained that the Executive Branch had acted "with explicit congressional approval" and that Hamdi's detention "falls squarely within the Federal Government's war powers."

Extracts from the various opinions follow:

Justice O'CONNOR announced the judgment of the Court and delivered an opinion in which the Chief Justice and Justices Kennedy and Breyer join:

"[The] threshold question before us is whether the Executive has the authority to detain citizens who qualify as 'enemy combatants.' There is some debate as to the proper scope of this term, and the Government has the authority to detain citizens who qualify as 'enemy combatants.' There is some debate as to the proper scope of this term, and the Government has never provided any court with the full criteria that it uses in classifying individuals as such. It has made clear, however, that, for purposes of this case, the 'enemy combatant' that it is seeking to detain is an individual who, it alleges, was 'part of or supporting forces hostile to the United States or coalition partners' in Afghanistan and who 'engaged in an armed conflict against the United States' there. We therefore answer only the narrow question before us: whether the detention of citizens falling within that definition is authorized.

"We do not reach the question whether Article II provides [the requisite] authority [even though the Non–Detention Act] states that '[n]o citizen shall be imprisoned or otherwise detained by the United States except pursuant to an Act of Congress.' [We conclude, however, that] the AUMF is explicit congressional authorization for the detention of individuals in the narrow category we describe (assuming, without deciding, that such authorization is required). [There] can be no doubt that individuals who fought against the United States in Afghanistan as part of the Taliban, [are] individuals Congress sought to target in passing the AUMF.

"[Even] in cases in which the detention of enemy combatants is legally authorized, [however,] there remains the question of what process is constitutionally due to a citizen who disputes his enemy-combatant status. [A]ll agree that, absent suspension, the writ of habeas corpus remains available to every individual detained within the United States. U.S. Const., Art. I, § 9, cl. 2. [All] agree suspension of the writ has not occurred here. Thus, it is undisputed that Hamdi was properly before an Article III court to challenge his detention under 28 U.S.C. § 2241, [which provides that the courts of the United States may 'within their respective jurisdictions' issue the writ to order the release of prisoners held 'in custody in violation of the Constitution, laws, or treaties of the United States']

"[The] simple outline of § 2241 makes clear both that Congress envisioned that habeas petitioners would have some opportunity to present and rebut facts and that courts in cases like this retain some ability to vary the ways in which they do so as mandated by due process. The Government recognizes the basic procedural protections required by the habeas statute, but asks us to hold that, given both the flexibility of the habeas mechanism and the circumstances presented in this case, the presentation of the Mobbs Declaration to the habeas court completed the required factual development.

"[The] ordinary mechanism that we use for balancing such serious competing interests, and for determining the procedures that are necessary to ensure that a citizen is not 'deprived of life, liberty, or property, without due process of law,' is the test that we articulated in *Mathews v. Eldridge*, 424 U.S. 319 (1976). *Mathews* dictates that the process due in any given instance is determined by weighing 'the private interest that will be affected by the official action' against the Government's asserted interest, 'including the function involved' and the burdens the Government would face in providing greater process.

"[It] is beyond question that substantial interests lie on both sides of the scale in this case. Hamdi's 'private interest [affected] by the official action,' is the most elemental of liberty interests—the interest in being free from physical detention by one's own government. * * * 'We have always been careful not to "minimize the importance and fundamental nature" of the individual's right to liberty,' and we will not do so today.

"Nor is the weight on this side of the *Mathews* scale offset by the circumstances of war or the accusation of treasonous behavior, for '[i]t is clear that commitment for *any* purpose constitutes a significant deprivation of liberty that requires due process protection,' and at this stage in the *Mathews* calculus, we consider the interest of the *erroneously* detained individual. [A]s critical as the Government's interest may be in detaining those who actually pose an immediate threat to the national security of the United States during ongoing international conflict, history and common sense teach us that an unchecked system of detention carries the potential to become a means for oppression and abuse of others who do not present that sort of threat. [We] reaffirm today the fundamental nature of a citizen's right to be free from involuntary confinement by his own government without due process of law, and we weigh the opposing governmental interests against the curtailment of liberty that such confinement entails.

"[We hold] that a citizen-detainee seeking to challenge his classification as an enemy combatant must receive notice of the factual basis for his classification, and a fair opportunity to rebut the Government's factual assertions before a neutral decisionmaker. [These] essential constitutional promises may not be eroded.

"At the same time, the exigencies of the circumstances may demand that, aside from these core elements, enemy combatant proceedings may be tailored to alleviate their uncommon potential to burden the Executive at a time of ongoing military conflict. Hearsay, for example, may need to be accepted as the most reliable available evidence from the Government in such a proceeding. Likewise, the Constitution would not be offended by a presumption in favor of the Government's evidence, so long as that presumption remained a rebuttable one and fair opportunity for rebuttal were provided. [A] burden-shifting scheme of this sort would meet the goal of ensuring that the errant tourist, embedded journalist, or local aid worker has a chance to prove military error while giving due regard to the Executive once it has put forth meaningful support for its conclusion that the detainee is in fact an enemy combatant. In the words of *Mathews,* process of this sort would sufficiently address the 'risk of erroneous deprivation' of a detainee's liberty interest while eliminating certain procedures that have questionable additional value in light of the burden on the Government.

"We think it unlikely that this basic process will have the dire impact on the central functions of warmaking that the Government forecasts. The parties agree that initial captures on the battlefield need not receive the process we have discussed here; that process is due only when the determination is made to *continue* to hold those who have been seized. The Government has made clear in its briefing that documentation regarding battlefield detainees already is kept in the ordinary course of military affairs. Any factfinding imposition created by requiring a knowledgeable affiant to summarize these records to an independent tribunal is a minimal one. [It] does not infringe on the core role of the military for the courts to exercise their own time-honored and constitutionally mandated roles of reviewing and resolving claims like those presented here.

"[There] remains the possibility that the standards we have articulated could be met by an appropriately authorized and properly constituted military tribunal. [In] the absence of such process, however, a court that receives a petition for a writ of habeas corpus from an alleged enemy combatant must itself ensure that the minimum requirements of due process are achieved.

"[Hamdi] asks us to hold that the [lower court] also erred by denying him immediate access to counsel upon his detention and by disposing of the case without permitting him to meet with an attorney. Since our grant of certiorari in this case, Hamdi has been appointed counsel, with whom he has met for consultation purposes on several occasions, and with whom he is now being granted unmonitored meetings. He unquestionably has the right to access to counsel in connection with the proceedings on remand. No further consideration of this issue is necessary at this stage of the case."

Justice SOUTER, joined by Ginsburg, J., concurred in part, dissented in part, and concurred in the judgment: "[It] is undisputed that the Government has not charged [Hamdi] with espionage, treason, or any other crime under domestic law. It is likewise undisputed that for one year and nine months, on the basis of an Executive designation of Hamdi as an 'enemy combatant,' the Government denied him the right to send or receive any communication beyond the prison where he was held and, in particular, denied him access to counsel to represent him.[1] The Government asserts a right to hold Hamdi under these conditions indefinitely, that is, until the Government determines that the United States is no longer threatened by the terrorism exemplified in the attacks of September 11, 2001.

"[The] plurality rejects [the Government's arguments trying to limit] the exercise of habeas jurisdiction and so far I agree with its opinion. The plurality does, however, accept the Government's position that if Hamdi's designation as an enemy combatant is correct, his detention (at least as to some period) is authorized by [the] AUMF. Here I disagree and respectfully dissent. [The] threshold issue is how broadly or narrowly to read the Non–Detention Act, the tone of which is severe: "No citizen shall be imprisoned or otherwise detained by the United States except pursuant to an Act of Congress." [For] a number of reasons, the

1. The Government has since February 2004 permitted Hamdi to consult with counsel as a matter of policy, but does not concede that it has an obligation to allow this.

prohibition within § 4001(a) has to be read broadly to accord the statute a long reach and to impose a burden of justification on the Government.

"First, the circumstances in which the Act was adopted point the way to this interpretation. The provision superseded a cold-war statute, the Emergency Detention Act of 1950, which had authorized the Attorney General, in time of emergency, to detain anyone reasonably thought likely to engage in espionage or sabotage. That statute was repealed in 1971 out of fear that it could authorize a repetition of the World War II internment of citizens of Japanese ancestry; Congress meant to preclude another episode like the one described in *Korematsu v. United States*, 323 U.S. 214, 65 S.Ct. 193, 89 L.Ed. 194 (1944).

"[Even] if history had spared us the cautionary example of the internments in World War II, [there] would be a compelling reason to read [the Non–Detention Act] to demand manifest authority to detain before detention is authorized. [For] reasons of inescapable human nature, the branch of the Government asked to counter a serious threat is not the branch on which to rest the Nation's entire reliance in striking the balance between the will to win and the cost in liberty on the way to victory.

"[Under] this principle of reading [the Non–Detention Act] robustly to require a clear statement of authorization to detain, none of the Government's arguments suffices to justify Hamdi's detention. [The] Government's [principal] claim, accepted by the Court, [is] that the terms of the [AUMF] are adequate to authorize detention of an enemy combatant under the circumstances described. [But the statute] never so much as uses the word detention, and there is no reason to think Congress might have perceived any need to augment Executive power to deal with dangerous citizens within the United States, given the well-stocked statutory arsenal of defined criminal offenses covering the gamut of actions that a citizen sympathetic to terrorists might commit.

"[Because] I find Hamdi's detention forbidden by § 4001(a) and unauthorized by the [AUMF], I would not reach any questions of what process he may be due in litigating disputed issues in a proceeding under the habeas statute or prior to the habeas enquiry itself. [Since] this disposition does not command a majority of the Court, however, the need to give practical effect to the conclusions of eight members of the Court rejecting the Government's position calls for me to join with the plurality in ordering remand on terms closest to those I would impose. Although I think litigation of Hamdi's status as an enemy combatant is unnecessary, the terms of the plurality's remand will allow Hamdi to offer evidence that he is not an enemy combatant, and he should at the least have the benefit of that opportunity."

Justice SCALIA, joined by Stevens, J., dissented. "[Where] the Government accuses a citizen of waging war against it, our constitutional tradition has been to prosecute him in federal court for treason or some other crime. Where the exigencies of war prevent that, the Constitution's Suspension Clause allows Congress to relax the usual protections temporarily. Absent suspension, however, the Executive's assertion of military exigency has not been thought sufficient to permit detention without charge.

"[The] writ of habeas corpus was preserved in the Constitution [as] a means to protect against 'the practice of arbitrary imprisonments [in] all ages, [one of] the favourite and most formidable instruments of tyranny.' Indeed, availability of the writ under the new Constitution (along with the requirement of trial by jury in criminal cases) was [Hamilton's] basis for arguing that additional, explicit procedural protections were unnecessary.

"[The] allegations here, of course, are no ordinary accusations of criminal activity. [Hamdi] has been imprisoned because the Government believes he participated in the waging of war against the United States. The relevant question, then, is whether there is a different, special procedure for imprisonment of a citizen accused of wrongdoing *by aiding the enemy in wartime.*

"Justice O'Connor, writing for a plurality of this Court, asserts that captured enemy combatants (other than those suspected of war crimes) have traditionally been detained until the cessation of hostilities and then released. That is probably an accurate description of wartime practice with respect to enemy *aliens.* The tradition with respect to American citizens, however, has been quite different. Citizens aiding the enemy have been treated as traitors subject to the criminal process.

"[The] plurality finds justification for Hamdi's imprisonment in the [AUMF]. [This] is not remotely a congressional suspension of the writ, and no one claims that it is. [If] the Suspension Clause does not guarantee the citizen that he will either be tried or released, unless the conditions for suspending the writ exist and the grave action of suspending the writ has been taken; if it merely guarantees the citizen that he will not be detained unless Congress by ordinary legislation says he can be detained; it guarantees him very little indeed."

Justice THOMAS, dissented: "The Executive Branch, acting pursuant to the powers vested in the President by the Constitution and with explicit congressional approval, has determined that Yaser Hamdi is an enemy combatant and should be detained. This detention falls squarely within the Federal Government's war powers, and we lack the expertise and capacity to second-guess that decision. As such, petitioners' habeas challenge should fail, and there is no reason to remand the case. The plurality reaches a contrary conclusion by failing adequately to consider basic principles of the constitutional structure as it relates to national security and foreign affairs and by using the balancing scheme of *Mathews v. Eldridge.* I do not think that the Federal Government's war powers can be balanced away by this Court. Arguably, Congress could provide for additional procedural protections, but until it does, we have no right to insist upon them. But even if I were to agree with the general approach the plurality takes, I could not accept the particulars. The plurality utterly fails to account for the Government's compelling interests and for our own institutional inability to weigh competing concerns correctly.

"[The] Government's asserted authority to detain an individual that the President has determined to be an enemy combatant, at least while hostilities continue, comports with the Due Process Clause. [The] Executive's decision that a detention is necessary to protect the public need not and should not be subjected to judicial second-guessing. Indeed, at least in the context of enemy-combatant determinations, this would defeat the unity, secrecy, and dispatch that the Founders believed to be so important to the warmaking function. I therefore cannot agree with Justice Scalia's conclusion that the Government must choose between using standard criminal processes and suspending the writ."

A Note on American, British and Israeli Experiences Fighting Terrorism

After examining the experience of two democratic nations, Britain and Israel, that confronted grave terrorist threats for extended periods before September 11, 2001, STEPHEN S. SCHULHOFER, *Checks and Balances in Wartime: American, British and Israeli Experiences*, 103 Mich.L.Rev. 1907, 1955 (2004), concludes:

"Confronted by acute contemporary threats of terrorism, both Britain and Israel * * * granted executive and military authorities some extraordinary powers but preserved a system of effective checks on the executive and the assurance of *prompt, fully independent* judicial review.

"In the current 'war on terrorism,' however, the U.S. government has claimed emergency powers that exceed by very large margins—indeed, by light years—the executive powers accepted as necessary and legitimate in Britain and Israel. Addressing measures far more cautious than those deployed by our own government, courts nonetheless struck down the executive and military actions as unacceptable erosions of necessary checks and balances.

"The fact that other nations reached such conclusions, and indeed that our own courts did so in previous national emergencies, cannot by itself refute empirical claims about the supposed effectiveness of greater executive power and the supposed need for fewer judicial checks. We can be confident, however, that contrary to conventional wisdom, the emergency powers the U.S. government now claims—and that the *Hamdi* plurality seems prepared to accept—are not *normal*, even for a situation of national crisis."

Chapter 3

SOME GENERAL REFLECTIONS ON LAW ENFORCEMENT OFFICIALS, THE LEGISLATURES, THE COURTS AND THE CRIMINAL PROCESS*

MICHAEL J. KLARMAN—THE RACIAL ORIGINS OF MODERN CRIMINAL PROCEDURE

99 Mich.L.Rev. 48, 52, 82–83, 93–94 (2000).

[*Moore v. Dempsey*, 261 U.S. 86 (1923), overturning a conviction obtained through a mob-dominated trial; the related cases of *Powell v. Alabama*, 287 U.S. 45 (1932) (holding that, under the circumstances of this capital case, due process required the appointed of counsel) and *Norris v. Alabama*, 294 U.S. 587 (1935) (reversing a conviction under the Equal Protection Clause where blacks had been intentionally excluded from the jury); and *Brown v. Mississippi*, 297 U.S. 278 (1936), marking the first time the Supreme Court overturned a state conviction based on coerced confessions] arose out of three quite similar episodes. Southern black defendants were charged with serious crimes against whites—either rape or murder. All three sets of defendants nearly were lynched before their cases could be brought to trial. * * * Lynchings were avoided only through the presence of state militiamen armed with machine guns surrounding the courthouse. There was a serious doubt—not just with the aid of historical hindsight, but at the time

* In addition to the articles extracted in this chapter, see Francis A. Allen, *The Judicial Quest for Penal Justice: The Warren Court and the Criminal Cases,* 1975 U.Ill.L.F. 518; Albert Alschuler, *Failed Pragmatism: Reflections on the Burger Court,* 100 Harv.L.Rev. 1436 (1987); Akhil Reed Amar, *The Constitution and Criminal Procedure: First Principles* (1997); Anthony Amsterdam, *The Supreme Court and the Rights of Suspects in Criminal Cases,* 45 N.Y.U.L.Rev. 785 (1970); Peter Arenella, *Rethinking the Functions of Criminal Procedure: The Warren and Burger Courts' Competing Ideologies,* 72 Geo.L.J. 185 (1983); Susan Bandes, *"We the People" and Our Enduring Values,* 96 Mich.L.Rev. 1376 (1998) (Book Review); Craig Bradley, *The Failure of the Criminal Procedure Revolution* (1993); Donald Dripps, *Akhil Amar on Criminal Procedure and Constitutional Law: "Here I Go Down that Wrong Road Again,"* 74 N.C.L.Rev. 1559 (1996); Jerold Israel, *Criminal Procedure, the Burger Court, and the Legacy of the Warren Court,* 75 Mich.L.Rev. 1319 (1977); Yale Kamisar, *The Warren Court and Criminal Justice,* in The Warren Court: A Retrospective 116 (Bernard Schwartz ed. 1996); Herbert Packer, *The Courts, the Police and the Rest of Us,* 57 J.Crim.L.C. & P.S. (1966); William Pizzi, *Punishment and Procedure: A Different View of the American Criminal Justice System,* 13 Const. Comm. 55 (1996); Stephen Saltzburg, *Foreword: The Flow and Ebb of Constitutional Criminal Procedure in the Warren and Burger Courts,* 69 Geo.L.J. 1512 (1980); Stephen Schulhofer, *The Constitution and the Police: Individual Rights and Law Enforcement,* 66 Wash.U.L.Q. 11 (1988); Louis Michael Seidman, *Criminal Procedure as the Servant of Politics,* 12 Const.Comm. 207 (1995); Carol Steiker, *Counter-Revolution in Constitutional Criminal Procedure? Two Audiences, Two Answers,* 94 Mich.L.Rev. 2466 (1996); George Thomas III, *Remapping the Criminal Procedure Universe,* 83 Va.L.Rev. 1819 (1997) (Book Review); Robert Weisberg, *Criminal Procedure Doctrine: Some Versions of the Skeptical,* 76 J.Crim.L. & C. 832 (1985); Charles Whitebread, *The Burger Court's Counter–Revolution in Criminal Procedure,* 24 Washburn L.J. 471 (1985).

of the trial—as to whether any of the defendants were in fact guilty of the crime charged. * * * Trials took place quickly after the alleged crimes in order to avoid a lynching. [The] trials were completed within a matter of hours [and] the jurors, from which blacks were intentionally excluded * * *, deliberated for only a matter of minutes before imposing death sentences. * * *

It is impossible to measure the amount of physical coercion employed by southern sheriffs to extract confessions from black suspects, and thus one cannot say for sure what effect *Brown v. Mississippi* had on this practice. Supreme Court cases from the 1940s, however, make it clear that beating blacks into confessing remained a common practice in the South after *Brown*. For a variety of reasons, *Brown* had, at most, a limited impact on southern police practices. First, it must be recalled that the deputy sheriff who had administered the beatings in *Brown* made no effort to hide his behavior. The likeliest effect of the Supreme Court's decision, then, was to reduce the candor of state law enforcement officials. * * * Tortured confessions, if detected, might eventually be reversed by the Supreme Court or even by a state appellate court, but the vast majority of criminal cases never made it that far in the system. Thus, most convictions based on coerced confessions were unlikely to be overturned. Moreover, the narrow construction provided to federal civil rights statutes at this time made it very difficult to prosecute law enforcement officials who used physical violence against black suspects. Even in those unusual cases where a federal violation could be established, convincing all-white southern jurors to indict and convict law enforcement officials who had mistreated black defendants proved virtually impossible. * * *

[The rulings in *Moore, Powell, Norris* and *Brown*] support the claim made by several recent commentators that the Supreme Court's constitutional interventions tend to be less countermajoritarian than is commonly supposed. [The four rulings] almost certainly were consonant with dominant national opinion at the time. Even within the South, significant support existed for the results in these cases. [These] rulings only bound the southern states to abstract norms of behavior that they generally had embraced on their own. In the North, meanwhile, although blacks suffered oppressive discrimination in housing, employment, and public accommodations, the criminal justice system approached somewhat nearer to the ideal of colorblindness. Thus, it is erroneous to conceive of these landmark criminal procedure cases as instances of judicial protection of minority rights from majoritarian oppression. Rather, they better exemplify the paradigm of judicial imposition of a national consensus on resistant state outliers (with the qualification that even the southern states generally accepted these norms in the abstract).

Relatedly, these criminal procedure decisions raise the interesting possibility that during the interwar period the Supreme Court reflected national opinion on racial issues better than did Congress. These rulings imposed constitutional constraints on southern lynch law at almost precisely the same time that the national legislature was debating the imposition of statutory constraints on lynching. The House of Representatives approved anti-lynching bills three times, in 1922, 1937, and 1940. But these measures never survived in the Senate, mainly because that institution's antimajoritarian filibuster rules enabled intensely committed southern Senators (with the aid of some largely indifferent westerners) to block passage. Similarly, the House approved anti-poll tax bills five times in the 1940s, but they never passed the Senate, while the Supreme Court that same decade struck a momentous blow for black suffrage by invalidating the white primary.

YALE KAMISAR—THE WARREN COURT AND CRIMINAL JUSTICE

Reprinted in The Warren Court: A Retrospective 116, 140–43 (B. Schwartz ed. 1996).

Did the Warren Court's Reform Effort Come at a Bad Time? Could It Have Come at a Better Time?

In his lively book, *The Self–Inflicted Wound* (1970) (an account of the Warren Court's revolution in criminal procedure), former *New York Times* Supreme Court reporter Fred Graham observes: "History has played cruel jokes before, but few can compare with the coincidence in timing between the rise in crime, violence and racial tensions [and] the Supreme Court's campaign to strengthen the rights of criminal suspects against the state. [The] Court's reform effort could have come at almost any time in the recent past * * * [at a time] when it could have taken root before crime became the problem that it has become."

When was that? According to the media, the claims of law enforcement officials, and the statements of politicians, we have *always* been experiencing a "crime crisis"—*at no time* in our recent, or not-so-recent, past has there *been a time* when "society" *could afford* a strengthening or expansion of the rights of the accused.

In 1943, the Court held in *McNabb v. United States* [p. 558], in the exercise of its supervisory authority over the administration of federal criminal justice, that voluntary confessions should be excluded from evidence if they were obtained while the suspect was being held in violation of federal requirements that arrestees be promptly taken before a committing magistrate. The *McNabb* Court tried to do for the federal courts what, a quarter-century later, *Miranda* was designed to do for state, as well as federal, courts: bypass the frustrating "swearing contests" over the nature of the secret interrogation and reduce, if not eliminate, both police temptations and opportunity to coerce incriminating statements. The *McNabb* doctrine sought to do so by focusing on a relatively objective factor—the length of time a suspect was held by the police before being brought to a judicial officer to be advised of his rights.

Although it placed lesser restrictions on federal police than *Miranda* was to place on all police a quarter-century later, the *McNabb* rule was severely criticized by many law enforcement authorities and many members of Congress for barring the use of voluntary confessions. For example, in his testimony before a House subcommittee, the then head of the District of Columbia Police Department called *McNabb* "one of the greatest handicaps that has ever confronted law enforcement officers."

Police officials and politicians were not the only ones unhappy with the *McNabb* decision. Most of the judges of the lower federal courts "were unsympathetic, if not openly hostile, toward a rule which suppressed evidence not only relevant but also cogent and often crucial in order to effectuate what seemed to them to be an exaggerated concern for individual rights."[206]

A year after the *McNabb* decision, at a time when a bill to repudiate it was gathering much support, the Court took another look at the doctrine in the *Mitchell* case.[207] With one eye on Congress, and stung by strong criticism from the bench and bar, as well as from police and prosecutors, the Court backed off; it wrote an opinion that could be read as limiting *McNabb* to its particular facts.

206. Hogan & Snee, *The McNabb–Mallory Rule: Its Rise, Rationale and Rescue*, 47 Geo. L.J. 1, 5 (1958).

207. Mitchell v. United States, 321 U.S. 756 (1944).

[Although the Supreme Court reaffirmed the *McNabb* rule fourteen years later in *Mallory v. United States* (p. 559)], the storm of controversy over the rule never subsided. * * * More bills were introduced to repeal, or at least soften, the doctrine, and in 1968 a law was finally enacted that badly crippled it. [See p. 680.] (Because the *McNabb-Mallory* doctrine was a rule of evidence formulated in the exercise of the Court's supervisory authority over the administration of federal criminal justice, it was subject to repeal or revision by the Congress.)

The experience with the *McNabb-Mallory* rule is strong evidence that the 1940s and 1950s were hardly auspicious times for the Court to do what it was to do in *Miranda*—deem custodial interrogation by state police, as well as federal, "inherently coercive." Indeed, when, in the 1944 case of *Ashcraft v. Tennessee* [p. 553], a majority of the Court called *thirty-six hours of continuous relay interrogation* "inherently coercive," it evoked a powerful dissent by three Justices who severely criticized the majority for departing from the traditional "voluntariness" test.

In another coerced confession case, one decided in 1949 (*Watts v. Indiana*), concurring Justice Robert Jackson warned that our Bill of Rights, as interpreted by the Court up to that time, imposed "the maximum restrictions upon the power of organized society over the individual that are compatible with the maintenance of organized society itself"—good reason for not indulging in any further expansion of them.[a]

Were the 1950s a good time to impose the search-and-seizure exclusionary rule on the states? When the California Supreme Court adopted the exclusionary rule on its own initiative in 1955,[217] the cries of protest were almost deafening. Prominent law enforcement officials called the exclusionary rule "the 'Magna Carta' for the criminals" and "catastrophic as far as efficient law enforcement is concerned" and warned that it had "broken the very backbone of narcotics enforcement."

What of the 1930s? In 1935 [New York] Governor Herbert Lehman opened a conference on crime by warning: "There is no question that in recent years there has come a substantial increase in organized crime. The professional criminal has become bolder. * * * We must take steps to increase the certainty of punishment following crime. * * * We must have fewer legal technical loopholes in trials and appeals."

The New York gathering on crime was not a unique event in those troubled times. The U.S. attorney general also called a conference on crime, and similar conferences were held in various states.[220] The public was so alarmed by the apparent increase in crime that a U.S. Senate investigating committee, chaired by Royal Copeland of New York, scoured the country for information and advice that could lead to a national legislative solution. At these 1933 congressional hearings, witnesses attacked virtually every procedural safeguard found in the Bill of Rights.

Going back still further, in 1931 the famous criminologist Harry Elmer Barnes voiced fear that the repeal of prohibition would trigger "an avalanche of crime"—as thousands of crooks, chased out of the booze business, would return to their old rackets.[223] He warned that "the only effective check we can think of

a. Consider that this observation was made—and many agreed—more than a decade *before* such cases as *Gideon v. Wainwright* (p. 85), *Mapp v. Ohio* (p. 219) and *Miranda* (p. 575) were decided.

217. People v. Cahan, 282 P.2d 905 (Cal. 1955).

220. See Wechsler, *A Caveat on Crime Control*, 27 J.Crim.L. & Criminology 629 (1937).

223. Barnes, *Battling the Crime Wave* 87–88 (1931).

[would] be to turn our cities over for the time being to the United States Army and Marines." Transferring the Marines from Central America to the streets of Chicago, added Barnes, "might not only promote the checking of the crime menace but also solve at one and the same time our diplomatic relations with Central America."

"Every generation supposes that its own problems are new, unknown to its forefathers."[226] To most of those who lived during that period, the 1930s (as usual) was *not* a time for strengthening the rights of the accused. Rather it seemed to be a period when (as usual) criminal procedure safeguards had already been stretched to the breaking point.

DONALD A. DRIPPS—CONSTITUTIONAL THEORY FOR CRIMINAL PROCEDURE: *DICKERSON, MIRANDA*, AND THE CONTINUING QUEST FOR BROAD—BUT—SHALLOW

43 Wm. & Mary L.Rev. 1, 45–46 (2001).

American legislatures consistently have failed to address defects in the criminal process, even when they rise to crisis-level proportions. For example, when the *Miranda* Court invited Congress and the states to experiment with alternatives to traditional backroom police interrogation, Congress responded by adopting Title II,[a] which stubbornly insisted on the traditional practice. To this day only two American jurisdictions, Alaska and Minnesota, require taping interrogations. In both instances the state courts, rather than the state legislature, were the sources of reform.

Legislatures across the United States have found billions of dollars for prisons, but the support for indigent defense is shamefully inadequate. No legislature has adopted reforms of police identification procedures, even though we have known since the 1930s that mistaken identification is the leading cause of false convictions. Legislatures have not filled the voids created by contemporary pro-government criminal procedure rulings. They have not, for instance, adopted statutory regulations of undercover operations, even though the Court has left such operations unregulated by the Fourth Amendment. They have not adopted statutory requirements for judicial warrants, or the preservation of exculpatory evidence, or plugged holes in the exclusionary rule, let alone delivered the effective tort remedy exclusionary rule critics have advocated for decades.

The record is not an accident, but the product of rational political incentives. Almost everyone has an interest in controlling crime. Only young men, disproportionately black, are at significant risk of erroneous prosecution for garden-variety felonies. Abuses of police search and seizure or interrogation powers rarely fall upon middle-aged, middle-class citizens. When powerful interest groups are subject to the exercise of police powers that pale in comparison to what is visited on young black men luckless enough to reside in a "high crime area," things are different. [But] so long as the vast bulk of police and prosecutorial power targets the relatively powerless (and when will that ever be otherwise?), criminal procedure rules that limit public power will come from the courts or they will come from nowhere.

PETER ARENELLA—FOREWORD: O. J. LESSONS

69 S.Cal.L.Rev. 1233, 1234–35 (1996).

Lawyers control adversarial trials. They decide what evidence to present and how to massage it into a story of guilt, innocence, or reasonable doubt. In such a

226. Sutherland, *Crime and Confession*, 79 Harv.L.Rev. 21, 32–33 (1965).

a. The relevant provision of Title II (which purported to "overrule" *Miranda* and reinstate the old due process-voluntariness test) is set forth at p. 679. The provision was struck down in *Dickerson v. United States* (2000), set forth at p. 680.

lawyer-dominated system, the trial's outcome may hinge on which side has the superior resources to pay for the best investigators, experts, and counsel. Money can have a greater impact on the verdict than the "facts" because it dictates how those "facts" are transformed into legally admissible and persuasive evidence.

This resource factor usually favors the state because most criminal defendants are poor. The prosecutor can use law enforcement agencies, state and private forensic laboratories, and experts on the public payroll to develop, shape, and present her evidence. Crime victims and witnesses usually cooperate with the prosecution. If they do not, the prosecutor can command their appearance before a grand jury and compel their testimony.

In contrast, a skilled and experienced public defender is lucky if she gets an investigator to spend a few hours investigating the "facts." Crime victims and civilian witnesses frequently refuse to answer the investigator's questions. If the public defender needs expert assistance, she must petition the court for funds to pay for the expert's time. The one or two state-funded experts she may obtain won't be [the caliber of O. J. Simpson's experts] and they will rarely spend hundreds of hours looking for flaws in the state's case.

This resource imbalance is particularly egregious in death penalty prosecutions. Given the horrific nature of these crimes, the defendant's life often depends on the defense's ability and capacity to make the client's humanity apparent to the jury deciding his fate at the sentencing phase of the trial.[4] Far too often, underpaid defense lawyers in capital cases spend less time and effort on death penalty cases than the Simpson defense team expended prepping for his preliminary hearing.

The "trial of the century" illustrated this resource imbalance problem in reverse. One of [O. J. Simpson's defense lawyer's] wisest decisions was to hire some of this country's leading medical, forensic, and legal experts before Simpson was even arrested. With the aid of [these experts], the defense's forensic attorney team * * * transformed incriminating hair, blood, DNA, and fiber data into evidence of police and criminalist incompetence and corruption. While defense counsel for the indigent can read the Simpson trial transcripts and learn new ways to attack forensic evidence, they lack the resources to buy the experts whose prestige and skills made the "garbage in-garbage out" strategy so effective.[a]

WILLIAM J. STUNTZ—THE UNEASY RELATIONSHIP BETWEEN CRIMINAL PROCEDURE AND CRIMINAL JUSTICE

107 Yale L.J. 1, 3–12, 72–76 (1997).

Most talk about the law of criminal procedure treats that law as a self-contained universe. The picture looks something like this: The Supreme Court

4. This is no easy task. Explaining how one's client became a killer will not work unless the defendant's life story includes factors that trigger the jury's compassion. Constructing such a story requires extensive investigation into the offender's past, documentation of whatever factors "victimized" the offender at an early age, evidence of how the "system" failed to address these factors, and expert testimony explaining why these factors diminished the offender's capacity to control his anti-social impulses. Accounts of the offender's early victimizations may well fall on deaf ears unless the defense can also make some showing of why the offender is not beyond redemption.

a. See also Deborah L. Rhodes, *Simpson Sound Bites: What Is and Isn't News About Domestic Violence*, in Postmortem: The O. J. Simpson Case 83, 84 (Jeffrey Abramson ed. 1996). After observing that a single public defender often handles hundreds of cases per year and usually lacks adequate time or resources for investigation and expert testimony, Professor Rhode continues: "By contrast, in the Simpson case, [the] complete defense bill, including legal fees, may have reached $10 million. That figure exceeds what some states spend on appointed counsel for thousands of indigent defendants."

says that suspects and defendants have a right to be free from certain types of police or prosecutorial behavior. Police and prosecutors, for the most part, then do as they're told. When they don't, and when the misconduct is tied to criminal convictions, the courts reverse the convictions, thereby sending a message to misbehaving officials. Within the bounds of this picture there is room for a lot of debate about the wisdom or constitutional pedigree of particular doctrines, and the literature is filled with debate of that sort. There is also room for theorizing about the optimal specificity of the rules the Supreme Court creates; the literature contains some of that, though less than it should. Finally, there is room for arguing about remedies—about whether reversing criminal convictions is an appropriate means of getting the police, prosecutors, and trial judges to do what the law says they ought to do. At least in the sphere of Fourth and Fifth Amendment law, a lively debate along those lines exists. But for all their variety, these debates take for granted the same basic picture of the process, a process whose only variables are the rules themselves and the remedies for their violation.

The picture is, of course, wrong. Criminal procedure's rules and remedies are embedded in a larger system, a system that can adjust to those rules in ways other than obeying them. And the rules can in turn respond to the system in a variety of ways, not all of them pleasant. The more one focuses on that dynamic, the more problematic the law of criminal procedure seems.

The heart of the problem is the system's structure. The criminal justice system is dominated by a trio of forces: crime rates, the definition of crime (which of course partly determines crime rates), and funding decisions—how much money to spend on police, prosecutors, defense attorneys, judges, and prisons. These forces determine the ratio of crimes to prosecutors and the ratio of prosecutions to public defenders, and those ratios in turn go far toward determining what the system does and how the system does it. But the law that defines what the criminal process looks like, the law that defines defendants' rights, is made by judges and Justices who have little information about crime rates and funding decisions, and whose incentives to take account of those factors may be perverse. High crime rates make it easy for prosecutors to substitute cases without strong procedural claims for cases with such claims. Underfunding of criminal defense counsel limits the number of procedural claims that can be pressed. Both phenomena make criminal procedure doctrines seem inexpensive to the appellate judges who define those doctrines. Unsurprisingly, given that regulating the criminal justice system has seemed cheap, the courts have done a lot of regulating—more, one suspects, than they would have done in a world where defendants could afford to litigate more often and more aggressively, or where prosecutors could not so easily substitute some cases for others. Criminal procedure is thus distorted by forces its authors probably do not understand.

The distortion runs both ways. As courts have raised the cost of criminal investigation and prosecution, legislatures have sought out devices to reduce those costs. Severe limits on defense funding are the most obvious example, but not the only one. Expanded criminal liability makes it easier for the government to induce guilty pleas, as do high mandatory sentences that serve as useful threats against recalcitrant defendants. And guilty pleas avoid most of the potentially costly requirements that criminal procedure imposes. These strategies would no doubt be politically attractive anyway, but the law of criminal procedure makes them more so. Predictably, underfunding, overcriminalization, and oversentencing have increased as criminal procedure has expanded.

Nor are the law's perverse effects limited to courts and legislatures. Constitutional criminal procedure raises the cost of prosecuting wealthier defendants by giving those defendants more issues to litigate. The result, at the margin, is to steer prosecutors away from such defendants and toward poorer ones. By giving defendants other, cheaper claims to raise, constitutional criminal procedure also raises the cost to defense counsel of investigating and litigating factual claims, claims that bear directly on their clients' innocence or guilt. The result is to steer defense counsel, again at the margin, away from those sorts of claims and toward constitutional issues. More Fourth, Fifth, and Sixth Amendment claims probably mean fewer self-defense claims and mens rea arguments. This turns the standard conservative criticism of the law of criminal procedure on its head. Ever since the 1960s, the right has argued that criminal procedure frees too many of the guilty. The better criticism may be that it helps to imprison too many of the innocent.

It also does little about the concern that, more than anything else, prompted its creation. The post–1960 constitutionalization of criminal procedure arose, in large part, out of the sense that the system was treating black suspects and defendants much worse than white ones. Warren-era constitutional criminal procedure began as a kind of antidiscrimination law. But the criminal justice system is characterized by extraordinary discretion—over the definition of crimes (legislatures can criminalize as much as they wish), over enforcement (police and prosecutors can arrest and charge whom they wish), and over funding (legislatures can allocate resources as they wish). In a system so dominated by discretionary decisions, discrimination is easy, and constitutional law has surprisingly little to say about it. * * *

Interestingly, judicial intervention in other aspects of the criminal justice system—the definition of crimes and the funding of criminal defense—does not seem likely to have these sorts of perverse effects. Constitutionalizing procedure, in a world where substantive law and funding are the province of legislatures, may tend to encourage bad substantive law and underfunding. But constitutionalizing some aspects of substantive criminal law and defense funding would not tend to encourage bad procedure, or bad anything else. Yet substance and funding are the areas where courts have most deferred to legislatures, where passivity rather than activism has been the judicial norm. It may be that the broad structure of constitutional regulation of criminal justice has it backward, that courts have been not too activist, but activist in the wrong places. * * *

Broader substantive criminal law allows the state to end-run much of criminal procedure. In a world where trivial crimes stay on the books, or one where routine traffic offenses count as crimes, the requirement of probable cause to arrest may mean almost nothing. Officers can arrest for a minor offense—everyone violates the traffic rules—in order to search or question a suspect on a major one.[6] This allows arrests and searches of suspected drug dealers without any ex ante support for the suspicion, the very thing the probable cause standard is supposed to forbid. In a world where sodomy laws remain valid long after their enforcement has ceased, prosecutors can induce guilty pleas in some problematic sexual assault cases—the need to prove nonconsent disappears, and with it (again, in some cases) the ability to mount a plausible defense. This amounts to convicting defendants of sexual assault without proving the crime, by pointing to another crime that serves as the excuse for punishment, but not the reason.

[Legislatures] fund the system. Legislatures decide how many police officers, prosecutors, and judges to have, and how much to pay them. They also decide how

6. See *Whren v. United States* (1996) [p. 339] (holding that police can detain motorists where there is a probable cause to believe that they have violated traffic laws, regardless of whether the stop is pretextual).

generously to fund criminal defense counsel in those cases (the majority) in which the court appoints counsel. * * *

Over the course of the past couple of decades, legislatures have exercised this funding power to expand substantially the resources devoted to law enforcement, though the budget increases appear less substantial in light of parallel increases in crime. * * * [N]otwithstanding nominal budget increases, spending on indigent defendants in constant dollars per case appears to have declined significantly between the late 1970s and the early 1990s.

The predictable result is public defenders' offices with very large ratios of cases to lawyers. One recent study found a jurisdiction in which some public defenders represented over four hundred felony defendants in an eight-month span, and the average representation was more than half that number. [Those familiar with the system agree:] Public defenders are terribly overburdened. The story is essentially the same in jurisdictions that use separately appointed defense counsel rather than public defenders. * * * [A] typical appointed defense lawyer faces something like the following pay scale: $30 or $40 an hour for the first twenty to thirty hours, and zero thereafter. * * *

[There] are a great many constitutional rules, most of which are highly contestable. The rules are produced by a court system that acts quite independently of legislative preference, at least in this area. (*Mapp v. Ohio* and *Miranda v. Arizona* were hardly examples of majoritarian lawmaking.) Perhaps more so than anywhere else in constitutional law, in criminal procedure the broad exercise of judicial power tends to be justified precisely by legislators' unwillingness to protect constitutional interests. Yet these judge-made rules are enforced through the efforts of criminal defense counsel who, in most cases, are paid by the state—the same state whose preferences the rules purport to trump. By buying less criminal defense, the state can buy less enforcement of constitutional criminal procedure. It can, to some degree, trump the trump. Of course, if it does so it necessarily also buys less of whatever else criminal defense counsel do. * * *

* * * Why has constitutional law focused so heavily on criminal procedure, and why has it so strenuously avoided anything to do with substantive criminal law and the funding of defense counsel? * * *

The real difficulty with regulating substantive criminal law and funding decisions may be [that there] is no nonarbitrary way to arrive at the proper legal rules, no way to get to sensible bottom lines by something that looks and feels like legal analysis. Whether proportionality review is lodged in appellate or trial courts, the only way to do it is to do it, to decide that this sentence is too great but not that one. There is no metric for determining right answers, no set of analytic tools that defines what a given sentence ought to be. That, after all, was the problem with discretionary sentencing regimes, the problem that produced the current infatuation with guidelines. Similarly, heightened mens rea requirements for overbroad crimes beg the question of which crimes are overbroad.

[The] only way to set funding floors is to set them—to say, states must spend this much on criminal defense, but need not spend more. There is no analytic structure that allows one to specify the right dollar amount. [A] good deal of constitutional law may consist of judicial policy preferences with a thin legal veneer, but here the veneer seems transparent.

That simple point may be the source of much of constitutional law's troubled relationship with criminal justice. Constitutional law has focused relentlessly on the sorts of issues that are susceptible to legal analysis—how to select juries, when to require warrants, which mistrials permit retrial and which ones mean the defendant must go free. These are classic lawyers' issues; they give rise to classic lawyers' arguments. But courts' decisions on those issues are embedded in a system shaped by more open-ended—and more flagrantly political—judgments: How bad should something be before we call it a crime? How much money should we spend on criminal defense? Perhaps courts would do a sufficiently poor job of making these open-ended political judgments that we are better off leaving them to other actors. That is the system's current premise, and the premise is entirely plausible. But if that premise is right, those other actors—chiefly legislators and prosecutors—are able to defeat courts' work on courts' own turf: All those judge-made procedural rules are likely not to work the way they are supposed to. In the criminal justice system's three-legged stool—procedure, substance, and money—procedure is the least stable leg, the one that most depends on the others for support.

So criminal procedure may be no more than an instance of courts properly recognizing the need to intervene in a system that imposes terrible costs on large numbers of people, and then doing what comes naturally, regulating the kinds of things courts are used to regulating. That includes avoiding a kind of decision-making that, for courts, seems unnatural. All of which might be fine if the judicially regulated sphere could be isolated from the rest of the system. Sadly, it cannot. * * *

[The law of criminal procedure prevents some serious wrongs and produces other benefits, some of which are quite familiar.] Yet there are substantial tradeoffs, and the tradeoffs are not so familiar. The criminal process is much harder to control than courts suppose; it is driven by forces the courts do not, and perhaps cannot, direct. When courts do act, their actions are shaped by those forces in ways the courts themselves may not understand, ways that are at best ambiguous and at worst bad. Some part of what the Fourth, Fifth, and Sixth Amendments protect has probably come at the cost of a criminal justice system that is less focused on the merits and hence more likely to convict innocents, a system that disproportionately targets the poor, and a system that convicts for "crimes" that cover vastly more than anyone would wish to punish. The merits of this bargain are at least open to question. * * *

[For] the past thirty-five years, the legal system's discussion of criminal defendants' rights has suffered from an air of unreality, a sense that all goals can be satisfied and all values honored—that we can, for example, have the jury selection process we want at no cost to anything else we might want. A sense of rank ordering, of assigning priority to some constitutional norms rather than treating all as equally deserving of regulatory attention, is absent.

That should change. It is time to acknowledge the tradeoffs, to take seriously the nature of the system the law of criminal procedure regulates and the ways in which that system can evade or undermine the regulation. In a regime like ours, countermajoritarian restraints on the criminal process can succeed only at a cost, the cost is probably substantial, and it is disproportionately imposed on those who least deserve to bear it. Leaving more of the process to majoritarian institutions might be better, not least for some of the defendants the process is designed to protect.

That need not mean leaving defendants to the mercies of state legislatures and local prosecutors. If constitutional law's response to criminal justice has failed, it has failed not just from too much intervention but from too little as well. Making *Gideon* a formal right only, without any ancillary funding requirements, has produced a criminal process that is, for poor defendants, a scandal. Courts' reluctance to police legislatures' criminalization and sentencing decisions—coupled with the way those legislative decisions can be used in a system that gives prosecutors blanket authority to choose whom to go after and for what—has produced its own scandals. Defendants' interests might best be protected by less procedure, coupled with a much more activist judicial posture toward funding, the definition of crime, and sentencing—all areas where judges have been loath to take dramatic stands.

This judicial reticence seems to have been motivated by a desire not to trench on the prerogatives of the politicians, a desire to stick to the more law-like and presumably less contentious ground of process. That the 1960s produced a revolution in criminal *procedure* may testify to the underrated conservatism of Warren Court constitutional thought, to that radical Court's willingness to confine its intervention to conventional categories. If so, in this area these conservative instincts may have been misplaced—as, perhaps, was the Court's reformist (procedural) zeal. The system might be better off today had Warren and his colleagues worried less about criminal procedure, and more about criminal justice.

TRACEY MACLIN—"BLACK AND BLUE ENCOUNTERS"—SOME PRELIMINARY THOUGHTS ABOUT FOURTH AMENDMENT SEIZURES: SHOULD RACE MATTER?[a]

26 Valparaiso U.L.Rev. 243, 250, 252–61, 265–70 (1991).

* * * I submit that the dynamics surrounding an encounter between a police officer and a black male are quite different from those that surround an encounter between an officer and the so-called average, reasonable person. My tentative proposal is that the Court should disregard the notion that there is an average, hypothetical, reasonable person out there by which to judge the constitutionality of police encounters. When assessing the coercive nature of an encounter, the Court should consider the race of the person confronted by the police, and how that person's race might have influenced his attitude toward the encounter.

* * * [The] Supreme Court has said over and over that *all citizens*—not just rich, white men from the suburbs—are free to ignore a police officer who accosts them. In *Florida v. Royer* [p. 425], Justice White explained that: "The person approached . . . need not answer any question put to him; indeed, he may decline to listen to the questions at all and may go on his way. He may not be detained even momentarily without reasonable, objective grounds for doing so; and his refusal to listen or answer does not, without more, furnish those grounds."[43]

This is what the law is supposed to be; black men, however, know that a different "law" exists on the street. Black men know they are liable to be stopped at anytime, and that when they question the authority of the police, the response from the cops is often swift and violent. This applies to black men of all economic strata, regardless of their level of education, and whatever their job status or place in the community.

If the stories of black men in Boston are not convincing, consider what happened to Don Jackson, a former police officer from southern California. Mr. Jackson was trying to document that the police in Long Beach, California were discriminating against and harassing minority citizens who lived and visited Long

a. See also Elizabeth A. Gaynes, *The Urban Criminal Justice System: Where Young + Black + Male = Probable Cause*, 20 Ford. Urb.L.J. 621 (1993); David A. Harris, *Factors for Reasonable Suspicion: When Black and Poor Means Stopped and Frisked*, 69 Ind.L.J. 659 (1994); David A. Harris, *Driving While Black and All Other Traffic Offenses: The Supreme Court and Pretextual Traffic Stops*, 87 J.Crim.L. & C. 554 (1997); Sheri Lynn Johnson, *Race and the Decision to Detain a Suspect*, 93 Yale L.J. 214 (1983); Sheri Lynn Johnson, *Unconscious Racism and the Criminal Law*, 73 Cornell L.Rev. 1016 (1988); Randall Kennedy, *The State, Criminal Law, and Racial Discrimination: A Comment*, 107 Harv.L.Rev. 1255 (1994); *Developments in the Law—Race and the Criminal Process*, 101 Harv.L.Rev. 1472 (1988).

43. Florida v. Royer [p. 425], (1983) (plurality opinion) * * *.

Beach. [When he asked the officers why they had stopped him while driving] an officer pushed Mr. Jackson through a plate glass store window. Unknown to the officers, an NBC camera crew filmed the entire incident.

In a *New York Times* op-ed article entitled, *Police Embody Racism To My People,* Mr. Jackson wrote: "Operating free of constitutional limitations, the police have long been the greatest nemesis of blacks, irrespective of whether we are complying with the law or not. We have learned that there are cars we are not supposed to drive, streets we are not supposed to walk. We may still be stopped and asked 'Where are you going, boy?' Whether we're in a Mercedes or a Volkswagen."

Mr. Jackson's remarks demonstrate the illusory quality of the Court's view that police encounters are not deserving of Fourth Amendment scrutiny because citizens will feel free to leave and *know* of their right to ignore a police officer who has accosted them. The Court's approach, as it is applied in the case of black men, is flawed not because black males have not been informed, as a technical matter, of their legal rights. I have spoken with a number of black lawyers and law students who know their constitutional rights but never feel free to ignore the police. The Court's view is wrong because it is out of touch with the reality on the streets of America. Most black men simply do not trust police officers to respect their rights.

* * * Black males learn at an early age that confrontations with the police should be avoided; black teenagers are advised never to challenge a police officer, even when the officer is wrong. Even if a police officer has arguable grounds for stopping a black male, such an encounter often engenders distinct feelings for the black man. Those feelings are fear of possible violence or humiliation.

To be sure, when whites are stopped by the police, they too feel uneasy and often experience fear. [But] I wonder whether the average white person worries that an otherwise routine police encounter may lead to a violent confrontation. When they are stopped by the police, do whites contemplate the possibility that they will be physically abused for questioning why an officer has stopped them? White teenagers who walk the streets or hang-out in the local mall, do they worry about being strip-searched by the police? Does the average white person ever see himself experiencing what Rodney King or Don Jackson went through during their encounters with the police?

Police officers have shown [that] they will not hesitate to "teach a lesson" to any black male who, even in the slightest way challenges his authority. For example, in Los Angeles, even before [the Rodney King beating], blacks knew not to argue with the police unless they wanted to risk death in a police choke-hold that seemed to be applied more frequently in the case of black males than other citizens.[56]

In addition to fear, distrust is another component that swirls around encounters between black males and the police. Over the years, black males have learned that police officers have little regard for their Fourth Amendment rights. Two years ago in Boston, for instance, a city learned what can happen when a police department is encouraged to ignore the constitutional rights of a targeted class of individuals—black males. In the aftermath of a tragic shooting of a white couple and the declaration of a "war" against teenage gangs and their associates, black

56. See City of Los Angeles v. Lyons, 461 U.S. 95, 116 n. 3 (1983) (Marshall, J., dissenting) ("[S]ince 1975 no less than sixteen persons have died following use of a chokehold by an LAPD police officer. Twelve have been Negro males. [Thus] in a city where Negro males constitute nine per cent of the population, they have accounted for seventy-five per cent of the deaths resulting from the use of chokehold."). * * *

males were subjected to what one state judge called "martial law"[57] tactics by a police department that offered no apologies for its disregard of constitutional liberties.[58] * * *

* * * [B]eing black constitutes a "double-brand" in the mind of the police. Black men are associated with "crimes against the person, with bodily harm to police officers, and with a general lack of support for the police."[67] Also, because of their race, black males "are bound to appear discordant to policemen in most of the environment of a middle-class white society. For this reason, black males doubly draw the attention of police officers."[68] In essence, the police officer "identif[ies] the black man with danger."[69]

From the perspective of the black man, however, these police attitudes only reinforce the view that " '[t]he police system is a dictatorship toward the black people.' "[70] * * * Black men are considered suspicious and targeted for questioning not because of any objective or empirical evidence that they are involved in criminality, but because of police bias and societal indifference to the plight of black males who are on the receiving-end of aggressive police tactics. In effect, black men are accorded "sub-citizen" status for Fourth Amendment purposes. * * *

* * * Currently, the Court assesses the coercive nature of a police encounter by considering the *totality of the circumstances* surrounding the confrontation. All I want the Court to do is to consider the role race might play, along with the other factors it considers, when judging the constitutionality of the encounter.

Some will no doubt object to the explicit use of race in deciding constitutional questions. Understandably, some will ask: If we really wish to live in a future non-racial society, shouldn't we be moving away from procedures and decisions in which people are classified by their race?

I too would like to see a future in which decision-makers will not have to consider the race of individuals in deciding important legal and constitutional questions. But in *today's* world, where the anger and distrust between black males and the police is rising, not decreasing, we must recall Justice Blackmun's familiar stance in the affirmative action debate. "In order to get beyond racism, we must first take account of race. There is no other way."[108]

RANDALL L. KENNEDY—RACE, CRIME, AND THE LAW

158–60 (1997).

When a Mexican–American motorist is selected for questioning in part on the basis of his perceived ancestry, he is undoubtedly being burdened more heavily at that moment on account of his race than his white Anglo counterpart. He is being

57. Commonwealth v. Phillips and Woody, No. 080275–6, Memorandum and Order, at 3 (Suffolk Sup.Ct. Sept. 17, 1989) (Judge Cortland Mathers found that a police order that all known gang members and their associates would be searched on sight was "a proclamation of martial law in Roxbury for a narrow class of people, young blacks, suspected of membership in a gang or perceived by the police to be in the company of someone thought to be a member."). * * *

58. Boston Police Deputy Superintendent William Celester had been quoted as saying: " 'People are going to say we're violating their [gang members'] constitutional rights, but we're not too concerned about that.... If we have to violate their rights, if that's what it takes, then that's what we're going to do." * * *

67. D. Bagley & H. Mendelsohn, *Minorities and the Police* 107 (1969).

68. Id.

69. J. Skolnick, *Justice Without Trial* 49 (1966).

70. B. Blauner, *Black Lives, White Lives* 110 (1989).

108. Regents of Univ. of Cal. v. Bakke, 438 U.S. 265, 407 (1978) (Blackmun, J., dissenting). * * *

made to pay a type of racial tax for the campaign against illegal immigration that whites, blacks, and Asians escape. Similarly, a young black man selected for questioning by police as he alights from an airplane or drives a car is being made to pay a type of racial tax for the war against drugs that whites and other groups escape. That tax is the cost of being subjected to greater scrutiny than others. But is that tax illegitimate?

One defense of it is that, under the circumstances, people of other races are simply not in a position to pay the tax effectively. In contrast to apparent Mexican ancestry, neither apparent white nor black nor Asian ancestry appreciably raises the risk that a person near the Mexican border is illegally resident in the United States. Similarly, the argument would run that in contrast to the young black man, the young white man is not as likely to be a courier of illicit drugs. The defense could go on to say that, in this context, race is *not* being used invidiously. It is not being used as a marker to identify people to harm through enslavement, or exclusion, or segregation. Rather, race is being used merely as a signal that facilitates efficient law enforcement. In this context, apparent Mexican ancestry or blackness is being used for unobjectionable ends in the same way that whiteness is used in the affirmative action context: as a marker that has the effect, though not the purpose, of burdening a given racial group. Whereas whites are make to pay a racial tax for the purpose of opening up opportunities for people of color in education and employment, Mexican–Americans and blacks are made to pay a racial tax for the purpose of more efficient law enforcement.

We need to pause here to consider the tremendous controversy that has surrounded affirmative action policies aimed at helping racial minorities. Many of the same arguments against race-based affirmative action are applicable as well in the context of race-based police stops. With affirmative action, many whites claim that they are victims of racial discrimination. With race-based police stops, many people of color complain that they are victims of racial discrimination. With affirmative action, many adversely affected whites claim that they are *innocent* victims of a policy that penalizes them for the misconduct of others who also happened to have been white. With race-based police stops, many adversely affected people of color maintain that they are *innocent* victims of a policy that penalizes them for the misconduct of others who also happen to be colored. Many whites claim that a major drawback of affirmative action which makes it more costly than valuable is the fact of their intense resentment against such programs. Many people of color claim that one of the drawbacks of race-based police stops that makes it more costly than valuable is their resentment against such policies.

There, exist, however, a remarkable difference in reactions to these racial policies, both of which involve race-dependent decisionmaking. While affirmative action is under tremendous pressure politically and legally, racial policing is not.[a] * * *

STUART TAYLOR JR.—POLITICALLY INCORRECT PROFILING: A MATTER OF LIFE OR DEATH

National Journal, March 3, 2001, p. 3406.

What would happen if another 19 well-trained al Qaeda terrorists, this time with 19 bombs in their bags, tried to board 19 airliners over the next 19 months? Many would probably succeed, blowing up lots of planes and thousands of people,

a. Consider, too, Randall L. Kennedy, *Suspect Policy: Racial profiling by the police isn't necessarily motivated by bigotry. In fact, it's quite rational. But whatever benefits it may produce in the war against crime are outweighed by the damage it does to the very legitimacy of law enforcement*, New Republic, Sept. 13 & 20, 1999, pp. 30, 33–34.

if the forces of head-in-the-sand political correctness prevail—as they did before Sept. 11—in blocking use of national origin as a factor in deciding which passengers' bags to search with extra care.

But a well-designed profiling system might well catch all 19. Such a system would not be race-based; indeed, most Arab–Americans would not fit the profile. It would factor in suspicious behavior, along with national origin, gender, and age. It could spread the burden by selecting at least one white (or black, or Asian) passenger to be searched for every Middle Easterner so selected. And it should be done politely and respectfully.

We have no good alternative. For the foreseeable future, the shortage of high-tech bomb-detection machines and the long delays required to search luggage by hand will make it impossible to effectively screen more than a small percentage of checked bags. The only real protection is to make national origin a key factor in choosing those bags. Otherwise, federalizing airport security and confiscating toenail clippers will be futile gestures.

I revisit this issue in part because research since my Sept. 24 column reinforces my conviction that national-origin profiling may be the only way (in the short term) to avoid hundreds or thousands of deaths.[a] At the same time, critics have persuaded me that the "racial" profiling of "Arab-looking" people that I previously advocated would be less effective than profiling based on apparent origin in any of the nations known to be exporters of anti-American terrorism—not only nations in the Arab world, but also most, or all, of the nations in the Muslim world. Millions of Arab–Americans would not fit the profile because their American roots would be apparent—from their accents and speech patterns—to trained security screeners.

We have heard a great deal about the dismay of Middle Eastern passengers who have been searched and (in some cases) rudely treated on flights or unjustifiably ejected from airliners. We have heard far less about the dangers of not searching. The reason is that "large and important parts of the American news media practice a virulent form of political correctness that is indistinguishable

a. In his September 22nd column, *The Case for Racial Profiling at Airports*, National Journal, p. 2877, Mr. Taylor contrasted racial profiling of people boarding airlines with the racial profiling that occurs when highway police pull over African–Americans in hugely disproportionate numbers to search for drugs. He thought racial profiling of that kind "should be deemed unconstitutional even where there is a statistically valid basis for believing that it will help catch more drug dealers or violent criminals." Taylor continued:

"Such racial profiling is hard to distinguish from—and sometimes involves—plain old racist harassment. It subjects thousands of innocent people to the kind of humiliation that characterizes police states. It hurts law enforcement by fomenting fear and distrust among potential witnesses, tipsters, and jurors. It is rarely justified by any risk of imminent violence. And it makes a mockery of conservative preachings that the Constitution is colorblind.

"Stopping hijacking is different. First, preventing mass murder is infinitely more important than finding illegal drugs or guns. Second, 100 percent of the people who have hijacked airplanes to mass-murder Americans have been Arab men. Third, a virulent perversion of Islam is the only mass movement in the world so committed to mass-murdering Americans that its fanatics are willing to kill themselves in the process. Fourth, this movement includes people who have lived legally in America for years—some of whom may be citizens—so the risk of weapons being smuggled onto airplanes cannot be eliminated by giving special scrutiny only to foreign nationals.

"In short, the mathematical probability that a randomly chosen Arab passenger might attempt a mass-murder-suicide hijacking—while tiny—is considerably higher than the probability that a randomly chosen white, black, Hispanic, or Asian passenger might. In constitutional law parlance, while racial profiling may be presumptively unconstitutional, that presumption is overcome in the case of airline passengers, because the government has a compelling interest in preventing mass-murder-suicide hijackings, and because close scrutiny of Arab-looking people is narrowly tailored to protect that interest."

from censorship," in the words of Richard Cohen, the mostly liberal *Washington Post* columnist.

Opponents of national-origin profiling claim it would be more effective to focus solely on suspicious behavior. They are wrong. Competent terrorists know how to avoid the suspicious-behavior trap. They are not likely to buy one-way tickets the next time. Or to pay in cash. Or to fly from Afghanistan to Pakistan to New York. Or to hang around airport security checkpoints with video cameras. These people are not stupid.

The hardest thing to hide if you are an Islamic terrorist is your Islamic-world origin, as evinced by speech patterns, facial characteristics, skin color, or (to a lesser extent) dress and travel documents. Sure, there is always the risk that the next attack will come from another homegrown Timothy McVeigh, or a Swedish Girl Scout, or (more likely) a mush-headed leftist French coed recruited by al Qaeda. But there are a lot more Islamic terrorists than there are Timothy McVeighs. And not many people from outside the Islamic world appear eager to volunteer for suicide missions. Many Arab–Americans—if not their purported leaders—now seem to understand this. In a *Detroit Free Press* poll of 527 local Arab–Americans, 61 percent supported extra scrutiny of people with Middle Eastern features or accents. * * *

It's unclear whether national-origin profiling would have prevented the hijackings, in part because FAA rules did not bar small knives—although some airlines have suggested that they would have confiscated any box cutters they detected. But politically correct profiling virtually guaranteed that the hijackers' weapons would go undetected.

The Bush administration's profiling policy, if any, is cloaked in politically cowardly and dangerous ambiguity. The FAA and Attorney General John Ashcroft have implied opposition to national-origin profiling, even as Ashcroft's subordinates have detained with minimal explanation more than 1,000 people, most Middle–Easterners against whom there appears to be scant evidence of terrorist activity. The administration should have the courage to preach what it practices. * * *

[If] considered unblinkingly, [national-origin profiling] is not a close call. It has nothing to do with prejudice. It is a matter of life or death.

SHARON L. DAVIES—PROFILING TERROR

1 Ohio St.J.Crim.L. 45, 46–48, 51–53, 85, 99–100 (2003).

Following the attack on the World Trade Center on September 11, 2001, the nation's debate over racial profiling turned an abrupt corner. [The] public's view of racial profiling lurched from dramatically against the practice to decidedly in its favor. * * *

Even as it became apparent that ethnicity figured most heavily into the government's post–9/11 investigation than it first cared to admit, one popular reaction was: so what? After all, nineteen of the 9/11 suicide hijackers were nationals of Middle Eastern states. Didn't simple common sense mandate that government investigators of the events factor the shared ethnicity of additional suspects into their decisions of whom to question, detain, arrest or search? Post 9/11 polls showed that many believed the answer was yes. * * *

This Article rejects the suggestion that Arab or Middle Eastern heritage provides an appropriate basis of suspicion of individuals in the aftermath of the September 11 attacks. In a nation that claims upwards of 3.5 million persons of Arab ancestry, the ethnic characteristic of Arab descent, standing alone, possesses no useful predictive power for separating the September 11 terrorists' accomplices and other terrorist wannabees from innocent Americans.[a] It is a variable that is incapable of sufficiently narrowing what I call the "circle of suspicion" to warrant the kind of reliance pro-profiling arguments would place upon it. * * *

[Even] were we to assume that Middle Eastern origin had some value for distinguishing terrorists from non-terrorists, that ethnic fact would have no value for distinguishing between law-abiding and non-law-abiding persons of Middle Eastern descent. Put slightly differently, even if it had some minimal value for excluding certain people from the "circle of suspicion" (a point that this Article contests), it would have no value for moving individual Middle Easterners inside that circle * * *.

A public convinced of its vulnerability might well be willing to endure greater police intrusions in exchange for greater security, even in the absence of hard evidence that the privacy-impairing measures it contemplates will actually deliver that security. But surely public acceptance cannot by itself supply the justification for a law enforcement policy that subscribes to racially-biased policing. The public "consented" to the forced relocation of over 100,000 persons of Japanese ancestry during World War II, but no thoughtful scholar today would defend the government's internment decisions on the basis of that consensus.

[Some have concluded that the Department of Justice's campaign to interview thousands of Middle Eastern men after 9/11] was *not* profiling "to the extent that the agents [were] pursuing case-specific information about the September 11 attacks, albeit in a dragnet fashion." This suggests that whenever an investigative effort derives in some (even remote) sense from an actual crime in which specific information about the racial or ethnic identity of the perpetrator (or perpetrators) is available, it will not technically be profiling, even if the police "dragnet" entire communities of persons with the same racial or ethnic characteristic in an effort to nab those responsible.[207]

a. See also Frank H. Wu, *Profiling in the Wake of September 11: The Precedent of the Japanese American Internment*, Criminal Justice, Summer 2002, pp. 52, 58: "Most Arab Americans are not Muslim; most Muslims in the United States are South Asian or African American; and the post-September 11 backlash of violence has revealed our collective carelessness in assaulting Indian Sikhs—neither Arab nor Muslim but persons who look like they might be Arab or Muslim because of skin color, accents, and dress. * * *

"[It] may well be that respective probabilities that a random older, white, Protestant American woman and the probability that a younger, Arab Muslim immigrant male are wrongdoers are not the same. But even were there a thousand sleeper agents of Arab descent or Muslim faith, ready to rise up in arms against democracy, they would constitute far less than a fraction of one-tenth of 1 percent of the Arab and Muslim populations of the United States. It is worth disputing whether the disparity in the chances are great enough to offset the tremendous cost to not just Arab Americans and Muslims but all of us is we relinquish our principle of individualism and presumption of innocence."

Consider, too, David A. Harris, *Racial Profiling Revisited: "Just Common Sense" in the Fight Against Terrorism?*, Criminal Justice, Summer 2002, pp. 36, 40–41: "[If] we are to avoid attacks in the future by al-Qaeda operatives based on our own soil, we need to do much better in the intelligence arena than we did before September 11. And that, of course, means we will have to get information from those likely to know the Arab, Muslim, and Middle Eastern men we might suspect. This information is going to have to come not from the population at large, but from the Middle Eastern communities themselves; there is simply no avoiding this. It stands to reason, then, that what we need most right now are good, solid relations with the Arab and Muslim communities in the United States. Profiling that focuses on Arab and Muslim heritage will effectively communicate to these very same communities that we regard all their members not as our partners in law enforcement and terror prevention, but just the opposite: as potential terrorists. * * * [It] is not hard to imagine the result: alienation and anger toward the authorities at a time when we can least afford it."

207. It is sheer fiction that the bulk of the ethnic focus of the government's post–9/11 investigation has been designed to bring to justice the perpetrators of the horrendous events of that single day. The plain focus of the government's ongoing law enforcement efforts is

Yet this argument surely excuses too much. [This] type of over-reliance on racial and ethnic information is extremely unlikely in a diverse society to yield those responsible for crimes. Even where such racial information is logically relevant to a criminal investigation, its value is largely limited to excluding groups of individuals from the circle of suspicion rather than moving any particular individual possessing that racial or ethnic characteristic inside that circle. Once we lose sight of this point, the door to using racial and ethnic information is opened far too wide: the police officer who has arrested a Latino male for involvement in a drug conspiracy can use this as a reason to stop other Latinos anywhere and everywhere.[b]

A Note on the Justice Department's Policy Guidance Regarding Racial Profiling

The Justice Department's June 2003 *Policy Guidance Regarding Racial Profiling* condemns racial profiling because it "sends the dehumanizing message to our citizens that they are judged by the color of their skin and harms the criminal justice system by eviscerating the trust that is necessary if law enforcement is to effectively protect our communities." The Justice Department guidelines point out that "even in the national security context, reliance upon generalized stereotypes is restricted by the Constitution." "Of course," adds a Justice Department release, "federal law enforcement officers may continue to rely upon specific descriptions of the physical appearance of criminal suspects, if a specific description exists in that particular case." One of the guidelines points out that when, as they often do, "federal officers have specific information [to] 'be on the lookout' for specific individuals identified at least in part by race or ethnicity, [the] officer is not acting based on a generalized assumption about persons of different races; rather, the officer is helping locate specific individuals previously identified as involved in crime."

Consider Jonathan Glater, *New Profile Policy: Is Less Really Less?*, N.Y. Times, June 2, 2003, § 4, p. 2: "The policy is the Bush administration's effort to deal with a controversial subject, racial profiling, in a way that earns points with members of minorities but that does not restrict the government's options in the battle against terrorism. But relying as it does on the difference between suspect descriptions (which it approves) and race-based profiles (which it doesn't), the policy restrictions on profiling may have little impact." After quoting a law professor, who comments that "the distinction falls apart very easily" because "most areas of law enforcement do not fall neatly into either [category]," the *Times* article continues: "The use of a suspect's description can have the same effect as racial profiling, either because the description is too broad or because the police use it to stop too many people."[a]

to investigate and prevent *future*, not past, terrorist conduct, and the question for legal thinkers is how far can it go in doing that, and down what sorts of paths?

b. Reasonable people can differ about "national-origin" or "ethnic" or "racial" profiling in the wake of the September 11 attacks—and a goodly number have. For other thoughtful views on this subject, see e.g., Sherry Colb, *Profiling With Apologies*, 1 Ohio St.J.Crim.L. (2004); Samuel R. Gross & Debra Livingston, *Racial Profiling Under Attack*, 102 Colum.L.Rev. 1413 (2002); William Stuntz, *Local Policing After the Terror*, 111 Yale L.J. 2137 (2002).

a. See *Brown v. City of Oneonta*, p. 416.

Chapter 4

THE RIGHT TO COUNSEL, "BY FAR THE MOST PERVASIVE" RIGHT OF THE ACCUSED; EQUALITY AND THE ADVERSARY SYSTEM

"Of all the rights that an accused person has, the right to be represented by counsel is by far the most pervasive, for it affects his ability to assert any other rights he may have. [Procedural rules] are designed for those who know [them], and they can become a source of entrapment for those who do not. Substantive criminal law also presents difficulties to the uniniated."

—Justice Walter V. Schaefer of the Supreme Court of Illinois, *Federalism and State Criminal Procedure*, 70 Harv.L.Rev. 1, 8 (1956).

REPORT OF THE ATTORNEY GENERAL'S COMMITTEE ON POVERTY AND THE ADMINISTRATION OF FEDERAL CRIMINAL JUSTICE 5–11 (1963)[a]

Poverty and criminal justice: The nature of government's obligation * * *

a. *The Concept of "Poverty."* [The] concept proved an elusive one and the difficulties of definition substantial.[b] It is apparent that a total absence in the accused of all means and resources cannot be adequate for these purposes. Even the constitutional rights to the appointment of counsel are not conditioned on a showing of total destitution. Rather, the criterion appears to be a lack of financial resources adequate to permit the accused to hire his own lawyer.[c] Reflection led the Committee to the conclusion that the poverty must be viewed as a relative concept with the consequence that the poverty of accused must be measured in each case by reference to the particular need or service under consideration.

Thus in the criminal process a problem of poverty may arise at each stage of the proceedings. There is a problem of poverty if the defendant is unable to obtain

a. The Report is often called *The Allen Report*, after the Chairman of the Committee, Professor Francis A. Allen.

b. "[F]ew statutory standards are available to guide the [trial court] in its determination of indigency sufficient to warrant court-appointed counsel; as a result, the courts have utilized various criteria for determining eligibility. While some courts have limited the scope of inquiry, for example, to whether the accused is working and has money to hire a lawyer, other courts have considered the accused's assets, debts, employment, ability to post bail, and responsibility for dependents. The confusion and lack of consistency that exist in federal indigency standards are mirrored in the state courts." Note, 12 U.S.F.L.Rev. 717, 720–21 (1978).

c. Should the test of eligibility for court-appointed counsel be whether a private attorney would be interested in representing the defendant in his present economic circumstances? Can this standard be applied with any uniformity?

pre-trial release by reason of financial inability to meet the bail requirements or to retain a lawyer to represent him at the trial. There is also a problem of poverty if the accused is unable to finance a pretrial investigation of the case or to obtain the services of expert witnesses when such investigation or testimony is essential to an adequate defense.[d] So, too, in the appellate process, there is a problem of poverty if through lack of means the accused is inhibited or prevented from presenting grounds of reversal to the appellate court or from making adequate presentation.

It follows that concern with poverty and the administration of criminal justice requires attention to be extended beyond those who are unable at the outset of the proceedings to obtain release on bail or to hire counsel.[e] It requires consideration, also, of those who, although possessing means to obtain some elements of an adequate defense (such as hiring a lawyer), lack means to secure other essential elements.[f] Indeed, it requires attention be given to the plight of the accused with substantial means rendered indigent by the levy of a jeopardy assessment and thus unable to hire the services of an accountant in defense of a net-worth tax prosecution.

[In] summary, the Committee believes that, for the purposes at hand, poverty must be conceived as a relative concept. An impoverished accused is not necessarily one totally devoid of means. A problem of poverty arises for the system of criminal justice when at any stage of the proceedings lack of means in the accused substantially inhibits or prevents the proper assertion of a right or a claim of right.

b. *The Obligation of "Equal Justice."*

[It] should be understood that governmental obligation to deal effectively with problems of poverty in the administration of criminal justice does not rest or depend upon some hypothetical obligation of government to indulge in acts of public charity. It does not presuppose a general commitment on the part of the federal government to relieve impoverished persons of the consequences of limited means, whenever or however manifested. It does not even presuppose that government is always required to take into account the means of the citizen when dealing directly with its citizens.

[The] obligation of government in the criminal cases rests on wholly different considerations and reflects principles of much more limited application. The essential point is that the problems of poverty with which this Report is concerned arise in a process *initiated* by government for the achievement of basic governmental purposes. It is, moreover, a process that has as one of its consequences the imposition of severe disabilities on the persons proceeded against. Duties arise from action. When a course of conduct, however legitimate, entails the possibility of serious injury to persons, a duty on the actor to avoid the reasonably avoidable injuries is ordinarily recognized. When government chooses to exert its powers in the criminal area, its obligation is surely no less than that of taking reasonable measures to eliminate those factors that are irrelevant to just administration of the law but which, nevertheless, may occasionally affect determinations of the accused's liability or penalty. While government may not be required to relieve the

d. On the indigent's right to investigatory, expert and other assistance in addition to counsel, see *Ake v. Oklahoma* (p. 106) and accompanying Notes.

e. *A.B.A. Standards* § 5–6.1 provides that assigned counsel "should not be denied merely because friends or relatives have resources adequate to retain counsel or because bond has been or can be posted."

f. *A.B.A. Standards* § 5–6.1 provides: "Supporting services necessary to an adequate defense should be available to all persons eligible for representation *and to the clients of retained counsel* who are financially unable to afford necessary supporting services." (Emphasis added.)

accused of his poverty, it may properly be required to minimize the influence of poverty on its administration of justice.

The Committee, therefore, conceives the obligation of government less as an undertaking to eliminate "discrimination" against a class of accused persons and more as a broad commitment by government to rid its processes of all influences that tend to defeat the ends a system of justice is intended to serve. Such a concept of "equal justice" does not confuse equality of treatment with identity of treatment. We assume that government must be conceded flexibility in devising its measures and that reasonable classifications are permitted. The crucial question is, has government done all that can reasonably be required of it to eliminate those factors that inhibit the proper and effective assertion of grounds relevant to the criminal liability of the accused or to the imposition of sanctions and disabilities on the accused at all stages of the criminal process?

c. *Poverty and the Adversary System.*

[The] essence of the adversary system is challenge. The survival of our system of criminal justice and the values which it advances depend upon a constant, searching, and creative questioning of official decisions and assertions of authority at all stages of the process. The proper performance of the defense function is thus as vital to the health of the system as the performance of the prosecuting and adjudicatory functions. It follows that insofar as the financial status of the accused impedes vigorous and proper challenges, it constitutes a threat to the viability of the adversary system. We believe that the system is imperiled by the large numbers of accused persons unable to employ counsel or to meet even modest bail requirements and by the large, but indeterminate, numbers of persons, able to pay some part of the costs of defense, but unable to finance a full and proper defense.[g] Persons suffering such disabilities are incapable of providing the challenges that are indispensable to satisfactory operation of the system. The loss to the interests of accused individuals, occasioned by these failures, are great and apparent. It is also clear that a situation in which persons are required to contest a serious accusation but are denied access to the tools of contest is offensive to fairness and equity. Beyond these considerations, however, is the fact that the conditions produced by the financial incapacity of the accused are detrimental to the proper functioning of the system of justice and that the loss in vitality of the adversary system, thereby occasioned, significantly endangers the basic interests of a free community.

Notes and Questions

1. ***The indigent defendant's "obligation" to repay the government for defense costs; reimbursement as a condition of probation.*** *Rinaldi v. Yeager,* 384 U.S. 305 (1966), invalidated a New Jersey statute which required only those indigent defendants who were sentenced to prison to reimburse the state for the cost of a transcript on appeal, finding an "invidious discrimination" between those convicted defendants and others sentenced only to pay fines or subject only to a suspended sentence or to probation. *James v. Strange,* 407 U.S. 128 (1972), held that a Kansas recoupment statute (which applied whether or not the indigent defendant was convicted) violated equal protection because the indigent defendant could not avail himself of restrictions on wage garnishments and other protective exemptions afforded to other civil judgment debtors.

g. The percentage of state felony cases in which defendants were given appointed counsel rose from just under 50% in the late 1970s to about 80% by 1992. See William J. Stuntz, *The Uneasy Relationship Between Criminal Procedure and Criminal Justice*, 107 Yale L.J. 1, 9 (1997).

Fuller v. Oregon, 417 U.S. 40 (1974), however, upheld an Oregon recoupment statute which, under certain circumstances, authorized repayment to the state of the costs of a free legal defense as a condition of probation. A 7–2 majority, per Stewart, J., stressed that "the recoupment statute is quite clearly directed only at those convicted defendants who are indigent at the time of the criminal proceedings against them but who subsequently gain the ability to pay the expenses of legal representation. Defendants with no likelihood of having the means to repay are not put under even a conditional obligation to do so, and those upon whom a conditional obligation is imposed are not subjected to collection procedures until their indigency has ended and no 'manifest hardship' [to defendant or his immediate family] will result."

Distinguishing *James* and *Rinaldi,* the Court rejected petitioner's equal protection challenge. It pointed out that Oregon had not denied exemptions from execution afforded to other judgment debtors. Unlike the classification struck down in *Rinaldi,* it deemed a distinction between defendants who are convicted, on the one hand, and those acquitted or whose convictions are reversed, on the other hand, "wholly noninvidious": "Oregon could surely decide with objective rationality that when a defendant has been forced to submit to a criminal prosecution that does not end in conviction, he will be freed of any potential liability to reimburse the state for the costs of his defense."

Nor was the Court impressed with the argument that a defendant's knowledge that he may be obligated to reimburse the state for expenses incurred in providing him a legal defense might lead him to reject the services of appointed counsel and thus "chill" his constitutional right to counsel: "The fact that an indigent who accepts [appointed counsel] knows that he might someday be required to repay the costs of these services in no way affects his eligibility to obtain counsel. The Oregon statute is carefully designed to insure that only those who actually become capable of repaying the State will ever be obliged to do so."

Dissenting Justice Marshall, joined by Brennan, J., protested that "the important fact which the majority ignores" is that because the repayment of the indigent defendant's debt to the state can be made a condition of his probation, as it was in this case, "[p]etitioner's failure to pay his debt can result in his being sent to prison. In this respect the indigent defendant in Oregon, like [his counterpart in *James*], is treated quite differently from other civil judgment debtors."

2. Notwithstanding the *Fuller* case, *A.B.A. Standards* § 5–6.2 (commentary) "recommends that defendants be ordered to [make reimbursement] for their defense only in instances where they have made fraudulent representations for purposes of being found eligible for counsel. [The] offer of free legal assistance is rendered hollow if defendants are required to make payments for counsel for several years following conviction. Reimbursement requirements also may serve to discourage defendants from exercising their right to counsel * * *."

SECTION 1. THE RIGHT TO APPOINTED COUNSEL AND RELATED PROBLEMS

A. The Right to Appointed Counsel in Criminal Proceedings

Introduction

A look at early English law reveals that the right to counsel had "surprisingly modest beginnings." James Tomkovicz, *The Right to the Assistance of Counsel* 1 (2002). Originally only those accused of minor offenses could be represented by counsel. (Evidently the monarch believed that permitting representation by defense counsel generally would prevent the successful prosecution of serious cases.) However, against a background of a decade of false treason charges against the Whigs, the Treason Act of 1695 provided that those prosecuted for high treason should be allowed to defend themselves by "counsel learned in the law." Thus, at the time of the adoption of the U.S. Constitution, England recognized a right to *retain* counsel to argue matters of fact only for those accused of misdemeanors or high treason.[a]

From the earliest times, the general practice in serious criminal cases in the American colonies was self-representation, not representation by counsel. But by the time the nation was about to ratify the Constitution, most states had granted criminal defendants the right to be represented by a lawyer. No state, however, guaranteed the right to *appointed* counsel. As Professor Tomkovicz has observed, "[i]t seems highly probable that the Sixth Amendment was designed to grant a legal representative of one's own choosing [thereby rejecting the restricted British approach], but no right to have counsel provided by the government."

One hundred and fifty-one years after the ratification of the Sixth Amendment and some sixty years after the adoption of the Fourteenth, the Supreme Court handed down its first significant opinion concerning the right to counsel—*Powell v. Alabama* (1932) (discussed infra). Although the *Powell* opinion contains sweeping, much-quoted language (such as "the right to be heard would be in many cases of little avail if it did not comprehend the right to be heard by counsel") the Court dwelt on the special circumstances—"above all that [the defendants] stood in peril of their lives." In a case *such as this* the Court told us, "the failure of the trial court to give [the defendants] reasonable time and opportunity to secure counsel was a clear denial of due process." *And in a case with these facts*, "the right to have counsel appointed [is] *a logical corollary of the constitutional right to be heard by counsel*." (Emphasis added.)

Powell, of course, was a state case. Six years later, in *Johnson v. Zerbst* (1938) (discussed infra), the Court held, without discussing the likely intent of the Sixth Amendment, that the Amendment guaranteed indigent *federal* defendants (at least all felony defendants) a right to *appointed* counsel. But it would take another twenty-five years before the Court would conclude that the Constitution guaranteed *state* defendants the same unqualified right.

BETTS v. BRADY

316 U.S. 455, 62 S.Ct. 1252, 86 L.Ed. 1595 (1942).

Justice ROBERTS delivered the opinion of the Court.

Petitioner, an indigent, was indicted for robbery. His request for counsel was denied because local practice permitted appointment only in rape and murder prosecutions. Petitioner then pled not guilty and elected to be tried without a jury. At the trial he chose not to take the stand. He was convicted and sentenced to eight years imprisonment.

[The] due process clause of the Fourteenth Amendment does not incorporate, as such, the specific guarantees found in the Sixth Amendment although a denial by a state of rights or privileges specifically embodied in that and others of the

a. At some point in the development of the right to counsel in England, retained counsel could appear on behalf of a felony defendant to argue, but only to argue, matters of law. "When it came to presenting evidence and arguing as to the strength of the evidence, the felony defendant was on his own." CRIMPROC § 1.5(b). However, the distinction between matters of fact and matters of law was hazy and by the middle of the nineteenth century "questions of law" seem to have been extended to include both direct examination and cross-examination. See id.

first eight amendments may, in certain circumstances, * * * deprive a litigant of due process of law in violation of the Fourteenth. [Due process] formulates a concept less rigid and more fluid than those envisaged in other specific and particular provisions of the Bill of Rights. Its application is less a matter of rule. Asserted denial is to be tested by an appraisal of the totality of facts in a given case.

[Petitioner] says the rule to be deduced from our former decisions is that, in every case, whatever the circumstances, one charged with crime, who is unable to obtain counsel, must be furnished counsel by the state. Expressions in the opinions of this court lend color to the argument, but, as the petitioner admits, none of our decisions squarely adjudicates the question now presented.

In *Powell v. Alabama,* 287 U.S. 45 [1932], ignorant and friendless negro youths, strangers in the community, without friends or means to obtain counsel, were hurried to trial for a capital offense without effective appointment of counsel on whom the burden of preparation and trial would rest, and without adequate opportunity to consult even the counsel casually appointed to represent them. [This] court held the resulting convictions were without due process of law. It said that, in the light of all the facts, the failure of the trial court to afford the defendants reasonable time and opportunity to secure counsel was a clear denial of due process. The court stated further that "under the circumstances [the] necessity of counsel was so vital and imperative that the failure of the trial court to make an effective appointment of counsel was likewise a denial of due process," but added: "whether this would be so in other criminal prosecutions, or under other circumstances, we need not determine. All that it is necessary now to decide, as we do decide, is that in a capital case, where the defendant is unable to employ counsel, and is incapable adequately of making his own defense because of ignorance, feeblemindedness, illiteracy, or the like, it is the duty of the court, whether requested or not, to assign counsel for him as a necessary requisite of due process of law * * *."

* * * We have construed the [Sixth Amendment] to require appointment of counsel in all [federal] cases where a defendant is unable to procure the services of an attorney, and where the right has not been intentionally and competently waived. [*Johnson v. Zerbst,* 304 U.S. 458 (1938)].[a] Though [the] amendment lays down no rule for the conduct of the states, the question recurs whether the constraint laid by the amendment upon the national courts expresses a rule so fundamental and essential to a fair trial, and so, to due process of law, that it is made obligatory upon the states by the Fourteenth Amendment. Relevant data on the subject are afforded by constitutional and statutory provisions subsisting in the colonies and the states prior to the inclusion of the Bill of Rights in the national Constitution, and in the constitutional, legislative, and judicial history of the states to the present date.

[I]n the great majority of the states, it has been the considered judgment of the people, their representatives and their courts that appointment of counsel is not a fundamental right, essential to a fair trial. On the contrary, the matter has generally been deemed one of legislative policy. In the light of this evidence we are

a. In holding that the Sixth Amendment required appointment of counsel, the Court, per Black, J., had reasoned: "The Sixth Amendment stands as a constant admonition that if the constitutional safeguards it provides be lost, justice will not 'still be done.' Cf. *Palko.* It embodies a realistic recognition of the obvious truth that the average defendant does not have the professional legal skill to protect himself when brought before a tribunal with power to take his life or liberty, wherein the prosecution is presented by experienced and learned counsel. [The] Sixth Amendment withholds from federal courts, in all criminal proceedings, the power and authority to deprive an accused of his life or liberty unless he has or waives the assistance of counsel."

unable to say that the concept of due process incorporated in the Fourteenth Amendment obligates the states, whatever may be their own views, to furnish counsel in every such case. Every court has power, if it deems proper, to appoint counsel where that course seems to be required in the interest of fairness.

The practice of the courts of Maryland gives point to the principle that the states should not be straight-jacketed in this respect, by a construction of the Fourteenth Amendment. Judge Bond's opinion states, and counsel at the bar confirmed the fact, that in Maryland the usual practice is for the defendant to waive a trial by jury. This the petitioner did in the present case. Such trials, as Judge Bond remarks, are much more informal than jury trials and it is obvious that the judge can much better control the course of the trial and is in a better position to see impartial justice done than when the formalities of a jury trial are involved.

In this case there was no question of the commission of a robbery. The State's case consisted of evidence identifying the petitioner as the perpetrator. The defense was an alibi. Petitioner called and examined witnesses to prove that he was at another place at the time of the commission of the offense. The simple issue was the veracity of the testimony for the State and that for the defendant. As Judge Bond says, the accused was not helpless, but was a man forty-three years old, of ordinary intelligence and ability to take care of his own interests on the trial of that narrow issue. He had once before been in a criminal court, pleaded guilty to larceny and served a sentence and was not wholly unfamiliar with criminal procedure. It is quite clear that in Maryland, if the situation had been otherwise and it had appeared that the petitioner was, for any reason, at a serious disadvantage by reason of the lack of counsel, a refusal to appoint would have resulted in the reversal of a judgment of conviction.

[To] deduce from the due process clause a rule binding upon the states in this matter would be to impose upon them, as Judge Bond points out, a requirement without distinction between criminal charges of different magnitude or in respect of courts of varying jurisdiction. As he says: "Charges of small crimes tried before justices of the peace and capital charges tried in the higher courts would equally require the appointment of counsel. Presumably it would be argued that trials in the Traffic Court would require it."

[While] want of counsel in a particular case may result in a conviction lacking [in] such fundamental fairness, we cannot say that the [Fourteenth Amendment] embodies an inexorable command that no trial for any offense, or in any court, can be fairly conducted and justice accorded a defendant who is not represented by counsel.

The judgment is affirmed.

Justice BLACK, dissenting, with whom Justice DOUGLAS and Justice MURPHY concur.

To hold that the petitioner had a constitutional right to counsel in this case does not require us to say that "no trial for any offense, or in any court, can be fairly conducted and justice accorded a defendant who is not represented by counsel." This case can be determined by resolution of a narrower question: whether in view of the nature of the offense and the circumstances of his trial and conviction, this petitioner was denied the procedural protection which is his right under the federal constitution. I think he was.

The petitioner [was] a farm hand, out of a job and on relief. [The] court below found that [he] had "at least an ordinary amount of intelligence." It is clear from his examination of witnesses that he was a man of little education.

If this case had come to us from a federal court, it is clear we should have to reverse it, because the Sixth Amendment makes the right to counsel in criminal cases inviolable by the federal government. I believe that the Fourteenth Amendment made the sixth applicable to the states. But this view [has] never been accepted by a majority of this Court and is not accepted today. * * * I believe, however, that under the prevailing view of due process, as reflected in the opinion just announced, a view which gives this Court such vast supervisory powers that I am not prepared to accept it without grave doubts, the judgment below should be reversed.

[The] right to counsel in a criminal proceeding is "fundamental." *Powell v. Alabama.* [A] practice cannot be reconciled with "common and fundamental ideas of fairness and right" which subjects innocent men to increased dangers of conviction merely because of their poverty. Whether a man is innocent cannot be determined from a trial in which as here, denial of counsel has made it impossible to conclude, with any satisfactory degree of certainty, that the defendant's case was adequately presented.[b] * * *

Denial to the poor of the request for counsel in proceedings based on charges of serious crime has long been regarded as shocking to the "universal sense of justice" throughout this country. In 1854, for example, the Supreme Court of Indiana said: "It is not to be thought of, in a civilized community, for a moment, that any citizen put in jeopardy of life or liberty should be debarred of counsel because he was too poor to employ such aid * * * " *Webb v. Baird,* 6 Ind. 13, 18. And most of the other states have shown their agreement by constitutional provisions, statutes, or established practice judicially approved which assure that no man shall be deprived of counsel merely because of his poverty. Any other practice seems to me to defeat the promise of our democratic society to provide equal justice under the law.

THE AFTERMATH OF BETTS v. BRADY—NOTES AND QUESTIONS

1. ***Was Betts "prejudiced"?*** When the Court reviewed Betts' case, he had appellate counsel, but his lawyer was confident—too confident—that the Court would apply the full measure of the Sixth Amendment right to counsel to the states. Thus he did not make any analysis of the trial and present any specific examples of how Betts might have been prejudiced by the absence of counsel. For the view that a number of such examples could have been shown and that competent trial counsel could have raised many more issues than "the simple issue [of] the veracity of the testimony for the State and that for the defendant," see Kamisar, *The Right to Counsel and the Fourteenth Amendment,* 30 U.Chi. L.Rev. 1, 42–56 (1962).

2. ***The "flat" requirement of counsel in capital cases.*** In *Bute v. Illinois,* 333 U.S. 640 (1948), and subsequent noncapital cases, the Court suggested that there was a "flat" requirement of counsel in capital cases. In *Hamilton v. Alabama,* 368 U.S. 52, (1961), holding that arraignment is so critical a stage in Alabama procedure that denial of counsel at that stage in a capital case violates due process, a unanimous Court declared, per Douglas, J., that "when one pleads

b. Consider William Beaney, *The Right to Counsel in American Courts* 163, 185 (1955): "Surely the [*Betts*] majority, in adopting [Judge] Bond's position that counsel could have done little or nothing for the defendant was pursuing a line of reasoning which would inevitably destroy all rights. Rights are agreed upon in order to insure that justice will be done prospectively, in the ordinary run of affairs. To hold that an individual can be deprived of rights except in those cases where a retrospective view of events reveals a shocking situation is to defeat the whole rationale of the rule of law." See also Note 1 infra.

to a capital charge without benefit of counsel, we do not stop to determine whether prejudice resulted. [T]he degree of prejudice can never be known." For an explanation and criticism of the Court's distinction between capital and noncapital cases, see Francis A. Allen, *The Supreme Court, Federalism, and State Systems of Criminal Justice,* 8 DePaul L.Rev. 213, 230–31 (1959).

3. ***The absolute right to retained counsel.*** During the *Betts* reign, the Court made it clear that denying a defendant the assistance of *his own lawyer* on *any* issue in the trial of *any* case, constituted a per se violation of "fundamental fairness." Thus, in *Chandler v. Fretag,* 348 U.S. 3 (1954), the Court stamped the right of petitioner "to be heard through his own counsel" as "unqualified." And *Ferguson v. Georgia,* 365 U.S. 570 (1961), held, in effect, that a state may not deny a criminal defendant the right to have his own counsel guide him on direct examination. Could these cases be reconciled with *Betts?* See Israel, *Gideon v. Wainwright: The "Art" of Overruling,* 1963 Sup.Ct.Rev. 211, 243; Kamisar, *Betts v. Brady Twenty Years Later,* 61 Mich.L.Rev. 219, 227?28, 256–60 (1962).

GIDEON v. WAINWRIGHT

372 U.S. 335, 83 S.Ct. 792, 9 L.Ed.2d 799 (1963).

Justice BLACK delivered the opinion of the Court.

Petitioner was charged in a Florida state court with having broken and entered a poolroom with intent to commit a misdemeanor. This offense is a felony under Florida law. Appearing in court without funds and without a lawyer, petitioner asked the court to appoint counsel for him, whereupon the following colloquy took place:

"The Court: Mr. Gideon, I am sorry, but I cannot appoint Counsel to represent you in this case. Under the laws of the State of Florida, the only time the Court can appoint Counsel to represent a Defendant is when that person is charged with a capital offense. * * *

"The Defendant: The United States Supreme Court says I am entitled to be represented by Counsel."

Put to trial before a jury, Gideon conducted his defense about as well as could be expected from a layman. He made an opening statement to the jury, cross-examined the State's witnesses, presented witnesses in his own defense, declined to testify himself, and made a short argument "emphasizing his innocence to the charge contained in the Information filed in this case." The jury returned a verdict of guilty, and petitioner was sentenced to serve five years in the state prison. Later, petitioner [unsuccessfully attacked his conviction and sentence in the state supreme court on the ground that the trial court's refusal to appoint counsel for him violated his constitutional rights]. Since 1942, when *Betts v. Brady* was decided by a divided Court, the problem of a defendant's federal constitutional right to counsel in a state court has been a continuing source of controversy and litigation in both state and federal courts. To give this problem another review here, we granted certiorari [and] appointed counsel to represent [petitioner].

We accept *Betts*'s assumption, based as it was on our prior cases, that a provision of the Bill of Rights which is "fundamental and essential to a fair trial" is made obligatory upon the States by the Fourteenth Amendment. We think the Court in *Betts* was wrong, however, in concluding that the Sixth Amendment's guarantee of counsel is not one of these fundamental rights. Ten years before *Betts,* this Court, after full consideration of all the historical data examined in *Betts,* had unequivocally declared that "the right to the aid of counsel is of this fundamental character." *Powell.* While the Court at the close of its *Powell* opinion did by its language, as this Court frequently does, limit its holding to the particular facts and circumstances of that case, its conclusions about the fundamental nature of the right to counsel are unmistakable. [The] fact is that in deciding as it did—that "appointment of counsel is not a fundamental right, essential to a fair trial"—the [*Betts* Court] made an abrupt break with its own well-considered precedents. In returning to these old precedents, sounder we believe than the new, we but restore constitutional principles established to achieve a fair system of justice. Not only these precedents but also reason and reflection require us to recognize that in our adversary system of criminal justice, any person haled into court, who is too poor to hire a lawyer, cannot be assured a fair trial unless counsel is provided for him. This seems to us to be an obvious truth. Governments, both state and federal, quite properly spend vast sums of money to establish machinery to try defendants accused of crime. Lawyers to prosecute are everywhere deemed essential to protect the public's interest in an orderly society. Similarly, there are few defendants charged with crime, few indeed, who fail to hire the best lawyers they can get to prepare and present their defenses. That government hires lawyers to prosecute and defendants who have the money hire lawyers to defend are the strongest indications of the widespread belief that lawyers in criminal courts are necessities, not luxuries. The right of one charged with crime to counsel may not be deemed fundamental and essential to fair trials in some countries, but it is in ours. From the very beginning, our state and national constitutions and laws have laid great emphasis on procedural and substantive safeguards designed to assure fair trials before impartial tribunals in which every defendant stands equal before the law. This noble ideal cannot be realized if the poor man charged with crime has to face his accusers without a lawyer to assist him. * * *

The Court in *Betts* departed from the sound wisdom upon which the Court's holding in *Powell* rested. Florida, supported by two other States, has asked that *Betts v. Brady* be left intact. Twenty-two States, as friends of the Court, argue that *Betts* was "an anachronism when handed down" and that it should now be overruled. We agree. * * *

Reversed.[a]

Justice CLARK, concurring in the result.

[T]he Constitution makes no distinction between capital and noncapital cases. The Fourteenth Amendment requires due process of law for the deprival of "liberty" just as for deprival of "life," and there cannot constitutionally be a difference in the quality of the process based merely upon a supposed difference in the sanction involved. How can the Fourteenth Amendment tolerate a procedure which it condemns in capital cases on the ground that deprival of liberty may be less onerous than deprival of life—a value judgment not universally accepted—or that only the latter deprival is irrevocable? * * *

Justice HARLAN, concurring.

I agree that *Betts* should be overruled, but consider it entitled to a more respectful burial than has been accorded, at least on the part of those of us who were not on the Court when that case was decided. I cannot subscribe to the view that *Betts* represented "an abrupt break with its own well-considered precedents." [In *Powell*] this Court declared that under the particular facts there presented—"the ignorance and illiteracy of the defendants, their youth, the circumstances of public hostility [and] above all that they stood in deadly peril of their lives"—the

a. Gideon was retried, this time with appointed counsel, and acquitted. See Anthony Lewis, *Gideon's Trumpet* 223–38 (1964).

state court had a duty to assign counsel for the trial as a necessary requisite of due process of law. It is evident that these limiting facts were not added to the opinion as an afterthought; they were repeatedly emphasized [and] were clearly regarded as important to the result.

Thus when this Court, a decade later, decided *Betts,* it did no more than to admit of the possible existence of special circumstances in noncapital as well as capital trials, while at the same time to insist that such circumstances be shown in order to establish a denial of due process. The right to appointed counsel had been recognized as being considerably broader in federal prosecutions, see *Johnson v. Zerbst,* but to have imposed these requirements on the States would indeed have been "an abrupt break" with the almost immediate past. The declaration that the right to appointed counsel in state prosecutions, as established in *Powell,* was not limited to capital cases was in truth not a departure from, but an extension of, existing precedent.

The principles declared in *Powell* and in *Betts,* however, had a troubled journey throughout the years that have followed first the one case and then the other.

[In] noncapital cases, the "special circumstances" rule has continued to exist in form while its substance has been substantially and steadily eroded. In the first decade after *Betts,* there were cases in which the Court found special circumstances to be lacking, but usually by a sharply divided vote. However, no such decision has been cited to us, and I have found none, [after] 1950. At the same time, there have been not a few cases in which special circumstances were found in little or nothing more than the "complexity" of the legal questions presented, although those questions were often of only routine difficulty. The Court has come to recognize, in other words, that the mere existence of a serious criminal charge constituted in itself special circumstances requiring the services of counsel at trial. In truth the *Betts* rule is no longer a reality.

This evolution, however, appears not to have been fully recognized by many state courts, in this instance charged with the front-line responsibility for the enforcement of constitutional rights. To continue a rule which is honored by this Court only with lip service is not a healthy thing and in the long run will do disservice to the federal system.

The special circumstances rule has been formally abandoned in capital cases, and the time has now come when it should be similarly abandoned in noncapital cases, at least as to offenses which, as the one involved here, carry the possibility of a substantial prison sentence. (Whether the rule should extend to *all* criminal cases need not now be decided.) * * *[b]

Notes and Questions

1. ***The significance of Powell v. Alabama and Johnson v. Zerbst.*** Did the Court in *Betts* make, as Justice Black asserts in *Gideon,* "an abrupt break with its own well-considered precedents"? Did *Powell* furnish a steppingstone to either a *Betts* or a *Gideon,* depending on how far and fast the Supreme Court was willing to use the opinion's potential for expansion? Did the *Palko* doctrine

b. Bruce Jacob is now Dean Emeritus and Professor at the Stetson University College of Law. Forty years ago, when he was almost fresh out of law school, he argued the *Gideon* case for the State of Florida. For his views on the *Gideon* case and what has happened to the *Gideon* principle, see Bruce R. Jacob, *Memories of and Reflections About Gideon v. Wainwright,* 33 Stetson L.Rev. 181 (2003). For another look back at *Gideon*, see Yale Kamisar, Abe Krash, Anthony Lewis & Ellen Podgor, *Gideon at 40: Facing the Crisis, Fulfilling the Promise,* 41 Am.Crim.L.Rev. 131 (2004).

constitute a clear warning that the Court would not impose the same requirements for appointed counsel upon the states as it had upon the federal government in *Johnson v. Zerbst?* See Israel, *Gideon v. Wainwright: The "Art" of Overruling,* 1963 Supreme Court Rev. 211, 234–38, 240–41.

2. ***Alternative techniques of overruling available in Gideon.*** Among the traditional arts of overruling are the arguments that (a) the old precedent has not withstood the "lessons of experience" and (b) that its rejection is required by later "inconsistent precedents." See e.g., *Mapp v. Ohio,* p. 219. Were these arguments available in *Gideon?* As to (b) reconsider, for example, the *Chandler* and *Ferguson* cases, establishing the unqualified right to the assistance of counsel *one can hire;* and the post-*Betts* development of the "automatic right" to appointed counsel in capital cases and its implicit admission of the unsoundness of the "fair trial" rule. As to (a), consider how, in the two decades since *Betts,* the assumption that a lawyerless defendant would usually be able to defend himself had fared in light of the constant expansion of the "special circumstances" concept; and how the assumption that a "special circumstances" test was more consistent with the "obligations of federalism" than an "absolute rule" had stood up in the face of the proliferation of federal habeas corpus cases produced by the *Betts* rule and the resulting friction between state and federal courts. See generally Israel, supra at 242–69.

3. ***Why did the Gideon opinion take the route it did?*** If the foregoing techniques of overruling were available in *Gideon,* why did Justice Black fail to utilize them? Would it have been most desirable to emphasize that the overruling of *Betts* was not attributable to recent changes in personnel, but that it constituted the product of a long line of Justices who, over two decades, participated in various decisions undermining *Betts?* See Israel, supra at 225, 269. Is the failure to employ the usual overruling "arts" in *Gideon* attributable to Justice Black's personal interest in vindicating his own dissenting opinion in *Betts?* Or his reluctance to admit even the *original validity* of a decision that exemplifies the evils (to him) of the "fundamental rights" interpretation of the fourteenth amendment? See id. at 270–72.

4. ***The unrealized dream of Gideon.*** For the view, spelled out at considerable length, that many years after *Gideon,* the dream of that landmark case—the dream of a country "in which every person charged with a crime will be capably defended, no matter what his economic circumstances"—remains largely unrealized, see Stephen B. Bright, *Counsel for the Poor: the Death Sentence not for the Worst Crime but for the Worst Lawyer*, 103 Yale L.J. 1835 (1994). According to Bright, id. at 1870, "a properly working adversary system will never be achieved unless defender organizations are established and properly funded to employ lawyers at wages and benefits equal to what is spent on the prosecution, to retain expert and investigative assistance, to assign lawyers to capital cases, to recruit and support local lawyers and to supervise the performance of counsel defending capital cases. Judges are not equipped to do this. Management of the defense is not a proper judicial function."

5. ***Our double standards of criminal defense.*** Consider the comments on the O.J. Simpson case by Professors Arenella and Rhodes at pp. 63–64.

In ARGERSINGER v. HAMLIN, 407 U.S. 25 (1972), the Court, per DOUGLAS, J., struck down a Florida rule (following the line marked out in the jury trial cases) requiring that counsel be appointed only "for nonpetty offenses punishable by more than six months imprisonment," and held that "absent a knowing and intelligent waiver, no person may be *imprisoned* for any offense, whether classified as petty, misdemeanor, or felony unless he was represented by counsel" (emphasis added):

"While there is historical support for limiting the [right] to trial by jury [to] 'serious criminal cases,' there is no such support for a similar limitation on the right to assistance of counsel. [Thus,] we reject [the] premise that since prosecutions for crimes punishable by imprisonment for less than six months may be tried without a jury, they may always be tried without a lawyer. [The] requirement of counsel may well be necessary for a fair trial even in a petty offense prosecution. We are by no means convinced that legal and constitutional questions involved in a case that actually leads to imprisonment even for a brief period are any less complex than when a person can be sent off for six months or more. * * *

"Beyond the problem of trials and appeals is that of the guilty plea, a problem which looms large in misdemeanor as well as in felony cases. Counsel is needed so that the accused may know precisely what he is doing, so that he is fully aware of the prospect of going to jail or prison, and so that he is treated fairly by the prosecution.

"In addition, the volume of misdemeanor cases, far greater in number than felony prosecutions, may create an obsession for speedy dispositions, regardless of the fairness of the result. * * *

"We must conclude, therefore, that the problems associated with misdemeanor and petty offenses often require the presence of counsel to insure the accused a fair trial. [In his concurring opinion,] Mr. Justice Powell suggests that these problems are raised even in situations where there is no prospect of imprisonment. We need not consider the requirements of the Sixth Amendment as regards the right to counsel where loss of liberty is not involved, however, for here, petitioner was in fact sentenced to jail * * *.

"Under the rule we announce today, every judge will know when the trial of a misdemeanor starts that no imprisonment may be imposed, even though local law permits it, unless the accused is represented by counsel. He will have a measure of the seriousness and gravity of the offense and therefore know when to name a lawyer to represent the accused before the trial starts."[a]

Analyzing the problem in terms of general due process rather than the sixth amendment right to counsel, concurring Justice POWELL, joined by Rehnquist, J., concluded that "there is a middle course, between the extremes of Florida's six month rule and the Court's rule, which comports with the requirements of the Fourteenth Amendment"—"fundamental fairness" requires that a defendant have the assistance of counsel in petty cases when, but only when, "necessary to assure a fair trial":

"Due process, perhaps the most fundamental concept in our law, embodies principles of fairness rather than immutable line-drawing as to every aspect of a criminal trial. While counsel is often essential to a fair trial, this is by no means a universal fact. Some petty offense cases are complex; others are exceedingly simple. [The] government often does not hire lawyers to prosecute petty offenses; instead the arresting police officer presents the case. Nor does every defendant who can afford to do so hire lawyers to defend petty charges. Where the possibility of a jail sentence is remote and the probable fine seems small, or where the

a. Burger, C.J., concurred in the result. Brennan, J., joined by Douglas and Stewart, JJ., joined the Court's opinion and, in a brief concurring opinion, added the observation that "law students as well as practicing attorneys may provide an important source of legal representation for the indigent. [M]ore than 125 of the country's 147 accredited law schools have established clinical programs in which faculty-supervised students aid clients in a variety of civil and criminal matters."

evidence of guilt is overwhelming, the costs of assistance of counsel may exceed the benefits. It is anomalous that the Court's opinion today will extend the right of appointed counsel to indigent defendants in cases where the right to counsel would rarely be exercised by nonindigent defendants.

"Indeed, one of the effects of this ruling will be to favor defendants classified as indigents over those not so classified yet who are in low income groups where engaging counsel in a minor petty offense case would be a luxury the family could not afford. The line between indigency and assumed capacity to pay for counsel is necessarily somewhat arbitrary, drawn differently from State to State and often resulting in serious inequities to accused persons. The Court's new rule will accent the disadvantage of being barely self-sufficient economically.

"[The] rule adopted today [is] limited to petty offense cases in which the sentence is some imprisonment. The thrust of the Court's position indicates, however, that when the decision must be made, the rule will be extended to all petty offense cases except perhaps the most minor traffic violations. If the Court rejects on constitutional grounds, as it has today, the exercise of any judicial discretion as to need for counsel if a jail sentence is imposed, one must assume a similar rejection of discretion in other petty offense cases. * * *

"I would hold that the right to counsel in petty offense cases is not absolute but is one to be determined by the trial courts exercising a judicial discretion on a case-by-case basis. * * * [T]hree general factors should be weighed. First, the court should consider the complexity of the offense charged. Second, the court should consider the probable sentence that will follow if a conviction is obtained. The more serious the likely consequences, the greater is the probability that a lawyer should be appointed. Third, the court should consider the individual factors peculiar to each case. These, of course, would be the most difficult to anticipate. One relevant factor would be the competency of the individual defendant to present his own case. The attitude of the community toward a particular defendant or particular incident would be another consideration. * * *

"Such a rule is similar in certain respects to the special circumstances rule applied to felony cases in *Betts,* which this Court overruled in *Gideon*. One of the reasons for seeking a more definitive standard in felony cases was the failure of many state courts to live up to their responsibilities in determining on a case-by-case basis whether counsel should be appointed. But this Court should not assume that the past insensitivity of some state courts to the rights of defendants will continue. Certainly if the Court follows the course of reading rigid rules into the Constitution, so that the state courts will be unable to exercise judicial discretion within the limits of fundamental fairness, there is little reason to think that insensitivity will abate."

Petitioner, an indigent, was charged with shoplifting merchandise valued at less than $150, punishable by as much as a $500 fine, or one year in jail, or both. He was not provided counsel. After a bench trial he was convicted of the offense and fined $50. The Supreme Court of Illinois declined to "extend *Argersinger*" to a case where one is charged with an offense for which imprisonment upon conviction is authorized but not actually imposed. A 5–4 majority of the Supreme Court, per REHNQUIST, J., agreed, SCOTT v. ILLINOIS, 440 U.S. 367 (1979):

"[W]e believe that the central premise of *Argersinger*—that actual imprisonment is a penalty different in kind from fines or the mere threat of imprisonment—is eminently sound and warrants adoption of actual imprisonment as the line defining the constitutional right to appointment of counsel. * * * We therefore hold that the Sixth and Fourteenth Amendments [require] only that no indigent criminal defendant be sentenced to a term of imprisonment unless the State has afforded him the right to assistance of appointed counsel in his defense."

Concurring Justice POWELL noted that "the drawing of a line based on whether there is imprisonment (even for overnight) can have the practical effect of precluding provision of counsel in other types of cases in which conviction can have more serious consequences." He also thought that an "actual imprisonment" rule "tends to impair the proper functioning of the criminal justice system in that trial judges, in advance of hearing any evidence and before knowing anything about the case except the charge, all too often will be compelled to forego the legislatively granted option to impose a sentence of imprisonment upon conviction." Nevertheless, Justice Powell joined the opinion of the Court because "[i]t is important that this Court provide clear guidance to the hundreds of courts across the country that confront this problem daily." He hoped, however, "that in due time a majority will recognize that a more flexible rule is consistent with due process and will better serve the cause of justice."

Justice BRENNAN, joined by Marshall and Stevens, JJ., dissented:

"[*Argersinger*] established a 'two dimensional' test for the right to counsel: the right attaches to any 'non-petty' offense punishable by more than six months in jail and in addition to any offense where actual incarceration is likely regardless of the maximum authorized penalty. See Steven B. Duke, *The Right to Appointed Counsel: Argersinger and Beyond,* 12 Am.Crim.L.Rev. 601 (1975).

"The offense of 'theft' with which Scott was charged is certainly not a 'petty' one. It is punishable by a sentence of up to one year in jail. Unlike many traffic or other 'regulatory' offenses, it carries the moral stigma associated with common-law crimes traditionally recognized as indicative of moral depravity. The State indicated at oral argument that the services of a professional prosecutor were considered essential to the prosecution of this offense. Likewise, nonindigent defendants charged with this offense would be well advised to hire the 'best lawyers they can get.' Scott's right to the assistance of appointed counsel is thus plainly mandated by the logic of the Court's prior cases, including *Argersinger* itself.

"Perhaps the strongest refutation of respondent's alarmist prophecies that an authorized imprisonment standard would wreak havoc on the States is that the standard has not produced that result in the substantial number of States that already provide counsel in all cases where imprisonment is authorized—States that include a large majority of the country's population and a great diversity of urban and rural environments. * * * It may well be that adoption by this Court of an authorized imprisonment standard would lead state and local governments to re-examine their criminal statutes. A state legislature or local government might determine that it no longer desired to authorize incarceration for certain minor offenses in light of the expense of meeting the requirements of the Constitution. In my view this re-examination is long overdue. In any event, the Courts actual imprisonment standard must inevitably lead the courts to make this re-examination, which plainly should more properly be a legislative responsibility."

In a separate dissent, Justice Blackmun maintained that the right to counsel "extends at least as far as the right to jury trial" and thus that "an indigent defendant in a state criminal case must be afforded appointed counsel whenever the defendant is prosecuted for a nonpetty criminal offense, that is, one punishable by more than six months' imprisonment, *or* whenever the defendant is actually subjected to a term of imprisonment."

Notes and Questions

1. Were Justice Powell's reasons for switching from his position in *Argersinger* to the "actual confinement" approach in *Scott*—to "provide clear guidance" to lower courts and to reach a result consistent with *Argersinger*—persuasive? Did Justice Powell explain why the "actual confinement" test provides clearer guidance than the alternative to it? Did he explain why he declined to join Justice Blackmun's dissenting opinion? Of all the opinions in *Scott,* does the Blackmun opinion diverge least from the views Powell expressed in *Argersinger?* See Lawrence Herman & Charles A. Thompson, *Scott v. Illinois and the Right to Counsel: A Decision in Search of a Doctrine?* 17 Am.Crim.L.Rev. 71, 94 (1979).

2. ***How important are misdemeanor cases when no imprisonment is actually imposed?*** Consider Bruce R. Jacob, *Memories of and Reflections about Gideon v. Wainwright*, 33 Stetson L.Rev. 180, 284 (2003) (writing forty years after he had argued the losing side in *Gideon*): "The stigma of any criminal conviction, including a misdemeanor conviction that results in a fine, is significant. Any misdemeanor conviction in a person's past, except for a minor traffic offense,[419] makes it difficult for that person to gain entry into medical school or law school, to obtain certain jobs, or to enter the military service. Imposing a fine is a taking of property under [Fourteenth Amendment Due Process]. [Now] that the right to counsel has been incorporated into the Fourteenth Amendment, an indigent defendant in a misdemeanor case, facing a possible fine as punishment, should be entitled to the appointment of counsel."

3. Are unrepresented defendants likely to waive their right to a jury trial, hoping that a judge who sits as factfinder will be able to provide assistance? If so, how in a *non-jury* case, can a judge *properly* make an intelligent pre-trial determination as to whether the sentence is likely to include incarceration, at least where he will hear the case? Isn't a considerable amount of potentially prejudicial information likely to be injected into the factfinding process? If an indigent defendant charged with an offense usually punished only by a fine is appointed counsel, would a *different* judge hearing the case assume that a colleague had found that the defendant had a "bad record" or had committed the minor offense in an egregious manner? See Commentary to Unif.R.Crim.P. 321(b); Note, 1979 U.Ill.L.F. 739, 752.

4. May the problems raised in Note 3 never be reached because of judicial reluctance to conduct pretrial inquiries about the likely sentence? Consider Note, 93 Harv.L.Rev. 82, 87 (1979): "It seems far more likely that, due to the sheer volume of misdemeanor cases, judges simply will not appoint counsel, thereby relinquishing their discretion to impose the penalty of imprisonment." If so, would this constitute improper judicial interference with the legislature's judgment concerning the appropriate range of penalties? See id.

5. ***Gideon revisited—and criticized.*** Although he recognizes that "probably no decision in the field of constitutional criminal procedure enjoys anything like the unqualified and unanimous approval" that *Gideon* has received, Professor Dripps criticizes the case for focusing on the language of the Sixth Amendment rather than taking a more general due process approach. DONALD A. DRIPPS, *About Guilt or Innocence* 117 (2003):

"[*Gideon*] took a Procrustean approach to the Sixth Amendment. Where the amendment says the defendant may appear through counsel, *Gideon* stretches the

419. I do not consider leaving the scene of an accident or driving while intoxicated to be minor offenses.

amendment to cover subsidizing counsel for the poor. Where the amendment says ['in *all* criminal prosecutions'], *Gideon* reduces the amendment to covering [felony cases and only those misdemeanor cases leading to incarceration]. Would the Court now or ever uphold a federal statute that forbade a misdemeanor defendant from appearing through privately-retained counsel? If not, how can 'all' mean 'all' when the issue is prohibiting appearance through counsel, but mean 'some' when the issue is providing indigent defense? * * * [By] relying on the Sixth Amendment (albeit in a distorted fashion) the Warren Court deflected attention from instrumental reliability in favor of a formalistic focus on the textually-referenced 'assistance of counsel.' The incorporation approach necessarily failed to describe Gideon's constitutional right with appropriate generality. There is nothing *intristically* valuable about lawyers; that is why subsequent cases have developed the idea, if not the reality, that defense counsel's assistance must be *effective*. * * * Gideon's right was not be a lawyer, but to a trial that ran no more than some practically irreducible risk of falsely convicting him."

6. *Can an uncounseled misdemeanor conviction still be used to enhance a prison sentence when, after being given counsel, a defendant is convicted of a second crime?* Overruling an earlier decision (*Baldasar v. Illinois*, 446 U.S. 222 (1980)), the Court, per REHNQUIST, C.J., held in NICHOLS v. UNITED STATES, 511 U.S. 738 (1994), that a "logical consequence" of *Scott* is that "an uncounseled conviction valid under *Scott* [because no prison term was imposed] may be relied upon to enhance the sentence for a subsequent offense, even though that sentence entails imprisonment. Enhancement statutes, whether in the nature of criminal history provisions such as those contained in the Sentencing Guidelines, or recidivist statutes that are commonplace in state criminal laws, do not change the penalty imposed for the earlier conviction." (Seven years earlier, when not represented by counsel, Nichols had pled *nolo contendere* to a state misdemeanor (DUI) and paid a $250 fine. This misdemeanor conviction was used to enhance his sentence when he was subsequently convicted of a federal drug offense.)

The Chief Justice pointed out: "[Nichols] could have been sentenced more severely based simply on evidence of the underlying conduct that gave rise to the previous DUI offense. And the state need prove such conduct only by a preponderance of the evidence. Surely, then, it must be constitutionally permissible to consider a prior uncounseled conviction based on the same conduct where that conduct must be proved beyond a reasonable doubt."[a]

BLACKMUN, J., joined by Stevens and Ginsburg, JJ., dissented: "It is more logical, and more consistent with the reasoning in *Scott*, to hold that a conviction that is invalid for imposing a sentence for the offense remains invalid for increasing the term of imprisonment imposed for a subsequent conviction. [That] the sentence in *Scott* was imposed in the first instance and the sentence here was the result of an enhancement statute is a distinction without a constitutional difference. [Moreover,] as a practical matter, introduction of a record of conviction generally causes greater weight than other evidence of pure conduct. * * * Realistically, then, the conclusion that a state may prove prior conduct in a sentencing proceeding [in a subsequent case] does not support, much less compel a

a. The Court also rejected the argument that due process requires a misdemeanor defendant to be warned that his conviction might be used for enhancement purposes should he later be convicted of another crime: "[A] large number of misdemeanor convictions take place in police or justice courts which are not courts of record"; therefore, "there would be no way to memorialize any such warning." "Nor is it at all clear how expansive the warning would have to be. [And] a warning at the completely general level—that if he is brought back into court on another criminal charge [he] will be treated more harshly—would merely tell him what he must surely already know."

conclusion that the state may, in lieu of proving directly the prior conduct, rely on a conviction obtained against an uncounseled defendant."[b]

7. ***If an indigent defendant is not provided counsel, can he be given a suspended sentence or placed on probation?*** Consider ALABAMA v. SHELTON, 535 U.S. 654 (2002), which arose as follows: After being convicted of a misdemeanor, third-degree assault, Shelton, an indigent defendant who had not been afforded counsel, was sentenced to a jail term of 30 days, which the trial court immediately suspended. Shelton was then placed on two years unsupervised probation. The Supreme Court of Alabama took the position that a suspended sentence constitutes a "term of imprisonment" within the meaning of *Argersinger* and *Scott* even though incarceration is not immediate or inevitable. Accordingly, the court affirmed Shelton's conviction and the monetary portion of his punishment, but invalidated "that aspect of his sentence imposing 30 days of suspended jail time." By reversing Shelton's suspended sentence, the court also vacated the two-year term of probation. A 5–4 majority, per GINSBURG, J., affirmed:

"[Where] the State provides no counsel to an indigent defendant, does the Sixth Amendment permit activation of a suspended sentence upon the defendant's violation of the terms of probation? We conclude that it does not. A suspended sentence is a prison term imposed for the offense of conviction. Once the prison term is triggered, the defendant is incarcerated not for the probation violation, but for the underlying offense. The uncounseled conviction at that point 'result[s] in imprisonment'; it 'ends up in the actual deprivation of a person's liberty.' This is precisely what the Sixth Amendment as interpreted in *Argersinger* and *Scott* does not allow.

"[*Amicus*] contends that 'practical considerations clearly weigh against' the extension of the Sixth Amendment appointed-counsel right to a defendant in Shelton's situation. [On the basis of figures suggesting that conditional sentences are commonly imposed but rarely activated,] *amicus* argues that a rule requiring appointed counsel in every case involving a suspended sentence would unduly hamper the States' attempts to impose effective probationary punishment. A more 'workable solution,' he contends, would permit imposition of a suspended sentence on an uncounseled defendant and require appointment of counsel, if at all, only at the probation revocation stage, when incarceration is imminent.

"[*Amicus*] does not describe the contours of the hearing, that, he suggests, might precede revocation of a term of probation imposed on an uncounseled defendant. [In] Alabama, however, the character of the probation revocation hearing currently afforded is not in doubt. The proceeding is an 'informal' one at which the defendant has no right to counsel, and the court no obligation to observe customary rules of evidence. More significant, the sole issue at the hearing—apart from determinations about the necessity of confinement—is whether the defendant breached the terms of probation. [The] validity or reliability of the underlying conviction is beyond attack. * * *

"We think it plain that a hearing so timed and structured cannot compensate for the absence of trial counsel, for it does not even address the key Sixth Amendment inquiry: whether the adjudication of guilt corresponding to the prison sentence is sufficiently reliable to permit incarceration. Deprived of counsel when tried, convicted, and sentenced, and unable to challenge the original judgment at a

b. Souter, J. concurred only in the judgment, concluding that the enhanced sentence was permissible because the Sentencing Guidelines do not provide for "automatic enhancement" based on prior uncounseled convictions. Therefore, "a defendant has the chance to convince the sentencing court of the unreliability of any prior valid but uncounseled convictions in reflecting the seriousness of his past criminal conduct or predicting the likelihood of recidivism."

subsequent probation revocation hearing, a defendant in Shelton's circumstances faces incarceration on a conviction that has never been subjected to 'the crucible of meaningful adversarial testing.'

"[The] dissent imagines a set of safeguards Alabama might provide at the probation revocation stage sufficient to cure its failure to appoint counsel prior to sentencing, including, perhaps, 'complete retrial of the misdemeanor violation with assistance of counsel.' But there is no cause for speculation about Alabama's procedures; they are established by Alabama statute and decisional law, and they bear no resemblance to those the dissent invents in its effort to sanction the prospect of Shelton's imprisonment on an uncounseled conviction.[5] Assessing the issue before us in light of actual circumstances, we do not comprehend how the procedures Alabama in fact provides at the probation revocation hearing could bring Shelton's sentence within constitutional bounds."

Justice SCALIA, joined by the Chief Justice and Justices Kennedy and Thomas, dissented:

"[What procedures the Alabama courts will adopt if Shelton someday violates the terms of probation and the state decides to deprive him of his liberty] is not the [question] before us, and the Court has no business offering an advisory opinion on its answer. We are asked to decide whether 'imposition of a suspended or conditional sentence in a misdemeanor case invoke[s] a defendant's Sixth Amendment right to counsel.' Since *imposition* of a suspended sentence does not deprive a defendant of his personal liberty, the answer to *that* question is plainly no. In the future, *if and when* the State of Alabama seeks to imprison respondent on the previously suspended sentence, we can ask whether the procedural safeguards attending the imposition of that sentence comply with the Constitution. But that question is *not* before us now.

"[Surely] the procedures attending reimposition of a suspended sentence would be adequate if they required, upon the defendant's request, complete retrial of the misdemeanor violation with assistance of counsel. By what right does the Court deprive the State of that option? It may well be a sensible option, since most defendants will be induced to comply with the terms of their probation by the mere threat of a retrial that could send them to jail, and since the expense of those rare, counseled retrials may be much less than the expense of providing counsel initially in all misdemeanor cases that bear a possible sentence of imprisonment. And it may well be that, in some cases, even procedures short of complete retrial will suffice."

B. THE "BEGINNINGS" OF THE RIGHT TO COUNSEL: HEREIN OF "CRIMINAL PROSECUTIONS" AND "CRITICAL STAGES"

The point at which the right to the assistance of counsel "begins" or first "attaches" is a question that arises in a number of different contexts and one that is considered at various parts of the book. See, e.g., *Miranda* (p. 575) ("custodial interrogation"); *United States v. Wade* (p. 757) (pretrial lineups); *Coleman v. Alabama* (p. 1047) (preliminary hearing).

Compelled self-incrimination considerations aside, a defendant is not entitled to the assistance of counsel unless (a) adversary judicial proceedings have commenced (the Sixth Amendment right to counsel is guaranteed only "in all criminal

5. In any event, the dissent is simply incorrect that our decision today effectively "deprive[s] the State of th[e] option" of placing an uncounseled defendant on probation, with incarceration conditioned on a guilty verdict following a trial *de novo*. That option is the functional equivalent of pretrial probation, as to which we entertain no constitutional doubt. * * *

prosecutions")[a] *and* (b) the encounter is a "critical stage" of the criminal proceeding. Two pretrial identifications make the point. In *Kirby v. Illinois* (1972) (p. 769), the Court held that defendant was not entitled to a lawyer at his lineup, because the lineup had been held *prior* to his indictment. In *United States v. Ash* (1973) (p. 772), in a successful effort to identify the defendant as the culprit, the prosecutor showed photographs of defendant and others to witnesses *after* adversary criminal proceedings had begun. Nevertheless, the Court held that defendant was still not entitled to the presence of counsel at the identification because, unlike a corporeal identification, a photographic display was not a "critical stage" of the prosecution.[b]

Although at one time the *Escobedo* case (p. 563) indicated otherwise, it is now clear that the right to counsel does not come into play simply because a person is or becomes the "prime suspect" or "focal point," or even when he is arrested (absent "interrogation" or its equivalent). "[A] person is entitled to the help of a lawyer"—assuming the stage of the "prosecution" is a "critical" one—"at or after the time that judicial proceedings have been initiated against him—'whether by way of formal charge, preliminary hearing, indictment, information, or arraignment [presumably as early as the first appearance before a judicial officer].' " *Brewer v. Williams* (p. 733) (the Court, per Stewart, J.).

As indicated by the cases dealing with the use of informants and other secret government agents to obtain incriminating statements (see, e.g., *Hoffa*, *Osborn* and *White,* all discussed in Ch. 7, § 4), when judicial proceedings have not been initiated against a person, the privilege against self-incrimination as interpreted in *Miranda*—and *Miranda* alone—strikes the appropriate balance. If and when the conditions surrounding or inherent in a "preformal charge" confrontation are sufficiently coercive, "interrogation" or its equivalent may bring the "*Miranda* right to counsel" into play. But the right to counsel as such, what might be called the "pure" right to counsel, is not brought into play. At the "pre-charge" stage, at least when the suspect neither has nor has expressed a desire for counsel, the right to counsel is triggered by, and dependent on, forces that "jeopardize" the privilege against compelled self-incrimination; it has no life it can call its own.

The importance of the commencement of adversary criminal proceedings for right to counsel purposes is underscored in UNITED STATES v. GOUVEIA, 467 U.S. 180 (1984). During the investigation of murders of fellow inmates in a federal

a. As Justice Stewart observed, concurring in a pretrial identification case, *United States v. Ash* (p. 772), "the requirement that there be a 'prosecution' means that [the] 'right to counsel attaches only at or after the time that the adversary proceedings have been initiated against [an accused].' 'It is this point [that] marks the commencement of the "criminal prosecution" to which alone the explicit guarantees of the Sixth Amendment are applicable.' "

b. The Court, per Blackmun, J., observed that the right to counsel has always been limited to "trial-like confrontations" between prosecuting authorities and the accused where the lawyer acts as "a spokesman for, or advisor to the accused." Concurring Justice Stewart emphasized that "a photographic identification is quite different from a lineup, for there are substantially fewer possibilities of impermissible suggestion when photographs are used, and those unfair influences can be readily constructed at trial."

Dissenting Justice Brennan, joined by Douglas and Marshall, JJ., insisted that, regardless of whether the accused is physically present, "a 'stage' of the prosecution must be deemed 'critical' for the purpose of the Sixth Amendment if it is one at which the presence of counsel is necessary 'to protect the fairness of *the trial itself.*' " Responding to Justice Stewart's argument, the dissenters maintained that "the risks [of misidentification] are obviously as great at a photographic display as at a lineup." In fact, " 'because of the inherent limitations of photography, . . . [a] photographic identification, even when properly obtained, is clearly inferior to a properly obtained corporeal identification.' "

prison, defendants were isolated in administrative detention for periods ranging from eight to nineteen months until their indictment on federal criminal charges. The Ninth Circuit reasoned that the administrative detention of prison inmates for more than 90 days because of a pending felony investigation constitutes an "accusation" for right to counsel purposes and required that the prisoners either be provided counsel or released back into the prison population. The Supreme Court, per REHNQUIST, J., disagreed:

"[O]ur cases have long recognized that the right to counsel attaches only at or after the initiation of adversary proceedings against the defendant [referring to *Kirby v. Illinois* and subsequent cases]. Although we have extended an accused's right to counsel to certain 'critical' pre-trial proceedings, we have done so recognizing that at those proceedings, 'the accused [is] confronted, just as at trial, by the procedural system, or by his expert adversary, or by both,' in a situation where the results of the confrontation 'might well settle the accused's fate and reduces the trial itself to a mere formality.' [But] our cases have never suggested that the purpose of the right to counsel is to provide a defendant with a pre-indictment private investigator, and we see no reason to adopt that novel interpretation of the right to counsel in this case."[a]

SECTION 2. THE *GRIFFIN-DOUGLAS* "EQUALITY" PRINCIPLE

GRIFFIN v. ILLINOIS: "THERE CAN BE NO EQUAL JUSTICE WHERE THE KIND OF TRIAL A MAN GETS DEPENDS ON THE MONEY HE HAS"

Prior to GRIFFIN v. ILLINOIS, 351 U.S. 12 (1956), full direct appellate review could only be had in Illinois by furnishing the appellate court with a bill of exceptions or report of the trial proceedings, certified by the trial judge. Preparation of these documents was sometimes impossible without a stenographic transcript of the trial proceedings, but such a transcript was furnished free only to indigent defendants sentenced to death. *Griffin* upheld by a 5–4 vote the contention that the due process and equal protection clauses of the fourteenth amendment require that *all* indigent defendants be furnished a transcript, at least where allegations that manifest errors occurred at the trial are not denied. See generally Francis A. Allen, *Griffin v. Illinois: Antecedents and Aftermath,* 25 U.Chi.L.Rev. 151, 152 (1957).

There was no opinion of the Court in *Griffin*. Justice Black announced the Court's judgment in a four-justice opinion; Justice Frankfurter concurred specially. In the course of his opinion, Justice BLACK observed: "In criminal trials a State can no more discriminate on account of poverty than on account of religion, race, or color. Plainly the ability to pay costs in advance bears no rational relationship to a defendant's guilt or innocence and could not be used as an excuse to deprive a defendant of a fair trial. [It] is true that a State is not required by the federal constitution to provide appellate courts or a right to appellate review at all. [But] that is not to say that a State that does grant appellate review can do so in a

a. Stevens, J., joined by Brennan, J., concurred in the result on the ground that under the circumstances defendants' administrative detention "did not serve an accusatorial function," but a concern for the welfare of other inmates or defendants themselves. Marshall, J. dissented.

In *United States v. Moody*, 206 F.3d 609 (6th Cir.2000), the Sixth Circuit relied on *Gouveia* to hold that the Sixth Amendment right to counsel does not "attach" during preindictment plea bargaining. Thus, defendant could not be given the benefit of the plea bargain he rejected due to the ineffective assistance of counsel.

way that discriminates against some convicted defendants on account of their poverty. * * *

"All of the States now provide some method of appeal from criminal convictions, recognizing the importance of appellate review to a correct adjudication of guilt or innocence. Statistics show that a substantial proportion of criminal convictions are reversed by state appellate courts. Thus to deny adequate review to the poor means that many of them may lose their life, liberty or property because of unjust convictions which appellate courts would set aside. Many States have recognized this and provided aid for convicted defendants who have a right to appeal and need a transcript but are unable to pay for it. A few have not. Such a denial is a misfit in a country dedicated to affording equal justice to all and special privileges to none in the administration of its criminal law. There can be no equal justice where the kind of trial a man gets depends on the amount of money he has. Destitute defendants must be afforded as adequate appellate review as defendants who have money enough to buy transcripts."

A. Application (or Extension) of *Griffin*

In the decade and a half following *Griffin,* its underlying principle was broadly applied. See *Burns v. Ohio,* 360 U.S. 252 (1959) (state cannot require indigent defendant to pay filing fee before permitting him to appeal); *Smith v. Bennett,* 365 U.S. 708 (1961) (extending ban on filing fees to state post-conviction proceedings); *Long v. District Court of Iowa,* 385 U.S. 192 (1966) (indigent must be furnished a free transcript of a state habeas corpus hearing for use on appeal from a denial of habeas corpus, although availability of transcript not a sine qua non to access to the appellate court); *Gardner v. California,* 393 U.S. 367 (1969) (indigent prisoner entitled to free transcript of lower court habeas proceeding for use in filing application for a new habeas proceeding before a higher state court, even though that application need contain only a "brief statement" of prior proceedings and need not assign errors or refer to testimony in the prior proceeding); *Roberts v. LaVallee,* 389 U.S. 40 (1967) (indigent defendant entitled to free transcript of preliminary hearing for use at trial, even though both defendant and his counsel attended preliminary hearing and no indication of use to which preliminary hearing transcript could be put—points stressed by dissenting Justice Harlan); *Williams v. Illinois,* 399 U.S. 235 (1970) (defendant unable to pay fine could not be incarcerated beyond maximum term fixed by statute; equal protection requires that "statutory ceiling" on imprisonment be same for all "irrespective of their economic status"); *Tate v. Short,* 401 U.S. 395 (1971) (indigent convicted of offenses punishable by fine only cannot be incarcerated a sufficient time to satisfy fines);[a] *Britt v. North Carolina,* 404 U.S. 226 (1971) (recognition that under ordinary circumstances indigent would be entitled to free transcript of previous trial ending with a hung jury because such a transcript would be "valuable to the defendant" as a discovery device and "as a tool at the [second] trial itself for the impeachment of prosecution witnesses").

In MAYER v. CHICAGO, 404 U.S. 189 (1971), a unanimous Court, per BRENNAN, J., carried the *Griffin* principle further than it ever has the *Gideon* principle by holding that an indigent appellant "cannot be denied a 'record of sufficient completeness' to permit proper consideration of his claims" because he was convicted of ordinance violations punishable by fine only. "The size of the

a. A decade later, the Court relied on *Williams* and *Tate* to hold that a sentencing court cannot "automatically revoke" probation because a defendant cannot pay his fine without determining that the defendant "had not made sufficient bona fide efforts to pay or that adequate alternative forms of punishment did not exist." *Bearden v. Georgia,* 461 U.S. 660 (1983).

defendant's pocketbook bears no more relationship to his guilt or innocence in a non-felony than in a felony case." Nor was the Court impressed with the argument that appellant's interest in a transcript in a case where he is not subject to imprisonment is outweighed by the State's fiscal and other interests in not burdening the appellate process:

"*Griffin* does not represent a balance between the needs of the accused and the interests of society; its principle is a flat prohibition against pricing indigent defendants out of as effective an appeal as would be available to others able to pay their own way. The invidiousness of the discrimination that exists when criminal procedures are made available only to those who can pay is not erased by any differences in the sentences that may be imposed. The State's fiscal interest is, therefore, irrelevant.

"We add that even approaching the problem in the terms the city suggests hardly yields the answer the city tenders. The practical effects of conviction of even petty offenses of the kind involved here are not to be minimized. A fine may bear as heavily on an indigent accused as forced confinement.[b] The collateral consequences of conviction may be even more serious, as when (as was apparently a possibility in this case) the impecunious medical student finds himself barred from the practice of medicine because of a conviction he is unable to appeal for lack of funds."[c]

B. The Impact of the "Equality" Principle on Those Who Cannot Afford Counsel or Other Forms of Assistance

Prior to *Gideon,* the *Griffin* case posed a challenge to *Betts:* How could the *Betts* line of cases be reconciled with the language, if not the holding, of *Griffin?* Since there was an unqualified right to have one's own paid counsel of his choosing at state trial, capital or not, did *Griffin* not imply that an indigent also has this unqualified right? By requiring *special circumstances* to exist before the indigent was entitled to appointed counsel in non-capital state cases, was the indigent not denied equal protection of the law? When the Supreme Court finally overruled the *Betts* case, somewhat surprisingly, it did not rely on *Griffin* at all, but *Douglas v. California,* infra, decided the same day, is another story.

DOUGLAS v. CALIFORNIA, 372 U.S. 353 (1963), arose as follows: Indigent defendants requested, and were denied, the assistance of counsel on appeal. In accordance with a California rule of criminal procedure, the California District Court of Appeals stated that it had "gone through" the record and had come to the conclusion that "no good whatever could be served by appointment of counsel." Under the California procedure, appellate courts had to appoint counsel only if in their opinion it would be helpful to the defendant or the court. A 6–3 majority, per DOUGLAS, viewed the denial of counsel on appeal to an indigent under these circumstances "a discrimination at least as invidious as that condemned in [*Griffin*]:

"[Whether the issue is a transcript on appeal or the assistance of counsel on appeal] the evil is the same: discrimination against the indigent. For there can be no equal justice where the kind of an appeal a man enjoys 'depends on the amount of money he has.' * * *

"When an indigent is forced to run this gantlet of a preliminary showing of merit, the right to appeal does not comport with fair procedure. [T]he discrimina-

b. But cf. *Argersinger v. Hamlin,* p. 88; *Scott v. Illinois,* p. 90.

c. Chief Justice Burger joined the Court's opinion, but in a separate opinion emphasized that "there are alternatives in the majority of cases to a full verbatim transcript of an entire trial."

tion is not between 'possibly good and obviously bad cases,' but between cases where the rich man can require the court to listen to argument of counsel before deciding on the merits, but a poor man cannot. There is lacking that equality demanded by the Fourteenth Amendment where the rich man, who appeals as of right, enjoys the benefit of counsel's examination into the record, research of the law, and marshalling of arguments on his behalf, while the indigent, already burdened by a preliminary determination that his case is without merit, is forced to shift for himself. The indigent, where the record is unclear or the errors are hidden, has only the right to a meaningless ritual, while the rich man has a meaningful appeal."[a]

Justice HARLAN, whom Stewart, J. joined, dissented,[b] maintaining that "the Equal Protection Clause is not apposite, and its application to cases like the present one can lead only to mischievous results." He thought the case "should be judged solely under the Due Process Clause" and that the California procedure did not violate that provision. In rejecting the equal protection argument, Harlan observed:

"Laws such as these do not deny equal protection to the less fortunate for one essential reason: the Equal Protection Clause does not impose on the States 'an affirmative duty to lift the handicaps flowing from differences in economic circumstances.' To so construe it would be to read into the Constitution a philosophy of leveling that would be foreign to many of our basic concepts of the proper relations between government and society. The State may have a moral obligation to eliminate the evils of poverty, but it is not required by the Equal Protection Clause to give to some whatever others can afford.

"[I]t should be noted that if the present problem may be viewed as one of equal protection, so may the question of the right to appointed counsel at trial, and the Court's analysis of that right in *Gideon* [is] wholly unnecessary. The short way to dispose of *Gideon,* in other words, would be simply to say that the State deprives the indigent of equal protection whenever it fails to furnish him with legal services, and perhaps with other services as well, equivalent to those that the affluent defendant can obtain."[c]

ROSS v. MOFFITT

417 U.S. 600, 94 S.Ct. 2437, 41 L.Ed.2d 341 (1974).

Justice REHNQUIST delivered the opinion of the Court.

[Like many other states, the North Carolina appellate system is multitiered, providing for both an intermediate Court of Appeals and a Supreme Court. North Carolina authorizes appointment of counsel for a convicted defendant appealing to the intermediate court of appeals, but not for a defendant who seeks either discretionary review in the state supreme court or a writ of certiorari in the U.S. Supreme Court. In one case, the Mecklenburg County forgery conviction, respondent sought appointed counsel for discretionary review in the state supreme court. In another case, the Guilford County forgery conviction, respondent was repre-

a. The Court pointed out it was dealing "only with the first appeal, granted as a matter of right," not deciding whether a state had to provide counsel for an indigent seeking discretionary review.

b. Justice Clark wrote a separate dissenting opinion.

c. One may ask, too, why the Court failed even to discuss the applicability of the *Griffin-Douglas* "equality" principle to the issue raised in *Scott v. Illinois* p. 90. Since it is plain that one charged with an offense *punishable* by incarceration may *retain* counsel for his defense, does not the "equality" principle suggest that the "actual imprisonment" standard, even if it defensibly defines the Sixth Amendment right to appointed counsel, is unsatisfactory under the equal protection clause?

sented by the public defender in the state supreme court, but sought court-appointed counsel to prepare a writ of certiorari to the U.S. Supreme Court. On federal habeas corpus, a unanimous panel of the U.S. Court of Appeals for the Fourth Circuit, per Haynsworth, C.J., held that the *Douglas* rationale required appointment of counsel in both instances.]

[*Griffin* and succeeding cases, such as *Burns v. Ohio* and *Smith v. Bennett* (the filing fee cases summarized at p. 98),] stand for the proposition that a State cannot arbitrarily cut off appeal rights for indigents while leaving open avenues of appeal for more affluent persons. In *Douglas,* however, [the] Court departed somewhat from the limited doctrine of [these] cases and undertook an examination of whether an indigent's access to the appellate system was adequate. [The *Douglas* Court] concluded that a State does not fulfill its responsibility toward indigent defendants merely by waiving its own requirements that a convicted defendant procure a transcript or pay a fee in order to appeal, and held that the State must go further and provide counsel for the indigent on his first appeal as of right. It is this decision we are asked to extend today.

[The] precise rationale for the *Griffin* and *Douglas* lines of cases has never been explicitly stated, some support being derived from the Equal Protection Clause of the Fourteenth Amendment, and some from the Due Process Clause of that Amendment. Neither clause by itself provides an entirely satisfactory basis for the result reached, each depending on a different inquiry which emphasizes different factors. "Due process" emphasizes fairness between the State and the individual dealing with the State, regardless of how other individuals in the same situation may be treated. "Equal protection," on the other hand, emphasizes disparity in treatment by a State between classes of individuals whose situations are arguably indistinguishable. We will address these issues separately in the succeeding sections.

Recognition of the due process rationale in *Douglas* is found both in the Court's opinion and in the dissenting opinion of Mr. Justice Harlan. The Court in *Douglas* stated that "[w]hen an individual is forced to run this gauntlet of a preliminary showing of merit, the right to appeal does not comport with fair procedure." Mr. Justice Harlan thought that the due process issue in *Douglas* was the only one worthy of extended consideration. * * *

We do not believe that the Due Process Clause requires North Carolina to provide respondent with counsel on his discretionary appeal to the State Supreme Court. At the trial stage of a criminal proceeding, the right of an indigent defendant to counsel [is] fundamental and binding upon the States by virtue of the Sixth and Fourteenth Amendments. But there are significant differences between the trial and appellate stages of a criminal proceeding. The purpose of the trial stage from the State's point of view is to convert a criminal defendant from a person presumed innocent to one found guilty beyond a reasonable doubt. To accomplish this purpose, the State employs a prosecuting attorney who presents evidence to the court, challenges any witnesses offered by the defendant, argues rulings of the court, and makes direct arguments to the court or jury seeking to persuade them of the defendant's guilt. Under these circumstances "* * * reason and reflection require us to recognize that in our adversary system of criminal justice, any person haled into court, who is too poor to hire a lawyer, cannot be assured a fair trial unless counsel is provided for him." *Gideon.*

By contrast, it is ordinarily the defendant, rather than the State, who initiates the appellate process, seeking not to fend off the efforts of the State's prosecutor but rather to overturn a finding of guilt made by a judge or jury below. The defendant needs an attorney on appeal not as a shield to protect him against being "haled into court" by the State and stripped of his presumption of innocence, but rather as a sword to upset the prior determination of guilt. This difference is significant for, while no one would agree that the State may simply dispense with the trial stage of proceedings without a criminal defendant's consent, it is clear that the State need not provide any appeal at all. *McKane v. Durston.* The fact that an appeal *has* been provided does not automatically mean that a State then acts unfairly by refusing to provide counsel to indigent defendants at every stage of the way. Unfairness results only if indigents are singled out by the State and denied meaningful access to that system because of their poverty. That question is more profitably considered under an equal protection analysis.

Language invoking equal protection notions is prominent both in *Douglas* and in other cases treating the rights of indigents on appeal. * * * Despite the tendency of all rights "to declare themselves absolute to their logical extreme," there are obviously limits beyond which the equal protection analysis may not be pressed without doing violence to principles recognized in other decisions of this Court. The Fourteenth Amendment "does not require absolute equality or precisely equal advantages," nor does it require the State to "equalize economic conditions." *Griffin* (Frankfurter, J., concurring). It does require [that] indigents have an adequate opportunity to present their claims fairly within the adversarial system. The State cannot adopt procedures which leave an indigent defendant "entirely cut off from any appeal at all," by virtue of his indigency, *Lane,* or extend to such indigent defendants merely a "meaningless ritual" while others in better economic circumstances have a "meaningful appeal." *Douglas.* The question is not one of absolutes, but one of degrees. In this case we do not believe that the Equal Protection Clause when interpreted in the context of these cases, requires North Carolina to provide free counsel for indigent defendants seeking to take discretionary appeals to the North Carolina Supreme Court, or to file petitions for certiorari in this Court.

[The] facts show that respondent, in connection with his Mecklenburg County conviction, received the benefit of counsel in examining the record of his trial and in preparing an appellate brief on his behalf for the state Court of Appeals. Thus, prior to his seeking discretionary review in the State Supreme Court, his claims "had once been presented by a lawyer and passed upon by an appellate court." *Douglas.* We do not believe that it can be said, therefore, that a defendant in respondent's circumstances is denied meaningful access to the North Carolina Supreme Court simply because the State does not appoint counsel to aid him in seeking review in that court. At that stage he will have, at the very least, a transcript or other record of trial proceedings, a brief on his behalf in the Court of Appeals setting forth his claims of error, and in many cases an opinion by the Court of Appeals disposing of his case. These materials, supplemented by whatever submission respondent may make *pro se,* would appear to provide the Supreme Court of North Carolina with an adequate basis on which to base its decision to grant or deny review.

We are fortified in this conclusion by our understanding of the function served by discretionary review in the North Carolina Supreme Court. The critical issue in that court, as we perceive it, is not whether there has been "a correct adjudication of guilt" in every individual case, but rather whether "the subject matter of the appeal has significant public interest," whether "the cause involves legal principles of major significance to the jurisprudence of the state," or whether the decision below is in probable conflict with a decision of the Supreme Court. The Supreme Court may deny certiorari even though it believes that the decision of the Court of Appeals was incorrect, since a decision which appears incorrect may nevertheless fail to satisfy any of the criteria discussed above. Once a defendant's claims of error are organized and presented in a lawyer-like fashion to the Court of Appeals, the justices of the Supreme Court of North Carolina who make the decision to grant or deny discretionary review should be able to ascertain whether his case satisfies the standards established by the legislature for such review.

This is not to say, of course, that a skilled lawyer, particularly one trained in the somewhat arcane art of preparing petitions for discretionary review, would not prove helpful to any litigant able to employ him. An indigent defendant seeking review in the Supreme Court of North Carolina is therefore somewhat handicapped in comparison with a wealthy defendant who has counsel assisting him in every conceivable manner at every stage in the proceeding. But both the opportunity to have counsel prepare an initial brief in the Court of Appeals and the nature of discretionary review in the Supreme Court of North Carolina make this relative handicap far less than the handicap borne by the indigent defendant denied counsel on his initial appeal as of right in *Douglas.* And the fact that a particular service might be of benefit to an indigent defendant does not mean that the service is constitutionally required. The duty of the State under our cases is not to duplicate the legal arsenal that may be privately retained by a criminal defendant in a continuing effort to reverse his conviction, but only to assure the indigent defendant an adequate opportunity to present his claims fairly in the context of the State's appellate process. We think respondent was given that opportunity under the existing North Carolina system.

Much of the discussion in the preceding section is equally relevant to the question of whether a State must provide counsel for a defendant seeking review of his conviction in this Court. North Carolina will have provided counsel for a convicted defendant's only appeal as of right, and the brief prepared by that counsel together with one and perhaps two North Carolina appellate opinions will be available to this Court in order that it may decide whether or not to grant certiorari. This Court's review, much like that of the Supreme Court of North Carolina, is discretionary and depends on numerous factors other than the perceived correctness of the judgment we are asked to review.

[The] suggestion that a State is responsible for providing counsel to one petitioning this Court simply because it initiated the prosecution which led to the judgment sought to be reviewed is unsupported by either reason or authority. It would be quite as logical under the rationale of *Douglas* and *Griffin,* and indeed perhaps more so, to require that the Federal Government or this Court furnish and compensate counsel for petitioners who seek certiorari here to review state judgments of conviction. Yet this Court has followed a consistent policy of denying applications for appointment of counsel by persons seeking to file jurisdictional statements or petitions for certiorari in this Court. In the light of these authorities, it would be odd, indeed, to read the Fourteenth Amendment to impose such a requirement on the States, and we decline to do so. * * *

Justice DOUGLAS, with whom Justice BRENNAN and Justice MARSHALL concur, dissenting.

[In his opinion below] Chief Judge Haynsworth could find "no logical basis for differentiation between appeals of right and permissive review procedures in the context of the Constitution and the right to counsel." More familiar with the functioning of the North Carolina criminal justice system than are we, he concluded that "in the context of constitutional questions arising in criminal prosecutions, permissive review in the state's highest court may be predictably the most meaningful review the conviction will receive." The North Carolina Court of Appeals, for example, will be constrained in diverging from an earlier opinion of the State Supreme Court, even if subsequent developments have rendered the earlier Supreme Court decision suspect. "[T]he state's highest court remains the ultimate arbiter of the rights of its citizens."

Chief Judge Haynsworth also correctly observed that the indigent defendant proceeding without counsel is at a substantial disadvantage relative to wealthy defendants represented by counsel when he is forced to fend for himself in seeking discretionary review from the State Supreme Court or from this Court. It may well not be enough to allege error in the courts below in layman's terms; a more sophisticated approach may be demanded:

"An indigent defendant is as much in need of the assistance of a lawyer in preparing and filing a petition for certiorari as he is in the handling of an appeal as of right. In many appeals, an articulate defendant could file an effective brief by telling his story in simple language without legalisms, but the technical requirement for applications for writs of certiorari are hazards which one untrained in the law could hardly be expected to negotiate. * * * "

[The] right to discretionary review is a substantial one, and one where a lawyer can be of significant assistance to an indigent defendant. It was correctly perceived below that the "same concepts of fairness and equality which require counsel in a first appeal of right, require counsel in other and subsequent discretionary appeals."

ON THE MEANING OF *ROSS v. MOFFITT*

1. Is *Mayer v. Chicago* (p. 98) "good law" after *Ross?* Are *Long v. District Court*, *Gardner v. California*, *Roberts v. LaVallee,* and *Britt v. North Carolina* (all summarized at p. 98) "good law" after *Ross?* Does the *Long-Gardner* line of cases (never mentioned by the *Ross* Court) constitute a significant "departure" from what the *Ross* Court calls the "limited doctrine" of *Griffin* and succeeding cases?

2. Consider Laurence H. Tribe, *American Constitutional Law* 1647 (2d ed.1988): "[The *Ross* Court] disengaged *Griffin* from *Douglas,* deftly rewove the *Griffin* transcript and filing fee decisions together as minimal access cases rather than equal protection cases, and neatly severed *Douglas* from this newly created body of law." See also Kamisar, *Poverty, Equality, and Criminal Procedure,* in National College of District Attorneys, *Constitutional Law Deskbook* 1–97 to 1–100 (1977).

3. ***Does the Ross opinion's "equal protection analysis" closely resemble a "due process analysis"?*** Indeed, now that *Ross* is on the books, does the "equality" principle *add anything* to what the indigent defendant or prisoner already has in his arsenal? Consider Kamisar, supra, at 1–101 to 1–108:

"[The *Ross* 'equal protection analysis'] seems to put to one side the admitted fact that an indigent seeking discretionary review is 'somewhat handicapped in comparison with a wealthy defendant who has counsel assisting him' and focuses instead on whether an indigent seeking discretionary review without counsel has a '*meaningful* opportunity' (emphasis added) to present his claims in the state supreme court—to provide the court 'with an *adequate* basis for its decision to grant or deny review' (emphasis added)—*regardless* of whether a wealthy defendant who has counsel at this stage has a *significantly better* opportunity to present his claims.

"[What *Ross*] really seems to be asking, and deciding, is whether an indigent in respondent's circumstances has a *fair chance,* a *fighting chance* (or the requisite *minimum* chance), to get the attention of the state supreme court. [This] is 'due process,' not 'equal protection' reasoning. * * *

"So long as the indigent defendant's 'brand of justice' satisfies certain minimal standards—passes government inspection, one might say—[*Ross* tells us that] *it need not be* the same brand of justice or the same 'choice' or 'prime' grade of justice as the wealthy man's. [In some phases of the criminal process an indigent will not have 'meaningful access' to the hearing body or an 'adequate opportunity' to present his claim], but in [such] cases 'fundamental fairness'—'due process'—will require the state to furnish counsel. In those cases where due process *does not* impose a duty on the state to provide counsel, *neither,* it seems, *will 'equal protection.'* "

4. ***Is there a right to appointed counsel on discretionary appeal from a plea of guilty?*** Under Michigan law, unless leave to appeal is granted by the intermediate appellate court, appointed counsel is not provided indigent defendants seeking discretionary appellate review of a guilty plea. A divided Michigan Supreme Court upheld the constitutionality of this practice, relying on the special character of the guilty plea conviction, but the U.S. Court of Appeals (sitting en banc and also divided) concluded that the practice was unconstitutional. *Tesmer v. Granholm*, 333 F.3d 683 (6th Cir.2003), reversed on procedural grounds, sub. nom. *Kowalski v. Tesmer*, 125 S.Ct. 564 (2004). The issue is expected to be resolved in *Halbert v. Michigan*, cert. granted, 125 S.Ct. 823 (2005). As the Sixth Circuit viewed the issue, the Michigan practice deprived the indigent guilty plea defendant of an adequate opportunity to present his claim within the state's appellate practice. A key factor in *Ross v. Moffitt*, emphasized the Sixth Circuit, was the presence of an earlier appeal of right, which provided a brief by defense counsel on the same issues that might be considered in a discretionary appeal.

5. ***What light, if any, is shed on the meaning of Ross by the MacCollom case?*** *United States v. MacCollom*, 426 U.S. 317 (1976) upheld the constitutionality of 28 U.S.C. § 753(f), which provides for a free transcript for indigent prisoners seeking relief under 28 U.S.C. § 2255 (the statutory counterpart to habeas corpus for federal prisoners) *only if* the trial judge certifies that (a) the claim is "not frivolous" and (b) the transcript is needed to decide the issues presented." The principal opinion was written by Rehnquist, J., joined by Burger, C.J., and Stewart and Powell, JJ.

Concurring Justice Blackmun, who provided the fifth vote for the Court's judgment, thought it clear that "there is no constitutional requirement that the [government] provide an indigent with a transcript when that transcript is not necessary in order for him to prove his claim, or when his claim is frivolous on its face. Nor does the Constitution require that an indigent be furnished every possible legal tool, no matter how devoid of assistance it may be, merely because a person of unlimited means might choose to waste his resources in a quest of that kind."

Dissenting Justice Brennan, joined by Marshall, J., maintained, that the government's refusal to furnish a free transcript in a § 2255 proceeding "upon merely a showing of indigency" violated the "equal protection" element of fifth amendment due process: "The *Griffin* principle of equality was not limited to transcripts for purposes of direct appellate review [discussing, e.g., *Lane v. Brown*, *Long v. District Court*, *Gardner v. California*]."[a]

6. What light, if any, is shed on the meaning of *Ross* by *Ake v. Oklahoma,* immediately below.

a. In a separate dissent, Stevens, J., joined by Brennan, White and Marshall, JJ., maintained that § 753(f) should be construed to make free transcripts available as a matter of course to § 2255 petitioners, as well as to convicted defendants pursuing direct appeals. The plurality's response was that Justice Stevens' construction of § 753(f) "would do violence to the intent of Congress."

C. The Indigent Defendant's Right to Expert Services in Addition to Counsel

In AKE v. OKLAHOMA, 470 U.S. 68 (1985), the Court broke its thirty-year silence on the issue of an indigent defendant's right to a psychiatrist and other expert assistance and held that (1) at least when a defendant has made a preliminary showing that his sanity at the time of the offense is likely to be a significant factor at trial, the state must provide access to "the psychiatric examination and assistance necessary to prepare an effective defense based on [the defendant's] mental condition" and (2) when, at a capital sentencing proceeding, the state presents psychiatric evidence of the defendant's future dangerousness, due process requires access to psychiatric assistance.

The case arose as follows: Ake, an indigent, was charged with first-degree murder. At his arraignment, Ake's behavior was so bizarre that the trial judge ordered him to be examined by a psychiatrist. The examining psychiatrist found Ake incompetent to stand trial. Six weeks after being committed to the state mental hospital, Ake was found to be competent to stand trial on the condition that he continue to be sedated with an antipsychotic drug. Petitioner's attorney informed the court that he would raise an insanity defense, but his motion for a psychiatric evaluation at state expense was denied. The jury rejected the insanity defense and petitioner was convicted of first-degree murder. At the capital sentencing proceeding, the state asked for the death penalty, relying on the examining psychiatrist's testimony to establish the likelihood of petitioner's future dangerousness. Petitioner had no expert witness to rebut this testimony or to give evidence in mitigation of his punishment, and he was sentenced to death. In reversing, the Court observed, per MARSHALL, J:

"This Court has long recognized that when a State brings its judicial power to bear on an indigent defendant in a criminal proceeding, it must take steps to assure that the defendant has a fair opportunity to present his defense. This elementary principle, grounded in significant part on the Fourteenth Amendment's due process guarantee of fundamental fairness, derives from the belief that justice cannot be equal where, simply as a result of his poverty, a defendant is denied the opportunity to participate meaningfully in a judicial proceeding in which his liberty is at stake. [Thus,] this Court held almost 30 years ago that once a State offers to criminal defendants the opportunity to appeal their cases, it must provide a trial transcript to an indigent defendant if the transcript is necessary to a decision on the merits of the appeal. *Griffin v. Illinois.* Indeed, in *Little v. Streater,* 452 U.S. 1 (1981), we extended this principle of meaningful participation to a 'quasi-criminal' proceeding and held that, in a paternity action, the State cannot deny the putative father blood grouping tests, if he cannot otherwise afford them.

"Meaningful access to justice has been the consistent theme of these cases. [A] criminal trial is fundamentally unfair if the State proceeds against an individual defendant without making certain that he has access to the raw materials integral to the building of an effective defense. Thus, while the Court has not held that a State must purchase for the indigent defendant all the assistance that his wealthier counterpart might buy, see *Ross v. Moffitt,* it has often reaffirmed that fundamental fairness entitles indigent defendants to 'an adequate opportunity to present their claims fairly within the adversary system,' id. To implement this principle, we have focused on identifying the 'basic tools of an adequate defense or appeal,' and we have required that such tools be provided to those defendants who cannot afford to pay for them.

"[W]ithout the assistance of a psychiatrist to conduct a professional examination on issues relevant to the defense, to help determine whether the insanity defense is viable to present testimony, and to assist in preparing the cross-examination of a State's psychiatric witnesses, the risk of an inaccurate resolution of sanity issues is extremely high. With such assistance, the defendant is fairly able to present at least enough information to the jury, in a meaningful manner, as to permit it to make a sensible determination.

"A defendant's mental condition is not necessarily at issue in every criminal proceeding, however, and it is unlikely that psychiatric assistance of the kind we have described would be of probable value in cases where it is not. The risk of error from denial of such assistance, as well as its probable value, are most predictably at their height when the defendant's mental condition is seriously in question. When the defendant is able to make an ex parte threshold showing to the trial court that his sanity is likely to be a significant factor in his defense, the need for the assistance of a psychiatrist is readily apparent. It is in such cases that a defense may be devastated by the absence of a psychiatric examination and testimony; with such assistance, the defendant might have a reasonable chance of success. In such a circumstance, where the potential accuracy of the jury's determination is so dramatically enhanced, and where the interests of the individual and the State in an accurate proceeding are substantial, the State's interest in its fisc must yield.

"We therefore hold that when a defendant demonstrates [that] his sanity at the time of the offense is to be a significant factor at trial, the State must, at a minimum, assure the defendant access to a competent psychiatrist who will conduct an appropriate examination and assist in evaluation, preparation, and presentation of the defense. This is not to say, of course, that the indigent defendant has a constitutional right to choose a psychiatrist of his personal liking or to receive funds to hire his own. Our concern is that the indigent defendant have access to a competent psychiatrist for the purpose we have discussed, and as in the case of provision of counsel we leave to the State the decision on how to implement this right.

"Ake also was denied the means of presenting evidence to rebut the State's evidence of his future dangerousness. The foregoing discussion compels a similar conclusion in the context of a capital sentencing proceeding, when the State presents psychiatric evidence of the defendants future dangerousness. * * *

"This Court has upheld the practice [in state capital sentencing proceedings] of placing before the jury psychiatric testimony on the question of future dangerousness, at least where the defendant has had access to an expert of his own. * * * Without a psychiatrist's assistance, the defendant cannot offer a well-informed expert's opposing view, and thereby loses a significant opportunity to raise in the jurors' minds questions about the State's proof of an aggravating factor. In such a circumstance, where the consequence of error is so great, the relevance of responsive psychiatric testimony so evident, and the burden on the State so slim, due process requires access to a psychiatric examination on relevant issues, to the testimony of the psychiatrist, and to assistance in preparation at the sentencing phase."[a]

a. Burger, C.J., concurred in the judgment, maintaining: "The facts of this case and the question presented confine the actual holding of the Court. In capital cases the finality of the sentence imposed warrants protections that may or may not be required in other cases. Nothing in the Court's opinion reaches non-capital cases." Can (should) the Court's opinion be limited to capital cases? See Note, 84 Mich.L.Rev. 1326 (1986).

Rehnquist, J., dissented. He did not believe that "the facts of this case warrant" the establishment of the constitutional rule announced by the Court and, in any event, he thought the rule "far too broad." He would limit it to capital cases and "make clear that the entitlement is to an independent psychiatric evaluation, not to a defense consultant." Is it clear that the entitlement *is* to a "defense consultant?"

Notes and Questions

1. ***The Sixth Amendment vs. Fourteenth Amendment due process.*** Although one might maintain that a right to a court-appointed psychiatrist under certain circumstances is implicit in the right to counsel or implements or effectuates that right, *Ake* is not written that way. It is a free-standing procedural due process decision; one that applies "the Fourteenth Amendment's due process guarantee of fundamental fairness." Consider Donald A. Dripps, *About Guilt or Innocence* 142 (2003): "The *Ake* Court described the appropriate inquiry as whether the defense had access to 'the basic tools' of an effective defense. This test has not been generously interpreted by the lower courts. Nonetheless, it is an illuminating comment on the power of doctrine that even a conservative majority could be moved to order the expenditure of public funds when faced with the prospect that a criminal trial ran a gratuitous risk of error, despite compliance with every specific safeguard in the Bill of Rights."

2. ***Ake's impact on the equality principle.*** How much of an exaggeration, if any, is it to say, as one commentator has, that "*Ake* represents the final and complete collapse of the equality principle into due process analysis" and "the full ascendancy of Justice Harlan's position in *Griffin* and *Douglas*"? See David Harris, *The Constitution and Truth Seeking: A New Theory on Expert Services for Indigent Defendants,* 83 J.Crim.L. & C. 469, 482, 488 (1992).

3. ***The breadth of the supporting services that may be needed.*** "Quality legal representation," emphasizes *A.B.A. Standards* § 5–1.4 (commentary), "cannot be rendered either by defenders or by assigned counsel unless the lawyers have available for their use adequate supporting services. These [include] expert witnesses * * *, personnel skilled in social work and related disciplines to provide assistance at pretrial release hearings and at sentencing, and trained investigators to interview witnesses and to assemble demonstrative evidence. The quality of representation at trial, for example, may be excellent and yet valueless to the defendant if the defense requires the assistance of a psychiatrist or handwriting expert and no such services are available. If the defense attorney must personally conduct factual investigations, the financial cost to the justice system is likely to be greater. Moreover, when an attorney personally interviews witnesses, [he] may be placed in the untenable position of either taking the stand to challenge their credibility if their testimony conflicts with statements previously given or withdrawing from the case."

4. ***The meaning of "basic tools."*** Under *Ake,* how basic does a tool have to be before a state is required to supply it to an indigent defendant? Consider Harris, Note 2 supra, at 486–87:

"As lower courts have struggled to define 'basic tools,' they have asked whether the particular resource requested by an indigent defendant is a 'virtual necessity' for the defense. Is the resource so important that the defense simply cannot do without it? Thus, 'basic tool' has come to mean not just something fundamental to a defendant's legal arsenal, but a resource without which the defense fails. Under this interpretation, most expert services remain luxuries for indigent defendants because the tasks experts perform and the issues with which they deal are not usually outcome determinative by themselves. Rather, the service any one expert or investigator provides is typically germane only to one or a few elements of the crime. If any one of the links in the evidentiary chain weakens, an acquittal may result, but this usually does not depend on the testimony of a single expert, such as the psychiatrist in *Ake.* Since lower courts have interpreted *Ake* to mean that the defense receives assistance only when the accused's case will fail without it, the basic tools standard does very little for most indigent defendants."

5. ***A new approach.*** Instead of trying to make indigent defendants "equal" or giving them "basic tools," Professor David Harris suggests, id. at 491–92, that courts use a theory that "targets the implications of economic disparity in criminal justice by focusing on whether the defendant's poverty could prevent the jury from hearing all of the relevant evidence on contested issues. Based on the Sixth Amendment, this theory would have judges ask two questions in deciding whether to grant a request for expert services. First, is the issue to which the requested resource pertains in dispute? Second, is the information that could be brought to trial as a result of granting the defendant's request for expert services helpful to the factfinder's decision? In other words, could this information, either by itself or in combination with other information, be the basis for a finding of reasonable doubt?"

6. ***The resource imbalance—a problem the Simpson case illustrated in reverse.*** Reconsider Professor Arenella's comments, set forth at p. 63, as to how, usually, the "resource factor" greatly favors the prosecution.

SECTION 3. WITHDRAWAL OF APPOINTED COUNSEL ON APPEAL: THE POTENTIAL TENSION BETWEEN THE INDIGENT DEFENDANT'S RIGHT TO COUNSEL ON FIRST APPEAL OF RIGHT AND THE LAWYER'S ETHICAL OBLIGATION NOT TO ASSERT FRIVOLOUS CLAIMS

If court appointed counsel believes an appeal should not be filed because it lacks any merit, how should she proceed? ANDERS v. CALIFORNIA, 386 U.S. 738 (1967), per CLARK, J., held a "no-merit letter"—counsel had stated in a letter to the state appellate court that he would not file a brief because he was "of the opinion that there is no merit to the appeal"—insufficient because it "affords neither the client nor the court any aid. The former must shift entirely for himself while the court has only the cold record which it must review without the help of an advocate." If, after a "conscientious examination" of his case, counsel finds an appeal to be "wholly frivolous," he should so advise the court and request permission to withdraw. "That request must, however, be accompanied by a brief referring to anything in the record that might arguably support the appeal. A copy of counsel's brief should be furnished the indigent and time allowed him to raise any points that he chooses; the court—not counsel—then proceeds, after a full examination of all the proceedings, to decide whether the case is wholly frivolous. If it so finds it may grant counsel's request to withdraw and dismiss the appeal insofar as federal requirements are concerned, or proceed to a decision on the merits, if state law so requires. On the other hand, if it finds any of the legal points arguable on their merits (and therefore not frivolous) it must, prior to decision, afford the indigent the assistance of counsel to argue the appeal."

Dissenting Justice STEWART, joined by Black and Harlan, JJ., expressed puzzlement as to why an appointed lawyer who considers an appeal "wholly frivolous" should be required to file "a brief reference to anything in the record that might arguably support the appeal." "[I]f the record did present any such 'arguable' issues, the appeal would not be frivolous and counsel would not have filed a 'non-merit' letter in the first place."

See also *Suggs v. United States,* 391 F.2d 971 (D.C.Cir.1968) (Leventhal, J.), stressing that appointed counsel should not ask to withdraw "unless in the same circumstances he would insist on withdrawal if he had been retained. As a general rule, the court will be greatly aided if appointed counsel remains in a case, even though he may be subjectively unimpressed with the merits of the available points." Adequate representation of an indigent appellant should include personal interviews "if in the same circumstances [they would be considered] useful or desirable were [counsel] representing a private client. Ordinarily at least one interview by counsel would appear to be useful."[a]

Notes and Questions

1. *Anders* has been sharply criticized by an assistant public defender who maintains that "it offers counsel the choice of filing a schizophrenic motion to withdraw (accompanied by a formal brief opposing the motion), or the alternative of writing the brief and not moving to withdraw. Human nature will force the selection of the latter alternative. [If tax-supported] groups of lawyers are forced to brief frivolous appeals, the people who will suffer the most are the indigent prisoners who have been *unjustly* convicted; they will languish in prison while the lawyers devote time and energy to hopeless causes on a first come-first served basis." James Doherty, *Wolf! Wolf!—The Ramifications of Frivolous Appeals,* 59 J.Crim.L.C. & P.S. 1, 2 (1968).

2. The egalitarian pronouncement in *Suggs* that appointed counsel should not seek to withdraw "unless in the same circumstances he would insist on withdrawal if he had been retained" has been criticized on the ground that it "glosses over the possibility that the two situations may not be comparable. It is likely that the need to pay a lawyer's fee and expenses is some deterrent to frivolous criminal appeals.[b] Retained counsel can also withdraw more readily and informally—usually by substitution of other counsel—than can assigned counsel and further, can more readily avoid prejudicing the defendant by alerting the court, and in some circuits the Government, to the weaknesses of the case." Robert Hermann, *Frivolous Criminal Appeals,* 47 N.Y.U.L.Rev. 701, 706 (1972). But compare the remarks of Judge Jack Day, *Proceedings of the National Conference on Standards for the Administration of Criminal Justice* (1972), 57 F.R.D. 303, 309 (1973): "I can never remember a case, really never, in a long life at the Bar, [where] if the money was there the appeal was so frivolous that the lawyer couldn't make it. I'm not suggesting nobody ever stood up and said grandly, 'Take away that $10,000; there's nothing to this case; I will not appeal

a. Cf. *Commonwealth v. Moffett,* 418 N.E.2d 585 (Mass.1981), prohibiting appointed counsel from withdrawing solely on the ground that the appeal is frivolous even when she files an "*Anders* brief" demonstrating that all possible arguments in favor of her client lack any merit: "As long as counsel must research and prepare an advocate's brief, he or she may as well submit it for the purpose of an ordinary appeal. Even if the appeal is frivolous, less time and energy will be spent directly reviewing the case on the merits. If the appeal is not frivolous, [prohibiting] withdrawal would also obviate any need to substitute counsel to argue the appeal." See also *State v. McKenney,* 568 P.2d 1213 (Idaho 1977) *State v. Gates,* 466 S.W.2d 681 (Mo.1971). See generally Mendelson, *Frivolous Criminal Appeals: The Anders Brief or the Idaho Rule,* 19 Crim.L.Bull. 22 (1983).

b. A major reason for "hopeless appeals," observe Paul Carrington, Daniel Meador & Maurice Rosenberg, *Justice on Appeal* 91–95 (1976), is that unlike the non-indigent convicted of crime, who has incentives *not* to appeal (he must balance benefit against cost), the indigent defendant is in "a no-lose situation, which provides every inducement to appeal, however forlorn the hope." In order to give the indigent "something to lose in the appeal similar to that which the non-indigent has," the authors propose establishing a fund, supplied out of tax money, that will cause the indigent to decide, with the aid of counsel, "whether there are any appealable issues that make the appeal worthwhile when balanced against the economic loss that will be involved." The indigent would be given an option: "he could purchase his appeal at public expense (as he can now) or he could elect instead to take a specified amount of money from the fund [at least several hundred dollars], either for himself [or for] persons he would designate [e.g., his spouse, children or bona fide creditors]. This plan would force the defendant to think about his case as a non-indigent must."

it.' Maybe that happened, but maybe there are angels in the balcony, too. [Moreover,] there is always the probability that unless there's an excellent reason, beyond being busy, the lawyer at least ought to be told that he might try to present what the client wanted. He doesn't have to argue as his own points matters that are stupid or ridiculous, but at least there ought to be some effort made to present the point the client believes important."[c]

3. ***May court-appointed appellate counsel be required to discuss why she believes her client's appeal lacks merit?*** Yes, answered a 5–3 majority (Kennedy, J., not participating) in McCOY v. COURT OF APPEALS OF WISCONSIN, 486 U.S. 429 (1988). A Wisconsin Supreme Court rule requires an *Anders* brief to include a discussion of why the appeal lacks merit. Court-appointed appellate counsel refused to comply with this requirement, maintaining that it would be both unethical and contrary to *Anders* to do so. The Court, per STEVENS, J., disagreed:

"[The Wisconsin rule] furthers the same interests that are served by *Anders*. Because counsel may discover previously unrecognized aspects of the law in the process of preparing a written explanation for his or her written conclusion [that the appeal is frivolous], the discussion requirement provides an additional safeguard against mistaken conclusions by counsel that the strongest arguments he or she can find are frivolous. Just like the reference to favorable aspects of the record required by *Anders,* the discussion requirement may forestall some motions to withdraw and will assist the court in passing on the soundness of the lawyer's conclusion that the appeal is frivolous. * * *

"We also do not find that the Wisconsin rule burdens an indigent defendant's right to effective representation on appeal. [A] supported conclusion that the appeal is frivolous does not implicate Sixth or Fourteenth Amendment concerns to any greater extent than does a bald conclusion."

Dissenting Justice BRENNAN, joined by Marshall and Blackmun, JJ., protested:

"[When] retained counsel in Wisconsin declines to appeal a case on the ground that he believes the appeal to be frivolous, the wealthy client can always seek a second opinion and might well find a lawyer who in good conscience believes it to have arguable merit. In no event, however, will any lawyer file in the wealthy client's name a brief that undercuts his position. In contrast, when appointed counsel harbors the same belief, the indigent client has no recourse to a second opinion, and (unless he withdraws his appeal) must respond in court to the arguments of his own defender.

"[The] Court looks at Wisconsin's regime and sees a friend of the client who 'assur[es] that the constitutional rights of indigent defendants are scrupulously honored.' I look at the same regime and see a friend of the court whose advocacy is so damning that the prosecutor never responds. Either way, with friends like that, the indigent criminal appellant is truly alone."[a]

4. ***New counsel on appeal.*** Should trial counsel be required to remain on the criminal defense for purposes of arguing the appeal? Presumably the trial counsel is already intimately familiar with the case and sometimes, at least, can start writing a brief even before a trial transcript is prepared. Thus, much time might be lost by a change in counsel. On the other hand, how, on appeal, can trial

c. See also Carrington, et al., fn. b supra at 77: "Several judges have reported to us the disheartening experience of reversing convictions after appointed counsel has filed an '*Anders*' brief explaining that his client's cause was entirely hopeless."

a. May an indigent defendant compel appointed counsel to argue all nonfrivolous points on appeal? See *Jones v. Barnes* (p. 147) (answering in the negative).

counsel be expected to explore the possibility of ineffective counsel? Moreover, might a good trial lawyer turn out to be a very poor appellate lawyer? See generally Carrington, et al., p. ___, fn. a, at 83–84 and authorities cited therein.

When an appellate court denies defense counsel's motion to be relieved because he is of the opinion that the appeal is frivolous, should the court continue present counsel's appointment or assign new counsel? See Hermann, Note 2 supra, at 714.

5. *Is a state free to adopt other procedures than Anders for handling indigent criminal appeals?* Consider SMITH v. ROBBINS, 528 U.S. 259 (2000), which grew out of the following facts: Twelve years after *Anders*, in *People v. Wende*, 600 P.2d 1071 (Cal.1979), California adopted a new procedure for dealing with potentially frivolous appeals, under which, upon concluding that an appeal would be frivolous, counsel (a) "files a brief with the appellate court that summarizes the procedural and factual history of the case, with citations of the record"; (b) "attests that he has reviewed the record, explained the evaluation of the case to his client, provided the client with a copy of the brief and informed the client of his right to file a *pro se* supplemental brief"; and (c) "requests that the court independently examine the record for arguable issues." Upon receiving a "*Wende* brief," the appellate court must "conduct a review of the entire record." If, after doing so, the appellate court finds the appeal to be frivolous, it may affirm. However, if it finds an arguable issue (*i.e.*, nonfrivolous) issue, it orders briefing on that issue.

Respondent Robbins was convicted of second-degree murder and grand theft in a California court. Concluding that an appeal would be frivolous, Robbins's appointed counsel filed a brief with the state appellate court that complied with *Wende*, not *Anders*. Agreeing with counsel's assessment of the case, the state appellate court affirmed. The Ninth Circuit granted federal habeas relief, viewing *Anders*, together with *Douglas v. California* [p. 99], as "setting forth the exclusive procedure through which appointed counsel's performance can pass constitutional muster."

A 5–4 majority of the Supreme Court, per THOMAS, J., reversed. The *Anders* procedure, held the majority, "is merely one method of satisfying the requirements of the Constitution for indigent criminal appeals"; a state is free to adopt other procedures if these procedures "afford adequate and effective appellate review to indigent defendants" and a state's procedure provides such review "so long as it reasonably ensures [as does the *Wende* procedure] that an indigent's appeal will be resolved in a way that is related to the merit of that appeal":

"In *Pennsylvania v. Finley* [p. 1632], we explained that the *Anders* procedure is not 'an independent constitutional command,' but rather is just 'a prophylactic framework' that was established to vindicate the constitutional right to appellate counsel announced in *Douglas*. We did not say that our *Anders* procedure was the *only* prophylactic framework that could adequately vindicate this right; instead, by making clear that the Constitution itself does not compel the *Anders* procedure, we suggested otherwise.

"* * * [I]t is more in keeping with our status as a court, and particularly with our status as a court in a federal system, to avoid imposing a single solution on the States from the top down. We should, and do, evaluate state procedures one at a time, as they come before us, while leaving 'the more challenging task of crafting appropriate procedures [to] the laboratory of the States in the first instance.'

"* * * We think the *Wende* procedure reasonably ensures that an indigent's appeal will be resolved in a way that is related to the merit of that appeal. Whatever the strengths or weaknesses as a matter of policy, we cannot say that it fails to afford indigents the adequate and effective appellate review that the Fourteenth Amendment requires. [Thus,] there was no constitutional violation in this case simply because the *Wende* procedure was used.

"On remand, the proper standard for evaluating Robbins's claim that appellate counsel was ineffective in neglecting to file a merits brief is that enunciated in *Strickland*. * * * Respondent must first show that his counsel was objectively unreasonable in failing to find arguable issues to appeal—that is, that counsel unreasonably failed to discover nonfrivolous issues and to file a merits brief raising them. If Robbins succeeds in such a showing, he then has the burden of demonstrating prejudice. That is, he must show a reasonable probability that, but for his counsel's unreasonable failure to file a merits brief, he would have prevailed on his appeal.

"[The] applicability of *Strickland*'s actual-prejudice prong to Robbins's claim of ineffective counsel follows from *Penson v. Ohio*, 488 U.S. 75 (1988), where we distinguished denial of counsel altogether on appeal, which warranted a presumption of prejudice, from mere ineffective assistance of counsel on appeal, which did not.[a] [But] where, as here, the defendant has received appellate counsel who has complied with a valid state procedure for determining whether the defendant's appeal is frivolous, and the State has not at any time left the defendant without counsel on appeal, there is no reason to assume that the defendant has been prejudiced."

"Believ[ing] [that] the procedure adopted in *Wende* fails to assure representation by counsel with the adversarial character demanded by the Constitution," Justice SOUTER, joined by Stevens, Ginsburg, and Breyer, JJ., dissented:

"We have not held the details of *Anders* to be exclusive, but it does make sense to read the case as exemplifying what substantial equality requires on behalf of indigent appellants entitled to an advocate's review and to reasonable certainty that arguable issues will be briefed on their merits. With *Anders* thus as a benchmark, California's *Wende* procedure fails to measure up. Its primary failing is in permitting counsel to refrain as a matter of course from mentioning possibly arguable issues in a no-merit brief; its second deficiency is a correlative of the first, in obliging an appellate court to search the record for arguable issues without benefit of an issue-spotting, no-merit brief to review.

"[In] an *amicus* brief filed in this case, 13 retired Justices of the Supreme Court or Courts of Appeal of California have pointed out the 'risk that the review of the cold record [under the *Wende* scheme] will be more perfunctory without the issue-spotting guidance, and associated record citations, of counsel.' The *amici* have candidly represented that '[w]hen a California appellate court receives a *Wende* brief, it assigns the case to a staff attorney who prepares a memorandum analyzing all possible legal issues in the case. Typically, the staff attorney then makes an oral presentation to the appellate panel. . . .' When the responsibility of counsel is thrown onto the court, the court gives way to a staff attorney; it could not be clearer that *Wende* is seriously at odds with the respective obligations of counsel and the courts as contemplated by the Constitution.

"[The] assumption behind *Strickland*'s prejudice requirement is that the defendant had a lawyer who was representing him as his advocate at least at some level, whereas that premise cannot be assumed when a defendant receives the

a. In *Penson*, where appellant's lawyer failed to satisfy *Anders*, the Court "emphasized that the denial of counsel in this case left petitioner completely without representation during the appellate court's actual decisional process. This is quite different from a case in which it is claimed that counsel's performance was ineffective. As we stated in *Strickland*, the '[a]ctual or constructive denial of the assistance of counsel altogether is legally presumed to result in prejudice.' "

benefit of nothing more than a *Wende* brief. In a *Wende* situation, nominal counsel is functioning merely as a friend of the court, helping the judge to grasp the structure of the record but not even purporting to highlight the record's nearest approach to supporting his client's hope to appeal. Counsel under *Wende* is doing less than the judge's law clerk (or staff attorney) might do, and he is doing nothing at all in the way of advocacy. When a lawyer abandons the role of advocate and adopts that of *amicus curiae,* he is no longer functioning as counsel or rendering assistance within the meaning of the Sixth Amendment. Since the apparently missing ingredient of the advocate's analysis goes to the very essence of the right to counsel, a lawyer who does nothing more than file a *Wende* brief is closer to being no counsel at all than to being subpar counsel under *Strickland.*

"This, I think, is the answer to any suggestion that a specific assessment of prejudice need be shown in order to get relief from *Wende*. A complete absence of counsel is a reversible violation of the constitutional right to representation, even when there is no question that at the end of the day the smartest lawyer in the world would have watched his client being led off to prison. We do not ask how the defendant would have fared if he had been given counsel, and we should not look to what sort of appeal might have ensued if an appellant's lawyer had flagged the points that came closest to appealable issues."[b]

SECTION 4. THE RIGHT TO APPOINTED COUNSEL IN PROCEEDINGS OTHER THAN CRIMINAL PROSECUTIONS: THE CONTINUED VITALITY OF THE *BETTS v. BRADY* APPROACH

A. PROBATION AND PAROLE REVOCATION HEARINGS: JUVENILE COURT PROCEEDINGS; PARENTAL STATUS TERMINATION PROCEEDINGS

GAGNON v. SCARPELLI, 411 U.S. 778 (1973), arose as follows: After pleading guilty to armed robbery, Scarpelli was sentenced to 15 years imprisonment. However, his sentence was suspended and he was placed on probation. A month later, he and a "known criminal" were apprehended while burglarizing a house. Probation was revoked without a hearing on the stated grounds that (a) Scarpelli had associated with known criminals in violation of probation conditions and (b) while associating with a known criminal he had been involved in a burglary. The Court held, per POWELL, J., that an indigent probationer or parolee has no unqualified due process right to be represented by counsel at revocation hearings:[a]

"In *Mempa v. Rhay,*[b] the Court held a probationer is entitled to be represented by appointed counsel at a combined revocation and sentencing hearing.

b. What light does *Smith v. Robbins* shed on the Court's use of "prophylactic rules"? Is *Robbins* consistent with *Dickerson v. United States*, p. 680, which struck down a federal statute purporting to replace the "prophylactic" *Miranda* rules with a more "police friendly" test because *Miranda* "is a constitutional decision" that "Congress may not legislatively supersede"? Compare Paul G. Cassell, *The Path Not Taken: The Supreme Court's Failure in Dickerson,* 99 Mich.L.Rev. 898, 904–05 (2001) with Yale Kamisar, *Miranda Thirty-Five Years Later: A Close Look at the Majority and Dissenting Opinions in Dickerson,* 33 Ariz. St.L.J. 387, 413 (2001).

a. Since Scarpelli did not attempt to *retain* counsel, the Court reserved judgment on "whether a probationer or parolee has a right to be represented at a revocation hearing by retained counsel in situations other than those where the State would be obliged to furnish counsel for an indigent."

b. In *Mempa,* 389 U.S. 128 (1967), petitioners' sentencing was deferred subject to probation. The prosecutor subsequently moved to

Reasoning that counsel is required 'at every stage of a criminal proceeding where substantial rights of a criminal accused may be affected,' and that sentencing is one such stage, the Court concluded that counsel must be provided an indigent at sentencing even when it is accomplished as part of a subsequent, probation revocation proceeding. But this line of reasoning does not require a hearing or counsel at the time of probation revocation in a case such as the present one, where the probationer was sentenced at the time of that trial.[c]

"[The] introduction of counsel into a revocation proceeding will alter significantly the nature of the proceeding. If counsel is provided for the probationer or parolee, the State in turn will normally provide its own counsel; lawyers, by training and disposition, are advocates and bound by professional duty to present all available evidence and arguments in support of their clients' positions and to contest with vigor all adverse evidence and views. The role of the hearing body itself, aptly described in *Morrissey* as being 'predictive and discretionary' as well as fact-finding, may become more akin to that of a judge at a trial, and less attuned to the rehabilitative needs of the individual probationer or parolee. In the greater self-consciousness of its quasi-judicial role, the hearing body may be less tolerant of marginal deviant behavior and feel more pressure to reincarcerate rather than continue nonpunitive rehabilitation. Certainly, the decision-making process will be prolonged, and the financial cost to the State—for appointed counsel, counsel for the State, a longer record, and the possibility of judicial review—will not be insubstantial.

"In some cases, these modifications in the nature of the revocation hearing must be endured and the costs borne because [the] probationer's or parolee's version of a disputed issue can fairly be represented only by a trained advocate. But due process is not so rigid as to require that the significant interests in informality, flexibility, and economy must always be sacrificed.

"In so concluding, we are of course aware that the case-by-case approach to the right to counsel in felony prosecutions adopted in *Betts* [was] later rejected in favor of a *per se* rule. [But we do not] draw from *Gideon* and *Argersinger* the conclusion that a case-by-case approach to furnishing counsel is necessarily inadequate to protect constitutional rights asserted in varying types of proceedings: there are critical differences between criminal trials and probation or parole revocation hearings, and both society and the probationer or parolee have stakes in preserving these differences.

"In a criminal trial, the State is represented by a prosecutor; formal rules of evidence are in force; a defendant enjoys a number of procedural rights which may be lost if not timely raised; and, in a jury trial, a defendant must make a presentation understandable to untrained jurors. In short, a criminal trial under our system is an adversary proceeding with its own unique characteristics. In a revocation hearing, on the other hand, the State is represented not by a prosecutor but by a parole officer with the orientation described above; formal procedures

have their probation revoked on the ground that petitioners had committed other crimes. At these hearings neither petitioner was represented by counsel or offered counsel. As a result of these hearings, each petitioner's probation was revoked and he was sentenced to a term of imprisonment. A unanimous Court, per Marshall, J., held that "a lawyer must be afforded at this [deferred sentencing] procedure whether it be labeled a revocation of probation or a deferred sentencing."

c. But see Fred Cohen, *Sentencing, Probation, and the Rehabilitative Ideal,* 47 Texas L.Rev. 1, 2–6 (1968), viewing *Mempa* as "the beginning of judicial activity in the sentencing-to-final discharge area of law, and not as a rear guard mopping-up operation in the natural evolution of right-to-counsel decisions," and stressing that "[t]here is no other area of law, except perhaps the civil commitment of the mentally ill, where the lives of so many people are so drastically affected by officials who exercise a virtually absolute, unreviewed discretion."

and rules of evidence are not employed; and the members of the hearing body are familiar with the problems and practice of probation or parole. The need for counsel at revocation hearings derives not from the invariable attributes of those hearings but rather from the peculiarities of particular cases. * * *

"We [find] no justification for a new inflexible constitutional rule with respect to the requirement of counsel. We think, rather, that the decision as to the need for counsel must be made on a case-by-case basis in the exercise of a sound discretion by the state authority charged with responsibility for administering the probation and parole system. * * * Presumptively, it may be said that counsel should be provided in cases where, after being informed of his right to request counsel, the probationer or parolee makes such a request, based on a timely and colorable claim (i) that he has not committed the alleged violation of the conditions upon which he is at liberty; or (ii) [that] there are substantial reasons which justified or mitigated the violation and make revocation inappropriate and that the reasons are complex or otherwise difficult to develop or present. In passing on a request for the appointment of counsel, the responsible agency also should consider, especially in doubtful cases, whether the probationer appears to be capable of speaking effectively for himself. * * *

"We return to the facts of the present case. Because respondent was not afforded either a preliminary hearing or a final hearing, the revocation of his probation did not meet the standards of due process prescribed in *Morrissey*.[d] [Accordingly,] respondent was entitled to a writ of habeas corpus. [Because of respondent's assertions regarding his confession to the crime] we conclude that the failure [to] provide[him] with the assistance of counsel should be reexamined in light of this opinion."[e]

Notes and Questions

1. ***Betts, Gideon and Gagnon compared.*** How likely is it that a probationer or parolee will be able to convince a court, *without* the benefit of counsel, on the basis of a record made *without* the assistance of counsel, that there are "substantial reasons which justified or mitigated the violation" or that "the reasons are complex or otherwise difficult to develop or present"? How many probationers or parolees will know *what* to point to or look for and *why?* How intelligent a decision can be made as to whether "the probationer appears to be capable of speaking effectively for himself" without knowing what justifications or mitigations a competent lawyer might have raised or developed? Can *Gagnon* escape the criticism of *Betts?* Consider, *ABA Standards* § 18–7.5 (commentary; Kamisar, *The Right to Counsel and the Fourteenth Amendment: A Dialogue on "the Most Pervasive Right" of an Accused,* 30 U.Chi.L.Rev. 53, 65 (1962).

2. ***Juvenile court proceedings.*** The *Gagnon* Court talked about "the rehabilitative needs of the individual probationer or parolee" and viewed the probation or parole officer's function "not so much to compel conformance to a strict code of behavior as to supervise a course of rehabilitation." But compare *In re Gault,* 387 U.S. 1 (1967), holding that, in respect to juvenile delinquency proceedings that may result in loss of the juvenile's freedom, fourteenth amend-

d. *Morrissey v. Brewer,* 408 U.S. 471 (1972), held that even though the revocation of parole is not a part of the criminal prosecution, the loss of liberty involved is a serious deprivation requiring that the parolee be accorded due process. That means a preliminary and a final revocation hearing under the conditions specified in *Morrissey.*

e. Dissenting in part, Justice Douglas maintained that "due process requires the appointment of counsel in this case because of the claim that respondent's confession of the burglary was made under coercion."

ment due process requires that "the child and his parent [be] notified of the child's right to be represented by [retained counsel] or, if they are unable to afford counsel that counsel will be appointed to represent the child." The Court stressed the need for counsel to assure a fair hearing in a proceeding "comparable in seriousness to a felony prosecution." It rejected the state's suggestion that the probation officers, parents, and judge might be relied on to "represent the child," finding "no material difference in this respect between adult and juvenile proceedings of the sort involved here."

Gault was hailed as demonstrating the Court's reluctance to be "hemmed in by such artificial labels as 'criminal,' 'civil', or 'quasi-administrative,'" and for taking the position that "a desire to help—the rehabilitation ideal—no longer will serve as the incantation before which procedural safeguards must succumb." Fred Cohen, *Sentencing, Probation, and the Rehabilitative Ideal,* 47 Texas L.Rev. 1, 2 (1968).

3. ***Summary courts-martial; loss of liberty does not trigger the Sixth Amendment right to counsel.*** In *Middendorf v. Henry,* 425 U.S. 25 (1976), a 7–2 majority held there is no right to appointed counsel at summary courts-martial, even though the officer conducting these proceedings can impose a maximum punishment of 30 days confinement at hard labor. In rejecting even the view that counsel must be provided in "special circumstances," the Court, per Rehnquist J., observed:

"[E]ven were the Sixth Amendment to be held applicable to court-martial proceedings, the summary court-martial provided for in these cases was not a 'criminal prosecution' within the meaning of that Amendment. [T]he fact that the outcome of a proceeding may result in loss of liberty does not by itself, even in civilian life, mean that the Sixth Amendment's guarantee of counsel is applicable. In *Gagnon,* the respondent faced the prospect of being sent to prison as a result of the revocation of his probation, but we held that the revocation proceeding was nonetheless not a 'criminal proceeding.' [In *Gault*] the juvenile faced possible initial confinement as a result of the proceeding in question, but the Court nevertheless based its conclusion that counsel was required on [Fourteenth Amendment due process], rather than on any determination that the hearing was a 'criminal prosecution' within the meaning of the Sixth Amendment."

4. ***Parental status termination proceedings; is potential loss of liberty a necessary, if not a sufficient, requirement, for the automatic right to appointed counsel?*** Over the dissenters' protest that "the unique importance of a parent's interest in the care and custody of his or her child cannot constitutionally be extinguished through formal judicial proceedings without the benefit of counsel" and the dissenters' charge that the Court was "reviv[ing] an ad hoc approach thoroughly discredited nearly 20 years ago in *Gideon,*" in *Lassiter v. Department of Social Services,* 452 U.S. 18 (1981), a 5–4 majority, per Stewart, J., rejected the view that due process requires the appointment of counsel in every parental status termination proceeding involving indigent parents. Thus, the Court left the appointment of counsel in such proceedings to be determined by the state courts on a case-by-case basis.

"The pre-eminent generalization that emerges from the Court's precedents on an indigent's right to appointed counsel," observed the Court, "is that such a right has been recognized to exist only where the litigant may lose his physical liberty if he loses the litigation. * * * Significantly, as a litigant's interest in personal liberty diminishes, so does his right to appointed counsel. [Thus, *Gagnon*] declined to hold that indigent probationers have, *per se*, a right to counsel at revocation hearings, and instead left the decision whether counsel should be appointed to be made on a case-by-case basis."

The Court then examined the termination hearing and found it to be fundamentally fair. "In light of the unpursued avenues of defense, and of the experiences petitioner underwent at this hearing," the dissenters found the Court's conclusion "virtually incredible." Consider Bruce R. Jacob, *Memories of and Reflections about Gideon v. Wainwright*, 33 Stetson L.Rev. 180, 287 (2003): "[Whether counsel is to be appointed in cases involving the termination of parental rights] is to be made on a case-by-case basis, in the same way decisions such as this were made under the *Betts* rule. The rule of *Betts* was considered unworkable by the Court. That was one of the main reasons for the decision in *Gideon* * * *. If *Betts* was not workable in 1963, why is it workable now?"

5. ***Where to draw the line.*** Was the *Lassiter* Court's greatest concern where to draw the line? If the state must provide indigents counsel in parental termination proceedings, why not in a child custody fight growing out of a divorce action when one parent is indigent? Why not in an eviction proceeding, when an indigent is about to lose his place of residence? Is there a stronger case for providing counsel in parental termination proceedings than in these other proceedings? Why (not)? See Kamisar, *Gideon v. Wainwright A Quarter–Century Later,* 10 Pace L.Rev. 343, 357–59 (1990).

B. Collateral Attack Proceedings

[As is discussed more extensively elsewhere in this book (see Ch. 29, § 1), an indigent prisoner has no federal constitutional right to assigned counsel in postconviction proceedings. See *Pennsylvania v. Finley* (1987) (p. 1632). A 5–4 majority held in *Murray v. Giarratano* (1989) (p. 1632) that this rules applies no differently in capital cases than in noncapital cases.]

Chapter 5

THE ROLE OF COUNSEL[aa]

SECTION 1. WAIVER OF THE RIGHT TO COUNSEL; THE RIGHT TO PROCEED *PRO SE*

FARETTA v. CALIFORNIA

422 U.S. 806, 95 S.Ct. 2525, 45 L.Ed.2d 562 (1975).

Justice STEWART delivered the opinion of the Court.

[Well before the date of his trial, Faretta, charged with grand theft, requested that he be allowed to represent himself. Questioning by the trial judge revealed that Faretta had once before represented himself in a criminal prosecution, that he had a high school education, and that he did not want to be represented by the public defender because he thought that office had too heavy a caseload. The trial judge subsequently held a hearing to inquire into Faretta's ability to conduct his own defense. In the course of that hearing, the judge questioned Faretta as to his knowledge of the hearsay rule and the law governing the challenge of jurors. Taking account of Faretta's answers, the judge ruled that Faretta had not made an intelligent and knowing waiver of his right to counsel. The judge also ruled that Faretta had no constitutional right to conduct his own defense. The judge then appointed the public defender to represent Faretta. Throughout the subsequent trial, the judge required that Faretta's defense be conducted only through the appointed lawyer. Faretta was found guilty as charged and sentenced to prison. The appellate court affirmed his conviction.]

* * * [This] Court's past recognition of the right of self-representation, the federal court authority holding the right to be of constitutional dimension, and the state constitutions pointing to the right's fundamental nature form a consensus not easily ignored. [This] consensus is soundly premised. The right of self-representation finds support in the structure of the Sixth Amendment, as well as in the English and colonial experience from which the Amendment emerged.

[The] Sixth Amendment does not provide merely that a defense shall be made for the accused; it grants to the accused personally the right to make his defense. It is the accused, not counsel, who must be "informed of the nature and cause of the accusation," who must be "confronted with witnesses against him," and who must be accorded "compulsory process for obtaining witnesses in his favor." [T]he right to self-representation—to make one's defense personally—is

aa. The issues presented in this chapter are loosely tied together by the common thread that, in resolving these issues, the Supreme Court has proceeded on certain assumptions as to that role of counsel which underlies the Sixth Amendment's guarantee of a right to the assistance of counsel. This is not to suggest that doctrine developed in resolving these issues is shaped only by that point of reference, or that the doctrine reflects a single view of the character of the assistance guaranteed by the Sixth Amendment.

thus necessarily implied by the structure of the Amendment.[15] The right to defend is given directly to the accused; for it is he who suffers the consequences if the defense fails.

The counsel provision supplements this design. It speaks of the "assistance" of counsel, and an assistant, however expert, is still an assistant. The language and spirit of the Sixth Amendment contemplate that counsel, like the other defense tools guaranteed by the Amendment, shall be an aid to a willing defendant—not an organ of the State interposed between an unwilling defendant and his right to defend himself personally. To thrust counsel upon the accused, against his considered wish, thus violates the logic of the Amendment. [It] is true that when a defendant chooses to have a lawyer manage and present his case, law and tradition may allocate to the counsel the power to make binding decisions of trial strategy in many areas.[a] This allocation can only be justified, however, by the defendant's consent, at the outset, to accept counsel as his representative. An unwanted counsel "represents" the defendant only through a tenuous and unacceptable legal fiction. Unless the accused has acquiesced in such representation, the defense presented is not the defense guaranteed by the Constitution, for, in a very real sense, it is not *his* defense.

The Sixth Amendment, when naturally read, thus implies a right of self-representation. This reading is reinforced by the Amendment's roots in English legal history. [After an extensive discussion of the right of self-representation in England and the American colonies, the Court concluded:]

In sum, there is no evidence that the colonists and the Framers ever doubted the right of self-representation, or imagined that this right might be considered inferior to the right of assistance of counsel. To the contrary, [they], as well as their English ancestors, always conceived of the right to counsel as an "assistance" for the accused, to be used at his option, in defending himself. The Framers selected in the Sixth Amendment a form of words that necessarily implies the right of self-representation. That conclusion is supported by centuries of history.

There can be no blinking the fact that the right of an accused to conduct his own defense seems to cut against the grain of this Court's decisions holding that the Constitution requires that no accused can be convicted and imprisoned unless he has been accorded the right to the assistance of counsel. For it is surely true that the basic thesis of those decisions is that the help of a lawyer is essential to assure the defendant a fair trial. And a strong argument can surely be made that the whole thrust of those decisions must inevitably lead to the conclusion that a State may constitutionally impose a lawyer upon even an unwilling defendant.

15. [The] inference of rights is not, of course, a mechanical exercise. In *Singer v. United States* (1965) [p. 1388], the Court held that an accused has no right to a bench trial, despite his capacity to waive his right to a jury trial. In so holding, the Court stated that "[t]he ability to waive a constitutional right does not ordinarily carry with it the right to insist upon the opposite of that right." But that statement was made only *after* the Court had concluded that the Constitution does not affirmatively protect any right to be tried by a judge. Recognizing that an implied right must arise independently from the design and history of the constitutional text, the Court searched for, but could not find, any "indication that the colonists considered the ability to waive a jury trial to be of equal importance to the right to demand one." Instead, the Court could locate only "isolated instances" of a right to trial by judge, and concluded that these were "clear departures from the common law."

We follow the approach of *Singer* here. Our concern is with an *independent* right of self-representation. We do not suggest that this right arises mechanically from a defendant's power to waive the right to the assistance of counsel. On the contrary, the right must be independently found in the structure and history of the constitutional text.

a. See Section 4 infra.

But it is one thing to hold that every [accused] has the right to the assistance of counsel, and quite another to say that a State may compel a defendant to accept a lawyer he does not want. The value of state-appointed counsel was not unappreciated by the Founders, yet the notion of compulsory counsel was utterly foreign to them. * * * [To] force a lawyer on a defendant can only lead him to believe that the law contrives against him. Moreover, it is not inconceivable that in some rare instances, the defendant might in fact present his case more effectively by conducting his own defense. Personal liberties are not rooted in the law of averages. The right to defend is personal. The defendant, and not his lawyer or the State, will bear the personal consequences of a conviction. It is the defendant, therefore, who must be free personally to decide whether in his particular case counsel is to his advantage. And although he may conduct his own defense ultimately to his own detriment, his choice must be honored out of "that respect for the individual which is the lifeblood of the law."[46]

When an accused manages his own defense, he relinquishes, as a purely factual matter, many of the traditional benefits associated with the right to counsel. For this reason, in order to represent himself, the accused must "knowingly and intelligently" forego those relinquished benefits. Johnson v. *Zerbst*, 304 U.S. 458 (1938). Although a defendant need not himself have the skill and experience of a lawyer in order competently and intelligently to choose self-representation, he should be made aware of the dangers and disadvantages of self-representation, so that the record will establish that "he knows what he is doing and his choice is made with eyes open." *Adams v. United States ex rel. McCann*, 317 U.S. 269 (1942).

Here, weeks before trial, Faretta clearly and unequivocally declared [that] he wanted to represent himself and did not want counsel. The record affirmatively shows that [defendant] was literate, competent, and understanding, and that he was voluntarily exercising his informed free will. The trial judge had warned [defendant] that he thought it was a mistake not to accept the assistance of counsel and that [defendant] would be required to follow all the "ground rules" of trial procedure. We need make no assessment of how well or poorly [defendant] had mastered the intricacies of the hearsay rule and the California code provisions that govern challenges of potential jurors on *voir dire* [matters about which the trial judge specifically questioned defendant before ruling that he had not made an intelligent and knowing waiver of his right to the assistance of counsel]. For [defendant's] technical legal knowledge, as such, was not relevant to an assessment of his knowing exercise of the right to defend himself. * * *

Chief Justice BURGER, with whom Justice BLACKMUN and Justice REHNQUIST join, dissenting.

* * * [The goal of achieving justice] is ill-served, and the integrity of and public confidence in the system are undermined, when an easy conviction is obtained due to the defendant's ill-advised decision to waive counsel. [The crimi-

46. We are told that many criminal defendants representing themselves may use the courtroom for deliberate disruption of their trials. But the right of self-representation has been recognized from our beginnings by federal law and by most of the States, and no such result has thereby occurred. Moreover, the trial judge may terminate self-representation by a defendant who deliberately engages in serious and obstructionist misconduct. Of course, a State may—even over objection by the accused—appoint a "standby counsel" to aid the accused if and when the accused requests help, and to be available to represent the accused in the event that termination of the defendant's self-representation is necessary.

The right of self-representation is not a license to abuse the dignity of the courtroom. Neither is it a license not to comply with relevant rules of procedural and substantive law. Thus, whatever else may or may not be open to him on appeal, a defendant who elects to represent himself cannot thereafter complain that the quality of his own defense amounted to a denial of "effective assistance of counsel."

nal justice system] should not be available as an instrument of self-destruction. [B]oth the "spirit and the logic" of the Sixth Amendment are that every person accused of crime shall receive the fullest possible defense; in the vast majority of cases this command can be honored only by means of the expressly-guaranteed right to counsel, and the trial judge is in the best position to determine whether the accused is capable of conducting his defense. True freedom of choice and society's interest in seeing that justice is achieved can be vindicated only if the trial court retains discretion to reject any attempted waiver of counsel and insist that the accused be tried according to the Constitution. This discretion is as critical an element of basic fairness as a trial judge's discretion to decline to accept a plea of guilty. * * *

If we were to assume that there will be widespread exercise of the newly-discovered constitutional right to self-representation, it would almost certainly follow that there will be added congestion in the courts and that the quality of justice will suffer. Moreover, [i]t is totally unrealistic [to] suggest that an accused will always be held to the consequences of a decision to conduct his own defense. Unless [most defendants] have more wit than to insist upon [self-representation], we can expect that many expensive and good-faith prosecutions will be nullified on appeal for reasons that trial courts are now deprived of the power to prevent.

Justice BLACKMUN, with whom The Chief Justice and Justice REHNQUIST join, dissenting. * * *

I cannot agree that there is anything in the [Constitution] that requires the States to subordinate the solemn business of conducting a criminal prosecution to the whimsical—albeit voluntary—caprice of every accused who wishes to use his trial as a vehicle for personal or political self-gratification. * * * I do not believe that any amount of *pro se* pleading can cure the injury to society of an unjust result, but I do believe that a just result should prove to be an effective balm for almost any frustrated *pro se* defendant.

* * * I note briefly the procedural problems that, I suspect, today's decision will visit upon trial courts in the future. * * * Must every defendant be advised of his right to proceed *pro se?* If so, when must that notice be given? Since the right to the assistance of counsel and the right to self-representation are mutually exclusive, how is the waiver of each right to be measured? If a defendant has elected to exercise his right to proceed *pro se,* does he still have a constitutional right to assistance of standby counsel? How soon in the criminal proceeding must a defendant decide between proceeding by counsel or *pro se?* Must he be allowed to switch in mid-trial? May a violation of the right to self-representation ever be harmless error? Must the trial court treat the *pro se* defendant differently than it would professional counsel? [The] procedural problems spawned by an absolute right to self-representation will far outweigh whatever tactical advantage the defendant may feel he has gained by electing to represent himself. * * *

Notes and Questions

1. ***The rationale of Faretta.*** In *Wheat v. United States*, p. 208, sustaining the disqualification of defendant's counsel (over defendant's objection), the Supreme Court noted that courts have "an independent interest" in ensuring that legal proceeding are fair and "appear fair to all who observe them." Is the *Faretta* majority saying that self-determination is an element of both fairness and the appearance of fairness, or that self-determination is a value that outweighs ensuring fairness and the appearance of fairness? Consider in this regard the description of the *Faretta* rationale in *Martinez v. Court of Appeal*, infra note 2.

Several lower courts have viewed *Faretta* as leaving open the possibility of denying self-representation, notwithstanding a waiver of the right to counsel that is both knowing and voluntary, where the trial court views representation by counsel as absolutely necessary to ensure a fair trial—in particular, where a physical disability (e.g., a speech impediment) or educational deficiency "may significantly affect [defendant's] ability to communicate a possibly defense to the jury." *Pickens v. State*, 292 N.W.2d 601 (1980). But see United States v. McDowell, 814 F.2d 245 (6th Cir.1987), disagreeing with this line of cases. The Sixth Circuit there noted: "To suggest that an accused who knows and appreciates what he is relinquishing and yet intelligently chooses to forego counsel and represent himself must still have some formal education or the ability to converse in English is, we think, to misunderstand *Faretta*. * * * Any limitations due to physical or educational impairments that do not affect the ability of the accused to choose self-representation over counsel can probably be overcome, if necessary, through the use of stand-by counsel or interpreters."

2. Does the principle of self-representation apply to appeals as well? In MARTINEZ v. COURT OF APPEAL OF CALIFORNIA, 528 U.S. 152 (2000), defendant (who described himself as a self-taught paralegal with 25 years experience) was convicted of embezzlement after representing himself at trial. He sought to represent himself on appeal as well, but was rebuffed by the state appellate courts. The Supreme Court, per STEVENS, J., held, without a dissent, that "neither the holding nor the reasoning in *Faretta* requires [a state] to recognize a constitutional right to self-representation on direct appeal from a criminal conviction." Justice Stevens reasoned:

"Appeals as of right in federal courts were nonexistent for the first century of our Nation, and appellate review of any sort was 'rarely allowed.' [Thus,] unlike the inquiry in *Faretta*, the historical evidence does not provide any support for an affirmative constitutional right to appellate self-representation. * * * The *Faretta* majority's reliance on the structure of the Sixth Amendment is also not relevant. The Sixth Amendment identifies the basic rights that the accused shall enjoy in 'all criminal prosecutions.' * * * [The] Sixth Amendment does not include any right to appeal. [It] necessarily follows that the Amendment itself does not provide any basis for finding a right to self-representation on appeal."

As for a right to self-representation based on a respect for individual autonomy grounded in the Due Process Clause, Justice Stevens noted: "[W]e are entirely unpersuaded that the risk of either disloyalty or suspicion of disloyalty is a sufficient concern to conclude that a constitutional right of self-representation is a necessary component of a fair appellate proceeding. * * * As the *Faretta* opinion recognized, the right to self-representation is not absolute. * * * [Even] at the trial level, therefore, the government's interest in ensuring the integrity and efficiency of the trial at times outweighs the defendant's interest in acting as his own lawyer. In the appellate context, the balance between the two competing interests surely tips in favor of the State. The status of the accused defendant, who retains a presumption of innocence throughout the trial process, changes dramatically when a jury returns a guilty verdict. * * * Considering the change in position from defendant to appellant, the autonomy interests that survive a felony conviction are less compelling than those motivating the decision in *Faretta*. Yet the overriding state interest in the fair and efficient administration of justice remains as strong as at the trial level."

Justice Steven's opinion also seemed to suggest second thoughts about *Faretta*: It noted: "The historical evidence relied upon by *Faretta* as identifying a right of self-representation is not always useful because it pertained to times when lawyers were scarce, often mistrusted, and not readily available to the average person accused of crime. For one who could not obtain a lawyer, self-representation was the only feasible alternative to asserting no defense at all. * * * [But] an individual's decision to represent himself is no longer compelled by the necessity of choosing self-representation over incompetent or nonexistent representation. * * * [Therefore,] while *Faretta* is correct in concluding that there is abundant support for the proposition that a right to self-representation has been recognized for centuries, the original reasons for protecting that right do not have the same force when the availability of competent counsel for every indigent defendant has displaced the need—although not always the desire—for self-representation. * * * No one, including Martinez and the *Faretta* majority, attempts to argue that as a rule *pro se* representation is wise, desirable or efficient. * * * Our experience has taught us that a 'pro se defense is usually a bad defense, particularly when compared to a defense provided by an experienced criminal defense attorney.' "

Justice SCALIA concurred in the judgment, noting that he did "not share the apparent skepticism of today's opinion" regarding *Faretta*. He explained:

"I have no doubt that the Framers of our Constitution, who were suspicious enough of governmental power—including judicial power—that they insisted upon a citizen's right to be judged by an independent jury of private citizens, would not have found acceptable the compulsory assignment of counsel *by the government* to plead a criminal defendant's case. * * * While I might have rested the [*Faretta*] decision upon the Due Process Clause rather than the Sixth Amendment, I believe it was correct. * * * That asserting the right of self-representation may often, or even usually, work to the defendant's disadvantage is no more remarkable—and no more a basis for withdrawing the right—than is the fact that proceeding without counsel in custodial interrogation, or confessing to the crime, usually works to the defendant's disadvantage. Our system of laws generally presumes that the criminal defendant, after being fully informed, knows his own best interests and does not need them dictated by the State. Any other approach is unworthy of a free people.

"In any event, *Faretta* is relevant to the question before us only to the limited extent that we must decide whether its holding applies to self-representation on appeal. [That] question is readily answered by the fact that there is no constitutional right to appeal. Since a State could, as far as the Federal Constitution is concerned, subject its trial-court determinations to no review whatever, it could *a fortiori* subject them to review which consists of a nonadversarial reexamination of convictions by a panel of government experts. Adversarial review with counsel appointed by the State is even less questionable than that."

Responding to Justice Scalia, Justice BREYER, who joined the Court's opinion, wrote separately to "note that judges closer to the firing line have sometimes expressed dismay about the practical consequences" of *Faretta*. However, he added "without some strong factual basis for believing that *Faretta*'s holding has proved counterproductive in practice, we are not in a position to reconsider the constitutional assumptions that underlie that case." But Justice KENNEDY, who also joined the opinion of the Court, wrote separately to observe that "[t]o resolve this case it is unnecessary to cast doubt upon the rationale of *Faretta*."

3. Answering Justice Blackmun's questions. In *McKaskle v. Wiggins* [Note 4 infra], the Court address one of the issues raised in Justice Blackmun's *Faretta* dissent, and concluded that the denial of the right to self-representation cannot constitute a "harmless error." See fn. 8 of *McKaskle* [p. 126]. The remaining questions have been addressed by various lower courts, which have concluded: (1) unlike the right to the assistance counsel, which demands notification of the right on the record where the defendant is not represented by counsel (see Note 3, p. 136), there is no constitutional obligation to inform the defendant of his right to proceed *pro se* in the absence of a clear indication on his part that he desires to consider that option; requiring automatic notification, the courts note, might undermine the "overriding constitutional policy" favoring the provision of counsel by suggesting that counsel is not needed; (2) since the waiver of the right to counsel must be "clear and unequivocal," the defendant, after being advised of his right, must explicitly and unconditionally choose to proceed *pro se*; (3) the defendant does not have a constitutional right to the assistance of standby counsel (although such an appointment is the preferred practice); (4) the defendant's right to self-representation is conditioned on a timely assertion of that right, which ordinarily is satisfied by a request made before the scheduled trial date (provided the defendant does not insist upon a continuance as a condition of proceeding *pro se*); the trial court has "broad discretion to reject as untimely a request made during the course of trial"; and (5) the trial court is not constitutionally required to provide direction to the *pro se* defendant as to the exercise of procedural rights (with the possible exception of notification as to the right not to testify), and as noted in *Faretta* (see fn.46 at p. 121), the defendant cannot complain as to the loss of trial rights due to his procedural errors (just as he cannot complain in general as to the ineffectiveness of his self-representation, even if it fell below the "ordinary skill of laymen"). See CRIMPROC § 11.5 (collecting and discussing the cases).

4. *"Standby counsel."* McKASKLE v. WIGGINS, 465 U.S. 168 (1984), made explicit "what is already implicit in *Faretta:* a defendant's Sixth Amendment rights are not violated when a trial judge appoints standby counsel—even over the defendant's objection[a]—to relieve the judge of the need to explain and enforce basic rules of courtroom protocol or to assist the defendant in overcoming routine obstacles that stand in the way of the defendant's achievement of his own clearly indicated goals."

The trial court permitted Wiggins to represent himself at his state robbery trial, but designated two appointed lawyers as "standby counsel." Before and during the trial, Wiggins frequently changed his mind regarding the standby attorneys' role, objecting to their participation on some occasions, but conferring with them or expressly adopting their initiatives on other occasions. Wiggins filed and argued numerous *pro se* motions both before and during the trial. He conducted the defense's voir dire of prospective jurors, made the opening statement for the defense and, throughout the trial, selected the witnesses for the defense. He cross-examined the prosecution's witnesses freely. He also filed his own requested charges to the jury and made his own objections to the court's suggested charge. On several occasions, however he strongly opposed the initiatives of counsel and sometimes indignantly demanded that counsel not participate further without invitation. At one point, an acrimonious exchange between Wiggins and one of his standby lawyers occurred over the questioning of a witness.

Wiggins was convicted and sentenced to life imprisonment as a recidivist. The Fifth Circuit granted habeas corpus relief, establishing a rule that "standby counsel is 'to be seen, but not heard' "; "his presence is there for advisory purposes only, to be used or not used as the defendant sees fit." The Supreme Court majority, per O'CONNOR, J., explicitly rejected the Fifth Circuit's rule and reversed its judgment:

"A defendant's right to self-representation plainly encompasses certain specific rights to have his voice heard. The *pro se* defendant must be allowed to control

a. Who should compensate the standby counsel in this situation? See Poulin, infra Note 5 ("no court has directly addressed how to compensate standby counsel forced upon a nonindigent defendant"; as for indigents, appointment of the public defender may be precluded by statutory language that does not "defin[e] the duties of the public defender broadly enough to include service as standby counsel"; one Circuit held that, in the federal system, the Criminal Justice Act "does not authorize payment of advisory or standby counsel requested by the indigent").

the organization and content of his own defense, to make motions, to argue points of law, to participate in voir dire, to question witnesses, and to address the court and the jury at appropriate points in the trial. The record reveals that Wiggins was in fact accorded all of these rights. * * * " Wiggins' complaint is directed not at limits placed on *his* participation in the trial, for there clearly were none. It is directed instead at the allegedly inadequate limits placed on standby counsel's participation. * * * Wiggins claims, and the Court of Appeals agreed, that the *pro se* defendant may insist on presenting his own case wholly free from interruption or other uninvited involvement by standby counsel.

"[In] our view, [*Faretta* indicates] that no absolute bar on standby counsel's unsolicited participation is appropriate or was intended. The right to appear *pro se* exists to affirm the dignity and autonomy of the accused and to allow the presentation of what may, at least occasionally, be the accused's best possible defense. Both of these objectives can be achieved without categorically silencing standby counsel. * * * [But] we recognize [that] the right to speak for oneself entails more than the opportunity to add one's voice to a cacophony of others. * * * Thus, the *Faretta* right must impose some limits on the extent of standby counsel's unsolicited participation.[8]

"First, the *pro se* defendant is entitled to preserve actual control over the case he chooses to present to the jury. This is the core of the *Faretta* right. If standby counsel's participation over the defendant's objection effectively allows counsel to make or substantially interfere with any significant tactical decisions, or to control the questioning of witnesses, or to speak *instead* of the defendant on any matter of importance, the *Faretta* right is eroded.

"Second, participation by standby counsel without the defendant's consent should not be allowed to destroy the jury's perception that the defendant is representing himself. The defendant's appearance in the status of one conducting his own defense is important in a criminal trial, since the right to appear *pro se* exists to affirm the accused's individual dignity and autonomy. * * *

"Participation by standby counsel outside the presence of the jury engages only the first of these two limitations. * * * The appearance of a *pro se* defendant's self-representation will not be unacceptably undermined by counsel's participation outside the presence of the jury. * * * Thus, *Faretta* rights are adequately vindicated in proceedings outside the presence of the jury if [as here] the *pro se* defendant is allowed to address the court freely on his own behalf and if [as here] disagreements between counsel and the *pro se* defendant are resolved in the defendant's favor whenever the matter is one that would normally be left to the discretion of counsel. * * * [Though several of the exchanges between Wiggins and standby counsel] are regrettable, we are satisfied that counsel's participation outside the presence of jury fully satisfied the first standard we have outlined. * * * Equally important, all conflicts between Wiggins and counsel were resolved in Wiggins' favor. The trial judge repeatedly explained to all concerned that Wiggins' strategic choices, not counsel's, would prevail. * * *

8. Since the right of self-representation is a right that when exercised usually increases the likelihood of a trial outcome unfavorable to the defendant, its denial is not amenable to "harmless error" analysis. The right is either respected or denied; its deprivation cannot be harmless.

As a corollary, however, a defendant who exercises his right to appear *pro se* "cannot thereafter complain that the quality of his own defense amounted to a denial of 'effective assistance of counsel.' " *Faretta.* Moreover, the defendant's right to proceed *pro se* exists in the larger context of the criminal trial designed to determine whether or not a defendant is guilty of the offense with which he is charged. The trial judge may be required to make numerous rulings reconciling the participation of standby counsel with a *pro se* defendant's objection to that participation; nothing in the nature of the *Faretta* right suggests that the usual deference to "judgment calls" on these issues by the trial judge should not obtain here as elsewhere.

"Participation by standby counsel in the presence of the jury is more problematic. It is here that the defendant may legitimately claim that excessive involvement by counsel will destroy the appearance that the defendant is acting *pro se.* * * * Nonetheless, we believe that a categorical bar on participation by standby counsel in the presence of the jury is unnecessary. * * * [The] record in this case reveals that Wiggins' *pro se* efforts were undermined primarily by his own, frequent changes of mind regarding counsel's role. * * * The only two long appearances by counsel at Wiggins' trial, one before the jury and one outside its presence, were both initiated with Wiggins' express approval. In these circumstances it is very difficult to determine how much of counsel's participation was in fact contrary to Wiggins' desires of the moment.

"*Faretta* does not require a trial judge to permit 'hybrid' representation of the type Wiggins was actually allowed. But if a defendant is given the opportunity and elects to have counsel appear before the court or jury, his complaints concerning counsel's subsequent unsolicited participation lose much of their force. A defendant does not have a constitutional right to choreograph special appearances by counsel. Once a *pro se* defendant invites or agrees to any substantial participation by counsel, subsequent appearances by counsel must be presumed to be with the defendant's acquiescence, at least until the defendant expressly and unambiguously renews his request that standby counsel be silenced. * * *

"*Faretta* affirmed the defendant's constitutional right to appear on stage at his trial. We recognize that a *pro se* defendant may wish to dance a solo, not a *pas de deux.* Standby counsel must generally respect that preference. But counsel need not be excluded altogether, especially when the participation is outside the presence of the jury or is with the defendant's express or tacit consent. The defendant in this case was allowed to make his own appearances as he saw fit. In our judgment counsel's unsolicited involvement was held within reasonable limits."[b]

Dissenting Justice WHITE, joined by Brennan and Marshall, JJ., protested:

"[Under] the Court's new test, it is necessary to determine whether the *pro se* defendant retained 'actual control over the case he [chose] to present to the jury' and whether standby counsel's participation 'destroy[ed] the jury's perception that the defendant [was] representing himself.' Although this test purports to protect all of the values underlying our holding in *Faretta,* it is unclear whether it can achieve this result.

"As long as the *pro se* defendant is allowed his say, the first prong of the Court's test accords standby counsel at a bench trial or any proceeding outside the presence of a jury virtually untrammeled discretion to present any factual or legal argument to which the defendant does not object. The limits placed on counsel's participation in this context by the 'actual control' test are more apparent than real. * * *

"Although the Court is more solicitous of a *pro se* defendant's interests when standby counsel intervenes before a jury, the test's second prong suffers from similar shortcomings. To the extent that trial and appellate courts can discern the point at which counsel's unsolicited participation substantially undermines a *pro se* defendant's appearance before the jury, a matter about which I harbor substantial doubts, their decisions will, to a certain extent, 'affirm the accused's individual dignity and autonomy.' But they will do so incompletely, for in focusing on how the jury views the defendant, the majority opinion ignores *Faretta's* emphasis on the defendant's own perception of the criminal justice system, and implies that

b. Justice Blackmun concurred in the result without opinion.

the Court actually adheres to the result-oriented harmless error standard it purports to reject. [See fn. 8 to the Court's opinion].

"As a guide for standby counsel and lower courts, moreover, the Court's two-part test is clearly deficient. [Trial courts] clearly must prevent standby counsel from overtly muzzling their *pro se* clients and resolve certain conflicts in defendants' favor. But the Court's opinion places few, if any, other clear limits on counsel's uninvited participation; instead it requires trial courts to make numerous subjective judgments concerning the effect of counsel's actions on defendants' *Faretta* rights.

"[In] short, I believe that the Court's test is unworkable and insufficiently protective of the fundamental interests we recognized in *Faretta*. * * * The inappropriateness of the Court's standard is made manifest by the Court's conclusion that the conduct of standby counsel in this case passes muster under that standard. In frequently and grievously exceeding the proper role of standby counsel, the more active of Wiggins' appointed attorneys distracted Wiggins and usurped his prerogatives, altered the tenor of the defense, disrupted the trial, undermined Wiggins' perception that he controlled his own fate, induced a belief—most assuredly unfounded, but sincerely held nevertheless—that 'the law contrive[d] against him,' and undoubtedly reduced Wiggins' credibility and prejudiced him in the eyes of the jury. In allowing such intervention to continue despite Wiggins' repeated requests that it cease, the trial court clearly denied Wiggins' right of self-representation."

5. ***Lower courts and standby counsel.*** Anne Bowen Poulin, *The Role of Standby Counsel in Criminal Cases: In the Twilight Zone of The Criminal Justice System*, 76 N.Y.U.L.Rev. 676 (2000), notes that "judicial decisions addressing pro se defendants' complaints," reveal several "troubling patterns" in current practice. These include:

(1) Some courts are "actually hostile" to *pro se* defendants' request for standby counsel, as reflected by an appellate court suggestion that "the defendant be given the stark choice of self-representation (with no standby counsel) or the assistance of counsel"—thereby ensuring that the decision to proceed *pro se* will not be made "with the comforting knowledge" that a back-up is always available.

(2) A common scenario leading to *pro se* representation involves: (1) an indigent defendant seeks replacement of his counsel, (2) the trial judge determines that the defendant's complaints against counsel do not present the extreme situation needed for mandatory replacement (see Note 3, p. 140); (3) the defendant is told that he must choose between continued representation by appointed counsel or proceeding *pro se*; (4) the defendant chooses to proceed *pro se*; and (5) the court then appoints as standby counsel the "very attorney whose representation precipitated the defendant's complaint."

(3) "In cases where the defendant is not irretrievably estranged from standby counsel," defendants quite naturally will drift towards asking counsel to make presentations (as occurred in *McKaskle*) as "defendants often assume that standby counsel is not merely a resource but also someone available to act for the defendant." However, in such a situation, some courts refuse to allow standby counsel to assume this "larger role" (particularly at trial), insisting that the defendant choose between waiving his "*Faretta* rights" or utilizing counsel strictly as an advisor.

(4) Many standby counsel will not (1) take it upon themselves to explore "factual investigations and legal options that the defendant might overlook" and then bring their findings to the attention of the defendant, (2) raise legal objections on their own initiative, or (3) present mitigating evidence at sentencing on their own initiative—all actions advocated by the author. This failure to

initiate assistance arguably is a product in part of various lower court opinions that characterize the role of standby counsel as simply "an observer, an attorney who attends the trial or other proceeding and who may offer advice, but who does not speak for the defendant or bear responsibility for his defense." *United States v. Taylor*, 933 F.2d 307 (5th Cir.1991).

To what extent does the acceptance of such practices follow from a "judicial perception that standby counsel serves the court's purpose rather than the defendant's"? Ibid. Did the Court in *McKaskle* approve of an "active role" for standby counsel, in which counsel acts as "part of the defense team," subject to the "defendant's right to actual control of the case and to the appearance of control in the presence of the factfinder"? Ibid.

6. ***Ineffective assistance of standby counsel.*** Lower courts generally have rejected claims of ineffective assistance by standby counsel. They note that the *pro se* defendant cannot complain of his own ineffective performance, (see *Faretta*, fn.46) and the final decisions are being made by the defendant. They also note that ineffective assistance claims are tied to a constitutional right to counsel's assistance (see Note 1, p. 153), and the defendant has no constitutional right to the assistance of standby counsel. See Poulin, supra Note 5. However, "some courts" have held that *pro se* defendants may claim ineffective assistance of standby counsel as to erroneous "legal advice." Ibid.

7. ***"Hybrid" representation.*** Under hybrid representation, defendant and counsel act, in effect, as co-counsel, with each speaking for the defense during different phases of the trial. Does footnote 15 of *Faretta* (p. 120), in its last paragraph, provide a constitutional grounding for hybrid representation in its description of both self-representation and representation by counsel as "independent constitutional rights." Looking in part to the *McKaskle* comment that *Faretta* did not "require the trial judge to permit 'hybrid' representation of the type Wiggins was actually allowed," and to Justice Blackmun's description (in *Faretta*) of the two rights as "mutually exclusive" (p. 122), lower courts have uniformly held that there is no constitutional right to hybrid representation. Trial courts may permit hybrid representation as "a matter of grace," but that permission is rarely granted. Courts express concern, in particular, that hybrid representation will be used by the defendant to gain the advantages of representation by counsel while at the same time using his participation to "testify" (by making the opening or closing argument) without being subject to cross-examination. See CRIMPROC. § 11.5(g).

8. ***Requisite warnings and judicial inquiry***. Appellate court opinions direct trial courts, once the defendant has indicated an interest in proceeding pro se (see Note 3 supra), to advise the defendant of the various disadvantages (and possible adverse consequences) of proceeding *pro se*, including the following: "(1) that 'presenting a defense is not a simple matter of telling one's story,' but requires adherence to various 'technical' rules governing the conduct of a trial; (2) that a lawyer has substantial experience and training in trial procedure and that the prosecution will be represented by an experienced lawyer; (3) that a person unfamiliar with legal procedures may allow the prosecutor an advantage by failing to make objections to inadmissible evidence, may not make effective use of such rights as the voir dire of jurors, and may make tactical decisions that produce unintended consequences; (4) that there may be possible defenses and other rights of which counsel would be aware and if those are not timely asserted, they may be lost permanently; (5) that a defendant proceeding pro se will not be allowed to complain on appeal about the competency of his representation; and (6) 'that the effectiveness of his defense may well be diminished by his dual role as attorney and accused.' " CRIMPROC. § 11.5(c). After providing such advice, the trial court is then directed to determine through a penetrating inquiry (which goes beyond

requiring "yes" and "no" answers) that the defendant understands and appreciates those disadvantages and consequences.

To what extent is such advice and the follow-up inquiry constitutionally required? Looking to various statements in *Faretta*, several appellate courts have concluded that the Sixth Amendment requires reference to "specific disadvantages," and not simply a "vague, general admonishment," and that must be followed by an "inquiry realistically 'designed to reveal [defendants] understanding.'" See CRIMPROC § 11.5(c) (collecting cases). Consider, however, UNITED STATES v. HILL, 252 F.3d 919 (7th Cir.2001), involving a challenge on appeal to the trial court having permitted the defendant to proceed *pro se* (a choice made by defendant after the trial refused to replace appointed counsel). In rejecting that challenge, Judge EASTERBROOK's opinion noted:

"Waiver does not depend on astute (or even rudimentary) understanding of how rights can be employed to best advantage. Defendants routinely plead guilty, waiving oodles of constitutional rights, in proceedings where rights are named but not explained. For example, the judge will tell the defendant that the plea waives the right to jury trial but will not describe how juries work, when they are apt to find a prosecutor's case insufficient, why the process of formulating and giving jury instructions creates issues for appeal, and so on. * * * The contention that 'knowing and intelligent' means something different when a defendant elects self-representation than when the same defendant elects a bench trial (or waives another constitutional right) has its genesis in *Faretta* * * * [where] the Court remarked: 'Although a defendant need not himself have the skill and experience of a lawyer in order competently and intelligently to choose self-representation, he should be made aware of the dangers and disadvantages of self-representation, so that the record will establish that he knows what he is doing and his choice is made with eyes wide open' [p. 121] * * *. From this statement of preference ('should' is not 'must') has grown a jurisprudence demanding more and more extensive advise and warnings to impress on the defendant the drawbacks of dispensing with counsel. * * * The Federal Judicial Center's *Benchbook* * * * propounds 15 questions. This litany is a means of discouraging self-representation * * *. But we doubt that any list can be mandated. *Faretta* adopted the waiver standard of *Johnson v. Zerbst*, which noted that the determination 'whether there has been an intelligent waiver of the right to counsel must depend, in each case, upon the particular facts and circumstances surrounding the case, including the background, experience, and conduct of the accused.' That standard can be met without a demonstration that the accused has a deep understanding of how counsel could assist him. After all, *Godinez* [Note 5 p. 136] * * * holds that any person competent to stand trial is able to waive counsel, [and] the competence standard is met by persons who are barely able to understand the proceedings, let alone recognize how lawyers navigate the legal shoals."

The *Hill* opinion added that "in or out of the criminal justice system, people freely assume risks that they do not fully understand * * * yet we do not call these decisions unintelligent; venturing into the unknown with a sketchy idea of what lies ahead may be the wisest choice even when the odds are beyond calculation." Here, it noted, the defendant had been told by the trial judge that: representing himself "was foolish"; the "stakes are very high"; "there are disadvantages in a person who is not a lawyer in representing himself"; and the "rules of evidence and procedure" would apply and not be changed "just because you are not skilled or learned in the law." The prosecutor "chimed in with some additional advice, which the judge seconded," warning defendant he would not get additional privileges in prison because he was representing himself, and that he would face "numerous burdens and roadblocks to defending himself." That was sufficient information to provide an understanding that met constitutional standards. After being told that he would have to comply with the rules of evidence, the defendant was asked whether he understood, and he responded "A little bit." That answer, the *Hill* opinion concluded, showed "a sound appreciation of his position (defendant did not pretend he had a legal education) rather than a lack of intelligent choice. If [defendant] was about to face hazards he could not fully understand, his election was nonetheless valid because he knew that he was in unchartered waters."

The *Hill* opinion also questioned the value, in any event, of a more extensive colloquy. Defendant had acted throughout in "a pig-headed fashion" and it was "hard to imagine" that by quoting the Benchbook list or "expatiating about the drawbacks of self-representation," the "district could have talked him out of his decision." "Lists," the opinion noted, "do not convey knowledge or change minds." It "is hard to image any defendant with even modest resolve responding: 'Oh, now that I know that something called the Sentencing Guidelines' exists, I see the foolishness of representing myself.' "

Hill was decided before *Iowa v. Tovar*, infra. Although *Tovar*, unlike *Hill* and *Faretta*, did not involve a defendant who desired to waive counsel so he could represent himself at trial, the opinion there did discuss that situation in distinguishing the case before it. Does the analysis of *Hill* survive the *Tovar* discussion?

IOWA v. TOVAR

541 U.S. 77, 124 S.Ct. 1379, 158 L.Ed.2d 209 (2004).

Justice GINSBURG delivered the opinion of the Court.

* * * This case concerns the extent to which a trial judge, before accepting a guilty plea from an uncounseled defendant, must elaborate on the right to representation [by counsel]. Beyond affording the defendant the opportunity to consult with counsel prior to entry of a plea and to be assisted by counsel at the plea hearing, must the court, specifically: (1) advise the defendant that "waiving the assistance of counsel in deciding whether to plead guilty [entails] the risk that a viable defense will be overlooked"; and (2) "admonis[h]" the defendant "that by waiving his right to an attorney he will lose the opportunity to obtain an independent opinion on whether, under the facts and applicable law, it is wise to plead guilty"? The Iowa Supreme Court held both warnings essential to the "knowing and intelligent" waiver of the Sixth Amendment right to the assistance of counsel. We hold that neither warning is mandated by the Sixth Amendment. The constitutional requirement is satisfied when the trial court informs the accused of the nature of the charges against him, of his right to be counseled regarding his plea, and of the range of allowable punishments attendant upon the entry of a guilty plea.

* * * [On November 2, 1996, after being arrested for operating a motor vehicle while under the influence of alcohol (OWI), respondent Tovar, then a 21–year-old college student, was brought before an Iowa district court judge for his first appearance]. The judge indicated on the Initial Appearance form that Tovar appeared without counsel and waived application for court-appointed counsel. The judge also marked on the form's checklist that Tovar was "informed of the charge and his . . . rights and receive[d] a copy of the Complaint." Arraignment was set for November 18, 1996. In the interim, Tovar was released from jail.

At the November 18 arraignment, the court's inquiries of Tovar began: "Mr. Tovar appears without counsel and I see, Mr. Tovar, that you waived application for a court appointed attorney. Did you want to represent yourself at today's hearing?" Tovar replied: "Yes, sir." The court soon after asked: "[H]ow did you wish to plead?" Tovar answered: "Guilty." * * * Conducting the guilty plea colloquy required by the Iowa Rules of Criminal Procedure, the court explained that, if Tovar pleaded not guilty, he would be entitled to a speedy and public trial by jury, and would have the right to be represented at that trial by an attorney, who "could help [Tovar] select a jury, question and cross-examine the State's witnesses, present evidence, if any, in [his] behalf, and make arguments to the judge and jury on [his] behalf." By pleading guilty, the court cautioned, "not only [would Tovar] give up [his] right to a trial [of any kind on the charge against him], [he would] give up [his] right to be represented by an attorney at that trial." The court further advised Tovar that, if he entered a guilty plea, he would relinquish the right to remain silent at trial, the right to the presumption of innocence, and the right to subpoena witnesses and compel their testimony. Turning to the particular offense with which Tovar had been charged, the court informed him that an OWI conviction carried a maximum penalty of a year in jail and a $1,000 fine, and a minimum penalty of two days in jail and a $500 fine. Tovar affirmed that he understood his exposure to those penalties. The court next explained that, before accepting a guilty plea, the court had to assure itself that Tovar was in fact guilty of the charged offense. To that end, the court [explained the elements of the offense—operating a motor vehicle and being intoxicated—and Tovar confirmed he had driven a motor vehicle and that the intoxilyzer test results, which he did not contest, showed a blood alcohol content nearly twice over the legal limit.] The court then accepted Tovar's plea, observing that there was "a factual basis" for it, and that Tovar had made the plea "voluntarily, with a full understanding of [his] rights, [and] . . . of the consequences of [pleading guilty]."

On December 30, 1996, Tovar appeared for sentencing on the OWI charge and, simultaneously, for arraignment on a subsequent charge of driving with a suspended license. Noting that Tovar was again in attendance without counsel, the court inquired: "Mr. Tovar, did you want to represent yourself at today's hearing or did you want to take some time to hire an attorney to represent you?" Tovar replied that he would represent himself. The court then engaged in essentially the same plea colloquy on the suspension charge as it had on the OWI charge the previous month. After accepting Tovar's guilty plea on the suspension charge, the court sentenced him on both counts: For the OWI conviction, the court imposed the minimum sentence of two days in jail and a $500 fine, plus a surcharge and costs; for the suspension conviction, the court imposed a $250 fine, plus a surcharge and costs.

On March 16, 1998, Tovar was convicted of OWI for a second time. He was represented by counsel in that proceeding, in which he pleaded guilty. On December 14, 2000, Tovar was again charged with OWI, this time as a third offense, and additionally with driving while license barred. Iowa law classifies first-offense OWI as a serious misdemeanor and second-offense OWI as an aggravated misdemeanor. Third-offense OWI, and any OWI offenses thereafter, rank as class "D" felonies. Represented by an attorney, Tovar pleaded not guilty to both December 2000 charges. * * * Through counsel, Tovar [subsequently] filed a * * * motion [arguing] that Tovar's first OWI conviction, in 1996, could not be used to enhance the December 2000 OWI charge from a second-offense aggravated misdemeanor to a third-offense felony. Significantly, Tovar did not allege that he was unaware at the November 1996 arraignment of his right to counsel prior to pleading guilty and at the plea hearing. Instead, he maintained that his 1996 waiver of counsel was invalid—not "full knowing, intelligent, and voluntary"—because he "was never made aware by the court . . . of the dangers and disadvantages of self-representation."

The [trial] court denied Tovar's motion in May 2001, explaining: "Where the offense is readily understood by laypersons and the penalty is not unduly severe, the duty of inquiry which is imposed upon the court is only that which is required to assure an awareness of [the] right to counsel and a willingness to proceed without counsel in the face of such awareness." Tovar then waived his right to a jury trial and was found guilty by the court of both the OWI third-offense charge and driving while license barred. * * * The Iowa Court of Appeals affirmed, but the Supreme Court of Iowa, by a 4 to 3 vote, reversed and remanded for entry of judgment without consideration of Tovar's first OWI conviction. Iowa's highest court acknowledged that "the dangers of proceeding *pro se* at a guilty plea proceeding will be different than the dangers of proceeding *pro se* at a jury trial, [therefore] the inquiries made at these proceedings will also be different." The court nonetheless held that the colloquy preceding acceptance of Tovar's 1996 guilty plea had been constitutionally inadequate, and instructed dispositively:

> "[A] defendant such as Tovar who chooses to plead guilty without the assistance of an attorney must be advised of the usefulness of an attorney and the dangers of self-representation in order to make a knowing and intelligent waiver of his right to counsel.... [T]he trial judge [must] advise the defendant generally that there are defenses to criminal charges that may not be known by laypersons and that the danger in waiving the assistance of counsel in deciding whether to plead guilty is the risk that a viable defense will be overlooked. The defendant should be admonished that by waiving his right to an attorney he will lose the opportunity to obtain an independent opinion on whether, under the facts and applicable law, it is wise to plead guilty. In addition, the court must ensure the defendant understands the nature of the charges against him and the range of allowable punishments."

We granted certiorari, in view of the division of [lower court] opinions on the requirements the Sixth Amendment imposes for waiver of counsel at a plea hearing, and we now reverse the judgment of the Iowa Supreme Court.

* * * Because Tovar received a two-day prison term for his 1996 OWI conviction, he had a right to counsel both at the plea stage and at trial had he elected to contest the charge.[10] A person accused of crime, however, may choose to forgo representation. While the Constitution "does not force a lawyer upon a defendant," *Adams v. United States ex rel. McCann*, 317 U.S. 269 (1942), it does require that any waiver of the right to counsel be knowing, voluntary, and intelligent, see *Johnson v. Zerbst,* 304 U.S. 458 (1938). * * * We have described a waiver of counsel as intelligent when the defendant "knows what he is doing and his choice is made with eyes open." We have not, however, prescribed any formula or script to be read to a defendant who states that he elects to proceed without counsel. The information a defendant must possess in order to make an intelligent election, our decisions indicate, will depend on a range of case-specific factors, including the defendant's education or sophistication, the complex or easily grasped nature of the charge, and the stage of the proceeding. See *Johnson*.

As to waiver of trial counsel, we have said that before a defendant may be allowed to proceed *pro se,* he must be warned specifically of the hazards ahead.

10. [transposed] The United States as *amicus curiae* reads our decision in *Scott v. Illinois,* [p. 90] to hold that a constitutionally defective waiver of counsel in a misdemeanor prosecution, although warranting vacation of any term of imprisonment, affords no ground for disturbing the underlying conviction. *Amicus* accordingly contends that the Constitution should not preclude use of an uncounseled misdemeanor conviction to enhance the penalty for a subsequent offense, regardless of the validity of the prior waiver. * * * The State, however, does not contest the Iowa Supreme Court's determination that a conviction obtained without an effective waiver of counsel cannot be used to enhance a subsequent charge. We therefore do not address arguments *amicus* advances questioning that premise.

Faretta v. California, [p. 119]. * * * Later, in *Patterson v. Illinois* [p. 740], we elaborated on "the dangers and disadvantages of self-representation" to which *Faretta* referred. "[A]t trial," we observed, "counsel is required to help even the most gifted layman adhere to the rules of procedure and evidence, comprehend the subtleties of *voir dire,* examine and cross-examine witnesses effectively . . ., object to improper prosecution questions, and much more." Warnings of the pitfalls of proceeding to trial without counsel, we therefore said, must be "rigorous[ly]" conveyed. We clarified, however, that at earlier stages of the criminal process, a less searching or formal colloquy may suffice. *Patterson* concerned postindictment questioning by police and prosecutor. At that stage of the case, we held, the warnings required by *Miranda v. Arizona* [p. 575] adequately informed the defendant not only of his Fifth Amendment rights, but of his Sixth Amendment right to counsel as well. * * * *Patterson* describes a "pragmatic approach to the waiver question," one that asks "what purposes a lawyer can serve at the particular stage of the proceedings in question, and what assistance he could provide to an accused at that stage," in order "to determine the scope of the Sixth Amendment right to counsel, and the type of warnings and procedures that should be required before a waiver of that right will be recognized." We require less rigorous warnings pretrial, *Patterson* explained, not because pretrial proceedings are "less important" than trial, but because, at that stage, "the full dangers and disadvantages of self-representation . . . are less substantial and more obvious to an accused than they are at trial."

In Tovar's case, the State maintains that, like the *Miranda* warnings we found adequate in *Patterson,* Iowa's plea colloquy suffices both to advise a defendant of his right to counsel, and to assure that his guilty plea is informed and voluntary. The plea colloquy, according to the State, "makes plain that an attorney's role would be to challenge the charge or sentence," and therefore adequately conveys to the defendant both the utility of counsel and the dangers of self-representation. Tovar, on the other hand, defends the precise instructions required by the Iowa Supreme Court as essential to a knowing, voluntary, and intelligent plea stage waiver of counsel.

To resolve this case, we need not endorse the State's position that nothing more than the plea colloquy was needed to safeguard Tovar's right to counsel. Preliminarily, we note that there were some things more in this case. Tovar first indicated that he waived counsel at his Initial Appearance, affirmed that he wanted to represent himself at the plea hearing, and declined the court's offer of "time to hire an attorney" at sentencing, when it was still open to him to request withdrawal of his plea. Further, the State does not contest that a defendant must be alerted to his right to the assistance of counsel in entering a plea. See Brief for Petitioner 19 (acknowledging defendant's need to know "retained or appointed counsel can assist" at the plea stage by "work[ing] on the issues of guilt and sentencing"). Indeed, the Iowa Supreme Court appeared to assume that Tovar was informed of his entitlement to counsel's aid or, at least, to have pretermitted that issue. Accordingly, the State presents a narrower question: "Does the Sixth Amendment require a court to give a rigid and detailed admonishment to a *pro se* defendant pleading guilty of the usefulness of an attorney, that an attorney may provide an independent opinion whether it is wise to plead guilty and that without an attorney the defendant risks overlooking a defense?" * * * We hold it does not.

This Court recently explained, in reversing a lower court determination that a guilty plea was not voluntary: "[T]he law ordinarily considers a waiver knowing, intelligent, and sufficiently aware if the defendant fully understands the nature of the right and how it would likely apply *in general* in the circumstances—even though the defendant may not know the *specific detailed* consequences of invoking it." *United States v. Ruiz*, 536 U.S. 622, (2002) (emphasis in original). We similarly observed in *Patterson:* "If [the defendant] . . . lacked a full and complete appreciation of all of the consequences flowing from his waiver, it does not defeat the State's showing that the information it provided to him satisfied the constitutional minimum." The Iowa Supreme Court gave insufficient consideration to these guiding decisions. In prescribing scripted admonitions and holding them necessary in every guilty plea instance, we further note, the Iowa high court overlooked our observations that the information a defendant must have to waive counsel intelligently will "depend, in each case, upon the particular facts and circumstances surrounding that case."

Moreover, as Tovar acknowledges, in a collateral attack on an uncounseled conviction, it is the defendant's burden to prove that he did not competently and intelligently waive his right to the assistance of counsel. In that light, we note that Tovar has never claimed that he did not fully understand the charge or the range of punishment for the crime prior to pleading guilty. Further, he has never "articulate[d] with precision" the additional information counsel could have provided, given the simplicity of the charge. Nor does he assert that he *was* unaware of his right to be counseled prior to and at his arraignment. Before this Court, he suggests only that he "*may have been* under the mistaken belief that he had a right to counsel at trial, but not if he was merely going to plead guilty." Brief for Respondent 16.

Given "the particular facts and circumstances surrounding [this] case," see *Johnson*, it is far from clear that warnings of the kind required by the Iowa Supreme Court would have enlightened Tovar's decision whether to seek counsel or to represent himself. In a case so straightforward, the United States as *amicus curiae* suggests, the admonitions at issue might confuse or mislead a defendant more than they would inform him: The warnings the Iowa Supreme Court declared mandatory might be misconstrued as a veiled suggestion that a meritorious defense exists or that the defendant could plead to a lesser charge, when neither prospect is a realistic one. If a defendant delays his plea in the vain hope that counsel could uncover a tenable basis for contesting or reducing the criminal charge, the prompt disposition of the case will be impeded, and the resources of either the State (if the defendant is indigent) or the defendant himself (if he is financially ineligible for appointed counsel) will be wasted. Brief for United States as *Amicus Curiae* 9.

We note, finally, that States are free to adopt by statute, rule, or decision any guides to the acceptance of an uncounseled plea they deem useful. See, *e.g.*, Alaska Rule Crim. Proc. 39(a) (2003); Fla. Rule Crim. Proc. 3.111(d) (2003); Md. Ct. Rule 4–215 (2002); Minn. Rule Crim. Proc. 5.02 (2003); Pa. Rule Crim. Proc. 121, comment (2003). We hold only that the two admonitions the Iowa Supreme Court ordered are not required by the Federal Constitution. * * *

Notes and Questions

1. ***What advice is essential?*** The Court speaks of the Sixth Amendment prerequisites for waiver being "satisfied" as to the defendant who desires to plead guilty, when the "trial court informs the accused of [1] the nature of the charges against him, [2] of his right to be counseled regarding his plea, and [3] of the range of allowable punishments attendant upon the entry of a guilty plea" (p. 131, brackets added). Items [1] and [3] are also viewed as prerequisites for the waiver of the various trial rights relinquished in connection with a guilty plea, and judicial discussions of the required content of the advice on those two items commonly focuses on the understanding need for a valid guilty plea. Courts here have noted that constitutional acceptability may be achieved without spelling out

all aspects of the allowable punishment or each and every element of the offense. See Ch. 22, § 4; CRIMPROC § 21.4. Where defendant waives the right to assistance of counsel at an earlier stage in the proceeding, involving a lesser consequence (e.g., waiver of counsel in connection with the waiver of a preliminary hearing), would the rationale of *Tovar* suggest that the court need not advise the defendant, in any respect, as to the nature of the offense charged or of possible punishments?

2. Does *Tovar* hold open the possibility that, under some circumstances, the judge accepting a waiver of counsel in connection with the entry of a guilty plea must advise the defendant of the possible benefits of counsel's assistance in considering whether to plead guilty? If so, what circumstances might require such advice? Would such advice be required where an element of the offense charged called for an arguably subjective jury determination (e.g., what constitutes negligence) and the facts presented in establishing a factual basis for the guilty plea were sufficient to convince a jury on that element, but not overwhelmingly so?

3. ***Collateral attack.*** As the Court notes, in a collateral attack on an uncounseled conviction, the burden shifts to the defendant to prove that he lacked the understanding needed for a constitutionally acceptable waiver. Does this mean that the defendant must go beyond establishing that the advice given by the trial court clearly failed to encompass some information that had to be understood for the waiver to be constitutionally acceptable? Must the defendant also show his actual ignorance of the particular information?

In *Carnley v. Cochrane*, 369 U.S. 506 (1962), also a habeas case, the Court warned against assuming that the defendant has the necessary knowledge to make an acceptable waiver. The Court there concluded that waiver could not be presumed from a "silent record." The "record must show, or there must be an allegation and evidence which show, that an accused was offered counsel, but intelligently and understandingly rejected the offer. * * * No amount of circumstantial evidence that the person may have been aware of his right will suffice to stand [in place of that showing]."

4. ***State requirements***. As noted in the last paragraph of *Tovar*, states often require more extensive advisements for the waiver of counsel as a matter of state law. Such state provisions commonly require, in addition to an explanation of the advantages that come with representation by counsel, the prerequisites set forth in Justice Black's opinion (for a four justice plurality) in *Von Moltke v. Gillies*, 332 U.S. 708 (1948): "To be valid such a waiver must be made with an apprehension of the nature of the charges, the statutory offenses included within them, the range of allowable punishments thereunder, possible defenses to the charges and circumstances in mitigation thereof and all other facts essential to a broad understanding of the whole matter." *Von Molthe*, like *Tovar*, involved a defendant who waived counsel in connection with the entry of a guilty plea.

5. ***The competency standard for waiving the right to counsel.*** In GODINEZ v. MORAN, 509 U.S. 389 (1993) (a case in which a capital defendant discharged his attorneys, pled guilty and was ultimately sentenced to death), a 7–2 majority, per THOMAS, J., rejected the notion that competency to plead guilty or to waive the right to counsel must be measured by a higher or different standard than the competency standard for standing trial—whether the defendant has "sufficient present ability to consult with his lawyer with a reasonable degree of rational understanding" and has "a rational as well as functional understanding of the proceedings against him." Observed Justice Thomas:

"[As for the guilty plea, a] defendant who stands trial is likely to be presented with choices [such as whether to testify, whether to waive a jury trial, and whether to cross-examine witnesses for the prosecution] that entail relinquishment of the same rights that are relinquished by a defendant who pleads guilty. [While] the decision to plead guilty is a profound one, it is not more complicated than the sum total of decisions that a defendant may be called upon to make during the course of a trial. [Thus,] we can conceive of no basis for demanding a higher level of competence for those defendants who choose to plead guilty.

"[As for waiving the right to counsel,] there is no reason to believe that [that] decision requires an appreciably higher level of mental functioning than the decision to waive other constitutional rights. [The] competence that is required of a defendant seeking to waive his right to counsel is the competence to *waive the right*, not the competence to represent himself. [A] defendant's ability to represent himself has no bearing upon his competence to *choose* self-representation."

The majority also warned, however, that a defendant being competent to stand trial would not in itself meet the prerequisites for pleading guilty or waiving the right to counsel: In such instances "a trial court must satisfy itself that the waiver [of] constitutional rights is knowing and voluntary. In this sense, there is a 'heightened' standard for pleading guilty and for waiving the right to counsel, but it is not a heightened standard of *competence.*" The purpose of a competency inquiry, explained the Court, is to determine whether a defendant "has the *ability* to understand the proceedings," but "the purpose of the 'knowing and voluntary' inquiry [is] to determine whether the defendant actually *does* understand the significance and consequences of a particular decision and whether the decision is uncoerced."[c]

6. *Forfeiture of the right to counsel.* A series of lower court cases have held that misconduct by the defendant can produce a forfeiture of the right to assistance of counsel, requiring defendant thereafter to proceed *pro se*. Two settings have most frequently led to findings of forfeiture: (1) defendant assaulted or threatened counsel, who then asked to withdraw; (2) defendant was given ample time to obtain counsel, and after assuring the court that he would obtain counsel by the date of the trial, appeared on that date without counsel and without a reasonable excuse for failing to have obtained counsel. See CRIMPROC §§ 11.3(c), 11.4(d). Other courts have refused to accept the concept of forfeiture in such situations, but will force the defendant to proceed *pro se* on the basis of a "waiver by conduct." They require that the defendant previously has been made aware that the misconduct at issue would result in the loss of his right to counsel. Ibid. But see *State v. Carruthers*, 35 S.W.3d 516 (Tenn.2000) (reviewing the cases that have "attempted" to distinguish the concepts of "implicit waiver by conduct" and "forfeiture," finding the distinction "slight", and concluding that the right to counsel may be forfeited by interactions with counsel (here threats) that seek to "manipulate, delay, or disrupt trial proceedings").

c. Justice Kennedy, joined by Scalia, J., wrote a concurring opinion. Justice Blackmun, joined by Stevens, J., dissented, pointing out that Moran had "presented no defense, called no witnesses and offered no mitigating evidence on his behalf." A finding that defendant is competent to stand trial, emphasized the dissent, "establishes only that he is capable of aiding his attorney in making critical decisions required at trial or in plea negotiations. The reliability or even relevancy of such a finding vanishes when its basic premise—that counsel will be present—ceases to exist. The question is no longer whether the defendant can proceed with an attorney, but whether he can proceed alone and uncounselled."

Thirty-three months after he lost his case in the U.S. Supreme Court, Moran was executed. See *Nevada Executes Man Who Killed 3 People*, N.Y. Times, Mar. 31, 1996, Sec. 1, at 27.

SECTION 2. THE RIGHT TO COUNSEL OF ONE'S OWN CHOICE

A. Appointed Counsel

1. **Selecting appointed counsel.** As noted in Chapter One (p. 13), three basic systems are used to provide counsel for the indigent defendant: (1) a public defender system; (2) court appointment of attorneys in private practice; and (3) a contract system. On occasion, a defendant in a jurisdiction utilizing appointed private attorneys will request that his case be assigned to a particular attorney (typically, an attorney who has represented the defendant in the past), who has expressed a willingness to accept the appointment. With only a few exceptions, lower courts have held that the court making the appointment need give no weight to the defendant's preference (or the grounds supporting that preference) in selecting appointed counsel. They note in this regard that the indigent has no constitutional right to selection of his choice of appointed counsel, even where the appointment of that attorney would not increase the state's costs in providing counsel. Since the Sixth Amendment guarantees the defendant a right only to representation that is competent, and not to that representation which the indigent believes (correctly or not) to be the best, the trial court is free to value over the defendant's choice such interests as: (1) the administrative convenience of utilizing a routine appointment process; (2) ensuring the "even handed distribution of assignments" (which would be disrupted if defendants frequently prefer the same attorneys); and (3) selecting attorneys who are familiar with the practice in the particular court. See CRIMPROC. 11.4(a) (collecting cases). Another concern arguably leading to this position is that giving legal recognition to the indigent's preference would undercut the public defender system by either requiring courts to override the executive authority of the public defender in assigning cases or requiring courts to make appointments of preferred attorneys outside of the public defender system.[a]

2. While the Supreme Court has not spoken directly to the lower court rulings rejecting any constitutional protection of the indigent defendant's preference in the selection of appointed counsel, its reasoning in MORRIS v. SLAPPY, 461 U.S. 1 (1983), is often cited as supporting those rulings. In that case, the trial court appointed the public defender to represent the indigent defendant Slappy, who was charged with rape, robbery, and burglary, all involving the same victim. Deputy Public Defender Goldfine was assigned to represent defendant. Goldfine represented defendant at the preliminary hearing and supervised an extensive investigation, but shortly before trial, was hospitalized for emergency surgery. Six days before the scheduled trial, the Public Defender assigned Hotchkiss, a senior trial attorney, to take over the representation of Slappy.

After the trial was under way, Slappy moved for a continuance, claiming his new attorney had not had enough time to prepare the case. But Hotchkiss told the court that he was "ready" for trial. The court denied a continuance. On the third day of trial, Slappy claimed that he was unrepresented by counsel, maintaining

a. Studies have noted widespread defendant distrust of public defenders (who are seen as "agents of the State"), which suggests that many defendants, if given the choice, would prefer appointment of private practitioners. See Jonathan Casper, *Criminal Courts: The Defendant's Perspective* (1978).

Stephen Schulhofer and David Friedman, *Rethinking Indigent Defense: Promoting Effective Representation through Consumer Sovereignty and Freedom of Choice for all Criminal Defendants*, 31 Am.Crim.L.Rev. 73 (1993), have proposed a system for selecting counsel that would give the defendant the fullest range of choice. They propose that "present institutions for providing criminal defense * * * be replaced with a voucher system, in order to provide indigent defendants with freedom of choice and to provide their attorneys with the same incentive to serve their clients that attorneys have always had when they represent client's other than the poor."

that Goldfine, not Hotchkiss, was his attorney. The court treated this as a motion for a continuance and denied it. Slappy then announced that he would not cooperate at all in the trial. Ignoring Hotchkiss' advice, Slappy refused to take the stand. The jury returned a verdict of guilty on some counts, but failed to reach a verdict on the sexual assault counts. A week later, a second trial was held on the charges left unresolved as a result of the mistrial. Hotchkiss again represented defendant. Again, defendant ignored Hotchkiss' advice and refused to testify. Indeed, defendant refused to even speak to Hotchkiss. The second jury returned a guilty verdict on the sexual assault counts.

The Court of Appeals for the Ninth Circuit subsequently granted federal habeas corpus relief, observing that the Sixth Amendment "would be without substance *if it did not include the right to a meaningful attorney-client relationship.*" (Emphasis added by the Supreme Court.) The Court of Appeals next stated that by failing to weigh defendant's interest in continued representation by Goldfine against the state's interest in proceeding with the scheduled trial (the trial court had not inquired about the probable length of Goldfine's absence), the trial court had ignored Slappy's Sixth Amendment right to a "meaningful attorney-client relationship" and that this violation required reversal without any need to show prejudice. The Supreme Court, per BURGER, C.J., disagreed. After finding no merit to the claim that the denial of a continuance prevented Hotchkiss from being fully prepared for trial and concluding that respondent's motion on the third day of trial for a continuance to permit Goldfine to continue to represent him was not timely, the Court observed:

"[The] Court of Appeals' conclusion that the Sixth Amendment right to counsel 'would be without substance if it did not include the right to a *meaningful attorney-client relationship*' (emphasis added) is without basis in the law. * * * No court could possibly guarantee that a defendant will develop the kind of rapport with his attorney—privately retained or provided by the public—that the Court of Appeals thought part of the Sixth Amendment guarantee of counsel. Accordingly, we reject the claim that the Sixth Amendment guarantees a 'meaningful relationship' between an accused and his counsel.[6]

"[In] its haste to create a novel Sixth Amendment right, the court wholly failed to take into account the interest of the victim of these crimes in not undergoing the ordeal of yet a third trial in this case. Of course, inconvenience and embarrassment to witnesses cannot justify failing to enforce constitutional rights of an accused: when prejudicial error is made that clearly impairs a defendant's constitutional rights, the burden of a new trial must be borne by the prosecution, the courts, and the witnesses; the Constitution permits nothing less. But in the administration of criminal justice, courts may not ignore the concerns of victims. Apart from all other factors, such a course would hardly encourage victims to report violations to the proper authorities; this is especially so when the crime is one calling for public testimony about a humiliating and degrading experience such as was involved here."

Although he concurred in the result (because he agreed with the Court that Slappy did not make a timely motion for continuance based on Goldfine's unavailability), Justice BRENNAN, joined by Marshall, J., disputed much of the Court's reasoning:

6. The Court of Appeals seems to have believed that an appointed counsel with whom the accused did not have a "meaningful relationship" was the equivalent of no counsel; as a consequence, it held that no prejudice need be shown for violations of the right to a "meaningful" attorney-client relationship. Our holding that there is no Sixth Amendment right to a "meaningful attorney-client relationship" disposes of that argument.

"[In] light of the importance of a defendant's relationship with his attorney to his Sixth Amendment right to counsel, recognizing a qualified right to continue that relationship is eminently sensible. The Court of Appeals simply held that where a defendant expresses a desire to continue to be represented by counsel who already has been appointed for him by moving for a continuance until that attorney again will be available, the trial judge has an obligation to inquire into the length of counsel's expected unavailability and to balance the defendant's interest against the public's interest in the efficient and expeditious administration of criminal justice. Contrary to the Court's suggestion, this does not require a trial court 'to guarantee' attorney-defendant 'rapport.'

"[The] defendant's interest in preserving his relationship with a particular attorney is not afforded absolute protection. If the attorney is likely to be unavailable for an extended period, or if other factors exist that tip the balance in favor of proceeding in spite of a particular attorney's absence, the defendant's motion for a continuance clearly may be denied. Such denials would be subject to review under the traditional 'abuse of discretion' standard. As the Court of Appeals suggested, however, the balancing is critical. In the absence of a balancing inquiry a trial court cannot discharge its 'duty to preserve the fundamental rights of an accused.' "[b]

3. Replacement of appointed counsel. Because the indigent defendant has no right to appointed counsel of choice, he also has no right to replace one appointed counsel with another even if that can be done without causing any delay in the proceedings. The defendant has a right to substitution only upon establishing "good cause, such as a conflict of interest, a complete breakdown of communication, or an irreconcilable conflict which [could] lead * * * to an apparently unjust verdict." CRIMPROC. § 11.4(b) The mere loss of confidence in his appointed counsel does not establish "good cause." Defendant must have some well founded reason for believing that the appointed attorney cannot or will not competently represent him, which does not include disagreements on matters of strategy, the failure of counsel to meet frequently with the defendant (where counsel is otherwise working on the case), or counsel's belief that defendant's defense probably will fail. Although an irreconcilable conflict does establish good cause, courts warn that defendant cannot manufacture good cause by abusive and uncooperative behavior See Note 6, p. 137.

B. Retained Counsel

CAPLIN & DRYSDALE, CHARTERED v. UNITED STATES

491 U.S. 617, 109 S.Ct. 2646, 105 L.Ed.2d 528 (1989).

Justice WHITE delivered the opinion of the Court.

[Christopher Reckmeyer was charged with running a massive drug importation and distribution scheme alleged to be a continuing criminal enterprise (CCE) in violation of 21 U.S.C. § 848. Relying on a provision of the CCE statute that authorizes forfeiture of "any property constituting, or derived from, any proceeds" obtained from drug law violations, § 853, the indictment sought forfeiture of specified assets in Reckmeyer's possession. Acting pursuant to § 853(e), the district court entered a restraining order forbidding Reckmeyer from transferring any of the potentially forfeitable assets.

b. Blackmun, J., joined by Stevens, J., concurred in the result agreeing with the Court that Slappy had not made a timely motion for continuance based on Goldfine's unavailability. He saw no occasion to consider the Sixth Amendment issue. For strong criticism of the majority opinion in *Slappy,* see Vivian O. Berger, *The Supreme Court and Defense Counsel: Old Roads, New Paths—A Dead End?,* 86 Colum.L.Rev. 9, 49–55 (1986).

[Notwithstanding the restraining order and the indictment, Reckmeyer transferred $25,000 to petitioner, a law firm, for pre-indictment legal services. Petitioner placed the sum in an escrow account and continued to represent Reckmeyer after his indictment. Reckmeyer moved to modify the restraining order to permit him to use some of the restrained assets to pay petitioner's fees and to exempt such assets from post-conviction forfeiture. Before the court ruled on his motion, however, Reckmeyer entered a plea agreement with the government in which, inter alia, he agreed to forfeit all of the specified assets. The court then denied Reckmeyer's motion and, subsequently, entered an order forfeiting virtually all of his assets to the government.

[The § 853 forfeiture provision includes a "relation-back" provision, which extends the forfeiture to third party recipients of forfeitable property. An exemption is created for the third party who entered into a "bona fide transaction" with the defendant, but only if the third party was "at the time of [the transaction] reasonably without cause to believe the [defendant's assets] were subject to forfeiture." That exemption did not apply to the petitioner since the $25,000 was received after the issuance of an indictment that included the forfeiture request, and the further funds sought were for legal services rendered after the issuance of the indictment. The petitioner requested an adjudication of its interest in the forfeited property, arguing that assets used to pay an attorney were not included under the forfeiture provisions, and if they were, the forfeiture violated the federal constitution. In the companion case of *United States v. Monsanto*, 491 U.S. 617 (1989), the Court majority rejected the contention that the forfeiture provisions, as written, did not apply to funds used to retain an attorney. In enacting the forfeiture provisions, the majority noted, "Congress decided to give force to the old adage that 'crime does not pay' " and there was no indication in the "plain and unambiguous" language of the statute or its legislative history that "Congress intended to modify the nostrum to read 'crime does not pay' except for attorneys' fees." That ruling set the stage for considering petitioner's constitutional claim, which had a parallel in arguments raised against a similar forfeiture position in the Racketeer Influenced and Corrupt Organization Act (RICO).]

* * * Petitioner contends that the statute infringes on criminal defendants' Sixth Amendment right to counsel of choice, and upsets the "balance of power" between the government and the accused in a manner contrary to the Due Process Clause of the Fifth Amendment. We consider these contentions in turn.

Petitioner's first claim is that the forfeiture law makes impossible, or at least impermissibly burdens, a defendant's right "to select and be represented by one's preferred attorney." *Wheat v. United States* [p. 208]. [N]othing in § 853 prevents a defendant from hiring the attorney of his choice, or disqualifies any attorney from serving as a defendant's counsel. Thus, unlike *Wheat* [which sustained the disqualification of a defense attorney subject to a possible conflict of interest, over the defendant's objection], this case does not involve a situation where the Government has asked a court to prevent a defendant's chosen counsel from representing the accused. Instead, petitioner urges that a violation of the Sixth Amendment arises here because of the forfeiture, at the instance of the Government, of assets that defendants intend to use to pay their attorneys.

Even in this sense, of course, the burden the forfeiture law imposes on a criminal defendant is limited. The forfeiture statute does not prevent a defendant who has nonforfeitable assets from retaining any attorney of his choosing. Nor is it necessarily the case that a defendant who possesses nothing but assets the Government seeks to have forfeited will be prevented from retaining counsel of choice. Defendants like Reckmeyer may be able to find lawyers willing to represent them, hoping that their fees will be paid in the event of acquittal, or via some other means that a defendant might come by in the future. The burden placed on defendants by the forfeiture law is therefore a limited one.

Nonetheless, there will be cases where a defendant will be unable to retain the attorney of his choice, when that defendant would have been able to hire that lawyer if he had access to forfeitable assets, and if there was no risk that fees paid by the defendant to his counsel would later be recouped under § 853(c). It is in these cases, petitioner argues, that the Sixth Amendment puts limits on the forfeiture statute.

This submission is untenable. Whatever the full extent of the Sixth Amendment's protection of one's right to retain counsel of his choosing, that protection does not go beyond "the individual's right to spend his own money to obtain the advice and assistance [of] counsel." A defendant has no Sixth Amendment right to spend another person's money for services rendered by an attorney, even if those funds are the only way that that defendant will be able to retain the attorney of his choice. A robbery suspect, for example, has no Sixth Amendment right to use funds he has stolen from a bank to retain an attorney to defend him if he is apprehended. The money, though in his possession, is not rightfully his; the government does not violate the Sixth Amendment if it seizes the robbery proceeds, and refuses to permit the defendant to use them to pay for his defense. * * *

There is no constitutional principle that gives one person the right to give another's property to a third party, even where the person seeking to complete the exchange wishes to do so in order to exercise a constitutionally protected right. [If] defendants have a right to spend forfeitable assets on attorney's fees, why not on exercises of the right to speak, practice one's religion, or travel? The full exercise of these rights, too, depends in part on one's financial wherewithal; and forfeiture, or even the threat of forfeiture, may similarly prevent a defendant from enjoying these rights as fully as he might otherwise. Nonetheless, we are not about to recognize an antiforfeiture exception for the exercise of each such right; nor does one exist for the exercise of Sixth Amendment rights, either.

Petitioner's "balancing analysis" to the contrary rests substantially on the view that the Government has only a modest interest in forfeitable assets that may be used to retain an attorney. Petitioner takes the position that, in large part, once assets have been paid over from client to attorney, the principal ends of forfeiture have been achieved: dispossessing a drug dealer or racketeer of the proceeds of his wrongdoing. We think that this view misses the mark for three reasons. * * * First, the Government has a pecuniary interest in forfeiture that goes beyond merely separating a criminal from his ill-gotten gains; that legitimate interest extends to recovering *all* forfeitable assets, for such assets are deposited in a Fund that supports law-enforcement efforts in a variety of important and useful ways. * * * [Second,] the statute permits "rightful owners" of forfeited assets to make claims for forfeited assets before they are retained by the government. The Government's interest in winning undiminished forfeiture thus includes the objective of returning property, in full, to those wrongfully deprived or defrauded of it. * * * Finally, as we have recognized previously, a major purpose motivating congressional adoption and continued refinement of the RICO and CCE forfeiture provisions has been the desire to lessen the economic power of organized crime and drug enterprises. [The] Court of Appeals put it aptly: "The modern day Jean Valjean must be satisfied with appointed counsel. Yet the drug merchant claims that his possession of huge sums of money ... entitles him to something more. We reject this contention, and any notion of a constitutional right to use the proceeds of crime to finance an expensive defense."[7]

7. We also reject the contention [that] a type of "*per se*" ineffective assistance of counsel results—due to the particular complexity of RICO or drug-enterprise cases—when a defen-

It is our view that there is a strong governmental interest in obtaining full recovery of all forfeitable assets, an interest that overrides any Sixth Amendment interest in permitting criminals to use assets adjudged forfeitable to pay for their defense. * * * We therefore reject petitioner's claim of a Sixth Amendment right of criminal defendants to use assets that are the government's—assets adjudged forfeitable, as Reckmeyer's were—to pay attorneys' fees, merely because those assets are in their possession.[10]

Petitioner's second constitutional claim is that the forfeiture statute is invalid under the Due Process Clause of the Fifth Amendment because it permits the Government to upset the "balance of forces between the accused and his accuser." We are not sure that this contention adds anything to petitioner's Sixth Amendment claim, because, while "[t]he Constitution guarantees a fair trial through the Due Process Clauses [it] defines the basic elements of a fair trial largely through the several provisions of the Sixth Amendment." Even [if] the Fifth Amendment provides some added protection not encompassed in the Sixth Amendment's more specific provisions, we find petitioner's claim based on the Fifth Amendment unavailing.

Forfeiture provisions are powerful weapons in the war on crime; like any such weapons, their impact can be devastating when used unjustly. But due process claims alleging such abuses are cognizable only in specific cases of prosecutorial misconduct (and petitioner has made no such allegation here) or when directed to

dant is not permitted to use assets in his possession to retain counsel of choice, and instead must rely on appointed counsel. If such an argument were accepted, it would bar the trial of indigents charged with such offenses, because those persons would have to rely on appointed counsel—which this view considers *per se* ineffective.

If appointed counsel is ineffective in a particular case, a defendant has resort to the remedies discussed in *Strickland v. Washington* [p. 158]. But we cannot say that the Sixth Amendment's guarantee of effective assistance of counsel is a guarantee of a privately-retained counsel in every complex case, irrespective of a defendant's ability to pay.

10. Petitioner advances three additional reasons for invalidating the forfeiture statute, all of which concern possible ethical conflicts created for lawyers defending persons facing forfeiture of assets in their possession.

Petitioner first notes the statute's exemption from forfeiture of property transferred to a bona fide purchaser who was "reasonably without cause to believe that the property was subject to forfeiture." 21 U.S.C. § 853(n)(6)(B). This provision, it is said, might give an attorney an incentive not to investigate a defendant's case as fully as possible, so that the lawyer can invoke it to protect from forfeiture any fees he has received. Yet given the requirement that any assets which the Government wishes to have forfeited must be specified in the indictment, the only way a lawyer could be a beneficiary of § 853(n)(6)(B) would be to fail to read the indictment of his client. In this light, the prospect that a lawyer might find himself in conflict with his client, by seeking to take advantage of § 853(n)(6)(B), amounts to very little. * * *

The second possible conflict arises in plea bargaining: petitioner posits that a lawyer may advise a client to accept an agreement entailing a more harsh prison sentence but no forfeiture—even where contrary to the client's interests—in an effort to preserve the lawyer's fee. Following such a strategy, however, would surely constitute ineffective assistance of counsel. [In] any event, there is no claim that such conduct occurred here, nor could there be, as Reckmeyer's plea agreement included forfeiture of virtually every asset in his possession. * * *

Finally, petitioner argues that the forfeiture statute, in operation, will create a system akin to "contingency fees" for defense lawyers: only a defense lawyer who wins acquittal for his client will be able to collect his fees, and contingent fees in criminal cases are generally considered unethical. But there is no indication here that petitioner, or any other firm, has actually sought to charge a defendant on a contingency basis; rather the claim is that a law firm's prospect of collecting its fee may turn on the outcome at trial. This, however, may often be in the case in criminal defense work. Nor is it clear why permitting contingent fees in criminal cases—if that is what the forfeiture statute does—violates a criminal defendant's Sixth Amendment rights. The fact that a federal statutory scheme authorizing contingency fees—again, if that is what Congress has created in § 853 (a premise we doubt)—is at odds with model disciplinary rules or state disciplinary codes hardly renders the federal statute invalid.

a rule that is inherently unconstitutional. * * * Petitioner's claim—that the power available to prosecutors under the statute *could* be abused—proves too much, for many tools available to prosecutors can be misused in a way that violates the rights of innocent persons. [Cases] involving particular abuses can be dealt with individually by the lower courts, when (and if) any such cases arise. * * *

Justice BLACKMUN, with whom Justice BRENNAN, Justice MARSHALL, and Justice STEVENS join, dissenting.

[T]he majority pauses hardly long enough to acknowledge "the Sixth Amendment's protection of one's right to retain counsel of his choosing," let alone to explore its "full extent." Instead, it moves rapidly from the observation that "a defendant may not insist on representation by an attorney he cannot afford" to the conclusion that the Government is free to deem the defendant indigent by declaring his assets "tainted" by criminal activity the Government has yet to prove. That the majority implicitly finds the Sixth Amendment right to counsel of choice so insubstantial that it can be outweighed by a legal fiction demonstrates, still once again, its " 'apparent unawareness of the function of the independent lawyer as a guardian of our freedom.' "

[The] right to retain private counsel serves to foster the trust between attorney and client that is necessary for the attorney to be a truly effective advocate. Not only are decisions crucial to the defendant's liberty placed in counsel's hands, but the defendant's perception of the fairness of the process, and his willingness to acquiesce in its results, depend upon his confidence in his counsel's dedication, loyalty, and ability. When the Government insists upon the right to choose the defendant's counsel for him, that relationship of trust is undermined: counsel is too readily perceived as the Government's agent rather than his own.

[The] right to retain private counsel also serves to assure some modicum of equality between the Government and those it chooses to prosecute. * * * When the Government provides for appointed counsel, there is no guarantee that levels of compensation and staffing will be even average. Where cases are complex, trials long, and stakes high, that problem is exacerbated. [Over] the long haul, the result of lowered compensation levels will be that talented attorneys will "decline to enter criminal practice. [This] exodus of talented attorneys could devastate the criminal defense bar." Winick, *Forfeiture of Attorney's Fees under RICO and CCE and The Right to Counsel of Choice: The Constitutional Dilemma and How to Avoid It*, 43 U. Miami L.Rev. 765, 781 (1989). Without the defendant's right to retain private counsel, the Government too readily could defeat its adversaries simply by outspending them.[12]

The right to privately chosen and compensated counsel also serves broader institutional interest. The "virtual socialization of criminal defense work in this country" that would be the result of a widespread abandonment of the right to retain chosen counsel, too readily would standardize the provision of criminal-defense services and diminish defense counsel's independence. There is a place in our system of criminal justice for the maverick and the risk-taker, for approaches that might not fit into the structured environment of a public defender's office, or that might displease a judge whose preference for nonconfrontational styles of advocacy might influence the judge's appointment decisions. [There] is also a place for the employment of "specialized defense counsel" for technical and complex cases. * * * The choice of counsel is the primary means for the defendant to

12. That the Government has this power when the defendant is indigent is unfortunate, but "[i]t is an irrelevancy once recognized."

establish the kind of defense he will put forward. Only a healthy, independent defense bar can be expected to meet the demands of the varied circumstances faced by criminal defendants, and assure that the interests of the individual defendant are not unduly "subordinat[ed] [to] the needs of the system."

[Had] it been Congress' express aim to undermine the adversary system as we know it, it could hardly have found a better engine of destruction than attorney's-fee forfeiture. The main effect of forfeitures under the Act, of course, will be to deny the defendant the right to retain counsel, and therefore the right to have his defense designed and presented by an attorney he has chosen and trusts. If the Government restrains the defendant's assets before trial, private counsel will be unwilling to continue or to take on the defense. Even if no restraining order is entered, the possibility of forfeiture after conviction will itself substantially diminish the likelihood that private counsel will agree to take the case. The "message [to private counsel] is 'Do not represent this defendant or you will lose your fee.' * * * "

Even if the defendant finds a private attorney who is "so foolish, ignorant, beholden or idealistic as to take the business," the attorney-client relationship will be undermined by the forfeiture statute. Perhaps the attorney will be willing to violate ethical norms by working on a contingent fee basis in a criminal case. See [majority opinion at] n. 10. But if he is not—and we should question the integrity of any criminal-defense attorney who would violate the ethical norms of the profession by doing so—the attorney's own interests will dictate that he remain ignorant of the source of the assets from which he is paid. [The] less an attorney knows, the greater the likelihood that he can claim to have been an "innocent" third party. The attorney's interest in knowing nothing is directly adverse to his client's interest in full disclosure.[c] The result of the conflict may be a less vigorous investigation of the defendant's circumstances, leading in turn to a failure to recognize or pursue avenues of inquiry necessary to the defense. Other conflicts of interest are also likely to develop. The attorney who fears for his fee will be tempted to make the Government's waiver of fee-forfeiture the *sine qua non* for any plea agreement, a position which conflicts with his client's best interests.

Perhaps most troubling is the fact that forfeiture statutes place the Government in the position to exercise an intolerable degree of power over any private attorney who takes on the task of representing a defendant in a forfeiture case. [The] Government will be ever tempted to use the forfeiture weapon against a defense attorney who is particularly talented or aggressive on the client's behalf—the attorney who is better than what, in the Government's view, the defendant deserves. The spectre of the Government's selectively excluding only the most talented defense counsel is a serious threat to the equality of forces necessary for the adversarial system to perform at its best.

[The] long-term effects of the fee-forfeiture practice will be to decimate the private criminal-defense bar. As the use of the forfeiture mechanism expands to new categories of federal crimes and spreads to the States, only one class of defendants will be free routinely to retain private counsel: the affluent defendant accused of a crime that generates no economic gain. As the number of private clients diminishes, only the most idealistic and the least skilled of young lawyers

c. Although the statutory exemption from forfeiture for bona fide transactions does not extend to a third party who "was reasonably with cause to believe" the received assets were forfeitable (21 U.S.C.A. 853), the Department of Justice Guidelines on Forfeiture (U.S.A.M. § 9–111,000 et seq.) direct federal prosecutors to seek forfeiture of assets transferred to a defense counsel only if there are "reasonable grounds to believe the attorney had *actual knowledge* that the asset was subject to challenge at the time of the transfer." (emphasis added)

will be attracted to the field, while the remainder seek greener pastures elsewhere. See Winick, supra, at 781–782.

In short, attorney's-fee forfeiture substantially undermines every interest served by the Sixth Amendment right to chosen counsel, on the individual and institutional levels, over the short term and the long haul. * * *

Notes and Questions

1. *Caplin* produced a diverse reaction from commentators. For some, it reflected the Court's refusal to place the forfeiture provision in context and recognize forfeiture's role as one of several tools being used by federal prosecutors to "discourage zealous representation" by some of their most capable opponents (the "high-priced private defense attorneys specializing in drug and white collar offenses"). See William J. Genego, *The New Adversary*, 54 Brook L.Rev. 781 (1988) (noting the need for courts to consider the combined systemic impact of such measures as forfeitures, motions to disqualify, grand jury subpoenas requiring attorney testimony, and application of IRS reporting requirements to require attorneys to report to cash payments from clients exceeding $10,000). Another commentator viewed *Caplin* as resting on the special context of legal representation for CCE and RICO offenses, one in which attorneys tend to perform as "house counsel" for an entity client involved in an ongoing revenue-generating enterprise and thereby enhance its continued operation by ensuring participants that they will have legal help available to "avoid investigation, prosecution, conviction or imprisonment." See Pamela S. Karlan, *Discrete and Relational Criminal Representation: The Changing Vision of the Right to Counsel*, 105 Harv.L.Rev. 670 (1992). Still other commentators viewed *Caplin* as reflecting the lesser status of the defendant's right to counsel of choice, evidenced in the Court's willingness to override the right in order to preserve the "mere possibility" that the funds involved may belong to the government. See Note, 103 Harv.L.Rev. 137, 146 (1989) (defendants without other assets will be unable to obtain representation by private counsel, particularly where assets are restrained before trial, even though, in the end, it may be decided that the assets were not subject to forfeiture).

2. In light of *Caplin*, should a trial court's interest in keeping to its schedule also prevail over the defendant's interest in being represented by counsel of choice? In particular, may a trial court refuse automatically to grant a continuance that is needed to discharge one defense counsel and substitute another, absent a good cause grounding (see Note 3, p. 140) for discharging counsel? Appellate decisions agree that trial courts cannot give scheduling concerns such per se priority, but must engage in a case-by-case balancing of interests. The leading Supreme Court ruling on the subject noted: "The matter of a continuance is traditionally within the trial court's discretion. * * * There are no mechanical tests for deciding when a denial of a continuance is so arbitrary as to violate [defendant's constitutional right to retain counsel of choice]. The answer must be found in the circumstances present in every case, particularly the reasons presented to the trial judge at the time the request is denied." *Ungar v. Sarafite*, 376 U.S. 575 (1964).

As noted in CRIMPROC. § 11.4(c), although appellate courts frequently note that they "will give considerable leeway to the trial court in its determination not to grant a continuance, a substantial body of cases have found abuses of discretion resulting in a denial of defendant's constitutional rights." Among the factors considered are whether the request came at a point sufficiently in advance of trial to permit the trial court to readily adjust its calendar, whether the continuance would carry the trial beyond the period specified in the speedy trial act, whether the continuance would inconvenience witnesses, and whether the defendant had some legitimate cause for dissatisfaction with counsel, even though it fell short of "good cause" for replacement. Ibid.

3. As to a court denying the defendant representation by defendant's retained counsel-of-choice because counsel is not a member of the local bar, consider *Leis v. Flynt*, 439 U.S. 438 (1979). Responding to the challenge of an out-of-state attorney excluded from appearing *pro hoc vice*, the Court majority (in a per curiam opinion) concluded that the attorney's claim did not rest on an interest protected by due process. The majority acknowledged that "the practice of courts in most states is to allow an out-of-state lawyer the privilege of appearing upon motion, especially when [as here] he is associated with a member of the local bar," but concluded that this "is not a right granted either by statute or the Constitution. Since the founding of the Republic, the licensing and regulation of lawyers has been left exclusively to the States * * *." The Court noted that it was not ruling on whether the constitutional rights of the defendant might be violated since that claim was not before it.

SECTION 3. THE CONSTITUTIONAL DIVISION OF AUTHORITY OVER DEFENSE DECISIONS

1. ***Self-representation vs. attorney control.*** Prior to *Faretta*, a long line of lower court decisions cases had held that a defense counsel had the authority to make various defense decisions on her or his own initiative. Those decisions, commonly characterized as relating to matters of "strategy" or "tactics," were said to be within the "exclusive province" of the lawyer. Counsel had no obligation to consult with the defendant, and if she did consult, had no obligation to follow the defendant's wishes. Other defense decisions, however, were said to rest in the ultimate authority of the defendant. As to those decisions, commonly said to require the "personal choice" of the defendant, counsel had to advise the client and abide by the client's directions.

The *Faretta* majority took note of these decisions in referring to the "law and tradition" that granted counsel the ultimate authority to make "binding decisions of trial strategy in many areas" (see p. 120). Indeed, the Court cited that law and tradition as a factor supporting the recognition of a right of self-representation, which allowed the defendant to exercise control over these decisions. The argument was advanced, however, that the overall perspective of the *Faretta* opinion required that the attorney's authority over tactical decisions be limited to "on the spot" decisions, where timing considerations precluded full consultation with the defendant. Apart from that administrative justification, it was argued, *Faretta's* recognition of the "personal character" of the defendant's "right to make a defense," as the person "who suffers the consequence if the defense fails," carries with it the ultimate authority over the various decisions which shape that defense.

2. In JONES v. BARNES, 463 U.S. 745 (1983), a divided Supreme Court rejected this view of *Faretta*. The *Jones* majority (per BURGER, C.J.) held that appellate counsel did not have to present a nonfrivolous claim that her client wished to press if counsel believed that the better strategy was to limit her argument and brief to other issues. Counsel was free to follow the time tested advice of countless advocates that inclusion of "every colorable claim" will "dilute and weaken a good case and will not save a bad one." It was for counsel to decide which claims were strong enough to be presented consistent with this strategy. The Court briefly took note of *Faretta*, noting that "the accused has ultimate authority to make certain fundamental decisions * * * [such] as whether to plead guilty, waive a jury, testify on his or her own behalf, or to take an appeal," and beyond that, under *Faretta*, the accused could gain control by "electing to act as his or her own advocate." But neither *Faretta* nor decisions defining the obligation of appointed appellate counsel had altered counsel's right to act upon her best professional judgment as to matters of strategy.

In dissent, JUSTICE BRENNAN, joined by Justice Marshall took a different view of *Faretta*:

"The right to counsel as *Faretta* and *Anders* [p. 109] conceive it is not an all-or-nothing right, under which a defendant must choose between forgoing the assistance of counsel altogether or relinquishing control over every aspect of his case beyond its most basic structure (*i.e.*, how to plead, whether to present a defense, whether to appeal). A defendant's interest in his case clearly extends to other matters. Absent exceptional circumstances, he is bound [in later proceedings] by the tactics used by his counsel at trial and on appeal. He may want to press the argument that he is innocent, even if other stratagems are more likely to result in the dismissal of charges or in a reduction of punishment. He may want to insist on certain arguments for political reasons. He may want to protect third parties. This is just as true on appeal as at trial, and the proper role of counsel is to *assist* him in these efforts, insofar as that is possible consistent with the lawyer's conscience, the law, and his duties to the court. * * * I cannot accept the notion that lawyers are one of the punishments a person receives merely for being accused of a crime. Clients, it they wish, are capable of making informed judgments about which issues to appeal, and when they exercise that prerogative their choices should be respected unless they would require lawyers to violate their consciences, the law, or their duties to the court."

3. *Identifying "strategic" and "personal" decisions.* In a series of decisions, both before and after *Jones*, "[t]he Supreme Court has stated, in dictum or holding, that it is for the defendant to decide whether to take each of the following steps: plead guilty or take action tantamount to entering a guilty plea; waive the right to jury trial; waive his right to be present at trial; testify on his own behalf; or forgo an appeal. * * * On the other side, the Supreme Court has indicated, in dictum or holding, that counsel has the ultimate authority in deciding whether or not to advance the following defense rights: barring prosecution use of unconstitutionally obtained evidence; obtaining dismissal of an indictment on the ground of racial discrimination in the selection of the grand jury; wearing civilian clothes, rather than prison garb, during the trial; striking an improper jury instruction; including a particular nonfrivolous claim among the issues briefed and argued on appeal; foregoing cross-examination; calling possible witness (other than defendant) to testify; providing discovery to the prosecution (even where the failure to do so risks possible sanctions of exclusion); and being tried within the 180 day time period specified in the Interstate Agreement on Detainers." CRIMPROC § 11.6(a)[a]

4. *Explaining the distinction.* The Supreme Court's explanations of why particular decisions are for counsel or client have been brief and conclusory. Decisions within the client's control are simply described as involving "fundamental rights," while those within the lawyer's control are said to involve matters

a. Where the ultimate decisionmaking authority rests with counsel and the defendant disagrees with counsel's decision, the defendant may, of course, seek to replace counsel with an attorney who favors the strategy that defendant prefers. However, the disagreement between defendant and counsel over such strategy does not constitute the "good cause" that would mandate the replacement of appointed counsel, or require a continuance for substitution of new retained counsel. See Note 3, p. 140. Of course, if counsel is retained and the defendant's requests for replacement does not cause a significant disruption in the trial schedule, the defendant's Sixth Amendment right to counsel of choice may require that defendant be allowed to replace current counsel. See Note 2, p. 146.

requiring the "superior ability of trained counsel" in assessing "strategy." Commentators have found such explanations lacking in substance. See e.g., CRIMPROC. § 11.6(b): "While the rights subject to defendant's 'personal choice' clearly are "fundamental," the Court has not explained why various rights subject to counsel's authority are not equally fundamental. Arguably, the decision to plead guilty has a special quality because it involves the relinquishment of so many basic rights. But it is more difficult to distinguish the right to be tried before a jury, for example, from the right to present a particular witness or to cross-examine an opposing witness. If the fundamental nature of a right is measured by its importance, its historic tradition, or its current status in constitutional or state law, those rights would appear to be on the same plane. * * * The Court's emphasis upon the strategic element in those decisions subject to counsel's control also fails to distinguish the different types of decisions. Certainly the decisions to waive a jury or not have the defendant testify also involve substantial strategic considerations. It may be argued that the elements of strategy involved in such decisions are more readily understood by the layman because they do not as frequently rest on technical concerns as many of the tactical decisions made by counsel. But they are hardly distinguishable in this regard from still other decisions made by counsel. For example, counsel's decision not to have a particular witness testify often rests on considerations of the same kind that would lead counsel, if he had such control, to keep the defendant from testifying. Similarly, much the same type of judgment is involved in deciding that a jury should be waived because the trial judge is likely to be the more sympathetic factfinder [a decision for defendant], as in deciding that an unconstitutionally composed jury should not be challenged because discriminatory jury selection has produced a more sympathetic group of jurors [counsel's decision]. In sum, just as the fundamental rights characterization could be applied to many of the rights subject to counsel's control, so could the characterization of a decision as strategic and requiring counsel's expertise be applied to certain basic determinations subject to defendant's control."

5. ***The Nixon ruling.*** Does the Court provide a better analytical framework for distinguishing between decisions within counsel's control and decisions with defendant's control in its latest decision in that issue FLORIDA v. NIXON, ___ U.S ___, 125 S.Ct. 551 (2004). In *Nixon*, defense counsel Corin was faced with the inevitability of going to trial on a capital charge (the prosecutor refused to recommend a lesser sentence, even on a guilty plea) with the state's evidence of guilt (which included defendant's confession) "not 'subject to any reasonable dispute'." Experienced in capital defense, Corin feared that "denying [defendant] Nixon's commission * * * [of the crime] during the guilty phase would compromise Corin's ability to persuade the jury, during the penalty phase, that Nixon's conduct was the product of his mental illness." Corin therefore adopted a strategy of "conceding guilt during the guilty phase, thereby preserving his credibility in urging leniency during the penalty phase." Corin "attempted to explain this strategy to Nixon at least three times," but, although he had represented Nixon previously and "the two had a good relationship in Corin's estimation," Nixon was "generally unresponsive during their discussions," and "never verbally approved or protested Corin's proposed strategy." At trial, Corin acknowledged Nixon's guilt in the opening statement, and urged the jury to focus on the penalty phase. Nixon was not present during the trial as his disruptive behavior during jury selection led to his "voluntary waiver" of his right to be present. During the guilt phase of the trial, Corin simply "cross-examined * * * witnesses only when he felt their statements needed clarification," and objected to the introduction of crime scene photographs as unduly prejudicial. After the jury found the defendant guilty, in the penalty phase, Corin presented a variety of evidence designed to establish that Nixon was "not normal organically, intellectually, emotionally or

educationally or in any other way," and advanced in his closing arguments a variety of reasons why the death penalty was inappropriate. That evidence and argument failed to convince the jury, as it sentenced Nixon to death.

The Florida Supreme Court subsequently reversed Nixon's conviction, holding that a defense attorney's concession that his client committed murder automatically constituted prejudicial ineffective assistance of counsel when that strategy was implemented without the "affirmative, explicit acceptance" of the defendant. A unanimous Supreme Court (per GINSBURG, J.) reversed. The Court reasoned:

"An attorney undoubtedly has a duty to consult with the client regarding 'important decisions,' including questions of overarching defense strategy. *Strickland v. Washington* [p. 160]. That obligation, however, does not require counsel to obtain the defendant's consent to 'every tactical decision.' *Taylor v. Illinois* [p. 1260] (an attorney has authority to manage most aspects of the defense without obtaining his client's approval). But certain decisions regarding the exercise or waiver of basic trial rights are of such moment that they cannot be made for the defendant by a surrogate. A defendant, this Court affirmed, has 'the ultimate authority' to determine 'whether to plead guilty, waive a jury, testify in his or her own behalf, or take an appeal.' *Jones v. Barnes* Note 2, [p. 147]. Concerning those decisions, an attorney must both consult with the defendant and obtain consent to the recommended course of action. * * *

"The Florida Supreme Court * * * required Nixon's 'affirmative, explicit acceptance' of Corin's strategy because it deemed Corin's statements to the jury 'the functional equivalent of a guilty plea.' We disagree with that assessment. * * * Despite Corin's concession, Nixon retained the rights accorded a defendant in a criminal trial. Cf. *Boykin v. Alabama* [Note 4, p. 1362] (a guilty plea is 'more than a confession which admits that the accused did various acts,' it is a 'stipulation that no proof by the prosecution need be advanced'). The State was obliged to present during the guilt phase competent, admissible evidence establishing the essential elements of the crimes with which Nixon was charged. That aggressive evidence would thus be separated from the penalty phase, enabling the defense to concentrate that portion of the trial on mitigating factors. Further, the defense reserved the right to cross-examine witnesses for the prosecution and could endeavor, as Corin did, to exclude prejudicial evidence. In addition, in the event of errors in the trial or jury instructions, a concession of guilt would not hinder the defendant's right to appeal.

"Nixon nevertheless urges, relying on *Brookhart v. Janis*, 384 U.S. 1 (1967), that this Court has already extended the requirement of 'affirmative, explicit acceptance' to proceedings 'surrender[ing] the right to contest the prosecution's factual case on the issue of guilty or innocence.' Defense counsel in *Brookhart* had agreed to a 'prima facie' bench trial at which the State would be relieved of its obligation to put on 'complete proof' of guilt or persuade a jury of the defendant's guilt beyond a reasonable doubt. In contrast to *Brookhart*, there was in Nixon's case no 'truncated' proceeding, shorn of the need to persuade the trier 'beyond a reasonable doubt,' and of the defendant's right to confront and cross-examine witnesses. While the 'prima facie' trial in *Brookhart* was fairly characterized as 'the equivalent of a guilty plea,' the full presentation to the jury in Nixon's case does not resemble that severely abbreviated proceeding. *Brookhart,* in short, does not carry the weight Nixon would place on it.

"Corin was obliged to, and in fact several times did, explain his proposed trial strategy to Nixon. Given Nixon's constant resistance to answering inquiries put to him by counsel and court, Corin was not additionally required to gain express consent before conceding Nixon's guilt. The two evidentiary hearings conducted by the Florida trial court demonstrate beyond doubt that Corin fulfilled his duty of consultation by informing Nixon of counsel's proposed strategy and its potential benefits. Nixon's characteristic silence each time information was conveyed to him, in sum, did not suffice to render unreasonable Corin's decision to concede guilt and to home in, instead, on the life or death penalty issue.

"The Florida Supreme Court's erroneous equation of Corin's concession strategy to a guilty plea led it to apply the wrong standard in determining whether counsel's performance ranked as ineffective assistance. * * * [T]he correct standard is the *Strickland* standard [p. 160], [and] * * * if counsel's strategy, given the evidence bearing on the defendant's guilt, satisfies the *Strickland* [performance] standard [of a "reasonably competent attorney], that is the end of the matter; no tenable claim of ineffective assistance would remain."

6. If Nixon had objected to Corin's authority, could Corin have insisted on pursuing that strategy as a decision within the control of the counsel? Does *Nixon* create a category of decisionmaking on which the defense counsel must consult, but need not abide by the defendant's decision? The Third Circuit has noted that consultation serves four important functions even where ultimate authority rests with the counsel. Consultation, the court noted, will: (1) ensure that counsel receives any factual information relevant to the issue that the defendant might have; (2) give the defendant the opportunity (depending on timing) to consider the possibility of seeking substitute counsel (see fn. a, p. 148) or proceeding *pro se*; (3) "promote and maintain a cooperative client-counsel relationship"; and (4) give to the attorney the opportunity to shape his or her decision in light of the client's views and desires concerning the best course to be followed.[b] *Government of Virgin Islands v. Weatherwax*, 77 F.3d 1425 (3d Cir.1996).

7. Prior to *Nixon*, lower courts had divided as to whether the defendant's consent was needed to pursue a partial defense (i.e., a defense that challenges only the higher level of multiple charges) or to adopt on "all or nothing approach" by waiving the right to a jury instruction on included offenses. The courts had generally agreed, however, that the defendant's decision controlled where a defendant held competent to standard trial refused to enter an insanity plea. See CRIMPROC § 11.6(a). What, if anything, does *Nixon* suggest as to the treatment of these issues?

8. ***Failing to consult and per se prejudice.*** Where the choice is within defendant's control, and counsel failed to even consult, does that establish per se ineffective assistance of counsel? That situation was presented in ROE v. FLORES–ORTEGA, 528 U.S. 470 (2000), where counsel had failed to consult with

b. See CRIMPROC § 11.6(a): "[W]here the client's preference is not based on a misunderstanding of law or an inability to understand why the lawyer favors an alternative tactic, and that alternative does not require the lawyer to forsake 'meaningful adversary testing' of the prosecution's case, *United States v. Cronic* [p. 184], a lawyer may find justification for following [the client's] preference in the client's position as the person who 'will bear the personal consequences of the conviction.' The North Carolina Supreme Court, looking to the principal-agent nature of the attorney-client relationship' has gone so far as to hold as a matter of state law that where lawyer and client are at an impasse on the exercise of a peremptory challenge, the client's wishes must control, notwithstanding the 'tactical' nature of that decision. *State v. Ali*, 407 S.E.2d 183 (1991)."

Various commentators have argued for client control over decisions that current constitutional precedent allows counsel to control. See Rodney J. Uphoff, *Who Should Control the Decision to Call a Certain Witness: Respecting a Criminal Defendant's Tactical Choices*, 68 U.Cin.L.Rev. 763 (2000) (very often, respect for the client's decisionmaking required "that the client be afforded the right to be foolish or wrong"); H. Richard Uviller, *Calling the Shots; The Allocation of Choice Between the Accused and Counsel in Defense of a Criminal Case*, 52 Rutgers L.Rev. 719 (2000) (defendant should have the final say as to the theory of defense–not only whether or not to plead guilty by reason of insanity, but also which (if any) of the various affirmative defenses or mitigating factors to assert).

client as to the filing of an appeal and did not file an appeal. The Court majority, per O'CONNOR, J., concluded that these facts alone did not establish incompetency.

Justice O'Connor noted initially that since the appeal involved was a first appeal of right, defendant had a constitutional right to the effective assistance of counsel. The Court had previously held that counsel's failure to file such an appeal, when an appeal had been requested by the defendant, constituted per se ineffective assistance of counsel as it inherently met both prongs of the *Strickland* standard (see p. 160) for establishing ineffective assistance–incompetent performance and prejudicial impact.[c] Where there was a failure to consult, however, neither prong inherently existed as the failure did not necessarily deny the defendant a right that counsel reasonably could have assumed to be of interest to the defendant, and that defendant would have exercised.

Justice O'Connor concluded that, to establish *Strickland's* first prong of professional unreasonableness based upon a failure to consult, it must be shown either that (1) the circumstances of the case were such that a "rational defendant would [have] want[ed] to appeal," or (2) that "this particular defendant reasonably demonstrated to counsel that he was interested in appealing." Thus, a "highly relevant factor would be whether the conviction follows a trial or a guilty plea, both because a guilty plea reduces the scope of potentially appealable issues and because such a plea may indicate that the defendant seeks an end to judicial proceedings." Where a guilty plea was entered, the court therefore should look to surrounding circumstances, including "whether the defendant received the sentence bargained for" and whether the plea "expressly reserved or waived some or all appeal rights."

As for the *Strickland* element of a prejudicial impact, Justice O'Connor concluded that the failure-to-consult was not inherently prejudicial. For even if "all the information counsel knew or should have known" establishes that the rational defendant would want to appeal or that this defendant demonstrated an interest in an appeal, that does not invariably establish that the failure to consult "actually caus[ed] the forfeiture of the appeal." To meet the prejudice prerequisite, the defendant must "demonstrate that there is a reasonable probability that, but for counsel's deficient failure to consult with him about an appeal, he would have timely appealed." Justice O'Connor acknowledged that this inquiry "is not wholly dissimilar from the inquiry into whether counsel performed deficiently" by failing to consult. Thus, where the defendant shows nonfrivolous grounds for appeal, that will establish both that a "rational defendant would [have] want[ed] to appeal" and a "reasonable probability" defendant would have chosen to appeal after consultation. On the other hand, where the failure to consult constituted deficient performance because defendant had "sufficiently demonstrated to counsel his interest in an appeal," the defendant must also be able to establish that after consultation (which might suggest an appeal was fruitless), he would have continued that interest and instructed his counsel to file the appeal.[d]

c. Explaining these rulings, Justice O'Connor noted that the failure to comply with the client's instruction clearly was "professionally unreasonable"–the failure was not a "strategic decision," but simply "reflect[ed] inattention to the defendant's wishes" as to a decision on which the "accused has ultimate authority." As for prejudice, as the Court noted in *Cronic* Note 2 (p. 184), "the complete denial of counsel during a critical stage of a judicial proceeding mandates a presumption of prejudice * * *, [and] the even more serious denial of the entire judicial proceeding itself, which the defendant wanted at the time, and to which he had a right, similarly demands a presumption of prejudice."

d. Justice Breyer, who provided the sixth vote for the majority noted that the question presented to the Court concerned only the "filing of a notice of appeal following a guilty plea," and the opinion of the Court "in my view, makes clear that counsel 'almost always' has a constitutional duty to consult with a defendant about an appeal after a trial." Jus-

SECTION 4. THE RIGHT TO "EFFECTIVE" ASSISTANCE OF COUNSEL

A. Basic Features of the Right

1. ***Prerequisite of a constitutional right.*** The Supreme Court first recognized a constitutional right to the effective assistance of counsel in *Powell v. Alabama* [p. 182]. *Powell* noted that where due process requires the state to provide counsel for an indigent defendant, "that duty is not discharged by an assignment at such a time or under such circumstances as to preclude the giving of effective aid in the preparation and trial of the case." Ten years later, in *Glasser v. United States*, [Note 5, p. 193], the Court held in a federal case that the Sixth Amendment was violated by judicial action that denied defendant's "right to have the effective assistance of counsel." Following its recognition of an equal protection right to appointed counsel on a first appeal of right, the Court held that the defendant also had a constitutional right to the effective assistance of that appointed appellate counsel. *Jones v. Barnes* [Note 2 p. 147]. As the Court later explained; "The promise of *Douglas* [p. 99] that a criminal defendant has a right to counsel on appeal–like the promise of *Gideon* [p. 85] that a criminal defendant has a right to counsel at trial–would be a futile gesture unless it comprehended the right to the effective assistance of counsel." *Evitts v. Lucey*, 469 U.S. 387 (1985). In *Evitts*, after concluding that the constitutional right to counsel on a first appeal of right also had a due process grounding and therefore encompassed representation by retained counsel, the Court noted that defendant was entitled *a fortiori* to effective representation by that retained counsel. For "a party whose counsel is unable to provide effective representation is in no better position that one who has no counsel at all."

2. All of the above cases involved proceedings at which an indigent defendant would be entitled to the appointment of counsel. Commentators have noted that even in proceedings as to which there is not a right to appointed counsel, due process may nonetheless recognize a constitutionally protected interest in being represented by retained counsel—recognizing the individual's interest in "defending himself in whatever manner he deems best, using every legitimate to resource at his command," *People v. Crovedi*, 417 P.2d 868 (Cal.1966)—absent some overriding state interest in precluding all counsel. See CRIMPROC § 11.1(b). Should defendant have a constitutional right to the effective assistance of such retained counsel?

WAINWRIGHT v. TORNA, 455 U.S. 586 (1982), flatly rejected an effective assistance right in one such situation. There, respondent Torna's felony convictions had been affirmed by an intermediate state appellate court. His subsequent application for a writ of certiorari was dismissed by the state supreme court because it had not been filed timely. Respondent contended that he had been denied the effective assistance of counsel by the failure of his retained counsel to file that application in time. Summarily reversing a federal habeas ruling that had sustained respondent's contention, the Court majority (per curiam) held that

tice Ginsburg, dissenting in part, also described the majority ruling as quite narrow. She described the issue before the Court as "whether, after a defendant pleads guilty or is convicted, the Sixth Amendment permits the defense counsel to simply walk away, leaving defendant uncounseled about his appeal rights," and she characterized the majority's answer as "effectively respond[ing]: hardly ever." Justice Souter, in dissent, similarly described the issue, but characterized the majority's answer as being "sometimes," while "mine is 'almost always' in cases in which a plea of guilty has not obviously waived any claims of error."

respondent had no constitutional right to retain counsel's effective assistance. It noted: "*Ross v. Moffitt* [p. 100] held that a criminal defendant does not have a constitutional right to counsel to pursue discretionary state appeals or applications for review in this Court. [Since] respondent had no constitutional right to counsel, he could not be deprived of the effective assistance of counsel by his retained counsel's failure to file the application timely."[a]

Torna's reference to the absence of a "constitutional right to counsel" centered on a right that would encompass the appointment of counsel for the indigent. It is not read as suggesting that the state constitutionally could have precluded Torna's use of retained counsel in filing an application for review, but simply as holding that he must "bear the consequences of his unwise choice of counsel." CRIMPROC § 11.7a.

3. Would the result in *Torna* have been different if the counsel there had been chosen and provided by the state? *Pennsylvania v. Finley*, 481 U.S. 551 (1987), arguably indicates that factor would be irrelevant. *Finley* involved counsel appointed to represent an indigent prisoner in challenging her conviction through a state postconviction procedure. The appointed counsel advised the habeas court that the prisoner's claim was totally without merit, which resulted in the court-approved withdrawal of counsel and the dismissal of the petition for postconviction relief. Counsel's action had been inconsistent with the withdrawal safeguards prescribed in *Anders v. California* [p. 109] to ensure that appellate counsel appointed pursuant to the constitutional mandate of *Douglas v. California* effectively represent their clients. *Finley* held, however, that the *Anders* safeguards were not constitutionally required in a postconviction proceeding because the state had no constitutional obligation to appoint counsel in such a proceeding. The *Finley* opinion contained language that arguably limited the Court's ruling (the Court noting that the *Anders* safeguards were "prophylactic" and that the procedures followed by counsel had "fully comported with 'fundamental fairness"). However, a later case, *Coleman v. Thompson*, 501 U.S. 722 (1991), recognized no such limitation in its analysis of *Finley*, and concluded that *Finley* rejects ineffective-assistance claims as a general matter for all proceedings in which there is no constitutional obligation to provide appointed counsel.

4. *Retained v. appointed counsel.* Prior to CUYLER v. SULLIVAN, 446 U.S. 335 (1980), many lower courts utilized different standards in reviewing ineffective assistance claims as to trial counsel, distinguishing between privately retained and appointed counsel. The distinction was based on the state-action requirement of the Fourteenth Amendment. A constitutional violation, it was argued, required state participation at a sufficient level to render the state responsible for counsel's inadequacies. That responsibility was seen as arising automatically from the trial court's selection of appointed counsel. As for retained counsel, the state bore responsibility for counsel's inadequacies only where they were so obvious that they should have been apparent to the trial court.

Cuyler put an end to drawing such a distinction. At issue there was alleged ineffectiveness due to retained attorneys having failed to take certain actions because of the potential harm to codefendants also represented by the attorneys. The state argued that the attorneys had not been ineffective, but in any event, "the alleged failings of * * * retained counsel cannot provide a basis for a [constitutional violation] because the conduct of retained counsel does not involve state action." Rejecting that contention, the Court (per POWELL, J.) noted:

a. Dissenting Justice Marshall "would hold that when [as here] a defendant can show that he reasonably relied on his attorney's promise to seek discretionary review, due process requires the State to consider his application, even when the application is untimely. To deny the right to seek discretionary review simply because of counsel's error is fundamentally unfair." Brennan, J., would set the case for oral argument.

"A proper respect for the Sixth Amendment disarms [the prosecution's] contention that defendants who retain their own lawyers are entitled to less protection than defendants for whom the State appoints counsel. * * * The vital guarantee of the Sixth Amendment would stand for little if the often uninformed decision to retain a particular lawyer could reduce or forfeit the defendant's entitlement to constitutional protection. Since the State's conduct of a criminal trial itself implicates the State in the defendant's conviction, we see no basis for drawing a distinction between retained and appointed counsel that would deny equal justice to defendants who must choose their own lawyers."

5. Does the analysis of *Cuyler v. Sullivan* open the door for establishment of a constitutional violation in at least some instances in which counsel was ineffective, but there is no constitutional right to effective assistance under *Torna* and *Finley* (Notes 2 and 3 supra)? Consider the analysis of CRIMPROC § 11.7(a): "Both *Torna* and *Finley* involved a proceeding that the state had no constitutional obligation to provide. Where the state has a constitutional obligation to provide a particular process, but that obligation does not include a duty to appoint counsel, the ineffective performance of counsel, whether retained or appointed, might be successfully challenged by reference to the adequacy of that process. Such a possibility would be presented, for example, by the ineffective assistance of retained counsel at a misdemeanor trial which resulted in the imposition only of a fine [and thus was a proceeding in which defendant was not constitutionally entitled to appointed counsel, see *Scott v. Illinois*, p. 90]. The defendant could argue here that ineffectiveness of counsel resulted in a proceeding in which defendant was so deprived of his ability to make use of the procedural rights constitutionally guaranteed to him in such a trial that the proceeding itself did not comport with due process. The state cannot be relieved of the responsibility to provide such a hearing by the fact that the counsel who contributed to the denial of the constitutional right was either retained by the defendant or provided without constitutional command by the state."

6. ***Raising an ineffectiveness claim.*** Two major obstacles restrict raising an ineffective assistance claim on direct appeal from a conviction: (1) very often, the attorney on appeal is the trial counsel (see Note 4, p. 111), and attorneys not only are unlikely to look to their own ineptitude in developing grounds for appeal, but they commonly are viewed as placing themselves in a conflict situation (requiring a withdrawal from representation) if they challenge their own performance; and (2) the record on appeal is limited to the actions taken in recorded proceedings, thus excluding from consideration various other circumstances that may be relevant in presenting an ineffective assistance claim. Because of these obstacles, almost all jurisdictions prefer that ineffective assistance claims be presented on collateral attack (where the opportunity is available to present evidence beyond the trial record and the defendant can raise the claim pro se or with a different attorney).[b] Some jurisdictions, have concluded that few ineffective assistance claims will not present either or both of the above obstacles, and there

b. *Pennsylvania v. Finley* (Note 3, p. 154) and *Murray v. Giarratano* 492 U.S. 1 (1989), both state that the indigent defendant has no constitutional right to assistance of counsel on collateral review. See Note 4(a), p. 1631. However, *Coleman v. Thompson*, 501 U.S. 722 (1991), left open the question of whether a constitutional right to counsel exists for the limited purpose of raising on collateral attack a claim of ineffective-assistant that state law prohibited from being raised on direct appeal.

In most jurisdictions, if an indigent defendant sets forth a cognizable claim on a petition for collateral relief, counsel will be appointed (and as to capital defendants, many jursidictions make an automatic appointment). See CRIMPROC § 28.11 and Note 4(b), p. 1632. In contrast to counsel appointed to represent the defendant on appeal (where the practice in many jurisdictions is to utilize the trial counsel or the same public defender office), counsel appointed for collateral attack tends to be different counsel (in part, because of the frequency of ineffective-assistance claims).

is greater benefit in ensuring that all aspects of potentially ineffective assistance are considered together than in allowing the exceptions to be raised on direct appeal. They accordingly have adopted the rule that all ineffective claims may be raised only on collateral attack. Others jurisdictions will allow such claims to be raised on appeal where the grounding for the claim appears on the trial court record. They warn the defendant, however, that the limited record impacts review of the claim. As noted in *United States v. Taglia*, 922 F.2d 413 (7th Cir.1991): "When the only record on which a claim of ineffective assistance is based is the trial record, every indulgence will be given to the possibility that a seeming lapse or error by defense counsel was in fact a tactical move flawed only in hindsight." Thus, the defendant must establish that there could be no explanation for counsel's performance other than counsel's ineptitude, and if the defendant fails to do that on the trial record, there will be no possibility of expanding the record on collateral attack, as rejection of a claim on appeal ordinarily precludes reconsideration on collateral attack.

When an ineffective assistance claim is presented on collateral attack, an evidentiary hearing permits the defendant to establish what occurred in counsel's pretrial preparation, what communications occurred between defendant and counsel, and what might have occurred if counsel had taken other actions (e.g., what further investigation would have revealed). In this connection, the defendant (or the prosecution) may require the trial counsel to testify. Moreover, that testimony may reveal conversations between the client and the lawyer, as the challenge to counsel's performance constitutes an implicit waiver of the lawyer-client privilege. See *Bittaker v. Woodford*, 331 F.3d 715 (9th Cir.2003) (viewing that waiver as limited to the adjudication of the ineffectiveness claim, so testimony as to such communications cannot be used in any subsequent proceedings): *Commonwealth v. Chmiel*, 738 A.2d 406 (1999) (viewing waiver as not so limited).

7. ***Federal habeas review of state claims.*** Although the Supreme Court occasionally considers a state defendant's ineffective assistance claim on a direct appeal from the conviction (the defendant having raised the issue on direct appeal within the state system and the Supreme Court then having granted certiorari), ineffective assistance claims usually are considered on review of a federal habeas corpus challenge to the defendant's state conviction. Prior to 1966, where a state court rejected an ineffective assistance claim and defendant subsequently presented that claim in a federal habeas challenge, federal courts treated the issue as involving a mixed question of law and fact and therefore subject to de novo review. See e.g., *Cuyler v. Sullivan*, Note 4, p. 154 . In 1996, Congress adopted the Antiterrorism and Effective Death Penalty Act, which changed the standard of review. See Ch. 29, § 4; CRIMPROC § 28.6. Under the AEDPA, where the state court applied (and properly interpreted) the correct legal standard for assessing an ineffective assistance claim (typically the *Strickland* standard discussed infra), the issue before the federal habeas court is not whether the state court's application of the standard was "correct," but whether the state court applied that standard in an "objectively unreasonable manner" to the facts of the case. See *Williams (Terry) v. Taylor*, 529 U.S. 362 (2000) (p. 1662). Thus, the habeas petitioner "must do more than show he would have satisfied *Strickland's* test if his claim were being analyzed in the first instance." *Bell v. Cone*, Note 3, p. 185. As to what is "objectively unreasonable," the Court has noted simply that (1) the term "unreasonable * * * is a common term in the legal world and, accordingly, federal judges are familiar with its meaning," and (2) since the test is "objective", an application is not reasonable simply because "one of the Nation's jurists has applied the relevant federal law in the same manner as the state court did." *Williams (Terry) v. Taylor*, supra.

8. ***The prevailing standard for judging ineffective assistance.*** Prior to the Court's decision in *Strickland*, infra, many state courts applied the "mockery of justice standard" to determine ineffectiveness. Under this test, a conviction was reversed only when counsel's performance was so poor as to "reduce the trial to a farce' or render it a mockery of justice." Judge David Bazelon of the D.C. Circuit, among others, was highly critical of this test, which he described as requiring "such a minimum level of performance from counsel" as to constitute a "mockery of the Sixth Amendment." David Bazelon, *The Defective Assistance of Counsel*, 42 U.Cin.L.Rev. 1, 28 (1973). The test failed to reach what he characterized as a massive problem of incompetency. Indeed, he noted, "I have often been told that if my court were to reverse every case in which there was inadequate counsel, we would have to send back half of the convictions in my jurisdiction." In light of the Supreme Court's ruling in *McMann v. Richardson*, Note 1, p. 1372, various state courts and a majority of federal courts had switched to an incompetency standard which asked whether the defense counsel's representation fell below a "reasonable" or "normal" or "customary" level of competence. Critical of such standards as well, Judge Bazelon noted that they "beg the question of what is customary or reasonable for a lawyer to do prior to or at arraignment, plea bargaining, trial, or sentencing." Bazelon, *The Realities of Gideon and Argersinger,* 64 Geo.L.J. 811, 819 (1976).

Both in his judicial opinions and in his law review articles, Judge Bazelon championed what has been called the "checklist" or "categorical" approach to the ineffective counsel problem. He attempted to give substantive content to the Sixth Amendment's mandate by setting forth specific minimum requirements of competent performance—a categorization of minimum duties owed by counsel to client, derived from *A.B.A. Standards Relating to the Defense Function* (1971). Dissenting in *United States v. Decoster,* 624 F.2d 196, 275 (D.C.Cir.1976) (en banc), Judge Bazelon (joined by Wright, C.J.), observed: "The heart of [the 'categorical'] approach lies in defining ineffective assistance in terms of the *quality of counsel's performance,* rather than looking to the effect of counsel's actions on the outcome of the case. If the Sixth Amendment is to serve a central role in eliminating second-class justice for the poor, then it must proscribe second-class performances by counsel, whatever the consequences in a particular case. Moreover, by focusing on the quality of representation and providing incentives in all cases for counsel to meet or exceed minimum standards, this approach reduces the likelihood that any particular defendant will be prejudiced by counsel's shortcomings. In this way, courts can safeguard the defendant's rights to a constitutionally adequate trial without engaging in the inherently difficult task of speculating about the precise effect of each error or omission by an attorney."

Although the categorical approach gained numerous supporters in the academy, it was adopted by only a small number of courts. In large part, the courts adhered to the position adopted in the plurality opinion in *Decoster*. Judge Leventhal argued in that opinion that a determination of whether counsel's performance amounted to ineffective assistance "cannot be divorced from consideration of the peculiar facts and circumstances that influenced counsel's judgement." Accordingly what was need was a "judgmental approach"—one that looks to the totality of the circumstances. Judge Leventhal argued that a categorical approach had a pernicious tendency to "torture" the "adversary system out of shape"—as it promoted "inevitable and increasing intrusion into the development and presentation of the defense case by the trial judge and (out of self-protection) by the prosecution," and failed to give adequate consideration to the lack of actual prejudice ("the realistic thrust [of a categorical approach] is a rule structured toward a conclusion of prejudice from any deviation from the checklist of standards, * * * whatever the likely or actual consequence").

In *Strickland*, the Court of Appeals noted that it adhered to a judgmental approach, but it also set forth fairly specific guidelines for judging the particular deficiency alleged in that case–counsel's failure to conduct a full factual investigation. The opinions for the Court in *Strickland* and *United States v. Cronic* (fn. b, p. 159, and Note 2, p. 184, decided on the same day, responded not only to the rulings below, but to the basic issues relating to determining ineffective assistance that had divided the lower courts. See also Note 1, p. 183.

STRICKLAND v. WASHINGTON

466 U.S. 668, 104 S.Ct. 2052, 80 L.Ed.2d 674 (1984).

Justice O'CONNOR delivered the opinion of the Court. * * *

[During a ten-day period, respondent Washington planned and committed three groups of crimes, including three brutal capital murders, torture, kidnapping and attempted murders. Against counsel's advice, Washington pled guilty to all charges, including the three capital murder charges.

[In the plea colloquy, Washington told the Florida trial judge that, although he had committed a string of burglaries, he had no significant prior criminal record and that at the time of his criminal spree he was under extreme stress caused by his inability to support his family. He also stated, however, that he accepted responsibility for the crimes. The trial judge told Washington that he had "a great deal of respect for people who are willing to step forward and admit their responsibility" but that he was making no statement at all about his likely sentencing decision.

[Against counsel's advice, Washington waived his state right to an advisory jury at his capital sentencing hearing and chose to be sentenced by the trial judge without a jury recommendation. In preparing for the sentencing hearing, counsel spoke on the phone with respondent's wife and mother, but did not otherwise seek out character witnesses for respondent. Nor did counsel request a psychiatric examination. Counsel later explained in the habeas hearing that his conversations with his client gave no indication that Washington had psychological problems. Counsel also decided not to present and hence not to look further for evidence concerning Washington's character and emotional state. This decision reflected counsel's sense of hopelessness about overcoming the impact of respondent's confessions to the gruesome crimes and his judgment that it was advisable to rely on the plea colloquy for character evidence. This strategy, he noted, avoided two drawbacks of using other sources–the state cross-examining Washington and the state presenting psychiatric evidence of its own. Finally, counsel explained that he did not request a presentence report because it would have included respondent's criminal history and thereby undermine the claim of no significant prior criminal record.

[Counsel's strategy was based primarily on the trial judge's remarks at the plea colloquy as well as on his reputation as a sentencing judge who thought it important for a convicted defendant to "own up" to his crime. However, trial judge, as the Supreme Court read the record, "found numerous aggravating circumstances and no (or a single comparatively insignificant) mitigating circumstance." He therefore sentenced Washington to death on each of the three counts of murder. The state supreme court upheld the convictions and sentences on direct appeal.

[Washington eventually sought federal habeas corpus relief on the ground, inter alia, that counsel had rendered ineffective assistance at the sentencing proceeding in several respects, including his failure to request a psychiatric report, to seek out and present character witnesses, and to request a presentence report.

The district court concluded that, although trial counsel had made errors in judgment in failing to investigate nonstatutory mitigating evidence further than he did, no prejudice to respondent's sentence resulted from any such error. On rehearing en banc, Unit B of the former Fifth Circuit, now the Eleventh Circuit, developed its own framework for analyzing ineffective assistance claims and reversed and remanded the case for new factfinding under the newly announced standards.]

[T]he Court has recognized that "the right to counsel is the right to the effective assistance of counsel." *McMann v. Richardson*, 397 U.S. 759 (1970). Government violates the right to effective counsel when it interferes in certain ways with the ability of counsel to make independent decisions about how to conduct the defense. See, e.g., *Geders v. United States,* 425 U.S. 80 (1976) (bar on attorney-client consultation during overnight recess);[a] *Herring v. New York,* 422 U.S. 853 (1975) (bar on summation at bench trial); *Brooks v. Tennessee,* 406 U.S. 605 (1972) (requirement that defendant be first defense witness); *Ferguson v. Georgia,* 365 U.S. 570 (1961) (bar on direct examination of defendant). Counsel, however, can also deprive a defendant of the right to effective legal assistance, simply by failing to render "adequate legal assistance," *Cuyler v. Sullivan,* 446 U.S. 335 (1980) (actual conflict of interest adversely affecting lawyer's performance renders assistance ineffective).

The Court has not elaborated on the meaning of the constitutional requirement of effective assistance in the latter class of cases—that is, those presenting claims of "actual ineffectiveness." In giving meaning to the requirement, however, we must take its purpose—to ensure a fair trial—as the guide. The benchmark for judging any claim of ineffectiveness must be whether counsel's conduct so undermined the proper functioning of the adversarial process that the trial cannot be relied on as having produced a just result.[b]

The same principle applies to a capital sentencing proceeding such as that provided by Florida law. We need not consider the role of counsel in an ordinary sentencing, which may involve informal proceedings and standardless discretion in the sentencer, and hence may require a different approach to the definition of constitutionally effective assistance. A capital sentencing proceeding like the one involved in this case, however, is sufficiently like a trial in its adversarial format and in the existence of standards for decision that counsel's role in the proceeding is comparable to counsel's role at trial—to ensure that the adversarial testing process works to produce a just result under the standards governing decision. For purposes of describing counsel's duties, therefore, Florida's capital sentencing proceeding need not be distinguished from an ordinary trial.

a. "[A] showing of prejudice," observed the Court, per Stevens, J., in *Perry v. Leeke,* 488 U.S. 272 (1989), "is not an essential element of a violation of the rule announced in *Geders*"; "our citation of *Geders* in [*Strickland*] was intended to make clear that '[a]ctual or constructive denial of the assistance of counsel altogether' is not subject to the kind of prejudice analysis that is appropriate in determining whether the quality of a lawyer's performance itself has been constitutionally ineffective." In *Perry*, a 6–3 majority held that the *Geders* rule does not apply to a trial court's order, at the conclusion of petitioner's direct testimony, that petitioner not talk to anyone, including his lawyer, during a 15–minute recess.

b. In *United States v. Cronic,* 466 U.S. 648 (1984) (also discussed in Note 2, p. 184), decided along with *Strickland*, the Court majority noted that the touchstone for measuring the constitutional adequacy of counsel's performance is the functioning of the adversary process: "The adversarial process protected by the Sixth Amendment requires that the accused have 'counsel acting in the role of an advocate.' The right to the effective assistance of counsel is thus the right of the accused to require the prosecution's case to survive the crucible of meaningful adversarial testing. When a true adversarial criminal trial has been conducted–even if defense counsel may have made demonstrable errors–the kind of testing envisioned by the Sixth Amendment has occurred. But if the process loses its character as a confrontation between adversaries, the constitutional guarantee is violated."

A convicted defendant's claim that counsel's assistance was so defective as to require reversal of a conviction or death sentence has two components. First, the defendant must show that counsel's performance was deficient. This requires showing that counsel made errors so serious that counsel was not functioning as the "counsel" guaranteed the defendant by the Sixth Amendment. Second, the defendant must show that the deficient performance prejudiced the defense. This requires showing that counsel's errors were so serious as to deprive the defendant of a fair trial, a trial whose result is reliable. Unless a defendant makes both showings, it cannot be said that the conviction or death sentence resulted from a breakdown in the adversary process that renders the result unreliable.

As all the Federal Courts of Appeals have now held, the proper standard for attorney performance is that of reasonably effective assistance. The Court indirectly recognized as much when it stated in *McMann* that a guilty plea cannot be attacked as based on inadequate legal advice unless counsel was not "a reasonably competent attorney" and the advice was not "within the range of competence demanded of attorneys in criminal cases." When a convicted defendant complains of the ineffectiveness of counsel's assistance, the defendant must show that counsel's representation fell below an objective standard of reasonableness.

More specific guidelines are not appropriate. The Sixth Amendment refers simply to "counsel," not specifying particular requirements of effective assistance. It relies instead on the legal profession's maintenance of standards sufficient to justify the law's presumption that counsel will fulfill the role in the adversary process that the Amendment envisions. The proper measure of attorney performance remains simply reasonableness under prevailing professional norms.

Representation of a criminal defendant entails certain basic duties. Counsel's function is to assist the defendant, and hence counsel owes the client a duty of loyalty, a duty to avoid conflicts of interest. From counsel's function as assistant to the defendant derive the overarching duty to advocate the defendant's cause and the more particular duties to consult with the defendant on important decisions and to keep the defendant informed of important developments in the course of the prosecution. Counsel also has a duty to bring to bear such skill and knowledge as will render the trial a reliable adversarial testing process.

These basic duties neither exhaustively define the obligations of counsel nor form a checklist for judicial evaluation of attorney performance. In any case presenting an ineffectiveness claim, the performance inquiry must be whether counsel's assistance was reasonable considering all the circumstances. Prevailing norms of practice as reflected in American Bar Association standards and the like are guides to determining what is reasonable, but they are only guides. No particular set of detailed rules for counsel's conduct can satisfactorily take account of the variety of circumstances faced by defense counsel or the range of legitimate decisions regarding how best to represent a criminal defendant. Any such set of rules would interfere with the constitutionally protected independence of counsel and restrict the wide latitude counsel must have in making tactical decisions. Indeed, the existence of detailed guidelines for representation could distract counsel from the overriding mission of vigorous advocacy of the defendant's cause. Moreover, the purpose of the effective assistance guarantee of the Sixth Amendment is not to improve the quality of legal representation, although that is a goal of considerable importance to the legal system. The purpose is simply to ensure that criminal defendants receive a fair trial.

Judicial scrutiny of counsel's performance must be highly deferential. It is all too tempting for a defendant to second-guess counsel's assistance after conviction or adverse sentence, and it is all too easy for a court, examining counsel's defense after it has proved unsuccessful, to conclude that a particular act or omission of counsel was unreasonable. A fair assessment of attorney performance requires that every effort be made to eliminate the distorting effects of hindsight, to reconstruct the circumstances of counsel's challenged conduct, and to evaluate the conduct from counsel's perspective at the time. Because of the difficulties inherent in making the evaluation, a court must indulge a strong presumption that counsel's conduct falls within the wide range of reasonable professional assistance; that is, the defendant must overcome the presumption that, under the circumstances, the challenged action "might be considered sound trial strategy." There are countless ways to provide effective assistance in any given case. Even the best criminal defense attorneys would not defend a particular client in the same way.

The availability of intrusive post-trial inquiry into attorney performance or of detailed guidelines for its evaluation would encourage the proliferation of ineffectiveness challenges. Criminal trials resolved unfavorably to the defendant would increasingly come to be followed by a second trial, this one of counsel's unsuccessful defense. Counsel's performance and even willingness to serve could be adversely affected.

[Thus,] a court deciding an actual ineffectiveness claim must judge the reasonableness of counsel's challenged conduct on the facts of the particular case, viewed as of the time of counsel's conduct. A convicted defendant making a claim of ineffective assistance must identify the acts or omissions of counsel that are alleged not to have been the result of reasonable professional judgment. The court must then determine whether, in light of all the circumstances, the identified acts or omissions were outside the wide range of professionally competent assistance. In making that determination, the court should keep in mind that counsel's function, as elaborated in prevailing professional norms, is to make the adversarial testing process work in the particular case. At the same time, the court should recognize that counsel is strongly presumed to have rendered adequate assistance and made all significant decisions in the exercise of reasonable professional judgment.

These standards require no special amplification in order to define counsel's duty to investigate, the duty at issue in this case. [S]trategic choices made after thorough investigation of law and facts relevant to plausible options are virtually unchallengeable; and strategic choices made after less than complete investigation are reasonable precisely to the extent that reasonable professional judgments support the limitations on investigation. [In] any ineffectiveness case, a particular decision not to investigate must be directly assessed for reasonableness in all the circumstances, applying a heavy measure of deference to counsel's judgments.

The reasonableness of counsel's actions may be determined or substantially influenced by the defendant's own statements or actions. Counsel's actions are usually based, quite properly, on informed strategic choices made by the defendant and on information supplied by the defendant. In particular, what investigation decisions are reasonable depends critically on such information. For example, when the facts that support a certain potential line of defense are generally known to counsel because of what the defendant has said, the need for further investigation may be considerably diminished or eliminated altogether. And when a defendant has given counsel reason to believe that pursuing certain investigations would be fruitless or even harmful, counsel's failure to pursue those investigations may not later be challenged as unreasonable. In short, inquiry into counsel's conversations with the defendant may be critical to a proper assessment of counsel's investigation decisions, just as it may be critical to a proper assessment of counsel's other litigation decisions.

An error by counsel, even if professionally unreasonable, does not warrant setting aside the judgment of a criminal proceeding if the error had no effect on the judgment. The purpose of the Sixth Amendment guarantee of counsel is to ensure that a defendant has the assistance necessary to justify reliance on the outcome of the proceeding. Accordingly, any deficiencies in counsel's performance must be prejudicial to the defense in order to constitute ineffective assistance under the Constitution.

In certain Sixth Amendment contexts, prejudice is presumed. Actual or constructive denial of the assistance of counsel altogether is legally presumed to result in prejudice. So are various kinds of state interference with counsel's assistance. Prejudice in these circumstances is so likely that case by case inquiry into prejudice is not worth the cost. Moreover, such circumstances involve impairments of the Sixth Amendment right that are easy to identify and, for that reason and because the prosecution is directly responsible, easy for the government to prevent.

One type of actual ineffectiveness claim warrants a similar, though more limited, presumption of prejudice. In *Cuyler v. Sullivan* [see fn. a, p. 198], the Court held that prejudice is presumed when counsel is burdened by an actual conflict of interest. In those circumstances, counsel breaches the duty of loyalty, perhaps the most basic of counsel's duties. Moreover, it is difficult to measure the precise effect on the defense of representation corrupted by conflicting interest. Given the obligation of counsel to avoid conflicts of interest and the ability of trial courts to make early inquiry in certain situations likely to give rise to conflicts, see e.g., Fed.R.Crim.P. 44(c), it is reasonable for the criminal justice system to maintain a fairly rigid rule of presumed prejudice for conflicts of interest. Even so, the rule is not quite the *per se* rule of prejudice that exists for the Sixth Amendment claims mentioned above. Prejudice is presumed only if the defendant demonstrates that counsel "actively represented conflicting interests" and "that an actual conflict of interest adversely affected his lawyer's performance." *Cuyler v. Sullivan.*

Conflict of interest claims aside, actual ineffectiveness claims alleging a deficiency in attorney performance are subject to a general requirement that the defendant affirmatively prove prejudice. [Attorney errors] cannot be classified according to likelihood of causing prejudice. Nor can they be defined with sufficient precision to inform defense attorneys correctly just what conduct to avoid. Representation is an art, and an act or omission that is unprofessional in one case may be sound or even brilliant in another. Even if a defendant shows that particular errors of counsel were unreasonable, therefore, the defendant must show that they actually had an adverse effect on the defense.

It is not enough for the defendant to show that the errors had some conceivable effect on the outcome of the proceeding. Virtually every act or omission of counsel would meet that test, and not every error that conceivably could have influenced the outcome undermines the reliability of the result of the proceeding. Respondent suggests requiring a showing that the errors "impaired the presentation of the defense." That standard, however, provides no workable principle. Since any error, if it is indeed an error, "impairs" the presentation of the defense, the proposed standard [provides] no way of deciding what impairments are sufficiently serious to warrant setting aside the outcome of the proceeding.

On the other hand, we believe that a defendant need not show that counsel's deficient conduct more likely than not altered the outcome in the case. [The] appropriate test for prejudice finds its roots in the test for materiality of exculpatory information not disclosed to the defense by the prosecution, *United States v. Agurs*, 427 U.S. 97 (1976), and in the test for materiality of testimony made unavailable to the defense by Government deportation of a witness, *United States v. Valenzuela–Bernal*, 458 U.S. 858 (1982). The defendant must show that there is a reasonable probability that, but for counsel's unprofessional errors, the result of the proceeding would have been different. A reasonable probability is a probability sufficient to undermine confidence in the outcome.

In making [this] determination, [a] court should presume, absent challenge to the judgment on grounds of evidentiary insufficiency, that the judge or jury acted according to law. An assessment of the likelihood of a result more favorable to the defendant must exclude the possibility of arbitrariness, whimsy, caprice, "nullification," and the like. A defendant has no entitlement to the luck of a lawless decisionmaker, even if a lawless decision cannot be reviewed. The assessment of prejudice should proceed on the assumption that the decisionmaker is reasonably, conscientiously, and impartially applying the standards that govern the decision. It should not depend on the idiosyncracies of the particular decisionmaker, such as unusual propensities toward harshness or leniency. Although these factors may actually have entered into counsel's selection of strategies and, to that limited extent, may thus affect the performance inquiry, they are irrelevant to the prejudice inquiry. Thus, evidence about the actual process of decision, if not part of the record of the proceeding under review, and evidence about, for example, a particular judge's sentencing practices, should not be considered in the prejudice determination.

The governing legal standard plays a critical role in defining the question to be asked in assessing the prejudice from counsel's errors. When a defendant challenges a conviction, the question is whether there is a reasonable probability that, absent the errors, the factfinder would have had a reasonable doubt respecting guilt. When a defendant challenges a death sentence such as the one at issue in this case, the question is whether there is a reasonable probability that, absent the errors, the sentencer—including an appellate court, to the extent it independently reweighs the evidence—would have concluded that the balance of aggravating and mitigating circumstances did not warrant death.

In making this determination, a court hearing an ineffectiveness claim must consider the totality of the evidence before the judge or jury. Some of the factual findings will have been unaffected by the errors, and factual findings that were affected will have been affected in different ways. Some errors will have had a pervasive effect on the inferences to be drawn from the evidence, altering the entire evidentiary picture, and some will have had an isolated, trivial effect. Moreover, a verdict or conclusion only weakly supported by the record is more likely to have been affected by errors than one with overwhelming record support. Taking the unaffected findings as given, and taking due account of the effect of the errors on the remaining findings, a court making the prejudice inquiry must ask if the defendant has met the burden of showing that the decision reached would reasonably likely have been different absent the errors.

A number of practical considerations are important for the application of the standards we have outlined. Most important, in adjudicating a claim of actual ineffectiveness of counsel, a court should keep in mind that the principles we have stated do not establish mechanical rules. Although those principles should guide the process of decision, the ultimate focus of inquiry must be on the fundamental fairness of the proceeding whose result is being challenged. In every case the court should be concerned with whether, despite the strong presumption of reliability, the result of the particular proceeding is unreliable because of a breakdown in the adversarial process that our system counts on to produce just results.

To the extent that this has already been the guiding inquiry in the lower courts, the standards articulated today do not require reconsideration of ineffectiveness claims rejected under different standards. Cf. *Trapnell v. United States*,

725 F.2d 149 (2d Cir.1983) (in several years of applying "farce and mockery" standard along with "reasonable competence" standard, court "never found that the result of a case hinged on the choice of a particular standard"). In particular, the minor differences in the lower courts' precise formulations of the performance standard are insignificant: the different formulations are mere variations of the overarching reasonableness standard. With regard to the prejudice inquiry, only the strict outcome-determinative test, among the standards articulated in the lower courts, imposes a heavier burden on defendants than the tests laid down today. The difference, however, should alter the merit of an ineffectiveness claim only in the rarest case.

Although we have discussed the performance component of an ineffectiveness claim prior to the prejudice component, there is no reason for a court deciding an ineffective assistance claim to approach the inquiry in the same order or even to address both components of the inquiry if the defendant makes an insufficient showing on one. In particular, a court need not determine whether counsel's performance was deficient before examining the prejudice suffered by the defendant as a result of the alleged deficiencies. The object of an ineffectiveness claim is not to grade counsel's performance. If it is easier to dispose of an ineffectiveness claim on the ground of lack of sufficient prejudice, which we expect will often be so, that course should be followed. Courts should strive to ensure that ineffectiveness claims not become so burdensome to defense counsel that the entire criminal justice system suffers as a result. * * *

Having articulated general standards for judging ineffectiveness claims, we think it useful to apply those standards to the facts of this case in order to illustrate the meaning of the general principles. The record makes it possible to do so. [The facts] make clear that the conduct of respondent's counsel at and before respondent's sentencing proceeding cannot be found unreasonable. They also make clear that, even assuming the challenged conduct of counsel was unreasonable, respondent suffered insufficient prejudice to warrant setting aside his death sentence.

With respect to the performance component, the record shows that respondent's counsel made a strategic choice to argue for the extreme emotional distress mitigating circumstance and to rely as fully as possible on respondent's acceptance of responsibility for his crimes. Although counsel understandably felt hopeless about respondent's prospects, nothing in the record indicates [that] counsel's sense of hopelessness distorted his professional judgment. Counsel's strategy choice was well within the range of professionally reasonable judgments, and the decision not to seek more character or psychological evidence than was already in hand was likewise reasonable.

[With] respect to the prejudice component, the lack of merit of respondent's claim is even more stark. The evidence that respondent says his trial counsel should have offered at the sentencing hearing would barely have altered the sentencing profile presented to the sentencing judge. As the state courts and District Court found, at most this evidence shows that numerous people who knew respondent thought he was generally a good person and that a psychiatrist and a psychologist believed he was under considerable emotional stress that did not rise to the level of extreme disturbance. Given the overwhelming aggravating factors, there is no reasonable probability that the omitted evidence would have changed the conclusion that the aggravating circumstances outweighed the mitigating circumstances and, hence, the sentence imposed. * * *

Failure to make the required showing of either deficient performance or sufficient prejudice defeats the ineffectiveness claim. Here there is a double failure. More generally, respondent has made no showing that the justice of his sentence was rendered unreliable by a breakdown in the adversary process caused by deficiencies in counsel's assistance. * * *

We conclude, therefore, that the District Court properly declined to issue a writ of habeas corpus. * * *

Justice BRENNAN, concurring in part and dissenting in part.

I join the Court's opinion but dissent from its judgment. * * * [As to the judgement, Justice Brennan noted that since he viewed the death penalty to be unconstitutional, he would vacate the death penalty, along with remanding for further proceedings.] * * *

I join the Court's opinion because I believe that the standards it sets out today will both provide helpful guidance to courts considering claims of actual ineffectiveness of counsel and also permit those courts to continue their efforts to achieve progressive development of this area of the law. * * * [The] standards announced today can and should be applied with concern for the special considerations that must attend review of counsel's performance in a capital sentencing proceeding. In contrast to a case in which a finding of ineffective assistance requires a new trial, a conclusion that counsel was ineffective with respect to only the penalty phase of a capital trial imposes on the state the far lesser burden of reconsideration of the sentence alone. On the other hand, the consequences to the defendant of incompetent assistance at a capital sentencing could not, of course, be greater. * * *

Justice MARSHALL, dissenting.

[The] opinion of the Court revolves around two holdings. First, the majority ties the constitutional minima of attorney performance to a simple "standard of reasonableness." Second, the majority holds that only an error of counsel that has sufficient impact on a trial to "undermine confidence in the outcome" is grounds for overturning a conviction. I disagree with both of these rulings.

My objection to the performance standard adopted by the Court is that it is so malleable that, in practice, it will either have no grip at all or will yield excessive variation in the manner in which the Sixth Amendment is interpreted and applied by different courts. To tell lawyers and the lower courts that counsel for a criminal defendant must behave "reasonably" and must act like "a reasonably competent attorney" is to tell them almost nothing.

[The] debilitating ambiguity of an "objective standard of reasonableness" in this context is illustrated by the majority's failure to address important issues concerning the quality of representation mandated by the Constitution. It is an unfortunate but undeniable fact that a person of means, by selecting a lawyer and paying him enough to ensure he prepares thoroughly, usually can obtain better representation than that available to an indigent defendant, who must rely on appointed counsel, who, in turn, has limited time and resources to devote to a given case. Is a "reasonably competent attorney" a reasonably competent adequately paid retained lawyer or a reasonably competent appointed attorney? It is also a fact that the quality of representation available to ordinary defendants in different parts of the country varies significantly. Should the standard of performance mandated by the Sixth Amendment vary by locale? The majority offers no clues as to the proper responses to these questions.

* * * I agree that counsel must be afforded "wide latitude" when making "tactical decisions" regarding trial strategy, but many aspects of the job of a criminal defense attorney are more amenable to judicial oversight [than the majority indicates]. For example, much of the work involved in preparing for a trial, applying for bail, conferring with one's client, making timely objections to significant, arguably erroneous rulings of the trial judge, and filing a notice of

appeal if there are colorable grounds therefor could profitably be made the subject of uniform standards. * * *

I object to the prejudice standard adopted by the Court for two independent reasons. First, it is often very difficult to tell whether a defendant convicted after a trial in which he was ineffectively represented would have fared better if his lawyer had been competent. Seemingly impregnable cases can sometimes be dismantled by good defense counsel. On the basis of a cold record, it may be impossible for a reviewing court confidently to ascertain how the government's evidence and arguments would have stood up against rebuttal and cross-examination by a shrewd, well prepared lawyer. The difficulties of estimating prejudice after the fact are exacerbated by the possibility that evidence of injury to the defendant may be missing from the record precisely because of the incompetence of defense counsel. In view of all these impediments to a fair evaluation of the probability that the outcome of a trial was affected by ineffectiveness of counsel, it seems to me senseless to impose on a defendant whose lawyer has been shown to have been incompetent the burden of demonstrating prejudice.

Second and more fundamentally, the assumption on which the Court's holding rests is that the only purpose of the constitutional guarantee of effective assistance of counsel is to reduce the chance that innocent persons will be convicted. In my view, the guarantee also functions to ensure that convictions are obtained only through fundamentally fair procedures. [A] proceeding in which the defendant does not receive meaningful assistance in meeting the forces of the state does not, in my opinion, constitute due process.

[In] my view, the right to *effective* assistance of counsel is entailed by the right to counsel, and abridgment of the former is equivalent to abridgment of the latter. I would thus hold that a showing that the performance of a defendant's lawyer departed from constitutionally prescribed standards requires a new trial regardless of whether the defendant suffered demonstrable prejudice thereby.

Even if I were inclined to join the majority's two central holdings, I could not abide the manner in which the majority elaborates upon its rulings. Particularly regrettable are the majority's discussion of the "presumption" of reasonableness to be accorded lawyers' decisions and its attempt to prejudge the merits of claims previously rejected by lower courts using different legal standards. [The majority suggests] that reviewing courts should "indulge a strong presumption that counsel's conduct" was constitutionally acceptable and should "apply[] a heavy measure of deference to counsel's judgments".

[The] adjectives "strong" and "heavy" might be read as imposing upon defendants an unusually weighty burden of persuasion. If that is the majority's intent, I must respectfully dissent. The range of acceptable behavior defined by "prevailing professional norms" seems to me sufficiently broad to allow defense counsel the flexibility they need in responding to novel problems of trial strategy. To afford attorneys more latitude, by "strongly presuming" that their behavior will fall within the zone of reasonableness, is covertly to legitimate convictions and sentences obtained on the basis of incompetent conduct by defense counsel.

[The] majority suggests that, "[f]or purposes of describing counsel's duties," a capital sentencing proceeding "need not be distinguished from an ordinary trial." I cannot agree. The Court has repeatedly acknowledged that the Constitution requires stricter adherence to procedural safeguards in a capital case than in other cases. * * *

The [above] views * * * oblige me to dissent from the majority's disposition of the case before us. It is undisputed that respondent's trial counsel made virtually no investigation of the possibility of obtaining testimony from respondent's relatives, friends, or former employers pertaining to respondent's character or background. Had counsel done so, he would have found several persons willing and able to testify that, in their experience, respondent was a responsible, nonviolent man, devoted to his family, and active in the affairs of his church. Respondent contends that his lawyer could have and should have used that testimony to "humanize" respondent, to counteract the impression conveyed by the trial that he was little more than a cold-blooded killer. Had this evidence been admitted, respondent argues, his chances of obtaining a life sentence would have been significantly better.

Measured against the standards outlined above, respondent's contentions are substantial. Experienced members of the death-penalty bar have long recognized the crucial importance of adducing evidence at a sentencing proceeding that establishes the defendant's social and familial connections. See Goodpaster, *The Trial for Life: Effective Assistance of Counsel in Death Penalty Cases*, 58 N.Y.U.L.Rev. 299 (1983). The State makes a colorable—though in my view not compelling—argument that defense counsel in this case might have made a reasonable "strategic" decision not to present such evidence at the sentencing hearing on the assumption that an unadorned acknowledgment of respondent's responsibility for his crimes would be more likely to appeal to the trial judge, who was reputed to respect persons who accepted responsibility for their actions.[19] But however justifiable such a choice might have been after counsel had fairly assessed the potential strength of the mitigating evidence available to him, counsel's failure to make any significant effort to find out what evidence might be garnered from respondent's relatives and acquaintances surely cannot be described as "reasonable." Counsel's failure to investigate is particularly suspicious in light of his candid admission that respondent's confession and conduct in the course of the trial gave him a feeling of "hopelessness" regarding the possibility of saving respondent's life.

[If] counsel had investigated the availability of mitigating evidence, he might well have decided to present some such material at the hearing. If he had done so, there is a significant chance that respondent would have been given a life sentence. In my view, those possibilities, conjoined with the unreasonableness of counsel's failure to investigate, are more than sufficient to establish a violation of the Sixth Amendment and to entitle respondent to a new sentencing proceeding. * * *

Notes and Questions

1. ***Commentator criticism.*** Commentators have been nearly unanimous in their criticism of the *Strickland* standard and the *Strickland* majority opinion. See CRIMPROC. § 11.10(a) (collecting citations). Major lines of criticism include: (1) the *Strickland* opinion reflects "at best an insensitive attitude toward a very serious problem," Vivian O. Berger, *The Supreme Court and Defense Counsel: Old Roads, New Paths—A Dead End?*, 86 Colum.L.Rev. 9, 86–87 (1986)[b]; (2) the *Strickland* standard, as applied, finds ineffectiveness in far too few instances of

19. Two considerations undercut the State's explanation of counsel's decision. First, it is not apparent why adducement of evidence pertaining to respondent's character and familial connections would have been inconsistent with respondent's acknowledgment that he was responsible for his behavior. Second, the Florida Supreme Court possesses—and frequently exercises—the power to overturn death sentences it deems unwarranted by the facts of a case. Even if counsel's decision not to try to humanize respondent for the benefit of the trial judge were deemed reasonable, counsel's failure to create a record for the benefit of the state Supreme Court might well be deemed unreasonable.

b. Professor Burger cites in this connection the Court's statement (p. 164) regarding lower courts finding it "easier to dispose of an ineffectiveness claim on the ground of lack of prejudice" (which she describes as a "not so subtle suggestion that virtually all challenges to counsel can be readily rejected") and the "stated strong presumption of competence." A com-

incompetent performance, see e.g., David Cole, *No Equal Justice* 78–79 (1999)[c]; (3) *Strickland* creates a major loophole with its extreme deference to strategic decisions, see e.g., Donald A. Dripps, *Ineffective Assistance of Counsel: The Case for an Ex Ante Parity Standard*, 88 J.Crim.L. & C. 242, 281 (1997)[d]; (4) the *Strickland* approach fails to "improve the defense function" because its inquiry focuses on an "*after the fact*" inquiry into the performance of counsel, based in large part on a record created by counsel, Dripps, supra[e]; (5) the *Strickland* standard confuses the Sixth Amendment right to effective assistance by counsel with the due process interest in a just outcome, see e.g., William J. Genego, *The Future Effective Assistance of Counsel: Performance Standards, and Competent Representation*, 22 Am.Crim.L.Rev. 181, 200 (1984)[f]; (6) *Strickland* applies a standard derived from due process cases (see pp. 162–63) to establish prejudice as an element of the ineffectiveness claim, rather than treating incompetent performance as a Sixth Amendment violation, which could then be subjected to the "harmless error" standard traditionally applied to constitutional violations, see Berger, supra; and (7) *Strickland* combines with *Cronic*, Note 2, p. 184, to ignore entirely the institutional factors that make inevitable widespread incompetent performance, see e.g., Richard Klein, *The Constitutionalization of Ineffective Assistance of Counsel*, 58 Md.L.Rev. 1433 (1999), and Note 1, p. 188.

mon theme of much of academic criticism is that incompetent performance is far more widespread than the Strickland Court apparently assumed. See also Note 1, p. 188.

c. Professor Cole notes that the *Strickland* test "has proved virtually impossible to meet. Courts have declined to find ineffective assistance where defense counsel slept during portions of the trial, where counsel used heroin and cocaine throughout the trial, where counsel allowed his client to wear the same sweatshirt and shoes in court that the perpetrator was alleged to have worn on the day of the crime, where counsel stated prior to trial that he was not prepared on the law or facts of the case, and where counsel appointed in a capital case could not name a single Supreme Court decision on the death penalty."

d. Professor Dripps notes: "Should we take the government's plea offer? Should we rely on self-defense, or on accident, or on insanity? Should we put the defendant on the stand? Can we trust witness X to testify as we expect? These are the kinds of judgments that people need defense lawyers to make. They are also the kinds of judgments that can rarely be challenged successfully under *Strickland*. As 'tactical choices' to which reviewing courts afford a 'heavy measure of deference,' the consequences of which are imponderable and thus presumptively not prejudicial, counsel's key decisions are virtually beyond review. It hardly follows, however, that typical indigent defenders make these decisions as well as they could be made." Professor Dripps advocates requiring a judicial inquiry "before proceedings commence" as to whether counsel can provide effective representation.

Consider also Cole, supra, at 79–80, noting that "as Strickland itself illustrated, * * * almost any deficiency in performance can in hindsight be described as tactical." As a result of the deference to tactical decisions, "as one [federal district] court has explained, 'even if many reasonable lawyers would not have done as defense counsel did at trial, no relief can be granted on ineffective grounds unless it is shown that *no* reasonable lawyer in the circumstances would have done so.' "

e. *Strickland*, Professor Dripps argues, rests on a "counter-factual—even Kafkaesque—assumption that when the prior performance of defense counsel undermines the fairness of the trial, the situation will be manifest to the reviewing court after the fact." See also Note 1, p. 188. Consider also Burger, supra, noting that, in allowing the lower court to dispose of a claim on lack of prejudice, without assessing counsel's performance, the Court ignores the fact that "decisions on the merits * * * may operate preventively, not only remedially * * * [by] teaching the bar in general about their duties."

f. Professor Genego notes: "The role of a [defense attorney] is not [to] see that his or her client received a fair trial and that a just outcome resulted. The attorney's role is to do everything ethically proper to see that the client receives the most favorable outcome possible—whether or not it produces an outcome which society considers just. Society relies on the adversary system to produce just results from partisan advocacy. The guiding principle in determining whether an attorney has provided effective representation must then be whether he or she discharged the role of partisan advocate faithfully and zealously, not whether the performance yielded what a court views as a just result."

2. ***Justice Marshall's criticism of the "reasonably competent attorney" standard.*** Many commentators find persuasive Justice Marshall's criticism of the "debilitating ambiguity" of Strickland's performance standard (p. 165). They argue that the Court should have allowed room for the categorical approach urged by Judge Bazelon, but since that approach appears to be forbidden by *Strickland* (see p. 160), the Court should at least provide answers to questions of the type posed by Justice Marshall, and thereby identify precise reference points for the concept of a "reasonably competent attorney." Does the *Strickland* performance standard lend itself to such reference points as the common practice of "adequately payed retained attorney[s]" (p. 165)? Consider CRIMPROC § 11.10(b) ("there was no suggestion in *Strickland* that reasonableness was to be judged by reference to any empirical survey of attorney practices" because such information, as the Court indicated in its discussion of "prevailing norms of practice" could serve only as a "helpful starting point"; "the ultimate point of reference is the performance * * * needed, under the circumstances of the case, to ensure 'the proper functioning of the adversarial process' (see *Strickland* at fn. b, p. 159)" and that must be case-specific). As for consideration of local practice, consider also the reference to such practice in *Wiggins v. Smith*, p. 178.

3. ***Strickland in other settings.*** As discussed in *Strickland* (p. 162) and in pt. C infra, there are exceptions to the application of the two-pronged *Strickland* standard. *Strickland* does provide however, the basic standard for assessing incompetent performance claims. In *Smith v. Murray*, 477 U.S. 527 (1986), the Court held that the "test of *Strickland v. Washington*" was not limited to trial counsel, but also applied to the alleged ineffective assistance of appellate counsel on a first appeal of right. *Hill v. Lockhart*, 474 U.S. 52 (1985), concluded that past precedent on counsel's ineffective assistance in a guilty plea case converted into the application of the *Strickland* standard. As for the "prejudice" prong of the *Strickland* standard, it would be sufficient in guilty plea cases that the defendant establish "a reasonable probability that, but for counsel's errors, he would not have pleaded guilty and would have insisted on going to trial." See also Ch.22, § 3 and § 5.

4. ***Strickland and capital cases.*** "In view of the Court's repeated statements that 'death is different,'" observes Welsh S. White, *Effective Assistance of Counsel in Capital Cases: The Evolving Standard of Care,* 1993 U.Ill.L.Rev. 323, 333, "[the *Strickland* Court] might have been expected to discuss such questions as whether the standard of effectiveness should be the same in a capital as a noncapital case, whether the meaning of *prejudice* should be the same in both situations, and whether a capital defense counsel's role at the penalty phase of a capital case is different than it is at the guilt phase. Without discussing any of these questions, however, the Court tersely stated [p. 159] that '[f]or purposes of describing counsel's duties [the] capital sentencing proceedings need not be distinguished from an ordinary trial.'"

Drawing upon the *ABA Guidelines for the Appointment and Performance of Counsel in Death Penalty Cases* (1989), the practice of experienced capital defense attorneys, and relevant lower court decisions, Professor White maintains, that "the failure of a capital defense attorney to take specific actions—in particular, failure to seek and introduce certain types of mitigating evidence, to seek a favorable plea bargain that will avoid the death sentence, and to try to establish a relationship of trust with the defendant—usually should be viewed as deficient representation." Consider also, Stephen B. Bright, *Counsel for the Poor: The Death Sentence Not for the Worst Crime but for the Worst Lawyer*, 103 Yale L.J. 1835, 1862–63 (1994): "The [*Strickland*] prejudice standard is particularly inappropriate for application to deficient representation at the penalty phase of a capital case. * * * [The Supreme Court has repeatedly said that the sentencer must consider any aspect of a capital defendant's life or background that the defense offers as a basis for a sentence less than death, but it] is impossible for reviewing courts to assess the difference that investigation into mitigating circumstances and the effective presentation of mitigating circumstances might make on a jury's sentencing decision."

Does the case for a different approach in capital cases find support in the leading study of error rates in capital cases, which found that a high percentage of capital cases were reversed on direct appeal or habeas review, and that the most common error was "egregiously incompetent" defense lawyer (accounting for "37% of the state post-conviction reversals"). See James Liebman, et. al., *A Broken System: Error Rates in Capital Cases, 1973–95* (2000), www.law.columbia.edu/brokensystem (over the period studied, 79% of the 5760 death sentence verdicts had reached a final decision on direct appellate review, with a reversal rate of 41% based on "serious-error," and roughly 10% had been reviewed on federal habeas corpus, with a reversal rate there of 40% on "serious error"). See also CRIMPROC § 1.7, fn. 82.1 (citing various discussions of the Broken System Reports).

Does the case for a different approach in capital cases find support in the application of the *Strickland* standard to the facts of the *Strickland* case? See Genego, Note 1, supra (challenging the *Strickland* analysis of counsel's performance: "Washington had everything to gain and nothing to lose from a defense-initiated psychiatric examination, and the defense attorney could not have known the value of the report before one was made," and as Justice Marshall noted, Washington's attorney was in no position to have "intelligently speculated" about the utility of the testimony of the 14 character witnesses, based simply on "telephone conversations with Washington's wife and mother"). See also the cases discussed in Note 8, p. 176.

B. Application of the Strickland Standard

NOTES ON APPLYING THE PERFORMANCE STANDARD

1. ***An immense body of precedent.*** Apart from one or two search-and-seizure issues, no criminal justice issue is more often the subject of appellate opinions than the question of what constitutes ineffective assistance of counsel under the *Strickland* standard. Such rulings cover almost every action that could be taken by defense counsel, with the challenges sometimes based on what counsel failed to do and sometimes based on what counsel actually did. The body of precedent is immense, with hundreds of opinion added each year. As might be expected with such a large body of precedent, "the rulings are hardly consistent in their treatment of even roughly similar fact situations." CRIMPROC § 11.10(c).

The number of issues considered in this large body of precedent is far too great to permit review here, even in a summary fashion. Our focus will be on several of the most significant issues that have attracted the attention of the Supreme Court in its application of *Strickland* to cases that ended in trial convictions. As to guilty pleas, see Ch. 22, §§ 3 and 5.

2. ***The role of the standards of professional responsibility.*** If a defense counsel takes an action adverse to his client, but counsel took that action to avoid a violation of the state's standards of professional responsibility, does that purpose render counsel's action per se acceptable under the performance prong of *Strickland*? If the attorney engages in action which violates the standards of professional responsibility, does that factor automatically render counsel's actions as beyond

the pale for a reasonably competent attorney? NIX v. WHITESIDE, 475 U.S. 157 (1986), offered answers to both these questions.

In that case, defendant Whiteside's counsel, upon learning that Whiteside intended to commit perjury, warned Whiteside that such action would (1) lead counsel to seek to withdraw, (2) require counsel to advise the trial court of the perjury, and (3) that counsel "probably would [then] be allowed to attempt to impeach that testimony." As a result of those warnings, Whiteside testified without perjuring himself. The Eighth Circuit, in reversing a denial of habeas relief, concluded that counsel's warning breached the "obligations of confidentially and zealous advocacy" imposed on defense counsel by the Sixth Amendment. Rejecting that conclusion, Chief Justice BURGER's opinion for the Court found counsel's assumption of an obligation to report known client perjury to be "wholly consistent with the Iowa standards of professional conduct and law, with the overwhelming majority of courts, and with codes of professional ethics [i.e., the Model Code of Professional Responsibility and the Model Rules of Professional Conduct]." His opinion also arguably suggested that action taken by an attorney to avoid a breach of professional responsibility automatically met *Strickland*'s performance prong. It noted: "Since there has been no breach of any recognized professional duty, it follows that there can be no deprivation of the right to assistance of counsel under the *Strickland* standard."

This suggestion led four justices [per BLACKMUN, J] to concur only in the judgement. They found it sufficient to reverse the ruling below on the ground that the action of counsel could not be deemed prejudicial based on the likelihood that a different result would have been reached if defendant had been able to present perjured testimony (a ground also stressed in the majority opinion). Justice Blackmun expressed concern as to the Court's "implicit adoption of a set of standards of professional responsibility for attorneys in state criminal proceedings" through its reliance upon counsel's adherence to the codes of professional responsibility. Justice Blackmun warned that "whether an attorney's response to what he sees as a client's plan to commit perjury" constitutes ineffective assistance depends upon a variety of factors (e.g., certainty that the client's testimony will be false, stage of the proceedings, means of dissuading the client), which therefore "makes inappropriate a blanket rule that defense attorneys must reveal, or threaten to reveal, a client's anticipated perjury to the trial court." Justice Blackmun did not suggest that the Sixth Amendment would require counsel to violate standards of professional responsibility, but that where several avenues were available for achieving compliance with those standards, the Sixth Amendment requirement of reasonably effective assistance should not invariably be met by whichever avenue counsel chose.

Chief Justice Burger's opinion for the Court in *Nix v. Whiteside*, also spoke to whether reasonably effective assistance could be provided where the attorney breached an "ethical standard of professional responsibility." It noted:

"Under the *Strickland* standard, breach of an ethical standard does not necessarily make out a denial of the Sixth Amendment guarantee of assistance of counsel. When examining attorney conduct, a court must be careful not to narrow the wide range of conduct acceptable under the Sixth Amendment so restrictively as to constitutionalize particular standards of professional conduct and thereby intrude into the State's proper authority to define and apply the standards of professional conduct applicable to those it admits to practice in its courts. In some future case challenging attorney conduct * * *, we may need to define with greater precision the weight to be given to recognized canons of ethics, the standards established by the State in statutes or professional codes, and the Sixth Amendment, in defining the proper scope and limits on that conduct."

3. In light of *Nix v. Whiteside*, how should *Strickland* have been applied to the fact situation presented in *McClure v. Thompson*, 323 F.3d 1233 (9th Cir. 2003). There, the defendant, at counsel's urging, revealed to counsel the locations at which the defendant had left the two children of the woman defendant had killed. Subsequently, counsel, with his client's permission, arranged for an anonymous telephone call to the police identifying those locations. Counsel later testified that he believed the children were probably dead, but he also thought "there was a chance they were alive" as defendant's statements to counsel were ambiguous. The police found the bodies of the dead children and additional charges were filed. The Ninth Circuit concluded that the client's authorization could not justify counsel's breach of confidentiality, because the consent was not sufficiently "informed" (counsel did not advise the defendant of the possible adverse consequences if the children were dead). However, counsel would not have violate *Strickland's* performance prong if the breach of client confidentiality had been permissible under the standards of professional responsibility, to prevent possible dangers to the children left unattended in remote locations (and to keep a kidnaping charge from becoming a possible homicide charge). Since the standards required that the attorney "reasonably believed" that disclosure could prevent future harm, whether the attorney's action constituted incompetent performance would rest on whether his belief that the children might be alive was reasonable. The majority found that belief reasonable in light of the lower court's "factual findings regarding the nature of [the attorney's] investigation and inquiry," but the dissent found it was not reasonable because counsel did not have "a firm factual basis" for believing the children were alive. Both opinions apparently concluded that a breach of client confidentially, even if made in a good faith belief that the circumstances justified the breach under the professional responsibility standards, constitutes per se incompetent performance for Sixth Amendment purposes if not actually justified under those standards.

4. ***Ignorance of the law.*** Where counsel's actions were a product of counsel's ignorance of well-established legal principles, does that factor standing alone, overcome the "strong presumption that counsel's conduct falls within the wide range of reasonable professional assistance." Consider KIMMELMAN v. MORRISON, 477 U.S. 365 (1986). During defendant Morrison's trial for rape, the state had introduced a sheet seized from his bed and expert testimony concerning stains and hair found on the sheet. Defense counsel had objected on Fourth Amendment grounds, but the trial court refused to consider that objection because there had been no pretrial motion to suppress. Counsel explained that he had not previously been aware of the seizure of the sheet, but the trial judge found that to be no excuse since counsel had not asked for pretrial discovery. Counsel then sought to justify that omission by asserting that it was the state's obligation to inform him of its case against his client and that he had not expected to go to trial since he had been told that the complainant was reluctant to testify. Both justifications were rejected by the trial judge. The first represented a clear misunderstanding of the law, and the second ignored the fact that it would have required a court order, not simply the victim's preference, to dismiss the rape indictment.

On a habeas challenge to his conviction, Morrison relied entirely on counsel's failure to successfully challenge the illegal search. The state responded that counsel's overall trial performance constituted reasonable representation; *Strickland* did not demand a flawless performance, and the mishandling of the Fourth Amendment issue was a minor error. Rejecting that argument, the Court (per BRENNAN, J.) concluded that counsel's failure to request pretrial discovery clearly fell below "prevailing professional norms." There had been "a total failure to conduct pretrial discovery" for which counsel offered only "implausible explanations" that reflected "a startling ignorance the law." Moreover, the state's attempt to "minimize the seriousness of counsel's errors by asserting that [its] case turned far more on the credibility of witnesses than on the bedsheet and related testimony" was not persuasive as to this issue. Counsel's performance would not be measured by a "hindsight" evaluation of the "relative importance of various components of the State's case"; at the time he failed to seek discovery, counsel "did not * * * know what the State's case would be." While "the relative importance of witness credibility vis-a-vis the bedsheet and related expert testimony [would be] pertinent to the determination of prejudice" (a determination left for lower court consideration on remand), it "shed no light on the reasonableness of counsel's decision not to request discovery."

5. Numerous lower court cases have similarly held that a counsel's misunderstanding of the law violated *Strickland*'s performance prong, but those opinions have uniformly insisted also that the error related to an issue of potential significance. See CRIMPROC § 11.10(c). The lower courts are divided, however, as to exactly what constitutes a "misunderstanding" of the law for this purpose. Consider *Smith v. Singletary*, 170 F.3d 1051 (11th Cir.1999) ("even if many reasonable lawyers at the pertinent time would not have interpreted the habitual-violent-felony-offender provision as Smith' counsel did, no relief can be granted unless it is shown that no reasonable lawyer, in the same circumstances, would have interpreted it as Smith's counsel did"); *Schnelle v. State*, 103 S.W.3d 165 (Mo.App.2003) (where a testifying defendant refused to answer a collateral question relating to a prior felony conviction, and prosecutor moved to strike the entire testimony, defense counsel believed that was the prescribed remedy, but caselaw "arguably" indicated that judge might fashion a less severe sanction; counsel's failure to recognize and urge such an alternative constituted ineffective assistance).

6. ***The classical "strategic decision".*** YARBOROUGH v. GENTRY, 540 U.S. 1 (2003), presented a federal habeas corpus challenge to alleged ineffective assistance of counsel in a traditional area of trial strategy—the content of a closing argument. Respondent Gentry was convicted in a state court of stabbing his girlfriend (Handy) with a deadly weapon. Handy had testified at trial that she recalled being stabbed, but could not remember the details of the incident. The prosecution then "confronted Handy with her testimony from a preliminary hearing that Gentry had placed his hand around her throat before stabbing her twice." Williams, a security guard in neighboring building, testified that he saw Gentry, Handy, and another man from his third-floor window, and saw Gentry swing his hand into Handy's left side with some object, causing her to lean forward and scream. On cross-examination, Williams was "inconsistent about the quality of light at the time." Gentry "testified in his own defense that he had stabbed Handy accidentally while pushing her out of the way. When asked about prior convictions, he falsely stated that he had been convicted only once; evidence showed he had been separately convicted of burglary, grand theft, battery on a peace officer, and being a felon in possession of a firearm. He attributed his error to confusion about whether a plea bargain counted as a conviction."

The prosecutor, in her closing argument "expressed sympathy for Handy's plight as a pregnant, drug-addicted mother of three and highlighted [Handy's] damaging preliminary hearing testimony." The prosecutor also "accused Gentry of telling the jury a 'pack of lies'." The defense counsel's response was relatively brief (nine paragraphs as quoted by the state court). The essence of the argument, as summarized by the Supreme Court was: "that William's testimony about the quality of light was inconsistent; that Handy's personal circumstances were irrelevant to Gentry's guilt; that the case turned on whether the stabbing was accidental, and the jury had to acquit if it believed Gentry's version of the events;

that Gentry's criminal history was irrelevant to his guilt, particularly given the seriousness of the charge compared to his prior theft offenses; and that Gentry's misstatement of the number of times he had been convicted could be explained by his lack of education. Woven through these issues was a unifying theme—that the jury, like the prosecutor and defense counsel himself, were not at the scene of the crime and so could only speculate about what had happened and who was lying."

On direct appeal, the California Court of Appeals applied *Strickland* and rejected Gentry's claim of ineffective assistance. On Gentry's petition for federal habeas relief, the Ninth Circuit sustained the ineffective assistance claim. A unanimous Supreme Court reversed in a per curiam opinion:

"Where, as here, the state court's application of governing federal law is challenged [in a habeas petition], it must be shown to be not only erroneous but objectively unreasonable [see Note 7, p. 156]. * * * The right to effective assistance extends to closing arguments. Nonetheless, counsel has wide latitude in deciding how best to represent a client, and deference to counsel's tactical decisions in his closing presentation is particularly important because of the broad range of legitimate defense strategy at that stage. Closing arguments should sharpen and clarify the issues for resolution by the trier of fact, but which issues to sharpen and how best to clarify them are questions with many reasonable answers. * * * Judicial review of a defense attorney's summation is therefore highly deferential—and doubly deferential when it is conducted through the lens of federal habeas. * * * In light of these principles, the Ninth Circuit erred in finding the California Court of Appeal's decision objectively unreasonable.

"The Ninth Circuit rejected the state court's conclusion in large part because counsel did not highlight various other potentially exculpatory pieces of evidence: that Handy had used drugs on the day of the stabbing and during the early morning hours of the day of her preliminary hearing; that William's inability to see the stabbing clearly was relevant to the issue of intent; that Gentry's testimony was consistent with William's in some respects; that the government did not call as a witness William's co-worker who also saw the stabbing; that the stab wound was only one inch deep, suggesting it may have been accidental; that Handy testified she had been stabbed twice, but only had one wound; and that Gentry, after being confronted by Williams, did not try to retrieve his weapon but instead moved toward Handy while repeating, 'she's my girlfriend.'

"These other potential arguments do not establish that the state court's decision was unreasonable. Some of the omitted items, such as Gentry's reaction to Williams, are thoroughly ambiguous. Some of the others might well have backfired. For example, although Handy claimed at trial she had used drugs before the preliminary hearing, she testified at the hearing that she was not under the influence and could remember exactly what had happened the day of the stabbing. And, although Handy's wound was only one inch deep, it still lacerated her stomach and diaphragm, spilling the stomach's contents into her chest cavity and requiring almost two hours of surgery. These are facts that the prosecutor could have exploited to great advantage in her rebuttal.

"Even if some of the arguments would unquestionably have supported the defense, it does not follow that counsel was incompetent for failing to include them. Focusing on a small number of key points may be more persuasive than a shotgun approach. * * * When counsel focuses on some issues to the exclusion of others, there is a strong presumption that he did so for tactical reasons rather than through sheer neglect. That presumption has particular force where a petitioner bases his ineffective-assistance claim solely on the trial record, creating a situation in which a court may have no way of knowing whether a seemingly unusual or misguided action by counsel had a sound strategic motive. Moreover, even if an omission is inadvertent, relief is not automatic. The Sixth Amendment guarantees reasonable competence, not perfect advocacy judged with the benefit of hindsight. To recall the words of Justice (and former Solicitor General) Jackson: "I made three arguments of every case. First came the one that I planned—as I thought, logical coherent, complete. Second was the one actually presented—interrupted, incoherent, disjointed, disappointing. The third was the utterly devastating argument that I though of after going to bed that night." *Advocacy Before the Supreme Court*, 37 A. B. A. J. 801, 803 (1951).

"The Ninth Circuit found other flaws in counsel's presentation. It criticized him for mentioning "a host of details that hurt his client's position, none of which mattered as a matter of law." Of course the reason counsel mentioned those details was precisely to remind the jury that they were legally irrelevant. That was not an unreasonable tactic. * * * As Judge Kleinfeld pointed out in dissenting from denial of rehearing en banc, the court's criticism applies just as well to Clarence Darrow's closing argument in the Leopold and Loeb case: 'I do not know how much salvage there is in these two boys.... Your Honor would be merciful if you tied a rope around their necks and let them die; merciful to them, but not merciful to civilization, and not merciful to those who would be left behind.'

"The Ninth Circuit rebuked counsel for making only a passive request that the jury reach some verdict, rather than an express demand for acquittal. But given a patronizing and overconfident summation by a prosecutor, a low-key strategy that stresses the jury's autonomy is not unreasonable. * * *

"Finally, the Ninth Circuit criticized counsel's approach on the ground that, by confessing that he too could not be sure of the truth, counsel 'implied that even he did not believe Gentry's testimony.' But there is nothing wrong with a rhetorical device that personalizes the doubts anyone but an eyewitness must necessarily have. Winning over an audience by empathy is a technique that dates back to Aristotle. See P. Lagarias, *Effective Closing Argument* §§ 2.05–2.06, pp. 99–101 (1989) (citing Aristotle's Rhetoric for the point that '[a] speech should indicate to the audience that the speaker shares the attitudes of the listener, so that, in turn, the listener will respond positively to the views of the speaker').

"To be sure, Gentry's lawyer was not Aristotle or even Clarence Darrow. But the Ninth Circuit's conclusion—not only that his performance was deficient, but that any disagreement with that conclusion would be objectively unreasonable–gives too little deference to the state courts that have primary responsibility for supervising defense counsel in state criminal trials."

7. Consider in light of *Yarborough v. Gentry*, the Florida Supreme Court ruling in *State v. Davis*, 872 So.2d 250 (Fla.2004). There, defense counsel, representing an African–American defendant accused of murdering a white woman, informed the jury on voir dire that he did not like black people, that he was ashamed of his prejudice, but it sometimes did make him "mad towards black people because they're black." He urged the jury, which was entirely white, to live up to its word not to let race become a factor, stressing the need, as he well knew, to be especially vigilant against some feelings they may have "deep down," as he did.

On direct appeal from defendant's conviction, the court held that counsel's remarks to the jury brought his assistance below the level required by *Strickland*. The court reasoned that counsel's statements as to his own racial prejudice simply was not a "legitimate tactical approach," for "whether or not counsel is in fact a racist, his expressions of prejudice against African–Americans cannot be tolerated." The "manner in which counsel approached the subject [of racial prejudice] unnecessarily tended either to alienate jurors who did not share his animus against African–Americans * * *, or to legitimizing racial prejudice without accomplishing counsel's stated objective of bringing latent bias out into the open."

8. ***The duty to investigate in capital cases.*** The ineffective assistance claim presented in *Strickland*—focusing on counsel's failure to further explore potential sources of mitigating evidence for possible presentation at a capital sentencing hearing—has been reexamined by the Court in several later cases. Excerpts from the most recent of these rulings, WIGGINS v. SMITH, 539 U.S. 510 (2003), are set forth below. In that case, a 7–2 majority, per O'CONNOR, J., held that the state court made an "unreasonable application of Strickland" (see Note 7, p. 156) in rejecting the defendant's ineffective assistance claim. Over the two decades that separated *Strickland* and *Wiggins*: (1) a series of rulings from different federal circuits had sustained ineffective assistance claims based on deficiencies in counsel's investigation of the possible presentation of mitigating evidence in a capital sentencing hearing, see CRIMPROC § 11.10(c) (collecting citations , and also noting numerous cases that had rejected such claims); (2) Justice Blackmun (who had joined Justice O'Connor's majority opinion in *Strickland*), shortly before he retired, offered a scathing denouncement of the failure of key capital-punishment states to appoint qualified trial attorneys in capital cases and noted the "impotence" of *Strickland* in dealing with the resulting in adequacies in representation, see *McFarland v. Scott*, 512 U.S. 1256 (1994) (Blackmun, J., dissenting from the denial of certiorari); and (3) academic commentary repeatedly pointed to the failure to investigate (and therefore to present) mitigating psychological and social history evidence as a common flaw in capital representation, see e.g., the articles cited in Note 4, p. 169. Whether any or all of these factors had an influence on the Supreme Court is debatable, but it has been suggested that *Wiggins* reflected a distinct shift from *Strickland* and the Court's earlier rulings applying *Strickland* "to a position that today gives somewhat less deference to counsel's decision not investigate [in capital cases]." CRIMPROC § 11.10(c). Would you agree that the reasoning and tenor of the *Wiggins* majority opinion effects such a shift?

EXCERPTS FROM THE MAJORITY OPINION, WIGGINS v. SMITH (O'CONNOR, J.)

[Defendant Wiggins was charged in Baltimore County, Maryland with the first degree murder of a 77 year old woman, drowned in her bathtub during the course of an apparent robbery. Represented by two public defenders (Schlaich and Nethercott), defendant elected to be tried before a judge and was convicted after a 4–day trial. Defendant then elected to be sentenced by a jury. Counsel filed a motion for bifurcation of sentencing, explaining that they intended first to prove that Wiggins did not act as a "principal in the first degree" (Maryland law requiring proof of direct responsibility for death eligibility), "and then intended, if necessary to present a mitigation case." Counsel argued that bifurcation was needed to avoid having mitigating evidence "dilut[e] their claim that Wiggins was not directly responsible for the murder." After the court denied that motion, counsel, apart from an opening statement reference to defendant's "difficult life" and "clean record," concentrated entirely on the direct-responsibility issue. To preserve bifurcation as an issue for appeal, counsel made a proffer of the mitigating evidence they would have introduced in a bifurcated proceeding. Counsel referred to psychological reports and expert testimony demonstrating Wiggins' limited intellectual capacities, but "did [not] proffer any evidence of [Wiggins'] life history or family background." The jury returned a sentence of death.

[Wiggins subsequently sought postconviction relief in the state court. With new counsel, he argued that his attorneys had rendered constitutionally defective assistance by failing to investigate and present mitigating evidence of his dysfunctional background. To support that claim, counsel presented the testimony of a licensed social worker (Selvog), who described "an elaborate social history report he had prepared containing evidence of the severe physical and sexual abuse Wiggins suffered at the hands of his mother and while in the care of a series of foster parents. Relying on state social services, medical, and school records, as well as interviews with petitioner and numerous family members, Selvog chornicled petitioner's bleak life history." Public defender Schlaich testified that "he did not remember retaining a forensic social worker to prepare a social history." Schlaich "explained that he and Nethercott, well in advance of the sentencing trial, decided to focus their efforts on 'retrying the factual case' and disputing Wiggins' direct responsibility for the murder." The postconviction hearing judge rejected Wiggins claim for relief, through noting that "he could not remember a capital case in which counsel had not compiled a social history" and anticipated that the Maryland Court of Appeals would view that failure as "absolute error." The Court of Appeals, however, affirmed the denial of relief, concluding that counsel had made "a deliberate tactical decision" to concentrate on the direct responsibility issue, notwithstanding their awareness of Wiggins unfortunate childhood. A federal district court granted a federal habeas petition, but the Fourth Circuit reversed. The Supreme Court majority held that the Fourth Circuit erred, as the writ should have been granted].

We have made clear that the "unreasonable application" prong of § 2254(d)(1) permits a federal habeas court to grant the writ if the state court identifies the correct governing legal principle * * * [as "clearly established" by our "precedents at the time"] but unreasonably applies that principle to the facts of petitioners case. *Williams (Terry) v. Taylor* [Note 7, p. 156]. * * * We established the legal principles that govern claims of ineffective assistance of counsel in *Strickland*. * * *

In this case, as in *Strickland*, petitioner's claim stems from counsel's decision to limit the scope of their investigation into potential mitigating evidence. Here, as in *Strickland*, counsel attempt to justify their limited investigation as reflecting a tactical judgment not to present mitigating evidence at sentencing and to pursue an alternative strategy instead. In rejecting the respondent's claim [in *Strickland*], we defined the deference owed such strategic judgments in terms of the adequacy of the investigations supporting those judgments:

> "[S]trategic choices made after thorough investigation of law and facts relevant to plausible options are virtually unchallengeable; and strategic choices made after less than complete investigation are reasonable precisely to the extent that reasonable professional judgments support the limitations on investigation. In other words, counsel has a duty to make reasonable investigations or to make a reasonable decision that makes particular investigations unnecessary. In any ineffectiveness case, a particular decision not to investigate must be directly assessed for reasonableness in all the circumstances, applying a heavy measure of deference to counsel's judgments" [p. 161].

Our opinion in *Williams v. Taylor* is illustrative of the proper application of these standards. In finding Williams' ineffectiveness claim meritorious, we applied *Strickland* and concluded that counsel's failure to uncover and present voluminous mitigating evidence at sentencing could not be justified as a tactical decision to focus on Williams' voluntary confessions, because counsel had not "fullfill[ed] their obligation to conduct a thorough investigation of the defendant's background." 529 U.S., at 396 (citing 1 ABA Standards for Criminal Justice 4–4.1, commentary, pp. 4–55 (2d ed.1980)). While *Williams* had not yet been decided at the time the Maryland Court of Appeals rendered the decision at issue in this case, Williams' case was before us on habeas review. Contrary to the dissent's contention, we therefore made no new law in resolving Williams' ineffectiveness claim. * * * In highlighting counsel's duty to investigate, and in referring to the ABA Standards for Criminal Justice as guides, we applied [in *Williams*] the same "clearly established" precedent of *Strickland* we apply today. * * *

In light of these standards, our principal concern in deciding whether Schlaich and Nethercott exercised "reasonable professional judgmen[t]," is not whether counsel should have presented a mitigation case. Rather, we focus on whether the investigation supporting counsel's decision not to introduce mitigating evidence of Wiggins' background *was itself reasonable.* * * * The record demonstrates that counsel's investigation drew from three sources. Counsel arranged for William Stejskal, a psychologist, to conduct a number of tests on petitioner. Stejskal concluded that petitioner had difficulty coping with demanding situations, and exhibited features of a personality disorder. These reports revealed nothing, however, of petitioner's life history.

With respect to that history, counsel had available to them the written PSI [a standard report prepared by the Division of Parole and Probation], which included a one-page account of Wiggins' "personal history" noting his "misery as a youth," quoting his description of his own background as " 'disgusting,' " and observing that he spent most of his life in foster care. Counsel also "tracked down" records kept by the Baltimore City Department of Social Services (DSS) documenting petitioner's various placements in the State's foster care system. In describing the scope of counsel's investigation into petitioner's life history, both the Fourth Circuit and the Maryland Court of Appeals referred only to these two sources of information.

Counsel's decision not to expand their investigation beyond the PSI and the DSS records fell short of the professional standards that prevailed in Maryland in 1989. As Schlaich acknowledged, standard practice in Maryland in capital cases at the time of Wiggins' trial included the preparation of a social history report. Despite the fact that the Public Defender's office made funds available for the retention of a forensic social worker, counsel chose not to commission such a report. Counsel's conduct similarly fell short of the standards for capital defense work articulated by the American Bar Association (ABA) standards to which we long have referred as "guides to determining what is reasonable." *Strickland*. The ABA Guidelines provide that investigations into mitigating evidence "should comprise efforts to discover all *reasonably available* mitigating evidence." Despite these well-defined norms, however, counsel abandoned their investigation after having a acquired only rudimentary knowledge of [Wiggins'] hirtory from a narrow set of sounds. * * *

The scope of their investigation was also unreasonable in light of what counsel actually discovered in the DSS records. The records revealed several facts: Petitioner's mother was a chronic alcoholic; Wiggins was shuttled from foster home and displayed some emotional difficulties while there; he had frequent, lengthy absences from school; and, on at least one occasion, his mother left him and his siblings along for days without food. * * * [Any] reasonably competent attorney would have realized that pursuing [the leads contained in these records] was necessary to making an informed choice among possible defenses, particularly given the apparent absence of any aggravating factors in petitioner's background. Indeed, counsel uncovered no evidence in their investigation to suggest that a mitigation case, in its own right, would have been counterproductive, or that further investigation would have been fruitless; this case is therefore distinguishable from our precedents in which we have found limited investigations into mitigating evidence to be reasonable. See, *e.g.*, *Strickland* concluding that counsel could "reasonably surmise . . . that character and psychological evidence would be of little help"); *Burger v. Kemp*, 483 U.S. 776, 794 (1987) (concluding counsel's limited investigation was reasonable because he interviewed all witnesses brought to his attention, discovering little that was helpful and much that was harmful).[a] * * *

The record of the actual sentencing proceedings underscores the unreasonableness of counsel's conduct by suggesting that their failure to investigate thoroughly resulted from inattention, not reasoned strategic judgment. * * * On the eve of sentencing, counsel represented to the court that they were prepared to come forward with mitigating evidence, and that they intended to present such evidence in the event the court granted their motion to bifurcate. In other words, prior to sentencing, counsel never actually abandoned the possibility that they would present a mitigation defense. Until the court denied their motion, then, they had every reason to develop the most powerful mitigation case possible.

What is more, during the sentencing proceeding itself, counsel did not focus exclusively on Wiggins' direct responsibility for the murder. * * * Though she told the jury it would "hear [that] Wiggins has had a difficult life," counsel never followed up on that suggestion with details of Wiggins' history. * * * Far from focusing exclusively on petitioner's direct responsibility, then, counsel put on a halfhearted mitigation case * * *. When viewed in this light, the "strategic decision" the state courts and respondents all invoke to justify counsel's limited pursuit of mitigating evidence resembles more a *post-hoc* rationalization of counsel's conduct than an accurate description of their deliberations prior to sentencing. * * *

In rejecting petitioner's ineffective assistance claim, the Maryland Court of Appeals appears to have assumed that because counsel had *some* information with respect to petitioner's background—the information in the PSI and the DSS records—they were in a position to make a tactical choice not to present a mitigation defense. In assessing the reasonableness of an attorney's investigation, however, a court must consider not only the quantum of evidence already known to counsel, but also whether the known evidence would lead a reasonable attorney to investigate further. Even assuming Schlaich and Nethercott limited the scope of their investigation for strategic reasons, *Strickland* does not establish that a cursory investigation automatically justifies a tactical decision with respect to sentencing strategy. * * *

The Maryland Court of Appeals' application of *Strickland*'s governing legal principles was objectively unreasonable. * * * Additionally, the court based its conclusion, in part, on a clear factual error—that the "social service records ... recorded incidences of ... sexual abuse." As the State and the United States now concede, the records contain no mention of sexual abuse, much less of the repeated molestations and rapes of petitioner detailed in the Selvog report. * * *

In finding that Schlaich and Nethercott's investigation did not meet *Strickland*'s performance standards, we emphasize that *Strickland* does not require counsel to investigate every conceivable line of mitigating evidence no matter how unlikely the effort would be to assist the defendant at sentencing. Nor does *Strickland* require defense counsel to present mitigating evidence at sentencing in every case. Both conclusions would interfere with the "constitutionally protected independence of counsel" at the heart of *Strickland*. We base our conclusion on the much more limited principle that "strategic choices made after less than

a. In *Burger*, counsel expressed concern that: (1) evidence of defendant's unhappy childhood would come primarily from defendant's mother, but her testimony would reveal that the defendant "had committed at least one petty offense" (while "as the record stood, there was absolutely no evidence that petitioner had any prior criminal record of any kind"); (2) the psychologist's testimony would suggest that petitioner "never expressed any remorse about his crime"; and (3) the psychologist's report indicated that placing the defendant on the stand was risky as defendant "might even have bragged about [the] crime."

complete investigation are reasonable'' only to the extent that ''reasonable professional judgments support the limitations on investigation.'' *Strickland*. A decision not to investigate thus ''must be directly assessed for reasonableness in all the circumstances.''[b]

NOTES ON APPLYING THE PREJUDICE STANDARD

1. ***"Structural" errors***. Consider CRIMPROC § 11.10(d): ''Application of the [*Strickland*] prejudice standard can call for quite difficult and subjective judgments, depending upon the character of counsel's alleged incompetency. Where counsel's performance relates to the introduction of evidence, the court can ask what bearing that evidence might have had on the jury's verdict, a question very much like that traditionally applied in harmless error analysis (although the standard is different). Where the allege incompetency relates to [the failure to present] some legal claim that could have produced a dismissal or new trial, the court can readily determine whether that objection would have been successful. However, where the alleged incompetency relates to a claim that would have changed the structure of the trial, as opposed to producing a dismissal or altering the evidence before the jury, the task of determining its impact (assuming the claim had merit) is quite different from traditional harmless error analysis. Where a court erred in denying a change of venue, or rejecting a challenge to jury composition, that error results in automatic reversal. If those claims were not presented due to counsel's incompetency, should the court then ask whether there is a reasonable probability that the outcome of the trial would have differed if the trial had been in a different district or before a different jury? Courts have divided in their approach to this issue, with some suggesting that here also prejudice should be automatic.''

2. ***Exclusionary rule errors.*** In KIMMELMAN v. MORRISON, 477 U.S. 365 (1986), the Court rejected the contention that a ineffective-assistance claim based on counsel's failure to timely present a Fourth Amendment suppression motion could not be presented in a federal habeas challenge to a conviction. The Supreme Court had held in *Stone v. Powell* [p. 1635] that Fourth Amendment exclusionary rule claims were not cognizable on collateral attack, and the state argued that the same was true of an ineffective-assistance claim based on

b. Justice Scalia's dissent, joined by Justice Thomas, argued: (1) under the applicable habeas provisions, the Maryland Court of Appeals was required only to apply Supreme Court rulings as of the time of its decision, which did not inlcude the ''new rule'' announced in *Williams* through its incorporation of the ABA standards (see p. 177); (2) contrary to the majority's reading of the record, attorney Schlaich testified that counsel were aware of incidences of sexual abuse in Wiggins' history when they decided to focus on the direct-responsibility issue, and the Maryland Court of Appeals did not assume that counsel's investigation ''began and ended with the P.S.T. and D.S.S. records'', but assumed that it went beyond those reports, which was consistent with other information in the record; (3) ''once one eliminates the Court's mischaracterization of the state-court opinion * * *, there is no basis for finding it ''unreasonable'' [in accepting] counsel's investigation * * * [as] adequate,'' as ''nothing in our clearly established precedents requires counsel to retain a social worker when he is largely aware of his client's background''; and (4) the Maryland court's error in assuming that the social service records included incidences of sexual abuse was irrelevant in light of that court's acceptance of Schlaich's testimony as to his knowledge of the sexual abuse (apparently obtained from other sources, such as Wiggins himself.)

The majority and dissent also disagreed as to the application of *Strickland's* prejudice prong. Among the areas of disagreement were: (1) whether the defense counsel would have decided to use the social history report, or have simply focused on the direct-responsibility issue; (2) whether that report would have been admissible in evidence; and (3) whether there was a reasonable probability that, had the jury been informed of the information in the social history report, ''at least one juror would have struck a difficult balance [on capital punishment]'' (which, under Maryland law, would have barred a capital sentence).

counsel's failure at trial to present such a Fourth Amendment claim. Rejecting that argument, Justice BRENNAN's opinion for the Court noted:

"In determining that federal courts should withhold habeas review where the State has provided an opportunity for full and fair litigation of a Fourth Amendment claim, [*Stone*] found it crucial that the remedy for Fourth Amendment violations provided by the exclusionary rule 'is not a personal constitutional right.' [The] right of an accused to counsel is beyond question a fundamental right. * * * Without counsel, the right to a fair trial itself would be of little consequence, for it is through counsel that the accused secures his other rights. * * *

"We also reject the suggestion that criminal defendants should not be allowed to vindicate through federal habeas corpus their right to effective assistance of counsel where counsel's primary error is failure to make a timely request for the exclusion of illegally seized evidence—evidence which is 'typically reliable and often the most probative information bearing on the guilt or innocence of the defendant.' *Stone*. * * * [W]e have never intimated that the right to counsel is conditioned upon actual innocence. The constitutional rights of criminal defendants are granted to the innocent and the guilty alike. Consequently, we decline to hold either that the guarantee of effective assistance of counsel belongs solely to the innocent or that it attaches only to matters affecting the determination of actual guilt."

Turning to the merits of the habeas petitioner's claim, the Court concluded that counsel's representation had fallen below the performance standard of *Strickland* [see Note 4, p. 172], but then also remanded to the lower court to consider the prejudice issue. That remand led to a concurring opinion by Justice POWELL (joined by Burger, C.J., and Rehnquist, J.). Justice Powell "agree[d] that *Stone* does not bar consideration of respondent's ineffective assistance of counsel claim on federal habeas corpus," but doubted whether "the admission of illegally seized but reliable evidence can ever constitute 'prejudice' under *Strickland*". He explained:

"[The reasoning of *Strickland*] strongly suggests that only errors that call into question the basic justice of the defendant's conviction suffice to establish prejudice under [that case]. The question, in sum, must be whether the particular harm suffered by the defendant due to counsel's incompetence rendered the defendant's trial fundamentally unfair. [The] admission of illegally seized but reliable evidence does not lead to an unjust or fundamentally unfair result. [Thus,] the harm suffered by respondent in this case is not the denial of a fair and reliable adjudication of his guilt, but rather the absence of a windfall.

"As we emphasized only last Term '[the] very premise of our adversary system of criminal justice is that partisan advocacy on both sides of a case will best promote *the ultimate objective that the guilty be convicted and the innocent go free.*' *Evitts v. Lucey*, 469 U.S. 387 (1985) [emphasis added by Powell, J.]. The right to effective assistance of counsel flows logically from this premise. But it would shake that right loose from its constitutional moorings to hold that the Sixth Amendment protects criminal defendants against errors that merely deny those defendants a windfall."[a]

Can Justice Powell's reasoning be squared with Justice Brennan's comments regarding "actual innocence" and the right to counsel. The Supreme Court has not had occasion to return to the issue raised by Justice Powell. Of the several circuits that have considered the issue, only one—the Seventh Circuit in *Holman*

a. Nevertheless, Justice Powell did not vote to reverse "because neither the parties nor the courts below have considered the issue I raise here." He cautioned, however, that "the Court's rhetoric" should not "mistakenly be read to answer a question that has not been asked."

v. Page, 95 F.3d 481 (7th Cir.1996)—has sided with Justice Powell and held that counsel's failure to gain suppression of reliable evidence cannot produce prejudice under *Strickland.*

3. *That the outcome would have been different but for counsel's deficient performance does not invariably establish "prejudice."* Although some language in *Strickland* suggests otherwise, a defendant claiming that she has been denied the effective assistance of counsel may not prevail even though she establishes that (a) her lawyer's performance was seriously deficient and (b) there is a reasonable probability that but for that deficiency the result of the proceeding could have been different. As the Court emphasized in LOCKHART v. FRETWELL, 506 U.S. 364 (1993), the "prejudice" component of the *Strickland* test involves more than a determination that the outcome would have been different. "It focuses on the question whether a counsel's deficient performance renders the result of the trial unreliable or the proceeding fundamentally unfair." And "unreliability or unfairness does not result if the ineffectiveness of counsel does not deprive the defendant of any substantive or procedural right to which the law entitles him."

The *Fretwell* case grew out of an unusual set of facts. An Arkansas jury convicted respondent of capital felony murder. During the death penalty phase of the case, the jury found an aggravating factor—that the murder, which occurred during a robbery, had been committed for pecuniary gain. But under *Collins v. Lockhart,* 754 F.2d 258 (8th Cir.1985) a then-existing (but subsequently overruled) Eighth Circuit precedent, an aggravating factor could not duplicate an element of the underlying felony—murder in the course of a robbery. However, respondent's lawyer failed to make any objection.

By the time the Eighth Circuit considered respondent's case on federal habeas corpus, it had already overruled *Collins.* Nevertheless, it held that respondent was entitled to relief, reasoning that had his lawyer objected to the use of the aggravating factor at the sentencing phase the trial judge would have sustained it and respondent would not have been sentenced to death. A 7–2 majority, per REHNQUIST, C.J., disagreed:

"To set aside a conviction or sentence solely because the outcome would have been different but for counsel's error may grant the defendant a windfall to which the law does not entitle him. Our decision in *Nix v. Whiteside* [Note 2 p. 170]. which held that a defendant was not prejudiced when his lawyer refused to cooperate in presenting perjured testimony, makes this very point. * * * Obviously, had [Whiteside] presented false testimony to the jury, there would have been a reasonable probability that the jury would not have returned a verdict of guilty. Sheer outcome determination, however, was not sufficient to make out a claim under the Sixth Amendment. * * * The touchstone of an ineffective assistance claim is the fairness of the adversary proceeding and [in determining that] 'a defendant has no entitlement to the luck of a lawless decisionmaker.' * * * [Defense counsel's failure to make an objection could not be prejudicial because the result of the sentencing proceeding] was rendered neither unreliable nor fundamentally unfair as a result of counsel's failure. [The] Court of Appeals, which had decided *Collins* in 1985, overruled [it] four years later. Had the trial court chosen to follow *Collins,* counsel's error would have 'deprived respondent of the chance to have the state court make an error in his favor.' "

In a concurring opinion, Justice O'CONNOR, wrote separately "only to point out that today's decision will, in the vast majority of cases, have no effect on the prejudice inquiry under *Strickland*": "The Court's ruling", she noted, "held only that the court making the prejudice determination may not consider the effect of an objection it knows to be wholly meritless under current governing law, even if the objection might have been considered meritorious at the time of its omission."

Dissenting Justice STEVENS, joined by Blackmun, J., expressed dismay at the Court's "astonishing conclusion that deficient performance by counsel does not prejudice a defendant even when it results in the erroneous imposition of a death sentence. The Court's aversion to windfalls seems to disappear, however, when the State is the favored recipient. For the end result in this case is that the State, through the coincidence of inadequate representation and fortuitous timing, may carry out a death sentence that was invalid when imposed." Continued the dissent:

"Hindsight has no place in a Sixth Amendment jurisprudence that focuses, quite rightly, on protecting the adversarial balance at trial. Respondent was denied 'the assistance necessary to justify reliance on the outcome of the proceeding,' *Strickland,* because his counsel's performance was so far below professional standards that it satisfied *Strickland*'s first prong, and so severely lacking that the verdict 'would reasonably likely have been different absent the errors.' It is simply irrelevant that we can now say, with hindsight, that had counsel failed to make a double-counting objection four years after the fact, his performance would have been neither deficient nor prejudicial. For as it happened, counsel's failure to object came at a time when it signified a breakdown in the adversarial process. A *post hoc* vision of what would have been the case years later has no bearing on the force of this showing."

4. In *Williams (Terry) v. Taylor*, 529 U.S. 362 (2000), the Virginia Supreme Court, relying on *Lockhart v. Fretwell*, held that the trial judge had erred in relying "on mere outcome determination" in assessing *Strickland* prejudice where counsel had failed to present available mitigation evidence in a capital sentencing proceeding. The state court held that, to establish prejudice, the defendant also had to "demonstrate that his sentencing proceeding was fundamentally unfair." The Supreme Court concluded that the state court was clearly in error. *Lockhart* did not require "a separate inquiry into fundamental fairness," but simply held that there are situations, such as that presented in *Nix* and *Lockhart*, in which "it would be unjust to characterize the likelihood of a different outcome as legitimate' prejudice'." Those cases "do not justify a departure from a straightforward application of *Strickland* when the ineffectiveness of counsel does deprive the defendant of a substantive or procedural right to which the law entitles him." Consider also *Glover v. United States*, 531 U.S. 198 (2001) (*Lockhart* lent no support to lower court's erroneous view that "an increase of 6 to 21 months in a defendant's sentence was not significant enough to amount to prejudice for purposes of *Strickland*:")

C. Strickland Exceptions

1. *Recognizing exceptions.* *Strickland* presents the dominant standard for resolving ineffective assistance claims, but as Strickland itself noted, that standard is not universal. Thus *Strickland* pointed to two settings in which the Court applied a standard other than the *Strickland* two-pronged test: (1) where the trial court had prevented counsel from utilizing certain adversarial procedures (commonly described as "interference cases") (p. 159)[a]; and (2) where counsel had been "burdened by an actual conflict of interest" as in *Cuyler v. Sullivan* (p. 162) (an exception further considered in *Mickens v. Taylor*, p. 198). The Court's ruling

a. As to interference with the counsel-client relationship through actions of enforcement agents, see pp. 494–96.

in *United States v. Cronic*, Note 2 infra, recognized additional exceptions while stressing the dominance of the *Strickland* decision. The Notes that follow discuss the scope of those additional exceptions, and the rejection of still broader exceptions.

2. ***Rejection of a broad inferential exception.*** In UNITED STATES v. CRONIC, 466 U.S. 648 (1984), decided on the same day as *Strickland*, the Court rejected an attempt to create a broad exception to the Strickland approach.

Respondent Cronic and two associates were indicted on mail fraud charges involving a "check kiting" scheme. When, shortly before the scheduled trial date, respondent's trial counsel withdrew, the district court appointed a young lawyer with a real estate practice who had never participated in a jury trial to represent respondent. Appointed counsel was allowed only 25 days for pretrial preparation, although it had taken the government over four and a half years to investigate the case and it had reviewed thousands of documents during that investigation. Without referring to any specific error or inadequacy in appointed counsel's performance, the U.S. Court of Appeals for the Tenth Circuit reversed respondent's conviction, inferring from the circumstances surrounding the representation of respondent that his right to the effective assistance of counsel had been violated. The court based this conclusion on five factors: (1) the limited time afforded counsel for investigation and preparation; (2) counsel's inexperience; (3) the gravity of the charge; (4) the complexity of possible defenses; and (5) the inaccessibility of witnesses to counsel. The Supreme Court, per STEVENS, J., disagreed:

"We begin by recognizing that the right to the effective assistance of counsel is recognized not for its own sake, but because of the effect it has on the ability of the accused to receive a fair trial. Absent some effect of challenged conduct on the reliability of the trial process, the Sixth Amendment guarantee is generally not implicated. Moreover, because we presume that the lawyer is competent to provide the guiding hand that the defendant needs, the burden rests on the accused to demonstrate a constitutional violation. There are, however, circumstances that are so likely to prejudice the accused that the cost of litigating their effect in a particular case is unjustified.

"Most obvious, of course, is the complete denial of counsel. The presumption that counsel's assistance is essential requires us to conclude that a trial is unfair if the accused is denied counsel at a critical stage of his trial.[b] Similarly, if counsel entirely fails to subject the prosecution's case to meaningful adversarial testing, then there has been a denial Sixth Amendment rights that makes the adversary process itself presumptively unreliable.* * * Circumstances of that magnitude also may be present on some occasions when, although counsel is available to assist the accused during trial, the likelihood that any lawyer, even a fully competent one, could provide effective assistance is so small that a presumption of prejudice is appropriate. without inquiry into the actual conduct of the trial. *Powell v. Alabama* [p. 82] was such a case.

"The defendants [in *Powell*] had been indicted for a highly publicized capital offense. Six days before trial, the trial judge appointed 'all the members of the bar' for purposes of arraignment. 'Whether they would represent the defendants thereafter if no counsel appeared in their behalf, was a matter of speculation only, or, as the judge indicated, of mere anticipation on the part of the court.' On the day of trial, a lawyer from Tennessee appeared on behalf of persons "interested"

b. *Roe v. Flores-Ortega*, Note 8, p. 151, concluded that a presumption of prejudice similarly was mandated where counsel denied the defendant his right to appeal as of right by refusing to file a requested appeal (see fn. c, p. 152), but not where the record shows only that counsel failed to consult and the defendant did not request an appeal.

in the defendants, but stated that he had not had an opportunity to prepare the case or to familiarize himself with local procedure, and therefore was unwilling to represent the defendants on such short notice. The problem was resolved when the court decided that the Tennessee lawyer would represent the defendants, with whatever help the local bar could provide. * * * This Court held that 'such designation of counsel as was attempted was either so indefinite or so close upon the trial as to amount to a denial of effective and substantial aid in that regard.' * * *

"But every refusal to postpone a criminal trial will not give rise to such a presumption. In *Avery v. Alabama*, 308 U.S. 444 (1940), counsel was appointed in a capital case only three days before trial, and the trial court denied counsel's request for additional time to prepare. Nevertheless, the Court held that since evidence and witnesses were easily accessible to defense counsel, the circumstances did not make it unreasonable to expect that counsel could adequately prepare for trial during that period of time. Similarly, in *Chambers v. Maroney*, 399 U.S. 42 (1970), the Court refused "to fashion a *per se* rule requiring reversal of every conviction following tardy appointment of counsel." Thus, only when surrounding circumstances justify a presumption of ineffectiveness can a Sixth Amendment claim be sufficient without inquiry into counsel's actual performance at trial. * * *

"The five factors listed in the Court of Appeals' opinion are relevant to an evaluation of a lawyer's effectiveness in a particular case, but neither separately nor in combination do they provide a basis for concluding that competent counsel was not able to provide this respondent with the guiding hand that the Constitution guarantees. * * * "

3. *The constructive denial of counsel.* Relying on *Cronic*'s discussion of *Powell* and its reference to counsel who "entirely fails to subject the prosecution's case to meaningful adversary testing, lower courts have developed a doctrine of "constructive denial" of counsel. Those cases held that where counsel's absence at a critical proceeding or lack of effort was so extensive as produce a "complete failure" of representation, a presumption of prejudice was justified. BELL v. CONE, 535 U.S. 685 (2002) was typical of such rulings.

At respondent's trial the prosecution provided overwhelming evidence that he had killed an elderly couple in brutal fashion. Respondent's defense was that he was not guilty by reason of insanity due to substance abuse and posttraumatic stress disorder related to his Vietnam military service. The jury found respondent guilty of the murders, and a sentencing hearing followed. The prosecution introduced evidence of aggravating factors and the defense called the jury's attention to the mitigating evidence already before it. The defense also cross-examined prosecution witnesses, but called no witnesses of its own. After the junior prosecutor made a closing argument, defense counsel waived final argument, which prevented the lead prosecutor from arguing in rebuttal. The jury found four aggravating factors and no mitigating factors. Under state law, these findings required the death penalty.

The Sixth Circuit granted federal habeas relief, concluding that counsel's failures at the sentencing hearing amounted to a constructive denial of counsel and that justified a presumption of prejudice under the analysis of *Cronic*. But an 8–1 majority, per REHNQUIST, C.J., held that the lower court's reliance on *Cronic* was misplaced:

"When we spoke in *Cronic* of the possibility of presuming prejudice based on an attorney's failure to test the prosecutor's case, we indicated that the attorney's failure must be complete. [Here] respondent's argument is not that his counsel failed to oppose the prosecution throughout the sentencing proceeding as a whole, but that his counsel failed to do so at specific points. For purposes of distinguishing between the rule of *Strickland* and that of *Cronic*, this difference is not of degree but of kind. The aspects of counsel's performance challenged by respondent—the failure to adduce mitigating evidence and the waiver of closing argument—are plainly of the same ilk as other specific attorney errors we have held subject to *Strickland*'s performance and prejudice components."[c]

4. BURDINE v. JOHNSON, 262 F.3d 336 (5th Cir.2001) (en banc) was decided before *Bell v. Cone*. Should *Bell v. Cone* require reconsideration of the majority's ruling in *Burdine*?

Petitioner Burdine was convicted of capital murder and sentenced to death. On the basis of evidence that Burdine's defense lawyer, Joe Cannon, "repeatedly dozed and/or actually slept during substantial portions" of the murder trial, the state habeas court granted relief. The court concluded that because defense counsel was, in effect, "absent," a showing of prejudice in accordance with *Strickland* was not required. The Texas Court of Criminal Appeals did not dispute the lower court's findings regarding the sleeping of Burdine's lawyer, but concluded that Burdine was not entitled to relief because he had failed to meet his burden of proof under *Strickland*. The federal habeas court concluded that Cannon's sleeping during the trial amounted to a constructive denial of counsel for substantial portions of the trial and therefore prejudice should be presumed in accordance with *Strickland* and *Cronic*. A 9–5 majority, per BENAVIDES, J., affirmed:

"[O]nce we have accepted as presumptively correct the state court finding that counsel slept 'during portions of [Burdine's] trial on the merits, in particular during the guilt-innocence phase when the State's sole prosecutor was questioning witnesses and presenting evidence,' there is no need to attempt to further scrutinize the record. * * * " The factual findings made during Burdine's state habeas proceedings demonstrate that Burdine's counsel was repeatedly asleep, and hence unconscious * * *. Unconscious counsel equates to no counsel at all. * * * When we have no basis for assuming that counsel exercised judgment on behalf of his client during critical stages of trial, we have insufficient basis for trusting that trial and consequently must presume prejudice. * * *

"An unconscious attorney does not, indeed cannot, perform at all. This fact distinguishes the sleeping lawyer from the drunk or drugged one. [The] unconscious attorney is in fact no different from an attorney that is physically absent from trial since both are equally unable to exercise judgment on behalf of their clients. Such absence of counsel at a critical stage of a proceeding makes the adversary process unreliable, and thus a presumption of prejudice is warranted pursuant to *Cronic*.

c. The Court also rejected respondent's argument that the state court's adjudication of his claim involved an "unreasonable application" of *Strickland*: "When the junior prosecutor delivered a matter-of-fact closing that did not dwell on any of the brutal aspects of the crime, counsel was faced with a choice. He could make a closing argument and reprise for the jury, perhaps in greater detail than his opening, the primary mitigating evidence concerning his client's drug dependency and post-traumatic stress from Vietnam. [But] he knew that if he took this opportunity, he would give the lead prosecutor, who all agreed was very persuasive, the chance to depict his client as a heartless killer just before the jurors began deliberation. Alternatively, counsel could prevent the lead prosecutor from arguing by waiving his own summation and relying on the jurors' familiarity with the case and his opening plea for life made just a few hours before. Neither option, it seems to us, so clearly outweighs the other that it was objectively unreasonable for the Tennessee Court of Appeals to deem counsel's choice to waive argument a tactical decision about which competent lawyers might disagree."

Dissenting Justice Stevens maintained that the defense counsel's shortcomings were so great that the Sixth Circuit correctly concluded that he " 'entirely fail[ed] to subject the prosecution's case to meaningful adversarial testing.' *Cronic*."

"* * * [W]e decline to adopt a per se rule that any dozing by defense counsel during trial merits a presumption of prejudice. Our holding, that the repeated unconsciousness of Burdine's counsel through not insubstantial portions of the critical guilt-innocence phase of Burdine's murder trial warrants a presumption of prejudice, is limited to the egregious facts found by the state habeas court in this case."

BARKSDALE, J., joined by three other judges, dissented:

"[Although the majority indicates otherwise,] there is no state-finding that Cannon was 'repeatedly unconscious' for either 'substantial' or 'not unsubstantial portions' [of the trial]. [The] only presumptively correct, and therefore binding, somewhat specific state-finding is that Cannon 'dozed and actually fell asleep during portions of [Burdine's] trial on the merits, in particular during the guilt-innocence phase when the state's sole prosecutor was questioning witnesses and presenting evidence.'

"[In] the light of the circumstances of this case, [none of the reasons articulated in *Strickland* for presuming, rather than requiring proof of, prejudice applies]. First, as the state court found, neither the prosecutor nor the trial judge was aware of Cannon's sleeping. [Accordingly,] the State could not have easily prevented the sleeping. * * *

"Second, the claimed prejudice is not easy to identify, just the opposite. The claim was not raised until over ten years after trial, after it was first raised by another death row inmate. Therefore, a determination of precisely when counsel slept has been rendered impossible due to the passage of time and the lack of any indication in the trial transcript [as] to when the conduct occurred. Nor can it be determined from the witnesses' testimony at the state evidentiary hearing. Accordingly, it is impossible to determine whether, for example, Cannon slept during the presentation of crucial, inculpatory evidence, or during the introduction of unobjectionable, uncontested evidence.[d]

"Finally, for circumstances where, as here, counsel sleeps for unidentified portions of a trial, prejudice is not so likely that case-by-case inquiry into prejudice is not worth the cost. [The] majority states that its rule 'is limited to the egregious facts found by the state habeas court in this case.' [But] the state habeas court made no finding that Cannon's dozing and sleeping rose to the level of unconsciousness, and, in any event, no finding quantifying the amount of sleeping or what evidence was then being presented. * * *

"Prejudice has not been presumed for claims of denial of effective-assistance due to counsel's alleged impairment because of alcohol, drug use, or a mental condition. [The] majority distinguishes those cases on the basis that, unlike a drunk or drugged lawyer, who 'exercises judgment, though perhaps impaired' (to say the least, such 'impaired judgment' may well be worse than none at all), an unconscious lawyer (according to the majority, because he is sleeping) is not capable of exercising any judgment. The majority maintains such an unconscious attorney is no different from one who is physically absent. The flaw in its analysis is that it assumes, without any state-finding or record evidence, that Cannon was always so deeply and soundly asleep that he was always 'unconscious.' [The] state-finding that Cannon 'dozed and actually fell asleep' does not support the majority's characterizing each episode as 'unconsciousness.' In any event, [in] the

d. In a separate dissenting opinion, Jolly, J. explained that because, inter alia, Burdine is "plainly guilty of murder beyond a reasonable doubt," his lawyer actually provided competent representation throughout the trial. Burdine "waited eleven years before he ever raised the 'sleeping lawyer' claim," and "there is no evidence in the record the counsel's sleeping occurred at a critical stage in the trial."

context of Cannon's otherwise quite meaningful assistance to Burdine, Burdine was not denied counsel.

"[Cannon's] sleeping during unidentified portions of Burdine's trial did not result in losing its character as a confrontation between adversaries, nor did it render the trial fundamentally unfair. Because Cannon provided meaningful assistance to Burdine, prejudice *vel non* to Burdine's defense, resulting from Cannon's sleeping, should be established under *Strickland*'s two-prong test: Burdine should be required to demonstrate a reasonable probability that the outcome of the trial would have been different if, during the periods in which the transcript reflects no activity by Cannon, he had taken some action."[e]

NOTES ON CHALLENGES TO INSTITUTIONAL DEFICIENCIES

1. Commentators over the years have argued that criminal defense systems are in "a state of perpetual crises." Schulhofer & Friedman, fn.a, p. 138. They argue that appointed counsel (especially public defenders) face such serious obstacles in the lack of funds and heavy caseloads that they will almost invariably render ineffective assistance in a significant portion of their cases. They argue that legislatures have been largely unresponsive to these difficulties,[a] and therefore the courts should expand their role in ensuring effective assistance of counsel, by insisting upon appropriate institutional responses to the caseload and funding difficulties.[b]

e. The Supreme Court denied certiorari in *Burdine*, 535 U.S. 1120 (2002) a ruling that came after *Bell v. Cone*. In seeking review of the case, the Texas attorney general had argued that the Fifth Circuit's ruling, if allowed to stand, would encourage many appeals by "imaginative" prisoners trying to convert a lawyers's "impaired trial performance" into an authentic ticket for a new trial. See Linda Greenhouse, *Inmate Whose Lawyer Slept Gets New Trial*, N.Y. Times, June 4, 2002, p.A16. "It was hard to avoid the sense," comments Greenhouse, "that whatever danger the justices thought the [Fifth Circuit's] ruling might pose for the legal system, they had decided that it would be even more dangerous for the Supreme Court to suggest that for a lawyer to sleep through a trial was acceptable."

a. Jurisdictions obviously vary in this regard. See U.S. Department of Justice, *Keeping Defender Workloads Manageable* (NCJ–185632, 2001) (listing caseload maximums imposed on public defenders in, 14 states, with 8 having felony maximums of 150 or less; also noting the adoption of plans for allocating indigency defense between defender officers and appointed counsel, taking into consideration the weighted caseload capacity of the defender office); Note, *Gideon*'s Promise Unfulfilled, 113 Harv.L.Rev. 2052 (2000) acknowledging that the federal system of assistance for indigent defendants "has generally been well supported," but describing state systems as suffering from severe deficiencies).

Consider also CRIMPROC § 1.4(j), fn. 309.7: "A major difficulty of almost all of the commentary is the reliance upon broad generalizations in describing the current setting, both as to funding and caseloads. With few national studies being available, shortcomings found in studies of a scattering of communities are taken to be the norm. * * * Admittedly, some commentators acknowledge that funding, caseloads, or performance may be adequate or even more than adequate in a particular jurisdiction. But none have gone so far as to suggest that these elements are satisfactory in a significant number of jurisdictions, notwithstanding efforts in many jurisdictions to limit caseloads and increase funding."

b. See e.g., Richard Klein, the Eleventh Commandment: Thou Shalt Not Be Compelled To Render the Ineffective Assistance of Counsel, 68 Indiana L.J. 363, 432 (1993): "Court officials, administrators of court-appointed counsel plans, and judges have rarely concerned themselves with the *quality* of counsel provided indigent defendants. Absent some completely unforeseeable event, the prognosis for any additional funding for defense services is poor indeed—it is almost inconceivable that elected politicians would call for or provide additional funding to represent indigents accused of crime. The responsibility of defense counsel, who are most aware of the egregious violations which result from inadequate funding, is clear. Neither habeas corpus petitions, nor appeals based on claims of ineffective assistance of counsel, nor attempts by private court-appointed counsel to unite and strike have been successful in bringing about the fundamental changes that are required. * * * Systematic litigation attacking the constitutionali-

2. The commentators acknowledge that *Cronic* appears to preclude a Sixth Amendment analysis that overturns a conviction based on institutional deficiencies, and that state courts have regularly denied such challenges, "holding that * * * ineffective assistance claims must be established on an individualized basis." They argue, however, that challenges brought prospectively should result in rulings holding that inadequate funding or heavy caseloads preclude fulfilling the constitutional mandate of effective assistance. Courts have, on occasion, required that appointed counsel receive greater compensation, or held that defender offices may no larger be required to carry a caseload beyond a particular maximum. However, they have done so on grounds other than presuming that the limited compensation or heavy caseload will produce a Sixth Amendment violation. See Robert Rigg, *The Constitution, Compensation, and Competence: A Case Study*, 27 Am.J.Crim.L. 1 (1999) (decisions commonly based on court's inherent power or undue burden placed on defense counsel). Consider also David Cole, *No Equal Justice*, 83 (1999) (noting that other courts have rejected challenges to unrealistically low statutory caps for compensating appointed counsel, reasoning that the "ineffective assistance of counsel" standard will ensure competent representation; in particular, a Missouri case sustained a cap of $1,000 plus out-of-pocket expenses for two experienced death penalty lawyers who had each worked more than 400 hours preparing for and trying a capital case).

3. An exceptional ruling, often praised by commentators, is in *State v. Peart*, 621 So.2d 780 (La.1993). Leonard Peart, an indigent defendant was charged with armed robbery, aggravated rape, aggravated burglary and murder. When Rick Teisser, a public defender in a section of the New Orleans Criminal District Court, was appointed to represent Peart against all charges, except murder, Teisser was handling 70 active felony cases. He had represented 418 defendants in the first seven months of the year (entering 130 guilty pleas at arraignment) and had at least one serious felony case set for trial for every trial date during the year. Moreover he had no funding for expert witnesses and had access to only three investigators, who were responsible for rendering assistance in 7000 cases annually. Teisser filed a pretrial motion asking the trial judge to declare that, under the conditions Teisser had to work, he could not possibly provide an effective legal defense.

The trial judge agreed, concluding that under the circumstances "not even a lawyer with an 'S' on his chest could effectively handle the docket." Unlike the trial court, the state supreme court declined to rule that the entire defender system was constitutionally inadequate, but it did adopt a rebuttable presumption that defendants represented by those in Teisser's public defender office were not receiving a constitutionally adequate defense, a presumption that would continue unless changes occurred in workloads and resources. "This step," reports Note, 113 Harv.L.Rev. 2062, 2074 (2000), "prompted the Louisiana legislature to increase indigent defense funding by $5 million over the next two years."

4. Consider also *Miranda v. Clark County, Nevada*, 319 F.3d 465 (9th Cir.2002). There, a 1983 civil rights action was brought against a county and its public defender by a former defendant whose capital murder conviction had been overturned on grounds of ineffective assistance of counsel. He claimed that two alleged allocation policies of the public defender office reflected a "deliberate indifference" to the Sixth Amendment requirement of adequate "representation" and therefore established a § 1983 cause of action. The first policy, under the majority's reading of the complaint, allocated resources based on a client's polygraph result, with clients who failed the test being provided "minimal

ty of the system for delivering defense services, however, offers hope and promise. The failures of states and counties to provide adequate funds to ensure the constitutionally mandated effective assistance of counsel are subject to, and call for, attack."

resources to develop a defense." That policy was viewed as contrary to the "constitutional guarantee * * * of effective representation of all defendants regardless of guilt or innocence." The second alleged policy involved "assigning the least-experience counsel to capital cases without providing any training." In finding "callous disregard of constitutional rights" in such a policy, the Ninth Circuit rejected the contention that attorneys who had graduated from law school and passed the bar thereby had sufficient competence to adequately represent defendants in capital murder cases.[c]

5. Many commentators have argued that the failure of courts generally to be more responsive to Sixth Amendment challenges to institutional deficiencies in the provision of appointed counsel reflects an unwillingness to challenge the legislative bodies (state or local) responsible for such deficiencies. Consider, however, the following possible concerns:

(1) Although the *ABA* Standards, *Providing Defense Services* 73 (3d.ed.1992) set forth caseload guidelines widely accepted by commentators, properly weighing caseloads involves considerable complexity and the assumptions underlying optimal resource levels (e.g., a caseload that permits full litigation in most cases) are subject to challenge. See e.g., Jerold Israel, *Excessive Criminal Justice Caseloads: Challenging the Conventional Wisdom*, 48 Fla.L.Rev. 761 (1996) (optimal resource levels should recognize that many defendants may desire to enter a guilty plea, and from a utilitarian perspective, must take account of the caseloads burden carried by the prosecutor).

(2) Disagreements exist as to what level of funding is adequate. One issue of dispute is whether the adequacy of the funding should be measured by reference only to what is spent on law enforcement. See Cole, Note 2 supra, at 64–65 (comparison also made to other government expenditures). Another is what constitutes a proper ratio of expenditures on defense to expenditures on prosecution. See CRIMPROC. § 1.4 at fn. 309.7 (collecting authorities).

(3) Studies indicate that "public counsel" (i.e., public defenders and appointed counsel) achieve outcomes that are largely the same (for similar types of offenses) as those achieved by retained counsel. See e.g., U.S. Department of Justice, Bureau of Justice Statistics, *Defense Counsel in Criminal Cases* (NCJ–179023, 2000) (1996) (survey of dispositions of all federal felony defendants and state felony defendants in the 75 largest counties; study considered both rate of conviction and sentences, type of offense charged, and criminal history of defendant);[d] CRIMPROC § 11.8 at 59.3 (citing other studies).[e]

c. A dissent disagreed with the majority's reading of the complaint. It argued that the complaint "actually pled that the public defender had a policy of using a lawyer with a year and a half of experience to prepare the case, but rather than send him into the courtroom alone, the office policy provided for experienced counsel to backup the green lawyer and give advice at trial." The dissent also noted: "The majority's reliance on the County's assignment of an inexperienced lawyer and policy of refusing to train lawyers is also surprising in light of the Supreme Court's holding in *United States v. Cronic* that ineffective assistance cannot be inferred from assignment of a young inexperienced lawyer to a major felony case, even though he had no criminal experience and had never tried a case to a jury."

d. The same study summarized the responses of representative samples of prison inmates as to their interactions with counsel. These responses indicated that defendants with public counsel had a longer interval between arrest and first contact with counsel in both the state system and the federal system. Far fewer spoke to counsel within 24 hours or within a week of arrest and a larger percentage stated that they first spoke to counsel at trial (13.6% vs. 3.5% for state prisoners). Those represented by public counsel also reported fewer conversations with counsel.

e. Floyd Feeney & Patrick G. Jackson, *Public Defenders, Assigned Counsel Retained Counsel: Does the Type of Counsel Matter?*, 22 Rutgers 361 (1991), agree that studies indicate that the type of lawyer (public defender, assigned, or retained) make very little difference as to outcome, but add that "the best lawyers do make a difference." They note that only a very few defendants of those retaining counsel

SECTION 5. CONFLICTS OF INTEREST

"An attorney appeared in a municipal court for the purpose of requesting a reduction of bail for four defendants jointly charged with possession of a large cache of drugs seized from a communal house. Referring to the first of his clients, the lawyer stated: 'The defendant should be released on his recognizance, Your Honor, because he has no rap sheet. Obviously he is not a hardened criminal and should not be locked up with others who are.' When the second defendant's case was called, counsel argued: 'No drugs were found in this defendant's bedroom, Your Honor. His chance for an acquittal is great and consequently it is highly likely that he will show up for trial.' On behalf of the third defendant, the lawyer began to argue that his client had lived in the area all of his life. The judge interrupted the lawyer, asking him if any drugs had been seized from the bedroom of defendant number three. The lawyer responded, 'No comment, Your Honor.' The judge countered with the remark: 'I suppose that this client also has a prior record, making him a hardened criminal,' evoking the response that although the defendant had a prior record, he certainly was not a hardened criminal. The fourth defendant then interrupted the proceedings by eagerly requesting to be represented by the public defender."

—G. Lowenthal, *Joint Representation in Criminal Cases: A Critical Appraisal,* 64 Va.L.Rev. 939, 941 (1978).

A. Potential Conflicts and The Duty to Inquire

1. ***Range of Conflicts.*** The Court first noted, in *Glasser v. United States,* 315 U.S. 60 (1942), that the right to the assistance of counsel is not satisfied by a counsel whose actions are influenced by a conflict of interest. The conflict in *Glasser*, arose out an attorney's joint representation of codefendants in the same trial. While that is the classic conflict setting, many other settings also can product an "actual conflict of interest"—i.e., a situation in which action taken (or not taken) on behalf of the defendant would work against an obligation the attorney owes to another person or the attorney's self-interest. Those other settings—commonly described as "potential conflict situations"—include: (1) joint representation of codefendants who will be tried separately; (2) defense counsel has previously represented, or is currently representing, in another matter or the same matter, a victim of the alleged offense; (3) defense counsel has previously represented, or is currently representing, in another matter or the same matter, a likely prosecution witness; (4) a third party with some interest in the case is paying defense counsel's fee; (5) a fee arrangement that creates a possible conflict between counsel's financial interests and the defendant's interests (e.g., a compensation agreement under which counsel has an interest in royalties received from a movie or book relating to the trial); (6) counsel was involved in the same transaction and fears possible criminal prosecution; (7) counsel is under investigation or being actively prosecuted by the same prosecutor's office as to another matter; (8) counsel is facing possible criminal or disciplinary consequences as a result of questionable behavior in representing the defendant; (9) counsel has

can afford the very best, resulting in such representation having no impact upon the studies. See also CRIMPROC. § 11.8(c) ("of course, [the outcome-similarity for public and retained attorneys] may be because retained counsel operate under similar funding constraints and caseload burdens, but the courts would find regulation of those factors as to retained counsel even more difficult than as to state-provided counsel). But compare Dripps, Note 1 p. 167 (arguing for an "ex ante parity standard" that compares appointed counsel and prosecutors, as "a comparison between appointed counsel and retained counsel is not necessarily a comparison between appointed counsel and effective counsel").

delivered, or has an obligation to deliver, to the police physical evidence that can be used against the defendant; and (10) counsel is to be called as a prosecution witness.[a]

2. ***Conflicts and professional responsibility standards.*** While the various settings described above all create a potential for inhibiting counsel's actions on behalf of his client, none do so inevitably. Indeed, few situations creating potential conflicts are viewed as so fraught with the danger of dividing counsel's loyalties as to be absolutely prohibited by prevailing standards of professional responsibility. The ABA's Model Rules of Professional Conduct, Rule 1.7 provides that where a defense counsel has another client whose interests are "directly adverse" to the defendant, the lawyer may nonetheless represent the defendant if the lawyer "reasonably believes that [he or she] will be able to provide competent and diligent representation to each affected client," and each client consents after full disclosure. So too, Rule 1.8 states that a lawyer is not prohibited from representing a client where the representation of that client "will be materially limited by the lawyer's responsibilities to another client, a former client, * * * or by a personal interest of the lawyer" if the lawyer believes the representation will be competent and diligent and there is adequate consultation and consent.

The profession's willingness to tolerate arrangements that create a high potential for dividing the attorney's loyalty is not based simply upon the fact that those arrangements will not inevitably create a conflict. Its decision not to absolutely prohibit such arrangements is also based in part on the potential value of many of these arrangements to the client. Initially, they may permit the client to obtain the services of the one lawyer that he wants to represent him. Some defendants put their trust in a particular lawyer and would want that lawyer even though she may have previously represented one of the prosecution's witnesses or even the victim. Some would prefer a privately retained lawyer and can afford one only if their employer, a codefendant, or some other interested person will pay that lawyer. Joint representation of codefendants, in particular, may have strategic advantages. Thus the Supreme has noted: "Joint representation is a means of ensuring against reciprocal recrimination. A common defense often gives strength against a common attack." Holloway v. Arkansas, Note 5, p. 193.

3. ***Prohibiting representation in potential-conflict situations.*** As one might anticipate, neither courts nor legislatures have been willing to adopt prophylactic rules that ban defense arrangements which create a potential conflict where the profession has been unwilling to do so in its regulations. Various states, by court rule or statute, have prohibited public defender offices from jointly representing codefendants (see fn. a, p. 192), but such prohibitions have not been

a. In many of the above situations, conflicts also arise where the potentially conflicting representation is by another attorney in the same law firm as the defendant's counsel. Under ethics codes, conflicts generally are vicariously imputed to all members of a law firm. While the Supreme Court has not ruled directly on this approach, *Burger v. Kemp*, (Note 2, p. 206) "assumed without deciding that two law partners are considered as one attorney" in analyzing the conflict potential of representing codefendants. Some states treat the lawyers in a public defender office in much the same manner. Many other jurisdictions, however, hold the "same firm" principle generally inapplicable to public defenders, in part because "the salaried government employee does not have the financial interest in the success of the departmental representation that is inherent in private practice." In these jurisdictions, where the defender office's potential conflict stems from confidential information received from a past client now a prosecution witness, the common solution is to utilize an internal ethical wall of separation which keeps that information away from the attorney representing the defendant. That device tends not to be viewed as sufficient, however, as to codefendants. Defender offices commonly are prohibited by state law from representing indigent codefendants, even when the codefendants, seek joint representation; representation is provided through a combination of the defender office representing one codefendant and separate appointed counsel representing each of the others. See CRIMPROC. § 11.9(a).

extended to joint representation by retained counsel. At least one state, however, has taken the position that multiple representation of codefendants is "inherently prejudicial," and therefore may be permitted only with an appropriate waiver by both codefendants. See *Asch v. State*, 62 P.3d 945 (2003). Would an absolute prohibition against multiple representation of codefendants be constitutional? Consider *Wheat v. United States*, p. 208, noting the difficulties presented in relying upon in client waivers.

4. ***Non-constitutional requirements of judicial inquiry.*** Federal Rule 44 requires the trial court to conduct an inquiry whenever defendants have been jointly charged under Rule 8(b) or joined for trial under Rule 13 and are represented by "the same counsel or counsel who are associated in the practice of law." The trial court is directed to "promptly inquire about the propriety of the joint representation," and to "personally advise each defendant of the right to the effective assistance of counsel, including separate representation." Moreover, "unless there is good cause to believe that no conflict of interest is likely to arise," the trial court "must take appropriate measures to protect each defendant's right to counsel." Several states impose similar obligations on their trial courts. The Advisory Committee Notes to Rule 44(c) clearly indicated that the failure to comply with Rule 44(c) should not in itself constitute a per se reversible error. Accordingly, on review after a conviction, appellate courts will look to whether the reversal is required under the Sixth Amendment. See Pt. B infra.

5. ***The initial recognition of a constitutional duty of inquiry.*** The Supreme Court first recognized a constitutional duty to inquire in HOLLOWAY v. ARKANSAS, 435 U.S. 475 (1978). Holloway presented the very common situation of codefendants represented by the same attorney in a joint trial, but it also presented the unusual situation of defense counsel requesting pretrial that the trial court appoint separate counsel for each defendant (counsel noting that the defendant's statements to him indicated "a possibility of conflict"), and the court basically ignoring that request without conducting an inquiry. The Supreme Court majority (per BURGER, C.J.) reversed the convictions of all three codefendants. *Glasser v. United States*, 315 U.S. 60 (1942), had found a Sixth Amendment violation where the trial court had required defendant's retained counsel to also represent a codefendant, leading counsel to take action adverse to the defendant's interests. (see fn. a, p. 198) The *Glasser* opinion had stated that the trial court has a duty not to insist that counsel "undertake to concurrently represent interests which might diverge." In failing to inquire into the possibility of a conflict, after that possibility was "brought home to the court" by the counsel's request for separate representation, the trial court here had violated that duty. The Court stressed that counsel's request did not require the trial court to automatically appoint separate counsel, but the trial court did have to "take adequate steps to ascertain whether the risk [of a conflict] was too remote to warrant separate counsel." That failure in itself violated the Sixth Amendment and required reversal of the defendant's convictions.

The *Holloway* ruling opened up a debate as to whether the constitutional duty to inquire extended beyond the unusual *Holloway* fact situation. The Supreme Court addressed that issue in Cuyler v. Sullivan, Note 6 infra.

6. ***Defining the scope of the duty.*** In CUYLER v. SULLIVAN,[c] 446 U.S. 335 (1980), defendant Sullivan had been indicted, along with two codefendants, for the first degree murders of two victims. Sullivan accepted representation from the two lawyers retained by his codefendants because he could not afford to retain a lawyer. Sullivan came to trial first and counsel challenged the prosecution's

c. Since appellant Cuyler was the prison warden, also involved in other litigation, the case is often referred to as *Sullivan*, although some judges prefer *Cuyler*.

case, but did not put on any defense evidence. The jury found Sullivan guilty and set his sentence at life imprisonment. Sullivan's two codefendants were later acquitted in separate trials. Sullivan then sought collateral relief under state law, raising for the first time a claim that his counsel had represented conflicting interests. Although the Third Circuit, on federal habeas corpus, held that there had been an actual conflict of interest, the Supreme Court first reviewed the contention that Sullivan was entitled to a reversal of his conviction, without examining whether an actual conflict had occurred, because, as in *Holloway*, the trial court had violated a constitutional duty to conduct an inquiry into the possibility of a conflict. the Court majority (per POWELL, J.) rejected that contention:.

"In *Holloway,* a single public defender represented three defendants at the same trial. The trial court refused to consider the appointment of separate counsel despite the defense lawyer's timely and repeated assertions that the interests of his clients conflicted. This Court recognized that a lawyer forced to represent codefendants whose interests conflict cannot provide the adequate legal assistance required by the Sixth Amendment. Given the trial court's failure to respond to timely objections, however, the Court did not consider whether the alleged conflict actually existed. It simply held that the trial court's error unconstitutionally endangered the right to counsel.

"*Holloway* requires state trial courts to investigate timely objections to multiple representation. But nothing in our precedents suggests that the Sixth Amendment requires state courts themselves to initiate inquiries into the propriety of multiple representation in every case. Defense counsel have an ethical obligation to avoid conflicting representations and to advise the court promptly when a conflict of interest arises during the course of trial. Absent special circumstances, therefore, trial courts may assume either that multiple representation entails no conflict or that the lawyer and his clients knowingly accept such risk of conflict as may exist. Indeed, as the Court noted in *Holloway,* trial courts necessarily rely in large measure upon the good faith and good judgment of defense counsel. 'An attorney representing two defendants in a criminal matter is in the best position professionally and ethically to determine when a conflict of interests exists or will probably develop at trial.' Id. Unless the trial court knows or reasonably should know that a particular conflict exists, the court need not initiate an inquiry.

"Nothing in the circumstances of this case indicates that the trial court had a duty to inquire whether there was a conflict of interest. The provision of separate trials for Sullivan and his codefendants significantly reduced the potential for a divergence in their interests. No participant in Sullivan's trial ever objected to the multiple representation. [Counsel's] opening argument for Sullivan outlined a defense compatible with the view that none of the defendants was connected with the murders. The opening arguments also suggested that counsel was not afraid to call witnesses whose testimony might be needed at the trials of Sullivan's codefendants. Finally counsel's critical decision to rest Sullivan's defense was on its face a reasonable tactical response to the weakness of the circumstantial evidence presented by the prosecutor. On these facts, we conclude that the Sixth Amendment imposed upon the trial court no affirmative duty to inquire into the propriety of multiple representation.

Justices Brennan and Marshall, in separate concurring opinions, disagreed with the Court's analysis on this issue. Justice BRENNAN noted: "[As the Court observes], 'a possible conflict inheres in almost every instance of multiple representation.' Therefore, upon discovery of joint representation, the duty of the trial court is to ensure that the defendants have not unwittingly given up their constitutional right to effective counsel. This is necessary since it is usually the case that defendants will not know what their rights are or how to raise them. This is surely true of the defendant who may not be receiving the effective assistance of counsel as a result of conflicting duties owed to other defendants. Therefore, the trial court cannot safely assume that silence indicates a knowledgeable choice to proceed jointly. The court must at least affirmatively advise the defendants that joint representation creates potential hazards which the defendants should consider before proceeding with the representation. * * * [Where, as here,] there is no evidence that the court advised respondent about the potential for conflict or that respondent made a knowing and intelligent choice to forego his right to separate counsel, I believe that respondent, who has shown a significant possibility of conflict, is entitled to a presumption that his representation in fact suffered. * * * ''

7. ***The "reasonably should know" standard.*** What circumstance present a situation in which the trial court "reasonably should know" that a conflict exists and therefore conduct an inquiry? In light of *Sullivan*'s explanation of why the multiple representation presented there did not present such a situation, would an inquiry be required where counsel representing codefendants did not suggest a conflict, but their unified defense clearly would favor one defendant over the other. See State v. Weese, 424 A.2d 705 (Me.1981) (united defense favored father over son). CRIMPROC. § 11.9(b) notes that the "reasonably should know" standard generally has been applied only to situations in which "actual conflicts were obvious," such as "where the record established that the defense counsel had previously represented a [prosecution] witness in connection with the same or a related waiver [or] that the defense counsel was facing a disciplinary complaint in connection to this case." The courts have held it not to apply "where indicators were ambiguous, or suggested no more than a potential conflict." Is this approach consistent with the Supreme Court's ruling in *Wood v. Georgia*, Note 8 infra. Consider also Mickens v. Taylor, p. 196.

8. Although the Court's ruling was far from clear, WOOD v. GEORGIA, 450 U.S. 261 (1981), appeared to conclude that the trial court reasonably should have known of a conflict (and the case was so interpreted in the subsequent decision of *Mickens v. Taylor*, p. 196). The Supreme Court granted certiorari in *Wood* to determine whether a state could constitutionally revoke the probation of defendants who were unable to pay fines imposed for a previous conviction. The case was remanded, however, for an evidentiary hearing on a conflict issue raised by the Court sua sponte. The defendants had been charged with an offense committed in the course of their employment and their counsel had been provided by their employer. They had been sentenced to pay substantial fines on the assumption that the employer would provide them with the necessary funds. When the employer refused to give them the funds, counsel did not immediately move for modification of the fines or ask for leniency. Instead, he pressed the argument that a probation revocation for the failure to pay fines that were beyond a defendant's means was unconstitutional, a contention which, if accepted, would work to the long range benefit of the employer. The Supreme Court (per POWELL, J.) noted that the record of the revocation proceedings was not sufficiently complete for it to determine whether a conflict actually existed. "Nevertheless," it noted, "the record does demonstrate that the possibility of a conflict of interest was sufficiently apparent at the time of the revocation hearing to impose upon the [state] court a duty to inquire further." All of the relevant facts relating to the employer's retention of counsel, the employer's failure to pay the fines, and "counsel's insistence upon pressing a constitutional attack" were known to the state court. Moreover, "any doubt as to whether th[at] court should have been aware of the problem [was] dispelled by the fact that the [prosecutor] had raised the conflict problem."

The *Wood* ruling created some confusion because the Court stated in footnote 18 that "*Sullivan* mandates a reversal when the trial court has failed to make an inquiry even though it knows or reasonably should know that a particular conflict exists," but it did not reverse the conviction. Rather, the Court remanded to the lower court with directions to grant a new revocation hearing only if it found that an actual conflict had existed and had not been waived. *Mickens v. Taylor* [p. 196] subsequently concluded that: *Wood* had held there was a *Sullivan* duty to inquire; the remand was the appropriate disposition, notwithstanding the violation; and the context of the footnote statement indicated that it should not be read literally (see fn.3, p. 198).

9. ***Scope of the inquiry.*** Appellate courts note that where an inquiry is required, it cannot be "perfunctory," but should include "probing and specific questions" regarding the apparent conflict. They also note, however, that the trial court is "entitled to rely on the attorney's representations" as to the "underlying facts." CRIMPROC. § 11.9(b). Some commentators are skeptical of the potential value of such inquiries. Consider John S. Geer, *Representation of Multiple Criminal Defendants: Conflict of Interest and Professional Responsibilities of the Defense Attorney*, 62 Minn.L.Rev. 119 (1978): "At the start of the trial, the judge will not know the defenses to be raised on behalf of each defendant, the potential defenses to be foregone, the weight and sufficiency of the evidence to be adduced against each defendant, or each defendant's personal history and past criminal record. Without such information, the trial judge cannot impress upon a defendant the significance of waiver, nor can he evaluate the defendant's appreciation of it."

B. Postconviction Review

MICKENS v. TAYLOR

535 U.S. 162, 122 S.Ct. 1237, 152 L.Ed.2d 291 (2002).

Justice SCALIA delivered the opinion of the Court.

The question presented in this case is what a defendant must show in order to demonstrate a Sixth Amendment violation where the trial court fails to inquire into a potential conflict of interest about which it knew or reasonably should have known.

I

[A Virginia jury convicted Mickens of the murder and sexual assault of Timothy Hall and sentenced him to death. The attorney preparing Mickens's federal habeas corpus petition learned that Bryan Saunders, Mickens' court-appointed trial attorney, had been representing Hall, the alleged victim of Mickens's crimes, at the time of the murder. The same judge who had appointed Saunders to represent Hall appointed him three weeks later to represent Mickens. Saunders did not disclose this potential conflict of interest to the trial judge, his co-counsel, or Mickens.

[Relying on *Cuyler v. Sullivan* [Note 6, p. 193], the U.S. Court of Appeals for the Fourth Circuit, sitting en banc, held that a defendant must show "both an actual conflict of interest and an adverse effect even if the trial court failed to inquire into a potential conflict about which it reasonably should have known." Concluding that Mickens had not demonstrated an adverse effect, the court affirmed the denial of habeas relief.]

II

* * * As a general matter, a defendant alleging a Sixth Amendment violation must demonstrate "a reasonable probability that, but for counsel's unprofessional

errors, the result of the proceeding would have been different." *Strickland*. There is an exception to this general rule. We have spared the defendant the need of showing probable effect upon the outcome, and have simply presumed such effect, where assistance of counsel has been denied entirely or during a critical stage of the proceeding. When that has occurred, the likelihood that the verdict is unreliable is so high that a case-by-case inquiry is unnecessary. But only in "circumstances of that magnitude" do we forgo individual inquiry into whether counsel's inadequate performance undermined the reliability of the verdict.

We have held in several cases that "circumstances of that magnitude" may also arise when the defendant's attorney actively represented conflicting interests. The nub of the question before us is whether the principle established by these cases provides an exception to the general rule of *Strickland* under the circumstances of the present case. To answer that question, we must examine those cases in some detail.[1]

Holloway [Note 5, p. 193] * * * creates an automatic reversal rule only where defense counsel is forced to represent codefendants over his timely objection, unless the trial court has determined that there is no conflict. * * * In *Sullivan*, the respondent was one of three defendants * * * tried separately, represented by the same counsel. Neither counsel nor anyone else objected to the multiple representation, and counsel's opening argument at Sullivan's trial suggested that the interests of the defendants were aligned. We declined to extend *Holloway*'s automatic reversal rule to this situation, and held that, absent objection, a defendant must demonstrate that "a conflict of interest actually affected the adequacy of his representation." In addition to describing the defendant's burden of proof, *Sullivan* addressed separately a trial court's duty to inquire into the propriety of a multiple representation, construing *Holloway* to require inquiry only when "the trial court knows or reasonably should know that a particular conflict exists"[2]—which is not to be confused with when the trial court is aware of a vague, unspecified possibility of conflict, such as that which "inheres in almost every instance of multiple representation." In *Sullivan*, no "special circumstances" triggered the trial court's duty to inquire.

Finally, in *Wood v. Georgia* [Note 8, p. 195], [we concluded that] the possibility that counsel was actively representing the conflicting interests of employers and defendants "was sufficiently apparent at the time of the revocation hearing to impose upon the court a duty to inquire further." Because "[o]n the record before us, we [could not] be sure whether counsel was influenced in his basic strategic decisions by the interests of the employer who hired him," we

1. * * * [Those cases,] *Holloway*, *Sullivan*, and *Wood*, establish the framework that they do precisely because that framework is thought to identify the situations in which the conviction will reasonably not be regarded as fundamentally fair. We believe it eminently performs that function in the case at hand, and that Justice Breyer is mistaken to think otherwise. But if he does think otherwise, a proper regard for the judicial function—and especially for the function of this Court, which must lay down rules that can be followed in the innumerable cases we are unable to review—would counsel that he propose some other "sensible and coherent framework," rather than merely saying that prior representation of the victim, plus the capital nature of the case, plus judicial appointment of the counsel, strikes him as producing a result that will not be regarded as fundamentally fair. This is not a rule of law but expression of an ad hoc "fairness" judgment (with which we disagree).

2. In order to circumvent *Sullivan*'s clear language, Justice Stevens suggests that a trial court must scrutinize representation by appointed counsel more closely than representation by retained counsel. But we have already rejected the notion that the Sixth Amendment draws such a distinction. "A proper respect for the Sixth Amendment disarms [the] contention that defendants who retain their own lawyers are entitled to less protection than defendants for whom the State appoints counsel. [The] vital guarantee of the Sixth Amendment would stand for little if the often uninformed decision to retain a particular lawyer could reduce or forfeit the defendant's entitlement to constitutional protection." *Cuyler v. Sullivan*. [Note 4, p. 154]

remanded for the trial court "to determine whether the conflict of interest that this record strongly suggests actually existed."

Petitioner argues that the remand instruction in *Wood* established an "unambiguous rule" that where the trial judge neglects a duty to inquire into a potential conflict, the defendant, to obtain reversal of the judgment, need only show that his lawyer was subject to a conflict of interest, and need not show that the conflict adversely affected counsel's performance.[3] He relies upon the language in the remand instruction directing the trial court to grant a new revocation hearing if it determines that "an actual conflict of interest existed," without requiring a further determination that the conflict adversely affected counsel's performance. As used in the remand instruction, however, we think "an actual conflict of interest" meant precisely a conflict *that affected counsel's performance*—as opposed to a mere theoretical division of loyalties. It was shorthand for the statement in *Sullivan* that "a defendant who shows that a conflict of interest *actually affected the adequacy of his representation* need not demonstrate prejudice in order to obtain relief" (emphasis added).[a] This is the only interpretation

3. Petitioner no longer argues, as he did below and as Justice Souter does now, that the Sixth Amendment requires reversal of his conviction without further inquiry into whether the potential conflict that the judge should have investigated was real. Some Courts of Appeals have read a footnote in *Wood* as establishing that outright reversal is mandated when the trial court neglects a duty to inquire into a potential conflict of interest. The *Wood* footnote says that *Sullivan* does not preclude "raising . . . a conflict-of-interest problem that is apparent in the record" and that "*Sullivan mandates* a reversal when the trial court has failed to make [the requisite] inquiry." *Wood*, at n. 18. These statements were made in response to the dissent's contention that the majority opinion had "gone beyond" *Cuyler v. Sullivan* in reaching a conflict-of-interest due-process claim that had been raised neither in the petition for certiorari nor before the state courts. To the extent the "*mandates* a reversal" statement goes beyond the assertion of mere jurisdiction to reverse, it is dictum—and dictum inconsistent with the disposition in *Wood*, which was *not* to reverse but to vacate and remand for the trial court to conduct the inquiry it had omitted.

Justice Souter labors to suggest that the *Wood* remand order is part of "a coherent scheme," in which automatic reversal is required when the trial judge fails to inquire into a potential conflict that was apparent before the proceeding was "held or completed," but a defendant must demonstrate adverse effect when the judge fails to inquire into a conflict that was not apparent before the end of the proceeding. The problem with this carefully concealed "coherent scheme" (no case has ever mentioned it) is that in *Wood* itself the court did not decree automatic reversal, even though it found that "the *possibility* of a conflict of interest was sufficiently apparent *at the time of* the revocation hearing to impose upon the court a duty to inquire further" (second emphasis added). Indeed, the State had actually notified the judge of a potential conflict of interest " '[d]uring the probation revocation hearing.' " Justice Souter's statement that "the signs that a conflict may have occurred were clear to the judge at the close of the probation revocation proceeding"—when it became apparent that counsel had neglected the "strategy more obviously in the defendants' interest, of requesting the court to reduce the fines or defer their collection"—would more accurately be phrased "the *effect of the conflict upon counsel's performance* was clear to the judge at the close of the probation revocation proceeding."

a. Relying on an earlier ruling, *Glasser v. United States*, 315 U.S. 60 (1942), the *Sullivan* Court stated that "unconstitutional multiple representation is never harmless error." In *Glasser*, *Sullivan* noted, "once the Court concluded that Glasser's lawyer had an actual conflict of interest [counsel failed to cross-examine a key witness and had failed to object to "arguably inadmissible evidence" because of his desire to diminish the jury's perception of guilt as to a codefendant also represented by counsel], it "refused to indulge in nice calculations as to the amount of prejudice attributable to the conflict. The conflict itself demonstrated a denial of the 'right to have the effective assistance of counsel'."

In *Strickland* [p. 158], the Court referred to this doctrine as presuming prejudice—a *presumption* justified because "counsel breaches the duty of loyalty, perhaps the most basic of duties" and "it is difficult to measure the precise effect on the defense of representation corrupted by conflicting interests." *Strickland* added (p. 162) that the *Sullivan* rule "is not quite the per se rule of prejudice that exists for the Sixth Amendment claims mentioned above [the interference cases]. Prejudice is presumed only if the defendant demonstrates that counsel 'actively represented conflicting interests' and an actual conflict of interest adversely

consistent with the *Wood* Court's earlier description of why it could not decide the case without a remand: "On the record before us, we cannot be sure whether counsel *was influenced in his basic strategic decisions* by the interests of the employer who hired him. *If this was the case*, the due process rights of petitioners were not respected...." (emphasis added). The notion that *Wood* created a new rule *sub silentio*—and in a case where certiorari had been granted on an entirely different question, and the parties had neither briefed nor argued the conflict-of-interest issue—is implausible.

Petitioner's proposed rule of automatic reversal when there existed a conflict that did not affect counsel's performance, but the trial judge failed to make the *Sullivan*-mandated inquiry, makes little policy sense. As discussed, the rule applied when the trial judge is not aware of the conflict (and thus not obligated to inquire) is that prejudice will be presumed only if the conflict has significantly affected counsel's performance—thereby rendering the verdict unreliable, even though *Strickland* prejudice cannot be shown. The trial court's awareness of a potential conflict neither renders it more likely that counsel's performance was significantly affected nor in any other way renders the verdict unreliable. Nor does the trial judge's failure to make the *Sullivan*-mandated inquiry often make it harder for reviewing courts to determine conflict and effect, particularly since those courts may rely on evidence and testimony whose importance only becomes established at the trial.

Nor, finally, is automatic reversal simply an appropriate means of enforcing *Sullivan*'s mandate of inquiry. Despite Justice Souter's belief that there must be a threat of sanction (to-wit, the risk of conferring a windfall upon the defendant) in order to induce "resolutely obdurate" trial judges to follow the law, we do not presume that judges are as careless or as partial as those police officers who need the incentive of the exclusionary rule.* * * And in any event, the *Sullivan* standard, which requires proof of effect upon representation but (once such effect is shown) presumes prejudice, already creates an "incentive" to inquire into a potential conflict. * * *

Since this was not a case in which (as in *Holloway*) counsel protested his inability simultaneously to represent multiple defendants; and since the trial court's failure to make the *Sullivan*-mandated inquiry does not reduce the petitioner's burden of proof; it was at least necessary, to void the conviction, for petitioner to establish that the conflict of interest adversely affected his counsel's performance. The Court of Appeals having found no such effect, the denial of habeas relief must be affirmed.

III

Lest today's holding be misconstrued, we note that the only question presented was the effect of a trial court's failure to inquire into a potential conflict upon the *Sullivan* rule that deficient performance of counsel must be shown. The case was presented and argued on the assumption that (absent some exception for failure to inquire) *Sullivan* would be applicable—requiring a showing of defective performance, but *not* requiring in addition (as *Strickland* does in other ineffectiveness-of-counsel cases), a showing of probable effect upon the outcome of trial. That assumption was not unreasonable in light of the holdings of Courts of Appeals, which have applied *Sullivan* "unblinkingly" to "all kinds of alleged attorney ethical conflicts," *Beets v. Scott*, 65 F.3d 1258, 1266 (CA5 1995) (en banc).[b] They have invoked the *Sullivan* standard not only when (as here) there is

affected his lawyer's performance' *Cuyler v. Sullivan*."

b. In *Beets*, a closely divided Fifth Circuit concluded that *Cuyler v. Sullivan*'s prejudice presumption should apply only to conflicts pre-a conflict rooted in counsels obligations to *former* clients, but even when representation of the defendant somehow implicates counsel's personal or financial interests, including a book deal, * * * a job with the prosecutor's office, * * * the teaching of classes to Internal Revenue Service agents, * * * a romantic "entanglement" with the prosecutor, * * * or fear of antagonizing the trial judge.

It must be said, however, that the language of *Sullivan* itself does not clearly establish, or indeed even support, such expansive application. "[U]ntil," it said, "a defendant shows that his counsel *actively represented* conflicting interests, he has not established the constitutional predicate for his claim of ineffective assistance" (emphasis added). Both *Sullivan* itself and *Holloway* stressed the high probability of prejudice arising from multiple concurrent representation, and the difficulty of proving that prejudice. Not all attorney conflicts present comparable difficulties. Thus, the Federal Rules of Criminal Procedure treat concurrent representation and prior representation differently, requiring a trial court to inquire into the likelihood of conflict whenever jointly charged defendants are represented by a single attorney (Rule 44(c)), but not when counsel previously represented another defendant in a substantially related matter, even where the trial court is aware of the prior representation.

This is not to suggest that one ethical duty is more or less important than another. The purpose of our *Holloway* and *Sullivan* exceptions from the ordinary requirements of *Strickland*, however, is not to enforce the Canons of Legal Ethics, but to apply needed prophylaxis in situations where *Strickland* itself is evidently inadequate to assure vindication of the defendant's Sixth Amendment right to counsel. [In] resolving this case on the grounds on which it was presented to us, we do not rule upon the need for the *Sullivan* prophylaxis in cases of successive representation. Whether *Sullivan* should be extended to such cases remains, as far as the jurisprudence of this Court is concerned, an open question. * * *

Justice KENNEDY, with whom Justice O'CONNOR joins, concurring.

In its comprehensive analysis the Court has said all that is necessary to address the issues raised by the question presented, and I join the opinion in full. The trial judge's failure to inquire into a suspected conflict is not the kind of error requiring a presumption of prejudice. We did not grant certiorari on a second question presented by petitioner: whether, if we rejected his proposed presumption, he had nonetheless established that a conflict of interest adversely affected his representation. I write separately to emphasize that the facts of this case well illustrate why a wooden rule requiring reversal is inappropriate for cases like this one.

At petitioner's request, the District Court conducted an evidentiary hearing on the conflict claim and issued a thorough opinion, which found that counsel's brief representation of the victim had no effect whatsoever on the course of petitioner's trial. The District Court's findings depend upon credibility judgments made after hearing the testimony of petitioner's counsel, Bryan Saunders, and other witnesses. As a reviewing court, our role is not to speculate about counsel's

sented by "multiple representation" situations (i.e., defense counsel represented codefendants or represented the defendant and witnesses or other interested parties), as opposed to conflicts arising from some self-interest of the attorney. In the latter situation, a claim of ineffective assistance based on a conflict should be treated no differently than any other ineffective assistance claim, with the court applying the *Strickland* standard, which requires a showing of prejudicial impact upon the outcome. The *Beets* majority reasoned that attorney ethical conflicts that do not result from obligations owed to current or former clients simply reflect another form of incompetent performance. To allow a "recharacterization of ineffectiveness claims to duty of loyalty claims," thereby importing "*Cuyler*'s lesser standard of prejudice" was to "blu[r] the *Strickland* standard" and undercut its role as the "uniform standard of constitutional ineffectiveness."

motives or about the plausibility of alternative litigation strategies. Our role is to defer to the District Court's factual findings unless we can conclude they are clearly erroneous. [The] District Court found that Saunders did not believe he had any obligation to his former client, Timothy Hall, that would interfere with the litigation. [Although] the District Court concluded that Saunders probably did learn some matters that were confidential, it found that nothing the attorney learned was relevant to the subsequent murder case. * * * Indeed, even if Saunders had learned relevant information, the District Court found that he labored under the impression he had no continuing duty at all to his deceased client. [While] Saunders' belief may have been mistaken, it establishes that the prior representation did not influence the choices he made during the course of the trial. This conclusion is a good example of why a case-by-case inquiry is required, rather than simply adopting an automatic rule of reversal.

Petitioner's description of roads not taken would entail two degrees of speculation. We would be required to assume that Saunders believed he had a continuing duty to the victim, and we then would be required to consider whether in this hypothetical case, the counsel would have been blocked from pursuing an alternative defense strategy. The District Court concluded that the prosecution's case, coupled with the defendant's insistence on testifying, foreclosed the strategies suggested by petitioner after the fact. According to the District Court, there was no plausible argument that the victim consented to sexual relations with his murderer, given the bruises on the victim's neck, blood marks showing the victim was stabbed before or during sexual intercourse, and, most important, petitioner's insistence on testifying at trial that he had never met the victim. [The] basic defense at the guilt phase was that petitioner was not at the scene; this is hardly consistent with the theory that there was a consensual encounter.

The District Court said the same for counsel's alleged dereliction at the sentencing phase. Saunder's failure to attack the character of the 17–year-old victim and his mother had nothing to do with the putative conflict of interest. This strategy was rejected as likely to backfire, not only by Saunders, but also by his co-counsel, who owed no duty to Hall. * * * These facts, and others relied upon by the District Court, provide compelling evidence that a theoretical conflict does not establish a constitutional violation, even when the conflict is one about which the trial judge should have known. * * *

Justice STEVENS, dissenting.

This case raises three uniquely important questions about a fundamental component of our criminal justice system—the constitutional right of a person accused of a capital offense to have the effective assistance of counsel for his defense. The first is whether a capital defendant's attorney has a duty to disclose that he was representing the defendant's alleged victim at the time of the murder. Second, is whether, assuming disclosure of the prior representation, the capital defendant has a right to refuse the appointment of the conflicted attorney. Third, is whether the trial judge, who knows or should know of such prior representation, has a duty to obtain the defendant's consent before appointing that lawyer to represent him. Ultimately, the question presented by this case is whether, if these duties exist and if all of them are violated, there exist "circumstances that are so likely to prejudice the accused that the cost of litigating their effect in a particular case is unjustified." *United States v. Cronic* [Note 2, p. 184].

The first critical stage in the defense of a capital case is the series of pretrial meetings between the accused and his counsel when they decide how the case should be defended. A lawyer cannot possibly determine how best to represent a new client unless that client is willing to provide the lawyer with a truthful account of the relevant facts. When an indigent defendant first meets his newly appointed counsel, he will often falsely maintain his complete innocence. Truthful disclosures of embarrassing or incriminating facts are contingent on the development of the client's confidence in the undivided loyalty of the lawyer. Quite obviously, knowledge that the lawyer represented the victim would be a substantial obstacle to the development of such confidence. * * *

Saunders' concealment of essential information about his prior representation of the victim was a severe lapse in his professional duty. The lawyer's duty to disclose his representation of a client related to the instant charge is not only intuitively obvious, it is as old as the profession. * * * Mickens' lawyer's violation of this fundamental obligation of disclosure is indefensible. The relevance of Saunders' prior representation of Hall to the new appointment was far too important to be concealed.

If the defendant is found guilty of a capital offense, the ensuing proceedings that determine whether he will be put to death are critical in every sense of the word. At those proceedings, testimony about the impact of the crime on the victim, including testimony about the character of the victim, may have a critical effect on the jury's decision. Because a lawyer's fiduciary relationship with his deceased client survives the client's death, Saunders necessarily labored under conflicting obligations that were irreconcilable. He had a duty to protect the reputation and confidences of his deceased client, and a duty to impeach the impact evidence presented by the prosecutor. Saunders' conflicting obligations to his deceased client, on the one hand, and to his living client, on the other, were unquestionably sufficient to give Mickens the right to insist on different representation. * * *

[When] an indigent defendant is unable to retain his own lawyer, the trial judge's appointment of counsel is itself a critical stage of a criminal trial. At that point in the proceeding, by definition, the defendant has no lawyer to protect his interests and must rely entirely on the judge. For that reason it is "the solemn duty of [a] judge before whom a defendant appears without counsel to make a thorough inquiry and to take all steps necessary to insure the fullest protection of this constitutional right at every stage of the proceedings." *Von Moltke v. Gillies*, [Note 4, p. 136]. * * * This duty with respect to indigent defendants is far more imperative than the judge's duty to investigate the possibility of a conflict that arises when retained counsel represents either multiple or successive defendants. It is true that in a situation of retained counsel, "[u]nless the trial court knows or reasonably should know that a particular conflict exists, the court need not initiate an inquiry." *Sullivan*.[8] But when, as was true in this case, the judge is not merely reviewing the permissibility of the defendant's choice of counsel, but is responsible for making the choice herself, and when she knows or should know that a conflict does exist, the duty to make a thorough inquiry is manifest and unqualified. Indeed, under far less compelling circumstances, we squarely held that when a record discloses the possibility of a conflict between the interests of the defendants and the interests of the party paying their counsel's fees, the

8. Part III of the Court's opinion is a foray into an issue that is not implicated by the question presented. In dicta, the Court states that *Sullivan* may not even apply in the first place to *successive* representations. Most Courts of Appeals, however, have applied *Sullivan* to claims of successive representation as well as to some insidious conflicts arising from a lawyer's self-interest. We have done the same. See *Wood* (applying *Sullivan* to a conflict stemming from a third-party payment arrangement). Neither we nor the Courts of Appeals have applied this standard "unblinkingly," as the Court accuses, but rather have relied upon principled reason. When a conflict of interest, whether multiple, successive, or otherwise, poses so substantial a risk that a lawyer's representation would be materially and adversely affected by diverging interests or loyalties and the trial court judge knows of this and yet fails to inquire, it is a "[c]ircumstanc[e] of [such] magnitude" that "the likelihood that any lawyer, even a fully competent one, could provide effective assistance is so small that a presumption of prejudice is appropriate without inquiry into the actual conduct of the trial." *Cronic*.

Constitution imposes a duty of inquiry on the state-court judge even when no objection was made. *Wood.*

Mickens had a constitutional right to the services of an attorney devoted solely to his interests. That right was violated. The lawyer who did represent him had a duty to disclose his prior representation of the victim to Mickens and to the trial judge. That duty was violated. When Mickens had no counsel, the trial judge had a duty to make a thorough inquiry and to take all steps necessary to insure the fullest protection of his right to counsel. *Von Moltke.* Despite knowledge of the lawyer's prior representation, she violated that duty.

We will never know whether Mickens would have received the death penalty if those violations had not occurred nor precisely what effect they had on Saunders' representation of Mickens. We do know that he did not receive the kind of representation that the Constitution guarantees. If Mickens had been represented by an attorney-impostor who never passed a bar examination, we might also be unable to determine whether the impostor's educational shortcomings "actually affected the adequacy of his representation" (emphasis deleted). We would, however, surely set aside his conviction if the person who had represented him was not a real lawyer. Four compelling reasons make setting aside the conviction the proper remedy in this case.

First, it is the remedy dictated by our holdings in *Holloway*, *Sullivan*, and *Wood*. * * * Second, it is the only remedy that responds to the real possibility that Mickens would not have received the death penalty if he had been represented by conflict-free counsel during the critical stage of the proceeding in which he first met with his lawyer. We should presume that the lawyer for the victim of a brutal homicide is incapable of establishing the kind of relationship with the defendant that is essential to effective representation. Third, it is the only remedy that is consistent with the legal profession's historic and universal condemnation of the representation of conflicting interests without the full disclosure and consent of all interested parties. The Court's novel and naive assumption that a lawyer's divided loyalties are acceptable unless it can be proved that they actually affected counsel's performance is demeaning to the profession. Finally, "justice must satisfy the appearance of justice." Setting aside Mickens' conviction is the only remedy that can maintain public confidence in the fairness of the procedures employed in capital cases. [A] rule that allows the State to foist a murder victim's lawyer onto his accused is not only capricious; it poisons the integrity of our adversary system of justice. * * *

Justice SOUTER, dissenting.

* * * The Court today holds, * * * that Mickens should be denied this remedy because Saunders failed to employ a formal objection [as in *Holloway*] as a means of bringing home to the appointing judge the risk of conflict. Without an objection, the majority holds, Mickens should get no relief absent a showing that the risk turned into an actual conflict with adverse effect on the representation provided to Mickens at trial. But why should an objection matter when even without an objection the state judge knew or should have known of the risk and was therefore obliged to enquire further? What would an objection have added to the obligation the state judge failed to honor? The majority says that in circumstances like those now before us, we have already held such an objection necessary for reversal, absent proof of actual conflict with adverse effect, so that this case calls simply for the application of precedent, albeit precedent not very clearly stated.

The majority's position is error, resting on a mistaken reading of our cases. Three are on point, *Holloway*, *Cuyler,* and *Wood.* * * * The different burdens [placed] on the *Holloway* and *Cuyler* defendants are consistent features of a coherent scheme for dealing with the problem of conflicted defense counsel; a prospective risk of conflict subject to judicial notice is treated differently from a retrospective claim that a completed proceeding was tainted by conflict, although the trial judge had not been derelict in any duty to guard against it. * * * The error [in *Holloway*] occurred when the judge failed to act, and the remedy restored the defendant to the position he would have occupied if the judge had taken reasonable steps to fulfill his obligation. But when the problem of conflict comes to judicial attention not prospectively, but only after the fact, the defendant must show an actual conflict with adverse consequence to him in order to get relief. Fairness requires nothing more, for no judge was at fault in allowing a trial to proceed even though fraught with hidden risk.

In light of what the majority holds today, it bears repeating that, in this coherent scheme established by *Holloway* and *Cuyler*, there is nothing legally crucial about an objection by defense counsel to tell a trial judge that conflicting interests may impair the adequacy of counsel's representation. * * * Since the District Court in this case found that the state judge was on notice of a prospective potential conflict, this case calls for nothing more than the application of the prospective notice rule * * *.

But in the majority's eyes, this conclusion takes insufficient account of *Wood*, whatever may have been the sensible scheme staked out by *Holloway* and *Cuyler*, * * *. *Wood* is not easy to read, and I believe the majority misreads it. * * * Careful attention to *Wood* shows that the case did not involve prospective notice of risk unrealized, and that it held nothing about the general rule to govern in such circumstances. What *Wood* did decide was how to deal with a possible conflict of interests that becomes known to the trial court only at the conclusion of the trial proceeding at which it may have occurred, * * *. Treating the case more like *Cuyler* and remanding was the correct choice. *Wood* was not like *Holloway*, in which the judge was put on notice of a risk before trial. * * * It was rather, much closer to *Cuyler* since any notice to a court went to a conflict, if there was one, that had pervaded a completed trial proceeding extending over two years. * * *

* * * Since the majority will not leave the law as it is, however, the question is whether there is any merit in the rule it now adopts, of treating breaches of a judge's duty to enquire into prospective conflicts differently depending on whether defense counsel explicitly objected. There is not. The distinction is irrational on its face, it creates a scheme of incentives to judicial vigilance that is weakest in those cases presenting the greatest risk of conflict and unfair trial, and it reduces the so-called judicial duty to enquire into so many empty words.

The most obvious reason to reject the majority's rule starts with the accepted view that a trial judge placed on notice of a risk of prospective conflict has an obligation then and there to do something about it. The majority does not expressly repudiate that duty, which is too clear for cavil. It should go without saying that the best time to deal with a known threat to the basic guarantee of fair trial is before the trial has proceeded to become unfair. It would be absurd, after all, to suggest that a judge should sit quiescent in the face of an apparent risk that a lawyer's conflict will render representation illusory and the formal trial a waste of time, emotion, and a good deal of public money. And as if that were not bad enough, a failure to act early raises the specter, confronted by the *Holloway* Court, that failures on the part of conflicted counsel will elude demonstration after the fact, simply because they so often consist of what did not happen. While a defendant can fairly be saddled with the characteristically difficult burden of proving adverse effects of conflicted decisions after the fact when the judicial system was not to blame in tolerating the risk of conflict, the burden is indefensible when a judge was on notice of the risk but did nothing. * * *

The Court's rule makes no sense unless, that is, the real point of this case is to eliminate the judge's constitutional duty entirely in no-objection cases, for that is certainly the practical consequence of today's holding. The defendant has the same burden to prove adverse effect (and the prospect of reversal is the same) whether the judge has no reason to know of any risk or every reason to know about it short of explicit objection. In that latter case, the duty explicitly described in *Cuyler* and *Wood* becomes just a matter of words, devoid of sanction; it ceases to be any duty at all. * * *

Justice BREYER, with whom Justice GINSBURG joins, dissenting.

* * * The parties spend a great deal of time disputing how this Court's precedents of *Holloway*, *Cuyler*, and *Wood* resolve the case. * * * Although I express no view at this time about how our precedents should treat *most* ineffective-assistance-of-counsel claims involving an alleged conflict of interest (or, for that matter, whether *Holloway*, *Sullivan*, and *Wood* provide a sensible or coherent framework for dealing with those cases at all), I am convinced that *this* case is not governed by those precedents, for the following reasons.

First, this is the kind of representational incompatibility that is egregious on its face. Mickens was represented by the murder victim's lawyer; that lawyer had represented the victim on a criminal matter; and that lawyer's representation of the victim had continued until one business day before the lawyer was appointed to represent the defendant.

Second, the conflict is exacerbated by the fact that it occurred in a capital murder case. In a capital case, the evidence submitted by both sides regarding the victim's character may easily tip the scale of the jury's choice between life or death. Yet even with extensive investigation in post-trial proceedings, it will often prove difficult, if not impossible, to determine whether the prior representation affected defense counsel's decisions regarding, for example: which avenues to take when investigating the victim's background; which witnesses to call; what type of impeachment to undertake; which arguments to make to the jury; what language to use to characterize the victim; and, as a general matter, what basic strategy to adopt at the sentencing stage. Given the subtle forms that prejudice might take, the consequent difficulty of proving actual prejudice, and the significant likelihood that it will nonetheless occur when the same lawyer represents both accused killer and victim, the cost of litigating the existence of actual prejudice in a particular case cannot be easily justified. * * *

Third, the Commonwealth itself *created* the conflict in the first place. Indeed, it was the *same judge* who dismissed the case against the victim who then appointed the victim's lawyer to represent Mickens one business day later. In light of the judge's active role in bringing about the incompatible representation, I am not sure why the concept of a judge's "duty to inquire" is thought to be central to this case. No "inquiry" by the trial judge could have shed more light on the conflict than was obvious on the face of the matter, namely, that the lawyer who would represent Mickens today is the same lawyer who yesterday represented Mickens' alleged victim in a criminal case.

This kind of breakdown in the criminal justice system creates, at a minimum, the appearance that the proceeding will not " 'reliably serve its function as a vehicle for determination of guilt or innocence,' " and the resulting "criminal punishment" will not "be regarded as fundamentally fair." * * * This appearance, together with the likelihood of prejudice in the typical case, are serious enough to warrant a categorical rule—a rule that does not require proof of prejudice in the individual case.

Notes and Questions

1. ***The "adverse impact" requirement.*** Dissenting in *Sullivan*, Justice Marshall questioned the Court's requirement that the defendant not only show the presence of an actual conflict (i.e., a situation in which conflicting loyalties pointed in opposite directions), but also that the conflict "adversely affected counsel's performance" (i.e., that counsel proceeded to act against the defendant's interest, favoring the conflicting loyalty). Justice Marshall noted that the Court was willing to presume prejudice where the conflict adversely affected counsel's performance because determining the impact of the conflict upon the outcome of the case its too speculative (see fn. a, p. 198). Why, he asked was not the same true of the impact of an actual conflict upon the counsel's performance?

Does the following explanation adequately respond to Justice Marshall's query? CRIMPROC. § 11.8(d) (describing the rationale suggested in various cases): "It would not be sufficient for reversal to show only that counsel had faced a situation in which action or inaction that might benefit his client would work to the detriment of another interest that divided counsel's loyalty. There would be no harm to the defendant if counsel actually pursued the route favoring his client, disregarding the conflicting interest. Moreover, even where counsel did not pursue that route, counsel's action or inaction may have been influenced solely by a reasonable determination that the route not taken was inferior to the alternative route, which was more beneficial to his client, putting aside any concern for the conflicting interest. Having identified an actual conflict of interest, defendant should be able to establish as well precisely how counsel acted in response to that conflict. However, once it is shown that counsel was actually influenced by the conflict in one aspect of his performance, it would be inappropriate to measure the impact of that conflict solely by reference to that action or inaction. A court could not assume that counsel so motivated had not also been influenced by the conflict in various other aspects of his representation."

2. ***Applying The "adverse impact" requirement.*** The leading Supreme Court ruling on the application of the adverse impact standard is BURGER v. KEMP, 483 U.S. 776 (1987). In that case Burger and Stevens were indicted for murder, but tried separately. Each made a confession that emphasized the culpability of the other. Leaphart, an experienced and well-respected criminal lawyer, was appointed to represent Burger. Leaphart's law partner was appointed to represent Stevens in his later, separate trial. Leaphart, however, did assist his partner in the representation of Stevens. Moreover, he prepared the briefs for both defendants on their second appeal to the Georgia Supreme Court.

At their separate trials, each of the defendants sought to underscore the culpability of the other in order to avoid the death penalty. Although he had relied on Burger's lesser culpability as a trial defense, Leaphart did not make a "lesser culpability" argument in his appellate brief on behalf of Burger. In a subsequent federal habeas petition, defendant Burger argued that this omission, along with others, established Leaphart's incompetency under the *Sullivan* standard. Two lower federal courts rejected that claim, and a divided Supreme Court, per STEVENS, J., affirmed:

"Assuming without deciding that two law partners are considered as one attorney, it is settled that '[r]equiring or permitting a single attorney to represent codefendants [is] not *per se* violative of constitutional guarantees of effective assistance of counsel.' *Holloway.* [W]e presume prejudice 'only if the defendant demonstrates that counsel "actively represented conflicting interests" and that "an actual conflict of interest adversely affected his lawyer's performance." ' *Strickland.* (quoting *Cuyler*) * * *

"In an effort to identify an actual conflict of interest, petitioner points out that Leaphart prepared the briefs for both Burger and Stevens on their second appeal to the Georgia Supreme Court, and that Leaphart did not make a 'lesser culpability' argument in his appellate brief on behalf of Burger even though he had relied on Burger's lesser culpability as a trial defense. Given the fact that it was petitioner who actually killed Honeycutt [and] the further fact that the Georgia Supreme Court expressed the opinion that petitioner's actions were 'outrageously and wantonly vile and inhuman under any reasonable standard of human conduct,' [the] decision to forgo this omission had a sound strategic basis. * * *

"In addition, determining that there was an actual conflict of interest requires the attribution of Leaphart's motivation for not making the 'lesser culpability' argument to the fact that his partner was Stevens' lawyer, or to the further fact that he assisted his partner in that representation. The District Court obviously credited his testimony to the contrary, and its findings were twice sustained by the Court of Appeals. It would thus be most inappropriate, and factually unsupportable, for this Court to speculate that the drafting of a brief on appeal was tainted by a lawyer's improper motivation. Our duty to search for constitutional error with painstaking care is never more exacting than it is in a capital case. Nevertheless, when the lower courts have found that a lawyer has performed his or her solemn duties in such a case at or above the lower boundary of professional competence, both respect for the bar and deference to the shared conclusion of two reviewing courts prevent us from substituting speculation for their considered opinions. The district judge, who presumably is familiar with the legal talents and character of the lawyers who practice at the local bar and who saw and heard the witness testify, is in a far better position than we are to evaluate a charge of this kind, and the regional courts of appeals are in a far better position than we are to conflict appellate review of these heavily fact-based rulings."

BLACKMUN, J., joined by Brennan and Marshall, J. J. dissented:

"[This] Court recognizes the unique nature of claims that arise out of a conflict of interest and does not impose on such claims the two-prong standard of inadequate performance and prejudice that applies to general claims of ineffective assistance. Instead, prejudice is presumed if a defendant demonstrates that his attorney 'actively represented conflicting interests' and that 'an actual conflict of interest adversely affected his lawyer's performance.' * * * It is difficult to imagine a more direct conflict than existed here, where counsel was preparing the appellate brief for petitioner at the same time that he was preparing the appellate brief for Stevens, and where the state statute specifies that one of the roles of that appellate process is to consider the comparative culpability and sentences of defendants involved in similar crimes. Counsel's abandonment of the lesser-culpability argument on appeal, the stage at which the two cases would be reviewed contemporaneously, is indicative of the 'struggle to serve two masters.' This record *compels* a finding that counsel's representation of the conflicting interests of petitioner and Stevens had an adverse effect on his performance as petitioner's counsel."

3. ***Presuming an adverse impact.*** Federal appellate rulings have held that an adverse impact on counsel's performance can be presumed in the instance of certain flagrant conflicts. See e.g., *United States v. Fulton*, 5 F.3d 605 (2d Cir.1993) (*per se* rule applies where the "attorney has engaged in the defendant's crimes," and also where a prosecution witness alleged that "he has direct

knowledge of criminal conduct by defense counsel"; "the danger arising from a counsel who has been implicated in related criminal activity by a government witness is of a different order of magnitude"); Walberg v. Israel, 766 F.2d 1071 (7th Cir.1985) (adverse impact presumed where trial judge indicated to appointed counsel that approval of his fee and future appointments would depend upon counsel "pulling his punches"). Does *Mickens* require reexamination of such rulings?

4. *Limiting the presumption of prejudice.* Post *Mickens*, several circuits have recognized the possible restriction of the presumption of prejudice but have not ruled on the issue. See *Moss v. United States*, 323 F.3d 445 (6th Cir.2003) (predicting that Court would limit the application of the presumption in cases of "successive representation;" but not as to the case before it, which posed concerns similar to those presented in multiple representations, as the successive representations here "occurred during the same proceedings and arose from identical facts"). Does the majority's suggested explanation for limiting application of the presumption (pp. 199–200) indicate that the presumption should not apply in one of situations in which *Beets* (fn. b, p. 199) found it acceptable—where the attorney also was represented witnesses or other interested parties—as the potential impact of the witness testimony can readily be evaluated under the prejudice standard of *Strickland*.

C. Disqualification of Counsel

WHEAT v. UNITED STATES

486 U.S. 153, 108 S.Ct. 1692, 100 L.Ed.2d 140 (1988).

Chief Justice REHNQUIST delivered the opinion of the Court.

[Petitioner, along with numerous codefendants, including Gomez–Barajas and Bravo, was charged with participating in a far-flung drug conspiracy. Both Gomez–Barajas and Bravo were represented by attorney Eugene Iredale. Gomez–Barajas was tried first and was acquitted on drug charges overlapping with those against petitioner. To avoid a second trial on other charges, Gomez–Barajas offered to plead guilty to certain offenses stemming from the conspiracy. At the commencement of petitioner's trial, the district court had not yet accepted the plea of Gomez–Barajas; thus he was free to withdraw his plea and proceed to trial. Bravo pled guilty.

[At the conclusion of Bravo's guilty plea proceedings and two court days before his trial was to commence, petitioner moved for the substitution of Iredale as his counsel as well. The government objected on the ground that Iredale's representation of the two other codefendants created a serious conflict of interest: (1) In the event that Gomez–Barajas's plea and the sentencing arrangement negotiated between him and the government were rejected by the court, petitioner was likely to be called as a witness for the prosecution at Gomez–Barajas's trial. This scenario would pose a conflict of interest for Iredale, who would be prevented from cross-examining petitioner and thereby from effectively representing Gomez–Barajas. (2) In the likely event that Bravo was called as a witness for the prosecution against petitioner, ethical proscriptions would prevent Iredale from cross-examining Bravo in any meaningful way. Thus, Iredale would be unable to provide petitioner with effective assistance of counsel.

[In response, petitioner emphasized his right to have counsel of his own choosing and his willingness, and the willingness of the other codefendants, to waive the right to conflict-free counsel. Moreover, maintained petitioner, the circumstances posited by the government that would create a conflict of interest were highly speculative and bore no connection to the true relationship among the co-conspirators. If called to testify against petitioner, Bravo would simply say that he did not know petitioner and had had no dealings with him. In the unlikely event that Gomez–Barajas went to trial, petitioner's lack of involvement in his alleged crimes made his appearance as a witness highly improbable. According to petitioner, the government was "manufacturing implausible conflicts" in an attempt to disqualify Iredale, who had already proved extremely effective in representing the other codefendants.

[The district court denied petitioner's request to substitute Iredale as his attorney, concluding, on the basis of the representation of the government, that it "really has no choice at this point other than to find that an irreconcilable conflict of interest exists." Petitioner proceeded to trial with his original counsel and was convicted of various drug offenses. The Court of Appeals for the Ninth Circuit affirmed.]

[While] the right to select and be represented by one's preferred attorney is comprehended by the Sixth Amendment, the essential aim of the Amendment is to guarantee an effective advocate for each criminal defendant rather than to ensure that a defendant will inexorably be represented by the lawyer whom he prefers.

The Sixth Amendment right to choose one's own counsel is circumscribed in several important respects. Regardless of his persuasive powers, an advocate who is not a member of the bar may not represent clients (other than himself) in court.[3] Similarly, a defendant may not insist on representation by an attorney he cannot afford or who for other reasons declines to represent the defendant. Nor may a defendant insist on the counsel of an attorney who has a previous or ongoing relationship with an opposing party, even when the opposing party is the Government. The question raised in this case is the extent to which a criminal defendant's right under the Sixth Amendment to his chosen attorney is qualified by the fact that the attorney has represented other defendants charged in the same criminal conspiracy.

[Petitioner] insists that the provision of waivers by all affected defendants cures any problems created by the multiple representation. But no such flat rule can be deduced from the Sixth Amendment presumption in favor of counsel of choice. Federal courts have an independent interest in ensuring that criminal trials are conducted within the ethical standards of the profession and that legal proceedings appear fair to all who observe them. Both the American Bar Association's Model Code of Professional Responsibility and its Model Rules of Professional Conduct, as well as the rules of the California Bar Association (which governed the attorneys in this case), impose limitations on multiple representation of clients. Not only the interest of a criminal defendant but the institutional interest in the rendition of just verdicts in criminal cases may be jeopardized by unregulated multiple representation.

For this reason, the Federal Rules of Criminal Procedure direct trial judges to investigate specially cases involving joint representation. In pertinent part, Rule 44(c) [requires an inquiry in cases of joint representation]: * * * Although Rule 44(c) does not specify what particular measures may be taken by a district court, one option suggested by the Notes of the Advisory Committee is an order by the court that the defendants be separately represented in subsequent proceedings in the case. This suggestion comports with our instructions in *Holloway* [Note 5, p. 193] and in *Glasser* [Note 5, p. 193] that the trial courts, when alerted by objection from one of the parties, have an independent duty to ensure that

3. Our holding in *Faretta* [p. 119] that a criminal defendant has a Sixth Amendment right to represent *himself* if he voluntarily elects to do so, does not encompass the right to choose any advocate if the defendant wishes to be represented by counsel.

criminal defendants receive a trial that is fair and does not contravene the Sixth Amendment.

To be sure, this need to investigate potential conflicts arises in part from the legitimate wish of district courts that their judgments remain intact on appeal. As the Court of Appeals accurately pointed out, trial courts confronted with multiple representations face the prospect of being "whip-sawed" by assertions of error no matter which way they rule. If a district court agrees to the multiple representation, and the advocacy of counsel is thereafter impaired as a result, the defendant may well claim that he did not receive effective assistance. On the other hand, a district court's refusal to accede to the multiple representation may result in a challenge such as petitioner's in this case. Nor does a waiver by the defendant necessarily solve the problem, for we note, without passing judgment on, the apparent willingness of Courts of Appeals to entertain ineffective assistance claims from defendants who have specifically waived the right to conflict-free counsel.

Thus, where a court justifiably finds an actual conflict of interest, there can be no doubt that it may decline a proffer of waiver, and insist that defendants be separately represented. * * *

Unfortunately for all concerned, a district court must pass on the issue of whether or not to allow a waiver of a conflict of interest by a criminal defendant not with the wisdom of hindsight after the trial has taken place, but the murkier pretrial context when relationships between parties are seen through a glass, darkly. The likelihood and dimensions of nascent conflicts of interest are notoriously hard to predict, even for those thoroughly familiar with criminal trials. It is a rare attorney who will be fortunate enough to learn the entire truth from his own client, much less be fully apprised before trial of what each of the Government's witnesses will say on the stand. A few bits of unforeseen testimony or a single previously unknown or unnoticed document may significantly shift the relationship between multiple defendants. These imponderables are difficult enough for a lawyer to assess, and even more difficult to convey by way of explanation to a criminal defendant untutored in the niceties of legal ethics. Nor is it amiss to observe that the willingness of an attorney to obtain such waivers from his clients may bear an inverse relation to the care with which he conveys all the necessary information to them.

For these reasons we think the District Court must be allowed substantial latitude in refusing waivers of conflicts of interest not only in those rare cases where an actual conflict may be demonstrated before trial, but in the more common cases where a potential for conflict exists which may or may not burgeon into an actual conflict as the trial progresses. In the circumstances of this case, with the motion for substitution of counsel made so close to the time of trial, the District Court relied on instinct and judgment based on experience in making its decision. We do not think it can be said that the court exceeded the broad latitude which must be accorded it in making this decision. Petitioner of course rightly points out that the government may seek to "manufacture" a conflict in order to prevent a defendant from having a particularly able defense counsel at his side; but trial courts are undoubtedly aware of this possibility, and must take it into consideration along with all of the other factors which inform this sort of a decision.

Here the District Court was confronted not simply with an attorney who wished to represent two coequal defendants in a straightforward criminal prosecution; rather, Iredale proposed to defend three conspirators of varying stature in a complex drug distribution scheme. The Government intended to call Bravo as a witness for the prosecution at petitioner's trial.[4] The Government might readily

4. Bravo was in fact called as a witness at petitioner's trial. His testimony was elicited to demonstrate the transportation of drugs that the prosecution hoped to link to petitioner.

have tied certain deliveries of marijuana by Bravo to petitioner, necessitating vigorous cross-examination of Bravo by petitioner's counsel. Iredale, because of his prior representation of Bravo, would have been unable ethically to provide that cross-examination.

Iredale had also represented Gomez–Barajas, one of the alleged kingpins of the distribution ring, and had succeeded in obtaining a verdict of acquittal for him. Gomez–Barajas had agreed with the Government to plead guilty to other charges, but the District Court had not yet accepted the plea arrangement. If the agreement were rejected, petitioner's probable testimony at the resulting trial of Gomez–Barajas would create an ethical dilemma for Iredale from which one or the other of his clients would likely suffer.

Viewing the situation as it did before trial, we hold that the District Court's refusal to permit the substitution of counsel in this case was within its discretion and did not violate petitioner's Sixth Amendment rights. Other district courts might have reached differing or opposite conclusions with equal justification, but that does not mean that one conclusion was "right" and the other "wrong." The District Court must recognize a presumption in favor of petitioner's counsel of choice, but that presumption may be overcome not only by a demonstration of actual conflict but by a showing of a serious potential for conflict. The evaluation [of the] circumstances of each case under this standard must be left primarily to the informed judgment of the trial court. * * *

Justice MARSHALL, with whom Justice BRENNAN joins, dissenting.

[I] disagree [with] the Court's suggestion that the trial court's decision as to whether a potential conflict justifies rejection of a defendant's chosen counsel is entitled to some kind of special deference on appeal. The Court grants trial courts "broad latitude" over the decision to accept or reject a defendant's choice of counsel; although never explicitly endorsing a standard of appellate review, the Court appears to limit such review to determining whether an abuse of discretion has occurred. [This approach] accords neither with the nature of the trial court's decision nor with the importance of the interest at stake.

[The] interest at stake in this kind of decision is nothing less than a criminal defendant's Sixth Amendment right to counsel of his choice. The trial court simply does not have "broad latitude" to vitiate this right. In my view, a trial court that rejects a criminal defendant's chosen counsel on the ground of a potential conflict should make findings on the record to facilitate review, and an appellate court should scrutinize closely the basis for the trial court's decision. Only in this way can a criminal defendant's right to counsel of his choice be appropriately protected.

The Court's resolution of the instant case flows from its deferential approach to the District Court's denial of petitioner's motion to add or substitute counsel; absent deference, a decision upholding the District Court's ruling would be inconceivable. Indeed, I believe that even under the Court's deferential standard, reversal is in order.

[At] the time of petitioner's trial, Iredale's representation of Gomez–Barajas was effectively completed. * * * Gomez–Barajas was not scheduled to appear as a witness at petitioner's trial; thus, Iredale's conduct of that trial would not require him to question his former client. The only possible conflict this Court can divine from Iredale's representation of both petitioner and Gomez–Barajas rests on the premise that the trial court would reject the negotiated plea agreement and that Gomez–Barajas then would decide to go to trial. In this event, the Court tells us, "petitioner's probable testimony at the resulting trial of Gomez–Barajas would create an ethical dilemma for Iredale."

This argument rests on speculation of the most dubious kind. The Court offers no reason to think that the trial court would have rejected Gomez–Barajas's plea agreement; neither did the Government posit any such reason in its argument or brief before this Court. The most likely occurrence at the time petitioner moved to retain Iredale as his defense counsel was that the trial court would accept Gomez–Barajas's plea agreement, as the court in fact later did. Moreover, even if Gomez–Barajas had gone to trial, petitioner probably would not have testified. [The] only alleged connection between petitioner and Gomez–Barajas sprang from the conspiracy to distribute marijuana, and a jury already had acquitted Gomez–Barajas of that charge. It is therefore disingenuous to say that representation of both petitioner and Gomez–Barajas posed a serious potential for a conflict of interest.

Similarly, Iredale's prior representation of Bravo was not a cause for concern. * * * Contrary to the Court's inference, Bravo could not have testified about petitioner's involvement in the alleged marijuana distribution scheme. As all parties were aware at the time, Bravo did not know and could not identify petitioner; indeed, prior to the commencement of legal proceedings, the two men never had heard of each other. Bravo's eventual testimony at petitioner's trial related to a shipment of marijuana in which petitioner was not involved; the testimony contained not a single reference to petitioner. Petitioner's counsel did not cross-examine Bravo, and neither petitioner's counsel nor the prosecutor mentioned Bravo's testimony in closing argument. All of these developments were predictable when the District Court ruled on petitioner's request that Iredale serve as trial counsel; the contours of Bravo's testimony were clear at that time. Given the insignificance of this testimony to any matter that petitioner's counsel would dispute, the proposed joint representation of petitioner and Bravo did not threaten a conflict of interest.

Moreover, even assuming that Bravo's testimony might have "necessitat[ed] vigorous cross-examination," the District Court could have insured against the possibility of any conflict of interest without wholly depriving petitioner of his constitutional right to the counsel of his choice. Petitioner's motion requested that Iredale either be substituted for petitioner's current counsel or be added to petitioner's defense team. Had the District Court allowed the addition of Iredale and then ordered that he take no part in the cross-examination of Bravo, any possibility of a conflict would have been removed. Especially in light of the availability of this precautionary measure, the notion that Iredale's prior representation of Bravo might well have caused a conflict of interest at petitioner's trial is nothing short of ludicrous. * * *

Justice STEVENS, with whom Justice BLACKMUN joins, dissenting.

[The] Court gives inadequate weight to the informed and voluntary character of the clients' waiver of their right to conflict-free representation. Particularly, the Court virtually ignores the fact that the additional counsel representing petitioner had provided him with sound advice concerning the wisdom of a waiver and would have remained available during the trial to assist in the defense. Thus, [the] question before [the District Judge] was whether petitioner should be permitted to have *additional* counsel of his choice. I agree with Justice Marshall that the answer to that question is perfectly clear.

Notes and Questions

1. ***Viewing Wheat from different perspectives.*** Commentators have approached the issue of disqualification from quite diverse perspectives, producing equally diverse evaluations of the *Wheat* ruling. Consider:

(a) William J. Stuntz, *Waiving Rights in Criminal Procedure*, 75 Va. L. Rev. 761 (1989): "One might try to explain *Wheat* as nothing more than a paternalistic attempt to protect Iredale's clients against their own irrationality * * * [but] that approach to the case seems strained. * * * [Professor Stuntz notes that Wheat was involved in a large-scale conspiracy, where defendants often are more "sophisticated."] * * * There are two reasons why the coconspirators [in Wheat] might have wished to use Iredale as common counsel. The first, offered by the defendants, is unobjectionable: the defendants believed Iredale to be a very good attorney, better than the likely alternatives. But the second is troubling. If the three defendants in question were guilty, they may well have faced a classic prisoners' dilemma: it may have been in each individual's interest to 'sell out' to the government and implicate his colleagues, but may have been far better for all if all either lied or remained silent. Common counsel may have removed the dilemma by facilitating the enforcement of an agreement not to finger each other. Obtaining the testimony of one conspirator against others may require careful negotiation with the would-be witness. If all the conspirators have the same lawyer, the government is, in effect, able to deal with one defendant only by dealing with all. One cannot be absolutely certain whether the codefendants wanted a common lawyer for good reasons or bad, but there is a fairly good proxy for that determination. If an objective observer familiar with the local bar would have concluded that Iredale was not any better than the lawyers who might have taken his place, then the defendants' motive for retaining him seems suspect. The district judge was in a good position to make that judgment.[116] The ability of district judges to make case-by-case assessments of defendants' counsel of choice may be why the Court left the matter in the district courts' discretion, rather than promulgate a blanket rule either barring or allowing waiver."

(b) Bruce A. Green, *"Through a Glass, Darkly": How the Court Sees Motions to Disqualify Criminal Defense Lawyers,* 89 Colum.L.Rev. 1201, 1215–16, 1221–22 (1989): "Because Wheat was the only client awaiting trial, the most significant ethical concern identified in *Wheat* was the possibility that, if codefendant Bravo's testimony was to tie Wheat to particular deliveries of marijuana, attorney Iredale 'would have been unable ethically to provide' the vigorous cross-examination that would have been needed to impeach Bravo. This was essentially the same problem that typically arises when a defense attorney is called upon to cross-examine a former, rather than a current client. [Under] the prevailing professional standards, a potential conflict arising out of the need to cross-examine a former client is appropriately deemed less serious than a conflict arising out of the joint representation of codefendants. * * *

"In light of the nature of the potential conflict in *Wheat* and the manner in which it is addressed by the prevailing ethical standards, the district judge in that case had no basis for concluding that, if Bravo were to be a government witness at Wheat's trial, Iredale's representation of Wheat would violate the prevailing ethical norms. To begin with, the trial judge had no reason to believe that Iredale

116. In some cases, defendants will have an interest in retaining common counsel because their case is factually complex, and the costs of bringing individual counsel up to speed would be high. As with the possibility that counsel is exceptionally skilled, the district judge is well situated to determine whether a particular case involves large economies of scale in legal representation.

had received confidential disclosures which Iredale would have to bend over backwards to avoid using in cross-examining Bravo. Moreover, as Justice Marshall noted in his dissent, Iredale could have permitted cocounsel to cross-examine Bravo, while himself conducting the remainder of the trial. Had Iredale agreed not to reveal Bravo's confidences to his cocounsel, this would have eliminated any possible conflict.

"Even if Iredale were called upon to cross-examine Bravo, the clients' consent to the potential conflict would have eliminated the ethical barrier to the representation, notwithstanding Iredale's possession of confidences that needed to be preserved. * * * Moreover, unlike cases involving joint representation at trial, the consent in this case would have eliminated not only the ethical barrier, but the conflict itself. By authorizing Iredale to make use of his confidences, or at least to err on the side of using them, Bravo would have eliminated any danger to Wheat's defense. At the same time, Wheat could have agreed that, insofar as possible, Iredale's cross-examination of Bravo would be based only on nonconfidential matters * * *. Thus, the *Wheat* decision is bottomed on the Court's misunderstanding of the ethical rules. [The] Court upheld the denial of Wheat's choice of counsel in a case where the ethical rules plainly would have permitted that choice."

(c) Note, 102 Harv.L.Rev. 143 (1988). "By allowing the government successfully to oppose Wheat's attempted waiver on the basis of institutional concerns external to Wheat, the Court in effect vested the right to conflict-free defense counsel in the state as well as in Wheat. * * * Recognizing such a right transforms the sixth amendment, presumably a shield to help criminal defendants receive fair treatment in their battle against a more powerful adversary, into an additional weapon for their prosecutors to use against them.[a] The state might now intentionally manufacture conflicts in order to disqualify a particularly formidable opposing attorney. Indeed, the relative insignificance of Bravo's testimony against Wheat, the late date at which the government expressed interest in that testimony, and the success of Iredale in representing Wheat's alleged co-conspirators together suggest that Wheat's prosecutor succeeded in doing just that."

(d) Pamela S. Karlan, *Discrete and Relational Representation: The Changing Vision of the Right to Counsel*, 105 Harv.L.Rev. 670 (1992) [Professor Karlan concludes that the original right to counsel decisions envisioned a "discrete criminal representation"—"lawyers [who] enter the picture only after * * * the prosecution has begun * * * to form an association with the client for a discrete purpose: providing technical legal assistance in defending against formal criminal charges." Cases like *Wheat* and *Caplin & Drysdale* (p. 140) reflect an alternative vision of the attorney-client relationship, that of "relational" criminal representation—where the attorney "has an ongoing association with her client" and often serves as "counsel to an enterprise rather than an individual." She notes that relational criminal representation may lead to the tactics noted by Professor

a. See William F. Genego, *The New Adversary*, 54 Brook.L.Rev. 781 (1988): "In recent years federal prosecutors have adopted practices, which respond to the special investigative and prosecutorial needs associated with drug and white collar offenses. Many of these practices directly affect criminal defense attorneys, and, in turn, the representation received by criminal defendants. Examples of third party enforcement practices utilized by the government include grand jury and trial subpoenas directed to defense counsel, * * * forfeiture of attorneys' fees, * * * and efforts to disqualify attorneys. * * * Criminal defense attorneys charge that federal prosecutors employ these third party enforcement practices not to fulfill legitimate prosecutorial need, but to discourage zealous representation by defense attorneys and to prevent particular attorneys from representing specific clients. * * * Prosecutors deny that they target [particular attorneys] or attempt to interfere with defendants' constitutional rights to representation. Further, prosecutors insist that such practices are not widespread but are used selectively in appropriate circumstances."

Stuntz, including "circumvent[ing] the prisoners dilemma." However, she adds it may also contribute to "false positives" (i.e., erroneous convictions)]:

"In another class of cases, relational representation may reduce the defendant's interest in avoiding a false positive. These cases involve so-called 'benefactor' payments—cases in which a benefactor pays the legal fees of another. In some benefactor cases, the interests of the benefactor and the defendant are identical. * * * But in other cases the benefactor's and defendant's interests diverge. Consider the fall guy: a low-level operative in an ongoing criminal enterprise who agrees to take the rap for crimes committed by his superiors within the organization or agrees not to use his knowledge about his superiors' activities in attempting to strike a deal for himself with the government. * * * [Here] a benefactor-paid lawyer may generate two potential advantages. First, for the defendant, it may represent one of the fringe benefits of employment by the enterprise. * * * Second, providing an attorney for subordinates may enable the benefactor to monitor the defendant's contacts with prosecutors to ensure that the defendant does not cooperate with the government to the benefactor's detriment."

2. ***"Manufactured conflicts."*** Assume that the defense claims, in responding to a motion to disqualify, that the prosecution has "manufactured a conflict" based on: (i) a prosecution offer of a plea bargain (in exchange for testifying for the government) to one of several jointly represented codefendants; (ii) the prosecution's current investigation of defense counsel as to events relating to the charges against the client; or (iii) the prosecution's intent to call the defense counsel as a witness. What type of inquiry, if any, is needed to satisfy *Wheat*'s directive that the trial court "must take * * * into consideration" the possibility that the conflict was "manufactured" by the prosecution to "prevent a defendant from having a particularly able defense counsel at his side" (p. 210). Consider *United States v. Diozzi*, 807 F.2d 10 (1st Cir.1986) (to ensure against a "manufactured conflict," where conflict is based on prosecution's use of defense counsel as a witness, the trial court should seek to determine whether the testimony of counsel is truly needed or whether the same facts could be established through other means, but the government should not be forced "to settle for less than its best evidence").

3. ***Disqualification in other conflict settings.*** "Recognizing [*Wheat*'s acceptance of trial court] discretion and applying a deferential standard of review, appellate courts have sustained the disqualification of counsel not only in cases involving multiple representation of codefendants (as in *Wheat*), but also in a broad range of other settings that present a realistic potential for a conflict of interest. These include cases in which: (1) defense counsel currently was representing an anticipated prosecution witness on either a related or different matter; (2) defense counsel had previously represented a prosecution witness on a related matter; (3) defense counsel was a potential witness for the prosecution; (4) defense counsel's participation in events that would be described before the jury could lead to calling him as a defense witness, and would make him an "unsworn" witness for the defense even if he were not called to testify; (5) defense counsel was a former member of the prosecution's staff who had participated in the bringing of these charges or otherwise had access through that position to confidential information relevant to the prosecution; (6) defense counsel was alleged to have been involved in criminal activity or professional misconduct that would bear upon his representation of the defendant; and (7) defense counsel also represented the entity with which defendant was associated (with that entity having interests separate from the defendant)." CRIMPOC. § 11.9(c) Do all of these situations present the justifications for broad judicial discretion that were cited in *Wheat*?

4. ***Waivers.*** Where the conflict creates the potential of giving the defendant an adversarial advantage (e.g., where defense counsel is a former prosecutor and

acquired confidential information relating to the prosecution's case), disqualification in all courts is virtually automatic. Where, however, the primary concern is that the particular conflict will adversely impact the defendant (or the related "judicial integrity" concern that such representation will appear less than fair), many trial courts will refuse to disqualify if they can obtain a satisfactory waiver of the conflict. Although *Wheat* spoke of federal appellate decisions that appeared to allow a defendant to press a postconviction conflict of interest challenge notwithstanding defendant's waiver of the right to conflict-free counsel, "post-*Wheat* circuit court rulings have established that a knowing and intelligent waiver precludes a subsequent competency challenge based on the conflict." CRIMPROC. § 11.9(c).

Various appellate courts have offered fairly detailed instructions for advising defendants of potential and actual conflicts in the course of obtaining a waiver, and some courts also insist that a defendant have consulted with independent counsel before entering the waiver. *United States v. Newell*, 315 F.3d 510 (5th Cir.2002), indicates, however, that even such precautions may not provide a waiver that is an acceptable response to a postconviction challenge.

In *Newell*, the trial judge followed the detailed instructions for obtaining a waiver set forth in Fifth Circuit precedent, and allowed continued representation of codefendants after receiving the waiver. The Fifth Circuit held, however, that the waiver was flawed. When the waiver was accepted, neither the trial judge nor the defendant anticipated that counsel's strategy eventually would include implicating the defendant in order to exonerate the codefendant. When this conflict emerged at trial, the trial judge did not reopen the waiver issue and undertake further inquiry (which the Fifth Circuit described as the trial court's obligation under Rule 44). Finding the waiver invalid, the Fifth Circuit noted: "We do not suggest that a trial court cannot at the outset * * * obtain a waiver of the right to conflict-free counsel, * * * [but] such a waiver * * * will be valid [only] against conflicts where they emerge at trial in cases that were sufficiently *forseeable* that the judge can bring them home to the defendants in concrete terms."

5. The Second Circuit has held that, no matter how extensive the warnings and inquiry, a valid defense waiver cannot be obtained where defense counsel is alleged to have personally participated in the crime charged (or a related crime) because that conflict "so permeate[s] the defense that no meaningful waiver can be obtained." *United States v. Fulton*, 5 F.3d 605 (2d Cir.1993). Building upon that ruling, the Second Circuit later held that similarly invalid were waivers where "the attorney suffers from a severe conflict—such that no rational defendant would knowingly and intelligently deserve the conflicted lawyer's representation." See e.g., *United States v. Schwarz*, 283 F.3d 76 (2d Cir.2002) (defense waiver invalid under this standard; defendant police officer was charged with violating the civil rights of arrestee Abner Louima in a case that attracted nationwide attention; defendant waived as to representation by a law firm that also represented police union, but the union's interests diverged from that of defendant; Louima in a civil suit had alleged that the union participated in a "coverup conspiracy," but the plausible defense strategy of implicating another officer, not pursued by defense counsel, would have worked against its interest in that suit).

Part Two
POLICE PRACTICES

Chapter 6
ARREST, SEARCH AND SEIZURE[a]

SECTION 1. THE EXCLUSIONARY RULE[b]

WOLF v. COLORADO

338 U.S. 25, 69 S.Ct. 1359, 93 L.Ed. 1782 (1949).

Justice FRANKFURTER delivered the opinion of the Court.

The precise question for consideration is this: Does a conviction by a State court for a State offense deny the "due process of law" required by the Fourteenth Amendment, solely because evidence that was admitted at the trial was obtained under circumstances which would have rendered it inadmissible in a prosecution for violation of a federal law in a court of the United States because there deemed to be an infraction of the Fourth Amendment as applied in *Weeks v. United States,* 232 U.S. 383 [1914]? * * *

The security of one's privacy against arbitrary intrusion by the police—which is at the core of the Fourth Amendment—is basic to a free society. It is therefore implicit in "the concept of ordered liberty" and as such enforceable against the States through the Due Process Clause. * * *

Accordingly, we have no hesitation in saying that were a State affirmatively to sanction such police incursion into privacy it would run counter to the guaranty of the Fourteenth Amendment. But the ways of enforcing such a basic right raise questions of a different order. How such arbitrary conduct should be checked, what remedies against it should be afforded, the means by which the right should be made effective, are all questions that are not to be so dogmatically answered as to preclude the varying solutions which spring from an allowable range of judgment on issues not susceptible of quantitative solution.

a. For detailed treatment of this subject and reference to other secondary sources, consult Wayne R. LaFave, *Search and Seizure: A Treatise on the Fourth Amendment* (6 vols., 4th ed.2004) [cited herein by its Westlaw database name SEARCHSZR].

b. The concern herein is with the exclusion of evidence obtained in violation of the Fourth Amendment. An arrest or search which passes Fourth Amendment muster may nonetheless violate state law, and the exclusionary sanction is also used when state constitutional provisions similar to the Fourth Amendment have been violated, though if a state chooses not to do so this does not violate federal due process. *California v. Greenwood,* p. 251. As for violations of statutes, court rules and administrative regulations, it is customary to require exclusion if the violation significantly affected the defendant's substantial rights.

In *Weeks v. United States,* this Court held that in a federal prosecution the Fourth Amendment barred the use of evidence secured through an illegal search and seizure. This ruling * * * was not derived from the explicit requirements of the Fourth Amendment; it was not based on legislation expressing Congressional policy in the enforcement of the Constitution. The decision was a matter of judicial implication. Since then it has been frequently applied and we stoutly adhere to it. But the immediate question is whether the basic right to protection against arbitrary intrusion by the police demands the exclusion of logically relevant evidence obtained by an unreasonable search and seizure because, in a federal prosecution for a federal crime, it would be excluded. As a matter of inherent reason, one would suppose this to be an issue as to which men with complete devotion to the protection of the right of privacy might give different answers. When we find that in fact most of the English-speaking world does not regard as vital to such protection the exclusion of evidence thus obtained, we must hesitate to treat this remedy as an essential ingredient of the right. The contrariety of views of the States is particularly impressive in view of the careful reconsideration which they have given the problem in the light of the *Weeks* decision.

* * * As of today 30 States reject the *Weeks* doctrine, 17 States are in agreement with it. * * * Of 10 jurisdictions within the United Kingdom and the British Commonwealth of Nations which have passed on the question, none has held evidence obtained by illegal search and seizure inadmissible. * * *

The jurisdictions which have rejected the *Weeks* doctrine have not left the right to privacy without other means of protection. Indeed, the exclusion of evidence is a remedy which directly serves only to protect those upon whose person or premises something incriminating has been found. We cannot, therefore, regard it as a departure from basic standards to remand such persons, together with those who emerge scatheless from a search, to the remedies of private action and such protection as the internal discipline of the police, under the eyes of an alert public opinion, may afford. Granting that in practice the exclusion of evidence may be an effective way of deterring unreasonable searches, it is not for this Court to condemn as falling below the minimal standards assured by the Due Process Clause a State's reliance upon other methods which, if consistently enforced, would be equally effective. * * * There are, moreover, reasons for excluding evidence unreasonably obtained by the federal police which are less compelling in the case of police under State or local authority. The public opinion of a community can far more effectively be exerted against oppressive conduct on the part of police directly responsible to the community itself than can local opinion, sporadically aroused, be brought to bear upon remote authority pervasively exerted throughout the country.

We hold, therefore, that in a prosecution in a State court for a State crime the Fourteenth Amendment does not forbid the admission of evidence obtained by an unreasonable search and seizure. * * *

Justice BLACK, concurring.

* * * I agree with what appears to be a plain implication of the Court's opinion that the federal exclusionary rule is not a command of the Fourth Amendment but is a judicially created rule of evidence which Congress might negate. * * *

Justice MURPHY, with whom Justice RUTLEDGE joins, dissenting.

[T]here is but one alternative to the rule of exclusion. That is no sanction at all.

* * * Little need be said concerning the possibilities of criminal prosecution. Self-scrutiny is a lofty ideal, but its exaltation reaches new heights if we expect a District Attorney to prosecute himself or his associates for well-meaning violations of the search and seizure clause during a raid the District Attorney or his associates have ordered. But there is an appealing ring in another alternative. A trespass action for damages is a venerable means of securing reparation for unauthorized invasion of the home. Why not put the old writ to a new use? When the Court cites cases permitting the action, the remedy seems complete.

But what an illusory remedy this is, if by "remedy" we mean a positive deterrent to police and prosecutors tempted to violate the Fourth Amendment. The appealing ring softens when we recall that in a trespass action the measure of damages is simply the extent of the injury to physical property. If the officer searches with care, he can avoid all but nominal damages—a penny, or a dollar. Are punitive damages possible? Perhaps. But a few states permit none, whatever the circumstances. In those that do, the plaintiff must show the real ill will or malice of the defendant, and surely it is not unreasonable to assume that one in honest pursuit of crime bears no malice toward the search victim. If that burden is carried, recovery may yet be defeated by the rule that there must be physical damages before punitive damages may be awarded. In addition, some states limit punitive damages to the actual expenses of litigation. * * * Even assuming the ill will of the officer, his reasonable grounds for belief that the home he searched harbored evidence of crime is admissible in mitigation of punitive damages. * * * The bad reputation of the plaintiff is likewise admissible. * * * If the evidence seized was actually used at a trial, that fact has been held a complete justification of the search, and a defense against the trespass action. * * * And even if the plaintiff hurdles all these obstacles, and gains a substantial verdict, the individual officer's finances may well make the judgment useless—for the municipality, of course, is not liable without its consent. Is it surprising that there is so little in the books concerning trespass actions for violation of the search and seizure clause? * * *

Justice DOUGLAS, dissenting.

* * * I agree with Justice Murphy that * * * in absence of [an exclusionary] rule of evidence the Amendment would have no effective sanction. * * *

MAPP v. OHIO

367 U.S. 643, 81 S.Ct. 1684, 6 L.Ed.2d 1081 (1961).

Justice CLARK delivered the opinion of the Court. * * *

On May 23, 1957, three Cleveland police officers arrived at appellant's residence in that city pursuant to information that "a person [was] hiding out in the home who was wanted for questioning in connection with a recent bombing, and that there was a large amount of policy paraphernalia being hidden in the home." Miss Mapp and her daughter by a former marriage lived on the top floor of the two-family dwelling. Upon their arrival at that house, the officers knocked on the door and demanded entrance but appellant, after telephoning her attorney, refused to admit them without a search warrant. * * *

The officers again sought entrance some three hours later when four or more additional officers arrived on the scene. When Miss Mapp did not come to the door immediately, at least one of the several doors to the house was forcibly opened and the policemen gained admittance. Meanwhile Miss Mapp's attorney arrived, but the officers, having secured their own entry, and continuing in their defiance of the law, would permit him neither to see Miss Mapp nor to enter the house. [When the officers broke into the hall, Miss Mapp] demanded to see the search warrant. A paper, claimed to be a warrant, was held up by one of the officers. She grabbed the "warrant" and placed it in her bosom. A struggle ensued in which the officers recovered the piece of paper and as a result of which they handcuffed appellant because she had been "belligerent" in resisting their official rescue of the "warrant" from her person. * * * Appellant, in handcuffs, was then forcibly taken upstairs to her bedroom where the officers searched a dresser, a chest of drawers, a closet and some suitcases. * * * The search spread to the rest of the second floor * * *. The basement of the building and a trunk found therein were also searched. The obscene materials for possession of which she was ultimately convicted were discovered in the course of that widespread search.

At the trial no search warrant was produced by the prosecution, nor was the failure to produce one explained or accounted for. At best [as the Ohio Supreme Court, which affirmed the conviction, expressed it], "there is, in the record, considerable doubt as to whether there ever was any warrant for the search of defendant's home." * * *

The State says that even if the search were made without authority, or otherwise unreasonably, it is not prevented from using the unconstitutionally seized evidence at trial, citing *Wolf v. Colorado,* * * *. On this appeal, * * * it is urged once again that we review that holding. * * *

The Court in *Wolf* first stated that "[t]he contrariety of views of the States" on the adoption of the exclusionary rule of *Weeks* was "particularly impressive" * * * While in 1949, prior to the *Wolf* case, almost two-thirds of the States were opposed to the use of the exclusionary rule, now, despite the *Wolf* case, more than half of those since passing upon it, by their own legislative or judicial decision, have wholly or partly adopted or adhered to the *Weeks* rule. * * * Significantly, among those now following the rule is California which, according to its highest court, was "compelled to reach that conclusion because other remedies have completely failed to secure compliance with the constitutional provisions * * *." In connection with this California case, we note that the second basis elaborated in *Wolf* in support of its failure to enforce the exclusionary doctrine against the States was that "other means of protection" have been afforded "the right to privacy." The experience of California that such other remedies have been worthless and futile is buttressed by the experience of other States. * * *

It, therefore, plainly appears that the factual considerations supporting the failure of the *Wolf* Court to include the *Weeks* exclusionary rule when it recognized the enforceability of the right to privacy against the States in 1949, while not basically relevant to the constitutional consideration, could not, in any analysis, now be deemed controlling.

* * * Today we once again examine *Wolf's* constitutional documentation of the right to privacy free from unreasonable state intrusion, and, after its dozen years on our books, are led by it to close the only courtroom door remaining open to evidence secured by official lawlessness in flagrant abuse of that basic right, reserved to all persons as a specific guarantee against that very same unlawful conduct. We hold that all evidence obtained by searches and seizures in violation of the Constitution is, by that same authority, inadmissible in a state court.

Since the Fourth Amendment's right of privacy has been declared enforceable against the States through the Due Process Clause of the Fourteenth, it is enforceable against them by the same sanction of exclusion as is used against the Federal Government. Were it otherwise then just as without the *Weeks* rule the assurance against unreasonable federal searches and seizures would be "a form of words," valueless and undeserving of mention in a perpetual charter of inestimable human liberties, so too, without that rule the freedom from state invasions of privacy would be so ephemeral and so neatly severed from its conceptual nexus with the freedom from all brutish means of coercing evidence as not to merit this Court's high regard as a freedom "implicit in 'the concept of ordered liberty.' "

* * * [I]n extending the substantive protections of due process to all constitutionally unreasonable searches—state or federal—it was logically and constitutionally necessary that the exclusion doctrine—an essential part of the right to privacy—be also insisted upon as an essential ingredient of the right newly recognized by the *Wolf* case. In short, the admission of the new constitutional right by *Wolf* could not consistently tolerate denial of its most important constitutional privilege, namely, the exclusion of the evidence which an accused had been forced to give by reason of the unlawful seizure. To hold otherwise is to grant the right but in reality to withhold its privilege and enjoyment. Only last year the Court itself recognized that the purpose of the exclusionary rule "is to deter—to compel respect for the constitutional guaranty in the only effectively available way—by removing the incentive to disregard it."

Indeed, we are aware of no restraint, similar to that rejected today, conditioning the enforcement of any other basic constitutional right. The right to privacy, no less important than any other right carefully and particularly reserved to the people, would stand in marked contrast to all other rights declared as "basic to a free society." * * * [N]othing could be more certain than that when a coerced confession is involved, "the relevant rules of evidence" are overridden without regard to "the incidence of such conduct by the police," slight or frequent. Why should not the same rule apply to what is tantamount to coerced testimony by way of unconstitutional seizure of goods, papers, effects, documents, etc.? We find that, as to the Federal Government the Fourth and Fifth Amendments and, as to the States, the freedom from unconscionable invasions of privacy and the freedom from convictions based upon coerced confessions do enjoy an "intimate relation" in their perpetuation of "principles of humanity and civil liberty * * *." They express "supplementing phases of the same constitutional purpose—to maintain inviolate large areas of personal privacy." The philosophy of each Amendment and of each freedom is complementary to, although not dependent upon, that of the other in its sphere of influence—the very least that together they assure in either sphere is that no man is to be convicted on unconstitutional evidence.

Moreover, our holding * * * is not only the logical dictate of prior cases, but it also makes very good sense. There is no war between the Constitution and common sense. Presently, a federal prosecutor may make no use of evidence illegally seized, but a State's attorney across the street may, although he supposedly is operating under the enforceable prohibitions of the same Amendment. Thus the State, by admitting evidence unlawfully seized, serves to encourage disobedience to the Federal Constitution which it is bound to uphold. * * *

There are those who say, as did Justice (then Judge) Cardozo, that under our constitutional exclusionary doctrine "[t]he criminal is to go free because the constable has blundered." *People v. Defore*, 150 N.E. 585 (N.Y.1926). In some cases this will undoubtedly be the result. But, "there is another consideration—the imperative of judicial integrity." The criminal goes free, if he must, but it is the law that sets him free. Nothing can destroy a government more quickly than its failure to observe its own laws, or worse, its disregard of the charter of its own existence. As Justice Brandeis, dissenting, said in *Olmstead v. United States* [p. 463]: "Our government is the potent, the omnipresent teacher. For good or for ill, it teaches the whole people by its example. * * * If the government becomes a lawbreaker, it breeds contempt for law; it invites every man to become a law unto himself; it invites anarchy." Nor can it lightly be assumed that, as a practical matter, adoption of the exclusionary rule fetters law enforcement. Only last year this Court expressly considered that contention and found that "pragmatic evidence of a sort" to the contrary was not wanting. *Elkins v. United States*, 364 U.S. 206 (1960). * * * The Court noted that:

"The federal courts themselves have operated under the exclusionary rule of *Weeks* for almost half a century; yet it has not been suggested either that the Federal Bureau of Investigation has thereby been rendered ineffective, or that the administration of criminal justice in the federal courts has thereby been disrupted. Moreover, the experience of the states is impressive * * *. The movement toward the rule of exclusion has been halting but seemingly inexorable."

The ignoble shortcut to conviction left open to the State tends to destroy the entire system of constitutional restraints on which the liberties of the people rest. Having once recognized that the right to privacy embodied in the Fourth Amendment is enforceable against the States, and that the right to be secure against rude invasions of privacy by state officers is, therefore, constitutional in origin, we can no longer permit that right to remain an empty promise. Because it is enforceable in the same manner and to like effect as other basic rights secured by the Due Process Clause, we can no longer permit it to be revocable at the whim of any police officer who, in the name of law enforcement itself, chooses to suspend its enjoyment. Our decision, founded on reason and truth, gives to the individual no more than that which the Constitution guarantees him, to the police officer no less than that to which honest law enforcement is entitled, and, to the courts, that judicial integrity so necessary in the true administration of justice. * * *

Reversed and remanded.[a]

Justice HARLAN, whom Justice FRANKFURTER and Justice WHITTAKER join, dissenting. * * *

I would not impose upon the States this federal exclusionary remedy. The reasons given by the majority for now suddenly turning its back on *Wolf* seem to me notably unconvincing.

First, it is said that "the factual grounds upon which *Wolf* was based" have since changed, in that more States now follow the *Weeks* exclusionary rule than was so at the time *Wolf* was decided. While that is true, a recent survey indicates that at present one half of the States still adhere to the common-law non-exclusionary rule, and one, Maryland, retains the rule as to felonies. * * * But in any case surely all this is beside the point, as the majority itself indeed seems to recognize. Our concern here, as it was in *Wolf*, is not with the desirability of that rule but only with the question whether the States are Constitutionally free to follow it or not as they may themselves determine, and the relevance of the disparity of views among the States on this point lies simply in the fact that the judgment involved is a debatable one. Moreover, the very fact on which the majority relies, instead of lending support to what is now being done, points away from the need of replacing voluntary state action with federal compulsion.

The preservation of a proper balance between state and federal responsibility in the administration of criminal justice demands patience on the part of those who might like to see things move faster among the States in this respect. Problems of criminal law enforcement vary widely from State to State. One State, in considering the totality of its legal picture, may conclude that the need for embracing the *Weeks* rule is pressing because other remedies are unavailable or inadequate to secure compliance with the substantive Constitutional principle involved. Another, though equally solicitous of Constitutional rights, may choose to pursue one purpose at a time, allowing all evidence relevant to guilt to be

a. Concurring opinions by Black and Douglas, JJ., and a memorandum by Stewart, J., are omitted.

brought into a criminal trial, and dealing with Constitutional infractions by other means. Still another may consider the exclusionary rule too rough and ready a remedy, in that it reaches only unconstitutional intrusions which eventuate in criminal prosecution of the victims. Further, a State after experimenting with the *Weeks* rule for a time may, because of unsatisfactory experience with it, decide to revert to a non-exclusionary rule. And so on. * * * For us the question remains, as it has always been, one of state power, not one of passing judgment on the wisdom of one state course or another. In my view this Court should continue to forbear from fettering the States with an adamant rule which may embarrass them in coping with their own peculiar problems in criminal law enforcement. * * *

* * * Our role in promulgating the *Weeks* rule and its extensions * * * was quite a different one than it is here. There, in implementing the Fourth Amendment, we occupied the position of a tribunal having the ultimate responsibility for developing the standards and procedures of judicial administration within the judicial system over which it presides. Here we review State procedures whose measure is to be taken not against the specific substantive commands of the Fourth Amendment but under the flexible contours of the Due Process Clause. I do not believe that the Fourteenth Amendment empowers this Court to mould state remedies effectuating the right to freedom from "arbitrary intrusion by the police" to suit its own notions of how things should be done * * *.

Finally, it is said that the overruling of *Wolf* is supported by the established doctrine that the admission in evidence of an involuntary confession renders a state conviction constitutionally invalid. Since such a confession may often be entirely reliable, and therefore of the greatest relevance to the issue of the trial, the argument continues, this doctrine is ample warrant in precedent that the way evidence was obtained and not just its relevance, is constitutionally significant to the fairness of a trial. I believe this analogy is not a true one. The "coerced confession" rule is certainly not a rule that any illegally obtained statements may not be used in evidence. I would suppose that a statement which is procured during a period of illegal detention is, as much as unlawfully seized evidence, illegally obtained, but this Court has consistently refused to reverse state convictions resting on the use of such statements. * * *

The point, then, must be that in requiring exclusion of an involuntary statement of an accused, we are concerned not with an appropriate remedy for what the police have done, but with something which is regarded as going to the heart of our concepts of fairness in judicial procedure. The operative assumption of our procedural system is that "ours is the accusatorial as opposed to the inquisitorial system. * * *." * * * The pressures brought to bear against an accused leading to a confession, unlike an unconstitutional violation of privacy, do not, apart from the use of the confession at trial, necessarily involve independent Constitutional violations. What is crucial is that the trial defense to which an accused is entitled should not be rendered an empty formality by reason of statements wrung from him, for then "a prisoner * * * [has been] made the deluded instrument of his own conviction." That this is a *procedural right,* and that its violation occurs at the time his improperly obtained statement is admitted at trial, is manifest.[b] * * *

This, and not the disciplining of the police, as with illegally seized evidence, is surely the true basis for excluding a statement of the accused which was unconstitutionally obtained. In sum, I think the coerced confession analogy works strongly *against* what the Court does today. * * *

b. Is this so? Would such an argument have carried more force after the privilege against self-incrimination was held applicable in the police station? See *Chavez v. Martinez*, p. 695.

UNITED STATES v. LEON

468 U.S. 897, 104 S.Ct. 3405, 82 L.Ed.2d 677 (1984).

Justice WHITE delivered the opinion of the Court. * * *

This case presents the question whether the Fourth Amendment exclusionary rule should be modified so as not to bar the use in the prosecution's case-in-chief of evidence obtained by officers acting in reasonable reliance on a search warrant issued by a detached and neutral magistrate but ultimately found to be unsupported by probable cause. * * *

The Fourth Amendment contains no provision expressly precluding the use of evidence obtained in violation of its commands, and an examination of its origin and purposes makes clear that the use of fruits of a past unlawful search or seizure "work[s] no new Fourth Amendment wrong." The wrong condemned by the Amendment is "fully accomplished" by the unlawful search or seizure itself, and the exclusionary rule is neither intended nor able to "cure the invasion of the defendant's rights which he has already suffered." The rule thus operates as "a judicially created remedy designed to safeguard Fourth Amendment rights generally through its deterrent effect, rather than a personal constitutional right of the person aggrieved."

Whether the exclusionary sanction is appropriately imposed in a particular case, our decisions make clear, is "an issue separate from the question whether the Fourth Amendment rights of the party seeking to invoke the rule were violated by police conduct." Only the former question is currently before us,[a] and it must be resolved by weighing the costs and benefits of preventing the use in the prosecution's case-in-chief of inherently trustworthy tangible evidence obtained in reliance on a search warrant issued by a detached and neutral magistrate that ultimately is found to be defective.

The substantial social costs exacted by the exclusionary rule for the vindication of Fourth Amendment rights have long been a source of concern. "Our cases have consistently recognized that unbending application of the exclusionary sanction to enforce ideals of governmental rectitude would impede unacceptably the truth-finding functions of judge and jury." An objectionable collateral consequence of this interference with the criminal justice system's truth-finding function is that some guilty defendants may go free or receive reduced sentences as a result of favorable plea bargains.[6] Particularly when law enforcement officers have acted

a. A large quantities of drugs were suppressed on the ground the warrant had not issued on probable cause, in that the affidavit reported only the allegations of an untested informant and limited corroboration by police surveillance of events themselves "as consistent with innocence as * * * with guilt." The Court earlier noted that whether this warrant would pass muster under the intervening and less demanding test of *Illinois v. Gates,* p. 280, "has not been briefed or argued," and thus chose "to take the case as it comes to us."

6. Researchers have only recently begun to study extensively the effects of the exclusionary rule on the disposition of felony arrests. One study suggests that the rule results in the nonprosecution or nonconviction of between 0.6% and 2.35% of individuals arrested for felonies. Davies, *A Hard Look at What We Know (and Still Need to Learn) About the "Costs" of the Exclusionary Rule: The NIJ Study and Other Studies of "Lost" Arrests,* 1983 A.B.F.Res.J. 611, 621. The estimates are higher for particular crimes the prosecution of which depends heavily on physical evidence. Thus, the cumulative loss due to nonprosecution or nonconviction of individuals arrested on felony drug charges is probably in the range of 2.8% to 7.1%. Davies' analysis of California data suggests that screening by police and prosecutors results in the release because of illegal searches or seizures of as many as 1.4% of all felony arrestees, id., at 650, that 0.9% of felony arrestees are released because of illegal searches or seizures at the preliminary hearing or after trial, *id.,* at 653, and that roughly 0.5% of all felony arrestees benefit from reversals on appeal because of illegal searches. * * *

Many of these researchers have concluded that the impact of the exclusionary rule is

in objective good faith or their transgressions have been minor, the magnitude of the benefit conferred on such guilty defendants offends basic concepts of the criminal justice system. Indiscriminate application of the exclusionary rule, therefore, may well "generat[e] disrespect for the law and the administration of justice." Accordingly, "[a]s with any remedial device, the application of the rule has been restricted to those areas where its remedial objectives are thought most efficaciously served."

Close attention to those remedial objectives has characterized our recent decisions concerning the scope of the Fourth Amendment exclusionary rule. The Court has, to be sure, not seriously questioned, "in the absence of a more efficacious sanction, the continued application of the rule to suppress evidence from the [prosecution's] case where a Fourth Amendment violation has been substantial and deliberate * * *." Nevertheless, the balancing approach that has evolved in various contexts—including criminal trials—"forcefully suggest[s] that the exclusionary rule be more generally modified to permit the introduction of evidence obtained in the reasonable good-faith belief that a search or seizure was in accord with the Fourth Amendment."

In *Stone v. Powell*, 428 U.S. 465 (1976), the Court emphasized the costs of the exclusionary rule, expressed its view that limiting the circumstances under which Fourth Amendment claims could be raised in federal habeas corpus proceedings would not reduce the rule's deterrent effect, and held that a state prisoner who has been afforded a full and fair opportunity to litigate a Fourth Amendment claim may not obtain federal habeas relief on the ground that unlawfully obtained evidence had been introduced at his trial. Proposed extensions of the exclusionary rule to proceedings other than the criminal trial itself have been evaluated and rejected under the same analytic approach[, as in *United States v. Calandra*, p. 241, and *United States v. Janis*, p. 243.]

[C]ases considering the use of unlawfully obtained evidence in criminal trials themselves [also] make clear [that] it does not follow from the emphasis on the exclusionary rule's deterrent value that "anything which deters illegal searches is thereby commanded by the Fourth Amendment." *Alderman v. United States* [p. 892]. * * * Standing to invoke the rule has thus been limited to cases in which the prosecution seeks to use the fruits of an illegal search or seizure against the victim of police misconduct. *Rakas v. Illinois* [p. 896]. Even defendants with standing to challenge the introduction in their criminal trials of unlawfully obtained evidence cannot prevent every conceivable use of such evidence. Evidence obtained in violation of the Fourth Amendment and inadmissible in the prosecution's case in chief may be used to impeach a defendant's direct testimony. *Walder v. United States* [p. 922]. * * *

When considering the use of evidence obtained in violation of the Fourth Amendment in the prosecution's case in chief, moreover, we have declined to adopt a *per se* or "but for" rule that would render inadmissible any evidence that came to light through a chain of causation that began with an illegal arrest. *Brown v. Illinois* [p. 908]; *Wong Sun v. United States* [p. 907]. We also have held that a witness' testimony may be admitted even when his identity was discovered in an unconstitutional search. *United States v. Ceccolini* [p. 915]. The perception underlying these decisions—that the connection between police misconduct and evidence of crime may be sufficiently attenuated to permit the use of that evidence at trial—is a product of considerations relating to the exclusionary rule and the

insubstantial, but the small percentages with which they deal mask a large absolute number of felons who are released because the cases against them were based in part on illegal searches or seizures. * * * Because we find that the rule can have no substantial deterrent effect in the sorts of situations under consideration in this case, we conclude that it cannot pay its way in those situations.

constitutional principles it is designed to protect. * * * Not surprisingly in view of this purpose, an assessment of the flagrancy of the police misconduct constitutes an important step in the calculus. *Brown v. Illinois*, supra. * * *

As yet, we have not recognized any form of good-faith exception to the Fourth Amendment exclusionary rule. But the balancing approach that has evolved during the years of experience with the rule provides strong support for the modification currently urged upon us. As we discuss below, our evaluation of the costs and benefits of suppressing reliable physical evidence seized by officers reasonably relying on a warrant issued by a detached and neutral magistrate leads to the conclusion that such evidence should be admissible in the prosecution's case in chief. * * *

Only [when a warrant is grounded upon an affidavit knowingly or recklessly false] has the Court set forth a rationale for suppressing evidence obtained pursuant to a search warrant;[b] in the other areas, it has simply excluded such evidence without considering whether Fourth Amendment interests will be advanced. To the extent that proponents of exclusion rely on its behavioral effects on judges and magistrates in these areas, their reliance is misplaced. First, the exclusionary rule is designed to deter police misconduct rather than to punish the errors of judges and magistrates. Second, there exists no evidence suggesting that judges and magistrates are inclined to ignore or subvert the Fourth Amendment or that lawlessness among these actors requires application of the extreme sanction of exclusion.[14]

Third, and most important, we discern no basis, and are offered none, for believing that exclusion of evidence seized pursuant to a warrant will have a significant deterrent effect on the issuing judge or magistrate. Many of the factors that indicate that the exclusionary rule cannot provide an effective "special" or "general" deterrent for individual offending law enforcement officers apply as well to judges or magistrates. And, to the extent that the rule is thought to operate as a "systemic" deterrent on a wider audience, it clearly can have no such effect on individuals empowered to issue warrants. Judges and magistrates are not adjuncts to the law enforcement team; as neutral judicial officers, they have no stake in the outcome of particular criminal prosecutions. The threat of exclusion thus cannot be expected significantly to deter them. Imposition of the exclusionary sanction is not necessary meaningfully to inform judicial officers of their errors, and we cannot conclude that admitting evidence obtained pursuant to a warrant while at the same time declaring that the warrant was somehow defective will in any way reduce judicial officers' professional incentives to comply with the Fourth Amendment, encourage them to repeat their mistakes, or lead to the granting of all colorable warrant requests.[18]

b. The reference is to the *Franks* case, p. 296, where the Court declared "it would be an unthinkable imposition upon [the magistrate's] authority if a warrant affidavit, revealed after the fact to contain a deliberately or recklessly false statement, were to stand beyond impeachment."

14. Although there are assertions that some magistrates become rubber stamps for the police and others may be unable effectively to screen police conduct, we are not convinced that this is a problem of major proportions.

18. Limiting the application of the exclusionary sanction may well increase the care with which magistrates scrutinize warrant applications. We doubt that magistrates are more desirous of avoiding the exclusion of evidence obtained pursuant to warrants they have issued than of avoiding invasions of privacy.

Federal magistrates, moreover, are subject to the direct supervision of district courts. They may be removed for "incompetency, misconduct, neglect of duty, or physical or mental disability." 28 U.S.C. § 631(i). If a magistrate serves merely as a "rubber stamp" for the police or is unable to exercise mature judgment, closer supervision or removal provides a more effective remedy than the exclusionary rule.

If exclusion of evidence obtained pursuant to a subsequently invalidated warrant is to have any deterrent effect, therefore, it must alter the behavior of individual law enforcement officers or the policies of their departments. One could argue that applying the exclusionary rule in cases where the police failed to demonstrate probable cause in the warrant application deters future inadequate presentations or "magistrate shopping" and thus promotes the ends of the Fourth Amendment. Suppressing evidence obtained pursuant to a technically defective warrant supported by probable cause also might encourage officers to scrutinize more closely the form of the warrant and to point out suspected judicial errors. We find such arguments speculative and conclude that suppression of evidence obtained pursuant to a warrant should be ordered only on a case-by-case basis and only in those unusual cases in which exclusion will further the purposes of the exclusionary rule.[19]

We have frequently questioned whether the exclusionary rule can have any deterrent effect when the offending officers acted in the objectively reasonable belief that their conduct did not violate the Fourth Amendment. "No empirical researcher, proponent or opponent of the rule, has yet been able to establish with any assurance whether the rule has a deterrent effect * * *." But even assuming that the rule effectively deters some police misconduct and provides incentives for the law enforcement profession as a whole to conduct itself in accord with the Fourth Amendment, it cannot be expected, and should not be applied, to deter objectively reasonable law enforcement activity. * * *[20]

This is particularly true, we believe, when an officer acting with objective good faith has obtained a search warrant from a judge or magistrate and acted within its scope. In most such cases, there is no police illegality and thus nothing to deter. It is the magistrate's responsibility to determine whether the officer's allegations establish probable cause and, if so, to issue a warrant comporting in form with the requirements of the Fourth Amendment. In the ordinary case, an officer cannot be expected to question the magistrate's probable-cause determination or his judgment that the form of the warrant is technically sufficient. "[O]nce the warrant issues, there is literally nothing more the policeman can do in seeking to comply with the law." Penalizing the officer for the magistrate's error, rather than his own, cannot logically contribute to the deterrence of Fourth Amendment violations.[22]

19. Our discussion of the deterrent effect of excluding evidence obtained in reasonable reliance on a subsequently invalidated warrant assumes, of course, that the officers properly executed the warrant and searched only those places and for those objects that it was reasonable to believe were covered by the warrant. * * *

20. We emphasize that the standard of reasonableness we adopt is an objective one. Many objections to a good-faith exception assume that the exception will turn on the subjective good faith of individual officers. "Grounding the modification in objective reasonableness, however, retains the value of the exclusionary rule as an incentive for the law enforcement profession as a whole to conduct themselves in accord with the Fourth Amendment." The objective standard we adopt, moreover, requires officers to have a reasonable knowledge of what the law prohibits. As Professor Jerold Israel has observed:

"The key to the [exclusionary] rule's effectiveness as a deterrent lies, I believe, in the impetus it has provided to police training programs that make officers aware of the limits imposed by the fourth amendment and emphasize the need to operate within those limits. [An objective good-faith exception] * * * is not likely to result in the elimination of such programs, which are now viewed as an important aspect of police professionalism. Neither is it likely to alter the tenor of those programs; the possibility that illegally obtained evidence may be admitted in borderline cases is unlikely to encourage police instructors to pay less attention to fourth amendment limitations. Finally, [it] * * * should not encourage officers to pay less attention to what they are taught, as the requirement that the officer act in 'good faith' is inconsistent with closing one's mind to the possibility of illegality."

22. * * * Our cases establish that the question whether the use of illegally obtained evidence in judicial proceedings represents judicial participation in a Fourth Amendment violation and offends the integrity of the courts

We conclude that the marginal or nonexistent benefits produced by suppressing evidence obtained in objectively reasonable reliance on a subsequently invalidated search warrant cannot justify the substantial costs of exclusion. We do not suggest, however, that exclusion is always inappropriate in cases where an officer has obtained a warrant and abided by its terms. [T]he officer's reliance on the magistrate's probable-cause determination and on the technical sufficiency of the warrant he issues must be objectively reasonable,[23] and it is clear that in some circumstances the officer[24] will have no reasonable grounds for believing that the warrant was properly issued.

Suppression therefore remains an appropriate remedy if the magistrate or judge in issuing a warrant was misled by information in an affidavit that the affiant knew was false or would have known was false except for his reckless disregard of the truth. The exception we recognize today will also not apply in cases where the issuing magistrate wholly abandoned his judicial role in the manner condemned in *Lo-Ji Sales, Inc. v. New York,* [p. 305 fn. a][c], in such circumstances, no reasonably well-trained officer should rely on the warrant. Nor would an officer manifest objective good faith in relying on a warrant based on an affidavit "so lacking in indicia of probable cause as to render official belief in its existence entirely unreasonable." Finally, depending on the circumstances of the particular case, a warrant may be so facially deficient—i.e., in failing to particularize the place to be searched or the things to be seized—that the executing officers cannot reasonably presume it to be valid.

* * * The good-faith exception for searches conducted pursuant to warrants is not intended to signal our unwillingness strictly to enforce the requirements of the Fourth Amendment, and we do not believe that it will have this effect. As we have already suggested, the good-faith exception, turning as it does on objective reasonableness, should not be difficult to apply in practice. When officers have acted pursuant to a warrant, the prosecution should ordinarily be able to establish objective good faith without a substantial expenditure of judicial time.

Nor are we persuaded that application of a good-faith exception to searches conducted pursuant to warrants will preclude review of the constitutionality of the search or seizure, deny needed guidance from the courts, or freeze Fourth Amendment law in its present state.[25] There is no need for courts to adopt the

"is essentially the same as the inquiry into whether exclusion would serve a deterrent purpose." * * * Absent unusual circumstances, when a Fourth Amendment violation has occurred because the police have reasonably relied on a warrant issued by a detached and neutral magistrate but ultimately found to be defective, "the integrity of the courts is not implicated."

23. [O]ur good-faith inquiry is confined to the objectively ascertainable question whether a reasonably well-trained officer would have known that the search was illegal despite the magistrate's authorization. In making this determination, all of the circumstances—including whether the warrant application had previously been rejected by a different magistrate—may be considered.

24. References to "officer" throughout this opinion should not be read too narrowly. It is necessary to consider the objective reasonableness, not only of the officers who eventually executed a warrant, but also of the officers who originally obtained it or who provided information material to the probable-cause determination. Nothing in our opinion suggests, for example, that an officer could obtain a warrant on the basis of a "bare bones" affidavit and then rely on colleagues who are ignorant of the circumstances under which the warrant was obtained to conduct the search.

c. There the magistrate was held not to have "manifest[ed] that neutrality and detachment demanded of a judicial officer when presented with a warrant application," where he went to the scene and made judgments there about what should be seized as obscene, as he "allowed himself to become a member, if not the leader of the search party which was essentially a police operation."

25. The argument that defendants will lose their incentive to litigate meritorious Fourth Amendment claims as a result of the good-faith exception we adopt today is unpersuasive. Although the exception might discourage presentation of insubstantial suppression motions, the magnitude of the benefit conferred on de-

inflexible practice of always deciding whether the officers' conduct manifested objective good faith before turning to the question whether the Fourth Amendment has been violated. Defendants seeking suppression of the fruits of allegedly unconstitutional searches or seizures undoubtedly raise live controversies which Article III empowers federal courts to adjudicate. * * *

If the resolution of a particular Fourth Amendment question is necessary to guide future action by law enforcement officers and magistrates, nothing will prevent reviewing courts from deciding that question before turning to the good-faith issue.[26] Indeed, it frequently will be difficult to determine whether the officers acted reasonably without resolving the Fourth Amendment issue. Even if the Fourth Amendment question is not one of broad import, reviewing courts could decide in particular cases that magistrates under their supervision need to be informed of their errors and so evaluate the officers' good faith only after finding a violation. In other circumstances, those courts could reject suppression motions posing no important Fourth Amendment questions by turning immediately to a consideration of the officers' good faith. We have no reason to believe that our Fourth Amendment jurisprudence would suffer by allowing reviewing courts to exercise an informed discretion in making this choice. * * *

In the absence of an allegation that the magistrate abandoned his detached and neutral role, suppression is appropriate only if the officers were dishonest or reckless in preparing their affidavit or could not have harbored an objectively reasonable belief in the existence of probable cause. Only respondent Leon has contended that no reasonably well-trained police officer could have believed that there existed probable cause to search his house; significantly, the other respondents advance no comparable argument. Officer Rombach's application for a warrant clearly was supported by much more than a "bare bones" affidavit. The affidavit related the results of an extensive investigation and, as the opinions of the divided panel of the Court of Appeals make clear, provided evidence sufficient to create disagreement among thoughtful and competent judges as to the existence of probable cause. Under these circumstances, the officers' reliance on the magistrate's determination of probable cause was objectively reasonable, and application of the extreme sanction of exclusion is inappropriate.

Accordingly, the judgment of the Court of Appeals is *reversed.*

Justice BLACKMUN, concurring. * * *

What must be stressed * * * is that any empirical judgment about the effect of the exclusionary rule in a particular class of cases necessarily is a provisional one. * * * If it should emerge from experience that, contrary to our expectations, the good faith exception to the exclusionary rule results in a material change in police compliance with the Fourth Amendment, we shall have to reconsider what we have undertaken here. The logic of a decision that rests on untested predictions about police conduct demands no less. * * *

Justice BRENNAN, with whom Justice MARSHALL joins, dissenting. * * *

[The majority's reading of the Fourth Amendment] appears plausible, because, as critics of the exclusionary rule never tire of repeating, the Fourth Amendment makes no express provision for the exclusion of evidence secured in violation of its commands. A short answer to this claim, of course, is that many of the Constitution's most vital imperatives are stated in general terms and the task

fendants by a successful motion makes it unlikely that litigation of colorable claims will be substantially diminished.

26. It has been suggested, in fact, that "the recognition of a 'penumbral zone,' within which an inadvertent mistake would not call for exclusion, * * * will make it less tempting for judges to bend fourth amendment standards to avoid releasing a possibly dangerous criminal because of a minor and unintentional miscalculation by the police."

of giving meaning to these precepts is therefore left to subsequent judicial decision-making in the context of concrete cases. * * *

* * * Because seizures are executed principally to secure evidence, and because such evidence generally has utility in our legal system only in the context of a trial supervised by a judge, it is apparent that the admission of illegally obtained evidence implicates the same constitutional concerns as the initial seizure of that evidence. Indeed, by admitting unlawfully seized evidence, the judiciary becomes a part of what is in fact a single governmental action prohibited by the terms of the Amendment. Once that connection between the evidence-gathering role of the police and the evidence-admitting function of the courts is acknowledged, the plausibility of the Court's interpretation becomes more suspect. Certainly nothing in the language or history of the Fourth Amendment suggests that a recognition of this evidentiary link between the police and the courts was meant to be foreclosed. It is difficult to give any meaning at all to the limitations imposed by the Amendment if they are read to proscribe only certain conduct by the police but to allow other agents of the same government to take advantage of evidence secured by the police in violation of its requirements. The Amendment therefore must be read to condemn not only the initial unconstitutional invasion of privacy—which is done, after all, for the purpose of securing evidence—but also the subsequent use of any evidence so obtained. * * *

[T]he question whether the exclusion of evidence would deter future police misconduct was never considered a relevant concern in the early cases from *Weeks* to *Olmstead*. In those formative decisions, the Court plainly understood that the exclusion of illegally obtained evidence was compelled not by judicially fashioned remedial purposes, but rather by a direct constitutional command. * * *

* * * Indeed, no other explanation suffices to account for the Court's holding in *Mapp,* since the only possible predicate for the Court's conclusion that the States were bound by the Fourteenth Amendment to honor the *Weeks* doctrine is that the exclusionary rule was "part and parcel of the Fourth Amendment's limitation upon [governmental] encroachment of individual privacy."

Despite this clear pronouncement, however, the Court * * * has gradually pressed the deterrence rationale for the rule back to center stage. The various arguments advanced by the Court in this campaign have only strengthened my conviction that the deterrence theory is both misguided and unworkable. First, the Court has frequently bewailed the "cost" of excluding reliable evidence. In large part, this criticism rests upon a refusal to acknowledge the function of the Fourth Amendment itself. If nothing else, the Amendment plainly operates to disable the government from gathering information and securing evidence in certain ways. In practical terms, of course, this restriction of official power means that some incriminating evidence inevitably will go undetected if the government obeys these constitutional restraints. It is the loss of that evidence that is the "price" our society pays for enjoying the freedom and privacy safeguarded by the Fourth Amendment. Thus, some criminals will go free *not*, in Justice (then Judge) Cardozo's misleading epigram, "because the constable has blundered," but rather because official compliance with Fourth Amendment requirements makes it more difficult to catch criminals. Understood in this way, the Amendment directly contemplates that some reliable and incriminating evidence will be lost to the government; therefore, it is not the exclusionary rule, but the Amendment itself that has imposed this cost.

In addition, the Court's decisions over the past decade have made plain that the entire enterprise of attempting to assess the benefits and costs of the exclusionary rule in various contexts is a virtually impossible task for the judiciary to perform honestly or accurately. Although the Court's language in those cases suggests that some specific empirical basis may support its analyses, the reality is that the Court's opinions represent inherently unstable compounds of intuition, hunches, and occasional pieces of partial and often inconclusive data. * * * To the extent empirical data is available regarding the general costs and benefits of the exclusionary rule, it has shown, on the one hand, as the Court acknowledges today, that the costs are not as substantial as critics have asserted in the past, and, on the other hand, that while the exclusionary rule may well have certain deterrent effects, it is extremely difficult to determine with any degree of precision whether the incidence of unlawful conduct by police is now lower than it was prior to *Mapp*. The Court has sought to turn this uncertainty to its advantage by casting the burden of proof upon proponents of the rule. "Obviously," however, "the assignment of the burden of proof on an issue where evidence does not exist and cannot be obtained is outcome determinative. [The] assignment of the burden is merely a way of announcing a predetermined conclusion."

By remaining within its redoubt of empiricism and by basing the rule solely on the deterrence rationale, the Court has robbed the rule of legitimacy. A doctrine that is explained as if it were an empirical proposition but for which there is only limited empirical support is both inherently unstable and an easy mark for critics. The extent of this Court's fidelity to Fourth Amendment requirements, however, should not turn on such statistical uncertainties. * * *

Even if I were to accept the Court's general approach to the exclusionary rule, I could not agree with today's result. * * *

At the outset, the Court suggests that society has been asked to pay a high price—in terms either of setting guilty persons free or of impeding the proper functioning of trials—as a result of excluding relevant physical evidence in cases where the police, in conducting searches and seizing evidence, have made only an "objectively reasonable" mistake concerning the constitutionality of their actions. But what evidence is there to support such a claim?

Significantly, the Court points to none, and, indeed, as the Court acknowledges, recent studies have demonstrated that the "costs" of the exclusionary rule—calculated in terms of dropped prosecutions and lost convictions—are quite low. Contrary to the claims of the rule's critics that exclusion leads to "the release of countless guilty criminals," these studies have demonstrated that federal and state prosecutors very rarely drop cases because of potential search and seizure problems. For example, a 1979 study prepared at the request of Congress by the General Accounting Office reported that only 0.4% of all cases actually declined for prosecution by federal prosecutors were declined primarily because of illegal search problems. If the GAO data are restated as a percentage of *all* arrests, the study shows that only 0.2% of all felony arrests are declined for prosecution because of potential exclusionary rule problems. Of course, these data describe only the costs attributable to the exclusion of evidence in all cases; the costs due to the exclusion of evidence in the narrower category of cases where police have made objectively reasonable mistakes must necessarily be even smaller. The Court, however, ignores this distinction and mistakenly weighs the aggregated costs of exclusion in *all* cases, irrespective of the circumstances that led to exclusion, against the potential benefits associated with only those cases in which evidence is excluded because police reasonably but mistakenly believe that their conduct does not violate the Fourth Amendment. When such faulty scales are used, it is little wonder that the balance tips in favor of restricting the application of the rule.

What then supports the Court's insistence that this evidence be admitted? Apparently, the Court's only answer is that even though the costs of exclusion are not very substantial, the potential deterrent effect in these circumstances is so marginal that exclusion cannot be justified. The key to the Court's conclusion in this respect is its belief that the prospective deterrent effect of the exclusionary rule operates only in those situations in which police officers, when deciding whether to go forward with some particular search, have reason to know that their planned conduct will violate the requirements of the Fourth Amendment.

* * * But what the Court overlooks is that the deterrence rationale for the rule is not designed to be, nor should it be thought of as, a form of "punishment" of individual police officers for their failures to obey the restraints imposed by the Fourth Amendment. Instead, the chief deterrent function of the rule is its tendency to promote institutional compliance with Fourth Amendment requirements on the part of law enforcement agencies generally. Thus, as the Court has previously recognized, "over the long term, [the] demonstration [provided by the exclusionary rule] that our society attaches serious consequences to violation of constitutional rights is thought to encourage those who formulate law enforcement policies, and the officers who implement them, to incorporate Fourth Amendment ideals into their value system." It is only through such an institution-wide mechanism that information concerning Fourth Amendment standards can be effectively communicated to rank and file officers.[13]

If the overall educational effect of the exclusionary rule is considered, application of the rule to even those situations in which individual police officers have acted on the basis of a reasonable but mistaken belief that their conduct was authorized can still be expected to have a considerable long-term deterrent effect. If evidence is consistently excluded in these circumstances, police departments will surely be prompted to instruct their officers to devote greater care and attention to providing sufficient information to establish probable cause when applying for a warrant, and to review with some attention the form of the warrant that they have been issued, rather than automatically assuming that whatever document the magistrate has signed will necessarily comport with Fourth Amendment requirements.

After today's decision, however, that institutional incentive will be lost. Indeed, the Court's "reasonable mistake" exception to the exclusionary rule will tend to put a premium on police ignorance of the law. Armed with the assurance provided by today's decision that evidence will always be admissible whenever an officer has "reasonably" relied upon a warrant, police departments will be encouraged to train officers that if a warrant has simply been signed, it is reasonable, without more, to rely on it. Since in close cases there will no longer be any incentive to err on the side of constitutional behavior, police would have every reason to adopt a "let's-wait-until-its-decided" approach in situations in which there is a question about a warrant's validity or the basis for its issuance.[14]

Although the Court brushes these concerns aside, a host of grave consequences can be expected to result from its decision to carve this new exception out of the exclusionary rule. A chief consequence of today's decision will be to convey a clear and unambiguous message to magistrates that their decisions to issue warrants are now insulated from subsequent judicial review. Creation of this new

13. * * * A former United States Attorney and now Attorney General of Maryland, Stephen Sachs, has described the impact of the rule on police practices in similar terms: "I have watched the rule deter, routinely, throughout my years as a prosecutor * * *. [P]olice-prosecutor consultation is customary in all our cases when Fourth Amendment concerns arise * * *. In at least three Maryland jurisdictions, for example, prosecutors are on twenty-four hour call to field search and seizure questions presented by police officers."

14. The authors of a recent study of the warrant process in seven cities concluded that application of a good faith exception where an officer relies upon a warrant "would further encourage police officers to seek out the less inquisitive magistrates and to rely on boilerplate formulae, thereby lessening the value of search warrants overall. * * *"

exception for good faith reliance upon a warrant implicitly tells magistrates that they need not take much care in reviewing warrant applications, since their mistakes will from now on have virtually no consequence: If their decision to issue a warrant was correct, the evidence will be admitted; if their decision was incorrect but the police relied in good faith on the warrant, the evidence will also be admitted. Inevitably, the care and attention devoted to such an inconsequential chore will dwindle. Although the Court is correct to note that magistrates do not share the same stake in the outcome of a criminal case as the police, they nevertheless need to appreciate that their role is of some moment in order to continue performing the important task of carefully reviewing warrant applications. Today's decision effectively removes that incentive.

Moreover, the good faith exception will encourage police to provide only the bare minimum of information in future warrant applications. The police will now know that if they can secure a warrant, so long as the circumstances of its issuance are not "entirely unreasonable," all police conduct pursuant to that warrant will be protected from further judicial review. The clear incentive that operated in the past to establish probable cause adequately because reviewing courts would examine the magistrate's judgment carefully, has now been so completely vitiated that the police need only show that it was not "entirely unreasonable" under the circumstances of a particular case for them to believe that the warrant they were issued was valid. The long-run effect unquestionably will be to undermine the integrity of the warrant process.

Finally, even if one were to believe, as the Court apparently does, that police are hobbled by inflexible and hypertechnical warrant procedures, today's decision cannot be justified. This is because, given the relaxed standard for assessing probable cause established just last Term in *Illinois v. Gates*, the Court's newly fashioned good faith exception, when applied in the warrant context, will rarely, if ever, offer any greater flexibility for police than the *Gates* standard already supplies.[d] In *Gates*, the Court held that "the task of an issuing magistrate is simply to make a practical, common-sense decision whether, given all the circumstances set forth in the affidavit before him, * * * there is a fair probability that contraband or evidence of a crime will be found in a particular place." The task of a reviewing court is confined to determining whether "the magistrate had a 'substantial basis' for concluding that probable cause existed." Given such a relaxed standard, it is virtually inconceivable that a reviewing court, when faced with a defendant's motion to suppress, could first find that a warrant was invalid under the new *Gates* standard, but then, at the same time, find that a police officer's reliance on such an invalid warrant was nevertheless "objectively reasonable" under the test announced today. * * *

Notes and Questions

1. Must (should) the Fourth Amendment be read, as dissenting Justice Brennan maintains, "to condemn not only the initial unconstitutional invasion of privacy" but "also the subsequent use of any evidence so obtained"? Consider Arnold H. Loewy, *Police-Obtained Evidence and the Constitution: Distinguishing Unconstitutionally Obtained Evidence from Unconstitutionally Used Evidence,* 87 Mich.L.Rev. 907, 909–11, 939 (1989):

d. Thus STEVENS, J., dissenting, objected: "It is probable, though admittedly not certain, that the Court of Appeals would now conclude that the warrant in *Leon* satisfied the Fourth Amendment if it were given the opportunity to reconsider the issue in the light of *Gates.* Adherence to our normal practice following the announcement of a new rule would therefore postpone, and probably obviate, the need for the promulgation of the broad new rule the Court announces today."

"[F]reedom from unreasonable searches and seizures is a substantive protection available to all inhabitants of the United States, whether or not charged with crime. The right thus differs from protections under most of the fifth amendment and all of the sixth amendment, which refers to persons charged with crime or the 'accused.' * * * [Because] the fourth amendment, in language and origin, is clearly substantive [the] Court was correct in holding the exclusionary rule to be simply a remedial device designed to make the substantive right more meaningful, rather than an independent procedural right.

"* * * Procedural rights are supposed to exclude evidence. Substantive rights need not. Consequently, fourth amendment rights should be deemed different from, but not less important than, the procedural rights protected by the fifth, sixth and fourteenth amendments. By way of comparison, first and third amendment rights are substantive, but nobody would deem them second class. * * *

"Whether evidence is unconstitutionally obtained or unconstitutionally used makes a difference. If the only constitutional wrong inheres in using the evidence, the Court has no business considering concepts of deterrence. The Court should prohibit use of such evidence. Conversely, when obtaining evidence is the constitutional wrong, exclusion should be subjected to a cost/benefit analysis."

2. Which of the Supreme Court's express or implicit assumptions in *Mapp* and *Leon* regarding the behavior of police and judges are correct? Consider Myron W. Orfield, *Deterrence, Perjury, and the Heater Factor: An Exclusionary Rule in the Chicago Criminal Courts,* 63 U.Colo.L.Rev. 75, 82–83 (1992), summarizing the views of interviewed actors in the Chicago criminal justice system:

"Respondents in the Courts Study[e] report the same perceptions of the deterrent effect of the rule as the officers in the Police Study.[f] First, respondents uniformly believe that officers care about convictions and experience adverse personal reactions when they lose evidence. Respondents report that police change their behavior in response to the suppression of evidence. They also believe that suppression effectively educates officers in the law of search and seizure and that the law is not too complicated for police officers to do their jobs effectively.

"The Courts Study respondents believe even more strongly than the Police Study respondents that the exclusionary rule's deterrent effect is greater when officers are working on big or important cases. They also believe the exclusionary rule has a greater deterrent effect on officers in specialized units like the Narcotics Section.

"Respondents also stated that the exclusionary rule fosters a closer working relationship between prosecutors and police. They note that prosecutors help police officers conduct proper searches and understand why evidence is suppressed. * * *

"Significantly, the Courts respondents outlined a pattern of pervasive police perjury intended to avoid the requirements of the Fourth Amendment. Dishonesty occurs in both the investigative process and the courtroom. The respondents report systematic fabrications in case reports and affidavits for search warrants, creating artificial probable cause which forms the basis of later testimony. Moreover, police keep dual sets of investigatory files; official files and 'street files.' Exculpatory material in the street files may be edited from the official record. Respondents, including prosecutors, estimate that police commit perjury between

e. 14 public defenders, 14 prosecutors and 13 judges, all assigned to the felony trial courtrooms in the Criminal Division of the Circuit Court of Cook County.

f. 26 police officers in the Narcotics Section of the Organized Crime Division, Chicago Police Department.

20 and 50% of the time they testify on Fourth Amendment issues. This perjury may be tolerated, or even encouraged, by prosecutors at each step in the process in both direct and indirect ways.

"The Courts respondents, including judges, also believe that judges may purposefully ignore the law to prevent evidence from being suppressed, and even more often, knowingly accept police perjury as truthful. When the crime is serious, this judicial 'cheating' is more likely to occur due to three primary reasons; first, the judge's sense that it is unjust to suppress the evidence under the circumstances of a particular case, second, the judge's fear of adverse publicity, and third, the fear that the suppression will hurt their chances in judicial elections. In addition, serious cases in Chicago are diverted to judges who are more likely to convict the defendant.

"However, even in the face of persistent police perjury and judicial abdication of function, the Courts respondents, like the police respondents, believe that the exclusionary rule, although imperfect and often avoided, clearly leads to increased police professionalism and greater observance of the law of the Fourth Amendment. They do not believe that the rule causes significant harm to police work. Although the Courts respondents acknowledge that the rule can sometimes be unjust to crime victims, they believe that the rule's benefits to society equal or exceed its costs. Respondents report that there is no more effective remedy for Fourth Amendment violations, and that a tort remedy would be less effective. Finally, they believe the rule should be retained."

3. Does (should) *Leon* mean that "when the Court speaks of the good faith of the police, it is talking about their good faith *before going* to the magistrate and not about their good faith *after* they have received the warrant"? Craig M. Bradley, *The "Good Faith Exception" Cases: Reasonable Exercises in Futility*, 60 Ind.L.J. 287, 297 (1985). Consider *Malley v. Briggs,* p. 238, fn. h, which the majority explained involved application of "the same standard of objective reasonableness that we applied in the context of a suppression hearing in *Leon.*"

4. Will (should) *Leon* be extended to warrantless arrests and searches? In *Lopez-Mendoza,* p. 243, involving a warrantless arrest, White, J., dissenting, asserted *Leon* was applicable, so that "if the agents neither knew nor should have known that they were acting contrary to the dictates of the Fourth Amendment, evidence will not be suppressed even if it is held that their conduct was illegal." If that is wrong, then does it follow, as concluded in *United States v. O'Neal*, 17 F.3d 239 (8th Cir.1994), that *Leon* cannot save a search warrant where it now appears that some of the facts essential to the probable cause showing in the affidavit were acquired in a prior illegal warrantless search?

5. In the companion case of MASSACHUSETTS v. SHEPPARD, 468 U.S. 981 (1984), a detective prepared an affidavit for a search warrant to search for specified evidence of a homicide but, because it was Sunday, could only find a warrant form for controlled substances. He presented his affidavit and that form to a judge and pointed out the problem to him, and the judge, unable to locate a more suitable form, told the detective that he would make the necessary changes to make it a proper warrant. He made some changes, but failed to change that part of the warrant which authorized a search only for controlled substances and related paraphernalia. The detective took the two documents and he and other officers then executed the warrant, seizing evidence of the homicide. That evidence was suppressed in the state court because the warrant failed to particularly describe the items to be seized, as required by the Fourth Amendment. The Supreme Court, per WHITE, J., held this situation fell within *Leon* because "there was an objectively reasonable basis for the officers' mistaken belief" that "the warrant authorized the search that they conducted." As for defendant's objection that the detective knew when he went to the judge that the warrant was defective, the Court stated: "Whatever an officer may be required to do when he executes a warrant without knowing beforehand what items are to be seized,[6] we refuse to rule that an officer is required to disbelieve a judge who has just advised him, by word and by action, that the warrant he possesses authorizes him to conduct the search he has requested."

What if the detective who obtained the warrant had simply turned it over to another officer for execution and that officer, after a careful reading of the warrant, had made a search for and found drugs within an envelope, a place he would not have been entitled to look had he been aware that the warrant should have described certain larger items which could not be concealed in the envelope?

6. What result under *Leon* and *Sheppard* on the following facts, essentially those in *People v. Deitchman,* 695 P.2d 1146 (Colo.1985)? Four teenage girls were sexually assaulted in the same area over a 10–day span, and they gave a similar general description of their assailant. One said he wore distinctively marked shoes; one said he had a red bandana; and two said his car license was CN–4714. Those facts were put into a search warrant affidavit, along with a statement that investigation "revealed that CN–4714 lists to Jerry M. Deitchman of 1755 South Pecos Street." The affidavit asserted, without explanation, that there was "reason to believe" that the shoes and bandana were at 3300 West Ohio Avenue; the magistrate issued a warrant to search that location for the shoes and bandana, which were found there in execution of the warrant. Police had earlier been unable to locate Deitchman until his employer said he had moved to 3300 West Ohio, and police arrested him there prior to obtaining the warrant, but those facts were not reported to the magistrate.

7. In GROH v. RAMIREZ, 540 U.S. 551 (2004), the affiant, who was also the executing officer, correctly stated the items to be seized in the search warrant application and the supporting affidavit, but in the search warrant itself mistakenly entered in the space for that specification a description of the place to be searched. That error was not noticed by the magistrate who issued the warrant, and was not noticed by the affiant/executing officer until after the warrant was executed; he instructed his search team on the basis of the items listed in the application and affidavit. In this action under *Bivens*, p. 238 fn. h, applying the same standard as used under the *Leon* "good faith" exception, the Court, 5–4, concluded per STEVENS, J.:

"Given that the particularity requirement is set forth in the text of the Constitution, no reasonable officer could believe that a warrant that plainly did not comply with that requirement was valid. * * * Moreover, because petitioner himself prepared the invalid warrant, he may not argue that he reasonably relied on the Magistrate's assurance that the warrant contained an adequate description of the things to be seized and was therefore valid. Cf. *Sheppard* * * *. And even a cursory reading of the warrant in this case—perhaps just a simple glance—would have revealed a glaring deficiency that any reasonable police officer would have known was constitutionally fatal. * * *

6. Normally, when an officer who has not been involved in the application stage receives a warrant, he will read it in order to determine the object of the search. In this case, Detective O'Malley, the officer who directed the search, knew what items were listed in the affidavit presented to the judge, and he had good reason to believe that the warrant authorized the seizure of those items. Whether an officer who is less familiar with the warrant application or who has unalleviated concerns about the proper scope of the search would be justified in failing to notice a defect like the one in the warrant in this case is an issue we need not decide. We hold only that it was not unreasonable for the police in this case to rely on the judge's assurances that the warrant authorized the search they had requested.

"Petitioner contends that the search in this case was the product, at worst, of a lack of due care, and that our case law requires more than negligent behavior before depriving an official of qualified immunity. * * * But as we observed in [*Leon*], 'a warrant may be so facially deficient—i.e., in failing to particularize the place to be searched or the things to be seized—that the executing officers cannot reasonably presume it to be valid.' "

The two dissenting opinions, collectively, made these points: (i) The case involves "a straightforward mistake of fact," as "the officer simply made a clerical error when he filled out the proposed warrant." (ii) "Given the sheer number of warrants prepared and executed by officers each year," it "is inevitable that officers acting reasonably and entirely in good faith will occasionally make such errors." (iii) The officer's later "failure to recognize his clerical error on a warrant form can be a reasonable mistake," and such was the case here, for "where the officer is already fully aware of the scope of the intended search and the magistrate gives no reason to believe that he has authorized anything other than the requested search," there is nothing unreasonable in the officer's failure "to proofread the warrant." (iv) The majority's reliance upon the *Leon* quote is in error, for it has to do with "a mistake of law"; that is, the "issue in this case is whether an officer can reasonably fail to recognize a clerical error, not whether an officer who recognizes a clerical error can reasonably conclude that a defective warrant is legally valid."

8. Are there other "limitations" which might well be imposed upon the exclusionary rule? Consider the two proposals made in John Kaplan, *The Limits of the Exclusionary Rule,* 26 Stan.L.Rev. 1027 (1974): (1) that "the rule not apply in the most serious cases—treason, espionage, murder, armed robbery, and kidnapping by organized groups" (where exclusion would occur only under the *Rochin*, p. 33, test), because "the political costs of the rule, the possibility of releasing serious and dangerous offenders into the community, and the disproportion between the magnitude of the policeman's constitutional violation and the crime in which the evidence is to be suppressed are sufficient reasons to modify the rule"; and (2) "to hold the exclusionary rule inapplicable to cases where the police department in question has taken seriously its responsibility to adhere to the fourth amendment," as reflected by "a set of published regulations giving guidance to police officers as to proper behavior in situations such as the one under litigation, a training program calculated to make violations of the fourth amendment rights isolated occurrences, and, perhaps most importantly, a history of taking disciplinary action where such violations are brought to its attention."[g]

9. Should the Court instead abolish the exclusionary rule entirely on the ground that the deterrence function stressed in *Leon* is more generally not served by exclusion? Consider Burger, C.J., dissenting in *Bivens v. Six Unknown Named Agents,* p. 238 fn. h, asserting a lack of deterrent efficacy because: (i) "The rule does not apply any direct sanction to the individual official whose illegal conduct results in the exclusion of evidence in a criminal trial." (ii) Police "have no * * * stake in successful prosecutions," and "the prosecutor who loses his case because of police misconduct is not an official in the police department; he can rarely set in motion any corrective action or administrative penalties." (iii) "Policemen do not have the time, inclination, or training to read and grasp the nuances of the

g. For strong criticism of Professor Kaplan's proposal that the exclusionary rule not apply in the most serious cases and of a similar proposal by James D. Cameron & Richard Lustiger, *The Exclusionary Rule: A Cost–Benefit Analysis,* 101 F.R.D. 109 (1984) that the rule apply neither in the most serious cases nor in any case where the reprehensibility of the defendant's crime is greater than the gravity of the officer's illegality, see Yale Kamisar, *"Comparative Reprehensibility" and the Fourth Amendment Exclusionary Rule,* 86 Mich.L.Rev. 1 (1987).

appellate opinions that ultimately define the standards of conduct they are to follow." (iv) "[T]here are large areas of police activity which do not result in criminal prosecutions—hence the rule has virtually no applicability and no effect in such situations." Would such abolition be more palatable if, as the Chief Justice also suggested in *Bivens*, Congress were to "develop an administrative or quasi-judicial remedy against the government itself to afford compensation and restitution for persons whose Fourth Amendment rights have been violated"?[h] Consider also Richard A. Posner, *Excessive Sanctions for Governmental Misconduct in Criminal Cases,* 57 Wash.L.Rev. 635 (1982) (applying an economic analysis to the problem and concluding it should suffice if the government were required to compensate the victim of an illegal search for his "cleanup costs"); Donald Dripps, *The Case for the Contingent Exclusionary Rule*, 38 Am.Crim.L.Rev.1, 2 (2001) (proposing "that courts should begin to experiment with suppression orders that are contingent on the failure of the police department to pay damages set by the court [in an amount] equal to the expected governmental gain from the violation").

10. In *Michigan v. DeFillippo*, 443 U.S. 31 (1979), the Court reaffirmed its earlier holdings "that the exclusionary rule required suppression of evidence obtained in searches carried out pursuant to statutes" subsequently held unconstitutional when the statutes, "by their own terms, authorized searches under circumstances which did not satisfy the traditional warrant and probable cause requirements of the Fourth Amendment." But after *Leon* the Court concluded otherwise in the 5–4 decision in ILLINOIS v. KRULL, 480 U.S. 340 (1987), concerning an unconstitutional search made pursuant to a statute authorizing warrantless inspection of the records of licensed motor vehicle and vehicular parts sellers. The Court, per BLACKMUN, J., reasoned:

h. As for existing federal remedies, 42 U.S.C. § 1983 provides: "Every person who, under color of any statute, ordinance, regulation, custom, or usage, of any State or Territory, subjects, or causes to be subjected, any citizen of the United States or other person within the jurisdiction thereof to the deprivation of any rights, privileges, or immunities secured by the Constitution and laws, shall be liable to the party injured in an action at law, suit in equity, or other proper proceeding for redress." State and local police officers thus may be sued for damages for violation of Fourth Amendment rights, but the officers have an objective good faith defense. This is so even with respect to a police officer's action in applying for an arrest warrant; notwithstanding the magistrate's issuance of the warrant, the question "is whether a reasonably well-trained officer in petitioner's position would have known that his affidavit failed to establish probable cause and that he should not have applied for the warrant." *Malley v. Briggs,* 475 U.S. 335 (1986). *Monell v. New York City Dep't of Social Services,* 436 U.S. 658 (1978), cautioned that the statute did not "impose liability vicariously on governing bodies solely on the basis of the existence of an employer-employee relationship with a tortfeasor," and thus concluded "that a local government may not be sued for an injury inflicted solely by its employees or agents. Instead, it is when execution of a government's policy or custom, whether made by its lawmakers or by those whose edicts or acts may fairly be said to represent official policy, inflicts the injury that the government as an entity is responsible under § 1983."

Section 1983 applies only to persons acting under color of state law, thus excluding federal officers acting under color of their authority. In *Bivens v. Six Unknown Named Agents*, 403 U.S. 388 (1971), the Court held that, although Congress had not provided a tort remedy under such circumstances, a complaint alleging that the Fourth Amendment had been violated by federal agents acting under color of their authority gives rise to a federal cause of action for damages. Here as well, there is personal liability only in the absence of "objective legal reasonableness.". *Anderson v. Creighton,* 483 U.S. 635 (1987). As for liability of the federal government, the Court in *Bivens* stated this issue was better left to Congress because "the federal purse was involved." In 1974 Congress amended the Federal Tort Claims Act to make it applicable "to acts or omissions of investigative or law enforcement officers of the United States Government" on any subsequent claim arising "out of assault, battery, false imprisonment, false arrest, abuse of process, or malicious prosecution. For the purpose of this subsection, 'investigative or law enforcement officer' means any officer of the United States who is empowered by law to execute searches, to seize evidence, or to make arrests for violations of Federal law." 28 U.S.C. § 2680(h).

"The approach used in *Leon* is equally applicable to the present case. The application of the exclusionary rule to suppress evidence obtained by an officer acting in objectively reasonable reliance on a statute would have as little deterrent effect on the officer's actions as would the exclusion of evidence when an officer acts in objectively reasonable reliance on a warrant. Unless a statute is clearly unconstitutional, an officer cannot be expected to question the judgment of the legislature that passed the law. * * *

"Any difference between our holding in *Leon* and our holding in the instant case, therefore, must rest on a difference between the effect of the exclusion of evidence on judicial officers and the effect of the exclusion of evidence on legislators. Although these two groups clearly serve different functions in the criminal justice system, those differences are not controlling for purposes of this case. We noted in *Leon* as an initial matter that the exclusionary rule was aimed at deterring police misconduct. Thus, legislators, like judicial officers, are not the focus of the rule. Moreover, to the extent we consider the rule's effect on legislators, our initial inquiry, as set out in *Leon,* is whether there is evidence to suggest that legislators 'are inclined to ignore or subvert the Fourth Amendment.' * * *

"There is no evidence suggesting that Congress or state legislatures have enacted a significant number of statutes permitting warrantless administrative searches violative of the Fourth Amendment. * * * Thus, we are given no basis for believing that legislators are inclined to subvert their oaths and the Fourth Amendment and that 'lawlessness among these actors requires application of the extreme sanction of exclusion.' *United States v. Leon.*

"Even if we were to conclude that legislators are different in certain relevant respects from magistrates, because legislators are not officers of the judicial system, the next inquiry necessitated by *Leon* is whether exclusion of evidence seized pursuant to a statute subsequently declared unconstitutional will 'have a significant deterrent effect' on legislators enacting such statutes. Respondents have offered us no reason to believe that applying the exclusionary rule will have such an effect. Legislators enact statutes for broad, programmatic purposes, not for the purpose of procuring evidence in particular criminal investigations. Thus, it is logical to assume that the greatest deterrent to the enactment of unconstitutional statutes by a legislature is the power of the courts to invalidate such statutes. Invalidating a statute informs the legislature of its constitutional error, affects the admissibility of all evidence obtained subsequent to the constitutional ruling, and often results in the legislature's enacting a modified and constitutional version of the statute, as happened in this very case. There is nothing to indicate that applying the exclusionary rule to evidence seized pursuant to the statute prior to the declaration of its invalidity will act as a significant, additional deterrent."

O'CONNOR, J., for the dissenters, emphasized: (1) "[B]oth the history of the Fourth Amendment and this Court's later interpretations of it, support application of the exclusionary rule to evidence gathered under the 20th century equivalent of the act authorizing the writ of assistance." (2) "The distinction drawn between the legislator and the judicial officer is sound" because "a legislature's unreasonable authorization of searches may affect thousands or millions" and thus "poses a greater threat to liberty." (3) "[L]egislators by virtue of their political role are more often subjected to the political pressures that may threaten Fourth Amendment values than are judicial officers." (4) "Providing legislatures a grace period during which the police may freely perform unreasonable searches in order to convict those who might have otherwise escaped creates a positive incentive to promulgate unconstitutional laws." (5) "The scope of the Court's good-faith exception is unclear," as "it is not apparent how much constitutional law the reasonable officer is expected to know. In contrast, *Leon* simply instructs courts that police officers may rely upon a facially valid search warrant. Each case is a fact-specific self-terminating episode. Courts need not inquire into the officer's probable understanding of the state of the law except in the extreme instance of a search warrant upon which no reasonable officer would rely. Under the decision today, however, courts are expected to determine at what point a reasonable officer should be held to know that a statute has, under evolving legal rules, become 'clearly' unconstitutional."

11. What if a police officer at the time of his search or seizure had relied upon law then authorizing such action, but that law was not in a statute (as in *Krull*) but rather in an appellate court decision since disapproved by a Supreme Court case which, per the Court's current retroactivity doctrine (see Ch. 2, § 3), relates back to the time of the officer's conduct? See *State v. Ward*, 604 N.W.2d 517 (Wis.2000), concluding such "good faith reliance upon the pronouncements of this court" is on a par with the "good faith reliance upon an apparently valid statute" in *Krull*.

12. Should the fruits of constitutional but yet illegal arrests and searches be excluded? Reconsider fn. b, p. 217, and consider UNITED STATES v. CACERES, 440 U.S. 741 (1979), holding that the failure of an IRS agent to follow IRS electronic surveillance regulations did not require suppression. STEVENS, J., for the majority, could not "ignore the possibility that a rigid application of an exclusionary rule to every regulatory violation could have a serious deterrent impact on the formulation of additional standards to govern prosecutorial and police procedures. Here, the Executive itself has provided for internal sanctions in cases of knowing violations of the electronic surveillance regulations. To go beyond that, and require exclusion in every case, would take away from the Executive Department the primary responsibility for fashioning the appropriate remedy for the violation of its regulations. But since the content, and indeed the existence, of the regulations would remain within the Executive's sole authority, the result might well be fewer and less protective regulations. In the long run, it is far better to have rules like those contained in the IRS Manual, and to tolerate occasional erroneous administration of the kind displayed by this record, than either to have no rules except those mandated by statute, or to have them framed in a mere precatory form."

13. Although an illegal arrest or other unreasonable seizure of the person is itself a violation of the Fourth and Fourteenth Amendments, the exclusionary sanction comes into play only when the police have obtained evidence as a result of the unconstitutional seizure. It is no defense to a state or federal criminal prosecution that the defendant was illegally arrested or forcibly brought within the jurisdiction of the court. The trial of such a defendant violates neither Fifth nor Fourteenth Amendment Due Process nor any federal legislation. *Frisbie v. Collins,* 342 U.S. 519 (1952); *Ker v. Illinois,* 119 U.S. 436 (1886).[i] In *Gerstein v. Pugh,* p. 326, the Court declined to "retreat from the established rule that illegal arrest or detention does not void a subsequent conviction." See also *United States v. Crews,* p. 910, holding an illegally arrested defendant "is not himself a suppressible 'fruit' and the illegality of his detention cannot deprive the Government of the opportunity to prove his guilt through the introduction of evidence wholly untainted by the police misconduct."

i. In *United States v. Alvarez–Machain,* 504 U.S. 655 (1992), the Court held that *Ker,* involving forcible abduction from a foreign country, was "fully applicable to this case" despite the fact that here the abduction was from Mexico, with whom the U.S. has an extradition treaty. "The Treaty says nothing about the obligations of the [parties] to refrain from forcible abductions of people from the territory of the other nation, or the consequences under the Treaty if such an abduction occurs."

NOTES ON THE "DIMENSIONS" OF THE EXCLUSIONARY RULE

1. ***Evidence obtained by government agents, used as basis for questions to grand jury witness.*** In UNITED STATES v. CALANDRA, 414 U.S. 338 (1974), the Court, per POWELL, J., held that a grand jury witness may not refuse to answer questions on the ground that they are based on evidence obtained from him in an earlier unlawful search. After observing that a contrary holding would unduly interfere with the effective and expeditious discharge of the grand jury's duties [see p. 823], the Court asserted: "Whatever deterrence of police misconduct may result from the exclusion of illegally-seized evidence from criminal trials, it is unrealistic to assume that application of the rule to grand jury proceedings would significantly further that goal. Such an extension would deter only police investigation consciously directed toward the discovery of evidence solely for use in a grand jury investigation. The incentive to disregard the requirement of the Fourth Amendment solely to obtain an indictment from a grand jury is substantially negated by the inadmissibility of the illegally-seized evidence in a subsequent criminal prosecution of the search victim. For the most part, a prosecutor would be unlikely to request an indictment where a conviction could not be obtained. We therefore decline to embrace a view that would achieve a speculative and undoubtedly minimal advance in the deterrence of police misconduct at the expense of substantially impeding the role of the grand jury."

BRENNAN, J., joined by Douglas and Marshall, JJ., dissenting, quoted from *Weeks* to show that "the twin goals of enabling the judiciary to avoid the taint of partnerships in official lawlessness and of assuring the people * * * that the government would not profit from its lawless behavior, * * * not the rule's possible deterrent effect, were uppermost in the minds of the framers of the rule," and then argued: "It is no answer, as the Court suggests, that the grand jury witnesses' Fourth Amendment rights will be sufficiently protected 'by the inadmissibility of the illegally-seized evidence in a subsequent criminal prosecution of the search victim.' This, of course, is no alternative for Calandra, since he was granted transactional immunity and cannot be criminally prosecuted. But the fundamental flaw of the alternative is that to compel Calandra to testify in the first place under penalty of contempt necessarily 'thwarts' his Fourth Amendment protection and 'entangle the courts in the illegal acts of Government agents' * * *."

2. ***Evidence obtained by government agents, used in criminal case after conviction.*** Should illegally seized evidence be admissible after conviction for consideration by the judge in determining the sentence to be imposed? *Verdugo v. United States,* 402 F.2d 599 (9th Cir.1968), holding no, was distinguished in *United States v. Schipani,* 315 F.Supp. 253 (E.D.N.Y.1970), aff'd, 435 F.2d 26 (2d Cir.1970), in that the decision in *Verdugo* was "predicated upon the fact that the search which had produced the improper evidence was conducted outside the course of the regular criminal investigation. It was undertaken, not to obtain evidence to support an indictment and conviction, but to recover contraband and thus to enhance the possibility of a heavier sentence after the basic investigation had been completed. [Under these circumstances,] law enforcement officials would have little to lose, but much to gain, in violating the Fourth Amendment." That situation was not present in *Schipani,* and thus the court concluded that "no appreciable increment in deterrence would result from applying a second exclusion at sentencing after the rule has been applied at the trial itself."

In PENNSYLVANIA BOARD OF PROBATION AND PAROLE v. SCOTT, 524 U.S. 357 (1998), parole officers made an illegal search of parolee Scott's residence and found weapons there, which were later admitted at his parole revocation hearing, resulting in Scott being recommitted to serve 36 months. Thereafter, the state supreme court, although following the prevailing general rule against application of the exclusionary rule at parole revocation hearings, carved out an exception for cases in which the officer who conducted the search was aware of the person's parole status. The Supreme Court, in a 5–4 decision, disagreed. THOMAS, J., for the majority, relying upon *Calandra*, supra, and *Janis* and *Lopez-Mendoza*, infra, declined "to extend the operation of the exclusionary rule beyond the criminal trial context" because "application of the exclusionary rule would both hinder the functioning of state parole systems and alter the traditionally flexible, administrative nature of parole revocation proceedings," but at the same time "would provide only minimal deterrence benefits in this context." On the matter of deterrence, the majority declared it would be "minimal" even in the special situation which concerned the state court, for if the searcher was a police officer he would be deterred by the risk of exclusion of evidence at a criminal trial and would be unaffected by what happened at the parole proceeding, which, in the words of *Janis*, "falls outside the offending officer's zone of primary interest." If the searcher was a parole officer, he will likewise be deterred by the risk of evidence exclusion at a criminal trial, and, in any event, is not "engaged in the often competitive enterprise of ferreting out crime" and thus can be sufficiently deterred by "departmental training and discipline and the threat of damages actions."

The dissenters, per SOUTER, J., noted "the police very likely do know a parolee's status when they go after him," which is significant because (1) police officers with such knowledge, "especially those employed by the same sovereign that runs the parole system, * * * have every incentive not to jeopardize a recommitment by rendering evidence inadmissible," and thus could be deterred by the threat of exclusion at a parole hearing; (2) "the actual likelihood of trial is often far less than the probability of a petition for parole revocation" because, as the Court itself noted on an earlier occasion, parole revocation "is often preferred to a new prosecution because of the procedural ease of recommitting the individual on the basis of a lesser showing by the State," and this means there will be "nothing 'marginal' about the deterrence provided by an exclusionary rule operating" in the parole revocation context, and (3) "the cooperation between parole and police officers * * * casts serious doubt upon the aptness of treating police officers differently from parole officers," who themselves "are considered police officers with respect to the offenders under their jurisdiction" and who, consequently, can no more than other police be thought to be adequately deterred by the risk of departmental discipline or the threat of damages actions.

3. *Evidence obtained by government agents, used in "quasi-criminal" or civil case.* In ONE 1958 PLYMOUTH SEDAN v. PENNSYLVANIA, 380 U.S. 693 (1965), a unanimous Court held that the *Weeks-Mapp* exclusionary rule applies to forfeiture proceedings. *Boyd v. United States*, p. 804 "the leading case on the subject of search and seizure * * * itself was not a criminal case," pointed out the majority, "but was a proceeding by the United States to forfeit 35 cases of plate glass which had allegedly been imported without payment of the customs duty * * *. [As] pointed out in *Boyd,* a forfeiture proceeding is quasi-criminal in character. Its object, like a criminal proceeding, is to penalize for the commission of an offense against the law. In this case * * * the driver and owner of the automobile was arrested and charged with a criminal offense against the Pennsylvania liquor laws. * * * In this forfeiture proceeding he was subject to the loss of his automobile, which at the time involved had an estimated value of approximately $1,000, a higher amount than the maximum fine in the criminal proceeding. It would be anomalous indeed, under these circumstances, to hold that in the criminal proceeding the illegally seized evidence is excludable, while in the forfeiture proceeding, requiring the determination that the criminal law has been violated, the same evidence would be admissible."

Los Angeles police seized wagering records and $4,940 in cash pursuant to a search warrant, and then notified the IRS, which made an assessment against Janis for wagering taxes and levied upon the seized cash in partial satisfaction. After Janis' motion to suppress was granted in the state criminal proceedings, he sued for refund of the money and to quash the assessment because it was based upon illegally seized evidence. The federal district court ruled for Janis, and the court of appeals affirmed. In UNITED STATES v. JANIS, 428 U.S. 433 (1976), the Court, per BLACKMUN, J., reversed: "Working, as we must, with the absence of convincing empirical data, common sense dictates that the deterrent effect of the exclusion of relevant evidence is highly attenuated when the 'punishment' imposed upon the offending criminal enforcement officer is the removal of that evidence from a civil suit by or against a different sovereign. In *Elkins* [p. 222] the Court indicated that the assumed interest of criminal law enforcement officers in the criminal proceedings of another sovereign counterbalanced this attenuation sufficiently to justify an exclusionary rule. Here, however, the attenuation is further augmented by the fact that the proceeding is one to enforce only the civil law of the other sovereign.

"This attenuation coupled with the existing deterrence effected by the denial of use of the evidence by either sovereign in the criminal trials with which the searching officer is concerned, creates a situation in which the imposition of the exclusionary rule sought in this case is unlikely to provide significant much less substantial, additional deterrence. It falls outside the offending officer's zone of primary interest."

BRENNAN and Marshall, JJ., dissented on the basis of their *Calandra* dissent. STEWART, J., dissenting, argued that the majority's deterrence theory compelled the opposite result in light of the fact that "federal and local law enforcement personnel regularly provide federal tax officials with information, obtained in criminal investigations, indicating liability under the wagering tax. The pattern is one of mutual cooperation and coordination, with the federal wagering tax provisions buttressing state and federal criminal sanctions." He noted that it was admitted by the local police officer in the instant case that he notified the IRS whenever he uncovered a gambling operation involving a substantial amount of cash.

Utilizing the *Janis* cost-benefit approach, the Court held 5–4 in I.N.S. v. LOPEZ–MENDOZA, 468 U.S. 1032 (1984), that the exclusionary rule is inapplicable in a civil deportation hearing. O'CONNOR, J., explained that the deterrent value of the exclusionary rule in this context was reduced because (i) "deportation will still be possible when evidence not derived directly from the arrest is sufficient to support deportation," (ii) INS agents know "that it is highly unlikely that any particular arrestee will end up challenging the lawfulness of his arrest," (iii) "the INS has its own comprehensive scheme for deterring Fourth Amendment violations" by training and discipline, and (iv) "alternative remedies" including the "possibility of declaratory relief" are available for institutional practices violating the Fourth Amendment. On the cost side, the Court continued, are these factors: (i) that application of the exclusionary rule "in proceedings that are intended not to punish past transgressions but to prevent their continuance or renewal would require courts to close their eyes to ongoing violations of the law," (ii) that invocation of the exclusionary rule at deportation hearings, where "neither the hearing officers nor the attorneys * * * are likely to be well versed in the intricacies of Fourth Amendment law," "might significantly change and complicate the character of these proceedings," and (iii) that because many INS arrests "occur in crowded and confused circumstances," application of the exclusionary rule "might well result in the suppression of large amounts of information that had been obtained entirely lawfully." WHITE, J., dissenting, objected that "unlike the situation in *Janis,* the conduct challenged here falls within 'the offending officer's zone of primary interest,' " and concluded that "the costs and benefits of applying the exclusionary rule in civil deportation proceedings do not differ in any significant way from the costs and benefits of applying the rule in ordinary criminal proceedings."

4. *Evidence obtained by private persons, used in criminal proceedings.* In *Burdeau v. McDowell,* 256 U.S. 465 (1921), the exclusionary rule was characterized "as a restraint upon the activities of sovereign authority and * * * not * * * a limitation upon other than governmental agencies," and on this basis courts have declined to exclude evidence in criminal cases when obtained by private persons. However, the Fourth Amendment *is* applicable "to private individuals who are acting as instruments or agents of the government. * * * Whether a private individual is an agent of the government is determined by a totality-of-the-circumstances test. Circumstances to be considered in this test include the motive of the private actor; any compensation or other benefit the private actor receives from the government; and the advice, direction, and level of participation given by the government. Using this test, if it is found that the private actor was sufficiently influenced and supported by the state, the exclusionary rule will apply to any evidence obtained by the private actor." Comment, 65 U.Cin.L.Rev. 665, 672 (1997).

One issue which frequently arises with respect to private person searches is whether, if that person then summons the police, police activity with respect to the same object is a separate "search" subject to Fourth Amendment constraints. For example, in UNITED STATES v. JACOBSEN, 466 U.S. 109 (1984), Federal Express employees opened a damaged box and found newspapers covering a tube which, when cut open, was found to contain plastic bags of white powder. Federal drug agents were summoned, but before their arrival the bags had been put back into the tube and the tube and newspapers back into the box, which was left open. A federal agent reopened the packaging to the extent necessary to expose the powder, which he field tested and found to be cocaine. The Court, per STEVENS, J., concluded the agent's actions were not a significant expansion of the earlier private search and that consequently no warrant was required. "Respondents could have no privacy interest in the contents of the package, since it remained unsealed and since the Federal Express employees had just examined the package and had, of their own accord, invited the federal agent to their offices for the express purpose of viewing its contents. The agent's viewing of what a private party had freely made available for his inspection did not violate the Fourth Amendment.

"Similarly, the removal of the plastic bags from the tube and the agent's visual inspection of their contents enabled the agent to learn nothing that had not previously been learned during the private search. It infringed no legitimate expectation of privacy and hence was not a 'search' within the meaning of the Fourth Amendment."[a]

Three members of the Court rejected that reasoning. WHITE, J., objected: "The majority opinion is particularly troubling when one considers its logical implications. I would be hard-pressed to distinguish this case, which involves a private search, from (1) one in which the private party's knowledge, later

a. As for the field test, see p. 264.

communicated to the government, that a particular container concealed contraband and nothing else arose from his presence at the time the container was sealed; (2) one in which the private party learned that a container concealed contraband and nothing else when it was previously opened in his presence; or (3) one in which the private party knew to a certainty that a container concealed contraband and nothing else as a result of conversations with its owner. In each of these cases, the approach adopted by the Court today would seem to suggest that the owner of the container has no legitimate expectation of privacy in its contents and that government agents opening that container without a warrant on the strength of information provided by the private party would not violate the Fourth Amendment."

5. *Evidence obtained by virtue of conduct of nonpolice government employee, used in criminal proceedings.* The *Burdeau* rule, grounded in the proposition that the Fourth Amendment is entirely inapplicable where there is no governmental action, must be distinguished from that recognized in ARIZONA v. EVANS, 514 U.S. 1 (1995): that some government searches covered by the Fourth Amendment are nonetheless inappropriate occasions for use of the exclusionary rule, considering the kind of government official who was at fault. After Evans was stopped for a traffic violation, the patrol car's computer indicated he had an outstanding arrest warrant, so Evans was arrested; incident thereto, the officer found marijuana. It was later learned that this warrant (issued because of Evans' nonappearance on several traffic violations) had been quashed upon Evans' voluntary appearance in court a few weeks earlier, but that apparently the court clerk had not thereafter followed the usual procedure of notifying the sheriff's department so that the warrant could be removed from the computer records. The state supreme court held this amounted to a violation of the Fourth Amendment and that consequently the evidence must be suppressed, but the Supreme Court, per REHNQUIST, C.J., considering only the latter point, disagreed:

"This holding is contrary to the reasoning of *Leon,* [p. 224]; *Massachusetts v. Sheppard* [p. 235]; and *Krull* [p. 238]. If court employees were responsible for the erroneous computer record, the exclusion of evidence at trial would not sufficiently deter future errors so as to warrant such a severe sanction. First, as we noted in *Leon,* the exclusionary rule was historically designed as a means of deterring police misconduct, not mistakes by court employees. Second, respondent offers no evidence that court employees are inclined to ignore or subvert the Fourth Amendment or that lawlessness among these actors requires application of the extreme sanction of exclusion. To the contrary, the Chief Clerk of the Justice Court testified at the suppression hearing that this type of error occurred once every three or four years.

"Finally, and most important, there is no basis for believing that application of the exclusionary rule in these circumstances will have a significant effect on court employees responsible for informing the police that a warrant has been quashed. Because court clerks are not adjuncts to the law enforcement team engaged in the often competitive enterprise of ferreting out crime, they have no stake in the outcome of particular criminal prosecutions. The threat of exclusion of evidence could not be expected to deter such individuals from failing to inform police officials that a warrant had been quashed.

"If it were indeed a court clerk who was responsible for the erroneous entry on the police computer, application of the exclusionary rule also could not be expected to alter the behavior of the arresting officer. * * * There is no indication that the arresting officer was not acting objectively reasonably when he relied upon the police computer record. Application of the *Leon* framework supports a categorical exception to the exclusionary rule for clerical errors of court employees.[5]"

O'CONNOR, J., joined by Souter and Bryer, concurring, cautioned: "Surely it would not be reasonable for the police to rely, say, on a recordkeeping system, their own or some other agency's, that has no mechanism to ensure its accuracy over time and that routinely leads to false arrests, even years after the probable cause for any such arrest has ceased to exist (if it ever existed)."

STEVENS, J., dissenting, objected: "Taken on its own terms, *Leon*'s logic does not extend to the time after the warrant has issued; nor does it extend to court clerks and functionaries, some of whom work in the same building with police officers and may have more regular and direct contact with police than with judges or magistrates."

GINSBURG, J., joined by Stevens, while mainly disagreeing with the majority's invocation of "the *Long* presumption" [see p. 51] to assert jurisdiction, made these comments on the merits: "In the Court's view, exclusion of evidence, even if capable of deterring police officer errors, cannot deter the carelessness of other governmental actors.[5] Whatever federal precedents may indicate—an issue on which I voice no opinion—the Court's conclusion is not the lesson inevitably to be drawn from logic or experience.

"In this electronic age, particularly with respect to recordkeeping, court personnel and police officers are not neatly compartmentalized actors. Instead, they serve together to carry out the State's information-gathering objectives. Whether particular records are maintained by the police or the courts should not be dispositive where a single computer database can answer all calls. Not only is it artificial to distinguish between court clerk and police clerk slips; in practice, it may be difficult to pinpoint whether one official, e.g., a court employee, or another, e.g., a police officer, caused the error to exist or to persist."

In *New Jersey v. T.L.O.*, p. 442, involving search of a student by a high school administrator, the Court reaffirmed that "the Fourth Amendment [is] applicable to the activities of civil as well as criminal authorities." However, because the search was found to be reasonable, the Court avoided expressing any opinion about the question which prompted the original grant of certiorari: whether the exclusionary rule is also applicable to searches by school authorities. In light of *Evans,* what is the answer to that question?

6. *Evidence obtained by foreign officials, used in domestic criminal proceedings.* Would any purpose be served by applying the exclusionary rule in such circumstances? What if American authorities requested or participated in the actions of the foreign police?

5. [Rehnquist opinion] The Solicitor General, as amicus curiae, argues that an analysis similar to that we apply here to court personnel also would apply in order to determine whether the evidence should be suppressed if police personnel were responsible for the error. As the State has not made any such argument here, we agree that "[t]he record in this case . . . does not adequately present that issue for the Court's consideration." Accordingly, we decline to address that question.

5. [Ginsburg opinion] It has been suggested that an exclusionary rule cannot deter carelessness, but can affect only intentional or reckless misconduct. This suggestion runs counter to a premise underlying all of negligence law—that imposing liability for negligence, i.e., lack of due care, creates an incentive to act with greater care. That the mistake may have been made by a clerical worker does not alter the conclusion that application of the exclusionary rule has deterrent value. Just as the risk of respondeat superior liability encourages employers to supervise more closely their employees' conduct, so the risk of exclusion of evidence encourages policymakers and systems managers to monitor the performance of the systems they install and the personnel employed to operate those systems. In the words of the trial court, the mistake in Evans' case was "perhaps the negligence of the Justice Court, or the negligence of the Sheriff's office. But it is still the negligence of the State."

Even if there has been direct U.S. involvement in the foreign search, the Fourth Amendment may be inapplicable for yet another reason. In *United States v. Verdugo–Urquidez,* 494 U.S. 259 (1990), the opinion of the Court, per Rehnquist, C.J., declared that the phrase "the people" in the Fourth Amendment (and the First, Second, Ninth and Tenth Amendments) "refers to a class of persons who are part of a national community or who have otherwise developed sufficient connection with this community to be considered part of that community." The defendant in the instant case was deemed not to be such a person; he was a Mexican citizen and resident who, to be sure, just two days before the search of his residence in Mexico had been turned over to U.S. authorities by Mexican police, but "this sort of presence—lawful but involuntary—is not the sort to indicate any substantial connection with our country." (The Court added it was an open question whether even the illegal aliens in *Lopez–Mendoza,* p. 243, were such persons, though their situation was different from the defendant's here because they "were in the United States voluntarily and presumably had accepted some societal obligations.") The three dissenters agreed, as Blackmun, J., put it, "that when a foreign national is held accountable for purported violations of United States criminal laws, he has effectively been treated as one of 'the governed' and therefore is entitled to Fourth Amendment protections." Because the two concurring Justices placed great emphasis upon the inapplicability of the Fourth Amendment's warrant clause to the search in the instant case (Kennedy, J., stressing this was not a case in which "the full protections of the Fourth Amendment would apply" because of the "absence of local judges or magistrates available to issue warrants"; Stevens, J., that "American magistrates have no power to authorize such searches"), the application of *Verdugo–Urquidez* to a foreign search of an alien's property made even without probable cause is not entirely clear.

Relying in part on *Verdugo-Urquidez,* the court in *United States v. Esparza–Mendoza*, 265 F.Supp.2d 1254 (D.Utah 2003), held "that previously deported alien felons" who reenter the U.S. "are not covered by the Fourth Amendment," meaning such a person "is not free to argue that, in his particular case, he possesses a sufficient connection to this country to receive Fourth Amendment coverage (unless, of course, he could prove he was in this country lawfully)."

SECTION 2. PROTECTED AREAS AND INTERESTS

KATZ v. UNITED STATES

389 U.S. 347, 88 S.Ct. 507, 19 L.Ed.2d 576 (1967).

Justice STEWART delivered the opinion of the Court.

The petitioner was convicted [of] transmitting wagering information by telephone from Los Angeles to Miami and Boston in violation of a federal statute. At trial the Government was permitted, over the petitioner's objection, to introduce evidence of the petitioner's end of telephone conversations, overheard by FBI agents who had attached an electronic listening and recording device to the outside of the public telephone booth from which he had placed his calls. In affirming his conviction, the Court of Appeals rejected the contention that the recordings had been obtained in violation of the Fourth Amendment, because "[t]here was no physical entrance into the area occupied by [the petitioner]." We granted certiorari in order to consider the constitutional questions thus presented.

The petitioner has phrased those questions as follows:

"A. Whether a public telephone booth is a constitutionally protected area so that evidence obtained by attaching an electronic listening recording device to the top of such a booth is obtained in violation of the right to privacy of the user of the booth.

"B. Whether physical penetration of a constitutionally protected area is necessary before a search and seizure can be said to be violative of the Fourth Amendment to the United States Constitution."

We decline to adopt this formulation of the issues. In the first place the correct solution of Fourth Amendment problems is not necessarily promoted by incantation of the phrase "constitutionally protected area." Secondly, the Fourth Amendment cannot be translated into a general constitutional "right to privacy." That Amendment protects individual privacy against certain kinds of governmental intrusion, but its protections go further, and often have nothing to do with privacy at all. Other provisions of the Constitution protect personal privacy from other forms of governmental invasion. But the protection of a person's *general* right to privacy—his right to be let alone by other people—is, like the protection of his property and of his very life, left largely to the law of the individual States.

Because of the misleading way the issues have been formulated, the parties have attached great significance to the characterization of the telephone booth from which the petitioner placed his calls. The petitioner has strenuously argued that the booth was a "constitutionally protected area." The Government has maintained with equal vigor that it was not. But this effort to decide whether or not a given "area," viewed in the abstract, is "constitutionally protected" deflects attention from the problem presented by this case. For the Fourth Amendment protects people, not places. What a person knowingly exposes to the public, even in his own home or office, is not a subject of Fourth Amendment protection. * * * But what he seeks to preserve as private, even in an area accessible to the public, may be constitutionally protected. * * *

The Government stresses the fact that the telephone booth from which the petitioner made his calls was constructed partly of glass, so that he was as visible after he entered it as he would have been if he had remained outside. But what he sought to exclude when he entered the booth was not the intruding eye—it was the uninvited ear. He did not shed his right to do so simply because he made his calls from a place where he might be seen. No less than an individual in a business office, in a friend's apartment, or in a taxicab, a person in a telephone booth may rely upon the protection of the Fourth Amendment. One who occupies it, shuts the door behind him, and pays the toll that permits him to place a call, is surely entitled to assume that the words he utters into the mouthpiece will not be broadcast to the world. To read the Constitution more narrowly is to ignore the vital role that the public telephone has come to play in private communication.

The Government contends, however, that the activities of its agents in this case should not be tested by Fourth Amendment requirements, for the surveillance technique they employed involved no physical penetration of the telephone booth from which the petitioner placed his calls.

* * * [A]lthough a closely divided Court supposed in *Olmstead* [p. 463] that surveillance without any trespass and without the seizure of any material object fell outside the ambit of the Constitution, we have since departed from the narrow view on which that decision rested. Indeed, we have expressly held that the Fourth Amendment governs not only the seizure of tangible items, but extends as well to the recording of oral statements overheard without any "technical trespass under * * * local property law." *Silverman v. United States* [p. 467]. Once this much is acknowledged, and once it is recognized that the Fourth Amendment protects people—and not simply "areas"—against unreasonable searches and seizures it becomes clear that the reach of that Amendment cannot turn upon the presence or absence of a physical intrusion into any given enclosure.

We conclude that the underpinnings of *Olmstead* and *Goldman* [p. 467] have been so eroded by our subsequent decisions that the "trespass" doctrine there enunciated can no longer be regarded as controlling. The Government's activities in electronically listening to and recording the petitioner's words violated the privacy upon which he justifiably relied while using the telephone booth and thus constituted a "search and seizure" within the meaning of the Fourth Amendment. The fact that the electronic device employed to achieve that end did not happen to penetrate the wall of the booth can have no constitutional significance.

The question remaining for decision, then, is whether the search and seizure conducted in this case complied with constitutional standards. In that regard, the Government's position is that its agents acted in an entirely defensible manner: They did not begin their electronic surveillance until investigation of the petitioner's activities had established a strong probability that he was using the telephone in question to transmit gambling information to persons in other States, in violation of federal law. Moreover, the surveillance was limited, both in scope and in duration to the specific purpose of establishing the contents of the petitioner's unlawful telephonic communications. The agents confined their surveillance to the brief periods during which he used the telephone booth, and they took great care to overhear only the conversations of the petitioner himself.

Accepting this account of the Government's actions as accurate, it is clear that this surveillance was so narrowly circumscribed that a duly authorized magistrate, properly notified of the need for such investigation, specifically informed of the basis on which it was to proceed, and clearly apprised of the precise intrusion it would entail, could constitutionally have authorized, with appropriate safeguards, the very limited search and seizure that the Government asserts in fact took place. * * *

The Government * * * urges the creation of a new exception to cover this case. It argues that surveillance of a telephone booth should be exempted from the usual requirement of advance authorization by a magistrate upon a showing of probable cause. We cannot agree. Omission of such authorization "bypasses the safeguards provided by an objective predetermination of probable cause, and substitutes instead the far less reliable procedure of an after-the-event justification for the * * * search, too likely to be subtly influenced by the familiar shortcomings of hindsight judgment." And bypassing a neutral predetermination of the *scope* of a search leaves individuals secure from Fourth Amendment violations "only in the discretion of the police."

These considerations do not vanish when the search in question is transferred from the setting of a home, an office, or a hotel room, to that of a telephone booth. Wherever a man may be, he is entitled to know that he will remain free from unreasonable searches and seizures. The government agents here ignored "the procedure of antecedent justification * * * that is central to the Fourth Amendment," procedure that we hold to be a constitutional precondition of the kind of electronic surveillance involved in this case. * * *

Judgment reversed.[a]

Justice HARLAN, concurring. * * *

As the Court's opinion states, "The Fourth Amendment protects people, not places." The question, however, is what protection it affords to those people. Generally, as here, the answer to that question requires reference to a "place." My understanding of the rule that has emerged from prior decisions is that there is a twofold requirement, first that a person have exhibited an actual (subjective)

a. Justice Marshall took no part in the case. Concurring opinions by Douglas, J., joined by Brennan, J., and by White, J., are omitted.

expectation of privacy and, second, that the expectation be one that society is prepared to recognize as "reasonable."[b] Thus a man's home is, for most purposes, a place where he expects privacy, but objects, activities, or statements that he exposes to the "plain view" of outsiders are not "protected" because no intention to keep them to himself has been exhibited. On the other hand, conversations in the open would not be protected against being overheard, for the expectation of privacy under the circumstances would be unreasonable. * * *

The critical fact in this case is that "[o]ne who occupies it, [a telephone booth] shuts the door behind him, and pays the toll that permits him to place a call, is surely entitled to assume" that his conversation is not being intercepted. The point is not that the booth is "accessible to the public" at other times, but that it is a temporarily private place whose momentary occupants' expectations of freedom from intrusion are recognized as reasonable. * * *

Justice BLACK, dissenting. * * *

Tapping telephone wires, of course, was an unknown possibility at the time the Fourth Amendment was adopted. But eavesdropping (and wiretapping is nothing more than eavesdropping by telephone) was * * * "an ancient practice which at common law was condemned as a nuisance. In those days the eavesdropper listened by naked ear under the eaves of houses or their windows, or beyond their walls seeking out private discourse." There can be no doubt that the Framers were aware of this practice, and if they had desired to outlaw or restrict the use of evidence obtained by eavesdropping, I believe that they would have used the appropriate language to do so in the Fourth Amendment. They certainly would not have left such a task to the ingenuity of language-stretching judges. * * *

* * * By clever word juggling the Court finds it plausible to argue that language aimed specifically at searches and seizures of things that can be searched and seized may, to protect privacy, be applied to eavesdropped evidence of conversations that can neither be searched nor seized. Few things happen to an individual that do not affect his privacy in one way or another. Thus, by arbitrarily substituting the Court's language, designed to protect privacy, for the Constitution's language, designed to protect against unreasonable searches and seizures, the Court has made the Fourth Amendment its vehicle for holding all laws violative of the Constitution which offend the Court's broadest concept of privacy. * * *

Notes and Questions

1. ***Fourth Amendment interests.*** In *Katz,* the Court held that the police conduct "constituted a 'search and seizure' within the meaning of the Fourth Amendment" because of the intrusion upon the defendant's privacy interest. But this does not mean that privacy is the *only* interest protected by the Fourth Amendment. The Fourth Amendment also protects the interests in possession of property and liberty of person, as in *United States v. Place,* p. 263 (detention of traveler's luggage 90 minutes was an unreasonable seizure in two respects, as it

b. Consider Anthony Amsterdam, *Perspectives on the Fourth Amendment,* 58 Minn. L.Rev. 349, 384 (1974): "But Justice Harlan himself [dissenting in *United States v. White,* p. 498] later expressed second thoughts about this conception, and rightly so. An actual, subjective expectation of privacy obviously has no place in a statement of what *Katz* held or in a theory of what the fourth amendment protects. It can neither add to, nor can its absence detract from, an individual's claim to fourth amendment protection. If it could, the government could diminish each person's subjective expectation of privacy merely by announcing half-hourly on television * * * that we were all forthwith being placed under comprehensive electronic surveillance."

constituted a deprivation of defendant's "possessory interest in his luggage" and his "liberty interest in proceeding with his itinerary").

In *Soldal v. Cook County,* 506 U.S. 56 (1992), a § 1983 action was commenced against sheriff's deputies who knowingly participated in an unlawful eviction which involved disconnecting the plaintiff's trailer home from its utilities and hauling it off the landlord's property, in the process of which the trailer was badly damaged. The court of appeals affirmed the officers motion for summary judgment on the ground that the Fourth Amendment offered no protection where, as here, the intrusion upon a possessory interest was unaccompanied by an intrusion upon a privacy interest or, for that matter, upon a liberty interest. A unanimous Supreme Court reversed, holding "that seizures of property are subject to Fourth Amendment scrutiny even though no search within the meaning of the Amendment has taken place."

2. ***Garbage.*** In CALIFORNIA v. GREENWOOD, 486 U.S. 35 (1988), police on two occasions had the neighborhood garbage collector pick up opaque plastic bags of garbage, which Greenwood had left at his curb for pick-up, and turn them over without mixing their contents with other garbage collected. On each occasion evidence of narcotics use was found, and each discovery served as the basis for a search warrant to search Greenwood's home which, upon execution, led to the discovery of narcotics. In reversing the state court's holding that these actions violated the Fourth Amendment, the Court, per WHITE, J., reasoned:

"It may well be that respondents did not expect that the contents of their garbage bags would become known to the police or other members of the public. An expectation of privacy does not give rise to Fourth Amendment protection, however, unless society is prepared to accept that expectation as objectively reasonable.[c]

"Here, we conclude that respondents exposed their garbage to the public sufficiently to defeat their claim to Fourth Amendment protection. It is common knowledge that plastic garbage bags left on or at the side of a public street are readily accessible to animals, children, scavengers, snoops, and other members of the public. Moreover, respondents placed their refuse at the curb for the express purpose of conveying it to a third party, the trash collector, who might himself have sorted through respondents' trash or permitted others, such as the police, to do so. Accordingly, having deposited their garbage 'in an area particularly suited for public inspection and, in a manner of speaking, public consumption, for the express purpose of having strangers take it,' respondents could have had no reasonable expectation of privacy in the inculpatory items that they discarded.

"Furthermore, as we have held, the police cannot reasonably be expected to avert their eyes from evidence of criminal activity that could have been observed by any member of the public. Hence, '[w]hat a person knowingly exposes to the public, even in his own home or office, is not a subject of Fourth Amendment protection.' *Katz.* We held in *Smith v. Maryland,* 442 U.S. 735 (1979), for example, that the police did not violate the Fourth Amendment by causing a pen register to be installed at the telephone company's offices to record the telephone numbers dialed by a criminal suspect. An individual has no legitimate expectation of privacy in the numbers dialed on his telephone, we reasoned, because he voluntarily conveys those numbers to the telephone company when he uses the telephone. Again, we observed that 'a person has no legitimate expectation of privacy in information he voluntarily turns over to third parties.'

c. As for the respondents' reliance upon their right to privacy in garbage recognized by California law, the Court later stated: "Respondent's argument is no less than a suggestion that concepts of privacy under the laws of each State are to determine the reach of the Fourth Amendment. We do not accept this submission."

"Similarly, we held in *California v. Ciraolo,* 476 U.S. 207 (1986) that the police were not required by the Fourth Amendment to obtain a warrant before conducting surveillance of the respondent's fenced backyard from a private plane flying at an altitude of 1,000 feet. We concluded that the respondent's expectation that his yard was protected from such surveillance was unreasonable because '[a]ny member of the public flying in this airspace who glanced down could have seen everything that these officers observed.'[d]"

BRENNAN, J., for the two dissenters, objected that a "trash bag, like any of the above-mentioned containers, 'is a common repository for one's personal effects' and, even more than many of them, is 'therefore ... inevitably associated with the expectation of privacy.' A single bag of trash testifies eloquently to the eating, reading, and recreational habits of the person who produced it. A search of trash, like a search of the bedroom, can relate intimate details about sexual practices, health, and personal hygiene. Like rifling through desk drawers or intercepting phone calls, rummaging through trash can divulge the target's financial and professional status, political affiliations and inclinations, private thoughts, personal relationships, and romantic interests. It cannot be doubted that a sealed trash bag harbors telling evidence of the 'intimate activity associated with the "sanctity of a man's home and the privacies of life," which the Fourth Amendment is designed to protect. * * *

"Nor is it dispositive that 'respondents placed their refuse at the curb for the express purpose of conveying it to a third party, ... who might himself have sorted through respondents' trash or permitted others, such as police, to do so.' In the first place, Greenwood can hardly be faulted for leaving trash on his curb when a county ordinance commanded him to do so, and prohibited him from disposing of it in any other way. More importantly, even the voluntary relinquishment of possession or control over an effect does not necessarily amount to a relinquishment of a privacy expectation in it. Were it otherwise, a letter or package would lose all Fourth Amendment protection when placed in a mail box or other depository with the 'express purpose' of entrusting it to the postal officer or a private carrier; those bailees are just as likely as trash collectors (and certainly have greater incentive) to 'sor[t] through' the personal effects entrusted to them, 'or permi[t] others, such as police to do so.' Yet, it has been clear for at least 110 years that the possibility of such an intrusion does not justify a warrantless search by police in the first instance. See *Ex parte Jackson,* 96 U.S. (6 Otto) 727 (1878)."

Should *Greenwood* apply even when the defendant has resorted to rather extraordinary means to ensure that the incriminating character of his garbage is not perceived by others? Yes is the answer given in *United States v. Scott,* 975 F.2d 927 (1st Cir.1992), where IRS agents painstakingly reassembled documents which defendant shredded into 5/32–inch strips before putting them in the garbage later placed outside his curtilage. The court offered this analogy: "A person who prepares incriminating documents in a secret code (or for that matter in some obscure foreign language), and thereafter blithely discards them as trash, relying on the premise or hope that they will not be deciphered [or translated] by the authorities could well be in for an unpleasant surprise if his code is 'broken' by the police [or a translator is found for the abstruse language], but he cannot make

d. *Ciraolo* was a 5–4 decision. The dissenters objected that "the actual risk to privacy from commercial or pleasure aircraft is virtually nonexistent. Travelers on commercial flights, as well as private planes used for business or personal reasons, normally obtain at most a fleeting, anonymous, and nondiscriminating glimpse of the landscape and buildings over which they pass. The risk that a passenger on such a plane might observe private activities, and might connect those activities with particular people, is simply too trivial to protect against."

a valid claim that his subjective expectation in keeping the contents private by use of the secret code [or language] was reasonable in a constitutional sense."

3. *"Curtilage" vs. "open fields."* After *Greenwood,* what result as to garbage left for pickup in a can well within the curtilage, if (i) the police merely enter and take the garbage, or (ii) the police have the garbage collector pick up and segregate the garbage from that can? More generally, what lands are protected by the Fourth Amendment from what kinds of police intrusions? Consider:

(a) In OLIVER v. UNITED STATES, 466 U.S. 170 (1984), the Court, per POWELL, J., held that the "open fields" doctrine of *Hester v. United States,* 265 U.S. 57 (1924), by which police entry and examination of a field is free of any Fourth Amendment restraints, had not been implicitly overruled by *Katz.* This was because the *Hester* rule "was founded upon the explicit language of the Fourth Amendment. That Amendment indicates with some precision the places and things encompassed by its protections. As Justice Holmes explained for the Court in his characteristically laconic style: '[T]he special protection accorded by the Fourth Amendment to the people in their "persons, houses, papers, and effects," is not extended to the open fields. The distinction between the latter and the house is as old as the common law.' "

The Court in *Oliver* reasoned that this interpretation of the Amendment was consistent with *Katz,* as "open fields do not provide the setting for those intimate activities that the Amendment is intended to shelter from government interference or surveillance. There is no societal interest in protecting the privacy of those activities, such as the cultivation of crops, that occur in open fields. Moreover, as a practical matter these lands usually are accessible to the public and the police in ways that a home, an office or commercial structure would not be. It is not generally true that fences or no trespassing signs effectively bar the public from viewing open fields in rural areas. And both petitioner Oliver and respondent Thornton concede that the public and police lawfully may survey lands from the air. For these reasons, the asserted expectation of privacy in open fields is not an expectation that 'society recognizes as reasonable.'

"The historical underpinnings of the 'open fields' doctrine also demonstrate that the doctrine is consistent with respect for 'reasonable expectations of privacy.' As Justice Holmes, writing for the Court, observed in *Hester,* the common law distinguished 'open fields' from the 'curtilage,' the land immediately surrounding and associated with the home. The distinction implies that only the curtilage, not the neighboring open fields, warrants the Fourth Amendment protections that attach to the home. At common law, the curtilage is the area to which extends the intimate activity associated with the 'sanctity of a man's home and the privacies of life,' and therefore has been considered part of home itself for Fourth Amendment purposes. Thus, courts have extended Fourth Amendment protection to the curtilage; and they have defined the curtilage, as did the common law, by reference to the factors that determine whether an individual reasonably may expect that an area immediately adjacent to the home will remain private.[e]

e. As the Court explained in *United States v. Dunn,* 480 U.S. 294 (1987), "curtilage questions should be resolved with particular reference to four factors: the proximity of the area claimed to be curtilage to the home, whether the area is included within an enclosure surrounding the home, the nature of the uses to which the area is put, and the steps taken by the resident to protect the area from observation by people passing by." Applying these factors, the Court then concluded the barn into which the police looked was not within the curtilage, as it was 60 yards from the house, was outside the area surrounding the house enclosed by a fence, did not appear to the police to be "used for intimate activities of the home," and the fences outside the barn were not of a kind "to prevent persons from observing what lay inside the enclosed area." The Court added that even assuming the barn was protected business premises, it still was no search to look into the open barn from an open fields vantage point.

Conversely, the common law implies, as we reaffirm today, that no expectation of privacy legitimately attaches to open fields."

As for the contention of Oliver and Thornton that the circumstances may sometimes show the existence of a reasonable expectation of privacy, the Court said it was answered by the "language of the Fourth Amendment," but added that such a case-by-case approach would in any event be unworkable because "police officers would have to guess before every search whether landowners had erected fences sufficiently high, posted a sufficient number of warning signs, or located contraband in an area sufficiently secluded to establish a right of privacy." The *Oliver* majority also asserted that it rejected "the suggestion that steps taken to protect privacy establish that expectations of privacy in an open field are legitimate. It is true, of course, that petitioner Oliver and respondent Thornton, in order to conceal their criminal activities, planted the marijuana upon secluded land and erected fences and no trespassing signs around the property. And it may be that because of such precautions, few members of the public stumbled upon the marijuana crops seized by the police. Neither of these suppositions demonstrates, however, that the expectation of privacy was *legitimate* in the sense required by the Fourth Amendment. The test of legitimacy is not whether the individual chooses to conceal assertedly 'private' activity. Rather, the correct inquiry is whether the government's intrusion infringes upon the personal and societal values protected by the Fourth Amendment. As we have explained, we find no basis for concluding that a police inspection of open fields accomplishes such an infringement."

MARSHALL, J., for the three dissenters, argued (1) that the Court's first ground could not be squared with earlier decisions, including *Katz* itself, for "neither a public telephone booth nor a conversation conducted therein can fairly be described as a person, house, paper, or effect"; and (2) that society *is* prepared to recognize as reasonable the expectations of Oliver and Thornton, which were supported by the law of criminal trespass, the private uses to which privately owned lands could be put, and the precautions which they had taken to manifest their privacy interest to others. From this the dissenters posited this "clear, easily administrable rule": "Private land marked in a fashion sufficient to render entry thereon a criminal trespass under the law of the state in which the land lies is protected by the Fourth Amendment's proscription of unreasonable searches and seizures."[f]

(c) FLORIDA v. RILEY, 488 U.S. 445 (1989), presented the question: "Whether surveillance of the interior of a partially covered greenhouse in a residential backyard from the vantage point of a helicopter located 400 feet above the greenhouse constitutes a 'search' for which a warrant is required under the Fourth Amendment." WHITE, J., for the 4–Justice plurality, concluded it did not "make a difference for Fourth Amendment purposes that the helicopter was flying at 400 feet when the officer saw what was growing in the greenhouse through the partially open roof and sides of the structure. We would have a different case if flying at that altitude had been contrary to law or regulation. But helicopters are not bound by the lower limits of the navigable airspace allowed to other aircraft. Any member of the public could legally have been flying over Riley's property in a helicopter at the altitude of 400 feet and could have observed Riley's greenhouse. The police officer did no more. This is not to say that an inspection of the curtilage of a house from an aircraft will always pass muster under the Fourth Amendment simply because the plane is within the navigable airspace specified by law. But it is of obvious importance that the helicopter in this case was *not* violating the law, and there is nothing in the record or before us to suggest that

f. See Stephen A. Saltzburg, *Another Victim of Illegal Narcotics: The Fourth Amendment (As Illustrated by the Open Fields Doctrine),* 48 U.Pitt.L.Rev. 1 (1986).

helicopters flying at 400 feet are sufficiently rare in this country to lend substance to respondent's claim that he reasonably anticipated that his greenhouse would not be subject to observation from that altitude. Neither is there any intimation here that the helicopter interfered with respondent's normal use of the greenhouse or of other parts of the curtilage. As far as this record reveals, no intimate details connected with the use of the home or curtilage were observed, and there was no undue noise, no wind, dust, or threat of injury. In these circumstances, there was no violation of the Fourth Amendment."

O'CONNOR, J., concurring only in the judgment because "the plurality's approach rests the scope of Fourth Amendment protection too heavily on compliance with FAA regulations whose purpose is to promote air safety not to protect" Fourth Amendment rights, concluded: "Because there is reason to believe that there is considerable public use of airspace at altitudes of 400 feet and above, and because Riley introduced no evidence to the contrary before the Florida courts, I conclude that Riley's expectation that his curtilage was protected from naked-eye aerial observation from that altitude was not a reasonable one. However, public use of altitudes lower than that—particularly public observations from helicopters circling over the curtilage of a home—may be sufficiently rare that police surveillance from such altitudes would violate reasonable expectations of privacy, despite compliance with FAA air safety regulations."

BRENNAN, J., joined by Marshall and Stevens, JJ., dissenting, objected: "Under the plurality's exceedingly grudging Fourth Amendment theory, the expectation of privacy is defeated if a single member of the public could conceivably position herself to see into the area in question without doing anything illegal. It is defeated whatever the difficulty a person would have in so positioning herself, and however infrequently anyone would in fact do so. In taking this view the plurality ignores the very essence of *Katz*. * * * Finding determinative the fact that the officer was where he had a right to be, at bottom, an attempt to analogize surveillance from a helicopter to surveillance by a police officer standing on a public road and viewing evidence of crime through an open window or a gap in a fence. In such a situation, the occupant of the home may be said to lack any reasonable expectation of privacy in what can be seen from that road—even if, in fact, people rarely pass that way.

"The police officer positioned 400 feet above Riley's backyard was not, however, standing on a public road. The vantage point he enjoyed was not one any citizen could readily share. His ability to see over Riley's fence depended on his use of a very expensive and sophisticated piece of machinery to which few ordinary citizens have access. In such circumstances it makes no more sense to rely on the legality of the officer's position in the skies than it would to judge the constitutionality of the wiretap in *Katz* by the legality of the officer's position outside the telephone booth. The simply inquiry whether the police officer had the legal right to be in the position from which he made his observations cannot suffice, for we cannot assume that Riley's curtilage was so open to the observations of passersby in the skies that he retained little privacy or personal security to be lost to police surveillance. The question before us must be not whether the police were where they had a right to be, but whether public observation of Riley's curtilage was so commonplace that Riley's expectation of privacy in his backyard could not be considered reasonable."

BLACKMUN, J., dissenting, first concluded that "a majority of this Court" (himself, the other three dissenters and O'Connor, J.) agreed "that the reasonableness of Riley's expectation depends, in large measure, on the frequency of nonpolice helicopter flights at an altitude of 400 feet." As for how this factual issue should be decided, he noted Brennan "suggests that we may resolve it ourselves without any evidence in the record on this point," while O'Connor "would impose the burden of proof on Riley" but would not now "allow Riley an opportunity to meet this burden." Blackmun, on the other hand, would impose upon the prosecution the burden of proving those "facts necessary to show that Riley lacked a reasonable expectation of privacy" and, "because our prior cases gave the parties little guidance on the burden of proof issue," would "remand this case to allow the prosecution an opportunity to meet this burden."

4. *Other premises.* (a) *Business and commercial premises* are covered by the Fourth Amendment. As stated in *See v. City of Seattle,* 387 U.S. 541 (1967), "[t]he businessman, like the occupant of a residence, has a constitutional right to go about his business free from unreasonable official entries upon his private commercial property."

(b) *Private areas in public places.* What if a police officer, positioned at an overhead vent above a rest room, looks down into an individual closed stall and observes criminal conduct? See *State v. Bryant,* 177 N.W.2d 800 (Minn.1970) (is a search). What, however, if the stalls had no doors?

(c) *Detention facilities.* In *Hudson v. Palmer,* 468 U.S. 517 (1984), involving a § 1983 action brought by a state prison inmate who alleged a prison guard had conducted a "shakedown" search of his cell and had destroyed his noncontraband property for purposes of harassment, the Court held, 5–4, "that the Fourth Amendment has no applicability to a prison cell." The Chief Justice reasoned: "A right of privacy in traditional Fourth Amendment terms is fundamentally incompatible with the close and continual surveillance of inmates and their cells required to ensure institutional security and internal order. We are satisfied that society would insist that the prisoner's expectation of privacy always yield to what must be considered the paramount interest in institutional security. We believe that it is accepted by our society that '[l]oss of freedom of choice and privacy are inherent incidents of confinement.'" The Court added that for "the same reasons" the seizure and destruction of a prisoner's effects did not fall within the protections of the Fourth Amendment. It is unclear whether *Hudson* applies to the search of the person of a prisoner[g] or, in any event, to a pretrial detention facility.[h]

5. *Vehicles.* (a) In *Cardwell v. Lewis,* 417 U.S. 583 (1974), police seized a car from a public parking lot and later took a small paint sample off the car and matched the tire tread with tracks at a crime scene. The Court divided on the propriety of the seizure of the car, but the plurality opinion seemed to view the later activity as no search: "With the 'search' limited to the examination of the tire on the wheel and the taking of paint scraping from the exterior of the vehicle left in the public parking lot, we fail to comprehend what expectation of privacy was infringed."

(b) In *New York v. Class,* 475 U.S. 106 (1986), an officer stopped a car for traffic violations and then, after the driver exited the car, opened the door and reached in to move papers obscuring the dashboard Vehicle Identification Number, at which time he saw a gun inside the car. Noting that "federal law requires that the VIN be placed in the plain view of someone *outside* the automobile," the

g. As the dissenters noted, the majority "appears to limit its holding to a prisoner's 'papers and effects' located in his cell" and apparently "believes that at least a prisoner's 'person' is secure from unreasonable search and seizure." In *Bell v. Wolfish,* 441 U.S. 520 (1979), where the Court declared that at best prisoners have a "reasonable expectation of privacy * * * of a diminished scope," it was held that neither strip searches nor body cavity inspections of pretrial detainees after contact visits with outsiders were unreasonable.

h. Much, but certainly not all, of the Court's analysis in *Hudson* has to do with circumstances existing in facilities housing those convicted of crime. But O'Connor, J., concurring, stated the broader proposition that the "fact of arrest and incarceration abates all legitimate Fourth Amendment privacy and possessory interests in personal effects."

Court concluded "there was no reasonable expectation of privacy in the VIN," so that the "mere viewing of the formerly obscured VIN was not" a search. But the Court then concluded that because "a car's interior [is] subject to Fourth Amendment protection," the officer's action in reaching inside the car "constituted a 'search' " (albeit a reasonable one in the circumstances).[i]

6. *Effects.* During a lawful stop of a Greyhound bus, federal agents walked through the bus and squeezed the soft luggage passengers had placed in the overhead storage spaces. An agent noticed thereby that one bag contained a brick-like object; passenger Downs admitted the bag was his and allowed the agent to open it, revealing a brick of methamphetamine. In BOND v. UNITED STATES, 529 U.S. 334 (2000), the Court, per REHNQUIST, C.J., preliminarily noted: (1) that a "traveler's personal luggage is clearly an 'effect' protected by the Fourth Amendment"; (2) that the government's reliance on such cases as *Riley* was misplaced because "[p]hysical invasive inspection is simply more intrusive than purely visual inspection"; and (3) that while Bond's "bag was not part of his person," "travelers are particularly concerned about their carry-on luggage; they generally use it to transport personal items that, for whatever reason, they prefer to keep close at hand." The Court then concluded: "When a bus passenger places a bag in an overhead bin, he expects that other passengers or bus employees may move it for one reason or another. Thus, a bus passenger clearly expects that his bag may be handled. He does not expect that other passengers or bus employees will, as a matter of course, feel the bag in an exploratory manner. But this is exactly what the agent did here. We therefore hold that the agent's physical manipulation of petitioner's bag violated the Fourth Amendment."

BREYER and Scalia, JJ., dissenting, objected: (1) that the squeezing did not "differ from the treatment that overhead luggage is likely to receive from strangers in a world of travel that is somewhat less gentle than it used to be"; (2) that whether "tactile manipulation * * * is more intrusive or less intrusive than visual observation * * * necessarily depends on the particular circumstances"; and (3) that "the decision will lead to a constitutional jurisprudence of 'squeezes,' thereby complicating further already complex Fourth Amendment law."

What is the significance of *Bond* with respect to tactile examination of the carry-on luggage of train and airplane passengers, and of the checked luggage of passengers on various forms of public transportation?

7. *Enhancing the senses.* Generally speaking, it is fair to say that it is not a search for an officer, lawfully present at a certain place, to detect something by one of his natural senses. *United States v. Mankani*, 738 F.2d 538 (2d Cir.1984) (no search where conversations in adjoining motel room "were overheard by the naked human ear"). The result ordinarily is the same when common means of enhancing the senses, such as a flashlight or binoculars, are used.[j] As for use of more sophisticated or less common means, consider the following material.

KYLLO v. UNITED STATES

533 U.S. 27, 121 S.Ct. 2038, 150 L.Ed.2d 94 (2001).

Justice SCALIA delivered the opinion of the Court. * * *

In 1991 Agent William Elliott of the United States Department of the Interior came to suspect that marijuana was being grown in the home belonging to

i. See Tracey Maclin, *New York v. Class: A Little–Noticed Case With Disturbing Implications,* 78 J.Crim.L. & C. 1 (1987).

j. But consider *Raettig v. State,* 406 So.2d 1273 (Fla.App.1981) (use of flashlight to look into camper through half-inch wide crack a search, as "a minute crack on the surface of such area can hardly be regarded as an implied invitation to any curious passerby to take a look"); *State v. Ward,* 617 P.2d 568 (Hawaii 1980) (use of binoculars to see crap game in 7th story apartment from closest vantage point an eighth of a mile away a search, as "the constitution does not require that in all cases a person, in order to protect his privacy, must shut himself off from fresh air, sunlight and scenery").

petitioner Danny Kyllo, part of a triplex on Rhododendron Drive in Florence, Oregon. Indoor marijuana growth typically requires high-intensity lamps. In order to determine whether an amount of heat was emanating from petitioner's home consistent with the use of such lamps, at 3:20 a.m. on January 16, 1992, Agent Elliott and Dan Haas used an Agema Thermovision 210 thermal imager[a] to scan the triplex. Thermal imagers detect infrared radiation, which virtually all objects emit but which is not visible to the naked eye. The imager converts radiation into images based on relative warmth—black is cool, white is hot, shades of gray connote relative differences; in that respect, it operates somewhat like a video camera showing heat images. The scan of Kyllo's home took only a few minutes and was performed from the passenger seat of Agent Elliott's vehicle across the street from the front of the house and also from the street in back of the house. The scan showed that the roof over the garage and a side wall of petitioner's home were relatively hot compared to the rest of the home and substantially warmer than neighboring homes in the triplex. Agent Elliott concluded that petitioner was using halide lights to grow marijuana in his house, which indeed he was. Based on tips from informants, utility bills, and the thermal imaging, a Federal Magistrate Judge issued a warrant authorizing a search of petitioner's home, and the agents found an indoor growing operation involving more than 100 plants. Petitioner was indicted on one count of manufacturing marijuana, in violation of 21 U. S. C. § 841(a)(1). He unsuccessfully moved to suppress the evidence seized from his home and then entered a conditional guilty plea[, and the court of appeals affirmed]. * * *

It would be foolish to contend that the degree of privacy secured to citizens by the Fourth Amendment has been entirely unaffected by the advance of technology. For example, * * * the technology enabling human flight has exposed to public view (and hence, we have said, to official observation) uncovered portions of the house and its curtilage that once were private. See *Ciraolo*, [p. 252]. The question we confront today is what limits there are upon this power of technology to shrink the realm of guaranteed privacy.

The *Katz* test—whether the individual has an expectation of privacy that society is prepared to recognize as reasonable—has often been criticized as circular, and hence subjective and unpredictable. While it may be difficult to refine *Katz* when the search of areas such as telephone booths, automobiles, or even the curtilage and uncovered portions of residences are at issue, in the case of the search of the interior of homes—the prototypical and hence most commonly litigated area of protected privacy—there is a ready criterion, with roots deep in the common law, of the minimal expectation of privacy that exists, and that is acknowledged to be reasonable. To withdraw protection of this minimum expectation would be to permit police technology to erode the privacy guaranteed by the Fourth Amendment. We think that obtaining by sense-enhancing technology any information regarding the interior of the home that could not otherwise have been obtained without physical "intrusion into a constitutionally protected area" constitutes a search—at least where (as here) the technology in question is not in general public use. This assures preservation of that degree of privacy against

a. As the Court later elaborated, "the District Court found that the Agema 210 'is a non-intrusive device which emits no rays or beams and shows a crude visual image of the heat being radiated from the outside of the house'; it 'did not show any people or activity within the walls of the structure'; '[t]he device used cannot penetrate walls or windows to reveal conversations or human activities'; and '[n]o intimate details of the home were observed.' "

government that existed when the Fourth Amendment was adopted. On the basis of this criterion, the information obtained by the thermal imager in this case was the product of a search.[2]

The Government maintains, however, that the thermal imaging must be upheld because it detected "only heat radiating from the external surface of the house." The dissent makes this its leading point, contending that there is a fundamental difference between what it calls "off-the-wall" observations and "through-the-wall surveillance." But just as a thermal imager captures only heat emanating from a house, so also a powerful directional microphone picks up only sound emanating from a house—and a satellite capable of scanning from many miles away would pick up only visible light emanating from a house. We rejected such a mechanical interpretation of the Fourth Amendment in *Katz*, where the eavesdropping device picked up only sound waves that reached the exterior of the phone booth. Reversing that approach would leave the homeowner at the mercy of advancing technology—including imaging technology that could discern all human activity in the home. While the technology used in the present case was relatively crude, the rule we adopt must take account of more sophisticated systems that are already in use or in development.[3] * * *

The Government also contends that the thermal imaging was constitutional because it did not "detect private activities occurring in private areas." * * * The Fourth Amendment's protection of the home has never been tied to measurement of the quality or quantity of information obtained. * * * In the home, our cases show, all details are intimate details, because the entire area is held safe from prying government eyes. Thus, in *Karo*, [p. 265], the only thing detected was a can of ether in the home; and in *Arizona v. Hicks*, [p. 358], the only thing detected by a physical search that went beyond what officers lawfully present could observe in "plain view" was the registration number of a phonograph turntable. These were intimate details because they were details of the home, just as was the detail of how warm—or even how relatively warm—Kyllo was heating his residence.

Limiting the prohibition of thermal imaging to "intimate details" would not only be wrong in principle; it would be impractical in application, failing to provide "a workable accommodation between the needs of law enforcement and the interests protected by the Fourth Amendment." To begin with, there is no necessary connection between the sophistication of the surveillance equipment

2. The dissent's repeated assertion that the thermal imaging did not obtain information regarding the interior of the home is simply inaccurate. A thermal imager reveals the relative heat of various rooms in the home. The dissent may not find that information particularly private or important, but there is no basis for saying it is not information regarding the interior of the home. The dissent's comparison of the thermal imaging to various circumstances in which outside observers might be able to perceive, without technology, the heat of the home—for example, by observing snowmelt on the roof—is quite irrelevant. The fact that equivalent information could sometimes be obtained by other means does not make lawful the use of means that violate the Fourth Amendment. The police might, for example, learn how many people are in a particular house by setting up year-round surveillance; but that does not make breaking and entering to find out the same information lawful. In any event, on the night of January 16, 1992, no outside observer could have discerned the relative heat of Kyllo's home without thermal imaging.

3. The ability to "see" through walls and other opaque barriers is a clear, and scientifically feasible, goal of law enforcement research and development. The National Law Enforcement and Corrections Technology Center, a program within the United States Department of Justice, features on its Internet Website projects that include a "Radar–Based Through-the-Wall Surveillance System," "Handheld Ultrasound Through the Wall Surveillance," and a "Radar Flashlight" that "will enable law officers to detect individuals through interior building walls." www.nlectc.org/techproj/ (visited May 3, 2001). Some devices may emit low levels of radiation that travel "through-the-wall," but others, such as more sophisticated thermal imaging devices, are entirely passive, or "off-the-wall" as the dissent puts it.

and the "intimacy" of the details that it observes—which means that one cannot say (and the police cannot be assured) that use of the relatively crude equipment at issue here will always be lawful. * * * We * * * would have to develop a jurisprudence specifying which home activities are "intimate" and which are not. And even when (if ever) that jurisprudence were fully developed, no police officer would be able to know in advance whether his through-the-wall surveillance picks up "intimate" details—and thus would be unable to know in advance whether it is constitutional.

The dissent's proposed standard—whether the technology offers the "functional equivalent of actual presence in the area being searched"—would seem quite similar to our own at first blush. The dissent concludes that *Katz* was such a case, but then inexplicably asserts that if the same listening device only revealed the volume of the conversation, the surveillance would be permissible. Yet if, without technology, the police could not discern volume without being actually present in the phone booth, Justice STEVENS should conclude a search has occurred. * * * The same should hold for the interior heat of the home if only a person present in the home could discern the heat. Thus the driving force of the dissent, despite its recitation of the above standard, appears to be a distinction among different types of information—whether the "homeowner would even care if anybody noticed." The dissent offers no practical guidance for the application of this standard, and for reasons already discussed, we believe there can be none. The people in their houses, as well as the police, deserve more precision.[6]

We have said that the Fourth Amendment draws "a firm line at the entrance to the house." That line, we think, must be not only firm but also bright—which requires clear specification of those methods of surveillance that require a warrant. While it is certainly possible to conclude from the videotape of the thermal imaging that occurred in this case that no "significant" compromise of the homeowner's privacy has occurred, we must take the long view, from the original meaning of the Fourth Amendment forward. * * *

Since we hold the Thermovision imaging to have been an unlawful search, it will remain for the District Court to determine whether, without the evidence it provided, the search warrant issued in this case was supported by probable cause—and if not, whether there is any other basis for supporting admission of the evidence that the search pursuant to the warrant produced. * * *

Justice STEVENS, with whom THE CHIEF JUSTICE, Justice, Justice O'CONNOR, and Justice KENNEDY join, dissenting. * * *

While the Court "take[s] the long view" and decides this case based largely on the potential of yet-to-be-developed technology that might allow "through-the-wall surveillance," this case involves nothing more than off-the-wall surveillance by law enforcement officers to gather information exposed to the general public from the outside of petitioner's home. All that the infrared camera did in this case was passively measure heat emitted from the exterior surfaces of petitioner's home; all that those measurements showed were relative differences in emission levels, vaguely indicating that some areas of the roof and outside walls were warmer than others. As still images from the infrared scans show, no details regarding the interior of petitioner's home were revealed. Unlike an x-ray scan, or other possible

6. The dissent argues that we have injected potential uncertainty into the constitutional analysis by noting that whether or not the technology is in general public use may be a factor. That quarrel, however, is not with us but with this Court's precedent. See *Ciraolo* ("In an age where private and commercial flight in the public airways is routine, it is unreasonable for respondent to expect that his marijuana plants were constitutionally protected from being observed with the naked eye from an altitude of 1,000 feet"). Given that we can quite confidently say that thermal imaging is not "routine," we decline in this case to reexamine that factor.

"through-the-wall" techniques, the detection of infrared radiation emanating from the home did not accomplish "an unauthorized physical penetration into the premises," nor did it "obtain information that it could not have obtained by observation from outside the curtilage of the house."

Indeed, the ordinary use of the senses might enable a neighbor or passerby to notice the heat emanating from a building, particularly if it is vented, as was the case here. Additionally, any member of the public might notice that one part of a house is warmer than another part or a nearby building if, for example, rainwater evaporates or snow melts at different rates across its surfaces. Such use of the senses would not convert into an unreasonable search if, instead, an adjoining neighbor allowed an officer onto her property to verify her perceptions with a sensitive thermometer. Nor, in my view, does such observation become an unreasonable search if made from a distance with the aid of a device that merely discloses that the exterior of one house, or one area of the house, is much warmer than another. Nothing more occurred in this case. * * *

Notwithstanding the implications of today's decision, there is a strong public interest in avoiding constitutional litigation over the monitoring of emissions from homes, and over the inferences drawn from such monitoring. Just as "the police cannot reasonably be expected to avert their eyes from evidence of criminal activity that could have been observed by any member of the public," *Greenwood*, [p. 251], so too public officials should not have to avert their senses or their equipment from detecting emissions in the public domain such as excessive heat, traces of smoke, suspicious odors, odorless gases, airborne particulates, or radioactive emissions, any of which could identify hazards to the community. In my judgment, monitoring such emissions with "sense-enhancing technology," and drawing useful conclusions from such monitoring, is an entirely reasonable public service.

On the other hand, the countervailing privacy interest is at best trivial. After all, homes generally are insulated to keep heat in, rather than to prevent the detection of heat going out, and it does not seem to me that society will suffer from a rule requiring the rare homeowner who both intends to engage in uncommon activities that produce extraordinary amounts of heat, and wishes to conceal that production from outsiders, to make sure that the surrounding area is well insulated. * * *

Despite the Court's attempt to draw a line that is "not only firm but also bright," the contours of its new rule are uncertain because its protection apparently dissipates as soon as the relevant technology is "in general public use." Yet how much use is general public use is not even hinted at by the Court's opinion, which makes the somewhat doubtful assumption that the thermal imager used in this case does not satisfy that criterion.[5] In any event, putting aside its lack of clarity, this criterion is somewhat perverse because it seems likely that the threat to privacy will grow, rather than recede, as the use of intrusive equipment becomes more readily available.

It is clear, however, that the category of "sense-enhancing technology" covered by the new rule is far too broad. It would, for example, embrace potential mechanical substitutes for dogs trained to react when they sniff narcotics. But in

5. The record describes a device that numbers close to a thousand manufactured units; that has a predecessor numbering in the neighborhood of 4,000 to 5,000 units; that competes with a similar product numbering from 5,000 to 6,000 units; and that is "readily available to the public" for commercial, personal, or law enforcement purposes, and is just an 800–number away from being rented from "half a dozen national companies" by anyone who wants one. Since, by virtue of the Court's new rule, the issue is one of first impression, perhaps it should order an evidentiary hearing to determine whether these facts suffice to establish "general public use."

United States v. Place, [p. 263], we held that a dog sniff that "discloses only the presence or absence of narcotics" does "not constitute a 'search' within the meaning of the Fourth Amendment," and it must follow that sense-enhancing equipment that identifies nothing but illegal activity is not a search either. Nevertheless, the use of such a device would be unconstitutional under the Court's rule, as would the use of other new devices that might detect the odor of deadly bacteria or chemicals for making a new type of high explosive * * *.

Because the new rule applies to information regarding the "interior" of the home, it is too narrow as well as too broad. Clearly, a rule that is designed to protect individuals from the overly intrusive use of sense-enhancing equipment should not be limited to a home. If such equipment did provide its user with the functional equivalent of access to a private place—such as, for example, the telephone booth involved in *Katz*, or an office building—then the rule should apply to such an area as well as to a home. * * *

The two reasons advanced by the Court as justifications for the adoption of its new rule are both unpersuasive. First, the Court suggests that its rule is compelled by our holding in *Katz*, because in that case, as in this, the surveillance consisted of nothing more than the monitoring of waves emanating from a private area into the public domain. Yet there are critical differences between the cases. In *Katz*, the electronic listening device attached to the outside of the phone booth allowed the officers to pick up the content of the conversation inside the booth, making them the functional equivalent of intruders because they gathered information that was otherwise available only to someone inside the private area; it would be as if, in this case, the thermal imager presented a view of the heat-generating activity inside petitioner's home. By contrast, the thermal imager here disclosed only the relative amounts of heat radiating from the house; it would be as if, in *Katz*, the listening device disclosed only the relative volume of sound leaving the booth, which presumably was discernible in the public domain. * * *

Second, the Court argues that the permissibility of "through-the-wall surveillance" cannot depend on a distinction between observing "intimate details" such as "the lady of the house [taking] her daily sauna and bath," and noticing only "the nonintimate rug on the vestibule floor" or "objects no smaller than 36 by 36 inches." This entire argument assumes, of course, that the thermal imager in this case could or did perform "through-the-wall surveillance" that could identify any detail "that would previously have been unknowable without physical intrusion." In fact, the device could not and did not enable its user to identify either the lady of the house, the rug on the vestibule floor, or anything else inside the house, whether smaller or larger than 36 by 36 inches. * * *

Although the Court is properly and commendably concerned about the threats to privacy that may flow from advances in the technology available to the law enforcement profession, it has unfortunately failed to heed the tried and true counsel of judicial restraint. Instead of concentrating on the rather mundane issue that is actually presented by the case before it, the Court has endeavored to craft an all-encompassing rule for the future. It would be far wiser to give legislators an unimpeded opportunity to grapple with these emerging issues rather than to shackle them with prematurely devised constitutional constraints. * * *

Notes and Questions

1. ***Katz vs. Kyllo.*** Is it a fair conclusion, as stated in Richard H. Seamon, *Kyllo v. United States and the Partial Ascendance of Justice Scalia's Fourth Amendment*, 79 Wash.U.L.Q. 1013, 1022 (2001), that "the *Kyllo* majority did not apply the *Katz* test to the case before it"? If so, has Justice Scalia thereby avoided

the faults he attributed to that test in *Minnesota v. Carter*, p. 900, namely that it "has no plausible foundation in the text of the Fourth Amendment," is "notoriously unhelpful" in identifying what government conduct constitutes a search, and is "self-indulgent" because it allows judges to decide what privacy expectations are "reasonable"?

2. ***The canine nose.*** In UNITED STATES v. PLACE, 462 U.S. 696 (1983), dealing with a temporary seizure of luggage at an airport so that it could be brought into contact with a drug detection dog, the majority declared "that a person possesses a privacy interest in the contents of personal luggage that is protected by the Fourth Amendment. A 'canine sniff' by a well-trained narcotics detection dog, however, does not require opening the luggage. It does not expose noncontraband items that otherwise would remain hidden from public view, as does, for example, an officer's rummaging through the contents of the luggage. Thus, the manner in which information is obtained through this investigative technique is much less intrusive than a typical search. Moreover, the sniff discloses only the presence or absence of narcotics, a contraband item. Thus, despite the fact that the sniff tells the authorities something about the contents of the luggage, the information obtained is limited. This limited disclosure also ensures that the owner of the property is not subjected to the embarrassment and inconvenience entailed in less discriminate and more intrusive investigative methods.

"In these respects, the canine sniff is *sui generis.* We are aware of no other investigative procedure that is so limited both in the manner in which the information is obtained and in the content of the information revealed by the procedure. Therefore, we conclude that the particular course of investigation that the agents intended to pursue here—exposure of respondent's luggage, which was located in a public place, to a trained canine—did not constitute a 'search' within the meaning of the Fourth Amendment."[a]

Is the notion that "the fourth amendment exists to protect the innocent and may normally be invoked by the guilty only when necessary to protect the innocent," so that "if a device could be invented that accurately detected weapons and did not disrupt the normal movement of people, there could be no fourth amendment objection to its use"? Arnold H. Loewy, *The Fourth Amendment as a Device for Protecting the Innocent,* 81 Mich.L.Rev. 1229, 1246, 1248 (1983). Is the use of these dogs nonetheless objectionable because people have a right to be free of unwanted suspicion, Martin R. Gardner, *Sniffing for Drugs in the Classroom,* 74 Nw.U.L.Rev. 803, 844–47 (1980), or is the answer that the innocent are benefited by "the dog that freed them from the unwarranted suspicion which otherwise would have continued"? Loewy, supra, at 1247. What then of other concerns about the use of such dogs: "To the extent that the dog is less than perfectly accurate, innocent people run the risk of being searched. Additionally, the very act of being subjected to a body sniff by a German Shepherd may be offensive at best or harrowing at worst to the innocent sniffee." Id. at 1246–47.

In ILLINOIS v. CABALLES, p. 428, *Place* was reaffirmed and applied to a dog sniff of a vehicle during a traffic stop, but dissenting Justice Souter argued for a contrary conclusion because the drug dog's "supposed infallibility is belied by judicial opinions describing well-trained animals sniffing and alerting with less

a. Brennan and Marshall, JJ., concurring in the result, objected that this issue, neither reached by the court of appeals nor briefed and argued in the Supreme Court, should not be decided in "a discussion unnecessary to the judgment." Blackmun, J., concurring separately, expressed the same concern and added: "While the Court has adopted one plausible analysis of the issue, there are others. For example, a dog sniff may be a search, but a minimally intrusive one that could be justified in this situation under *Terry* upon mere reasonable suspicion."

than perfect accuracy, whether owing to errors by their handlers, the limitations of the dogs themselves, or even the pervasive contamination of currency by cocaine": "Once the dog's fallibility is recognized, however, that ends the justification claimed in *Place* for treating the sniff as sui generis under the Fourth Amendment: the sniff alert does not necessarily signal hidden contraband, and opening the container or enclosed space whose emanations the dog has sensed will not necessarily reveal contraband or any other evidence of crime. This is not, of course, to deny that a dog's reaction may provide reasonable suspicion, or probable cause, to search the container or enclosure; the Fourth Amendment does not demand certainty of success to justify a search for evidence or contraband. The point is simply that the sniff and alert cannot claim the certainty that *Place* assumed, both in treating the deliberate use of sniffing dogs as sui generis and then taking that characterization as a reason to say they are not searches subject to Fourth Amendment scrutiny. And when that aura of uniqueness disappears, there is no basis in *Place*'s reasoning, and no good reason otherwise, to ignore the actual function that dog sniffs perform. They are conducted to obtain information about the contents of private spaces beyond anything that human senses could perceive, even when conventionally enhanced. The information is not provided by independent third parties beyond the reach of constitutional limitations, but gathered by the government's own officers in order to justify searches of the traditional sort, which may or may not reveal evidence of crime but will disclose anything meant to be kept private in the area searched. Thus in practice the government's use of a trained narcotics dog functions as a limited search to reveal undisclosed facts about private enclosures, to be used to justify a further and complete search of the enclosed area. And given the fallibility of the dog, the sniff is the first step in a process that may disclose 'intimate details' without revealing contraband, just as a thermal-imaging device might do, as described in *Kyllo*."

Place was relied upon in *United States v. Jacobsen,* p. 244, holding that where police lawfully came upon a white powder in a package originally opened by private parties, an on-the-spot chemical test of a trace of the powder which would reveal only whether or not it was cocaine was not a search. "Here, as in *Place,* the likelihood that official conduct of the kind disclosed by the record will actually compromise any legitimate interest in privacy seems much too remote to characterize the testing as a search subject to the Fourth Amendment." Brennan and Marshall, JJ., dissenting, objected that "under the Court's analysis in these cases, law enforcement officers could release a trained cocaine-sensitive dog * * * to roam the streets at random, alerting the officers to people carrying cocaine. Or, if a device were developed that, when aimed at a person, would detect instantaneously whether the person is carrying cocaine, there would be no Fourth Amendment bar, under the Court's approach, to the police setting up such a device on a street corner and scanning all passersby. In fact, the Court's analysis is so unbounded that if a device were developed that could detect, from the outside of a building, the presence of cocaine inside, there would be no constitutional obstacle to the police cruising through a residential neighborhood and using the device to identify all homes in which the drug is present."[b]

3. *Weapons detector.* The device imagined by Prof. Loewy back in 1983 may now be a reality. As a result of Department of Justice funding, several organizations are developing concealed weapons detection technology in order to

b. What if a dog were utilized for this purpose? Compare *United States v. Thomas,* 757 F.2d 1359 (2d Cir.1985) (reading *Place* with *United States v. Karo,* p. 265, and concluding such use of those dogs is a search); with *United States v. Colyer,* 878 F.2d 469 (D.C.Cir.1989) (questioning and distinguishing *Thomas* in holding there was no search where a drug dog in the public corridor of a train "alerted" to a particular sleeper compartment). Is *Kyllo* irrelevant on this issue because, as asserted in *State v. Bergmann,* 633 N.W.2d 328 (Iowa 2001), "a drug sniffing dog is not 'technology' of the type addressed in *Kyllo*."

produce a commercially and technologically viable device that can do an "electronic frisk" of a suspect from a distance of ten to twenty feet. Two of the detectors use magnetic fields, albeit in quite different ways. Raytheon's device illuminates the subject with a low intensity electromagnetic pulse and then measures the time decay of the radiated energy from metal objects carried by the person. The device detects only metal objects, but produces no images. Rather, by measurement of the intensity and the time decay of the secondary radiation, there are produced "signatures" which can be identified as indicating whether the detected metal object is or is not a gun. By comparison, the INEL system uses magnetic gradiometers to measure fluctuations produced when anything made of ferromagnetic material moves through the earth's magnetic field. No electronic energy is directed at the subject, as these instruments merely measure what certain objects do to the earth's magnetic field. By use of target recognition software, the readings are compared with known "signatures" of weapons of similar mass, shape and density to determine the likelihood that the device has focused upon a weapon. The third device, the Millitech system, uses passive millimeter wave imaging technology. The amplitude of radiation at which the waves are emitted varies with the object's temperature and other properties, and thus the Millitech detector scans the waves emitted by the human body and any objects concealed on the person and produces a small image on the back of the device in which the outlines of concealed objects, usually dark, are clearly visible against the much brighter image of the body.

Would the use of any or all of these systems constitute a Fourth Amendment search? Would the answer be the same in those twenty-five jurisdictions which have enacted some variety of a concealed weapon permit statute? See David Harris, *Superman's X–Ray Vision and the Fourth Amendment: The New Gun Detection Technology*, 69 Temple L.Rev. 1 (1996).

4. ***Electronic tracking.*** With the consent of a chemical company, police installed a "beeper," a battery operated radio transmitter, into a container of chloroform, a chemical used to manufacture illicit drugs, prior to its purchase. By a combination of visual surveillance and monitoring of the beeper signal the police tracked the container as it was carried in Petschen's automobile to Knotts' cabin in a rural area. On that evidence and other information, a search warrant for the cabin was issued, and an illicit drug lab was discovered within. In *United States v. Knotts,* 460 U.S. 276 (1983), the Court held that the use of the "beeper" did not constitute a Fourth Amendment search:

"Visual surveillance from public places along Petschen's route or adjoining Knotts' premises would have sufficed to reveal all of these facts to the police. The fact that the officers in this case relied not only on visual surveillance, but on the use of the beeper to signal the presence of Petschen's automobile to the police receiver, does not alter the situation. Nothing in the Fourth Amendment prohibited the police from augmenting the sensory faculties bestowed upon them at birth with such enhancement as science and technology afforded them in this case." To Knotts' objection that under such a view "twenty-four hour surveillance of any citizen of this country will be possible, without judicial knowledge or supervision," the Court responded that "if such dragnet type law enforcement practices as respondent envisions should eventually occur, there will be time enough then to determine whether different constitutional principles may be applicable."

In UNITED STATES v. KARO, 468 U.S. 705 (1984), the Court was "called upon to address two questions left unresolved in *Knotts:* (1) whether installation of a beeper in a container of chemicals with the consent of the original owner constitutes a search or seizure within the meaning of the Fourth Amendment when the container is delivered to a buyer having no knowledge of the presence of the beeper, and (2) whether monitoring of a beeper falls within the ambit of the

Fourth Amendment when it reveals information that could not have been obtained through visual surveillance." The Court, per WHITE, J., answered the first question in the negative, reasoning that the mere transfer of the can containing an unmonitored beeper "infringed no privacy interest" because it "conveyed no information that [the recipient] wished to keep private, for it conveyed no information at all," and thus was no search, and that "it cannot be said that anyone's possessory interest was interfered with in a meaningful way," and thus there was no seizure. (STEVENS, Brennan and Marshall, JJ., dissenting on this branch of the case, argued that by "attaching the beeper and using the container to conceal it, the Government in the most fundamental sense was asserting 'dominion and control' over the property," which "is a 'seizure' in the most basic sense of the term.")

The Court answered the second question in the affirmative, first noting that unquestionably it would be an unreasonable search to surreptitiously enter a residence without a warrant to verify that the container was there. "For purpose of the Amendment, the result is the same where, without a warrant, the Government surreptitiously employs an electronic device to obtain information that it could not have obtained by observation from outside the curtilage of the house. The beeper tells the agent that a particular article is actually located at a particular time in the private residence and is in the possession of the person or persons whose residence is being surveilled. Even if visual surveillance has revealed that the article to which the beeper is attached has entered the house, the later monitoring not only verifies the officers' observations but also establishes that the article remains on the premises." The Court next concluded that absent "truly exigent circumstances" such use of the beeper was governed by "the general rule that a search of a house should be conducted pursuant to a warrant."[c] Such monitoring was characterized by the Court as "less intrusive than a full-scale search," but the Court did not have occasion to decide whether as a consequence such a warrant could issue upon reasonable suspicion rather than probable cause.[d]

5. *Cellular phone tracking.* An FCC rule requires cellular telephone companies to have the capability of determining the location from which a cellular phone call originates to within 125 meters. "The cellular telephone call location technology now mandated by the FCC will turn each of the more than fifty million cell phones in the United States into a tracking device. It will enable police not just to pinpoint the location of cell phone calls to 911 operators, but to track the location of all cellular phone users, no matter who they are calling, both as they are actually making calls and after the fact through phone company computer records. Moreover, because cellular telephones send out signals to the cellular system every few minutes to keep the system informed of their location, police will be able to remotely track any individual with a cellular telephone that is turned on, whether or not they are actually placing a call. Cellular telephone location technology thus will provide law enforcement with an extraordinarily powerful new tool for monitoring the movement of individuals."[e] In light of *Smith v. Maryland*, p. 251, and *Karo*, p. 265, is law enforcement use of this technology a search?

c. In response to the government's claim that a warrant should not be required because of the difficulty in satisfying the particularity requirement of the Fourth Amendment, in that it is usually not known in advance to what place the container with the beeper in it will be taken, the Court concluded that it would suffice if the warrant were "to describe the object into which the beeper is to be placed, the circumstances that led agents to wish to install the beeper, and the length of time for which beeper surveillance is requested."

d. See Clifford Fishman, *Electronic Tracking Devices and the Fourth Amendment: Knotts, Karo, and the Questions Still Unanswered,* 34 Cath.U.L.Rev. 277 (1985).

e. Note, 10 Stan.L. & Pol'y Rev. 103, 104 (1998).

6. ***Photographic magnification.*** In DOW CHEMICAL CO. v. UNITED STATES, 476 U.S. 227 (1986), the Court, per BURGER, C.J., held that aerial photography of a chemical company's industrial complex was not a Fourth Amendment "search": "It may well be, as the Government concedes, that surveillance of private property by using highly sophisticated surveillance equipment not generally available to the public, such as satellite technology, might be constitutionally proscribed absent a warrant. But the photographs here are not so revealing of intimate details as to raise constitutional concerns. Although they undoubtedly give EPA more detailed information than naked-eye views, they remain limited to an outline of the facility's buildings and equipment. The mere fact that human vision is enhanced somewhat, at least to the degree here, does not give rise to constitutional problems.[6] An electronic device to penetrate walls or windows so as to hear and record confidential discussions of chemical formulae or other trade secrets would raise very different and far more serious questions; other protections such as trade secret laws are available to protect commercial activities from private surveillance by competitors.

"We conclude that the open areas of an industrial plant complex with numerous plant structures spread over an area of 2,000 acres are not analogous to the 'curtilage' of a dwelling for purposes of aerial surveillance; such an industrial complex is more comparable to an open field and as such it is open to the view and observation of persons in aircraft lawfully in the public airspace immediately above or sufficiently near the area for the reach of cameras."

POWELL, J., for the dissenters, objected that "Dow has taken every feasible step to protect information claimed to constitute trade secrets from the public and particularly from its competitors," and accordingly "has a reasonable expectation of privacy in its commercial facility in the sense required by the Fourth Amendment." Moreover, the rationale of *Ciraolo,* [p. 252], is inapplicable here, for "the camera used in this case was highly sophisticated in terms of its capability to reveal minute details of Dow's confidential technology and equipment. The District Court found that the photographs revealed details as 'small as ½ inch in diameter.' Satellite photography hardly could have been more informative about Dow's technology. Nor are 'members of the public' likely to purchase $22,000.00 cameras."

7. ***Enclosed space detection system.*** "The ESDS, or heartbeat detector, is a surveillance tool designed to detect the presence of people 'hiding in enclosed spaces of vehicles' by identifying the presence of a 'human ballistocardiogram.' With each beat of the human heart, a ballistocardiogram or a small mechanical shock wave propagates through the body. This shock wave, in turn, causes the entire vehicle holding the person to vibrate 'at a frequency dissimilar from any other source.'

"The heart's ability to move an entire vehicle, even a big truck, provides law enforcement with a previously unavailable window through which to view the contents of vehicles passing at various checkpoints. Officers can merely require known occupants to turn off the engine and exit the vehicle. Then, such officers

6. The partial dissent emphasizes Dow's claim that under magnification power lines as small as ½-inch diameter can be observed. But a glance at the photographs in issue shows that those power lines are observable only because of their stark contrast with the snow-white background. No objects as small as ½—inch diameter such as a class ring, for example, are recognizable, nor are there any identifiable human faces or secret documents captured in such a fashion as to implicate more serious privacy concerns. Fourth Amendment cases must be decided on the facts of each case, not by extravagant generalizations. "[W]e have never held that potential, as opposed to actual, invasions of privacy constitute searches for purposes of the Fourth Amendment." *United States v. Karo,* [p. 265]. On these facts, nothing in these photographs suggests that any reasonable expectations of privacy have been infringed.

temporarily can place 'sensitive seismic geophones' on the 'roof, bumper, or other flat surface' of the vehicle. When a heartbeat's vibrations move a weight suspended in an electromagnetic field of a geophone, the reaction generates an electrical signal. This signal then transmits to a computer that determines whether a beating heart concealed within the vehicle caused the small vibrations."[f] Does detection of a person in this way sometimes/always not constitute a search because "the heartbeat detector is as limited as a canine sniff both in manner of obtaining facts and in the content of the information it reveals"?[g]

8. *Interception of computer communications.* By use of an Internet surveillance software originally known as Carnivore but now denominated DCS1000, the FBI has the capability to intercept e-mail communications by using an access point of an Internet service provider to access and then filter all traffic from a suspect.[h] Such interception is a search, it is argued, as "e-mail offers security equal to or greater than U.S. and commercial mail, faxes, and land-line telephone conversations," and hence "an e-mail user's expectation of privacy should be equal to or greater than those forms of communications."[i] The seminal case on this issue, *United States v. Maxwell*, 45 M.J.406 (A.F.Ct.Crim.App.1996), drew upon those parallels and then concluded without hesitation "that the transmitter of an e-mail message enjoys a reasonable expectation that police officials will not intercept the transmission without probable cause and a search warrant." *Maxwell* cautions that once e-mail "transmissions are received by another person, the transmitter no longer controls its destiny," meaning the sender has no valid Fourth Amendment complaint should the recipient turn the message over to the police, forward it on to others, or turn out to be an undercover police officer. How important to the result in *Maxwell* is the fact that the e-mail service was provided by AOL, which contractually agreed with subscribers not to read or disclose the content of their e-mail? See *United States v. Monroe*, 52 M.J. 326 (A.F.Ct.Crim.App.2000). Should *Maxwell* apply to chat-room conversations? See *Commonwealth v. Proetto,* 771 A.2d 823 (Pa.Super.2001).

9. *Decryption.* Especially because of the development of this technology, more sophisticated criminals have undertaken to safeguard their data and communications by encryption, whereby plain text is encrypted with one key and then can be decrypted only by the person who has the other key, which is itself encrypted on the recipent's machine using a password or secret key. That development prompted the proposal in the mid–1990s of "key escrow" legislation, whereby all developers of encryption software would be required to provide a key to the code, retained by "trusted third parties," who could turn the information over to law enforcement authorities in specified circumstances. Had such legislation been enacted, would decryption via "key escrow" itself constitute a search? Cf. *United States v. Scott*, p. 252.

Absent such legislation, law enforcement looked to new technology, namely, a "keystroke logging" system which, when embedded in the host computer, captures each keystroke made when no communications device is being simultaneously used, providing the information needed to decrypt any encrypted communication. As originally developed, it was necessary for law enforcement agents to surreptitiously physically enter the premises where the computer in question was located and physically install the device on that computer, a process deemed in its entirety unquestionably to constitute a search, *United States v. Scarfo*, 180

f. George M. Dery, *The Loss of Privacy is Just a Heartbeat Away: An Exploration of Government Heartbeat Detection Technology and Its Impact on Fourth Amendment Protections*, 7 Wm. & Mary Bill Rts. J. 401, 403–04 (1999).

g. Id. at 424.

h. See John Lewis, *Carnivore—The FBI's Internet Surveillance System*, 23 Whittier L.Rev. 317 (2001).

i. Comment, 80 N.C.L.Rev. 315, 342 (2001).

F.Supp.2d 572 (D.N.J.2001). But more recently the FBI has developed a software version of such a system (called "Magic Lantern") that uses a computer virus for remote installation of the device, which then records keystrokes typed on the computer and e-mails the data out to law enforcement personnel. Is that activity not a search because it is merely "the cyber-equivalent of the dog sniff in *Place*"? Ku, *The Founder's Privacy: The Fourth Amendment and the Power of Technological Surveillance*, 86 Minn.L.Rev. 1325, 1352 (2002). Is it relevant that such "software versions of a keystroke logging system are commercially available on the Internet"?[j]

10. ***CRT Microspy.*** "Due to the electromagnetic nature of computer equipment it is possible to monitor computer activity from a location as remote as five hundred feet with specialized electronic surveillance equipment. Computers, monitors, keyboards, and printers leak electronic signals in all directions in the form of radio frequency energy. A receiver specifically designed for the task can pick up these radio waves and display the captured images on a monitor screen. * * * Computers can be shielded from remote surveillance, but such protection is quite expensive [and thus] it seems unlikely that ordinary computer users would take this precaution, making their computer activity vulnerable to microspy scanning. * * * Computers and their peripherals broadcast radio signals in all directions, just like waves emanating from a stone dropped in water. Also, computer monitors bear an FCC warning alerting users to the fact that they are unintentional radiators."[k] Does the presence of those two factors, similar to those relied upon in denying Fourth Amendment protection to the earlier, unsophisticated cordless telephones, e.g., *State v. Smith*, 438 N.W.2d 571 (Wis.1989), mean that law enforcement use of CRT Microspy to obtain copies of images a person displays on his office or home computer does not constitute a search?

11. ***Digital contraband detector.*** Another "special technique for acquiring otherwise-private computer data * * * is unique because it discovers only 'digital contraband' (that is, 'any computer file that, outside of very specific authorized exceptions, cannot be legally possessed,' such as 'digital videos of child pornography' or 'a "cracked" copy of a commercial program—one that has been illegally modified to remove licensing protection'). Apparently a computer program can be designed to search through any hard drive connected to the Internet for a file matching one already in possession of the person making such a search. Indeed, it even may be possible to run such a search program on a large number of networked hard drives simultaneously. And thus a law enforcement officer who had come into possession of one specific piece of digital contraband might then run a Net-wide search for that very contraband. In doing so, he might 'identify dozens, hundreds, or even thousands of individuals who did have a copy on their computer and for whom he would then have probable cause to request a search warrant.' Such a search, to be sure, 'presents a novel set of characteristics: As part of a dragnet search, individuals' hard drives are searched without their permission and without any particularized cause to believe them guilty, and the search scans through a vast amount of very personal information located within people's offices and homes. At the same time, however, the search has a minimal impact on property, produces no false positives, need not be noticeable, and reveals nothing to officials beyond the identity of some individuals who possess

j. Note, 2002 U.Ill.J.L.Tech & Pol'y 193, 199. "Hundreds of these products are available, and the most frequent civilian consumers are companies who monitor employees' computer habits while on the job, parents interested in knowing what their children do online, and suspicious spouses who try to short-circuit the dreaded on-line love affair." Note, 70 U.M.K.C.L.Rev. 751, 768 (2002).

k. Note, 60 U.M.K.C.L.Rev. 139, 143, 164 (1991).

this particular piece of digital contraband.' "[l] Would use of such a computer program constitute a search?

12. ***Facial character recognition.*** "Although few spectators at last Sunday's Super Bowl were aware of it, surveillance cameras photographed their faces as they filed into Raymond James Stadium. Those images were then relayed instantly by cable to computers that scanned and compared them with images in a police database of criminals and criminal suspects. A Tampa Bay police spokesman described the system as a potentially 'priceless' tool for detecting dangerous individuals and preventing terrorist acts. * * * Citizens do accept surveillance cameras at, say, automated teller machines to help deter robbery and provide a sense of safety. But the Super Bowl snooping represented random surveillance of a huge public event, exploiting not one but two potentially invasive technologies. One is video surveillance, which has become increasingly common throughout American society. The other is what is known as facial character recognition, a technology that allows computers to create and compare digital images using 128 facial characteristics."[m] Is such use of this technology a search, or, as a Tampa councilman said when the police placed three dozen cameras with face-recognition software in a downtown district popular with locals and tourists. is it "no different than having a cop walking around with a mug shot"[n]? What then of what might be called "vehicle character recognition," a digital license plate reader[o] which can read a license plate from 250 feet away and thus identify a vehicle as being at a certain place (e.g., an airport parking lot) at a particular time or as being involved in a videotaped offense (e.g., running a red light)?

13. ***Gas chromatography*** involves using an extremely sensitive filtering machine to break down a gas sample or a liquid mixture into its molecular subcomponents. The sample to be tested is forced through a column, which is a glass tube filled with special filtration material, and a detector attached at the outgoing end of the column records the quantity and concentration of each particular molecular compound contained in the sample. Government-funded product development in recent years has turned GC from simply "a scientific laboratory technique" to one that is also used "on the streets." A law enforcement agent can use an eight-pound sampling unit, which resembles a large flashlight and works like a vacuum, to suck in vapors and particles from the immediate vicinity of a suspected container or individual. The analytical unit, also at the scene, then takes this sample and produces a chemical sketch of it, which is then compared to the make-up of known explosives (under one version of the equipment) or drugs (under another). The assumption is that a positive GC report establishes the presence of explosives or drugs, as the case may be, upon the object person or within the object container. Is such use of a portable unit, sometimes characterized as an "electronic canine," governed by the *Place* decision, p. 263? See Peter J. Bober, *The "Chemical Signature" of the Fourth Amendment: Gas Chromatography/Mass Spectometry and the War on Drugs*, 8 Seton Hall Const.L.J. 75 (1997).

14. ***Passive alcohol sensor.*** "The latest invention in fighting crime is the P.A.S. III. Developed under the direction of various insurance and highway safety organizations and touted as non-intrusive, this innocuous looking flashlight with a

l. SEARCHSZR § 2.6, quoting Note, 105 Yale L.J. 1093 (1996).

m. *Super Bowl Snooping*, N.Y.Times, Feb. 4, 2001, at § 4, p. 16. There has also been discussion of using such equipment at airport checkins, with the cameras linked to a database of potential terrorists. Barnaby J. Feder, *Exploring Technology to Protect Passengers With Fingerprint or Retina Scans*, N.Y. Times, Sept. 19, 2001, at B3.

n. Dana Canedy, *TV Cameras Seek Criminals in Tampa's Crowds*, N.Y.Times, July 4, 2001, at A1.

o. See Catherine Greenman, *Zeroing In on the Suspicious Number Above the State Motto*, N.Y.Times, Oct. 25, 2001, at D11.

built-in breathalyzer is being used to analyze a driver's breath without their participation or consent. The sensor that is attached to the flashlight is an electrochemical fuel cell that detects the presence of alcohol in the air of the car.

"In order to analyze a driver's breath, the tool needs to be held within ten inches from the driver as the driver is exhaling. In order to obtain a sample of exhaled air, the Sniffer's manufacturer, PAS Systems International, suggests that the officer request the driver to give their name, address, and date of birth. A pump within the sensor draws in a sample of the exhaled breath as well as the air in the car and the fuel cell analyzes the amount of alcohol in the sample. A bar display on the flashlight indicates the possible blood alcohol content detected. The display ranges from green to red, which corresponds to an approximate blood alcohol content range of .01 to .12. For daytime use, an innocuous looking clipboard with an attached breathalyzer serves the same function." Note, 9 J.L. & Pol'y 835, 857–58 (2001).

Assuming a lawfully stopped vehicle, should use of this device "be deemed to constitute a search," id. at 866, or do such cases as *Place*, p. 263, *Knotts*, p. 265, *Dionisio* and *Mara*, both p. 437, mean "there is ample precedent for finding use of the sensor is not a search," Michele Fields & Andrew R. Hricko, *Passive Alcohol Sensor—Constitutional Implications*, 20 The Prosecutor 45 (Summer, 1986). Of what relevance, if any, is *Kyllo*, p. 257?

In *Gouled v. United States,* 255 U.S. 298 (1921), the Court held that search warrants "may not be used as a means of gaining access to a man's house or office and papers solely for the purpose of making search to secure evidence to be used against him in a criminal or penal proceeding." The Court derived from *Boyd v. United States,* p. 804, the proposition that warrants may be resorted to "only when a primary right to such search and seizure may be found in the interest which the public or the complainant may have in the property to be seized, or in the right to the possession of it, or when a valid exercise of the police power renders possession of the property by the accused unlawful and provides that it may be taken," that is, when the property is an instrumentality or fruit of crime or contraband. This "mere evidence" rule, as it came to be called, was finally repudiated in *Warden v. Hayden,* 387 U.S. 294 (1967). Stressing that "the principal object of the Fourth Amendment is the protection of privacy rather than property," the Court noted that "privacy 'would be just as well served by a restriction on search to the even-numbered days of the month. * * * And it would have the extra advantage of avoiding hair-splitting questions.' " The government need not have a property interest in the property to be seized, as "government has an interest in solving crime," and that interest and the protection of privacy are best accommodated, the Court reasoned, by merely requiring probable cause that "the evidence sought will aid in a particular apprehension or conviction." But the Court cautioned:

"The items of clothing involved in this case are not 'testimonial' or 'communicative' in nature, and their introduction therefore did not compel respondent to become a witness against himself in violation of the Fifth Amendment. This case thus does not require that we consider whether there are items of evidential value whose very nature precludes them from being the object of a reasonable search and seizure."

ANDRESEN v. MARYLAND

427 U.S. 463, 96 S.Ct. 2737, 49 L.Ed.2d 627 (1976).

Justice BLACKMUN delivered the opinion of the Court.

[State authorities obtained search warrants to search petitioner's law office and also corporate offices for specified documents pertaining to a fraudulent sale of land. The papers found in the execution of the warrants were admitted against the petitioner at his trial, and he was convicted.]

The Fifth Amendment * * * provides that "[n]o person * * * shall be compelled in any criminal case to be a witness against himself." * * * The "historic function" of the privilege has been to protect a " 'natural individual from compulsory incrimination through his own testimony or personal records.' " There is no question that the records seized from petitioner's offices and introduced against him were incriminating. Moreover, it is undisputed that some of these business records contain statements made by petitioner. The question, therefore, is whether the seizure of these business records, and their admission into evidence at his trial, compelled petitioner to testify against himself in violation of the Fifth Amendment. This question may be said to have been reserved in *Warden v. Hayden.*

Petitioner contends that "the Fifth Amendment prohibition against compulsory self-incrimination applies as well to personal business papers seized from his offices as it does to the same papers being required to be produced under a subpoena." He bases his argument, naturally, on dicta in a number of cases which imply, or state, that the search for and seizure of a person's private papers violate the privilege against self-incrimination. Thus, in *Boyd v. United States* the Court said: "[W]e have been unable to perceive that the seizure of a man's private books and papers to be used in evidence against him is substantially different from compelling him to be a witness against himself." And in *Hale v. Henkel* [p. 809], it was observed that "the substance of the offense is the compulsory production of private papers, whether under a search warrant or a *subpoena duces tecum,* against which the person * * * is entitled to protection."

We do not agree, however, that these broad statements compel suppression of this petitioner's business records as a violation of the Fifth Amendment. In the very recent case of *Fisher v. United States* [p. 857], the Court held that an attorney's production, pursuant to a lawful summons, of his client's tax records in his hands did not violate the Fifth Amendment privilege of the taxpayer "because enforcement against a taxpayer's lawyer would not 'compel' the taxpayer to do anything—and certainly would not compel him to be a 'witness' against himself." We recognized that the continued validity of the broad statements contained in some of the Court's earlier cases had been discredited by later opinions. In those earlier cases, the legal predicate for the inadmissibility of the evidence seized was a violation of the Fourth Amendment; the unlawfulness of the search and seizure was thought to supply the compulsion of the accused necessary to invoke the Fifth Amendment. Compulsion of the accused was also absent in *Couch v. United States,* 409 U.S. 322 (1973), where the Court held that a summons served on a taxpayer's accountant requiring him to produce the taxpayer's personal business records in his possession did not violate the taxpayer's Fifth Amendment rights.

Similarly, in this case, petitioner was not asked to say or to do anything. The records seized contained statements that petitioner had voluntarily committed to writing. The search for and seizure of these records were conducted by law enforcement personnel. Finally, when these records were introduced at trial, they were authenticated by a handwriting expert, not by petitioner. Any compulsion of petitioner to speak, other than the inherent psychological pressure to respond at trial to unfavorable evidence, was not present.

This case thus falls within the principle stated by Mr. Justice Holmes: "A party is privileged from producing the evidence but not from its production." * * * Thus, although the Fifth Amendment may protect an individual from complying with a subpoena for the production of his personal records in his possession because the very act of production may constitute a compulsory authentication of incriminating information, a seizure of the same materials by law enforcement officers differs in a crucial respect—the individual against whom the search is directed is not required to aid in the discovery, production, or authentication of incriminating evidence. * * *

Moreover, a contrary determination would prohibit the admission of evidence traditionally used in criminal cases and traditionally admissible despite the Fifth Amendment. For example, it would bar the admission of an accused's gambling records in a prosecution for gambling; a note given temporarily to a bank teller during a robbery and subsequently seized in the accused's automobile or home in a prosecution for bank robbery; and incriminating notes prepared, but not sent, by an accused in a kidnapping or blackmail prosecution. * * *

In this case, petitioner, at the time he recorded his communication, at the time of the search, and at the time the records were admitted at trial, was not subjected to "the cruel trilemma of self-accusation, perjury or contempt." Indeed, he was never required to say or to do anything under penalty of sanction. Similarly, permitting the admission of the records in question does not convert our accusatorial system of justice into an inquisitorial system. * * *

Justice BRENNAN, dissenting. * * *

Until today, no decision by this Court had held that the seizure of testimonial evidence by legal process did not violate the Fifth Amendment. Indeed, with few exceptions, the indications were strongly to the contrary. * * * These cases all reflect the root understanding of *Boyd v. United States:* "It is not the breaking of his doors, and the rummaging of his drawers, that constitutes the essence of the offence [to the Fifth Amendment]; but it is the invasion of his indefeasible right of personal security, personal liberty and private property. * * * [A]ny forcible and compulsory extortion of a man's own testimony or his private papers to be used as evidence to convict him of crime * * *, is within the condemnation of [the Amendment]. In this regard the fourth and fifth amendments run almost into each other."[a]

Notes and Questions

1. If the item to be seized was a diary instead of the business records in *Andresen,* would there be a stronger Fourth Amendment[b] or Fifth Amendment[c] argument against permitting the seizure? Consider *Model Pre–Arraignment Code* § SS 210.3(2): "With the exception of handwriting samples, and other writings or recordings of evidentiary value for reasons other than their testimonial content, things subject to seizure * * * shall not include personal diaries, letters, or other writings or recordings, made solely for private use or communication to an

a. Marshall, J., dissented on other grounds and thus found it unnecessary to reach the Fifth Amendment issue.

b. In *Fisher,* relied upon in *Andresen,* the Court, after stating that the taxpayers "have not raised arguments of a Fourth Amendment nature * * * and could not be successful if they had," cautioned that the "[s]pecial problems of privacy which might be presented by subpoena of a personal diary * * * are not involved here." See also fn. 7 on p. 859.

c. "[I]t has been thought that a diary in which its author has recited his criminal conduct, seized in an otherwise lawful search, should not be used against him, just as any other kind of involuntary confession is unusable under the Fifth Amendment." *United States v. Boyette,* 299 F.2d 92 (4th Cir.1962).

individual occupying a family, personal, or other confidential relation, other than a relation in criminal enterprise, unless such things have served or are serving a substantial purpose in furtherance of a criminal enterprise."

2. In ZURCHER v. STANFORD DAILY, 436 U.S. 547 (1978), police obtained and executed a warrant to search the offices of the Stanford Daily for negatives, film and pictures relevant to identification of those who had injured nine policemen during a campus demonstration. The Daily later brought a civil action in federal district court, where declaratory relief was granted. That court held (i) that the Fourth Amendment forbade the issuance of a warrant to search for materials in the possession of one not suspected of crime except upon a showing of probable cause a subpoena *duces tecum* would be impracticable; and (ii) that the First Amendment bars search of newspaper offices except upon a clear showing that important materials would otherwise be destroyed or removed and that a restraining order would be futile.

The Supreme Court, per WHITE, J., concluded that "it is untenable to conclude that property may not be searched unless its occupant is reasonably suspected of crime and is subject to arrest. * * * The Fourth Amendment has itself struck the balance between privacy and public need, and there is no occasion or justification for a court to revise the Amendment and strike a new balance by denying the search warrant in the circumstances present here and by insisting that the investigation proceed by subpoena *duces tecum,* whether on the theory that the latter is a less intrusive alternative, or otherwise. * * *

"In any event, the reasons presented by the District Court and adopted by the Court of Appeals for arriving at its remarkable conclusion do not withstand analysis. First, as we have said, it is apparent that whether the third-party occupant is suspect or not, the State's interest in enforcing the criminal law and recovering the evidence remains the same; and it is the seeming innocence of the property owner that the District Court relied on to foreclose the warrant to search. But as respondents themselves now concede, if the third party knows that contraband or other illegal materials are on his property, he is sufficiently culpable to justify the issuance of a search warrant. Similarly, if his ethical stance is the determining factor, it seems to us that whether or not he knows that the sought-after articles are secreted on his property and whether or not he knows that the articles are in fact the fruits, instrumentalities, or evidence of crime, he will be so informed when the search warrant is served, and it is doubtful that he should then be permitted to object to the search, to withhold, if it is there, the evidence of crime reasonably believed to be possessed by him or secreted on his property, and to forbid the search and insist that the officers serve him with a subpoena *duces tecum.*

"Second, we are unpersuaded that the District Court's new rule denying search warrants against third parties and insisting on subpoenas would substantially further privacy interests without seriously undermining law enforcement efforts. As the District Court understands it, denying third-party search warrants would not have substantial adverse effects on criminal investigations because the nonsuspect third party, once served with a subpoena, will preserve the evidence and ultimately, lawfully respond. The difficulty with this assumption is that search warrants are often employed early in an investigation, perhaps before the identity of any likely criminal and certainly before all the perpetrators are or could be known. The seemingly blameless third party in possession of the fruits or evidence may not be innocent at all; and if he is, he may nevertheless be so related to or so sympathetic with the culpable that he cannot be relied upon to retain and preserve the articles that may implicate his friends, or at least not to notify those who would be damaged by the evidence that the authorities are aware of its location. In any event, it is likely that the real culprits will have access to the property, and the delay involved in employing the subpoena *duces tecum,* offering as it does the opportunity to litigate its validity, could easily result in the disappearance of the evidence, whatever the good faith of the third party. * * *[8]

"We are also not convinced that the net gain to privacy interests by the District Court's new rule would be worth the candle.[9] In the normal course of events, search warrants are more difficult to obtain than subpoenas, since the latter do not involve the judiciary and do not require proof of probable cause. Where, in the real world, subpoenas would suffice, it can be expected that they will be employed by the rational prosecutor. On the other hand, when choice is available under local law and the prosecutor chooses to use the search warrant, it is unlikely that he has needlessly selected the more difficult course. His choice is more likely to be based on the solid belief, arrived at through experience but difficult, if not impossible, to sustain a specific case, that the warranted search is necessary to secure and to avoid the destruction of evidence.

"[The Framers] did not forbid warrants where the press was involved, did not require special showings that subpoenas would be impractical, and did not insist that the owner of the place to be searched, if connected with the press, must be shown to be implicated in the offense being investigated. Further, the prior cases do no more than insist that the courts apply the warrant requirements with particular exactitude when First Amendment interests would be endangered by the search.[d] As we see it, no more than this is required where the warrant requested is for the seizure of criminal evidence reasonably believed to be on the premises occupied by a newspaper. Properly administered, the pre-conditions for a warrant—probable cause, specificity with respect to the place to be searched and the things to be seized, and overall reasonableness—should afford sufficient

8. It is also far from clear, even apart from the dangers of destruction and removal, whether the use of the subpoena *duces tecum* under circumstances where there is probable cause to believe that a crime has been committed and that the materials sought constitute evidence of its commission will result in the production of evidence with sufficient regularity to satisfy the public interest in law enforcement. Unlike the individual whose privacy is invaded by a search, the recipient of a subpoena may assert the Fifth Amendment privilege against self-incrimination in response to a summons to produce evidence or give testimony. See *Maness v. Meyers,* 419 U.S. 449 (1975). This privilege is not restricted to suspects. We have construed it broadly as covering any individual who might be incriminated by the evidence in connection with which the privilege is asserted. *Hoffman v. United States,* 341 U.S. 479 (1951). The burden of overcoming an assertion of the Fifth Amendment privilege, even if prompted by a desire not to cooperate rather than any real fear of self-incrimination, is one which prosecutors would rarely be able to meet in the early stages of an investigation despite the fact they did not regard the witness as a suspect. Even time spent litigating such matters could seriously impede criminal investigations.

9. We reject totally the reasoning of the District Court that additional protections are required to assure that the Fourth Amendment rights of third parties are not violated because of the unavailability of the exclusionary rule as a deterrent to improper searches of premises in the control of nonsuspects. * * * It is probably seldom that police during the investigatory stage when most searches occur will be so convinced that no potential defendant will have standing to exclude evidence on Fourth Amendment grounds that they will feel free to ignore constitutional restraints. * * *

d. This does *not* mean, the Court later held in *New York v. P.J. Video, Inc.,* 475 U.S. 868 (1986), that a higher probable cause standard applies in such cases. The Court deemed sufficient "the longstanding special protections" established in its earlier cases, namely: (a) "that the police may not rely on the 'exigency' exception to the Fourth Amendment's warrant requirement in conducting a seizure of allegedly obscene materials, under circumstances where such a seizure would effectively constitute a 'prior restraint' "; (b) "that the large-scale seizure of books or films constituting a 'prior restraint' must be preceded by an adversary hearing on the question of obscenity"; (c) "that, even where a seizure of allegedly obscene materials would not constitute a 'prior restraint,' but instead would merely preserve evidence for trial, the seizure must be made pursuant to a warrant and there must be an opportunity for a prompt post-seizure judicial determination of obscenity"; and (d) "that a warrant authorizing the seizure of materials presumptively protected by the First Amendment may not issue based solely on the conclusory allegations of a police officer that the sought-after materials are obscene."

protection against the harms that are assertedly threatened by warrants for searching newspaper offices."

Justices STEWART and Marshall, dissenting, raised a First Amendment objection because of the "serious burden on a free press imposed by an unannounced police search of a newspaper office: the possibility of disclosure of information received from confidential sources, or of the identity of the sources themselves. Protection of those sources is necessary to ensure that the press can fulfill its constitutionally designated function of informing the public, because important information can often be obtained only by an assurance that the source will not be revealed.

Justice STEVENS, dissenting, raised a Fourth Amendment objection, namely, that a "showing of probable cause that was adequate to justify the issuance of a warrant to search for stolen goods in the 18th century does not automatically satisfy the new dimensions of the Fourth Amendment in the post-*Hayden* era. * * * The only conceivable justification for an unannounced search of an innocent citizen is the fear that, if notice were given, he would conceal or destroy the object of the search. Probable cause to believe that the custodian is a criminal, or that he holds a criminal's weapons, spoils, or the like, justifies that fear, and therefore such a showing complies with the Clause. But if nothing said under oath in the warrant application demonstrates the need for an unannounced search by force, the probable cause requirement is not satisfied. In the absence of some other showing of reasonableness, the ensuing search violates the Fourth Amendment."

3. Compare *O'Connor v. Johnson,* 287 N.W.2d 400 (Minn.1979), involving a warrant issued for an attorney's office to search for and seize a certain client's business records: "Even the most particular warrant cannot adequately safeguard client confidentiality, the attorney-client privilege, the attorney's work product, and the criminal defendant's constitutional right to counsel of all of the attorney's clients. It is unreasonable, in any case, to permit law enforcement officers to peruse miscellaneous documents in an attorney's office while attempting to locate documents listed in a search warrant. Even if it were possible to meet the particularity requirement regarding the place to be searched, the file would still contain some confidential information that is immune from seizure under the attorney-client privilege or the work product doctrine. Once that information is revealed to the police, the privileges are lost, and the information cannot be erased from the minds of the police. * * *

"It will not unreasonably burden prosecutors' offices and effective law enforcement to require officers to proceed by subpoena duces tecum in seeking documents held by an attorney. Attorneys are required by statute, the Code of Professional Responsibility, and the oath of admission to the bar to preserve and protect the judicial process. Thus, attorneys must respond faithfully and promptly, while still being allowed the opportunity to assert applicable privileges by a motion to quash."

4. It is noted in 67 A.B.A.J. 33 (1981) "that California's legislative response to the problem of surprise searches of offices of 'privilege-holders' may serve as a model for other states. The law calls for appointment of a special master to spearhead the search. * * *

"The California solution hasn't satisfied everyone, however. John Cleary, head of the federal public defender office in San Diego, said the law is 'unhealthy. There is an illusion of protection.' Robert Philibosian, chief assistant California attorney general, said: 'We vigorously opposed [the law].' He said it impairs law enforcement, especially in the white-collar crime area: 'We have to jump through hoops [to obtain evidence].' "[e]

5. Compare *Model Pre–Arraignment Code* §§ 220.5(2) & (3) providing that if the documents to be seized "cannot be searched for or identified without examining the contents of other documents, or if they constitute items or entries in account books, diaries, or other documents containing matter not specified in the warrant, the executing officer shall not examine the documents but shall either impound them under appropriate protection where found, or seal and remove them for safekeeping pending further proceedings." At a later adversary judicial hearing, a motion may be made for return of the documents or for "specification of such conditions and limitations on the further search for the documents to be seized as may be appropriate to prevent unnecessary or unreasonable invasion of privacy." If return is not ordered, "the search shall proceed under such conditions and limitations as the order shall prescribe."

6. In *Tattered Cover, Inc. v. City of Thornton*, 44 P.3d 1044 (Colo.2002), a bookseller brought suit to restrain the police from executing a search warrant for records of the books purchased by a particular customer. The court first concluded that such a warrant "intrudes into areas protected by" the First Amendment, which "embraces the individual's right to purchase and read whatever books she wishes to, without fear that the government will take steps to discover which books she buys, reads, or intends to read." Then, acknowledging that "the import of *Zurcher*" arguably foreclosed such a holding under the federal Constitution, the court ruled as a matter of state constitutional law "that an innocent, third-party bookstore must be afforded an opportunity for a hearing prior to the execution of any search warrant that seeks to obtain its customers' book-purchasing records"; and that at the hearing the court must "determine whether law enforcement officials have a sufficiently compelling need for the book purchase record that outweighs the harms associated with enforcement of the search warrant."

Consider in this regard a provision of the PATRIOT Act, 50 U.S.C.A. § 1861, set out in App. B, which it is contended "gives the FBI the power to seize all of the circulation, purchasing and other records of library users and bookstore customers on no stronger a claim than an FBI official's statement that they are part of a terrorism investigation," "new powers [that] appear to have been used already—a University of Illinois survey shows libraries were targeted at least 175 times in the year after 9/11."[f] "Hoping to stop criticism and embarrass the critics, the Justice Department has declassified information about the Patriot Act, saying it has never been used to monitor what the public is reading and viewing."[g] "[A]n amendment to an appropriations bill that would have prohibited funds from being used to get court orders requesting 'library circulation records, library patron lists, library Internet records, book sales records, or book customer lists' * * * seemed sure to pass, but House Republicans extended the voting time, giving them a chance to convince enough representatives to change their votes. The amendment failed on a 210–210 vote"[h] on the use of grand jury subpoenas to obtain such material, see p. 831.

e. See Ronald Goldstock & Steven Chananie, *"Criminal" Lawyers: The Use of Electronic Surveillance and Search Warrants in the Investigation and Prosecution of Attorneys Suspected of Criminal Wrongdoing*, 136 U.Pa.L.Rev. 1855 (1988).

f. Congressman Bernie Sanders, *Pulling FBI's Nose Out of Your Books*, http://bernie.house.gov/documents/opeds/20030508100516.asp

g. *No Patriot Check Out at Libraries*, http://www.cbsnews.com/stories/2003/08/19/national/main569135.shtml

h. *Despite Federal Assurances, Critics Still Worry About the Patriot Act's Reach*, http://news.minnesota.publicradio.org/features/2004/07/15_straumanisa_patriotfolo/

SECTION 3. "PROBABLE CAUSE"

SPINELLI v. UNITED STATES

393 U.S. 410, 89 S.Ct. 584, 21 L.Ed.2d 637 (1969).

Justice HARLAN delivered the opinion of the Court.

William Spinelli was convicted * * of traveling to St. Louis, Missouri, from a nearby Illinois suburb with the intention of conducting gambling activities proscribed by Missouri law. At every appropriate stage in the proceedings in the lower courts, the petitioner challenged the constitutionality of the warrant which authorized the FBI search that uncovered the evidence necessary for his conviction. * * * Believing it desirable that the principles of [*Aguilar v. Texas,* 378 U.S. 108 (1964)] should be further explicated, we granted certiorari * * *.

In *Aguilar,* a search warrant had issued upon an affidavit of police officers who swore only that they had "received reliable information from a credible person and do believe" that narcotics were being illegally stored on the described premises. While recognizing that the constitutional requirement of probable cause can be satisfied by hearsay information, this Court held the affidavit inadequate for two reasons. First, the application failed to set forth any of the "underlying circumstances" necessary to enable the magistrate independently to judge of the validity of the informant's conclusion that the narcotics were where he said they were. Second, the affiant-officers did not attempt to support their claim that their informant was " 'credible' or his information 'reliable.' " The Government is, however, quite right in saying that the FBI affidavit in the present case is more ample than that in *Aguilar.* Not only does it contain a report from an anonymous informant, but it also contains a report of an independent FBI investigation which is said to corroborate the informant's tip. We are, then, required to delineate the manner in which *Aguilar's* two-pronged test should be applied in these circumstances.

In essence, the affidavit * * * contained the following allegations:

1. The FBI had kept track of Spinelli's movements on five days during the month of August 1965. On four of these occasions, Spinelli was seen crossing one of two bridges leading from Illinois into St. Louis, Missouri, between 11 a.m. and 12:15 p.m. On four of the five days, Spinelli was also seen parking his car in a lot used by residents of an apartment house at 1108 Indian Circle Drive in St. Louis, between 3:30 p.m. and 4:45 p.m. On one day, Spinelli was followed further and seen to enter a particular apartment in the building.

2. An FBI check with the telephone company revealed that this apartment contained two telephones listed under the name of Grace P. Hagen, and carrying the numbers WYdown 4–0029 and WYdown 4–0136.

3. The application stated that "William Spinelli is known to this affiant and to federal law enforcement agents and local law enforcement agents as a bookmaker, an associate of bookmakers, a gambler, and an associate of gamblers."

4. Finally, it was stated that the FBI "has been informed by a confidential reliable informant that William Spinelli is operating a handbook and accepting wagers and disseminating wagering information by means of the telephones which have been assigned the numbers WYdown 4–0029 and WYdown 4–0136."

There can be no question that the last item mentioned, detailing the informant's tip, has a fundamental place in this warrant application. Without it, probable cause could not be established. The first two items reflect only innocent-seeming activity and data. Spinelli's travels to and from the apartment building and his entry into a particular apartment on one occasion could hardly be taken as bespeaking gambling activity; and there is surely nothing unusual about an apartment containing two separate telephones. Many a householder indulges himself in this petty luxury. Finally, the allegation that Spinelli was "known" to the affiant and to other federal and local law enforcement officers as a gambler and an associate of gamblers is but a bald and unilluminating assertion of suspicion that is entitled to no weight in appraising the magistrate's decision. *Nathanson v. United States,* 290 U.S. 41, 46 (1933).

So much indeed the Government does not deny. Rather, following the reasoning of the Court of Appeals, the Government claims that the informant's tip gives a suspicious color to the FBI's reports detailing Spinelli's innocent-seeming conduct and that, conversely, the FBI's surveillance corroborates the informant's tip, thereby entitling it to more weight. * * * We believe, however, that the "totality of circumstances" approach taken by the Court of Appeals paints with too broad a brush. Where, as here, the informer's tip is a necessary element in a finding of probable cause, its proper weight must be determined by a more precise analysis.

The informer's report must first be measured against *Aguilar's* standards so that its probative value can be assessed. If the tip is found inadequate under *Aguilar,* the other allegations which corroborate the information contained in the hearsay report should then be considered. At this stage as well, however, the standards enunciated in *Aguilar* must inform the magistrate's decision. He must ask: Can it fairly be said that the tip, even when certain parts of it have been corroborated by independent sources, is as trustworthy as a tip which would pass *Aguilar's* tests without independent corroboration? * * *

Applying these principles to the present case, we first consider the weight to be given the informer's tip when it is considered apart from the rest of the affidavit. It is clear that a Commissioner could not credit it without abdicating his constitutional function. Though the affiant swore that his confidant was "reliable," he offered the magistrate no reason in support of this conclusion. Perhaps even more important is the fact that *Aguilar's* other test has not been satisfied. The tip does not contain a sufficient statement of the underlying circumstances from which the informer concluded that Spinelli was running a bookmaking operation. We are not told how the FBI's source received his information—it is not alleged that the informant personally observed Spinelli at work or that he had ever placed a bet with him. Moreover, if the informant came by the information indirectly, he did not explain why his sources were reliable. In the absence of a statement detailing the manner in which the information was gathered, it is especially important that the tip describe the accused's criminal activity in sufficient detail so that the magistrate may know that he is relying on something more substantial than a casual rumor circulating in the underworld or an accusation based merely on an individual's general reputation.

The detail provided by the informant in *Draper v. United States,* 358 U.S. 307 (1959), provides a suitable benchmark. While Hereford, the FBI's informer in that case, did not state the way in which he had obtained his information, he reported that Draper had gone to Chicago the day before by train and that he would return to Denver by train with three ounces of heroin on one of two specified mornings. Moreover, Hereford went on to describe, with minute particularity, the clothes that Draper would be wearing upon his arrival at the Denver station. A magistrate, when confronted with such detail, could reasonably infer that the informant had gained his information in a reliable way. Such an inference cannot be made in the present case. Here, the only facts supplied were that Spinelli was using two specified telephones and that these phones were being used in gambling operations. This meager report could easily have been obtained from an off-hand remark heard at a neighborhood bar.

Nor do we believe that the patent doubts *Aguilar* raises as to the report's reliability are adequately resolved by a consideration of the allegations detailing the FBI's independent investigative efforts. At most, these allegations indicated that Spinelli could have used the telephones specified by the informant for some purpose. This cannot by itself be said to support both the inference that the informer was generally trustworthy and that he had made his charge against Spinelli on the basis of information obtained in a reliable way. Once again, *Draper* provides a relevant comparison. Independent police work in that case corroborated much more than one small detail that had been provided by the informant. There, the police, upon greeting the inbound Denver train on the second morning specified by informer Hereford, saw a man whose dress corresponded precisely to Hereford's detailed description. It was then apparent that the informant had not been fabricating his report out of whole cloth; since the report was of the sort which in common experience may be recognized as having been obtained in a reliable way, it was perfectly clear that probable cause had been established.

We conclude, then, that in the present case the informant's tip—even when corroborated to the extent indicated—was not sufficient to provide the basis for a finding of probable cause. * * *

The judgment of the Court of Appeals is reversed * * *.

Justice WHITE, concurring. * * *

The tension between *Draper* and the *Nathanson-Aguilar* line of cases is evident from the course followed by the majority opinion. * * * Since [the informant's] specific information about Spinelli using two phones with particular numbers had been verified, did not his allegation about gambling thereby become sufficiently more believable if the *Draper* principle is to be given any scope at all? I would think so, particularly since the information from the informant which was verified was not neutral, irrelevant information but was material to proving the gambling allegation: two phones with different numbers in an apartment used away from home indicates a business use in an operation, like bookmaking, where multiple phones are needed. The *Draper* approach would reasonably justify the issuance of a warrant in this case, particularly since the police had some awareness of Spinelli's past activities. The majority, however, while seemingly embracing *Draper,* confines that case to its own facts. Pending full scale reconsideration of that case, on the one hand, or of the *Nathanson-Aguilar* cases on the other, I join the opinion of the Court and the judgment of reversal especially since a vote to affirm would produce an equally divided Court.[a]

ILLINOIS v. GATES

462 U.S. 213, 103 S.Ct. 2317, 76 L.Ed.2d 527 (1983).

Justice REHNQUIST delivered the opinion of the Court.

* * * A chronological statement of events usefully introduces the issues at stake. Bloomingdale, Ill., is a suburb of Chicago located in DuPage County. On May 3, 1978, the Bloomingdale Police Department received by mail an anonymous handwritten letter which read as follows:

> "This letter is to inform you that you have a couple in your town who strictly make their living on selling drugs. They are Sue and Lance Gates,

a. Black, Fortas, and Stewart, JJ., dissented separately; Marshall, J., took no part in the case.

they live on Greenway, off Bloomingdale Rd. in the condominiums. Most of their buys are done in Florida. Sue his wife drives their car to Florida, where she leaves it to be loaded up with drugs, then Lance flys down and drives it back. Sue flys back after she drops the car off in Florida. May 3 she is driving down there again and Lance will be flying down in a few days to drive it back. At the time Lance drives the car back he has the trunk loaded with over $100,000.00 in drugs. Presently they have over $100,000.00 worth of drugs in their basement.

"They brag about the fact they never have to work, and make their entire living on pushers.

"I guarantee if you watch them carefully you will make a big catch. They are friends with some big drugs dealers, who visit their house often. * * *"

The letter was referred by the Chief of Police of the Bloomingdale Police Department to Detective Mader, who decided to pursue the tip. Mader learned, from the office of the Illinois Secretary of State, that an Illinois driver's license had been issued to one Lance Gates, residing at a stated address in Bloomingdale. He contacted a confidential informant, whose examination of certain financial records revealed a more recent address for the Gates, and he also learned from a police officer assigned to O'Hare Airport that "L. Gates" had made a reservation on Eastern Airlines flight 245 to West Palm Beach, Fla., scheduled to depart from Chicago on May 5 at 4:15 p.m.

Mader then made arrangements with an agent of the Drug Enforcement Administration for surveillance of the May 5 Eastern Airlines flight. The agent later reported to Mader that Gates had boarded the flight, and that federal agents in Florida had observed him arrive in West Palm Beach and take a taxi to the nearby Holiday Inn. They also reported that Gates went to a room registered to one Susan Gates and that, at 7:00 a.m. the next morning, Gates and an unidentified woman left the motel in a Mercury bearing Illinois license plates and drove northbound on an interstate frequently used by travelers to the Chicago area. In addition, the DEA agent informed Mader that the license plate number on the Mercury registered to a Hornet station wagon owned by Gates. The agent also advised Mader that the driving time between West Palm Beach and Bloomingdale was approximately 22 to 24 hours.

Mader signed an affidavit setting forth the foregoing facts, and submitted it to a judge of the Circuit Court of DuPage County, together with a copy of the anonymous letter. The judge of that court thereupon issued a search warrant for the Gates' residence and for their automobile. The judge, in deciding to issue the warrant, could have determined that the *modus operandi* of the Gates had been substantially corroborated. As the anonymous letter predicted, Lance Gates had flown from Chicago to West Palm Beach late in the afternoon of May 5th, had checked into a hotel room registered in the name of his wife, and, at 7:00 a.m. the following morning, had headed north, accompanied by an unidentified woman, out of West Palm Beach on an interstate highway used by travelers from South Florida to Chicago in an automobile bearing a license plate issued to him.

At 5:15 a.m. on May 7th, only 36 hours after he had flown out of Chicago, Lance Gates, and his wife, returned to their home in Bloomingdale, driving the car in which they had left West Palm Beach some 22 hours earlier. The Bloomingdale police were awaiting them, searched the trunk of the Mercury, and uncovered approximately 350 pounds of marijuana. A search of the Gates' home revealed marijuana, weapons, and other contraband. The Illinois Circuit Court ordered suppression of all these items, on the ground that the affidavit submitted to the Circuit Judge failed to support the necessary determination of probable cause to believe that the Gates' automobile and home contained the contraband in question. This decision was affirmed in turn by the Illinois Appellate Court and by a divided vote of the Supreme Court of Illinois.

The Illinois Supreme Court concluded—and we are inclined to agree—that, standing alone, the anonymous letter sent to the Bloomingdale Police Department would not provide the basis for a magistrate's determination that there was probable cause to believe contraband would be found in the Gates' car and home. The letter provides virtually nothing from which one might conclude that its author is either honest or his information reliable; likewise, the letter gives absolutely no indication of the basis for the writer's predictions regarding the Gates' criminal activities. Something more was required, then, before a magistrate could conclude that there was probable cause to believe that contraband would be found in the Gates' home and car.

The Illinois Supreme Court also properly recognized that Detective Mader's affidavit might be capable of supplementing the anonymous letter with information sufficient to permit a determination of probable cause. In holding that the affidavit in fact did not contain sufficient additional information to sustain a determination of probable cause, the Illinois court applied a "two-pronged test," derived from our decision in *Spinelli v. United States*. The Illinois Supreme Court, like some others, apparently understood *Spinelli* as requiring that the anonymous letter satisfy each of two independent requirements before it could be relied on. According to this view, the letter, as supplemented by Mader's affidavit, first had to adequately reveal the "basis of knowledge" of the letter writer—the particular means by which he came by the information given in his report. Second, it had to provide facts sufficiently establishing either the "veracity" of the affiant's informant, or, alternatively, the "reliability" of the informant's report in this particular case.

The Illinois court, alluding to an elaborate set of legal rules that have developed among various lower courts to enforce the "two-pronged test,"[4] found that the test had not been satisfied. First, the "veracity" prong was not satisfied because, "there was simply no basis [for] * * * conclud[ing] that the anonymous person [who wrote the letter to the Bloomingdale Police Department] was credible." The court indicated that corroboration by police of details contained in the letter might never satisfy the "veracity" prong, and in any event, could not do so if, as in the present case, only "innocent" details are corroborated. In addition, the letter gave no indication of the basis of its writer's knowledge of the Gates' activities. The Illinois court understood *Spinelli* as permitting the detail contained in a tip to be used to infer that the informant had a reliable basis for his statements, but it thought that the anonymous letter failed to provide sufficient detail to permit such an inference. Thus, it concluded that no showing of probable cause had been made.

We agree with the Illinois Supreme Court that an informant's "veracity," "reliability" and "basis of knowledge" are all highly relevant in determining the value of his report. We do not agree, however, that these elements should be understood as entirely separate and independent requirements to be rigidly exacted in every case, which the opinion of the Supreme Court of Illinois would

4. In summary, these rules posit that the "veracity" prong of the *Spinelli* test has two "spurs"—the informant's "credibility" and the "reliability" of his information. Various interpretations are advanced for the meaning of the "reliability" spur of the "veracity" prong. Both the "basis of knowledge" prong and the "veracity" prong are treated as entirely separate requirements, which must be independently satisfied in every case in order to sustain a determination of probable cause. Some ancillary doctrines are relied on to satisfy certain of the foregoing requirements. For example, the "self-verifying detail" of a tip may satisfy the "basis of knowledge" requirement, although not the "credibility" spur of the "veracity" prong. Conversely, corroboration would seem not capable of supporting the "basis of knowledge" prong, but only the "veracity" prong. * * *

imply. Rather, as detailed below, they should be understood simply as closely intertwined issues that may usefully illuminate the common sense, practical question whether there is "probable cause" to believe that contraband or evidence is located in a particular place.

This totality of the circumstances approach is far more consistent with our prior treatment of probable cause than is any rigid demand that specific "tests" be satisfied by every informant's tip. Perhaps the central teaching of our decisions bearing on the probable cause standard is that it is a "practical, nontechnical conception." *Brinegar v. United States,* 338 U.S. 160 (1949). "In dealing with probable cause, * * * as the very name implies, we deal with probabilities. These are not technical; they are the factual and practical considerations of everyday life on which reasonable and prudent men, not legal technicians, act." Our observation in *United States v. Cortez,* [p. 417], regarding "particularized suspicion," is also applicable to the probable cause standard:

> The process does not deal with hard certainties, but with probabilities. Long before the law of probabilities was articulated as such, practical people formulated certain common-sense conclusions about human behavior; jurors as factfinders are permitted to do the same—and so are law enforcement officers. Finally, the evidence thus collected must be seen and weighed not in terms of library analysis by scholars, but as understood by those versed in the field of law enforcement.

As these comments illustrate, probable cause is a fluid concept—turning on the assessment of probabilities in particular factual contexts—not readily, or even usefully, reduced to a neat set of legal rules. Informants' tips doubtless come in many shapes and sizes from many different types of persons. * * * Rigid legal rules are ill-suited to an area of such diversity. "One simple rule will not cover every situation."[7]

7. The diversity of informants' tips, as well as the usefulness of the totality of the circumstances approach to probable cause, is reflected in our prior decisions on the subject. In *Jones v. United States,* 362 U.S. 257 (1960), we held that probable cause to search petitioners' apartment was established by an affidavit based principally on an informant's tip. The unnamed informant claimed to have purchased narcotics from petitioners at their apartment; the affiant stated that he had been given correct information from the informant on a prior occasion. This, and the fact that petitioners had admitted to police officers on another occasion that they were narcotics users, sufficed to support the magistrate's determination of probable cause.

Likewise, in *Rugendorf v. United States,* 376 U.S. 528 (1964), the Court upheld a magistrate's determination that there was probable cause to believe that certain stolen property would be found in petitioner's apartment. The affidavit submitted to the magistrate stated that certain furs had been stolen, and that a confidential informant, who previously had furnished confidential information, said that he saw the furs in petitioner's home. Moreover, another confidential informant, also claimed to be reliable, stated that one Schweihs had stolen the furs. Police reports indicated that petitioner had been seen in Schweihs' company and a third informant stated that petitioner was a fence for Schweihs.

Finally, in *Ker v. California,* 374 U.S. 23 (1963), we held that information within the knowledge of officers who searched the Ker's apartment provided them with probable cause to believe drugs would be found there. The officers were aware that one Murphy had previously sold marijuana to a police officer; the transaction had occurred in an isolated area, to which Murphy had led the police. The night after this transaction, police observed Ker and Murphy meet in the same location. Murphy approached Ker's car, and, although police could see nothing change hands, Murphy's *modus operandi* was identical to what it had been the night before. Moreover, when police followed Ker from the scene of the meeting with Murphy he managed to lose them after performing an abrupt U-turn. Finally, the police had a statement from an informant who had provided reliable information previously, that Ker was engaged in selling marijuana, and that his source was Murphy. We concluded that "To say that this coincidence of information was sufficient to support a reasonable belief of the officers that Ker was illegally in possession of marijuana is to indulge in understatement."

Moreover, the "two-pronged test" directs analysis into two largely independent channels—the informant's "veracity" or "reliability" and his "basis of knowledge." There are persuasive arguments against according these two elements such independent status. Instead, they are better understood as relevant considerations in the totality of circumstances analysis that traditionally has guided probable cause determinations: a deficiency in one may be compensated for, in determining the overall reliability of a tip, by a strong showing as to the other, or by some other indicia of reliability.

If, for example, a particular informant is known for the unusual reliability of his predictions of certain types of criminal activities in a locality, his failure, in a particular case, to thoroughly set forth the basis of his knowledge surely should not serve as an absolute bar to a finding of probable cause based on his tip. Likewise, if an unquestionably honest citizen comes forward with a report of criminal activity—which if fabricated would subject him to criminal liability—we have found rigorous scrutiny of the basis of his knowledge unnecessary. Conversely, even if we entertain some doubt as to an informant's motives, his explicit and detailed description of alleged wrongdoing, along with a statement that the event was observed first-hand, entitles his tip to greater weight than might otherwise be the case. Unlike a totality of circumstances analysis, which permits a balanced assessment of the relative weights of all the various indicia of reliability (and unreliability) attending an informant's tip, the "two-pronged test" has encouraged an excessively technical dissection of informants' tips, with undue attention being focused on isolated issues that cannot sensibly be divorced from the other facts presented to the magistrate. * * *

We also have recognized that affidavits "are normally drafted by non-lawyers in the midst and haste of a criminal investigation. Technical requirements of elaborate specificity once exacted under common law pleading have no proper place in this area." Likewise, search and arrest warrants long have been issued by persons who are neither lawyers nor judges, and who certainly do not remain abreast of each judicial refinement of the nature of "probable cause." The rigorous inquiry into the *Spinelli* prongs and the complex superstructure of evidentiary and analytical rules that some have seen implicit in our *Spinelli* decision, cannot be reconciled with the fact that many warrants are—quite properly—issued on the basis of nontechnical, common-sense judgments of laymen applying a standard less demanding than those used in more formal legal proceedings. Likewise, given the informal, often hurried context in which it must be applied, the "built-in subtleties" of the "two-pronged test" are particularly unlikely to assist magistrates in determining probable cause.

Similarly, we have repeatedly said that after-the-fact scrutiny by courts of the sufficiency of an affidavit should not take the form of *de novo* review. A magistrate's "determination of probable cause should be paid great deference by reviewing courts." "A grudging or negative attitude by reviewing courts toward warrants" is inconsistent with the Fourth Amendment's strong preference for searches conducted pursuant to a warrants; "courts should not invalidate * * * warrant[s] by interpreting affidavit[s] in a hypertechnical, rather than a commonsense, manner."

If the affidavits submitted by police officers are subjected to the type of scrutiny some courts have deemed appropriate, police might well resort to warrantless searches, with the hope of relying on consent or some other exception to the warrant clause that might develop at the time of the search. In addition, the possession of a warrant by officers conducting an arrest or search greatly reduces the perception of unlawful or intrusive police conduct, by assuring "the individual whose property is searched or seized of the lawful authority of the executing officer, his need to search, and the limits of his power to search." Reflecting this preference for the warrant process, the traditional standard for review of an issuing magistrate's probable cause determination has been that so long as the magistrate had a "substantial basis for * * * conclud[ing]" that a search would uncover evidence of wrongdoing, the Fourth Amendment requires no more. We think reaffirmation of this standard better serves the purpose of encouraging recourse to the warrant procedure and is more consistent with our traditional deference to the probable cause determinations of magistrates than is the "two-pronged test."

Finally, the direction taken by decisions following *Spinelli* poorly serves "the most basic function of any government": "to provide for the security of the individual and of his property". The strictures that inevitably accompany the "two-pronged test" cannot avoid seriously impeding the task of law enforcement. If, as the Illinois Supreme Court apparently thought, that test must be rigorously applied in every case, [anonymous tips would be] of greatly diminished value in police work. Ordinary citizens, like ordinary witnesses, generally do not provide extensive recitations of the basis of their everyday observations. Likewise, as the Illinois Supreme Court observed in this case, the veracity of persons supplying anonymous tips is by hypothesis largely unknown, and unknowable. As a result, anonymous tips seldom could survive a rigorous application of either of the *Spinelli* prongs. Yet, such tips, particularly when supplemented by independent police investigation, frequently contribute to the solution of otherwise "perfect crimes." While a conscientious assessment of the basis for crediting such tips is required by the Fourth Amendment, a standard that leaves virtually no place for anonymous citizen informants is not.

For all these reasons, we conclude that it is wiser to abandon the "two-pronged test" established by our decisions in *Aguilar* and *Spinelli*.[11] In its place we reaffirm the totality of the circumstances analysis that traditionally has informed probable cause determinations. The task of the issuing magistrate is simply to make a practical, common-sense decision whether, given all the circumstances set forth in the affidavit before him, including the "veracity" and "basis of knowledge" of persons supplying hearsay information, there is a fair probability that contraband or evidence of a crime will be found in a particular place. And the duty of a reviewing court is simply to ensure that the magistrate had a "substantial basis for * * * conclud[ing]" that probable cause existed. We are convinced that this flexible, easily applied standard will better achieve the accommodation of public and private interests that the Fourth Amendment requires than does the approach that has developed from *Aguilar* and *Spinelli.*

Our earlier cases illustrate the limits beyond which a magistrate may not venture in issuing a warrant. A sworn statement of an affiant that "he has cause to suspect and does believe that" liquor illegally brought into the United States is located on certain premises will not do. *Nathanson v. United States.* An affidavit must provide the magistrate with a substantial basis for determining the existence of probable cause, and the wholly conclusory statement at issue in *Nathanson* failed to meet this requirement. An officer's statement that "affiants have received reliable information from a credible person and believe" that heroin is stored in a home, is likewise inadequate. *Aguilar v. Texas.* As in *Nathanson,* this is a mere conclusory statement that gives the magistrate virtually no basis at all

11. * * * Whether the allegations submitted to the magistrate in *Spinelli* would, under the view we now take, have supported a finding of probable cause, we think it would not be profitable to decide. There are so many variables in the probable cause equation that one determination will seldom be a useful "precedent" for another. Suffice it to say that while we in no way abandon *Spinelli's* concern for the trustworthiness of informers and for the principle that it is the magistrate who must ultimately make a finding of probable cause, we reject the rigid categorization suggested by some of its language.

for making a judgment regarding probable cause. Sufficient information must be presented to the magistrate to allow that official to determine probable cause; his action cannot be a mere ratification of the bare conclusions of others. In order to ensure that such an abdication of the magistrate's duty does not occur, courts must continue to conscientiously review the sufficiency of affidavits on which warrants are issued. But when we move beyond the "bare bones" affidavits present in cases such as *Nathanson* and *Aguilar,* this area simply does not lend itself to a prescribed set of rules, like that which had developed from *Spinelli.* Instead, the flexible, common-sense standard articulated in *Jones, Ventresca,* and *Brinegar* better served the purposes of the Fourth Amendment's probable cause requirement.

Justice Brennan's dissent suggests in several places that the approach we take today somehow downgrades the role of the neutral magistrate, because *Aguilar* and *Spinelli* "preserve the role of magistrates as independent arbiters of probable cause * * *." Quite the contrary, we believe, is the case. Nothing in our opinion in any way lessens the authority of the magistrate to draw such reasonable inferences as he will from the material supplied to him by applicants for a warrant; indeed, he is freer than under the regime of *Aguilar* and *Spinelli* to draw such inferences, or to refuse to draw them if he is so minded.

The real gist of Justice Brennan's criticism seems to be a second argument, somewhat at odds with the first, that magistrates should be restricted in their authority to make probable cause determinations by the standards laid down in *Aguilar* and *Spinelli* and that such findings "should not be authorized unless there is some assurance that the information on which they are based has been obtained in a reliable way by an honest or credible person." However, under our opinion magistrates remain perfectly free to exact such assurances as they deem necessary, as well as those required by this opinion, in making probable cause determinations. Justice Brennan would apparently prefer that magistrates be restricted in their findings of probable cause by the development of an elaborate body of case law dealing with the "veracity" prong of the *Spinelli* test, which in turn is broken down into two "spurs"—the informant's "credibility" and the "reliability" of his information, together with the "basis of knowledge" prong of the *Spinelli* test. That such a labyrinthine body of judicial refinement bears any relationship to familiar definitions of probable cause is hard to imagine. * * *

Justice Brennan's dissent also suggests that "words such as 'practical,' 'nontechnical,' and 'common sense,' as used in the Court's opinion, are but code words for an overly permissive attitude towards police practices in derogation of the rights secured by the Fourth Amendment." * * * "Fidelity" to the commands of the Constitution suggests balanced judgment rather than exhortation. The highest "fidelity" is achieved neither by the judge who instinctively goes furthest in upholding even the most bizarre claim of individual constitutional rights, any more than it is achieved by a judge who instinctively goes furthest in accepting the most restrictive claims of governmental authorities. The task of this Court, as of other courts, is to "hold the balance true," and we think we have done that in this case.

Our decisions applying the totality of circumstances analysis outlined above have consistently recognized the value of corroboration of details of an informant's tip by independent police work.

Our decision in *Draper v. United States,* however, is the classic case on the value of corroborative efforts of police officials. There, an informant named Hereford reported that Draper would arrive in Denver on a train from Chicago on one of two days, and that he would be carrying a quantity of heroin. The informant also supplied a fairly detailed physical description of Draper, and predicted that he would be wearing a light colored raincoat, brown slacks and black shoes, and would be walking "real fast." Hereford gave no indication of the basis for his information.[12]

On one of the stated dates police officers observed a man matching this description exit a train arriving from Chicago; his attire and luggage matched Hereford's report and he was walking rapidly. We explained in *Draper* that, by this point in his investigation, the arresting officer "had personally verified every facet of the information given him by Hereford except whether petitioner had accomplished his mission and had the three ounces of heroin on his person or in his bag. And surely with every other bit of Hereford's information being thus personally verified, [the officer] had 'reasonable grounds' to believe that the remaining unverified bit of Hereford's information—that Draper would have the heroin with him—was likewise true."

The showing of probable cause in the present case was fully as compelling as that in *Draper*. Even standing alone, the facts obtained through the independent investigation of Mader and the DEA at least suggested that the Gates were involved in drug trafficking. In addition to being a popular vacation site, Florida is well-known as a source of narcotics and other illegal drugs. Lance Gates' flight to Palm Beach, his brief, overnight stay in a motel, and apparent immediate return north to Chicago in the family car, conveniently awaiting him in West Palm Beach, is as suggestive of a prearranged drug run, as it is of an ordinary vacation trip.

In addition, the magistrate could rely on the anonymous letter, which had been corroborated in major part by Mader's efforts—just as had occurred in *Draper*.[13] The Supreme Court of Illinois reasoned that *Draper* involved an informant who had given reliable information on previous occasions, while the honesty and reliability of the anonymous informant in this case were unknown to the Bloomingdale police. While this distinction might be an apt one at the time the police department received the anonymous letter, it became far less significant after Mader's independent investigative work occurred. The corroboration of the letter's predictions that the Gates' car would be in Florida, that Lance Gates would fly to Florida in the next day or so, and that he would drive the car north

12. The tip in *Draper* might well not have survived the rigid application of the "two-pronged test" that developed following *Spinelli*. The only reference to Hereford's reliability was that he had "been engaged as a 'special employee' of the Bureau of Narcotics at Denver for about six months, and from time to time gave information to [the police] for small sums of money, and that [the officer] had always found the information given by Hereford to be accurate and reliable." Likewise, the tip gave no indication of how Hereford came by his information. At most, the detailed and accurate predictions in the tip indicated that, however Hereford obtained his information, it was reliable.

13. The Illinois Supreme Court thought that the verification of details contained in the anonymous letter in this case amounted only to "the corroboration of innocent activity," and that this was insufficient to support a finding of probable cause. We are inclined to agree, however, with the observation of Justice Moran in his dissenting opinion that "In this case, just as in *Draper*, seemingly innocent activity became suspicious in the light of the initial tip." And it bears noting that *all* of the corroborating detail established in *Draper, supra*, was of entirely innocent activity—a fact later pointed out by the Court in both *Jones v.* United States, *and* Ker v. California.

This is perfectly reasonable. As discussed previously, probable cause requires only a probability or substantial chance of criminal activity, not an actual showing of such activity. By hypothesis, therefore, innocent behavior frequently will provide the basis for a showing of probable cause; to require otherwise would be to *sub silentio* impose a drastically more rigorous definition of probable cause than the security of our citizens demands. We think the Illinois court attempted a too rigid classification of the types of conduct that may be relied upon in seeking to demonstrate probable cause. In making a determination of probable cause the relevant inquiry is not whether particular conduct is "innocent" or "guilty," but the degree of suspicion that attaches to particular types of non-criminal acts.

toward Bloomingdale all indicated, albeit not with certainty, that the informant's other assertions also were true. "Because an informant is right about some things, he is more probably right about other facts," *Spinelli, supra* (White, J., concurring)—including the claim regarding the Gates' illegal activity. This may well not be the type of "reliability" or "veracity" necessary to satisfy some view of the "veracity prong" of *Spinelli,* but we think it suffices for the practical, commonsense judgment called for in making a probable cause determination. It is enough, for purposes of assessing probable cause, that "corroboration through other sources of information reduced the chances of a reckless or prevaricating tale," thus providing "a substantial basis for crediting the hearsay."

Finally, the anonymous letter contained a range of details relating not just to easily obtained facts and conditions existing at the time of the tip, but to future actions of third parties ordinarily not easily predicted. The letter writer's accurate information as to the travel plans of each of the Gates was of a character likely obtained only from the Gates themselves, or from someone familiar with their not entirely ordinary travel plans. If the informant had access to accurate information of this type a magistrate could properly conclude that it was not unlikely that he also had access to reliable information of the Gates' alleged illegal activities.[14] Of course, the Gates' travel plans might have been learned from a talkative neighbor or travel agent; under the "two-pronged test" developed from *Spinelli,* the character of the details in the anonymous letter might well not permit a sufficiently clear inference regarding the letter writer's "basis of knowledge." But, as discussed previously, probable cause does not demand the certainty we associate with formal trials. It is enough that there was a fair probability that the writer of the anonymous letter had obtained his entire story either from the Gates or someone they trusted. And corroboration of major portions of the letter's predictions provides just this probability. It is apparent, therefore, that the judge issuing the warrant had a "substantial basis for * * * conclud[ing]" that probable cause to search the Gates' home and car existed. The judgment of the Supreme Court of Illinois therefore must be

Reversed.

Justice WHITE, concurring in the judgment.[a]

14. The dissent seizes on one inaccuracy in the anonymous informant's letter—its statement that Sue Gates would fly from Florida to Illinois, when in fact she drove—and argues that the probative value of the entire tip was undermined by this allegedly "material mistake." We have never required that informants used by the police be infallible, and can see no reason to impose such a requirement in this case. Probable cause, particularly when police have obtained a warrant, simply does not require the perfection the dissent finds necessary.

Likewise, there is no force to the dissent's argument that the Gates' action in leaving their home unguarded undercut the informant's claim that drugs were hidden there. Indeed, the line-by-line scrutiny that the dissent applies to the anonymous letter is akin to that we find inappropriate in reviewing magistrate's decisions. The dissent apparently attributes to the magistrate who issued the warrant in this case the rather implausible notion that persons dealing in drugs always stay at home, apparently out of fear that to leave might risk intrusion by criminals. If accurate, one could not help sympathizing with the self-imposed isolation of people so situated. In reality, however, it is scarcely likely that the magistrate ever thought that the anonymous tip "kept one spouse" at home, much less that he relied on the theory advanced by the dissent. The letter simply says that Sue would fly from Florida to Illinois, without indicating whether the Gates' made the bitter choice of leaving the drugs in their house, or those in their car, unguarded. The magistrate's determination that there might be drugs or evidence of criminal activity in the Gates' home was well-supported by the less speculative theory, noted in text, that if the informant could predict with considerable accuracy the somewhat unusual travel plans of the Gates, he probably also had a reliable basis for his statements that the Gates' kept a large quantity of drugs in their home and frequently were visited by other drug traffickers there.

a. In an omitted portion of his opinion, Justice White argued for adoption of a "good-faith" exception to the exclusionary rule.

* * * Although I agree that the warrant should be upheld, I reach this conclusion in accordance with the *Aguilar-Spinelli* framework.

For present purposes, the *Aguilar-Spinelli* rules can be summed up as follows. First, an affidavit based on an informer's tip, standing alone, cannot provide probable cause for issuance of a warrant unless the tip includes information that apprises the magistrate of the informant's basis for concluding that the contraband is where he claims it is (the "basis of knowledge" prong), *and* the affiant informs the magistrate of his basis for believing that the informant is credible (the "veracity" prong).[20] Second, if a tip fails under either or both of the two prongs, probable cause may yet be established by independent police investigatory work that corroborates the tip to such an extent that it supports "both the inference that the informer was generally trustworthy and that he made his charge on the basis of information obtained in a reliable way." In instances where the officers rely on corroboration, the ultimate question is whether the corroborated tip "is as trustworthy as a tip which would pass *Aguilar's* tests without independent corroboration."

In the present case, it is undisputed that the anonymous tip, by itself, did not furnish probable cause. The question is whether those portions of the affidavit describing the results of the police investigation of the respondents, when considered in light of the tip, "would permit the suspicions engendered by the informant's report to ripen into a judgment that a crime was probably being committed." * * *

In my view, the lower court's characterization of the Gates' activity here as totally "innocent" is dubious. In fact, the behavior was quite suspicious. I agree with the Court that Lance Gates' flight to Palm Beach, an area known to be a source of narcotics, the brief overnight stay in a motel, and apparent immediate return North, suggest a pattern that trained law-enforcement officers have recognized as indicative of illicit drug-dealing activity.

Even, however, had the corroboration related only to completely innocuous activities, this fact alone would not preclude the issuance of a valid warrant. The critical issue is not whether the activities observed by the police are innocent or suspicious. Instead, the proper focus should be on whether the actions of the suspects, whatever their nature, give rise to an inference that the informant is credible and that he obtained his information in a reliable manner.

20. The "veracity" prong is satisfied by a recitation in the affidavit that the informant previously supplied accurate information to the police, see *McCray v. Illinois,* [p. 297], or by proof that the informant gave his information against his penal interest, see *United States v. Harris,* 403 U.S. 573 (1971) (plurality opinion). [Editor's Note: In *Harris,* the informant said that he had purchased illicit whiskey from defendant for two years, most recently within the past two weeks, and had often seen defendant get the whiskey for him and others from a certain building. The plurality opinion concluded that because "people do not lightly admit a crime and place critical evidence in the hands of the police in the form of their own admissions," such admissions "carry their own indicia of credibility—sufficient at least to support finding of probable cause to search" when, as here, the basis of knowledge is also indicated (as almost inevitably will be the case when there is such an admission). The four dissenters objected that "the effect of adopting such a rule would be to encourage the Government to prefer as informants participants in criminal enterprises rather than ordinary citizens, a goal the Government specifically eschews in its brief in this case upon the explicit premise that such persons are often less reliable than those who obey the law."] The "basis of knowledge" prong is satisfied by a statement from the informant that he personally observed the criminal activity, or, if he came by the information indirectly, by a satisfactory explanation of why his sources were reliable, or, in the absence of a statement detailing the manner in which the information was gathered, by a description of the accused's criminal activity in sufficient detail that the magistrate may infer that the informant is relying on something more substantial than casual rumor or an individual's general reputation. *Spinelli v. United States.*

Thus, in *Draper v. United States* an informant stated on Sept. 7 that Draper would be carrying narcotics when he arrived by train in Denver on the morning of Sept. 8 or Sept. 9. The informant also provided the police with a detailed physical description of the clothes Draper would be wearing when he alighted from the train. The police observed Draper leaving a train on the morning of Sept. 9, and he was wearing the precise clothing described by the informant. The Court held that the police had probable cause to arrest Draper at this point, even though the police had seen nothing more than the totally innocent act of a man getting off a train carrying a briefcase. As we later explained in *Spinelli,* the important point was that the corroboration showed both that the informant was credible, *i.e.* that he "had not been fabricating his report out of whole cloth," and that he had an adequate basis of knowledge for his allegations, "since the report was of the sort which in common experience may be recognized as having been obtained in a reliable way." The fact that the informer was able to predict, two days in advance, the exact clothing Draper would be wearing dispelled the possibility that his tip was just based on rumor or "an off-hand remark heard at a neighborhood bar." Probably Draper had planned in advance to wear these specific clothes so that an accomplice could identify him. A clear inference could therefore be drawn that the informant was either involved in the criminal scheme himself or that he otherwise had access to reliable, inside information.[22]

As in *Draper,* the police investigation in the present case satisfactorily demonstrated that the informant's tip was as trustworthy as one that would alone satisfy the *Aguilar* tests. The tip predicted that Sue Gates would drive to Florida, that Lance Gates would fly there a few days after May 3, and that Lance would then drive the car back. After the police corroborated these facts, the magistrate could reasonably have inferred, as he apparently did, that the informant, who had specific knowledge of these unusual travel plans, did not make up his story and that he obtained his information in a reliable way. * * * I therefore conclude that the judgment of the Illinois Supreme Court invalidating the warrant must be reversed.

The Court agrees that the warrant was valid, but, in the process of reaching this conclusion, it overrules the *Aguilar-Spinelli* tests and replaces them with a "totality of the circumstances" standard. As shown above, it is not at all necessary to overrule *Aguilar-Spinelli* in order to reverse the judgment below. Therefore, because I am inclined to believe that, when applied properly, the *Aguilar-Spinelli* rules play an appropriate role in probable cause determinations, and because the

22. Thus, as interpreted in *Spinelli,* the Court in *Draper* held that there was probable cause because "the kind of information related by the informant [was] not generally sent ahead of a person's arrival in a city except to those who are intimately connected with making careful arrangements for meeting him." *Spinelli* (White, J., concurring). As I said in *Spinelli,* the conclusion that *Draper* itself was based on this fact is far from inescapable. Prior to *Spinelli, Draper* was susceptible to the interpretation that it stood for the proposition that "the existence of the tenth and critical fact is made sufficiently probable to justify the issuance of a warrant by verifying nine other facts coming from the same source." *Spinelli* (White, J., concurring). But it now seems clear that the Court in *Spinelli* rejected this reading of *Draper.*

Justice Brennan erroneously interprets my *Spinelli* concurrence as espousing the view that "corroboration of certain details in a tip may be sufficient to satisfy the veracity, but not the basis of knowledge, prong of *Aguilar.*" I did not say that corroboration could *never* satisfy the basis of knowledge prong. My concern was, and still is, that the prong might be deemed satisfied on the basis of corroboration of information that does not in any way suggest that the informant had an adequate basis of knowledge for his report. If, however, as in *Draper,* the police corroborate information from which it can be inferred that the informant's tip was grounded on inside information, this corroboration is sufficient to satisfy the basis of knowledge prong. *Spinelli* (White, J., concurring). The rules would indeed be strange if, as Justice Brennan suggests, the basis of knowledge prong could be satisfied by detail in the tip alone, but not by independent police work.

Court's holding may foretell an evisceration of the probable cause standard, I do not join the Court's holding.

The Court reasons that the "veracity" and "basis of knowledge" tests are not independent, and that a deficiency as to one can be compensated for by a strong showing as to the other. Thus, a finding of probable cause may be based on a tip from an informant "known for the unusual reliability of his predictions" or from "an unquestionably honest citizen," even if the report fails thoroughly to set forth the basis upon which the information was obtained. If this is so, then it must follow *a fortiori* that "the affidavit of an officer, known by the magistrate to be honest and experienced, stating that [contraband] is located in a certain building" must be acceptable. It would be "quixotic" if a similar statement from an honest informant, but not one from an honest officer, could furnish probable cause. But we have repeatedly held that the unsupported assertion or belief of an officer does not satisfy the probable cause requirement. Thus, this portion of today's holding can be read as implicitly rejecting the teachings of these prior holdings.

The Court may not intend so drastic a result. Indeed, the Court expressly reaffirms the validity of cases such as *Nathanson* that have held that, no matter how reliable the affiant-officer may be, a warrant should not be issued unless the affidavit discloses supporting facts and circumstances. The Court limits these cases to situations involving affidavits containing only "bare conclusions" and holds that, if an affidavit contains anything more, it should be left to the issuing magistrate to decide, based solely on "practical[ity]" and "common-sense," whether there is a fair probability that contraband will be found in a particular place.

Thus, as I read the majority opinion, it appears that the question whether the probable cause standard is to be diluted is left to the common-sense judgments of issuing magistrates. I am reluctant to approve any standard that does not expressly require, as a prerequisite to issuance of a warrant, some showing of facts from which an inference may be drawn that the informant is credible and that his information was obtained in a reliable way. * * * Hence, I do not join the Court's opinion rejecting the *Aguilar-Spinelli* rules.

Justice BRENNAN, with whom Justice MARSHALL joins, dissenting.

Although I join Justice Stevens' dissenting opinion and agree with him that the warrant is invalid even under the Court's newly announced "totality of the circumstances" test, I write separately to dissent from the Court's unjustified and ill-advised rejection of the two-prong test for evaluating the validity of a warrant based on hearsay announced in *Aguilar v. Texas,* and refined in *Spinelli v. United States.* * * *

The [*Spinelli*] Court held that the *Aguilar* test should be applied to the tip, and approved two additional ways of satisfying that test. First, the Court suggested that if the tip contained sufficient detail describing the accused's criminal activity it might satisfy *Aguilar's* basis of knowledge prong. Such detail might assure the magistrate that he is "relying on something more substantial than a casual rumor circulating in the underworld or an accusation based merely on an individual's general reputation." Although the tip in the case before it did not meet this standard, "[t]he detail provided by the informant in *Draper v. United States* provide[d] a suitable benchmark" because "[a] magistrate, when confronted with such detail, could reasonably infer that the informant had gained his information in a reliable way."

Second, the Court stated that police corroboration of the details of a tip could provide a basis for satisfying *Aguilar.* The Court's opinion is not a model of clarity on this issue since it appears to suggest that corroboration can satisfy both the basis of knowledge and veracity prongs of *Aguilar.* Justice White's concurring opinion, however, points the way to a proper reading of the Court's opinion. After reviewing the Court's decision in *Draper v. United States,* Justice White concluded that "[t]he thrust of *Draper* is not that the verified facts have independent significance with respect to proof of [another unverified fact]." In his view, "[t]he argument instead relates to the reliability of the source: because an informant is right about some things, he is more probably right about other facts, usually the critical, unverified facts." Justice White then pointed out that prior cases had rejected "the notion that the past reliability of an officer is sufficient reason for believing his current assertions." Justice White went on to state:

> "Nor would it suffice, I suppose, if a reliable informant states there is gambling equipment in Apartment 607 and then proceeds to describe in detail Apartment 201, a description which is verified before applying for the warrant. He was right about 201, but that hardly makes him more believable about the equipment in 607. But what if he states that there are narcotics locked in a safe in Apartment 300, which is described in detail, and the apartment manager verifies everything but the contents of the safe? I doubt that the report about the narcotics is made appreciably more believable by the verification. The informant could still have gotten his information concerning the safe from others about whom nothing is known or could have inferred the presence of narcotics from circumstances which a magistrate would find unacceptable."

I find this reasoning persuasive. Properly understood, therefore, *Spinelli* stands for the proposition that corroboration of certain details in a tip may be sufficient to satisfy the veracity, but not the basis of knowledge, prong of *Aguilar.* As noted, *Spinelli* also suggests that in some limited circumstances considerable detail in an informant's tip may be adequate to satisfy the basis of knowledge prong of *Aguilar.* * * *

[O]ne can concede that probable cause is a "practical, nontechnical" concept without betraying the values that *Aguilar* and *Spinelli* reflect. As noted, *Aguilar* and *Spinelli* require the police to provide magistrates with certain crucial information. They also provide structure for magistrates' probable cause inquiries. In so doing, *Aguilar* and *Spinelli* preserve the role of magistrates as independent arbiters of probable cause, insure greater accuracy in probable cause determinations, and advance the substantive value of precluding findings of probable cause, and attendant intrusions, based on anything less than information from an honest or credible person who has acquired his information in a reliable way. Neither the standards nor their effects are inconsistent with a "practical, nontechnical" conception of probable cause. Once a magistrate has determined that he has information before him that he can reasonably say has been obtained in a reliable way by a credible person, he has ample room to use his common sense and to apply a practical, nontechnical conception of probable cause. * * *

The Court also insists that the *Aguilar-Spinelli* standards must be abandoned because they are inconsistent with the fact that non-lawyers frequently serve as magistrates. To the contrary, the standards help to structure probable cause inquiries and, properly interpreted, may actually help a non-lawyer magistrate in making a probable cause determination. * * *

Justice STEVENS, with whom Justice BRENNAN joins, dissenting.

* * * The informant had indicated that "Sue drives their car to Florida *where she leaves it to be loaded up with drugs * * *. Sue flies back after she drops the car off in Florida.*" (emphasis added). Yet Detective Mader's affidavit reported that she "left the West Palm Beach area driving the Mercury northbound."

The discrepancy between the informant's predictions and the facts known to Detective Mader is significant for three reasons. First, it cast doubt on the informant's hypothesis that the Gates already had "over $100,000 worth of drugs in their basement." The informant had predicted an itinerary that always kept one spouse in Bloomingdale, suggesting that the Gates did not want to leave their home unguarded because something valuable was hidden within. That inference obviously could not be drawn when it was known that the pair was actually together over a thousand miles from home.

Second, the discrepancy made the Gates' conduct seem substantially less unusual than the informant had predicted it would be. It would have been odd if, as predicted, Sue had driven down to Florida on Wednesday, left the car, and flown right back to Illinois. But the mere facts that Sue was in West Palm Beach with the car,[1] that she was joined by her husband at the Holiday Inn on Friday,[2] and that the couple drove north together the next morning[3] are neither unusual nor probative of criminal activity.

Third, the fact that the anonymous letter contained a material mistake undermines the reasonableness of relying on it as a basis for making a forcible entry into a private home.

Of course, the activities in this case did not stop when the magistrate issued the warrant. The Gates drove all night to Bloomingdale, the officers searched the car and found 400 pounds of marijuana, and then they searched the house. However, none of these subsequent events may be considered in evaluating the warrant, and the search of the house was legal only if the warrant was valid. I cannot accept the Court's casual conclusion that, *before the Gates arrived in Bloomingdale,* there was probable cause to justify a valid entry and search of a private home. No one knows who the informant in this case was, or what motivated him or her to write the note. Given that the note's predictions were faulty in one significant respect, and were corroborated by nothing except ordinary innocent activity, I must surmise that the Court's evaluation of the warrant's validity has been colored by subsequent events. * * *

Notes and Questions

1. In MASSACHUSETTS v. UPTON, 466 U.S. 727 (1984), police Lt. Beland assisted in the execution of a search warrant for a motel room reserved by one Richard Kelleher, which produced several items of identification belonging to two persons whose homes had recently been burglarized. Other items taken in the burglaries, such as jewelry, silver and gold, were not found. A few hours later Beland received a call from an unidentified female who told him that there was "a motor home full of stolen stuff," including jewelry, silver and gold, at George Upton's premises. After verifying that a motor home was parked there, Beland prepared an application for a search warrant, to which he attached the police reports on the two prior burglaries, along with lists of the stolen property, and his affidavit with the above information and the following:

1. The anonymous note suggested that she was going down on Wednesday, but for all the officers knew she had been in Florida for a month.

2. Lance does not appear to have behaved suspiciously in flying down to Florida. He made a reservation in his own name and gave an accurate home phone number to the airlines. And Detective Mader's affidavit does not report that he did any of the other things drug couriers are notorious for doing, such as paying for the ticket in cash, dressing casually, looking pale and nervous, improperly filling out baggage tags, carrying American Tourister luggage, not carrying any luggage, or changing airlines en route.

3. Detective Mader's affidavit hinted darkly that the couple had set out upon "that interstate highway commonly used by travelers to the Chicago area." But the same highway is also commonly used by travelers to Disney World, Sea World, and Ringling Brothers and Barnum and Bailey Circus World. It is also the road to Cocoa Beach, Cape Canaveral, and Washington, D.C. I would venture that each year dozens of perfectly innocent people fly to Florida, meet a waiting spouse, and drive off together in the family car.

"She further stated that George Upton was going to move the motor home any time now because of the fact that Ricky Kelleher's motel room was raided and that George Upton had purchased these stolen items from Ricky Kelleher. This unidentified female stated that she had seen the stolen items but refused to identify herself because 'he'll kill me,' referring to George Upton. I then told this unidentified female that I knew who she was, giving her the name of Lynn Alberico, who I had met on May 16, 1980, at George Upton's repair shop off Summer St., in Yarmouthport. She was identified to me by George Upton as being his girlfriend, Lynn Alberico. The unidentified female admitted that she was the girl that I had named, stating that she was surprised that I knew who she was. She then told me that she'd broken up with George Upton and wanted to burn him. She also told me that she wouldn't give me her address or phone number but that she would contact me in the future, if need be."

A magistrate issued the warrant, and a subsequent search of the motor home produced the described items. The Supreme Court, per curiam upheld the warrant:

"Examined in light of *Gates*, Lt. Beland's affidavit provides a substantial basis for the issuance of the warrant. No single piece of evidence in it is conclusive. But the pieces fit neatly together and, so viewed, support the magistrate's determination that there was 'a fair probability that contraband or evidence of crime' would be found in Upton's motor home. The informant claimed to have seen the stolen goods and gave a description of them which tallied with the items taken in recent burglaries. She knew of the raid on the motel room—which produced evidence connected to those burglaries—and that the room had been reserved by Kelleher. She explained the connection between Kelleher's motel room and the stolen goods in Upton's motor home. And she provided a motive both for her attempt at anonymity—fear of Upton's retaliation—and for furnishing the information—her recent breakup with Upton and her desire 'to burn him.' "[a]

2. While the Fourth Amendment expressly requires probable cause for a valid arrest warrant or search warrant, police are often permitted to make arrests and searches without first obtaining a warrant, in which case the Fourth Amendment's protection against "unreasonable searches and seizures" applies. But, because a "principal incentive" for the procurement of warrants would be destroyed if police needed less evidence when acting without a warrant, the requirements in such instances "surely cannot be less stringent" than when a warrant is obtained, *Wong Sun v. United States*, 371 U.S. 471 (1963), meaning probable cause is also required for warrantless arrests and searches.[b]

3. It is generally assumed that the same quantum of evidence is required whether one is concerned with probable cause to arrest or probable cause to search. However, probable cause for search requires a somewhat different kind of conclusion than probable cause for arrest. For arrest, there must be a substantial probability that a crime has been committed and that the person to be arrested committed it; for search, there must be a substantial probability that certain items are the fruits, instrumentalities or evidence of crime and that these items are presently to be found at a certain place.

a. Brennan and Marshall, JJ., dissented from the summary disposition of the case and would have denied the petition for certiorari. After remand, *Commonwealth v. Upton,* 476 N.E.2d 548 (Mass.1985), held that *Aguilar* and *Spinelli* "provide a more appropriate structure for probable cause inquiries" under the *state* constitution, and concluded that the affidavit failed to establish probable cause.

b. However, as discussed in §§ 7, 8 of this chapter, certain kinds of searches and seizures, because they involve a lesser degree of intrusion or interference, are permitted upon less than the traditional amount of probable cause.

Because the latter type of probable cause has to do with the *present* location of certain objects, it may be found to be lacking because the time of the facts relied upon is unknown or highly uncertain. Does this mean, as held in *Schmidt v. State*, 659 S.W.2d 420 (Tex.Crim.App.1983), that there was no probable cause to search defendant's car for drugs when the affidavit said defendant, "presently under medical attention," had been found in that vehicle in need of medical attention and had said then that he "had been sniffing cocaine," in that the only reference to time is ambiguous because it is not clear whether defendant had been under medical attention "for a few hours or a few months"? When the time of the facts is given probable cause will sometimes be lacking because that information has become "stale."[c] See, e.g., *United States v. Steeves,* 525 F.2d 33 (8th Cir.1975) (warrant to search for clothing, ski mask, hand gun, money and money bag, all sought as evidence of bank robbery which occupant of premises participated in three months earlier; held, there was no probable cause the money or bag would still be there, but there was probable cause the other items would be there, as "a highly incriminating or consumable item of personal property is less likely to remain in one place as long as an item of property which is not consumable or which is innocuous in itself or not particularly incriminating"). Finally, even if no such problems are present, it must be remembered that to have probable cause to search there must be a sufficient connection of the items sought with a particular place. Thus, while a valid search warrant can sometimes issue even when the perpetrator of the crime is unknown, it does not necessarily follow that probable cause to arrest a person will likewise constitute probable cause to search that person's residence for evidence of that crime. See, e.g., *United States v. Lalor*, 996 F.2d 1578 (4th Cir.1993) (where informants gave information re defendant's drug sales at certain street corner, probable cause to search defendant's residence elsewhere lacking where affidavit does not "explain the geographic relationship between the area where the drug sales occurred" and defendant's residence).

4. When the police act without a warrant, they initially make the probable cause decision themselves, although it is subject to after-the-fact review by a judicial officer upon a motion to suppress evidence found because of the arrest or search. When the police act with a warrant, the probable cause decision is made by a magistrate in the first instance, but his decision may likewise be challenged in an adversary setting upon a motion to suppress (except insofar as the question is avoided entirely by reliance on *United States v. Leon,* p. 224). In a warrant case, the issue upon the motion to suppress is usually cast in terms of whether the facts set out in the complaint or affidavit upon which the warrant was issued establish probable cause.[d] However, the dissenters in *Aguilar* suggested that a defective affidavit might be cured by what the judge was told at the time the warrant was sought, and they would also resuscitate the affidavit on the basis of the officer's subsequent testimony on the motion to suppress.

As to the first possibility, consider *United States v. Clyburn,* 24 F.3d 613 (4th Cir.1994) (the "Fourth Amendment does not require that the basis for probable cause be established in a written affidavit," and thus "magistrates may consider

c. In contrast to the "stale" information problem, the question is sometimes raised whether the information is premature, in the sense that it only shows that certain goods are to be at a certain place at some future time. Most courts agree with *People v. Glen,* 282 N.E.2d 614 (N.Y.1972), noted in 19 Wayne L.Rev. 1339 (1973) (search warrant issued on information that package containing narcotics would arrive at designated premises on future date; held: "as long as the evidence creates substantial probability that the seizable property will be on the premises when searched, the warrant should be sustained").

d. But consider *United States v. Marin–Buitrago*, 734 F.2d 889 (2d Cir.1984), holding that police are required "to report [to the magistrate who issued the warrant] any material changes in the facts contained in a warrant affidavit that occur before the warrant is executed."

sworn, unrecorded oral testimony in making probable cause determinations during warrant proceedings," even though "presentation of written affidavits or recorded testimony provides a preferable way of securing a search warrant"; Fed.R.Crim.P. 41(c)(1) requirement that all information showing probable cause be in affidavit not applicable here, as warrant at issue obtained by local police from local magistrate). As to the second possibility, consider *Whiteley v. Warden,* 401 U.S. 560 (1971): "Under the cases of this Court, an otherwise insufficient affidavit cannot be rehabilitated by testimony concerning information possessed by the affiant when he sought the warrant but not disclosed to the issuing magistrate. * * * A contrary rule would, of course, render the warrant requirements of the Fourth Amendment meaningless."

5. Does it follow that the defendant may not challenge an affidavit which is sufficient on its face? No, the Court answered in FRANKS v. DELAWARE, 438 U.S. 154 (1978). Reasoning that (i) "a flat ban on impeachment of veracity could denude the probable cause requirement of all real meaning," (ii) "the hearing before the magistrate not always will suffice to discourage lawless or reckless misconduct," (iii) "the alternative sanctions of a perjury prosecution, administrative discipline, contempt, or a civil suit are not likely to fill the gap," (iv) "allowing an evidentiary hearing, after a suitable preliminary proffer of material falsity, will not diminish the importance and solemnity of the warrant-issuing process," (v) "the claim that a post-search hearing will confuse the issue of the defendant's guilt with the issue of the State's possible misbehavior is footless," and (vi) allowing impeachment does not really extend the exclusionary rule "to a 'new' area," the Court, per BLACKMUN, J., held "that, where the defendant makes a substantial preliminary showing that a false statement knowingly and intentionally, or with reckless disregard for the truth, was included by the affiant in the warrant affidavit, and if the allegedly false statement is necessary to the finding of probable cause, the Fourth Amendment requires that a hearing be held at the defendant's request. In the event that at that hearing the allegation of perjury or reckless disregard is established by the defendant by a preponderance of the evidence, and, with the affidavit's false material set to one side, the affidavit's remaining content is insufficient to establish probable cause, the search warrant must be voided and the fruits of the search excluded to the same extent as if probable cause was lacking on the face of the affidavit."[e]

Shouldn't the same result obtain if the false statement was negligently made, as reasoned in *Theodor v. Superior Court,* 501 P.2d 234 (Cal.1972), given "the overriding principle of reasonableness which governs the application of the Fourth Amendment"? Shouldn't the same result follow even as to innocently made falsehoods, where "[a]n honestly-erring individual * * * has substituted his erroneous judgment for that of the magistrate," as argued in Comment, 19 U.C.L.A.L.Rev. 96, 140 (1971)? If there was a deliberate false statement, then why shouldn't this *always* invalidate the warrant because, as stated in *United States v. Carmichael,* 489 F.2d 983 (7th Cir.1973), "[t]he fullest deterrent sanctions of the exclusionary rule should be applied to such serious and deliberate government wrongdoing"?

Should *Franks* apply where defendant's objection is that the police left out of the affidavit some additional information which would have put into question the probable cause shown by the information included? If so, what constitutes a material omission for this purpose, and what is the applicable mental state regarding the affiant's failure to include that information?

e. Rehnquist, J., joined by the Chief Justice, dissenting, argued: "If the function of the warrant requirement is to obtain the determination of a neutral magistrate as to whether sufficient grounds have been urged to support the issuance of a warrant, that function is fulfilled at the time the magistrate concludes that the requirement has been met."

NOTES ON THE INFORMER'S PRIVILEGE

1. In McCRAY v. ILLINOIS, 386 U.S. 300 (1967), petitioner was arrested and found to have heroin on his person. At the suppression hearing, the arresting officers testified that an informant who had supplied reliable information in about 20 previous cases told them that he had observed McCray selling narcotics at a certain corner and then accompanied them to that corner and pointed him out. Both officers were asked for the name and address of the informant, but objections to these questions were sustained. Petitioner's motion was denied, and he was subsequently convicted. The Court, per STEWART, J., affirmed:

"When the issue is not guilt or innocence, but, as here, the question of probable cause for an arrest or search, the Illinois Supreme Court has held that police officers need not invariably be required to disclose an informant's identity if the trial judge is convinced, by evidence submitted in open court and subject to cross-examination, that the officers did rely in good faith upon credible information supplied by a reliable informant. This Illinois evidentiary rule is consistent with the law of many other States. * * *

"The reasoning of the Supreme Court of New Jersey in judicially adopting the same basic evidentiary rule was instructively expressed by Chief Justice Weintraub in *State v. Burnett*, 201 A.2d 39 [N.J.1964]:

" 'If a defendant may insist upon disclosure of the informant in order to test the truth of the officer's statement that there is an informant or as to what the informant related or as to the informant's reliability, we can be sure that every defendant will demand disclosure. He has nothing to lose and the prize may be the suppression of damaging evidence if the State cannot afford to reveal its source, as is so often the case. And since there is no way to test the good faith of a defendant who presses the demand, we must assume the routine demand would have to be routinely granted. The result would be that the State could use the informant's information only as a lead and could search only if it could gather adequate evidence of probable cause apart from the informant's data. Perhaps that approach would sharpen investigatorial techniques, but we doubt that there would be enough talent and time to cope with crime upon that basis. Rather we accept the premise that the informer is a vital part of society's defensive arsenal. The basic rule protecting his identity rests upon that belief. * * *

" 'We must remember also that we are not dealing with the trial of the criminal charge itself. There the need for a truthful verdict outweighs society's need for the informer privilege. Here, however, the accused seeks to avoid the truth. The very purpose of a motion to suppress is to escape the inculpatory thrust of evidence in hand, not because its probative force is diluted in the least by the mode of seizure, but rather as a sanction to compel enforcement officers to respect the constitutional security of all of us under the Fourth Amendment. * * * If the motion to suppress is denied, defendant will still be judged upon the untarnished truth. * * *

" 'The Fourth Amendment is served if a judicial mind passes upon the existence of probable cause. Where the issue is submitted upon an application for a warrant, the magistrate is trusted to evaluate the credibility of the affiant in an *ex parte* proceeding. As we have said, the magistrate is concerned, not with whether the informant lied, but with whether the affiant is truthful in his recitation of what he was told. If the magistrate doubts the credibility of the affiant, he may require that the informant be identified or even produced. It seems to us that the same approach is equally sufficient where the search was without a warrant, that is to say, that it should rest entirely with the judge who hears the motion to suppress to decide whether he needs such disclosure as to the informant in order to decide whether the officer is a believable witness.' * * *

"[W]e are now asked to hold that the Constitution somehow compels Illinois to abolish the informer's privilege from its law of evidence, and to require disclosure of the informer's identity in every such preliminary hearing where it appears that the officers made the arrest or search in reliance upon facts supplied by an informer they had reason to trust . . . * * *

"Nothing in the Due Process Clause of the Fourteenth Amendment requires a state court judge in every such hearing to assume the arresting officers are committing perjury."

DOUGLAS, J., joined by The Chief Justice, and Justices Brennan and Fortas, dissented:

"There is no way to determine the reliability of Old Reliable, the informer, unless he is produced, at the trial and cross-examined. Unless he is produced, the Fourth Amendment is entrusted to the tender mercies of the police. What we do today is to encourage arrests and searches without warrants. The whole momentum of criminal law administration should be in precisely the opposite direction, if the Fourth Amendment is to remain a vital force. Except in rare and emergency cases, it requires magistrates to make the findings of 'probable cause.' We should be mindful of its command that a judicial mind should be interposed between the police and the citizen. We should also be mindful that 'disclosure, rather than suppression, of relevant materials ordinarily promotes the proper administration of criminal justice.' "

2. How valid is the following criticism of *McCray* by Irving Younger, a former federal prosecutor, in *The Perjury Routine,* The Nation, May 8, 1967, pp. 596–97:

"[The *McCray* majority] said that 'nothing in the Due Process Clause of the Fourteenth Amendment requires a state court judge in every such hearing to assume the arresting officers are committing perjury.' Why not? Every lawyer who practices in the criminal courts knows that police perjury is commonplace.

"The reason is not hard to find. Policemen see themselves as fighting a two-front war—against criminals in the street and against 'liberal' rules of law in court. All's fair in this war, including the use of perjury to subvert 'liberal' rules of law that might free those who 'ought' to be jailed. * * *

"Far from adopting a presumption of perjury, the *McCray* case almost guarantees wholesale police perjury. When his conduct is challenged as constituting an unreasonable search and seizure, all the policeman need say is that an unnamed 'reliable informant' told him that the defendant was committing a crime. Henceforth, every policeman will have a genie-like informer to legalize his master's arrests."

3. Appellate decisions reversing a trial judge's denial of disclosure are extremely rare, and typically involve a situation in which the court could have simply said that probable cause had not been shown. But a growing number of cases are to be found along the lines of *People v. Darden,* 313 N.E.2d 49 (N.Y.1974), concluding it is "fair and wise, in a case such as this, where there is insufficient evidence to establish probable cause apart from the testimony of the arresting officer as to communications received from an informer, when the issue of identity of the informer is raised at the suppression hearing, for the suppression judge then to conduct an in camera inquiry. The prosecution should be required to make the informer available for interrogation before the Judge. The prosecutor may be present but not the defendant or his counsel. Opportunity should be afforded counsel for defendant to submit in writing any questions which he may desire the Judge to put to the informer. The Judge should take testimony, with recognition of the special need for protection of the interests of the absent defendant, and make a summary report as to the existence of the informer and with respect to the communications made by the informer to the police to which the police testify. That report should be made available to the defendant and to the People and the transcript of testimony should be sealed to be available to the appellate courts if the occasion arises." Contra: *State v. Richardson*, 529 A.2d 1236 (Conn.1987): "Requiring an informant to attend an in camera hearing involves a substantial risk that his identity will be discovered."

MARYLAND v. PRINGLE

540 U.S. 366, 124 S.Ct. 795, 157 L.Ed.2d 769 (2003).

Chief Justice REHNQUIST delivered the opinion of the Court. * * *

At 3:16 a.m. on August 7, 1999, a Baltimore County Police officer stopped a Nissan Maxima for speeding. There were three occupants in the car: Donte Partlow, the driver and owner, respondent Pringle, the front-seat passenger, and Otis Smith, the back-seat passenger. The officer asked Partlow for his license and registration. When Partlow opened the glove compartment to retrieve the vehicle registration, the officer observed a large amount of rolled-up money in the glove compartment. The officer returned to his patrol car with Partlow's license and registration to check the computer system for outstanding violations. The computer check did not reveal any violations. The officer returned to the stopped car, had Partlow get out, and issued him an oral warning.

After a second patrol car arrived, the officer asked Partlow if he had any weapons or narcotics in the vehicle. Partlow indicated that he did not. Partlow then consented to a search of the vehicle. The search yielded $763 from the glove compartment and five plastic glassine baggies containing cocaine from behind the back-seat armrest. When the officer began the search the armrest was in the upright position flat against the rear seat. The officer pulled down the armrest and found the drugs, which had been placed between the armrest and the back seat of the car.

The officer questioned all three men about the ownership of the drugs and money, and told them that if no one admitted to ownership of the drugs he was going to arrest them all. The men offered no information regarding the ownership of the drugs or money. All three were placed under arrest and transported to the police station.

Later that morning, Pringle * * * gave an oral and written confession in which he acknowledged that the cocaine belonged to him, that he and his friends were going to a party, and that he intended to sell the cocaine or "[u]se it for sex." Pringle maintained that the other occupants of the car did not know about the drugs, and they were released.

The trial court denied Pringle's motion to suppress his confession as the fruit of an illegal arrest, holding that the officer had probable cause to arrest Pringle. A jury convicted Pringle of possession with intent to distribute cocaine and possession of cocaine. He was sentenced to 10 years' incarceration without the possibility of parole. * * *

The Court of Appeals of Maryland, by divided vote, reversed, holding that, absent specific facts tending to show Pringle's knowledge and dominion or control over the drugs, "the mere finding of cocaine in the back armrest when [Pringle] was a front seat passenger in a car being driven by its owner is insufficient to establish probable cause for an arrest for possession." * * *

It is uncontested in the present case that the officer, upon recovering the five plastic glassine baggies containing suspected cocaine, had probable cause to believe a felony had been committed. The sole question is whether the officer had probable cause to believe that Pringle committed that crime.[1] * * *

The probable-cause standard is incapable of precise definition or quantification into percentages because it deals with probabilities and depends on the totality of the circumstances. We have stated, however, that "[t]he substance of all the definitions of probable cause is a reasonable ground for belief of guilt," and that the belief of guilt must be particularized with respect to the person to be searched or seized. * * *

In this case, Pringle was one of three men riding in a Nissan Maxima at 3:16 a.m. There was $763 of rolled-up cash in the glove compartment directly in front of Pringle.[2] Five plastic glassine baggies of cocaine were behind the back-seat armrest and accessible to all three men. Upon questioning, the three men failed to offer any information with respect to the ownership of the cocaine or the money.

We think it an entirely reasonable inference from these facts that any or all three of the occupants had knowledge of, and exercised dominion and control over, the cocaine. Thus a reasonable officer could conclude that there was probable cause to believe Pringle committed the crime of possession of cocaine, either solely or jointly.

Pringle's attempt to characterize this case as a guilt-by-association case is unavailing. His reliance on *Ybarra v. Illinois*, [p. 312], and *United States v. Di Re*, [p. 318 fn. 8], is misplaced. In *Ybarra*, police officers obtained a warrant to search a tavern and its bartender for evidence of possession of a controlled substance. Upon entering the tavern, the officers conducted patdown searches of the customers present in the tavern, including Ybarra. Inside a cigarette pack retrieved from Ybarra's pocket, an officer found six tinfoil packets containing heroin. We stated:

> "[A] person's mere propinquity to others independently suspected of criminal activity does not, without more, give rise to probable cause to search that person. Where the standard is probable cause, a search or seizure of a person must be supported by probable cause particularized with respect to that person. This requirement cannot be undercut or avoided by simply pointing to the fact that coincidentally there exists probable cause to search or seize another or to search the premises where the person may happen to be."

We held that the search warrant did not permit body searches of all of the tavern's patrons and that the police could not pat down the patrons for weapons, absent individualized suspicion.

This case is quite different from *Ybarra*. Pringle and his two companions were in a relatively small automobile, not a public tavern. In *Wyoming v. Houghton*, [p. 384], we noted that "a car passenger—unlike the unwitting tavern patron in *Ybarra*—will often be engaged in a common enterprise with the driver, and have the same interest in concealing the fruits or the evidence of their wrongdoing." Here we think it was reasonable for the officer to infer a common enterprise among the three men. The quantity of drugs and cash in the car indicated the likelihood of drug dealing, an enterprise to which a dealer would be unlikely to admit an innocent person with the potential to furnish evidence against him.

1. Maryland law defines "possession" as "the exercise of actual or constructive dominion or control over a thing by one or more persons."

2. The Court of Appeals of Maryland dismissed the $763 seized from the glove compartment as a factor in the probable-cause determination, stating that "[m]oney, without more, is innocuous." The court's consideration of the money in isolation, rather than as a factor in the totality of the circumstances, is mistaken in light of our precedents. * * * We think it is abundantly clear from the facts that this case involves more than money alone.

In *Di Re*, a federal investigator had been told by an informant, Reed, that he was to receive counterfeit gasoline ration coupons from a certain Buttitta at a particular place. The investigator went to the appointed place and saw Reed, the sole occupant of the rear seat of the car, holding gasoline ration coupons. There were two other occupants in the car: Buttitta in the driver's seat and Di Re in the front passenger's seat. Reed informed the investigator that Buttitta had given him counterfeit coupons. Thereupon, all three men were arrested and searched. After noting that the officers had no information implicating Di Re and no information pointing to Di Re's possession of coupons, unless presence in the car warranted that inference, we concluded that the officer lacked probable cause to believe that Di Re was involved in the crime. We said "[a]ny inference that everyone on the scene of a crime is a party to it must disappear if the Government informer singles out the guilty person." No such singling out occurred in this case; none of the three men provided information with respect to the ownership of the cocaine or money.

We hold that the officer had probable cause to believe that Pringle had committed the crime of possession of a controlled substance. Pringle's arrest therefore did not contravene the Fourth and Fourteenth Amendments. Accordingly, the judgment of the Court of Appeals of Maryland is reversed, and the case is remanded for further proceedings not inconsistent with this opinion. * * *

Notes and Questions

1. Note that the "any or all three" and "solely or jointly" language makes it apparent that the Court has accepted *both* of the following propositions: (i) there is probable cause that the three men were jointly in possession of the drugs; and (ii) there is probable cause that Pringle alone was in possession of the drugs. Are you convinced as to both, one or neither?

2. On what basis can an inference of *sole* possession by Pringle be drawn? Can such an inference be squared with the common assertion that the "person who owns or exercises dominion and control over a motor vehicle in which contraband is concealed, is deemed to possess the contraband," *Leavell v. Commonwealth*, 737 S.W.2d 695 (Ky.1987)? Is this because Partlow consented to the search that uncovered the cocaine? Because, as the Court notes at one point, there "was $763 of rolled-up cash in the glove compartment directly in front of Pringle"? Because, as the Court also notes, the hidden cocaine was "accessible to all three men"?

3. If drawing an inference of sole possession by Pringle is otherwise problematical, may it be said then that the point of *Pringle* is that when the presence of drugs has been established beyond question and it is a virtual certainty that the possession was by one of the three men in the vehicle at the time it was stopped, none of whom admitted possession, so that there is no clear basis for selecting one of the three to the exclusion of the two others, there is consequently a 33 1/3% possibility as to each of them, which should be deemed sufficient to establish probable cause as to each of them?

Is this branch of *Pringle* supported by *State v. Thomas,* 421 S.E.2d 227 (W.Va.1992), where police, investigating a sexual assault-murder apparently committed by one person acting alone, obtained separate search warrants to search the homes and cars of Mosier and Thomas, each of whom was known to have had contact with the victim on the night of her death and to fit the FBI psychological profile of a possible perpetrator of such crimes. As the court recognized, such facts starkly present this issue: "If the same facts can be used to implicate more than one person in a crime that could have been committed by one of them, can probable cause be found to exist?" Relying on the *Gates* assertion that no "numerically precise degree of certainty" is required to show probable cause, the *Thomas* court answered in the affirmative and thus upheld the search warrant which resulted in discovery of a minute portion of the victim's type of blood in defendant's car. Does the *Pringle* Court's assertion that the probable cause standard "is incapable of precise definition or quantification into percentages" manifest an acceptance or rejection of the *Thomas* approach, considering that such a version of probable cause was both championed and condemned in the various briefs in *Pringle* and was questioned as to its limits during oral argument of the case (e.g., as to what the outcome then would be if there were, say, 5 or 10 occupants of the vehicle)?

4. What then of the Court's alternative conclusion in *Pringle*, namely, that there was probable cause that the three occupants of the vehicle were in joint possession of the cocaine: "it was reasonable for the officer to infer a common enterprise among the three men" because the "quantity of drugs and cash in the car indicated the likelihood of drug dealing, an enterprise to which a dealer would be unlikely to admit an innocent person with the potential to furnish evidence against him"? Is such an inference more readily drawn in *Pringle*, where the drugs were not in view and it was unknown whether the drug dealing would occur 10 minutes, 10 hours, or 10 days in the future, as compared to *Di Re*, where the driver brought Di Re with him to the very place and time of the prearranged sale of counterfeit rationing coupons, which were in plain view in the vehicle (albeit perhaps not readily recognizable as contraband)? Can *Di Re* be distinguished on the basis of what *Pringle* calls the "singling out" of the guilty party, considering that *Di Re* itself only says that "Reed, on being asked [about the ration coupons in his hand], said he obtained them from Buttitta" but said nothing one way or another about Di Re?

5. Given the Court's conclusion that an inference of a "common enterprise" was permissible in *Pringle,* in what other situations is such an inference likewise permissible? Does the Court's reliance on *Houghton* mean *Pringle* is only a vehicle case, or does it also apply when drugs and money are uncovered in an apartment where three persons are present? Does the inference apply only when there is a "relatively small automobile," as the Court characterized the situation in *Pringle,* or also to SUVs, vans, and buses? Does it apply only when large sums of money and substantial quantities of drugs are *both* present? Also, what if in *Pringle* (a) the vehicle had been a taxi; (b) the vehicle was private but Pringle asserted he was a hitchhiker, which the other occupants did not dispute; or (c) the vehicle was private but Pringle asserted, without contradiction, that he was being driven home?

NOTES ON OTHER SOURCES OF PROBABLE CAUSE

The probable cause decisions of the United States Supreme Court, mostly concerned with when information from an informant, with or without some corroborating facts, is sufficient for arrest or search, are not fairly representative of the full range of probable cause issues confronted by the police. Consider these situations:

1. ***Information from an alleged victim of, or witness to, a crime.*** A major distinction between the victim-witness cases and the informant cases is that prior reliability need not be shown as to the former. As explained in *State v. Paszek,* 184 N.W.2d 836 (Wis.1971), "an ordinary citizen who reports a crime which has been committed in his presence, or that a crime is being or will be committed, stands on much different ground than a police informer. He is a witness to criminal activity who acts with an intent to aid the police in law enforcement because of his concern for society or for his own safety. He does not expect any gain or concession in exchange for his information. An informer of this type usually would not have more than one opportunity to supply information to the police, thereby precluding proof of his reliability by pointing to previous accurate information which he has supplied."

In the victim-witness cases, the critical question usually is whether the general description given by the victim or witness is sufficient to justify the arrest of any one person. For example, in *Brown v. United States,* 365 F.2d 976 (D.C.Cir.1966), the police received a radio report at 4:30 a.m. of a recent armed robbery, and were told to be on the lookout for a heavily built black male driving a maroon 1954 Ford. Shortly thereafter, 20 blocks from the robbery scene, the police saw what they thought to be such a car (actually, it was a 1952 Ford), and radioed for details about the robber. They were told that the robber was about five feet five inches, and that he was wearing a brown jacket and cream-colored straw hat. The suspect was about five feet eleven inches, was wearing blue, and had only a felt hat, but he was nonetheless arrested. Held: "These discrepancies, which can be the result of the victim's excitement or poor visibility or of the suspect's changing clothes, did not destroy the ascertainment made on the basis of the accurate portion of the identification, which was by itself enough to constitute probable cause."

2. ***Direct observations by police.*** Most troublesome, because the situations are so varied, are those cases in which the probable cause determination must be made solely upon suspicious conduct observed by police. For example, in *Brooks v. United States,* 159 A.2d 876 (D.C.Mun.App.1960), an officer observed two men, both known to have prior convictions for larceny, carrying a console-type record player in the commercial area at 6:30 p.m. The officer noted that the player was new and still bore store tags. Upon questioning, one of the suspects said the machine belonged to his mother and that he was taking it in to be repaired. When the officer pointed out the tags, the suspect changed his story and said that the machine had been given to him by an unknown person, whom he was unable to describe. The officer then placed the two men under arrest. The court, noting that "the probabilities must be measured by the standards of the reasonable, cautious and prudent peace officer as he sees them, and not those of the casual passerby," held that the officer had acted on probable cause.

What if the officer had not known of the suspects' past records? What if the suspects had refused to answer any questions? Or, what if the suspect had not changed his first story? If the officer had been aware of the fact that larcenies were common in that area, would this be relevant?[a] What if the suspects had taken flight upon being stopped? Cf. Note 7, p. 422. What if they had engaged in "furtive gestures" upon seeing the police? To what extent, if at all, should account

a. Consider *United States v. Davis,* 458 F.2d 819 (D.C.Cir.1972): "Although no presumption of guilt arises from the activities of inhabitants of an area in which the police know that narcotics offenses frequently occur, the syndrome of criminality in those areas cannot realistically go unnoticed by the judiciary. It too is a valid consideration when coupled with other reliable indicia or suspicious circumstances. We make this statement warily, for it is all too clear that few live in these areas by choice."

Compare Jerome H. Skolnick, *Justice Without Trial* 217–18 (1966): "If an honest citizen resides in a neighborhood heavily populated by criminals, just as the chances are high that he might be one, so too are the chances high that he might be mistaken for one. The probabilities, from the point of view of the individual, are always the same—either he is or is not culpable. Thus, behavior which seems 'reasonable' to the police because of the character of the neighborhood is seen by the honest citizen in it as irresponsible and unreasonable. About *him,* more errors will necessarily be made under a 'reasonableness' standard."

be taken of the expertise of the police in ascertaining what is probably criminal conduct?[b]

3. ***Information and orders from official channels.*** In *Whiteley v. Warden,* 401 U.S. 560 (1971), Laramie, Wyoming police arrested two men fitting a description given in a police bulletin emanating from the office of the Carbon County Sheriff and transmitted over the state police radio network, indicating that the two described men were wanted for breaking and entering and that a warrant had been issued for their arrest. Although the warrant had not issued on probable cause, the state claimed that the arrests made by the Laramie officers were nonetheless legal because "they reasonably assumed that whoever authorized the bulletin had probable cause to direct Whiteley's and Daley's arrest." The Court, per Justice Harlan, disagreed: "We do not of course question that the Laramie police were entitled to act on the strength of the radio bulletin. Certainly police officers called upon to aid other officers in executing arrest warrants are entitled to assume that the officers requesting aid offered the magistrate the information requisite to support an independent judicial assessment of probable cause. Where, however, the contrary turns out to be true, an otherwise illegal arrest cannot be insulated from challenge by the decision of the instigating officer to rely on fellow officers to make the arrest."[c] What is the status of *Whiteley* after *Evans,* p. 245, where the Court distinguished *Whiteley,* relied upon by the defendant, because it mistakenly "treated identification of a Fourth Amendment violation as synonymous with application of the exclusionary rule to evidence secured incident to that violation"?

SECTION 4. SEARCH WARRANTS

A. Issuance of the Warrant

1. ***The "neutral and detached magistrate" requirement.*** Consider *Coolidge v. New Hampshire,* 403 U.S. 443 (1971) (where State Attorney General, authorized by state law to issue search warrants as a justice of the peace, issued search warrant for defendant's car in course of murder investigation of which he had taken personal charge and for which he later served as chief prosecutor at trial, this procedure "violated a fundamental premise of both the Fourth and Fourteenth Amendments" because "the state official who was the chief investigator and prosecutor in this case * * * was not the neutral and detached magistrate required by the Constitution"); *Connally v. Georgia,* 429 U.S. 245 (1977) (search warrant not issued by a "neutral and detached magistrate" where issuing justice of the peace was unsalaried and, so far as search warrants were concerned, was paid a fee of $5 if he issued a warrant but nothing if he denied the application); *Rooker v. Commonwealth,* 508 S.W.2d 570 (Ky.App.1974) (in ruling that evidence obtained in execution of a search warrant must be suppressed, court held that where "a judge issues a search warrant based upon an affidavit which he does not read, he makes no determination of probable cause but merely serves as a rubber stamp for the police. Such action is improper even though the affidavit actually shows probable cause for the issuance of the warrant").

b. Compare *United States v. 1964 Ford Thunderbird,* 445 F.2d 1064 (3d Cir.1971) ("The standard is not what a police officer trained in a particular field would conclude, but rather it is what a reasonable prudent man would conclude"); with *United States v. Hoyos,* 892 F.2d 1387 (9th Cir.1989) (the "experience and expertise of the officers involved in the investigation and arrest may be considered in determining probable cause").

c. Compare *United States v. Webster,* 750 F.2d 307 (5th Cir.1984) (arrest illegal notwithstanding probable cause at the source of the request, as defendant was arrested in response to a request which merely asked that anyone discovered in the area of the crime be picked up).

Compare *Shadwick v. City of Tampa,* 407 U.S. 345 (1972), where a unanimous Court, per Powell, J., upheld a city charter provision authorizing municipal court clerks to issue *arrest* warrants for municipal ordinance violations. Rejecting the notion "that all warrant authority must reside exclusively in a lawyer or judge" (and noting that "even within the federal system warrants were until recently widely issued by nonlawyers"), the Court concluded that "an issuing magistrate must meet two tests. He must be neutral and detached, and he must be capable of determining whether probable cause exists for the requested arrest or search." The clerk possesses the requisite detachment, as he "is removed from prosecutor or police and works within the judicial branch subject to the supervision of the municipal court judge."[a] As to capacity: "We presume from the nature of the clerk's position that he would be able to deduce from the facts on an affidavit before him whether there was probable cause to believe a citizen guilty of impaired driving, breach of peace, drunkenness, trespass or the multiple other common offenses covered by a municipal code. There has been no showing that this is too difficult a task for a clerk to accomplish. Our legal system has long entrusted nonlawyers to evaluate more complex and significant factual data than that in the case at hand. Grand juries daily determine probable cause prior to rendering indictments, and trial juries assess whether guilt is proved beyond a reasonable doubt." On the basis of *Shadwick,* could court clerks be authorized to issue arrest warrants in all cases? To issue search warrants? If so, can *Shadwick* be reconciled with *Leon*, p. 224?

United States v. Davis, 346 F.Supp. 435 (S.D.Ill.1972), involved these facts: A Treasury agent, accompanied by an assistant U.S. attorney, went to Magistrate Ghiglieri and presented an affidavit for a search warrant. The agent did not swear to the affidavit, but the magistrate dated and signed the affidavit and indicated that it was denied. The following day the agent, again accompanied by the assistant, went to Magistrate Giffin and presented the same affidavit. Giffin, after being apprised of the proceedings before Ghiglieri, issued a search warrant. The court found this procedure to be "highly improper" and concluded: "Magistrate Ghiglieri's decision was final and binding, and his denial of the application * * * equitably estopped Magistrate Giffin from issuing a search warrant on the exact same showing." Is this a desirable result, in that it limits magistrate-shopping? If the first magistrate was in error, what recourse should be open to the affiant-officer?

2. *Particular description of the place to be searched.* As for the Fourth Amendment requirement of particularity in the description of the place to be searched, it "is enough if the description is such that the officer with a search warrant can, with reasonable effort ascertain and identify the place intended." *Steele v. United States,* 267 U.S. 498 (1925). The common practice is to identify premises in an urban area by street address, which is sufficient. Less particularity is required for rural premises; for example, description of a farm by the name of the owner and general directions for reaching the farm is adequate.

Most of the problems which arise concerning the particularity of description occur not because the warrant description is facially vague, but rather because upon execution it proves to be not as certain as theretofore assumed. One possibility is that the description will turn out not to be sufficiently precise, as where the warrant refers to apartment 3 in a certain building but the officers find apartments with that number on each floor. In this kind of case, courts are receptive to a showing that the executing officers had other information (e.g., the

a. Is the magistrate sufficiently detached from the police if it is his practice to assist the police in the preparation of search warrant affidavits? See *United States v. Steed,* 465 F.2d 1310 (9th Cir.1972); *Albitez v. Beto,* 465 F.2d 954 (5th Cir.1972). If he assists the police in execution of the warrant? See *Lo-Ji Sales, Inc. v. New York,* 442 U.S. 319 (1979).

occupant's name), via the affidavit or otherwise, which made it apparent which place was intended.

Another type of case is that in which the executing officers find that some but not all of the descriptive facts fit the same place. Illustrative is *State v. Blackburn,* 511 P.2d 381 (Or.1973), where the apartment in a particular building was said to be apartment number 2 with "the letters ECURB on the door," but the officer found one apartment with the numeral 2 on the door and another with no numeral but the letters ECURB on the door. In upholding the search of the latter apartment, the court held that "there could be no real doubt as to which of the premises was intended" because "[n]o one could have made a mistake or been confused about a word like ECURB, but anyone could easily have made a mistake about a numeral."

In the absence of a probable cause showing as to all the separate living units in a multiple-occupancy structure, the warrant for such a building must describe the particular unit to be searched. But, if the building in question from its outward appearance would be taken to be a single-occupancy structure and neither the affiant nor other investigating officers nor the executing officers knew or had reason to know otherwise until execution of the warrant was under way, then the warrant is not defective for failure to specify a unit within the building.

A similar situation, was involved in MARYLAND v. GARRISON, 480 U.S. 79 (1987), where police obtained a search warrant to search the person of one McWebb and "the premises known as 2036 Park Avenue third floor apartment," but discovered only after uncovering contraband during execution that they were in respondent's separate apartment. The Court, per STEVENS, J., concluded: (i) that the search warrant authorized search of the entire third floor but yet "was valid when it issued," for such validity "must be assessed on the basis of the information that the officers disclosed, or had a duty to discover and to disclose, to the issuing magistrate"; (ii) that the execution of the search warrant was valid because "the officers' failure to realize the overbreadth of the warrant was objectively understandable and reasonable." BLACKMUN, J., for the three dissenters, objected: (i) that the search warrant did not authorize search of the entire third floor, but only the apartment on that floor belonging to McWebb; and (ii) that the police knew the building was a multiple-occupancy structure and should have known before obtaining the search warrant and did know before executing it that there were seven apartments in the 3-story building, and thus unreasonably assumed the third floor was but one apartment.

3. *Particular description of the things to be seized.* The Fourth Amendment requirement of particularity in the description of the persons[b] or things to be seized is intended to prevent general searches, to prevent the seizure of objects on the mistaken assumption that they fall within the magistrate's authorization, and to prevent "the issuance of warrants on loose, vague or doubtful bases of fact." *Go-Bart Importing Co. v. United States,* 282 U.S. 344 (1931). As noted in SEARCHSZR § 4.6:

"Consistent with these three purposes are certain general principles which may be distilled from the decided cases in this area. They are: (1) A greater degree of ambiguity will be tolerated when the police have done the best that could be expected under the circumstances, by acquiring all the descriptive facts which reasonable investigation of this type of crime could be expected to uncover and by ensuring that all of those facts were included in the warrant.[19] (2) A more general

b. Search warrants are usually issued to search for and seize evidence of crimes, but are sometimes issued to seek "a person to be arrested [see *Steagald v. United States*, p. 370] or a person who is unlawfully restrained." Fed. R.Crim.P. 41(c)(4).

19. * * * Compare * * * *United States v. Blakeney*, 942 F.2d 1001 (6th Cir.1991) ("jewel-type of description will be sufficient when the nature of the objects to be seized are such that they could not be expected to have more specific characteristics.[20] (3) A less precise description is required of property which is, because of its particular character, contraband. (4) Failure to provide all of the available descriptive facts is not a basis for questioning the adequacy of the description when the omitted facts could not have been expected to be of assistance to the executing officer.[22] (5) An error in the statement of certain descriptive facts is not a basis for questioning the adequacy of the description if the executing officer was nonetheless able to determine, from the other facts provided, that the object seized was that intended by the description.[23] (6) Greater care in description is ordinarily called for when the type of property sought is generally in lawful use in substantial quantities.[24] (7) A more particular description than otherwise might be necessary is required when other objects of the same general classification are likely to be found at the particular place to be searched.[25] (8) The greatest care in description is required when the consequences of a seizure of innocent articles by mistake is most substantial, as when the objects to be seized are books or films or indicia of membership in an association, or where the place to be searched is an attorney's office. (9) The mere fact that some items were admittedly improperly seized in execution of the warrant 'does not mean that the warrant was not sufficiently particular.' (10) The Fourth Amendment's particularity requirement does *not* 'require particularity with respect to the criminal activity suspected.' (11) Some leeway will be tolerated where it appears additional time could have resulted in a more particularized description, where there was 'some urgency to conduct a search * * * before the defendant had the opportunity to remove or destroy the evidence' sought."

4. ***Particular description, reliance on affidavit.*** Courts have frequently been confronted with the question of whether a particularity defect in a warrant can be overcome by a sufficient description in the supporting affidavit, and the Supreme Court had occasion to deal with a rather unusual fact situation in this regard in GROH v. RAMIREZ, described at p. 236. On whether there had been a valid with-warrant search, the Court concluded:

"The fact that the *application* adequately described the 'things to be seized' does not save the *warrant* from its facial invalidity. The Fourth Amendment by its terms requires particularity in the warrant, not in the supporting documents. * * * And for good reason: 'The presence of a search warrant served a high function,' * * * and that high function is not necessarily vindicated when some other document, somewhere, says something about the objects of the search, but the contents of that document are neither known to the person whose home is being searched nor available for her inspection. We do not say that the Fourth Amendment forbids a warrant from cross-referencing other documents. Indeed, most Courts of Appeals have held that a court may construe a warrant with reference to a supporting application or affidavit if the warrant uses appropriate words of incorporation, and if the supporting document accompanies the warrant.

ry" insufficient where inventory available of what taken in jewelry store robbery) * * *.

20. * * * *State v. Salsman,* 290 A.2d 618 (N.H.1972) (description of 42 sheets of plywood sufficient, "considering the nature of these items"). * * *

22. * * * *United States v. Scharfman,* 448 F.2d 1352 (2d Cir.1971) (any effort to describe more particularly which furs in fur stores were stolen "would have required a legion of fur experts" to execute the warrant).

23. *United States v. Rytman,* 475 F.2d 192 (5th Cir.1973) (compressor of described brand and with serial number approximating that stated in the warrant could be seized); * * *

24. * * * *People v. Prall,* 145 N.E. 610 (Ill.1924) (thus description of "certain automobile tires and tubes" insufficient); * * *

25. * * * *United States v. Cook,* 657 F.2d 730 (5th Cir.1981) ("cassettes onto which * * * copyrighted films * * * have been electronically transferred" insufficient as to place with many other cassettes). * * *

* * * But in this case the warrant did not incorporate other documents by reference, nor did either the affidavit or the application * * * accompany the warrant. Hence, we need not further explore the matter of incorporation."

The Court in *Groh* then turned to the question of whether petitioner Groh was correct in asserting that the case was one in which it could be concluded a reasonable warrantless search was made because the search "was functionally equivalent to a search authorized by a valid warrant," in that "the goals served by the particularity requirement are otherwise satisfied." In examining that premise, the Court first considered the assertion that because the executing officers acted upon the basis of the sufficient description in the supporting documents, "the scope of the search did not exceed the limits set forth in the application." As to this, the Court concluded: "But unless the particular items described in the affidavit are also set forth in the warrant itself (or at least incorporated by reference, and the affidavit present at the search), there can be no written assurance that the Magistrate actually found probable cause to search for, and to seize, every item mentioned in the affidavit. * * * In this case, for example, it is at least theoretically possible that the Magistrate was satisfied that the search for weapons and explosives was justified by the showing in the affidavit, but not convinced that any evidentiary basis existed for rummaging through respondents' files and papers for receipts pertaining to the purchase or manufacture of such items. * * * Or, conceivably, the Magistrate might have believed that some of the weapons mentioned in the affidavit could have been lawfully possessed and therefore should not be seized. * * * The mere fact that the Magistrate issued a warrant does not necessarily establish that he agreed that the scope of the search should be as broad as the affiant's request." Two Justices disagreed on this branch of the case because "the more reasonable inference is that the Magistrate intended to authorize everything in the warrant application, as he signed the application and did not make any written adjustments to the application or the warrant itself."

Groh is an atypical case, quite unlike the usual case of this genre, and the majority seized upon its unique character as the fundamental reason for rejecting the contention that the search "was functionally equivalent to a search authorized by a valid warrant." "We disagree," the majority unequivocally responded, because the warrant "did not simply omit a few items from a list of many to be seized, or misdescribe a few of several items," nor "did it make what fairly could be characterized as a mere technical mistake or typographical error," but instead "did not describe the items to be seized *at all*." *Groh* thus covers the latter situation only, and leaves open the possibility that at least some of the other situations mentioned may justify affiant/executing officer reliance upon elaborating language in an unincorporated, unaccompanying affidavit.

5. *Neutrality, particularity, and "good faith."* Consider the impact of *United States v. Leon,* p. 224, and *Massachusetts v. Sheppard,* p. 235, in this context.

B. Execution of the Warrant

1. *Time of execution.* Statutes and court rules commonly provide that a search warrant must be executed within a certain time, such as 10 days. Execution within that time is proper, "provided that the probable cause recited in the affidavit continues until the time of execution, giving consideration to the intervening knowledge of the officers and the passage of time." *United States v. Nepstead,* 424 F.2d 269 (9th Cir.1970) (execution of warrant, for seizure of equipment used to manufacture LSD, 6 days after issuance timely, as premises under daily surveillance and no activity noted until after first 5 days).[c] Compare *State v. Neely,* 862 P.2d 1109 (Mont.1993) (where probable cause for search warrant not stale when it issued, warrant may be lawfully executed any time within 10–day statutory period); and consider the somewhat reverse situation in *State v. Miller,* 429 N.W.2d 26 (S.D.1988) (where violation of statutory 10–day rule but probable cause had not dissipated, suppression not necessary, as "the letter, not the spirit, of the law was broken").

Also, in many jurisdictions a search warrant may be served only in the daytime unless it expressly states to the contrary, and a warrant so stating often can be obtained only by meeting special requirements—e.g., obtaining the concurrence of two magistrates, showing that the property is definitely in the place to be searched, or showing some need for prompt action. In GOODING v. UNITED STATES, 416 U.S. 430 (1974), holding that the federal statute relating to searches for controlled substances required no special showing for a nighttime search other than that the contraband is likely to be on the property at that time, Justice MARSHALL, joined by Douglas and Brennan, JJ., noted in dissent that while the "constitutional question is not presented in this case and need not be resolved here," the principle that nighttime searches "involve a greater intrusion than ordinary searches and therefore require a greater justification * * * may well be a constitutional imperative. It is by now established Fourth Amendment doctrine that increasingly severe standards of probable cause are necessary to justify increasingly intrusive searches [citing *Camara v. Municipal Court,* p. 440]. In some situations—and the search of a private home during nighttime would seem to be a paradigm example—this principle requires a showing of additional justification for a search over and above the ordinary showing of probable cause."

In *United States v. Gervato,* 474 F.2d 40 (3d Cir.1973), the court emphasized the various protections provided by Fed.R.Crim.P. 41 in rejecting the district court's holding "that a search warrant executed in the absence of the occupant constitutes an unreasonable search because there exists the possibility of a general search and 'pilferage by officers of the law.' " So-called "sneak-and-peak" search warrants, authorizing police to enter premises, look around (e.g., to determine the status of a clandestine drug lab) and then depart without leaving any notice of the search, are deliberately executed when it is known no one is present. Given the Fourth Amendment requirement of notice of a search absent "some showing of special facts," *Berger v. New York,* p. 467, courts have imposed two limitations on such warrants: (i) "the court should not allow the officers to dispense with advance or contemporaneous notice of the search unless they have made a showing of reasonable necessity for the delay"; and (ii) "the court should nonetheless require the officers to give the appropriate person notice of the search within a reasonable time of the covert entry." *United States v. Villegas,* 899 F.2d 1324 (2d Cir.1990). What then of the much-disputed provision in the PATRIOT Act, 18 U.S.C.A. § 3103a(b), App. B, for a delayed notice search warrant?

2. *Gaining entry.* In *Wilson v. Arkansas,* 514 U.S. 927 (1995), a unanimous Court, per Thomas, J., proceeded "to resolve the conflict among the lower courts" by holding that the common law doctrine which "recognized a law enforcement officer's authority to break open the doors of a dwelling, but generally indicated that he first ought to announce his presence and authority," "forms a part of the reasonableness inquiry under the Fourth Amendment." The Court cautioned that the "Fourth Amendment's flexible requirement of reasonableness should not be read to mandate a rigid rule of announcement that ignores countervailing law enforcement interests," for "the common-law principle of announcement was never stated as an inflexible rule."

c. See also *United States v. Marin–Buitrago,* fn. d at p. 295.

In RICHARDS v. WISCONSIN, 520 U.S. 385 (1997), a unanimous Court, per STEVENS, J., rejected the state supreme court's holding that police officers are *never* required to knock and announce their presence when executing a search warrant in a felony drug investigation:

"The Wisconsin court explained its blanket exception as necessitated by the special circumstances of today's drug culture, and the State asserted at oral argument that the blanket exception was reasonable in 'felony drug cases because of the convergence in a violent and dangerous form of commerce of weapons and the destruction of drugs.' But creating exceptions to the knock-and-announce rule based on the 'culture' surrounding a general category of criminal behavior presents at least two serious concerns.

"First, the exception contains considerable overgeneralization. For example, while drug investigation frequently does pose special risks to officer safety and the preservation of evidence, not every drug investigation will pose these risks to a substantial degree. For example, a search could be conducted at a time when the only individuals present in a residence have no connection with the drug activity and thus will be unlikely to threaten officers or destroy evidence. Or the police could know that the drugs being searched for were of a type or in a location that made them impossible to destroy quickly. In those situations, the asserted governmental interests in preserving evidence and maintaining safety may not outweigh the individual privacy interests intruded upon by a no-knock entry. Wisconsin's blanket rule impermissibly insulates these cases from judicial review.

"A second difficulty with permitting a criminal-category exception to the knock-and-announce requirement is that the reasons for creating an exception in one category can, relatively easily, be applied to others. Armed bank robbers, for example, are, by definition, likely to have weapons, and the fruits of their crime may be destroyed without too much difficulty. If a per se exception were allowed for each category of criminal investigation that included a considerable—albeit hypothetical—risk of danger to officers or destruction of evidence, the knock-and-announce element of the Fourth Amendment's reasonableness requirement would be meaningless.

"Thus, the fact that felony drug investigations may frequently present circumstances warranting a no-knock entry cannot remove from the neutral scrutiny of a reviewing court the reasonableness of the police decision not to knock and announce in a particular case. Instead, in each case, it is the duty of a court confronted with the question to determine whether the facts and circumstances of the particular entry justified dispensing with the knock-and-announce requirement.

"In order to justify a 'no-knock' entry, the police must have a reasonable suspicion that knocking and announcing their presence, under the particular circumstances, would be dangerous or futile, or that it would inhibit the effective investigation of the crime by, for example, allowing the destruction of evidence. This standard—as opposed to a probable cause requirement—strikes the appropriate balance between the legitimate law enforcement concerns at issue in the execution of search warrants and the individual privacy interests affected by no-knock entries. * * * This showing is not high, but the police should be required to make it whenever the reasonableness of a no-knock entry is challenged."

The Court concluded with two additional points: (1) The trial judge had correctly concluded that the police were excused from the knock-and-announce requirement because of the facts of the particular case. The officer who knocked at the door of defendant's hotel room claimed to be a maintenance man, defendant opened the door slightly and upon seeing a uniformed officer slammed the door, at which the police kicked the door in and entered. As the Court explained, once "the officers reasonably believed that Richards knew who they were * * * it was reasonable for them to force entry immediately given the disposable nature of the drugs." (2) The refusal of the magistrate issuing the search warrant to issue a no-knock warrant[d] did not alter this conclusion, as "a magistrate's decision not to authorize a no-knock entry should not be interpreted to remove the officers authority to exercise independent judgment concerning the wisdom of a no-knock entry at the time the warrant is being executed."

In light of the test set out in *Richards* and the illustrations therein of what would *not* suffice, which of the following bits of information would justify an unannounced entry to execute a search warrant for drugs: (a) that the small amount of narcotics was always kept near a toilet; (b) that there was but a small amount of drugs; (c) that there was an unknown quantity of drugs; (d) that the person who planned to sell the drugs was present; (e) that the person who used the drugs was present; (f) that a person whose relationship to the drugs was unknown was present.

In UNITED STATES v. RAMIREZ, 523 U.S. 65 (1998), the Court, per REHNQUIST, C.J., unanimously held that whether the *Richards* reasonable suspicion test has been met "depends in no way on whether police must destroy property in order to enter." The Court then concluded that no Fourth Amendment violation had occurred in the instant case, where police executing a search warrant authorizing entry to seize a wanted person broke a garage window in order to deter the occupants of the premises (who thereafter exited and surrendered) from entering the garage to obtain weapons thought to be stored there: "A reliable confidential informant had notified the police that Alan Shelby might be inside respondent's home, and an officer had confirmed this possibility. Shelby was a prison escapee with a violent past who reportedly had access to a large supply of weapons. He had vowed that he would 'not do federal time.' The police certainly had a 'reasonable suspicion' that knocking and announcing their presence might be dangerous to themselves or to others."

In UNITED STATES v. BANKS, 540 U.S. 31 (2003), a unanimous Court, per SOUTER, J., decided two issues regarding the *Wilson* notice requirement: (i) how long a wait is necessary before the police may reasonably conclude they have been refused admittance; and (ii) what shorter wait will suffice because of what kind of exigent circumstances. As to the first, the Court declared that in the absence of exigent circumstances, the issue is simply whether the occupant's "failure to admit [the police] fairly suggested a refusal to let them in," which means the question would be whether it reasonably appeared to the police that "an occupant has had time to get to the door." This judgment, the Court emphasized, is to be made upon the facts known by the police at the time (so that it would not be relevant that, as in *Banks*, the occupant "was actually in the shower and did not hear the officers"). The amount of time needed would vary, the Court added, depending on "the size of the establishment," as it would take "perhaps five seconds to open a motel room door, or several minutes to move through a townhouse." But, the Court cautioned, "in the case with no reason to suspect an immediate risk of frustration or futility in waiting at all, the reasonable wait time

d. Wisconsin is among those few jurisdictions specifically authorizing magistrates to issue such search warrants, allowing entry without prior announcement, upon a sufficient showing to the magistrate of a need to do so. A "reverse twist" on the *Richards* view regarding a magistrate's *refusal* to issue such a warrant is the position, stated in *Parsley v. Superior Court*, 513 P.2d 611 (Cal.1973), that a magistrate's *issuance* of such a warrant is of no effect because "unannounced entry is excused only on the basis of exigent circumstances existing at the time an officer approached a site to make an arrest or execute a warrant," and thus "can be judged only in light of circumstances of which the officer is aware at the latter moment."

may well be longer when police make a forced entry, since they ought to be more certain the occupant has had time to answer the door."

But, as to the second question, where "the police claim exigent need to enter" and such claim is deemed legitimate when assessed under essentially "the same criteria" that apply to whether announcement is excused under *Richards,* then the "crucial fact" is "not time to reach the door but the particularly exigency claimed." The risk in *Banks,* re execution of a search warrant at Banks's apartment for cocaine, was that once the police announced their authority and purpose, the defendant would attempt to "flush away the easily disposable cocaine," which the Court concluded made it "reasonable to suspect imminent loss of evidence" after the 15–20 second wait. This was because such a lapse of time would suffice "for getting to the bathroom or the kitchen to start flushing cocaine down the drain," considering that "a prudent dealer will keep [the drugs] near a commode or kitchen sink," and also that the warrant was being executed "during the day, when anyone inside would probably have been up and around." The Court added that "since the bathroom and kitchen are usually in the interior of a dwelling, not the front hall, there is no reason generally to peg the travel time to the location of the door, and no reliable basis for giving the proprietor of a mansion a longer wait than the resident of a bungalow, or an apartment like Banks's." Moreover, once "the exigency had matured, * * * the officers were not bound to learn anything more or wait any longer before going in, even though their entry entailed some harm to the building."

3. ***Search of persons on the premises.*** On the basis of information from an informant that he had frequently and recently observed tinfoil packets of heroin behind the bar and on the person of the bartender of a certain tavern and that the bartender told him he would that day have heroin for sale, a warrant authorizing search of the tavern and bartender for heroin was issued. The warrant was executed during the late afternoon by 7–8 officers, who proceeded to pat down each of the 9–13 customers then present. A cigarette package was located and retrieved from customer Ybarra's pocket, and tinfoil packets of heroin were found therein. State courts held the heroin admissible because found in a search authorized by a statute[e] deemed constitutional as applied in the instant case. In YBARRA v. ILLINOIS, 444 U.S. 85 (1979), the Court, in a 6–3 decision, reversed. STEWART, J., for the majority, stated:

"There is no reason to suppose that, when the search warrant was issued on March 1, 1976, the authorities had probable cause to believe that any person found on the premises of the Aurora Tap Tavern, aside from [bartender] 'Greg,' would be violating the law. The Complaint for Search Warrant did not allege that the bar was frequented by persons illegally purchasing drugs. It did not state that the informant had ever seen a patron of the tavern purchase drugs from 'Greg' or from any other person. Nowhere, in fact, did the complaint even mention the patrons of the Aurora Tap Tavern.

"Not only was probable cause to search Ybarra absent at the time the warrant was issued; it was still absent when the police executed the warrant. Upon entering the tavern, the police did not recognize Ybarra and had no reason to believe that he had committed, was committing or was about to commit any offense under state or federal law. Ybarra made no gestures indicative of criminal conduct, made no movements that might suggest an attempt to conceal contraband, and said nothing of a suspicious nature to the police officers. * * *

e. This statute, Ill.Comp.Stat. ch. 725, § 5/108–9, reads: "In the execution of the warrant the person executing the same may reasonably detain to search any person in the place at the time: (a) To protect himself from attack, or (b) To prevent the disposal or concealment of any instruments, articles or things particularly described in the warrant."

"It is true that the police possessed a warrant based on probable cause to search the tavern in which Ybarra happened to be at the time the warrant was executed. But, a person's mere propinquity to others independently suspected of criminal activity does not, without more, give rise to probable cause to search that person. * * *[7]"

As for the state's claim "that the first patdown search of Ybarra constituted a reasonable frisk for weapons under the doctrine of *Terry v. Ohio,*" p. 401, the Court responded that the frisk was "not supported by a reasonable belief that he was armed and presently dangerous, a belief which this Court has invariably held must form the predicate to a patdown of a person for weapons. * * * Upon seeing Ybarra, [the police] neither recognized him as a person with a criminal history nor had any particular reason to believe that he might be inclined to assault them. Moreover, as police agent Johnson later testified, Ybarra, whose hands were empty, gave no indication of possessing a weapon, made no gestures or other actions indicative of an intent to commit an assault, and acted generally in a manner that was not threatening."

Emphasizing "the ease with which the evidence of narcotics possession may be concealed or moved around from person to person," the State next contended that the *Terry* standard "should be made applicable to aid the evidence-gathering function of the search warrant." The Court answered: "The 'long prevailing' constitutional standard of probable cause embodies "the best compromise that has been found for accommodating the [ ] often opposing interests" in "safeguard[ing] citizens from rash and unreasonable interferences with privacy" and in "seek[ing] to give fair leeway for enforcing the law in the community's protection.' "

REHNQUIST, J., for the dissenters, reasoned that the *Terry* individualized suspicion standard, "important in the case of an on-the-street stop, where the officer must articulate some reason for singling the person out of the general population," was of "less significance in the present situation" for two reasons: (i) "in place of the requirement of 'individualized suspicion' as a guard against arbitrary exercise of authority, we have here the determination of a neutral and detached magistrate that a search was necessary"; and (ii) "the task performed by the officers executing a search warrant is inherently more perilous than is a momentary encounter on the street."

4. ***Detention of persons on the premises.*** MICHIGAN v. SUMMERS, 452 U.S. 692 (1981), involved these facts: "As Detroit police officers were about to execute a warrant to search a house for narcotics, they encountered respondent descending the front steps. They requested his assistance in gaining entry and detained him while they searched the premises. After finding narcotics in the basement and ascertaining that respondent owned the house, the police arrested him, searched his person, and found in his coat pocket an envelope containing 8.5 grams of heroin." The Court, per STEVENS, J., upheld the seizure on the basis of the principle derived from *Terry* and related cases, namely, that "some seizures * * * constitute such limited intrusions on the personal security of those detained and are justified by such substantial law enforcement interests that they may be made on less than probable cause, so long as police have an articulable basis for suspecting criminal activity":

"Of prime importance in assessing the intrusion is the fact that the police had obtained a warrant to search respondent's house for contraband. A neutral and detached magistrate had found probable cause to believe that the law was being violated in that house and had authorized a substantial invasion of the privacy of

7. [W]e need not consider situations where the warrant itself authorizes the search of unnamed persons in a place and is supported by probable cause to believe that persons who will be in the place at the time of the search will be in possession of illegal drugs.

the persons who resided there. The detention of one of the residents while the premises were searched, although admittedly a significant restraint on his liberty, was surely less intrusive than the search itself. Indeed, we may safely assume that most citizens—unless they intend flight to avoid arrest—would elect to remain in order to observe the search of their possessions. Furthermore, the type of detention imposed here is not likely to be exploited by the officer or unduly prolonged in order to gain more information, because the information the officers seek normally will be obtained through the search and not through the detention. Moreover, because the detention in this case was in respondent's own residence, it could add only minimally to the public stigma associated with the search itself and would involve neither the inconvenience nor the indignity associated with a compelled visit to the police station. * * *

"In assessing the justification for the detention of an occupant of premises being searched for contraband pursuant to a valid warrant, both the law enforcement interest and the nature of the "articulable facts" supporting the detention are relevant. Most obvious is the legitimate law enforcement interest in preventing flight in the event that incriminating evidence is found. Less obvious, but sometimes of greater importance, is the interest in minimizing the risk of harm to the officers. Although no special danger to the police is suggested by the evidence in this record, the execution of a warrant to search for narcotics is the kind of transaction that may give rise to sudden violence or frantic efforts to conceal or destroy evidence. The risk of harm to both the police and the occupants is minimized if the officers routinely exercise unquestioned command of the situation. Finally, the orderly completion of the search may be facilitated if the occupants of the premises are present. Their self-interest may induce them to open locked doors or locked containers to avoid the use of force that is not only damaging to property but may also delay the completion of the task at hand.

"It is also appropriate to consider the nature of the articulable and individualized suspicion on which the police base the detention of the occupant of a home subject to a search warrant. We have already noted that the detention represents only an incremental intrusion on personal liberty when the search of a home has been authorized by a valid warrant. The existence of a search warrant, however, also provides an objective justification for the detention. A judicial officer has determined that police have probable cause to believe that someone in the home is committing a crime. Thus a neutral magistrate rather than an officer in the field has made the critical determination that the police should be given a special authorization to thrust themselves into the privacy of a home. The connection of an occupant to that home gives the police officer an easily identifiable and certain basis for determining that suspicion of criminal activity justifies a detention of that occupant."

STEWART, J., joined by Brennan and Marshall, JJ., dissenting, objected that *Terry* and related cases required "some governmental interest independent of the ordinary interest in investigating crime and apprehending suspects," which was not present here, and also that the majority's "view that the detention here is of the limited, unintrusive sort" required under *Terry* was in error, as "a detention 'while a proper search is being conducted' can mean a detention of several hours."

5. ***Intensity and duration of the search.*** Although a search under a search warrant may extend to all parts of the premises described in the warrant, it does not follow that the executing officers may look everywhere within the described premises; they may only look where the items described in the warrant might be concealed. For example, if a search warrant indicated that the items sought were stolen television sets, the officer would not be authorized to rummage through desk drawers and other places too small to hold these items. Once the items named in the search warrant have been found, the search must cease.

6. ***Seizure of items not named in the search warrant.*** In HORTON v. CALIFORNIA, 496 U.S. 128 (1990), a police officer's affidavit established probable cause to search defendant's home for the proceeds of a robbery (including three specified rings) and for the weapons used in that robbery, but the magistrate issued a warrant only for the proceeds. They were not found in execution of the warrant, but the guns were; they were seized. The defendant claimed this seizure did not come within Justice Stewart's plurality decision in *Coolidge v. New Hampshire,* 403 U.S. 443 (1971), that items found in "plain view" may be seized "where it is immediately apparent to the police that they have evidence before them," because he also required "that the discovery of evidence in plain view must be inadvertent." The Court in *Horton,* per STEVENS, J., disagreed, finding "two flaws" in the reasoning underlying the latter requirement: "First, evenhanded law enforcement is best achieved by the application of objective standards of conduct, rather than standards that depend upon the subjective state of mind of the officer. The fact that an officer is interested in an item of evidence and fully expects to find it in the course of a search should not invalidate its seizure if the search is confined in area and duration by the terms of a warrant or a valid exception to the warrant requirement. If the officer has knowledge approaching certainty that the item will be found, we see no reason why he or she would deliberately omit a particular description of the item to be seized from the application for a search warrant. Specification of the additional item could only permit the officer to expand the scope of the search. On the other hand, if he or she has a valid warrant to search for one item and merely a suspicion concerning the second, whether or not it amounts to probable cause, we fail to see why that suspicion should immunize the second item from seizure if it is found during a lawful search for the first. * * *

"Second, the suggestion that the inadvertence requirement is necessary to prevent the police from conducting general searches, or from converting specific warrants into general warrants, is not persuasive because that interest is already served by the requirements that no warrant issue unless it 'particularly describ[es] the place to be searched and the persons or things to be seized,' and that a warrantless search be circumscribed by the exigencies which justify its initiation. Scrupulous adherence to these requirements serves the interests in limiting the area and duration of the search that the inadvertence requirement inadequately protects. Once those commands have been satisfied and the officer has a lawful right of access, however, no additional Fourth Amendment interest is furthered by requiring that the discovery of evidence be inadvertent. If the scope of the search exceeds that permitted by the terms of a validly issued warrant or the character of the relevant exception from the warrant requirement, the subsequent seizure is unconstitutional without more."

In determining whether the discovered article is incriminating in nature, how carefully may the police examine it? See *Stanley v. Georgia,* 394 U.S. 557 (1969) (obscene films suppressed where police found reels of film while searching for gambling paraphernalia and then viewed the film on a projector and screen found in another room); cf. *Arizona v. Hicks*, p. 358; and compare *State v. Ruscoe*, 563 A.2d 267 (Conn.1989) (where in executing warrant for silver "candlesticks, napkin holders and a silver mug" police moved a TV, 2 VCR's and a tape deck and noticed they without serial numbers, this a lawful discovery under *Hicks*, as "the police moved items in the course of searching for items listed in the warrant").

7. ***Presence of third parties.*** Police executing search warrants are sometimes accompanied by others. The most common situation was noted in *Wilson v. Layne*, 526 U.S. 603 (1999): "Where the police enter a home under the authority of a warrant to search for stolen property, the presence of third parties for the purpose of identifying the stolen property has long been approved by this Court

and our common-law tradition.'' But in *Wilson*, which involved execution of an *arrest* warrant within premises, the police were accompanied by a reporter and a photographer from the Washington Post. Citing such cases as *Summers*, p. 313, and *Horton*, p. 315, in support of the proposition that the Fourth Amendment requires ''that police actions in execution of a warrant be related to the objectives of the authorized intrusion,'' a unanimous Court concluded the presence of members of the media was unconstitutional because it ''was not in aid of the execution of the warrant.'' Had the media representatives been present during execution of a *search* warrant, would any evidence first discovered by them be inadmissible? Would all the evidence found by the police be inadmissible? In *Wilson*, which was a § 1983 case, the Court, speaking of the media presence, dropped this footnote: ''Even though such actions might violate the Fourth Amendment, if the police are lawfully present, the violation of the Fourth Amendment is the presence of the media and not the presence of the police in the home. We have no occasion here to decide whether the exclusionary rule would apply to any evidence discovered or developed by the media representatives.''

8. ***Delivery of warrant.*** Many jurisdictions have statutes or court rules declaring that an officer executing a search warrant must delivery a copy of the warrant at the place searched; see, e.g., Fed.R.Crim.P. 41(d), App. C. Although it had often been assumed that these provisions were not grounded in the Fourth Amendment, the Supreme Court in *Groh v. Ramirez*, p. 236, indicated otherwise. In rejecting Groh's claim that what had occurred was a reasonable warrantless search because the goals of the warrant process had been ''otherwise satisfied,'' the Court gave as an added reason the fact that yet another purpose of the particularity requirement—that it ''also 'assures the individual whose property is searched or seized of the lawful authority of the executing officer, his need to search, and the limits of his power to search' ''—had not been met. The unstated conclusion in *Groh* apparently is that the Fourth Amendment was violated when the police handed over at the conclusion of the search[6] a copy of a warrant that did not in fact specify the things to be seized.

C. The ''Preference'' for Warrants

1. The Supreme Court has long expressed a strong preference for searches made pursuant to a search warrant, e.g., *United States v. Ventresca*, 380 U.S. 102 (1965), and on occasion has even asserted ''that the police must, whenever practicable, obtain advance judicial approval of searches and seizures.'' *Terry v. Ohio*, p. 401. But this is far from being an accurate portrayal of current law or practice; the fact of the matter is that a great majority of police seizures and searches are made and upheld notwithstanding the absence of a warrant.

This is so because, as elaborated later in this Chapter, the Supreme Court has recognized a considerable variety of circumstances in which the police may lawfully make a search or a seizure without the prior approval of a magistrate. A warrant is excused in situations other than those in which there existed genuine exigent circumstances making it unfeasible for the police to utilize the often time-

6. The Court did say that the Fourth Amendment does *not* require ''serving the warrant on the owner before commencing the search,'' but went on to caution that it was not decided whether ''it would be unreasonable to refuse a request to furnish the warrant at the outset of the search when, as in this case, an occupant of the premises is present and poses no threat to the officers' safe and effective performance of their mission.''

When property is seized pursuant to a warrant, there is also a *due process* requirement that police ''take reasonable steps to give notice that the property has been taken so that the owner can pursue remedies for the return,'' which can be met when no one is present by leaving a ''notice of service'' with a list of the property seized attached. *City of West Covina v. Perkins*, 525 U.S. 234 (1999).

consuming warrant process. Sometimes this is explained by the Court on the ground that the police activity being permitted without a warrant intrudes only upon lesser Fourth Amendment values. Illustrative is *California v. Carney*, p. 371, allowing warrantless search of vehicles because of the "diminished expectation of privacy" in them. Sometimes warrant excusal is rationalized on the ground that the permitted police activity is merely "routine," as with the inventory allowed in *Colorado v. Bertine*, p. 395. On other occasions the Supreme Court has recognized an exception to the warrant requirement because of a purported need for "bright lines" in the rules governing police conduct. Illustrative is *United States v. Watson*, p. 318, holding a warrant is never needed to arrest in a public place because a contrary holding would "encumber criminal prosecutions with endless litigation with respect to the existence of exigent circumstances, whether it was practicable to get a warrant, whether the suspect was about to flee, and the like." The tension between these and other considerations has not always produced predictable or consistent results in the Court's decisions concerning what is permissible warrantless police action.

2. The preference for the warrant process is commonly explained on the ground that it, more so than the post-search suppression process, *prevents* illegal searches. Compare William S. Stuntz, *Warrants and Fourth Amendment Remedies,* 77 Va.L.Rev. 881, 893 (1991): "Unfortunately, given our existing system, warrants may not have the desired preventive effect. Police officers are not the only ones who can get the relevant legal standards wrong; other actors in the system make mistakes as well. And while requiring warrants does reduce the odds of police mistake in applying the relevant legal standards, it also creates additional opportunities for error by magistrates. This is no small problem. Magistrates (1) may do a bad job of applying the probable cause standard because of deficiencies in the warrant process (review is ex parte and cursory), and (2) nevertheless receive a great deal of deference by judges after the fact. Requiring warrants therefore may lead to many *more* bad searches than would a simple system of police decisionmaking followed by after-the-fact review.

"And even if warrants do prevent bad searches, so do after-the-fact sanctions. An ounce of prevention may indeed be worth a pound of cure, but the pound of cure—after-the-fact sanctions—is itself a preventive device, since the threat of ex post penalties affects behavior ex ante. This is a simple point, but an important one. Police officers, like other regulated actors, respond to legal signals and alter their behavior in order to avoid after-the-fact sanctions. In most other contexts, that is thought to be the cheapest means of achieving a given level of deterrence * * *. Thus, to defend warrants, one must point to some reason why after-the-fact deterrence will work unusually poorly in the search and seizure context—some argument that explains why search and seizure law should be treated *differently* than most other regulatory regimes."

Stuntz, id. at 884, suggests some other reasons—that "the exclusionary rule generates an additional pair of problems for fourth amendment law, problems that warrants might plausibly help solve. Exclusion * * * may bias judges' after-the-fact probable cause determinations by requiring that they be made in cases where the officer actually found incriminating evidence. Similarly, the lack of a credible opponent (the defendant has, after all, been found with incriminating evidence) invites the police to subvert the governing legal standard by testifying falsely at suppression hearings. Warrants can reduce both problems by forcing the necessary judicial decision to be made, and the police officer's account of the facts to be given, before the evidence is found."

SECTION 5. WARRANTLESS ARRESTS AND SEARCHES OF THE PERSON

UNITED STATES v. WATSON

423 U.S. 411, 96 S.Ct. 820, 46 L.Ed.2d 598 (1976).

Justice WHITE delivered the opinion of the Court.

[Reliable informant Khoury told a federal postal inspector that Watson had supplied him with a stolen credit card and had agreed to furnish additional cards at their next meeting, scheduled for a few days later. At that meeting, which occurred in a restaurant, Khoury signaled the inspector that Watson had the cards, at which point the inspector arrested Watson without a warrant, as he was authorized to do under 18 U.S.C. § 3061 and applicable postal regulations. The court of appeals held the arrest unconstitutional because the inspector had failed to secure an arrest warrant although he concededly had time to do so, and this was a significant factor in the court's additional holding that Watson's consent to a search of his car was not voluntary.]

* * * Section 3061 represents a judgment by Congress that it is not unreasonable under the Fourth Amendment for postal inspectors to arrest without a warrant provided they have probable cause to do so. This was not an isolated or quixotic judgment of the legislative branch. Other federal law enforcement officers have been expressly authorized by statute for many years to make felony arrests on probable cause but without a warrant. * * *

Because there is a "strong presumption of constitutionality due to an Act of Congress, especially when it turns on what is 'reasonable,' * * * [o]bviously the Court should be reluctant to decide that a search thus authorized by Congress was unreasonable and that the Act was therefore unconstitutional." Moreover, there is nothing in the Court's prior cases indicating that under the Fourth Amendment a warrant is required to make a valid arrest for a felony. Indeed, the relevant prior decisions are uniformly to the contrary. * * *[a]

The cases construing the Fourth Amendment thus reflect the ancient common-law rule that a peace officer was permitted to arrest without a warrant for a misdemeanor or felony committed in his presence as well as for a felony not committed in his presence if there was reasonable grounds for making the arrest. This has also been the prevailing rule under state constitutions and statutes. * * *

Because the common-law rule authorizing arrests without warrant generally prevailed in the States, it is important for present purposes to note that in 1792 Congress invested United States Marshals and their deputies with "the same powers in executing the laws of the United States, as sheriffs and their deputies in their several states have by law, in executing the laws of their respective states." The Second Congress thus saw no inconsistency between the Fourth Amendment and giving United States Marshals the same power as local peace officers to arrest for a felony without a warrant.[8] * * *

a. The Court noted by way of footnote that because the arrest here was in a public place, it did not have to resolve the "still unsettled question" of whether a warrant is needed to enter private premises to make an arrest. This issue is considered at p. 364.

8. Of equal import is the rule recognized by this Court that even in the absence of a federal statute granting or restricting the authority of federal law enforcement officers, "the law of the state where an arrest without warrant takes place determines its validity." *United States v. Di Re,* 332 U.S. 581 (1948). * * *

The balance struck by the common law in generally authorizing felony arrests on probable cause, but without a warrant, has survived substantially intact. It appears in almost all of the States in the form of express statutory authorization. * * *

This is the rule Congress has long directed its principal law enforcement officers to follow. Congress has plainly decided against conditioning warrantless arrest power on proof of exigent circumstances. Law enforcement officers may find it wise to seek arrest warrants where practicable to do so, and their judgments about probable cause may be more readily accepted where backed by a warrant issued by a magistrate. But we decline to transform this judicial preference into a constitutional rule when the judgment of the Nation and Congress has for so long been to authorize warrantless public arrests on probable cause rather than to encumber criminal prosecutions with endless litigation with respect to the existence of exigent circumstances, whether it was practicable to get a warrant, whether the suspect was about to flee, and the like. * * *

Reversed.

Justice STEVENS took no part in the consideration or decision of this case.

Justice POWELL, concurring. * * *

On its face, our decision today creates a certain anomaly. There is no more basic constitutional rule in the Fourth Amendment area than that which makes a warrantless search unreasonable except in a few "jealously and carefully drawn" exceptional circumstances. * * * In short, the course of judicial development of the Fourth Amendment with respect to searches has remained true to the principles so well expressed by Justice Jackson:

> "Any assumption that evidence sufficient to support a magistrate's disinterested determination to issue a search warrant will justify the officers in making a search without a warrant would reduce the Amendment to a nullity and leave the people's homes secure only in the discretion of police officers. * * * When the right of privacy must reasonably yield to the right of search is, as a rule, to be decided by a judicial officer, not by a policeman or Government enforcement agent." *Johnson v. United States,* 333 U.S. 10, 14 (1948).

Since the Fourth Amendment speaks equally to both searches and seizures, and since an arrest, the taking hold of one's person, is quintessentially a seizure, it would seem that the constitutional provision should impose the same limitations upon arrests that it does upon searches. Indeed, as an abstract matter an argument can be made that the restrictions upon arrest perhaps should be greater. A search may cause only annoyance and temporary inconvenience to the law-abiding citizen, assuming more serious dimension only when it turns up evidence of criminality. An arrest, however, is a serious personal intrusion regardless of whether the person seized is guilty or innocent. Although an arrestee cannot be held for a significant period without some neutral determination that there are grounds to do so, no decision that he should go free can come quickly enough to erase the invasion of his privacy that already will have occurred. Logic therefore would seem to dictate that arrests be subject to the warrant requirement at least to the same extent as searches.

But logic sometimes must defer to history and experience. The Court's opinion emphasizes the historical sanction accorded warrantless felony arrests. * * *

Moreover, a constitutional rule permitting felony arrests only with a warrant or in exigent circumstances could severely hamper effective law enforcement. Good police practice often requires postponing an arrest, even after probable cause has been established, in order to place the suspect under surveillance or otherwise develop further evidence necessary to prove guilt to a jury. Under the holding of the Court of Appeals such additional investigative work could imperil the entire prosecution. Should the officers fail to obtain a warrant initially, and later be required by unforeseen circumstances to arrest immediately with no chance to procure a last-minute warrant, they would risk a court decision that the subsequent exigency did not excuse their failure to get a warrant in the interim since they first developed probable cause. If the officers attempted to meet such a contingency by procuring a warrant as soon as they had probable cause and then merely held it during their subsequent investigation, they would risk a court decision that the warrant had grown stale by the time it was used.[5] Law enforcement personnel caught in this squeeze could ensure validity of their arrests only by obtaining a warrant and arresting as soon as probable cause existed, thereby foreclosing the possibility of gathering vital additional evidence from the suspect's continued actions. * * *

Justice STEWART, concurring in the result. * * *

Justice MARSHALL, with whom Justice BRENNAN joins, dissenting. * * *

The signal of the reliable informant that Watson was in possession of stolen credit cards gave the postal inspectors probable cause to make the arrest. * * * When law enforcement officers have probable cause to believe that an offense is taking place in their presence and that the suspect is at that moment in possession of the evidence, exigent circumstances exist. Delay could cause the escape of the suspect or the destruction of the evidence. Accordingly, Watson's warrantless arrest was valid under the recognized exigent circumstances exception to the warrant requirement, and the Court has no occasion to consider whether a warrant would otherwise be necessary. * * *

[T]he substance of the ancient common-law rule provides no support for the far-reaching modern rule that the Court fashions on its model. * * *

* * * Only the most serious crimes were felonies at common law, and many crimes now classified as felonies under federal or state law were treated as misdemeanors. * * * To make an arrest for any of these crimes at common law, the police officer was required to obtain a warrant, unless the crime was committed in his presence. Since many of these same crimes are commonly classified as felonies today however, under the Court's holding a warrant is no longer needed to make such arrests, a result in contravention of the common law.

[T]he only clear lesson of history is contrary to the one the Court draws: the common law considered the arrest warrant far more important than today's decision leaves it. * * *

[W]e must now consider (1) whether the privacy of our citizens will be better protected by ordinarily requiring a warrant to be issued before they may be arrested; and (2) whether a warrant requirement would unduly burden legitimate governmental interests.

The first question is easily answered. Of course the privacy of our citizens will be better protected by a warrant requirement. We have recognized that "the Fourth Amendment protects people, not places." Indeed, the privacy guaranteed by the Fourth Amendment is quintessentially personal. Thus a warrant is re-

5. The probable cause to support issuance of an arrest warrant normally would not grow stale as easily as that which supports a warrant to search a particular place for particular objects. This is true because once there is probable cause to believe that someone is a felon the passage of time often will bring new supporting evidence. But in some cases the original grounds supporting the warrant could be disproved by subsequent investigation that at the same time turns up wholly new evidence supporting probable cause on a different theory. In those cases the warrant could be stale because based upon discredited information.

quired in search situations not because of some high regard for property, but because of our regard for the individual, and *his* interest in his possessions and person. * * *

The Government's assertion that a warrant requirement would impose an intolerable burden stems, in large part, from the specious supposition that procurement of an arrest warrant would be necessary as soon as probable cause ripens. There is no requirement that a search warrant be obtained the moment police have probable cause to search. The rule is only that present probable cause be shown and a warrant obtained before a search is undertaken. The same rule should obtain for arrest warrants, where it may even make more sense. Certainly, there is less need for prompt procurement of a warrant in the arrest situation. Unlike probable cause to search, probable cause to arrest, once formed will continue to exist for the indefinite future, at least if no intervening exculpatory facts come to light.

This sensible approach obviates most of the difficulties that have been suggested with an arrest warrant rule. Police would not have to cut their investigation short the moment they obtain probable cause to arrest, nor would undercover agents be forced suddenly to terminate their work and forfeit their covers. Moreover, if in the course of the continued police investigation exigent circumstances develop that demand an immediate arrest, the arrest may be made without fear of unconstitutionality, so long as the exigency was unanticipated and not used to avoid the arrest warrant requirement. Likewise, if in the course of the continued investigation police uncover evidence tying the suspect to another crime, they may immediately arrest him for that crime if exigency demands it, and still be in full conformity with the warrant rule. This is why the arrest in this case was not improper.[15] Other than where police attempt to evade the warrant requirement, the rule would invalidate an arrest only in the obvious situation: where police, with probable cause but without exigent circumstances, set out to arrest a suspect. Such an arrest must be void, even if exigency develops in the course of the arrest that would ordinarily validate it; otherwise the warrant requirement would be reduced to a toothless prescription. * * *

It is suggested, however, that even if application of this rule does not require police to secure a warrant as soon as they obtain probable cause, the confused officer would nonetheless be prone to do so. If so, police "would risk a court decision that the warrant had grown stale by the time it was used." (Powell, J., concurring). This fear is groundless. First, as suggested above, the requirement that police procure a warrant before an arrest is made is rather simple of application. Thus, there is no need for the police to find themselves in this "squeeze." Second, the "squeeze" is nonexistent. Just as it is virtually impossible for probable cause for an arrest to grow stale between the time of formation and the time a warrant is procured, it is virtually impossible for probable cause to become stale between procurement and arrest. Delay by law enforcement officers in executing an arrest warrant does not ordinarily affect the legality of the arrest. * * *

Notes and Questions

1. Consider SEARCHSZR § 5.1: "A study conducted for the President's Commission on Law Enforcement and Administration of Justice indicated that, while nearly fifty percent of all arrests are made within two hours of the crime as

15. Although the postal inspectors here anticipated the occurrence of the second crime, they could not have obtained a warrant for Watson's arrest for that crime until probable cause formed, just moments before the arrest. A warrant based on anticipated facts is premature and void. *United States v. Roberts,* 333 F.Supp. 786 (E.D.Tenn.1971).

a result of a 'hot' search of the crime scene or a 'warm' search of the general vicinity of the crime, very few additional arrests occur immediately thereafter. Rather, there is a delay while further investigation is conducted; about 45 percent of all arrests occur more than a day after the crime, and nearly 35 percent of all arrests are made after the passage of over a week. In these latter instances, * * * the risk is negligible that the defendant will suddenly flee between the time the police solve the case and the time which would be required to obtain and serve an arrest warrant. Indeed, in such cases the need to arrest before an arrest warrant can be obtained is likely to be considerably less apparent than the need to search before a search warrant can be acquired and executed; the defendant is unlikely suddenly to decide to flee or go into hiding at that point, but he well might have reached the stage where he is about to dispose of the fruits of his crime or destroy or abandon items of physical evidence which might link him with the crime."

2. As for the *Watson* dissenters' conclusion that "the privacy of our citizens will be better protected by ordinarily requiring a warrant to be issued before they may be arrested," consider Edward Barrett, *Criminal Justice: The Problem of Mass Production,* in The American Assembly, Columbia University, The Courts, the Public, and the Law Explosion 85, 117–18 (H.W. Jones ed. 1965): "How can a magistrate be more than a 'rubber stamp' in signing warrants unless he devotes at least some minutes in each case to reading the affidavits submitted to him in support of the request for a warrant, and inquiring into the background of the conclusions stated therein? And where is the judicial time going to be found to make such inquiries in the generality of cases? The Los Angeles Municipal Court with annual filings of about 130,000 (excluding parking and traffic) *finds itself so pressed that in large areas of its caseload it averages but a minute per case in receiving pleas and imposing sentence.* How could it cope with the added burden that would be involved in the issuance of warrants to govern the approximately 200,000 arrests made per year in Los Angeles for offenses other than traffic"?

3. Is the "preference" for arrest warrants nonetheless justified on the ground that, at least the police must make a record before the event of the basis for their actions? Consider Jerome H. Skolnick, *Justice Without Trial* 214–15 (1966): "[T]he policeman perceives * * * the need to be able to reconstruct a set of complex happenings in such a way that, subsequent to the arrest, probable cause can be found according to appellate court standards. In this way, as one district attorney expressed it, 'the policeman fabricates probable cause.' By saying this, he did not mean to assert that the policeman is a liar, but rather that he finds it necessary to construct an *ex post facto* description of the preceding events so that these conform to legal arrest requirements, whether in fact the events actually did so or not at the time of the arrest. Thus, the policeman respects the necessity for 'complying' with the arrest laws. His 'compliance,' however, may take the form of *post hoc* manipulation of the facts rather than before-the-fact behavior."

4. Given the concern regarding "*post hoc* manipulation of the facts," should the arrest of a person stated at arrest to be for one offense or resulting in booking for that offense be upheld on the ground that the police actually had sufficient evidence of a quite different offense? Compare Chief Justice Warren, dissenting from the dismissal of the writ of certiorari in *Wainwright v. New Orleans,* 392 U.S. 598 (1968) ("I see no more justification for permitting the State to disregard its own booking record than for permitting any other administrative body to disregard its own records. * * * If the police in this case really believed that petitioner was the murder suspect, and if they had probable cause to so believe, all they had to do was to arrest and book him for murder"); with *Devenpeck v. Alford,* ___ U.S. ___, 125 S.Ct. 588 (2004) (unanimous Court, per Scalia, J., rejects court of appeals) position that probable cause can only be shown as to the offense stated at the time of arrest or as to another offense "closely related" to it, for that position is inconsistent with precedent in, e.g., *Whren v. United States*, p. 339, "that an arresting officer's state of mind (except for the facts that he knows) is irrelevant to the existence of probable cause"; moreover, a "closely related" limitation would not ensure "that officers will cease making sham arrests on the hope that such arrests will later be validated, but rather that officers will cease providing reasons for arrest" or "would simply give every reason for which probable cause could conceivably exist").

5. Some but by no means all relevant authorities have described the common law warrantless arrest power of police regarding misdemeanors as having two limitations: (i) that the offense have occurred in the officer's presence; and (ii) that the offense constitute a "breach of the peace." These authorities were relied upon by the plaintiff in the § 1983 case of ATWATER v. CITY OF LAGO VISTA, 532 U.S. 318 (2001), involving these facts:

"In March 1997, Petitioner Gail Atwater was driving her pickup truck in Lago Vista, Texas, with her 3–year-old son and 5–year-old daughter in the front seat. None of them was wearing a seatbelt. Respondent Bart Turek, a Lago Vista police officer at the time, observed the seatbelt violations and pulled Atwater over. According to Atwater's complaint (the allegations of which we assume to be true for present purposes), Turek approached the truck and 'yell[ed]' something to the effect of '[w]e've met before' and '[y]ou're going to jail.'[1] He then called for backup and asked to see Atwater's driver's license and insurance documentation, which state law required her to carry. When Atwater told Turek that she did not have the papers because her purse had been stolen the day before, Turek said that he had 'heard that story two-hundred times.'

"Atwater asked to take her 'frightened, upset, and crying' children to a friend's house nearby, but Turek told her, '[y]ou're not going anywhere.' As it turned out, Atwater's friend learned what was going on and soon arrived to take charge of the children. Turek then handcuffed Atwater, placed her in his squad car, and drove her to the local police station, where booking officers had her remove her shoes, jewelry, and eyeglasses, and empty her pockets. Officers took Atwater's 'mug shot' and placed her, alone, in a jail cell for about one hour, after which she was taken before a magistrate and released on $310 bond.

"Atwater was charged with driving without her seatbelt fastened, failing to secure her children in seatbelts, driving without a license, and failing to provide proof of insurance. She ultimately pleaded no contest to the misdemeanor seatbelt offenses and paid a $50 fine; the other charges were dismissed."

Although Texas law at that time gave the officer total discretion to choose between a custodial arrest and issuance of a citation in such circumstances, Atwater claimed the arrest was contrary to common law and hence in violation of the Fourth Amendment. The Court, per SOUTER, J., agreed that the common law view was "obviously relevant, if not entirely dispositive," as to what the Fourth Amendment's framers thought was reasonable, but then concluded that her "historical argument * * * ultimately fails" because the English and American cases and commentators reached "divergent conclusions" regarding any breach-of-the-peace requirement. Moreover, the post-Amendment history "is of two centuries of uninterrupted (and largely unchallenged) state and federal practice permit-

1. Turek had previously stopped Atwater for what he had thought was a seatbelt violation, but had realized that Atwater's son, although seated on the vehicle's armrest, was in fact belted in. Atwater acknowledged that her son's seating position was unsafe, and Turek issued a verbal warning.

ting warrantless arrests for misdemeanors not amounting to or involving breach of the peace."[a]

6. *Atwater* is one of several recent cases in which the Supreme Court has made the principal criterion for identifying violations of the Fourth Amendment "whether a particular governmental action * * * was regarded as an unlawful search or seizure under the common law when the Amendment was framed," *Wyoming v. Houghton*, p. 384. This approach, which "departs dramatically from the largely ahistorical approach the Court has taken to the Fourth Amendment for most of the past thirty years," has been criticized as "find[ing] support neither in the constitutional text, nor in what we know of the intentions of the 'Framers,'" and as obscuring the fact "that the Fourth Amendment places on courts a burden of judgment, and that the burden cannot be relieved by the common law's sporadic, contradictory, and necessarily time-bound rules of search and seizure." David A. Sklansky, *The Fourth Amendment and Common Law,* 100 Colum.L.Rev. 1739, 1813–14 (2000). As for use of the technique in *Atwater*, a leading Fourth Amendment historian has concluded that Justice "Souter's claims bear little resemblance to authentic framing-era arrest doctrine," and "that his supposed historical analysis consisted almost entirely of rhetorical ploys and distortions of the historical sources. * * * A robust comparison of the analysis and holding in *Atwater* with the pertinent historical sources reveals that the Framers neither expected nor intended for officers to exercise the sort of unfettered arrest authority that *Atwater* permits." Thomas Y. Davies, *The Fictional Character of Law-and-Order Originalism: A Case Study of the Distortions and Evasions of Framing–Era Arrest Doctrine in Atwater v. Lago Vista*, 37 Wake Forest L.Rev. 239, 246–47 (2002).

7. The common law "in presence" requirement for a warrantless misdemeanor arrest has sometimes caused the courts difficulties. Consider *People v. Burdo,* 223 N.W.2d 358 (Mich.App.1974) (officer could not arrest for misdemeanor of driving under influence of liquor when he came on scene of auto accident and found defendant there, even though defendant obviously was intoxicated and admitted he had been driving); *People v. Dixon,* 222 N.W.2d 749 (Mich.1974) (after stopping noisy vehicle, officer could arrest driver for misdemeanor of driving without a license after being advised via police radio that defendant's license had been suspended).

8. Some states use the felony-arrest rule for *all* offenses, and when such provisions have been challenged as unconstitutional it has been held that the Fourth Amendment should not "be interpreted to prohibit warrantless arrests for misdemeanors committed outside an officer's presence." *Street v. Surdyka*, 492 F.2d 368 (4th Cir.1974). Is this so after *Atwater*? Consider that in *Atwater* the Court dropped this footnote: "We need not, and thus do not, speculate whether the Fourth Amendment entails an 'in the presence' requirement for purposes of misdemeanor arrests. Cf. *Welsh v. Wisconsin*, p. 369 (White, J., dissenting) ('[T]he requirement that a misdemeanor must have occurred in the officer's presence to justify a warrantless arrest is not grounded in the Fourth Amendment')."

9. Rejecting the contention that if the *Watson* probable cause "requirement is satisfied the Fourth Amendment has nothing to say about *how* that seizure is made," the Court in TENNESSEE v. GARNER, 471 U.S. 1 (1985), held that the use of deadly force to arrest a fleeing felon is sometimes unreasonable under the Fourth Amendment. WHITE, J., stated for the majority:

a. Four members of the Court dissented on another branch of the case, discussed at p. 335, but as to the above matter agreed "that warrantless misdemeanor arrests were not the subject of a clear and consistently applied rule at common law."

"The use of deadly force to prevent the escape of all felony suspects, whatever the circumstances, is constitutionally unreasonable. It is not better that all felony suspects die than that they escape. Where the suspect poses no immediate threat to the officer and no threat to others, the harm resulting from failing to apprehend him does not justify the use of deadly force to do so. It is no doubt unfortunate when a suspect who is in sight escapes, but the fact that the police arrive a little late or are a little slower afoot does not always justify killing the suspect. A police officer may not seize an unarmed, nondangerous suspect by shooting him dead. The Tennessee statute is unconstitutional insofar as it authorizes the use of deadly force against such fleeing suspects.

"It is not, however, unconstitutional on its face. Where the officer has probable cause to believe that the suspect poses a threat of serious physical harm, either to the officer or to others, it is not constitutionally unreasonable to prevent escape by using deadly force. Thus, if the suspect threatens the officer with a weapon or there is probable cause to believe that he has committed a crime involving the infliction or threatened infliction of serious physical harm, deadly force may be used if necessary to prevent escape, and if, where feasible, some warning has been given. As applied in such circumstances, the Tennessee statute would pass constitutional muster."

O'CONNOR, J., joined by the Chief Justice and Rehnquist, J., dissenting, objected: "A proper balancing of the interests involved suggests that use of deadly force as a last resort to apprehend a criminal suspect fleeing from the scene of a nighttime burglary is not unreasonable within the meaning of the Fourth Amendment. Admittedly, the events giving rise to this case are in retrospect deeply regrettable. No one can view the death of an unarmed and apparently nonviolent 15–year old without sorrow, much less disapproval. Nonetheless, the reasonableness of Officer Hymon's conduct for purposes of the Fourth Amendment cannot be evaluated by what later appears to have been a preferable course of police action. The officer pursued a suspect in the darkened backyard of a house that from all indications had just been burglarized. The police officer was not certain whether the suspect was alone or unarmed; nor did he know what had transpired inside the house. He ordered the suspect to halt, and when the suspect refused to obey and attempted to flee into the night, the officer fired his weapon to prevent escape. The reasonableness of this action for purposes of the Fourth Amendment is not determined by the unfortunate nature of this particular case; instead, the question is whether it is constitutionally impermissible for police officers, as a last resort, to shoot a burglary suspect fleeing the scene of the crime."[b]

The Fourth Amendment reasonableness standard, the Court later declared in *Graham v. Connor,* 490 U.S. 386 (1989), (1) applies to "*all* claims that law enforcement officers have used excessive force—deadly or not—in the course of an arrest, investigatory stop, or other 'seizure' of a free citizen";[c] (2) "requires careful attention to the facts and circumstances of each particular case, including the severity of the crime at issue, whether the suspect poses an immediate threat to the safety of the officers or others, and whether he is actively resisting arrest or attempting to evade arrest by flight"; (3) "must embody allowance for the fact that police officers are often forced to make split-second judgments—in circumstances that are tense, uncertain, and rapidly evolving—about the amount of force that is necessary in a particular situation"; and (4) asks "whether the officers'

b. See H. Richard Uviller, *Seizure by Gunshot: The Riddle of the Fleeing Felon,* 14 N.Y.U.Rev.L. & Soc.Chg. 705 (1986).

c. If the police conduct causing death or bodily harm was not a search or seizure, then the Fourteenth Amendment due process shocks-the-conscience test, rather than the Fourth Amendment reasonableness test, applies. See *County of Sacramento v. Lewis,* p. 36.

actions are 'objectively reasonable' in light of the facts and circumstances confronting them, without regard to their underlying intent or motivation."

What is the meaning of the term "deadly force" in *Garner*? In *Vera Cruz v. City of Escondido*, 139 F.3d 659 (9th Cir.1997), an officer acting solely to terminate a person's flight released his "K–9 companion," who bit the fleeing party on the arm and held him until the officer took away the arrestee's knife, resulting in wounds requiring surgery and eight days of hospitalization. In a § 1983 action, plaintiff argued for the Model Penal Code definition, "force that the actor uses with the purpose of causing or that he knows to create a substantial risk of causing death or serious bodily injury," but the court ruled that "deadly force is that force which is reasonably likely to cause death." Which is correct?

10. In GERSTEIN v. PUGH, 420 U.S. 103 (1975), the Court, per POWELL, J., held that a "policeman's on-the-scene assessment of probable cause provides legal justification for arresting a person suspected of crime, and for a brief period of detention to take the administrative steps incident to arrest. Once the suspect is in custody, however, the reasons that justify dispensing with the magistrate's neutral judgment evaporate. There no longer is any danger that the suspect will escape or commit further crimes while the police submit their evidence to a magistrate. And, while the State's reasons for taking summary action subside, the suspect's need for a neutral determination of probable cause increases significantly. The consequences of prolonged detention may be more serious than the interference occasioned by arrest. Pretrial confinement may imperil the suspect's job, interrupt his source of income, and impair his family relationships. Even pretrial release may be accompanied by burdensome conditions that effect a significant restraint on liberty. When the stakes are this high, the detached judgment of a neutral magistrate is essential if the Fourth Amendment is to furnish meaningful protection from unfounded interference with liberty. Accordingly, we hold that the Fourth Amendment requires a judicial determination of probable cause as a prerequisite to extended restraint on liberty following arrest.[d]

"This result has historical support in the common law that has guided interpretation of the Fourth Amendment. At common law it was customary, if not obligatory, for an arrested person to be brought before a justice of the peace shortly after arrest. The justice of the peace would 'examine' the prisoner and the witnesses to determine whether there was reason to believe the prisoner had committed a crime. If there was, the suspect would be committed to jail or bailed pending trial. If not, he would be discharged from custody. The initial determination of probable cause also could be reviewed by higher courts on a writ of habeas corpus. This practice furnished the model for criminal procedure in America immediately following the adoption of the Fourth Amendment, and there are indications that the Framers of the Bill of Rights regarded it as a model for a 'reasonable' seizure."

The Court then concluded the Court of Appeals had erred in holding "that the determination of probable cause must be accompanied by the full panoply of adversary safeguards—counsel, confrontation, cross-examination, and compulsory process for witnesses." The Court of Appeals had required that the state provide, in effect, a "full preliminary hearing * * * modeled after the procedure used in

d. In a subsequent footnote, the Court indicated that a grand jury determination to indict would provide such a "judicial determination." In distinguishing the prosecutor's determination that probable cause exists, the Court noted: "By contrast, the Court has held that an indictment, 'fair upon its face,' and returned by a 'properly constituted grand jury' conclusively determines the existence of probable cause and requires issuance of an arrest warrant without further inquiry. The willingness to let a grand jury judgment substitute for that of a neutral and detached magistrate is attributable to the grand jury's relationship to the courts and its historical role of protecting individuals from unjust prosecution."

many States to determine whether the evidence justifies going to trial under an information or presenting the case to a grand jury." The Fourth Amendment, the Court noted, did not require such an adversary proceeding:

"The sole issue is whether there is probable cause for detaining the arrested person pending further proceedings. This issue can be determined reliably without an adversary hearing. That standard—probable cause to believe the suspect has committed a crime—traditionally has been decided by a magistrate in a nonadversary proceeding on hearsay and written testimony, and the Court has approved these informal modes of proof. * * * The use of an informal procedure is justified not only by the lesser consequences of a probable cause determination but also by the nature of the determination itself. It does not require the fine resolution of conflicting evidence that a reasonable-doubt or even a preponderance standard demands, and credibility determinations are seldom crucial in deciding whether the evidence supports a reasonable belief in guilt. This is not to say that confrontation and cross-examination might not enhance the reliability of probable cause determinations in some cases. In most cases, however, their value would be too slight to justify holding, as a matter of constitutional principle, that these formalities and safeguards designed for trial must also be employed in making the Fourth Amendment determination of probable cause."[e]

"* * * There is no single preferred pretrial procedure, and the nature of the probable cause determination usually will be shaped to accord with a State's pretrial procedure viewed as a whole. * * * It may be found desirable, for example, to make the probable cause determination at the suspect's first appearance before a judicial officer,[24] the determination may be incorporated into the procedure for setting bail or fixing other conditions of pretrial release. * * * Whatever procedure a State may adopt, it must provide a fair and reliable determination of probable cause as a condition for any significant pretrial restraint on liberty,[26] and this determination must be made by a judicial officer either before or promptly after arrest.[27]"

e. Stewart, J., joined by Douglas, Brennan and Marshall, JJ., refused to join this portion of the Court's opinion. Justice Stewart noted: "I see no need in this case for the Court to say that the Constitution extends less procedural protection to an imprisoned human being than is required to test the propriety of garnishing a commercial bank account, *North Georgia Finishing, Inc. v. Di–Chem, Inc.,* 419 U.S. 601 [(1975)], the custody of a refrigerator, *Mitchell v. W. T. Grant Co.,* 416 U.S. 600 [(1974)], the temporary suspension of a public school student, *Goss v. Lopez,* 419 U.S. 565 [(1975)], or the suspension of a driver's license, *Bell v. Burson,* 402 U.S. 535 [(1971)]. Although it may be true that the Fourth Amendment's 'balance between individual and public interests always has been thought to define the "process that is due" for seizures of person or property in criminal cases,' this case does not involve an initial arrest, but rather the continuing incarceration of a presumptively innocent person. Accordingly, I cannot join the Court's effort to foreclose any claim that the traditional requirements of constitutional due process are applicable in the context of pretrial detention."

24. Several States already authorize a determination of probable cause at this stage or immediately thereafter. This Court has interpreted the Federal Rules of Criminal Procedure to require a determination of probable cause at the first appearance.

26. Because the probable cause determination is not a constitutional prerequisite to the charging decision, it is required only for those suspects who suffer restraints on liberty other than the condition that they appear for trial. There are many kinds of pretrial release and many degrees of conditional liberty. We cannot define specifically those that would require a prior probable cause determination, but the key factor is significant restraint on liberty. [Editors' note: Consider *In re Walters,* 543 P.2d 607 (Cal.1975): "As the posting of bail may impose an unwarranted burden on an accused if probable cause to detain is lacking, the accused is entitled to have that determination made prior to electing to post or not to post bail."]

27. In his concurring opinion, Mr. Justice Stewart objects to the Court's choice of the Fourth Amendment as the rationale for decision and suggests that the Court offers less procedural protection to a person in jail than it requires in certain civil cases. Here we deal with the complex procedures of a criminal case and a threshold right guaranteed by the Fourth Amendment. The historical basis of the

11. In COUNTY OF RIVERSIDE v. McLAUGHLIN, 500 U.S. 44 (1991), the Court confronted the question of "what is 'prompt' under *Gerstein*" and concluded, 5–4, per O'CONNOR, J., that "it is important to provide some degree of certainty so that States and counties may establish procedures with confidence that they fall within constitutional bounds. Taking into account the competing interests articulated in *Gerstein,* we believe that a jurisdiction that provides judicial determinations of probable cause within 48 hours of arrest will, as a general matter, comply with the promptness requirement of *Gerstein.*[f] For this reason, such jurisdictions will be immune from systemic challenges.

"This is not to say that the probable cause determination in a particular case passes constitutional muster simply because it is provided within 48 hours. Such a hearing may nonetheless violate *Gerstein* if the arrested individual can prove that his or her probable cause determination was delayed unreasonably. Examples of unreasonable delay are delays for the purpose of gathering additional evidence to justify the arrest, a delay motivated by ill will against the arrested individual, or delay for delay's sake. In evaluating whether the delay in a particular case is unreasonable, however, courts must allow a substantial degree of flexibility. Courts cannot ignore the often unavoidable delays in transporting arrested persons from one facility to another, handling late-night bookings where no magistrate is readily available, obtaining the presence of an arresting officer who may be busy processing other suspects or securing the premises of an arrest, and other practical realities.

"Where an arrested individual does not receive a probable cause determination within 48 hours, the calculus changes. In such a case, the arrested individual does not bear the burden of proving an unreasonable delay. Rather, the burden shifts to the government to demonstrate the existence of a bona fide emergency or other extraordinary circumstance. The fact that in a particular case it may take longer than 48 hours to consolidate pretrial proceedings does not qualify as an extraordinary circumstance. Nor, for that matter, do intervening weekends. A jurisdiction that chooses to offer combined proceedings must do so as soon as is reasonably feasible, but in no event later than 48 hours after arrest."

12. Assuming a *Gerstein* violation, what bearing should it have if the individual is later prosecuted? In *Powell v. Nevada,* 511 U.S. 79 (1994), holding *McLaughlin* retroactive to that case, the Court, per Ginsburg, J., noted: "It does not necessarily follow, however, that Powell must 'be set free' or gain other relief, for several questions remain open for decision on remand," including "the appropriate remedy for a delay in determining probable cause (an issue not resolved by *McLaughlin*)." In *Powell,* an untimely probable cause determination was made four days after defendant's arrest, shortly after he gave the police an incriminating statement. In declaring that "whether a suppression remedy applies in that setting remains an unresolved question," Justice Ginsburg took note of

probable cause requirement is quite different from the relatively recent application of variable procedural due process in debtor-creditor disputes and termination of government-created benefits. The Fourth Amendment was tailored explicitly for the criminal justice system, and its balance between individual and public interests always has been thought to define the "process that is due" for seizures of person or property in criminal cases, including the detention of suspects pending trial. Moreover, the Fourth Amendment probable cause determination is in fact only the *first* stage of an elaborate system, unique in jurisprudence, designed to safeguard the rights of those accused of criminal conduct. The relatively simple civil procedures (e.g., prior interview with school principal before suspension) presented in the cases cited in the concurring opinion are inapposite and irrelevant in the wholly different context of the criminal justice system. * * *

f. SCALIA, J., dissenting, reasoned that "the only element bearing upon the reasonableness of delay was * * * the arresting officer's ability, once the prisoner had been secured, to reach a magistrate who could issue the needed warrant for further detention," and that consequently the time at which the presumption should shift ought to be only 24 hours.

two arguably analogous rules pointing in opposite directions: (i) that an after-the-fact judicial determination of probable cause does not make admissible evidence obtained in a search in violation of the Fourth Amendment's search warrant requirement; and (ii) that under *Harris*, p. 911, suppression of a statement subsequently obtained elsewhere is not required because of defendant's warrantless arrest inside premises in violation of the Fourth Amendment.

13. The governor of Michigan issued an arrest warrant for Doran pursuant to a request for extradition from the governor of Arizona. Attached to the Arizona requisition were an arrest warrant for theft, two supporting affidavits, and the original complaint on which the charge was based. Relying upon *Gerstein* and language of the Uniform Criminal Extradition Act that the "indictment, information, or affidavit made before the magistrate must substantially charge the person demanded with having committed a crime," the state supreme court held that Doran could not be extradited because the "complaint and arrest warrant are both phrased in conclusory language" and "the two supporting affidavits fail to set out facts which could justify a Fourth Amendment finding of probable cause." But in *Michigan v. Doran*, 439 U.S. 282 (1978), the Court, per Burger, C.J., held "that once the governor of the asylum state has acted on a requisition for extradition based on the demanding state's judicial determination that probable cause existed, no further judicial inquiry may be had on that issue in the asylum state." Emphasizing that the Extradition Clause[g] "was intended to enable each state to bring offenders to trial as swiftly as possible in the state where the alleged offense was committed," the Court concluded that to "allow plenary review in the asylum state of issues that can be fully litigated in the charging state would defeat the plain purposes of the summary and mandatory procedure authorized by" the Clause.

Three concurring Justices, after noting the absence of any discussion in the majority opinion of the significance of the Fourth Amendment, reasoned that the "extradition process involves an 'extended restraint of liberty following arrest' even more severe than that accompanying detention within a single State. [T]herefore, the Amendment's language and the holding in *Gerstein* mean that, even in the extradition context, where the demanding State's 'charge' rests upon something less than an indictment, there must be a determination of probable cause by a detached and neutral magistrate, and that the asylum State need not grant extradition unless that determination has been made. The demanding State, of course, has the burden of so demonstrating." They then concluded that this burden had been met in the instant case because the Arizona arrest warrant declared that a probable cause finding had been made.

UNITED STATES v. ROBINSON

414 U.S. 218, 94 S.Ct. 467, 38 L.Ed.2d 427 (1973).

Justice REHNQUIST delivered the opinion of the Court. * * *

On April 23, 1968, at approximately 11 o'clock p.m., Officer Richard Jenks, a 15–year veteran of the District of Columbia Metropolitan Police Department, observed the respondent driving a 1965 Cadillac near the intersection of 8th and C Streets, Southeast, in the District of Columbia. Jenks, as a result of previous investigation following a check of respondent's operator's permit four days earlier, determined there was reason to believe that respondent was operating a motor

g. U.S. Const., Art. IV, § 2: "A Person charged in any State with Treason, Felony, or other Crime, who shall flee from Justice, and be found in another State, shall on Demand of the executive Authority of the State from which he fled, be delivered up, to be removed to the State having Jurisdiction of the Crime."

vehicle after the revocation of his operator's permit. This is an offense defined by statute in the District of Columbia which carries a mandatory minimum jail term, a mandatory minimum fine, or both.

Jenks signaled respondent to stop the automobile, which respondent did, and all three of the occupants emerged from the car. At that point Jenks informed respondent that he was under arrest for "operating after revocation and obtaining a permit by misrepresentation." It was assumed by the majority of the Court of Appeals, and is conceded by the respondent here, that Jenks had probable cause to arrest respondent, and that he effected a full custody arrest.

In accordance with procedures prescribed in Police Department instructions,[2] Jenks then began to search respondent. He explained at a subsequent hearing that he was "face to face" with the respondent, and "placed [his] hands on [the respondent], my right hand to his left breast like this (demonstrating) and proceeded to pat him down thus (with the right hand)." During this patdown, Jenks felt an object in the left breast pocket of the heavy coat respondent was wearing, but testified that he "couldn't tell what it was" and also that he "couldn't actually tell the size of it." Jenks then reached into the pocket and pulled out the object, which turned out to be a "crumpled up cigarette package." Jenks testified that at this point he still did not know what was in the package: "As I felt the package I could feel objects in the package but I couldn't tell what they were. * * * I knew they weren't cigarettes."

The officer then opened the cigarette pack and found 14 gelatin capsules of white powder which he thought to be, and which later analysis proved to be, heroin. Jenks then continued his search of respondent to completion, feeling around his waist and trouser legs, and examining the remaining pockets. The heroin seized from the respondent was admitted into evidence at the trial which resulted in his conviction in the District Court[, which was reversed by the Court of Appeals].

It is well settled that a search incident to a lawful arrest is a traditional exception to the warrant requirement of the Fourth Amendment. This general exception has historically been formulated into two distinct propositions. The first is that a search may be made of the *person* of the arrestee by virtue of the lawful arrest. The second is that a search may be made of the area within the control of the arrestee.

Examination of this Court's decisions in the area show that these two propositions have been treated quite differently. The validity of the search of a person incident to a lawful arrest has been regarded as settled from its first enunciation, and has remained virtually unchallenged until the present case. The validity of the second proposition, while likewise conceded in principle, has been subject to differing interpretations as to the extent of the area which may be searched. * * *

2. The government introduced testimony at the evidentiary hearing upon the original remand by the Court of Appeals as to certain standard operating procedures of the Metropolitan Police Department. Sergeant Dennis C. Donaldson, a Training Division Instructor, testified that when a police officer makes "a full custody arrest" which he defined as where an officer "would arrest a subject and subsequently transport him to a police facility for booking," the officer is trained to make a full "field type search" * * *. Sergeant Donaldson testified that officers are instructed to examine the "contents of all of the pockets" of the arrestee in the course of the field search. * * * Those regulations also provide that in the case of some traffic offenses, including the crime of operating a motor vehicle after revocation of an operator's permit, the officer shall make a summary arrest of the violator and take the violator, in custody, to the stationhouse for booking. D.C.Metropolitan Police Department General Order No. 3, series 1959 (April 24, 1959). Such operating procedures are not, of course, determinative of the constitutional issues presented by this case.

Thus the broadly stated rule, and the reasons for it, have been repeatedly affirmed in the decisions of this Court since *Weeks v. United States* nearly 60 years ago. Since the statements in the cases speak not simply in terms of an exception to the warrant requirement, but in terms of an affirmative authority to search, they clearly imply that such searches also meet the Fourth Amendment's requirement of reasonableness. * * *

Virtually all of the statements of this Court affirming the existence of an unqualified authority to search incident to a lawful arrest are dicta. We would not therefore be foreclosed by principles of *stare decisis* from further examination into history and practice in order to see whether the sort of qualifications imposed by the Court of Appeals in this case were in fact intended by the Framers of the Fourth Amendment or recognized in cases decided prior to *Weeks*. Unfortunately such authorities as exist are sparse. * * *

While these earlier authorities are sketchy, they tend to support the broad statement of the authority to search incident to arrest found in the successive decisions of this Court, rather than the restrictive one which was applied by the Court of Appeals in this case. * * *

The Court of Appeals in effect determined that the *only* reason supporting the authority for a *full* search incident to lawful arrest was the possibility of discovery of evidence or fruits. Concluding that there could be no evidence or fruits in the case of an offense such as that with which respondent was charged, it held that any protective search would have to be limited by the conditions laid down in *Terry* [*v. Ohio*, p. 401] for a search upon less than probable cause to arrest. Quite apart from the fact that *Terry* clearly recognized the distinction between the two types of searches, and that a different rule governed one than governed the other, we find additional reason to disagree with the Court of Appeals.

The justification or reason for the authority to search incident to a lawful arrest rests quite as much on the need to disarm the suspect in order to take him into custody as it does on the need to preserve evidence on his person for later use at trial. The standards traditionally governing a search incident to lawful arrest are not, therefore, commuted to the stricter *Terry* standards by the absence of probable fruits or further evidence of the particular crime for which the arrest is made.

Nor are we inclined, on the basis of what seems to us to be a rather speculative judgment, to qualify the breadth of the general authority to search incident to a lawful custodial arrest on an assumption that persons arrested for the offense of driving while their license has been revoked are less likely to be possessed of dangerous weapons than are those arrested for other crimes.[5] It is scarcely open to doubt that the danger to an officer is far greater in the case of the extended exposure which follows the taking of a suspect into custody and transporting him to the police station than in the case of the relatively fleeting contact resulting from the typical *Terry*-type stop. This is an adequate basis for treating all custodial arrests alike for purposes of search justification.

5. Such an assumption appears at least questionable in light of the available statistical data concerning assaults on police officers who are in the course of making arrests. The danger to the police officer flows from the fact of the arrest, and its attendant proximity, stress and uncertainty, and not from the grounds for arrest. One study concludes that approximately 30% of the shootings of police officers occur when the officer approaches a person seated in a car. Bristow, *Police Officer Shootings—A Tactical Evaluation,* 54 J.Crim.L.C. & P.S. 93 (1963). The Government in its brief notes that the Uniform Crime Reports, prepared by the Federal Bureau of Investigation, indicate that a significant percentage of murders of police officers occurs when the officers are making traffic stops. Brief for the United States, at 23. Those reports indicate that during January–March, 1973, 35 police officers were murdered; 11 of those officers were killed while engaged in traffic stops. Ibid.

But quite apart from these distinctions, our more fundamental disagreement with the Court of Appeals arises from its suggestion that there must be litigated in each case the issue of whether or not there was present one of the reasons supporting the authority for a search of the person incident to a lawful arrest. We do not think the long line of authorities of this Court dating back to *Weeks,* nor what we can glean from the history of practice in this country and in England, requires such a case by case adjudication. A police officer's determination as to how and where to search the person of a suspect whom he has arrested is necessarily a quick *ad hoc* judgment which the Fourth Amendment does not require to be broken down in each instance into an analysis of each step in the search. The authority to search the person incident to a lawful custodial arrest, while based upon the need to disarm and to discover evidence, does not depend on what a court may later decide was the probability in a particular arrest situation that weapons or evidence would in fact be found upon the person of the suspect. A custodial arrest of a suspect based on probable cause is a reasonable intrusion under the Fourth Amendment; that intrusion being lawful, a search incident to the arrest requires no additional justification. It is the fact of the lawful arrest which establishes the authority to search, and we hold that in the case of a lawful custodial arrest a full search of the person is not only an exception to the warrant requirement of the Fourth Amendment, but is also a "reasonable" search under that Amendment.

The search of respondent's person conducted by Officer Jenks in this case and the seizure from him of the heroin, were permissible under established Fourth Amendment law. * * * Since it is the fact of custodial arrest which gives rise to the authority to search, it is of no moment that Jenks did not indicate any subjective fear of the respondent or that he did not himself suspect that respondent was armed.[7] Having in the course of a lawful search come upon the crumpled package of cigarettes, he was entitled to inspect it; and when his inspection revealed the heroin capsules, he was entitled to seize them as "fruits, instrumentalities, or contraband" probative of criminal conduct. The judgment of the Court of Appeals holding otherwise is reversed.

Reversed.

Justice MARSHALL, with whom Justice DOUGLAS and Justice BRENNAN join, dissenting. * * *

The majority's attempt to avoid case-by-case adjudication of Fourth Amendment issues is not only misguided as a matter of principle, but is also doomed to fail as a matter of practical application. As the majority itself is well aware, the powers granted the police in this case are strong ones, subject to potential abuse. Although, in this particular case, Officer Jenks was required by Police Department regulation to make an in-custody arrest rather than to issue a citation, in most jurisdictions and for most traffic offenses the determination of whether to issue a citation or effect a full arrest is discretionary with the officer. There is always the possibility that a police officer, lacking probable cause to obtain a search warrant, will use a traffic arrest as a pretext to conduct a search. I suggest this possibility not to impugn the integrity of our police, but merely to point out that case-by-case adjudication will always be necessary to determine whether a full arrest was effected for purely legitimate reasons or, rather, as a pretext for searching the arrestee. * * *

7. The United States concedes that "in searching respondent, [Officer Jenks] was not motivated by a feeling of imminent danger and was not specifically looking for weapons." Brief for the United States. Officer Jenks testified, "I just searched him [Robinson]. I didn't think about what I was looking for. I just searched him." Officer Jenks also testified that upon removing the cigarette package from the respondent's custody, he was still unsure what was in the package, but that he knew it was not cigarettes.

The Government does not now contend that the search of respondent's pocket can be justified by any need to find and seize evidence in order to prevent its concealment or destruction, for as the Court of Appeals found, there are no evidence or fruits of the offense with which respondent was charged. The only rationale for a search in this case, then, is the removal of weapons which the arrestee might use to harm the officer and attempt an escape. This rationale, of course, is identical to the rationale of the search permitted in *Terry*. * * *

Since the underlying rationale of a *Terry* search and the search of a traffic violator are identical, the Court of Appeals held that the scope of the searches must be the same. * * *

The problem with this approach, however, is that it ignores several significant differences between the context in which a search incident to arrest for a traffic violation is made, and the situation presented in *Terry*. Some of these differences would appear to suggest permitting a more thorough search in this case than was permitted in *Terry;* other differences suggest a narrower, more limited right to search than was there recognized.

The most obvious difference between the two contexts relates to whether the officer has cause to believe that the individual he is dealing with possesses weapons which might be used against him. *Terry* did not permit an officer to conduct a weapons frisk of anyone he lawfully stopped on the street, but rather, only where "he has reason to believe that he is dealing with an armed and dangerous individual. * * * "While the policeman who arrests a suspected rapist or robber may well have reason to believe he is dealing with an armed and dangerous person, certainly this does not hold true with equal force with respect to persons arrested for motor vehicle violations of the sort involved in this case.

Nor was there any particular reason in this case to believe that respondent was dangerous. He had not attempted to evade arrest, but had quickly complied with the police both in bringing his car to a stop after being signalled to do so and in producing the documents Officer Jenks requested. In fact, Jenks admitted that he searched respondent face-to-face rather than in spread-eagle fashion because he had no reason to believe respondent would be violent.

While this difference between the situation presented in *Terry* and the context presented in this case would tend to suggest a lesser authority to search here than was permitted in *Terry,* other distinctions between the two contexts suggest just the opposite. As the Court of Appeals noted, a crucial feature distinguishing the in-custody arrest from the *Terry* context "is not the greater likelihood that a person taken into custody is armed, but rather the increased likelihood of danger to the officer *if* in fact the person is armed." A *Terry* stop involves a momentary encounter between officer and suspect, while an in-custody arrest places the two in close proximity for a much longer period of time. If the individual happens to have a weapon on his person, he will certainly have much more opportunity to use it against the officer in the in-custody situation. The prolonged proximity also makes it more likely that the individual will be able to extricate any small hidden weapon which might go undetected in a weapons frisk, such as a safety pin or razor blade. In addition, a suspect taken into custody may feel more threatened by the serious restraint on his liberty than a person who is simply stopped by an officer for questioning, and may therefore be more likely to resort to force.

Thus, in some senses there is less need for a weapons search in the in-custody traffic arrest situation than in a *Terry* context, while in other ways, there is a greater need. Balancing these competing considerations in order to determine what is a reasonable warrantless search in the traffic arrest context is a difficult process, one for which there may be no easy analytical guideposts. We are dealing in factors not easily quantified and, therefore, not easily weighed one against the other. And the competing interests we are protecting—the individual's interest in remaining free from unnecessarily intrusive invasions of privacy and society's interest that police officers not take unnecessary risks in the performance of their duties—are each deserving of our most serious attention and do not themselves tip the balance in any particular direction. * * *

The majority opinion fails to recognize that the search conducted by Officer Jenks did not merely involve a search of respondent's person. It also included a separate search of effects found on his person. And even were we to assume, *arguendo,* that it was reasonable for Jenks to remove the object he felt in respondent's pocket, clearly there was no justification consistent with the Fourth Amendment which would authorize his opening the package and looking inside.

To begin with, after Jenks had the cigarette package in his hands, there is no indication that he had reason to believe or did in fact believe that the package contained a weapon. More importantly, even if the crumpled up cigarette package had in fact contained some sort of small weapon, it would have been impossible for respondent to have used it once the package was in the officer's hands. Opening the package therefore did not further the protective purpose of the search. * * *

It is suggested, however, that since the custodial arrest itself represents a significant intrusion into the privacy of the person, any additional intrusion by way of opening or examining effects found on the person is not worthy of constitutional protection. But such an approach was expressly rejected by the Court in *Chimel* [p. 351. There it was suggested that since the police had lawfully entered petitioner's house to effect an arrest, the additional invasion of privacy stemming from an accompanying search of the entire house was inconsequential. The Court answered: "[W]e see no reason why, simply because some interference with an individual's privacy and freedom of movement has lawfully taken place, further intrusions should automatically be allowed despite the absence of a warrant that the Fourth Amendment would otherwise require." * * *

The Government argues that it is difficult to see what constitutionally protected "expectation of privacy" a prisoner has in the interior of a cigarette pack. One wonders if the result in this case would have been the same were respondent a businessman who was lawfully taken into custody for driving without a license and whose wallet was taken from him by the police. Would it be reasonable for the police officer, because of the possibility that a razor blade was hidden somewhere in the wallet, to open it, remove all the contents, and examine each item carefully? Or suppose a lawyer lawfully arrested for a traffic offense is found to have a sealed envelope on his person. Would it be permissible for the arresting officer to tear open the envelope in order to make sure that it did not contain a clandestine weapon—perhaps a pin or a razor blade? Would it not be more consonant with the purpose of the Fourth Amendment and the legitimate needs of the police to require the officer, if he has any question whatsoever about what the wallet or letter contains, to hold onto it until the arrestee is brought to the precinct station? * * *

NOTES AND QUESTIONS ON UNNECESSARY, PRETEXTUAL, AND ARBITRARY ARRESTS

1. In the companion case of *Gustafson v. Florida*, 414 U.S. 260 (1973), marijuana cigarettes were found on petitioner's person in a search incident to his custodial arrest for failure to have his operator's license with him while driving. Petitioner contended his case was different from *Robinson* in that (a) the offense for which he was arrested was "benign or trivial in nature," carrying with it no mandatory minimum sentence; and (b) there were no police regulations which required the officer to take petitioner into custody[a] or which required full scale body searches upon arrest in the field. The Court did "not find these differences determinative of the constitutional issue," and thus upheld the search on the basis of *Robinson.* Stewart, J., concurring, stated "that a persuasive claim might have been made in this case that the custodial arrest of the petitioner for a minor traffic offense violated his rights under the Fourth and Fourteenth Amendments," but since petitioner had "fully conceded the constitutional validity of his custodial arrest," the search of his person should be accepted as incidental to that arrest.

Nearly thirty years later, the issue noted by Justice Stewart was addressed in ATWATER v. CITY OF LAGO VISTA, p. 323, where the Court, per SOUTER, J., responded to plaintiff's second argument, "for a modern arrest rule, one not necessarily requiring violent breach of the peace, but nonetheless forbidding custodial arrest, even upon probable cause, when conviction could not ultimately carry any jail time and when the government shows no compelling need for immediate detention.

"If we were to derive a rule exclusively to address the uncontested facts of this case, Atwater might well prevail. She was a known and established resident of Lago Vista with no place to hide and no incentive to flee, and common sense says she would almost certainly have buckled up as a condition of driving off with a citation. In her case, the physical incidents of arrest were merely gratuitous humiliations imposed by a police officer who was (at best) exercising extremely poor judgment. Atwater's claim to live free of pointless indignity and confinement clearly outweighs anything the City can raise against it specific to her case.

"But we have traditionally recognized that a responsible Fourth Amendment balance is not well served by standards requiring sensitive, case-by-case determinations of government need, lest every discretionary judgment in the field be converted into an occasion for constitutional review. See, e.g., *United States v. Robinson*, [p. 329]. Often enough, the Fourth Amendment has to be applied on the spur (and in the heat) of the moment, and the object in implementing its command of reasonableness is to draw standards sufficiently clear and simple to be applied with a fair prospect of surviving judicial second-guessing months and years after an arrest or search is made. Courts attempting to strike a reasonable Fourth Amendment balance thus credit the government's side with an essential interest in readily administrable rules.

"At first glance, Atwater's argument may seem to respect the values of clarity and simplicity, so far as she claims that the Fourth Amendment generally forbids warrantless arrests for minor crimes not accompanied by violence or some demonstrable threat of it (whether 'minor crime' be defined as a fine-only traffic offense, a fine-only offense more generally, or a misdemeanor). But the claim is not ultimately so simple, nor could it be, for complications arise the moment we begin to think about the possible applications of the several criteria Atwater

a. Note, in this regard, the variation in state law governing traffic "arrests." Some states require that persons halted for violations of misdemeanor traffic laws be released upon issuance of a citation unless they fall within certain exceptions. The exceptions usually are divided into two categories: (1) persons who must be arrested and taken before a magistrate—usually those violating several specified laws (e.g., driving with a suspended license, or driving under the influence of alcohol); and (2) person who may be released on citation or taken before a magistrate at the option of the police officer—e.g., those who have violated several other specified laws (e.g., reckless driving or failure to submit to vehicle inspection), who fail to have a license in their possession, or who fail to furnish satisfactory evidence of identification. Other states require that persons in certain categories be taken into custody, but grant the officer discretion as to whether to take other misdemeanor violators into custody or to release them upon issuance of a citation. Special requirements are often imposed for release of nonresident drivers.

proposes for drawing a line between minor crimes with limited arrest authority and others not so restricted.

"One line, she suggests, might be between 'jailable' and 'fine-only' offenses, between those for which conviction could result in commitment and those for which it could not. The trouble with this distinction, of course, is that an officer on the street might not be able to tell. It is not merely that we cannot expect every police officer to know the details of frequently complex penalty schemes, but that penalties for ostensibly identical conduct can vary on account of facts difficult (if not impossible) to know at the scene of an arrest. Is this the first offense or is the suspect a repeat offender? Is the weight of the marijuana a gram above or a gram below the fine-only line? Where conduct could implicate more than one criminal prohibition, which one will the district attorney ultimately decide to charge? And so on.

"But Atwater's refinements would not end there. She represents that if the line were drawn at nonjailable traffic offenses, her proposed limitation should be qualified by a proviso authorizing warrantless arrests where 'necessary for enforcement of the traffic laws or when [an] offense would otherwise continue and pose a danger to others on the road.' (Were the line drawn at misdemeanors generally, a comparable qualification would presumably apply.) The proviso only compounds the difficulties. Would, for instance, either exception apply to speeding? * * *

"There is no need for more examples to show that Atwater's general rule and limiting proviso promise very little in the way of administrability. It is no answer that the police routinely make judgments on grounds like risk of immediate repetition; they surely do and should. But there is a world of difference between making that judgment in choosing between the discretionary leniency of a summons in place of a clearly lawful arrest, and making the same judgment when the question is the lawfulness of the warrantless arrest itself. It is the difference between no basis for legal action challenging the discretionary judgment, on the one hand, and the prospect of evidentiary exclusion or (as here) personal § 1983 liability for the misapplication of a constitutional standard, on the other. Atwater's rule therefore would not only place police in an almost impossible spot but would guarantee increased litigation over many of the arrests that would occur. * * *

"One may ask, of course, why these difficulties may not be answered by a simple tie breaker for the police to follow in the field: if in doubt, do not arrest. The first answer is that in practice the tie breaker would boil down to something akin to a least-restrictive-alternative limitation, which is itself one of those 'ifs, ands, and buts' rules, generally thought inappropriate in working out Fourth Amendment protection. Beyond that, whatever help the tie breaker might give would come at the price of a systematic disincentive to arrest in situations where even Atwater concedes that arresting would serve an important societal interest. * * *

"Just how easily the costs could outweigh the benefits may be shown by asking, as one Member of this Court did at oral argument, 'how bad the problem is out there.' The very fact that the law has never jelled the way Atwater would have it leads one to wonder whether warrantless misdemeanor arrests need constitutional attention, and there is cause to think the answer is no. So far as such arrests might be thought to pose a threat to the probable-cause requirement, anyone arrested for a crime without formal process, whether for felony or misdemeanor, is entitled to a magistrate's review of probable cause within 48 hours, and there is no reason to think the procedure in this case atypical in giving the suspect a prompt opportunity to request release. Many jurisdictions, moreover, have chosen to impose more restrictive safeguards through statutes limiting warrantless arrests for minor offenses. It is of course easier to devise a minor-offense limitation by statute than to derive one through the Constitution, simply because the statute can let the arrest power turn on any sort of practical consideration without having to subsume it under a broader principle. It is, in fact, only natural that States should resort to this sort of legislative regulation, for * * * it is in the interest of the police to limit petty-offense arrests, which carry costs that are simply too great to incur without good reason. Finally, and significantly, under current doctrine the preference for categorical treatment of Fourth Amendment claims gives way to individualized review when a defendant makes a colorable argument that an arrest, with or without a warrant, was 'conducted in an extraordinary manner, unusually harmful to [his] privacy or even physical interests.' *Whren v. United States*, [p. 339].

"The upshot of all these influences, combined with the good sense (and, failing that, the political accountability) of most local lawmakers and law-enforcement officials, is a dearth of horribles demanding redress. Indeed, when Atwater's counsel was asked at oral argument for any indications of comparably foolish, warrantless misdemeanor arrests, he could offer only one. We are sure that there are others, but just as surely the country is not confronting anything like an epidemic of unnecessary minor-offense arrests. That fact caps the reasons for rejecting Atwater's request for the development of a new and distinct body of constitutional law."

O'CONNOR, J., for the four dissenters, responded: "A custodial arrest exacts an obvious toll on an individual's liberty and privacy, even when the period of custody is relatively brief. The arrestee is subject to a full search of her person and confiscation of her possessions. *United States v. Robinson*, supra. If the arrestee is the occupant of a car, the entire passenger compartment of the car, including packages therein, is subject to search as well. See *New York v. Belton*, [p. 389]. The arrestee may be detained for up to 48 hours without having a magistrate determine whether there in fact was probable cause for the arrest. See *County of Riverside v. McLaughlin*, [p. 328]. Because people arrested for all types of violent and nonviolent offenses may be housed together awaiting such review, this detention period is potentially dangerous. And once the period of custody is over, the fact of the arrest is a permanent part of the public record.

"We have said that 'the penalty that may attach to any particular offense seems to provide the clearest and most consistent indication of the State's interest in arresting individuals suspected of committing that offense.' *Welsh v. Wisconsin*, [p. 369]. If the State has decided that a fine, and not imprisonment, is the appropriate punishment for an offense, the State's interest in taking a person suspected of committing that offense into custody is surely limited, at best. This is not to say that the State will never have such an interest. A full custodial arrest may on occasion vindicate legitimate state interests, even if the crime is punishable only by fine. Arrest is the surest way to abate criminal conduct. It may also allow the police to verify the offender's identity and, if the offender poses a flight risk, to ensure her appearance at trial. But when such considerations are not present, a citation or summons may serve the State's remaining law enforcement interests every bit as effectively as an arrest.

"Because a full custodial arrest is such a severe intrusion on an individual's liberty, its reasonableness hinges on 'the degree to which it is needed for the promotion of legitimate governmental interests.' In light of the availability of citations to promote a State's interests when a fine-only offense has been committed, I cannot concur in a rule which deems a full custodial arrest to be reasonable in every circumstance. Giving police officers constitutional carte blanche to effect an arrest whenever there is probable cause to believe a fine-only misdemeanor has been committed is irreconcilable with the Fourth Amendment's command that seizures be reasonable. Instead, I would require that when there is probable cause to believe that a fine-only offense has been committed, the police officer should issue a citation unless the officer is 'able to point to specific and articulable facts which, taken together with rational inferences from those facts, reasonably warrant [the additional] intrusion' of a full custodial arrest.

"The majority insists that a bright-line rule focused on probable cause is necessary to vindicate the State's interest in easily administrable law enforcement rules. Probable cause itself, however, is not a model of precision. * * * The rule I propose—which merely requires a legitimate reason for the decision to escalate the seizure into a full custodial arrest—thus does not undermine an otherwise 'clear and simple' rule.

"While clarity is certainly a value worthy of consideration in our Fourth Amendment jurisprudence, it by no means trumps the values of liberty and privacy at the heart of the Amendment's protections. * * *

"The Court's error, however, does not merely affect the disposition of this case. The per se rule that the Court creates has potentially serious consequences for the everyday lives of Americans. A broad range of conduct falls into the category of fine-only misdemeanors. * * *

"To be sure, such laws are valid and wise exercises of the States' power to protect the public health and welfare. My concern lies not with the decision to enact or enforce these laws, but rather with the manner in which they may be enforced. Under today's holding, when a police officer has probable cause to believe that a fine-only misdemeanor offense has occurred, that officer may stop the suspect, issue a citation, and let the person continue on her way. Or, if a traffic violation, the officer may stop the car, arrest the driver, search the driver, search the entire passenger compartment of the car including any purse or package inside, and impound the car and inventory all of its contents. Although the Fourth Amendment expressly requires that the latter course be a reasonable and proportional response to the circumstances of the offense, the majority gives officers unfettered discretion to choose that course without articulating a single reason why such action is appropriate.

"Such unbounded discretion carries with it grave potential for abuse. The majority takes comfort in the lack of evidence of 'an epidemic of unnecessary minor-offense arrests.' But the relatively small number of published cases dealing with such arrests proves little and should provide little solace. Indeed, as the recent debate over racial profiling demonstrates all too clearly, a relatively minor traffic infraction may often serve as an excuse for stopping and harassing an individual. After today, the arsenal available to any officer extends to a full arrest and the searches permissible concomitant to that arrest. An officer's subjective motivations for making a traffic stop are not relevant considerations in determining the reasonableness of the stop. See *Whren v. United States*, supra. But it is precisely because these motivations are beyond our purview that we must vigilantly ensure that officers' poststop actions—which are properly within our reach—comport with the Fourth Amendment's guarantee of reasonableness."

2. Would/should the result in *Atwater* be different had there been a state law proscribing custodial arrest in the case of seat belt violations? Consider *United States v. Mota,* 982 F.2d 1384 (9th Cir.1993), where state officers found counterfeit money in the search of two brothers incident to their custodial arrest for the municipal ordinance violation of operating a food cart without a license. Because a state statute required that such violators merely be given a citation, the court ruled the Fourth Amendment required suppression of their money. Is this because the *arrest* (not claimed to be pretextual) violated the Fourth Amendment? The

Mota court seemed to think so, stating: "Given the state's expression of disinterest in allowing warrantless arrests for mere infractions, we conclude that a custodial arrest for such infractions is unreasonable, and thus unlawful under the Fourth Amendment." Given that there is considerable authority to the contrary,[b] should the court in *Mota* instead have said that it was the search and not the arrest which violated the Fourth Amendment because *Robinson* upholds a search on incident-to-arrest grounds only when the arrest is a "lawful custodial arrest," which must mean lawful as a matter of state law?

3. Compare with *Atwater* the situation regarding arrest of a person as a material witness (a tactic used with some frequency in the investigation immediately following the 9/11/01 attack). In *Bacon v. United States*, 449 F.2d 933 (9th Cir.1971), the court held that the power to arrest and detain a person as a material witness was "fairly inferable" from what is now 18 U.S.C. § 3144, App. B, but then relied upon the Fourth Amendment in concluding that such arrest was permissible only upon a need-for-custody showing. *Bacon* thus concluded that a material witness arrest warrant must be based upon probable cause, which must be tested by two criteria: (1) "that the testimony of a person is material," and (2) "that it may become impracticable to secure his presence by subpoena." The court's added observation that the first of these could be met by "a mere statement by a responsible official, such as the United States Attorney," was later subjected to a Fourth Amendment challenge on the ground that it "permits a much lower standard than that required for the issuance of a standard arrest warrant," *United States v. Oliver*, 683 F.2d 224 (7th Cir.1982), to which the court responded: "We believe requiring a materiality representation by a responsible official of the United States Attorney's Office strikes a proper and adequate balance between protecting the secrecy of the grand jury's investigation and subjecting an individual to an unjustified arrest."[c]

In *United States v. Awadallah*, 349 F.3d 42 (2d Cir.2003), the district court had concluded that the affidavit for a material witness warrant did not pass the *Bacon/Oliver* two-pronged test because, as for the first prong, "the affidavit fails * * * because it was submitted by [FBI] Agent Plunkett based solely upon his personal knowledge," but "he could not have made an informed judgment about the materiality of Awadallah's testimony to the grand jury's investigation as he was never present in the grand jury." The court of appeals disagreed, concluding that while "the person preparing the affidavit" should "have had at least some personal knowledge of what had transpired," "an FBI agent who works closely with a prosecutor in a grand jury investigation may satisfy the 'personal knowledge' requirement," as was the case as to Plunkett.

4. As for the pretext arrest issue raised by the *Robinson* dissenters, it was finally addressed by the Supreme Court in WHREN v. UNITED STATES, 517 U.S. 806 (1996). Plainclothes vice-squad officers patrolling a "high drug area" of the District of Columbia in an unmarked car became suspicious of a certain truck, and when they made a U-turn in order to head back toward the truck it turned right suddenly without signaling and then sped off at an unreasonable speed. The police caught up with the vehicle when it was stopped at a red light; one officer approached and told the driver to put the vehicle in park and then saw through the window that passenger Whren had in his hands two large plastic bags of what

b. See, e.g., *Barry v. Fowler*, 902 F.2d 770 (9th Cir.1990), holding that in a § 1983 action claiming an unconstitutional arrest, the plaintiff cannot prevail if the arrest was made on probable cause but was in violation of state law.

c. On the constitutionality and wisdom of the statutes to be found in all jurisdictions permitting severe restrictions on the liberty of persons needed as witnesses in criminal proceedings, see Ronald L. Carlson & Mark S. Voepel, *Material Witness and Material Injustice*, 58 Wash.U.L.Q. 1 (1980).

appeared to be crack cocaine. The occupants of the truck were arrested, and the illegal drugs retrieved from the vehicle led to their conviction notwithstanding the claim of a pretextual stop. Justice SCALIA delivered the opinion of a unanimous Court: "As a general matter, the decision to stop an automobile is reasonable where the police have probable cause to believe that a traffic violation has occurred.

"Petitioners accept that Officer Soto had probable cause to believe that various provisions of the District of Columbia traffic code [regarding inattentive driving, speeding, and turning without signalling] had been violated. They argue, however, that 'in the unique context of civil traffic regulations' probable cause is not enough. Since, they contend, the use of automobiles is so heavily and minutely regulated that total compliance with traffic and safety rules is nearly impossible, a police officer will almost invariably be able to catch any given motorist in a technical violation. This creates the temptation to use traffic stops as a means of investigating other law violations, as to which no probable cause or even articulable suspicion exists. Petitioners, who are both black, further contend that police officers might decide which motorists to stop based on decidedly impermissible factors, such as the race of the car's occupants. To avoid this danger, they say, the Fourth Amendment test for traffic stops should be, not the normal one (applied by the Court of Appeals) of whether probable cause existed to justify the stop; but rather, whether a police officer, acting reasonably, would have made the stop for the reason given.

"Petitioners contend that the standard they propose is consistent with our past cases' disapproval of police attempts to use valid bases of action against citizens as pretexts for pursuing other investigatory agendas. We are reminded that in *Florida v. Wells,* [p. 400], we stated that 'an inventory search must not be used as a ruse for a general rummaging in order to discover incriminating evidence'; that in *Colorado v. Bertine,* [p. 395], in approving an inventory search, we apparently thought it significant that there had been 'no showing that the police, who were following standard procedures, acted in bad faith or for the sole purpose of investigation'; and that in *New York v. Burger,* [p. 441], we observed, in upholding the constitutionality of a warrantless administrative inspection, that the search did not appear to be 'a "pretext" for obtaining evidence of . . . violation of . . . penal laws.' But only an undiscerning reader would regard these cases as endorsing the principle that ulterior motives can invalidate police conduct that is justifiable on the basis of probable cause to believe that a violation of law has occurred. In each case we were addressing the validity of a search conducted in the absence of probable cause. Our quoted statements simply explain that the exemption from the need for probable cause (and warrant), which is accorded to searches made for the purpose of inventory or administrative regulation, is not accorded to searches that are not made for those purposes.

"* * * Not only have we never held, outside the context of inventory search or administrative inspection (discussed above), that an officer's motive invalidates objectively justifiable behavior under the Fourth Amendment; but we have repeatedly held and asserted the contrary. In *United States v. Villamonte–Marquez,* 462 U.S. 579 (1983), we held that an otherwise valid warrantless boarding of a vessel by customs officials was not rendered invalid 'because the customs officers were accompanied by a Louisiana state policeman, and were following an informant's tip that a vessel in the ship channel was thought to be carrying marihuana.' We flatly dismissed the idea that an ulterior motive might serve to strip the agents of their legal justification. In *United States v. Robinson,* [p. 329], we held that a traffic-violation arrest (of the sort here) would not be rendered invalid by the fact that it was 'a mere pretext for a narcotics search,' and that a lawful postarrest search of the person would not be rendered invalid by the fact that it was not motivated by the officer-safety concern that justifies such searches. And in *Scott v. United States,* [p. 484], in rejecting the contention that wiretap evidence was subject to exclusion because the agents conducting the tap had failed to make any effort to comply with the statutory requirement that unauthorized acquisitions be minimized, we said that '[s]ubjective intent alone ... does not make otherwise lawful conduct illegal or unconstitutional.' We described *Robinson* as having established that 'the fact that the officer does not have the state of mind which is hypothecated by the reasons which provide the legal justification for the officer's action does not invalidate the action taken as long as the circumstances, viewed objectively, justify that action.'

"We think these cases foreclose any argument that the constitutional reasonableness of traffic stops depends on the actual motivations of the individual officers involved. We of course agree with petitioners that the Constitution prohibits selective enforcement of the law based on considerations such as race. But the constitutional basis for objecting to intentionally discriminatory application of laws is the Equal Protection Clause, not the Fourth Amendment. Subjective intentions play no role in ordinary, probable-cause Fourth Amendment analysis.

"Recognizing that we have been unwilling to entertain Fourth Amendment challenges based on the actual motivations of individual officers, petitioners disavow any intention to make the individual officer's subjective good faith the touchstone of 'reasonableness.' They insist that the standard they have put forward—whether the officer's conduct deviated materially from usual police practices, so that a reasonable officer in the same circumstances would not have made the stop for the reasons given—is an 'objective' one.

"But although framed in empirical terms, this approach is plainly and indisputably driven by subjective considerations. Its whole purpose is to prevent the police from doing under the guise of enforcing the traffic code what they would like to do for different reasons. Petitioners' proposed standard may not use the word 'pretext,' but it is designed to combat nothing other than the perceived 'danger' of the pretextual stop, albeit only indirectly and over the run of cases. Instead of asking whether the individual officer had the proper state of mind, the petitioners would have us ask, in effect, whether (based on general police practices) it is plausible to believe that the officer had the proper state of mind.

"Why one would frame a test designed to combat pretext in such fashion that the court cannot take into account actual and admitted pretext is a curiosity that can only be explained by the fact that our cases have foreclosed the more sensible option. If those cases were based only upon the evidentiary difficulty of establishing subjective intent, petitioners' attempt to root out subjective vices through objective means might make sense. But they were not based only upon that, or indeed even principally upon that. Their principal basis—which applies equally to attempts to reach subjective intent through ostensibly objective means—is simply that the Fourth Amendment's concern with 'reasonableness' allows certain actions to be taken in certain circumstances, whatever the subjective intent. See, e.g., *Robinson,* supra ('Since it is the fact of custodial arrest which gives rise to the authority to search, it is of no moment that [the officer] did not indicate any subjective fear of the [arrestee] or that he did not himself suspect that [the arrestee] was armed'). But even if our concern had been only an evidentiary one, petitioners' proposal would by no means assuage it. Indeed, it seems to us somewhat easier to figure out the intent of an individual officer than to plumb the collective consciousness of law enforcement in order to determine whether a 'reasonable officer' would have been moved to act upon the traffic violation. While police manuals and standard procedures may sometimes provide objective assistance, ordinarily one would be reduced to speculating about the hypothetical reaction of a hypothetical constable—an exercise that might be called virtual subjectivity.

"Moreover, police enforcement practices, even if they could be practicably assessed by a judge, vary from place to place and from time to time. We cannot accept that the search and seizure protections of the Fourth Amendment are so variable, and can be made to turn upon such trivialities. The difficulty is illustrated by petitioners' arguments in this case. Their claim that a reasonable officer would not have made this stop is based largely on District of Columbia police regulations which permit plainclothes officers in unmarked vehicles to enforce traffic laws 'only in the case of a violation that is so grave as to pose an immediate threat to the safety of others.' This basis of invalidation would not apply in jurisdictions that had a different practice. And it would not have applied even in the District of Columbia, if Officer Soto had been wearing a uniform or patrolling in a marked police cruiser.

"Petitioners argue that our cases support insistence upon police adherence to standard practices as an objective means of rooting out pretext. They cite no holding to that effect, and dicta in only two cases. In *Abel v. United States,* 362 U.S. 217 (1960), the petitioner had been arrested by the Immigration and Naturalization Service (INS), on the basis of an administrative warrant that, he claimed, had been issued on pretextual grounds in order to enable the Federal Bureau of Investigation (FBI) to search his room after his arrest. We regarded this as an allegation of 'serious misconduct,' but rejected Abel's claims on the ground that '[a] finding of bad faith is . . . not open to us on th[e] record' in light of the findings below, including the finding that ' "the proceedings taken by the [INS] differed in no respect from what would have been done in the case of an individual concerning whom [there was no pending FBI investigation]." ' But it is a long leap from the proposition that following regular procedures is some evidence of lack of pretext to the proposition that failure to follow regular procedures proves (or is an operational substitute for) pretext. *Abel,* moreover, did not involve the assertion that pretext could invalidate a search or seizure for which there was probable cause—and even what it said about pretext in other contexts is plainly inconsistent with the views we later stated in [the cases summarized above]. In the other case claimed to contain supportive dicta, *United States v. Robinson,* in approving a search incident to an arrest for driving without a license, we noted that the arrest was 'not a departure from established police department practice.' That was followed, however, by the statement that '[w]e leave for another day questions which would arise on facts different from these.' This is not even a dictum that purports to provide an answer, but merely one that leaves the question open.

"In what would appear to be an elaboration on the 'reasonable officer' test, petitioners argue that the balancing inherent in any Fourth Amendment inquiry requires us to weigh the governmental and individual interests implicated in a traffic stop such as we have here. That balancing, petitioners claim, does not support investigation of minor traffic infractions by plainclothes police in unmarked vehicles; such investigation only minimally advances the government's interest in traffic safety, and may indeed retard it by producing motorist confusion and alarm—a view said to be supported by the Metropolitan Police Department's own regulations generally prohibiting this practice. And as for the Fourth Amendment interests of the individuals concerned, petitioners point out that our cases acknowledge that even ordinary traffic stops entail 'a possibly unsettling show of authority'; that they at best 'interfere with freedom of movement, are inconvenient, and consume time' and at worst 'may create substantial anxiety.' That anxiety is likely to be even more pronounced when the stop is conducted by plainclothes officers in unmarked cars.

"It is of course true that in principle every Fourth Amendment case, since it turns upon a 'reasonableness' determination, involves a balancing of all relevant factors. With rare exceptions not applicable here, however, the result of that balancing is not in doubt where the search or seizure is based upon probable cause. That is why petitioners must rely upon cases like *Prouse* to provide examples of actual 'balancing' analysis. There, the police action in question was a random traffic stop for the purpose of checking a motorist's license and vehicle registration, a practice that—like the practices at issue in the inventory search and administrative inspection cases upon which petitioners rely in making their 'pretext' claim—involves police intrusion without the probable cause that is its traditional justification. Our opinion in *Prouse* expressly distinguished the case from a stop based on precisely what is at issue here: 'probable cause to believe that a driver is violating any one of the multitude of applicable traffic and equipment regulations.' It noted approvingly that '[t]he foremost method of enforcing traffic and vehicle safety regulations ... is acting upon observed violations,' which afford the ' "quantum of individualized suspicion' " necessary to ensure that police discretion is sufficiently constrained. What is true of *Prouse* is also true of other cases that engaged in detailed 'balancing' to decide the constitutionality of automobile stops: the detailed 'balancing' analysis was necessary because they involved seizures without probable cause.

"Where probable cause has existed, the only cases in which we have found it necessary actually to perform the 'balancing' analysis involved searches or seizures conducted in an extraordinary manner, unusually harmful to an individual's privacy or even physical interests—such as, for example, seizure by means of deadly force, see *Tennessee v. Garner,* [p. 324], unannounced entry into a home, see *Wilson v. Arkansas,* [p. 309], entry into a home without a warrant, see *Welsh v. Wisconsin,* [p. 369, or physical penetration of the body, see *Winston v. Lee,* [p. 349]. The making of a traffic stop out-of-uniform does not remotely qualify as such an extreme practice, and so is governed by the usual rule that probable cause to believe the law has been broken 'outbalances' private interest in avoiding police contact.

"Petitioners urge as an extraordinary factor in this case that the 'multitude of applicable traffic and equipment regulations' is so large and so difficult to obey perfectly that virtually everyone is guilty of violation, permitting the police to single out almost whomever they wish for a stop. But we are aware of no principle that would allow us to decide at what point a code of law becomes so expansive and so commonly violated that infraction itself can no longer be the ordinary measure of the lawfulness of enforcement. And even if we could identify such exorbitant codes, we do not know by what standard (or what right) we would decide, as petitioners would have us do, which particular provisions are sufficiently important to merit enforcement.

"For the run-of-the-mine case, which this surely is, we think there is no realistic alternative to the traditional common-law rule that probable cause justifies a search and seizure."

5. As the Supreme Court was advised in the briefs of the petitioners and amici, the tactic at issue in *Whren* is one which has been commonly employed by police in recent years in their "war against drugs." Both in urban areas and on the interstates, police are on the watch for "suspicious" travellers, and once one is spotted it is only a matter of time before some technical or trivial offense produces the necessary excuse for pulling him over. Perhaps because the offenses are so often insignificant, the driver is typically told at the outset that he will merely be given a warning. But then things often turn ugly. The driver and passengers are usually closely questioned about their identities, the reason for their travels, their intended destination, and the like. The subject of drugs comes up, and often the driver is induced to "consent" to a full search of the vehicle and all effects therein for drugs. If such consent is not forthcoming, another police vehicle with a drug-sniffing dog may appear on the scene. See, e.g., *United States v. Mesa,* 62 F.3d 159 (6th Cir.1995); *United States v. Roberson,* 6 F.3d 1088 (5th Cir.1993) (noting the trooper's "remarkable record" of turning traffic stops into drug arrests on 250 prior occasions); *State v. Dominguez–Martinez,* 895 P.2d 306 (Or.1995).[d]

6. Two illustrations from the many reported cases of this genre reveal how little it takes to supply grounds for a traffic stop acceptable to the courts. In one, a Texas state trooper passing a van noticed it had four black occupants, so the officer crested a hill, pulled onto the shoulder and doused his lights. When the van approached, the driver cautiously changed lanes to distance the van from the vehicle on the shoulder, but failed to signal—hardly surprising considering that the van was the only moving vehicle on that stretch of road. Yet the stop for an illegal lane change was upheld. *United States v. Roberson,* supra. In the other case, the stop occurred after a Utah deputy patrolling Interstate 70 saw an automobile driven by a black man straddle the center line for about one second before proceeding to the other lane of traffic. The stop was upheld on the grounds that the officer had sufficient suspicion the operator was driving while impaired. *United States v. Lee,* 73 F.3d 1034 (10th Cir.1996).

7. The dissent by Chief Judge Seymour in *United States v. Botero–Ospina,* 71 F.3d 783 (10th Cir.1995), a pre-*Whren* decision which squares with the *Whren* holding, provides an interesting contrast to the later Scalia opinion in *Whren.* That dissent states in part:

"In addition to producing the intrusion any individual experiences when subjected to a traffic stop, the majority's standard frees a police officer to target members of minority communities for the selective enforcement of otherwise unenforced statutes. The Supreme Court recognized in *Terry [v. Ohio,* p. 401] that the harassment of minority groups by certain elements of the police population does occur, and that 'the degree of community resentment aroused by particular practices is clearly relevant to an assessment of the quality of the intrusion upon reasonable expectations of personal security caused by those practices.' By refusing to examine either the arbitrariness with which a particular statute is enforced or the motivation underlying its enforcement in a particular case, the majority standard does nothing to curb the ugly reality that minority groups are sometimes targeted for selective enforcement.[e] As a result, the majority standard adds the onus of discrimination and resentment to the already significant burden imposed by traffic stops generally. * * *

d. A recent study estimates that in 1999 19.3 millions persons were subjected to a traffic stop; that in 1.3 million of these stops the police conducted a search (including, 80% of the time, a search of the vehicle); that about a third of the searches were with consent, while the rest were made without seeking consent or, occasionally, after consent had been denied; and that most drivers who consented to a search felt the police lacked a legitimate reason for the search. Patrick A. Langan et al., *Contacts between Police and the Public* (U.S. Dep't of Justice, 2001).

e. "As part of the settlement of a civil rights lawsuit, the Maryland State Police tracked the race of drivers stopped since January 1995.

"Statistics released last November showed that 73 percent of drivers who were stopped and searched on Interstate 95 between Baltimore and Delaware were African–American. A corresponding American Civil Liberties Union study concluded that only 14 percent of drivers on the highway were black.

"And in central Florida, black drivers on the Florida Turnpike were 6.5 times more likely to be searched than white drivers, according to an analysis by the *Orlando Sentinel,* which studied more than 3,800 traffic stops between January 1996 and April 1997." Michael Higgins, *Looking the Part,* 48 A.B.A.J. 48, 49 (Nov. 1997). See also David A. Harris, *"Driving While Black" and All Other Traffic Offenses: The Supreme Court and Pretextual Traffic Stops,* 87 J.Crim.L. & Criminology 544 (1997).

"The Supreme Court held in *Terry* that to justify a particular intrusion, a 'police officer must be able to point to specific and articulable facts which, taken together with the rational inferences from those facts, reasonably warrant that intrusion.' It is difficult to justify a stop as reasonable, even if supported by an observed violation, if the undisputed facts indicate that the violation does not ordinarily result in a stop. Moreover, the Court in *Terry* described in detail the appropriate reasonableness inquiry in language that is utterly irreconcilable with the majority standard. The Court stated that in assessing the reasonableness of a particular stop 'it is imperative that the facts be judged against an objective standard: would the facts available to the officer at the moment of the seizure or the search "warrant a man of reasonable caution in the belief" that the action taken was appropriate?' It would hardly seem necessary to point out that the Court's mandate to determine what a reasonable officer would do in the circumstances cannot be fulfilled by merely ascertaining in a vacuum what a particular officer could do under state law.

"Given the 'multitude of applicable traffic and equipment regulations' in any jurisdiction, upholding a stop on the basis of a regulation seldom enforced opens the door to the arbitrary exercise of police discretion condemned in *Terry* and its progeny. 'Anything less [than the reasonable officer standard] would invite intrusions upon constitutionally guaranteed rights based on nothing more substantial than inarticulate hunches, a result this Court has consistently refused to sanction.' *Terry.*"

8. Is Chief Judge Seymour's concern about harassment of minorities met by Justice Scalia's observation that selective enforcement based on race is barred by the Equal Protection Clause? How could the petitioners in *Whren* have proved such an equal protection violation? Does/should the "rigorous standard for discovery" against the government upon a defendant's claim of race-based selective prosecution, see *United States v. Armstrong,* Ch. 13, § 3, also apply in this setting? And even if the *Whren* petitioners *did* prove that the traffic stop was itself a violation of the Equal Protection Clause, would that bar prosecution on the *drug* charges? Would it require suppression of the drugs? Cf. *United States v. Jennings,* 985 F.2d 562 (6th Cir.1993) (dictum by majority that if defendant had proved he had been selected for a consensual encounter solely because of his race, then the evidence obtained in a consent search during that encounter ought to be excluded, as "evidence seized in violation of the Equal Protection Clause should be suppressed"; concurring opinion notes that the case cited in support by the majority, *Elkins v. United States,* p. 222, "provides absolutely no support for the majority's position").

9. Does Justice Scalia ever respond directly to the *Whren* petitioners' argument that probable cause is not enough "in the unique context of civil traffic regulations" because it is possible for a police officer to catch any given motorist in a technical violation? Is the proper response, as Scalia says at one point, that the matter of police purpose is relevant only in situations represented by *Wells, Bertine* and *Burger,* where the search is allowed without probable cause? Is the risk of pretext greater in those situations, where the police must show they complied with "standard procedures" or "reasonable legislative or administrative standards," than as to traffic stops?

Where does *Whren* end and *Bertine* begin? Consider *State v. Sullivan,* 16 S.W.3d 551 (Ark.2000), where the Court declined "to sanction conduct where a police officer can trail a targeted vehicle with a driver merely suspected of criminal activity, wait for the driver to exceed the speed limit by one mile per hour, arrest the driver for speeding, and conduct a full-blown inventory search of the vehicle with impunity." The Supreme Court summarily reversed because of the Arkansas court's erroneous claim that it could "interpret[] the U.S. Constitution more broadly than the United States Supreme Court," and added that *Whren*, itself a traffic stop case, also applied to custodial arrests. *Arkansas v. Sullivan*, 532 U.S. 769 (2001). The four concurring Justices said the above quotation from the state court opinion manifested "a concern rooted in the Fourth Amendment," but then concluded that "such exercises of official discretion are unlimited by the Fourth Amendment" in light of *Whren*. Is that a correct reading of *Whren*?

NOTES AND QUESTIONS ON OTHER SEARCHES OF THE PERSON

1. Full searches of an arrested person are more typically made when that person has been delivered to the place of his forthcoming detention. These searches are typically upheld on two bases: (1) as a delayed *Robinson* search incident to arrest; and (2) as an inventory incident to booking to safeguard the property of the accused and to ensure that weapons and contraband are not introduced into the jail. However, some jurisdictions have rejected the *Robinson* rule and have also limited the extent of permissible inventory. See, e.g., *State v. Kaluna,* 520 P.2d 51 (Hawaii 1974) (police matron subjected female arrested for armed robbery to strip search, resulting in discovery of packet of drugs in her bra; held, not a valid search incident to arrest because no reason to believe weapons or evidence of the crime there, and not valid inventory because the packet could have been inventoried without opening it). Also, in some jurisdictions a search at the station is deemed unlawful if the defendant was not afforded a sufficient opportunity to gain his release. See, e.g., *Zehrung v. State,* 569 P.2d 189 (Alaska 1977), on rehearing, 573 P.2d 858 (1978) ("when one is arrested and brought to a jail for a minor offense for which bail has already been set in a bail schedule, he should be allowed a reasonable opportunity to attempt to raise bail before being subjected to remand and booking procedures and the incidental inventory search"; but on rehearing court admits state may be correct in saying this impractical in smaller communities with no separate holding cells in unsecured area, and that there the search may be proper unless defendant presently has the bail money).

2. ILLINOIS v. LAFAYETTE, 462 U.S. 640 (1983), concerned the admissibility of amphetamines found in respondent's shoulder bag during an at-the-station inventory of his effects following his arrest for disturbing the peace. The Court, per BURGER, C.J., concluded:

"The governmental interests underlying a stationhouse search of the arrestee's person and possessions may in some circumstances be even greater than those supporting a search immediately following arrest. Consequently, the scope of a stationhouse search will often vary from that made at the time of arrest. Police conduct that would be impractical or unreasonable—or embarrassingly intrusive—on the street can more readily—and privately—be performed at the station. For example, the interests supporting a search incident to arrest would hardly justify disrobing an arrestee on the street, but the practical necessities of routine jail administration may even justify taking a prisoner's clothes before confining him, although that step would be rare. This was made clear in *United States v. Edwards,* [p. 347].[2]

"At the stationhouse, it is entirely proper for police to remove and list or inventory property found on the person or in the possession of an arrested person who is to be jailed. A range of governmental interests support an inventory process. It is not unheard of for persons employed in police activities to steal property taken from arrested persons; similarly, arrested persons have been

2. We were not addressing in *Edwards,* and do not discuss here, the circumstances in which a strip search of an arrestee may or may not be appropriate.

known to make false claims regarding what was taken from their possession at the stationhouse. A standardized procedure for making a list or inventory as soon as reasonable after reaching the stationhouse not only deters false claims but also inhibits theft or careless handling of articles taken from the arrested person. Arrested persons have also been known to injure themselves—or others—with belts, knives, drugs or other items on their person while being detained. Dangerous instrumentalities—such as razor blades, bombs, or weapons—can be concealed in innocent-looking articles taken from the arrestee's possession. The bare recital of these mundane realities justifies reasonable measures by police to limit these risks—either while the items are in the police possession or at the time they are returned to the arrestee upon his release. Examining all the items removed from the arrestee's person or possession and listing or inventorying them is an entirely reasonable administrative procedure. It is immaterial whether the police actually fear any particular package or container; the need to protect against such risks arises independent of a particular officer's subjective concerns. Finally, inspection of an arrestee's personal property may assist the police in ascertaining or verifying his identity. In short, every consideration of orderly police administration benefiting both police and the public points toward the appropriateness of the examination of respondent's shoulder bag prior to his incarceration. * * *

"The Illinois court held that the search of respondent's shoulder bag was unreasonable because 'preservation of the defendant's property and protection of police from claims of lost or stolen property, "could have been achieved in a less intrusive manner." For example, * * * the defendant's shoulder bag could easily have been secured by sealing it within a plastic bag or box and placing it in a secured locker.' Perhaps so, but the real question is not what 'could have been achieved,' but whether the Fourth Amendment *requires* such steps; it is not our function to write a manual on administering routine, neutral procedures of the stationhouse. Our role is to assure against violations of the Constitution.

" * * * We are hardly in a position to second-guess police departments as to what practical administrative method will best deter theft by and false claims against its employees and preserve the security of the stationhouse. It is evident that a stationhouse search of every item carried on or by a person who has lawfully been taken into custody by the police will amply serve the important and legitimate governmental interests involved.

"Even if less intrusive means existed of protecting some particular types of property, it would be unreasonable to expect police officers in the everyday course of business to make fine and subtle distinctions in deciding which containers or items may be searched and which must be sealed as a unit. * * * "[3]

3. UNITED STATES v. EDWARDS, 415 U.S. 800 (1974), concerned the admissibility of paint chips obtained from defendant's clothing, taken from him without a warrant while he was in jail about 10 hours after his arrest for attempted breaking and entering. The clothing was seized because investigation subsequent to the arrest showed that paint had been chipped from a window when entry was attempted with a pry bar. The Court, per WHITE, J., concluded "that once the defendant is lawfully arrested and is in custody, the effects in his possession at the place of detention that were subject to search at the time and place of his arrest may lawfully be searched and seized without a warrant even though a substantial period of time has elapsed between the arrest and subsequent administrative processing on the one hand and the taking of the property for use as evidence on the other. This is true where the clothing or effects are immediately seized upon arrival at the jail, held under the defendant's name in

3. The record is unclear as to whether respondent was to have been incarcerated after being booked for disturbing the peace. That is an appropriate inquiry on remand.

the 'property room' of the jail and at a later time searched and taken for use at the subsequent criminal trial. The result is the same where the property is not physically taken from the defendant until sometime after his incarceration."[a] The Court added it was not holding "that the warrant clause of the Fourth Amendment is never applicable to postarrest seizures of the effects of an arrestee," and by footnote to that caveat stated it was expressing no view "concerning those circumstances surrounding custodial searches incident to incarceration which might 'violate the dictates of reason either because of their number or their manner of perpetration.' "

STEWART, J., joined by Douglas, Brennan, and Marshall, JJ., dissented, arguing that they could "see no justification for dispensing with the warrant requirement here. The police had ample time to seek a warrant, and no exigent circumstances were present to excuse their failure to do so," as the government "has not even suggested that [the defendant] was aware of the presence of the paint chips on his clothing."

4. After *Robinson*, *Lafayette* and *Edwards,* is a person in custody following a lawful arrest "fair game" for a search for evidence of crimes other than the crime for which the arrest was made? Compare *People v. Trudeau,* 187 N.W.2d 890 (Mich.1971) (defendant was under arrest for breaking and entering, in recent attempted burglary with similar modus operandi watchman was killed and heel print was left at scene, police subsequently took defendant's shoe and matched it with heel print; held, seizure illegal because police "had no probable cause to believe that the seized shoes were evidence linked to the crime").

5. In SCHMERBER v. CALIFORNIA, [the facts and other aspects of which are discussed at p. 35], the Court per BRENNAN, J., observed:

"Although the facts which established probable cause to arrest in this case also suggested the required relevance and likely success of a test of petitioner's blood for alcohol, the question remains whether the arresting officer was permitted to draw these inferences himself, or was required instead to procure a warrant before proceeding with the test. Search warrants are ordinarily required for searches of dwellings, and, absent an emergency, no less could be required where intrusions into the human body are concerned. * * *

"The officer in the present case, however, might reasonably have believed that he was confronted with an emergency, in which the delay necessary to obtain a warrant, under the circumstances, threatened 'the destruction of evidence' * * *. We are told that the percentage of alcohol in the blood begins to diminish shortly after drinking stops, as the body functions to eliminate it from the system. Particularly in a case such as this, where time had to be taken to bring the accused to a hospital and to investigate the scene of the accident, there was no time to seek out a magistrate and secure a warrant. Given these special facts, we conclude that the attempt to secure evidence of blood-alcohol content in this case was an appropriate incident to petitioner's arrest."[b]

a. A search incident to arrest made at the station is deemed unlawful if the grounds for the arrest have dissipated prior to the time of the search. See *United States v. Coughlin,* 338 F.Supp. 1328 (E.D.Mich.1972) (defendant arrested upon leaving house at which mailman had just delivered package containing narcotics; at the station, police put his hands under fluorescent light and determined that defendant had handled the narcotics which the police had previously dusted with fluorescent powder; held, search illegal because promptly after arrest police learned that defendant was not the addressee of the package, so that there was not probable cause for further detention).

b. Is it essential that this be characterized as a search incident to arrest? What if the defendant had not been arrested and the blood sample was taken while he was in the emergency room of the hospital for treatment of injuries he received in an accident in which he was involved, because it reasonably appeared to the police investigating the accident that he

6. Applying the *Schmerber* balancing test, the Court in WINSTON v. LEE, 470 U.S. 753 (1985), held that the proposed court-ordered surgery on defendant, for the purpose of removing a bullet expected to show that defendant was the robber hit by the victim's gunfire, would constitute an unreasonable search. "The reasonableness of surgical intrusions beneath the skin," the Court stated per BRENNAN, J., "depends on a case-by-case approach, in which the individual's interests in privacy and security are weighed against society's interests in conducting the procedure." Taking into account medical evidence that the operation would require a general anesthetic, might last over two hours, and could require probing of muscle tissue which might cause injury to the muscle as well as to nerves, blood vessels and other tissue, the Court concluded the "operation sought will intrude substantially on respondent's protected interests." Such an intrusion would not be reasonable, the Court then decided, given the state's failure "to demonstrate a compelling need for it." No such need was deemed to be present, as the state had considerable other evidence connecting defendant with the robbery, including a prompt identification of him by the victim and his location near the robbery shortly after it occurred.[c]

7. In light of *Schmerber* and *Winston,* what about other scientific tests and intrusions into the body after arrest? Consider *United States ex rel. Guy v. McCauley,* 385 F.Supp. 193 (E.D.Wis.1974), concerning a stationhouse search of the vagina of an incarcerated female which resulted in the discovery of a packet of narcotics. The court held the search violated due process because not conducted "by skilled medical technicians." But what if it had been so conducted? In *Guy,* the defendant also objected that the search was not made upon probable cause, but the court, while noting that the search was apparently prompted by "vague information several years old that [she] was known to carry heroin in her vagina," asserted that this objection "missed the mark" in light of *Robinson* and *Edwards.* Is that so? What then of other warrantless searches of the body of an arrestee which have been upheld, including "the placing of the arrestee's hands under an ultraviolet lamp; examining the arrestee's arms to determine the age of burn marks; swabbing the arrestee's hands with a chemical substance; taking scrapings from under the arrestee's fingernails; taking a small sample of hair from the arrestee's head; obtaining a urine sample from the arrestee; taking a saliva sample from the arrestee; giving the arrestee a breathalyzer examination; swabbing the arrestee's penis; taking dental impressions from the arrestee; or taking pubic hair combings from him." SEARCHSZR § 5.3(c).

8. In KNOWLES v. IOWA, 525 U.S. 113 (1998), a policeman stopped Knowles for speeding and then, pursuant to a statute authorizing (but not requiring) him to issue a citation in lieu of arrest for most bailable offenses, issued Knowles a citation. The officer then made a full search of Knowles car and found a bag of marijuana. That search was upheld by the state courts on the ground that because an Iowa statute declared that issuance of a citation in lieu of arrest "does not affect the officer's authority to conduct an otherwise lawful search," it sufficed here that the officer had probable cause to make a custodial arrest. A unanimous Supreme Court, per REHNQUIST, C.J., reversed. Looking at the two historical rationales for search incident to arrest discussed in *Robinson*, the Court reasoned: (i) The "threat to officer safety from issuing a traffic citation * * * is a good deal less than in the case of a custodial arrest," where (as it was put in *Robinson*) there is "the extended exposure which follows the taking of a suspect into custody and transporting him to the police station," and thus the "concern for officer

was intoxicated? Is this issue resolved by *Cupp v. Murphy,* discussed in Note 9 infra?

c. See Ronald J. Bacigal, *Dodging a Bullet, But Opening Old Wounds in Fourth Amendment Jurisprudence,* 16 Seton Hall L.Rev. 597 (1986).

safety'' incident to a traffic stop is sufficiently met by the officer's authority to order the driver and passengers out of the car,[d] to "perform a 'patdown' of a driver and any passengers upon reasonable suspicion that they may be armed and dangerous,"[e] and to conduct a patdown "of the passenger compartment of a vehicle upon reasonable suspicion that an occupant is dangerous and may gain immediate control of a weapon."[f] (ii) The "need to discover and preserve evidence" does not exist here, as "no further evidence of excessive speed was going to be found either on the person of the offender or in the passenger compartment of the car," and any concern with destruction of evidence as to identity can be met by arresting the driver whenever the officer is not satisfied with his identification.

Considering that Knowles "did not argue * * * that the statute could never be lawfully applied" and that the Court only passed upon "the search at issue," are there circumstances in which a search made under this statute would be lawful? Consider *State v. Greenslit*, 559 A.2d 672 (Vt.1989) (upholding search of person incident to issuance of notice to appear for present use of marijuana). What if Iowa reformulated its statute to conform to language used in some other states, i.e., that if an officer makes an arrest, the lawfulness of a search incident thereto is not affected by a subsequent decision at the scene to issue a citation and release the arrestee? Or, even absent such reformulation, may Iowa police, given their broad statutory authority to elect either citation or arrest as they wish, merely delay that decision until after a search, and then justify productive searches under the principle of the *Rawlings* case, note g infra?

In *United States v. Jackson*, 377 F.3d 715 (7th Cir.2004), after a driver was stopped for a traffic offense, he was found not to be carrying a driver's license, and a check of identifying details via computer implied the driver might not be who he claimed to be, so the officer decided to detain him further in the squad car until his identity could be established. The officer told the driver he was not "under arrest" and was merely being "detained," and then, presumably without reasonable suspicion the driver was armed, conducted a frisk, resulting in discovery of 50 grams of crack cocaine. Is this case governed by *Knowles* or *Robinson*? What if instead the driver said he had proper identification at home and offered to show the officer where he lived, and upon their arrival there the officer followed the driver inside (where he observed evidence of a bogus-ID mill), relying upon his authority under *Washington v. Chrisman*, p. 357, as in *United States v. Garcia*, 376 F.3d 648 (7th Cir.2004)?

9. As for search of the person without any prior seizure, consider CUPP v. MURPHY, 412 U.S. 291 (1973). The Court, per STEWART, J., held that where Murphy voluntarily appeared at the station for questioning concerning the strangulation of his wife, at which time the police noticed what appeared to be blood on his finger, and the police had probable cause to arrest him but did not formally

d. In *Pennsylvania v. Mimms*, 434 U.S. 106 (1977), officers stopped a vehicle with an expired license plate for the purpose of issuing a traffic summons and then ordered the driver out of the car, which resulted in the observation of a large bulge under his pocket, and this prompted a frisk and discovery of a gun. Rejecting the state court's holding that the driver could be directed to get out of the car only upon a reasonable suspicion he "posed a threat to police safety," the Court reasoned that "this additional intrusion can only be described as de minimis" and was justified because it "reduces the likelihood that the officer will be the victim of an assault." In *Maryland v. Wilson*, 519 U.S. 408 (1997), the Court held "that an officer making a traffic stop may order passengers to get out of the car pending completion of the stop." The Court agreed that "there is not the same basis for ordering the passengers out of the car as there is for ordering the driver out," but yet deemed "the additional intrusion on the passenger" to be "minimal" and justified in light of the fact that "danger to an officer from a traffic stop is likely to be greater when there are passengers in addition to the driver in the stopped car."

e. As authorized by *Terry v. Ohio*, p. 401.

f. As authorized by *Michigan v. Long*, p. 435.

place him under arrest,[g] the warrantless taking of scrapings from his fingernails "was constitutionally permissible." Noting that Murphy was aware of the police suspicion and tried to wipe his fingers clean, the Court concluded that "the rationale of *Chimel* [p. 351] justified the police in subjecting him to the very limited search necessary to preserve the highly evanescent evidence they found under his fingernails." But, because a person not under formal arrest "might well be less hostile to the police and less likely to take conspicuous, immediate steps to destroy incriminating evidence on his person," the Court emphasized it was *not* holding "that a full *Chimel* search would have been justified in this case without a formal arrest and without a warrant." MARSHALL, J., concurring, noted that the police could not have preserved the evidence by "close surveillance" and that detaining Murphy while a warrant was sought "would have been as much a seizure as detaining him while his fingernails were scraped." DOUGLAS, J., dissenting, argued: "There was time to get a warrant; Murphy could have been detained while one was sought; and that detention would have preserved the perishable evidence the police sought."

SECTION 6. WARRANTLESS ENTRIES AND SEARCHES OF PREMISES

CHIMEL v. CALIFORNIA

395 U.S. 752, 89 S.Ct. 2034, 23 L.Ed.2d 685 (1969).

Justice STEWART delivered the opinion of the Court. * * *

The relevant facts are essentially undisputed. Late in the afternoon of September 13, 1965, three police officers arrived at the Santa Ana, California, home of the petitioner with a warrant authorizing his arrest for the burglary of a coin shop. The officers knocked on the door, identified themselves to the petitioner's wife, and asked if they might come inside. She ushered them into the house, where they waited 10 or 15 minutes until the petitioner returned home from work. When the petitioner entered the house, one of the officers handed him the arrest warrant and asked for permission to "look around." The petitioner objected, but was advised that "on the basis of the lawful arrest," the officers would nonetheless conduct a search. No search warrant had been issued.

Accompanied by the petitioner's wife, the officers then looked through the entire three-bedroom house, including the attic, the garage, and a small workshop. In some rooms the search was relatively cursory. In the master bedroom and sewing room, however the officers directed the petitioner's wife to open drawers and "to physically move contents of the drawers from side to side so that [they] might view any items that would have come from [the] burglary." After completing the search, they seized numerous items—primarily coins, but also several medals, tokens, and a few other objects. The entire search took between 45 minutes and an hour.

At the petitioner's subsequent state trial on two charges of burglary, the items taken from his house were admitted into evidence against him, over his objection that they had been unconstitutionally seized. He was convicted, and the judgments * * * affirmed * * *.

g. Murphy was not arrested until over a month later, and thus the case is unlike those in which the arrest followed the search by a matter of minutes. The prevailing view is that a search "incident" to arrest may actually come before the formal making of an arrest if the police had grounds to arrest at the time the search was made. As stated in *Rawlings v. Kentucky* (other aspects of which are discussed at p. 898): "Where the formal arrest followed quickly on the heels of the challenged search of petitioner's person, we do not believe it particularly important that the search preceded the arrest rather than vice versa."

Without deciding the question, we proceed on the hypothesis that the California courts were correct in holding that the arrest of the petitioner was valid under the Constitution. This brings us directly to the question whether the warrantless search of the petitioner's entire house can be constitutionally justified as incident to that arrest. The decisions of this Court bearing upon that question have been far from consistent, as even the most cursory review makes evident.[a]

In 1950 * * * came *United States v. Rabinowitz,* 339 U.S. 56 (1950), the decision upon which California primarily relies in the case now before us. In *Rabinowitz,* federal authorities had been informed that the defendant was dealing in stamps bearing forged overprints. On the basis of that information they secured a warrant for his arrest, which they executed at his one-room business office. At the time of the arrest, the officers "searched the desk, safe, and file cabinets in the office for about an hour and a half," and seized 573 stamps with forged overprints. The stamps were admitted into evidence at the defendant's trial, and this Court affirmed his conviction, rejecting the contention that the warrantless search had been unlawful. The Court held that the search in its entirety fell within the principle giving law enforcement authorities "[t]he right 'to search the place where the arrest is made in order to find and seize things connected with the crime * * *.' " * * * The test, said the Court, "is not whether it is reasonable to procure a search warrant, but whether the search was reasonable."

Rabinowitz has come to stand for the proposition, inter alia, that a warrantless search "incident to a lawful arrest" may generally extend to the area that is considered to be in the "possession" or under the "control" of the person arrested. And it was on the basis of that proposition that the California courts upheld the search of the petitioner's entire house in this case. That doctrine, however, at least in the broad sense in which it was applied by the California courts in this case, can withstand neither historical nor rational analysis.

Even limited to its own facts, the *Rabinowitz* decision was, as we have seen, hardly founded on an unimpeachable line of authority. * * *

Nor is the rationale by which the State seeks here to sustain the search of the petitioner's house supported by a reasoned view of the background and purpose of the Fourth Amendment. Justice Frankfurter wisely pointed out in his *Rabinowitz* dissent that the Amendment's proscription of "unreasonable searches and seizures" must be read in light of "the history that gave rise to the words"—a history of "abuses so deeply felt by the Colonies as to be one of the potent causes of the Revolution * * *." The Amendment was in large part a reaction to the general warrants and warrantless searches that had so alienated the colonists and had helped speed the movement for independence. In the scheme of the Amend-

a. In an omitted portion of the opinion, the Court described how dictum on search incident to arrest broadened from search of the "person," *Weeks v. United States,* 232 U.S. 383 (1914), to search for what is "upon his person or in his control," *Carroll v. United States,* 267 U.S. 132 (1925), to search of "persons lawfully arrested" and "the place where the arrest is made," *Agnello v. United States,* 269 U.S. 20 (1925). Then, in *Marron v. United States,* 275 U.S. 192 (1927), concerning seizure of evidence at a place where illegal liquor sales were occurring, the Court held that because the police had made an arrest on the premises they "had a right without a warrant contemporaneously to search the place in order to find and seize the things used to carry on the criminal enterprise." But in *Go-Bart Importing Co. v. United States,* 282 U.S. 344 (1931), *Marron* was limited to where the items seized "were visible and accessible and in the offender's immediate custody" and there "was no threat of force or general search or rummaging of the place." This limitation was reiterated in *United States v. Lefkowitz,* 285 U.S. 452 (1932), which, like *Go-Bart,* held unlawful a search of a desk despite the fact the search had accompanied a lawful arrest, but was abandoned in *Harris v. United States,* 331 U.S. 145 (1947), upholding the search of a four-room apartment as "incident to arrest." But *Harris* was not followed in *Trupiano v. United States,* 334 U.S. 699 (1948), declaring that "law enforcement agents must secure and use search warrants wherever reasonably practicable."

ment, therefore, the requirement that "no Warrants shall issue, but upon probable cause," plays a crucial part. * * * Even in the *Agnello* case the Court relied upon the rule that "[b]elief, however well founded, that an article sought is concealed in a dwelling house furnishes no justification for a search of that place without a warrant. And such searches are held unlawful notwithstanding facts unquestionably showing probable cause." Clearly, the general requirement that a search warrant be obtained is not lightly to be dispensed with, and "the burden is on those seeking [an] exemption [from the requirement] to show the need for it * * *."

* * * When an arrest is made, it is reasonable for the arresting officer to search the person arrested in order to remove any weapons that the latter might seek to use in order to resist arrest or effect his escape. Otherwise, the officer's safety might well be endangered, and the arrest itself frustrated. In addition, it is entirely reasonable for the arresting officer to search for and seize any evidence on the arrestee's person in order to prevent its concealment or destruction. And the area into which an arrestee might reach in order to grab a weapon or evidentiary items must, of course, be governed by a like rule. A gun on a table or in a drawer in front of one who is arrested can be as dangerous to the arresting officer as one concealed in the clothing of the person arrested. There is ample justification, therefore, for a search of the arrestee's person and the area "within his immediate control"—construing that phrase to mean the area from within which he might gain possession of a weapon or destructible evidence.

There is no comparable justification, however, for routinely searching rooms other than that in which an arrest occurs—or, for that matter, for searching through all the desk drawers or other closed or concealed areas in that room itself. Such searches, in the absence of well-recognized exceptions, may be made only under the authority of a search warrant. The "adherence to judicial processes" mandated by the Fourth Amendment requires no less. * * *

It is argued in the present case that it is "reasonable" to search a man's house when he is arrested in it. But that argument is founded on little more than a subjective view regarding the acceptability of certain sorts of police conduct, and not on considerations relevant to Fourth Amendment interests. Under such an unconfined analysis, Fourth Amendment protection in this area would approach the evaporation point. It is not easy to explain why, for instance, it is less subjectively "reasonable" to search a man's house when he is arrested on his front lawn—or just down the street—than it is when he happens to be in the house at the time of arrest. * * *

It would be possible, of course, to draw a line between *Rabinowitz* and *Harris* on the one hand, and this case on the other. For *Rabinowitz* involved a single room, and *Harris* a four-room apartment, while in the case before us an entire house was searched. But such a distinction would be highly artificial. The rationale that allowed the searches and seizures in *Rabinowitz* and *Harris* would allow the searches and seizures in this case. No consideration relevant to the Fourth Amendment suggests any point of rational limitation, once the search is allowed to go beyond the area from which the person arrested might obtain weapons or evidentiary items. The only reasoned distinction is one between a search of the person arrested and the area within his reach on the one hand, and more extensive searches on the other.[12]

12. It is argued in dissent that so long as there is probable cause to search the place where an arrest occurs, a search of that place would be permitted even though no search warrant has been obtained. This position seems to be based principally on two premises: first, that once an arrest has been made, the additional invasion of privacy stemming from the accompanying search is "relatively minor"; and second, that the victim of the search may

The petitioner correctly points out that one result of decisions such as *Rabinowitz* and *Harris* is to give law enforcement officials the opportunity to engage in searches not justified by probable cause, by the simple expedient of arranging to arrest suspects at home rather than elsewhere. We do not suggest that the petitioner is necessarily correct in his assertion that such a strategy was utilized here, but the fact remains that had he been arrested earlier in the day, at his place of employment rather than at home, no search of his house could have been made without a search warrant. * * *

Rabinowitz and *Harris* have been the subject of critical commentary for many years, and have been relied upon less and less in our own decisions. It is time, for the reasons we have stated, to hold that on their own facts, and insofar as the principles they stand for are inconsistent with those that we have endorsed today, they are no longer to be followed.

Application of sound Fourth Amendment principles to the facts of this case produces a clear result. The search here went far beyond the petitioner's person and the area from within which he might have obtained either a weapon or something that could have been used as evidence against him. There was no constitutional justification, in the absence of a search warrant, for extending the search beyond that area. The scope of the search was, therefore, "unreasonable" under the Fourth and Fourteenth Amendments, and the petitioner's conviction cannot stand.

Reversed.

Justice HARLAN, concurring. * * *

The only thing that has given me pause in voting to overrule *Harris* and *Rabinowitz* is that as a result of *Mapp v. Ohio,* every change in Fourth Amendment law must now be obeyed by state officials facing widely different problems of local law enforcement. We simply do not know the extent to which cities and towns across the Nation are prepared to administer the greatly expanded warrant system which will be required by today's decision; nor can we say with assurance that in each and every local situation, the warrant requirement plays an essential role in the protection of those fundamental liberties protected against state infringement by the Fourteenth Amendment. * * *

Justice WHITE, with whom Justice BLACK joins, dissenting.

* * * The Court has always held, and does not today deny, that when there is probable cause to search and it is "impracticable" for one reason or another to get a search warrant, then a warrantless search may be reasonable. This is the case whether an arrest was made at the time of the search or not. * * *

This case provides a good illustration of my point that it is unreasonable to require police to leave the scene of an arrest in order to obtain a search warrant when they already have probable cause to search and there is a clear danger that the items for which they may reasonably search will be removed before they

"shortly thereafter" obtain a judicial determination of whether the search was justified by probable cause. With respect to the second premise, one may initially question whether all of the States in fact provide the speedy suppression procedures the dissent assumes. More fundamentally, however, we cannot accept the view that Fourth Amendment interests are vindicated so long as "the rights of the criminal" are "protect[ed] * * * against introduction of evidence seized without probable cause." The Amendment is designed to prevent, not simply to redress, unlawful police action. In any event, we cannot join in characterizing the invasion of privacy that results from a top-to-bottom search of a man's house as "minor." And we can see no reason why, simply because some interference with an individual's privacy and freedom of movement has lawfully taken place, further intrusions should automatically be allowed despite the absence of a warrant that the Fourth Amendment would otherwise require.

return with a warrant. Petitioner was arrested in his home after an arrest whose validity will be explored below, but which I will now assume was valid. There was doubtless probable cause not only to arrest petitioner, but to search his house. He had obliquely admitted both to a neighbor, and to the owner of the burglarized store, that he had committed the burglary. In light of this, and the fact that the neighbor had seen other admittedly stolen property in petitioner's house, there was surely probable cause on which a warrant could have issued to search the house for the stolen coins. Moreover, had the police simply arrested petitioner, taken him off to the station house, and later returned with a warrant,[5] it seems very likely that petitioner's wife, who in view of petitioner's generally garrulous nature must have known of the robbery, would have removed the coins. For the police to search the house while the evidence they had probable cause to search out and seize was still there cannot be considered unreasonable.

This line of analysis, supported by the precedents of this Court, hinges on two assumptions. One is that the arrest of petitioner without a valid warrant[7] was constitutional as the majority assumes;[b] the other is that the police were not required to obtain a search warrant in advance, even though they knew that the effect of the arrest might well be to alert petitioner's wife that the coins had better be removed soon.

* * * It must very often be the case that by the time probable cause to arrest a man is accumulated, the man is aware of police interest in him or for other good reasons is on the verge of flight. Moreover, it will likely be very difficult to determine the probability of his flight. Given this situation, it may be best in all cases simply to allow the arrest if there is probable cause, especially since that issue can be determined very shortly after the arrest. * * *

If circumstances so often require the warrantless arrest that the law generally permits it, the typical situation will find the arresting officers lawfully on the premises without arrest or search warrant. * * * [W]here as here the existence of probable cause is independently established and would justify a warrant for a broader search for evidence, I would follow past cases and permit such a search to be carried out without a warrant, since the fact of arrest supplies an exigent circumstance justifying police action before the evidence can be removed, and also alerts the suspect to the fact of the search so that he can immediately seek judicial determination of probable cause in an adversary proceeding, and appropriate redress. * * *

NOTES ON SEARCH OF PREMISES INCIDENT TO AND AFTER ARREST THEREIN

1. Is the *Chimel* dissent strengthened or weakened by the Court's later decision in *Watson*, p. 318?

2. Some of the cases which have applied the *Chimel* "immediate control" test seem to assume that defendants maintain control over a considerable area

5. There were three officers at the scene of the arrest, one from the city where the coin burglary had occurred, and two from the city where the arrest was made. Assuming that one policeman from each city would be needed to bring the petitioner in and obtain a search warrant, one policeman could have been left to guard the house. However, if he not only could have remained in the house against petitioner's wife's will, but followed her about to assure that no evidence was being tampered with, the invasion of her privacy would be almost as great as that accompanying an actual search. Moreover, had the wife summoned an accomplice, one officer could not have watched them both.

7. An arrest warrant was in fact issued, but it was issued on an inadequate supporting affidavit and was therefore invalid, so that the case must be considered as though no warrant had issued.

b. But see the later decision in *Payton v. New York*, p. 364.

even after they have been arrested. See, e.g., *People v. Perry,* 266 N.E.2d 330 (Ill.1971) (4 officers broke into a 10 by 12 foot motel room, saw defendant place something in a dresser drawer, handcuffed him, and took him out into the corridor; their immediately subsequent search of the partially open dresser drawer and a purse on the bed was within *Chimel* rule, "since it was within the area from which defendant could have obtained a weapon or something that could have been used as evidence against him"). Are such cases best explained on the ground that *Chimel* should be construed so as to give the police a "bright line" rule (cf. *New York v. Belton,* p. 389), one which, as concluded in *People v. Hufnagel,* 745 P.2d 242 (Colo.1987), makes it irrelevant whether "the arrestee was physically able to reach the exact place searched at the exact second it was searched"?

3. *Chimel* also requires attention to the question of when, if ever, officers may look into other areas of the defendant's home *after* the defendant has been placed under arrest there. Consider:

(a) *When it is necessary for the arrestee to put on street clothes.* See, e.g., *Giacalone v. Lucas,* 445 F.2d 1238 (6th Cir.1971) (defendant arrested at front door went into bedroom to change into street clothes; held, police could look into dresser drawer defendant was about to open, and gun found therein admissible; dissent argues defendant initially told police he was ready to go immediately, thereby expressing "his desire to limit the officers' intrusion into the privacy of his home," and that he went to get dressed upon order of the police).

(b) *When the officers are acting for their own protection.* The question of when a "protective sweep" is permissible reached the Court in MARYLAND v. BUIE, 494 U.S. 325 (1990), where the state court had required full probable cause of a dangerous situation. By analogy to *Terry v. Ohio,* p. 401, and *Michigan v. Long,* p. 435, the Court opted for a less demanding reasonable suspicion test. The state had argued for a "bright-line rule" to the effect that "police should be permitted to conduct a protective sweep whenever they make an in-home arrest for a violent crime"; the Court responded that *Terry* requires individualized suspicion, but then adopted a two-part sweep rule which included another kind of bright line. Specifically, the Court (7–2), per WHITE, J., concluded:

"We agree with the State, as did the court below, that a warrant was not required. We also hold that as an incident to the arrest the officers could, as a precautionary matter and without probable cause or reasonable suspicion, look in closets and other spaces immediately adjoining the place of arrest from which an attack could be immediately launched. Beyond that, however, we hold that there must be articulable facts which, taken together with the rational inferences from those facts, would warrant a reasonable prudent officer in believing that the area to be swept harbors an individual posing a danger to those on the arrest scene. * * *

"We should emphasize that such a protective sweep, aimed at protecting the arresting officers, if justified by the circumstances, is nevertheless not a full search of the premises, but may extend only to a cursory inspection of those spaces where a person may be found. The sweep lasts no longer than is necessary to dispel the reasonable suspicion of danger and in any event no longer than it takes to complete the arrest and depart the premises."

The Court remanded for application of this test. The facts, as stated in the Supreme Court opinions, are these: Two men (one wearing a red running suit) committed an armed robbery of a restaurant on Feb. 3; warrants for them (Buie and Allen) were issued that day, and Buie's home was immediately placed under surveillance. On Feb. 5, after a police department secretary called the residence and verified that Buie was there, 6 or 7 officers proceeded to the house and fanned out through the first and second floors. Officer Rozar said he would "freeze" the basement so that no one could come up; he drew his weapon and twice shouted into the basement for anyone there to come out, and Buie then emerged from the basement. He was arrested, searched and handcuffed by Rozar. Once Buie was outside the house, Officer Frolich entered the basement, noticed a red running suit in plain view and seized it. Rozar testified he was not worried about any possible danger when he arrested Buie; Frolich said he entered the basement "in case there was someone else" down there, though he "had no idea who lived there." What should the result be on remand?

(c) *When the officers are seeking other offenders.* See, e.g., *People v. Block,* 499 P.2d 961 (Cal.1971) (officers knocked on door to check out tip concerning narcotics suspect, when door was opened they detected smell of burning marijuana, five persons in living room and two in dining room with odor of marijuana on their breath were arrested, after which one of the officers went upstairs and looked into bedrooms, where he found marijuana; held, in view of "undetermined number of participants" and fact upstairs light was on, officers had "reasonable cause to believe" other participants might be present; dissent objects there was not probable cause here and distinguishes *Guevara v. Superior Court,* 86 Cal.Rptr. 657 (App.1970), where informant had told police confederates were probably present). If a "potential accomplice" is located, should the police then be allowed to search areas within *his* immediate control?

4. In some circumstances, the Court concluded in WASHINGTON v. CHRISMAN, 455 U.S. 1 (1982), a warrantless *entry* of premises will be permissible incident to and following an arrest elsewhere. There, a campus policeman arrested an apparently underage student as he left a campus dormitory carrying a half-gallon bottle of gin, accompanied the student back to his room so that he could obtain his identification, and there observed marijuana seeds and a marijuana pipe. The state court had held that the entry was unlawful, but the Supreme Court, per BURGER, C.J., disagreed:

"Every arrest must be presumed to present a risk of danger to the arresting officer. Cf. *United States v. Robinson,* [p. 329], n. 5. There is no way for an officer to predict reliably how a particular subject will react to arrest or the degree of the potential danger. Moreover, the possibility that an arrested person will attempt to escape if not properly supervised is obvious. Although the Supreme Court of Washington found little likelihood that Overdahl could escape from his dormitory room, an arresting officer's custodial authority over an arrested person does not depend upon a reviewing court's after-the-fact assessment of the particular arrest situation. Cf. *New York v. Belton* [p. 389].

"We hold, therefore, that it is not 'unreasonable' under the Fourth Amendment for a police officer, as a matter of routine, to monitor the movements of an arrested person, as his judgment dictates, following the arrest."[c]

NOTES ON WARRANTLESS SEIZURES WHILE IN PREMISES TO ARREST

1. If an officer is lawfully present within premises to make an arrest, he may observe certain items not within the "immediate control" of the arrestee which will nonetheless be subject to warrantless seizure under the so-called "plain view" doctrine. But, as cautioned in *Coolidge v. New Hampshire,* 403 U.S. 443 (1971), such "extension of the original justification is legitimate only where it is immedi-

c. White, Brennan and Marshall, JJ., dissenting, could "perceive no justification for what is in effect a per se rule that an officer in Daugherty's circumstances could always enter the room and stay at the arrestee's elbow."

ately apparent[a] to the police that they have evidence before them; the 'plain view' doctrine may not be used to extend a general exploratory search from one object to another until something incriminating at last emerges."

2. In ARIZONA v. HICKS, 480 U.S. 321 (1987), police lawfully entered premises from which a weapon was fired, and within one officer "noticed two sets of expensive stereo components, which seemed out of place in the squalid and otherwise ill-appointed four-room apartment. Suspecting that they were stolen, he read and recorded their serial numbers—moving some of the components, including a Bang and Olufsen turntable, in order to do so—which he then reported by phone to his headquarters. On being advised that the turntable had been taken in an armed robbery, he seized it immediately. It was later determined that some of the other serial numbers matched those on other stereo equipment taken in the same armed robbery, and a warrant was obtained and executed to seize that equipment as well." SCALIA, J., for a 6–3 majority, concluded the moving of the equipment was an unreasonable search, while the dissenters relied on the fact that "the overwhelming majority of both state and federal courts have held that probable cause is not required for a minimal inspection of an item in plain view." The majority responded:

"Justice O'Connor's dissent suggests that we uphold the action here on the ground that it was a cursory inspection rather than a full-blown search, and could therefore be justified by reasonable suspicion instead of probable cause. As already noted, a truly cursory inspection—one that involves merely looking at what is already exposed to view, without disturbing it—is not a 'search' for Fourth Amendment purposes, and therefore does not even require reasonable suspicion. We are unwilling to send police and judges into a new thicket of Fourth Amendment law, to seek a creature of uncertain description that is neither a plain-view inspection nor yet a full-blown search. Nothing in the prior opinions of this Court supports such a distinction * * *.

"Justice Powell's dissent reasonably asks what it is we would have had Officer Nelson do in these circumstances. The answer depends, of course, upon whether he had probable cause to conduct a search, a question that was not preserved in this case. If he had, then he should have done precisely what he did. If not, then he should have followed up his suspicions, if possible, by means other than a search—just as he would have had to do if, while walking along the street, he had noticed the same suspicious stereo equipment sitting inside a house a few feet away from him, beneath an open window. It may well be that, in such circumstances, no effective means short of a search exist. But there is nothing new in the realization that the Constitution sometimes insulates the criminality of a few in order to protect the privacy of us all. Our disagreement with the dissenters pertains to where the proper balance should be struck; we choose to adhere to the textual and traditional standard of probable cause."

NOTES ON WARRANTLESS SEARCH OF PREMISES UNDER EXIGENT CIRCUMSTANCES

1. In VALE v. LOUISIANA, 399 U.S. 30 (1970), officers possessing two warrants for Vale's arrest and having information that he was residing at a specified address set up a surveillance of the house in an unmarked car. After about 15 minutes they observed a car drive up and sound the horn twice. A man

a. In *Texas v. Brown,* p. 387, the plurality opinion asserted that this phrase "was very likely an unhappy choice of words, since it can be taken to imply that an unduly high degree of certainty as to the incriminating character of evidence is necessary for an application of the 'plain view' doctrine," and then concluded it was intended to be merely a "statement of the rule * * * requiring probable cause for seizure in the ordinary case."

they recognized as Vale then came out of the house and walked up to the car, had a brief conversation with the driver, looked up and down the street and then returned to the house. A few minutes later he reappeared on the porch, looked cautiously up and down the street, and then proceeded to the car and leaned through the window. Convinced that a narcotics sale had just occurred, the officers approached. Vale retreated toward the house while the driver of the car began driving off. The police blocked the car and saw the driver, one Saucier, place something in his mouth. Vale was then arrested on his front steps and the police advised him they were going to search the house. An officer made a cursory inspection of the house to ascertain if anyone else was present, after which Vale's mother and brother entered the house and were told of the arrest and impending search. A quantity of narcotics were found in a rear bedroom. The Court, per STEWART, J., concluded (without deciding whether *Chimel* should be accorded retroactive effect[a]) that "no precedent of this Court can sustain the constitutional validity of the search in the case before us":

"A search may be incident to an arrest 'only if it is substantially contemporaneous with the arrest and is confined to the *immediate* vicinity of the arrest.' If a search of a house is to be upheld as incident to an arrest, that arrest must take place *inside* the house, not somewhere outside—whether two blocks away, twenty feet away, or on the sidewalk near the front steps. 'Belief, however well founded, that an article sought is concealed in a dwelling house furnishes no justification for a search of that place without a warrant.' That basic rule 'has never been questioned in this Court.'

"The Louisiana Supreme Court thought the search independently supportable because it involved narcotics, which are easily removed, hidden, or destroyed. It would be unreasonable, the Louisiana court concluded, 'to require the officers under the facts of the case to first secure a search warrant before searching the premises, as time is of the essence inasmuch as the officers never know whether there is anyone on the premises to be searched who could very easily destroy the evidence.' Such a rationale could not apply to the present case, since by their own account the arresting officers satisfied themselves that no one else was in the house when they first entered the premises. But entirely apart from that point, our past decisions make clear that only in 'a few specifically established and well-delineated' situations, may a warrantless search of a dwelling withstand constitutional scrutiny, even though the authorities have probable cause to conduct it. The burden rests on the State to show the existence of such an exceptional situation. And the record before us discloses none. * * *

"The officers were able to procure two warrants for the appellant's arrest. They also had information that he was residing at the address where they found him. There is thus no reason, so far as anything before us appears, to suppose that it was impracticable for them to obtain a search warrant as well. We decline to hold that an arrest on the street can provide its own 'exigent circumstance' so as to justify a warrantless search of the arrestee's house."

Justice BLACK, joined by The Chief Justice, dissented:

"[When Vale and Saucier were arrested,] the police had probable cause to believe that Vale was engaged in a narcotics transfer, and that a supply of narcotics would be found in the house, to which Vale had returned after his first conversation, from which he had emerged furtively bearing what the police could readily deduce was a supply of narcotics, and toward which he hurried after seeing the police. But the police did not know then who else might be in the house. Vale's

a. *Chimel* was later held not to be retroactive in *Williams v. United States,* 401 U.S. 646 (1971).

arrest took place near the house, and anyone observing from inside would surely have been alerted to destroy the stocks of contraband which the police believed Vale had left there. The police had already seen Saucier, the narcotics addict, apparently swallow what Vale had given him. Believing that some evidence had already been destroyed and that other evidence might well be, the police were faced with the choice of risking the immediate destruction of evidence or entering the house and conducting a search. I cannot say that their decision to search was unreasonable. Delay in order to obtain a warrant would have given an accomplice just the time he needed.

"That the arresting officers did, in fact, believe that others might be in the house is attested to by their actions upon entering the door left open by Vale. The police at once checked the small house to determine if anyone else was present. Just as they discovered the house was empty, however, Vale's mother and brother arrived. Now what had been a suspicion became a certainty: Vale's relatives were in possession and knew of his arrest. To have abandoned the search at this point, and left the house with Vale, would not have been the action of reasonable police officers. * * *

"Moreover, the circumstances here were sufficiently exceptional to justify a search, even if the search was not strictly 'incidental' to an arrest. The Court recognizes that searches to prevent the destruction or removal of evidence have long been held reasonable by this Court. Whether the 'exceptional circumstances' justifying such a search exist or not is a question which may be, as it is here, quite distinct from whether or not the search was incident to a valid arrest. It is thus unnecessary to determine whether the search was valid as incident to the arrest * * *.

"[T]he Court seems to argue that the search was unreasonable because the police officers had time to obtain a warrant. I agree that the opportunity to obtain a warrant is one of the factors to be weighed in determining reasonableness. But the record conclusively shows that there was no such opportunity here. As I noted above, once the officers had observed Vale's conduct in front of the house they had probable cause to believe that a felony had been committed and that immediate action was necessary. At no time after the events in front of Mrs. Vale's house would it have been prudent for the officers to leave the house in order to secure a warrant.

"The Court asserts, however, that because the police obtained two warrants for Vale's arrest there is 'no reason * * * to suppose that it was impracticable for them to obtain a search warrant as well.' The difficulty is that the two arrest warrants on which the Court seems to rely so heavily were not issued because of any present misconduct of Vale's; they were issued because the bond had been increased for an earlier narcotics charge then pending against Vale. When the police came to arrest Vale, they knew only that his bond had been increased. There is nothing in the record to indicate that, absent the increased bond, there would have been probable cause for an arrest, much less a search. Probable cause for the search arose for the first time when the police observed the activity of Vale and Saucier in and around the house."

2. What *should* the officers have done in *Vale?* Consider *United States v. Grummel,* 542 F.2d 789 (9th Cir.1976) (defendant picked up package known to contain heroin at post office; 10 minutes after taking the package into his home he was arrested there; because his mother was home, agent gave her the option of leaving the premises or remaining inside with him while another agent left to get a search warrant; held, it was proper on these facts to "secure the premises to the extent necessary to prevent destruction of the evidence until a warrant could be obtained"). Consider, in assessing the reasonableness of this alternative, the possibility of obtaining a warrant very promptly via telephone, as authorized in some jurisdictions (see, e.g., Fed.R.Crim.P. 41(d)(3), (e)(3)).

In SEGURA v. UNITED STATES, 468 U.S. 796 (1984), the police, upon confirming that they had in fact observed a drug sale by Colon and Segura, went to their apartment building. Segura was arrested in the lobby, and when Colon answered a knock on the door she was also arrested. Police made a warrantless entry of the apartment and remained there until a search warrant was issued, which occurred some 19 hours later because of "administrative delay." The Court held "that where officers, having probable cause, enter premises, and with probable cause, arrest the occupants who have legitimate possessory interests in its contents and take them into custody and, for no more than the period here involved, secure the premises from within to preserve the status quo while others, in good faith, are in the process of obtaining a warrant, they do not violate the Fourth Amendment's proscription against unreasonable seizures." The Court also held that the evidence first discovered in execution of the warrant was not a fruit of the illegal entry. (See p. 913.) The first holding was explicated in a portion of an opinion by BURGER, C.J., in which only O'Connor, J., joined. Without deciding whether the petitioners were correct in characterizing the police action as a seizure of the entire contents of the apartment, they concluded any such seizure was not unreasonable. Noting that in other contexts the Court had approved warrantless seizures in circumstances where a warrantless search could not have been held (see the *Chadwick* and *Sanders* cases, discussed in *California v. Acevedo,* p. 377), they could see "no reason * * * why the same principle should not apply when a dwelling is involved." These two Justices continued:

"In this case, the agents entered and secured the apartment from within. Arguably, the wiser course would have been to depart immediately and secure the premises from the outside by a 'stakeout' once the security check revealed that no one other than those taken into custody were in the apartment. But the method actually employed does not require a different result under the Fourth Amendment, insofar as the *seizure* is concerned. As the Court of Appeals held, absent exigent circumstances, the entry may have constituted an illegal *search,* or interference with petitioners' privacy interests, requiring suppression of all evidence observed during the entry. Securing of the premises from within, however, was no more an interference with the petitioners' possessory interests in the contents of the apartment than a perimeter 'stakeout.' In other words, the initial entry—legal or not—does not affect the reasonableness of the seizure. Under either method—entry and securing from within or a perimeter stakeout—agents control the apartment pending arrival of the warrant; both an internal securing and a perimeter stakeout interfere to the same extent with the possessory interests of the owners. * * *

"Of course, a seizure reasonable at its inception because based upon probable cause may become unreasonable as a result of its duration or for other reasons. Here, because of the delay in securing the warrant, the occupation of the apartment continued throughout the night and into the next day. Such delay in securing a warrant in a large metropolitan center unfortunately is not uncommon; this is not, in itself, evidence of bad faith. And there is no suggestion that the officers, in bad faith, purposely delayed obtaining the warrant. The asserted explanation is that the officers focused first on the task of processing those whom they had arrested before turning to the task of securing the warrant. It is not unreasonable for officers to believe that the former should take priority, given, as was the case here, that the proprietors of the apartment were in the custody of the officers throughout the period in question.

"There is no evidence that the agents in any way exploited their presence in the apartment; they simply awaited issuance of the warrant. Moreover, more than half of the 19–hour delay was between 10 p.m. and 10 a.m. the following day, when it is reasonable to assume that judicial officers are not as readily available for consideration of warrant requests. Finally, and most important, we observed in *United States v. Place,* [p. 263], that '[t]he intrusion on possessory interests occasioned by a seizure * * * can vary both in its nature and extent. The seizure may be made after the owner has relinquished control of the property to a third party or * * * from the immediate custody and control of the owner.' Here, of course, Segura and Colon, whose possessory interests were interfered with by the occupation, were under arrest and in the custody of the police throughout the entire period the agents occupied the apartment. The actual interference with their possessory interests in the apartment and its contents was, thus, virtually nonexistent. We are not prepared to say under these limited circumstances that the seizure was unreasonable under the Fourth Amendment."

The four dissenters, per STEVENS, J., argued that the occupation was an unreasonable search, infringing upon a reasonable expectation of privacy, and an unreasonable seizure, involving exercise of "complete dominion and control over the apartment and its contents"; that the Fourth Amendment protects possessory interests in a residence even when the occupants are in custody; and that "what is even more strange about the Chief Justice's conclusion is that it permits the authorities to benefit from the fact that they had unlawfully arrested" an occupant of the apartment.[b]

In ILLINOIS v. McARTHUR, 531 U.S. 326 (2001), two police officers stood by outside to keep the peace while defendant's wife removed her effects from the family residence, a trailer. Upon exiting, she told the officers her husband had hidden marijuana under the couch, so the officers sought his permission to search the premises. When he refused, one officer left to obtain a search warrant, while another officer remained on the porch with defendant, who was told he could not reenter unless he was accompanied by the officer. A warrant was obtained and executed two hours later, but in the interim defendant entered the trailer two or three times, and on each occasion the officer stood just inside the door and observe his actions. The Court, per BREYER, J., held:

"We conclude that the restriction at issue was reasonable, and hence lawful, in light of the following circumstances, which we consider in combination. First, the police had probable cause to believe that McArthur's trailer home contained evidence of a crime and contraband, namely, unlawful drugs. The police had had an opportunity to speak with Tera McArthur and make at least a very rough assessment of her reliability. They knew she had had a firsthand opportunity to observe her husband's behavior, in particular with respect to the drugs at issue. And they thought, with good reason, that her report to them reflected that opportunity.

"Second, the police had good reason to fear that, unless restrained, McArthur would destroy the drugs before they could return with a warrant. They reasonably might have thought that McArthur realized that his wife knew about his marijuana stash; observed that she was angry or frightened enough to ask the police to accompany her; saw that after leaving the trailer she had spoken with the police; and noticed that she had walked off with one policeman while leaving the other outside to observe the trailer. They reasonably could have concluded that McArthur, consequently suspecting an imminent search, would, if given the chance, get rid of the drugs fast.

b. For criticism of *Segura,* see Joshua Dressler, *A Lesson in Caution, Overwork, and Fatigue: The Judicial Miscraftsmanship of Segura v. United States,* 26 Wm. & Mary L.Rev. 375 (1985).

"Third, the police made reasonable efforts to reconcile their law enforcement needs with the demands of personal privacy. They neither searched the trailer nor arrested McArthur before obtaining a warrant. Rather, they imposed a significantly less restrictive restraint, preventing McArthur only from entering the trailer unaccompanied. They left his home and his belongings intact—until a neutral Magistrate, finding probable cause, issued a warrant.

"Fourth, the police imposed the restraint for a limited period of time, namely, two hours. As far as the record reveals, this time period was no longer than reasonably necessary for the police, acting with diligence, to obtain the warrant. Given the nature of the intrusion and the law enforcement interest at stake, this brief seizure of the premises was permissible.[c]

3. Although in *Vale* the Court noted in passing that "the goods ultimately seized were not in the process of destruction," many lower courts have not taken that language too seriously in light of the Court's assumption that not even a threat of destruction was present.[d] In *United States v. Rubin,* 474 F.2d 262 (3d Cir.1973), the court upheld a warrantless search[e] pursuant to this test:

"When Government agents, however, have probable cause to believe contraband is present and, in addition, based on the surrounding circumstances or the information at hand, they reasonably conclude that the evidence will be destroyed or removed before they can secure a search warrant, a warrantless search is justified. The emergency circumstances will vary from case to case, and the inherent necessities of the situation at the time must be scrutinized. Circumstances which have seemed relevant to courts include (1) the degree of urgency involved and the amount of time necessary to obtain a warrant * * *; (2) reasonable belief that the contraband is about to be removed * * *; (3) the possibility of danger to police officers guarding the site of the contraband while a search warrant is sought * * *; (4) information indicating the possessors of the contraband are aware that the police are on their trail * * *; and (5) the ready destructibility of the contraband and the knowledge 'that efforts to dispose of

c. Justice Souter, concurring, reasoned that had defendant remained inside the trailer then the "probability of destruction" of the marijuana "in anticipation of a warrant * * * would have justified the police in entering McArthur's trailer promptly to make a lawful, warrantless search," that this risk "abated and so did the reasonableness of entry by the police" once he came outside, but that once he came outside it was reasonable for the police to keep him from reentering not because "the law officiously insists on safeguarding a suspect's privacy from search," but rather because of "the law's strong preference for warrants, which underlies the rule that a search with a warrant has a stronger claim to justification on later, judicial review than a search without one. * * * The law can hardly raise incentives to obtain a warrant without giving the police a fair chance to take their probable cause to a magistrate and get one."

As for defendant's reliance upon *Welsh v. Wisconsin*, p. 369, the *McArthur* majority distinguished *Welsh* because (a) the offense involved here was punishable by up to 30 days in jail, and (b) "the restriction at issue here is less serious." Justice Stevens dissented as to the applicability of the *Welsh* doctrine.

d. See Barbara Salken, *Balancing Exigency and Privacy in Warrantless Searches to Prevent Destruction of Evidence,* 39 Hastings L.J. 283 (1988).

e. The facts in *Rubin* were as follows: Customs agents received reliable information that a bronze statute containing a large shipment of illicit drugs would be shipped to a hospital in a certain area. Agents were posted at the airport and waterfront, and finally a crate answering the general description given by the informant arrived at the airport from abroad. It was inspected and found to contain narcotics. Agents observed one Agnes pick up the crate and take it to a certain address, where it was unloaded at about 5 p.m. After one agent was dispatched to secure a search warrant, Agnes left the premises in his car but without the crate. He was tailed for a short distance, but when his evasive actions led agents to believe he was aware of the tail, they arrested him. When he was placed under arrest about six blocks from the house in question, he yelled to spectators to call his brother. At this point the agents, fearing disposal of the narcotics if they waited for the search warrant, entered the house and searched for and seized the narcotics.

narcotics and to escape are characteristic behavior of persons engaged in the narcotics traffic.' "

4. Assuming no such exigent circumstances, is it permissible for police to engage in a subterfuge which causes an occupant to remove the evidence to another place where warrantless search is permissible? See *State v. Hendrix,* 782 S.W.2d 833 (Tenn.1989) (proper for police to telephone residence with anonymous false "tip" that police were on their way there with search warrant, causing defendant to leave with drugs in car, which was then stopped and searched). What if the telephoning police had falsely reported a gas leak and likely explosion?

5. Although several courts had held that when the police are summoned to the scene of a homicide they may remain on those premises without a warrant (and, perhaps, return after a brief absence) to conduct a general investigation into the cause of the death, in *Mincey v. Arizona,* 437 U.S. 385 (1978), the Court, confronted with a rather broad variation of the so-called homicide scene exception to the warrant requirement (the criminal nature and perpetrator of the homicide were known from the outset, no occupant of the premises had summoned the police, and the searches upheld by the lower court continued for four days), "decline[d] to hold that the seriousness of the offense under investigation itself creates exigent circumstances of the kind that under the Fourth Amendment justify a warrantless search." *Mincey* was later applied in *Thompson v. Louisiana,* 469 U.S. 17 (1984), to invalidate a two-hour general search of premises to which police were summoned because of defendant's attempt to get medical assistance after shooting her husband. The Court noted the authorities, "while they were in petitioner's house to offer her assistance," could have seized evidence in plain view and could also have made a limited search for a suspect or for other victims.

In *Flippo v. West Virginia*, 528 U.S. 11 (1999), after defendant's 911 call that he and his wife had been attacked at a cabin in a state park, police arrived at the scene and found defendant outside wounded and his wife inside dead. The contents of a briefcase near the body, found upon a warrantless police reentry and search several hours later, were held admissible by the trial judge because found "within the crime scene area," a position the Court unanimously concluded "squarely conflicts with *Mincey*." As for the state's contention "that the trial court's ruling is supportable on the theory that petitioner's direction of the police to the scene of the attack implied consent to search as they did," the Court expressed no opinion because this "factual" issue had not been raised below.

6. When evidence of crime is fortuitously discovered by the police without a warrant while they are performing other functions, courts find it necessary to assess the reasonableness of the police conduct under the Fourth Amendment. Compare *Geimer v. State*, 591 N.E.2d 1016 (Ind.1992) (evidence admissible, as entry was on "a reasonable belief that a person within the premises is in need of aid" where one of missing person's sons said "it was unlike his father to leave town for a period of time without notifying anyone" and other son, who lived with father, "told various persons differing stories regarding the victim's sudden absence"); with *State v. Geisler*, 610 A.2d 1225 (Conn.1992) (evidence suppressed, as where car at accident scene suffered minor damage, key left in ignition, car door left open, and no response when officer rang bell and knocked at home of car owner, such "facts could not reasonably lead to the conclusion that the driver might have suffered the type of injury that would require emergency aid").

PAYTON v. NEW YORK

445 U.S. 573, 100 S.Ct. 1371, 63 L.Ed.2d 639 (1980).

Justice STEVENS delivered the opinion of the Court. * * *

On January 14, 1970, after two days of intensive investigation, New York detectives had assembled evidence sufficient to establish probable cause to believe that Theodore Payton had murdered the manager of a gas station two days earlier. At about 7:30 a.m. on January 15, six officers went to Payton's apartment in the Bronx, intending to arrest him. They had not obtained a warrant. Although light and music emanated from the apartment, there was no response to their knock on the metal door. They summoned emergency assistance and, about 30 minutes later, used crowbars to break open the door and enter the apartment. No one was there. In plain view, however, was a 30–caliber shell casing that was seized and later admitted into evidence at Payton's murder trial. * * *

On March 14, 1974, Obie Riddick was arrested for the commission of two armed robberies that had occurred in 1971. He had been identified by the victims in June of 1973 and in January 1974 the police had learned his address. They did not obtain a warrant for his arrest. At about noon on March 14, a detective, accompanied by three other officers, knocked on the door of the Queens house where Riddick was living. When his young son opened the door, they could see Riddick sitting in bed covered by a sheet. They entered the house and placed him under arrest. Before permitting him to dress, they opened a chest of drawers two feet from the bed in search of weapons and found narcotics and related paraphernalia. Riddick was subsequently indicted on narcotics charges. * * *

The New York Court of Appeals, in a single opinion, affirmed the convictions of both Payton and Riddick. * * *[a]

It is a "basic principle of Fourth Amendment law" that searches and seizures inside a home without a warrant are presumptively unreasonable. Yet it is also well-settled that objects such as weapons or contraband found in a public place may be seized by the police without a warrant. The seizure of property in plain view involves no invasion of privacy and is presumptively reasonable, assuming that there is probable cause to associate the property with criminal activity. * * *

As the late Judge Leventhal recognized, this distinction has equal force when the seizure of a person is involved. Writing on the constitutional issue now before us for the United States Court of Appeals for the District of Columbia Circuit sitting en banc, *Dorman v. United States,* 435 F.2d 385 (D.C.Cir.1970), Judge Leventhal first noted the settled rule that warrantless arrests in public places are valid. He immediately recognized, however, that

> "[a] greater burden is placed [ ] on officials who enter a home or dwelling without consent. Freedom from intrusion into the home or dwelling is the archetype of the privacy protection secured by the Fourth Amendment."

His analysis of this question then focused on the long-settled premise that, absent exigent circumstances, a warrantless entry to search for weapons or contraband is unconstitutional even when a felony has been committed and there is probable cause to believe that incriminating evidence will be found within. He reasoned that the constitutional protection afforded to the individual's interest in the privacy of his own home is equally applicable to a warrantless entry for the purpose of arresting a resident of the house; for it is inherent in such an entry that a search for the suspect may be required before he can be apprehended. Judge Leventhal concluded that an entry to arrest and an entry to search for and

a. At this point, the Court "put to one side other related problems that are *not* presented today": whether there were exigent circumstances justifying a warrantless entry; whether police can "enter a third party's home to arrest a suspect"; whether "the police lacked probable cause to believe that the suspect was at home when they entered"; and whether the entry was consented to.

to seize property implicate the same interest in preserving the privacy and the sanctity of the home, and justify the same level of constitutional protection. * * * We find this reasoning to be persuasive and in accord with this Court's Fourth Amendment decisions.

The majority of the New York Court of Appeals, however, suggested that there is a substantial difference in the relative intrusiveness of an entry to search for property and an entry to search for a person. It is true that the area that may legally be searched is broader when executing a search warrant than when executing an arrest warrant in the home. See *Chimel v. California,* [p. 351]. This difference may be more theoretical than real, however, because the police may need to check the entire premises for safety reasons, and sometimes they ignore the restrictions on searches incident to arrest.

But the critical point is that any differences in the intrusiveness of entries to search and entries to arrest are merely ones of degree rather than kind. The two intrusions share this fundamental characteristic: the breach of the entrance to an individual's home. * * * In terms that apply equally to seizures of property and to seizures of persons, the Fourth Amendment has drawn a firm line at the entrance to the house. Absent exigent circumstances, that threshold may not reasonably be crossed without a warrant. * * *[b]

The parties have argued at some length about the practical consequences of a warrant requirement as a precondition to a felony arrest in the home. In the absence of any evidence that effective law enforcement has suffered in those States that already have such a requirement, we are inclined to view such arguments with skepticism. More fundamentally, however, such arguments of policy must give way to a constitutional command that we consider to be unequivocal.

Finally, we note the State's suggestion that only a search warrant based on probable cause to believe the suspect is at home at a given time can adequately protect the privacy interests at stake, and since such a warrant requirement is manifestly impractical, there need be no warrant of any kind. We find this ingenious argument unpersuasive. It is true that an arrest warrant requirement may afford less protection than a search warrant requirement, but it will suffice to interpose the magistrate's determination of probable cause between the zealous officer and the citizen. If there is sufficient evidence of a citizen's participation in a felony to persuade a judicial officer that his arrest is justified, it is constitutionally reasonable to require him to open his doors to the officers of the law. Thus, for Fourth Amendment purposes, an arrest warrant founded on probable cause

b. At this point, Stevens, J., observed that New York argued that "the reasons supporting the *Watson* [p. 318] holding require a similar result here. In *Watson* the Court relied on (a) the well-settled common-law rule that a warrantless arrest in a public place is valid if the arresting officer had probable cause to believe the suspect is a felon; (b) the clear consensus among the States adhering to that well-settled common-law rule; and (c) the expression of the judgment of Congress that such an arrest is 'reasonable.' We consider each of these reasons as it applies to a warrantless entry into a home for the purpose of making a routine felony arrest."

In an extended analysis, the *Payton* majority concluded (a) that "the relevant common law does not provide the same guidance that was present in *Watson,*" as there is "no direct authority supporting forcible entries into a home to make a routine arrest and the weight of the scholarly opinion is somewhat to the contrary"; (b) that presently 24 states permit such warrantless entries, 15 prohibit them, and 11 have taken no position, with "a significant decline during the last decade in the number of States permitting warrantless entries for arrest"; and (c) that "no congressional determination that warrantless entries into the home are 'reasonable' has been called to our attention." While the majority then concluded from this that "neither history nor this Nation's experience" lent support to the New York position, the *Payton* dissenters read essentially the same data as supporting their position.

implicitly carries with it the limited authority to enter a dwelling in which the suspect lives when there is reason to believe the suspect is within.

Because no arrest warrant was obtained in either of these cases, the judgments must be reversed * * *.

Justice BLACKMUN, concurring. * * *

Justice WHITE, with whom THE CHIEF JUSTICE and Justice REHNQUIST join, dissenting. * * *

Today's decision ignores the carefully crafted restrictions on the common-law power of arrest entry and thereby overestimates the dangers inherent in that practice. At common law, absent exigent circumstances, entries to arrest could be made only for felony. Even in cases of felony, the officers were required to announce their presence, demand admission, and be refused entry before they were entitled to break doors. Further, it seems generally accepted that entries could be made only during daylight hours. And, in my view, the officer entering to arrest must have reasonable grounds to believe, not only that the arrestee has committed a crime, but also that the person suspected is present in the house at the time of the entry.[13]

These four restrictions on home arrests—felony, knock and announce, daytime, and stringent probable cause—constitute powerful and complementary protections for the privacy interests associated with the home. * * * In short, these requirements, taken together, permit an individual suspected of a serious crime to surrender at the front door of his dwelling and thereby avoid most of the humiliation and indignity that the Court seems to believe necessarily accompany a house arrest entry. Such a front door arrest, in my view, is no more intrusive on personal privacy than the public warrantless arrests which we found to pass constitutional muster in *Watson*.[14]

All of these limitations on warrantless arrest entries are satisfied on the facts of the present cases. * * * Today's decision, therefore, sweeps away any possibility that warrantless home entries might be permitted in some limited situations other than those in which exigent circumstances are present. The Court substitutes, in one sweeping decision, a rigid constitutional rule in place of the common-law approach, evolved over hundreds of years, which achieved a flexible accommodation between the demands of personal privacy and the legitimate needs of law enforcement.

A rule permitting warrantless arrest entries would not pose a danger that officers would use their entry power as a pretext to justify an otherwise invalid warrantless search. A search pursuant to a warrantless arrest entry will rarely, if ever, be as complete as one under authority of a search warrant. If the suspect surrenders at the door, the officers may not enter other rooms. Of course, the suspect may flee or hide, or may not be at home, but the officers cannot anticipate the first two of these possibilities and the last is unlikely given the requirement of probable cause to believe that the suspect is at home. Even when officers are justified in searching other rooms, they may seize only items within the arrestee's

13. I do not necessarily disagree with the Court's discussion of the quantum of probable cause necessary to make a valid home arrest. The Court indicates that only an arrest warrant, and not a search warrant, is required. To obtain the warrant, therefore, the officers need only show probable cause that a crime has been committed and that the suspect committed it. However, under today's decision, the officers apparently need an extra increment of probable cause when executing the arrest warrant, namely grounds to believe that the suspect is within the dwelling.

14. If the suspect flees or hides, of course, the intrusiveness of the entry will be somewhat greater; but the policeman's hands should not be tied merely because of the possibility that the suspect will fail to cooperate with legitimate actions by law enforcement personnel.

position [sic] or immediate control or items in plain view discovered during the course of a search reasonably directed at discovering a hiding suspect. Hence a warrantless home entry is likely to uncover far less evidence than a search conducted under authority of a search warrant. Furthermore, an arrest entry will inevitably tip off the suspects and likely result in destruction or removal of evidence not uncovered during the arrest. I therefore cannot believe that the police would take the risk of losing valuable evidence through a pretextual arrest entry rather than applying to a magistrate for a search warrant.

While exaggerating the invasion of personal privacy involved in home arrests, the Court fails to account for the danger that its rule will "severely hamper effective law enforcement." The policeman on his beat must now make subtle discriminations that perplex even judges in their chambers. As Justice Powell noted, concurring in *United States v. Watson,* police will sometimes delay making an arrest, even after probable cause is established, in order to be sure that they have enough evidence to convict. Then, if they suddenly have to arrest, they run the risk that the subsequent exigency will not excuse their prior failure to obtain a warrant. This problem cannot effectively be cured by obtaining a warrant as soon as probable cause is established because of the chance that the warrant will go stale before the arrest is made.

Further, police officers will often face the difficult task of deciding whether the circumstances are sufficiently exigent to justify their entry to arrest without a warrant. This is a decision that must be made quickly in the most trying of circumstances. If the officers mistakenly decide that the circumstances are exigent, the arrest will be invalid and any evidence seized incident to the arrest or in plain view will be excluded at trial. On the other hand, if the officers mistakenly determine that exigent circumstances are lacking, they may refrain from making the arrest, thus creating the possibility that a dangerous criminal will escape into the community. The police could reduce the likelihood of escape by staking out all possible exits until the circumstances become clearly exigent or a warrant is obtained. But the costs of such a stakeout seem excessive in an era of rising crime and scarce police resources.

The uncertainty inherent in the exigent circumstances determination burdens the judicial system as well. In the case of searches, exigent circumstances are sufficiently unusual that this Court has determined that the benefits of a warrant outweigh the burdens imposed, including the burdens on the judicial system. In contrast, arrests recurringly involve exigent circumstances, and this Court has heretofore held that a warrant can be dispensed with without undue sacrifice in Fourth Amendment values. The situation should be no different with respect to arrests in the home. Under today's decision, whenever the police have made a warrantless home arrest there will be the possibility of "endless litigation with respect to the existence of exigent circumstances, whether it was practicable to get a warrant, whether the suspect was about to flee, and the like." * * *

Notes and Questions

1. The Supreme Court has approved of warrantless entries to arrest under some circumstances. In *Warden v. Hayden,* 387 U.S. 294 (1967), where police were reliably informed that an armed robbery had taken place and that the perpetrator had entered a certain house five minutes earlier, the Court concluded they "acted reasonably when they entered the house and began to search for a man of the description they had been given and for weapons which he had used in the robbery or might use against them.[15] The Fourth Amendment does not require

15. Thus, the Court held admissible clothing found in a washing machine, where an officer looked for weapons "prior to or immediately contemporaneous with Hayden's arrest."

police officers to delay in the course of an investigation if to do so would gravely endanger their lives or the lives of others." And in *United States v. Santana,* 427 U.S. 38 (1976), it was held that *United States v. Watson,* p. 318, permitted the police to attempt a warrantless arrest of the defendant when she was found "standing directly in the doorway—one step forward would have put her outside, one step backward would have put her in the vestibule of her residence." The Court reasoned that she "was in a public place," as she "was not merely visible to the public but was exposed to public view, speech, hearing and touch as if she had been standing completely outside her house." Thus, under the *Hayden* "hot pursuit" rule the police could pursue her without a warrant when she sought refuge within upon their approach. What then if the person to be arrested answers a knock on the door by the police but does not step onto or over the threshold? What if he does because of a police request or subterfuge which conceals their purpose in being there? Or, what if the police use such tactics to gain entry into the premises?

2. In *Dorman,* relied upon in *Payton,* the court found that exceptional circumstances were present by assessing these considerations: (1) "that a grave offense is involved, particularly one that is a crime of violence"; (2) "that the suspect is reasonably believed to be armed"; (3) "that there exists not merely the minimum of probable cause, that is requisite even when a warrant has been issued, but beyond that a clear showing of probable cause, including 'reasonably trustworthy information,' to believe that the suspect committed the crime involved"; (4) "strong reason to believe that the suspect is in the premises being entered"; (5) "a likelihood that the suspect will escape if not swiftly apprehended"; (6) "the circumstance that the entry, though not consented, is made peaceably"; and (7) "time of entry—whether it is made at night," which however "works in more than one direction," as "the late hour may underscore the delay (and perhaps impracticability of) obtaining a warrant and hence serve to justify proceeding without one," while "the fact that an entry is made at night raises a particular concern over its reasonableness * * * and may elevate the degree of probable cause required, both as implicating the suspect, and as showing that he is in the place entered."

3. The Supreme Court focused upon the first *Dorman* factor in WELSH v. WISCONSIN, 466 U.S. 740 (1984), where Welsh was arrested within his own home minutes after a witness had seen him nearby driving erratically and then departing on foot in an apparently inebriated condition after driving off the road into a field. The Court, per BRENNAN, J., held "that an important factor to be considered when determining whether any exigency exists is the gravity of the underlying offense for which the arrest is being made. Moreover, although no exigency is created simply because there is probable cause to believe that a serious crime has been committed, see *Payton,* application of the exigent-circumstances exception in the context of a home entry should rarely be sanctioned when there is probable cause to believe that only a minor offense, such as the kind at issue in this case, has been committed.

"Application of this principle to the facts of the present case is relatively straightforward. The petitioner was arrested in the privacy of his own bedroom for a noncriminal, traffic offense. The State attempts to justify the arrest by relying on the hot-pursuit doctrine, on the threat to public safety, and on the need to preserve evidence of the petitioner's blood-alcohol level. On the facts of this case, however, the claim of hot pursuit is unconvincing because there was no immediate or continuous pursuit of the petitioner from the scene of a crime. Moreover, because the petitioner had already arrived home, and had abandoned his car at the scene of the accident, there was little remaining threat to the public safety. Hence, the only potential emergency claimed by the State was the need to ascertain the petitioner's blood-alcohol level.

"Even assuming, however, that the underlying facts would support a finding of this exigent circumstance, mere similarity to other cases involving the imminent destruction of evidence is not sufficient. The State of Wisconsin has chosen to classify the first offense for driving while intoxicated as a noncriminal, civil forfeiture offense for which no imprisonment is possible. This is the best indication of the state's interest in precipitating an arrest, and is one that can be easily identified both by the courts and by officers faced with a decision to arrest. Given this expression of the state's interest, a warrantless home arrest cannot be upheld simply because evidence of the petitioner's blood-alcohol level might have dissipated while the police obtained a warrant. To allow a warrantless home entry on these facts would be to approve unreasonable police behavior that the principles of the Fourth Amendment will not sanction."

WHITE, J., joined by Rehnquist, J., dissenting, agreed that the gravity of the offense is "a factor to be considered," but asserted that "if, under all the circumstances of a particular case, an officer has probable cause to believe that the delay involved in procuring an arrest warrant will gravely endanger the officer or other persons or will result in the suspect's escape, I perceive no reason to disregard those exigencies on the ground that the offense for which the suspect is sought is a 'minor' one." By like reasoning, they concluded that "nothing in our previous decisions suggests that the fact that a State has defined an offense as a misdemeanor for a variety of social, cultural, and political reasons necessarily requires the conclusion that warrantless in-home arrests designed to prevent the imminent destruction or removal of evidence of that offense are always impermissible. * * * A test under which the existence of exigent circumstances turns on the perceived gravity of the crime would significantly hamper law enforcement and burden courts with pointless litigation concerning the nature and gradation of various crimes."

Would the result in *Welsh* have been different if the police were in immediate hot pursuit? See *State v. Bolte,* 560 A.2d 644 (N.J.1989) (rejecting state's argument answer is yes because "citizens should not be encouraged to elude arrest by retreating into their homes").

4. In STEAGALD v. UNITED STATES, 451 U.S. 204 (1981), police entered Steagald's home in an effort to find one Lyons, for whom they had an arrest warrant; they did not find Lyons but did find drugs in plain view, resulting in Steagald's prosecution and conviction. In reversing the conviction, the Court, per MARSHALL, J., reasoned that "whether the arrest warrant issued in this case adequately safeguarded the interests protected by the Fourth Amendment depends upon what the warrant authorized the agents to do. To be sure, the warrant embodied a judicial finding that there was probable cause to believe that Ricky Lyons had committed a felony, and the warrant therefore authorized the officers to seize Lyons. However, the agents sought to do more than use the warrant to arrest Lyons in a public place or in his home; instead, they relied on the warrant as legal authority to enter the home of a third person based on their belief that Ricky Lyons might be a guest there. Regardless of how reasonable this belief might have been, it was never subjected to the detached scrutiny of a judicial officer. Thus, while the warrant in this case may have protected Lyons from an unreasonable seizure, it did absolutely nothing to protect petitioner's privacy interest in being free from an unreasonable invasion and search of his home. Instead, petitioner's only protection from an illegal entry and search was the agent's personal determination of probable cause. In the absence of exigent circumstances, we have consistently held that such judicially untested determinations are not reliable enough to justify an entry into a person's home to arrest him without a warrant, or a search of a home for objects in the absence of a search warrant. We see no reason to depart from this settled course when the search of a home is for a person rather than an object.

"A contrary conclusion—that the police, acting alone and in the absence of exigent circumstances, may decide when there is sufficient justification for searching the home of a third party for the subject of an arrest warrant—would create a significant potential for abuse. Armed solely with an arrest warrant for a single person, the police could search all the homes of that individual's friends and acquaintances. See, e.g., *Lankford v. Gelston,* 364 F.2d 197 (C.A.4 1966) (enjoining police practice under which 300 homes searched pursuant to arrest warrants for two fugitives). Moreover, an arrest warrant may serve as the pretext for entering a home in which the police have a suspicion, but not probable cause to believe, that illegal activity is taking place."

Though the majority went on to conclude that this result was not contrary to common law precedent and "will not significantly impede effective law enforcement efforts," in that "the situations in which a search warrant will be necessary are few" and in those situations "the inconvenience incurred by the police is simply not that significant," REHNQUIST and White, JJ., dissenting, argued that "the common law as it existed at the time of the framing of the Fourth Amendment" did not support such a result, and concluded:

"The genuinely unfortunate aspect of today's ruling is not that fewer fugitives will be brought to book, or fewer criminals apprehended, though both of these consequences will undoubtedly occur; the greater misfortune is the increased uncertainty imposed on police officers in the field, committing magistrates, and trial judges, who must confront variations and permutations of this factual situation on a day-to-day basis. They will, in their various capacities, have to weigh the time during which a suspect for whom there is an outstanding arrest warrant has been in the building, whether the dwelling is the suspect's home, how long he has lived there, whether he is likely to leave immediately, and a number of related and equally imponderable questions. Certainty and repose, as Justice Holmes said, may not be the destiny of man, but one might have hoped for a higher degree of certainty in this one narrow but important area of the law than is offered by today's decision."

5. An unannounced entry of premises to make an arrest therein is subject to Fourth Amendment limitations like those regarding unannounced entry to execute a search warrant, as set out in *Richards v. Wisconsin*, p. 310. See, e.g., *United States v. Fields*, 113 F.3d 313 (2d Cir.1997). State statutes declaring an officer may not enter to arrest unless he has been denied admittance after giving "notice of his office and purpose" have usually been interpreted as codifying the common law exception for "exigent circumstances" when there is a reasonable belief compliance "would increase his peril, frustrate an arrest, or permit the destruction of evidence." *People v. Rosales*, 437 P.2d 489 (Cal.1968).

SECTION 7. WARRANTLESS SEIZURES AND SEARCHES OF VEHICLES AND CONTAINERS

CALIFORNIA v. CARNEY

471 U.S. 386, 105 S.Ct. 2066, 85 L.Ed.2d 406 (1985).

Chief Justice BURGER delivered the opinion of the Court. * * *

On May 31, 1979, Drug Enforcement Agency Agent Robert Williams watched respondent, Charles Carney, approach a youth in downtown San Diego. The youth accompanied Carney to a Dodge Mini Motor Home parked in a nearby lot. Carney and the youth closed the window shades in the motor home, including one across the front window. Agent Williams had previously received uncorroborated information that the same motor home was used by another person who was exchanging marihuana for sex. Williams, with assistance from other agents, kept the motor home under surveillance for the entire one and one-quarter hours that Carney and the youth remained inside. When the youth left the motor home, the agents followed and stopped him. The youth told the agents that he had received marijuana in return for allowing Carney sexual contacts.

At the officers' request, the youth returned to the motor home and knocked on its door; Carney stepped out. The agents identified themselves as law enforcement officers. Without a warrant or consent, one agent entered the motor home and observed marihuana, plastic bags, and a scale of the kind used in weighing drugs on a table. Agent Williams took Carney into custody and took possession of the motor home. A subsequent search of the motor home at the police station revealed additional marihuana in the cupboards and refrigerator.

Respondent was charged with possession of marihuana for sale. At a preliminary hearing, he moved to suppress the evidence discovered in the motor home. The Magistrate denied the motion, [but later the state supreme court reversed the conviction, holding the search was unreasonable because no warrant was obtained.]

* * * There are, of course, exceptions to the general rule that a warrant must be secured before a search is undertaken; one is the so-called "automobile exception" at issue in this case. This exception to the warrant requirement was first set forth by the Court 60 years ago in *Carroll v. United States,* 267 U.S. 132 (1925). There, the Court recognized that the privacy interests in an automobile are constitutionally protected; however, it held that the ready mobility of the automobile justifies a lesser degree of protection of those interests. The Court rested this exception on a long-recognized distinction between stationary structures and vehicles:

> "[T]he guaranty of freedom from unreasonable searches and seizures by the Fourth Amendment has been construed, practically since the beginning of Government, as recognizing a necessary difference between a search of a store, dwelling house or other structure in respect of which a proper official warrant readily may be obtained, and a search of a ship, motor boat, wagon or automobile, for contraband goods, where it is not practicable to secure a warrant because the vehicle can be *quickly moved* out of the locality or jurisdiction in which the warrant must be sought."

The capacity to be "quickly moved" was clearly the basis of the holding in *Carroll,* and our cases have consistently recognized ready mobility[a] as one of the principal bases of the automobile exception. * * *

a. The Court's earlier cases make it clear that "ready mobility" does *not* refer to the actual likelihood that the vehicle would be moved if a search warrant were sought. *Chambers v. Maroney,* 399 U.S. 42 (1970) (police stopped station wagon on probable cause occupants had just committed a robbery; occupants were arrested and car was driven to police station, where thorough search revealed a revolver under dashboard; search upheld over dissent's reasoning that there was no need for a warrantless search because the car could have been held in police custody until a warrant was obtained); *Colorado v. Bannister,* 449 U.S. 1 (1980) (unanimous Court concludes that where probable cause to search developed after car stopped for a traffic violation, "it would be especially unreasonable to require a detour to a magistrate before the unanticipated evidence could be lawfully seized"); *Michigan v. Thomas,* 458 U.S. 259 (1982) ("the justification to conduct such a warrantless search does not vanish once the car has been immobilized; nor does it depend upon a reviewing court's assessment of the likelihood in each particular case that the car would have been driven away, or that its contents would have been tampered

However, although ready mobility alone was perhaps the original justification for the vehicle exception, our later cases have made clear that ready mobility is not the only basis for the exception. The reasons for the vehicle exception, we have said, are twofold. "Besides the element of mobility, less rigorous warrant requirements govern because the expectation of privacy with respect to one's automobile is significantly less than that relating to one's home or office."

Even in cases where an automobile was not immediately mobile, the lesser expectation of privacy resulting from its use as a readily mobile vehicle justified application of the vehicular exception. In some cases, the configuration of the vehicle contributed to the lower expectations of privacy; for example, we held in *Cardwell v. Lewis,* 417 U.S. [583 (1974)], that, because the passenger compartment of a standard automobile is relatively open to plain view, there are lesser expectations of privacy. But even when enclosed "repository" areas have been involved, we have concluded that the lesser expectations of privacy warrant application of the exception. We have applied the exception in the context of a locked car trunk, *Cady v. Dombrowski,* 413 U.S. 433 (1973), a sealed package in a car trunk, *United States v. Ross,* [p. 377], a closed compartment under the dashboard, *Chambers v. Maroney,* [p. 377], the interior of a vehicle's upholstery, *Carroll, supra,* or sealed packages inside a covered pickup truck, *United States v. Johns,* [p. 379].

These reduced expectations of privacy derive not from the fact that the area to be searched is in plain view, but from the pervasive regulation of vehicles capable of traveling on the public highways. As we explained in *South Dakota v. Opperman,* [p. 395], an inventory search case:

> "Automobiles, unlike homes, are subjected to pervasive and continuing governmental regulation and controls, including periodic inspection and licensing requirements. As an everyday occurrence, police stop and examine vehicles when license plates or inspection stickers have expired, or if other violations, such as exhaust fumes or excessive noise, are noted, or if headlights or other safety equipment are not in proper working order."

The public is fully aware that it is accorded less privacy in its automobiles because of this compelling governmental need for regulation. Historically, "individuals always [have] been on notice that movable vessels may be stopped and searched on facts giving rise to probable cause that the vehicle contains contraband, without the protection afforded by a magistrate's prior evaluation of those facts." In short, the pervasive schemes of regulation, which necessarily lead to reduced expectations of privacy, and the exigencies attendant to ready mobility justify searches without prior recourse to the authority of a magistrate so long as the overriding standard of probable cause is met.

When a vehicle is being used on the highways, or if it is readily capable of such use and is found stationary in a place not regularly used for residential purposes—temporary or otherwise—the two justifications for the vehicle exception come into play. First, the vehicle is obviously readily mobile by the turn of a switch key, if not actually moving. Second, there is a reduced expectation of privacy stemming from its use as a licensed motor vehicle subject to a range of police regulation inapplicable to a fixed dwelling. At least in these circumstances, the overriding societal interests in effective law enforcement justify an immediate search before the vehicle and its occupants become unavailable.

with, during the period required for the police to obtain a warrant"); *Florida v. Meyers,* 466 U.S. 380 (1984) (lower court erred in concluding warrantless search of car improper where, as here, the car had been impounded eight hours earlier and was presently stored in a secure area).

While it is true that respondent's vehicle possessed some, if not many of the attributes of a home, it is equally clear that the vehicle falls clearly within the scope of the exception laid down in *Carroll* and applied in succeeding cases. Like the automobile in *Carroll,* respondent's motor home was readily mobile. Absent the prompt search and seizure, it could readily have been moved beyond the reach of the police. Furthermore, the vehicle was licensed to "operate on public streets; [was] serviced in public places; * * * and [was] subject to extensive regulation and inspection." And the vehicle was so situated that an objective observer would conclude that it was being used not as a residence, but as a vehicle.

Respondent urges us to distinguish his vehicle from other vehicles within the exception because it was *capable of functioning as a home.* In our increasingly mobile society, many vehicles used for transportation can be and are being used not only for transportation but for shelter, i.e., as a "home" or "residence." To distinguish between respondent's motor home and an ordinary sedan for purposes of the vehicle exception would require that we apply the exception depending upon the size of the vehicle and the quality of its appointments. Moreover, to fail to apply the exception to vehicles such as a motor home ignores the fact that a motor home lends itself easily to use as an instrument of illicit drug traffic and other illegal activity. In *United States v. Ross,* we declined to distinguish between "worthy" and "unworthy" containers, noting that "the central purpose of the Fourth Amendment forecloses such a distinction." We decline today to distinguish between "worthy" and "unworthy" vehicles which are either on the public roads and highways, or situated such that it is reasonable to conclude that the vehicle is not being used as a residence.

Our application of the vehicle exception has never turned on the other uses to which a vehicle might be put. The exception has historically turned on the ready mobility of the vehicle, and on the presence of the vehicle in a setting that objectively indicates that the vehicle is being used for transportation.[3] These two requirements for application of the exception ensure that law enforcement officials are not unnecessarily hamstrung in their efforts to detect and prosecute criminal activity, and that the legitimate privacy interests of the public are protected. Applying the vehicle exception in these circumstances allows the essential purposes served by the exception to be fulfilled, while assuring that the exception will acknowledge legitimate privacy interests. * * *

This search was not unreasonable; it was plainly one that the magistrate could authorize if presented with these facts. * * *

The judgment of the California Supreme Court is reversed * * *.

Justice STEVENS, with whom Justice BRENNAN and Justice MARSHALL join, dissenting. * * *

As we explained in *Ross,* the automobile exception * * * has been developed to ameliorate the practical problems associated with the search of vehicles that have been stopped on the streets or public highways because there was probable cause to believe they were transporting contraband. Until today, however, the Court has never decided whether the practical justifications that apply to a vehicle that is stopped in transit on a public way apply with the same force to a vehicle

3. We need not pass on the application of the vehicle exception to a motor home that is situated in a way or place that objectively indicates that it is being used as a residence. Among the factors that might be relevant in determining whether a warrant would be required in such a circumstance is its location, whether the vehicle is readily mobile or instead, for instance, elevated on blocks, whether the vehicle is licensed, whether it is connected to utilities, and whether it has convenient access to a public road.

parked in a lot near a court house where it could easily be detained while a warrant is issued.[15]

In this case, the motor home was parked in an off-the-street lot only a few blocks from the courthouse in downtown San Diego where dozens of magistrates were available to entertain a warrant application.[16] The officers clearly had the element of surprise with them, and with curtains covering the windshield, the motor home offered no indication of any imminent departure. The officers plainly had probable cause to arrest the petitioner and search the motor home, and on this record, it is inexplicable why they eschewed the safe harbor of a warrant.

In the absence of any evidence of exigency in the circumstances of this case, the Court relies on the inherent mobility of the motor home to create a conclusive presumption of exigency. This Court, however, has squarely held that mobility of the place to be searched is not a sufficient justification for abandoning the warrant requirement. In *United States v. Chadwick,* 433 U.S. 1 (1977), the Court held that a warrantless search of a footlocker violated the Fourth Amendment even though there was ample probable cause to believe it contained contraband. The Government had argued that the rationale of the automobile exception applied to movable containers in general, and that the warrant requirement should be limited to searches of homes and other "core" areas of privacy. We categorically rejected the Government's argument observing that there are greater privacy interests associated with containers than with automobiles, and that there are less practical problems associated with the temporary detention of a container than with the detention of an automobile.

* * * It is perfectly obvious that the citizen has a much greater expectation of privacy concerning the interior of a mobile home than of a piece of luggage such as a footlocker. If "inherent mobility" does not justify warrantless searches of containers, it cannot rationally provide a sufficient justification for the search of a person's dwelling place.

Unlike a brick bungalow or a frame Victorian, a motor home seldom serves as a permanent lifetime abode. The motor home in this case, however, was designed to accommodate a breadth of ordinary everyday living. Photographs in the record indicate that its height, length and beam provided substantial living space inside: stuffed chairs surround a table; cupboards provide room for storage of personal effects; bunk-beds provide sleeping space; and a refrigerator provides ample space for food and beverages. Moreover, curtains and large opaque walls inhibit viewing the activities inside from the exterior of the vehicle. The interior configuration of

15. In *Coolidge v. New Hampshire,* 403 U.S. 443 (1971), a plurality refused to apply the automobile exception to an automobile that was seized while parked in the driveway of the suspect's house, towed to a secure police compound, and later searched:

"The word 'automobile' is not a talisman in whose presence the Fourth Amendment fades away and disappears. And surely there is nothing in this case to invoke the meaning and purpose of the rule of *Carroll v. United States*—no alerted criminal bent on flight, no fleeting opportunity on an open highway after a hazardous chase, no contraband or stolen goods or weapons, no confederates waiting to move the evidence, not even the inconvenience of a special police detail to guard the immobilized automobile. In short, by no possible stretch of the legal imagination can this be made into a case where 'it is not practicable to secure a warrant,' and the 'automobile exception' despite its label, is simply irrelevant." (opinion of Stewart, J., joined by Douglas, Brennan and Marshall, JJ.).

In *Cardwell v. Lewis,* 417 U.S. 583 (1974), a different plurality approved the seizure of an automobile from a public parking lot, and a later examination of its exterior. (opinion of Blackmun, J.). Here, of course, we are concerned with the reasonableness of the search, not the seizure. Even if the diminished expectations of privacy associated with an automobile justify the warrantless search of a parked automobile notwithstanding the diminished exigency, the heightened expectations of privacy in the interior of motor home require a different result.

16. In addition, a telephonic warrant was only 20 cents and the nearest phone booth away.

the motor home establishes that the vehicle's size, shape, and mode of construction should have indicated to the officers that it was a vehicle containing mobile living quarters.

The State contends that officers in the field will have an impossible task determining whether or not other vehicles contain mobile living quarters. It is not necessary for the Court to resolve every unanswered question in this area in a single case, but common English usage suggests that we already distinguish between a "motor home" which is "equipped as a self-contained traveling home," a "camper" which is only equipped for "casual travel and camping," and an automobile which is "designed for passenger transportation." Surely the exteriors of these vehicles contain clues about their different functions which could alert officers in the field to the necessity of a warrant.[21] * * *

In my opinion, searches of places that regularly accommodate a wide range of private human activity are fundamentally different from searches of automobiles which primarily serve a public transportation function. Although it may not be a castle, a motor home is usually the functional equivalent of a hotel room, a vacation and retirement home, or a hunting and fishing cabin. These places may be as spartan as a humble cottage when compared to the most majestic mansion, but the highest and most legitimate expectations of privacy associated with these temporary abodes should command the respect of this Court. In my opinion, a warrantless search of living quarters in a motor home is "presumptively unreasonable absent exigent circumstances."

I respectfully dissent.

Notes and Questions

1. In *Maryland v. Dyson*, 527 U.S. 465 (1999), the Court, per curiam, summarily reversed a state court decision holding "that in order for the automobile exception to the warrant requirement to apply, there must not only be probable cause to believe that evidence of a crime is contained in the automobile, but also a separate finding of exigency precluding the police from obtaining a warrant." That holding, the Court declared, "rests upon an incorrect interpretation of the automobile exception to the Fourth Amendment's warrant requirement," which "does not have a separate exigency requirement."

2. In *Florida v. White*, 526 U.S. 559 (1999), upholding the warrantless *seizure* of a car under the state forfeiture law on probable cause that the vehicle was contraband, the Court took note of "the special considerations recognized in the context of movable items" in the *Carroll-Carney* line of cases, and then concluded the need was "equally weighty when the *automobile*, as opposed to its contents, is the contraband that the police seek to secure." The Court also emphasized that "our Fourth Amendment jurisprudence has consistently accorded law enforcement officials greater latitude in exercising their duties in public places," and deemed the instant case "nearly indistinguishable" in this respect from *G.M. Leasing Corp. v. United States*, 429 U.S. 338 (1977), upholding the warrantless seizure from a public area of automobiles in partial satisfaction of income tax assessments. Two dissenting Justices in *White* objected (i) that an exigent circumstances rationale has no application "when the seizure is based upon a belief that the automobile may have been used at some time in the past to

21. In refusing to extend the California Supreme Court's decision in *Carney* beyond its context, the California Courts of Appeals have had no difficulty in distinguishing the motor home involved there from a Ford van and a cab-high camper shell on the back of a pick-up truck. There is no reason to believe that trained officers could not make similar distinctions between different vehicles, especially when state vehicle laws already require them to do so.

assist in illegal activity and the owner is already in custody," and (ii) that a warrant requirement "is bolstered by the inherent risks of hindsight at post-seizure hearings and law enforcement agencies' pecuniary interest in the seizure of such property."

3. In *Chambers v. Maroney,* 399 U.S. 42 (1970), the Court stated that what is required, even if no warrant need first be obtained, is "probable cause to search a particular auto for particular articles." This probable cause must be assessed in order to ascertain whether an otherwise lawful warrantless search of a vehicle was properly limited in scope and intensity, as is illustrated by *Maldonado v. State,* 528 S.W.2d 234 (Tex.Crim.1975) (truck searched on probable cause it was stolen, officers pulled up flooring and found false compartment containing 650 packages of marijuana; held, that part of search illegal because it "could not reasonably be expected that evidence of theft might be uncovered by these means"); *Wimberly v. Superior Court,* 547 P.2d 417 (Cal.1976) (after vehicle stopped for traffic violation, officer saw pipe and 12 marijuana seeds on floor and smelled odor of marijuana, passenger compartment was searched and bag with very small amount of marijuana was found in jacket pocket, trunk of car then searched and several pounds of marijuana found there; held, latter search illegal, as police had probable cause occupants of car were occasional users rather than dealers, and thus "it was not reasonable to infer that petitioners had additional contraband hidden in the trunk"). Compare *United States v. Loucks,* 806 F.2d 208 (10th Cir.1986) (such user-dealer distinction is "illogical and unreasonable").

4. Assuming grounds to make a warrantless search of a car, but the absence of grounds to arrest some occupant of the car, may that occupant also be searched if the items sought are of such a nature that they could be concealed on his person? No, the Supreme Court held in *United States v. Di Re,* p. 318 fn. 8. However, *Model Pre–Arraignment Code* § SS 260.3 provides otherwise (except as to passengers in a common carrier) if the officer has not found the items sought in the vehicle and has "reason to suspect that one or more of the occupants of the vehicle may have the things subject to seizure so concealed." The Reporters argue that "it seems absurd to say that the occupants can take the narcotics out of the glove compartment and stuff them in their pockets, and drive happily away after the vehicle has been fruitlessly searched." Can that position be squared with *Ybarra v. Illinois,* p. 312?

CALIFORNIA v. ACEVEDO

500 U.S. 565, 111 S.Ct. 1982, 114 L.Ed.2d 619 (1991).

Justice BLACKMUN delivered the opinion of the Court.

[One Daza picked up from a Federal Express office a package the police knew contained marijuana and took it to his apartment. About two hours later, Acevedo entered that apartment and shortly thereafter left carrying a brown paper bag the size of one of the wrapped marijuana packages. He placed the bag in the trunk of his car and drove off; the police then stopped him, opened the trunk and bag, and found marijuana. The California Court of Appeal held the marijuana should have been suppressed, the state supreme court denied review, and the Supreme Court then granted certiorari.]

In *United States v. Ross,* 456 U.S. 798, decided in 1982, we held that a warrantless search of an automobile under the *Carroll* doctrine could include a search of a container or package found inside the car when such a search was supported by probable cause. The warrantless search of Ross' car occurred after an informant told the police that he had seen Ross complete a drug transaction using drugs stored in the trunk of his car. The police stopped the car, searched it, and discovered in the trunk a brown paper bag containing drugs. We decided that the search of Ross' car was not unreasonable under the Fourth Amendment: "The scope of a warrantless search based on probable cause is no narrower—and no broader—than the scope of a search authorized by a warrant supported by probable cause." Thus, "[i]f probable cause justifies the search of a lawfully stopped vehicle, it justifies the search of every part of the vehicle and its contents that may conceal the object of the search." In *Ross,* therefore, we clarified the scope of the *Carroll* doctrine as properly including a "probing search" of compartments and containers within the automobile so long as the search is supported by probable cause.

In addition to this clarification, *Ross* distinguished the *Carroll* doctrine from the separate rule that governed the search of closed containers. The Court had announced this separate rule, unique to luggage and other closed packages, bags, and containers, in *United States v. Chadwick,* 433 U.S. 1 (1977). In *Chadwick,* federal narcotics agents had probable cause to believe that a 200–pound double-locked footlocker contained marijuana. The agents tracked the locker as the defendants removed it from a train and carried it through the station to a waiting car. As soon as the defendants lifted the locker into the trunk of the car, the agents arrested them, seized the locker, and searched it. In this Court, the United States did not contend that the locker's brief contact with the automobile's trunk sufficed to make the *Carroll* doctrine applicable. Rather, the United States urged that the search of movable luggage could be considered analogous to the search of an automobile.

The Court rejected this argument because, it reasoned, a person expects more privacy in his luggage and personal effects than he does in his automobile. Moreover, it concluded that as "may often not be the case when automobiles are seized," secure storage facilities are usually available when the police seize luggage.

In *Arkansas v. Sanders,* 442 U.S. 753 (1979), the Court extended *Chadwick*'s rule to apply to a suitcase actually being transported in the trunk of a car. In *Sanders,* the police had probable cause to believe a suitcase contained marijuana. They watched as the defendant placed the suitcase in the trunk of a taxi and was driven away. The police pursued the taxi for several blocks, stopped it, found the suitcase in the trunk, and searched it. Although the Court had applied the *Carroll* doctrine to searches of integral parts of the automobile itself, (indeed, in *Carroll,* contraband whiskey was in the upholstery of the seats), it did not extend the doctrine to the warrantless search of personal luggage "merely because it was located in an automobile lawfully stopped by the police." Again, the *Sanders* majority stressed the heightened privacy expectation in personal luggage and concluded that the presence of luggage in an automobile did not diminish the owner's expectation of privacy in his personal items.

In *Ross,* the Court endeavored to distinguish between *Carroll,* which governed the *Ross* automobile search, and *Chadwick,* which governed the *Sanders* automobile search. It held that the *Carroll* doctrine covered searches of automobiles when the police had probable cause to search an entire vehicle but that the *Chadwick* doctrine governed searches of luggage when the officers had probable cause to search only a container within the vehicle. Thus, in a *Ross* situation, the police could conduct a reasonable search under the Fourth Amendment without obtaining a warrant, whereas in a *Sanders* situation, the police had to obtain a warrant before they searched.

The dissent is correct, of course, that *Ross* involved the scope of an automobile search. *Ross* held that closed containers encountered by the police during a warrantless search of a car pursuant to the automobile exception could also be searched. Thus, this Court in *Ross* took the critical step of saying that closed containers in cars could be searched without a warrant because of their presence within the automobile. Despite the protection that *Sanders* purported to extend to closed containers, the privacy interest in those closed containers yielded to the broad scope of an automobile search. * * *

This Court in *Ross* rejected *Chadwick*'s distinction between containers and cars. It concluded that the expectation of privacy in one's vehicle is equal to one's expectation of privacy in the container, and noted that "the privacy interests in a car's trunk or glove compartment may be no less than those in a movable container." It also recognized that it was arguable that the same exigent circumstances that permit a warrantless search of an automobile would justify the warrantless search of a movable container. In deference to the rule of *Chadwick* and *Sanders,* however, the Court put that question to one side. It concluded that the time and expense of the warrant process would be misdirected if the police could search every cubic inch of an automobile until they discovered a paper sack, at which point the Fourth Amendment required them to take the sack to a magistrate for permission to look inside. We now must decide the question deferred in *Ross:* whether the Fourth Amendment requires the police to obtain a warrant to open the sack in a movable vehicle simply because they lack probable cause to search the entire car. We conclude that it does not.

Dissenters in *Ross* asked why the suitcase in *Sanders* was "more private, less difficult for police to seize and store, or in any other relevant respect more properly subject to the warrant requirement, than a container that police discover in a probable-cause search of an entire automobile?" We now agree that a container found after a general search of the automobile and a container found in a car after a limited search for the container are equally easy for the police to store and for the suspect to hide or destroy. In fact, we see no principled distinction in terms of either the privacy expectation or the exigent circumstances between the paper bag found by the police in *Ross* and the paper bag found by the police here. Furthermore, by attempting to distinguish between a container for which the police are specifically searching and a container which they come across in a car, we have provided only minimal protection for privacy and have impeded effective law enforcement.

The line between probable cause to search a vehicle and probable cause to search a package in that vehicle is not always clear, and separate rules that govern the two objects to be searched may enable the police to broaden their power to make warrantless searches and disserve privacy interests. * * * At the moment when officers stop an automobile, it may be less than clear whether they suspect with a high degree of certainty that the vehicle contains drugs in a bag or simply contains drugs. If the police know that they may open a bag only if they are actually searching the entire car, they may search more extensively than they otherwise would in order to establish the general probable cause required by *Ross.*

Such a situation is not far fetched. In *United States v. Johns,* 469 U.S. 478 (1985), customs agents saw two trucks drive to a private airstrip and approach two small planes. The agents drew near the trucks, smelled marijuana, and then saw in the backs of the trucks packages wrapped in a manner that marijuana smugglers customarily employed. The agents took the trucks to headquarters and searched the packages without a warrant. Relying on *Chadwick,* the defendants argued that the search was unlawful. The defendants contended that *Ross* was inapplicable because the agents lacked probable cause to search anything but the packages themselves and supported this contention by noting that a search of the entire vehicle never occurred. We rejected that argument and found *Chadwick* and *Sanders* inapposite because the agents had probable cause to search the entire body of each truck, although they had chosen not to do so.[a] We cannot see the benefit of a rule that requires law enforcement officers to conduct a more intrusive search in order to justify a less intrusive one.

To the extent that the *Chadwick–Sanders* rule protects privacy, its protection is minimal. Law enforcement officers may seize a container and hold it until they obtain a search warrant. "Since the police, by hypothesis, have probable cause to seize the property, we can assume that a warrant will be routinely forthcoming in the overwhelming majority of cases." And the police often will be able to search containers without a warrant, despite the *Chadwick–Sanders* rule, as a search incident to a lawful arrest [under] *Belton* [p. 389]. * * *

Finally, the search of a paper bag intrudes far less on individual privacy than does the incursion sanctioned long ago in *Carroll*. In that case, prohibition agents slashed the upholstery of the automobile. This Court nonetheless found their search to be reasonable under the Fourth Amendment. If destroying the interior of an automobile is not unreasonable, we cannot conclude that looking inside a closed container is. In light of the minimal protection to privacy afforded by the *Chadwick–Sanders* rule, and our serious doubt whether that rule substantially serves privacy interests, we now hold that the Fourth Amendment does not compel separate treatment for an automobile search that extends only to a container within the vehicle.

The *Chadwick–Sanders* rule not only has failed to protect privacy but it has also confused courts and police officers and impeded effective law enforcement. * * *

The discrepancy between the two rules has led to confusion for law enforcement officers. For example, when an officer, who has developed probable cause to believe that a vehicle contains drugs, begins to search the vehicle and immediately discovers a closed container, which rule applies? The defendant will argue that the fact that the officer first chose to search the container indicates that his probable cause extended only to the container and that *Chadwick* and *Sanders* therefore require a warrant. On the other hand, the fact that the officer first chose to search in the most obvious location should not restrict the propriety of the search. The *Chadwick* rule, as applied in *Sanders,* has developed into an anomaly such that the more likely the police are to discover drugs in a container, the less authority they have to search it. * * *

The interpretation of the *Carroll* doctrine set forth in *Ross* now applies to all searches of containers found in an automobile. In other words, the police may search without a warrant if their search is supported by probable cause. * * * In the case before us, the police had probable cause to believe that the paper bag in the automobile's trunk contained marijuana. That probable cause now allows a warrantless search of the paper bag. The facts in the record reveal that the police did not have probable cause to believe that contraband was hidden in any other

a. However, "the central issue" in *Johns* was whether the warrantless search was permissible in light of the fact that the packages were not opened until three days after they had been removed from the trucks. The majority answered in the affirmative:

"We do not suggest that police officers may indefinitely retain possession of a vehicle and its contents before they complete a vehicle search. Nor do we foreclose the possibility that the owner of a vehicle or its contents might attempt to prove that delay in the completion of a vehicle search was unreasonable because it adversely affected a privacy or possessory interest. We note that in this case there was probable cause to believe that the trucks contained contraband and there is no plausible argument that the object of the search could not have been concealed in the packages. Respondents do not challenge the legitimacy of the seizure of the trucks or the packages, and they never sought return of the property. Thus, respondents have not even alleged, much less proved, that the delay in the search of packages adversely affected legitimate interests protected by the Fourth Amendment."

part of the automobile and a search of the entire vehicle would have been without probable cause and unreasonable under the Fourth Amendment. * * *

Justice SCALIA, concurring in the judgment.

I agree with the dissent that it is anomalous for a briefcase to be protected by the "general requirement" of a prior warrant when it is being carried along the street, but for that same briefcase to become unprotected as soon as it is carried into an automobile. On the other hand, I agree with the Court that it would be anomalous for a locked compartment in an automobile to be unprotected by the "general requirement" of a prior warrant, but for an unlocked briefcase within the automobile to be protected. I join in the judgment of the Court because I think its holding is more faithful to the text and tradition of the Fourth Amendment, and if these anomalies in our jurisprudence are ever to be eliminated that is the direction in which we should travel. * * *

Although the Fourth Amendment does not explicitly impose the requirement of a warrant, it is of course textually possible to consider that implicit within the requirement of reasonableness. For some years after the (still continuing) explosion in Fourth Amendment litigation that followed our announcement of the exclusionary rule in *Weeks v. United States,* [p. 217], our jurisprudence lurched back and forth between imposing a categorical warrant requirement and looking to reasonableness alone. * * *

In my view, the path out of this confusion should be sought by returning to the first principle that the "reasonableness" requirement of the Fourth Amendment affords the protection that the common law afforded. I have no difficulty with the proposition that that includes the requirement of a warrant, where the common law required a warrant; and it may even be that changes in the surrounding legal rules (for example, elimination of the common-law rule that reasonable, good-faith belief was no defense to absolute liability for trespass), may make a warrant indispensable to reasonableness where it once was not. But the supposed "general rule" that a warrant is always required does not appear to have any basis in the common law, and confuses rather than facilitates any attempt to develop rules of reasonableness in light of changed legal circumstances, as the anomaly eliminated and the anomaly created by today's holding both demonstrate.

And there are more anomalies still. Under our precedents (as at common law), a person may be arrested outside the home on the basis of probable cause, without an arrest warrant. *United States v. Watson* [p. 318]. Upon arrest, the person, as well as the area within his grasp, may be searched for evidence related to the crime. *Chimel v. California* [p. 351]. Under these principles, if a known drug dealer is carrying a briefcase reasonably believed to contain marijuana (the unauthorized possession of which is a crime), the police may arrest him and search his person on the basis of probable cause alone. And, under our precedents, upon arrival at the station house, the police may inventory his possessions, including the briefcase, even if there is no reason to suspect that they contain contraband. *Illinois v. Lafayette* [p. 346]. According to our current law, however, the police may not, on the basis of the same probable cause, take the less intrusive step of stopping the individual on the street and demanding to see the contents of his briefcase. That makes no sense *a priori,* and in the absence of any common-law tradition supporting such a distinction, I see no reason to continue it.

I would reverse the judgment in the present case, not because a closed container carried inside a car becomes subject to the "automobile" exception to the general warrant requirement, but because the search of a closed container, outside a privately owned building, with probable cause to believe that the container contains contraband, and when it in fact does contain contraband, is not one of those searches whose Fourth Amendment reasonableness depends upon a warrant. For that reason I concur in the judgment of the Court.

Justice WHITE, dissenting.

Agreeing as I do with most of Justice Stevens' opinion and with the result he reaches, I dissent and would affirm the judgment below.

Justice STEVENS, with whom Justice MARSHALL joins, dissenting.

At the end of its opinion, the Court pays lip service to the proposition that should provide the basis for a correct analysis of the legal question presented by this case: It is " 'a cardinal principle that "searches conducted outside the judicial process, without prior approval by judge or magistrate, are *per se* unreasonable under the Fourth Amendment—subject only to a few specifically established and well-delineated exceptions." ' * * * "

[The warrant] requirement * * * reflects the sound policy judgment that, absent exceptional circumstances, the decision to invade the privacy of an individual's personal effects should be made by a neutral magistrate rather than an agent of the Executive. * * *

In *Chadwick,* the Department of Justice had mounted a frontal attack on the warrant requirement. The Government's principal contention was that "the Fourth Amendment Warrant Clause protects only interests traditionally identified with the home." We categorically rejected that contention, relying on the history and text of the amendment, the policy underlying the warrant requirement, and a line of cases spanning over a century of our jurisprudence. We also rejected the Government's alternative argument that the rationale of our automobile search cases demonstrated the reasonableness of permitting warrantless searches of luggage.

We concluded that neither of the justifications for the automobile exception could support a similar exception for luggage. We first held that the privacy interest in luggage is "substantially greater than in an automobile." Unlike automobiles and their contents, we reasoned, "[l]uggage contents are not open to public view, except as a condition to a border entry or common carrier travel; nor is luggage subject to regular inspections and official scrutiny on a continuing basis." Indeed, luggage is specifically intended to safeguard the privacy of personal effects, unlike an automobile, "whose primary function is transportation."

We then held that the mobility of luggage did not justify creating an additional exception to the Warrant Clause. Unlike an automobile, luggage can easily be seized and detained pending judicial approval of a search. Once the police have luggage "under their exclusive control, there [i]s not the slightest danger that the [luggage] or its contents could [be] removed before a valid search warrant could be obtained.... With the [luggage] safely immobilized, it [i]s unreasonable to undertake the additional and greater intrusion of a search without a warrant" (footnote omitted). * * *

[W]e recognized in *Ross* that *Chadwick* and *Sanders* had not created a special rule for container searches, but rather had merely applied the cardinal principle that warrantless searches are per se unreasonable unless justified by an exception to the general rule. *Ross* dealt with the scope of the automobile exception; *Chadwick* and *Sanders* were cases in which the exception simply did not apply.

In its opinion today, the Court recognizes that the police did not have probable cause to search respondent's vehicle and that a search of anything but the paper bag that respondent had carried from Daza's apartment and placed in the trunk of his car would have been unconstitutional. Moreover, as I read the opinion, the Court assumes that the police could not have made a warrantless inspection of the bag before it was placed in the car. Finally, the Court also does not question the fact that, under our prior cases, it would have been lawful for the police to seize the container and detain it (and respondent) until they obtained a search warrant. Thus, all of the relevant facts that governed our decisions in *Chadwick* and *Sanders* are present here whereas the relevant fact that justified the vehicle search in *Ross* is not present.

The Court does not attempt to identify any exigent circumstances that would justify its refusal to apply the general rule against warrantless searches. Instead, it advances these three arguments: First, the rules identified in the foregoing cases are confusing and anomalous. Second, the rules do not protect any significant interest in privacy. And, third, the rules impede effective law enforcement. None of these arguments withstands scrutiny. * * *

The Court summarizes the alleged "anomaly" created by the coexistence of *Ross*, *Chadwick*, and *Sanders* with the statement that "the more likely the police are to discover drugs in a container, the less authority they have to search it." This juxtaposition is only anomalous, however, if one accepts the flawed premise that the degree to which the police are likely to discover contraband is correlated with their authority to search *without a warrant.* Yet, even proof beyond a reasonable doubt will not justify a warrantless search that is not supported by one of the exceptions to the warrant requirement. And, even when the police have a warrant or an exception applies, once the police possess probable cause, the extent to which they are more or less certain of the contents of a container has no bearing on their authority to search it.

To the extent there was any "anomaly" in our prior jurisprudence, the Court has "cured" it at the expense of creating a more serious paradox. For, surely it is anomalous to prohibit a search of a briefcase while the owner is carrying it exposed on a public street yet to permit a search once the owner has placed the briefcase in the locked trunk of his car. One's privacy interest in one's luggage can certainly not be diminished by one's removing it from a public thoroughfare and placing it—out of sight—in a privately owned vehicle. Nor is the danger that evidence will escape increased if the luggage is in a car rather than on the street. In either location, if the police have probable cause, they are authorized to seize the luggage and to detain it until they obtain judicial approval for a search. Any line demarking an exception to the warrant requirement will appear blurred at the edges, but the Court has certainly erred if it believes that, by erasing one line and drawing another, it has drawn a clearer boundary.

The Court's statement that *Chadwick* and *Sanders* provide only "minimal protection to privacy" is also unpersuasive. Every citizen clearly has an interest in the privacy of the contents of his or her luggage, briefcase, handbag or any other container that conceals private papers and effects from public scrutiny. That privacy interest has been recognized repeatedly in cases spanning more than a century.

Under the Court's holding today, the privacy interest that protects the contents of a suitcase or a briefcase from a warrantless search when it is in public view simply vanishes when its owner climbs into a taxicab. Unquestionably the rejection of the *Sanders* line of cases by today's decision will result in a significant loss of individual privacy.

To support its argument that today's holding works only a minimal intrusion on privacy, the Court suggests that "[i]f the police know that they may open a bag only if they are actually searching the entire car, they may search more extensively than they otherwise would in order to establish the general probable cause required by *Ross*." As I have already noted, this fear is unexplained and inexplicable. Neither evidence uncovered in the course of a search nor the scope of the search conducted can be used to provide *post hoc* justification for a search unsupported by probable cause at its inception. * * *

Despite repeated claims that *Chadwick* and *Sanders* have "impeded effective law enforcement," the Court cites no authority for its contentions. * * *

Notes and Questions

1. After police stopped a vehicle for speeding, the driver admitted that he had used the syringe visible in his shirt pocket to take drugs. The police then ordered the two female passengers out of the car and searched the passenger compartment for contraband. On the back seat they found a purse that passenger Houghton claimed as hers; the police searched it and found drugs and drug paraphernalia. Houghton was convicted after her efforts to have the drugs suppressed failed, but the state supreme court overturned the conviction, reasoning that the search violated the Fourth Amendment because the officer "knew or should have known that the purse did not belong to the driver, but to one of the passengers," and because "there was no probable cause to search the passengers' personal effects and no reason to believe that contraband had been placed within the purse." But in WYOMING v. HOUGHTON, 526 U.S. 295 (1999), the Supreme Court, per SCALIA, J., reversed, reasoning that "neither *Ross* itself nor the historical evidence it relied upon admits of a distinction among packages or containers based on ownership. When there is probable cause to search for contraband in a car, it is reasonable for police officers—like customs officials in the Founding era—to examine packages and containers without a showing of individualized probable cause for each one. A passenger's personal belongings, just like the driver's belongings or containers attached to the car like a glove compartment, are 'in' the car, and the officer has probable cause to search for contraband in the car.

"Even if the historical evidence, as described by *Ross*, were thought to be equivocal, we would find that the balancing of the relative interests weighs decidedly in favor of allowing searches of a passenger's belongings. Passengers, no less than drivers, possess a reduced expectation of privacy with regard to the property that they transport in cars, which 'trave[l] public thoroughfares,' 'seldom serv[e] as ... the repository of personal effects,' are subjected to police stop and examination to enforce 'pervasive' governmental controls '[a]s an everyday occurrence,' and, finally, are exposed to traffic accidents that may render all their contents open to public scrutiny.

"In this regard—the degree of intrusiveness upon personal privacy and indeed even personal dignity—the two cases the Wyoming Supreme Court found dispositive differ substantially from the package search at issue here. *United States v. Di Re*, [p. 377], held that probable cause to search a car did not justify a body search of a passenger. And *Ybarra v. Illinois*, [p. 312], held that a search warrant for a tavern and its bartender did not permit body searches of all the bar's patrons. These cases turned on the unique, significantly heightened protection afforded against searches of one's person. 'Even a limited search of the outer clothing ... constitutes a severe, though brief, intrusion upon cherished personal security, and it must surely be an annoying, frightening, and perhaps humiliating experience.' Such traumatic consequences are not to be expected when the police examine an item of personal property found in a car.[34]

34. The dissent begins its analysis with an assertion that this case is governed by our decision in *United States v. Di Re*, which held, as the dissent describes it, that the automobile exception to the warrant requirement did not justify "searches of the passenger's pockets and the space between his shirt and underwear." It attributes that holding to "the set-

"Whereas the passenger's privacy expectations are, as we have described, considerably diminished, the governmental interests at stake are substantial. Effective law enforcement would be appreciably impaired without the ability to search a passenger's personal belongings when there is reason to believe contraband or evidence of criminal wrongdoing is hidden in the car. As in all car-search cases, the 'ready mobility' of an automobile creates a risk that the evidence or contraband will be permanently lost while a warrant is obtained. In addition, a car passenger—unlike the unwitting tavern patron in *Ybarra*—will often be engaged in a common enterprise with the driver, and have the same interest in concealing the fruits or the evidence of their wrongdoing. A criminal might be able to hide contraband in a passenger's belongings as readily as in other containers in the car—perhaps even surreptitiously, without the passenger's knowledge or permission. (This last possibility provided the basis for respondent's defense at trial; she testified that most of the seized contraband must have been placed in her purse by her traveling companions at one or another of various times, including the time she was 'half asleep' in the car.)

"To be sure, these factors favoring a search will not always be present, but the balancing of interests must be conducted with an eye to the generality of cases. To require that the investigating officer have positive reason to believe that the passenger and driver were engaged in a common enterprise, or positive reason to believe that the driver had time and occasion to conceal the item in the passenger's belongings, surreptitiously or with friendly permission, is to impose requirements so seldom met that a 'passenger's property' rule would dramatically reduce the ability to find and seize contraband and evidence of crime. Of course these requirements would not attach (under the Wyoming Supreme Court's rule) until the police officer knows or has reason to know that the container belongs to a passenger. But once a 'passenger's property' exception to car searches became widely known, one would expect passenger-confederates to claim everything as their own. And one would anticipate a bog of litigation—in the form of both civil lawsuits and motions to suppress in criminal trials—involving such questions as whether the officer should have believed a passenger's claim of ownership, whether he should have inferred ownership from various objective factors, whether he had probable cause to believe that the passenger was a confederate, or to believe that the driver might have introduced the contraband into the package with or without the passenger's knowledge.[35] When balancing the competing

tled distinction between drivers and passengers," rather than to a distinction between search of the person and search of property, which the dissent claims is "newly minted" by today's opinion—a "new rule that is based on a distinction between property contained in clothing worn by a passenger and property contained in a passenger's briefcase or purse."

In its peroration, however, the dissent quotes extensively from Justice Jackson's opinion in *Di Re*, which makes it very clear that it is precisely this distinction between search of the person and search of property that the case relied upon: "The Government says it would not contend that, armed 'with a search warrant for a residence only, it could search all persons found in it. But an occupant of a house could be used to conceal this contraband on his person quite as readily as can an occupant of a car.' " Does the dissent really believe that Justice Jackson was saying that a house-search could not inspect property belonging to persons found in the house—say a large standing safe or violin case belonging to the owner's visiting godfather? Of course that is not what Justice Jackson meant at all. He was referring precisely to that "distinction between property contained in clothing worn by a passenger and property contained in a passenger's briefcase or purse" that the dissent disparages. This distinction between searches of the person and searches of property is assuredly not "newly minted." And if the dissent thinks "pockets" and "clothing" do not count as part of the person, it must believe that the only searches of the person are strip searches.

35. The dissent is "confident in a police officer's ability to apply a rule requiring a warrant or individualized probable cause to search belongings that are . . . obviously owned by and in the custody of a passenger." If this is the dissent's strange criterion for warrant protection ("obviously owned by and in the custody of") its preceding paean to the importance of preserving passengers' privacy rings a little

interests, our determinations of "reasonableness" under the Fourth Amendment must take account of these practical realities. We think they militate in favor of the needs of law enforcement, and against a personal-privacy interest that is ordinarily weak.

"Finally, if we were to invent an exception from the historical practice that *Ross* accurately described and summarized, it is perplexing why that exception should protect only property belonging to a passenger, rather than (what seems much more logical) property belonging to anyone other than the driver. Surely Houghton's privacy would have been invaded to the same degree whether she was present or absent when her purse was searched. And surely her presence in the car with the driver provided more, rather than less, reason to believe that the two were in league. It may ordinarily be easier to identify the property as belonging to someone other than the driver when the purported owner is present to identify it—but in the many cases (like *Ross* itself) where the car is seized, that identification may occur later, at the station-house; and even at the site of the stop one can readily imagine a package clearly marked with the owner's name and phone number, by which the officer can confirm the driver's denial of ownership. The sensible rule (and the one supported by history and caselaw) is that such a package may be searched, whether or not its owner is present as a passenger or otherwise, because it may contain the contraband that the officer has reason to believe is in the car."

STEVENS, J., for the three dissenters, objected that in "all of our prior cases applying the automobile exception to the Fourth Amendment's warrant requirement, either the defendant was the operator of the vehicle and in custody of the object of the search, or no question was raised as to the defendant's ownership or custody. In the only automobile case confronting the search of a passenger defendant—*United States v. Di Re*—the Court held that the exception to the warrant requirement did not apply. In *Di Re*, as here, the information prompting the search directly implicated the driver, not the passenger. Today, instead of adhering to the settled distinction between drivers and passengers, the Court fashions a new rule that is based on a distinction between property contained in clothing worn by a passenger and property contained in a passenger's briefcase or purse. In cases on both sides of the Court's newly minted test, the property is in a 'container' (whether a pocket or a pouch) located in the vehicle. Moreover, unlike the Court, I think it quite plain that the search of a passenger's purse or briefcase involves an intrusion on privacy that may be just as serious as was the intrusion in *Di Re*. * * *[a]

hollow on rehearing. Should it not be enough if the passenger says he owns the briefcase, and the officer has no concrete reason to believe otherwise? Or would the dissent consider that an example of "obvious" ownership? On reflection, it seems not at all obvious precisely what constitutes obviousness—and so even the dissent's on-the-cheap protection of passengers' privacy interest in their property turns out to be unclear, and hence unadministrable. But maybe the dissent does not mean to propose an obviously-owned-by-and-in-the-custody-of test after all, since a few sentences later it endorses, simpliciter, "a rule requiring a warrant or individualized probable cause to search passenger belongings." For the reasons described in text, that will not work.

a. Compare BREYER, concurring: "Purses are special containers. They are repositories of especially personal items that people generally like to keep with them at all times. So I am tempted to say that a search of a purse involves an intrusion so similar to a search of one's person that the same rule should govern both. However, given this Court's prior cases, I cannot argue that the fact that the container was a purse automatically makes a legal difference, for the Court has warned against trying to make that kind of distinction. But I can say that it would matter if a woman's purse, like a man's billfold, were attached to her person. It might then amount to a kind of 'outer clothing' which under the Court's cases would properly receive increased protection. In this case, the purse was separate from the person, and no one has claimed that, under those circumstances, the type of container makes a difference. For that reason, I join the Court's opinion."

"Nor am I persuaded that the mere spatial association between a passenger and a driver provides an acceptable basis for presuming that they are partners in crime or for ignoring privacy interests in a purse. Whether or not the Fourth Amendment required a warrant to search Houghton's purse, at the very least the trooper in this case had to have probable cause to believe that her purse contained contraband. The Wyoming Supreme Court concluded that he did not.

"Finally, in my view, the State's legitimate interest in effective law enforcement does not outweigh the privacy concerns at issue. I am as confident in a police officer's ability to apply a rule requiring a warrant or individualized probable cause to search belongings that are—as in this case—obviously owned by and in the custody of a passenger as is the Court in a 'passenger-confederate[']s' ability to circumvent the rule. Certainly the ostensible clarity of the Court's rule is attractive. But that virtue is insufficient justification for its adoption. Moreover, a rule requiring a warrant or individualized probable cause to search passenger belongings is every bit as simple as the Court's rule; it simply protects more privacy. * * *[2]"

2. Reassess the law and facts of *Chadwick*, p. 375 in light of *Acevedo*. Absent true exigent circumstances, is a search warrant still required for a container having no connection with a vehicle? If so, is there actually a sufficient container-vehicle connection in *Chadwick* to make the *Acevedo* no-warrant rule applicable?

3. If there *is* a general rule that absent exigent circumstances search warrants are needed for the search of containers not sufficiently connected with vehicles, are there exceptions? Consider:

(a) Fn. 13 in *Sanders:* "Not all containers and packages found by police during the course of a search will deserve the full protection of the Fourth Amendment. Thus, some containers (for example a kit of burglar tools or a gun case) by their very nature cannot support any reasonable expectation of privacy because their contents can be inferred from their outward appearance. Similarly, in some cases the contents of a package will be open to 'plain view,' thereby obviating the need for a warrant."

(b) In *Texas v. Brown,* 460 U.S. 730 (1983), involving a warrantless search of a knotted opaque party balloon found with several plastic vials, a quantity of loose white powder, and a bag of balloons, Stevens, J., for three members of the Court, after characterizing the plurality's explanation for why no search warrant was needed to search the balloon as "incomplete," speculated that the balloon "could be one of those rare single-purpose containers which 'by their very nature cannot support any reasonable expectation of privacy because their contents can be inferred from their outward appearance.' Whereas a suitcase or a paper bag may contain an almost infinite variety of items, a balloon of this kind might be used only to transport drugs. Viewing it where he did could have given the officer a degree of certainty that is equivalent to the plain view of the heroin itself. If that be true, I would conclude that the plain view doctrine supports the search as well as the seizure even though the contents of the balloon were not actually visible to the officer.

"This reasoning leads me to the conclusion that the Fourth Amendment would not require exclusion of the balloon's contents in this case if, but only if,

2. In response to this dissent the Court has crafted an imaginative footnote suggesting that the *Di Re* decision rested, not on Di Re's status as a mere occupant of the vehicle and the importance of individualized suspicion, but rather on the intrusive character of the search. That the search of a safe or violin case would be less intrusive than a strip search does not, however, persuade me that the *Di Re* case would have been decided differently if Di Re had been a woman and the gas coupons had been found in her purse. * * *

there was probable cause to search the entire vehicle or there was virtual certainty that the balloon contained a controlled substance.[5]"

(c) After customs agents found marijuana inside a table shipped into the country, it was repackaged and delivered to defendant by police posing as delivery men. Surveilling police saw defendant pull the container into his apartment, and when he reemerged with it 30 to 45 minutes later he was arrested and the package searched without a warrant. The state court, relying upon *Sanders* and *Chadwick,* held the marijuana inadmissible, but the Supreme Court, in ILLINOIS v. ANDREAS, 463 U.S. 765 (1983), disagreed. The Court, per BURGER, C.J., first addressed the threshold question of "whether an individual has a legitimate expectation of privacy in the contents of a previously lawfully searched container. It is obvious that the privacy interest in the contents of a container diminishes with respect to a container that law enforcement authorities have already lawfully opened and found to contain illicit drugs. No protected privacy interest remains in contraband in a container once government officers lawfully have opened that container and identified its contents as illegal. The simple act of resealing the container to enable the police to make a controlled delivery does not operate to revive or restore the lawfully invaded privacy rights.

"This conclusion is supported by the reasoning underlying the 'plain view' doctrine. The plain view doctrine authorizes seizure of illegal or evidentiary items visible to a police officer whose access to the object has some prior Fourth Amendment justification and who has probable cause to suspect that the item is connected with criminal activity. The plain view doctrine is grounded on the proposition that once police are lawfully in a position to observe an item first-hand, its owner's privacy interest in that item is lost; the owner may retain the incidents of title and possession but not privacy. That rationale applies here; once a container has been found to a certainty to contain illicit drugs, the contraband becomes like objects physically within the plain view of the police, and the claim to privacy is lost. Consequently the subsequent opening is not a 'search' within the intendment of the Fourth Amendment."

The Court then noted that "perfect" controlled deliveries are often impossible, so that there may result "a gap in surveillance" during which "it is possible that the container will be put to other uses—for example, the contraband may be removed or other items may be placed inside." On the resulting question of "at what point after an interruption of control or surveillance, courts should recognize the individual's expectation of privacy in the container as a legitimate right protected by the Fourth Amendment," the Court adopted the "workable," "reasonable" and "objective" standard of "whether there is a substantial likelihood that the contents of the container have been changed during the gap in surveillance. We hold that absent a substantial likelihood that the contents have been changed, there is no legitimate expectation of privacy in the contents of a container previously opened under lawful authority." The Court then concluded there was no substantial likelihood in the instant case. "The unusual size of the container, its specialized purpose, and the relatively short break in surveillance, combine to make it substantially unlikely that the respondent removed the table or placed new items inside the container while it was in his apartment."

BRENNAN and Marshall, JJ., dissenting, objected that while after the customs search "any reasonable expectation respondent may have had that the

5. Sometimes there can be greater certainty about the identity of a substance within a container than about the identity of a substance that is actually visible. One might actually see a white powder without realizing that it is heroin, but be virtually certain a balloon contains such a substance in a particular context. It seems to me that in evaluating whether a person's privacy interests are infringed, "virtual certainty" is a more meaningful indicator than visibility.

existence of the contraband would remain secret was lost, and could not be regained," he still had a Fourth Amendment right "to be 'let alone' " which "is, at the very least, the right not to have one's repose and possessions disturbed" without a warrant. Moreover, "if a person has no reasonable expectation of privacy in a package whose contents are already legally known to the authorities, a reasonable expectation of privacy should reattach if the person has unobserved access to the package and any opportunity to change its contents." STEVENS, J., dissenting separately, would remand for reconsideration under his "virtual certainty" test in *Texas v. Brown.*

THORNTON v. UNITED STATES

541 U.S. 615, 124 S.Ct. 2127, 158 L.Ed.2d 905 (2004).

Chief Justice REHNQUIST delivered the opinion of the Court except as to footnote 4.

[Just as a patrol officer running a check on Thornton's license tags learned they had been issued for another vehicle, Thornton drove into a parking lot, parked, and got out of the vehicle. The officer then accosted him, asked him for his driver's license, told him of the tags violation, and asked if he had any illegal narcotics on him. Thornton produced "three bags of marijuana" plus "a large amount of crack cocaine." The officer then arrested and handcuffed Thornton and placed him in the back seat of the patrol car, and then searched Thornton's car and found a handgun under the driver's seat. The search was upheld below on the basis of *New York v. Belton*, 453 U.S. 454 (1981).]

In *Belton,* an officer overtook a speeding vehicle on the New York Thruway and ordered its driver to pull over. Suspecting that the occupants possessed marijuana, the officer directed them to get out of the car and arrested them for unlawful possession. He searched them and then searched the passenger compartment of the car. We considered the constitutionally permissible scope of a search in these circumstances and sought to lay down a workable rule governing that situation.

We first referred to *Chimel v. California,* [p. 351], a case where the arrestee was arrested in his home, and we had described the scope of a search incident to a lawful arrest as the person of the arrestee and the area immediately surrounding him. This rule was justified by the need to remove any weapon the arrestee might seek to use to resist arrest or to escape, and the need to prevent the concealment or destruction of evidence. Although easily stated, the *Chimel* principle had proved difficult to apply in specific cases. We pointed out that in *United States v. Robinson,* [p. 329], a case dealing with the scope of the search of the arrestee's person, we had rejected a suggestion that " 'there must be litigated in each case the issue of whether or not there was present one of the reasons supporting the authority' " to conduct such a search. Similarly, because "courts ha[d] found no workable definition of the 'area within the immediate control of the arrestee' when that area arguably include[d] the interior of an automobile and the arrestee [wa]s its recent occupant,"we sought to set forth a clear rule for police officers and citizens alike. We therefore held that "when a policeman has made a lawful custodial arrest of the occupant of an automobile, he may, as a contemporaneous incident of that arrest, search the passenger compartment of that automobile."

In so holding, we placed no reliance on the fact that the officer in *Belton* ordered the occupants out of the vehicle, or initiated contact with them while they remained within it. Nor do we find such a factor persuasive in distinguishing the current situation, as it bears no logical relationship to *Belton's* rationale. There is simply no basis to conclude that the span of the area generally within the arrestee's immediate control is determined by whether the arrestee exited the vehicle at the officer's direction, or whether the officer initiated contact with him while he remained in the car. * * *

In all relevant aspects, the arrest of a suspect who is next to a vehicle presents identical concerns regarding officer safety and the destruction of evidence as the arrest of one who is inside the vehicle. An officer may search a suspect's vehicle under *Belton* only if the suspect is arrested. A custodial arrest is fluid and "[t]he danger to the police officer flows from *the fact of the arrest,* and its attendant proximity, stress, and uncertainty." The stress is no less merely because the arrestee exited his car before the officer initiated contact, nor is an arrestee less likely to attempt to lunge for a weapon or to destroy evidence if he is outside of, but still in control of, the vehicle. In either case, the officer faces a highly volatile situation. It would make little sense to apply two different rules to what is, at bottom, the same situation.

In some circumstances it may be safer and more effective for officers to conceal their presence from a suspect until he has left his vehicle. Certainly that is a judgment officers should be free to make. But under the strictures of petitioner's proposed "contact initiation" rule, officers who do so would be unable to search the car's passenger compartment in the event of a custodial arrest, potentially compromising their safety and placing incriminating evidence at risk of concealment or destruction. The Fourth Amendment does not require such a gamble.

Petitioner argues, however, that *Belton* will fail to provide a "bright-line" rule if it applies to more than vehicle "occupants." But *Belton* allows police to search the passenger compartment of a vehicle incident to a lawful custodial arrest of both "occupants" and "recent occupants." Indeed, the respondent in *Belton* was not inside the car at the time of the arrest and search; he was standing on the highway. In any event, while an arrestee's status as a "recent occupant" may turn on his temporal or spatial relationship to the car at the time of the arrest and search,[2] it certainly does not turn on whether he was inside or outside the car at the moment that the officer first initiated contact with him.

To be sure, not all contraband in the passenger compartment is likely to be readily accessible to a "recent occupant." It is unlikely in this case that petitioner could have reached under the driver's seat for his gun once he was outside of his automobile. But the firearm and the passenger compartment in general were no more inaccessible than were the contraband and the passenger compartment in *Belton*. The need for a clear rule, readily understood by police officers and not depending on differing estimates of what items were or were not within reach of an arrestee at any particular moment, justifies the sort of generalization which *Belton* enunciated.[3] Once an officer determines that there is probable cause to

2. Petitioner argues that if we reject his proposed "contact initiation" rule, we should limit the scope of *Belton* to "recent occupants" who are within "reaching distance" of the car. We decline to address petitioner's argument, however, as it is outside the question on which we granted certiorari, and was not addressed by the Court of Appeals. We note that it is unlikely that petitioner would even meet his own standard as he apparently conceded in the Court of Appeals that he was in "close proximity, both temporally and spatially," to his vehicle when he was approached by Nichols.

3. Justice Stevens contends that *Belton's* bright-line rule "is not needed for cases in which the arrestee is first accosted when he is a pedestrian, because *Chimel* itself provides all the guidance that is necessary." Under Justice Stevens' approach, however, even if the car itself was within the arrestee's reaching distance under *Chimel,* police officers and courts would still have to determine whether a particular object within the passenger compartment was also within an arrestee's reaching distance under *Chimel*. This is exactly the type of unworkable and fact-specific inquiry that *Belton* rejected by holding that the entire passenger compartment may be searched when " 'the area within the immediate control of the arrestee' ... arguably includes the interior of an automobile and the arrestee is its recent occupant."

make an arrest, it is reasonable to allow officers to ensure their safety and to preserve evidence by searching the entire passenger compartment.

Rather than clarifying the constitutional limits of a *Belton* search, petitioner's "contact initiation" rule would obfuscate them. Under petitioner's proposed rule, an officer approaching a suspect who has just alighted from his vehicle would have to determine whether he actually confronted or signaled confrontation with the suspect while he remained in the car, or whether the suspect exited his vehicle unaware of, and for reasons unrelated to, the officer's presence. This determination would be inherently subjective and highly fact specific, and would require precisely the sort of ad hoc determinations on the part of officers in the field and reviewing courts that *Belton* sought to avoid. Experience has shown that such a rule is impracticable, and we refuse to adopt it. So long as an arrestee is the sort of "recent occupant" of a vehicle such as petitioner was here, officers may search that vehicle incident to the arrest.[4] * * *

Justice O'CONNOR, concurring in part. I join all but footnote 4 of the Court's opinion.

Although the opinion is a logical extension of the holding of *New York v. Belton*, I write separately to express my dissatisfaction with the state of the law in this area. * * * While the approach Justice SCALIA proposes appears to be built on firmer ground, I am reluctant to adopt it in the context of a case in which neither the Government nor the petitioner has had a chance to speak to its merit.

Justice SCALIA, with whom Justice GINSBURG joins, concurring in the judgment. * * *

When petitioner's car was searched in this case, he was neither in, nor anywhere near, the passenger compartment of his vehicle. Rather, he was handcuffed and secured in the back of the officer's squad car. The risk that he would nevertheless "grab a weapon or evidentiary ite[m]" from his car was remote in the extreme. The Court's effort to apply our current doctrine to this search stretches it beyond its breaking point, and for that reason I cannot join the Court's opinion.

I see three reasons why the search in this case might have been justified to protect officer safety or prevent concealment or destruction of evidence. None ultimately persuades me.

The first is that, despite being handcuffed and secured in the back of a squad car, petitioner might have escaped and retrieved a weapon or evidence from his vehicle * * *. The United States, endeavoring to ground this seemingly speculative fear in reality, points to a total of seven instances over the past 13 years in which state or federal officers were attacked with weapons by handcuffed or formerly handcuffed arrestees. These instances do not, however, justify the search authority claimed. Three involved arrestees who retrieved weapons concealed *on their own person*. Three more involved arrestees who seized a weapon *from the arresting officer*. Authority to search the arrestee's own person is beyond question; and of course no search could prevent seizure of the officer's gun. Only one of the seven instances involved a handcuffed arrestee who escaped from a squad car to retrieve a weapon from somewhere else: the suspect jumped out of the squad car

4. Whatever the merits of Justice Scalia's opinion concurring in the judgment, this is the wrong case in which to address them. Petitioner has never argued that *Belton* should be limited "to cases where it is reasonable to believe evidence relevant to the crime of arrest might be found in the vehicle," nor did any court below consider Justice Scalia's reasoning. * * *. And the United States has never had an opportunity to respond to such an approach. Under these circumstances, it would be imprudent to overrule, for all intents and purposes, our established constitutional precedent, which governs police authority in a common occurrence such as automobile searches pursuant to arrest, and we decline to do so at this time.

and ran through a forest to a house, where (still in handcuffs) he struck an officer on the wrist with a fireplace poker before ultimately being shot dead.

Of course, the Government need not document specific instances in order to justify measures that avoid obvious risks. But the risk here is far from obvious, and in a context as frequently recurring as roadside arrests, the Government's inability to come up with even a single example of a handcuffed arrestee's retrieval of arms or evidence from his vehicle undermines its claims. The risk that a suspect handcuffed in the back of a squad car might escape and recover a weapon from his vehicle is surely no greater than the risk that a suspect handcuffed in his residence might escape and recover a weapon from the next room—a danger we held insufficient to justify a search in *Chimel*.

The second defense of the search in this case is that, since the officer could have conducted the search at the time of arrest (when the suspect was still near the car), he should not be penalized for having taken the sensible precaution of securing the suspect in the squad car first. * * * The weakness of this argument is that it assumes that, one way or another, the search must take place. But conducting a *Chimel* search is not the Government's right; it is an exception—justified by necessity—to a rule that would otherwise render the search unlawful. If "sensible police procedures" require that suspects be handcuffed and put in squad cars, then police should handcuff suspects, put them in squad cars, and not conduct the search. Indeed, if an officer leaves a suspect unrestrained nearby just to manufacture authority to search, one could argue that the search is unreasonable *precisely because* the dangerous conditions justifying it existed only by virtue of the officer's failure to follow sensible procedures.

The third defense of the search is that, even though the arrestee posed no risk here, *Belton* searches in general are reasonable, and the benefits of a bright-line rule justify upholding that small minority of searches that, on their particular facts, are not reasonable. The validity of this argument rests on the accuracy of *Belton*'s claim that the passenger compartment is "in fact generally, even if not inevitably," within the suspect's immediate control. By the United States' own admission, however, "[t]he practice of restraining an arrestee on the scene before searching a car that he just occupied is so prevalent that holding that *Belton* does not apply in that setting would ... 'largely render *Belton* a dead letter.' " * * *

If *Belton* searches are justifiable, it is not because the arrestee might grab a weapon or evidentiary item from his car, but simply because the car might contain evidence relevant to the crime for which he was arrested. This more general sort of evidence-gathering search is not without antecedent. For example, in *United States v. Rabinowitz,* [p. 352], we upheld a search of the suspect's place of business after he was arrested there. We did not restrict the officers' search authority to "the area into which [the] arrestee might reach in order to grab a weapon or evidentiary ite[m]," and we did not justify the search as a means to prevent concealment or destruction of evidence.[1] Rather, we relied on a more general interest in gathering evidence relevant to the crime for which the suspect had been arrested.

Numerous earlier authorities support this approach, referring to the general interest in gathering evidence related to the crime of arrest with no mention of the more specific interest in preventing its concealment or destruction. * * * Only in the years leading up to *Chimel* did we start consistently referring to the narrower interest in frustrating concealment or destruction of evidence.

1. We did characterize the entire office as under the defendant's "immediate control," but we used the term in a broader sense than the one it acquired in *Chimel.*

There is nothing irrational about broader police authority to search for evidence when and where the perpetrator of a crime is lawfully arrested. The fact of prior lawful arrest distinguishes the arrestee from society at large, and distinguishes a search for evidence of *his* crime from general rummaging. Moreover, it is not illogical to assume that evidence of a crime is most likely to be found where the suspect was apprehended.

Nevertheless, *Chimel*'s narrower focus on concealment or destruction of evidence also has historical support. And some of the authorities supporting the broader rule address only searches of the arrestee's *person,* as to which *Chimel*'s limitation might fairly be implicit. Moreover, carried to its logical end, the broader rule is hard to reconcile with the influential case of *Entick v. Carrington,* 19 How. St. Tr. 1029, 1031, 1063–1074 (C.P. 1765) (disapproving search of plaintiff's private papers under general warrant, despite arrest).

In short, both *Rabinowitz* and *Chimel* are plausible accounts of what the Constitution requires, and neither is so persuasive as to justify departing from settled law. But if we are going to continue to allow *Belton* searches on *stare decisis* grounds, we should at least be honest about why we are doing so. *Belton* cannot reasonably be explained as a mere application of *Chimel.* Rather, it is a return to the broader sort of search incident to arrest that we allowed before *Chimel*—limited, of course, to searches of motor vehicles, a category of "effects" which give rise to a reduced expectation of privacy, see *Wyoming v. Houghton,* [p. 384], and heightened law enforcement needs.

Recasting *Belton* in these terms would have at least one important practical consequence. * * * When officer safety or imminent evidence concealment or destruction is at issue, officers should not have to make fine judgments in the heat of the moment. But in the context of a general evidence-gathering search, the state interests that might justify any overbreadth are far less compelling. A motorist may be arrested for a wide variety of offenses; in many cases, there is no reasonable basis to believe relevant evidence might be found in the car. I would therefore limit *Belton* searches to cases where it is reasonable to believe evidence relevant to the crime of arrest might be found in the vehicle.

In this case, as in *Belton,* petitioner was lawfully arrested for a drug offense. It was reasonable for Officer Nichols to believe that further contraband or similar evidence relevant to the crime for which he had been arrested might be found in the vehicle from which he had just alighted and which was still within his vicinity at the time of arrest. I would affirm the decision below on that ground.[3]

Justice STEVENS, with whom Justice SOUTER joins, dissenting.

[*Belton*] expanded the authority of the police in two important respects. It allowed the police to conduct a broader search than our decision in *Chimel v. California* would have permitted, and it authorized them to open closed containers that might be found in the vehicle's passenger compartment.[2] * * * I remain convinced that this [second] aspect of the *Belton* opinion was both unnecessary and erroneous.

3. The Court asserts that my opinion goes beyond the scope of the question presented, citing this Court's Rule 14.1(a). That Rule, however, does not constrain our authority to reach issues presented by the case, and in any event does not apply when the issue is necessary to an intelligent resolution of the question presented.

2. Because police lawfully may search the passenger compartment of the automobile, the Court reasoned, it followed "that the police may also examine the contents of any containers found within the passenger compartment, for if the passenger compartment is within reach of the arrestee, so also will containers in it be within his reach.... Such a container may, of course, be searched whether it is open or closed, since the justification for the search is not that the arrestee has no privacy interest in the container, but that the lawful custodial arrest justifies the infringement of any privacy interest the arrestee may have."

* * * *Belton* was demonstrably concerned only with the narrow but common circumstance of a search occasioned by the arrest of a suspect who was seated in or driving an automobile at the time the law enforcement official approached. Normally, after such an arrest has occurred, the officer's safety is no longer in jeopardy, but he must decide what, if any, search for incriminating evidence he should conduct. *Belton* provided previously unavailable and therefore necessary guidance for that category of cases.

The bright-line rule crafted in *Belton* is not needed for cases in which the arrestee is first accosted when he is a pedestrian, because *Chimel* itself provides all the guidance that is necessary. The only genuine justification for extending *Belton* to cover such circumstances is the interest in uncovering potentially valuable evidence. In my opinion, that goal must give way to the citizen's constitutionally protected interest in privacy when there is already in place a well-defined rule limiting the permissible scope of a search of an arrested pedestrian. The *Chimel* rule should provide the same protection to a "recent occupant" of a vehicle as to a recent occupant of a house.

Unwilling to confine the *Belton* rule to the narrow class of cases it was designed to address, the Court extends *Belton's* reach without supplying any guidance for the future application of its swollen rule. We are told that officers may search a vehicle incident to arrest "[s]o long as [the] arrestee is the sort of 'recent occupant' of a vehicle such as petitioner was here." But we are not told how recent is recent, or how close is close, perhaps because in this case "the record is not clear." As the Court cautioned in *Belton* itself, "[w]hen a person cannot know how a court will apply a settled principle to a recurring factual situation, that person cannot know the scope of his constitutional protection, nor can a policeman know the scope of his authority." Without some limiting principle, I fear that today's decision will contribute to "a massive broadening of the automobile exception" when officers have probable cause to arrest an individual but not to search his car. * * *

Notes and Questions

1. Does the Chief Justice make a good case for a "bright lines" approach to the problem? What then of the view of Rehnquist, J., dissenting in *Robbins v. California,* 453 U.S. 420 (1981), that "any search for 'bright lines' * * * is apt to be illusory" because lawyers are "trained to attack 'bright lines' the way hounds attack foxes"? If there are to be bright lines here, which is the brightest, the Rehnquist version or the Stevens version?

2. The majority in *Thornton* acknowledges that an arrestee's status as a "recent occupant" may "turn on his temporal or spatial relationship to the car at the time of the arrest and search." But, was the time of arrest and time of search in *Thornton* the same? If different, does the majority agree with Scalia as to which time is relevant? In any event, exactly what kind of "temporal or spatial relationship" should be required? Is any such "temporal or spatial relationship" limitation inconsistent with the bright-line justification in *Belton* and *Thornton*?

3. Could the search in *Thornton* have been upheld under *Carney*, p. 371? If so, is that relevant? Is that what Justice Scalia's new theory for *Belton* is all about, or is he proposing that vehicle searches for evidence be permitted incident to arrest absent *both* probable cause and any exigencies relating to evidence destruction or weapon acquisition by the arrestee? Do even the dissenters accept the latter notion in some circumstances? How can that position be distinguished from Scalia's analysis in *Arizona v. Hicks,* p. 358? Does *Rabinowitz* provide the basis for distinction, considering its treatment in *Chimel*?

COLORADO v. BERTINE

479 U.S. 367, 107 S.Ct. 738, 93 L.Ed.2d 739 (1987).

Chief Justice REHNQUIST delivered the opinion of the Court.

On February 10, 1984, a police officer in Boulder, Colorado arrested respondent Steven Lee Bertine for driving while under the influence of alcohol. After Bertine was taken into custody and before the arrival of a tow truck to take Bertine's van to an impoundment lot,[1] a backup officer inventoried the contents of the van. The officer opened a closed backpack in which he found controlled substances, cocaine paraphernalia, and a large amount of cash. Bertine was subsequently charged with driving while under the influence of alcohol, unlawful possession of cocaine with intent to dispense, sell, and distribute, and unlawful possession of methaqualone. We are asked to decide whether the Fourth Amendment prohibits the State from proving these charges with the evidence discovered during the inventory of Bertine's van[, as concluded by the Colorado Supreme Court]. The court recognized that in *South Dakota v. Opperman,* 428 U.S. 364 (1976), we had held inventory searches of automobiles to be consistent with the Fourth Amendment, and that in *Illinois v. Lafayette,* [p. 346], we had held that the inventory search of personal effects of an arrestee at a police station was also permissible under that Amendment. The Supreme Court of Colorado felt, however, that our decisions in *Arkansas v. Sanders,* [p. 378], and *United States v. Chadwick,* [p. 378], holding searches of closed trunks and suitcases to violate the Fourth Amendment, meant that *Opperman* and *Lafayette* did not govern this case.

[I]nventory searches are now a well-defined exception to the warrant requirement of the Fourth Amendment. The policies behind the warrant requirement are not implicated in an inventory search, nor is the related concept of probable cause:

> "The standard of probable cause is peculiarly related to criminal investigations, not routine, noncriminal procedures.... The probable-cause approach is unhelpful when analysis centers upon the reasonableness of routine administrative caretaking functions, particularly when no claim is made that the protective procedures are a subterfuge for criminal investigations."

For these reasons, the Colorado Supreme Court's reliance on *Arkansas v. Sanders* and *United States v. Chadwick* was incorrect. Both of these cases concerned searches solely for the purpose of investigating criminal conduct, with the validity of the searches therefore dependent on the application of the probable cause and warrant requirements of the Fourth Amendment.

By contrast, an inventory search may be "reasonable" under the Fourth Amendment even though it is not conducted pursuant to warrant based upon probable cause. In *Opperman,* this Court assessed the reasonableness of an inventory search of the glove compartment in an abandoned automobile impounded by the police. We found that inventory procedures serve to protect an owner's property while it is in the custody of the police, to insure against claims of lost, stolen, or vandalized property, and to guard the police from danger. In light of these strong governmental interests and the diminished expectation of privacy in

1. Section 7–7–2(a)(4) of the Boulder Revised Code authorizes police officers to impound vehicles when drivers are taken into custody. Section 7–7–2(a)(4) provides:

"A peace officer is authorized to remove or cause to be removed a vehicle from any street, parking lot, or driveway when:

. . .

(4) The driver of a vehicle is taken into custody by the police department." Boulder Rev.Code § 7–7–2(a)(4) (1981).

an automobile, we upheld the search. In reaching this decision, we observed that our cases accorded deference to police caretaking procedures designed to secure and protect vehicles and their contents within police custody.

In our more recent decision, *Lafayette,* a police officer conducted an inventory search of the contents of a shoulder bag in the possession of an individual being taken into custody. In deciding whether this search was reasonable, we recognized that the search served legitimate governmental interests similar to those identified in *Opperman.* We determined that those interests outweighed the individual's Fourth Amendment interests and upheld the search.

In the present case, as in *Opperman* and *Lafayette,* there was no showing that the police, who were following standardized procedures, acted in bad faith or for the sole purpose of investigation. In addition, the governmental interests justifying the inventory searches in *Opperman* and *Lafayette* are nearly the same as those which obtain here. In each case, the police were potentially responsible for the property taken into their custody. By securing the property, the police protected the property from unauthorized interference. Knowledge of the precise nature of the property helped guard against claims of theft, vandalism, or negligence. Such knowledge also helped to avert any danger to police or others that may have been posed by the property.[5]

The Supreme Court of Colorado opined that *Lafayette* was not controlling here because there was no danger of introducing contraband or weapons into a jail facility. Our opinion in *Lafayette,* however, did not suggest that the station-house setting of the inventory search was critical to our holding in that case. Both in the present case and in *Lafayette,* the common governmental interests described above were served by the inventory searches.

The Supreme Court of Colorado also expressed the view that the search in this case was unreasonable because Bertine's van was towed to a secure, lighted facility and because Bertine himself could have been offered the opportunity to make other arrangements for the safekeeping of his property. But the security of the storage facility does not completely eliminate the need for inventorying; the police may still wish to protect themselves or the owners of the lot against false claims of theft or dangerous instrumentalities. And while giving Bertine an opportunity to make alternate arrangements would undoubtedly have been possible, we said in *Lafayette:*

> "[t]he real question is not what 'could have been achieved,' but whether the Fourth Amendment *requires* such steps ... The reasonableness of any particular governmental activity does not necessarily or invariably turn on the existence of alternative 'less intrusive' means."

We conclude that here, as in *Lafayette,* reasonable police regulations relating to inventory procedures administered in good faith satisfy the Fourth Amendment, even though courts might as a matter of hindsight be able to devise equally reasonable rules requiring a different procedure.[6]

5. In arguing that the latter two interests are not implicated here, the dissent overlooks the testimony of the back-up officer who conducted the inventory of Bertine's van. According to the officer, the vehicle inventory procedures of the Boulder Police Department are designed for the "[p]rotection of the police department" in the event that an individual later claims that "there was something of value taken from within the vehicle." The officer added that inventories are also conducted in order to check "[f]or any dangerous items such as explosives [or] weapons." The officer testified that he had found such items in vehicles.

6. We emphasize that, in this case, the trial court found that the police department's procedures mandated the opening of closed containers and the listing of their contents. Our decisions have always adhered to the requirement that inventories be conducted according to standardized criteria.

By quoting a portion of the Colorado Supreme Court's decision out of context, the dis-

The Supreme Court of Colorado also thought it necessary to require that police, before inventorying a container, weigh the strength of the individual's privacy interest in the container against the possibility that the container might serve as a repository for dangerous or valuable items. We think that such a requirement is contrary to our decisions in *Opperman* and *Lafayette:*

> "Even if less intrusive means existed of protecting some particular types of property, it would be unreasonable to expect police officers in the everyday course of business to make fine and subtle distinctions in deciding which containers or items may be searched and which must be sealed as a unit." *Lafayette,* supra.

Bertine finally argues that the inventory search of his van was unconstitutional because departmental regulations gave the police officers discretion to choose between impounding his van and parking and locking it in a public parking place. The Supreme Court of Colorado did not rely on this argument in reaching its conclusion, and we reject it. Nothing in *Opperman* or *Lafayette* prohibits the exercise of police discretion so long as that discretion is exercised according to standard criteria and on the basis of something other than suspicion of evidence of criminal activity. Here, the discretion afforded the Boulder police was exercised in light of standardized criteria, related to the feasibility and appropriateness of parking and locking a vehicle rather than impounding it.[7] There was no showing that the police chose to impound Bertine's van in order to investigate suspected criminal activity. * * *

Reversed.

Justice BLACKMUN, with whom Justice POWELL and Justice O'CONNOR join, concurring. * * * I join the Court's opinion, but write separately to underscore [that] it is permissible for police officers to open closed containers in an inventory search only if they are following standard police procedures that mandate the opening of such containers in every impounded vehicle. * * *

Justice MARSHALL, with whom Justice BRENNAN joins, dissenting. * * *

As the Court acknowledges, inventory searches are reasonable only if conducted according to standardized procedures. In both *Opperman* and *Lafayette,* the Court relied on the absence of police discretion in determining that the inventory searches in question were reasonable. * * *

The Court today attempts to evade these clear prohibitions on unfettered police discretion by declaring that "the discretion afforded the Boulder police was exercised in light of standardized criteria, related to the feasibility and appropriateness of parking and locking a vehicle rather than impounding it." This vital assertion is flatly contradicted by the record in this case. The officer who conducted the inventory, Officer Reichenbach, testified at the suppression hearing that the decision not to "park and lock" respondent's vehicle was his "own

sent suggests that the inventory here was not authorized by the standard procedures of the Boulder Police Department. Yet that court specifically stated that the procedure followed here was "officially authorized." In addition, the court did not disturb the trial court's finding that the police procedures for impounding vehicles required a detailed inventory of Bertine's van.

7. In arguing that the Boulder Police Department procedures set forth no standardized criteria guiding an officer's decision to impound a vehicle, the dissent selectively quotes from the police directive concerning the care and security of vehicles taken into police custody. The dissent fails to mention that the directive establishes several conditions that must be met before an officer may pursue the park and lock alternative. For example, police may not park and lock the vehicle where there is reasonable risk of damage or vandalism to the vehicle or where the approval of the arrestee cannot be obtained. Not only do such conditions circumscribe the discretion of individual officers, but they also protect the vehicle and its contents and minimize claims of property loss.

individual discretionary decision." Indeed, application of these supposedly standardized "criteria" upon which the Court so heavily relies would have yielded a different result in this case. Since there was ample public parking adjacent to the intersection where respondent was stopped, consideration of "feasibility" would certainly have militated in favor of the "park and lock" option, not against it. I do not comprehend how consideration of "appropriateness" serves to channel a field officer's discretion; nonetheless, the "park and lock" option would seem particularly appropriate in this case, where respondent was stopped for a traffic offense and was not likely to be in custody for a significant length of time.

Indeed, the record indicates that *no* standardized criteria limit a Boulder police officer's discretion. According to a departmental directive,[1] after placing a driver under arrest, an officer has three options for disposing of the vehicle. First, he can allow a third party to take custody. Second, the officer or the driver (depending on the nature of the arrest) may take the car to the nearest public parking facility, lock it, and take the keys.[3] Finally, the officer can do what was done in this case: impound the vehicle, and search and inventory its contents, including closed containers.[4]

Under the first option, the police have no occasion to search the automobile. Under the "park and lock" option, "[c]losed containers that give no indication of containing either valuables or a weapon *may not be opened and the contents searched* (i.e., inventoried)." Only if the police choose the third option are they entitled to search closed containers in the vehicle. Where the vehicle is not itself evidence of a crime, as in this case, the police apparently have totally unbridled discretion as to which procedure to use. Consistent with this conclusion, Officer Reichenbach testified that such decisions were left to the discretion of the officer on the scene.

Once a Boulder police officer has made this initial completely discretionary decision to impound a vehicle, he is given little guidance as to which areas to search and what sort of items to inventory. The arresting officer, Officer Toporek,

1. Subsections 7–7–2(a)(1) and 7–7–2(a)(4) of the Boulder Revised Code authorize police to impound a vehicle if the driver is taken into custody or if the vehicle obstructs traffic. A departmental directive authorizes inventory searches of impounded vehicles. See General Procedure issued from the office of the Chief of Police, Boulder Police Department, concerning Motor Vehicle Impounds, effective September 7, 1977.

3. If the vehicle and its contents are not evidence of a crime and the owner consents, § III of the General Procedure provides, in relevant part:

"A. Upon placing the operator of a motor vehicle in custody, Officers *may* take the following steps in securing the arrestee's vehicle and property . . .:

. . .

"4. The Officer shall drive the vehicle off the roadway and legally park the vehicle in the nearest PUBLIC parking area. The date, time, and location where the vehicle is parked shall be indicated on the IMPOUND FORM.

"5. The Officer shall remove the ignition keys, and lock all doors of the vehicle.

"6. During the booking process, the arrestee shall be given a continuation form for his signature which indicates the location of his vehicle. One copy of the continuation form is to be retained in the case file." (emphasis added).

4. Section II(A) of the General Procedure establishes the following impoundment procedures:

"1. If the vehicle or its contents have been used in the commission of a crime or are themselves the fruit of a crime, the Officer shall conduct a detailed vehicle inspection and inventory and record it upon the VEHICLE IMPOUND FORM.

"2. Personal items of value should be removed from the vehicle and subsequently placed into Property for safekeeping.

"3. The Officer shall request a Tow Truck, and upon its arrival have the Tow Truck operatory sign the IMPOUND FORM, keeping one copy in his possession, before the Officer releases the vehicle for impoundment in the City of Boulder impoundment facility."

Subsection (B) of the directive provides that this procedure is also to be followed when a vehicle involved in a traffic accident is to be held for evidentiary purposes.

testified at the suppression hearing as to what items would be inventoried: "That would I think be very individualistic as far as what an officer may or may not go into. I think whatever arouses his suspicious [*sic*] as far as what may be contained in any type of article in the car." In application, these so-called procedures left the breadth of the "inventory" to the whim of the individual officer. Clearly, "[t]he practical effect of this system is to leave the [owner] subject to the discretion of the official in the field." * * *

In *South Dakota v. Opperman,* and *Illinois v. Lafayette,* both of which involved inventories conducted pursuant to standardized procedures, we balanced the individual's expectation of privacy against the government's interests to determine whether the search was reasonable. Even if the search in this case did constitute a legitimate inventory, it would nonetheless be unreasonable under this analysis.

The Court greatly overstates the justifications for the inventory exception to the Fourth Amendment. Chief Justice Burger, writing for a plurality in *Opperman,* relied on three governmental interests to justify the inventory search of an unlocked glove compartment in an automobile impounded for overtime parking: (i) "the protection of the owner's property while it remains in police custody"; (ii) "the protection of the police against claims or disputes over lost or stolen property"; and (iii) "the protection of the police from potential danger." The majority finds that "nearly the same" interests obtain in this case. As Justice Powell's concurring opinion in *Opperman* reveals, however, only the first of these interests is actually served by an automobile inventory search.

The protection-against-claims interest did not justify the inventory search either in *Opperman* or in this case. As the majority apparently concedes, the use of secure impoundment facilities effectively eliminates this concern.[6] As to false claims, "inventories are [not] a completely effective means of discouraging false claims, since there remains the possibility of accompanying such claims with an assertion that an item was stolen prior to the inventory or was intentionally omitted from the police records." * * *

The third interest—protecting the police from potential danger—failed to receive the endorsement of a majority of the Court in *Opperman.* After noting that "there is little danger associated with impounding unsearched vehicles," Justice Powell recognized that "there does not appear to be any effective way of identifying in advance those circumstances or classes of automobile impoundments which represent a greater risk." As with the charge of overtime parking in *Opperman,* there is nothing in the nature of the offense for which respondent was arrested that suggests he was likely to be carrying weapons, explosives, or other dangerous items.

Thus, only the government's interest in protecting the owner's property actually justifies an inventory search of an impounded vehicle. While I continue to believe that preservation of property does not outweigh the privacy and security interests protected by the Fourth Amendment, I fail to see how preservation can even be asserted as a justification for the search in this case. In *Opperman,* the owner of the impounded car was not available to safeguard his possessions, and it could plausibly be argued that, in his absence, the police were entitled to act for his presumed benefit. When the police conducted the inventory in *Opperman,* they could not predict how long the car would be left in their possession. In this case, however, the owner was "present to make other arrangements for the safekeeping of his belongings," yet the police made no attempt to ascertain whether in fact he

6. The impoundment lot in *South Dakota v. Opperman* was "the old county highway yard. It ha[d] a wooden fence partially around part of it, and kind of a dilapidated wire fence, a makeshift fence."

wanted them to "safeguard" his property. Furthermore, since respondent was charged with a traffic offense, he was unlikely to remain in custody for more than a few hours. He might well have been willing to leave his valuables unattended in the locked van for such a short period of time.

Thus, the government's interests in this case are weaker than in *Opperman,* but the search here is much more intrusive. *Opperman* did not involve a search of closed containers or other items that " 'touch upon intimate areas of an individual's personal affairs' "; nor can the Court's opinion be read to authorize the inspection of "containers which might themselves be sealed, removed and secured without further intrusion." To expand the *Opperman* rationale to include containers in which the owner clearly has a reasonable expectation of privacy, the Court relies on *Illinois v. Lafayette.* Such reliance is fundamentally misplaced, however; the inventory in *Lafayette* was justified by considerations which are totally absent in this context.

In *Lafayette,* we upheld a station house inventory search of an arrestee's shoulder bag. Notwithstanding the Court's assertions to the contrary, the inventory in that case *was* justified primarily by compelling governmental interests unique to the station house, preincarceration context. There is a powerful interest in preventing the introduction of contraband or weapons into a jail.

Notes and Questions

1. A narrower view is taken in some jurisdictions. For example, the South Dakota Supreme Court held on remand in *Opperman* that the inventory search violated the search and seizure guarantee of the South Dakota Constitution, the language of which "is almost identical to that found in the Fourth Amendment." *State v. Opperman,* 247 N.W.2d 673 (S.D.1976). Under the state constitutional provision, warrantless inventory searches of automobiles "must be restricted to safeguarding those articles which are within plain view of the officer's vision."

2. Consider the dissent of Ely, J., in *United States v. Mitchell,* 458 F.2d 960 (9th Cir.1972), suggesting that an "effective compromise" would be "to permit extensive inventory searches of seized vehicles, so as fully to protect the police, but to forbid, over the objection of one having standing, the use of any item seized in the search as evidence against the objector."

3. Evidence found in an otherwise lawful inventory must be suppressed if the prior impoundment of the vehicle was not justified. See, e.g., *Dyke v. Taylor Implement Mfg. Co.,* 391 U.S. 216 (1968) (search of car outside courthouse while driver, arrested for reckless driving, inside to post bond was improper, as "there is no indication that the police had purported to impound or to hold the car [or] that they were authorized by any state law to do so"); *State v. Simpson,* 622 P.2d 1199 (Wash.1980) (where defendant arrested at home, impoundment of his truck lawfully parked in front of house illegal).

4. In *Florida v. Wells,* 495 U.S. 1 (1990), all members of the Court agreed that the inventory of a locked suitcase found in an impounded vehicle was unlawful under *Bertine* because "the Florida Highway Patrol had no policy whatever with respect to the opening of closed containers encountered during an inventory search." The Chief Justice, for five members of the Court, went on to say that the state court erred in saying *Bertine* requires a policy either mandating or barring inventory of all containers:

"But in forbidding uncanalized discretion to police officers conducting inventory searches, there is no reason to insist that they be conducted in a totally mechanical 'all or nothing' fashion. * * * A police officer may be allowed sufficient latitude to determine whether a particular container should or should not be opened in light of the nature of the search and characteristics of the container itself. Thus, while policies of opening all containers or of opening no containers are unquestionably permissible, it would be equally permissible, for example, to allow the opening of closed containers whose contents officers determine they are unable to ascertain from examining the containers' exteriors. The allowance of the exercise of judgment based on concerns related to the purposes of an inventory search does not violate the Fourth Amendment."

Brennan and Marshall, JJ., concurring, declined to join the majority opinion because, in "pure dictum given the disposition of the case," it "goes on to suggest that a State may adopt an inventory policy that vests individual police officers with *some* discretion to decide whether to open such containers." Blackmun, J., concurring, agreed that the Fourth Amendment did not impose an "all or nothing" requirement, so that a state "probably could adopt a policy which requires the opening of all containers that are not locked, or a policy which requires the opening of all containers over or under a certain size, even though these policies do not call for the opening of all or no containers," but objected it was "an entirely different matter, however, to say, as this majority does, that an individual policeman may be afforded discretion in conducting an inventory search." Stevens, J., concurring separately, agreed with the Blackmun opinion.

5. If the inventory cannot be upheld when the department has no policy (as in *Wells*) or when the only standard practice identified is that of the individual officer (as in *United States v. Kordosky,* 909 F.2d 219 (7th Cir.1990)), then what if (unlike *Bertine*) the purported department policy followed was not in writing but was merely testified to by the inventorying officer? Most courts, e.g., *United States v. Ford,* 986 F.2d 57 (4th Cir.1993), have held that is sufficient, but this result has been questioned: "A primary concern, of course, is the possibility of undetected arbitrariness, a risk which takes on much greater proportions when the supposed 'standardized procedures' are established only by the self-serving and perhaps inaccurate oral statements of a police officer, and are not memorialized in the department's previous written instructions to its officers. Another * * * is that what is represented as department policy may constitute nothing more than a custom, hardly deserving the deference which an actual policy receives." Wayne R. LaFave, *Controlling Discretion by Administrative Regulations: The Use, Misuse, and Nonuse of Police Rules and Policies in Fourth Amendment Adjudication,* 89 Mich.L.Rev. 442, 456–57 (1990).

6. *Ex parte Boyd,* 542 So.2d 1276 (Ala.1989), held a vehicle inventory invalid where there was a four-day lapse of time between the impoundment and the inventory, reasoning that the "justifications for the intrusion—protecting the owner's property, protecting the police from false claims or disputes, and protecting the police from danger—are simply not served, however, when the inventory is inexcusably postponed; in that circumstance, the inventory becomes unreasonable."

SECTION 8. STOP AND FRISK

TERRY v. OHIO

392 U.S. 1, 88 S.Ct. 1868, 20 L.Ed.2d 889 (1968).

Chief Justice WARREN delivered the opinion of the court.

[Officer McFadden, a Cleveland plainclothes detective, became suspicious of two men standing on a street corner in the downtown area at about 2:30 in the afternoon. One of the suspects walked up the street, peered into a store, walked on, started back, looked into the same store, and then joined and conferred with his companion. The other suspect repeated this ritual, and between them the two men went through this performance about a dozen times. They also talked with a third man, and then followed him up the street about ten minutes after his departure. The officer, thinking that the suspects were "casing" a stickup and might be armed, followed and confronted the three men as they were again conversing. He identified himself and asked the suspects for their names. The men only mumbled something, and the officer spun Terry around and patted his breast pocket. He felt a pistol, which he removed. A frisk of Terry's companion also uncovered a pistol; a frisk of the third man did not disclose that he was armed, and he was not searched further. Terry was charged with carrying a concealed weapon, and he moved to suppress the weapon as evidence. The motion was denied by the trial judge, who upheld the officer's actions on a stop-and-frisk theory. The Ohio court of appeals affirmed, and the state supreme court dismissed Terry's appeal.]

* * * The question is whether in all the circumstances of this on-the-street encounter, [Terry's] right to personal security was violated by an unreasonable search and seizure.

We would be less than candid if we did not acknowledge that this question thrusts to the fore difficult and troublesome issues regarding a sensitive area of police activity—issues which have never before been squarely presented to this Court. * * *

On the one hand, it is frequently argued that in dealing with the rapidly unfolding and often dangerous situations on city streets the police are in need of an escalating set of flexible responses, graduated in relation to the amount of information they possess. For this purpose it is urged that distinctions should be made between a "stop" and an "arrest" (or a "seizure" of a person), and between a "frisk" and a "search." Thus, it is argued, the police should be allowed to "stop" a person and detain him briefly for questioning upon suspicion that he may be connected with criminal activity. Upon suspicion that the person may be armed, the police should have the power to "frisk" him for weapons. If the "stop" and the "frisk" give rise to probable cause to believe that the suspect has committed a crime, then the police should be empowered to make a formal "arrest," and a full incident "search" of the person. This scheme is justified in part upon the notion that a "stop" and a "frisk" amount to a mere "minor inconvenience and petty indignity," which can properly be imposed upon the citizen in the interest of effective law enforcement on the basis of a police officer's suspicion.

On the other side the argument is made that the authority of the police must be strictly circumscribed by the law of arrest and search as it has developed to date in the traditional jurisprudence of the Fourth Amendment. It is contended with some force that there is not—and cannot be—a variety of police activity which does not depend solely upon the voluntary cooperation of the citizen and yet which stops short of an arrest based upon probable cause to make such an arrest. The heart of the Fourth Amendment, the argument runs, is a severe requirement of specific justification for any intrusion upon protected personal security, coupled with a highly developed system of judicial controls to enforce upon the agents of the State the commands of the Constitution. * * *

* * * The State has characterized the issue here as "the right of a police officer * * * to make an on-the-street stop, interrogate and pat down for weapons (known in the street vernacular as 'stop and frisk')." But this is only partly accurate. For the issue is not the abstract propriety of the police conduct, but the admissibility against petitioner of the evidence uncovered by the search and seizure. * * * [I]n our system evidentiary rulings provide the context in which the

judicial process of inclusion and exclusion approves some conduct as comporting with constitutional guarantees and disapproves other actions by state agents. A ruling admitting evidence in a criminal trial, we recognize, has the necessary effect of legitimizing the conduct which produced the evidence, while an application of the exclusionary rule withholds the constitutional imprimatur.

The exclusionary rule has its limitations, however, as a tool of judicial control. It cannot properly be invoked to exclude the products of legitimate police investigative techniques on the ground that much conduct which is closely similar involves unwarranted intrusions upon constitutional protections. Moreover, in some contexts the rule is ineffective as a deterrent. Street encounters between citizens and police officers are incredibly rich in diversity. They range from wholly friendly exchanges of pleasantries or mutually useful information to hostile confrontations of armed men involving arrests, or injuries, or loss of life. Moreover, hostile confrontations are not all of a piece. Some of them begin in a friendly enough manner, only to take a different turn upon the injection of some unexpected element into the conversation. Encounters are initiated by the police for a wide variety of purposes, some of which are wholly unrelated to a desire to prosecute for crime. Doubtless some police "field interrogation" conduct violates the Fourth Amendment. But a stern refusal by this Court to condone such activity does not necessarily render it responsive to the exclusionary rule. Regardless of how effective the rule may be where obtaining convictions is an important objective of the police, it is powerless to deter invasions of constitutionally guaranteed rights where the police either have no interest in prosecuting or are willing to forego successful prosecution in the interest of serving some other goal.

Proper adjudication of cases in which the exclusionary rule is invoked demands a constant awareness of these limitations. The wholesale harassment by certain elements of the police community, of which minority groups, particularly Negroes, frequently complain, will not be stopped by the exclusion of any evidence from any criminal trial. Yet a rigid and unthinking application of the exclusionary rule, in futile protest against practices which it can never be used effectively to control, may exact a high toll in human injury and frustration of efforts to prevent crime. No judicial opinion can comprehend the protean variety of the street encounter, and we can only judge the facts of the case before us. * * *

[W]e turn our attention to the quite narrow question posed by the facts before us: whether it is always unreasonable for a policeman to seize a person and subject him to a limited search for weapons unless there is probable cause for an arrest.

* * * It is quite plain that the Fourth Amendment governs "seizures" of the person which do not eventuate in a trip to the station house and prosecution for crime—"arrests" in traditional terminology. It must be recognized that whenever a police officer accosts an individual and restrains his freedom to walk away, he has "seized" that person. And it is nothing less than sheer torture of the English language to suggest that a careful exploration of the outer surfaces of a person's clothing all over his or her body in an attempt to find weapons is not a "search." Moreover, it is simply fantastic to urge that such a procedure performed in public by a policeman while the citizen stands helpless, perhaps facing a wall with his hands raised, is a "petty indignity."[13] It is a serious intrusion upon the sanctity of the person, which may inflict great indignity and arouse strong resentment, and it is not to be undertaken lightly.

13. Consider the following apt description: "[T]he officer must feel with sensitive fingers every portion of the prisoner's body. A thorough search must be made of the prisoner's arms and armpits, waistline and back, the groin and area about the testicles, and entire surface of the legs down to the feet." Priar & Martin, *Searching and Disarming Criminals,* 45 J.Crim.L.C. & P.S. 481 (1954).

* * * We therefore reject the notions that the Fourth Amendment does not come into play at all as a limitation upon police conduct if the officers stop short of something called a "technical arrest" or a "full-blown search."

In this case there can be no question, then, that Officer McFadden "seized" petitioner and subjected him to a "search" when he took hold of him and patted down the outer surfaces of his clothing. We must decide whether at that point it was reasonable for Officer McFadden to have interfered with petitioner's personal security as he did.[16] And in determining whether the seizure and search were "unreasonable" our inquiry is a dual one—whether the officer's action was justified at its inception, and whether it was reasonably related in scope to the circumstances which justified the interference in the first place.

If this case involved police conduct subject to the Warrant Clause of the Fourth Amendment, we would have to ascertain whether "probable cause" existed to justify the search and seizure which took place. However, that is not the case. We do not retreat from our holdings that the police must, whenever practicable, obtain advance judicial approval of searches and seizures through the warrant procedure, * * * or that in most instances failure to comply with the warrant requirement can only be excused by exigent circumstances. * * * But we deal here with an entire rubric of police conduct—necessarily swift action predicated upon the on-the-spot observations of the officer on the beat—which historically has not been, and as a practical matter could not be, subjected to the warrant procedure. Instead, the conduct involved in this case must be tested by the Fourth Amendment's general proscription against unreasonable searches and seizures.

Nonetheless, the notions which underlie both the warrant procedure and the requirement of probable cause remain fully relevant in this context. In order to assess the reasonableness of Officer McFadden's conduct as a general proposition, it is necessary "first to focus upon the governmental interest which allegedly justifies official intrusion upon the constitutionally protected interests of the private citizen," for there is "no ready test for determining reasonableness other than by balancing the need to search [or seize] against the invasion which the search [or seizure] entails." *Camara v. Municipal Court* [p. 440]. And in justifying the particular intrusion the police officer must be able to point to specific and articulable facts which, taken together with rational inferences from those facts, reasonably warrant that intrusion. The scheme of the Fourth Amendment becomes meaningful only when it is assured that at some point the conduct of those charged with enforcing the laws can be subjected to the more detached, neutral scrutiny of a judge who must evaluate the reasonableness of a particular search or seizure in light of the particular circumstances. And in making that assessment it is imperative that the facts be judged against an objective standard: would the facts available to the officer at the moment of the seizure or the search "warrant a man of reasonable caution in the belief" that the action taken was appropriate? * * * Anything less would invite intrusions upon constitutionally guaranteed rights based on nothing more substantial than inarticulate hunches, a result this Court has consistently refused to sanction. * * *

16. We thus decide nothing today concerning the constitutional propriety of an investigative "seizure" upon less than probable cause for purposes of "detention" and/or interrogation. Obviously, not all personal intercourse between policemen and citizens involves "seizures" of persons. Only when the officer, by means of physical force or show of authority, has in some way restrained the liberty of a citizen may we conclude that a "seizure" has occurred. We cannot tell with any certainty upon this record whether any such "seizure" took place here prior to Officer McFadden's initiation of physical contact for purposes of searching Terry for weapons, and we thus may assume that up to that point no intrusion upon constitutionally protected rights had occurred.

Applying these principles to this case, we consider first the nature and extent of the governmental interests involved. One general interest is of course that of effective crime prevention and detection; it is this interest which underlies the recognition that a police officer may in appropriate circumstances and in an appropriate manner approach a person for purposes of investigating possibly criminal behavior even though there is no probable cause to make an arrest. It was this legitimate investigative function Officer McFadden was discharging when he decided to approach petitioner and his companions. He had observed Terry, Chilton, and Katz go through a series of acts, each of them perhaps innocent in itself, but which taken together warranted further investigation. There is nothing unusual in two men standing together on a street corner, perhaps waiting for someone. Nor is there anything suspicious about people in such circumstances strolling up and down the street, singly or in pairs. Store windows, moreover, are made to be looked in. But the story is quite different where, as here, two men hover about a street corner for an extended period of time, at the end of which it becomes apparent that they are not waiting for anyone or anything; where these men pace alternately along an identical route, pausing to stare in the same store window roughly 24 times; where each completion of this route is followed immediately by a conference between the two men on the corner; where they are joined in one of these conferences by a third man who leaves swiftly; and where the two men finally follow the third and rejoin him a couple of blocks away. It would have been poor police work indeed for an officer of 30 years' experience in the detection of thievery from stores in this same neighborhood to have failed to investigate this behavior further.

The crux of this case, however, is not the propriety of Officer McFadden's taking steps to investigate petitioner's suspicious behavior, but rather, whether there was justification for McFadden's invasion of Terry's personal security by searching him for weapons in the course of that investigation. We are now concerned with more than the governmental interest in investigating crime; in addition, there is the more immediate interest of the police officer in taking steps to assure himself that the person with whom he is dealing is not armed with a weapon that could unexpectedly and fatally be used against him. Certainly it would be unreasonable to require that police officers take unnecessary risks in the performance of their duties. American criminals have a long tradition of armed violence, and every year in this country many law enforcement officers are killed in the line of duty, and thousands more are wounded. Virtually all of these deaths and a substantial portion of the injuries are inflicted with guns and knives.

In view of these facts, we cannot blind ourselves to the need for law enforcement officers to protect themselves and other prospective victims of violence in situations where they may lack probable cause for an arrest. When an officer is justified in believing that the individual whose suspicious behavior he is investigating at close range is armed and presently dangerous to the officer or to others, it would appear to be clearly unreasonable to deny the officer the power to take necessary measures to determine whether the person is in fact carrying a weapon and to neutralize the threat of physical harm. * * *

Petitioner * * * does not say that an officer is always unjustified in searching a suspect to discover weapons. Rather, he says it is unreasonable for the policeman to take that step until such time as the situation evolves to a point where there is probable cause to make an arrest. * * *

There are two weaknesses in this line of reasoning however. First, it fails to take account of traditional limitations upon the scope of searches, and thus recognizes no distinction in purpose, character, and extent between a search incident to an arrest and a limited search for weapons. The former, although justified in part by the acknowledged necessity to protect the arresting officer from assault with a concealed weapon, is also justified on other grounds, and can therefore involve a relatively extensive exploration of the person. A search for weapons in the absence of probable cause to arrest, however, must, like any other search, be strictly circumscribed by the exigencies which justify its initiation. Thus it must be limited to that which is necessary for the discovery of weapons which might be used to harm the officer or others nearby, and may realistically be characterized as something less than a "full" search, even though it remains a serious intrusion.

A second, and related, objection to petitioner's argument is that it assumes that the law of arrest has already worked out the balance between the particular interests involved here—the neutralization of danger to the policeman in the investigative circumstance and the sanctity of the individual. But this is not so. An arrest is a wholly different kind of intrusion upon individual freedom from a limited search for weapons, and the interests each is designed to serve are likewise quite different. An arrest is the initial stage of a criminal prosecution. It is intended to vindicate society's interest in having its laws obeyed, and it is inevitably accompanied by future interference with the individual's freedom of movement, whether or not trial or conviction ultimately follows. The protective search for weapons, on the other hand, constitutes a brief, though far from inconsiderable intrusion upon the sanctity of the person. It does not follow that because an officer may lawfully arrest a person only when he is apprised of facts sufficient to warrant a belief that the person has committed or is committing a crime, the officer is equally unjustified, absent that kind of evidence, in making any intrusions short of an arrest. Moreover, a perfectly reasonable apprehension of danger may arise long before the officer is possessed of adequate information to justify taking a person into custody for the purpose of prosecuting him for a crime. * * *

Our evaluation of the proper balance that has to be struck in this type of case leads us to conclude that there must be a narrowly drawn authority to permit a reasonable search for weapons for the protection of the police officer, where he has reason to believe that he is dealing with an armed and dangerous individual, regardless of whether he has probable cause to arrest the individual for a crime. The officer need not be absolutely certain that the individual is armed; the issue is whether a reasonably prudent man in the circumstances would be warranted in the belief that his safety or that of others was in danger. * * * And in determining whether the officer acted reasonably in such circumstances, due weight must be given, not to his inchoate and unparticularized suspicion or "hunch", but to the specific reasonable inferences which he is entitled to draw from the facts in light of his experience.

We must now examine the conduct of Officer McFadden in this case to determine whether his search and seizure of petitioner were reasonable, both at their inception and as conducted. He had observed Terry, together with Chilton and another man, acting in a manner he took to be preface to a "stick-up." We think on the facts and circumstances Officer McFadden detailed before the trial judge a reasonably prudent man would have been warranted in believing petitioner was armed and thus presented a threat to the officer's safety while he was investigating his suspicious behavior. The actions of Terry and Chilton were consistent with McFadden's hypothesis that these men were contemplating a daylight robbery—which, it is reasonable to assume, would be likely to involve the use of weapons—and nothing in their conduct from the time he first noticed them until the time he confronted them and identified himself as a police officer gave him sufficient reason to negate that hypothesis. Although the trio had departed the original scene, there was nothing to indicate abandonment of an intent to commit a robbery at some point. Thus, when Officer McFadden approached the three men gathered before the display window at Zucker's store he had observed enough to make it quite reasonable to fear that they were armed; and nothing in their response to his hailing them, identifying himself as a police officer, and asking their names served to dispel that reasonable belief. We cannot say his decision at that point to seize Terry and pat his clothing for weapons was the product of a volatile or inventive imagination, or was undertaken simply as an act of harassment; the record evidences the tempered act of a policeman who in the course of an investigation had to make a quick decision as to how to protect himself and others from possible danger, and took limited steps to do so.

The manner in which the seizure and search were conducted is, of course, as vital a part of the inquiry as whether they were warranted at all. The Fourth Amendment proceeds as much by limitations upon the scope of governmental action as by imposing preconditions upon its initiation. The entire deterrent purpose of the rule excluding evidence seized in violation of the Fourth Amendment rests on the assumption that "limitations upon the fruit to be gathered tend to limit the quest itself." * * * Thus, evidence may not be introduced if it was discovered by means of a seizure and search which were not reasonably related in scope to the justification for their initiation.

[A protective search for weapons,] unlike a search without a warrant incident to a lawful arrest, is not justified by any need to prevent the disappearance or destruction of evidence of crime. The sole justification of the search in the present situation is the protection of the police officer and others nearby, and it must therefore be confined in scope to an intrusion reasonably designed to discover guns, knives, clubs, or other hidden instruments for the assault of the police officer.

The scope of the search in this case presents no serious problem in light of these standards. Officer McFadden patted down the outer clothing of petitioner and his two companions. He did not place his hands in their pockets or under the outer surface of their garments until he had felt weapons, and then he merely reached for and removed the guns. He never did invade Katz's person beyond the outer surfaces of his clothes, since he discovered nothing in his pat down which might have been a weapon. Officer McFadden confined his search strictly to what was minimally necessary to learn whether the men were armed and to disarm them once he discovered the weapons. He did not conduct a general exploratory search for whatever evidence of criminal activity he might find.

We conclude that the revolver seized from Terry was properly admitted in evidence against him. At the time he seized petitioner and searched him for weapons, Officer McFadden had reasonable grounds to believe that petitioner was armed and dangerous, and it was necessary for the protection of himself and others to take swift measures to discover the true facts and neutralize the threat of harm if it materialized. The policeman carefully restricted his search to what was appropriate to the discovery of the particular items which he sought. Each case of this sort will, of course, have to be decided on its own facts. We merely hold today that where a police officer observes unusual conduct which leads him reasonably to conclude in light of his experience that criminal activity may be afoot and that the persons with whom he is dealing may be armed and presently dangerous; where in the course of investigating this behavior he identifies himself as a policeman and makes reasonable inquiries; and where nothing in the initial stages of the encounter serves to dispel his reasonable fear for his own or others' safety, he is entitled for the protection of himself and others in the area to conduct a carefully limited search of the outer clothing of such persons in an attempt to discover weapons which might be used to assault him. Such a search is a reasonable search under the Fourth Amendment, and any weapons seized may properly be introduced in evidence against the person from whom they were taken.

Affirmed.

Justice HARLAN, concurring.

* * * The holding has * * * two logical corollaries that I do not think the Court has fully expressed.

In the first place, if the frisk is justified in order to protect the officer during an encounter with a citizen, the officer must first have constitutional grounds to insist on an encounter, to make a *forcible* stop. Any person, including a policeman, is at liberty to avoid a person he considers dangerous. If and when a policeman has a right instead to disarm such a person for his own protection, he must first have a right not to avoid him but to be in his presence. That right must be more than the liberty (again, possessed by every citizen) to address questions to other persons, for ordinarily the person addressed has an equal right to ignore his interrogator and walk away; he certainly need not submit to a frisk for the questioner's protection. I would make it perfectly clear that the right to frisk in this case depends upon the reasonableness of a forcible stop to investigate a suspected crime.

Where such a stop is reasonable, however, the right to frisk must be immediate and automatic if the reason for the stop is, as here, an articulable suspicion of a crime of violence. Just as a full search incident to a lawful arrest requires no additional justification, a limited frisk incident to a lawful stop must often be rapid and routine. There is no reason why an officer, rightfully but forcibly confronting a person suspected of a serious crime, should have to ask one question and take the risk that the answer might be a bullet. * * *

Justice WHITE, concurring.

* * * I think an additional word is in order concerning the matter of interrogation during an investigative stop. There is nothing in the Constitution which prevents a policeman from addressing questions to anyone on the streets. Absent special circumstances, the person approached may not be detained or frisked but may refuse to cooperate and go on his way. However, given the proper circumstances, such as those in this case, it seems to me the person may be briefly detained against his will while pertinent questions are directed to him. Of course, the person stopped is not obliged to answer, answers may not be compelled, and refusal to answer furnishes no basis for an arrest, although it may alert the officer to the need for continued observation. * * *

Justice DOUGLAS, dissenting.

* * * Had a warrant been sought, a magistrate would * * * have been unauthorized to issue one, for he can act only if there is a showing of "probable cause." We hold today that the police have greater authority to make a "seizure" and conduct a "search" than a judge has to authorize such action. We have said precisely the opposite over and over again. * * *

THE SIGNIFICANCE OF THE STOP-AND-FRISK CASES[a]

A. The Utility of the Balancing Test

1. What qualifies a particular police practice for assessment under the *Terry* balancing test?[b] In *Michigan v. Summers,* p. 313, Stewart, J., joined by Brennan and Marshall, JJ., dissenting, objected to the majority's use of the balancing test in holding that a warrant to search premises for contraband authorizes police to detain the occupants while the warrant is executed. They reasoned "that before a court can uphold a detention on less than probable cause on the ground that it is 'reasonable' in the light of the competing interests, the government must demonstrate an important purpose beyond the normal goals of criminal investigation,[c] or must demonstrate an extraordinary obstacle to such investigation," which they believed had not been done in the instant case.

2. Should the balancing test also be used to keep the evidentiary requirements for a given police practice "flexible," so that, for example, less evidence would be required when the crime being investigated is a serious one? Consider Justice Jackson, dissenting in *Brinegar v. United States,* 338 U.S. 160 (1949): "If we assume, for example, that a child is kidnapped and the officers throw a roadblock about the neighborhood and search every outgoing car, it would be a drastic and undiscriminating use of the search. The officers might be unable to show probable cause for searching any particular car. However, I should candidly strive hard to sustain such an action, executed fairly and in good faith, because it might be reasonable to subject travelers to that indignity if it was the only way to save a threatened life[d] and detect a vicious crime. But I should not strain to sustain such a roadblock and universal search to salvage a few bottles of bourbon and catch a bootlegger."[e]

B. Police Action Short of a Seizure

1. FLORIDA v. BOSTICK, 501 U.S. 429 (1991), involved these facts, as stated by the state supreme court: "Two officers, complete with badges, insignia and one of them holding a recognizable zipper pouch, containing a pistol, boarded a bus bound from Miami to Atlanta during a stopover in Fort Lauderdale. Eyeing the passengers, the officers admittedly without articulable suspicion, picked out the defendant passenger and asked to inspect his ticket and identification. The ticket, from Miami to Atlanta, matched the defendant's identification and both

a. For an exhaustive assessment of *Terry* by over 30 analysts, reflecting an interesting variety of viewpoints, see Symposium, *Terry v. Ohio 30 Years Later*, 72 St.John's L.Rev. 721–1524 (1998). Especially intriguing is John Q. Barrett, *Deciding the Stop and Frisk Cases: A Look Inside the Supreme Court's Conference*, id. at 749, which uses the available papers of former Justices to illuminate the role of individual members of the Court in resolving these cases.

b. See Scott E. Sundby, *A Return to Fourth Amendment Basics: Undoing the Mischief of Camara and Terry,* 72 Minn.L.Rev. 383 (1988).

c. See § 9 of this Chapter.

d. How great a departure from traditional probable cause would be permissible to save *thousands* of lives? See Ronald M. Gould & Simon Stern, *Catastrophic Threats and the Fourth Amendment,* 77 S.Cal.L.Rev. 777 (2004), inquiring on what Fourth Amendment theory a search of 100 separate homes could be justified on reliable information that a suitcase-sized atomic bomb had been smuggled into that part of a major city.

e. Compare *Dunaway v. New York,* p. 438.

On the use of roadblocks, consider *Model Pre-Arraignment Code* § 110.2, providing in part:

"(2) *Stopping of Vehicles at Roadblock.* A law enforcement officer may, if

"(a) he has reasonable cause to believe that a felony has been committed; and

"(b) stopping all or most vehicles moving in a particular direction or directions is reasonably necessary to permit a search for the perpetrator or victim of such felony in view of the seriousness and special circumstances of such felony, order the drivers of such vehicles to stop, and may search such vehicles to the extent necessary to accomplish such purpose. Such action shall be accomplished as promptly as possible under the circumstances."

were immediately returned to him as unremarkable. However, the two police officers persisted and explained their presence as narcotics agents on the lookout for illegal drugs. In pursuit of that aim, they then requested the defendant's consent to search his luggage. Needless to say, there is a conflict in the evidence about whether the defendant consented to the search of the second bag in which the contraband was found and as to whether he was informed of his right to refuse consent. However, any conflict must be resolved in favor of the state, it being a question of fact decided by the trial judge." That court ruled that "an impermissible seizure result[s] when police mount a drug search on buses during scheduled stops and question boarded passengers without articulable reasons for doing so, thereby obtaining consent to search the passengers' luggage." The Supreme Court reversed; O'CONNOR, J., for the majority, stated:

"Our cases make it clear that a seizure does not occur simply because a police officer approaches an individual and asks a few questions. So long as a reasonable person would feel free 'to disregard the police and go about his business,' the encounter is consensual and no reasonable suspicion is required. The encounter will not trigger Fourth Amendment scrutiny unless it loses its consensual nature. * * *

"There is no doubt that if this same encounter had taken place before Bostick boarded the bus or in the lobby of the bus terminal, it would not rise to the level of a seizure. The Court has dealt with similar encounters in airports and has found them to be 'the sort of consensual encounter[s] that implicat[e] no Fourth Amendment interest.' We have stated that even when officers have no basis for suspecting a particular individual, they may generally ask questions of that individual, ask to examine the individual's identification, and request consent to search his or her luggage—as long as the police do not convey a message that compliance with their requests is required.

"Bostick insists that this case is different because it took place in the cramped confines of a bus. A police encounter is much more intimidating in this setting, he argues, because police tower over a seated passenger and there is little room to move around. Bostick claims to find support in cases indicating that a seizure occurs when a reasonable person would believe that he or she is not 'free to leave.' Bostick maintains that a reasonable bus passenger would not have felt free to leave under the circumstances of this case because there is nowhere to go on a bus. Also, the bus was about to depart. Had Bostick disembarked, he would have risked being stranded and losing whatever baggage he had locked away in the luggage compartment.

"The Florida Supreme Court found this argument persuasive, so much so that it adopted a *per se* rule prohibiting the police from randomly boarding buses as a means of drug interdiction. The state court erred, however, in focusing on whether Bostick was 'free to leave', rather than on the principle that those words were intended to capture. When police attempt to question a person who is walking down the street or through an airport lobby, it makes sense to inquire whether a reasonable person would feel free to continue walking. But when the person is seated on a bus and has no desire to leave, the degree to which a reasonable person would feel that he or she could leave is not an accurate measure of the coercive effect of the encounter. * * *

"In this respect, the Court's decision in *INS v. Delgado,* [466 U.S. 210 (1984)] is dispositive. At issue there was the INs' practice of visiting factories at random and questioning employees to determine whether any were illegal aliens. Several INS agents would stand near the building's exits, while other agents walked through the factory questioning workers. The Court acknowledged that the workers may not have been free to leave their worksite, but explained that this was not the result of police activity: 'Ordinarily, when people are at work their freedom to move about has been meaningfully restricted, not by the actions of law enforcement officials, but by the workers' voluntary obligations to their employers.' We concluded that there was no seizure because, even though the workers were not free to leave the building without being questioned, the agents' conduct should have given employees 'no reason to believe that they would be detained if they gave truthful answers to the questions put to them or if they simply refused to answer.'

"The present case is analytically indistinguishable from *Delgado.* Like the workers in that case, Bostick's freedom of movement was restricted by a factor independent of police conduct—*i.e.,* by his being a passenger on a bus. Accordingly, the 'free to leave' analysis on which Bostick relies is inapplicable. In such a situation, the appropriate inquiry is whether a reasonable person would feel free to decline the officers' requests or otherwise terminate the encounter. * * * Where the encounter takes place is one factor, but it is not the only one. And, as the Solicitor General correctly observes, an individual may decline an officer's request without fearing prosecution. We have consistently held that a refusal to cooperate, without more, does not furnish the minimal level of objective justification needed for a detention or seizure.

"The facts of this case, as described by the Florida Supreme Court, leave some doubt whether a seizure occurred. Two officers walked up to Bostick on the bus, asked him a few questions, and asked if they could search his bags. As we have explained, no seizure occurs when police ask questions of an individual, ask to examine the individual's identification, and request consent to search his or her luggage—so long as the officers do not convey a message that compliance with their requests is required. Here, the facts recited by the Florida Supreme Court indicate that the officers did not point guns at Bostick or otherwise threaten him and that they specifically advised Bostick that he could refuse consent.

"Nevertheless, we refrain from deciding whether or not a seizure occurred in this case. The trial court made no express findings of fact, and the Florida Supreme Court rested its decision on a single fact—that the encounter took place on a bus—rather than on the totality of the circumstances. We remand so that the Florida courts may evaluate the seizure question under the correct legal standard. We do reject, however, Bostick's argument that he must have been seized because no reasonable person would freely consent to a search of luggage that he or she knows contains drugs. This argument cannot prevail because the 'reasonable person' test presupposes an *innocent* person."

MARSHALL, J., for the three dissenters, interpreted the state court holding as not a "*per se* rule" but rather as a decision based on all the facts, but then added that in any event the Supreme Court could determine the "question of law" of whether *all* the facts set forth in the state court opinion add up to a Fourth Amendment seizure. Accepting the majority's "free to decline" test, Marshall continued:

"Unlike the majority, I have no doubt that the answer to this question is no. Apart from trying to accommodate the officers, respondent had only two options. First, he could have remained seated while obstinately refusing to respond to the officers' questioning. But in light of the intimidating show of authority that the officers made upon boarding the bus, respondent reasonably could have believed that such behavior would only arouse the officers' suspicions and intensify their interrogation. Indeed, officers who carry out bus sweeps like the one at issue here frequently admit that this is the effect of a passenger's refusal to cooperate. The majority's observation that a mere refusal to answer questions, 'without more,' does not give rise to a reasonable basis for seizing a passenger, is utterly beside the point, because a passenger unadvised of his rights and otherwise unversed in constitutional law *has no reason to know* that the police cannot hold his refusal to cooperate against him.

"Second, respondent could have tried to escape the officers' presence by leaving the bus altogether. But because doing so would have required respondent to squeeze past the gun-wielding inquisitor who was blocking the aisle of the bus, this hardly seems like a course that respondent reasonably would have viewed as available to him. The majority lamely protests that nothing in the stipulated facts shows that the questioning officer '*point[ed]* [his] gu[n] at [respondent] or otherwise *threatened* him' with the weapon. Our decisions recognize the obvious point, however, that the choice of the police to 'display' their weapons during an encounter exerts significant coercive pressure on the confronted citizen. We have never suggested that the police must go so far as to put a citizen in immediate apprehension of *being shot* before a court can take account of the intimidating effect of being questioned by an officer with weapon in hand.

"Even if respondent had perceived that the officers would *let* him leave the bus, moreover, he could not reasonably have been expected to resort to this means of evading their intrusive questioning. For so far as respondent knew, the bus' departure from the terminal was imminent. Unlike a person approached by the police on the street or at a bus or airport terminal after reaching his destination, a passenger approached by the police at an intermediate point in a long bus journey cannot simply leave the scene and repair to a safe haven to avoid unwanted probing by law-enforcement officials. The vulnerability that an intrastate or interstate traveler experiences when confronted by the police outside of his 'own familiar territory' surely aggravates the coercive quality of such an encounter."

2. In UNITED STATES v. DRAYTON, 536 U.S. 194 (2002), the Court split 6–3 on the application of *Bostick* to another instance of on-bus drug interdiction activity. During a scheduled stop, the driver turned the bus over to three police officers; one knelt on the driver's seat and faced back, a second stayed in the rear and faced forward, and the third worked his way from back to front, speaking with individual passengers without first advising them of their right to refuse to cooperate. Upon reaching the row in which Drayton and Brown were seated, the officer declared that the police were looking for drugs and weapons and asked if the two had any bags. Both pointed to a bag overhead, the officer asked if he could check it, Brown agreed, and the subsequent search revealed no contraband. The officer then asked Brown whether he minded if the officer checked his person, Brown agreed, and when a pat-down revealed hard objects similar to drug packages in both thigh areas Brown was arrested. The same procedure with the same results was followed as to Drayton, and a further search revealed that both men had taped cocaine between their shorts. The officer testified that passengers who declined to cooperate or who chose to exit the bus would have been allowed to do so, and that five or six times in the previous year passengers had done so.

KENNEDY, J., for the majority, concluded there had been no seizure, as there "was no application of force, no intimidating movement, no overwhelming show of force, no brandishing of weapons, no blocking of exits, no threat, no command, not even an authoritative tone of voice. It is beyond question that had this encounter occurred on the street, it would be constitutional. The fact that an encounter takes place on a bus does not on its own transform standard police questioning of citizens into an illegal seizure. Indeed, because many fellow passengers are present to witness officers' conduct, a reasonable person may feel even more secure in his or her decision not to cooperate with police on a bus than in other circumstances. * * * Finally, the fact that in Officer Lang's experience only a few passengers have refused to cooperate does not suggest that a reasonable person would not feel free to terminate the bus encounter. [B]us passengers answer officers' questions and otherwise cooperate not because of coercion but because the passengers know that their participation enhances their own safety and the safety of those around them."

SOUTER, J., for the three dissenters, questioned the majority's assumption as to a comparable "on the street" situation, stating that if a pedestrian were similarly the object of attention by three officers in equally-confined space, say, a small alley, then "there is every reason to believe that the pedestrian would have understood, to his considerable discomfort, what Justice Stewart described as the 'threatening presence of several officers.' [which] may overbear a normal person's ability to act freely, even in the absence of explicit commands or the formalities of detention." Stressing that "the driver with the tickets entitling the passengers to travel had yielded his custody of the bus and its seated travelers to three police officers, whose authority apparently superseded the driver's own," the dissenters concluded: "The reasonable inference was that the 'interdiction' was not a consensual exercise, but one the police would carry out whatever the circumstances; that they would prefer "cooperation" but would not let the lack of it stand in their way. There was no contrary indication that day, since no passenger had refused the cooperation requested, and there was no reason for any passenger to believe that the driver would return and the trip resume until the police were satisfied."

3. In CALIFORNIA v. HODARI D., 499 U.S. 621 (1991), Hodari fled upon seeing an approaching police car, only to be pursued on foot by Officer Pertoso, after which Hodari tossed away what appeared to be a small rock but which when retrieved by the police proved to be crack cocaine. The state court suppressed the cocaine as the fruit of a seizure made without reasonable suspicion, but the Supreme Court, per SCALIA, J., reversed:

"To say [as the common law authorities do] that an arrest is effected by the slightest application of physical force, despite the arrestee's escape, is not to say that for Fourth Amendment purposes there is a *continuing* arrest during the period of fugitivity. If, for example, Pertoso had laid his hands upon Hodari to arrest him, but Hodari had broken away and had *then* cast away the cocaine, it would hardly be realistic to say that that disclosure had been made during the course of an arrest. Cf. *Thompson v. Whitman,* 18 Wall. 457, 471 (1874) ('A seizure is a single act, and not a continuous fact'). The present case, however, is even one step further removed. It does not involve the application of any physical force; Hodari was untouched by Officer Pertoso at the time he discarded the cocaine. His defense relies instead upon the proposition that a seizure occurs 'when the officer, by means of physical force *or show of authority,* has in some way restrained the liberty of a citizen.' *Terry v. Ohio,* [p. 401]. Hodari contends (and we accept as true for purposes of this decision) that Pertoso's pursuit qualified as a 'show of authority' calling upon Hodari to halt. The narrow question before us is whether, with respect to a show of authority as with respect to application of physical force, a seizure occurs even though the subject does not yield. We hold that it does not.

"The language of the Fourth Amendment, of course, cannot sustain respondent's contention. The word 'seizure' readily bears the meaning of a laying on of hands or application of physical force to restrain movement, even when it is ultimately unsuccessful. ('She seized the purse-snatcher, but he broke out of her grasp.') It does not remotely apply, however, to the prospect of a policeman yelling 'Stop, in the name of the law!' at a fleeing form that continues to flee. That is no seizure. Nor can the result respondent wishes to achieve be produced—indirectly, as it were—by suggesting that Pertoso's uncomplied-with show of authority was a common-law arrest, and then appealing to the principle that all common-law arrests are seizures. An arrest requires *either* physical force (as described above) *or,* where that is absent, *submission* to the assertion of authority. * * *

"We do not think it desirable, even as a policy matter, to stretch the Fourth Amendment beyond its words and beyond the meaning of arrest, as respondent urges. Street pursuits always place the public at some risk, and compliance with police orders to stop should therefore be encouraged. Only a few of those orders, we must presume, will be without adequate basis, and since the addressee has no ready means of identifying the deficient ones it almost invariably is the responsible course to comply. Unlawful orders will not be deterred, moreover, by sanctioning through the exclusionary rule those of them that are *not* obeyed. Since policemen do not command 'Stop!' expecting to be ignored, or give chase hoping to be outrun, it fully suffices to apply the deterrent to their genuine, successful seizures."

STEVENS, J., for the two dissenters, objected: "The deterrent purposes of the exclusionary rule focus on the conduct of law enforcement officers, and on discouraging improper behavior on their part, and not on the reaction of the citizen to the show of force. In the present case, if Officer Pertoso had succeeded in tackling respondent before he dropped the rock of cocaine, the rock unquestionably would have been excluded as the fruit of the officer's unlawful seizure. Instead, under the Court's logic-chopping analysis, the exclusionary rule has no application because an attempt to make an unconstitutional seizure is beyond the coverage of the Fourth Amendment, no matter how outrageous or unreasonable the officer's conduct may be.

"It is too early to know the consequences of the Court's holding. If carried to its logical conclusion, it will encourage unlawful displays of force that will frighten countless innocent citizens into surrendering whatever privacy rights they may still have. It is not too soon, however, to note the irony in the fact that the Court's own justification for its result is its analysis of the rules of the common law of arrest that antedated our decisions in *Katz* [p. 247] and *Terry*. Yet, even in those days the common law provided the citizen with protection against an attempt to make an unlawful arrest. The central message of *Katz* and *Terry* was that the protection the Fourth Amendment provides to the average citizen is not rigidly confined by ancient common-law precept. The message that today's literal-minded majority conveys is that the common law, rather than our understanding of the Fourth Amendment as it has developed over the last quarter of a century, defines, and limits, the scope of a seizure. The Court today defines a seizure as commencing, not with egregious police conduct, but rather, with submission by the citizen. Thus, it both delays the point at which 'the Fourth Amendment becomes relevant' to an encounter and limits the range of encounters that will come under the heading of 'seizure.' Today's qualification of the Fourth Amendment means that innocent citizens may remain 'secure in their persons ... against unreasonable searches and seizures' only at the discretion of the police."[f]

4. After citing *Hodari D.* to support the conclusion "that a police pursuit in attempting to seize a person does not amount to a 'seizure' within the meaning of the Fourth Amendment," the Court in *County of Sacramento v. Lewis,* p. 36, also concluded "that no Fourth Amendment seizure would take place where a 'pursuing police car sought to stop the suspect only by the show of authority represented by flashing lights and continuing pursuit,' but accidentally stopped the suspect by crashing into him." This is because for a Fourth Amendment seizure there must be "a governmental termination of freedom of movement *through means intentionally applied.*"

5. What result would the Court have reached if, before Hodari threw away the cocaine, Officer Pertoso had (a) fired his pistol at Hodari, barely missing him; (b) fired his pistol at Hodari, causing a wound which slowed down but did not stop him; (c) cornered Hodari in a dead-end alley; or (d) grabbed the collar of Hodari's

f. For criticism of *Bostick* and *Hodari D.,* see Wayne R. LaFave, *Pinguitudinous Police, Pachydermatous Prey: Whence Fourth Amendment "Seizures"?,* 1991 U.Ill.L.Rev. 729.

jacket, only to have him slip out of the garment? Compare *United States v. Lender,* 985 F.2d 151 (4th Cir.1993) (officer called defendant to stop, defendant responded "you don't want me" and continued walking, officer again called defendant to stop and defendant did stop, at which loaded pistol fell to the ground, which officer prevented defendant from picking up; no prior seizure of defendant, as court refuses "to characterize as capitulation conduct that is fully consistent with preparation to whirl and shoot the officers"); with *United States v. Wood,* 981 F.2d 536 (D.C.Cir.1992) (when officer ordered defendant to stop, defendant "froze in his tracks and immediately dropped the [theretofore unobserved] weapon between his feet," there was a prior seizure; court "cannot imagine a more submissive response"). Compare *Tom v. Voida,* 963 F.2d 952 (7th Cir.1992) (where flight and pursuit and, when suspect fell on ice, officer kneeled on him but suspect violently resisted and broke away, seizure occurred when officer "overtook him on the ice and physically touched him"); with *United States v. Holloway,* 962 F.2d 451 (5th Cir.1992) (where after defendant's car boxed in by police cars defendant accelerated into police car behind him, no prior seizure, as no "touching" of defendant and no submission given that he then "decided to flee").

6. What result under *Bostick* and *Hodari D.* if, when an intercity bus has stopped for an equipment change, necessitating that all passengers leave the bus with their luggage, the police board the bus and announce that they have a narcotics canine outside the bus and that the dog will "alert" to anyone carrying narcotics? Does it depend upon whether "the tenor and tone of [the] announcement was informative rather than confrontational"? On whether the passengers are told to exit "in a normal fashion with your carry-on," or instead to disembark "with all their carry-on luggage in their right hand so that the luggage would pass by the dog"? Compare *United States v. Jones,* 914 F.Supp. 421 (D.Colo.1996); with *United States v. Brumfield,* 910 F.Supp. 1528 (D.Colo.1996).

7. In *United States v. Wilson,* 953 F.2d 116 (4th Cir.1991), involving an airport encounter between a DEA agent and a drug courier suspect, Wilson granted the agent's request to speak with him and submitted to questioning, produced identification upon request, and allowed the agent and an associate to search his bag and his person. But when the agent asked to search the two coats Wilson was carrying, Wilson angrily refused and walked away. The agent stayed with him, repeatedly requesting that Wilson consent to search of the coats and repeatedly asking Wilson to explain why he would not allow the search. Wilson continued walking through the terminal and then outside on the sidewalk, objecting the entire time to the harassment, but he finally consented to the search, which uncovered a bag of cocaine. If Wilson claims his consent to the search was the fruit of an illegal seizure, what result under *Bostick* and *Hodari D.?*

8. In *Bostick* and *Hodari D.* the defendants were black. Is that relevant? Consider Tracey Maclin, *"Black and Blue Encounters"—Some Preliminary Thoughts About Fourth Amendment Seizures: Should Race Matter?,* 26 Val. U.L.Rev. 243, 250 (1991): "I submit that the dynamics surrounding an encounter between a police officer and a black male are quite different from those that surround an encounter between an officer and the so-called average, reasonable person. My tentative proposal is that the Court should disregard the notion that there is an average, hypothetical, reasonable person out there by which to judge the constitutionality of police encounters. When assessing the coercive nature of an encounter, the Court should consider the race of the person confronted by the police, and how that person's race might have influenced his attitude toward the encounter."

Cf. *In re J.M.,* 619 A.2d 497 (D.C.App.1992) (majority, applying *Bostick* objective standard, concludes 14–year–old bus passenger had not been seized during his on-bus interrogation which culminated in the youth's supposed consent to a search of his bag and pat-down of his person; two concurring judges argue it "consistent with the teaching of the Supreme Court opinions that specific, objectively observable characteristics of the person who is the object of police conduct be considered by a court in determining whether a seizure has occurred," so that issue here is "whether a reasonable person who is a child would have thought that he or she was free to leave under the circumstances"; another judge "would factor into the totality of the circumstances the relevant characteristics of age and race," and suggests "that no reasonable innocent black male (with any knowledge of American history) would feel free to ignore or walk away from a drug interdicting team"). For the Supreme Court's more recent treatment of a comparable issue under *Miranda, see Yarborough v. Alvarado*, p. 608.

9. Is the fact the encountered suspect is black relevant in another sense? Reconsider Note 8, p. 345; and consider *Brown v. City of Oneonta*, 221 F.3d 329 (2d Cir.2000). Oneonta has about 10,000 full-time residents plus some 7,500 students who attend the local branch of the state university; fewer than 300 blacks live in the town, and 2% of the students are black. A 77-year-old woman attacked in her home at 2 a.m. told police her assailant was black and young and had cut himself on the hand with his knife. A police canine unit tracked the assailant's scent from the scene of the crime toward the campus, but lost the trail after several hundred yards. Police obtained from the university a list of its black male students and then attempted to locate and question each of them. When that endeavor produced no suspects, over the next several days police conducted a "sweep" of Oneonta, approaching and questioning non-white persons on the streets and inspecting their hands for cuts. More than two hundred persons were questioned during that period, but no suspect was apprehended. Some of those affected then brought a § 1983 action based upon both the Fourth Amendment and the Equal Protection Clause. The court of appeals concluded that only four plaintiffs had established that a seizure had occurred under the *Bostick* test, and then dismissed the equal protection claims on the pleadings, distinguishing the *Oneonta* investigation from racial profiling and concluding that the plaintiffs' pleadings failed to identify "any law or policy that contains an express racial classification." See R. Richard Banks, *Race-Based Suspect Selection and Colorblind Equal Protection Doctrine and Discourse*, 48 UCLA L.Rev. 1075 (2001), critiquing *Oneonta* and concluding that "law enforcement use of race-based suspect description is as much of a racial classification as is racial profiling"; and Sharon L. Davies, *Profiling Terror*, 1 Ohio St J Crim L 45, 70 (2003), concluding that the "police conduct in *Oneonta* demonstrates why it would be helpful to train the police to see that the probative value of racial or ethnic information is often minimal, even where that information is provided by a crime victim."

C. Grounds for Temporary Seizure for Investigation

1. Under *Terry,* what grounds are needed for a stop, and how do they differ from those needed for a full-fledged arrest? Shortly after *Terry,* one commentator suggested that for arrest it must be "more probable than not that the person is the offender," while for a *Terry* stop "it should be sufficient that there is a substantial possibility that a crime has been or is about to be committed and that the suspect is the person who committed or is planning the offense."[g] Compare

g. Wayne R. LaFave, *"Street Encounters" and the Constitution: Terry, Sibron, Peters and Beyond,* 67 Mich.L.Rev. 40, 73–75 (1968). An excellent illustration is provided by *Luckett v. State,* 284 N.E.2d 738 (Ind.1972), where an officer stopped for investigation a green car bearing a license plate prefix 82J upon information that such a car had been used by persons fleeing from a burglary earlier in the evening. The court concluded that the officer

the Court's later elaboration in UNITED STATES v. CORTEZ, 449 U.S. 411 (1981):

"Courts have used a variety of terms to capture the elusive concept of what cause is sufficient to authorize police to stop a person. Terms like 'articulable reasons' and 'founded suspicion' are not self-defining; they fall short of providing clear guidance dispositive of the myriad factual situations that arise. But the essence of all that has been written is that the totality of the circumstances—the whole picture—must be taken into account.[h] Based upon that whole picture the detaining officers must have a particularized and objective basis for suspecting the particular person stopped of criminal activity.

"The idea that an assessment of the whole picture must yield a particularized suspicion contains two elements, each of which must be present before a stop is permissible. First, the assessment must be based upon all the circumstances. The analysis proceeds with various objective observations, information from police reports, if such are available, and consideration of the modes or patterns of operation of certain kinds of lawbreakers. From these data, a trained officer draws inferences and makes deductions—inferences and deductions that might well elude an untrained person.

"The process does not deal with hard certainties, but with probabilities. Long before the law of probabilities was articulated as such, practical people formulated certain common sense conclusions about human behavior; jurors as factfinders are permitted to do the same—and so are law enforcement officers. Finally, the evidence thus collected must be seen and weighed not in terms of library analysis by scholars, but as understood by those versed in the field of law enforcement.

"The second element contained in the idea that an assessment of the whole picture must yield a particularized suspicion is the concept that the process just described must raise a suspicion that the particular individual being stopped is engaged in wrongdoing."

2. In SIBRON v. NEW YORK, 392 U.S. 40 (1968), a companion case to *Terry,* the facts as stated by the Court were as follows: "At the hearing on the motion to suppress, Officer Martin testified that while he was patrolling his beat in uniform on March 9, 1965, he observed Sibron 'continually from the hours of 4:00 P.M. to 12:00, midnight * * * in the vicinity of 742 Broadway.' He stated that during this period of time he saw Sibron in conversation with six or eight persons whom he (Patrolman Martin) knew from past experience to be narcotics addicts. The officer testified that he did not overhear any of these conversations, and that he did not see anything pass between Sibron and any of the others. Late in the evening Sibron entered a restaurant. Patrolman Martin saw Sibron speak with three more known addicts inside the restaurant. Once again, nothing was overheard and nothing was seen to pass between Sibron and the addicts. Sibron sat down and ordered pie and coffee, and as he was eating, Patrolman Martin approached him and told him to come outside. Once outside, the officer said to Sibron, 'You know what I am after.' According to the officer, Sibron 'mumbled

had grounds to stop the automobile even though it was "readily apparent" that he "did not have probable cause to stop every green automobile with an 82J license prefix and formally arrest its occupants."

h. Hence, in *United States v. Arvizu*, 534 U.S. 266 (2002), where the court of appeals, in examining the factors relied upon by the officer and district court, assessed them one-by-one, dismissed some as entitled to "no weight" because individually susceptible to an innocent explanation, and found those remaining insufficient to show a reasonable suspicion, a unanimous Supreme Court reversed, reasoning that the court of appeals' approach would "seriously undercut the 'totality of the circumstances' principle which governs the existence *vel non* of 'reasonable suspicion,' " and that such "divide-and-conquer analysis" was precluded by *Terry*, where a series of acts each "perhaps innocent in itself" was deemed to add up to reasonable suspicion.

something and reached into his pocket.' Simultaneously, Patrolman Martin thrust his hand into the same pocket, discovering several glassine envelopes, which, it turned out, contained heroin."

Though the Court, per WARREN, C.J., focused primarily upon the lack of grounds for and the improper manner of the frisk (see Notes 1 and 3, pp. 434–35, it was intimated that there were not even grounds for a stop because "Patrolman Martin was completely ignorant regarding the content of these conversations, and * * * he saw nothing pass between Sibron and the addicts. So far as he knew, they might indeed 'have been talking about the World Series.' The inference that persons who talk to narcotics addicts are engaged in the criminal traffic in narcotics is simply not the sort of reasonable inference required to support an intrusion by the police upon an individual's personal security."

Do you believe that Officer Martin was less certain of what Sibron was up to than Officer McFadden was as to what Terry and his companions were up to? Are there other considerations at play here? HARLAN, J., concurring in *Sibron,* observed that "in *Terry,* the police officer judged that his suspect was about to commit a violent crime and that he had to assert himself in order to prevent it. Here there was no reason for Officer Martin to think that an incipient crime, or flight, or the destruction of evidence would occur if he stayed his hand; indeed, there was no more reason for him to intrude upon Sibron at the moment when he did than there had been four hours earlier, and no reason to think the situation would have changed four hours hence. While no hard-and-fast rule can be drawn, I would suggest that one important factor, missing here, that should be taken into account in determining whether there are reasonable grounds for a forcible intrusion is whether there is any need for immediate action." What then of the conclusion in *United States v. Botero–Ospina*, 71 F.3d 783 (10th Cir.1995), that "a traffic stop is valid under the Fourth Amendment if the stop is based on an observed traffic violation or if the police officer has reasonable articulable suspicion that a traffic or equipment violation has occurred or is occurring."[i]

3. In FLORIDA v. J.L., 529 U.S. 266 (2000), an anonymous caller reported to police than a young black male standing at a particular bus stop and wearing a plaid shirt was carrying a gun; officers went there and saw such a person but did not see a firearm or any unusual movements, and had no reason to suspect him apart from the tip. A frisk of the suspect, which produced a firearm, was held by the Court, per GINSBURG, J., to be unreasonable: "Unlike a tip from a known informant whose reputation can be assessed and who can be held responsible if her allegations turn out to be fabricated, 'an anonymous tip alone seldom demonstrates the informant's basis of knowledge or veracity,' *Alabama v. White*, [496 U.S. 325 (1990)]. As we have recognized, however, there are situations in which an anonymous tip, suitably corroborated, exhibits 'sufficient indicia of reliability to provide reasonable suspicion to make the investigatory stop.' The question we here confront is whether the tip pointing to J.L. had those indicia of reliability.

"In *White*, the police received an anonymous tip asserting that a woman was carrying cocaine and predicting that she would leave an apartment building at a specified time, get into a car matching a particular description, and drive to a named motel. Standing alone, the tip would not have justified a *Terry* stop. Only after police observation showed that the informant had accurately predicted the woman's movements, we explained, did it become reasonable to think the tipster had inside knowledge about the suspect and therefore to credit his assertion about the cocaine. Although the Court held that the suspicion in *White* became reason-

i. See Wayne R. LaFave, *The "Routine Traffic Stop" From Start to Finish: Too Much "Routine," Not Enough Fourth Amendment,* 102 Mich.L.Rev. 1843, 1846-52 (2004).

able after police surveillance, we regarded the case as borderline. Knowledge about a person's future movements indicates some familiarity with that person's affairs, but having such knowledge does not necessarily imply that the informant knows, in particular, whether that person is carrying hidden contraband. We accordingly classified *White* as a 'close case.'

"The tip in the instant case lacked the moderate indicia of reliability present in *White* and essential to the Court's decision in that case. The anonymous call concerning J.L. provided no predictive information and therefore left the police without means to test the informant's knowledge or credibility. That the allegation about the gun turned out to be correct does not suggest that the officers, prior to the frisks, had a reasonable basis for suspecting J.L. of engaging in unlawful conduct: The reasonableness of official suspicion must be measured by what the officers knew before they conducted their search. All the police had to go on in this case was the bare report of an unknown, unaccountable informant who neither explained how he knew about the gun nor supplied any basis for believing he had inside information about J.L. If *White* was a close case on the reliability of anonymous tips, this one surely falls on the other side of the line. * * *

"An accurate description of a subject's readily observable location and appearance is of course reliable in this limited sense: It will help the police correctly identify the person whom the tipster means to accuse. Such a tip, however, does not show that the tipster has knowledge of concealed criminal activity. The reasonable suspicion here at issue requires that a tip be reliable in its assertion of illegality, not just in its tendency to identify a determinate person. * * *

"Firearms are dangerous, and extraordinary dangers sometimes justify unusual precautions. Our decisions recognize the serious threat that armed criminals pose to public safety; *Terry's* rule, which permits protective police searches on the basis of reasonable suspicion rather than demanding that officers meet the higher standard of probable cause, responds to this very concern. But an automatic firearm exception to our established reliability analysis [advanced by Florida and the United States as *amicus*] would rove too far. Such an exception would enable any person seeking to harass another to set in motion an intrusive, embarrassing police search of the targeted person simply by placing an anonymous call falsely reporting the target's unlawful carriage of a gun. Nor could one securely confine such an exception to allegations involving firearms. Several Courts of Appeals have held it per se foreseeable for people carrying significant amounts of illegal drugs to be carrying guns as well. If police officers may properly conduct *Terry* frisks on the basis of bare-boned tips about guns, it would be reasonable to maintain under the above-cited decisions that the police should similarly have discretion to frisk based on bare-boned tips about narcotics. * * *

"The facts of this case do not require us to speculate about the circumstances under which the danger alleged in an anonymous tip might be so great as to justify a search even without a showing of reliability. We do not say, for example, that a report of a person carrying a bomb need bear the indicia of reliability we demand for a report of a person carrying a firearm before the police can constitutionally conduct a frisk. Nor do we hold that public safety officials in quarters where the reasonable expectation of Fourth Amendment privacy is diminished, such as airports and schools, cannot conduct protective searches on the basis of information insufficient to justify searches elsewhere.

"Finally, the requirement that an anonymous tip bear standard indicia of reliability in order to justify a stop in no way diminishes a police officer's prerogative, in accord with *Terry*, to conduct a protective search of a person who has already been legitimately stopped. We speak in today's decision only of cases in which the officer's authority to make the initial stop is at issue. In that context, we hold that an anonymous tip lacking indicia of reliability of the kind contemplated in *Adams* [p. 434] and *White* does not justify a stop and frisk whenever and however it alleges the illegal possession of a firearm."

Justice KENNEDY, joined by The Chief Justice, concurring., added: "It seems appropriate to observe that a tip might be anonymous in some sense yet have certain other features, either supporting reliability or narrowing the likely class of informants, so that the tip does provide the lawful basis for some police action. One such feature, as the Court recognizes, is that the tip predicts future conduct of the alleged criminal. There may be others. For example, if an unnamed caller with a voice which sounds the same each time tells police on two successive nights about criminal activity which in fact occurs each night, a similar call on the third night ought not be treated automatically like the tip in the case now before us. In the instance supposed, there would be a plausible argument that experience cures some of the uncertainty surrounding the anonymity, justifying a proportionate police response. In today's case, however, the State provides us with no data about the reliability of anonymous tips. Nor do we know whether the dispatcher or arresting officer had any objective reason to believe that this tip had some particular indicia of reliability.

"If an informant places his anonymity at risk, a court can consider this factor in weighing the reliability of the tip. An instance where a tip might be considered anonymous but nevertheless sufficiently reliable to justify a proportionate police response may be when an unnamed person driving a car the police officer later describes stops for a moment and, face to face, informs the police that criminal activity is occurring. This too seems to be different from the tip in the present case.

"Instant caller identification is widely available to police, and, if anonymous tips are proving unreliable and distracting to police, squad cars can be sent within seconds to the location of the telephone used by the informant. Voice recording of telephone tips might, in appropriate cases, be used by police to locate the caller. It is unlawful to make false reports to the police, and the ability of the police to trace the identity of anonymous telephone informants may be a factor which lends reliability to what, years earlier, might have been considered unreliable anonymous tips."

4. In UNITED STATES v. SOKOLOW, 490 U.S. 1 (1989), the defendant was stopped at the Honolulu airport by agents who knew "that (1) he paid $2,100 for two airplane tickets from a roll of $20 bills; (2) he traveled under a name that did not match the name under which his telephone number was listed; (3) his original destination was Miami, a source city for illicit drugs; (4) he stayed in Miami for only 48 hours, even though a round-trip flight from Honolulu to Miami takes 20 hours; (5) he appeared nervous during his trip; and (6) he checked none of his luggage." The Court, per REHNQUIST, C.J., held this amounted to reasonable suspicion (said to be a level of suspicion "considerably less than proof of wrongdoing by a preponderance of the evidence") defendant was a drug courier:

"We do not agree with respondent that our analysis is somehow changed by the agents' belief that his behavior was consistent with one of the DEA's 'drug courier profiles.' A court sitting to determine the existence of reasonable suspicion must require the agent to articulate the factors leading to that conclusion, but the fact that these factors may be set forth in a 'profile' does not somehow detract from their evidentiary significance as seen by a trained agent."

MARSHALL, J., joined by Brennan, J., dissenting, objected: "It is highly significant that the DEA agents stopped Sokolow because he matched one of the DEA's 'profiles' of a paradigmatic drug courier. In my view, a law enforcement officer's mechanistic application of a formula of personal and behavioral traits in deciding whom to detain can only dull the officer's ability and determination to make sensitive and fact-specific inferences 'in light of his experience,' *Terry*, particularly in ambiguous or borderline cases. Reflexive reliance on a profile of drug courier characteristics runs a far greater risk than does ordinary, case-by-case police work, of subjecting innocent individuals to unwarranted police harassment and detention. This risk is enhanced by the profile's 'chameleon-like way of adapting to any particular set of observations.' "

5. Should either the seriousness of the suspected crime or the time of its apparent commission have any bearing on whether a *Terry* stop is permissible? In UNITED STATES v. HENSLEY, 469 U.S. 221 (1985), the Court, per O'CONNOR, J., held by analogy to *Whiteley v. Warden,* p. 304, "that, if a flyer or bulletin has been issued on the basis of articulable facts supporting a reasonable suspicion that the wanted person has committed an offense, then reliance on that flyer or bulletin justifies a stop to check identification, to pose questions to the person, or to detain the person briefly while attempting to obtain further information." But the Court first rejected the lower court's position that *Terry* is limited to ongoing criminal activity:

"* * * The precise limits on investigatory stops to investigate past criminal activity are more difficult to define. The proper way to identify the limits is to apply the same test already used to identify the proper bounds of intrusions that further investigations of imminent or ongoing crimes. That test, which is grounded in the standard of reasonableness embodied in the Fourth Amendment, balances the nature and quality of the intrusion on personal security against the importance of the governmental interests alleged to justify the intrusion. When this balancing test is applied to stops to investigate past crimes, we think that probable cause to arrest need not always be required.

"The factors in the balance may be somewhat different when a stop to investigate past criminal activity is involved rather than a stop to investigate ongoing criminal conduct. This is because the governmental interest and the nature of the intrusions involved in the two situations may differ. As we noted in *Terry,* one general interest present in the context of ongoing or imminent criminal activity is 'that of effective crime prevention and detection.' A stop to investigate an already completed crime does not necessarily promote the interest of crime prevention as directly as a stop to investigate suspected ongoing criminal activity. Similarly, the exigent circumstances which require a police officer to step in before a crime is committed or completed are not necessarily as pressing long afterwards. Public safety may be less threatened by a suspect in a past crime who now appears to be going about his lawful business than it is by a suspect who is currently in the process of violating the law. Finally, officers making a stop to investigate past crimes may have a wider range of opportunity to choose the time and circumstances of the stop.

"Despite these differences, where police have been unable to locate a person suspected of involvement in a past crime, the ability to briefly stop that person, ask questions, or check identification in the absence of probable cause promotes the strong government interest in solving crimes and bringing offenders to justice. Restraining police action until after probable cause is obtained would not only hinder the investigation, but might also enable the suspect to flee in the interim and to remain at large. Particularly in the context of felonies or crimes involving a threat to public safety, it is in the public interest that the crime be solved and the suspect detained as promptly as possible. The law enforcement interests at stake in these circumstances outweigh the individual's interest to be free of a stop and detention that is no more extensive than permissible in the investigation of imminent or ongoing crimes.

"We need not and do not decide today whether *Terry* stops to investigate all past crimes, however serious, are permitted. It is enough to say that, if police have a reasonable suspicion, grounded in specific and articulable facts, that a person they encounter was involved in or is wanted in connection with a completed felony, then a *Terry* stop may be made to investigate that suspicion."[j]

6. Are there grounds for the stops made on the following facts, essentially those in *United States v. Feliciano,* 45 F.3d 1070 (7th Cir.1995)? An officer on patrol near a train station at midnight saw *F* and *M* walking in an area of a parking lot where there were no cars and which led to the river embankment. *M* then approached *K,* who was standing near the tracks with a suitcase, spoke with him for a while, and then left, rejoined *F,* and departed the scene in a direction opposite of that *K* then headed. The officer approached *K,* who told the officer that *M* had tried to lure him to the embankment to help an injured friend, but that *K* had refused. *K* explained that he had also seen *F* earlier and thus knew he was not injured; *K* surmised that the two had been planning to mug him. The officer asked his backup officer to stop *F* and *M.* The backup officer, who recognized *F* as a gang member recently released from prison, where *F* had served time for robbery, then stopped *F* and *M* as they walked toward their homes through the apparently deserted downtown area.

7. In ILLINOIS v. WARDLOW, 528 U.S. 119 (2000), a Chicago police officer in the last car of a 4–car caravan, which was converging on an area known for heavy narcotics trafficking in order to investigate drug transactions, saw defendant look in the direction of the officers and then run away; defendant was stopped and frisked and found to be carrying a handgun. The Court, per REHNQUIST, C.J., held "that the officer's stop did not violate the Fourth Amendment," reasoning: "An individual's presence in an area of expected criminal activity, standing alone, is not enough to support a reasonable, particularized suspicion that the person is committing a crime. But officers are not required to ignore the relevant characteristics of a location in determining whether the circumstances are sufficiently suspicious to warrant further investigation. Accordingly, we have previously noted the fact that the stop occurred in a 'high crime area' among the relevant contextual considerations in a *Terry* analysis.

"In this case, moreover, it was not merely respondent's presence in an area of heavy narcotics trafficking that aroused the officers' suspicion but his unprovoked flight upon noticing the police. Our cases have also recognized that nervous, evasive behavior is a pertinent factor in determining reasonable suspicion. Headlong flight—wherever it occurs—is the consummate act of evasion; it is not necessarily indicative of wrongdoing, but it is certainly suggestive of such." The Court emphasized in addition that while it had previously held that "refusal to cooperate, without more, does not furnish the minimal level of objective justification needed for a detention or seizure," "unprovoked flight is simply not a mere refusal to cooperate"; and that while it "is undoubtedly true" that "there are innocent reasons for flight from police," *Terry* "recognized that the officers could detain the individuals to resolve the ambiguity."

STEVENS, J., for the four Justices concurring in part and dissenting in part, first noted the majority had "wisely" not endorsed either the state's per se rule that flight at the sight of police is always grounds for a stop or the defendant's

j. But, what if the stop is made other than at a crime scene because the individual is thought to have information about the criminal activity of others? A stop for such a purpose was involved in *United States v. Ward,* 488 F.2d 162 (9th Cir.1973), where FBI agents used their siren to stop a person driving a car, after which he displayed a false draft card. The court held that the seizure was improper because there was no emergency requiring the interview of that person at that particular time, and went on to note that *Terry* "cannot be stretched so far as to allow detentive stops for generalized criminal inquiries."

rule that such flight is never grounds for a stop, for the "inference we can reasonably draw about the motivation for a person's flight * * * will depend on a number of different circumstances. Factors such as the time of day, the number of people in the area, the character of the neighborhood, whether the officer was in uniform, the way the runner was dressed, the direction and speed of flight, and whether the person's behavior was otherwise unusual might be relevant in specific cases." (As for the State's claim "for a *per se* rule regarding 'unprovoked flight upon seeing a clearly identifiable police officer,' the four Justices responded that even this 'described a category of activity too broad and varied to permit a *per se* reasonable inference regarding the motivation for the activity.' ") Noting that instead "the totality of the circumstances, as always, must dictate the result," the dissenters found the record as a whole failed to establish reasonable suspicion, considering that it did not show whether any vehicles in the caravan were marked, whether any other officers in the group were in uniform, where the intended destination of the officers was in relation to where defendant was seen, whether the caravan had passed before defendant ran, etc., and then concluded:

"The State, along with the majority of the Court, relies as well on the assumption that this flight occurred in a high crime area. Even if that assumption is accurate, it is insufficient because even in a high crime neighborhood unprovoked flight does not invariably lead to reasonable suspicion. On the contrary, because many factors providing innocent motivations for unprovoked flight are concentrated in high crime area, the character of the neighborhood arguably makes an inference of guilt less appropriate, rather than more so.[k] Like unprovoked flight itself, presence in a high crime neighborhood is a fact too generic and susceptible to innocent explanation to satisfy the reasonable suspicion inquiry."

Regarding the scope of the majority opinion: What kind of movement away from the police, short of what the majority calls "headlong flight" in *Wardlow*, will qualify as "flight"? What police conduct would make the flight other than "unprovoked"? Does only flight "upon noticing the police" count, and if so what evidence is needed to establish that element? If the flight must coexist with presence in a "high crime area," what if anything needs to be shown about the nature of the crime problem in the area and where the area is vis-a-vis the suspect's location?

Considering the kinds of things the dissenters listed as shortcomings in the record, how would they have come out if the record had shown that the vehicles were marked, the officers were uniformed, the destination was nearby, and the caravan had not passed yet when defendant ran? In what way do the other "factors" listed by the dissenters (e.g., "time of day") manifest the likely presence or absence of an innocent motivation?

Consider Tracey L. Meares & Bernard E. Harcourt, *Transparent Adjudication and Social Science Research in Constitutional Criminal Procedure*, 90 J.Crim.L. & Criminology 733, 786–92 (2000), concluding that a "pathbreaking study of street stops in New York City released on December 1, 1999, about six weeks before *Wardlow* was published, provides critical insight to the central question in *Wardlow*." The overall ratio of stops to arrests was 9:1 (i.e., there were 9 stops for

k. As the dissenters elsewhere stated: "Among some citizens, particularly minorities and those residing in high crime areas, there is also the possibility that the fleeing person is entirely innocent, but, with or without justification, believes that contact with the police can itself be dangerous, apart from any criminal activity associated with the officer's sudden presence. For such a person, unprovoked flight is neither 'aberrant' nor 'abnormal.' Moreover, these concerns and fears are known to the police officers themselves, and are validated by law enforcement investigations into their own practices. Accordingly the evidence supporting the reasonableness of these beliefs is too pervasive to be dismissed as random or rare, and too persuasive to be disparaged as inconclusive or insufficient."

every 1 eventual arrest), but the stop/arrest ratio for blacks was twice as high as for whites, "suggest[ing] that minority individuals have a relationship with the police that makes interpretation of flight extremely difficult." The stop/arrest ratio for all cases where the stop was undertaken because of the suspect's flight was 26:1, but as to stops in the more discrete category of flight to elude the police the ratio was 15.8:1, but if that category was narrowed down further by considering only such stops in a high crime area the ratio was 45:1, which "is suggestive that in high-crime urban communities where the population is disproportionately minority, flight from an identifiable police officer is a very poor indicator that crime is afoot."

8. *Terry* relied upon the *Camara* case, p. 440, allowing safety inspections of buildings without such individualized suspicion when pursuant to an established scheme or plan. And in *Brown v. Texas,* 443 U.S. 47 (1979), a unanimous Court declared that the Fourth Amendment requires that a brief detention for investigation "be based on specific, objective facts indicating that society's legitimate interests require the seizure of the particular individual, or that the seizure must be carried out pursuant to a plan embodying explicit, neutral limitations on the conduct of individual officers." Does this mean that such a plan is a sufficient substitute for individualized suspicion? How might such a plan be drafted?

D. Permissible Extent and Scope of Temporary Seizure

1. When courts decide whether a *Terry* stop was sufficiently limited, sometimes (especially when the concern is with a threat or show of force in making the seizure or movement of the suspect from the scene thereafter) the focus may be upon whether, in light of such aggravating circumstances, the seizure was sufficiently distinguishable from a full-fledged custodial arrest. Usually, however, the focus is upon the declaration in *Terry* that the seizure "must be 'strictly tied to and justified by' the circumstances which rendered its initiation permissible," so that the inquiry is "whether it was reasonably related in scope to the circumstances which justified the interference in the first place." But the Supreme Court's later discussions of that requirement in, e.g., *Royer*, Note 2 infra, *Hensley*, p. 421, and *McArthur*, p. 362, indicate that "scope" in the broad sense actually includes two factors, one variously called "time," "duration" or "length," and the other variously called "scope" in a narrower sense or "intrusiveness." Despite the "in the first place" language in *Terry*, lower courts have understandably taken the position that in judging the length or intrusiveness of a *Terry* stop it is proper to take into account the offense reasonably suspected at the outset and also other offenses reasonably suspected as a result of information previously obtained lawfully during the stop. See, e.g., *Medrano v. State*, 914 P.2d 804 (Wyo.1996) (officer did not exceed scope of stop by inquiring if defendant possessed drugs, as while stop was on reasonable suspicion of robbery, there then developed reasonable suspicion of drug possession).

2. While a *Terry* stop may be rendered unlawful because the officer used a threat or show of force suggestive of the making of a full-fledged arrest, such as drawing a weapon, handcuffing the suspect, or placing him in a squad car, such tactics do not inevitably establish that the officer exceeded his authority under *Terry*. Although such tactics are hardly "standard procedures" for *Terry* stops, their use has been upheld when the facts of the particular case show that the decision to utilize them was reasonable. See, e.g., *Flowers v. Fiore*, 359 F.3d 24 (1st Cir.2004) (officers properly drew their guns, as they "were faced with a report of an armed threat"); *State v. Munson*, 594 N.W.2d 128 (Minn.1999) ("brief handcuffing" proper here, as stop was late at night, involved multiple suspects, and was on information vehicle carrying large amount of drugs and that occupants might be armed); *Commonwealth v. Gwynn*, 723 A.2d 143 (Pa.1998) ("placing appellant in the police car during this nighttime street encounter in a high-crime area while his identification was checked" proper).

Movement of the suspect to another location may also indicate that the officer has exceeded his *Terry* authority, especially if, as in *Dunaway*, p. 438, the suspect is taken to the police station and subjected to a detention "in important respects indistinguishable from a traditional arrest." In FLORIDA v. ROYER, 460 U.S. 491 (1983), detectives questioned Royer on an airport concourse and then asked him to accompany them to a small room about 40 feet away. His luggage was retrieved from the airline and brought to that room, and Royer was then asked to consent to a search of the suitcases, which he did. About 15 minutes had elapsed since the initial encounter. The *Royer* plurality then concluded "that at the time Royer produced the key to his suitcase, the detention to which he was then subjected was a more serious intrusion on his personal liberty than is allowable on mere suspicion of criminal activity." They stressed: (i) that the situation "had escalated into an investigatory procedure in a police interrogation room," so that "[a]s a practical matter, Royer was under arrest"; and (ii) that "the officers' conduct was more intrusive than necessary to effectuate an investigative detention otherwise authorized by the *Terry* line of cases," as while "there are undoubtedly reasons of safety and security that would justify moving a suspect from one location to another during an investigatory detention, such as from an airport concourse to a more private area," there was "no indication in this case that such reasons prompted the officers to transfer the site of the encounter from the concourse to the interrogation room. It appears, rather, that the primary interest of the officers was not in having an extended conversation with Royer but in the contents of his luggage, a matter which the officers did not pursue orally with Royer until after the encounter was relocated to the police room. The record does not reflect any facts which would support a finding that the legitimate law enforcement purposes which justified the detention in the first instance were furthered by removing Royer to the police room prior to the officer's attempt to gain his consent to a search of his luggage. As we have noted, had Royer consented to a search on the spot, the search could have been conducted with Royer present in the area where the bags were retrieved by Officer Johnson and any evidence recovered would have been admissible against him. If the search proved negative, Royer would have been free to go much earlier and with less likelihood of missing his flight, which in itself can be a very serious matter in a variety of circumstances."

What then if the suspect was transported to a nearby crime scene for possible identification as the perpetrator? Consider *People v. Harris*, 540 P.2d 632 (Cal. 1975) (such action "violated defendant's constitutional rights," as officers failed to pursue "less intrusive and more reasonable alternatives to pre-arrest transportation," such as "escort[ing] the witness to the detention scene for an immediate viewing of the suspect, or [making] arrangements * * * for a subsequent confrontation with the witness"); *People v. Bloyd*, 331 N.W.2d 447 (Mich.1982) (because transportation of suspect even a short distance more intrusive than a mere stop, it "should be dependent upon knowledge that a crime has been committed" and impermissible when the defendant's conduct was suspicious but "there has not been any report of a crime" recently in the vicinity).

3. As for the time limits on a *Terry* stop, consider UNITED STATES v. SHARPE, 470 U.S. 675 (1985). There, a federal drug agent, patrolling in an unmarked car in a highway area under surveillance for drug trafficking, saw an apparently overloaded camper truck traveling in tandem with a Pontiac. He radioed for assistance, and when a highway patrolman responded they attempted to stop the two vehicles. The Pontiac pulled over, but the truck continued on, pursued by the patrolman. Once the drug agent obtained identification from the driver of the Pontiac, he sought without success to reach the patrolman by radio. He then radioed for more assistance, and when local police appeared he left them with the Pontiac and drove ahead to where the patrolman had stopped the truck. After smelling the odor of marijuana coming from the vehicle, he opened it and saw bales of marijuana and then arrested the driver of the truck, one Savage. The Court of Appeals held that the 20–minute detention of Savage "failed to meet the [Fourth Amendment's] requirement of brevity," but the Supreme Court, per BURGER, C.J., disagreed:

"* * * Obviously, if an investigative stop continues indefinitely, at some point it can no longer be justified as an investigative stop. But our cases impose no rigid time limitation on *Terry* stops. * * * Much as a 'bright line' rule would be desirable, in evaluating whether an investigative detention is unreasonable, common sense and ordinary human experience must govern over rigid criteria.[l]

"In assessing whether a detention is too long in duration to be justified as an investigative stop, we consider it appropriate to examine whether the police diligently pursued a means of investigation that was likely to confirm or dispel their suspicions quickly, during which time it was necessary to detain the defendant. A court making this assessment should take care to consider whether the police are acting in a swiftly developing situation, and in such cases the court should not indulge in unrealistic second-guessing. A creative judge engaged in *post hoc* evaluation of police conduct can almost always imagine some alternative means by which the objectives of the police might have been accomplished. But '[t]he fact that the protection of the public might, in the abstract, have been accomplished by "less intrusive" means does not, in itself, render the search unreasonable.' The question is not simply whether some other alternative was available, but whether the police acted unreasonably in failing to recognize or to pursue it."

Stressing that the "delay in this case was attributable almost entirely to the evasive actions of Savage," that most of the 20 minutes was consumed by the agent trying to reach the patrolman and to obtain additional assistance, and that when the agent reached Savage "he proceeded expeditiously," the majority in *Sharpe* concluded the delay was not unreasonable. MARSHALL, J., though concurring because the "prolonged encounter" was attributable to "the evasive actions" of Savage, argued that "fidelity to the rationales that justify *Terry* stops require that the intrusiveness of the stop be measured independently of law enforcement needs. A stop must first be found not unduly intrusive, particularly in its length, before it is proper to consider whether law enforcement aims warrant limited investigation." BRENNAN, J., dissenting, objected that record did not clearly show that Savage had tried to elude the police, and that the government had not met its burden under *Royer* to "show at a minimum that the 'least intrusive means reasonably available' were used in carrying out the stop."

4. In HIIBEL v. SIXTH JUDICIAL DISTRICT COURT, 542 U.S. 177 (2004), defendant was convicted of obstructing an officer in his duties for not complying with the command in Nevada's "stop and identify" statute that a person lawfully stopped under *Terry* "shall identify himself." The Court held, 5–4, that defendant's conviction did not violate either the Fourth Amendment or (see Note 10, p. 628) the Fifth Amendment's privilege against self-incrimination. On the Fourth Amendment issue, the majority declared Justice White's statement in *Terry* (p. 408) meant only that "the Fourth Amendment itself cannot require a suspect to answer questions," while the instant case posed the "different issue" of

l. Compare *Model Code of Pre–Arraignment Procedure* § 110.2(1), recommending a maximum of 20 minutes for a *Terry* stop.

whether state law could impose such a requirement without violating the Fourth Amendment. Using a *Terry*-style balancing of interests, the Court answered the latter question in the affirmative, reasoning (i) that the "request for identity has an immediate relation to the purpose, rationale, and practical demands of a *Terry* stop"; (ii) that the "threat of criminal sanction helps ensure that the request for identity does not become a legal nullity"; and (iii) that such threat "does not alter the nature of the stop itself" provided (as is essential under *Terry*) that the "the request for identification was 'reasonably related in scope to the circumstances which justified' the stop." (The dissenters objected there was "no good reason now to reject" a "generation-old statement of law," the "strong dicta" in *Berkemer v. McCarty*, p. 608, that a *Terry* detainee "is not obliged to respond" to any questions.) Does the *Terry* scope limitation mean that sometimes a request for identity will be outside the scope of the stop? Consider *Carey v. Nevada Gaming Control Board,* 279 F.3d 873 (9th Cir.2002) (asking Carey, detained in a Nevada casino because he was suspected of cheating while gambling, for identification made the detention unlawful, as "Carey's name was not related to determining whether Carey had cheated").

Hiibel has limited Fourth Amendment significance; it does not affect when a *Terry* stop may be made or how a post-stop investigation may be conducted, and only approves a crime definition permitting arrest in the rare event a suspect refuses to give a name. *Hiibel* is so limited because the Court, relying upon a sentence in the state court decision asserting that the suspect is only required "to state his name," assumed that "the statute does not require a suspect to give the officer a driver's license or any other document," and thus limited its holding to the "question whether a State can compel a suspect to disclose his name during a *Terry* stop." But the facts of the case as recited by the Court appear to indicate that Hiibel was repeatedly asked "to produce a driver's license or some other form of written identification," which he repeatedly refused to do, but was never asked (and thus never refused) merely to state his name. Would/should the Court come out the same way had it focused upon those facts rather than the state court's representation? Is requiring production of written identification actually the preferred investigative technique during a *Terry* stop because of its greater reliability, or is that offset by the fact any written identification tendered is likely to reveal additional information about the suspect? A dissent in *Hiibel* asks: "Can a State, in addition to requiring a stopped individual to answer 'What's your name?' also require an answer to 'What's your license number?' or 'Where do you live?' "

5. Often relying upon the Supreme Court's statement in *Berkemer v. McCarty*, p. 608, that "the usual traffic stop is more analogous to a so-called '*Terry* stop' than to a formal arrest," defendants subjected to the pretext traffic stop tactic discussed in Notes 5–8, pp. 343–45, have often relied upon the temporal and scope limitations in the *Terry* line of cases as a basis for seeking to suppress evidence (usually narcotics) found by police employing various investigative techniques after a traffic stop. As a consequence, some courts have held certain investigative activities improper because conducted after all legitimate actions relating to the traffic stop had been completed, e.g., *Harris v. Commonwealth*, 581 S.E.2d 206 (Va.2003), or because they were directed at criminal activity for which reasonable suspicion was then lacking, e.g., *State v. Fort*, 660 N.W.2d 415 (Minn.2003), while other courts have been unwilling or less willing to do so (sometimes noting the *Berkemer* statement has a qualifying footnote: "We of course do not suggest that a traffic stop supported by probable cause may not exceed the bounds set by the Fourth Amendment on the scope of a *Terry* stop"). See Wayne R. LaFave, *The "Routine Traffic Stop" From Start to Finish: Too Much "Routine," Not Enough Fourth Amendment*, 102 Mich.L.Rev. 1843 (2004).

Then came ILLINOIS v. CABALLES, ___ U.S. ___, 125 S.Ct. 834 (2005), where defendant was stopped by a state trooper for doing 71 m.p.h. on an interstate highway with a posted speed limit of 65. Another trooper assigned to the Drug Interdiction Team heard a radio transmission reporting the stop and without any request immediately traveled to the scene and walked his drug dog around defendant's car while defendant was in the patrol car awaiting a warning ticket. The dog alerted, and in a subsequent search of the car's trunk marijuana was found. The state supreme court overturned defendant's conviction on the ground that use of the dog "unjustifiably enlarge[ed] the scope of a routine traffic stop into a drug investigation." The *total* response by the Supreme Court to that conclusion[m] was, per STEVENS, J., as follows:

"Here, the initial seizure of respondent when he was stopped on the highway was based on probable cause, and was concededly lawful. It is nevertheless clear that a seizure that is lawful at its inception can violate the Fourth Amendment if its manner of execution unreasonably infringes interests protected by the Constitution. A seizure that is justified solely by the interest in issuing a warning ticket to the driver can become unlawful if it is prolonged beyond the time reasonably required to complete that mission. In an earlier case involving a dog sniff that occurred during an unreasonably prolonged traffic stop, the Illinois Supreme Court held that use of the dog and the subsequent discovery of contraband were the product of an unconstitutional seizure. We may assume that a similar result would be warranted in this case if the dog sniff had been conducted while respondent was being unlawfully detained.

"In the state-court proceedings, however, the judges carefully reviewed the details of Officer Gillette's conversations with respondent and the precise timing of his radio transmissions to the dispatcher to determine whether he had improperly extended the duration of the stop to enable the dog sniff to occur. We have not recounted those details because we accept the state court's conclusion that the duration of the stop in this case was entirely justified by the traffic offense and the ordinary inquiries incident to such a stop.

"Despite this conclusion, the Illinois Supreme Court held that the initially lawful traffic stop became an unlawful seizure solely as a result of the canine sniff that occurred outside respondent's stopped car. That is, the court characterized the dog sniff as the cause rather than the consequence of a constitutional violation. In its view, the use of the dog converted the citizen-police encounter from a lawful traffic stop into a drug investigation, and because the shift in purpose was not supported by any reasonable suspicion that respondent possessed narcotics, it was unlawful. In our view, conducting a dog sniff would not change the character of a traffic stop that is lawful at its inception and otherwise executed in a reasonable manner, unless the dog sniff itself infringed respondent's constitutionally protected interest in privacy. Our cases hold that it did not."

In light of *Caballes*, what is the status of various other investigative techniques commonly utilized incident to traffic stops, theretofore challenged with varied results, see LaFave, supra, at 1874–98, such as running a warrant check on the driver, running a criminal history check on the driver, questioning the driver about whether there are narcotics in the vehicle, questioning the driver about whether there are weapons in the vehicle, questioning the driver in detail about his travels (beginning, destination, route, purpose, contacts, etc.), seeking consent from the driver to conduct a search of the vehicle, or doing any of the above with respect to a mere passenger in the vehicle? Are all of them unobjectionable because they too are not searches? Even assuming that is so, is their occurrence always irrelevant? What if in *Caballes* the defendant had spent more time in the squad car because of such investigative activities and only because of that was still being detained when the dog arrived? That is, does the conclusion a particular

m. The Court devoted an equal amount of space to explaining why it was not abandoning its prior holdings to the effect that a drug dog sniff is not a Fourth Amendment search; see p. 263. The state court had never claimed otherwise, although counsel for Caballes did.

investigative technique is permissible during a traffic stop necessarily means is it a permissible basis for extending the length of that stop?

6. SEARCHSZR § 9.3(b) (pending revision) takes a dim view of *Caballes*: "For all one would conclude from the *Caballes* majority opinion,[51.6] the Illinois supreme court had fancied up out of whole cloth a concept so wanting in bona fides that it could be dismissed out of hand. But in actuality, the state court opinion, as with the state and federal cases in general accord cited earlier, was grounded in the straightforward proposition that the temporal and scope limitations adopted in *Terry* and its progeny are equally applicable to traffic stops. It is odd, to say the least, that the Supreme Court, in overturning the state court ruling, never even cited *Terry* or any of the post-*Terry* stop-and-frisk cases discussing those limitations, and, for that matter, *never cited any prior Supreme Court decision at all* to justify its holding!

"The abruptness of the Court's decision and the virtually total lack of analysis might appear even to raise some doubt as to what the basis of the decision actually is. But, * * * the *Caballes* decision seems to be grounded in nothing other than the bald assertion that only such conduct as itself constitutes a Fourth Amendment search can qualify as investigative activity amounting to a scope violation under the *Terry* line of cases. If this is so, then the Court's failure to cite a single precedent in support becomes quite understandable, for the Supreme Court's relevant prior decisions consistently point in the other direction.

"For one thing, if the *Terry* scope limitation was only a no-search command, it would amount to nothing more than an unnecessary redundancy, as all the search limitations upon the police were otherwise spelled out in *Terry* and related decisions. *Terry* made it unmistakably clear, in another branch of the case not dealing with the scope limits, that the only exception to the usual rule that a search for evidence requires full probable cause is that an officer in a *Terry* context could upon reasonable suspicion that the suspect was armed and dangerous make a limited 'frisk' of the suspect's person (extended to the suspect's car in *Michigan v Long* [p. 435]).

"For another, the Supreme Court has time and again pursued a scope inquiry as to challenged *Terry*-like stops even when the questioned investigative activity was *not* a search. In *Illinois v. McArthur* [p. 362], the Court upheld a brief seizure of defendant pending issuance of a search warrant for his residence, and though the seizure was deemed to involve merely '[t]emporarily keeping a person from entering his home, a consequence * * * considerably less intrusive than police entry into the home,' the Court still declined to uphold that seizure until it had determined that it was sufficiently 'limited in time and scope.' And in *Hiibel v. Sixth Judicial District Court* [p. 426], the investigative technique at issue was merely asking the suspect's name during a *Terry* stop, obviously not itself a search, but the Court nonetheless declined to uphold such an inquiry until it had determined that 'the request for identification was "reasonably related in scope to the circumstances which justified" the stop.' Moreover, *Hiibel* relied upon *Hayes v. Florida* [p. 436], suggesting fingerprinting might sometimes be justified incident to a *Terry* stop, where the Court cautiously added such action would be permissible only if there was 'a reasonable basis for believing that fingerprinting will establish or negate the suspect's connection with that crime' justifying the stop, notwithstanding the Court's earlier characterization of fingerprinting as a non-search obtaining of 'physical characteristics . . . constantly exposed to the public.'

"Had the Supreme Court in *Caballes* been true to these precedents, the Court would have held that use of the drug dog, albeit no search, was unreasonable because it was beyond the scope limitation of that traffic stop and constituted something more than the 'non-event' the petitioner claimed it was. While petition-

51.6 However, the dissent by Justice Ginsburg, joined by Justice Souter, clearly indicates the *Terry* groundings of the state court's decision and correctly concludes that the *Terry* limits deserve to be followed in the instant case.

er contended that use of a drug dog is not governed by the *Terry* scope limitation because it is essentially a 'non-event,' no different than if the officer, standing by to receive the driver's license and registration, were instead handed a bag of cocaine, there are two answers to this. The first is that it is not really necessary that the investigative technique have some profound effect upon the detainee in order to fall outside the scope limitation. It is the very fact that the technique does not serve the purposes of traffic law enforcement (or whatever purposes relate to the offense reasonably suspected in the case of a traditional *Terry* stop) that alone establishes a scope violation. This is apparent from the Court's most recent pre-*Caballes* discussion of the subject in *Hiibel*, which recognized that an act as insignificant as speaking four words ('What is your name?') could be a *Terry* scope violation. The Court imposed a scope limitation even as to the investigative technique of seeking a name, concluded the identity inquiry 'in this case' was proper because 'the request for identification was "reasonably related in scope to the circumstances which justified" the stop,' and thus by implication recognized there could be instances in which such a brief and limited inquiry would be constitutionally impermissible as a Fourth Amendment matter because beyond the scope of the temporary detention.

"The second answer is that what happened in *Caballes* is profoundly different from the situation put by Petitioner where an officer standing by to receive the driver's credentials happens to see drugs in the driver's hand. This latter situation truly involves a non-event, as the plain view of drugs was accomplished without any intrusive activity by the police officer. But if one asks whether use of the drug dog is such a non-event, the answer is most certainly no, even from the perspective of a traffic violator who is *not* violating the drug laws. * * * If a driver innocent of drug possession had the option of a traffic stop with a dog sniff or a traffic stop without a dog sniff, surely he or she would opt for the latter. This is because 'a dog sniff around a motor vehicle stopped only for a routine ... violation is intrusive to some degree,' for use of the dog produces many unpleasant and adverse consequences even for the innocent driver."[n]

7. Should the Supreme Court in *Caballes* instead have distinguished *Terry* and the other stop-and-frisk cases simply on the ground that in the instant case the traffic stop was made on probable cause rather than reasonable suspicion? Consider *United States v. Childs*, 256 F.3d 559 (7th Cir.2001), where upon stopping a vehicle having a cracked windshield, the officer asked passenger Childs, whose seat belt was not fastened, whether he was carrying marijuana (Childs said no) and whether he would consent to a search (Childs agreed), resulting in discovery of cocaine. While the panel decision concluded that "inquiries falling outside the scope of the detention constitute unlawful seizure," on rehearing en banc, 277 F.3d 947 (7th Cir.2002), the court concluded otherwise because (a) the asking of questions is not itself an independent seizure, and (b) the questioning did not make the pre-existing seizure unreasonable. With regard to the latter conclusion, the majority noted the oft-quoted statement from *Berkemer*, set out in Note 6 supra, but then declared that "it does not follow that the Constitution requires all traffic stops to be treated as if they were unsupported by probable cause." The en banc dissenters objected: "What the majority seems to be saying is that, because [the officer] *could* have gone on to a custodial arrest, he may instead (and without subjecting Childs to custodial arrest) elect to inquire into crimes for which there is neither probable cause nor reasonable suspicion." Taking into account *Atwater*, p. 335, *Knowles*, p. 349, *Cupp*, p. 350, and *Sharpe*, p. 425, what

n. This last point is elaborated in SEARCHSZR § 9.3(f) (pending revision): "(1) The use of large dogs in the immediate proximity of persons has an intimidating character to

would be the correct holding on this point under the facts of *Childs* or *Caballes*? See LaFave, Note 5 supra, at 1862–74.

8. If, as *Caballes* appears to acknowledge, the *Terry* temporal limitation has application in traffic cases, then it will be necessary in many instances to determine whether a traffic stop was extended or instead terminated at a certain point. Even if it is apparent to the defendant that the officer has completed writing up the ticket or warning, that does not terminate the stop if the officer continues to hold the defendant's license, vehicle registration, or other credentials. *United States v. Fernandez*, 18 F.3d 874 (10th Cir.1994). But if the officer *has* returned those credentials, does this mean that the seizure has terminated even if the officer then uses the Lt. Colombo gambit ("Oh, one more thing, . . . ") in order to question the defendant about drugs, as concluded in *United States v. Werking*, 915 F.2d 1404 (10th Cir.1990)?

Consider OHIO v. ROBINETTE, 519 U.S. 33 (1996), which involved these facts: a sheriff's deputy on "drug interdiction patrol" stopped defendant for speeding. The deputy examined defendant's license, ran a computer check indicating no previous violations, issued a verbal warning and returned defendant's license, and then immediately asked defendant if he had drugs in the car; when defendant answered in the negative, the deputy asked to search the car and defendant consented, resulting in a search which uncovered a small amount of marijuana and a single pill which was a controlled substance. The state supreme court concluded the evidence must be suppressed, reasoning that the "right to be secure in one's person and property requires that citizens stopped for traffic offenses be clearly informed by the detaining officer when they are free to go after a valid detention, before an officer attempts to engage in a consensual interrogation." The Supreme Court, per REHNQUIST, C.J., focused on the issue stated in the certiorari petition, whether such a warning is a prerequisite to a voluntary consent, and answered in the negative. The state court's per se rule was deemed inconsistent with the approach to Fourth Amendment issues by the Supreme Court, which has "consistently eschewed bright-line rules, instead emphasizing the fact-specific nature of the reasonableness inquiry." Moreover, the Court reasoned in *Robinette*, requiring such warnings would be just as impractical as the right-to-refuse-consent warnings held unnecessary by the Court in *Schneckloth v. Bustamonte* [p. 447].

it, whether it occurs in Abu Graib prison or alongside an interstate. * * * (2) Use of a drug dog on the vehicle of a motorist stopped for a traffic violation is an accusatory act, one which will be upsetting to the innocent motorist because it will appear that he has been singled out as a drug suspect for reasons about which he can only speculate. * * * (3) Use of a drug dog incident to a traffic stop is likely to be humiliating to the driver of the vehicle, for such use manifests police suspicion of the driver as a drug courier to all those who may pass by while the scenario is being played out on the side of an interstate highway or city street. * * * (4) Use of a drug dog on a vehicle stopped for a traffic violation will in many instances cause the driver and his passengers to be delayed in their journey longer than would have been the case absent this type of investigative activity[, as when] a dog and handler are being summoned to the scene of a traffic stop, the stopping officer is tempted to engage in stalling regarding his proper functions during the stop (e.g., checking registration and driver's license credentials, writing up a citation or warning notice) in order to give the appearance that the time for the stop has not expired in the interim. * * * (5) Use of drug dogs in wholesale fashion without individualized suspicion creates an unnecessary and unjustified risk that many motorists totally innocent of any wrongdoing regarding drugs will be subjected to an extended and exhaustive roadside search of their vehicles[, as d]rug dogs and drug handlers do make mistakes." For more on the fallibility of drug dogs, see Justice Souter's *Caballes* dissent at p. 263.

Only Justice STEVENS, dissenting, fully considered an alternative characterization of the state court's holding, namely, that (i) the officer's failure to tell defendant he was free to leave meant that a reasonable person would continue to believe he was not free to leave, so that the seizure had not yet ended at the time the consent was obtained; (ii) the seizure by that time was illegal, as it had exceeded its lawful purpose, the giving of a warning about the traffic offense; and (iii) consequently the evidence obtained via the voluntary consent was a suppressible fruit of that poisonous tree. He concluded that the evidence in the case (including the fact that this deputy had used this tactic to make 786 consent searches in one year) supported that conclusion, so that the suppression of evidence by the state court was justified.

The *Robinette* majority was not totally silent regarding this theory. The defendant argued the Court could not reach the voluntariness issue because the state court decision set out a valid alternative ground in the following language: "When the motivation behind a police officer's continued detention of a person stopped for a traffic violation is not related to the purpose of the original, constitutional stop, and when that continued detention is not based on articulable facts giving rise to a suspicion of some separate illegal activity justifying an extension of the detention, the continued detention constitutes an illegal seizure." Relying on the *Whren* case, p. 339, the Chief Justice declared that the state court was in error because "the subjective intentions of the officer did not make the continued detention of respondent illegal under the Fourth Amendment." Is this a proper application of *Whren*? Does it mean that in applying the *Terry* scope limitation, the fact the officer decided only to give a warning instead of a ticket is irrelevant? Or, is Justice Stevens correct in concluding that the irrelevant subjective motivation was drug interdiction, but that the subjective purpose of giving a warning bears on the justification for the continued detention, so that by the time the consent was obtained "the lawful traffic stop had come to an end" because the defendant "had been given his warning"?

E. Temporary Seizure of Effects

1. In *United States v. Van Leeuwen,* 397 U.S. 249 (1970) a postal clerk in Mt. Vernon, Washington, advised a policeman that he was suspicious of two packages of coins just mailed. The policeman immediately noted that the return address was fictitious and that the individual who mailed the packages had Canadian license plates, and later investigation disclosed that the addressees (one in California, the other in Tennessee) were under investigation for trafficking in illegal coins. Upon this basis a search warrant for both packages was obtained, but not until the packages had been held for slightly more than a day. A unanimous Court, although acknowledging that "detention of mail could at some point become an unreasonable seizure of 'papers' or 'effects' within the meaning of the Fourth Amendment," cited *Terry* in upholding this "detention, without a warrant, while an investigation was made." The Court emphasized that the investigation was conducted promptly and that most of the delay was attributable to the fact that because of the time differential the Tennessee authorities could not be reached until the following day.

2. In UNITED STATES v. PLACE, 462 U.S. 696 (1983), federal agents stopped respondent, a suspected drug courier, at LaGuardia Airport, seized his luggage for the purported purpose of taking it to a judge while a warrant was sought, and then allowed respondent to go his way. They took the bags to Kennedy Airport, where a trained narcotics dog reacted positively to one of them and ambiguously to the other, but because it was late Friday afternoon held the bags until Monday morning, when a warrant was obtained for the first bag and cocaine was found in execution of the warrant. The Court, per O'CONNOR, J., first recognized "the reasonableness under the Fourth Amendment of warrantless seizures of personal luggage from the custody of the owner on the basis of less than probable cause for the purpose of pursuing a limited course of investigation, short of opening the luggage, that would quickly confirm or dispel the authorities' suspicion." Applying the *Terry* balancing of interests approach, the Court concluded that "the governmental interest in seizing the luggage briefly to pursue further investigation is substantial," and that because "seizures of property can vary in intrusiveness, some brief detentions of personal effects may be so minimally intrusive of Fourth Amendment interests that strong countervailing governmental interests will justify a seizure based only on specific articulable facts that the property contains contraband or evidence of a crime.

" * * * Particularly in the case of detention of luggage within the traveler's immediate possession, the police conduct intrudes on both the suspect's possessory interest in his luggage as well as his liberty interest in proceeding with his itinerary. The person whose luggage is detained is technically still free to continue his travels or carry out other personal activities pending release of the luggage. Moreover, he is not subjected to the coercive atmosphere of a custodial confinement or to the public indignity of being personally detained. Nevertheless, such a seizure can effectively restrain the person since he is subjected to the possible disruption of his travel plans in order to remain with his luggage or to arrange for its return.[8] Therefore, when the police seize luggage from the suspect's custody, we think the limitations applicable to investigative detentions of the person should define the permissible scope of an investigative detention of the person's luggage on less than probable cause. Under this standard, it is clear that the police conduct here exceeded the permissible limits of a *Terry*-type investigative stop.

"The length of the detention of respondent's luggage alone precludes the conclusion that the seizure was reasonable in the absence of probable cause. Although we have recognized the reasonableness of seizures longer than the momentary ones involved in *Terry,* the brevity of the invasion of the individual's Fourth Amendment interests is an important factor in determining whether the seizure is so minimally intrusive as to be justifiable on reasonable suspicion. Moreover, in assessing the effect of the length of the detention, we take into account whether the police diligently pursue their investigation. We note that here the New York agents knew the time of Place's scheduled arrival at LaGuardia, had ample time to arrange for their additional investigation at that location, and thereby could have minimized the intrusion on respondent's Fourth Amendment interests. Thus, although we decline to adopt any outside time limitation for a permissible *Terry* stop, we have never approved a seizure of the person for the prolonged 90–minute period involved here and cannot do so on the facts presented by this case.

"Although the 90–minute detention of respondent's luggage is sufficient to render the seizure unreasonable, the violation was exacerbated by the failure of the agents to accurately inform respondent of the place to which they were

8. "At least when the authorities do not make it absolutely clear how they plan to reunite the suspect and his possessions at some future time and place, seizure of the object is tantamount to seizure of the person. This is because that person must either remain on the scene or else seemingly surrender his effects permanently to the police." 3 W. LaFave, *Search and Seizure* § 9.6, p. 61 (1982 Supp.).

transporting his luggage, of the length of time he might be dispossessed, and of what arrangements would be made for return of the luggage if the investigation dispelled the suspicion."

F. PROTECTIVE SEARCH

1. After *Terry,* what is the test for determining whether an officer may conduct a "frisk"? Consider *Sibron,* p. 417, where the Court stated: "In the case of the self-protective search for weapons, [the officer] must be able to point to particular facts from which he reasonably inferred that the individual was armed and dangerous. Patrolman Martin's testimony reveals no such facts. The suspect's mere act of talking with a number of known narcotics addicts over an eight-hour period no more gives rise to reasonable fear of life or limb on the part of the police officer than it justifies an arrest for committing a crime. Nor did Patrolman Martin urge that when Sibron put his hand in his pocket, he feared that he was going for a weapon and acted in self-defense. His opening statement to Sibron—'You know what I am after'—made it abundantly clear that he sought narcotics, and his testimony at the hearing left no doubt that he thought there were narcotics in Sibron's pocket."

Compare *Adams v. Williams,* 407 U.S. 143 (1972), where the majority concluded the officer "had ample reason to fear for his own safety"[o] upon being told by an informant that defendant, seated in a nearby car, was carrying narcotics and had a gun at his waist. Marshall, J., joined by Douglas, J., dissenting, objected: "The fact remains that Connecticut specifically authorizes persons to carry guns so long as they have a permit. Thus, there was no reason for the officer to infer from anything that the informant said that the respondent was dangerous."

Is the quantum and reliability of information needed to support a frisk the same or less than that needed to support a stop? For example, what if the stop was made on a reliable informant's information the suspect possessed illegal gambling paraphernalia, and the officer had also received a report from an anonymous informant that this same person regularly carries a gun? Reconsider the final paragraph of Justice Ginsburg's opinion in *J. L.*, p. 418.

2. Consider David A. Harris, *Frisking Every Suspect: The Withering of* Terry, 28 U.C. Davis L.Rev. 1, 5, 43–44 (1994): "Perhaps as a result of the high-visibility use of frisks as a contemporary crime control device, or because of general public antipathy to crime, lower courts have stretched the law governing frisks to the point that the Supreme Court might find it unrecognizable. Lower courts have consistently expanded the *types of offenses* always considered violent regardless of the individual circumstances. At the same time, lower courts have also found that certain *types of persons and situations* always pose a danger of armed violence to police [e.g., those present in a high-crime or drug-involved location who engage in allegedly evasive behavior toward the police]. When confronted with these offenses, persons, or situations, police may *automatically* frisk, whether or not any individualized circumstances point to danger. * * *

"* * * African–Americans and Hispanic–Americans pay a higher personal price for [these] contemporary stop and frisk practices than whites do."

o. The Court footnoted that statement with the following: "Figures reported by the Federal Bureau of Investigation indicate that 125 policemen were murdered in 1971, with all but five of them having been killed by gunshot wounds. Federal Bureau of Investigation *Law Enforcement Bulletin,* February 1972, p. 33. According to one study, approximately 30% of police shootings occurred when a police officer approached a suspect seated in an automobile. Bristow, *Police Officer Shootings—A Tactical Evaluation,* 54 J.Crim.L.C. & P.S. 93 (1963)."

3. As for the requisite search procedure, the Court in *Sibron* stated: "The search for weapons approved in *Terry* consisted solely of a limited patting of the outer clothing of the suspect for concealed objects which might be used as instruments of assault. Only when he discovered such objects did the officer in *Terry* place his hands in the pockets of the men he searched. In this case, with no attempt at an initial limited exploration for arms, Patrolman Martin thrust his hand into Sibron's pocket and took from him envelopes of heroin. His testimony shows that he was looking for narcotics, and he found them. The search was not reasonably limited in scope to the accomplishment of the only goal which might conceivably have justified its inception—the protection of the officer by disarming a potentially dangerous man."

Compare *Adams v. Williams,* where the officer immediately reached into the car and removed a theretofore concealed gun from defendant's waistband. The Court stated: "When Williams rolled down his window, rather than complying with the policeman's request to step out of the car so that his movements could more easily be seen, the revolver allegedly at Williams' waist became an even greater threat. Under these circumstances the policeman's action in reaching to the spot where the gun was thought to be hidden constituted a limited intrusion designed to insure his safety, and we conclude that it was reasonable."

4. Assuming that there are grounds for a protective search, how extensive a "patting down" of the suspect is permissible? Consider the description quoted in note 13 of *Terry.* Is the right to make a protective search limited to the person of the suspect? What if the suspect is carrying an attache case, a shopping bag, a purse, or similar object?

In *Minnesota v. Dickerson,* 508 U.S. 366 (1993), the frisking officer felt a small lump in the suspect's front pocket and then, upon further tactile examination, concluded the lump was crack cocaine in a plastic or cellophane bag, which the officer removed from the suspect's pocket. Noting the state court's findings that the officer "determined that the lump was contraband only after 'squeezing, sliding and otherwise manipulating the outside of the defendant's pocket' " *after* the officer knew it contained no weapon, the Supreme Court held the state court "was correct in holding that the police officer in this case overstepped the bounds of the 'strictly circumscribed' search for weapons allowed under *Terry.*"

5. In MICHIGAN v. LONG, 463 U.S. 1032 (1983), two deputies saw a car swerve into a ditch and stopped to investigate. Long, the only occupant of the car, met the deputies at the rear of the car, supplied his driver's license upon demand, and started back toward the open door when asked for his vehicle registration. The officers saw a large hunting knife on the floorboard, so Long was frisked and one officer then entered the vehicle and found an open pouch of marijuana under an armrest. The Supreme Court, per O'CONNOR, J., held:

"Our past cases indicate then that protection of police and others can justify protective searches when police have a reasonable belief that the suspect poses a danger, that roadside encounters between police and suspects are especially hazardous, and that danger may arise from the possible presence of weapons in the area surrounding a suspect. These principles compel our conclusion that the search of the passenger compartment of an automobile, limited to those areas in which a weapon may be placed or hidden, is permissible if the police officer possesses a reasonable belief based on 'specific and articulable facts which, taken together with the rational inferences from those facts, reasonably warrant' the officers in believing that the suspect is dangerous and the suspect may gain immediate control of weapons. * * *

"The Michigan Supreme Court appeared to believe that it was not reasonable for the officers to fear that Long could injure them, because he was effectively under their control during the investigative stop and could not get access to any weapons that might have been located in the automobile. This reasoning is mistaken in several respects. * * * Just as a *Terry* suspect on the street may, despite being under the brief control of a police officer, reach into his clothing and retrieve a weapon, so might a *Terry* suspect in Long's position break away from police control and retrieve a weapon from his automobile. In addition, if the suspect is not placed under arrest, he will be permitted to reenter his automobile, and he will then have access to any weapons inside. Or, as here, the suspect may be permitted to reenter the vehicle before the *Terry* investigation is over, and again, may have access to weapons. In any event, we stress that a *Terry* investigation, such as the one that occurred here, involves a police investigation 'at close range,' when the officer remains particularly vulnerable in part *because* a full custodial arrest has not been effected, and the officer must make a 'quick decision as to how to protect himself and others from possible danger * * *.' In such circumstances, we have not required that officers adopt alternate means to ensure their safety in order to avoid the intrusion involved in a *Terry* encounter."

BRENNAN and Marshall, JJ., dissenting, objected: "Putting aside the fact that the search at issue here involved a far more serious intrusion than that 'involved in a *Terry* encounter,' and as such might suggest the need for resort to 'alternate means,' the Court's reasoning is perverse. The Court's argument in essence is that the *absence* of probable cause to arrest compels the conclusion that a broad search, traditionally associated in scope with a search incident to arrest, must be permitted based on reasonable suspicion."

6. Can a limited search for any other reason ever be undertaken incident to a lawful stop? In *State v. Flynn,* 285 N.W.2d 710 (Wis.1979), one of two suspects lawfully stopped for investigation of a just-completed burglary admitted he had identification in his wallet but refused to identify himself, so the officer removed the wallet and examined it to the extent necessary to find the suspect's name and then arrested the suspect when a radio check revealed he was wanted for an earlier crime. Reasoning that "unless the officer is entitled to at least ascertain the identity of the suspect, the right to stop him can serve no useful purpose at all," that the search was a very limited one, and "that defendant could himself have substantially avoided the intrusion simply by producing the identification himself as his companion did," the court held the officer's actions reasonable under the *Terry* balancing test. Compare *People v. Williams,* 234 N.W.2d 541 (Mich.App.1975) (even though officer had good reason to believe lawfully stopped suspect was lying when he said he had no identification, looking in his wallet at driver's license violated the Fourth Amendment). Cf. *Arizona v. Hicks,* p. 358; and *Ybarra v. Illinois,* p. 312. Consider also the *Hiibel* case, Note 4, p. 426.

What then of on-the-scene fingerprinting? In *Hayes v. Florida,* 470 U.S. 811 (1985), the majority in dictum opined this would be permissible "if there is reasonable suspicion that the suspect has committed a criminal act, if there is a reasonable basis for believing that fingerprinting will establish or negate the suspect's connection with that crime, and if the procedure is carried out with dispatch." Brennan and Marshall, JJ., concurring, responded "that on-site fingerprinting (apparently undertaken in full view of any passerby) would involve a singular intrusion on the suspect's privacy, an intrusion that would not be justifiable (as was the patdown in *Terry*) as necessary for the officer's protection."

G. Other Brief Detention for Investigation

1. In DAVIS v. MISSISSIPPI, 394 U.S. 721 (1969), petitioner and 24 other black youths were detained for questioning and fingerprinting in connection with a rape for which the only leads were a general description given by the victim and a set of fingerprints around the window through which the assailant entered. Petitioner's prints were found to match those at the scene of the crime, and this evidence was admitted at his trial. The Court, per BRENNAN, J., held that the prints should have been excluded as the fruits of a seizure of petitioner in violation of the Fourth Amendment, but intimated that a detention for such a purpose might sometimes be permissible on evidence insufficient for arrest:

"Detentions for the sole purpose of obtaining fingerprints are no less subject to the constraints of the Fourth Amendment. It is arguable, however, that because of the unique nature of the fingerprinting process, such detentions might, under narrowly defined circumstances, be found to comply with the Fourth Amendment even though there is no probable cause in the traditional sense. Detention for fingerprinting may constitute a much less serious intrusion upon personal security than other types of police searches and detentions. Fingerprinting involves none of the probing into an individual's private life and thoughts which marks an interrogation or search. Nor can fingerprint detention be employed repeatedly to harass any individual, since the police need only one set of each person's prints. Furthermore, fingerprinting is an inherently more reliable and effective crime-solving tool than eyewitness identifications or confessions and is not subject to such abuses as the improper line-up[p] and the 'third degree.' Finally, because there is no danger of destruction of fingerprints, the limited detention need not come unexpectedly or at an inconvenient time. For this same reason, the general requirement that the authorization of a judicial officer be obtained in advance of detention would seem not to admit of any exception in the fingerprinting context.

"We have no occasion in this case, however, to determine whether the requirements of the Fourth Amendment could be met by narrowly circumscribed procedures for obtaining, during the course of a criminal investigation, the fingerprints of individuals for whom there is no probable cause to arrest. For it is clear that no attempt was made here to employ procedures which might comply with the requirements of the Fourth Amendment: the detention at police headquarters of petitioner and the other young Negroes was not authorized by a judicial officer; petitioner was unnecessarily required to undergo two fingerprinting sessions; and petitioner was not merely fingerprinted during the December 3 detention but also subjected to interrogation."[q]

2. *United States v. Dionisio,* p. 816, holds that the Fourth Amendment was not violated by subpoenaing witnesses to appear before a grand jury to give voice exemplars. No preliminary showing of "probable cause" or "reasonableness" is required in such a case, as: (a) "a subpoena to appear before a grand jury is not a 'seizure' in the Fourth Amendment sense," and thus "*Davis* is plainly inapposite"; and (b) the requirement that the witness give exemplars does not infringe upon Fourth Amendment rights, as "the physical characteristics of a person's voice, its tone and manner, as opposed to the content of a specific conversation, are constantly exposed to the public," so that "no person can have a reasonable expectation that others will not know the sound of his voice." *United States v. Mara,* p. 819 fn. b, reached the same result as to the subpoenaing of a witness to give handwriting exemplars.

p. In *Wise v. Murphy,* 275 A.2d 205 (D.C.App.1971), the court noted the negative reference in *Davis* was only to an "improper line-up" and thus concluded that upon a proper showing, lacking in the instant case, a court could order a person to appear in a lineup even if grounds for arrest were lacking, at least for investigation of "serious felonies involving grave personal injuries."

q. *Davis* was reaffirmed in *Hayes v. Florida,* p. 436, where the Court again suggested "the Fourth Amendment might permit the judiciary to authorize the seizure of a person on less than probable cause and his removal to the police station for the purpose of fingerprinting."

3. A few jurisdictions have adopted statutes or rules of court which authorize brief detention at the station (usually pursuant to court order), on less than the grounds needed to arrest, for the purpose of conducting certain identification procedures. Such provisions have been upheld by the courts, and some other cases have upheld similar procedures even absent such a provision. For example, in *In re Fingerprinting of M.B.*, 309 A.2d 3 (N.J.Super.1973), the court affirmed an order requiring all 22 male members of the eighth grade class of a particular school to submit to fingerprinting. A ring of that elementary school's graduating class was found near the body of a homicide victim, and later the victim's car was located. Fingerprints other than those of the victim were found both inside and outside the vehicle. Upon request of the prosecutor, the court ordered all male members of that graduating class to submit to fingerprinting; the order permitted the pupils to be accompanied by a parent, guardian or attorney, directed that the prints be used only in the investigation of the homicide, and specified further that upon completion of the investigation the prints should be destroyed. The appellate court, in affirming commented:

"[T]here [is] a substantial basis to suspect that a member of the school class in question may have had some implication in or material knowledge of the homicide such that fingerprinting of all the male members of the class was reasonable, having in mind the protective provision of the order for destruction of the prints after completion of the investigation. Under all the circumstances extant and the terms of the order below we find the existence of such 'narrowly circumscribed procedures' as render the order reasonable within the view of the Fourth Amendment adumbrated in *Davis*."

4. In DUNAWAY v. NEW YORK, 442 U.S. 200 (1979), the police, lacking grounds to arrest petitioner but suspecting he was implicated in an attempted robbery and homicide, had him "picked up" for questioning. He was placed in an interrogation room at police headquarters, where he was questioned by officers after being given the *Miranda* warnings. Petitioner waived counsel and within an hour gave incriminating statements. His conviction following a trial at which those statements were admitted was affirmed by the state court on the ground that officers "may detain an individual upon reasonable suspicion for questioning for a reasonable and brief period of time under carefully controlled conditions which are ample to protect the individual's Fifth and Sixth Amendment Rights." The Supreme Court, per BRENNAN, J., reversed:

"In contrast to the brief and narrowly circumscribed intrusions involved in [*Terry* and its progeny], the detention of petitioner was in important respects indistinguishable from a traditional arrest. Petitioner was not questioned briefly where he was found. Instead, he was taken from a neighbor's home to a police car, transported to a police station, and placed in an interrogation room. He was never informed that he was 'free to go'; indeed, he would have been physically restrained if he had refused to accompany the officers or had tried to escape their custody. The application of the Fourth Amendment's requirement of probable cause does not depend on whether an intrusion of this magnitude is termed an 'arrest' under state law. The mere facts that petitioner was not told he was under arrest, was not 'booked,' and would not have had an arrest record if the interrogation had proved fruitless, * * * obviously do not make petitioner's seizure even roughly analogous to the narrowly defined intrusions involved in *Terry* and its progeny. Indeed, any 'exception' that could cover a seizure as intrusive as that in this case would threaten to swallow the general rule that Fourth Amendment seizures are 'reasonable' only if based on probable cause. * * *

"In effect, respondents urge us to adopt a multifactor balancing test of 'reasonable police conduct under the circumstances' to cover all seizures that do not amount to technical arrests. But the protections intended by the Framers could all too easily disappear in the consideration and balancing of the multifarious circumstances presented by different cases, especially when that balancing may be done in the first instance by police officers engaged in the 'often competitive enterprise of ferreting out crime.' A single, familiar standard is essential to guide police officers, who have only limited time and expertise to reflect on and balance the social and individual interests involved in the specific circumstances they confront. Indeed, our recognition of these dangers, and our consequent reluctance to depart from the proven protections afforded by the general rule, is reflected in the narrow limitations emphasized in the cases employing the balancing test. For all but those narrowly defined intrusions, the requisite 'balancing' has been performed in centuries of precedent and is embodied in the principle that seizures are 'reasonable' only if supported by probable cause."

Justice Brennan then concluded "that the treatment of petitioner, whether or not it is technically characterized as an arrest, must be supported by probable cause" because "detention for custodial interrogation—regardless of its label—intrudes so severely on interests protected by the Fourth Amendment as necessarily to trigger the traditional safeguards against illegal arrest."[r]

WHITE, J., concurring, cautioned that the majority opinion should not be read to mean that *Terry* "is an almost unique exception to a hard-and-fast standard of probable cause," and added that it was "enough, for me, that the police conduct here is similar enough to an arrest that the normal level of probable cause is necessary before the interests of privacy and personal security must give way." REHNQUIST, J., joined by the Chief Justice in dissent, indicated he "would have little difficulty joining" the opinion of the Court but for his conclusion that no Fourth Amendment seizure had occurred: "After learning that the person who answered the door was petitioner, the officer asked him if he would accompany the officers to police headquarters for questioning, and petitioner responded that he would. Petitioner was not told that he was under arrest or in custody and was not warned not to resist or flee. No weapons were displayed and petitioner was not handcuffed. Each officer testified that petitioner was not touched or held during the trip downtown; his freedom of action was not in any way restrained by the police. In short, the police behavior in this case was entirely free of 'physical force or show of authority.' "

SECTION 9. ADMINISTRATIVE INSPECTIONS AND REGULATORY SEARCHES: MORE ON BALANCING THE NEED AGAINST THE INVASION OF PRIVACY

The Supreme Court has upheld a rather broad range of searches and seizures even when conducted without the traditional quantum of probable cause. These decisions manifest further application of the *Camara* balancing test, also used by the Court in *Terry*, p. 401, to assay the discrete police practice of stop-and-frisk. But *Camara* itself was an administrative inspection type of case, and thus it is not

r. In *Kaupp v. Texas*, 538 U.S. 626 (2003), the state court's no-seizure holding was summarily vacated by a unanimous Court because the following "evidence points to arrest even more starkly than the facts of *Dunaway*": "A 17-year-old boy was awakened in his bedroom at three in the morning by at least three police officers, one of whom stated 'we need to go and talk.' He was taken out in handcuffs, without shoes, dressed only in his underwear in January, placed in a patrol car, driven to the scene of a crime and then to the sheriff's offices, where he was taken into an interrogation room and questioned."

surprising that this balancing process has since been utilized most often regarding various other administrative inspections and regulatory searches, where the Court has often emphasized certain "special needs" beyond those present in the more typical law enforcement context.

Collectively, the cases briefly summarized below reflect two kinds of departures from the traditional probable cause requirement. One, as in *Terry,* is to require individualized suspicion (typically referred to as reasonable suspicion) less compelling than is need for the usual arrest or search. (In contrast to the rule in a regular law enforcement context, see *Ybarra,* p. 312, and *Hicks,* p. 358, such reasonable suspicion sometimes suffices even to search for incriminating evidence.) Another kind of departure is to require no individualized suspicion whatsoever, but instead to require that the seizure or search be conducted pursuant to some neutral criteria which guard against arbitrary selection of those subjected to such procedures (similar to the impoundment-inventory process approved in *Bertine,* p. 395).

1. ***Safety inspections***. In *Camara v. Municipal Court,* 387 U.S. 523 (1967), dealing with fire, health, and housing code inspection programs directed at dwellings, the Court concluded that if an occupant did not consent to an inspection the authorities would ordinarily have to get a warrant,[a] but "that 'probable cause' to issue a warrant to inspect must exist if reasonable legislative or administrative standards for conducting an area inspection are satisfied with respect to a particular dwelling. Such standards, which will vary with the municipal program being enforced, may be based upon the passage of time, the nature of the building (e.g., a multi-family apartment house), or the condition of the entire area, but they will not necessarily depend upon specific knowledge of the condition of the particular dwelling." Among the "persuasive factors" identified by the Court "to support the reasonableness of area code-enforcement inspections" were (i) doubt "that any other canvassing technique would achieve acceptable results," and (ii) that the contemplated inspections "involve a relatively limited invasion of the urban citizen's privacy" as compared to execution of the more traditional search warrant.[b]

A *Camara*-type warrant "showing that a specific business has been chosen * * * on the basis of a general administrative plan * * * derived from neutral sources" also suffices for inspection of business premises. *Marshall v. Barlow's, Inc.,* 436 U.S. 307 (1978). But the Court has often upheld warrantless business inspections by emphasizing the "closely regulated" nature of the business and

a. Three dissenters objected: "This boxcar warrant will be identical as to every dwelling in the area, save the street number itself. I daresay they will be printed up in pads of a thousand or more—with space for the street number to be inserted—and issued by magistrates in broadcast fashion as a matter of course."

b. Another type of safety inspection is that conducted after a fire. In *Michigan v. Clifford,* 464 U.S. 287 (1984), four Justices concluded that a burning building creates exigent circumstances justifying authorities to enter to fight the blaze and to remain a reasonable time to investigate the cause of the fire, but that later entries without consent require a warrant—an administrative warrant "to determine the cause and origin of a recent fire" on the showing "that a fire of undetermined origin has occurred on the premises, that the scope of the proposed search is reasonable and will not intrude unnecessarily on the fire victim's privacy, and that the search will be executed at a reasonable and convenient time"; or a conventional search warrant on probable cause if the "primary objective of the search is to gather evidence of criminal activity." A fifth Justice, concurring, opined that a "traditional criminal search warrant" should be required for any later entry without advance notice to the owner. The four dissenters agreed that a conventional warrant was required to search the balance of the home, but declared that a warrantless inspection of the fire scene was permissible because "the utility of requiring a magistrate to evaluate the grounds for a search following a fire is so limited that the incidental protection of an individual's privacy interests simply does not justify imposing a warrant requirement."

that the inspection permitted by statute or regulations is "carefully limited in time, place, and scope," as in *New York v. Burger,* 482 U.S. 691 (1987). In *Burger,* the Court upheld such warrantless inspections of junkyards even though the administrative scheme concerned a social problem (stolen property) also addressed in the penal law, police officers were allowed to make the inspections, and the inspections would often uncover evidence of crime. (But see Note 7.)

2. *Border searches.* In *United States v. Ramsey,* 431 U.S. 606 (1977), upholding a customs inspection of mail entering the United States (which, by regulation, could not extend to reading of correspondence), the Court stressed (i) that the search was constitutional under the longstanding rule generally applicable to border searches, namely, that such searches are "considered to be 'reasonable' by the single fact that the person or item in question had entered into our country from outside"; and (ii) that the lower court was wrong in concluding a warrant would be needed as to mail, for "the 'border search' exception is not based on the doctrine of 'exigent circumstances' at all."

As for nonroutine border inspections, lower courts have generally held that "a real suspicion" is needed for a strip search, and the "clear indication" of *Schmerber,* p. 35, for a body cavity search. See, e.g., *Henderson v. United States,* 390 F.2d 805 (9th Cir.1967). In *United States v. Montoya de Hernandez,* 473 U.S. 531 (1985), the Court held that when customs agents "reasonably suspect that the traveler is smuggling contraband in her alimentary canal" she may be detained so long as is "necessary to either verify or dispel the suspicion" (i.e., if the suspect declines to submit to an x-ray, until a bowel movement occurs).

"But the reasons that might support a requirement of some level of suspicion in the case of highly intrusive searches of the person—dignity and privacy interests of the person being searched—simply do not carry over to vehicles," and thus removal and disassembling of a vehicle's gas tank does not require reasonable suspicion, though "it may be true that some searches of property are so destructive as to require a different result." *United States v. Flores–Montano,* 541 U.S. 149 (2004).

3. *Vehicle checkpoints.* In a series of cases dealing with the stopping of vehicles away from the border to see if they were occupied by illegal aliens, the Court held that while roving patrols could stop and search vehicles for illegal aliens only on probable cause, *Almeida–Sanchez v. United States,* 413 U.S. 266 (1973), only *Terry*-type reasonable suspicion was needed for such patrols to engage in the more "modest" interference with Fourth Amendment interests which attends the stopping of motorists and inquiring briefly as to their residential status. Even at a permanent checkpoint away from the border, search of a vehicle for aliens is not permissible absent probable cause, *United States v. Ortiz,* 422 U.S. 891 (1975), but the brief questioning of vehicle occupants at such checkpoints is permissible without any individualized suspicion whatsoever. *United States v. Martinez–Fuerte,* 428 U.S. 543 (1976). As to the latter practice, the Court emphasized (i) that "the potential interference with legitimate traffic is minimal"; and (ii) that such checkpoint operations "involve less discretionary enforcement activity," as "the officer may stop only those cars passing the checkpoint," which "is not chosen by officers in the field, but by officials responsible for making overall decisions as to the most effective allocation of limited enforcement resources."[c] The Court in *Martinez–Fuerte* also concluded that if more than the briefest inquiry was needed in a particular instance the vehicle could be referred to a

c. The Court also rejected the argument "that routine stops at a checkpoint are permissible only if a warrant has given judicial authorization to the particular checkpoint location." As for defendant's reliance on *Camara* in this connection, the Court answered that there but not here a warrant was necessary to provide assurance to the individual involved that the government agent was acting under proper authorization.

secondary inspection area "on the basis of criteria that would not sustain a roving-patrol stop."

Consistent with those cases, the Court held in *Delaware v. Prouse,* 440 U.S. 648 (1979), that absent reasonable suspicion the police may not stop individual vehicles for the purpose of checking the driver's license and the registration of the automobile. But the Court stressed it was not precluding states "from developing methods for spot checks that involve less intrusion or that do not involve the unconstrained exercise of discretion," and gave as "one possible alternative" the "questioning of all oncoming traffic at roadblock-type stops."

Then came *Michigan Dep't of State Police v. Sitz,* 496 U.S. 444 (1990), upholding the sobriety checkpoint program there at issue. Important ingredients in that conclusion were: (i) the intrusion upon motorists is "slight"; (ii) the program sufficiently limited officers' discretion, as "checkpoints are selected pursuant to [established] guidelines, and uniformed police officers stop every approaching vehicle"; (iii) the program addressed the very serious "drunken driving problem"; and (iv) there was support in the record for the law enforcement judgment that such checkpoints were among the "reasonable alternatives" available for dealing with that problem. The Court emphasized it was addressing "only the initial stop of each motorist passing through a checkpoint and the associated preliminary questioning and observation by checkpoint officers," and cautioned that "detention of particular motorists for more extensive field sobriety testing may require satisfaction of an individualized suspicion standard."

4. ***Search of students.*** Utilizing the *Camara* balancing test, the Court in *New Jersey v. T.L.O.,* 469 U.S. 325 (1985), struck "the balance between the school child's legitimate expectations of privacy and the school's equally legitimate needs to maintain an environment in which learning can take place" by holding: (i) "that school officials need not obtain a warrant before searching a student who is under their authority"; (ii) that ordinarily "a search of a student by a teacher or other school official will be 'justified at its inception' when there are reasonable grounds for suspecting that the search will turn up evidence that the student has violated or is violating either the law or the rules of the school"; and (iii) that such a search "will be permissible in its scope when the measures adopted are reasonably related to the objectives of the search and not excessively intrusive in light of the age and sex of the student and the nature of the infraction."

5. ***Supervision of parolees and probationers.*** In *Griffin v. Wisconsin,* 483 U.S. 868 (1987), the Court concluded that a "State's operation of a probation system * * * likewise presents 'special needs' beyond normal law enforcement that may justify departures from the usual warrant and probable cause requirements." No warrant was required for search of the probationer's home, for it would not only "make it more difficult for probation officials to respond quickly to evidence of misconduct," but also would interfere with the probation officer's judgment as to "how close a supervision the probationer requires." Moreover, full probable cause was not required either, as such a requirement would also "reduce the deterrent effect of the supervisory arrangement" and would be "both unrealistic and destructive of the * * * continuing probation relationship."

6. ***Drug testing.*** While lower courts have approved government-mandated drug testing of government or private employees upon individualized reasonable suspicion, two programs not requiring such suspicion have been upheld by the Supreme Court. In *National Treasury Employees Union v. Von Raab,* 489 U.S. 656 (1989), the Court held "that the suspicionless testing of employees who apply for promotion to positions directly involving the interdiction of illegal drugs, or to positions which require the incumbent to carry a firearm, is reasonable." The Court reasoned that because the testing program at issue "is not designed to serve the ordinary needs of law enforcement," a balancing process was proper, in which the "Government's compelling interests in preventing the promotion of drug users to positions where they might endanger the integrity of our Nation's borders or the life of the citizenry" outweighed the "diminished expectation of privacy" of "those who seek promotion to these positions."[d]

By similar balancing, the Court in *Skinner v. Railway Labor Executives' Ass'n,* 489 U.S. 602 (1989), upheld blood and urine testing of railroad employees following major train accidents or incidents and the breath and urine testing of railroad employees who violate certain safety rules. In allowing such testing even "in the absence of * * * reasonable suspicion that any particular employee may be impaired," the Court emphasized (i) the special danger presented by the performance of "certain sensitive tasks while under the influence"; (ii) the "diminished expectation of privacy that attaches to information pertaining to the fitness of covered employees"; and (iii) "the limited discretion" railroad employers had regarding who and when to test.

In *Vernonia School District 47J v. Acton*, 515 U.S. 646 (1995), the Court upheld the district's policy under which each week 10% of the students then participating in school athletics were randomly selected for urinalysis. In reaching this conclusion, the Court emphasized (i) that "the schools' custodial and tutelary responsibility for children" means "students within the school environment have a lesser expectation of privacy than members of the population generally," especially as to medical examinations and procedures; (ii) that "legitimate privacy expectations are even less with regard to student athletes," who by going out for a team "voluntarily subject themselves to a degree of regulation even higher than that imposed on students generally"; (iii) that the "privacy-invasive aspect of urinalysis" was kept at a minimum; (iv) that the district court's findings that a large segment of the student body was "in a state of rebellion * * * fueled by alcohol and drug abuse" manifested "an immediate crisis of greater proportions than existed" in *Skinner* or *Von Raab*; and (v) "that a drug problem largely fueled by the 'role model' effect of athletes' drug use, and of particular danger to athletes, is effectively addressed by making sure that athletes do not use drugs." But the Court in *Acton* then "caution[ed] against the assumption that suspicionless drug testing will readily pass constitutional muster in other contexts."[e]

Acton was applied in the 5–4 decision in *Board of Education of Independent School District No. 92 of Pottawatomie County v. Earls,* 536 U.S. 822 (2002), upholding a random testing policy applicable to middle and high school students participating in *any* extracurricular activity. The majority reasoned: (a) as for the *Acton* emphasis upon the especially low privacy expectations of student-athletes, this factor "was not essential to our decision" in the earlier case and, "in any event," all students who "voluntarily subject themselves" to additional regulations by opting for extracurricular activities have as a consequence "a limited

d. Two Justices who joined the Court's decision in *Skinner* because of "the demonstrated frequency of drug and alcohol use by the targeted class of employees, and the demonstrated connection between such use and grave harm," dissented in *Von Raab* because the government was unable to cite "even a single instance" of such use or connection to harm.

e. Compare *Chandler v. Miller*, 520 U.S. 305 (1997), invalidating a Georgia statute requiring each candidate for public office to submit to drug testing, where the Court stated: "Georgia asserts no evidence of a drug problem among the State's elected officials, those officials typically do not perform high-risk, safety-sensitive tasks, and the required certification immediately aids no interdiction effort. The need revealed, in short, is symbolic, not 'special,' as that term draws meaning from our case law." As for the state's reliance on *Von Raab*, the Court noted that there the affected employees and their work product were not amenable to "day-to-day scrutiny," and then concluded: "Candidates for public office, in contrast, are subject to relentless scrutiny—by their peers, the public, and the press. Their day-to-day conduct attracts attention notable beyond the norm in ordinary work environments."

expectation of privacy"; (b) as for the "nature and immediacy of the government's concern," it suffices that "the nationwide epidemic makes the war against drugs a pressing concern in every school" and that, in addition, there was "specific evidence of drug use" at the schools; and (c) as for the efficacy of the policy in meeting the government's concerns, the policy in question "is a reasonably effective means of * * * preventing, deterring, and detecting drug use," and the fact that in *Acton* the athletes were at the heart of the drug problem there "was not essential to the holding" in that case, which "did not require the school to test the group of students most likely to use drugs."

7. *"Special needs" vs. ordinary law enforcement.* Whenever departure from the usual warrant and/or probable cause requirements is claimed to be justified on the basis of some "special need," it is necessary that this need be sufficiently different from and divorced from the state's general law enforcement interest, as is highlighted in two recent cases: *City of Indianapolis v. Edmond*, 531 U.S. 32 (2000); and *Ferguson v. City of Charleston*, 532 U.S. 67 (2001).

In *Edmond*, the Court held that city-operated vehicle checkpoints, complete with drug dogs, undertaken to interdict unlawful drugs, contravened the Fourth Amendment. As for the city's reliance on *Martinez-Fuerte*, *Prouse* and *Sitz*, the *Edmond* majority, per O'Connor, J., distinguished those cases because in none of them "did we indicate approval of a checkpoint program whose primary purpose was to detect evidence of ordinary criminal wrongdoing."[f] As for the city's response that securing the border and apprehending drunk drivers "are * * * law enforcement activities, and law enforcement officers employ arrests and criminal prosecutions in pursuit of these goals," the Court responded that analysis at that "high level of generality" would mean there "would be little check on the ability of the authorities to construct roadblocks for almost any conceivable law enforcement purpose."[g]

In *Ferguson*, a task force made up of representatives of the Charleston public hospital, police and other public officials developed a policy for identifying and testing pregnant patients suspected of drug use and then turning the results over to law enforcement agents without the knowledge or consent of the patients. This policy, which also contained procedures for arresting patients and for prosecuting them for drug offenses and/or child neglect, was challenged by a group of obstetrical patients at that hospital who had been arrested after testing positive for cocaine. The question, as the Court, per Stevens, J., put it, was "whether the interest in using the threat of criminal sanctions to deter pregnant women from using cocaine can justify a departure from the general rule that an official nonconsensual search is unconstitutional if not authorized by a valid warrant."

f. But the Court did add: "Of, course, there are circumstances that may justify a law enforcement checkpoint where the primary purpose would otherwise, but for some emergency, relate to ordinary crime control. For example, * * * the Fourth Amendment would almost certainly permit an appropriately tailored roadblock set up to thwart an imminent terrorist attack or to catch a dangerous criminal who is likely to flee by way of a particular route."

g. Rehnquist, C.J., for the three dissenters, argued that the checkpoints at issue shared the critical characteristics of those previously approved by the Court: they "effectively serve the State's legitimate interests; they are executed in a regularized and neutral manner, and they only minimally intrude upon the privacy of the motorists."

Illinois v. Lidster, 540 U.S. 419 (2004), involved a highway checkpoint set up by police to seek information from motorists about a hit-and-run accident a week earlier the same time of night. The Court rejected the state court's conclusion that this checkpoint was unconstitutional under *Edmond,* reasoning that the instant case did not fall within the "general interest in crime control" category of that case, as here the "stop's primary law enforcement purpose was *not* to determine whether a vehicle's occupants were committing a crime, but to ask vehicle occupants, as members of the public, for their help in providing information about a crime in all likelihood committed by others."

The majority noted that the instant case was different from *Acton* and the Court's other prior drug testing cases in several material respects: for one, in the previous cases "there was no misunderstanding about the purpose of the test or the potential use of the test results, and there were protections against the dissemination of the results to third parties." But the "critical difference" between the earlier cases and the instant one, the Court emphasized, "lies in the nature of the 'special need' asserted as justification for the warrantless searches," for in all the earlier cases the "special need" advanced was "one divorced from the State's general interest in law enforcement," while here "the central and indispensable feature of the policy from its inception was the use of law enforcement to coerce the patients into substance abuse treatment." As for the respondents' argument that their ultimate purpose of protecting both the mother and child was "a beneficent one," the majority responded that the policy itself "plainly reveals" that the purpose actually served "is ultimately indistinguishable from the general interest in crime control," for "an initial and continuing focus of the policy was on the arrest and prosecution of drug-abusing mothers," and local "prosecutors and police were extensively involved in the day-to-day administration of the policy." And it made no difference that the "threat of law enforcement" may have been "a means to an end," for if that did make a difference then "virtually any nonconsensual suspicionless search could be immunized under the special needs doctrine by defining the search solely in terms of its ultimate, rather than immediate purpose."[h]

8. Circumventing the *Edmond–Ferguson* limitation: probation searches revisited. While the emphasis upon the probation officer-probationer relationship in *Griffin*, Note 5 supra, itself suggested that a totally independent search of a known probationer by a police officer as part of a criminal investigation could not qualify under the *Griffin* "special needs" analysis, this seemed even more certainly the case after the decisions in *Edmond* and *Ferguson*. But when the Supreme Court revisited the subject of probation searches in UNITED STATES v. KNIGHTS, 534 U.S. 112 (2001), the Court came up with a purportedly different rationale for probation searches which was deemed to encompass such police searches.

After Knights was convicted in California of a drug offense, he was placed on probation subject to a "common California probation condition," namely, that he "[s]ubmit his . . . person, property, place of residence, vehicle, personal effects, to search at any time, with or without a search warrant, warrant of arrest or reasonable cause by any probation officer or law enforcement officer." Three days later, a sheriff's detective, without the knowledge or participation of probation officials, made a warrantless search of Knights residence on reasonable suspicion he was involved in vandalism, resulting in federal charges being lodged against Knights. The district court granted his motion to suppress the evidence found in his home on the ground that the search had been "investigatory" rather than "probationary," and the court of appeals affirmed. In response to the contention that such a limitation followed from *Griffin*, a unanimous Supreme Court, per the Chief Justice, noted that *Griffin* expressly declared that its "special needs" holding made it "unnecessary to consider whether" warrantless searches of

h. Kennedy, J., concurring, questioned the latter point and would have rested the decision solely on the fact that none of the Court's "special needs precedents has sanctioned the routine inclusion of law enforcement, both in the design of the policy and in using arrests, either threatened or real, to implement the system designed for the special needs objectives." Scalia, J., for the three dissenters, objected that it was not so that "the addition of a law-enforcement related purpose to a legitimate medical purpose destroys applicability of the 'special-needs' doctrine," "since the special-needs doctrine was developed, and is ordinarily employed, precisely to enable searches by law enforcement officials who, of course, ordinarily have a law enforcement objective," as illustrated by *Griffin*.

probationers were otherwise reasonable within the meaning of the Fourth Amendment.

The Court in *Knights* then proceeded to answer the reserved question in the affirmative, declaring that the search in the instant case passed muster "under our general Fourth Amendment approach of 'examining the totality of the circumstances' " and then determining reasonableness "by assessing, on the one hand, the degree to which it intrudes upon an individual's privacy and, on the other, the degree to which it is needed for the promotion of legitimate government interests." Proceeding with the balancing of interests,[i] the Court concluded (a) that the "probation order clearly expressed the search condition and Knights was unambiguously informed of it," meaning the "probation condition thus significantly diminished Knights's reasonable expectation of privacy"; (b) that because a probationer "will be more likely to engage in criminal conduct than an ordinary member of the community," the State's "interest in apprehending violators of the criminal law * * * may therefore justifiably focus on probationers in a way that it does not on the ordinary citizen"; and (c) that "the balance of these considerations requires no more than reasonable suspicion to conduct a search of this probationer's house"[j] and "render[s] a warrant requirement unnecessary." Distinguishing *Edmond*, the Court then concluded: "Because our holding rests on ordinary Fourth Amendment analysis that considers all the circumstances of a search, there is no basis for examining official purpose."

As for just when the "balancing of interests" approach may be used instead of the "special needs" approach, consider the en banc case of *United States v. Kincade*, 379 F.3d 813 (9th Cir.2004), concerning "whether the Fourth Amendment permits compulsory DNA profiling of certain conditionally-released federal offenders in the absence of individualized suspicion that they have committed additional crimes." One group of judges, after "balanc[ing] the degree to which DNA profiling interferes with the privacy interests of qualified federal offenders against the significance of the public interests served by such profiling," concluded that "reliance on a totality of the circumstances analysis to uphold compulsory DNA profiling of convicted offenders both comports with the Supreme Court's recent precedents and resolves this appeal in concert with the requirements of the Fourth Amendment." Another group of judges, on the other hand, deemed it inappropriate "to apply a totality of the circumstances test to a suspicionless law enforcement search," and then concluded that because "the primary purpose of the DNA Act is to collect information for ordinary law enforcement purposes—to help law enforcement authorities determine whether specific individuals have committed particular crimes," the Act did not pass muster under the "special needs" approach. Another judge provided the deciding vote; he agreed the "special needs" approach applied, but concluded that here just as in *Griffin* the challenged activity "serves the special needs of a supervised release system," for the person who refused to supply a DNA sample had not completed his period of such release.

SECTION 10. CONSENT SEARCHES

Consent searches are frequently relied upon by the police because they involve no time-consuming paper work and offer an opportunity to search even when probable cause is lacking. Thus, the constitutional protection against unreasonable search and seizure widens or narrows, depending on the difficulty or

i. In light of the use of a balancing test in this context, reconsider Notes 1 and 2, pp. 408–09.

j. In a footnote the Court added: "We do not decide whether the probation condition so diminished, or completely eliminated, Knights's reasonable expectation of privacy * * * that a search by a law enforcement officer without any individualized suspicion would have satisfied the reasonableness requirement of the Fourth Amendment."

ease with which the prosecution can establish that the defendant (or some other authorized person) has "consented" to what would otherwise be an unconstitutional invasion of his privacy.

A. The Nature of "Consent"

SCHNECKLOTH v. BUSTAMONTE

412 U.S. 218, 93 S.Ct. 2041, 36 L.Ed.2d 854 (1973).

Justice STEWART delivered the opinion of the Court. * * *

[A police officer stopped a car containing six men when he observed that one headlight and the license plate light were burned out. After the driver could not produce a license, the officer asked a passenger who claimed he was the vehicle owner's brother if he could search the car, and the passenger replied, "Sure, go ahead." The driver "helped in the search of the car, by opening the trunk and glove compartment." Stolen checks were found under a seat, leading to charges against passenger Bustamonte, whose motion to suppress was denied. His conviction was affirmed on appeal; the federal district court denied his petition for a writ of habeas corpus, but the 9th Circuit court of appeals set aside the district court's order.]

The precise question in this case, then, is what must the state prove to demonstrate that a consent was "voluntarily" given. * * *

The most extensive judicial exposition of the meaning of "voluntariness" has been developed in those cases in which the Court has had to determine the "voluntariness" of a defendant's confession for purposes of the Fourteenth Amendment. * * * It is to that body of case law to which we turn for initial guidance on the meaning of "voluntariness" in the present context. * * *

The significant fact about all of these decisions is that none of them turned on the presence or absence of a single controlling criterion; each reflected a careful scrutiny of all the surrounding circumstances. In none of them did the Court rule that the Due Process Clause required the prosecution to prove as part of its initial burden that the defendant knew he had a right to refuse to answer the questions that were put. While the state of the accused's mind, and the failure of the police to advise the accused of his rights, were certainly factors to be evaluated in assessing the "voluntariness" of an accused's responses, they were not in and of themselves determinative.

Similar considerations lead us to agree with the courts of California that the question whether a consent to a search was in fact "voluntary" or was the product of duress or coercion, express or implied, is a question of fact to be determined from the totality of all the circumstances. While knowledge of the right to refuse consent is one factor to be taken into account, the government need not establish such knowledge as the *sine qua non* of an effective consent. As with police questioning, two competing concerns must be accommodated in determining the meaning of a "voluntary" consent—the legitimate need for such searches and the equally important requirement of assuring the absence of coercion.

In situations where the police have some evidence of illicit activity, but lack probable cause to arrest or search, a search authorized by a valid consent may be the only means of obtaining important and reliable evidence. In the present case for example, while the police had reason to stop the car for traffic violations, the State does not contend that there was probable cause to search the vehicle or that the search was incident to a valid arrest of any of the occupants. Yet, the search yielded tangible evidence that served as a basis for a prosecution, and provided some assurance that others, wholly innocent of the crime, were not mistakenly brought to trial. And in those cases where there is probable cause to arrest or search, but where the police lack a warrant, a consent search may still be valuable. If the search is conducted and proves fruitless, that in itself may convince the police that an arrest with its possible stigma and embarrassment is unnecessary, or that a far more extensive search pursuant to a warrant is not justified. In short a search pursuant to consent may result in considerably less inconvenience for the subject of the search, and, properly conducted, is a constitutionally permissible and wholly legitimate aspect of effective police activity.

But the Fourth and Fourteenth Amendments require that a consent not be coerced, by explicit or implicit means, by implied threat or covert force. For, no matter how subtly the coercion were applied, the resulting "consent" would be no more than a pretext for the unjustified police intrusion against which the Fourth Amendment is directed. * * *

The problem of reconciling the recognized legitimacy of consent searches with the requirement that they be free from any aspect of official coercion cannot be resolved by an infallible touchstone. To approve such searches without the most careful scrutiny would sanction the possibility of official coercion; to place artificial restrictions upon such searches would jeopardize their basic validity. Just as was true with confessions, the requirement of a "voluntary" consent reflects a fair accommodation of the constitutional requirements involved. In examining all the surrounding circumstances to determine if in fact the consent to search was coerced, account must be taken of subtly coercive police questions, as well as the possibly vulnerable subjective state of the person who consents. Those searches that are the product of police coercion can thus be filtered out without undermining the continuing validity of consent searches. In sum, there is no reason for us to depart in the area of consent searches, from the traditional definition of "voluntariness."

The approach of the Court of Appeals for the Ninth Circuit finds no support in any of our decisions that have attempted to define the meaning of "voluntariness." Its ruling, that the State must affirmatively prove that the subject of the search knew that he had a right to refuse consent, would, in practice, create serious doubt whether consent searches could continue to be conducted. There might be rare cases where it could be proved from the record that a person in fact affirmatively knew of his right to refuse—such as a case where he announced to the police that if he didn't sign the consent form, "you [police] are going to get a search warrant;" or a case where by prior experience and training a person had clearly and convincingly demonstrated such knowledge. But more commonly where there was no evidence of any coercion, explicit or implicit, the prosecution would nevertheless be unable to demonstrate that the subject of the search in fact had known of his right to refuse consent.

The very object of the inquiry—the nature of a person's subjective understanding—underlines the difficulty of the prosecution's burden under the rule applied by the Court of Appeals in this case. Any defendant who was the subject of a search authorized solely by his consent could effectively frustrate the introduction into evidence of the fruits of that search by simply failing to testify that he in fact knew he could refuse to consent. And the near impossibility of meeting this prosecutorial burden suggests why this Court has never accepted any such litmus-paper test of voluntariness. * * *

One alternative that would go far towards proving that the subject of a search did know he had a right to refuse consent would be to advise him of that right before eliciting his consent. That, however, is a suggestion that has been almost universally repudiated by both federal and state courts, and, we think, rightly so. For it would be thoroughly impractical to impose on the normal consent search the detailed requirements of an effective warning.[a] Consent searches are part of the standard investigatory techniques of law enforcement agencies. They normally occur on the highway, or in a person's home or office, and under informal and unstructured conditions. The circumstances that prompt the initial request to search may develop quickly or be a logical extension of investigative police questioning. The police may seek to investigate further suspicious circumstances or to follow up leads developed in questioning persons at the scene of a crime. These situations are a far cry from the structured atmosphere of a trial where, assisted by counsel if he chooses, a defendant is informed of his trial rights. And, while surely a closer question, these situations are still immeasurably far removed from "custodial interrogation" where, in *Miranda v. Arizona* [p. 575], we found that the Constitution required certain now familiar warnings as a prerequisite to police interrogation. * * *

It is said, however, that a "consent" is a "waiver" of a person's rights under the Fourth and Fourteenth Amendments. The argument is that by allowing the police to conduct a search, a person "waives" whatever right he had to prevent the police from searching. It is argued that under the doctrine of *Johnson v. Zerbst,* 304 U.S. 458 (1938), to establish such a "waiver" the state must demonstrate "an intentional relinquishment or abandonment of a known right or privilege." * * *

Almost without exception the requirement of a knowing and intelligent waiver has been applied only to those rights which the Constitution guarantees to a criminal defendant in order to preserve a fair trial. Hence, and hardly surprisingly in view of the facts of *Johnson* itself, the standard of a knowing and intelligent waiver has most often been applied to test the validity of a waiver of counsel, either at trial, or upon a guilty plea. And the Court has also applied the *Johnson* criteria to assess the effectiveness of a waiver of other trial rights such as the right to confrontation, to a jury trial, and to a speedy trial, and the right to be free from twice being placed in jeopardy. Guilty pleas have been carefully scrutinized to determine whether the accused knew and understood all the rights to which he would be entitled at trial, and that he had intentionally chosen to forgo them. And the Court has evaluated the knowing and intelligent nature of the waiver of trial rights in trial-type situations, such as the waiver of the privilege against compulsory self-incrimination before an administrative agency or a congressional committee, or the waiver of counsel in a juvenile proceeding.

The guarantees afforded a criminal defendant at trial also protect him at certain stages before the actual trial, and any alleged waiver must meet the strict standard of an intentional relinquishment of a "known" right. But the "trial" guarantees that have been applied to the "pretrial" stage of the criminal process are similarly designed to protect the fairness of the trial itself. * * *[b]

The standards of *Johnson* were, therefore, found to be a necessary prerequisite to a finding of a valid waiver.[29] * * *

a. Relying upon this language, the Court later held in *Ohio v. Robinette,* 519 U.S. 33 (1996), that if a person has been lawfully seized, for example, because of commission of a traffic violation, and following the point at which the detainee would be free to go he consents to a search, that consent is not involuntary because the officer failed to specifically advise the detainee that he was free to go, as a requirement of such warnings would be equally "unrealistic."

b. At this point, the Court noted that "the standard of a knowing and intelligent waiver" applies to waiver of counsel at a line-up under *United States v. Wade,* p. 757, and *Gilbert v. California,* p. 758 fn. b, because counsel is provided to protect the right of cross-examination at trial; and that the same standard applies to waiver of counsel at custodial interrogation under *Miranda v. Arizona,* p. 575, because counsel is provided to ensure that the safeguards concerning the giving of testimony at trial do not "become empty formalities."

29. As we have already noted, *Miranda* itself involved interrogation of a suspect detained in custody and did not concern the

A strict standard of waiver has been applied to those rights guaranteed to a criminal defendant to insure that he will be accorded the greatest possible opportunity to utilize every facet of the constitutional model of a fair criminal trial. Any trial conducted in derogation of that model leaves open the possibility that the trial reached an unfair result precisely because all the protections specified in the Constitution were not provided. A prime example is the right to counsel. For without that right, a wholly innocent accused faces the real and substantial danger that simply because of his lack of legal expertise he may be convicted. * * *

The protections of the Fourth Amendment are of a wholly different order, and have nothing whatever to do with promoting the fair ascertainment of truth at a criminal trial. Rather, as Justice Frankfurter's opinion for the Court put it in *Wolf v. Colorado* [p. 217], the Fourth Amendment protects the "security of one's privacy against arbitrary intrusion by the police. . . ." * * *

Nor can it even be said that a search, as opposed to an eventual trial, is somehow "unfair" if a person consents to a search. While the Fourth and Fourteenth Amendments limit the circumstances under which the police can conduct a search, there is nothing constitutionally suspect in a person voluntarily allowing a search. The actual conduct of the search may be precisely the same as if the police had obtained a warrant. And, unlike those constitutional guarantees that protect a defendant at trial, it cannot be said every reasonable presumption ought to be indulged against voluntary relinquishment. We have only recently stated: "[I]t is no part of the policy underlying the Fourth and Fourteenth Amendments to discourage citizens from aiding to the utmost of their ability in the apprehension of criminals." *Coolidge v. New Hampshire,* [p. 304]. Rather the community has a real interest in encouraging consent, for the resulting search may yield necessary evidence for the solution and prosecution of crime, evidence that may insure that a wholly innocent person is not wrongly charged with a criminal offense.

Those cases that have dealt with the application of the *Johnson v. Zerbst* rule make clear that it would be next to impossible to apply to a consent search the standard of "an intentional relinquishment or abandonment of a known right or privilege." To be true to *Johnson* and its progeny, there must be examination into the knowing and understanding nature of the waiver, an examination that was designed for a trial judge in the structured atmosphere of a courtroom. * * * It would be unrealistic to expect that in the informal, unstructured context of a consent search, a policeman, upon pain of tainting the evidence obtained, could make the detailed type of examination demanded by *Johnson.* And, if for this reason a diluted form of "waiver" were found acceptable, that would itself be ample recognition of the fact that there is no universal standard that must be applied in every situation where a person forgoes a constitutional right.[33]

investigatory procedures of the police in general on-the-scene questioning. By the same token, the present case does not require a determination of the proper standard to be applied in assessing the validity of a search authorized solely by an alleged consent that is obtained from a person after he has been placed in custody. We do note, however, that other courts have been particularly sensitive to the heightened possibilities for coercion when the "consent" to a search was given by a person in custody.

33. It seems clear that even a limited view of the demands of "an intentional relinquishment or abandonment of a known right or privilege" standard would inevitably lead to a requirement of detailed warnings before any consent search—a requirement all but universally rejected to date. As the Court stated in *Miranda* with respect to the privilege against compulsory self-incrimination: "[W]e will not pause to inquire in individual cases whether the defendant was aware of his rights without a warning being given. Assessments of the knowledge the defendant possessed, based on information as to his age, education, intelligence, or prior contact with authorities, can never be more than speculation; a warning is a clearcut fact."

Similarly, a "waiver" approach to consent searches would be thoroughly inconsistent with our decisions that have approved "third party consents." In *Coolidge v. New Hampshire,* where a wife surrendered to the police guns and clothing belonging to her husband, we found nothing constitutionally impermissible in the admission of that evidence at trial since the wife had not been coerced. *Frazier v. Cupp,* [p. 462], held that evidence seized from the defendant's duffel bag in a search authorized by his cousin's consent was admissible at trial. We found that the defendant had assumed the risk that his cousin with whom he shared the bag would allow the police to search it. And in *Hill v. California,* 401 U.S. 797 (1971), we held that the police had validly seized evidence from the petitioner's apartment incident to the arrest of a third party, since the police had probable cause to arrest the petitioner and reasonably though mistakenly believed the man they had arrested was he. Yet it is inconceivable that the Constitution could countenance the waiver of a defendant's right to counsel by a third party, or that a waiver could be found because a trial judge reasonably though mistakenly believed a defendant had waived his right to plead not guilty. * * *

Much of what has already been said disposes of the argument that the Court's decision in the *Miranda* case requires the conclusion that knowledge of a right to refuse is an indispensable element of a valid consent. The considerations that informed the Court's holding in *Miranda* are simply inapplicable in the present case. In *Miranda* the Court found that the techniques of police questioning and the nature of custodial surroundings produce an inherently coercive situation. The Court concluded that "[u]nless adequate protective devices are employed to dispel the compulsion inherent in custodial surroundings, no statement obtained from the defendant can truly be the product of his free choice." And at another point the Court noted that "without proper safeguards the process of in-custody interrogation of persons suspected or accused of crime contains inherently compelling pressures which work to undermine the individual's will to resist and to compel him to speak where he would not otherwise do so freely."

In this case there is no evidence of any inherently coercive tactics—either from the nature of the police questioning or the environment in which it took place. Indeed, since consent searches will normally occur on a person's own familiar territory, the spectre of incommunicado police interrogation in some remote station house is simply inapposite. There is no reason to believe, under circumstances such as are present here, that the response to a policeman's question is presumptively coerced; and there is, therefore, no reason to reject the traditional test for determining the voluntariness of a person's response. *Miranda,* of course, did not reach investigative questioning of a person not in custody, which is most directly analogous to the situation of a consent search, and it assuredly did not indicate that such questioning ought to be deemed inherently coercive.

It is also argued that the failure to require the Government to establish knowledge as a prerequisite to a valid consent, will relegate the Fourth Amendment to the special province of "the sophisticated, the knowledgeable, and the privileged." We cannot agree. The traditional definition of voluntariness we accept today has always taken into account evidence of minimal schooling, low intelligence, and the lack of any effective warnings to a person of his rights; and the voluntariness of any statement taken under those conditions has been carefully scrutinized to determine whether it was in fact voluntarily given.

Our decision today is a narrow one. We hold only that when the subject of a search is not in custody and the State attempts to justify a search on the basis of his consent, the Fourth and Fourteenth Amendments require that it demonstrate that the consent was in fact voluntarily given, and not the result of duress or coercion, express or implied. Voluntariness is a question of fact to be determined from all the circumstances, and while the subject's knowledge of a right to refuse is a factor to be taken into account, the prosecution is not required to demonstrate such knowledge as a prerequisite to establishing a voluntary consent.[c]

Justice MARSHALL, dissenting. * * *

The Fifth Amendment, in terms, provides that no person "shall be compelled in any criminal case to be a witness against himself." Nor is the interest protected by the Due Process Clause of the Fourteenth Amendment any different. The inquiry in a case where a confession is challenged as having been elicited in an unconstitutional manner is, therefore, whether the behavior of the police amounted to compulsion of the defendant. * * *

In contrast, this case deals not with "coercion," but with "consent," a subtly different concept to which different standards have been applied in the past. Freedom from coercion is a substantive right, guaranteed by the Fifth and Fourteenth Amendments. Consent, however, is a mechanism by which substantive requirements, otherwise applicable, are avoided. * * * Thus, consent searches are permitted not because such an exception to the requirements of probable cause and warrant is essential to proper law enforcement, but because we permit our citizens to choose whether or not they wish to exercise their constitutional rights. Our prior decisions simply do not support the view that a meaningful choice has been made solely because no coercion was brought to bear on the subject. * * *

If consent to search means that a person has chosen to forego his right to exclude the police from the place they seek to search, it follows that his consent cannot be considered a meaningful choice unless he knew that he could in fact exclude the police. * * * I would therefore hold, at a minimum, that the prosecution may not rely on a purported consent to search if the subject of the search did not know that he could refuse to give consent. Where the police claim authority to search yet in fact lack such authority, the subject does not know that he may permissibly refuse them entry, and it is this lack of knowledge that invalidates the consent. * * *

The burden on the prosecutor would disappear, of course, if the police, at the time they requested consent to search, also told the subject that he had a right to refuse consent and thus his decision to refuse would be respected. The Court's assertions to the contrary notwithstanding, there is nothing impractical about this method of satisfying the prosecution's burden of proof. * * *

The Court contends that if an officer paused to inform the subject of his rights, the informality of the exchange would be destroyed. I doubt that a simple statement by an officer of an individual's right to refuse consent would do much to alter the informality of the exchange, except to alert the subject to a fact that he surely is entitled to know. It is not without significance that for many years the agents of the Federal Bureau of Investigation have routinely informed subjects of their right to refuse consent, when they request consent to search. The reported cases in which the police have informed subject of their right to refuse consent show, also, that the information can be given without disrupting the casual flow of events. What evidence there is, then, rather strongly suggests that nothing disastrous would happen if the police, before requesting consent, informed the

c. Powell, J., joined by the Chief Justice and Rehnquist, J., concurred on the ground "that federal collateral review of a state prisoner's Fourth Amendment claims—claims which rarely bear on innocence—should be confined solely to the question of whether the petitioner was provided a fair opportunity to raise and have adjudicated the question in state courts." Blackmun, J., concurred to express substantial agreement with the Powell opinion. Douglas, J., dissenting, would have remanded for a determination of whether Alcala knew he had the right to refuse. Brennan, J., dissenting, declared: "It wholly escapes me how our citizens can meaningfully be said to have waived something as precious as a constitutional guarantee without ever being aware of its existence."

subject that he had a right to refuse consent and that his refusal would be respected.[12]

I must conclude, with some reluctance, that when the Court speaks of practicality, what it really is talking of is the continued ability of the police to capitalize on the ignorance of citizens so as to accomplish by subterfuge what they could not achieve by relying only on the knowing relinquishment of constitutional rights. * * *

NOTES ON THE RELEVANT FACTORS IN DETERMINING THE VALIDITY OF A CONSENT

1. ***What is the issue?*** Some courts, as did the court of appeals in *Bustamonte,* 448 F.2d 699 (9th Cir.1971), characterize a consent to search as "a waiver of a constitutional right" and thus focus upon the state of mind of the person allegedly giving the consent. Some other courts look instead to the state of mind of the officer seeking the consent; the question is said to be whether "the officers, as reasonable men, could conclude that defendant's consent was given," e.g., *People v. Henderson,* 210 N.E.2d 483 (Ill.1965). Does *Bustamonte* clearly indicate a choice of either of these theories? Cf. *Florida v. Jimeno,* p. 455, and *Illinois v. Rodriguez,* p. 456. An illustration of how the choice of one of these theories over the other might affect the outcome is provided by *United States v. Elrod,* 441 F.2d 353 (5th Cir.1971), holding: "No matter how genuine the belief of the officers is that the consenter is apparently of sound mind and deliberately acting, the search depending upon his consent fails if it is judicially determined that he lacked mental capacity. It is not that the actions of the officers were imprudent or unfounded. It is that the key to validity—consent—is lacking for want of mental capacity, no matter how much concealed."

2. ***Claim or show of authority.*** In *Bumper v. North Carolina,* 391 U.S. 543 (1968), defendant's grandmother allowed the police to search her house after one of them announced, "I have a search warrant to search your house." At the hearing on the motion to suppress the rifle found therein, the prosecutor did not rely upon a warrant to justify the search. The Supreme Court was advised that the officers did have a warrant, but none was ever returned and nothing was known about the conditions under which it was issued. The Court held, 7–2, per Stewart, J., that a search cannot be justified on the basis of consent "when that 'consent' has been given only after the official conducting the search has asserted that he possesses a warrant," as when "a law enforcement officer claims authority to search a home under a warrant, he announces in effect that the occupant has no right to resist the search. The situation is instinct with coercion—albeit colorably lawful coercion. Where there is coercion there cannot be consent."

What if the grandmother had responded to the police, "You don't need a search warrant, go ahead"? What if the officer in *Bumper* had merely threatened to obtain a search warrant? Consider *United States v. Boukater,* 409 F.2d 537 (5th Cir.1969) (coercive unless the officer actually had grounds to obtain a warrant or he merely said he would seek a search warrant). The "claim of lawful authority" referred to in *Bumper* need not involve mention of a search warrant; a flat

12. The Court's suggestion that it would be "unrealistic" to require the officers to make "the detailed type of examination" involved when a court considers whether a defendant has waived a trial right, deserves little comment. The question before us relates to the inquiry to be made in court when the prosecution seeks to establish that consent was given. I therefore do not address the Court's strained argument that one may waive constitutional rights without making a knowing and intentional choice so long as the rights do not relate to the fairness of a criminal trial. I would suggest, however, that that argument is fundamentally inconsistent with the law of unconstitutional conditions.

assertion by the police that they have come to search will suffice. *Amos v. United States,* 255 U.S. 313 (1921).

3. *Threat of incarceration.* In *United States v. Knights*, p. 445, Knights signed the probation order containing the search condition and a declaration he agreed "to abide by same." "The Government, advocating the approach of the Supreme Court of California, * * * contends that the search satisfied the Fourth Amendment under the 'consent' rationale of * * * *Schneckloth* * * *. In the Government's view, Knights's acceptance of the search condition was voluntary because he had the option of rejecting probation and going to prison instead, which the Government argues is analogous to the voluntary decision defendants often make to waive their right to a trial and accept a plea bargain." Had the Court found it necessary to decide the consent issue, what conclusion should it have reached?

4. *Prior illegal police action*. Under the "fruit of the poisonous tree" doctrine of *Wong Sun,* p. 907, a consent may be held ineffective because obtained in exploitation of a prior illegal arrest.

5. *Mental or emotional state of the person.* Compare *United States v. Elrod,* Note 1 supra; and *Commonwealth v. Angivoni,* 417 N.E.2d 422 (Mass.1981) (voluntary consent of defendant in hospital emergency room with dislocated hip not established, as "defendant's understanding and ability to reason reflectively may have been impaired by intoxication or as a result of his injuries or an emotional trauma attendant to his just having been in an accident"); with the Supreme Court's more recent application of the voluntariness test in *Colorado v. Connelly,* p. 726.

6. *Denial of guilt.* Doesn't the ready discovery of incriminating evidence pursuant to the "consent" of a person who has denied his guilt manifest that the consent must have been involuntary? Yes, concluded the court in *Higgins v. United States,* 209 F.2d 819 (D.C.Cir.1954): "No sane man who denies his guilt would actually be willing that policemen search his room for contraband which is certain to be discovered." But in *Florida v. Bostick,* p. 409, in response to the defendant's contention that "no reasonable person would freely consent to a search of luggage that he or she knows contains drugs," the Court responded that such an "argument cannot prevail because the 'reasonable person' test presupposes an *innocent* person."

7. *Custody; Warning of Fourth Amendment rights.* In *United States v. Watson,* p. 318, the majority concluded that the failure to give the defendant Fourth Amendment warnings "is not to be given controlling significance" where, as there, the defendant "had been arrested and was in custody, but his consent was given while on a public street, not in the confines of the police station." Marshall and Brennan, JJ., dissenting, objected that the case should be remanded for reconsideration of the consent issue by the court of appeals in light of the fact that the "lack of custody was of decisional importance in *Schneckloth,* which repeatedly distinguished the case before it from one involving a suspect in custody."

In *Gentile v. United States,* 419 U.S. 979 (1974), where consent was obtained from the defendant during stationhouse custodial interrogation after the giving of the *Miranda* warnings but without Fourth Amendment warnings, Douglas and Marshall, JJ., dissenting from the denial of certiorari, noted: "When a suspect is in custody the situation is in control of the police. The pace of events will not somehow deny them an opportunity to give a warning, as the [*Schneckloth*] Court apparently feared would happen in noncustodial settings. Moreover, the custodial setting will permit easy documentation of both the giving of a warning and the arrestee's response."

8. ***Warning of Fifth Amendment rights.*** It has sometimes been held that a valid consent to search, given by a person in custody, must be preceded by *Miranda* warnings because "the request to search is a request that defendant be a witness against himself which he is privileged to refuse under the Fifth Amendment." *State v. Williams,* 432 P.2d 679 (Or.1967). But the prevailing view, as stated in *United States v. LaGrone*, 43 F.3d 332 (7th Cir.1994), is that "because requesting consent to search is not likely to elicit an incriminating statement, such questioning is not interrogation, and thus *Miranda* warnings are not required."

9. ***Right to counsel.*** In *Tidwell v. Superior Court,* 95 Cal.Rptr. 213 (App. 1971), the police asked petitioner, who was in jail, if they could search his car, which had been impounded. Petitioner allegedly replied, "Go ahead and search." The court held that petitioner's consent was ineffective since at the time he had been arraigned on a burglary charge and counsel had been appointed, yet the police had asked him to consent to the search without notifying his lawyer. Rejecting the argument that *Massiah* [p. 561] should apply only to "statements elicited and not to consents given," the court observed: "This distinction is very thin considering the incriminating effect a consent to search may have. The reasoning of [the cases protecting] defendants' right to effective aid of counsel applies equally to a consent given at the instigation of the police."

10. ***"Consent" by deception.*** In contrast to the type of deception allegedly used in *Bumper,* Note 3 supra, the police sometimes obtain evidence of criminal activity by acting in an undercover capacity and obtaining a "consent" which the defendant would not have given had he known the officer's true identity; see *Lewis v. United States,* p. 490, upholding this practice upon the facts presented. A third situation is that in which the officer's true identity is known but he misleads the suspect as to his intentions. Compare *Graves v. Beto,* 424 F.2d 524 (5th Cir.1970) (rape defendant's consent to blood test which resulted in matching his blood with that at crime scene not freely and intelligently given where his acquiescence was obtained by intimating that test was to be taken simply to determine whether he had a sufficient quantity of alcohol in his blood stream to be detained on a charge of public drunkenness); with *United States v. Andrews,* 746 F.2d 247 (5th Cir.1984) (federal agents asked to see shotgun on ruse they were trying to connect it with robberies, actual purpose was to establish defendant's crime of illegal possession of firearm by convicted felon; consent voluntary, *Graves* distinguished because "there is no evidence indicating that Andrews was assured his production of the guns would only be used to investigate the robberies").

11. ***Scope of consent.*** The standard for measuring the scope of a suspect's consent, the Court concluded in *Florida v. Jimeno,* 500 U.S. 248 (1991), is neither the suspect's intent nor the officer's perception thereof but rather "that of 'objective' reasonableness—what would the typical reasonable person have understood by the exchange between the officer and the suspect?" Given the officer's statement in *Jimeno* that he would be looking for narcotics, "it was objectively reasonable for the police to conclude that the general consent to search respondent's car included consent to search containers within that car which might bear drugs." But, the nature of the container is also relevant. "It is very unreasonable to think that a suspect, by consenting to the search of his trunk, has agreed to the breaking open of a locked briefcase within the trunk, but it is otherwise with respect to a closed paper bag."

Does the *Jimeno* principle, that "the scope of the search is generally defined by its expressed object," suffice as to consent searches of the person? Consider *United States v. Rodney,* 956 F.2d 295 (D.C.Cir.1992) (sweeping motion over crotch area during consent search for drugs lawful, as it no more intrusive than a

Terry frisk; court distinguishes *United States v. Blake,* 888 F.2d 795 (11th Cir.1989), suppressing drugs found on person, as that case involved "a direct 'frontal touching' of the defendant's private parts").

Does a consent, voluntary when given, justify a second search of the same place at a later time after a fruitless first search? Compare *People v. Nawrocki,* 150 N.W.2d 516 (Mich.App.1967) (defendant's consent to search his car construed as "permission to search the car at any time," thus justifying second search hours later after the car was impounded and the defendant was in jail); with *State v. Brochu,* 237 A.2d 418 (Me.1967) (contra where passage of time was greater, second search involved re-entry of defendant's home, and defendant's status had changed from suspect to accused in interim).

12. ***The proper place of consent searches in law enforcement.*** Compare: (a) "In a society based on law, the concept of agreement and consent should be given a weight and dignity of its own. Police officers act in full accord with the law when they ask citizens for consent. It reinforces the rule of law for the citizen to advise the police of his or her wishes and for the police to act in reliance on that understanding. When this exchange takes place, it dispels inferences of coercion." *United States v. Drayton,* 536 U.S. 194 (2002).

(b) "Every year, I witness the same mass incredulity. Why, one hundred criminal procedure students jointly wonder, would someone 'voluntarily' consent to allow a police officer to search the trunk of his car, knowing that massive amounts of cocaine are easily visible there? The answer, I have come to believe, is that most people don't willingly consent to police searches. Yet, absent extraordinary circumstances, chances are that a court nonetheless will conclude that the consent was valid and the evidence admissible under the Fourth Amendment. * * *

"Eliminating consent would require a huge leap of faith, but a worthy one. It would reaffirm a belief that the police can solve crime by focusing not on hunches, but on suspicion and probable cause. It would mean police cannot target minorities by stopping them on the public streets, and then intimidating them into agreeing to a search of their car—a search that only rarely yields incriminating evidence, but almost always leaves the consenter feeling diminished and angry. It would mean that the dignity of the individual is not overpowered by the authority and power of the police officer. It would mean that the Fourth Amendment's concern for the privacy of each citizen would be restored to its rightful place—to be interfered with only when the government has the proper justification for doing so. It would be the right thing to do." Marcy Strauss, *Reconstructing Consent,* 92 J.Crim.L. & Crimin. 211–12, 271–72 (2002).

B. Third Party Consent[a]

ILLINOIS v. RODRIGUEZ

497 U.S. 177, 110 S.Ct. 2793, 111 L.Ed.2d 148 (1990).

Justice SCALIA delivered the opinion of the Court. * * *

[Gail Fischer, who showed signs of a severe beating, told police that she had been assaulted by Rodriguez earlier that day in an apartment on South California. Fischer stated that Rodriguez was then asleep in the apartment, and she consented to travel there with the police in order to unlock the door with her key so that

a. See Mary I. Coombs, *Shared Privacy and the Fourth Amendment, or the Right of Relationships,* 75 Calif.L.Rev. 1593 (1987).

the officers could enter and arrest him. During this conversation, Fischer several times referred to the apartment on South California as "our" apartment, and said that she had clothes and furniture there. The police drove to the apartment accompanied by Fischer, who unlocked the door with her key and gave the officers permission to enter. Inside they observed in plain view drug paraphernalia and containers filled with cocaine. The officers arrested Rodriguez and seized the drugs and related paraphernalia. Rodriguez, charged with possession of a controlled substance with intent to deliver, moved to suppress all evidence seized at the time of his arrest. The court granted the motion, holding that at the time she consented to the entry Fischer did not have common authority over the apartment.]

The Fourth Amendment generally prohibits the warrantless entry of a person's home, whether to make an arrest or to search for specific objects. The prohibition does not apply, however, to situations in which voluntary consent has been obtained, either from the individual whose property is searched, or from a third party who possesses common authority over the premises, see *United States v. Matlock,* [415 U.S. 164 (1974)]. The State of Illinois contends that that exception applies in the present case.

As we stated in *Matlock,* "[c]ommon authority" rests "on mutual use of the property by persons generally having joint access or control for most purposes."[b] The burden of establishing that common authority rests upon the State. On the basis of this record, it is clear that burden was not sustained. The evidence showed that although Fischer, with her two small children, had lived with Rodriguez beginning in December 1984, she had moved out on July 1, 1985, almost a month before the search at issue here, and had gone to live with her mother. She took her and her children's clothing with her, though leaving behind some furniture and household effects. During the period after July 1 she sometimes spent the night at Rodriguez's apartment, but never invited her friends there, and never went there herself when he was not home. Her name was not on the lease nor did she contribute to the rent. She had a key to the apartment, which she said at trial she had taken without Rodriguez's knowledge (though she testified at the preliminary hearing that Rodriguez had given her the key). On these facts the State has not established that, with respect to the South California apartment, Fischer had "joint access or control for most purposes." To the contrary, the Appellate Court's determination of no common authority over the apartment was obviously correct.

[R]espondent asserts that permitting a reasonable belief of common authority to validate an entry would cause a defendant's Fourth Amendment rights to be "vicariously waived." We disagree.

We have been unyielding in our insistence that a defendant's waiver of his trial rights cannot be given effect unless it is "knowing" and "intelligent." We would assuredly not permit, therefore, evidence seized in violation of the Fourth Amendment to be introduced on the basis of a trial court's mere "reasonable belief"—derived from statements by unauthorized persons—that the defendant has waived his objection. But one must make a distinction between, on the one hand, trial rights that *derive* from the violation of constitutional guarantees and, on the other hand, the nature of those constitutional guarantees themselves. * * *

What Rodriguez is assured by the trial right of the exclusionary rule, where it applies, is that no evidence seized in violation of the Fourth Amendment will be

b. Where there is such "common authority," the Court went on to say in *Matlock,* "it is reasonable to recognize that any of the co-inhabitants has the right to permit the inspection in his own right and that the others have assumed the risk that one of their number might permit the common area to be searched."

introduced at his trial unless he consents. What he is assured by the Fourth Amendment itself, however, is not that no government search of his house will occur unless he consents; but that no such search will occur that is "unreasonable." There are various elements, of course, that can make a search of a person's house "reasonable"—one of which is the consent of the person or his cotenant. The essence of respondent's argument is that we should impose upon this element a requirement that we have not imposed upon other elements that regularly compel government officers to exercise judgment regarding the facts: namely, the requirement that their judgment be not only responsible but correct.[c]

[I]n order to satisfy the "reasonableness" requirement of the Fourth Amendment, what is generally demanded of the many factual determinations that must regularly be made by agents of the government—whether the magistrate issuing a warrant, the police officer executing a warrant, or the police officer conducting a search or seizure under one of the exceptions to the warrant requirement—is not that they always be correct, but that they always be reasonable. As we put it in *Brinegar v. United States,* [p. 409]:

> "Because many situations which confront officers in the course of executing their duties are more or less ambiguous, room must be allowed for some mistakes on their part. But the mistakes must be those of reasonable men, acting on facts leading sensibly to their conclusions of probability."

We see no reason to depart from this general rule with respect to facts bearing upon the authority to consent to a search. Whether the basis for such authority exists is the sort of recurring factual question to which law enforcement officials must be expected to apply their judgment; and all the Fourth Amendment requires is that they answer it reasonably. The Constitution is no more violated when officers enter without a warrant because they reasonably (though erroneously) believe that the person who has consented to their entry is a resident of the premises, than it is violated when they enter without a warrant because they reasonably (though erroneously) believe they are in pursuit of a violent felon who is about to escape.

Stoner v. California, [p. 460] is in our view not to the contrary. There, in holding that police had improperly entered the defendant's hotel room based on the consent of a hotel clerk, we stated that "the rights protected by the Fourth Amendment are not to be eroded ... by unrealistic doctrines of 'apparent authority.'" It is ambiguous, of course, whether the word "unrealistic" is descriptive or limiting—that is, whether we were condemning as unrealistic all reliance upon apparent authority, or whether we were condemning only such reliance upon apparent authority as is unrealistic. Similarly ambiguous is the opinion's earlier statement that "there [is no] substance to the claim that the search was reasonable because the police, relying upon the night clerk's expressions of consent, had a reasonable basis for the belief that the clerk had authority to consent to the search." Was there no substance to it because it failed as a matter of law, or because the facts could not possibly support it? At one point the opinion does seem to speak clearly:

> "It is important to bear in mind that it was the petitioner's constitutional right which was at stake here, and not the night clerk's nor the hotel's. It was a right, therefore, which only the petitioner could waive by word or deed, either directly or through an agent."

c. In an omitted portion of the opinion, illustrations were given: (i) the probable cause requirement for a warrant, as to which the magistrate may act on "seemingly reliable but factually inaccurate information"; (ii) the warrant requirement, as to which the officer may be reasonably mistaken as to the warrant's scope, *Maryland v. Garrison,* p. 306; and (iii) the search incident to arrest doctrine, where the officer may be reasonably mistaken as to the person to be arrested, *Hill v. California,* p. 451.

But as we have discussed, what is at issue when a claim of apparent consent is raised is not whether the right to be free of searches has been *waived,* but whether the right to be free of *unreasonable* searches has been *violated.* Even if one does not think the *Stoner* opinion had this subtlety in mind, the supposed clarity of its foregoing statement is immediately compromised, as follows:

> "It is true that the night clerk clearly and unambiguously consented to the search. But there is nothing in the record to indicate that *the police had any basis whatsoever to believe that* the night clerk had been authorized by the petitioner to permit the police to search the petitioner's room."

The italicized language should have been deleted, of course, if the statement two sentences earlier meant that an appearance of authority could never validate a search. In the last analysis, one must admit that the rationale of *Stoner* was ambiguous—and perhaps deliberately so. It is at least a reasonable reading of the case, and perhaps a preferable one, that the police could not rely upon the obtained consent because they knew it came from a hotel clerk, knew that the room was rented and exclusively occupied by the defendant, and could not reasonably have believed that the former had general access to or control over the latter. * * *

As *Stoner* demonstrates, what we hold today does not suggest that law enforcement officers may always accept a person's invitation to enter premises. Even when the invitation is accompanied by an explicit assertion that the person lives there, the surrounding circumstances could conceivably be such that a reasonable person would doubt its truth and not act upon it without further inquiry. As with other factual determinations bearing upon search and seizure, determination of consent to enter must "be judged against an objective standard: would the facts available to the officer at the moment ... 'warrant a man of reasonable caution in the belief' " that the consenting party had authority over the premises? If not, then warrantless entry without further inquiry is unlawful unless authority actually exists. But if so, the search is valid.

In the present case, the Appellate Court found it unnecessary to determine whether the officers reasonably believed that Fischer had the authority to consent, because it ruled as a matter of law that a reasonable belief could not validate the entry. Since we find that ruling to be in error, we remand for consideration of that question. * * *

Justice MARSHALL, with whom Justice BRENNAN and Justice STEVENS join, dissenting. * * *

Unlike searches conducted pursuant to the recognized exceptions to the warrant requirement, third-party consent searches are not based on an exigency and therefore serve no compelling social goal. Police officers, when faced with the choice of relying on consent by a third party or securing a warrant, should secure a warrant, and must therefore accept the risk of error should they instead choose to rely on consent. * * *

Acknowledging that the third party in this case lacked authority to consent, the majority seeks to rely on cases suggesting that reasonable but mistaken factual judgments by police will not invalidate otherwise reasonable searches. The majority reads these cases as establishing a "general rule" that "what is generally demanded of the many factual determinations that must regularly be made by agents of the government—whether the magistrate issuing a warrant, the police officer executing a warrant, or the police officer conducting a search or seizure under one of the exceptions to the warrant requirement—is not that they always be correct, but that they always be reasonable."

The majority's assertion, however, is premised on the erroneous assumption that third-party consent searches are generally reasonable. The cases the majority cites thus provide no support for its holding. In *Brinegar v. United States,* for example, the Court confirmed the unremarkable proposition that police need only probable cause, not absolute certainty, to justify the arrest of a suspect on a highway. As *Brinegar* makes clear, the possibility of factual error is built into the probable cause standard, and such a standard, by its very definition, will in some cases result in the arrest of a suspect who has not actually committed a crime. Because probable cause defines the reasonableness of searches and seizures outside of the home, a search is reasonable under the Fourth Amendment whenever that standard is met, notwithstanding the possibility of "mistakes" on the part of police. In contrast, our cases have already struck the balance against warrantless home intrusions in the absence of an exigency. Because reasonable factual errors by law enforcement officers will not validate unreasonable searches, the reasonableness of the officer's mistaken belief that the third party had authority to consent is irrelevant. * * *[d]

NOTES ON WHO MAY CONSENT

1. ***Husband-wife.*** In *United States v. Duran,* 957 F.2d 499 (7th Cir.1992), holding defendant's wife could consent to search of a separate building on their farm which he used as a gym, the court concluded the requisite access was established by the wife's testimony that she could have entered that building at any time, though the wife had not theretofore done so and had none of her personal effects there. This is not to say, the court cautioned, that there is "a per se rule that common spousal authority extends to every square inch of property upon which a couple's residence is built"; such an approach "presumes that spouses, in forging a marital bond, remove any and all boundaries between them," which "does not reflect reality, either in practice or in the eyes of the law." The *Duran* court thus opted for this position: "In the context of a more intimate marital relationship [as compared to other co-occupants], the burden upon the government should be lighter. We hold that a spouse presumptively has authority to consent to a search of all areas of the homestead; the nonconsenting spouse may rebut this presumption only by showing that the consenting spouse was denied access to the particular area searched." Query, what is the effect of the rebuttal in light of *Rodriguez?*

2. ***Parent-child.*** If a child is living at the home of his parents, the courts are in agreement that the head of the household may give consent to a search of the child's living quarters. A contrary result is sometimes reached if the "child" living with his parents has reached adulthood. A child may not give consent to a full search of the parent's house. However, where it is not unusual or unauthorized for the child to admit visitors into the home, the mere entry of police on the premises with the consent of the child is not improper.

3. ***Landlord-tenant; co-tenants.*** A landlord may not consent to a search of his tenant's premises (as compared to areas of common usage), and this is so even though the landlord may have some right of entry for purposes of inspecting or cleaning the premises. *Chapman v. United States,* 365 U.S. 610 (1961). Hotel employees may not consent to the search of a particular room during the period in which it has been rented by a guest. *Stoner v. California,* 376 U.S. 483 (1964). But

d. As for the other illustrations given by the majority, the dissenters explained that "*Hill* should be understood no less than *Brinegar* as simply a gloss on the meaning of 'probable cause,' " while *Garrison* "was premised on the [fact that] searches based on warrants are generally reasonable," and "like *Brinegar,* thus tells us nothing about the reasonableness under the Fourth Amendment of a warrantless arrest."

"where two or more persons occupy a dwelling place jointly, the general rule is that a joint tenant can consent to police entry and search of the entire house or apartment, even though they occupy separate bedrooms." *State v. Thibodeau,* 317 A.2d 172 (Me.1974).

4. ***Employer-employee.*** As to consent by defendant's employer, compare *Gillard v. Schmidt,* 579 F.2d 825 (3d Cir.1978) (consent invalid as to search of defendant's desk; protection of the Fourth Amendment "does not turn on the nature of the property interest in the searched premises, but on the reasonableness of the person's privacy expectation," and defendant had a high expectation concerning his desk because he worked "in an office secured by a locked door and a desk containing psychological profiles and other confidential student records"); with *Commonwealth v. Glover,* 405 A.2d 945 (Pa.Super.1979) (factory owner could consent to search of items on top of work bench, as it not an area assigned to defendant or used exclusively by him).

Whether an employee can give a valid consent to a search of his employer's premises depends upon the scope of his authority. Generally, the courts have been of the view that the average employee, such as a clerk, janitor, driver, or other person temporarily in charge, may not give consent. However, if the employee is a manager or other person of considerable authority who is left in complete charge for a substantial period of time, then the prevailing view is that such a person can waive his employer's rights.

5. ***Bailor-bailee.*** If a person leaves his car at a garage for repairs, does he assume the risk that the repairman might permit police to look inside the car to determine whether it is stolen, as held in *State v. Baker,* 310 S.E.2d 101 (N.C.App.1983)? If so, is a different result called for if the repairman turns the vehicle over to the police so that they can inspect it more closely at another location, as in *State v. Farrell,* 443 A.2d 438 (R.I.1982)?

NOTES ON LIMITS ON THIRD–PARTY CONSENT

Even if the consent was given by a third party who, at least in some circumstances, could give effective consent, it may still be questioned whether other circumstances of the particular case made that person's consent ineffective vis-a-vis the defendant. Consider:

1. ***Antagonism.*** What if, for example, a wife calls the police into the house and points out incriminating evidence because she is angry at her husband? Compare *State v. Gonzalez–Valle,* 385 So.2d 681 (Fla.App.1980) (where "the motive of the defendant's wife in consenting to the search was clearly one of spite," she "had no right to waive her husband's protection against unreasonable searches and seizures"); with *Commonwealth v. Martin,* 264 N.E.2d 366 (Mass. 1970) ("while they are both living in the premises the equal authority does not lapse and revive with the lapse and revival of amicable relations between the spouses").

2. ***Defendant's instructions.*** If the defendant had previously instructed the third party not to allow a search, should those instructions be controlling? In *People v. Fry,* 76 Cal.Rptr. 718 (App.1969), the court held: "When the officers solicited consent of the wife to enter for the purpose of seizing property they knew her husband had instructed her not to consent and, under these circumstances, were not entitled to rely upon her consent as justification for their conduct" in searching the family home. *Fry* was distinguished in *People v. Reynolds,* 127 Cal.Rptr. 561 (App.1976), because in the later case the police were unaware of the husband's instructions to his wife. Is the *Matlock* test relevant on this issue?

3. ***Defendant's refusal or failure to consent.*** In *Matter of Welfare of D.A.G.,* 484 N.W.2d 787 (Minn.1992), the court concluded: "The 'waiver' and 'assumption of risk' rationales, however, are not compelling in a case such as this, where the person against whom the search is directed is present and the consenting joint occupant is not. First, an absent third-party's consent should not be used to 'waive' another individual's constitutional rights when that individual is present at the search to give or withhold consent in his or her own right. Similarly, the risk that one co-inhabitant might permit the common area of a jointly occupied premises to be searched in the absence of another is qualitatively different from the risk that a warrantless search will be conducted over the objection of a present joint occupant: A present, objecting joint occupant cannot be said to have assumed the risk that an absent third party will vicariously waive his or her constitutional rights. We agree that 'the risk assumed by joint occupancy is merely an inability to control access to the premises during one's absence.' * * * We do not, however, decide what the result would be where both consenting and non-consenting joint occupants are present when the police request permission to search a premises."

4. ***Exclusive control by defendant of effects or areas within shared premises or objects.*** In *State v. Evans,* 372 P.2d 365 (Hawaii 1962), the court held the wife could not consent to a search of personal items found in a cuff link case located in her husband's dresser drawer. Is this holding consistent with the *Matlock* test? Consider also the relevance of *Frazier v. Cupp,* 394 U.S. 731 (1969), where the Court concluded that one of petitioner's contentions, namely, that the police illegally searched and seized clothing from his duffel bag, could "be dismissed rather quickly":

"This duffel bag was being used jointly by petitioner and his cousin Rawls and it had been left in Rawls' home. The police, while arresting Rawls, asked him if they could have his clothing. They were directed to the duffel bag and both Rawls and his mother consented to its search. During this search, the officers came upon petitioner's clothing and it was seized as well. Since Rawls was a joint user of the bag, he clearly had authority to consent to its search. The officers therefore found evidence against petitioner while in the course of an otherwise lawful search. * * * Petitioner argues that Rawls only had actual permission to use one compartment of the bag and that he had no authority to consent to a search of the other compartments. We will not, however, engage in such metaphysical subleties in judging the efficacy of Rawls' consent. Petitioner, in allowing Rawls to use the bag and in leaving it in his house, must be taken to have assumed the risk that Rawls would allow someone else to look inside."

5. ***Seizure vs. search.*** "Up to now, [the third-party consent] principle has found expression only in the context of consent to the search of property—but there is no sound reason to restrict the principle rigidly to that milieu," as "the logic of third-party consent can be adapted to seizures in some instances." *United States v. Woodrum,* 202 F.3d 1 (1st Cir.2000) (relying on third-party consent in upholding a program whereby police may stop to check on the safety of drivers of those cabs bearing a decal indicating the owner is voluntarily participating in a program contemplating such stops, reasoning that "these decals symbolized both the owner's and the driver's consent to future stops," that "the driver's command of the taxi allows him to maintain control over the vehicle's speed and route of travel," and that "the driver has the authority to consent to a stop in his own right, and that the passenger, by entering the cab, assumes the risk that the driver may exercise his right to stop briefly along the way").

Chapter 7

WIRETAPPING, ELECTRONIC EAVES-DROPPING, THE USE OF SECRET AGENTS TO OBTAIN INCRIMINATING STATEMENTS, AND THE FOURTH AMENDMENT[a]

SECTION 1. HISTORICAL BACKGROUND

A. CONSTITUTIONAL PERMISSION

OLMSTEAD v. UNITED STATES, 277 U.S. 438 (1928), held (5–4), per Chief Justice TAFT, that wiretapping did not amount to a search and seizure for reasons that have since been rejected by the Court. The Fourth Amendment itself, observed Taft, "shows that the search is to be of material things—the person, the house, his papers or his effects. The description of the warrant necessary to make the proceeding lawful, is that it must specify the place to be searched and the person or *things* to be seized." Moreover, not only did the police fail to violate the amendment by tapping, as such, but neither did they do so at any point along the way, in the course of gaining access to the wiretap evidence: "The evidence was secured by the use of the sense of hearing and that only. There was no entry of the houses or offices of the defendants."

Although the evidence which led to the conviction for conspiracy to violate the National Prohibition Act was obtained by federal prohibition agents in violation of a statute of the state of Washington, which made it a misdemeanor to "intercept" telegraphic or telephonic messages, the Chief Justice pointed out that "this statute does not declare that evidence obtained by such interception shall be inadmissible, and by the common law [it] would not be." Moreover, "clearly a [state statute] cannot affect the rules of evidence applicable in courts of the United States."[b]

a. This chapter does not attempt to cover in detail Title III of the Crime Control Act of 1968, as amended by the Electronic Communication Privacy Act of 1986, and the extensive litigation these statutes have generated. For more comprehensive treatment, see James Carr, *The Law of Electronic Surveillance* (2d ed. 1986); Clifford S. Fishman and A. McKenna, *Wiretapping and Eavesdropping* (2d ed. 1995); Michael Goldsmith, *The Supreme Court and Title III: Rewriting the Law of Electronic Surveillance*, 74 J.Crim.L. & C. 1 (1983). For a fairly brief but very helpful examination of various aspects of Title III, and of electronic surveillance generally, see Chapter 14 of Charles H. Whitebread & Christopher Slobogin, *Criminal Procedure* (4th ed. 2000).

b. "Taft did not challenge the fourth amendment exclusionary rule; he *confined* it. Rejecting the argument that 'unethically,' as well as unconstitutionally, secured evidence should be barred, he concluded that 'the exclusion of evidence should be confined to cases where *rights under the Constitution* would be violated by *admitting* it' "(emphasis added.) Kamisar, *Does (Did) (Should) the Exclusionary Rule Rest on a "Principled Basis" Rather than an "Empirical Proposition"*?, 16 Creighton L.Rev. 565, 603 (1983).

In an exhaustive dissenting opinion, Justice BRANDEIS observed:

"The progress of science in furnishing the government with means of espionage is not likely to stop with wire tapping. Ways may some day be developed by which the government, without removing papers from secret drawers, can reproduce them in court, and by which it will be enabled to expose to a jury the most intimate occurrences of the home. Advances in the psychic and related sciences may bring means of exploring unexpressed beliefs, thoughts and emotions. * * * Can it be that the Constitution affords no protection against such invasions of individual security?

"[In] *Ex parte Jackson,* 96 U.S. 727 [1877], it was held that a sealed letter intrusted to the mail is protected by the amendments. The mail is a public service furnished by the government. The telephone is a public service furnished by its authority. There is, in essence, no difference between the sealed letter and the private telephone message.

"[The] evil incident to invasion of the privacy of the telephone is far greater than that involved in tampering with the mails. Whenever a telephone line is tapped, the privacy of the persons at both ends of the line is invaded, and all conversations between them upon any subject, and although proper, confidential, and privileged, may be overheard. Moreover, the tapping of one man's telephone line involves the tapping of the telephone of every other person whom he may call, or who may call him. As a means of espionage, writs of assistance and general warrants are but puny instruments of tyranny and oppression when compared with wire tapping.

"Time and again this court, in giving effect to the principle underlying the Fourth Amendment, has refused to place an unduly literal construction upon it. * * * No court which looked at the words of the amendment rather than at its underlying purpose would hold, as this court did in *Ex parte Jackson,* that its protection extended to letters in the mails.

"[The] makers of our Constitution * * * conferred, as against the government, the right to be let alone—the most comprehensive of rights and the right most valued by civilized men. To protect that right, every unjustifiable intrusion by the government upon the privacy of the individual, whatever the means employed, must be deemed a violation of the Fourth Amendment. And the use, as evidence in a criminal proceeding, of facts ascertained by such intrusion must be deemed a violation of the Fifth. * * *

"Independently of the constitutional question, I am of opinion that the judgment should be reversed. By the laws of Washington, wire tapping is a crime. To prove its case, the government was obliged to lay bare the crimes committed by its officers on its behalf. A federal court should not permit such a prosecution to continue. * * *

"Decency, security, and liberty alike demand that government officials shall be subjected to the same rules of conduct that are commands to the citizen. In a government of laws, existence of the government will be imperiled if it fails to observe the law scrupulously. Our government is the potent, the omnipresent teacher. For good or for ill, it teaches the whole people by its example. Crime is contagious. If the government becomes a lawbreaker, it breeds contempt for law; it invites every man to become a law unto himself; it invites anarchy. To declare that in the administration of the criminal law the end justifies the means—to declare that the government may commit crimes in order to secure the conviction of a private criminal—would bring terrible retribution. Against that pernicious doctrine this court should resolutely set its face."

In a brief separate dissent, Justice HOLMES commented:

"While I do not deny it I am not prepared to say that the penumbra of the Fourth and Fifth Amendments covers the defendants, although I fully agree that courts are apt to err by sticking too closely to the words of a law where these words import a policy that goes beyond them. [But] I think, as Justice Brandeis says, that apart from the Constitution the government ought not to use evidence obtained and only obtainable by a criminal act. * * * It is desirable that criminals should be detected, and to that end that all available evidence should be used. It also is desirable that the government should not itself foster and pay for other crimes, when they are the means by which the evidence is to be obtained. * * * We have to choose, and for my part I think it is a less evil that some criminals should escape than that the government should play an ignoble part.

"For those who agree with me no distinction can be taken between the government as prosecutor and the government as judge. If the existing code does not permit district attorneys to have a hand in such dirty business it does not permit the judge to allow such iniquities to succeed. [And] if all that I have said so far be accepted it makes no difference that in this case wire tapping is made a crime by the law of the state, not by the law of the United States. * * * I am aware of the often-repeated statement that in a criminal proceeding the court will not take notice of the manner in which papers offered in evidence have been obtained. But that somewhat rudimentary mode of disposing of the question has been overthrown by *Weeks*. [T]he reason for excluding evidence obtained by violating the Constitution seems to me logically to lead to excluding evidence obtained by a crime of the officers of the law."

Notes and Questions

1. ***Different views of constitutional interpretation.*** For a close study of the opinions of Chief Justice Taft and Justice Brandeis in the *Olmstead* case and an insightful discussion of the two Justices' different views of constitutional interpretation, see James Boyd White, *Judicial Criticism,* 20 Ga.L.Rev. 835, 847–70 (1986).

2. ***Shedding light on the original bases of the exclusionary rule.*** Although often quoted by proponents of the fourth amendment exclusionary rule, the most famous passages in the Holmes–Brandeis dissents are arguments for extending the exclusionary rule to situations where the federal government has not violated the Constitution, or even federal law, but only a state anti-wiretapping law. "Nevertheless," observes Kamisar, fn. b, p. 348, "these famous dissents shed light on the original bases and purposes of the exclusionary rule. [They] underscore that the exclusionary rule is [or at least was thought to be] based on principle—one might also say that it has an important symbolic quality—not on estimates of how substantially the exclusion of evidence affects police behavior."

B. Statutory Prohibition: § 605 of the 1934 Federal Communications Act[a]

Chief Justice Taft noted in his *Olmstead* opinion that "Congress may of course protect the secrecy of telephone messages by making them when intercepted, inadmissible in evidence in federal criminal trials, by direct legislation, and thus depart from the common law of evidence." Such a development occurred with the passage of the Federal Communications Act of 1934. Section 605 of the Act

a. Section 605 of the 1934 Act was "amended" by Title III of the Crime Control Act of 1968, permitting court-approved wiretapping and electronic eavesdropping by federal and state law enforcement officials in the investigation of many listed offenses.

read in part: "[N]o person not being authorized by the sender shall intercept any communication and divulge or publish the existence, contents, substance, purport, effect, or meaning of such intercepted communication to any person * * *." This wording was held to cover wiretapping by state or federal officers as well as by private persons, *Nardone v. United States,* 302 U.S. 379 (1937), 308 U.S. 338 (1939); *Benanti v. United States,* 355 U.S. 96 (1957); and to apply to intrastate as well as interstate communications, *Weiss v. United States,* 308 U.S. 321 (1939).

The Department of Justice and the FBI took the position that Section 605 did not prohibit wiretapping *alone,* only tapping *followed by* "divulgence," and, further, that it was not a "divulgence" when one member of the government communicated to another, but only when he communicated outside the government, e.g., sought to introduce the wiretap information into evidence. See e.g., William P. Rogers, *The Case for Wire Tapping,* 63 Yale L.J. 792, 793 (1954). For sharp criticism of this view see, e.g., Edward Bennett Williams, *The Wiretapping–Eavesdropping Problem; A Defense Counsel's View,* 44 Minn.L.Rev. 855, 860 (1960).

C. Wiretapping, § 605 and Federal–State Relations

Since it involved the use of state-gathered wiretap evidence in a state prosecution, *Schwartz v. Texas,* 344 U.S. 199 (1952), posed the wiretapping counterpart of *Wolf v. Colorado.* Although the Court recognized that "the problem under '605 is somewhat different [than *Wolf*] because the introduction of the intercepted communication would itself be a violation of the statute," i.e., a prohibited "divulgence," it nevertheless relied on *Wolf* to hold the evidence admissible. Only Douglas, J., dissented.

More weight was given to the Federal Communication Act's "built-in" exclusionary rule in *Benanti v. United States,* supra, which barred state-gathered wiretap evidence proffered in a *federal* prosecution, even though at the time the great weight of authority (later overruled in *Elkins,* pp. 112, 134) allowed federal prosecutors to use evidence obtained by illegal state searches so long as there was no "collusion" between the two "sovereignties."

Two days before the electronic surveillance provisions of the Crime Control Act of 1968 were signed into law, *Schwartz* was overruled by *Lee v. Florida,* 392 U.S. 378 (1968): "*Schwartz* cannot survive the demise of *Wolf.* [*Mapp*] imposed a judicially devised exclusionary rule. [In] the present case the federal law itself explicitly protects intercepted communications from divulgence, in a court or any other place."

D. Non-Telephonic Electronic Eavesdropping

1. ***Brandeis' fears become a reality***. Several studies in the 1950s and 60s, e.g., Samuel Dash, Robert Knowlton & Richard Schwartz, *The Eavesdroppers* 339–79 (1959); Allan F. Westin, *Privacy and Freedom* 69–89 (1967); indicated that modern developments in electronic eavesdropping had made the prophetic fears voiced by Justice Brandeis in his *Olmstead* dissent a reality. According to these studies: Tiny microphones can be secreted behind a picture or built into a coat button. Highly directive microphones known as "parabolic microphones" are capable of eavesdropping on a conversation taking place in an office on the *opposite side of a busy street* or on a park bench or outdoor restaurant terrace hundreds of feet away. Laser beams can pick sound waves off closed windows. A small, continuously operating transmitter can be placed beneath the fender of an automobile and its signal picked up by a receiver in another car or in a fixed plant.

A special gun developed for American military authorities can shoot a small dart containing a wireless radio microphone into a tree, window pane, awning or any other object near the subject of investigation.

However, while electronic eavesdropping appeared to be "the ultimate invasion of privacy," Williams, supra, at 866, for decades the law furnished much less protection against this danger than it did against wiretapping. The Federal Communications Act applied only when telephone, telegraph, or radiotelegraph conversations were overheard and until the 1960's the constitutional protection against unreasonable search and seizure applied only when electronic snooping was accomplished by a physical invasion or "trespass". No such "trespass" occurred in *Olmstead* (the taps from house lines were made in the streets near the house) or in *Goldman v. United States,* 316 U.S. 129 (1942) (where federal officers placed a detectaphone *against the wall* of a private office) or in *On Lee v. United States* (1952) (Sec. 3, infra) (where incriminating statements were picked up via a "wired for sound" former acquaintance of petitioner).

2. ***The Constitution did furnish some protection***. That the Constitution did furnish *some* protection against the electronic seizure of conversations as well as the seizure of "papers and effects" was made plain by *Silverman v. United States,* 365 U.S. 505 (1961). There, a unanimous Court, per Stewart, J., held that listening to incriminating conversations within a house by inserting an electronic device (a so-called "spike mike") into a party wall and making contact with a heating duct serving the house occupied by petitioners, "thus converting their entire heating system into a conductor of sound," amounted to an illegal search and seizure.

Justice Douglas concurred, maintaining: "The depth of the penetration of the electronic device—even the degree of its remoteness from the inside of the house—is not measure of the injury. * * * Our concern should not be with the trivialities of the local law of trespass, as the opinion of the Court indicates. But neither should the command of the Fourth Amendment be limited by nice distinctions turning on the kind of electronic equipment employed. Rather our sole concern should be with whether the privacy of the home was invaded."

Silverman not only established that conversations could be "seized" within the meaning of the Fourth Amendment, but suggested that a Fourth Amendment "search" for them might occur without any trespass. This seemed even more certain when three years later, in *Clinton v. Virginia,* 377 U.S. 158 (1964) (per curiam), the Court summarily rejected the state court's holding that *Silverman* did not apply where the spike mike "was not driven into the wall but was 'stuck in' it." Any lingering doubts were dispelled by *Katz v. United States* (p. 247).

SECTION 2. *BERGER, KATZ* AND THE LEGISLATION THAT FOLLOWED

A. The Implications of *Berger* and *Katz*

BERGER v. NEW YORK, 388 U.S. 41 (1967),[a] left the dissenting Justices (and many others) wondering whether *any* wiretapping or electronic eaves-

a. The case grew out of a state investigation of alleged bribery of state liquor authority officials. Pursuant to the challenged New York statute, a court order was obtained permitting the installation of a recording device in a lawyer's office for up to 60 days. On the basis of information gathered from this eavesdrop, a second order was obtained, authorizing the installation of a recording device in another person's office. As a result of evidence obtained from the second eavesdrop, petitioner was indicted for, and convicted of, conspiracy to bribe the chairman of the state liquor authority.

dropping statute could pass constitutional muster. The Court, per CLARK, J., struck down a New York electronic surveillance statute, calling it a "blanket grant of permission to eavesdrop * * * without adequate supervision or protective procedures."

The statute, observed Justice Clark, (1) permitted a court order to issue merely on reasonable grounds to believe that evidence of crime may be obtained, without specifying what crime has been or is being committed and without describing what conversations are to be overheard—thus failing to "particularly [describe] the place to be searched, and the person or things to be seized," as required by the Fourth Amendment[b]—(2) permitted installation and operation of surveillance equipment for 60 days—"the equivalent of a series of intrusions, searches and seizures pursuant to a single showing of probable cause"—(3) permitted renewal of the order on the basis of the original grounds on which the initial order was issued—"this we believe insufficient without a showing of present probable cause for continuance of the eavesdrop"—(4) placed no termination on the eavesdrop once the conversation sought is seized—"this is left entirely to the discretion of the officer"—and (5) did not provide for a return on the warrant—"thereby leaving full discretion in the officer as to the use of seized conversations of innocent as well as guilty parties."

The Court contrasted the New York statute's "broadside authorization" of electronic surveillance with the "precise and discriminate" procedures followed in *Osborn v. United States,* 385 U.S. 323 (1966), where, on the basis of a detailed affidavit alleging that an attorney was attempting to bribe a juror, two federal judges authorized a tape recorder to be concealed on the person of the attorney's "employee" (actually a secret government agent) for a specific meeting with the attorney.[c] Because *Osborn* involved such a rare fact situation, one atypical of police electronic surveillance, the Court's reference to this case raised further doubts about the constitutionality of most electronic surveillance.[d]

DOUGLAS, J., concurred in the result, maintaining that electronic surveillance is "a search for 'mere evidence,' "which is a violation of the Fourth and Fifth Amendments regardless of "the nicety and precision with which a warrant may be drawn."[e] "If a statute were to authorize placing a policeman in every home or office where it was shown that there was probable cause to believe that evidence would be obtained," he observed, "there is little doubt that it would be struck down as a bald invasion of privacy, far worse than the general warrants prohibited by the Fourth Amendment. I can see no difference between such a statute and one authorizing electronic surveillance, which, in effect, places an

b. The statute did require the naming of "the person or persons whose communications, conversations or discussions are to be overheard or recorded," but, said the Court, "this does no more than identify the person whose constitutionally protected area is to be invaded rather than 'particularly describing' the communications, conversations, or discussions to be seized. As with general warrants, this leaves too much to the discretion of the officer executing the order."

c. Is there a "certain irony" in the *Berger* Court's approval of *Osborn?* If the *Osborn* order was properly issued without any statutory authorization, why didn't the *Berger* Court consider the particularity of the order issued in this case without regard to the constitutionality of the New York statute? See Kent Greenawalt, *The Consent Problem in Wiretapping and Eavesdropping,* 68 Colum.L.Rev. 189, 201–02 (1968).

d. See Samuel Dash, *Katz—Variations on a Theme by Berger,* 17 Cath.L.Rev. 296, 311–13 (1968).

e. Since *Berger* was briefed and argued prior to *Warden v. Hayden* (p. 271), petitioner argued at some length that the New York statute authorized "general searches" for "mere evidence." But the Court, per Clark, J., rejected the contention in a brisk footnote (fn. 2), stating that it had been "disposed of in *Hayden* adversely to petitioner's assertion here." For the view that it had not, that *Hayden* had been careful to leave open the possibility of some "testimonial limit" on the permissible objects of seizure, see Telford Taylor, *Two Studies in Constitutional Interpretation* 68–71, 101–03 (1969).

invisible policeman in the home. If anything, the latter is more offensive because the homeowner is completely unaware of the invasion of privacy."[f]

STEWART, J., concurred in the result. He fully agreed with the dissenters that the challenged New York law was constitutional, but he concluded that "the affidavits on which the judicial order issued in this case did not constitute a showing of probable cause adequate to justify the authorizing order." The standard of reasonableness embodied in the Fourth Amendment, "he observed," demands that the showing of justification match the degree of intrusion."The affidavits" "might be enough to satisfy the standards of the Fourth Amendment for a conventional search or arrest," but not "an intrusion of the scope and duration that was permitted in this case."[g]

Responding to the contentions that court-ordered electronic surveillance fails to specify with adequate particularity the conversations to be seized and allows a general and indiscriminate search and seizure, Justice HARLAN observed: "Just as some exercise of dominion, beyond mere perception, is necessary for the seizure of tangibles, so some use of the conversation beyond the initial listening process is required for the seizure of the spoken word."

Similarly, dissenting Justice WHITE maintained that an electronic surveillance that is continued over a span of time is no more a "general search" barred by the Fourth Amendment than the typical execution of a search warrant over a described area: "Petitioner suggests that the search is inherently overbroad because the eavesdropper will overhear conversations which do not relate to criminal activity. But the same is true of almost all searches of private property which the Fourth Amendment permits. In searching for seizable matters, the police must necessarily see or hear, and comprehend, items which do not relate to the purpose of the search. That this occurs, however, does not render the search invalid, so long as it is authorized by a suitable search warrant and so long as the police, in executing that warrant, limit themselves to searching for items which may constitutionally be seized."

A short time after *Berger,* the Court, per STEWART, J., made plain in KATZ v. UNITED STATES (p. 247) that the "trespass" doctrine enunciated in *Olmstead* and *Goldman* was no longer viable and that the "penetration" of the governmental intrusion "can have no constitutional significance." But the *Katz* Court thought it "clear that [the surveillance involved in this case] was so narrowly circumscribed that a duly authorized magistrate, properly notified of the need for such investigation, specifically informed of the basis on which it was to proceed, and clearly apprised of the precise intrusion it would entail, could constitutionally have authorized, with appropriate safeguards, the very limited search and seizure that the Government asserts in fact took place."[a]

f. How can this argument be met? Could a police officer lawfully hide in the closet of a suspect's home for 30 days? Ten? Twenty-four hours? Does it matter whether the officer looks through the keyhole as well as listens? As you limit the area of the search, may the time be increased? May a tap be distinguished from a bug on the ground that the former is a "search" of a much narrower "area"?

g. Justice Stewart's argument, however, has not prevailed. Illustrative is *United States v. Falcone*, 505 F.2d 478 (3d Cir.1974): "Probable cause is not a matter of degree. Although *Berger* and *Katz* call for extra vigilance in the supervision of electronic eavesdropping, neither case separates probable cause into degrees. Moreover, no special probable case requirement can be found in the statutory scheme." But consider Posner, J., in *United States v. Torres*, p. 480; Whitebread & Slobogin, p. 481.

a. FBI agents had attached an electronic listening and recording device to the outside of the public phone booth from which petitioner had placed his calls. The agents "did not begin their electronic surveillance until investigation

The Court likened the "discriminate circumstances" of the electronic surveillance in *Katz* to those in *Osborn* where, the *Berger* Court had said, the court order "afforded similar protections to those [of] conventional warrants authorizing the seizure of tangible evidence." "Here, too," observed the *Katz* Court, "a similar judicial order could have accommodated 'the legitimate needs of law enforcement' by authorizing the carefully limited use of electronic surveillance."

Although he dissented in *Katz,* Justice Black was encouraged: "[T]oday's opinion differs sharply from *Berger,* [which] set up what appeared to be insuperable obstacles to the valid passage [of] wiretapping laws. [The] Court's opinion [in] this case [removes] the doubts about state power in this field and abates to a large extent the confusion and near paralyzing effect of the *Berger* holding."

The basis for Justice Black's view that the *Katz* opinion "differs sharply from *Berger*" is unclear. *Both opinions* referred to *Osborn* with approval. And the surveillance in *Katz* itself, as well as in *Osborn,* was very narrowly circumscribed. But the Congress seemed to read *Katz* the same way Justice Black did. Within seven months of *Katz,* in Title III of the Omnibus Crime Control and Safe Streets Act of 1968 (commonly referred to as Title III), discussed immediately below, Congress adopted legislation granting law enforcement officials extensive powers to conduct wiretapping and electronic surveillance.

B. Title III of the Omnibus Crime Control and Safe Streets Act of 1968 (Title III), the Electronic Communications Privacy Act of 1986 (the ECPA) and the USA Patriot Act of 2001: An Overview

The relevant statutory provisions are set forth in App. B of the Annual Supplement to this casebook. For useful summaries or discussions of Title III and subsequent legislation, on which the following "overview" heavily relies, see Wayne R. LaFave, Jerold H. Israel & Nancy J. King, Criminal Procedure Treatise Ch. 4 (2nd ed. 1999) (hereafter cited as CRIMPROC); Charles H. Whitebread & Christopher Slobogin, *Criminal Procedure* Ch. 14 (4th ed. 2000) (hereafter cited as Whitebread & Slobogin); Michael Goldsmith, *The Supreme Court and Title III: Rewriting the Law of Electronic Surveillance*, 74 J. Crim.L. & Criminology 1 (1983) (hereafter Michael Goldsmith); Orin S. Kerr, *Internet Surveillance Law after the USA Patriot Act: The Big Brother that Isn't*; 97 Nw.U.L.Rev. 607 (2003) (hereafter Orin Kerr); and Daniel J. Solove, *Reconstructing Electronic Surveillance Law*, 72 G.W.L.Rev. 1264 (2004) (hereafter Daniel Solove).

In the wake of *Berger* and *Katz,* Congress enacted Title III of the Omnibus Crime Control Act of 1968. Eighteen years later, Congress amended Title III by passing the ECPA. A major reason was that new technologies seemed to be posing an increasing threat to privacy. ECPA expanded the coverage of Title III to include new forms of communication, such as e-mail. It also provided protection beyond communications in transmission (sometimes called "prospective" surveillance) to those stored in computer systems (sometimes called "retrospective" surveillance).

had established a strong possibility that he was using the telephone in question to transmit gambling information [in] violation of federal law. Moreover, the surveillance was limited, both in scope and in duration, to the specific purpose of establishing the contents of the petitioner's unlawful telephone communications. The agents confined their surveillance to the brief periods during which he used the telephone booth, and they took great care to overhear only the conversations of the petitioner himself."

ECPA restructures Title III into three parts: The Wiretap Act, which deals with prospective surveillance; the Stored Communications Act, which covers retrospective surveillance; and The Pen Register Act, which deals with "pen registers" and "trap and trace" devices.[a] These devices were not covered by the 1968 Act.

The USA Patriot Act of 2001 (enacted six weeks after the September 11 attacks)[b] has also affected surveillance law in various ways. Among other things, it makes the pen register provisions of the ECPA applicable to the Internet;[c] provides for "roving wiretaps" under the Foreign Intelligence Surveillance Act of 1978 (FISA);[d] and subjects "U.S. citizens and foreign nationals to broad FISA surveillance when the government's primary purpose is *not* to gather foreign intelligence but instead to gather evidence for use at a criminal trial."[e] Moreover, according to many critics of the Patriot Act, it encourages the use of Carnivore (recently renamed DSC–1000), a controversial Internet surveillance device developed by the FBI.[f]

The Patriot Act's changes to surveillance law "were not directly linked to September 11. [The] Act [was] actually a Department of Justice [DOJ] wish list from before September 11." Daniel Solove 1277–78. As one commentator, who worked in the Computer Crime Section of the Justice Department from 1998–01, has observed (Orin Kerr 637):

"By the time [September 11, 2001] arrived, amendments that had been proposed and debated within the Justice Department for several years were already drafted and provided an obvious starting point for amendments to the electronic surveillance laws. [These] proposals formed the basis for the electronic surveillance portions of the Justice Department's proposed Anti–Terrorism bill [which] in turn provided the basis for the USA Patriot Act passed on October 26."

1. *The scope of Title III.* As amended in 1986, Title III prohibits the "interception" of "wire, oral or electronic communications" unless such interception is authorized by the statute.[a] The prohibition covers electronic mail, computer-to-computer communications and cellular telephones among other modern communication techniques. Protected, too, are electronic storage and processing of information. (As pointed out by Whitebread & Slobogin 331, "to the extent such storage or processing is under the auspices of a third party computer operator, the [1986 amendments] provide protection the Fourth Amendment may not, since the Fourth Amendment is not implicated when information is sought from a party to whom it has voluntarily been surrendered."[b]

An "oral" communication is one "uttered by a person exhibiting an expectation that such communication is not subject to interception under circumstances justifying such expectation, but such term does not include any electronic communication" (§ 2510(2)). The mode of communication here is "sound waves" as

a. See Note 2, p. 472.

b. As observed in Orin Kerr 624, the Patriot Act is not a single coherent law. Rather, "the Act collects hundreds of minor amendments to federal law, grouped into ten subparts or 'Titles,' on topics ranging from immigration to money laundering. With many of these amendments, the devil is in the details: especially in the electronic surveillance context, the complex relationship among sections of statutory text means that the changes often defy easy sound bites."

c. See Note 2, p. 472.

d. See Note 10, p. 479.

e. Steven J. Schulhofer, *The Enemy Within* 45 (2002). See also pp. 478–79.

f. See Note 5, p. 474.

a. 28 U.S.C. § 2510(4).

b. "However, the core Title III protection extends only to the 'interception' of the aural transfer, which occurs as the voice mail transfer is made and placed in storage. To gain access to completed voice mail messages already held in storage, law enforcement officers only need comply with [18 U.S.C. §§ 2701–2711], which is not enforced by an exclusionary remedy." CRIMPROC § 4.3(a).

opposed to an "electronic medium." As noted in CRIMPROC, § 4.3(a), "the critical element of [the] definition is its limitation to persons having a justifiable expectation that their conversations would not be intercepted. The legislative history indicates that this limitation was intended 'to reflect existing law' and it follows the Fourth Amendment 'reasonable expectation of privacy standard' as set forth in *Katz v. United States*."

2. *The definition of "interception"; herein of "pen registers," "trap and trace" devices and, more generally, of "content information" and "envelope information"; application of the pen register laws to the Internet; silent video surveillance.* As amended in 1986, Title III defines "intercept" as meaning "the *aural* or other acquisition of the *contents* of any *communication* through the use of any electronic, mechanical or other device." § 2510(4) (emphasis added).

Thus, "pen registers" (which do not record phone conversations, but only the numbers dialed from a given phone and the times the number was dialed) were not covered by the Title III definition of "intercept." As the Court observed in *United States v. New York Telephone Co.*, 434 U.S. 159 (1977), these devices "do not acquire the 'contents' of communications" as that term is used in Title III and, because they do not hear sound, they "do not accomplish the 'aural acquisition' of anything." (The Court subsequently held, *Smith v. Maryland* (1979) (p. 251), that the use of a pen register did not constitute a "search" within the meaning of the Fourth Amendment either.) Nor were "trap and trace" devices (which capture impulses identifying the originating number of an instrument or device from which a wire or electronic communication was transmitted) covered by the Title III definition of "intercept."

However, the ECPA of 1986 prohibits the use of pen registers and trap and trace devices without a court order. (See 18 U.S.C. § 3127). To obtain such an order, though, a government attorney need only certify that the information sought is "relevant" to an ongoing criminal investigation and identify the possible relevant offenses. The court's function is to determine the completeness of the application; it need not make an independent investigation of the facts. Moreover, although a violation of the pen register law may lead to a prosecution, it does not result in suppression of the evidence.

Every communication network involves two types of information: "content information" (the contents of the communication) and "envelope information" (the addressing and routing information used to deliver the contents of communications). The "content information" for a telephone call is the actual conversation. The "envelope information" includes the number the caller dials, the number from which the caller dials, the time of the call, and its duration. As Professor Kerr has noted (Orin Kerr 612), "[t]hese principles translate to the Internet quite readily in the case of email. The content information for an email is the message in the body of the email itself [The] email also carries addressing information in a "mail header." The Patriot Act's amendments made the pen register laws applicable to the Internet. (See 18 U.S.C. §§ 3121–27).

Before the Patriot Act, it was unclear whether the definition of the terms "pen register" and "trap and trace" device applied to the Internet. The Department of Justice (DOJ) believed that they did apply to the Internet and acted on that basis.[a]

a. The DOJ's conclusion "created a double-edged sword" (Orin Kerr 634): "Without the pen register statute, the government could conduct envelope surveillance without a court order. The government or anybody else could wiretap the Internet and collect any noncontent information it wished without restriction. Applying the pen register laws to the Internet denied the government the power to conduct envelope surveillance without a

After 9/11, the DOJ sought to amend the pen register laws so they clearly applied to the Internet by describing envelope information as "dialing, routing, addressing, or signaling information" and amending the definition of pen register and trap and trace device to incorporate this new definition. Congress adopted the DOJ's approach with one modification—a caveat that "such information shall not include the contents of any communication." See 18 U.S.C.A § 3127(3)-(4). Email headers, Internet Protocal (IP) addresses and Uniform Resource locators (URLs) fall under the new definition.

Professor Kerr agrees with civil libertarian critics of the pen register laws that the standard for obtaining "envelope information" should be raised, but he emphasizes that it should be raised for *both* the Internet *and* the telephone.[b] (Orin Kerr 642–43). Although some critics of the Patriot Act maintain that Internet envelope surveillance poses a much greater threat to privacy than telephone envelope surveillance, Professor Kerr strongly disagrees. According to him, internet and telephone envelope surveillance "usually provide equally sensitive information, and in some key ways, Internet envelope surveillance provides much less sensitive information" (id. at 634). He also notes that if the pen register laws were not made applicable to the Internet, "then email and packet envelope surveillance would be totally unregulated by federal privacy law" (id. at 638).

It is worth noting that although it may well be the most invasive type of technological surveillance of all, surreptitious video surveillance is not covered by Title III or any of it's amendments. As pointed out in *United States v. Torres* (p. 480), a person televised while silently making a bomb "is not engaged in any form of communication"; nor is a visual observation in any sense 'an aural acquisition.'" However, some courts have applied Title III's provisions by analogy.[c]

3. *Nonconsensual electronic surveillance.* Title III only regulates "nonconsensual" electronic surveillance (i.e., electronic surveillance where *none* of the parties overheard have consented to the interception).[a] Thus, as pointed out in CRIMPROC, § 4.3(c), "law enforcement authorities are free to make consensual

court order, which limited government power and blocked private entities from conducting prospective envelope surveillance, thus protecting privacy. At the same time, applying the pen register statute to the Internet benefited law enforcement by giving the government a relatively easy way of obtaining orders compelling [internet service providers (ISPs] to conduct prospective envelope surveillance on the government's behalf. Absent that authority, the government would need to install monitoring devices itself, rely on the voluntary cooperation of ISPs, or try to use other laws requiring a higher factual showing than the pen register laws to obtain court orders compelling ISPs to conduct envelope surveillance."

b. Kerr points out that "envelope information" for a telephone call can reveal quite a bit—"activity from within the suspects' homes that tell the police where they were, at what time, and how long they spoke"—and, if it's a long call—that the two people on the phone probably knew each other "or at least had something substantial to discuss." *Id.* at 643. See also Daniel Solove 1286–88.

c. See Notes 11–13, pp. 480–482.

a. §§ 2511(2)(c) & (d) provide that "it shall not be unlawful under this chapter for a person [to] intercept a wire, oral or electronic communication where such person is a party to the communication or *one of the parties* to the communication has given prior consent to such interception." (Emphasis added.) Consensual electronic surveillance is not restricted by the Fourth Amendment. See *Lopez v. United States* (1963) (p. 488); *United States v. White* (1971) (p. 496).

The National Wiretap Commission, *Majority Report* (1976) found that consensual electronic surveillance "is especially vital for the investigation of certain criminal activities, particularly official corruption, extortion, and loansharking," and that "it also serves to protect police officers, informants, and complainants, or whoever is the consenting participant to the conversation." The Majority Report deemed court authorization for such surveillance "unnecessary for the protection of privacy because it is not a 'search' within the meaning of the Fourth Amendment" and because "it serves not to intercept conversations, but merely to corroborate them, improving the accuracy of evidence for use in court."

interceptions in a variety of ways: (1) by having the consenting party wear or carry a tape recorder with which he records his face-to-face conversations with another; (2) by having the consenting party wear a transmitter which broadcasts his conversations to agents equipped with a receiver; or (3) by having the consenting party to a telephone conversation record it or permit another to listen in on an extension."

4. *Title III's "exclusionary rule."* Title III has a general exclusion provision, § 2515, which applies to private, as well as government, interceptions. Section 2515 also states that no part of the contents of any communication intercepted in violation of the statute "may be received in evidence in any trial, hearing or other proceeding in or before any court, grand jury, * * * agency, regulatory body, legislative committee" or any federal or state authority. Thus, Title III's exclusionary rule has been called one that "transcends its constitutional counterpart by being applicable to all governmental, judicial, quasi-judicial, and administrative proceedings." Michael Goldsmith 40.[a] As the Supreme Court has construed Title III, however, exclusion of the evidence is not the consequence of *every* failure to comply with the statute's provisions. Exclusion is required only when the particular statutory provision violated "was intended to play a central role in the statutory scheme." Compare *United States v. Giordano*, 416 U.S. 505 (1974) with *United States v. Chavez*, 416 U.S. 562 (1974).

Moreover, although Title III of the 1968 Act was amended in 1986 to cover the interception of any "electronic communication," the exclusionary rule of Title III continues to be limited only to violations having to do with wire or oral communications. The legislative history expressly declares that the Title II exclusionary rule has no application to the interception of electronic communications. See *United States v. Steiger*, 318 F.3d 1039 (11th Cir.2003). The result is that, although e-mail has become a central means of communication, "a defendant can suppress evidence obtained by the illegal interception of a phone conversation, but not an e-mail"—a discrepancy Professor Solove calls "baseless" (Daniel Solove 1282). Finally, neither the pen register laws nor the Stored Communication Act (part of the ECPA) have an "exclusionary rule" remedy.

5. "Carnivore" (a.k.a. DCS–1000). Once a court order is obtained under Title III, "Carnivore" (recently renamed DCS–1000), an Internet-surveillance program developed by the FBI, is used to filter through Internet communications, including e-mail messages, to select the relevant ones. Carnivore checks its programming to determine whether it is supposed to collect the "contents" of communication or whether it is only supposed to collect "envelope information." Carnivore does its work without altering data or preventing messages from continuing to their intended destination. Moreover, the FBI maintains that no record is kept of any unrelated message sent by innocent customers of the same Internet provider.

Although the Patriot Act does not explicitly mention Carnivore, the press frequently reported that the Patriot Act provided for its expanded use. See, e.g., John Schwartz, *Privacy Debate Focuses on F.B.I. Use of an Internet Wiretap*, N.Y. Times, Oct. 13, 2001, at A14 (the use of Carnivore is "at the heart of the debate" over the Patriot Act).

In retrospect, the menacing name "Carnivore" was an obvious mistake. But as pointed out in Orin Kerr 653, the name was originally intended to reflect how privacy friendly the surveillance tool was designed to be. The first-generation tool

a. *Calandra* (1974) (p. 241), it will be recalled, refused to allow a grand jury witness to invoke the Fourth Amendment exclusionary rule. In *Gelbard v. United States,* 408 U.S. 41 (1972), however, a 5–4 majority, per Brennan, J., held that grand jury witnesses may refuse to testify where their testimony is sought on the basis of illegal electronic surveillance.

the FBI developed before Carnivore was one that utilized a primitive filter that sometimes collected more information than a court order allowed. Because this tool "ate" more than it should have, the FBI dubbed it "Omnivore." Because the second-generation tool only devoured the "meat" it was programmed to record, the FBI called it "Carnivore." "In an apparent attempt to remove associations of bloodthirstiness and improve the sniffer's image," reports David Wilson, *Sniffing Out the Unsavory on the Internet*, South China Morning Post, Dec. 5, 2001, at 7, the FBI named the third-generation tool DCS–1000. However, in some quarters at least, the change in name has only aroused more suspicion—"as one commentator said, even if Carnivore had been renamed Bambi, the fears would remain."

Carnivore's critics complain that since the FBI adamantly opposes disclosing the "blueprints" for how its software works—even to Congress—there is no way of knowing how broad the FBI "snooping" really is. See Ted Bridis & Neil King, Jr., *Carnivore E–Mail Tool Won't Eat Up Privacy, Says FBI*, Wall St.J., July 20, 2000, at A28. An ACLU spokesperson testified that the Carnivore is "roughly the equivalent to a wiretap capable of assessing the contents of all the phone company's customers with the assurance that the FBI will record only conversations of the specific target." Morever, added Cong. Jerold Nader, even if civilian experts could look at Carnivore's blueprints, they would only be looking at something that is continually being upgraded and modified. "It could change at any time," observe the Congressman. "You can't trust a police agency forever." Id.

Professor Kerr maintains that the broad criticism the Patriot Act has received for encouraging the use and expanding the use of Carnivore is unfounded. Moreover, emphasizes Kerr, Carnivore was really designed to protect privacy and to encourage compliance with court orders, not evade privacy. He concludes (Orin Kerr 655–56):

"Carnivore is merely one particular tool among many that could be used to conduct electronic surveillance, and there is no reason to think that the Patriot Act encourages the use of Carnivore as compared to any other tool * * *. Whether the government uses Carnivore or some other tool to conduct prospective surveillance, the legal questions remain the same. Unless an exception to the statute applies, the government must obtain a pen register order to obtain 'dialing, routing, addressing, and signaling information,' and must obtain a Wiretap Order to obtain 'contents.' This was true before the Patriot Act (although the first part was uncertain), and it is true after the Patriot Act. If the government does not obtain the right court orders, it violates the statute regardless of whether it has used Carnivore or Fluffy Bunny."

After this book went to press, an FBI spokesperson disclosed that the bureau had effectively abandoned its custom-built Internet technology, once known as Carnivore, and switched to unspecified commercial software and has increasingly asked Internet providers to wiretap targeted customers on the government's behalf, reimbursing companies for their costs. See Ted Bridis, *FBI Drops Custom Eavesdrop Hardware for Ready–Made*, San Diego Union, Jan. 19, 2005, p. A7. The bureau moved to popular commercial wiretap software because it was cheaper and because it had improved its ability to copy e-mail and other communications of a targeted Internet account without affecting other subscribers.

A spokesperson for the FBI stated that the FBI performed only eight Internet wiretaps in fiscal 2003 and five in fiscal 2002. According to FBI documents submitted to Senate and House oversight committees, none of the wiretaps used Carnivore/DCS–1000. See id. The FBI, which once claimed Carnivore was "far better" than commercial products, had previously reported that it had used the technology about 25 times between 1998 and 2000. Id.

6. ***Applications for court orders.*** Federal applications for a court order authorizing the interception of communications may be authorized only by the Attorney General or a specially designated Assistant Attorney General, see § 2516(1), a requirement designed to ensure that discretion is exercised by a senior and politically accountable executive official before a court is asked to pass on an application. (When authorized by state law, the "principal prosecuting attorney of any state or political subdivision thereof" may apply to a state judge for an electronic surveillance order. The state provisions are thus less centralized, but this was deemed necessitated by realities of state law enforcement systems.) Only federal district and appellate judges and their state counterparts may issue surveillance orders. See § 2510(9).

Except for "emergencies"—§ 2518(7) permits warrantless electronic surveillance when "an emergency situation exists" involving "conspiratorial activities threatening the national security interest" or "conspiratorial activities characteristic of organized crime" or (pursuant to a 1984 amendment) "immediate danger of death or serious physical injury to any person"[a]—no electronic surveillance is permitted without a properly authorized application. See § 2518(1).

Each application must be in writing and under oath; disclose the identity of the officer making the application and the officer authorizing it (see *United States v. Chavez,* supra); and include a "full and complete" statement of the circumstances justifying the belief that an order should be issued, including (i) details as to the particular offense, (ii) a particular description of the communication facility, (iii) a particular description of "the type of communication" sought to be intercepted, and (iv) "the identity of the person, if known, committing the offense, and whose conversation is to be intercepted."[b] "In other words," comments Goldsmith at 42, "there must be probable cause to believe that a particular person involved in a designated crime will have discussion pertinent to that crime using a particular phone (or at a particular place) during a specified time period."

Moreover, to discourage routine use of tapping or electronic eavesdropping, the application must include "full and complete" statements as to "whether or not other investigative procedures have been tried or failed or why they reasonably appear to be unlikely to succeed if tried or to be too dangerous"[c] and of the facts concerning all previous applications "involving any of the same persons, facilities or places specified in the application, and the action taken by the judge on each such application." See § 2518(1)(c), (e).

7. ***Entering an order.*** The judge may enter an order as requested or as modified upon determining, on the basis of the facts submitted, that "normal investigative procedures" are not a viable alternative and that there is probable cause for believing three things: an individual has committed or is about to commit a particular offense enumerated in the statute; "particular communications concerning that offense will be obtained through such interception"; and the facilities or place where the communications are to be intercepted are being, or

a. There must be "grounds upon which an order could be entered under this chapter to authorize such interception"; the situation must require an interception before a court order "can with due diligence be obtained"; and, within 48 hours after the interception has begun to occur, an application must be filed seeking retroactive approval for such interception.

See generally Clifford Fishman, *Interception of Communications in Exigent Circumstances,* 22 Ga.L.Rev. 1, 35–48 (1987). The "emergency surveillance" provision "has been invoked only rarely, and there has been virtually no judicial discussion or interpretation of it." Id. at 35.

b. On the obligation of the government to discover and name the person to be heard, see *United States v. Kahn,* 415 U.S. 143 (1974). For the consequences of noncompliance with this provision, see *United States v. Donovan,* 429 U.S. 413 (1977).

c. In practice, maintains James Carr, *The Law of Electronic Surveillance* 179 (1977), this requirement has been watered down to "one of investigatory utility, rather than necessity."

about to be, used in connection with the offense or "are leased to, listed in the name of, or commonly used by such person." See § 2518(3).

The court order must designate the personnel authorized to conduct the surveillance, identify both the person (if known) and the facilities or place targeted for interception, specify the period of surveillance, and furnish a "particular description of the type of communication sought to be intercepted, and a statement of the particular offense to which it relates."[a] See § 2518(4). In addition, each order must provide, § 2518(5), that the authorization to intercept "shall be executed as soon as practicable, shall be conducted in such a way as to *minimize the interception of communications not otherwise subject to interception*" (emphasis added),[b] and "must terminate upon attainment of the authorized objective, or in any event in thirty days."

8. ***"National security" surveillance and the FISA.*** When Title III was originally enacted, it contained a provision, § 2511(3), stating that nothing in the statute "shall limit the constitutional power of the President to take such measures as he deems necessary to protect the Nation against actual or potential attack or other hostile acts or a foreign power, to obtain foreign intelligence deemed essential to the security of the United States, or to protect national security information against foreign intelligence activities." In addition, the provision stated that nothing in the statute "shall [be] deemed to limit the constitutional power of the President to take such measures as he deems necessary to protect the United States against the overthrow of the Government [by] unlawful means or against any other clear and present danger to the structure or existence of the Government." In *United States v. United States District Court*, 407 U.S. 297 (1972) (often called *Keith*, after then District Judge Damon Keith), the government contended that this provision allowed it to conduct a warrantless surveillance of a purely domestic radical group engaged in a conspiracy to destroy federal government property. But, without a dissent, the Court, per Powell, J., held that the circumstances did not "justify departure [from] the customary Fourth Amendment requirement of judicial approval prior to initiation of a search or surveillance." The Court emphasized that the warrantless surveillance had been directed at a "domestic organization," i.e., one "composed of citizens of the United states and which has no significant connection with a foreign power, its agents or agencies." (However, the Court saw no occasion to spell out what kind of connection with a foreign power would suffice to distinguish the instant case.)

The Court, however, did observe that "domestic security surveillance may involve different policy and practical consideration from the surveillance of 'ordinary crime.'" Therefore, the Court continued, "different domestic standards" for acquiring domestic security intelligence "may be compatible with the Fourth Amendment if they are reasonable both in relation to the legitimate need of Government for intelligence information and the protected rights of our citizens." The Court's suggestion that it might be permissible to relax standards when national security was directly implicated did not escape Congress's attention. As a response to the *Keith* case and extensive Congressional hearings and reports about governmental surveillance abuses over a nearly forty-year span

a. What was intended by "type of communication" is unclear. It now "appears to be generally accepted that [this requirement] can be fulfilled by indicating the offense under investigation, without further details about the anticipated conversations," Carr, fn. i supra, at 173.

b. But see *Scott v. United States* (1978) (p. 1501), rejecting the contention that the failure of the surveilling officers to make any effort to comply with a minimization requirement was alone a basis for suppression. The Court took the position that "subjective intent alone does not make otherwise lawful conduct illegal," meaning that the officers' presumed failure to make even a good-faith effort to comply with the requirement was not itself a reason for excluding the evidence obtained.

(from 1936–75), the Foreign Intelligence Surveillance Act of 1978 (FISA) emerged, (50 U.S.C. §§ 1801–1811). See Daniel Solove 1275–77. See also CRIMPROC § 4.3(d).

FISA establishes the Foreign Intelligence Surveillance Court (FISC), a special court of eleven federal district judges designated by the Chief Justice of the United States,[a] and three other federal judges who shall "comprise a court of review," one which shall review the denial of any application made under the law.

Upon a proper application a judge of this court is to enter an ex parte order approving electronic surveillance for 90 days (or until its purpose is achieved, whichever is less) on finding "probable cause to believe" that "the target" of the electronic surveillance is "a foreign power or an agent of a foreign power" and that each of the places at which the electronic surveillance is directed is being used, or is about to be used by "a foreign power or an agent of a foreign power." The judge *need not* find probable cause to believe that the requested surveillance will in fact lead to the gathering of foreign intelligence information.

What is a "foreign power"? Who is a "foreign agent"? As Stephen J. Schulhofer, *The Enemy Within* 44 (2002) has observed: "[FISA] does not require actual or even suspected ties to a terrorist group or a hostile foreign government, and it does not require that the person targeted be suspected of any illicit activity whatever. A foreign power under FISA includes any 'foreign-based political organization not substantially comprised of United States persons,' and a foreign agent includes any foreign national employed by such an organization. Thus, a non-American spokesperson or fund-raiser for the British Labour Party or for a German environmental activist group is considered a foreign agent and while in the United States can be targeted for several months of eavesdropping, wiretapping, and clandestine physical searches to gain 'foreign intelligence information,' a term defined so broadly that it includes any information [that] relates [to] the conduct of the foreign affairs of the United States. U.S. citizens having (or reasonably believed to have) links to such organizations can be considered foreign agents and targeted for similar FISA surveillance under certain circumstances as well."

According to one commentator (Daniel Solove 1290), "[the] problem with FISA is its secrecy": "Under FISA, the entire proceedings are held *ex parte*, with nobody permitted to argue the opposing side. Only the government has the opportunity to appeal. The government thus gets two bites at the apple, and the courts only hear the government's side. [There] is little to ensure against abuses of power."

As we have seen, FISA has been severely criticized. Nevertheless, the Act has been upheld against a variety of challenges by the lower federal courts. Some might ask, what happened to the Fourth Amendment? Professor Kerr provides an answer. See p. 482.

9. *The USA Patriot Act expands FISA's applicability.* Prior to 2001, FISA required that a senior official certify that the collection of foreign intelligence was "*the* purpose" (emphasis added) of the FISA search or surveillance. The provision was designed to prevent the much more loosely regulated FISA surveillance power from becoming a tool for domestic law enforcement. However, the Patriot Act changed the language of FISA so that obtaining foreign intelligence need only be "*a significant* purpose" (emphasis added) of the investigation. Thus, the government may utilize the broad FISA surveillance power even when foreign intelligence gathering is *not* the primary purpose or when it is only one of several purposes. Professor Schulhofer, supra, calls the change in FISA "a momentous

a. This court originally consisted of seven judges, but the Patriot Act raised the number to eleven.

expansion of government power to conduct wide-ranging surveillance and secret physical searches." But he adds:

"Yet the change seeks to address a genuine and extremely difficult problem. September 11 made tragically clear that the traditional division between law enforcement and foreign intelligence operations, always somewhat artificial, has lost virtually all meaning in the context of large-scale international groups such as al Quaeda.

"That development puts two vital, deeply grounded principles of American government on a collision course. On the one hand, the president has an unquestioned responsibility to protect the nation against foreign attack and to prevent hostile foreign powers from conducting covert intelligence activity within our borders. On the other hand, law enforcement power, always potentially dangerous to a free society, may operate only within boundaries established by the Bill of Rights. And one of those boundaries, emphatically reaffirmed in the *Keith* case, is that law enforcement agents must submit to judicial scrutiny of the basis and scope of any surveillance that seeks evidence for criminal prosecutions—national security prosecutions included."

10. ***"Roving wiretaps" and the Patriot Act's expansion of this authority to FISA cases.*** A "roving wiretap" permits electronic surveillance of an individual rather than a specific telephone, cell phone or computer terminal. Prior to the ECPA amendments, Title III required that all eavesdropping warrants specify the facility or place of the anticipated communication. As amended in 1986, however, Title III orders need not designate the surveillance site—

(a) if in the case of an application with respect to the interception of an *oral* communication "the application contains a full and complete statement as to why such specification is *not practical*" and the judge finds such specification "*not practical*," § 2518(11)(a) (emphasis added); and

(b) if "in the case of an application with respect to a *wire* or *electronic* communication, [the] applicant makes a showing that there is probable cause to believe that the person's actions *could have the effect of thwarting interception* from a specified facility and the judge finds that such showing has been adequately made," § 2518(11)(b) (emphasis added).

Michael Goldsmith, *Eavesdropping Reform: The Legality of Roving Surveillance,* 1987 U.Ill.L.Rev. 401, 413, notes that "[t]he legislative history's only attempt to illustrate [the meaning of the 'not practical'] concept involves 'a suspect who moves from room to room in a hotel to avoid a bug and who sets up a meeting with another suspect for a beach or field." [This] observation is undoubtedly accurate, but fails to provide guidance in other situations."

Why did the 1986 amendment impose more stringent requirements on roving *wiretapping* interceptions than on roving *oral* interceptions? According to Clifford Fishman, *Interception of Communications in Exigent Circumstances,* 22 Ga.L.Rev. 1, 55–56 (1987) (hereinafter Fishman), it was "because of concerns expressed by lobbyists for the nation's telephone companies, [who] wanted statutory protection for their clients, who might suddenly be told to 'wire up' large numbers of pay telephones on short notice." Goldsmith 414 regards the "thwarting interception" requirement unduly restrictive and voices concern that "courts may interpret the 'thwart' restriction for wiretaps as evincing congressional intent to construe the term 'not practical' [the term governing roving oral interceptions] narrowly as well."

At the time of the 1986 Amendments, serious questions were raised about the constitutionality of roving surveillance. See Fishman, supra, at 66–69; Goldsmith, supra, at 416–28. (However, these laws were upheld by several lower federal courts.) Constitutional questions were raised again when § 206 of the USA PATRIOT Act of 2001 amended the FISA to allow "roving wiretaps" on the same showing that they are obtainable under Title III. This was done so that this tool could be used in terrorism investigations as well as criminal investigations.

Tracey Maclin, *Amending the Fourth: Another Grave Threat to Liberty*, National L. J., Nov. 12, 2001, maintains that "a wiretap that follows a person instead of a phone is at odds with the text and history of the Fourth Amendment"[a] and that "the requirement that a search warrant particularly describe the place to be searched was designed to bar multiple-specific search warrants that identified the target or object of a search or arrest, but authorized many places to be searched."[b] See also David Markus, *Fourth Amendment Forum*, The Champion (publication of the National Association of Criminal Defense Lawyers), Dec. 2001, pp. 36, 40. But see Milton Hirsch, *Fourth Amendment Forum*, The Champion, Dec. 2001, pp. 37–38: "[Roving wiretaps reflect] the facts of modern life [:] nowadays, more people spend more time sending and receiving more information over more phones and phone lines. Changes in technology have inevitably necessitated judicial and legislative responses. We do not live in the world of horse-drawn carriages, and we do not apply the Constitution as if we did."

"[To] a large extent," observes Orin Kerr 607 n.75, the public debate over the roving wiretap provisions of the Patriot Act concerned whether the events of September 11th justified a law that Congress had already enacted fifteen years earlier. Of course, the fact that Congress enacted a law in 1986 does not in itself justify its existence today, but it does seem relevant to whether the amendment broke new ground."

11. ***Secret video surveillance of private places: United States v. Torres.***[c] Title III does not cover video surveillance (and various attempts to legislate such surveillance have failed). Yet "[n]othing more dramatically conjures up the image of an 'Orwellian society' than a surreptitiously planted government 'eye' in one's living room." Whitebread & Slobogin 352.

Consider UNITED STATES v. TORRES, 751 F.2d 875 (7th Cir.1984), which arose as follows: The FBI obtained judicial authorization to install cameras in "safehouses" being used by members of FALN, a Puerto Rico separatist group suspected of making explosives for terrorist purposes. (The government had not invoked the Foreign Intelligence Surveillance Act.) The videotapes had no soundtracks, but at the same time that the FBI was televising the interior of the house (in some respects more like a business than a home) it was recording the sounds on different equipment. (The admissibility of the sound tapes was not an issue in this appeal.) As Judge Posner, author of the Seventh Circuit majority opinion in the case, explained, "the FBI wanted to see as well as hear because it had reason to believe that the [suspects], concerned that they might be bugged, would play the radio loudly when they were speaking to each other and also would speak in code and that the actual assembly of the bombs would be carried out in silence." The district court held that Title III did not authorize such surveillance and in the absence of any statutory basis for the authorizing order, the videotaping had violated the Fourth Amendment.

a. As Professor Maclin notes, the second clause of the Fourth Amendment states: "no Warrants shall issue, but upon probable cause, * * * and particularly describing the place to be searched and the persons or things to be seized." Adds Maclin: "The warrant clause requires greater precision for a search than for a seizure."

b. "The Framers," observes Professor Maclin, "were well aware of the danger associated with multiple-specific search warrants. In 1706, for example, colonial officials used such warrants to search every home in New Hampshire."

c. For video surveillance in public places, see p. 270.

The Seventh Circuit reversed. A majority of the court, per POSNER, J., agreed that there was no statutory authorization for the court order to install the cameras, but held that the district court nevertheless had the authority—under both Fed.R.Crim.P. 41(b) and its inherent judicial power to issue warrants—to issue a warrant authorizing the television surveillance. Although the court concluded that Title III neither authorized nor prohibited silent video surveillance, it made clear that, "because television surveillance is potentially so menacing to personal privacy," a warrant that failed to satisfy (as the government *did* satisfy in this case) the provisions of Title III would violate the Fourth Amendment.

"The usual way in which judges interpreting the Fourth Amendment take account of the fact that searches vary in the degree to which they invade personal privacy," observed Judge Posner, "is by requiring a higher degree of probable cause (to believe that the search will yield incriminating evidence), and by being more insistent that a warrant be obtained if at all feasible, the more intrusive the search is. But maybe in dealing with so intrusive a technique as television surveillance, other methods of control as well, such as banning the technique outright from use in the home in connection with minor crimes, will be required in order to strike a proper balance between public safety and personal privacy. That question is not before us, but we mention it to make clear that in declining to hold television surveillance unconstitutional *per se* we do not suggest that the Constitution must be interpreted to allow it to be used as generally as less intrusive techniques can be. [A] search could be unreasonable, though conducted pursuant to an otherwise valid warrant, by intruding on personal privacy to an extent disproportionate to the likely benefits from obtaining fuller compliance with the law. '[T]here can be no ready test for determining reasonableness other than by balancing the need to search against the invasion which the search entails.' *Camara v. Municipal Court* [p. 440]."

12. ***Considering its heightened level of intrusion, should video surveillance be subject to greater restriction than electronic surveillance?*** Professor Charles Whitehead and Christopher Slobogin answer in the affirmative (supra at 353):

"First, because minimization is particularly difficult to enforce where cameras are involved, a stringent prohibition [against] bad faith viewing of activities which are innocent or which do not involve the suspects is appropriate. * * * One appropriate minimization method [is] prohibition of video surveillance until audio surveillance indicates criminal activity is taking place.

"Indeed, one can argue that a warrant for video surveillance should not be issued unless no other method, including eavesdropping, can accomplish the investigative objective. In *Torres*, for instance, there may have been probable cause sufficient to obtain a search warrant authorizing entry of the safehouses while the bombs were being made. This alternative may not have produced as much evidence as video surveillance but may still have been preferable to it. In *People v. Teicher*,[133] on the other hand, there probably was no alternative to installing a camera focused on the dental chair of a dentist suspected of sexually abusing his patients. [Furthermore,] stated the court, 'the use of a police decoy without the protection of visual surveillance would not have produced the needed evidence in this case, since the decoy, of necessity, would have been heavily sedated and might not have been able to relate what transpired.' * * *

"[S]hortening the duration of video surveillance under each warrant is also a worthwhile idea. Given the intrusiveness of video surveillance, if evidence of criminal activity sufficient to make a case is not obtained within a very short time, police should have to justify further surveillance."

133. 422 N.E.2d 506 (N.Y.1981).

13. ***Have the courts which attempted to create constitutional standards for covert video surveillance by borrowing statutory standards from the audio surveillance field abdicated their responsibilities?*** Yes, maintains Ric Simmons, *Can Winston Save Us from Big Brother? The Need for Judicial Consistency in Regulating Hyper–Intrusive Searches*, 55 Rutgers L.Rev. 547 (2003). After noting that since *Torres*, "six other federal circuits have used the Title III safeguards to define the scope of the Fourth Amendment warrant in the context on video surveillance" (p. 558), Professor Simmons charges (id. at 589):

"By slavishly following the Title III guidelines, *Torres* and its progeny have relinquished their judicial duty to interpret the Constitution, an abdication which would be troubling in any area of the law, but is especially problematic when it occurs in the context of surveillance techniques that are both extraordinarily intrusive and becoming more common and more technologically sophisticated with every year. Defining the relationship between the Fourth Amendment and the newest surveillance techniques ought to be a careful judicial exercise in balancing the privacy interest of the citizens against the legitimate investigatory duties of the state. Instead, the courts appear to be adopting wholesale warrant requirements that were set by a federal statute intended to regulate a very specific field."

C. Is "Wiretapping Law" Constitutional in Theory, but Statutory in Practice? Are Legislatures Better Situated to Deal with New Technology than Courts?

ORIN S. KERR—THE FOURTH AMENDMENT AND NEW TECHNOLOGIES: CONSTITUTIONAL MYTHS AND THE CASE FOR CAUTION

102 Mich.L.Rev. 801, 854–55, 869–70, 888 (2004).

The same deference to legislative standards [that appears in electronic surveillance cases generally][a] appears in cases exploring how the Fourth Amendment applies to covert video surveillance specifically exempted from the Wiretap Act. Rather than create new judicial standards from scratch, courts have held that the Fourth Amendment is satisfied if the government complies with equivalent statutory standards that Title III enacted to regulate audio wiretapping. When called to formulate Fourth Amendment standards in areas that Congress has left unregulated, courts have set them by adopting the nearest statutory requirements. Even when the Supreme Court held that the Fourth Amendment applied to domestic wiretapping conducted for national security reasons, the Court specifically called on Congress to enact a new statute to set up the legal standards.

As these cases suggest, wiretapping law may be constitutional in theory, but it is statutory in practice. For prosecutors and defense attorneys, complying with wiretapping law means complying with statutory law; challenging wiretapping practices means challenging practices on statutory grounds. When wiretapping occurs inside the United States, courts generally refuse to construe the Fourth

a. It is noteworthy that although the constitutionality of Title III of the Crime Control of 1968 seemed questionable (for one thing, as pointed out in Herman Schwartz, *The Legitimation of Electronic Eavesdropping: The Politics of "Law and Order,"* 67 Mich.L.Rev. 455, 461 (1969), the lengthy electronic surveillance allowed by the statute on the basis of a single showing of probable cause seemed hard to reconcile with *Berger*), the U.S. Supreme Court has never explicitly considered the facial validity of Title III. But there is no hint in the Court's many decisions interpreting various provisions of Title III that the statute is facially invalid. Moreover, the lower federal courts have consistently upheld the statute against constitutional challenge. See, e.g., *United States v. Cafero*, 473 F.2d 489 (3d Cir.1973).

Amendment as going beyond the scope of the Wiretap Act; when wiretapping occurs outside the United States, courts often equate the Fourth Amendment with compliance with foreign statutory law. Berger and Katz helped shape the statutory structure at the time of the key statute's enactment. But despite their impact, the sources of wiretapping law have remained largely statutory. * * *

The history of Fourth Amendment law reflects [the lag between technological developments and judicial decisions]. The Supreme Court first considered the Fourth Amendment implications of wiretaps almost six decades after the invention of the telephone. Pen registers were in widespread use by the 1960s, but the Supreme Court did not pass on whether their use violated the Fourth Amendment until 1979. Even today, no Article III court at any level has decided whether an Internet user has a reasonable expectation of privacy in their e-mails stored with an Internet service provider; whether encryption creates a reasonable expectation of privacy;[b] or what the Fourth Amendment implications of the "Carnivore" Internet surveillance tool might be. The technologies exist, and in the case of encryption and e-mail, are used by millions of Americans everyday. But no one really knows how the Fourth Amendment applies to them.

* * * Legislative rules are different. Legislatures can act at any time, even when a technology is new. As a practical matter, legislatures often will wait for public concern to surface before regulating a new technology. But recent history suggests that legislatures usually act at a surprisingly early stage, and certainly long before the courts. For example, while the courts have not yet decided how the Fourth Amendment protects stored e-mails, Congress enacted a comprehensive regime to protect the privacy of e-mails in 1986 in the form of the Electronic Communications Privacy Act. Congress regulated the privacy of e-mail before most Americans had even heard of e-mail. Similarly, Congress enacted laws to regulate the "Carnivore" Internet surveillance system in 2001 before any Fourth Amendment challenges were raised to its use. * * *

As technology advances and the difficulty courts face regulating privacy in new technologies becomes clearer, [the] trend toward statutory protections will likely accelerate. In time, we may understand the law of criminal procedure as a bifurcated field, with constitutional rules governing most traditional cases and statutory rules governing most cases involving new technologies. New technolo-

b. As pointed out in another article by Professor Kerr, *The Fourth Amendment in Cyberspace: Can Encryption Create A "Reasonable Expectation of Privacy?,"* 33 Conn. L.Rev. 503 (2001), when a computer file is encrypted using software such as P.G.P. (for Pretty Good Privacy), the file is scrambled into an unreadable form (known at "ciphertext"). At this point, without the encryption key, it becomes virtually impossible for anyone (including law enforcement authorities) to convert the message back into readable form (known as "plaintext").

Speculation that those who attacked the World Trade Center and the Pentagon may have used encryption to cloak their communications have led some lawmakers to seek legislation requiring encryption companies to include a "back door" that would allow law enforcement agencies access when a suspected terrorist may have used encryption. See John Schwartz, *Disputes on Electronic Message Encryption Take on New Urgency*, N.Y. Times, Sept. 25, 2001, at C1. Proposals for such access systems are known as "key escrow" because a key that unlocks encrypted messages would be stored and made available to law enforcement. These proposals were the subject of a bitter debate in the mid–1990s when the Clinton Administration proposed a back-door access technology, popularly known as the "Clipper Chip." See id.

"The privacy implications of encryption," notes Kerr, supra, "have led many Internet law scholars to declare encryption regulation constitutionally off-limits" on the ground that "encrypting an electronic communication creates a 'reasonable expectation of privacy' in the communication's content, triggering Fourth Amendment protection." Some commentators, adds Professor Kerr, have analogized encryption to a lock and key: just as locking a box with a key creates a reasonable expectation of privacy in its contents, locking a communication by encrypting it with an encryption key does the same." Professor Kerr strongly disagrees with this view.

gies may reveal the limits of the modern enterprise of constitutional criminal procedure, making the field part constitutional and part statutory. The potential bifurcation of criminal procedure will pose a significant challenge to scholars of criminal procedure. Increasingly, an understanding of criminal procedure may require an understanding of complicated statutory provisions.[c]

SECTION 3. SOME APPLICATIONS OF TITLE III

After considerable discussion, Professor Michael Goldsmith concludes that Title III is constitutional on its face, Goldsmith at 55, but he quickly adds: "The real question today * * * is not Title III's facial validity, but the manner in which it has been applied. Congress intended that the statute be strictly enforced under careful judicial supervision. Indeed, given the many questions raised about its facial validity, the law's ultimate constitutionality was said by some to depend upon such enforcement. Yet, ironically, the Supreme Court, which originally took the initiative in advising Congress as to the drafting of electronic surveillance legislation, has since failed to enforce Title III in a consistently scrupulous manner." Consider the following:

A. "MINIMIZ[ING] THE INTERCEPTION OF COMMUNICATIONS NOT OTHERWISE SUBJECT TO INTERCEPTION"; WHAT WEIGHT, IF ANY, SHOULD BE GIVEN TO THE OFFICER'S UNDERLYING INTENT OR MOTIVATION?

One of the limiting provisions of Title III is found in § 2518(5), requiring every order to contain a provision that the authorization to intercept "be conducted in such a way as to minimize the interception of communications not otherwise subject to interception." In SCOTT v. UNITED STATES, 436 U.S. 128 (1978), pursuant to a court wiretap order requiring "minimization," government agents

c. As Professor Kerr recognizes, see his article at 857–58, a goodly number of commentators strongly disagree with him. These commentators maintain, inter alia, that courts understand the criminal process better than legislators and are not subject to the same political pressures to reduce basic liberties; that judges are better able than legislators to preserve and effectuate original values of liberty in a new context; and that statutory privacy protections are weak and growing weaker because the Justice Department controls the legislative process. See, e.g., CRIMPROC § 2.1; LAWRENCE LESSIG, *Code and Other Laws of Cyberspace*, 116–18, 222–23 (1999); Marc Jonathan Blitz, *Video Surveillance and the Constitution of Public Space: Fitting the Fourth Amendment to a World that Tracks Image and Identity*, 82 Texas L.Rev. 1349 (2004); Sherry F. Colb, *A World Without Privacy: Why Property Does Not Define the Limits of the Right Against Unreasonable Searches and Seizures*, 102 Mich.L.Rev. 888 (2004); Tracey Maclin, *Katz, Kyllo, and Technology: Virtual Fourth Amendment Protection in the Twenty–First Century*, 72 Miss. L.J. 51 (2002); Peter P. Swire, *Katz is Dead. Long Live Katz*, 102 Mich.L.Rev. 904 (2004). For Professor Kerr's reply to two of his critics, see Orin S. Kerr, *Technology, Privacy, and the Courts: A Reply to Colb and Swire*, 102 Mich. L.Rev. 933 (2004).

In his reply, id. at 939–40, Kerr acknowledges: "At the federal level, the constitutional structure gives law-enforcement agencies an important advantage in congressional negotiations in the form of the presidential veto power. Law-enforcement powers are executive-branch powers, and most presidents will be more willing to expand executive-branch powers than reduce them. This dynamic allows presidents to use threats of vetoes (and in unusual cases, vetoes themselves) as tools to block legislative enactments that law enforcement interests view as threatening. If, over time, the veto threat creates an institutional bias in legislation in favor of law-enforcement interests, that may create an important role for the judiciary to play. In effect, the judicial branch could act as a counter to the executive branch; while a President could use the veto power to nullify legislation that excessively narrows executive power, the courts could use their power of judicial review to nullify legislation that excessively broadens it."

intercepted for a one-month period virtually all conversations over a particular telephone suspected of being used in furtherance of a conspiracy to import and distribute narcotics. Only forty percent of the conversations were shown to be narcotics related and the Special Agent who conducted the wiretap testified that "he and the agents working under him knew of the minimization requirement but made no attempt to comply therewith." Rejecting petitioners' argument that the failure to make good-faith efforts to comply with the minimization requirement is itself a violation of § 2518(5), a 7–2 majority per REHNQUIST, J., agreed with the Court of Appeals that an evaluation of compliance with the minimization requirement, like evaluation of all alleged violations of the Fourth Amendment, should "be based on the reasonableness of the actual interceptions and not on whether the agents subjectively intended to minimize their interceptions." Observed the Court:

"The Government [contends] that petitioners' argument fails to properly distinguish between what is necessary to establish a statutory or constitutional violation and what is necessary to support a suppression remedy once a violation has been established. In view of the deterrent purposes of the exclusionary rule, consideration of official motives may play some part in determining whether application of the exclusionary rule is appropriate *after* a statutory or constitutional violation has been established. But the existence *vel non* of such a violation turns on an objective assessment of the officer's actions in light of the facts and circumstances confronting him at the time. Subjective intent alone, the Government contends, does not make otherwise lawful conduct illegal or unconstitutional.

"[The Government's position] embodies the proper approach for evaluating compliance with the minimization requirement. [A]lmost without exception in evaluating alleged violations of the Fourth Amendment the Court has first undertaken an objective assessment of an officer's actions in light of the facts and circumstances then known to him. The language of the Amendment itself proscribes only 'unreasonable' searches and seizures.

"[In] the very section in which it directs minimization, Congress, by its use of the word 'conducted,' made it clear that the focus was to be on the agents' actions, not their motives. Any lingering doubt is dispelled by the legislative history [which declares that] § 2515 was not 'intended generally to press the scope of the suppression role beyond present search and seizure law.' "[a]

Analyzing the reasonableness of the agents' conduct, the Court observed: "[B]lind reliance on the percentage of nonpertinent calls intercepted is not a sure guide to the correct answer. Such percentages may provide assistance, but there are surely cases, such as the one at bar, where the percentage of nonpertinent calls is relatively high and yet their interception was still reasonable. The reasons for this may be many. Many of the nonpertinent calls may have been very short. Others may have been one-time only calls. Still others may have been ambiguous in nature or involve guarded or coded language. In all these circumstances agents can hardly be expected to know that their calls are not pertinent prior to their termination.

"[We] find nothing to persuade us that the Court of Appeals was wrong in its rejection of [the minimization] claims. Forty percent of the calls were clearly narcotics related * * *. Many of the remaining calls were very short, such as

a. This is not to say, of course, that the question of motive plays absolutely no part in the suppression inquiry. On occasion, the motive with which the officer conducts an illegal search may have some relevance in determining the propriety of applying the exclusionary rule. [This] focus on intent, however, becomes relevant only after it has been determined that the Constitution was in fact violated. * * *

wrong number calls [and] calls to persons who were not available to come to the phone. [In] a case such as this, involving a wide-ranging conspiracy with a large number of participants, even a seasoned listener would have been hard pressed to determine with any precision the relevancy of many of the calls before they were completed. A large number were ambiguous in nature, making characterization virtually impossible until the completion of these calls. * * *

"We are thus left with the seven calls between [petitioner] Jenkins and her mother. [After pointing out that most of the calls were intercepted at the beginning of the surveillance and that several indicated that the mother may have known of the conspiracy, the Court concluded that] [a]lthough none of these conversations turned out to be material to the investigation at hand, we cannot say that the Court of Appeals was incorrect in concluding that the agents did not act unreasonably at the time they made these interceptions."

Dissenting Justice BRENNAN, joined by Marshall, J., maintained that the Court's reasoning "is thrice flawed":

"First, and perhaps most significant, it totally disregards the explicit congressional command that the wiretap be *conducted* so as to minimize interception of communications not subject to interception. Second, it blinks reality by accepting as a substitute for the good-faith exercise of judgment as to which calls should not be intercepted by the agent most familiar with the investigation, the *post hoc* conjectures of the Government as to how the agent would have acted had he exercised his judgment. [In] the nature of things it is impossible to know how many fewer interceptions would have occurred had a good-faith judgment been exercised, and it is therefore totally unacceptable to permit the failure to exercise the congressionally imposed duty to be excused by the difficulty in predicting what might have occurred had the duty been exercised. Finally, the Court's holding permits government agents deliberately to flout the duty imposed upon them by Congress. In a linguistic *tour de force* the Court converts the mandatory language that the interception shall be conducted to a precatory suggestion."

Notes and Questions

1. ***Commentary on Scott.*** For criticism of *Scott*, see John Burkoff, *The Court that Devoured the Fourth Amendment: The Triumph of an Inconsistent Exclusionary Doctrine,* 58 Or.L.Rev. 151, 187–88 (1979) ("[i]ronically, the *Scott* Court's use of one test for determining the existence of a fourth amendment violation and a second test for application of an exclusionary remedy appears to have as its casuistic end the exclusion of deterrence from the first test although deterrence is the key element of the second test"); Goldsmith at 108–09 ("[g]iven the greater intrusion occasioned by electronic surveillance, [the] fourth amendment's reasonableness clause would seem to require such searches to be undertaken in good faith"). But see CRIMPROC § 3.1(d), maintaining that *Scott* properly rejected the contention that "lack of good faith efforts" required suppression even if no minimization would have been feasible in this case.

2. ***Should the minimization provision be amended?*** Consider Clifford Fishman, *The "Minimization" Requirement in Electronic Surveillance: Title III, the Fourth Amendment and the Dread Scott Decision,* 28 Am.U.L.Rev. 315, 354–55 (1979):

"[A] purely objective analysis of reasonableness may be adequate to decide whether an officer was justified in making an isolated arrest, stop, frisk, search or seizure, [but]is wholly inadequate when several weeks of continuous, surreptitious interceptions of otherwise private conversations are at issue. Particularly in complex investigations, where the government, with superficial plausibility can retroactively defend total interception, it is unlikely that any minimization will be achieved unless a good-faith effort is made to do so. [The] minimization provision should be amended to read: 'Every order and extension thereof shall contain a provision that the [interception] shall be conducted in a *good faith and reasonable manner in order to* minimize the interception of communications not otherwise subject to interception under this chapter.''

B. Electronic Surveillance Which Involves Covert Entry Into Private Premises to Install Equipment; Has the Court's Statutory Perspective Undergone a Fundamental Change?

DALIA v. UNITED STATES, 441 U.S. 238 (1979), arose as follows: Finding reasonable cause to believe that petitioner was conspiring to steal goods being shipped in interstate commerce and that his business office was being used by petitioner and others in connection with the alleged conspiracy, a federal district court authorized the interception of all oral communications concerning the conspiracy at petitioner's office. Although the court order did not explicitly authorize entry into petitioner's office, FBI agents secretly entered the office one midnight by prying open a window and spent three hours in the building installing a listening device in the ceiling. All electronic surveillance of petitioner ended some six weeks later, at which time the agents secretly re-entered petitioner's office and removed the bug. Partly on the basis of conversations intercepted pursuant to this order, petitioner was convicted of receiving stolen goods and related charges. The Court, per POWELL, J., upheld the electronic surveillance:

First, ''[t]he Fourth Amendment does not prohibit *per se* a covert entry performed for the purpose of installing otherwise legal electronic bugging equipment.'' *Second,* the Court rejected the contention [that] Congress had not given the courts statutory authority to approve covert entries for electronic surveillance purposes: ''Those considering the surveillance legislation understood that, by authorizing electronic interception of oral communications in addition to wire communications, they were necessarily authorizing surreptitious entries.''

Third, the Court rejected the contention that, because the authorizing court did not explicitly set forth its approval of covert entries, the entry violated petitioner's Fourth Amendment privacy rights: The Warrant Clause of the Fourth Amendment requires only that warrants be issued by ''neutral, disinterested magistrates''; that they be based on probable cause [and] that they ''particularly describe'' the things to be seized as well as the place to be searched. Nothing in [the] Fourth Amendment or the Court's decisions ''suggests that, in addition to [these three requirements], search warrants also must include a specification of the precise manner in which they are to be executed.''

Dissenting Justice STEVENS, joined by Brennan and Marshall, JJ., maintained: ''Only one relevant conclusion can be drawn from a review of the entire legislative history of Title III. The legislators never even considered the possibility that they were passing a statute that would authorize federal agents to break into private premises without any finding of necessity by a neutral and detached magistrate. * * * Without a legislative mandate that is both explicit and specific, I would presume that this flagrant invasion of the citizen's privacy is prohibited.''

In a separate opinion, concurring in part and dissenting in part, Justice BRENNAN, joined by Stewart, J., maintained that ''even reading Title III to authorize covert entries, the Justice Department's present practice of securing specific authorization for covert entries is not only preferable, but also constitutionally required'': ''Breaking and entering into private premises for the purpose of planting a bug cannot be characterized as a mere mode of warrant execution to be left to the discretion of the executing officer. The practice entails an invasion of privacy of constitutional significance distinct from that which attends nontrespassory surveillance; indeed, it is tantamount to an independent search and seizure."

Notes and Questions

1. Consider, Comment, 70 J.Crim.L. & C. 510, 526–27 (1979): "[The *Dalia* majority's approach] is inconsistent with the overall emphasis of Title III—an emphasis upon minimizing the intrusiveness of an intercept order. [By] construing the statutory language—or the absence thereof—so as to require that breaking and entering be employed only when alternative means have been tried and have failed or else reasonably appear too unlikely to succeed if tried, the Supreme Court would merely have been extending the express requirement of sections 2518(1)(c) and 2518(3)(c)."

2. "In all likelihood," observes Goldsmith at 116–18, "the [*Dalia*] majority's pragmatic analysis more closely reflected congressional intent; [it] is inconceivable that, after years of debate, Congress would have failed to realize that most bugs necessitate covert entries. * * * Nevertheless, as enacted the statute contained a potential defect which had to be remedied. Ultimately, in *Dalia,* judicial process was used to rectify this legislative interstice. Hence, the true significance of *Dalia* lay not in the Court's holding that Title III conferred authority to effect covert entries, but in the manner in which this decision was made. * * * *Dalia* abandoned the mode of analysis adopted in *District Court* [p. 477] to remedy what Congress might otherwise have made explicit. In the process, the Court's statutory perspective seems to have undergone a fundamental change; although Title III had been designed to constitute a blanket prohibition against electronic surveillance, subject to narrowly tailored statutory exceptions, Justice Powell's analysis now suggested that the law conferred a general grant of authority subject to narrowly tailored prohibitions. Thus, analytically and perhaps philosophically, *Dalia* symbolized the extent to which the Supreme Court had changed direction since 1968 when Title III was enacted."

SECTION 4. THE USE OF SECRET AGENTS (WITH AND WITHOUT ELECTRONIC DEVICES) TO OBTAIN INCRIMINATING STATEMENTS

In LOPEZ v. UNITED STATES, 373 U.S. 427 (1963), petitioner made an unsolicited bribe offer to Davis, an IRS agent, who, following his superiors' instructions to "pretend to play along with the scheme," met petitioner in the latter's office and recorded his subsequent bribe offers by means of a concealed wire recorder. Relying heavily on *On Lee v. United States*[a] and *Rathbun v. United*

a. In *On Lee,* 343 U.S. 747 (1952), Chin Poy, an old acquaintance and former employee of defendant, entered the latter's laundry and engaged him in conversation, in the course of which defendant made incriminating statements. Unknown to defendant, Chin Poy was a "wired for sound" secret government agent, and the microphone concealed on his person transmitted all sounds to a narcotics agent stationed outside. Chin Poy was not called to testify about defendant's incriminating statements—probably because "the very defects of character and blemishes of record which [led defendant to confide in him] would make a jury distrust his testimony"—but the narcotics agent was allowed to relate the conversations he overheard. A 5–4 majority, per Jackson, J., rejected the claim that Chin Poy had committed a trespass because consent to enter defendant's laundry was obtained by fraud. And the Court dismissed as "verging on the frivolous" the further contention that the agent stationed outside the laundry was "a trespasser" because, by virtue of the microphone concealed on Chin Poy, he overheard what went on inside. "It would be a dubious service to the genuine liberties protected by the Fourth

States,[b] the Court, per HARLAN, J., rejected the argument that considering the agent's falsification of his mission, he gained access to Lopez's office by misrepresentation and consequently illegally "seized" Lopez's words:

"[T]his case involves no 'eavesdropping' whatever in any proper sense of that term. The Government did not use an electronic device to listen in on conversations it could not otherwise have heard. Instead, the device was used only to obtain the most reliable evidence possible of a conversation in which the Government's own agent was a participant and which that agent was fully entitled to disclose. And the device was not planted by means of an unlawful physical invasion of petitioner's premises under circumstances which would violate the Fourth Amendment. It was carried in and out by an agent who was there with petitioner's assent, and it neither saw nor heard more than the agent himself. * * *

"Stripped to its essentials, petitioner's argument amounts to saying that he has a constitutional right to rely on possible flaws in the agent's memory, or to challenge the agent's credibility without being beset by corroborating evidence that is not susceptible of impeachment. For no other argument can justify excluding an accurate version of a conversation that the agent could testify to from memory. We think the risk that petitioner took in offering a bribe to Davis fairly included the risk that the offer would be accurately reproduced in court, whether by faultless memory or mechanical recording."

Chief Justice WARREN concurred separately, agreeing with the *Lopez* dissenters that *On Lee* was wrongly decided, but finding *On Lee* and the instant case "quite dissimilar constitutionally":

"The only purpose the recording served [in the instant case] was to protect the credibility of [Agent] Davis against that of a man who wished to corrupt a public servant in the performance of his public trust. I find nothing unfair in this procedure. [The] use and purpose of the transmitter in *On Lee* was substantially different from the use of the recorder here. Its advantage was not to corroborate the testimony of Chin Poy, but rather, to obviate the need to put him on the stand. [Had] Chin Poy been available for cross-examination, [the defense could have explored] the possibility of entrapments, police pressure brought to bear to persuade Chin Poy to turn informer, and Chin Poy's own recollection of the contents of the conversation. His testimony might not only have seriously discredited the prosecution, but might also have raised questions of constitutional proportions."

Justice BRENNAN, joined by Douglas and Goldberg, JJ., dissented, finding *On Lee* indistinguishable from the instant case and maintaining that the evidence should have been excluded in both cases:

"[Not] all communications are privileged. On Lee assumed the risk that his acquaintance would divulge their conversation; Lopez assumed the same risk *vis-à-vis* Davis. The risk inheres in all communications which are not in the sight of the law privileged. [But] the risk which both *On Lee* and today's decision impose is of a different order. It is the risk that third parties, whether mechanical auditors

Amendment," observed the Court, "to make them bedfellows with spurious liberties improvised by farfetched analogies which would liken eavesdropping on a conversation, with the connivance of one of the parties, to an unreasonable search and seizure."

b. In *Rathbun,* 355 U.S. 107 (1957), the Court held, per Warren, C.J., that the overhearing of a conversation on a regularly used telephone extension with the consent of one party to the conversation was not a violation of § 605 of the Federal Communications Act: "Each party to a telephone conversation takes the risk that the other party may have an extension telephone and may allow another to overhear the conversation. When such takes place there has been no violation of any privacy of which the parties may complain. Consequently, one element of Section 605, *interception,* has not occurred."

like the Minifon or human transcribers of mechanical transmissions as in *On Lee*—third parties who cannot be shut out of a conversation as conventional eavesdroppers can be, merely by a lowering of voices, or withdrawing to a private place—may give independent evidence of any conversation. There is only one way to guard against such a risk, and that is to keep one's mouth shut on all occasions.

"[There] is a qualitative difference between electronic surveillance [and] conventional police stratagems such as eavesdropping and disguise. The latter do not so seriously intrude upon the right of privacy. The risk of being overheard by an eavesdropper or betrayed by an informer or deceived as to the identity of one with whom one deals is probably inherent in the conditions of human society. It is the kind of risk we necessarily assume whenever we speak. But as soon as electronic surveillance comes into play, the risk changes crucially. There is no security from that kind of eavesdropping, no way of mitigating the risk, and so not even a residuum of true privacy."

Notes and Questions

1. If conversations are within the protection of the Fourth Amendment, why should it matter whether the conversation was "seized" by an electronic device? Was the police practice involved in *On Lee* any dirtier business than it would have been had the defendant's old acquaintance simply elicited the incriminating admissions and then testified? Why does the fact that On Lee would have been better able to attack the acquaintance's credibility than he was to challenge that of the narcotics bureau agent make the original deceit more moral? See Kent Greenawalt, *The Consent Problem in Wiretapping and Eavesdropping,* 68 Colum.L.Rev. 189, 193 (1968); Edmund W. Kitch, *Katz v. United States: The Limits of the Fourth Amendment,* 1968 Supreme Court Rev. 133, 141–42.

2. Is the issue not whether secret agents and informers can be monitored, but whether a warrant is necessary for such monitoring? To what extent is Justice Brennan's position based on the premise that "the warrant procedure can be adapted to electronic surveillance of specific persons at specific places for a limited period of time," but—inasmuch as informers and secret agents "must be developed or placed over a long period of time and the objectives of their 'search' will almost always be broad and impossible to delineate with any precision in advance"?the Fourth Amendment warrant requirement would "prevent altogether the use of informers and secret agents"? See Kitch, supra, at 142.

In LEWIS v. UNITED STATES, 385 U.S. 206 (1966), decided the same day as *Hoffa,* infra, a federal narcotics agent, by misrepresenting his identity as "Jimmy the Pollack [sic]" and expressing a willingness to purchase narcotics, was invited into petitioner's home where an unlawful narcotics transaction took place. At petitioner's trial, the agent testified as to what occurred in petitioner's home and the narcotics were introduced. Petitioner relied on *Gouled v. United States,* 255 U.S. 298 (1921) (other aspects of which are discussed at p. 271), which excluded incriminating documents obtained when, acting under federal officers' orders, a business acquaintance of defendant obtained entry into defendant's office by pretending that he intended only to pay a social visit, but in defendant's absence searched the office. The *Gouled* Court held that "whether entrance to the home or office of a [suspect] be obtained by a [government agent] by stealth or through social acquaintance, or in the guise of a business call, and whether the owner be present or not when he enters, any search and seizure subsequently and secretly made in his absence falls within the scope of the prohibition of the Fourth Amendment * * * "

Distinguishing *Gouled,* the Court, per WARREN, C.J., stressed that "in the instant case [the] petitioner invited the undercover agent to his home for the specific purpose of executing a felonious sale of narcotics. [During] neither of his visits to petitioner's home did the agent see, hear, or take anything that was not contemplated and in fact intended by petitioner as a necessary part of his illegal business. Were we to hold the deceptions of the agent in this case constitutionally prohibited, we would come near to a rule that the use of undercover agents in any manner is virtually unconstitutional per se.[a] [W]hen, as here, the home is converted into a commercial center to which outsiders are invited for purposes of transacting unlawful business, that business is entitled to no greater sanctity than if it were carried on in a store, a garage, a car or on the street. [This case has been well summarized by the Government as follows:] '[T]he only statements repeated were those that were willingly made to the agent and the only things taken were the packets of marihuana voluntarily transferred to him. The pretense resulted in no breach of privacy; it merely encouraged the suspect to say things which he was willing and anxious to say to anyone who would be interested in purchasing marihuana.' "[b]

Why didn't the *Lewis* Court dismiss petitioner's argument out of hand with a citation to *Lopez?* Why instead, in a case in which no electronic device was used, did the Court assume that the use of a secret agent raised a serious Fourth Amendment problem. See Kitch, supra, at 141–43.

James Hoffa was convicted for endeavoring to bribe members of a jury, during the so-called Test Fleet trial, which ended in a hung jury. A substantial element in the government's proof was the testimony of one Partin, a local union official. After being released from jail where he had been held pending state and federal charges, Partin had made frequent visits to the Hoffa hotel suite, on which occasions he was continually in the company of Hoffa and his associates. Proceeding upon the premise that Partin was a "governmental informer" from the time he first arrived on the scene in the Test Fleet and that the government had

a. Consider Daniel Rotenberg, *The Police Detection Practice of Encouragement: Lewis v. United States and Beyond,* 4 Houston L.Rev. 609, 614 (1967): "To say that public encouragement [the author defines 'encouragement' as the activity of police or their agents acting in the capacity of 'victims' and communicating this feigned willingness to be a victim to the suspect] is proper, but private encouragement is not, is to tell narcotics sellers to 'move indoors.' [Where] the *modus operandi* of the criminal includes both public and private places, the encouraging officer, if he is to complete the encouragement detection, has no choice except to enter the defendant's private quarters. Observations of the practices of prostitutes show that some of them operate out of hotel rooms or private residences using the telephone to make appointments. If a policeman is to detect the prostitute's commission of a solicitation he must, playing the role of a client, enter her private room or residence and encourage her. It follows that, if the narcotics seller were, in effect, told to 'move indoors,' he would. Copying the homosexual [in a jurisdiction where only public solicitation by a homosexual is criminal] and prostitute, he would use the telephone to set up sales, or would roam the streets locating buyers and then retreat into privacy before making the outlawed sale. The [*Lewis*] Court obviously appreciated the inseparable relationship of public and private encouragement."

As Professor Rotenberg has observed, id. at 612, "the practice [of police encouragement], although not the label," was before the Court in *Lewis,* but what significance, if any, the case has for police encouragement and the defense of entrapment is unclear for, as the Court noted, "petitioner does not argue that he was entrapped, as he could not on the facts of this case." See generally Ch. 8, infra.

b. Only Justice Douglas dissented. See p. 493.

compensated him for his services as such, the Court nevertheless affirmed the conviction, HOFFA v. UNITED STATES, 385 U.S. 293 (1966),[a] in an opinion by Justice STEWART:

"The argument is that Partin's failure to disclose his role as a government informer vitiated the consent that the petitioner gave to Partin's repeated entries into [Hoffa's hotel] suite, and that by listening to the petitioner's statements Partin conducted an illegal 'search' for verbal evidence. [Where] the argument falls is in its misapprehension of the fundamental nature and scope of Fourth Amendment protection. What the Fourth Amendment protects is the security a man relies upon when he places himself or his property within a constitutionally protected area, be it his home or his office, his hotel room or his automobile.[b]

"[In] the present case, however, it is evident that no interest legitimately protected by the Fourth Amendment is involved. [Partin] was in the suite by invitation, and every conversation which he heard was either directed to him or knowingly carried on in his presence. The petitioner, in a word, was not relying on the security of the hotel room; he was relying upon his misplaced confidence that Partin would not reveal his wrongdoing. * * * Neither this Court nor any member of it has ever expressed the view that the Fourth Amendment protects a wrongdoer's misplaced belief that a person to whom he voluntarily confides his wrongdoing will not reveal it. Indeed, the Court unanimously rejected that very contention less than four years ago in *Lopez.* [The] Court was divided [on the admissibility of the surreptitious recording]. But there was no dissent from the view that testimony about the conversation by Davis himself was clearly admissible. [In] the words of the dissenting opinion in *Lopez,* 'the risk of being overheard by an eavesdropper or betrayed by an informer or deceived to the identity of one with whom one deals is probably inherent in the conditions of human society. It is the kind of risk we necessarily assume whenever we speak.' "[c]

Chief Justice WARREN dissented, deeming it unnecessary to reach any constitutional questions "for the affront to the quality and fairness of federal law which this case presents is sufficient to require an exercise of our supervisory powers":

"Here, Edward Partin, a jailbird languishing in a Louisiana jail under indictments for such state and federal crimes as embezzlement, kidnapping, and manslaughter (and soon to be charged with perjury and assault), contacted federal authorities and told them he was willing to become, and would be useful as, an informer against Hoffa who was then about to be tried in the Test Fleet case. A motive for his doing this is immediately apparent—namely, his strong desire to work his way out of jail and out of his various legal entanglements with the State and Federal Governments. And it is interesting to note that, if this was his motive, he has been uniquely successful in satisfying it. In the four years since he first volunteered to be an informer against Hoffa he has not been prosecuted on any of the serious federal charges for which he was at that time jailed, and the state charges have apparently vanished into thin air. This type of informer and the uses to which he was put in this case evidence a serious potential for undermining the integrity of the truth-finding process in the federal courts. Given the incentives and background of Partin, no conviction should be allowed to stand

a. *Hoffa* was decided the same day as *Lewis* and *Osborn* (p. 468), where, on the basis of a tape recorded meeting between defendant and his "employee" (a secret government agent), one of Hoffa's lawyers was convicted of attempting to bribe a juror.

b. But compare the same Justice's analysis for the Court a year later in *Katz,* p. 247.

c. Note well that at the time the meetings at which Partin was present occurred Hoffa had not been indicted for bribing a juror nor had judicial proceedings otherwise commenced against him with respect to this crime. If they had, Hoffa would have had the benefit of the *Massiah* doctrine. See generally Ch. 9, § 5.

when based heavily on his testimony. And that is exactly the quicksand upon which these convictions rest.

"[In] performing its duty to prosecute crime the Government must take the witnesses as it finds them. [But here] the Government reaches into the jailhouse to employ a man who was himself facing indictments far more serious (and later including one for perjury) than the one confronting the man against whom he offered to inform. It employed him not for the purpose of testifying to something that had already happened, but rather for the purpose of infiltration to see if crimes would in the future be committed. * * * Certainly if a criminal defendant insinuated his informer into the prosecution's camp in this manner he would be guilty of obstructing justice. * * *"

Justice Clark, joined by Justice Douglas, would have dismissed the writs of certiorari as improvidently granted for the reason that the district court's finding that the government did *not* "place" Partin in the defendant's midst could not be regarded "clearly erroneous." However, in the companion case of *Osborn,* fn. a, p. 468, Justice DOUGLAS, the lone dissenter in that case, made it plain that if he had been satisfied in *Hoffa* that the government had "placed" Partin in Hoffa's councils he would have voted to reverse the conviction: "[A] person may take the risk that a friend will turn on him and report to the police. But that is far different from the Government's 'planting' a friend in a person's entourage so that he can secure incriminating evidence. In the one case the Government has merely been the willing recipient of information supplied by a fickle friend. In the other, the Government has actively encouraged and participated in a breach of privacy by sending in an undercover agent. [T]he Government unlawfully enters a man's home when its agent crawls through a window, breaks down a door, enters surreptitiously, or, as alleged here, gets in by trickery and fraud."[d]

Notes and Questions

1. Had Hoffa opened his hotel suite for the conduct of any business? Did any specificity of purpose or duration limit Partin's presence there? Why "while so carefully limiting its holding in *Lewis,*" did the Court "at the same time approve the extensive intrusion in *Hoffa* without even acknowledging the substantial differences in the breadth of the searches involved in the two cases"? See *The Supreme Court, 1966 Term,* 81 Harv.L.Rev. 69, 192–93 (1967).

2. Was Hoffa, as the majority put it, "relying upon his misplaced confidence that Partin would not reveal his wrongdoing" or also on the assumption that the government would not attempt to spy on him in the privacy of his hotel room? Was Partin a friend who later "revealed wrongdoing" or was he working for the government at the very time Hoffa spoke? Must people take the risk that their "friends" or associates are "government agents," i.e., have been "planted" by the government or have already promised to report whatever they see or hear to the government? See Kitch, supra, at 151–52; Note, 76 Yale L.J. 994, 1009–13 (1967).

If so, then why does one using the phone not "assume the risk" that the police will be tapping the wire? And why does one using the mails not assume that the police will be reading his letters? Are these other risks small only because the Court has made them so? Should the inquiry be not whether a person has "assumed the risk," but what risks of governmental intrusion citizens of a free society *should have to assume?* Is the view that one "assumes the risk" that the friend in whom he confides is a "government agent" anything more than a conclusion that the probability of accomplishing some social good by such a tactic

d. Justices Fortas and White took no part in the case.

outweighs the invasion of privacy and therefore the risk is tolerable in a free society? Consider Harlan, J., dissenting in *United States v. White,* p. 496.

3. Consider Note, 76 Yale L.J. 994, 1010 (1967):

"Though rejected by the Court in Lopez, Brennan's dichotomy between bugging and secret agents became in *Hoffa* the basis of the Court's decision that secret agents do not threaten privacy enough to merit Fourth Amendment limitation. But it is difficult to accept, at least without explanation, [this reasoning]. Consider, for example, the likely reactions of the citizenry if asked to rank the offensiveness of three practices:

> "(1) the police will be allowed to search your home, without force during daylight hours;
>
> "(2) the police will be allowed to offer your friends very strong inducements to report to them any illegal activities on your part;
>
> "(3) the police will be allowed to employ agents, who may be strangers, business associates or friends, to invite or encourage you to take part in a criminal venture.

"The clear state of the constitutional law after *Hoffa* and its companion cases is that (1) represents an invasion of privacy abhorrent to the American way of life, but (2) and (3) are quite proper. The average citizen would hardly agree."

Does an undercover agent's participation in a pretrial meeting between defendant and his lawyer constitute a *per se* violation of defendant's right to the effective assistance of counsel with respect to the pending criminal action? If not, under what circumstances does such governmental activity fatally taint the trial? Consider WEATHERFORD v. BURSEY, 429 U.S. 545 (1977): Bursey and Weatherford (a state undercover agent) vandalized a selective service office. Weatherford reported the incident to the police, but in order to maintain his undercover status and his usefulness on other current matters in that capacity, he was arrested and charged along with Bursey. Both were released on bond and retained separate attorneys. Then, at the request of Bursey's attorney, who sought Weatherford's presence in order to discuss his client's defense, Weatherford attended two pretrial meetings with Bursey and his attorney. Weatherford had no discussions either with his superiors or the prosecution concerning anything said at the attorney-client meetings. Although Weatherford had not expected to be a witness at the trial, and had so told Bursey, on the day of the trial (because Weatherford had been seen in the company of police officers shortly before and his effectiveness as an undercover agent thus impaired), the prosecution decided to call him as a witness. Weatherford's testimony related only to events prior to the meetings with Bursey and his lawyer and did not refer to anything said at these meetings. Nor was there any evidence that any of Weatherford's testimony was the product of anything said at these meetings. Bursey was convicted. After he had served his sentence, he brought an action against Weatherford under 42 U.S.C. § 1983, alleging that the latter's participation in the pretrial meetings had deprived him of the effective assistance of counsel as well as his right to a fair trial. The Court, per WHITE, J., held that Bursey's constitutional rights were not violated and that the right to counsel establishes no *per se* rule forbidding an undercover agent to meet with a defendant's counsel:

"[As] long as the information possessed by Weatherford remained uncommunicated, he posed no substantial threat to Bursey's Sixth Amendment rights. Nor do we believe [that] prosecutors will be so prone to lie or the difficulties of proof so great that we must always assume not only that an informant communicates what he learns from an encounter with the defendant and his counsel but also that what he communicates has the potential for detriment or benefit to the prosecutor's case.

"[That a *per se* rule] would operate prophylactically and effectively is very likely true; but it would require the informant to refuse to participate in attorney-client meetings, even though invited, and thus for all practical purposes to unmask himself. Our cases, however, have recognized the unfortunate necessity of undercover work and the value it often is to effective law enforcement.

"[There] being no tainted evidence in this case, no communication of defense strategy to the prosecution, and no purposeful intrusion by Weatherford, there was no violation of the [right to counsel]."

Justice MARSHALL, joined by Brennan, J., dissented, unable to "join in providing even the narrowest of openings to the practice of spying upon attorney-client communications":

"[E]ven if I could agree that unintended and undisclosed interceptions by government witness-employers [violate no constitutional rights], I still could not join in upholding the practice. For [the] precious constitutional rights at stake here, like other constitutional rights, need 'breathing space to survive' and a prophylactic prohibition on all intrusions of this sort is therefore essential. A rule that offers defendants relief only when they can prove 'intent' or 'disclosure' is, I fear, little better than no rule at all. Establishing [an intent or desire to spy] will seldom be possible * * *. Proving that an informer reported to the prosecution on defense strategy will be equally difficult * * *."

Is a Justice Department Order Permitting the Monitoring of Communications Between Federal Prisoners and Their Lawyers Supported by Weatherford v. Bursey?

On October 31, 2001, Attorney General John Ashcroft, issued a Bureau of Prisons order (see *Prevention of Acts of Violence and Terrorism*, 28 C.F.R. § 501.3(d) (2003)) permitting attorney-client communications to be monitored in federal prison facilities where "reasonable suspicion exists to believe that a particular inmate may use communications with attorneys or their agents to further or facilitate acts of terrorism." This regulation does not require "probable cause" in order to initiate monitoring. Nor does it necessarily require any prior judicial approval. See generally, Ellen S. Podgor & John Wesley Hall, *Government Surveillance of Attorney–Client Communications: Invoked in the Name of Fighting Terrorism*, 17 Geo.J.Legal Ethics 145 (2003). See also Charlie Cassidy & Cassandra Porsch, *Government Monitoring of Attorney–Client Communications in Terrorism–Related Cases: Ethical Implications for Defense Attorneys*, 17 Geo.J.Legal Ethics 681 (2004).

The Attorney General's order establishes procedures designed to ameliorate the intrusiveness of this action. The monitoring of attorney-client prison conversations is to be limited to those instances where there is court approval *or* where notice has been given to the inmate and the attorneys involved. This notice must explain that all communications between inmate and attorney(s) may be monitored to the extent determined to be reasonably necessary to deter "future acts of violence or terrorism" and that no attorney-client privilege exists if the communications "would facilitate criminal acts or a conspiracy to commit criminal acts." The order also requires the notice to explain that appropriate procedures will be employed to ensure that all attorney-client communications are reviewed for privilege claims.

The government must establish a "taint team"—composed of individuals not involved in the underlying investigation—to review materials. According to the Attorney General, the use of a "taint team" and the building of a "firewall" between teams monitoring attorney-client conversations and government lawyers prosecuting the monitored defendants will adequately protect the attorney-client privilege.[a]

In defending the Bureau of Prisons order, Attorney General relied specifically on *Weatherford v. Bursey*, where, as he put it, the Supreme Court held that "when the government possesses a legitimate law enforcement interest in monitoring [conversations between a defendant and his attorney] no Sixth Amendment violation occurs so long as privileged communications are protected from disclosure and no information recovered through monitoring is used by the government in a way that deprives the defendant of a fair trial."

Consider, however, David Moran, *Ashcroft's Monitoring Violates Attorney–Client Rights*, Detroit News, Nov. 28, 2001, p. 13A: "It is true [that] the Supreme Court once held that the Sixth Amendment was not necessarily violated when a defendant unwittingly brought along an undercover informant to a meeting with his lawyer. But that case * * * is a far cry from an order requiring the attorney and client to meet under the government's watchful eyes and listening ears."

As pointed out in Podgor & Hall, supra, the National Association of Criminal Defense Lawyers (NACDL) also criticized the Attorney General for failing to mention footnote four in the *Weatherford v. Bursey* opinion. In that footnote Justice White observed that "a fear that some third party may turn out to be a government agent will inhibit attorney-client communications to a lesser degree than the fear that the government is monitoring those communications through electronic eavesdropping, because the former intrusion may be avoided by excluding third parties from defense meetings or refraining from divulging defense strategy when third parties are present at those meetings."

UNITED STATES v. WHITE

401 U.S. 745, 91 S.Ct. 1122, 28 L.Ed.2d 453 (1971).

Justice WHITE announced the judgment of the Court and an opinion in which The Chief Justice, Justice STEWART, and Justice BLACKMUN join.

[On numerous occasions a government informer, carrying a concealed radio transmitter, engaged defendant in conversations which were electronically overheard by federal narcotics agents. The conversations in a restaurant, defendant's home and in the informer's car were overheard by the use of radio equipment. A number of conversations in the informer's home were not only electronically overheard by an agent stationed outside the house but by another agent who, with the informer's consent, concealed himself in the latter's kitchen closet.[a] At no time did the agents obtain a warrant or court order. The informer was not produced at the trial, but the testimony of the "eavesdropping" agents was admitted and led to defendant's conviction of narcotics violations. The U.S. Court of Appeals for the Seventh Circuit read *Katz* as overruling *On Lee* and interpreted the Fourth Amendment as prohibiting testimony about the electronically overheard statements.]

a. Some defense lawyers doubted that the "firewall" constructed would prove very substantial, ridiculing the notion that the "taint team" would not share information with the prosecutors. See David Rovella, *Ashcroft Rule Puts Defenders in a Bind*, Nat'l.L.J., Dec. 3, 2001, p.1.

a. No testimony by this agent was offered at trial. See Note 4 following this case.

[The *Hoffa* case], left undisturbed by *Katz,* held that however strongly a defendant may trust an apparent colleague, his expectations in this respect are not protected by the Fourth Amendment when it turns out that the colleague is a government agent regularly communicating with the authorities. * * *

Conceding that *Hoffa, Lewis,* and *Lopez* remained unaffected by *Katz,* the Court of Appeals nevertheless read both *Katz* and the Fourth Amendment to require a different result if the agent not only records his conversations with the defendant but instantaneously transmits them electronically to other agents equipped with radio receivers.

[To] reach this result it was necessary for the Court of Appeals to hold that *On Lee* was no longer good law. In that case, [the] Court first rejected claims of a Fourth Amendment violation because the informer had not trespassed when he entered the defendant's premises and conversed with him. To this extent the Court's rationale cannot survive *Katz.* But the Court announced a second and independent ground for its decision; for it went on to say that overruling *Olmstead* and *Goldman* [which the Court subsequently did in *Katz*] would be of no aid to On Lee since he "was talking confidentially and indiscreetly with one he trusted, and he was overheard. * * * " We see no indication in *Katz* that the Court meant to disturb that understanding of the Fourth Amendment or to disturb the result reached in the *On Lee* case, nor are we now inclined to overturn this view of the Fourth Amendment.

Concededly a police agent who conceals his police connections may write down for official use his conversations with a defendant and testify concerning them, without a warrant authorizing his encounters with the defendant and without otherwise violating the latter's Fourth Amendment rights. *Hoffa.* For constitutional purposes, no different result is required if the agent instead of immediately reporting and transcribing his conversations with defendant, either (1) simultaneously records them with electronic equipment which he is carrying on his person, *Lopez;* (2) or carries radio equipment which simultaneously transmits the conversations either to recording equipment located elsewhere or to other agents monitoring the transmitting frequency. *On Lee.* If the conduct and revelations of an agent operating without electronic equipment do not invade the defendant's constitutionally justifiable expectations of privacy, neither does a simultaneous recording of the same conversations made by the agent or by others from transmissions received from the agent to whom the defendant is talking and whose trustworthiness the defendant necessarily risks.

Our problem is not what the privacy expectations of particular defendants in particular situations may be or the extent to which they may in fact have relied on the discretion of their companions. Very probably, individual defendants neither know nor suspect that their colleagues have gone or will go to the police or are carrying recorders or transmitters. Otherwise, conversation would cease and our problem with these encounters would be nonexistent or far different from those now before us. Our problem, in terms of the principles announced in *Katz,* is what expectations of privacy are constitutionally "justifiable"—what expectations the Fourth Amendment will protect in the absence of a warrant. So far, the law permits the frustration of actual expectations of privacy by permitting authorities to use the testimony of those associates who for one reason or another have determined to turn to the police, as well as by authorizing the use of informants in the manner exemplified by *Hoffa* and *Lewis.* If the law gives no protection to the wrongdoer whose trusted accomplice is or becomes a police agent, neither should it protect him when that same agent has recorded or transmitted the conversations which are later offered in evidence to prove the State's case.

Inescapably, one contemplating illegal activities must realize and risk that his companions may be reporting to the police. If he sufficiently doubts their trustworthiness, the association will very probably end or never materialize. But if he has no doubts, or allays them, or risks what doubt he has, the risk is his. In terms of what his course will be, what he will or will not do or say, we are unpersuaded that he would distinguish between probable informers on the one hand and probable informers with transmitters on the other.

[It is] untenable to consider the activities and reports of the police agent himself, though acting without a warrant, to be a "reasonable" investigative effort and lawful under the Fourth Amendment but to view the same agent with a recorder or transmitter as conducting an "unreasonable" and unconstitutional search and seizure. * * * No different result should obtain where, as in *On Lee* and the instant case, the informer disappears and is unavailable at trial; for the issue of whether specified events on a certain day violate the Fourth Amendment should not be determined by what later happens to the informer. [R]eversed.[b]

Justice DOUGLAS, dissenting. * * *

On Lee and *Lopez* are of a vintage opposed to *Berger* and *Katz.* However they may be explained, they are products of the old common-law notions of trespass. *Katz,* on the other hand, emphasized that with few exceptions "searches conducted outside the judicial process, without prior approval by judge or magistrate, are *per se* unreasonable under the Fourth Amendment. * * * "

Monitoring, if prevalent, certainly kills free discourse and spontaneous utterances. Free discourse—a First Amendment value—may be frivolous or serious, humble or defiant, reactionary or revolutionary, profane or in good taste; but it is not free if there is surveillance. Free discourse liberates the spirit, though it may produce only froth. The individual must keep some facts concerning his thoughts within a small zone of people. At the same time he must be free to pour out his woes or inspirations or dreams to others. He remains the sole judge as to what must be said and what must remain unspoken. This is the essence of the idea of privacy implicit in the First and Fifth Amendments as well as in the Fourth. * * *

Justice HARLAN, dissenting.

[The] plurality opinion seeks to erase the crucial distinction between the facts before us and [the holdings in *Lopez, Lewis* and *Hoffa*] by the following reasoning: if A can relay verbally what is revealed to him by B (as in *Lewis* and *Hoffa*), or record and later divulge it (as in *Lopez*), what difference does it make if A conspires with another to betray B by contemporaneously transmitting to the other all that is said? The contention is, in essence, an argument that the distinction between third-party monitoring and *other* undercover techniques is one of form and not substance. The force of the contention depends on the evaluation of two separable but intertwined assumptions: first, that there is no greater invasion of privacy in the third-party situation, and, second, that uncontrolled consensual surveillance in an electronic age is a tolerable technique of law enforcement, given the values and goals of our political system.

b. The plurality opinion also upheld the admissibility of the evidence of defendant's incriminating statements on another ground: the events in question took place long prior to *Katz* and *Desist,* p. 39, had held that *Katz* applied only to those electronic surveillances which occurred subsequent to the date of that decision. Justice Brennan, whose concurring opinion is summarized infra, concurred in the result, agreeing that *Desist* required affirmance, but differing on the issue of the continued viability of *On Lee.* Justice Black concurred in the result for the reasons set forth in his *Katz* dissent, but adhered to his view that *Katz* should be applied retroactively. Dissenting Justices Douglas, Harlan and Marshall would apply *Katz* retroactively and viewed it as overruling *On Lee.*

The first of these assumptions takes as a point of departure the so-called "risk analysis" approach of *Lewis,* and *Lopez,* and to a lesser extent *On Lee,* or the expectations approach of *Katz.* While these formulations represent an advance over the unsophisticated trespass analysis of the common law, they too have their limitations and can, ultimately, lead to the substitution of words for analysis. The analysis must, in my view, transcend the search for subjective expectations or legal attribution of assumptions of risk. Our expectations, and the risks we assume, are in large part reflections of laws that translate into rules the customs and values of the past and present.

Since it is the task of the law to form and project, as well as mirror and reflect, we should not, as judges, merely recite the expectations and risks without examining the desirability of saddling them upon society. The critical question, therefore, is whether under our system of government, as reflected in the Constitution, we should impose on our citizens the risks of the electronic listener or observer without at least the protection of a warrant requirement.

[The] impact of the practice of third-party bugging, must, I think, be considered such as to undermine that confidence and sense of security in dealing with one another that is characteristic of individual relationships between citizens in a free society. It goes beyond the impact on privacy occasioned by the ordinary type of "informer" investigation upheld in *Lewis* and *Hoffa.* The argument of the plurality opinion, to the effect that it is irrelevant whether secrets are revealed by the mere tattletale or the transistor, ignores the differences occasioned by third-party monitoring and recording which insures full and accurate disclosure of all that is said, free of the possibility of error and oversight that inheres in human reporting.

[I]t is too easy to forget—and, hence, too often forgotten—that the issue here is whether to interpose a search warrant procedure between law enforcement agencies engaging in electronic eavesdropping and the public generally. By casting its "risk analysis" solely in terms of the expectations and risks that "wrongdoers" or "one contemplating illegal activities" ought to bear, the plurality opinion, I think, misses the mark entirely. *On Lee* does not simply mandate that criminals must daily run the risk of unknown eavesdroppers prying into their private affairs; it subjects each and every law-abiding member of society to that risk. * * * Abolition of *On Lee* would not end electronic eavesdropping. It would prevent public officials from engaging in that practice unless they first had probable cause to suspect an individual of involvement in illegal activities and had tested their version of the facts before a detached judicial officer. The interest *On Lee* fails to protect is the expectation of the ordinary citizen, who has never engaged in illegal conduct in his life, that he may carry on his private discourse freely, openly, and spontaneously without measuring his every word against the connotations it might carry when instantaneously heard by others unknown to him and unfamiliar with his situation or analyzed in a cold, formal record played days, months, or years after the conversation. Interposition of a warrant requirement is designed not to shield "wrongdoers," but to secure a measure of privacy and a sense of personal security throughout our society. * * *

Justice MARSHALL, dissenting.

I am convinced that the correct view of the Fourth Amendment in the area of electronic surveillance is one that brings the safeguards of the warrant requirement to bear on the investigatory activity involved in this case. In this regard I agree with the dissents of Justice Douglas and Justice Harlan. In short, I believe that *On Lee* cannot be considered viable in light of the constitutional principles articulated in *Katz* and other cases. * * *

[Justice BRENNAN concurred in the result, agreeing that *Katz* should not be applied retroactively but emphasizing that on the issue of the viability of *On Lee,* neither the dissenters' views nor Justice White's "commands the support of a majority of the Court."[c] He would "go further" than the dissenters; their reasoning "compels the conclusion" that *Lopez,* as well as *On Lee,* is "no longer sound law. [C]urrent Fourth Amendment jurisprudence interposes a warrant requirement not only in cases of third-party electronic monitoring (the situation in *On Lee* and in this case) but also in cases of electronic recording by a government agent of a face-to-face conversation with a criminal suspect, which was the situation in *Lopez.*" As he viewed it, *Katz* had adopted the "doctrinal basis" of his *Lopez* dissent and that meant that both *On Lee* and *Lopez,* which presented "rationally indistinguishable" situations,[d] should now be regarded as overruled.[e]]

Notes and Questions

1. After *White,* what, if anything, is left of anyone's "justifiable reliance" on the privacy of his conversation (*Katz*)? Did *Katz* mean that a citizen must adjust his expectations of privacy to new laws and electronic techniques or that these new laws and techniques should conform to present expectations? Did *Katz* mean, or should it be read as meaning, that the individual only "assumes the risk" that he objectively perceives and no more? That *reasonable* reliance on the privacy of one's conversation suffices to invoke the protection of the Fourth Amendment? See Note, 52 B.U.L.Rev. 831, 838–44 (1972).

Didn't defendant White take reasonable steps to protect against governmental intrusion by choosing the locations he did for his private conversations? Didn't federal agents employ an informer and conceal a radio transmitter on his person for the very reason that they anticipated defendant White would make reasonable efforts to avoid being overheard? Does the *White* plurality opinion mean the privacy of one's conversation is unprotected if one can anticipate *any* risk that his words might be disclosed to third parties? If so, how does the Fourth Amendment protect the privacy of one's conversations unless one *completely stops* communicating to others? See Note, 85 Harv.L.Rev. 250, 254 (1971). See also Hufstedler, J., dissenting in *Holmes v. Burr,* 486 F.2d 55, 61, 71–76 (9th Cir.1973).

2. Did the *White* plurality opinion refuse to recognize normal expectations of privacy because to do so would restrict a "normal" police stratagem? Is the "reasonableness" of privacy expectations to be measured by how the average person views a given situation or by whether affording Fourth Amendment protection would "unreasonably" impede the police? See 52 B.U.L.Rev. at 838; Note, Harv.L.Rev. 63, 192–93 (1968).

3. ***Drawing lines***. The *White* plurality opinion observes that "the law gives no protection to the wrongdoer whose trusted accomplice [*unequipped* with an electronic device] *is* or *becomes* a police agent." (Emphasis added.) Should the law

c. Aren't there "five votes" in *White* sustaining *On Lee?* Recall that the "fifth Justice," Black, concurred in the *White* result for the reasons advanced in his *Katz* dissent, where he viewed Fourth Amendment protection of privacy as extending only to "unreasonable searches and seizures of 'persons, houses, papers and effects.' " Recall, too, Justice Black's *Berger* dissent, where he could not read the Fourth Amendment as applying to "the spoken word" as well as "tangible things." Justice Black did dissent in *On Lee*—solely on the ground that the Court should reject the evidence in the exercise of its supervisory authority over federal criminal justice. Why didn't he make that argument in *White?*

d. Did they?

e. As to whether the government has a constitutional obligation to retain tapes of conversations for the defendant's possible use, consider pp. 1296–99.

distinguish between (1) a "trusted accomplice" who, absent prior arrangements with the police, *subsequently* supplies them with evidence; and (2) a "trusted accomplice" who was a "police agent" all along, who was "planted" by the government to secure incriminating evidence? Reconsider Chief Justice Warren's dissenting opinion in *Hoffa,* p. 492; and Justice Douglas' dissenting opinion in *Osborn* and *Lewis,* p. 493.

Might the *White* dissenters have read *Katz* more broadly than they did? Might they have argued, alternatively, that if, as the *White* plurality opinion maintains, "the difference between the electronically equipped [governmental 'plant'] and the unequipped [governmental 'plant'] is [not] substantial enough to require discrete constitutional recognition," then *Katz* should be read as overruling *Hoffa* as well as *On Lee?* May it be said of the *Hoffa* case—using the language in *Katz*—that the government's use of defendant's trusted friend to obtain evidence against him "violated the privacy upon which [defendant] justifiably relied" and thus constituted a "search" or "seizure"?

4. Both the Seventh Circuit and Supreme Court opinions in *White* dealt only with the use of *electronically* overheard conversations because only such evidence was offered at trial. If the *White* dissenters had prevailed, would their reasoning also have led to the exclusion of the testimony of the narcotics agent (not equipped with an electronic device) who had overheard defendant's conversations from his hiding place in the informer's kitchen closet? Why (not)?

5. ***Renewed doubts about the validity of* White.** In *Marshall v. Barlow's* (p. 440), the government maintained that the pervasiveness of state and national safety regulations refuted the view that an employer can have a "realistic privacy interest" in employee work areas. Rejecting this argument, the Court, per White, J., observed: "Employees are not prohibited from reporting OSHA violations. What they observe in their daily functions is undoubtedly beyond the employer's reasonable expectation of privacy. The Government inspector, however, is not an employee. Without a warrant he stands in no better position than a member of the public. [That] an employee is free to report, and the Government is free to use, any evidence of noncompliance with OSHA that the employee observes furnishes no justification for federal agents to enter a place of business from which the public is restricted and to conduct their own warrantless search."

Does *Barlow's* raise serious questions and renewed doubts about the validity of *White* and other cases dealing with participant monitoring? By talking to a confidant, did the defendant in *White* consent to government information-gathering any more than the defendant in *Barlow's* did, by permitting employees to observe his premises? See Joseph D. Grano, *Perplexing Questions About Three Basic Fourth Amendment Issues,* 69 J.Crim.L. & C. 425, 435–38 (1978).

Chapter 8

POLICE "ENCOURAGEMENT" AND THE DEFENSE OF ENTRAPMENT

"The mode adopted [to] bring to light the malfeasance of the defendant, had no necessary connection with his violation of law. He exercised his own volition * * *. Even if inducements to commit crime could be assumed to exist in this case, the allegation of the defendant would be but the repetition of the plea as ancient as the world, and first interposed in Paradise: 'The serpent beguiled me and I did eat.' That defense was overruled by the great Lawgiver, and whatever estimate we may form, or whatever judgment pass upon the character or conduct of the tempter, this plea has never since availed to shield crime or give indemnity to the culprit, and it is safe to say that under any code of civilized, not to say christian ethics, it never will."

—Bacon, J., in *Board of Commissioners v. Backus,* 29 How.Pr. 33, 42 (N.Y.Sup.Ct.1864).

"[T]wo deeply seated and widely shared intuitive judgments [explain the creation and survival of the entrapment defense]. The first is that a person is somewhat less culpable if tempted into crime by certain kinds of inducements. The second is that it is extremely dangerous to allow government the power to stress test the morality of ordinary citizens by dangling substantial inducements before them. [But] where do [these] intuitions come from?"

—Louis Michael Seidman, *The Supreme Court, Entrapment, and Our Criminal Justice Dilemma,* 1981 Sup.Ct.Rev. 111, 146.

" 'Encouragement' is descriptive of an intentional technique of police agencies used in the detection of a certain class of crimes. [It] denotes activity of the police or their agent: (1) acting in the capacity of a victim, (2) intending by his actions to suggest his willingness to be a victim, (3) actually communicating this feigned willingness to the suspect, and (4) thereby having some influence upon his commission of the crime. It is not necessarily a single act; it usually consists of a series of acts by the officer which are part of the normal interplay between victim and suspect in the specific crime. It is utilized as a device in dealing with certain crimes having the common element of vice—prostitution, homosexuality, liquor sales, narcotics, and gambling. The reason that the same technique is adapted to all these crimes is suggested by the 'vice' label applicable to all of them, that these offenses are committed privately with a willing victim who will not complain, making normal detection virtually impossible. 'Encouragement,' to state it more succinctly, is a process of persuasion. * * *

"[It] is by no means a wholesome police practice. It is founded upon deception. Not only must the participating officer deliberately deceive, but he must often say and do things that are vulgar, profane and indecent. However, to condemn the characteristics is to condemn the practice, because deception, vulgarity, profanity, and indecency are often essential to the simulation of reality which encouragement attempts to achieve. When to these characteristics is added the unfortunate fact that on occasion encouragement induces persons to commit crime who ordinarily would not, it is understandable that the practice is roundly criticized. But if there is no way to protect society effectively from certain criminal harms except through detection by encouragement, then it is as idle to criticize the practice continually as it would be to criticize surgery for its efforts to eliminate disease because the surgical method, of necessity, cuts and hurts the body. The fact should not be overlooked that the fault lies more with the social harm and the human hurt and their causes than with the methods of eradication."

—Daniel Rotenberg, *The Police Detection Practice of Encouragement,* 49 Va.L.Rev. 871, 874 (1963).

"Manifestly, [the function of law enforcement] does not include the manufacturing of crime. Criminal activity is such that stealth and strategy are necessary weapons in the arsenal of the police officer. However, 'A different question is presented when the criminal design originates with the officials of the government, and they implant in the mind of an innocent person the disposition to commit the alleged offense and induce its commission in order that they may prosecute.' Then stealth and strategy become as objectionable police methods as the coerced confession and the unlawful search. * * * To determine whether entrapment has been established a line must be drawn between the trap for the unwary innocent and the trap for the unwary criminal."

—Warren, C.J., for the Court in *Sherman v. United States,* 356 U.S. 369 (1958).

"The purpose of the entrapment defense * * * must be to prohibit unlawful governmental activity in instigating crime. [If] so, then whether the particular defendant was 'predisposed' or 'otherwise innocent' is irrelevant; and the important question becomes whether the Government's conduct in inducing the crime was beyond judicial toleration."

—Stewart, J., dissenting in *United States v. Russell,* 411 U.S. 423, 442 (1973).

"If the police entice someone to commit a crime who would not have done so without their blandishments, and then arrest him and he is prosecuted, convicted, and punished, law enforcement resources are squandered in the following sense: resources that could and should have been used in an effort to reduce the nation's unacceptably high crime rate are used instead in the entirely sterile activity of first inciting and then punishing a crime. However, if the police are just inducing someone to commit sooner a crime he would have committed eventually, but to do so in controlled circumstances where the costs to the criminal justice system of apprehension and conviction are minimized, the police are economizing on resources. It is particularly difficult to catch arsonists, so if all the police were doing here was making it easier to catch an arsonist—not inducing someone to become an arsonist—they were using law enforcement resources properly and there is no occasion for judicial intervention. * * *

"Thus in my view 'entrapment' is merely the name we give to a particularly unproductive use of law enforcement resources, which our system properly condemns. If this is right, the implementing concept of 'predisposition to crime' calls less for psychological conjecture than for a common-sense assessment of whether it is likely that the defendant would have committed the crime anyway—without the blandishments the police used on him—but at a time and place where it would have been more difficult for them to apprehend him and the state to convict him, or whether the police used threats or promises so powerful that a law-abiding individual was induced to commit a crime. If the latter is the case, the police tactics do not merely affect the timing and location of a crime; they cause crime."

—Posner, J., concurring in *United States v. Kaminski,* 703 F.2d 1004, 1010 (7th Cir.1983).

"If the investigators were too creative or squandered their limited resources, this is a political problem. Congress can hold oversight hearings or pass a law; we shouldn't apply a chancellor's foot veto. Dissipating law enforcement resources injures persons who become victims of crime when the deterrent force of the law declines. Reversing convictions of the guilty cannot apply balm to these wounds. Those who protest that social interests would have been served by prosecuting someone else (or some additional, similarly situated persons) routinely lose. We deem it enough to support punishment that this person committed this offense, leaving to other institutions the redirection of investigative or prosecutorial resources. So it should be here."

—Easterbrook, J., concurring in *United States v. Miller,* 891 F.2d 1265, 1271–72 (7th Cir.1989).

"Our national integrity has been on a downhill slide for seven years; we really don't need the FBI to grease the skids with Operation ABSCAM.[a] Where no crime has been contemplated, the FBI has, through entrapment, induced to crime men who were previously involved in no wrongdoing. Aren't there enough naturally

a. "Abscam" is an acronym combining the first two letters of Abdul Enterprises, a fictitious Middle Eastern corporation, and "scam," a slang term for swindle or confidence game. Abscam began as a standard "sting" operation, i.e., an FBI undercover scheme to recover stolen securities and paintings. In 1978, the operation shifted to political corruption in the New Jersey area. A year later, it had turned its attention to the "Asylum Scenario"; unsuspecting "middlemen" (private persons unaware that they were part of a government undercover operation) passed the word to various Congressmen, or to their aides and acquaintances, that wealthy Arabs were willing to bribe members of Congress in order to ensure that they would introduce private immigration bills on the Arabs' behalf if and when necessary. In early 1980, shortly before shutting down, the operation shifted to political corruption in Philadelphia.

As a result of Abscam, a U.S. Senator, six U.S. Representatives and a number of other public officials and lawyers were convicted of various corrupt acts. Although many of the defendants (and many critics of the operation both in and out of Congress) charged that the FBI's methods constituted entrapment and/or violated the due process rights of the individuals caught in the operation, not a single Abscam defendant prevailed in the courts. See, e.g., *United States v. Kelly* (D.C.Cir.1983), p. 520, which discusses one phase of the Abscam operation at considerable length.

encouraging crimes to keep the FBI busy? Must they spend astronomical sums creating crime?"

—Letter to the Editor, Newsweek, Mar. 1, 1980, p. 5.

"House Speaker Thomas P. (Tip) O'Neill may have thundered that '[Operation ABSCAM] was a setup, a goddam setup,' but a crook is a crook is a crook. Whether set up or not, honest people do not take bribes."

—Letter to the Editor, Newsweek Mar. 1, 1980, p. 5.

"We assume that there are a few people who would not commit any criminal acts no matter what the provocation or enticement. We will not refer further to such saintly or misguided individuals. Everyone else, we assume has a price. [If] this assumption is true, then everyone except saints is predisposed to commit crimes. But that in turn means that 'predisposition' cannot usefully distinguish anyone from anyone else. The only salient question is whether a person's price has been met, not whether he has one, since by hypothesis everyone but the saintly does. * * * [T]he person who does not take the bait almost surely would take a higher, even if greatly higher, bait. The failure to take this one is evidence of his price, but not of predisposition."

—Ronald J. Allen, Melissa Luttrell & Anne Kreeger, *Clarifying Entrapment*, 89 J. Crim. L. & Criminology 407, 413 (1999).

SECTION 1. THE TESTS FOR ENTRAPMENT[a]

UNITED STATES v. RUSSELL

411 U.S. 423, 93 S.Ct. 1637, 36 L.Ed.2d 366 (1973).

Justice REHNQUIST delivered the opinion of the Court.

[After] a jury trial in the District Court, in which his sole defense was entrapment, respondent was convicted [of] having unlawfully manufactured and processed methamphetamine ("speed") and of having unlawfully sold and delivered that drug. [On] appeal, the United States Court of Appeals for the Ninth Circuit [reversed] the conviction solely for the reason that an undercover agent supplied an essential chemical for manufacturing the methamphetamine which formed the basis of respondent's conviction.

[There] is little dispute concerning the essential facts in this case. On December 7, 1969, Joe Shapiro, an undercover agent for the Federal Bureau of Narcotics and Dangerous Drugs, went to respondent's home [where] he met with respondent and his two codefendants, John and Patrick Connolly. Shapiro's

a. "Entrapment" is sometimes confused with, but should be distinguished from, "estoppel," which occurs when defendants rely on the assurances of government authorities that their contemplated conduct is lawful only to be prosecuted for such conduct. See *Cox v. Louisiana*, 379 U.S. 559 (1965) (to sustain appellant's conviction "for demonstrating where [public officials] told him he could 'would be to sanction an indefensible sort of entrapment by the State * * * ' "); *Raley v. Ohio*, 360 U.S. 423 (1959); *People v. Donovan*, 279 N.Y.S.2d 404 (Ct.Spec.Sess.1967), 81 Harv.L.Rev. 895 (1968).

assignment was to locate a laboratory where it was believed that methamphetamine was being manufactured illicitly. He told the respondent and the Connollys that he represented an organization [that] was interested in controlling the manufacture and distribution of methamphetamine. He then made an offer to supply the defendants with the chemical phenyl–2–propanone, an essential ingredient in the manufacture of methamphetamine, in return for one-half of the drug produced. This offer was made on the condition that Agent Shapiro be shown a sample of the drug which they were making and the laboratory where it was being produced.

During the conversation, Patrick Connolly revealed that he had been making the drug since May 1969 and since then had produced three pounds of it. John Connolly gave the agent a bag containing a quality of methamphetamine that he represented as being from "the last batch that we made." Shortly thereafter, Shapiro and Patrick Connolly left respondent's house to view the laboratory which was located in the Connolly house on Whidbey Island. At the house, Shapiro observed an empty bottle bearing the chemical label phenyl–2–propanone.

By prearrangement, Shapiro returned to the Connolly house on December 9, 1969, to supply 100 grams of propanone and observe the manufacturing process. When he arrived he observed Patrick Connolly and the respondent cutting up pieces of aluminum foil and placing them in a large flask. There was testimony that some of the foil pieces accidentally fell on the floor and were picked up by the respondent and Shapiro and put into the flask. Thereafter, Patrick Connolly added all of the necessary chemicals, including the propanone brought by Shapiro, to make two batches of methamphetamine. The manufacturing process having been completed the following morning, Shapiro was given one-half of the drug and respondent kept the remainder. Shapiro offered to buy, and the respondent agreed to sell, part of the remainder for $60.

About a month later, Shapiro returned to the Connolly house and met with Patrick Connolly to ask if he was still interested in their "business arrangement." Connolly replied that he was interested but that he had recently obtained two additional bottles of phenyl–2–propanone and would not be finished with them for a couple of days. He provided some additional methamphetamine to Shapiro at that time. Three days later Shapiro returned to the Connolly house with a search warrant and, among other items, seized an empty 500–gram bottle of propanone and a 100–gram bottle, not the one he had provided, that was partially filled with the chemical.

There was testimony at the trial of respondent and Patrick Connolly that phenyl–2–propanone was generally difficult to obtain. At the request of the Bureau of Narcotics and Dangerous Drugs, some chemical supply firms had voluntarily ceased selling the chemical.

At the close of the evidence, and after receiving the District Judge's standard entrapment instruction,[4] the jury found the respondent guilty on all counts charged. On appeal, the respondent conceded that the jury could have found him predisposed to commit the offenses, but argued that on the facts presented there was entrapment as a matter of law. The Court of Appeals agreed, although it did not find the District Court had misconstrued or misapplied the traditional standards governing the entrapment defense. Rather, the court in effect expanded

4. The District Judge stated the governing law on entrapment as follows: "Where a person already has the willingness and the readiness to break the law, the mere fact that the government agent provides what appears to be a favorable opportunity is not entrapment." He then instructed the jury to acquit respondent if it had a "reasonable doubt whether the defendant had the previous intent or purpose to commit the offense * * * and did so only because he was induced or persuaded by some officer or agent of the government." No exception was taken by respondent to this instruction.

the traditional notion of entrapment, which focuses on the predisposition of the defendant, to mandate dismissal of a criminal prosecution whenever the court determines that there has been "an intolerable degree of governmental participation in the criminal enterprise." In this case the court decided that the conduct of the agent in supplying a scarce ingredient essential for the manufacture of a controlled substance established that defense.

This new defense was held to rest on either of two alternative theories. One theory is based on two lower court decisions which have found entrapment, regardless of predisposition, whenever the government supplies contraband to the defendants. The second theory, a non-entrapment rationale, is based on a recent Ninth Circuit decision that reversed a conviction because a government investigator was so enmeshed in the criminal activity that the prosecution of the defendants was held to be repugnant to the American criminal justice system. The court below held that these two rationales constitute the same defense, and that only the label distinguishes them. In any event, it held that "[b]oth theories are premised on fundamental concepts of due process and evince the reluctance of the judiciary to countenance 'overzealous law enforcement.' "

This Court first recognized and applied the entrapment defense in *Sorrells v. United States,* 287 U.S. 435 (1932), [where] a federal prohibition agent visited the defendant while posing as a tourist and engaged him in conversation about their common war experiences. After gaining the defendant's confidence, the agent asked for some liquor, was twice refused, but upon asking a third time the defendant finally capitulated, and was subsequently prosecuted for violating the National Prohibition Act.

Chief Justice Hughes, speaking for the Court, held that as a matter of statutory construction the defense of entrapment should have been available to the defendant. Under the theory propounded by the Chief Justice, the entrapment defense prohibits law enforcement officers from instigating a criminal act by persons "otherwise innocent in order to lure them to its commission and to punish them." Thus, the thrust of the entrapment defense was held to focus on the intent or predisposition of the defendant to commit the crime. "[I]f the defendant seeks acquittal by reason of entrapment he cannot complain of an appropriate and searching inquiry into his own conduct and predisposition as bearing upon that issue."

Justice Roberts concurred but was of the view "that courts must be closed to the trial of a crime instigated by the government's own agents." The difference in the view of the majority and the concurring opinions is that in the former the inquiry focuses on the predisposition of the defendant, whereas in the latter the inquiry focuses on whether the government "instigated the crime."

In *Sherman v. United States,* 356 U.S. 369 (1958) the Court again considered the theory underlying the entrapment defense and expressly reaffirmed the view expressed by the *Sorrells* majority. In *Sherman* the defendant was convicted of selling narcotics to a Government informer. As in *Sorrells,* it appears that the Government agent gained the confidence of the defendant and, despite initial reluctance, the defendant finally acceded to the repeated importunings of the agent to commit the criminal act. On the basis of *Sorrells,* this Court [overturned the] conviction.

In affirming the theory underlying *Sorrells,* [the Court, per Chief Justice Warren] held that "[t]o determine whether entrapment has been established, a line must be drawn between the trap for the unwary innocent and the trap for the unwary criminal." Justice Frankfurter [maintained in a concurring opinion that] Justice Roberts had the better view in *Sorrells* and [thus] would have framed the question to be asked in an entrapment defense in terms of "whether the police conduct revealed in the particular case falls below standards [for] the proper use of governmental power."

In the instant case, [respondent] argues that the level of Shapiro's involvement in the manufacture of the methamphetamine was so high that a criminal prosecution for the drug's manufacture violates the fundamental principles of due process. [He] contends that the same factors that led this Court to apply the exclusionary rule to illegal searches and seizures [and] confessions should be considered here. But he would have the Court go further in deterring undesirable official conduct by requiring that any prosecution be barred absolutely because of the police involvement in criminal activity. The analogy is imperfect in any event, for the principal reason behind the adoption of the exclusionary rule was the Government's "failure to observe its own laws." [Here, however, the government's conduct] violated no independent constitutional right of the respondent. Nor did Shapiro violate any federal statute or rule or commit any crime in infiltrating the respondent's drug enterprise.

Respondent would overcome this basic weakness in his analogy to the exclusionary rule cases by having the Court adopt a rigid constitutional rule that would preclude any prosecution when it is shown that the criminal conduct would not have been possible had not an undercover agent "supplied an indispensable means to the commission of the crime that could not have been obtained otherwise, through legal or illegal channels." Even if we were to surmount the difficulties attending the notion that due process of law can be embodied in fixed rules, and those attending respondent's particular formulation, the rule he proposes would not appear to be of significant benefit to him. For, on the record presented, it appears that he cannot fit within the terms of the very rule he proposes.

[The] defendants admitted making the drug both before and after those batches made with the propanone supplied by Shapiro. [Thus, the record amply demonstrates] that the propanone used in the illicit manufacture of methamphetamine not only *could* have been obtained without the intervention of Shapiro but was in fact obtained by these defendants.

While we may some day be presented with a situation in which the conduct of law enforcement agents is so outrageous that due process principles would absolutely bar the government from invoking judicial processes to obtain a conviction, the instant case is distinctly not of that breed. Shapiro's contribution of propanone to the criminal enterprise already in process was scarcely objectionable. The chemical is by itself a harmless substance and its possession is legal. While the Government may have been seeking to make it more difficult for drug rings [to] obtain the chemical, the evidence described above shows that it nonetheless was obtainable. The law enforcement conduct here stops far short of violating that "fundamental fairness, shocking to the universal sense of justice," mandated by the Due Process Clause of the Fifth Amendment.

The illicit manufacture of drugs is not a sporadic, isolated criminal incident, but a continuing, though illegal, business enterprise. In order to obtain convictions for illegally manufacturing drugs, the gathering of evidence of past unlawful conduct frequently proves to be an all but impossible task. Thus in drug-related offenses law enforcement personnel have turned to one of the only practicable means of detection: the infiltration of drug rings and a limited participation in their unlawful present practices. Such infiltration is a recognized and permissible means of investigation; if that be so, then the supply of some item of value that the drug ring requires must, as a general rule, also be permissible. For an agent will not be taken into the confidence of the illegal entrepreneurs unless he has something of value to offer them. Law enforcement tactics such as this can hardly be said to violate "fundamental fairness" or "shocking to the universal sense of justice."

[This] Court's opinions in *Sorrells* and *Sherman* held that the principal element in the defense of entrapment was the defendant's predisposition to commit the crime. Respondent conceded [that] "he may have harbored a predisposition to commit the charged offenses." Yet he argues that the jury's refusal to find entrapment under the charge submitted to it by the trial court should be overturned and the views of Justices Roberts and Frankfurter, in *Sorrells* and *Sherman,* respectively, which make the essential element of the defense turn on the type and degree of governmental conduct, be adopted as the law. We decline to overrule these cases. [Since] the defense is not of a constitutional dimension, Congress may address itself to the question and adopt any substantive definition of the defense that it may find desirable.

Critics of the rule laid down in *Sorrells* and *Sherman* have suggested that its basis in the implied intent of Congress is largely fictitious, and have pointed to what they conceive to be the anomalous difference between the treatment of a defendant who is solicited by a private individual and one who is entrapped by a government agent. Questions have been likewise raised as to whether "predisposition" can be factually established with the requisite degree of certainty. [Such arguments] have been twice previously made to this Court, and twice rejected by it, first in *Sorrells* and then in *Sherman.*

We believe that at least equally cogent criticism has been made of the concurring views in these cases. Commenting in *Sherman* on Mr. Justice Roberts' position in *Sorrells* that "although the defendant could claim that the Government had induced him to commit the crime, the Government could not reply by showing that the defendant's criminal conduct was due to his own readiness and not to the persuasion of government agents," Mr. Chief Justice Warren quoted the observation of Judge Learned Hand in an earlier stage of that proceeding:

> " 'Indeed, it would seem probable that, if there were no reply [to the claim of inducement], it would be impossible ever to secure convictions of any offences which consist of transactions that are carried on in secret.' "

Nor does it seem particularly desirable for the law to grant complete immunity from prosecution to one who himself planned to commit a crime, and then committed it, simply because government undercover agents subjected him to inducements which might have seduced a hypothetical individual who was not so predisposed.

[Several lower federal court decisions] have undoubtedly gone beyond this Court's opinions in *Sorrells* and *Sherman* in order to bar prosecutions because of what they thought to be, for want of a better term, "overzealous law enforcement." But the defense of entrapment enunciated in those opinions was not intended to give the federal judiciary a "chancellor's foot" veto over law enforcement practices of which it did not approve. The execution of the federal laws under our Constitution is confided primarily to the Executive Branch of the Government, subject to applicable constitutional and statutory limitations and to judicially fashioned rules to enforce those limitations. We think that the decision of the Court of Appeals in this case quite unnecessarily introduces an unmanageably subjective standard which is contrary to the holdings of this Court in *Sorrells* and *Sherman.*

[In light of *Sorrells* and *Sherman,* respondent's concession] that the jury finding as to predisposition was supported by the evidence [is], therefore, fatal to his claim of entrapment. He was an active participant in an illegal drug manufacturing enterprise which began before the Government agent appeared on the scene, and continued after the Government agent had left the scene. He was, in the words of *Sherman,* not an "unwary innocent" but an "unwary criminal." * * *

Reversed.

Justice STEWART, with whom Justice BRENNAN and Justice MARSHALL join, dissenting.

[In] *Sorrells* and *Sherman* the Court took what might be called a "subjective" approach to the defense of entrapment. [This] approach focuses on the conduct and propensities of the particular defendant in each individual case: if he is "otherwise innocent," he may avail himself of the defense; but if he had the "predisposition" to commit the crime, or if the "criminal design" originated with him, then—regardless of the nature and extent of the Government's participation—there has been no entrapment. And, in the absence of a conclusive showing one way or the other, the question of the defendant's "predisposition" to the crime is a question of fact for the jury. The Court today adheres to this approach.

The concurring opinion of Justice Roberts, joined by Justices Brandeis and Stone, in the *Sorrells* case, and that of Justice Frankfurter, joined by Justices Douglas, Harlan, and Brennan, in the *Sherman* case, took a different view of the entrapment defense. In their concept, the defense is [grounded] on the belief that "the methods employed on behalf of the Government to bring about conviction cannot be countenanced." Thus, the focus of this approach is [on] "whether the police conduct revealed in the particular case falls below standards, to which common feelings respond, for the proper use of governmental power." Phrased another way, the question is whether—regardless of the predisposition to crime of the particular defendant involved—the governmental agents have acted in such a way as is likely to instigate or create a criminal offense. Under this approach, the determination of the lawfulness of the Government's conduct must be made—as it is on all questions involving the legality of law enforcement methods—by the trial judge, not the jury.

In my view, this objective approach to entrapment [is] the only one truly consistent with the underlying rationale of the defense.[1] * * * I find it impossible to believe that the purpose of the defense is to effectuate some unexpressed congressional intent to exclude from its criminal statutes persons who committed a prohibited act, but would not have done so except for the Government's inducements.

[Furthermore,] to say that such a defendant is "otherwise innocent" or not "predisposed" to commit the crime is misleading, at best. The very fact that he has committed an [illegal act] demonstrates conclusively that he is not innocent of the offense. He may not have originated the precise plan or the precise details, but he was "predisposed" in the sense that he has proved to be quite capable of committing the crime. That he was induced, provoked, or tempted to do so by government agents does not make him any more innocent or any less predisposed than he would be if he had been induced, provoked, or tempted by a private person—which, of course, would not entitle him to cry "entrapment." Since the only difference between these situations is the identity of the tempter, it follows that the significant focus must be on the conduct of the government agents, and not on the predisposition of the defendant.

[Moreover,] a test that makes the entrapment defense depend on whether the defendant had the requisite predisposition permits the introduction into evidence

1. Both the Proposed New Federal Criminal Code (1971), Final Report of the National Commission on Reform of Federal Criminal Laws § 702, and the American Law Institute's Model Penal Code § 2.13 (Proposed Official Draft, 1962), adopt this objective approach.

of all kinds of hearsay, suspicion, and rumor—all of which would be inadmissible in any other context—in order to prove the defendant's predisposition. It allows the prosecution, in offering such proof, to rely on the defendant's bad reputation or past criminal activities, including even rumored activities of which the prosecution may have insufficient evidence to obtain an indictment, and to present the agent's suspicions as to why they chose to tempt this defendant. This sort of evidence is not only unreliable, [but] is also highly prejudicial, especially if the matter is submitted to the jury, for, despite instructions to the contrary, the jury may well consider such evidence as probative not simply of the defendant's predisposition, but of his guilt of the offense with which he stands charged.

More fundamentally, focusing on the defendant's innocence or predisposition has the direct effect of making what is permissible or impermissible police conduct depend upon the past record and propensities of the particular defendant involved. Stated another way, this subjective test means that the Government is permitted to entrap a person with a criminal record or bad reputation, and then to prosecute him for the manufactured crime, confident that his record or reputation itself will be enough to show that he was predisposed to commit the offense anyway.

* * * [G]overnment agents may engage in conduct that is likely, when objectively considered, to afford a person ready and willing to commit the crime an opportunity to do so. But when the agents' involvement in criminal activities goes beyond the mere offering of such an opportunity, and when their conduct is of a kind that could induce or instigate the commission of a crime by one not ready and willing to commit it, then—regardless of the character or propensities of the particular person induced—I think entrapment has occurred. For in that situation, the Government has engaged in the impermissible manufacturing of crime, and the federal courts should bar the prosecution in order to preserve the institutional integrity of the system of federal criminal justice.

[What] the agent did here was to meet with a group of suspected producers of methamphetamine, including the respondent; to request the drug; to offer to supply the chemical phenyl–2–propanone in exchange for one-half of the methamphetamine to be manufactured therewith; and, when that offer was accepted, to provide the needed chemical ingredient, and to purchase some of the drug from the respondent. [Although] the Court of Appeals found that the phenyl–2–propanone could not have been obtained without the agent's intervention * * * the Court today rejects this finding as contradicted by the facts revealed at trial. The record, as the Court states, discloses that one of the respondent's accomplices, though not the respondent himself, had obtained phenyl–2–propanone from independent sources both before and after receiving the agent's supply, and had used it in the production of methamphetamine. This demonstrates, it is said, that the chemical was obtainable other than through the government agent; and hence the agent's furnishing it for the production of the methamphetamine involved in this prosecution did no more than afford an opportunity for its production to one ready and willing to produce it. Thus, the argument seems to be, there was no entrapment here, any more than there would have been if the agent had furnished common table salt, had that been necessary to the drug's production.

It cannot be doubted that if phenyl–2–propanone had been wholly unobtainable from other sources, the agent's undercover offer to supply it to the respondent in return for part of the illicit methamphetamine produced therewith—an offer initiated and carried out by the agent for the purpose of prosecuting the respondent for producing methamphetamine—would be precisely the type of governmental conduct that constitutes entrapment under any definition. For the agent's conduct in that situation would make possible the commission of an otherwise totally impossible crime, and, I should suppose, would thus be a textbook example of instigating the commission of a criminal offense in order to prosecute someone for committing it.[a]

[The] chemical ingredient was available only to licensed persons, and the Government itself had requested suppliers not to sell that ingredient even to people with a license. Yet the Government agent readily offered, and supplied, that ingredient to an unlicensed person and asked him to make a certain illegal drug with it. The Government then prosecuted that person for making the drug produced *with the very ingredient* which its agent had so helpfully supplied. This strikes me as the very pattern of conduct that should be held to constitute entrapment as a matter of law. * * *[b]

COMMENTARY ON THE "SUBJECTIVE" AND "OBJECTIVE" TESTS

1. ***Support for the "hypothetical person" or "objective" test.*** As pointed out in CRIMPROC § 5.2(b), "the objective test is favored by most commentators, and is reflected in the formulation of the entrapment defense appearing in the *Model Penal Code* § 2.13. Its first authoritative acceptance came by judicial decision in *Grossman v. State,* 457 P.2d 226 (Alaska 1969), and now a dozen other states have adopted it either by statute or case law. See Michael Piccaretta & Jefferson Keenan, *Entrapment Targets and Tactics: Jacobson v. United States,* 29 Crim.L.Bull. 241, 252 (1993).

See, e.g., *People v. Barraza,* 591 P.2d 947 (Cal.1979), per Mosk, J., holding that the proper test of entrapment in California is: "was the [police conduct] likely to induce a normally law-abiding person to commit the offense?" Observed the court:

"[W]e presume that [a normally law-abiding] person would resist the temptation to commit a crime presented by the simple opportunity to act unlawfully. [But] it is impermissible for the police or their agents to pressure the suspect by overbearing conduct such as badgering, cajoling, importuning, or other affirmative acts likely to induce a normally law-abiding person to commit the crime."

"[G]uidance will generally be found in the application of one or both of two principles. First, if the [police conduct] would generate in a normally law-abiding person a motive for the crime other than ordinary criminal intent, entrapment will be established. An example of such conduct would be an appeal by the police that would induce such a person to commit the act because of friendship or sympathy, instead of a desire for personal gain or other typical criminal purpose. Second, affirmative police conduct that would make commission of the crime unusually attractive to a normally law-abiding person will likewise constitute entrapment. Such conduct would include, for example, a guarantee that the act is not illegal or the offense will go undetected, an offer of exorbitant consideration, or any similar enticement."[a]

2. ***Doubts about the efficacy of the "objective" test.*** Roger Park, *The Entrapment Controversy,* 60 Minn.L.Rev. 163, 270–71 (1976), voices doubts that the "hypothetical person" test could control the conduct of police and informers:

a. But see *Hampton v. United States,* p. ___.

b. In a separate dissent, Justice Douglas, joined by Brennan, J., maintained that "[f]ederal agents play a debased role when they become the instigators of the crime, or partners in its commission, or the creative brain behind the illegal scheme. That is what the federal agent did here when he furnished the accused with one of the chemical ingredients needed to manufacture the unlawful drug."

a. Under this test, emphasized the court, "the character of the suspect, his predisposition to commit the offense, and his subjective intent are irrelevant." On this point, see Note 3 infra.

"Standardized procedures cannot govern the sundry and unpredictable events that occur during encounters between target and tempter. Moreover, even if such procedures could be formulated and somehow taught to the army of addicts and criminals used by police to set up controlled offenses, it is doubtful that they would be followed—particularly since the rules would inevitably become known to targets as well as police agents.

"* * * Because many targets are professional criminals, judges will be reluctant to rule that entrapment has occurred simply because an agent found it necessary to appeal to friendship, make multiple requests, or offer a substantial profit. Yet approval of such conduct would lead to unfair results in cases where the target was law-abiding but ductile. For example, conviction of someone who has been solicited by a friend may be fair enough in the general run of cases, but unfair if the target was a nondisposed person who would not have committed the type of crime charged but for a request from that particular friend.

"The danger of acquitting wolves and convicting lambs would be ameliorated if courts following the hypothetical-person test allow predisposition evidence to be introduced for its bearing on the propriety of the agent's inducement. The degree of persistence permitted would then depend upon whether the agent had sound reasons to believe that his target was already engaged in criminal enterprise. However, this approach would create even greater uncertainty about the boundaries of permissible inducement and further limit the defense's utility as a guide to police conduct.

"[The federal defense] attempts to distinguish between persons who are blameworthy and persons who are not. In the absence of extraordinary circumstances, that should be the goal of our law of crimes."

3. ***Should the "subjective" test be retained, but stripped of its indiscriminate attitude toward "predisposition" evidence?*** The "subjective" test, protested Stewart, J., dissenting in *United States v. Russell,* permits the use of otherwise inadmissible "hearsay, suspicion and rumor" to prove defendant's predisposition.[b] The defendant, in effect, is "put on trial for his past offenses and character." *Grossman v. State,* 457 P.2d 226, 229 (Alaska 1969) (adopting the objective test).

But, maintains Park, supra, at 272, "the indiscriminate attitude toward predisposition evidence"—"the greatest fault" of the subjective test—"is by no means a necessary feature of the subjective test. If the accused was already engaged in a course of criminal conduct, the prosecution should be able to develop an arsenal of reliable predisposition evidence. If it cannot, the danger of wrongful acquittal is outweighed by the danger of convicting a person whose only real vice is a bad reputation. Reputation and other hearsay evidence should not become admissible merely because the accused has raised the defense of entrapment. If construed to exclude such testimony, the subjective defense should present more reliable evidence to the fact-finder than the hypothetical-person defense. The latter focuses upon the nature of the inducement offered; consequently, trials are likely to be reduced to a swearing match between unreliable witnesses about words said in private."

4. ***Is the distinction between the objective and subjective approaches overstated?*** Consider Louis Michael Seidman, *The Supreme Court, Entrapment, and Our Criminal Justice Dilemma,* 1981 Sup.Ct.Rev. 111, 118–20:

b. Not only prior convictions, but prior arrests, acts of prior misconduct, "reputation testimony" and "suspicious conduct" have been admitted on this issue. See CRIMPROC, § 5.2(c).

"The [subjective test] is premised on the notion that it is possible to isolate the class of 'unwary criminals' who are 'ready and willing' to engage in crime apart from the inducements offered by the government. But whether a person is 'ready and willing' to break the law depends on what the person expects to get in return—that is, on the level of inducement. Like the rest of us, criminals do not generally work for free. Their willingness to take the risks of crime varies with the incentive which is provided. To be sure, the less cynical among us may believe that there is still a class of people who 'have no price.' [But] even if one concedes that such people can be found somewhere, they are, by definition, not among the ranks of entrapped defendants, since such defendants must have succumbed to some inducement in order to be entrapped.

"Consequently, so long as one equates 'predisposition' with a readiness to commit crime, no definition of 'predisposition' can be complete without an articulation of the level of inducement to which a 'predisposed' defendant would respond. Furthermore, the 'predisposed' cannot be distinguished from the 'nondisposed' without focusing on the propriety of the government's conduct—the very factor that the subjective approach professes to ignore. This is true because a defendant who responds favorably to a 'proper' inducement has thereby conclusively demonstrated that he is disposed to crime when such an inducement is offered.[c] It would seem, then, that so long as government agents restrict themselves to 'proper' inducements, they run no risk of violating the entrapment rules. The entrapment test is 'subjective' only in the sense that even if the government offers an 'excessive' inducement, the defendant may nonetheless be convicted under such a test if he would have responded favorably to a proper one."[d]

5. ***Was the distinction between the subjective and objective tests smudged in the DeLorean case?*** Because John DeLorean was prosecuted for drug violations in federal court, the judge instructed the jury to consider the entrapment claim in accordance with the subjective test. However, points out Maura Whelan, *Lead Us Not Into (Unwarranted) Temptation: A Proposal to Replace the Entrapment Defense with a Reasonable Suspicion Requirement,* 133 U.Pa.L.Rev. 1193, 1199–1200 (1985), "it seems from the jurors' remarks" after the acquittal that "they followed the objective approach instead. Those jurors who discussed the entrapment issue with reporters emphasized the impropriety of the operation, not DeLorean's character. One juror expressed the view that the FBI went after DeLorean only because he was an influential person. There were several indications that the agents viewed DeLorean as a highly desirable arrest. [It] was undoubtedly the spirit of the hunt that led [one agent] to report to FBI headquarters that DeLorean was 'involved in large scale narcotics transactions, in addition to the laundering [of] large amounts of illegally received income,' although he knew it wasn't true. His explanation for this message? 'I thought it sounded pretty good.' "[e]

c. In the Abscam cases, observes Bennett Gershman, *Abscam, the Judiciary, and the Ethics of Entrapment,* 91 Yale L.J. 1565, 1581 (1982), "the jury was allowed to infer predisposition simply from the defendant's affirmative response to the government's inducements. For instance, that [two defendants] readily accepted cash payments was found to constitute sufficient evidence that they had a *preexisting* intention to take a bribe. In other words, the defendant is said to be predisposed because he committed the act, and then is held responsible for the act because he was predisposed. The pernicious circularity of this approach is obvious."

d. Reconsider the extract from the Allen–Luttrell–Kreeger article at p. 505.

e. According to newspaper accounts of the DeLorean trial, summarized in Whelan, supra, at 1197–99, by 1980 DeLorean desperately needed ten million dollars to save his automobile company. About this time, he was invited to participate in a major cocaine transaction by FBI informant James Hoffman, a former neighbor of DeLorean and an admitted perjurer and occasional drug dealer. The FBI had no reason to believe that DeLorean was involved in drugs in any way until Hoffman came forward with his allegation that DeLorean wanted to make money quickly in a big narcotics deal

OTHER ISSUES RAISED BY THE ENTRAPMENT DEFENSE[a]

1. ***Contingent fee arrangements.*** In *Williamson v. United States,* 311 F.2d 441 (5th Cir.1962), the informer had been promised $200 and $100, respectively, for producing legally admissible evidence that two specified persons were engaged in illicit liquor dealings. Using its supervisory powers over the administration of federal criminal justice,[b] the court held that absent a special justification for its use in a particular case, a conviction is invalid if it rests on evidence of informants hired on such a basis. *Williamson* "could have been construed to limit the widespread practice of offering leniency to arrested persons who agree to incriminate others by making purchases of contraband," but the case "has had virtually no impact. Courts faced with a defense based on it have almost invariably found a way to distinguish it." Park, supra, at 175.

Williamson was, in effect, disapproved in *United States v. Grimes,* 438 F.2d 391 (6th Cir.1971), reasoning that a contingent fee informer is "no more likely to [lie and manufacture crimes] than witnesses acting for other, more common reasons," such as a codefendant hoping for leniency or an informant who feels that his future employment may depend upon success on this occasion. But are not contingent fee informers likely to be more desperate then informers generally? Are they not likely to have a stronger incentive for overreaching and falsification? See CRIMPROC, § 5.4(a).

2. ***"Inconsistent" defenses.*** The traditional view had been that the defense of entrapment is not available to one who denies commission of the criminal act with which he is charged, for the reason that the denial is inconsistent with the assertion of such a defense. But *Mathews v. United States,* 485 U.S. 58 (1988) holds that "even if the defendant denies one or more elements of the crime, he is entitled to an entrapment instruction whenever there is sufficient evidence from which a reasonable jury could find entrapment."

3. ***Triable by court or jury.*** Recall that *Sorrells* rejected, and *Sherman* declined to reconsider, the argument that the issue of entrapment should be tried separately to the court without a jury. Although most commentators favor a judicial determination of the issue, the defense has traditionally been regarded as a matter for the jury, except in those unusual cases where entrapment is established as a matter of law. It has been argued, in support of this position, that a jury has special, or at least traditional, competence to judge matters of credibility and motivation and to assess the subjective response to the stimulus of police

and hoped that Hoffman could arrange something.

According to the original scenario, DeLorean would invest two million dollars toward the purchase of the cocaine and make as much as sixty million dollars. When DeLorean reported that he would have to withdraw from the operation because of his inability to raise the money, either Hoffman or an FBI agent proposed an alternative: simply put up two million dollars of collateral, which included various property. DeLorean also signed over the entire voting stock of his company to the federal agents who were posing as drug dealers. An FBI agent recommended that DeLorean "launder" any profits from the operation through one of his companies.

The jury's acquittal of DeLorean was based both on disapproval of the FBI's methods and the conclusion that the government had failed to prove that DeLorean had committed a crime.

a. Because three issues—(1) when a private person should be considered a "government agent" for purposes of the entrapment defense; (2) whether a government agent should be allowed to solicit an offense absent "probable cause" or at least "reasonable suspicion" that his target is engaged in criminal activity; and (3) whether judicial authorization should be required for an undercover operation—received prominent attention as a result of the Abscam cases, treatment of these issues is postponed until the Notes and Questions following *United States v. Kelly*, p. 520.

b. See generally pp. 44–48.

encouragement. Moreover, if the matter is placed in the hands of the jury, there is an opportunity for "jury nullification" if the police conduct evokes "moral revulsion." See generally CRIMPROC § 5.3(b).

On the other hand, it has been said that where the subjective test prevails "the most urgent considerations" support judicial determination of the issue—to avoid the great impact on the jury of prior convictions, prior arrests and "reputation testimony"—but that in those jurisdictions that follow the objective approach "the case for separate trial to the court is more evenly balanced." See Comment to *Model Penal Code* § 2.10(2) (Tent. Draft No. 9, 1959). It has been argued, however, that here, too, the case for having the matter decided by the court is a strong one: It is the function of the court to preserve its own purity; to the extent that the objective approach is based on a deterrence-of-police rationale, this is the function of the court, just as it is when the court rules on suppression motions; and, as Frankfurter, J., maintained in *Sherman,* only the court can provide government agents with the necessary guidance. See CRIMPROC, supra.

4. ***Burden of proof.*** In those jurisdictions following the subjective approach, it is generally agreed that the defendant must establish the fact of inducement by a government agent. Once the defendant satisfies this threshold requirement (and it is unclear whether he need only produce "some evidence" of inducement or sustain a burden of persuasion by a preponderance of the evidence), the burden is then on the government to negate the defense by establishing the defendant's "predisposition" beyond a reasonable doubt. See CRIMPROC, § 5.3(d).

In states where the objective test prevails, entrapment is viewed as an "affirmative defense" rather than something that negates the existence of an element of the crime charged, and the entire burden of production and persuasion is on the defendant. The defendant must establish the defense by a preponderance of the evidence. The *Model Penal Code* § 2.13(2) also takes this position. For criticism of this approach, see Park, supra, at 265–67, suggesting that the real basis for placing the burden of persuasion on the defendant is that entrapment is a disfavored defense.

SECTION 2. MORE ON THE DUE PROCESS DEFENSE TO GOVERNMENT "OVERINVOLVEMENT" IN A CRIMINAL ENTERPRISE[a]

HAMPTON v. UNITED STATES, 425 U.S. 484 (1976), grew out of the following facts: Petitioner was convicted of distributing heroin in violation of federal law. The district court refused to give petitioner's requested instruction that if it were found, as he claimed, that the narcotics he sold to government agents (posing as narcotics buyers) had been supplied to him by a government informant[b] he must be acquitted as a matter of law regardless of his predisposi-

a. Although the claim that the government has unduly "dominated" or become impermissibly "overinvolved" in the criminal activity has often been viewed as a species of the objective test entrapment, it seems preferable to view it as the basis for a separate test for entrapment or as a due process defense independent of general entrapment theory.

b. According to petitioner's version of the events, the informant not only supplied the narcotics but was the first to propose the criminal enterprise. Petitioner alleged that when he stated that he was short of cash, the informant responded by proposing they sell drugs that he could get from a pharmacist friend. Evidently, petitioner did not deem this particular aspect of his version of the facts significant. Evidently, too, a majority of the Court considered it irrelevant so long as petitioner was "predisposed" to commit the offense and the governmental activity had not "implant[ed] in the mind of an *innocent* person the disposition to commit the alleged offense." (Emphasis added.) No member of the majority disputed distion to commit the offense charged. On appeal, petitioner conceded that he was "predisposed." A majority of the Court rejected petitioner's contention, but there was no opinion of the Court. Justice REHNQUIST, who announced the judgment of the Court in an opinion in which Burger, C.J., and White, J., joined, observed:

"In *Russell* [we] ruled out the possibility that the defense of entrapment could ever be based upon governmental misconduct in a case, such as this one, where the predisposition of the defendant to commit the crime was established. [Petitioner] correctly recognizes that his case does not qualify as one involving 'entrapment' at all, [but] relies on the language in *Russell* that 'we may some day be presented with a situation in which the conduct of law enforcement agents is so outrageous that due process principle would absolutely bar the government from invoking judicial processes to obtain a conviction.'

"[In] urging that this [is such a case], petitioner misapprehends the meaning of the quoted language in *Russell.* Admittedly petitioner's case is different from Russell's but the difference is one of degree, not of kind. In *Russell* the ingredient supplied by the government agent was a legal drug which the defendants demonstrably could have obtained from other sources besides the Government. Here the drug which the government informant allegedly supplied [was] both illegal and constituted the *corpus delicti* for the sale of which the petitioner was convicted. The Government obviously played a more significant role in enabling petitioner to sell contraband in this case than it did in *Russell.*

"But in each case the government agents were acting in concert with the defendant, and in each case either the jury found or the defendant conceded that he was predisposed to commit the crime for which he was convicted. The remedy of the criminal defendant with respect to the acts of government agents, which, far from being resisted, are encouraged by him, lies solely in the defense of entrapment. But, as noted, petitioner's conceded predisposition rendered this defense unavailable to him.

"To sustain petitioner's contention here would run directly contrary to our statement in *Russell* that the defense of entrapment is not intended 'to give the federal judiciary a "chancellor's foot" veto over law enforcement practices of which it did not approve. * * * ' " [The] limitations of the Due Process Clause of the Fifth Amendment come into play only when the Government activity in question violates some protected right of the defendant. [If] the police engage in illegal activity in concert with a defendant beyond the scope of their duties the remedy lies, not in freeing the equally culpable defendant, but in prosecuting the police under the applicable provisions of state or federal law. But the police conduct here no more deprived defendant of any right secured to him by the United States Constitution than did the police conduct in *Russell* deprive Russell of any rights."

Concurring Justice POWELL, joined by Blackmun, J., agreed that "this case is controlled completely by *Russell,*" but was "unwilling to join the plurality in concluding that, no matter what the circumstances, neither due process principles nor our supervisory power could support a bar to conviction in any case where the Government is able to prove disposition": "[Disposition of the claims in *Russell* and earlier cases] did not require the Court to consider whether overinvolvement of government agents in contraband offenses could ever reach such proportions as to bar conviction of a predisposed defendant as a matter of due process. Nor have

senting Justice Brennan's characterization of the case as one where "the two sales for which petitioner was convicted were allegedly instigated by Government agents." See also Judge Adams's dissent in *United States v. Twigg* (p. 405, fn. a infra) (describing *Hampton* as a case where the government "suggested the operation"). But see the majority opinion in *Twigg* and Note, 67 Geo.L.J. 1455, 1464 & fn. 73, 1466 (1979).

we had occasion yet to confront Government overinvolvement in areas outside the realm of contraband offenses."[c]

Justice BRENNAN, joined by Stewart and Marshall, JJ., dissented, urging that conviction be "barred as a matter of law where the subject of the criminal charge is the sale of contraband provided to the defendant by a Government agent."[d] The dissenters reiterated their support for the "objective" approach to entrapment, under which, they maintained, petitioner's claims "would plainly be held to constitute entrapment as a matter of law," but considered reversal compelled even "for those who follow the 'subjective' approach." Where the Government's agent "deliberately sets up the accused by supplying him with contraband and then bringing him to another agent as a potential purchaser," protested the dissent, "the Government's role has passed the point of toleration. The Government is doing nothing less than buying contraband from itself through an intermediary and jailing the intermediary."[e]

Notes and Questions

1. "The depth of our confusion concerning the proper limits on government power in this area," observes Louis Michael Seidman, *The Supreme Court, Entrapment, and Our Criminal Justice Dilemma,* 1981 Sup.Ct.Rev. 111, 116 n. 20, "is illustrated by comparing the intuitions of Justice Powell with those of the authors of the Model Penal Code. Justice Powell hints that his objective, due process test would be violated if the government induced beatings or armed robberies. [See fn. c to his concurring opinion in *Hampton.*] Yet the Model Penal Code [§ 2.13(3)] makes an entrapment defense unavailable in precisely those cases where the defendant causes or threatens bodily injury."

2. Leslie Abramson & Lisa Lindeman, *Entrapment and Due Process in the Federal Courts,* 8 Am.J.Crim.Law 139, 180–82 (1980), concludes, inter alia: "Many courts treat the constitutional due process defense as an illegitimate offspring of entrapment, and recognize the issue reluctantly when it is presented in the pleadings. It is then granted only cursory review. The better approach, therefore, is to plead the defense independently of the general entrapment defense, with police misconduct as the exclusive basis. In that case, the due process defense cannot later be dismissed by a finding of predisposition, because a defendant can prove police misconduct and overreaching without having to disprove his own predisposition. The trial court can then decide the due process question as a matter of law." [The] due process defense requires a stricter scrutiny of government conduct than the traditional entrapment defense. Possibly, as in *United States v. Twigg,*[a] lower courts will soon accept the need for a constitutional due

c. At this point Justice Powell quoted from Judge Friendly's view in *United States v. Archer,* 486 F.2d 670, 676 (2d Cir.1973), that "it would be unthinkable, for example, to permit government agents to instigate robberies and beatings merely to gather evidence to convict other members of a gang of hoodlums."

d. The dissent deemed it sufficient "for present purposes" to adopt this rule "under our supervisory power and leave to another day whether it ought to be made applicable to the States under the Due Process Clause." For a general discussion of the federal courts' supervisory power over criminal justice, see pp. 44–48.

e. Stevens, J., took no part in the consideration or decision of the case.

a. 588 F.2d 373 (3d Cir.1978). In *Twigg,* apparently the only post-*Hampton* federal court of appeals decision to invalidate a conviction on the basis of the due process defense, the informant contacted an old acquaintance, defendant Neville, and proposed that they set up a "speed" laboratory. Neville assumed responsibility for raising the capital and arranging for distribution of the product. The informant assumed responsibility for acquiring the necessary equipment, raw materials, and a production site. The DEA assisted the informant in carrying out his part of the operation by providing two and one-half gallons of the essential and hard to obtain ingredient, propanone; some glassware; and a rented farmhouse for the laboratory site. Defendant Twigg joined

process defense independent of the general entrapment theory. To protect the constitutional rights of an individual does not necessarily require application of a 'chancellor's foot.' "

3. ***Is the due process defense in entrapment cases so unruly and so subjective that it should no longer be considered?*** As a strong proponent of the due process defense in entrapment cases, Paul Marcus, recognizes, *The Due Process Defense in Entrapment Cases: The Journey Back,* 27 Am.Crim.L.Rev. 457, 458 (1990): "It will take a great deal to persuade courts that entrapment-like schemes violate due process. Some courts have announced that they have *never* overturned convictions on this basis."

See, e.g., *United States v. Simpson,* 813 F.2d 1462 (9th Cir.1987), holding that (1) the FBI's "manipulation" of a prostitute (Helen Miller), who was a heroin user and a fugitive from drug charges, into becoming an informant; (2) the fact that Ms. Miller continued to use heroin and engage in acts of prostitution during the investigation of defendant; (3) Ms. Miller's "use of sex" to deceive defendant into believing she was "an intimate friend" so that she could "lure him into selling heroin to undercover FBI agents"; and (4) the FBI's continued use of Ms. Miller as an informant even after learning of her sexual involvement with defendant was "not so shocking as to violate the due process clause." Although Simpson "may have suffered severe emotional trauma and felt stripped of his dignity upon learning that [Ms. Miller's] apparent affection for him was contrived," his treatment by her "falls short of the brutality and coercion underlying previous successful outrageous conduct challenges."

See also *United States v. Miller* 891 F.2d 1265 (7th Cir.1989), where the undercover agent had a contingent fee arrangement with the government, had been a cocaine addict both before and during her employment and had earlier

the operation, at the invitation of Neville. The laboratory operated for one week, producing about six pounds of speed. The informant alone had the expertise to manufacture the drug and thus was completely in charge of the laboratory.

Neville and Twigg were convicted of conspiracy to manufacture speed. On appeal, a 2–1 majority, per Rosenn, J., reversed. Distinguishing *Russell* as a case in which the defendant was an active participant before the government agent arrived on the scene, and *Hampton* as concerned with the sale of an illegal drug—"a much more fleeting and elusive crime to detect than the operation of an illicit drug laboratory"—the *Twigg* majority concluded that the government involvement was so "overreaching," "egregious" and "outrageous" as to bar prosecution as a matter of due process. The court emphasized (a) that the "illicit plan did not originate with the criminal defendants"; (b) that the informant's expertise was "an indispensable requisite to this criminal enterprise"; and (c) that Neville was "lawfully and peacefully minding his own affairs" until approached by the defendant.

As dissenting Judge Adams read the relevant Supreme Court cases, due process analysis "was not intended simply to reestablish the objective approach to entrapment under a new name." He dissented because he did not believe that "this situation presents the intolerable set of circumstances necessary to warrant resort to the due process clause." He thought the facts less persuasive for reversal than were those in *Hampton* because none of the chemicals, equipment or skill provided by the government "was itself contraband." The government, through its agent, did suggest the operation, "but that is the situation in many undercover operations, and was the case in *Hampton.*"

Twigg suggests that the oft-proposed but rarely applied "reasonable suspicion" requirement (see p. 525) "may on occasion emerge as an aspect of the due process limits upon encouragement activity. The point seems to be that overinvolvement by the government to the extent reflected in *Twigg* is permissible, if at all, only against a person who is 'reasonably suspected of criminal conduct or design.' " CRIMPROC § 5.4(c). See also Note, 67 Geo. L.J. 1455, 1461, 1467 (1979).

Another important principle recognized in *Twigg* is that "the practicalities of combatting" a certain type of criminal activity must be considered in determining whether "more extreme methods of investigation" are constitutionally permissible. But *Twigg* may have misapplied this principle. Consider Note, 67 Geo.L.J. at 1463: "[A] drug laboratory, which by nature is sophisticated and covert, arguably is *more* difficult to detect than the sale of drugs."

been sexually intimate with the defendant. But these factors "neither separately or combined" amounted to " 'truly outrageous' government conduct." Concurring Judge Easterbrook would have gone farther. He argued that there should not even be a due process defense in entrapment cases:

" 'Outrageousness' " as a defense * * * creates serious problems of consistency. [How] much is 'too much'? The nature of the question exposes it as (a) unanswerable, and (b) political. What, if anything, could separate stirring up of crime in unpalatable ways here [from] Operation Greylord [or] the 'creative' endeavors in Abscam? From any of the 'sting' operations? [Any] line we draw would be unprincipled and therefore not judicial in nature. More likely there would be no line; judges would vote their lower intestines. Such a meandering, personal approach is the antithesis of justice under law, and we ought not indulge it. Inability to describe in general terms just what makes tactics too outrageous to tolerate suggests that there is no definition?—and 'I know it when I see it' is not a rule of any kind, let alone a command of the Due Process Clause.

"The kinds of prosecution that trouble me most are not those like Operation Greylord or offers of sex in exchange for cocaine, but those that impose costs on the innocent. Take for example a sting in which the FBI sets up a fence and buys stolen goods. The money the government pumps into the business must lead people to steal things to sell to the FBI—with misery for the victims of the burglary and potential violence in the process. Stings have been upheld consistently, however * * *. Methods such as those used to ensnare [the defendant in this case] do not trouble me. Other judges are offended by immorality (such as sponsoring an informant's use of sexual favors as currency) or by acts that endanger informants (such as supplying them with drugs for personal use) but not by a traditional sting. This shows the subjective basis of the concern—all the more reason not to have such a doctrine in our law."[b]

But consider Marcus, supra, at 465: "[The due process defense in entrapment cases] is important because it creates outer limits on appropriate law enforcement techniques and because it clearly demonstrates to the legal and law enforcement communities, and to society at large, that courts are indeed willing to draw some lines that cannot be crossed even in pursuit of criminals. [As for Judge Easterbrook's argument that the inability of reasonable people to agree on the application of the defense indicates that it is not a rule of any kind,] it is not factually accurate. There will be fact situations where reasonable people could agree that the law enforcement behavior was utterly outrageous. Certainly, Judge Friendly's hypothetical problem of government agents beating some members of a gang in order to get to other members of a gang is just such a case."

UNITED STATES v. KELLY

707 F.2d 1460 (D.C.Cir.1983).

[The phase of the Abscam operation that resulted in the indictment of Kelly and other Congressmen was conceived by convicted confidence man Weinberg and approved by the FBI. It was to spread the word that wealthy Arabs were willing to bribe members of Congress to ensure that they would introduce private immigration legislation on the Arabs' behalf if and when necessary.

[Among those to whom the word was passed was codefendant Ciuzio, an acquaintance of Congressman Kelly. At a November, 1979 meeting, Ciuzio told Kelly that he had some Arab clients with immigration difficulties and asked Kelly

b. Some courts have followed Judge Easterbrook's lead in rejecting or greatly restricting the "outrageous governmental conduct" defense. See *United States v. Gaviria*, 116 F.3d 1498 (D.C.Cir.1997); *United States v. Tucker*, 28 F.3d 1420 (6th Cir.1994).

if he could help them. Kelly indicated that he would be glad to do so, particularly since Ciuzio indicated the Arabs might invest in his district. Ciuzio told Kelly that he—Ciuzio—would receive a large fee if Kelly helped the Arabs. Kelly replied that the fee would cause no difficulties. Ciuzio then told codefendant Weisz, who was a business associate of Rosenberg (who was helping Weinberg locate politicians willing to assist the latter's "Arab-employers"), that Kelly would be happy to help the Arabs. The word was passed via the Abscam "middlemen" to Weinberg that a "candidate" was available who would assist with the Arabs' immigration problems and that he wanted $250,000. Weinberg suggested that the Congressman be paid $25,000 down, with the balance paid when legislation was required.

[At a December 19 meeting among Ciuzio, Weinberg and FBI agent Amoroso (Weinberg's immediate supervisor), Ciuzio was told what assistance would be expected of the Congressman. Ciuzio indicated that the Congressman was Kelly and intimated that he and Kelly had had previous dealings of a similar nature. Ciuzio suggested that he had told Kelly of the offer and claimed that Kelly had left the arrangements to him. But Ciuzio opposed direct payment to Kelly and suggested that the money instead be escrowed through Weisz.

[A January 8, 1980 meeting was arranged between Kelly and the "Arabs' representatives" at the FBI's townhouse in Washington, D.C. Soon after his arrival, Ciuzio, in a private meeting with Weinberg and Amoroso, sought to dissuade them from attempting to bribe Kelly directly. It was ultimately agreed that Kelly would acknowledge that the money was in exchange for his agreement to assist the Arabs, but that Ciuzio would actually take the money from the meeting.

[Finally, later that evening, Congressman Kelly met with Amoroso alone. When Amoroso proposed a payoff, Kelly told him that he was interested in the investment in his district, that he didn't "know anything about" Amoroso's arrangement with Ciuzio and others—"I'm not involved with it"—but that Amoroso's arrangement with Ciuzio and others was "fine."

[After Amoroso received a phone call from an Assistant United States Attorney who was monitoring the meeting and who told Amoroso that Kelly was "being cute," Amoroso sought to clarify Kelly's position. Kelly maintained that he wanted the money given to Ciuzio. Amoroso indicated that all of the money was supposed to go to Kelly, that Ciuzio would be compensated separately, and that giving the money directly to Kelly would avoid witnesses, thus protecting Kelly. The Congressman then agreed that that was "the best way of doing it." Amoroso then gave Kelly $25,000 in packets of $100 bills and Kelly stuffed the money in the pockets of his suit.]

PER CURIAM: Judge MacKinnon files an opinion in Parts I, II, III(A), and IV of which Chief Judge Robinson concurs.[a] Judge Ginsburg files an opinion in which Chief Judge Robinson concurs. Thus Parts I, II, III(A) and IV of Judge MacKinnon's opinion together with Judge Ginsburg's opinion constitute the opinion of the court. * * *

MacKINNON, Circuit Judge. [On] January 8, 1980, Congressman Richard Kelly accepted $25,000 from an agent of the FBI who was posing as a representative of two wealthy Arabs as part of the FBI's elaborate Abscam investigation. In return, Kelly agreed to use his position in Congress to assist the Arabs to become permanent residents of the United States. Unbeknownst to Kelly, the FBI recorded the entire illegal transaction on video tape.

a. Part I, a detailed discussion of the facts, and Part II, a discussion of the district court opinion dismissing the indictment, are omitted.

On the basis of this and other evidence, Kelly and [Ciuzio and Weisz] were charged with [bribery and other federal offenses]. A jury found each defendant guilty on all counts. However, the district court granted Kelly's motion to dismiss the indictment, entering a judgment of acquittal in his favor, because it concluded that the FBI's actions in furtherance of Abscam were so outrageous that prosecution of Kelly was barred by principles of due process. * * *

III. Analysis

A. The Due Process Defense

"[Our task]" is to assess whether the FBI's conduct in Abscam reached a "demonstrable level of outrageousness" [Powell, J., concurring in *Hampton*], while keeping in mind the difficulties inherent in detecting corrupt public officials. Measured against this standard, the FBI's conduct did not violate due process.

B. Abscam

[S]tripped of [its] trappings of wealth, Abscam was no more than an "opportunity for the commission of crime by those willing to do so." *United States v. Myers,* 692 F.2d 823, 837 (2d Cir.1982). Amoroso and Weinberg let it be known that they would pay substantial sums of money to congressmen willing to promise to assist the wealthy Arabs with their immigration difficulties. Thereafter, the FBI operatives simply waited for the grapevine to work and to see who appeared to take bribes. No congressmen were targeted for investigation; rather, Abscam pursued all who were brought to the operation by the grapevine.[50] In essence, then, Abscam was *not* significantly different from an undercover drug or fencing operation offering to buy from all who appear at its door.[51] Instead of buying stolen goods or contraband drugs, Abscam bought corrupt official influence in Congress. Such government involvement in crime does not violate principles of due process.

We need not determine the exact limits on government involvement in crime imposed by the due process clause for it is clear that the FBI's involvement in Abscam was less than that government involvement found unobjectionable by the Supreme Court.[52]

50. However, not all officials brought to Abscam were offered bribes. The Abscam operatives recognized that they had no control over the representations made by intermediaries such as Ciuzio, Rosenberg, and Weisz. Accordingly, the FBI *always* discussed the asylum scenario with the officials prior to the offer of a bribe. That was certainly the case with Kelly; Amoroso carefully discussed the details of the asylum scenario with Kelly *before* any bribe money was paid. See discussion infra. In one instance, where this discussion revealed that the official was unaware of the corrupt nature of the proposal, the FBI terminated the meeting.

51. The district court concluded that Abscam was unlike ordinary, "passive" undercover operations because it used "recruiting agents" to spread the word that bribes were available. I disagree. I seriously doubt that the government would establish an undercover drug or fencing operation without spreading the word, through informants and criminal elements (labeled "recruiting agents" by the district court), that its services were available. The Abscam investigators did no more.

My colleagues term Abscam an extraordinary operation. It was extraordinary only in the positions of some of the individuals involved and in the intangible nature of the "commodity" purchased. Otherwise, it is strikingly similar to ordinary undercover operations. * * *

My colleagues also criticize the failure of the FBI to closely supervise the Abscam operation. To the extent that this criticism extends to the non-FBI middlemen, such as Ciuzio, Rosenberg and Weisz, involved in Abscam, their activities could hardly be "supervised" because they did not know Abscam was an undercover investigation. The FBI took considerable precautions to compensate for its inability to control the representations of the middlemen. See note 50 supra. * * *

52. For this reason, we need not decide the validity of the due process test formulated by the district court—whether the temptation offered is "one which the individual is likely to encounter in the ordinary course." It is sug-

[In *Russell* and *Hampton*] the government not only provided an *opportunity* to commit a crime, but also provided the *means* to commit that crime. Nevertheless, in each case the Supreme Court concluded that the government's conduct did not violate due process. Where, as in Abscam, the government simply provides the opportunity to commit a crime, prosecution of a defendant does not violate principles of due process. This conclusion is in accord with decisions of the Second and Third Circuits upholding Abscam convictions challenged on due process grounds. *United States v. Williams,* 705 F.2d 603 (2d Cir.1983); *Myers,* supra; *United States v. Alexandro,* 675 F.2d 34 (2d Cir.); *United States v. Jannotti,* 673 F.2d 578 (3d Cir.) (en banc).[53]

C. Specific Claims

1. Reasonable Suspicion[b]

Nor do any of the specifically challenged FBI actions in furtherance of Abscam reach that "demonstrable level of outrageousness" which would bar Kelly's prosecution. The district court stressed that Abscam's asylum scenario was not triggered by any suspicion of corruption in government. [But] prior to the January 8 meeting with Kelly, the Abscam operatives had evidence from which they could conclude that Kelly was, in fact, corrupt. [Thus,] the FBI had [the requisite reasonable suspicion] to justify pursuing the asylum scenario and Kelly, if such suspicion was necessary.[58] * * *

2. Utilization of Weinberg

[The] argument that the FBI violated due process by utilizing the services of an admitted confidence man, Melvin Weinberg, in Abscam should likewise be rejected. Successful creation of an "elaborate hoax" such as Abscam may well *require* employment of "experts" such as Weinberg to give the operation an aura of "credibility" and "contacts" with criminal elements. The employment of a convicted confidence man in Abscam is analogous to the entirely proper employment of a convicted seller of drugs to purchase drugs from a suspected distributor. * * *

4. Multiple Bribe Offers

Finally, Kelly contends that the FBI operatives violated due process when they persisted in offering a bribe after what he characterizes as his initial rejection. *Kelly asserts that he rejected the bribe at his meeting with Ciuzio on December 23, that Ciuzio informed Amoroso and Weinberg of that fact at the townhouse on January 8, and that he rejected the bribe several times in his meeting with Amoroso.* Kelly argues, and the district court agreed, that under these circumstances Amoroso's several bribe offers to Kelly were outrageous and violated due process. I cannot agree.

The evidence in this case clearly demonstrates that at no time did Kelly reject Abscam's corrupt immigration proposal. On both December 23 and January 8, Kelly agreed to assure the wealthy Arabs that he would help them with their immigration problems as a favor to Ciuzio, despite the fact that Kelly knew that in

gested, however, that criminal conduct being as highly varied as it is that such test is unduly speculative.

53. The Third Circuit's decision in *Jannotti* is particularly significant because it held that *Twigg,* the only post-*Hampton* case to uphold a due process challenge to prosecution because of excessive government involvement, did not control its consideration of Abscam. Thus Kelly's reliance on *Twigg* is misplaced.

b. See Notes 1–3 following this case.

58. Although we need not decide the question, both the Second and Third Circuits have rejected the argument that the government must have reasonable suspicion of wrongdoing before proceeding with an undercover operation such as Abscam.

return the Arabs would pay substantial sums to Ciuzio [and others]. It is also clear that Kelly understood that part of the arrangement was that the Arabs would make substantial investments in his district. Such agreements, which would benefit Kelly indirectly, constitute violations of the bribery statute. Furthermore, the discussions between Ciuzio, Kelly, and the Abscam operatives at the townhouse of January 8 focused on the *manner* in which the bribe would be paid, not on whether it would be paid. Ciuzio told Weinberg not to bribe Kelly directly, but agreed that he would take the money for Kelly. After agreeing that Amoroso was going to give him some money at the meeting, Kelly asked Amoroso to pay the bribe to Ciuzio—to "deal with [Ciuzio] about it." In my view, Congressman Kelly "did not reject a bribe, he [initially] rejected its payment under circumstances he feared would be incriminating." *Myers.*

I likewise reject Kelly's characterization of his conversation with Amoroso on January 8 as a *series* of bribe offers. Although the terms of the corrupt Abscam proposal were mentioned several times during that conversation, Amoroso's discussion reflects the evasive and circumspect negotiation to be expected of a person seeking to corrupt a public official. In my view, Amoroso's conversation with Kelly on January 8 can be fairly characterized only as a *single offer* of a corrupt proposal to Kelly. For these reasons I reject Kelly's contention that he initially rejected a bribe, that the Abscam agents persisted in offering him a bribe, and that they thus violated due process.

IV. Conclusion

[The] Supreme Court has made it clear that "a successful due process defense must be predicated on *intolerable government conduct* which goes beyond that necessary to sustain an entrapment defense." *Jannotti* (emphasis added). Considering the genuine need to detect corrupt public officials, as well as the difficulties inherent in doing so, we conclude that the FBI's conduct in furtherance of its Abscam operation, insofar as it involved Kelly, simply did not reach intolerable levels. * * *

RUTH BADER GINSBURG, Circuit Judge: ["Abscam"] was an extraordinary operation. The investigation was steered in large part by a convicted swindler; it relied upon con men to identify and attract targets, to whom legitimate as well as illegitimate inducements were offered; it proceeded without close supervision by responsible officials.[1]

[The] District Court stated and attempted to apply an objective test to determine when government investigation exceeds tolerable limits: Was the crime-inducing conduct in which the government engaged, the temptation presented to the target, modeled on reality? This test, the District Court indicated, should apply when the government had no knowledge of prior wrongdoing by the target and no reason to believe the target was about to commit a crime; it would serve as a check against government creation (rather than apprehension) of criminals by offers or importuning that would never occur in the real world.

1. * * * We do not share Judge MacKinnon's view that, apart from "trappings of wealth," Abscam "was *not* significantly different from" run-of-the-mill "passive" undercover operations. As the District Court's opinion sets out in painstaking detail, the Abscam actors did a good deal more than simply "spread the word." Nor can we agree with Judge MacKinnon that the FBI "had ample suspicion of corruption to justify pursuing * * * Kelly." That suspicion, as Judge MacKinnon recites, was based on Ciuzio's report to Amoroso and Weinberg that "Kelly was, in fact, corrupt." But as the District Court observed:

> "Ciuzio went to great lengths to make it appear that he had virtual control over the Congressman, indicating at the time that Kelly was dishonest and was already taking money and had various other weaknesses. He indicated that he had known and cultivated Kelly for about 2 1/2 years. None of this was true. No attempt was made to verify it; and there is no indication that Weinberg and Amoroso believed it."

The real-world test, as applied by the District Court, is speculative. The District Judge assumed that a person who offers a bribe would retreat upon encountering an initial rejection and would not "have the audacity" to press on "for fear of being reported." But the first overture renders the party offering the bribe vulnerable to prosecution. "In for a calf," such a person might press on if he perceives any chance of ultimate success.[9] Nonetheless, were the slate clean, we might be attracted to an approach similar to the District Court's, and would perhaps ask whether, in real-world circumstances, the person snared would ever encounter bait as alluring as the offer the government tendered.

However, our slate contains references that lower courts are not positioned to erase. We may not alter the contours of the entrapment defense under a due process cloak,[11] and we lack authority, where no *specific* constitutional right of the defendant has been violated, to dismiss indictments as an exercise of supervisory power over the conduct of federal law enforcement agents. *See United States v. Payner* [p. 46]. Precedent dictates that we refrain from applying the general due process constraint to bar a conviction except in the rare instance of "[p]olice overinvolvement in crime" that reaches "a demonstrable level of outrageousness." *Hampton* (Powell, J., concurring) * * *; *Russell.* The requisite level of outrageousness, the Supreme Court has indicated, is not established [unless there is] "coercion, violence or brutality to the person."[c]

The importuning of Congressman Kelly and the offers made to him, extraordinary and in excess of real-world opportunities as they appear to have been, did not involve the infliction of pain or physical or psychological coercion. We are therefore constrained to reverse, although we share the District Court's grave concern that the Abscam drama, both in its general tenor, and in "the [particular] manner in which Kelly was handled," unfolded as "an unwholesome spectacle."

Notes and Questions

1. ***The "reasonable suspicion" requirement.*** A number of commentators have maintained that the government should not be permitted to solicit an offense absent "probable cause" or at least "reasonable suspicion" that the target is engaged in criminal activity, but current lower federal court authority "overwhelmingly holds that no 'reasonable cause' requirement exits." Note, 67 Geo.L.J. 1455, 1467 (1979). Moreover, "*Russell* seems to have sapped [this theory] of any remaining vitality by indicating that the entrapment defense is intended to protect nondisposed defendants rather than to control police conduct." Roger Park, *The Entrapment Controversy,* 60 Minn.L.Rev. 163, 197 (1976).[a]

Operation Abscam, however, has prompted renewed interest in this issue, for there a convicted swindler and other "middlemen," themselves under investigation, decided which politicians would be offered bribes. Congressman Don Edwards, a former FBI agent, voiced concern about "free-floating surveyors, middlemen, who work with the FBI and are the ones who finger people," and his

9. As the government points out, parties to real-world transactions could readily adjust to a one-refusal rule: the bribe taker would always resist the first overture.

11. See *Twigg* (Adams, J., dissenting).

c. See Note 3, p. ___.

a. It should be noted, however, that in *United States v. Luttrell,* 889 F.2d 806 (9th Cir.1989), a panel opinion by Judge Dorothy Nelson of the Ninth Circuit took the position that government agents violate due process when, lacking "reasoned grounds" for believing their targets are involved in crime, they approach them and provide them with a specific opportunity to engage in criminal conduct. But the Ninth Circuit, sitting en banc, vacated the portion of the panel opinion discussing a "reasoned grounds" or "reasonable suspicion" requirement, noting that a number of other circuits had explicitly rejected such a requirement. See 923 F.2d 764 (9th Cir.1991).

colleague, Representative John Seiberling, balked at "the idea of giving some people of dubious ethical standards free rein to entice anyone they can entice to commit a crime." See N.Y. Times, Feb. 17, 1980, pp. 1, 20. Indeed, Professor Paul Chevigny maintains that "Abscam shows [that the] central evil of entrapment is discriminatory law enforcement, whether the police zero in on a 'politician' or a 'drug dealer.' " *A Rejoinder,* The Nation, Feb. 23, 1980, p. 205[b]. Consider, too, Bennett Gershman, *Abscam, the Judiciary, and the Ethics of Entrapment,* 91 Yale L.J. 1565, 1584–85 (1982), who emphasizes that, although Operation Abscam intruded on people's privacy and autonomy to a much greater degree than the typical search and seizure, the operation was not restricted by procedural safeguards such as the requirement of a warrant: "Government agents secretly monitored the Abscam defendants for many months, recorded their intimate conversations and surreptitiously videotaped meetings they attended. No judge authorized such procedures; indeed it is unlikely that any judge would have authorized this type of surveillance absent prior suspicion."

Professor Gershman proposes a federal entrapment statute that, inter alia, requires government agents to offer inducements "only to individuals currently engaged in, or reasonably suspected of engaging in, criminal activity." Id. at 1588. Such a requirement would allow courts "to dispense with the predisposition inquiry and to use instead the concept of 'reasonable suspicion' to test whether an individual is 'nondisposed.' "Id.

2. ***Are official corruption investigations different?*** Katherine Goldwasser, *After Abscam: An Examination of Congressional Proposals to Limit Targeting Discretion in Federal Undercover Investigations,* 36 Emory L.J. 75, 124–25 (1987); balks at imposing a probable cause or reasonable suspicion requirement for undercover targeting: "[D]eterrence is not the only societal benefit to be derived from targeting [public officials] without a factual basis. Such targeting—integrity testing—usually provides no other societal benefit because the integrity of most potential undercover targets is not particularly important to society. But integrity testing of public officials is different. Public officials routinely are confronted with tests of their corruptibility because of the official power they wield. Those who 'fail' cause considerable harm to society. In short, [the] testing of public officials does serve significant societal ends. [Such testing] without a factual basis would provide a strong deterrent against corruption, but would pose little risk to the personal privacy of public officials and would generate no generalized atmosphere of suspicion and mistrust throughout society."

3. ***When is a private person a "government agent" for entrapment purposes? The use of "unwitting agents."*** Defending Operation Abscam, then Assistant Attorney General Phillip Heymann emphasized: "No one associated with the United States ever picked any politician for the investigation. The middlemen did all that." N.Y. Times, Mar. 5, 1980 p. 18. But this raises another problem. Many of the people involved in Abscam were "unsuspecting middlemen," i.e., private persons who were unaware that they were working with, or for, government agents. But because entrapment is ultimately concerned with government conduct, it offers no defense to those who succumb to the inducements of private individuals acting alone. For entrapment purposes, should "unsuspecting middlemen," such as those utilized in Abscam, be regarded as agents of the government, albeit "unwitting agents"?

When government agents have persuaded a "middleman" to induce *a particular target selected by the agents* to commit a crime, the courts generally extend the entrapment defense to the ultimate targets. See, e.g., *People v. McIntire,* 591 P.2d

b. But compare the views of Chevigny's colleague, Professor Stephen Gillers, *In Defense of Abscam: Entrapment, Where is Thy Sting?,* The Nation, Feb. 23, 1980, p. 203.

527 (Cal.1979), where a narcotics agent, posing as a high school student, importuned a classmate, the brother of the defendant, to obtain marijuana from his sister. Rejecting the prosecution's argument that entrapment cannot be effected through an "unwitting agent" (in this case, the defendant's brother), the court, per Mosk, J., observed: "The purposes of the entrapment defense can be fulfilled only if it is understood that one can act as a [government agent] without realizing the identity of his principal; the unwitting agent, though he may not appreciate the true nature of his role, is nonetheless being manipulated as the officer's tool in a plan to foster a crime and entrap its perpetrator."

However, when investigations are not aimed at a specific target, even though there is "substantial certainty that the person solicited by the police for the commission of a crime will seek the participation of another," such as when the agent requests the middleman to seek unidentified public officials who will accept bribes, the federal courts have "sharply disagreed" on how to apply the law of entrapment. See Note, 95 Harv.L.Rev. 1122, 1126–27 (1982). "Whenever it is reasonable to expect that the investigation will result in a secondary target's committing an offense," maintains the Harvard Note, "whether the secondary target was selected by [a government agent] or [the unsuspecting middleman], the additional offense must be considered 'the creature of [the agent's] purpose' unless the government can prove that the defendant was predisposed to commit a similar crime." Id. at 1128.

Moreover, "even when the government has no reason to expect that [the initial target] of an investigation will induce a nonessential [third party] to join in criminal activity, the third party should still be able to plead entrapment if it is found that the initial target was himself entrapped. If the original target was entrapped, the government has by definition created the actions that the initial target took in pursuing the illegal activity." Id. at 1129.

SECTION 3. CONTINUING CONTROVERSY OVER THE ENTRAPMENT DEFENSE

JACOBSON v. UNITED STATES

503 U.S. 540, 112 S.Ct. 1535, 118 L.Ed.2d 174 (1992).

Justice WHITE delivered the opinion of the Court.

On September 24, 1987, [petitioner] was indicted for violating a provision of the Child Protection Act of 1984, which criminalizes the knowing receipt through the mails of a "visual depiction [that] involves the use of a minor engaging in sexually explicit conduct...." Petitioner defended on the ground that the Government entrapped him into committing the crime through a series of communications from undercover agents that spanned the 26 months preceding his arrest. [He was found guilty after a jury trial. The Eighth Circuit, sitting en banc, affirmed, concluding that "Jacobson was not entrapped as a matter of law."]

Because the Government overstepped the line between setting a trap for the "unwary innocent" and the "unwary criminal," and as a matter of law failed to establish that petitioner was independently predisposed to commit the crime for which he was arrested, we reverse * * *.

[In] February 1984, petitioner, a 56–year-old veteran-turned-farmer who supported his elderly father in Nebraska, ordered two magazines and a brochure from a California adult bookstore. The magazines, entitled *Bare Boys I* and *Bare Boys II,* contained photographs of nude preteen and teenage boys. The contents of the magazines startled petitioner, who testified that he had expected to receive photographs of "young men 18 years or older." [The] young men depicted in the magazines were not engaged in sexual activity, and petitioner's receipt of the magazines was legal under both federal and Nebraska law. Within three months, the law with respect to child pornography changed; Congress passed the Act illegalizing the receipt through the mails of sexually explicit depictions of children. In the very month that the new provision became law, postal inspectors found petitioner's name on the mailing list of the California bookstore that had mailed him *Bare Boys I* and *II*. There followed over the next 2½ years, repeated efforts by two Government agencies, through five fictitious organizations and a bogus pen pal, to explore petitioner's willingness to break the new law by ordering sexually explicit photographs of children through the mail.

The Government began its efforts in January 1985 when a postal inspector sent petitioner a letter supposedly from the American Hedonist Society, which in fact was a fictitious organization. The letter included a membership application and stated the Society's doctrine: that members had the "right to read what we desire, the right to discuss similar interests with those who share our philosophy, and finally that we have the right to seek pleasure without restrictions being placed on us by outdated puritan morality." Petitioner enrolled in the organization and returned a sexual attitude questionnaire that asked him to rank on a scale of one to four his enjoyment of various sexual materials, with one being "really enjoy," two being "enjoy," three being "somewhat enjoy," and four being "do not enjoy." Petitioner ranked the entry "[p]re-teen sex" as a two, but indicated that he was opposed to pedophilia.

For a time, the Government left petitioner alone. But then a new "prohibited mail specialist" in the Postal Service found petitioner's name in a file and in May 1986 petitioner received a solicitation from a second fictitious consumer research company, "Midlands Data Research," seeking a response from those who "believe in the joys of sex and the complete awareness of those lusty and youthful lads and lasses of the neophite *[sic]* age." The letter never explained whether "neophite" referred to minors or young adults. Petitioner responded: "Please feel free to send me more information, I am interested in teenage sexuality. Please keep my name confidential."

Petitioner then heard from yet another Government creation, "Heartland Institute for a New Tomorrow" (HINT), which proclaimed that it was "an organization founded to protect and promote sexual freedom and freedom of choice. We believe that arbitrarily imposed legislative sanctions restricting your sexual freedom should be rescinded through the legislative process." The letter also enclosed a second survey. Petitioner indicated that his interest in "[p]reteen sex-homosexual" material was above average, but not high. In response to another question, petitioner wrote: "Not only sexual expression but freedom of the press is under attack. We must be ever vigilant to counter attack right wing fundamentalists who are determined to curtail our freedoms."

"HINT" replied, portraying itself as a lobbying organization seeking to repeal "all statutes which regulate sexual activities, except those laws which deal with violent behavior, such as rape. HINT is also lobbying to eliminate any legal definition of 'the age of consent'." These lobbying efforts were to be funded by sales from a catalog to be published in the future "offering the sale of various items which we believe you will find to be both interesting and stimulating." HINT also provided computer matching of group members with similar survey responses; and, although petitioner was supplied with a list of potential "pen pals," he did not initiate any correspondence.

Nevertheless, the Government's "prohibited mail specialist" began writing to petitioner, using the pseudonym "Carl Long." The letters employed a tactic known as "mirroring," which the inspector described as "reflect[ing] whatever the interests are of the person we are writing to." Petitioner responded at first, indicating that his interest was primarily in "male-male items." Inspector "Long" wrote back:

> "My interests too are primarily male-male items. Are you satisfied with the type of VCR tapes available? Personally, I like the amateur stuff better if its [sic] well produced as it can get more kinky and also seems more real. I think the actors enjoy it more."

Petitioner responded:

> "As far as my likes are concerned, I like good looking young guys (in their late teens and early 20's) doing their thing together."

Petitioner's letters to "Long" made no reference to child pornography. After writing two letters, petitioner discontinued the correspondence.

By March 1987, 34 months had passed since the Government obtained petitioner's name from the mailing list of the California bookstore, and 26 months had passed since the Postal Service had commenced its mailings to petitioner. Although petitioner had responded to surveys and letters, the Government had no evidence that petitioner had ever intentionally possessed or been exposed to child pornography. The Postal Service had not checked petitioner's mail to determine whether he was receiving questionable mailings from persons—other than the Government—involved in the child pornography industry.

At this point, a second Government agency, the Customs Service, included petitioner in its own child pornography sting, "Operation Borderline," after receiving his name on lists submitted by the Postal Service. Using the name of a fictitious Canadian company called "Produit Outaouais," the Customs Service mailed petitioner a brochure advertising photographs of young boys engaging in sex. Petitioner placed an order that was never filled.

The Postal Service also continued its efforts in the Jacobson case, writing to petitioner as the "Far Eastern Trading Company Ltd." The letter began:

> "As many of you know, much hysterical nonsense has appeared in the American media concerning 'pornography' and what must be done to stop it from coming across your borders. This brief letter does not allow us to give much comments; however, why is your government spending millions of dollars to exercise international censorship while tons of drugs, which makes yours the world's most crime ridden country are passed through easily."

The letter went on to say:

> "[W]e have devised a method of getting these to you without prying eyes of U.S. Customs seizing your mail.... After consultations with American solicitors, we have been advised that once we have posted our material through your system, it cannot be opened for any inspection without authorization of a judge."

The letter invited petitioner to send for more information. [He] responded. A catalogue was sent and petitioner ordered *Boys Who Love Boys,* a pornographic magazine depicting young boys engaged in various sexual activities. Petitioner was arrested after a controlled delivery of a photocopy of the magazine.

When petitioner was asked at trial why he placed such an order, he explained that the Government had succeeded in piquing his curiosity:

> "Well, the statement was made of all the trouble and the hysteria over pornography and I wanted to see what the material was. * * * I didn't know for sure what kind of sexual action they were referring to in the Canadian letter...."

In petitioner's home, the Government found the *Bare Boys* magazines and materials that the Government had sent to him in the course of its protracted investigation, but no other materials that would indicate that petitioner collected or was actively interested in child pornography. * * *

The trial court instructed the jury on [the] entrapment defense,[1] petitioner was convicted, and [the] Eighth Circuit affirmed * * *.

[In] their zeal to enforce the law [the Government] may not originate a criminal design, implant in an innocent person's mind the disposition to commit a criminal act, and then induce commission of the crime so that the Government may prosecute. Where the Government has induced an individual to break the law and the defense of entrapment is at issue, as it was in this case, the prosecution must prove beyond reasonable doubt that the defendant was disposed to commit the criminal act prior to first being approached by Government agents.[2]

Thus, an agent deployed to stop the traffic in illegal drugs may offer the opportunity to buy or sell drugs, and, if the offer is accepted, make an arrest on the spot or later. In such a typical case, or in a more elaborate "sting" operation involving government-sponsored fencing where the defendant is simply provided with the opportunity to commit a crime, the entrapment defense is of little use because the ready commission of the criminal act amply demonstrates the defendant's predisposition. Had the agents in this case simply offered petitioner the opportunity to order child pornography through the mails, and petitioner—who must be presumed to know the law—had promptly availed himself of this criminal opportunity, it is unlikely that his entrapment defense would have warranted a jury instruction.

But that is not what happened here. By the time petitioner finally placed his order, he had already been the target of 26 months of repeated mailings and communications from Government agents and fictitious organizations. Therefore,

1. The jury was instructed:

"As mentioned, one of the issues in this case is whether the defendant was entrapped. If the defendant was entrapped he must be found not guilty. The government has the burden of proving beyond a reasonable doubt that the defendant was not entrapped.

"If the defendant before contact with law-enforcement officers or their agents did not have any intent or disposition to commit the crime charged and was induced or persuaded by law-enforcement officers o[r] their agents to commit that crime, then he was entrapped. On the other hand, if the defendant before contact with law-enforcement officers or their agents did have an intent or disposition to commit the crime charged, then he was not entrapped even though law-enforcement officers or their agents provided a favorable opportunity to commit the crime or made committing the crime easier or even participated in acts essential to the crime."

2. Inducement is not at issue in this case. The Government does not dispute that it induced petitioner to commit the crime. The sole issue is whether the Government carried its burden of proving that petitioner was predisposed to violate the law *before* the Government intervened. The dissent is mistaken in claiming that this is an innovation in entrapment law and in suggesting that the Government's conduct prior to the moment of solicitation is irrelevant. * * * Indeed, the proposition that the accused must be predisposed prior to contact with law enforcement officers is so firmly established that the Government conceded the point at oral argument, submitting that the evidence it developed during the course of its investigation was probative because it indicated petitioner's state of mind *prior* to the commencement of the Government's investigation.

This long-established standard in no way encroaches upon Government investigatory activities. Indeed, the Government's internal guidelines for undercover operations provide that an inducement to commit a crime should not be offered unless:

"(a) there is a reasonable indication, based on information developed through informants or other means, that the subject is engaging, has engaged, or is likely to engage in illegal activity of a similar type; *or*

"(b) The opportunity for illegal activity has been structured so that there is reason for believing that persons drawn to the opportunity, or brought to it, are predisposed to engage in the contemplated illegal activity." *Attorney General's Guidelines on FBI Undercover Operations* (Dec. 31, 1980).

although he had become predisposed to break the law by May 1987, it is our view that the Government did not prove that this predisposition was independent and not the product of the attention that the Government had directed at petitioner since January 1985.

The prosecution's evidence of predisposition falls into two categories: evidence developed prior to the Postal Service's mail campaign, and that developed during the course of the investigation. The sole piece of preinvestigation evidence is petitioner's 1984 order and receipt of the Bare Boys magazines. But this is scant if any proof of petitioner's predisposition to commit an illegal act, the criminal character of which a defendant is presumed to know. It may indicate a predisposition to view sexually-oriented photographs that are responsive to his sexual tastes; but evidence that merely indicates a generic inclination to act within a broad range, not all of which is criminal, is of little probative value in establishing predisposition.

Furthermore, petitioner was acting within the law at the time he received these magazines. * * * Evidence of predisposition to do what once was lawful is not, by itself, sufficient to show predisposition to do what is now illegal, for there is a common understanding that most people obey the law even when they disapprove of it. [Hence,] the fact that petitioner legally ordered and received the *Bare Boys* magazines does little to further the Government's burden of proving that petitioner was predisposed to commit a criminal act. This is particularly true given petitioner's unchallenged testimony was that he did not know until they arrived that the magazines would depict minors.

The prosecution's evidence gathered during the investigation also fails to carry the Government's burden. Petitioner's responses to the many communications prior to the ultimate criminal act were at most indicative of certain personal inclinations, including a predisposition to view photographs of preteen sex and a willingness to promote a given agenda by supporting lobbying organizations. Even so, petitioner's responses hardly support an inference that he would commit the crime of receiving child pornography through the mails.[3]

[On] the other hand, the strong arguable inference is that, by waving the banner of individual rights and disparaging the legitimacy and constitutionality of efforts to restrict the availability of sexually explicit materials, the Government not only excited petitioner's interest in sexually explicit materials banned by law but also exerted substantial pressure on petitioner to obtain and read such material as part of a fight against censorship and the infringement of individual rights. * * *

Petitioner's ready response to these solicitations cannot be enough to establish beyond reasonable doubt that he was predisposed, prior to the Government acts intended to create predisposition, to commit the crime of receiving child pornography through the mails. The evidence that petitioner was ready and willing to commit the offense came only after the Government had devoted 2½ years to convincing him that he had or should have the right to engage in the very behavior proscribed by law. Rational jurors could not say beyond a reasonable doubt that petitioner possessed the requisite predisposition prior to the Government's investigation and that it existed independent of the Government's many and varied approaches to petitioner. As was explained in *Sherman,* where entrapment was found as a matter of law, "the Government [may not] pla[y] on the

3. We do not hold, as the dissent suggests, that the Government was required to prove that petitioner knowingly violated the law. We simply conclude that proof that petitioner engaged in legal conduct and possessed certain generalized personal inclinations is not sufficient evidence to prove beyond a reasonable doubt that he would have been predisposed to commit the crime charged independent of the Government's coaxing.

weaknesses of an innocent party and beguil[e] him into committing crimes which he otherwise would not have attempted."

Law enforcement officials go too far when they "implant in the mind of an innocent person the *disposition* to commit the alleged offense and induce its commission in order that they may prosecute." *Sorrells* (emphasis added). [When] the Government's quest for convictions leads to the apprehension of an otherwise law-abiding citizen who, if left to his own devices, likely would have never run afoul of the law, the courts should intervene. * * *

Justice O'CONNOR, with whom The Chief Justice and Justice KENNEDY join, and with whom Justice SCALIA joins except as to Part II, dissenting.

Keith Jacobson was offered only two opportunities to buy child pornography through the mail. Both times, he ordered. Both times, he asked for opportunities to buy more. He needed no Government agent to coax, threaten, or persuade him; no one played on his sympathies, friendship, or suggested that his committing the crime would further a greater good. In fact, no Government agent even contacted him face-to-face. The Government contends that from the enthusiasm with which Mr. Jacobson responded to the chance to commit a crime, a reasonable jury could permissibly infer beyond a reasonable doubt that he was predisposed to commit the crime. I agree.

[The] first time the Government sent Mr. Jacobson a catalog of illegal materials, he ordered a set of photographs advertised as picturing "young boys in sex action fun." He enclosed the following note with his order: "I received your brochure and decided to place an order. If I like your product, I will order more later." For reasons undisclosed in the record, Mr. Jacobson's order was never delivered.

The second time the Government sent a catalog of illegal materials, Mr. Jacobson ordered a magazine called "Boys Who Love Boys," described as: "11 year old and 14 year old boys get it on in every way possible. Oral, anal sex and heavy masturbation. If you love boys, you will be delighted with this." Along with his order, Mr. Jacobson sent the following note: "Will order other items later. I want to be discreet in order to protect you and me."

Government agents admittedly did not offer Mr. Jacobson the chance to buy child pornography right away. Instead, they first sent questionnaires in order to make sure that he was generally interested in the subject matter. Indeed, a "cold call" in such a business would not only risk rebuff and suspicion, but might also shock and offend the uninitiated, or expose minors to suggestive materials. Mr. Jacobson's responses to the questionnaires gave the investigators reason to think he would be interested in photographs depicting preteen sex.

The Court, however, concludes that a reasonable jury could not have found Mr. Jacobson to be predisposed beyond a reasonable doubt on the basis of his responses to the Government's catalogs, even though it admits that, by that time, he was predisposed to commit the crime. The Government, the Court holds, failed to provide evidence that Mr. Jacobson's obvious predisposition at the time of the crime "was independent and not the product of the attention that the Government had directed at petitioner." In so holding, I believe the Court fails to acknowledge the reasonableness of the jury's inference from the evidence, redefines "predisposition," and introduces a new requirement that Government sting operations have a reasonable suspicion of illegal activity before contacting a suspect.

This Court has held previously that a defendant's predisposition is to be assessed as of the time the Government agent first suggested the crime, not when the Government agent first became involved. * * * [Even] in *Sherman,* [where entrapment was found] as a matter of law, the Government agent had repeatedly and unsuccessfully coaxed the defendant to buy drugs, ultimately succeeding only by playing on the defendant's sympathy. The Court found lack of predisposition based on the Government's numerous unsuccessful attempts to induce the crime, not on the basis of preliminary contacts with the defendant.

Today, the Court holds that Government conduct may be considered to create a predisposition to commit a crime, even before any Government action to induce the commission of the crime. In my view, this holding changes entrapment doctrine. Generally, the inquiry is whether a suspect is predisposed before the Government induces the commission of the crime, not before the Government makes initial contact with him. There is no dispute here that the Government's questionnaires and letters were not sufficient to establish inducement; they did not even suggest that Mr. Jacobson should engage in any illegal activity. If all the Government had done was to send these materials, Mr. Jacobson's entrapment defense would fail. Yet the Court holds that the Government must prove not only that a suspect was predisposed to commit the crime before the opportunity to commit it arose, but also before the Government came on the scene.

The rule that preliminary Government contact can create a predisposition has the potential to be misread by lower courts as well as criminal investigators as requiring that the Government must have sufficient evidence of a defendant's predisposition *before it ever seeks to contact him.* Surely the Court cannot intend to impose such a requirement, for it would mean that the Government must have a reasonable suspicion of criminal activity before it begins an investigation, a condition that we have never before imposed. The Court denies that its new rule will affect run-of-the-mill sting operations and one hopes that it means what it says. Nonetheless, after this case, every defendant will claim that something the Government agent did before soliciting the crime "created" a predisposition that was not there before. For example, a bribe taker will claim that the description of the amount of money available was so enticing that it implanted a disposition to accept the bribe later offered. A drug buyer will claim that the description of the drug's purity and effects was so tempting that it created the urge to try it for the first time. In short, the Court's opinion could be read to prohibit the Government from advertising the seductions of criminal activity as part of its sting operation, for fear of creating a predisposition in its suspects. That limitation would be especially likely to hamper sting operations such as this one, which mimic the advertising done by genuine purveyors of pornography. No doubt the Court would protest that its opinion does not stand for so broad a proposition, but the apparent lack of a principled basis for distinguishing these scenarios exposes a flaw in the more limited rule the Court today adopts.

The Court's rule is all the more troubling because it does not distinguish between Government conduct that merely highlights the temptation of the crime itself, and Government conduct that threatens, coerces, or leads a suspect to commit a crime in order to fulfill some other obligation. For example, in *Sorrells,* the Government agent repeatedly asked for illegal liquor, coaxing the defendant to accede on the ground that "one former war buddy would get liquor for another." In *Sherman,* the Government agent played on the defendant's sympathies, pretending to be going through drug withdrawal and begging the defendant to relieve his distress by helping him buy drugs.

The Government conduct in this case is not comparable. While the Court states that the Government "exerted substantial pressure on petitioner to obtain and read such material as part of a fight against censorship and the infringement of individual rights," one looks at the record in vain for evidence of such "substantial pressure." The most one finds is letters advocating legislative action to liberalize obscenity laws, letters which could easily be ignored or thrown away.

* * * Nowhere did the Government suggest that the proceeds of the sale of the illegal materials would be used to support legislative reforms. * * * Mr. Jacobson's curiosity to see what " 'all the trouble and the hysteria' "was about is certainly susceptible of more than one interpretation. And it is the jury that is charged with the obligation of interpreting it. In sum, the Court fails to construe the evidence in the light most favorable to the Government, and fails to draw all reasonable inferences in the Government's favor. It was surely reasonable for the jury to infer that Mr. Jacobson was predisposed beyond a reasonable doubt, even if other inferences from the evidence were also possible.

The second puzzling thing about the Court's opinion is its redefinition of predisposition. The Court acknowledges that "[p]etitioner's responses to the many communications prior to the ultimate criminal act [were] indicative of certain personal inclinations, including a predisposition to view photographs of preteen sex...." If true, this should have settled the matter; Mr. Jacobson was predisposed to engage in the illegal conduct. Yet, the Court concludes, "petitioner's responses hardly support an inference that he would commit the crime of receiving child pornography through the mails."

The Court seems to add something new to the burden of proving predisposition. Not only must the Government show that a defendant was predisposed to engage in the illegal conduct, here, receiving photographs of minors engaged in sex, but also that the defendant was predisposed to break the law knowingly in order to do so. The statute violated here, however, does not require proof of specific intent to break the law; it requires only knowing receipt of visual depictions produced by using minors engaged in sexually explicit conduct. Under the Court's analysis, however, the Government must prove *more* to show predisposition than it need prove in order to convict.

[The] crux of the Court's concern in this case is that the Government went too far and "abused" the "processes of detection and enforcement" by luring an innocent person to violate the law. Consequently, the Court holds that the Government failed to prove beyond a reasonable doubt that Mr. Jacobson was predisposed to commit the crime. It was, however, the jury's task, as the conscience of the community, to decide whether or not Mr. Jacobson was a willing participant in the criminal activity here or an innocent dupe. [There] is no dispute that the jury in this case was fully and accurately instructed on the law of entrapment, and nonetheless found Mr. Jacobson guilty. Because I believe there was sufficient evidence to uphold the jury's verdict, I respectfully dissent.

Notes and Questions

1. ***Is behavior in an artificial world largely uninformative of behavior in this one?*** To what extent does the following commentary by Ronald J. Allen, Melissa Luttrell & Anne Kreeger, *Clarifying Entrapment*, 89 J. Crim. L. & Criminology 407, 415–16 (1999), reflect the view of the *Jacobson* majority: "None of [the primary relevant objectives of the criminal law] is likely to be accomplished by the punishment of an individual who accepted an extra-market inducement to act. The concern of deterrence surely is to reduce the occurrence of criminal acts in the world we actually inhabit, not some hypothetically different one. That a person responds to extra-market prices [including both financial and emotional markets] is uninformative of how he will respond to market prices, and thus is uninformative on the justification for incapacitation. A person who accepts extra-market prices provides evidence that indeed virtually everybody has a price, but not that this person is in need of rehabilitation, given the world we actually inhabit. The point generalized is that criminal acts occur in the real world, not an

artificial one, and behavior in an artificial world is largely uninformative of behavior in this one."

2. ***Unproductive use of law enforcement resources.*** Consider Note, 61 U.Cin.L.Rev. 1067, 1090–91 (1993): "To allow law enforcement officials to go on 'fishing expeditions' based on only the most generalized suspicion is to allow a tremendous waste of resources and to risk the targeting of unpopular groups, such as gay men. Judge Posner has indicated that entrapment is, at its most basic, a label given to the unproductive use of law enforcement resources. [*United States v. Kaminski,* 703 F.2d 1004, 1010 (7th Cir.1983) (concurring opinion.)][a] [The] *Jacobson* case exemplifies this inefficient use of law enforcement resources, in that an individual with no apparent history of dealing in child pornography became the focus of an investigation lasting two and one-half years, culminating in his arrest and conviction for receiving a single magazine that was supplied by the government. The government's stated purpose in investigations of this sort is to eliminate child pornography, yet the only child pornography present in this case was that manufactured and distributed by the government."

Should second-guessing the government's use of its law enforcement resources be the business of the courts? See Adams, J., dissenting in *United States v. Twigg,* 588 F.2d 373 (3d Cir.1978). If government investigators squander their limited resources, should this be regarded as a political problem to be addressed by oversight hearings? See Easterbrook, J., concurring in *United States v. Miller,* 891 F.2d 1265, 1271–72 (7th Cir.1989).[b]

3. ***"Reasonable suspicion" that the target was predisposed to commit the crime.*** Is *Jacobson* likely, as Justice O'Connor suggests, to be interpreted by lower courts and criminal investigators "as requiring that the Government must have sufficient evidence of a defendant's predisposition *before it ever seeks to contact him*"? The majority observes that when Jacobson was arrested the government found no evidence—aside from the *Bare Boys* magazines and the material the government had sent him—indicating that he "collected or was actively interested in child pornography." Suppose government agents *had* found other material establishing that Jacobson collected child pornography *even though they were unaware* that such evidence existed before they arrested him? Wouldn't the prosecution have been able to defeat Jacobson's entrapment claim by establishing that his predisposition was independent and not the product of the government's many and varied approaches to him?

Note, too, the majority points out that if, absent any prior dealings between the government and Jacobson, federal agents had simply offered him the opportunity to order child pornography through the mails and he had promptly agreed, Jacobson's entrapment defense would have failed. For in such a case "the ready commission of the criminal act amply demonstrates the defendant's predisposition." But wouldn't this be so *regardless* of whether government agents had any indication of Jacobson's predisposition before they offered him the opportunity to obtain child pornography?

4. ***What must the government prove before it "comes on the scene"?*** Does *Jacobson* hold, as the dissenters maintain, that "the Government must prove not only that a suspect was predisposed to commit the crime before the opportunity to [do so] arose, but also before the Government came on the scene"?

If an undercover agent gradually became a close friend of a target but never brought up the subject of drugs in the first ten months of their acquaintanceship (during which time the agent simply socialized with, and gained the confidence of,

a. For an extract from Judge Posner's opinion see p. 503.

b. For an extract from Judge Easterbrook's opinion see p. 504.

the target), would it matter whether there was any evidence that the target was predisposed to commit a drug offense when the government agent initiated contact with the target or first "came on the scene"? Is *Jacobson* a different case because when a fictitious organization first sent Jacobson a mailing, the government had not *merely* initiated contact with him or arrived on the scene but (as far as a majority of the Court was concerned) had begun "working on" Jacobson?

5. ***Did the Jacobson Court blend the "subjective" and "objective" entrapment tests?*** As noted by Michael L. Piccarreta & Jefferson Keenan, *Entrapment Targets and Tactics: Jacobson v. United States*, 29 Crim.L.Bull. 241, 249 (1993), *Jacobson* "is the first Supreme Court opinion concerning entrapment in which none of the Justices even adverted to the 'objective' theory of entrapment." However, although the *Jacobson* majority purported to be applying the "subjective" test of entrapment, it also seemed quite offended by the tactics used by the government to induce Jacobson to order pornographic material. As the majority described it, some of the literature sent to Jacobson by the fictitious organizations created by the government disparaged the legitimacy of efforts to restrict the availability of sexually explicit material and came close to *challenging* Jacobson to assert his right to obtain and read such material. Does this feature of the case fit more easily within the framework of the "objective" test? Might it even constitute reprehensible or offensive conduct under that test?

But consider Note, 68 Wash.L.Rev. 185, 198–99 (1993): "Although the fictitious organizations did decry the criminalization of some forms of pornography, that very message signaled the illegality of the material. That Jacobson was aware that he was committing an unlawful act was not disputed. As the [Court's] opinion states, 'there is a common understanding that most people obey the law even when they disapprove of it.' If we analogize this fact pattern to a bribery sting, it is fantastic to suggest that a defendant could support an entrapment claim by avowing that the undercover agent avouched, 'Bribery is illegal—but it really shouldn't be.' "

6. ***In "reverse sting" cases, should the objective and subjective approaches be combined?*** Unlike the traditional "sting" (where undercover agents pose as buyers of illicit goods or services), in "reverse sting" cases, such as *Jacobson,* government agents act as sellers. According to Damon D. Camp, *Out of the Quagmire after Jacobson v. United States: Toward a More Balanced Entrapment Standard,* 83 J.Crim.L. & C. 1055, 1056 (1993), the subjective entrapment test works reasonably well in traditional sting cases. In such cases proclivity to engage in criminal conduct is difficult to deny because the defendant actually provides contraband to a government agent. In reverse stings, however, "the notion of predisposition becomes a significant issue, and the role of enforcement officers in securing cooperation becomes critical." In such cases, maintains Professor Camp, the key question should be whether predisposition to commit the crime or the government's conduct was a more important influence on the defendant's participation in crime.

HOW ARE THE FEDERAL COURTS INTERPRETING *JACOBSON*?

In UNITED STATES v. GENDRON, 18 F.3d 955 (1st Cir.1994), in the course of holding that defendant was not entrapped into receiving child pornography, Chief Judge (now Supreme Court Justice) BREYER observed:

"As the Supreme Court has recently stated: 'When the Government's quest for conviction leads to the apprehension of an *otherwise law-abiding citizen* who, *if left to his own devices*, likely would never have been afoul of the law, the courts should intervene.' *Jacobson v. United States* (emphasis added). Since the Court has repeatedly expressed concern about *both* government 'abuse' of its enforcement powers (or the like) *and* the 'otherwise law-abiding citizen' (or the like), it is not surprising that the defense has two parts, one that focuses upon government 'inducement' and the other upon the defendant's 'predisposition.'

"[The Supreme Court] saw in the entrapment defense not so much a sanction used to control police conduct, but rather a protection of the ordinary law-abiding citizen against government overreaching. Consequently, it saw no need to permit a defendant to take advantage of that defense unless he himself was such a citizen. The upshot is that we must find out just who that 'innocent person' is. Who is the '*otherwise* law-abiding citizen' who would not 'otherwise' have committed the crime?

"[The] right way to ask the question, it seems to us, is to abstract from—to assume away—the present circumstances *insofar as they reveal government overreaching*. That is to say, we should ask how the defendant likely would have reacted to an *ordinary* opportunity to commit the crime. *See Jacobson*, n. 2. By using the word 'ordinary,' we mean an opportunity that lacked those special features of the government's conduct that made of it an 'inducement,' or an 'overreaching.' Was the defendant 'predisposed' to respond affirmatively to a *proper*, not to an *improper*, lure? * * *

"We turn now to *Jacobson* * * *. In three respects [government agents] did more than provide an ordinary opportunity to buy child pornography: First, the solicitations reflected a psychologically 'graduated' set of responses to Jacobson's own noncriminal responses, beginning with innocent lures and progressing to frank offers. [Second,] the government's soliciting letters sometimes depicted their senders as 'free speech' lobbying organizations and fighters for the 'right to read what we desire'; they asked Jacobson to 'fight against censorship and the infringement of individual rights.' Third, the government's effort to provide an 'opportunity' to buy child pornography stretched out over two and a half years. Taken together, one might find in these three sets of circumstances—the graduated response, the long time period, the appeal to a proper (free speech) motive—a substantial risk of inducing an ordinary law-abiding person to commit the crime. Indeed, the government conceded in *Jacobson*, that its methods amounted, for entrapment purposes, to an improper 'inducement.' Id. at n. 2.

"*Jacobson's* importance, however, concerns the 'predisposition' part of the entrapment defense. The Court held that the evidence, as a matter of law, required acquittal because a reasonable jury would have had to doubt Jacobson's predisposition. [The government] failed to show 'predisposition' (beyond a reasonable doubt). That means (as we understand it) that the government's evidence did not show how Jacobson would have acted had he been faced with an ordinary 'opportunity' to commit the crime rather than a special 'inducement.'

"[The evidence in this case,] taken together, reveals a defendant who met an initial opportunity to buy child pornography with enthusiasm, who responded to each further government initiative with a purchase order, and who, unlike Jacobson, showed no particular interest in an anti-censorship campaign. [This evidence] permits a jury to find (beyond a reasonable doubt) that Gendron would have responded affirmatively to the most ordinary of opportunities, and hence, was 'predisposed' to commit the crime. We therefore find the jury's entrapment decision lawful."

Compare UNITED STATES v. HOLLINGSWORTH, 27 F.3d 1196 (7th Cir. 1994) (en banc). In the course of holding that the defendants, Pickard (an orthodontist) and Hollingsworth (a farmer), had been entrapped as a matter of law into engaging in a money laundering scheme, a 6–5 majority, per POSNER, C.J., observed:

"[Had] the Court in *Jacobson* believed that the legal concept of predisposition is exhausted in the demonstrated willingness of the defendant to commit the crime without threats or promises by the government, then Jacobson was predisposed, in which event the Court's reversal of his conviction would be difficult to explain. The government did not offer Jacobson any inducements to buy pornographic magazines or threaten him with harm if he failed to buy them. It was not as if the government had had to badger Jacobson for 26 months in order to overcome his resistance to committing a crime. He *never* resisted.

"* * * [W]e are naturally reluctant to suppose that [*Jacobson*] is limited to the precise facts before the Court, or to ignore the Court's definition of entrapment, which concludes the analysis portion of the opinion and is not found in previous opinions, as 'the apprehension of an otherwise law-abiding citizen who, if left to his own devices, likely would have never run afoul of the law.' That was Jacobson. However impure his thoughts, he was law abiding. A farmer in Nebraska, his access to child pornography was limited. As far as the government was aware, over the period of more than two years in which it was playing cat and mouse with him, he did not receive any other solicitations to buy pornography. So, had he been 'left to his own devices,' in all likelihood he would 'have never run afoul of the law.' If the same can be said of [the defendants in this case,] Pickard and Hollingsworth, they too are entitled to be acquitted. * * *

"Recently the First Circuit, struggling as are we to understand the scope of *Jacobson*, suggested that all it stands for is that the government may not, in trying to induce the target of a sting to commit a crime, confront him with circumstances that are different from the ordinary or typical circumstances of a private inducement. *Gendron*. The [First Circuit] thought that the government's attempt to persuade Jacobson that he had a First Amendment right to consume child pornography had departed from typicality. We are not so sure. Just as the gun industry likes to wrap itself in the mantle of the Second Amendment, so the pornography industry likes to wrap itself in the mantle of the First Amendment. But however that may be, the government made no effort in *this* case to show that a real customer for money laundering would have responded to an advertisement to sell a Grenadan bank * * *.

"We put the following hypothetical case to the government's lawyer at the reargument. Suppose the government went to someone and asked him whether he would like to make money as a counterfeiter, and the reply was, 'Sure, but I don't know anything about counterfeiting.' Suppose the government then bought him a printer, paper, and ink, showed him how to make the counterfeit money, hired a staff for him, and got everything set up so that all he had to do was press a button to print the money; and then offered him $10,000 for some quantity of counterfeit bills. The government's lawyer acknowledged that the counterfeiter would have a strong case that he had been entrapped, even though he was perfectly willing to commit the crime once the government planted the suggestion and showed him how and the government neither threatened him nor offered him an overwhelming inducement.[a]

"We do not suggest that *Jacobson* adds a new element to the entrapment defense—'readiness' or 'ability' or 'dangerousness' on top of inducement and, most important, predisposition. Predisposition is not a purely mental state, the state of being willing to swallow the government's bait. It has positional as well as dispositional force. [The] defendant must be so situated by reason of previous training or experience or occupation or acquaintances that it is likely that if the

a. Did the government's lawyer concede too much?

government had not induced him to commit the crime some criminal would have done so; only then does a sting or other arranged crime take a dangerous person out of circulation. A public official is in a position to take bribes; a drug addict to deal drugs; a gun dealer to engage in illegal gun sales. For these and other traditional targets of stings all that must be shown to establish the predisposition and thus defeat the defense of entrapment is willingness to violate the law without extraordinary inducements; ability can be presumed. It is different when the defendant is not in a position without the government's help to become involved in illegal activity. * * *

"There is no evidence that before 'Hinch' began his campaign to inveigle them into a money-laundering scheme either Pickard or Hollingsworth had contemplated engaging in such behavior. [When] the opportunity to become *crooked* international financiers beckoned, they were willing enough, though less willing than Jacobson had been to violate the federal law against purchasing child pornography through the mails—Jacobson never evinced reluctance, even though he had received no financial inducements. Pickard and Hollingsworth had no prayer of becoming money launderers without the government's aid.

"[The] point is not that Pickard and Hollingsworth were *incapable* of engaging in the act of money laundering. Obviously they were capable of the act. [But] to get into the international money-laundering business you need underworld contacts, financial acumen or assets, access to foreign banks or bankers, or other assets. Pickard and Hollingsworth had none. [They] were objectively harmless.

"We do not wish to be understood as holding that lack of *present* means to commit a crime is alone enough to establish entrapment if the government supplies the means. [Suppose] that before Hinch chanced on the scene (for *Jacobson* makes clear [that] a predisposition *created* by the government cannot be used to defeat a defense of entrapment), Pickard had decided to smuggle arms to Cuba but didn't know where to buy a suitable boat. On a hunch, a government agent sidles up to Pickard and gives him the address of a boat dealer; and Pickard is arrested after taking possession of the boat and setting sail, and is charged with attempted smuggling. That would be a case in which the defendant had the idea for the crime all worked out and lacked merely the present means to commit it, and if the government had not supplied them someone else very well might have. It would be a case in which the government had merely furnished the opportunity to commit the crime to someone already predisposed to commit it. * * *

"Our two would-be international financiers were at the end of their tether, making it highly unlikely that if Hinch had not providentially appeared someone else would have guided them into money laundering. No real criminal would do business with such tyros. Or so it appears * * *."[b]

Consider, too, UNITED STATES v. KNOX, 112 F.3d 802 (5th Cir.1997), which arose as follows: Defendant Brace was the pastor of a church that was heavily in debt. In an effort to raise $10 million to pay the church's creditors, Brace hired a financial advisor, who in turn contacted other people. At the same time, undercover federal agents were conducting a sting operation designed to catch money launderers. Brace's financial advisor and the advisor's contacts told the undercover agents that they knew of a minister who would be interested in laundering drug money. Finally, the undercover agents met with Brace himself and told him that he was being asked to launder money that came from the sale of cocaine. Brace replied that he had no trouble with that. The jury rejected the entrapment defense and convicted Brace of laundering drug proceeds. "Because the government failed to prove that the preacher was likely to engage in money

b. In three separate dissents, Judges Coffey, Easterbrook and Ripple voiced strong disagreement with the majority's interpretation of *Jacobson.*

laundering absent the government's conduct,'' the Fifth Circuit, per DeMOSS, J., held that Brace was entrapped ''as a matter of law'':

''The en banc Seventh Circuit recently wrestled with the meaning of *Jacobson* [in the *Hollingsworth* case]. Writing for the majority, Chief Judge Posner stated that in examining predisposition, we must ask ourselves what the defendant would have done had the government not been involved. To properly answer the question, we must look to more than the defendant's mental state; we must also consider the defendant's skills, background and contacts. * * *

''We recognize that the Seventh Circuit's reading of *Jacobson* has not been universally embraced. The Ninth Circuit has rejected the Seventh Circuit's positional predisposition requirement and the First Circuit has adopted a different test. In *Gendron,* then Chief Judge (now Justice) Breyer held that *Jacobson* stands for the proposition that in trying to induce the target of a sting to commit a crime, the government may not confront him with circumstances that are different from the ordinary circumstances a real criminal would use in inducing one to engage in wrongdoing. [Thus,] the Government must show that a defendant would have committed the crime when 'faced with an ordinary ''opportunity'' to commit the crime rather than a special 'inducement.' ''

''Nonetheless, we are persuaded that the Seventh Circuit's Hollingsworth decision is correct. See Paul Marcus, *Presenting, Back From the [Almost] Dead, the Entrapment Defense*, 47 Fla.L.Rev. 205, 233–34 (1995) (arguing *Hollingsworth* is proper approach to entrapment law). The Supreme Court instructs that in determining predisposition we are to ask what the defendant would have done absent government involvement. To give effect to that command, we must look not only to the defendant's mental state (his 'disposition'), but also to whether the defendant was able and likely, based on experience, training, and contacts, to actually commit the crime (his 'position').[c]

''[We] are called upon to determine whether the government proved beyond a reasonable doubt that Brace was predisposed to launder money. Following *Hollingsworth*, we look to Brace's position, as well as his mental disposition. [The] government failed to prove that Brace, absent government involvement, was in a position to launder money. Therefore, the evidence is insufficient to prove that Brace was predisposed to launder money.

''[When] we ask the question of what Brace would have done if he had never met the undercover agents, we cannot answer 'launder money for real drug dealers.' In all likelihood, Brace never would have laundered money * * *.''

c. The court noted that ''in this case the result would not differ under the First Circuit's *Gendron* test. The government failed to prove that real drug dealers would provide the same, or even similar, terms to a launderer as the undercover agents offered Brace. Thus, the government failed to offer any evidence that Brace would accept an 'ordinary opportunity' to launder money.''

Chapter 9

POLICE INTERROGATION AND CONFESSIONS

SECTION 1. SOME DIFFERENT PERSPECTIVES

FRED E. INBAU: POLICE INTERROGATION—A PRACTICAL NECESSITY

52 J.Crim.L.C. & P.S. 16 (1961), reprinted in Police Power and Individual Freedom 147 (Sowle ed. 1962).

One completely false assumption accounts for most of the legal restrictions on police interrogations. It is this, and the fallacy is certainly perpetuated to a very considerable extent by mystery writers, the movies, and TV: whenever a crime is committed, if the police will only look carefully at the crime scene they will almost always find some clue that will lead them to the offender and at the same time establish his guilt; and once the offender is located, he will readily confess or disclose his guilt by trying to shoot his way out of the trap. But this is pure fiction; in actuality the situation is quite different. As a matter of fact, the art of criminal investigation has not developed to a point where the search for and the examination of physical evidence will always, or even in most cases, reveal a clue to the identity of the perpetrator or provide the necessary proof of his guilt. In criminal investigations, even of the most efficient type, there are many, many instances where physical clues are entirely absent, and the only approach to a possible solution of the crime is the interrogation of the criminal suspect himself, as well as others who may possess significant information. Moreover, in most instances these interrogations, particularly of the suspect himself, must be conducted under conditions of privacy and for a reasonable period of time; and they frequently require the use of psychological tactics and techniques that could well be classified as "unethical," if we are to evaluate them in terms of ordinary, everyday social behavior.

To protect myself from being misunderstood, I want to make it unmistakably clear that I am not an advocate of the so-called "third degree," for I am unalterably opposed to the use of any interrogation tactic or technique that is apt to make an innocent person confess. I am opposed, therefore, to the use of force, threats, or promises of leniency—all of which might well induce *an innocent person* to confess; but I do approve of such psychological tactics and techniques as trickery and deceit that are not only helpful but frequently necessary in order to secure incriminating information from the guilty, or investigate leads from otherwise uncooperative witnesses or informants.

My position, then, is this, and it may be presented in the form of three separate points, each accompanied by case illustrations:

1. *Many criminal cases, even when investigated by the best qualified police departments, are capable of solution only by means of an admission or confession*

from the guilty individual or upon the basis of information obtained from the questioning of other criminal suspects.

As to the validity of this statement, I suggest that consideration be given to the situation presented by cases such as these. A man is hit on the head while walking home late at night. He did not see his assailant, nor did anyone else. A careful and thorough search of the crime scene reveals no physical clues. Then take the case of a woman who is grabbed on the street at night and dragged into an alley and raped. Here, too, the assailant was unaccommodating enough to avoid leaving his hat or other means of identification at the crime scene; and there are no other physical clues. All the police have to work on is the description of the assailant given by the victim herself. She described him as about six feet tall, white, and wearing a dark suit. Or consider this case, an actual recent one in Illinois. Three women are vacationing in a wooded resort area. Their bodies were found dead alongside a foot trail, the result of physical violence, and no physical clues are present.

In cases of this kind—and they all typify the difficult investigation problem that the police frequently encounter—how else can they be solved, if at all, except by means of the interrogation of suspects or of others who may possess significant information?

There are times, too, when a police interrogation may result not only in the apprehension and conviction of the guilty, but also in the release of the innocent from well-warranted suspicion. Here is one such actual case within my own professional experience.

The dead body of a woman was found in her home. Her skull had been crushed, apparently with some blunt instrument. A careful police investigation of the premises did not reveal any clues to the identity of the killer. No fingerprints or other significant evidence were located; not even the lethal instrument itself could be found. None of the neighbors could give any helpful information. Although there was some evidence of a slight struggle in the room where the body lay, there were no indications of a forcible entry into the home. The deceased's young daughter was the only other resident of the home and she had been away in school at the time of the crime. The daughter could not give the police any idea of what, if any, money or property had disappeared from the home.

For several reasons the police considered the victim's husband a likely suspect. He was being sued for divorce; he knew his wife had planned on leaving the state and taking their daughter with her; and the neighbors reported that the couple had been having heated arguments, and that the husband was of a violent temper. He also lived conveniently near—in a garage adjoining the home. The police interrogated him and although his alibi was not conclusive his general behavior and the manner in which he answered the interrogator's questions satisfied the police of his innocence. Further investigation then revealed that the deceased's brother-in-law had been financially indebted to the deceased; that he was a frequent gambler; that at a number of social gatherings which he had attended money disappeared from some of the women's purses; that at his place of employment there had been a series of purse thefts; and that on the day of the killing he was absent from work. The police apprehended and questioned him. As the result of a few hours of competent interrogation—unattended by any abusive methods, but yet conducted during a period of delay in presenting the suspect before a committing magistrate as required by state statute—the suspect confessed to the murder. * * *

Without an opportunity for interrogation the police could not have solved this case. The perpetrator of the offense would have remained at liberty, perhaps to repeat his criminal conduct.

2. *Criminal offenders, except, of course, those caught in the commission of their crimes, ordinarily will not admit their guilt unless questioned under conditions of privacy, and for a period of perhaps several hours.*

* * * Self-condemnation and self-destruction not being normal behavior characteristics, human beings ordinarily do not utter unsolicited, spontaneous confessions. They must first be questioned regarding the offense. In some instances, a little bit of information inadvertently given to a competent interrogator by the suspect may suffice to start a line of investigation which might ultimately establish guilt. Upon other occasions, a full confession, with a revelation of details regarding a body, the loot, or the instruments used in the crime, may be required to prove the case. But whatever the possible consequences may be, it is impractical to expect any but a very few confessions to result from a guilty conscience unprovoked by an interrogation. It is also impractical to expect admissions or confessions to be obtained under circumstances other than privacy. Here again recourse to our everyday experience will support the basic validity of this requirement. For instance, in asking a personal friend to divulge a secret, or embarrassing information, we carefully avoid making the request in the presence of other persons, and seek a time and place when the matter can be discussed in private. The very same psychological factors are involved in a criminal interrogation, and even to a greater extent. For related psychological considerations, if an interrogation is to be had at all, it must be one based upon an unhurried interview, the necessary length of which will in many instances extend to several hours, depending upon various factors such as the nature of the case situation and the personality of the suspect. * * *

If the right to counsel arises only at the time of trial, or even when the judicial process begins, as at a preliminary hearing or at the time of indictment, the police have at least some opportunity for an interrogation. On the other hand, if the right is considered to exist immediately upon arrest, the interrogation opportunity, for all practical purposes, is gone—because of the prevailing concept that the role of defense counsel is to advise his client, "keep your mouth shut; don't say anything to anybody." * * *

In my judgment the right to counsel at the time of trial, or even at the very start of the judicial process, should be accorded *and provided* to all indigent defendants, insofar as practicable, regardless of whether the case involves a capital or non-capital offense, or even if it amounts only to a misdemeanor. What I do object to is an extension of the right to arrestees, indigent or non-indigent, prior to the start of the judicial process. It is not constitutionally required, and practical considerations will not tolerate such an extension, and particularly so if the extension is supplemented by a rule of court that would nullify, as a violation of due process, a confession obtained during a period of police detention before the start of the judicial process. Moreover, sometime in the near future we will have to come to grips with this interrogation problem and consider the passage of legislation, by all the states as well as the federal government, which will specifically provide for a reasonable period of police detention for the interrogation of suspects who are not otherwise unwilling to talk. * * *

Regarding the routine advice of counsel to an arrestee to remain silent and refuse to answer questions put to him by the police, it is my suggestion that the legal profession give serious consideration to the adoption of an alternative practice, which would require counsel to say to his client, the arrestee: "Although you do not have to say anything, my advice to you is that you discuss this matter with the police and that you tell them the truth; I'll stand by to protect you from any harm or abuse." With the advent of such a change in the ethical concept of the role of counsel, we might then be able to say that all arrestees should be entitled to counsel from the time of their arrest. As matters now stand, however, public protection and safety require that we adhere to the present viewpoint that there is no right to counsel during the investigative, non-judicial stage of the case.

3. *In dealing with criminal offenders, and consequently also with criminal suspects who may actually be innocent, the interrogator must of necessity employ less refined methods than are considered appropriate for the transaction of ordinary, everyday affairs by and between law-abiding citizens.*

To illustrate this point, permit me to revert to the previously discussed case of the woman who was murdered by her brother-in-law. His confession was obtained largely as a result of the interrogator adopting a friendly attitude in questioning the suspect, when concededly no such genuine feeling existed; by pretending to sympathize with the suspect because of his difficult financial situation; by suggesting that perhaps the victim had done or said something which aroused his anger and which would have aroused the anger of anyone else similarly situated to such an extent as to provoke a violent reaction; and by resorting to other similar expressions, or even overtures of friendliness and sympathy such as a pat on the suspect's shoulder or knee. In all of this, of course, the interrogation was "unethical" according to the standards usually set for professional, business and social conduct. But the pertinent issue in this case was no ordinary, lawful, professional, business or social matter. It involved the taking of a human life by one who abided by no code of fair play toward his fellow human beings. The killer would not have been moved one bit toward a confession by subjecting him to a reading or lecture regarding the morality of his conduct. It would have been futile merely to give him a pencil and paper and trust that his conscience would impel him to confess. Something more was required—something which was in its essence an "unethical" practice on the part of the interrogator. But, under the circumstances involved in this case, how else would the murderer's guilt have been established? Moreover, let us bear this thought in mind. From the criminal's point of view, *any* interrogation of him is objectionable. To *him* it may be a "dirty trick" to be talked into a confession, for surely it was not done for his benefit. Consequently, any interrogation of him might be labeled as deceitful or unethical.

Of necessity, criminal interrogators must deal with criminal offenders on a somewhat lower moral plane than that upon which ethical, law-abiding citizens are expected to conduct their everyday affairs. That plane, in the interest of innocent suspects need only be subject to the following restriction: Although both "fair" and "unfair" interrogation practices are permissible, nothing shall be done or said to the subject that will be apt to make an innocent person confess.

If all this be so, why then the withholding of this essential interrogation opportunity from the police? And we do, insofar as the stated law is concerned. It comes in the form of statutes or rules that require the prompt delivery of an arrested person before a magistrate for a preliminary hearing or arraignment. Moreover, the United States Supreme Court has decreed that in federal cases no confession is to be received in evidence, regardless of its voluntariness or trustworthiness, if it was obtained during a period of unnecessary delay in delivering the arrestee to a federal commissioner or judge for arraignment. In the federal jurisdiction of Washington, D.C., which must cope with a variety of criminal offenses and problems similar to any other city of comparable size, this federal court rule has had a very crippling effect on police investigations.[6]

6. In addition, some concern should be exhibited over the risk involved in freeing obviously guilty offenders as a result of the courts' efforts to discipline the police. For instance, following the Supreme Court's reversal of his rape conviction, and his release from custody, the defendant in *Mallory* [p. 559] committed two other offenses against female victims. For the latest one he was found guilty and sentenced to the penitentiary by a Pennsylvania Court. * * *

One incongruity of the prompt arraignment rule is this. It is lawful for the police to arrest upon *reasonable belief* that the arrestee has committed the offense, following which they must take him before a magistrate, without unnecessary delay, and charge him with the crime; but for legal proof of the charge, his guilt at the time of trial must be established *beyond reasonable doubt.* Moreover, when the accused gets into the hands of a magistrate for the preliminary hearing, the opportunity for an effective interrogation is ended, many times because of the advice he receives from his attorney to keep his mouth shut.

If we view this whole problem realistically, we must come to the conclusion that an interrogation opportunity is necessary and that legislative provision ought to be made for a privately conducted police interrogation, covering a reasonable period of time, of suspects who are not unwilling to be interviewed, and that the only tactics or techniques that are to be forbidden are those which are apt to make an innocent person confess. * * *

The only real, practically attainable protection we can set up for ourselves against police interrogation abuses (just as with respect to arrest and detention abuses) is to see to it that our police are selected and promoted on a merit basis, that they are properly trained, adequately compensated, and that they are permitted to remain substantially free from politically inspired interference. In the hands of men of this competence there will be a minimum degree of abusive practices. And once again I suggest that the real interest that should be exhibited by the legislatures and the courts is with reference to the protection of the innocent from the hazards of tactics and techniques that are apt to produce confessions of guilt or other false information. Individual civil liberties can survive in such an atmosphere, alongside the protective security of the public.[a]

YALE KAMISAR—EQUAL JUSTICE IN THE GATEHOUSES AND MANSIONS OF AMERICAN CRIMINAL PROCEDURE

In Kamisar, Inbau & Arnold, Criminal Justice in Our Time 19–36 (Howard ed. 1965).

THE SHOW IN THE "GATEHOUSE" VS. THE SHOW IN THE "MANSION" * * *

The courtroom is a splendid place where defense attorneys bellow and strut and prosecuting attorneys are hemmed in at many turns. But what happens before an accused reaches the safety and enjoys the comfort of this veritable mansion? Ah, there's the rub. Typically he must first pass through a much less pretentious edifice, a police station with bare back rooms and locked doors.

In this "gatehouse" of American criminal procedure—through which most defendants journey and beyond which many never get—the enemy of the state is a depersonalized "subject" to be "sized up" and subjected to "interrogation tactics and techniques most appropriate for the occasion";[55] he is "game" to be stalked and cornered.[56]

a. See also Inbau, Reid & Buckley, Criminal Interrogation and Confessions xiii (3d ed. 1986) (introduction); Grano, *Selling the Idea to Tell the Truth: The Professional Interrogator and Modern Confessions Law,* 84 Mich.L.Rev. 662 (1986) (essay review of Inbau, Reid & Buckley, supra) (new edition of Inbau book is "a manual for successful interrogation that a free, civilized, and just society can and should endorse without apology").

55. Inbau & Reid, *Criminal Interrogation and Confessions* 20 (1962).

56. "[T]he interrogator's task is somewhat akin to that of a hunter stalking his game. Each must patiently maneuver himself into a position from which the desired objective may be attained; and in the same manner that the hunter may lose his game by a noisy dash through the bush, can the interrogator fail by not exercising the proper degree of patience." Inbau & Reid, *Lie Detection and Criminal Interrogation* 185 (3d ed. 1953). The authors have dropped this graphic language from their later work.

Here, ideals are checked at the door, "realities" faced, and the prestige of law enforcement vindicated. Once he leaves the "gatehouse" and enters the "mansion"—if he ever gets there—the enemy of the state is repersonalized, even dignified, the public invited, and a stirring ceremony in honor of individual freedom from law enforcement celebrated.

I suspect it is not so much that society knows and approves of the show in the gatehouse, but that society does not know or care. "[S]ociety, by its insouciance, has divested itself of a moral responsibility and unloaded it on to the police. Society doesn't want to know about criminals, but it does want them put away, and it is incurious how this can be done provided it is done. Thus society, in giving the policeman power and wishing to ignore what his techniques must be, has made over to him part of its own conscience."[57]

True, the man in the street would have considerable difficulty explaining why the Constitution requires so much in the courtroom and means so little in the police station, but that is not his affair. "The task of keeping the two shows going at the same time without losing the patronage or the support of the Constitution for either," as Thurman Arnold once observed, is "left to the legal scholar."[58] Perhaps this is only fitting and proper, for as Thomas Reed Powell used to say, if you can think about something that is related to something else without thinking about the thing to which it is related, then you have the legal mind.

That the legal mind passes by or shuts out the *de facto* inquisitorial system which has characterized our criminal procedure for so long is bad enough. What is worse is that such an attitude leads many—perhaps requires many—to recoil with horror and dismay at any proposal which recognizes the grim facts of the criminal process and seeks to do something about them.

[At this point, the author discusses suggestions in the late 1920's that (rather than a police officer) a magistrate, or a prosecutor in the presence of a magistrate, do the interrogation, and a proposal in the early 1940's that in federal cases a commissioner do the interrogation at preliminary hearings, but only after advising the suspect of his right to counsel and his right to remain silent. Both proposals were "beaten down to the accompaniment of cries" that they were "opposed to our traditions of fair play," "contrary to the basic traditions of Anglo–American procedure" and violative of the constitutional guarantee against self-incrimination.]

Evidently, so long as neither the proceedings nor the presiding officer is "judicial," basic traditions are honored and self-incrimination problems avoided. * * *

Four score years ago, Sir James Fitzjames Stephen noted with pride that the fact that "the prisoner is absolutely protected against all judicial questioning before or at the trial * * * contributes greatly to the dignity and apparent humanity of a criminal trial. It effectually avoids the appearance of harshness, not to say cruelty, which often shocks an English spectator in a French court of justice." Whatever the case then, one would have to underscore the "apparent" and "the appearance" in that statement today. Stephen also told us that "the fact that the prisoner cannot be questioned stimulates the search for independent evidence." Whatever the case then, one cannot but wonder today how often the only thing "stimulated" by the inability of judicial officers to question a prisoner is questioning by police officers. One cannot but wonder how often the availability of the privilege (or, perhaps more aptly, the inability of the State to undermine the privilege), once the accused reaches the safety and comfort of the mansion,

57. MacInnes, *The Criminal Society,* in The Police and the Public 101 (Rolph ed. 1962).

58. Arnold, *The Symbols of Government* 156 (Harbinger ed. 1962).

only furnishes the State with an *additional incentive* for proving the charge against him out of his own mouth before he leaves the gatehouse.

IS THE PRIVILEGE CHECKED AT THE "GATEHOUSE" DOOR?

[O]ne who would apply the privilege to the police station may select from the vast conglomerate of determinants which form its history the fact that the maxim "no man shall be compelled to accuse himself" first meant (and until the seventeenth century probably only meant) that no man shall be compelled to make the *first charge* against himself, to submit to a "fishing" interrogation about his crimes, to furnish his own indictment from his own lips. Until the 1600's all parties concerned seemed to have operated on the premise that *after* pleading to the indictment, the accused could be compelled to incriminate himself. * * * When we apply the privilege to "arrests for investigation" or "routine pickups," do we disguise a revolutionary idea in the garb of the past or do we restore the privilege to its primordial state?

Nor should it be forgotten that for many centuries there were simply no "police interrogators" to whom the privilege could be applied. Although what Dean Wigmore calls "the first part" of the history of the privilege, the opposition to the ex officio oath of the ecclesiastical courts, began in the 1200's "criminal investigation by the police, with its concomitant of police interrogation, is a product of the late nineteenth century";[82] in eighteenth-century America as in eighteenth-century England "there were no police [in the modern sense] and, though some states seem to have had prosecutors, private prosecution was the rule rather than the exception."[83] In fact as well as in theory, observes Professor Edmond M. Morgan, "there can be little question that the modern American police have taken over the functions performed originally by the English committing magistrates [and at least by some colonial magistrates]; they are in a real sense administrative officers and their questioning of the person under arrest is an investigative proceeding in which testimony is taken." If modern police are permitted to interrogate under the coercive influence of arrest and secret detention, then, insists Professor Albert R. Beisel, "they are doing the very same acts which historically the judiciary was doing in the seventeenth century but which the privilege against self-incrimination abolished."

I do not contend that "the implications of a tangled and obscure history" dictate that the privilege apply to the police station, only that they permit it. I do not claim that this long and involved history displaces judgment, only that it liberates it. I do not say that the distinct origins of the confession and self-incrimination rules are irrelevant, only that it is more important (if we share Dean Charles T. McCormick's views) that "the kinship of the two rules is too apparent for denial" and that "such policy as modern writers are able to discover as a basis for the self-incrimination privilege * * * pales to a flicker beside the flaming demands of justice and humanity for protection against extorted confessions."

Those who applaud the show in the mansion without hissing the show in the gatehouse may also:

Find refuge in the notion that compulsion to testify means *legal* compulsion. Since he is threatened neither with perjury for testifying falsely nor contempt for refusing to testify at all, it cannot be said, runs the argument, that the man in the back room of the police station is being "compelled" to be a "witness against

82. Note, *An Historical Argument for the Right to Counsel During Police Interrogation,* 73 Yale L.J. 1000, 1034 (1964).

83. Id. at 1041. See also Barrett, *Police Practices and the Law—From Arrest to Release or Charge,* 50 Calif.L.Rev. 11, 16–19 (1962). * * *

himself" within the meaning of the privilege. Since the police have no legal right to make him answer, "there is no legal obligation to which a privilege in the technical sense can apply."[91]

Can we accept this analysis without forgetting as lawyers and judges what we know as men? Without permitting logic to triumph over life? So long as "what on their face are merely words of request take on color from the officer's badge, gun and demeanor";[94] so long as his interrogators neither advise him of his rights nor permit him to consult with a lawyer who will; can there be any doubt that many a "subject" will *assume* that the police have a legal right to an answer? That many an incriminating statement will be extracted under "color" of law? So long as the interrogator is instructed to "get the idea across [that he] has 'all the time in the world' "; so long as "the power [legal or otherwise] to extract answers begets a forgetfulness of the just limitations of the power" and "the simple and peaceful process of questioning breeds a readiness to resort to bullying and to physical force"; can there be any doubt that many a subject will assume that there is an *illegal* sanction for contumacy?

If these inferences are unfair, if very few "subjects" are misled to believe that there is either a legal obligation to talk or unlimited time and illegal means available to make them do so—if, in short, they know they can "shut up"—why are the police so bent on preventing counsel from telling them what they already know? Why, at least, don't the officers themselves tell their "subjects" plainly and emphatically that they need not and cannot be made to answer? That they will be permitted to consult with counsel, or be brought before a magistrate in short order? And why is the "subject" questioned in *secret?* Why does the modest proposal that a suspect be interrogated by or before an impartial functionary immediately after arrest "meet with scant favor in police circles, even from the most high-minded and highly respected elements in those circles"?[99]

Finally, those who have learned to live with the widespread practices in the gatehouse may take the "waiver" tack. They may:

Concede that the privilege against self-incrimination exists in the police station, but maintain that when (instead of exercising his right to remain silent or to make only self-serving remarks) a suspect "volunteers" damaging statements he has *waived* his rights. This is not much of a concession for "if the privilege is easily waived, there is really no privilege at all."[100] However, if "when the state is putting questions, the answers to which will disclose criminal activities by the witness, there is likely to be an especially high insistence checked by an especially high reluctance," then there is likely to be an especially low incidence of valid waiving of the privilege.

So long as "the classic definition of waiver enumerated in *Johnson v. Zerbst*—'an intelligent relinquishment or abandonment of a known right or privilege'—furnishes the controlling standard,"[102] so long as the courts "indulge every reasonable presumption against [such] waiver," it is difficult to see how the contention that an unadvised suspect waives the privilege simply by talking even presents a substantial question. "The Fourteenth Amendment," announced the Supreme Court only a year ago, "secures against state invasion the same privilege that the Fifth Amendment guarantees against federal infringement—the right of a

91. See Mayers, *Shall We Amend the Fifth Amendment?* 82–83, 223–33 (1959); 8 Wigmore, *Evidence* 329 n. 27 (McNaughton rev. 1961). But both authors are quick to marshal the contrary arguments.

94. Foote, *The Fourth Amendment: Obstacle or Necessity in the Law of Arrest?* in Police Power and Individual Freedom 29, 30 (Sowle ed. 1962).

99. Mayers 90.

100. Note, 5 Stan.L.Rev. 459, 477 (1953).

102. *Fay v. Noia* [Ch. 28, § 2].

person to remain silent unless he chooses to speak in the unfettered exercise of his own will."[104] Can it seriously be said of the routine police interrogation that the suspect so speaks? Again, only a year ago, the Court pointed out that "no system of criminal justice can, or should, survive if it comes to depend for its continued effectiveness on the citizens' abdication through unawareness of their constitutional rights."[105] On what else does the existing system depend?

[The] trouble with both the "waiver" and "no legal compulsion" rationalizations of the existing *de facto* inquisitorial system is this: when we expect the police dutifully to notify a suspect of the very means he may utilize to frustrate them—when we rely on them to advise a suspect unbegrudgingly and unequivocally of the very rights he is being counted on *not* to assert—we demand too much of even our best officers. As Dean Edward L. Barrett has asked: "[I]s it the duty of the police to persuade the suspect to talk or persuade him not to talk? They cannot be expected to do both."[110]

Suspects there are who feel in a "pleading guilty" mood, for some of the many reasons most defendants do plead guilty. Suspects there are who would intentionally relinquish their rights for some hoped-for favor from the state. I do not deny this. I do deny that such suspects do not need a lawyer.

Surely the man who, in effect, is pleading guilty in the gatehouse needs a lawyer no less than one who arrives at the same decision only after surviving the perilous journey through that structure.[a]

JOSEPH D. GRANO—CONFESSIONS, TRUTH, AND THE LAW

129–36 (1993).

[Professor Laurence Benner] correctly noted that English judges in the nineteenth century came to regard it as their duty to advise suspects at the pretrial examination that they need not respond to questions, a requirement ultimately codified in 1848.[90] Because these developments occurred after the Fifth Amendment's adoption, however, they do not shed much light on the principle that the framers thought they were constitutionalizing. Moreover, judicial questioning of the accused at the preliminary examination persisted in some American states, such as New York, until the middle of the nineteenth century. At least one commentator has speculated that the privilege came to be viewed as a bar to judicial questioning at the pretrial examination only after the examination court ceased to perform an investigatory function and assumed more of an ordinary judicial role. This thesis finds support in the observation of a British Home Office working group that the nineteenth-century development of organized police forces made possible the separation of the investigative and judicial functions that had previously been combined in the pretrial examination court.

[It] should not be surprising [that] the mid-nineteenth-century statutory restrictions on judicial questioning of the accused created in some quarters "a

104. *Malloy v. Hogan* [p. 569].

105. *Escobedo v. Illinois* [p. 563].

110. Brief Amicus Curiae, p. 9, *People v. Dorado,* 398 P.2d 361 (1965) (on rehearing).

a. Compare Stephen A. Saltzburg, *Miranda v. Arizona Revisited: Constitutional Law or Judicial Fiat,* 26 Washburn L.J. 1, 14 (1986) (drafters of self-incrimination clause could not have intended to prohibit any magistrate or judge from compelling a person to answer questions, but to permit other officials to do so in secret sessions and without any judicial protection against the nature and manner of questioning) with Joseph D. Grano, *Selling the Idea to Tell the Truth: The Professional Interrogator and Modern Confessions Law,* 84 Mich.L.Rev. 662, 683–84, 686 (1986) (in an historical sense, no "compulsion" within meaning of self-incrimination clause is present in the stationhouse; moreover, "mere questioning by itself" is hardly equivalent to compulsion).

90. Benner, *Requiem for Miranda: The Rehnquist Court's Voluntariness Doctrine in Historical Perspective,* 67 Wash. U.L.Q. 59, 81–82.

sense of resistance to police interrogation"; in Professor Mark Berger's words, "[h]aving given up the role of interrogator, the justices of the peace were uncertain whether police could be allowed to perform that function."[99] As already seen, however, the development of organized police forces and the concomitant ban on judicial questioning, at least at the pretrial examination, did not take hold either in Britain or in this country until well after the Fifth Amendment was adopted. In any event, uncertainty about the propriety of police interrogation and a ban on police interrogation are two different matters, and the former never evolved into the latter. On the contrary, as Professor George Dix has documented, nineteenth-century voluntariness law in England tolerated confessions induced by trickery and made exceptions to the rule excluding confessions induced by promises, while American courts displayed even "less enthusiasm" for the common-law rules.[100]

[Thus, the *Miranda* Court] erred, at least from a historical perspective, in perceiving an "intimate connection"[a] between the privilege, which prohibited compulsory oaths and mandatory judicial questioning of the accused, and the issues pertaining to the admissibility of extrajudicial confessions. [Although] the common law had developed a voluntariness requirement for confessions prior to the adoption of the Fifth Amendment, neither the voluntariness rule nor its underlying trustworthiness rationale referred to the protection against compulsory self-incrimination. Concededly, some voices did question how police interrogation could be deemed consistent with the mid-nineteenth-century ban on mandatory judicial questioning of the accused at the pretrial examination, but in neither Great Britain nor the United States did the voluntariness rule or the privilege evolve to the point of prohibiting police interrogation. Indeed, not even [the *Miranda* case] went that far. * * *

Some may contend that the privilege, if applied to the police station, should make police-initiated interrogation unlawful. This would make the privilege in the police station coextensive with the privilege at trial, where both the prosecutor and judge are forbidden from questioning an accused who does not "waive" Fifth Amendment rights by taking the stand in his own defense. If this is the privilege to be applied, however, the "kinship" between it and the common-law voluntariness rule, far from being "too apparent for denial," is difficult to fathom, for the common-law voluntariness rule, as the previous section indicated, never condemned police interrogation as such.

Still, some may find it incongruous to bar interrogation at trial but to permit police questioning before trial. [Some 30 years ago] Bernard Weisberg complained in an influential article that we "would be hard put to explain to visitors from a legal Mars how ... secret questioning in a police station fits into a system of criminal law which recognizes the privilege against self-incrimination," and he specifically contrasted the scope of an accused's protections at trial with the absence of corresponding protections in the police station.[106] Building on this theme, Professor Kamisar similarly contrasted in colorful, metaphoric prose the "show in the gatehouse," where "ideals are checked at the door and 'realities'

99. Berger, *Legislating Confession Law in Great Britain: A Statutory Approach to Police Interrogations,* 24 U.Mich.J.L.Ref. 1, 10 n. 34 (1990).

100. Dix, *Mistake, Ignorance, Expectation of Benefit, and the Modern Law of Confessions,* 1975 Wash.U.L.Q. 275, 282–84.

a. After quoting extensively from several police interrogation manuals which recommended and spelled out various methods of obtaining incriminating statements from a suspect taken into custody, the *Miranda* Court commented (384 U.S. at 458, 86 S.Ct. at 1619): "From the foregoing, we can readily perceive an intimate connection between the privilege against self-incrimination and police custodial questioning."

106. Weisberg, *Police Interrogation of Arrested Persons: A Skeptical View,* 52 J.Crim.L. & P.S. 21 (1961).

faced," and the "show in the mansion," where "the defendant is 'even dignified, the public invited, and a stirring ceremony in honor of individual freedom from law enforcement celebrated.' "

[The] answer to the charge of incongruity is rooted both in history and in the "realities" that Professor Kamisar disparagingly referred to. Despite the questions that were raised, nineteenth-century courts in both Great Britain and this country refused to prohibit police interrogation or to render it ineffective by onerous restrictions. Although debate has never abated, courts in both countries, particularly in recent years, have continued to recognize the importance of police interrogation. Indeed, [the] transformation of the judicial role that occurred in the nineteenth century was probably made possible by the development of police forces that assumed the investigative function previously performed by the pretrial examination court.

[The] division of the investigative and adjudicative functions makes sense from a separation of powers perspective. Moreover, reflecting their own perceptions of fairness, American criminal justice systems in particular have deemed it important to separate the prosecutorial and the judicial roles. Whatever a system's structure or underlying ideology, however, the investigative authority must be lodged somewhere for the system to be viable. Because successful investigation often depends on the questioning of reluctant witnesses and suspects, and on other intrusive strategies as well, the investigative stage, as a practical matter, cannot be subject to the same restraints that govern the adjudicative stage. The operative rules will be different because the institutions that dominate the successive stages of the process have dissimilar functions and responsibilities. Simply put, an investigation is not, and cannot be, a trial. * * *

One might still object [that] an argument invoking history and practical considerations does not provide a principled response to the gatehouse-mansion dichotomy. After all, the fact remains that the accused is not subject to interrogation at trial unless he elects to testify, and on principle the institution of police interrogation seems inconsistent with this limitation. The answer to this is that the alleged inconsistency is not nearly as obvious as it seems. Rather than referring to a single rule, the "privilege . . . embraces several distinct rules of law, each having an independent development." Nonetheless, in most situations, the "privilege is merely an *option of refusal,* not a prohibition of inquiry."

Thus, * * * a grand jury may subpoena even a target of its investigation, and the targeted individual has the burden of invoking the privilege on a question-by-question basis. Similarly, even under *Miranda,* targets of police interrogation who are not in custody are not entitled to warnings and have the burden of affirmatively invoking the privilege when questioned.

[If] the privilege cannot plausibly be viewed as a ban on police-initiated questioning, what can it mean in the context of police interrogation, and what establishes its "kinship" to the voluntariness rule for confessions? [O]ne might concede that the privilege would prohibit any attempt formally to require suspects, in custody or not, to answer questions. Such a prohibition would be vacuous, however, if governmental officials could force suspects to answer questions by the use of physical or psychological coercion. Not surprisingly, therefore, although the privilege did not play a significant role in the abolition of torture to secure statements in English procedure, various individuals on both sides of the Atlantic came to regard torture as inconsistent with the privilege. Viewed in this light, an obvious kinship exists between the privilege and the voluntariness requirement; indeed, had a voluntariness requirement not independently developed, one might early have been inferred as a logical imperative of the privilege. All this leads, however, to the unremarkable conclusion that the Fifth Amendment, if properly applied to police interrogation at all, prohibits coerced or involuntary confessions. That is, in the context of police interrogation, to "compel" a suspect to become a witness against himself can only mean to "coerce" a suspect to become a witness against himself.

This conclusion, however, is bothersome for *Miranda*'s supporters. For example, Professors Irene and Yale Rosenberg have asserted that "it seems unlikely that the long struggle culminating in the incorporation of the Fifth Amendment prohibition against compelled testimony could have been simply an heroic effort to provide an official synonym for involuntariness."[128] Likewise, regarding it as almost self-evident that the privilege was "more than the 'voluntary' test masquerading under a different label," Professor Kamisar has declared that it takes "real dexterity" to purport to apply the Fifth Amendment to the police station and "yet conclude that [this] does not change things very much." But, to repeat, unless the Fifth Amendment is read as a prohibition on all police questioning, custodial and noncustodial, it can be read in the context of police interrogation only as providing protection against involuntariness or coercion. Indeed, the *Miranda* Court read the Fifth Amendment this way, for it found the Fifth Amendment applicable to the "informal compulsion" exerted by the police, concluded that "custodial" interrogation was "inherently compelling," and distinguished on-the-scene questioning, which it exempted from its holding, on the ground that "the compelling atmosphere inherent in the process of in-custody interrogation is not necessarily present."

The possibility remains, of course, that *coercion* for Fifth Amendment purposes should be a less demanding concept than *coercion* for due process purposes and that, accordingly, *involuntariness* should have different meanings under the two amendments. The Court in *Miranda* took such an approach, for none of its previous due process voluntariness cases had sought to protect the suspect merely from the inherent pressures of custodial questioning. Indeed, the Court candidly admitted, even if it understated the point, that it "might not find the defendants' statements to have been involuntary in traditional terms." The question that *Miranda* did not answer, however, is why the concepts of coercion and involuntariness should have different meanings in the Fifth Amendment and due process contexts.

SECTION 2. HISTORICAL BACKGROUND[a]

A. The Interests Protected by the Due Process "Voluntariness" Test for Admitting Confessions

The first rules governing the admissibility of confessions were laid down in the eighteenth and nineteenth centuries, a time when illegal police methods were relevant only insofar as they affected the trustworthiness of the evidence. Whatever the meaning of the elusive terms "involuntary" and "coerced" confessions

128. Rosenberg & Rosenberg, *A Modest Proposal for the Abolition of Custodial Confessions,* 68 N.C.L.Rev. 69, 108–9 (1989).

a. For a much more detailed treatment of the subject matter of this Note, see Mark Berger, Taking the Fifth 99–124 (1980); Joseph D. Grano, Confessions, Truth, and the Law 59–172 (1993); Otis Stephens, The Supreme Court and Confessions of Guilt 17–119 (1973); 3 Wigmore, Evidence §§ 817–26 (Chadbourn rev. 1970); Anthony G. Amsterdam, The Supreme Court and the Rights of Suspects in Criminal Cases, 45 N.Y.U. L.Rev. 785, 803–10 (1970); Laurence A. Benner, Requiem for Miranda: The Rehnquist Court's Voluntariness Doctrine in Historical Perspective, 67 Wash. U.L.Q. 59 (1989); Gerald M. Caplan, Questioning Miranda, 38 Vand.L.Rev. 1417, 1427–43 (1985); Catherine Hancock, Due Process before Miranda, 70 Tul.L.Rev. 2195 (1996); Yale Kamisar, What is an *"Involuntary" Confession?*, 17 Rutgers L.Rev. 728 (1963); Welsh S. White, *What is an Involuntary Confession Now?*, 50 Rutgers L.Rev. 2001 (1998).

since 1940, for centuries the rule that a confession was admissible so long as it was "voluntary" was more or less an alternative statement of the rule that a confession was admissible so long as it was free of influence which made it untrustworthy or "probably untrue." See generally Charles T. McCormick, *Evidence* 226 (1954); 3 John Henry Wigmore, *Evidence* § 822 (3d ed. 1940).

Indeed, Dean Wigmore condemned the use of the "voluntary" terminology for the reason that "there is nothing in the mere circumstance of compulsion to speak in general * * * which create any risk of untruth." 3 Wigmore, § 843. But the courts' continued reference to the term "voluntariness" in enunciating the requisites for the admissibility of a confession under the due process clause was defended by Dean McCormick, who suggested that it might be prompted "not only by a liking for its convenient brevity, but also by a recognition that there is an interest here to be protected closely akin to the interest of a witness or of an accused person which is protected by the privilege against compulsory self-incrimination." McCormick, *The Scope of Privilege in the Law of Evidence,* 16 Texas L.Rev. 447, 453 (1938).

At least in its advanced stage (the early 1960s), the "due process" or "involuntariness" test appeared to have *three* underlying values or goals. It barred the use of confessions (a) which were of doubtful reliability because of the police methods used to obtain them;[b] (b) which were produced by offensive methods even though the reliability of the confession was not in question; and (c) which were involuntary *in fact* (e.g., obtained from a drugged person) even though the confession was entirely trustworthy and not the product of any conscious police wrongdoing.[c]

At the outset, however, the primary (and perhaps the exclusive) basis for excluding confessions under the due process "voluntariness" test was the "untrustworthiness" rationale, the view that the confession rule was designed merely to protect the integrity of the fact-finding process. This rationale sufficed to explain the exclusion of the confession in *Brown v. Mississippi,* 297 U.S. 278 (1936), the first fourteenth amendment due process confession case (where the deputy who had presided over the beating of the defendants conceded that one prisoner had been whipped but "not too much for a Negro; not as much as I would have done if it were left to me"), and the cases which immediately followed for they, too, were pervaded by threats of, or outright, physical violence. "But when cases involving the more subtle 'psychological' pressures began to appear—usually instances of prolonged interrogation [it] was no longer possible easily to assume that the confessions exacted were unreliable as evidence of guilt. [In *Ashcraft v. Tennessee,* 322 U.S. 143 (1944)] a conviction was reversed where a confession had been obtained after some thirty-six hours of continuous interrogation of the defendant by the police. In effect, the Court ruled that the extended questioning raised a conclusive presumption of 'coercion.' Considering the facts as revealed in the record of the *Ashcraft* case, it is fair to suggest that the result reached by the Court reflected less a concern with the reliability of the confession as evidence of

b. But see *Colorado v. Connelly* (1986) (p. 726), viewing the unreliability of a confession as "a matter to be governed by the evidentiary laws of the forum and not by the Due Process Clause."

c. As for the third underlying value, see *Townsend v. Sain,* 372 U.S. 293 (1963), excluding a confession obtained from one given a drug with the properties of a truth serum, even though the police were unaware of the drug's effect and had engaged in no conscious wrongdoing (although they may have been negligent), and even though the confession was apparently reliable. "Any questioning by police officers which *in fact* produces a confession which is not the product of free intellect," observed the Court, "renders the confession inadmissible."

However, in *Colorado v. Connelly* (1986) (p. 726), the Court looked back at *Townsend* as a case that "presented [an] instance of police wrongdoing."

guilt in the particular case than disapproval of police methods which a majority of the Court conceived as generally dangerous and subject to serious abuse." Francis Allen, *The Supreme Court, Federalism, and State Systems of Criminal Justice,* 8 DePaul L.Rev. 213, 235 (1959). See also Monrad Paulsen, *The Fourteenth Amendment and the Third Degree,* 6 Stan.L.Rev. 411, 418–19 (1954).

As Professor Catherine Hancock has recently observed, *Due Process Before Miranda,* 70 Tul. 2195, 2226 (1996), "*Ashcraft* was a milestone because it prefigured *Miranda*'s recognition of the coercion inherent in all custodial interrogations. [In] a prophetic dictum, [dissenting Justice Jackson] declared that 'even one hour' of interrogation would be inherently coercive, and so there could be no stopping point to the *Ashcraft* doctrine. However, more than twenty years elapsed before this prophecy came to pass in the form of *Miranda*'s presumption that even a few moments of custodial interrogation are inherently coercive."

In *Watts v. Indiana,* 338 U.S. 49 (1949) and the companion cases of *Harris v. South Carolina,* 338 U.S. 68 (1949) and *Turner v. Pennsylvania,* 338 U.S. 62 (1949), the Court reversed three convictions resting on coerced confessions without disputing the accuracy of Justice Jackson's observation (concurring in *Watts* and dissenting in the other cases) that "checked with external evidence they [the confessions in each case] are inherently believable and were not shaken as to truth by anything that occurred at the trial."

The majority, per Frankfurter, J., commented: "In holding that the Due Process Clause *bars police procedure* which violates the basic notions of our accusatorial mode of prosecuting crime and vitiates a conviction based on the fruits of such procedure, we apply the Due Process Clause to its historic function of *assuring appropriate procedure* before liberty is curtailed or life is taken." (Emphasis added.) And three years later, in the famous "stomach-pumping" case of *Rochin v. California,* p. 33, the Court, again speaking through Justice Frankfurter, viewed the coerced confession cases as "only instances of the general requirement that States in their prosecutions respect certain decencies of civilized conduct," pointing out: "Use of involuntary verbal confessions in State criminal trials is constitutionally obnoxious not only because of their unreliability. They are inadmissible under the Due Process Clause even though statements contained in them may be independently established as true. Coerced confessions offend the community's sense of fair play and decency."

That the Court was applying a "police methods"—as well as a "trustworthiness"—test was made clear by *Spano v. New York,* 360 U.S. 315 (1959); *Blackburn v. Alabama,* 361 U.S. 199 (1960) and *Rogers v. Richmond,* 365 U.S. 534 (1961). Thus, the Court, per Warren, C.J., pointed out in *Spano* that the ban against "involuntary" confessions turns not only on their reliability but on the notion that "*the police must obey the law while enforcing the law.*" And the Court, again speaking through the Chief Justice, acknowledged in *Blackburn* that "a *complex of values* underlies the strictures against use by the state of confessions which, by way of *convenient shorthand,* this Court terms involuntary." (Emphasis added.)

Perhaps the most emphatic statement of the point that the untrustworthiness of a confession was not (or no longer) the principal reason for excluding it appears in one of Justice Frankfurter's last opinions on the subject. Writing for the Court in *Rogers,* he observed: "Our decisions under [the Fourteenth Amendment] have made clear that convictions following the admission into evidence of [involuntary confessions] cannot stand * * * not so much because such confessions are unlikely to be true but because the methods used to extract them offend an underlying principle in the enforcement of our criminal law: that ours is an accusatorial and not an inquisitorial system. * * * Indeed, in many of the cases [reversing] state convictions involving the use of confessions obtained by impermissible methods, independent corroborating evidence left little doubt of the truth of what the defendant had confessed."[d]

Although, theoretically, the "police methods" and "trustworthiness" standards for admitting confessions are to be applied independently of each other, in practice they often overlap. Even though it might be conclusively demonstrated that "offensive" police interrogation methods did not produce an "untrustworthy" confession *in the particular case* before the Court, the continued use of such methods is likely to create a substantial risk that other suspects subjected to similar tactics would falsely confess. See Kamisar, *What is an "Involuntary" Confession?,* 17 Rutgers L.Rev. 728, 754–55 (1963), reprinted in Kamisar, Police Interrogation and Confessions 1, 20–22 (1980) (hereinafter referred to as Kamisar Essays).

What *are* the objectionable police methods which render a resulting confession "involuntary"? In the advanced stages of the test, at least, the use or threatened use of physical violence or the kind of protracted relay interrogation that occurred in *Ashcraft,* supra, rendered any resulting confession inadmissible *per se.* In the main, however, it is difficult to isolate any particular interrogation tactic and say that, standing alone, it is so "coercive" or so "offensive" that it requires the exclusion of any resulting confession. For the significant fact about the great bulk of the "involuntary confessions" cases is that "none of them turned on the presence or absence of a single controlling criterion; each reflected a careful scrutiny of all the surrounding circumstances" *Schneckloth v. Bustamonte* (p. 447). And the totality of the surrounding circumstances included "both the characteristics of the accused [many of whom were uneducated, of low mentality or emotionally unstable] and the details of the interrogation." Ibid.

Nevertheless, the pre-*Escobedo,* pre-*Miranda* cases reveal numerous police practices which, if not impermissible *per se,* certainly militate heavily against the "voluntariness" of any resulting confession: stripping off defendant's clothes and keeping him naked for several hours, *Malinski v. New York,* 324 U.S. 401 (1945); informing defendant that state financial aid for her infant children would be cut off, and her children taken from her, if she failed to "cooperate" with police, *Lynumn v. Illinois,* 372 U.S. 528 (1963); after defendant persisted in his denial of guilt, pretending to "bring in" defendant's wife (who suffered from arthritis) for questioning, *Rogers v. Richmond,* supra; repeatedly rejecting defendant's requests to phone his wife and repeatedly informing him that he would not be able to call her or anyone else unless and until he gave the police a statement, *Haynes v. Washington,* 373 U.S. 503 (1963); removing defendant from jail to a distant place in order to thwart the efforts of his friends or relatives to secure his release, or at least to contact him, *Ward v. Texas,* 316 U.S. 547 (1942); utilization of a state-employed psychiatrist, with considerable knowledge of hypnosis, who posed as a "general practitioner" who would provide defendant with the medical relief he needed and succeeded in obtaining a confession from defendant by skillful and suggestive questioning, *Leyra v. Denno,* 347 U.S. 556 (1954); utilization of defendant's "childhood friend," then a fledgling police officer, who, pursuant to his superiors' instructions, pretended that defendant's phone call had gotten his "friend" "in a lot of trouble," so much so that his "friend's" job was in jeopardy,

d. In admitting the confession, the *Rogers* trial court had found that the interrogation tactics "had no tendency to produce a confession that was not in accord with the truth." The Supreme Court did not consider the finding *unwarranted,* but *irrelevant.* The admissibility of the confession had been decided "by reference to a legal standard which took into account the circumstance of probable truth or falsity"—"and this is not a permissible standard under the Due Process Clause." See Stephen J. Schulhofer, *Confessions and the Court,* 79 Mich.L.Rev. 865, 867 (1981).

and loss of his job would prove disastrous to his "friend's" wife and children, *Spano,* supra.

Consider Albert Alschuler, *Constraint and Confessions*, 74 Denv.U.L.Rev. 957 (1997): "The Court should define the term coerced confession to mean a confession caused by offensive governmental conduct, period. * * * Shifting their attention almost entirely from the minds of suspects to the conduct of government officers, courts should abandon the search for 'overborne wills' and attempts to assess the quality of individual choices."

B. The Shortcomings of the "Voluntariness" Test

Although the Supreme Court customarily used the terms "voluntariness" and "involuntariness" in explaining and applying the due process test for the admissibility of confessions, the "voluntariness" concept seems to be at once too wide and too narrow. In one sense, in the sense of wanting to confess, or doing so in a completely spontaneous manner, "in the sense of a confession to a priest merely to rid one's soul of a sense of guilt" (Jackson, J., dissenting in *Ashcraft v. Tennessee*), few criminal confessions reviewed by the courts, if any, had been "voluntary." On the other hand, in the sense that the situation always presents a "choice" between two alternatives, either one disagreeable, to be sure, *all* confessions are "voluntary." See 3 Wigmore, § 824.

Moreover, as the rationales for the Court's coerced confession cases evolved, it became increasingly doubtful that terms such as "voluntariness," "coercion," and "breaking the will" were very helpful in resolving the issue. For such terms do not focus directly on either the risk of untrue confessions or the offensiveness of police interrogation methods employed in eliciting the confession. See Paulsen, supra, at 429–30.

As the Court, per O'Connor, J., observed in *Miller v. Fenton,* 474 U.S. 104 (1985) (holding that the "voluntariness" of a confession is not a "factual issue" but "a legal question meriting independent consideration in a federal habeas corpus proceeding"): "[T]he admissibility of a confession turns as much on whether the techniques for extracting the statements, as applied to *this* suspect, are compatible with a system that presumes innocence and assures that a conviction will not be secured by inquisitorial means as on whether the defendant's will was in fact overborne. [The] hybrid quality of the voluntariness inquiry, subsuming, as it does, a 'complex of values,' *Blackburn,* itself militates against treating the question as one of simple historical fact." As the *Miller* Court also noted, "[t]he voluntariness rubric has been variously condemned as 'useless,' 'perplexing,' and 'legal 'double-talk.' "[a]

Nor was "the elusive, measureless standard of psychological coercion heretofore developed in this Court by accretion on almost an ad hoc, case-by-case basis," as Justice Clark described it, dissenting in *Reck v. Pate,* 367 U.S. 433 (1961); a test which seemed to permit constitutionally permissible police interrogation to vary widely according to how dull or alert or soft or tough the particular suspect, see e.g., Maguire, *Evidence of Guilt* 134 fn. 5 (1959); likely to guide or to shape police conduct very much, if at all.

Moreover, as pointed out in Schulhofer, fn. d supra, at 869–70, because of its ambiguity and "its subtle mixture of factual and legal elements," the "voluntariness" test "virtually invited [trial judges] to give weight to their subjective preferences" and "discouraged review even by the most conscientious appellate judges." See also Kamisar Essays at 12–25, 69–76; CRIMPROC § 6.2(d); Herman,

a. See also Notes 3 & 4 following *Colorado v. Connelly*, p. 730–32.

The Supreme Court, the Attorney General, and the Good Old Days of Police Interrogation, 48 Ohio St.L.J. 733, 745–55 (1987); Stone, *The Miranda Doctrine in the Burger Court,* 1977 Sup.Ct.Rev. 99, 102–03; W. White, *Defending Miranda: A Reply to Professor Caplan,* 39 Vand.L.Rev. 1, 7–9, 11–16 (1986).[b]

As police interrogators made greater use of "psychological" techniques over the years, the always difficult problems of proof confronting the alleged victims of improper interrogation practices became increasingly arduous. Disputes over whether physical violence occurred are not always easy to resolve, but evidence of "mental" or "psychological" coercion is especially elusive. Frequently, the defendant was inarticulate, which aggravated the difficulties of recreating the tenor and atmosphere of the police questioning or the *manner* in which the appropriate advice about the suspect's rights might have been given or, if properly given, subsequently undermined.

Moreover, the local courts almost always resolved the almost inevitable "swearing contest" over what happened behind the closed doors in favor of the police, perhaps for the reasons suggested by Walter Schaefer, *Federalism and State Criminal Procedure,* 70 Harv.L.Rev. 1, 7 (1956): "In the field of criminal procedure [a] strong local interest competes only against an ideal. Local interest is concerned with the particular case and with the guilt or innocence of the particular individual. * * * While it is hard indeed for any judge to set apart the question of the guilt or innocence of a particular defendant and focus solely upon the procedural aspect of the case, it becomes easier [in] a reviewing court where the impact of the evidence is diluted. The more remote the court, the easier it is to consider the case in terms of a hypothetical defendant accused of crime, instead of a particular man whose guilt has been established."[c]

b. But consider Gerald Caplan, *Questioning Miranda,* 38 Vand.L.Rev. 1417, 1433–34 (1985): "[The voluntariness test] allowed the Court to move carefully, to feel its way, and to make its judgments without fear of prematurely constitutionalizing interrogation practices. [The] Court's failure to state the basis for a particular decision or its blurring of a holding in the veiled attire of the 'totality of the circumstances' can be seen as shrewd and responsible pragmatism. Pragmatism may have been preferable to principles at a time when there was little general agreement on the principles to be applied. [If] the development of the voluntariness test had not come to a near end with the advent of *Miranda,* perhaps the test would have continued to achieve definition and improved serviceability."

c. This may help to explain the strikingly different reactions of the state courts and the U.S. Supreme Court to the situation in *Mincey v. Arizona,* 437 U.S. 385 (1978) (other aspects of which are discussed at pp. 364, 930. Just a few hours before the interrogation occurred, Mincey had been seriously wounded during a narcotics raid which resulted in the death of a police officer. According to the attending physician, Mincey had arrived at the hospital "depressed almost to the point of coma." At the time Detective Hust questioned him, Mincey's condition was still sufficiently serious that he was in the intensive care unit. Lying on his back on a hospital bed, encumbered by tubes, needles and breathing apparatus, Mincey (according to the Supreme Court) clearly and repeatedly expressed his wish not to be interrogated, but Hust continued to question him. Unable to speak because of the tube in his mouth, Mincey responded to Hust's questions by writing answers on pieces of paper provided by the hospital, at one point writing: "This is all I can say without a lawyer." (In a written report dated about a week later, Hust transcribed Mincey's answers and added the questions he believed he had asked.)

Under these circumstances, the trial court found "with unmistakable clarity" that Mincey's statements were "voluntary" and thus, despite being obtained in violation of *Miranda,* admissible for impeachment purposes. (On this point, see p. 922). The state supreme court unanimously affirmed. On the basis of its independent evaluation of the record, the Court, per Stewart, J., reversed. It noted, inter alia, that "the reliability of Hust's report [reconstructing the interrogation] is uncertain." It concluded that "the undisputed evidence makes clear that Mincey wanted *not* to answer Detective Hust" but that—"weakened by pain and shock, isolated from family, friends and legal counsel, and barely conscious"—Mincey's "will was simply overborne."

Rehnquist, J., dissented from the holding that Mincey's statements were involuntary and—as was true of so many of the older "involuntariness" cases—disputed the Court's reading of the record: "[The Court] ignores entirely some evidence of voluntariness and

Under the old case-by-case approach, however, the defendant could not often avail himself of the "remoteness" of the U.S. Supreme Court. In the thirty years since *Brown v. Mississippi,* the Court had taken an average of about one state confession case per year and *two-thirds of these* had been "death penalty" cases. Indeed, the Court's workload was so great that it even denied a hearing in most "death penalty" cases. See Kamisar Essays 75. Almost no garden-variety criminal defendant who cried "coerced confession" but lost the "swearing contest" below was likely to survive the winnowing process above. Not surprisingly, Justice Black remarked in the course of the oral arguments in *Miranda:* "[I]f you are going to determine [the admissibility of the confession] each time on the circumstances, [if] this Court will take them one by one [it] is more than we are capable of doing."

Although the 1964 *Massiah* and *Escobedo* cases and the 1966 *Miranda* case (all discussed infra) were to catch heavy criticism, "[g]iven the Court's inability to articulate a clear and predictable definition of 'voluntariness,' the apparent persistence of state courts in utilizing the ambiguity of the concept to validate confessions of doubtful constitutionality, and the resultant burden on its own workload, it seemed inevitable that the Court would seek 'some automatic device by which the potential evils of incommunicado interrogation [could] be controlled.' " Geoffrey R. Stone, *The Miranda Doctrine in the Burger Court,* 1977 Sup.Ct.Rev. 102–03 (quoting from Schaefer, *The Suspect and Society* 10 (1967)).[d]

C. The *McNabb–Mallory* Rule: Supervisory Authority Over Federal Criminal Justice vs. Fourteenth Amendment Due Process

As Justice FRANKFURTER pointed out for the majority in the famous case of McNABB v. UNITED STATES, 318 U.S. 332, 63 S.Ct. 608, 87 L.Ed. 819 (1943), while the power of the Court to upset *state* convictions is limited to the enforcement of fourteenth amendment due process, the standards of *federal* criminal justice "are not satisfied merely by observance of those minimal historic safeguards." Rather, the Court can, and has, formulated rules of evidence in the exercise of its "supervisory authority" over the administration of federal criminal

distinguishes away yet other testimony. * * * Despite the contrary impression given by the Court, [the state supreme court's] opinion casts no doubt on the testimony or report of Detective Hust. The Court is thus left solely with its own conclusions as to the reliability of various witnesses based on a re-examination of the record on appeal. * * * I believe that the trial court was entitled to conclude that, notwithstanding Mincey's medical condition, his statements in the intensive care unit were admissible. [T]hat the same court might have been equally entitled to reach the opposite conclusion does not justify this Court's adopting the opposite conclusion."

d. *The continued vitality of the pre-Miranda voluntariness test.* Since the landmark *Miranda* case, the police must give a suspect the now familiar warnings and obtain a waiver of his rights before subjecting him to "custodial interrogation." However, the "old" due process-voluntariness test is still important in a number of situations, e.g., when the police question a suspect not in "custody"; when the police question a suspect who waives his rights and agrees to talk, but denies any involvement in the crime. See generally pp. 715–24. Moreover, the distinction between an "involuntary" confession and one obtained only in violation of *Miranda* is important in a number of procedural contexts, e.g., use of the confession for impeachment purposes. See generally pp. 922–25.

Thus, "[c]areful attention to the voluntariness issue remains an imperative, though sometimes overlooked, obligation of court and counsel," Schulhofer, supra, at 878. To illustrate his point, Professor Schulhofer refers to *United States v. Mesa,* discussed at pp. 607, 633. The *Mesa* court's rejection of a *Miranda* challenge, observes Schulhofer, id. at 878 n. 58, was "based on particularities of *Miranda's* rationale and would by no means preclude a voluntariness claim. Yet the defense never argued, and so the [Third Circuit] never considered, whether the statements made by this psychologically distraught suspect, on the verge of suicide, [who had barricaded himself in a motel room and threatened that he would not surrender peacefully], in the course of a three-and-one-half-hour conversation [with an FBI crisis negotiator] under highly charged circumstances, were admissible under the due process test."

justice which go well beyond due process requirements.[a] A good example was the significance given to the fact that incriminating statements were obtained during illegal detention, i.e., while the suspect was held in violation of federal statutory requirements that he be promptly taken before a committing magistrate to ascertain whether good cause exists to hold him for trial. Although, during this period, an otherwise voluntary confession was not rendered inadmissible in a *state* prosecution solely because it was elicited during prolonged and hence illegal precommitment detention (this was only *one* of many factors in determining whether a confession was voluntary), the 1943 *McNabb* case, although hardly free from ambiguity, seemed to hold that such a confession had to be excluded from *federal* prosecutions.

The *McNabb* rule was heavily criticized by law enforcement spokesmen and many members of Congress and begrudgingly interpreted by most lower federal courts. See generally James E. Hogan & Joseph M. Snee, *The McNabb–Mallory Rule: Its Rise, Rationale and Rescue,* 47 Geo.L.J. 1 (1958). However, it was emphatically reaffirmed in MALLORY v. UNITED STATES, 354 U.S. 449 (1957), where, speaking for a unanimous Court, Justice FRANKFURTER observed:

"We cannot sanction this extended delay [some seven hours], resulting in confession, without subordinating [Fed.R.Crim.P. 5(a), requiring that an arrestee be taken 'without unnecessary delay' to the nearest available committing officer] to the discretion of arresting officers in finding exceptional circumstances for its disregard. [There is no escape] from the constraint laid upon the police by that Rule in that two other suspects were involved for the same crime. Presumably, whomever the police arrest they must arrest on 'probable cause.' It is not the function of the police to arrest, as it were, at large and to use an interrogating process at police headquarters in order to determine whom they should charge before a committing magistrate on 'probable cause.' "

Only a handful of states adopted the *McNabb–Mallory* rule or its equivalent on their own initiative.[b] But many hoped (and many others feared) that some day the Court would apply the rule to the states as a matter of fourteenth amendment due process. The Court never did. Instead, in the years since the 1957 *Mallory*

a. For a long, hard look at the federal courts' exercise of "supervisory powers" over the administration of federal criminal justice generally and a look back at *McNabb,* regarded by many as the first supervisory power decision, see Sara Sun Beale, *Reconsidering Supervisory Power in Criminal Cases: Constitutional and Statutory Limits on the Authority of the Federal Courts,* 84 Colum.L.Rev. 1433 (1984). Extracts from Professor Beale's article appear at p. 47.

b. It was not until 1960 that the states' unanimity in refusing to follow the Supreme Court's lead in the *McNabb–Mallory* line of cases was broken. See *People v. Hamilton,* 102 N.W.2d 738, 741–43 (Mich.1960); Rothblatt & Rothblatt, *Police Interrogation: The Right to Counsel and to Prompt Arraignment,* 27 Brooklyn L.Rev. 24, 40–44 (1960). On the eve of *Miranda,* two more states adopted an equivalent of the rule, Delaware, see *Webster v. State,* 213 A.2d 298, 301 (Del.1965); and Connecticut, by legislation, see *State v. Vollhardt,* 244 A.2d 601, 607 (Conn.1968) (subsequent case construing statute). In recent years at least three more state courts—Maryland, Montana, and Pennsylvania—adopted some equivalent of the rule. See *Johnson v. State,* 384 A.2d 709, 714–18 (Md.1978); *State v. Benbo,* 570 P.2d 894, 899–900 (Mont.1977); *Commonwealth v. Davenport,* 370 A.2d 301, 306 (Pa.1977); *Commonwealth v. Futch,* 290 A.2d 417, 418–19 (Pa. 1972).

The life of Maryland's version of the *McNabb–Mallory* rule, adopted in the 1978 *Johnson* case, "was short and unhappy." Donald E. Wilkes, *The New Federalism in Criminal Procedure in 1984: Death of the Phoenix?,* in Developments in State Constitutional Law 166, 170 (B. McGraw ed. 1985). The *Johnson* rule was usually interpreted begrudgingly and—in a "legislative blow to the new federalism"—repealed by statute in 1981. See id. at 169–171.

For a close examination and strong criticism of the "state court revival" *McNabb–Mallory* rule, see Note, 72 J.Crim.L. & C. 204 (1981). The Note maintains, id. at 241, that "current constitutional law addresses many of the original concerns underlying delay statutes, obviating the need for reliance on a doctrine of implied statutory exclusion."

decision, the last of the *McNabb* line of cases, the Court closed in on the state confession problem by making increasing resort to the right to counsel and the privilege against self-incrimination. By such means the state confession rules were eventually to *go beyond* the *McNabb–Mallory* doctrine in a number of respects.[c]

D. THE RIGHT TO COUNSEL AND THE ANALOGY TO THE ACCUSATORIAL, ADVERSARY TRIAL

CROOKER v. CALIFORNIA, 357 U.S. 433 (1958), involved a petitioner who attended one year of law school, during which time he studied criminal law, and who indicated in his dealings with the police that he was fully aware of his right to remain silent. On the basis of a challenged confession, he was convicted of murder of his paramour and sentenced to death. He contended that by persisting in interrogating him after denying his specific request to contact his lawyer the police violated his due process right to legal representation and advice and that therefore use of any confession obtained from him under these circumstances should be barred even though "freely" and "voluntarily" made under traditional standards. Such a rule retorted the Court, per CLARK, J., "would have [a] devastating effect on enforcement of criminal law, for it would effectively preclude police questioning—*fair as well as unfair*—until the accused was afforded opportunity to call his attorney. Due process, a concept 'less rigid and more fluid than those envisaged in other specific and particular provisions of the Bill of Rights,' *Betts v. Brady,* demands no such rule."

In his dissenting opinion, Justice DOUGLAS, with whom Warren, C.J., and Black and Brennan, JJ., joined, insisted: "The right to have counsel at the pretrial stage is often necessary to give meaning and protection to the right to be heard at the trial itself. It may also be necessary as a restraint on the coercive power of the police. [The] demands of our civilization expressed in the Due Process Clause require that the accused who wants a counsel should have one at any time after the moment of arrest."

In the companion case of CICENIA v. LA GAY, 357 U.S. 504 (1958), not only did petitioner unsuccessfully ask to see his lawyer while he was being questioned by the police, but his lawyer, who arrived at the police station while petitioner was being interrogated, repeatedly (and unsuccessfully) asked to see his client. Moreover, petitioner was not well educated as was Crooker. Nevertheless, the Court affirmed the murder conviction (which led to a life sentence), disposing of petitioner's contention that he had a constitutional right to confer with counsel on the authority of *Crooker*. With the exception of Justice Brennan, who took no part in the case, the Court split along the same lines it had in *Crooker*.

The following year, however, by virtue of SPANO v. NEW YORK, it appeared that the Court had reached the view that once a person was *formally charged* by indictment or information his constitutional right to counsel had "begun"—at least his right to the assistance of counsel he himself had retained. Four concurring Justices took this position in *Spano:* Justices Black, Douglas and Brennan, all of whom had dissented in *Crooker;* and newly appointed Justice Stewart, who had replaced Justice Burton.

In separate concurring opinions both Justice Douglas (joined by Black and Brennan, JJ.) and Justice Stewart (joined by Douglas and Brennan, JJ.) stressed that *Spano* was not a case where the police were questioning a suspect in the

c. Title II of the Omnibus Crime Control and Safe Streets Act of 1968 purports to repeal (among other judicial doctrines) the *McNabb–Mallory* rule. Because the possible constitutional vulnerability of this 1968 provision turns in part on an appraisal of *Miranda,* treatment of this point is postponed until p. 560.

course of investigating an unsolved crime but one where the subject of interrogation was already under indictment for murder when he surrendered to the authorities. Both concurring opinions also measured the proceedings in the "interrogation" room against the standard of a public trial and formal judicial proceedings. Thus Justice STEWART observed: "Under our system of justice an indictment is supposed to be followed by an arraignment and a trial. * * * What followed the petitioner's surrender in this case was not arraignment in a court of law, but an all-night inquisition in a prosecutor's office, a police station, and an automobile. * * * Our Constitution guarantees the assistance of counsel to a man on trial for his life in an orderly courtroom, presided over by a judge, open to the public, and protected by all the procedural safeguards of the law. Surely a Constitution which promises that much can vouchsafe no less to the same man under midnight inquisition in the squad room of a police station."

As we have already seen, a majority of the *Spano* Court did not go off on "right to counsel" grounds, finding the confession inadmissible on straight "coerced confession" grounds, but the Chief Justice, who wrote the majority opinion, had taken the position, a year earlier in *Crooker,* that the right to counsel should "begin" even earlier than at the point of indictment. Thus, counting heads, it appeared that by 1959 the view of the concurring Justices in *Spano* commanded a majority of the Court.

E. *Massiah and Escobedo*: The Court Closes in on the "Confession Problem"

"There is a case in the Supreme Court now from Illinois, *People v. Escobedo,* that involves this very issue [of when the right to counsel begins] and I am scared that the Court is going to hold that this right exists from the time of arrest—if a person asks for counsel and he is not given counsel, anything you get from him after that has to be excluded."

—Fred E. Inbau, *A Forum on the Interrogation of the Accused,* 49 Corn.L.Q. 382, 401 (January 31, 1964).

Five years after *Spano,* in MASSIAH v. UNITED STATES, 377 U.S. 201 (1964), a 6–3 majority (consisting of the four concurring Justices in *Spano,* Chief Justice Warren, and newly appointed Justice Goldberg) adopted the view advanced in the *Spano* concurring opinions. *Massiah* arose as follows: After he had been indicted for federal narcotics violations, Massiah retained a lawyer, pled not guilty, and was released on bail. A codefendant, Colson, invited him to discuss the pending case in Colson's car, parked on a city street. Unknown to Massiah, Colson had decided to cooperate with federal agents in their continuing investigation of the case. A radio transmitter was installed under the front seat of Colson's car, enabling a nearby agent (Murphy), who was equipped with a recording device, to overhear the Massiah–Colson conversation. As expected, Massiah made several damaging admissions.

It is hardly surprising that the *Massiah* dissenters considered the facts of the case a "peculiarly inappropriate" setting for a major breakthrough on the "police interrogation"-"confession" front. Even if the *Spano* concurring opinions had come to represent the majority view, argued then Solicitor General Archibald Cox, Massiah's statements should still be admissible because at the time he made them he was neither in "custody"—not even in the loosest sense—nor undergoing "police interrogation." He was under no "official pressure" to answer questions or even to engage in conversation; his conversation "was not affected by even that degree of constraint which may result from a suspect's knowledge that he is talking to a law enforcement officer."[a] Moreover, Colson, a layman unskilled in the art of interrogation, did not and probably could not utilize any of the standard techniques to induce Massiah to incriminate himself.[b]

Nevertheless, as the *Massiah* majority, per STEWART, J., saw it, the decisive feature of the case was that after he had been indicted—"and therefore at a time when he was clearly entitled to a lawyer's help" and at a time when he was awaiting trial "in an orderly courtroom, presided over by a judge, open to the public, and protected by all the procedural safeguards of the law"—Massiah had been subjected to a "completely extrajudicial" police-orchestrated proceeding designed to obtain incriminating statements from him. Besides, if in one respect—the lack of an inherently or potentially "coercive atmosphere"—Massiah had been less seriously imposed upon than the average "confession" defendant, he was more seriously imposed upon in another respect—he did not, and could not be expected to, keep his guard up because he was not even aware that he was dealing with a government agent[c]: "We hold that the petitioner was denied the basic protections of [the right to counsel] when there was used against him at his trial evidence of his own incriminating words, which federal agents had deliberately elicited from him after he had been indicted and in the absence of his counsel. It is true that in the *Spano* case the defendant was interrogated in a police station, while here the damaging testimony was elicited from [him] without his knowledge while he was free on bail. But, as Judge Hays pointed out in his dissent in the [Second Circuit], 'if such a rule is to have any efficacy it must apply to indirect and surreptitious interrogations as well as those conducted in the jailhouse. In this case, Massiah was more seriously imposed upon * * * because he did not even know that he was under interrogation by a government agent.' * * *

"We do not question that in this case, as in many cases, it was entirely proper to continue an investigation of the suspected criminal activities of the defendant and his alleged confederates, even though the defendant had already been indicted. All that we hold is that the defendant's own incriminating statements, obtained by federal agents under the circumstances here disclosed, could not constitutionally be used by the prosecution as evidence against *him* at his trial."

Dissenting Justice WHITE, joined by Clark and Harlan, JJ., protested: "[H]ere there was no substitution of brutality for brains, no inherent danger of police coercion justifying the prophylactic effect of another exclusionary rule. Massiah was not being interrogated in a police station, was not surrounded by numerous officers or questioned in relays, and was not forbidden access to others. Law enforcement may have the elements of a contest about it, but it is not a game."

The dissenters were "unable to see how this case presents an unconstitutional interference with Massiah's right to counsel. Massiah was not prevented from consulting with counsel as often as he wished. No meetings with counsel were

a. Extensive extracts from the Government's brief and oral argument in *Massiah* appear in Kamisar Essays 171–73.

b. The Massiah–Colson conversation was not only broadcast to a nearby federal agent, but secretly tape-recorded by Colson. In the district court, however, Massiah successfully objected to the admission of these tapes on the ground that they implicated other defendants and contained privileged matters. The Government maintained that the recording confirmed the testimony of Agent Murphy that Colson did not coerce Massiah into making any incriminating statements or even induce him by appeals to talk in the guise of friendship and filed the recording with the clerk of the Court. Colson did not testify himself. Massiah did not testify either or otherwise contradict Murphy's testimony about the meeting. See Kamisar Essays at 278 fn. 202.

c. Massiah's unawareness that he was, in effect, talking to the police, and thus his inability to protect himself, "was a nice point (or counterpoint), but it was hardly the decisive one." Kamisar Essays 174. Any doubts that the *Massiah* doctrine also applies when the suspect realizes he is in the presence of the police were removed in *Brewer v. Williams* (1977), p. ___.

disturbed or spied upon. Preparation for trial was in no way obstructed. It is only a sterile syllogism—an unsound one besides—to say that because Massiah had a right to counsel's aid before and during the trial, his out-of-court conversations and admissions must be excluded if obtained without counsel's consent or presence."

"This case," maintained the dissenters, "cannot be analogized to [Canon 9 of the ABA's Canons of Professional Ethics] forbidding an attorney to talk to the opposing party litigant outside the presence of his counsel.[d] Aside from the fact that [the canons] are not of constitutional dimensions, [Canon 9] deals with the conduct of lawyers and not with the conduct of investigators.[e] Lawyers are forbidden to interview the opposing party because of the supposed imbalance of legal skill and acumen between the lawyer and the party litigant; the reason for the rule does not apply to nonlawyers and certainly not to Colson, Massiah's codefendant."

Were the *Massiah* dissenters right when they observed that "the reason given for the result here—the admissions were obtained in the absence of counsel—would seem equally pertinent to statements obtained at any time after the right to counsel attaches, whether there has been an indictment or not"? Does a suspect who has not yet been indicted need "a lawyer's help" every bit as much as one who has been formally charged? By drawing the line at the initiation of formal judicial proceedings, had Justice Stewart (author of *Massiah,* but a dissenter in *Escobedo,* infra) "painted himself into a corner [from] which he could extricate himself only by a highly formalistic reading of the Sixth Amendment"? See Lawrence Herman, *The Supreme Court and Restrictions on Police Interrogation,* 25 Ohio St.L.J. 449, 491 (1964).

As made plain a short five weeks later in the same Term, ESCOBEDO v. ILLINOIS, 378 U.S. 478 (1964), a majority of the Court was not about to give the Sixth Amendment a formalistic reading. Escobedo's interrogation had occurred before "judicial" or "adversary" proceedings had commenced against him, but, as dissenting Justice Stewart characterized the *Escobedo* majority's reasoning, "[t]he Court disregards this basic difference between the present case and Massiah's, with the bland assertion that 'that fact should make no difference.' "

Escobedo arose as follows: On the night of January 19, petitioner's brother-in-law was fatally shot. A few hours later petitioner was taken into custody for questioning, but he made no statement and was released the following afternoon pursuant to a writ of habeas corpus obtained by his retained counsel. On January 30, one Di Gerlando, who was then in police custody and who was later indicted for the murder along with petitioner, stated that petitioner had fired the shots which killed his brother-in-law. That evening petitioner was again arrested and taken to police headquarters. En route to the police station he was told that Di Gerlando had named him as the one who fired the fatal shots and that he might as well admit it, but petitioner replied (probably because his attorney had obtained his release from police custody only 11 days earlier or because he had consulted with his attorney in the meantime): "I am sorry but I would like to have advice from my lawyer." Shortly after petitioner reached police headquarters, his re-

d. Does (should) this ethical rule apply to criminal proceedings? See Note 6, p. 743.

e. But consider Breitel, C.J., in *People v. Hobson,* 348 N.E.2d 894, 898 (N.Y.1976): "[I]t would not be rational, logical, moral or realistic to make any distinction between a lawyer acting for the State who [by seeking a waiver of the right to counsel from a suspect in the absence of, and without notification to, his lawyer] violates [the Code of Professional Responsibility] directly and one who indirectly uses the admissions improperly obtained by a police officer, who is the badged and uniformed representative of the State." See also *United States v. Springer,* 460 F.2d 1344, 1354–55 (7th Cir.1972) (Judge (now Justice) Stevens, dissenting).

tained lawyer arrived and spent the next several hours trying unsuccessfully to speak to his client. He talked to every officer he could find, but was repeatedly told that he could not see his client and that he would have to get a writ of habeas corpus. In the meantime, petitioner repeatedly but unsuccessfully asked to speak to his lawyer. Instead, the police arranged a confrontation between petitioner and Di Gerlando. Petitioner denied that he had fired the fatal shots, claiming that Di Gerlando had done so, but thereby implicated himself in the murder plot. Petitioner's subsequent statement, to an assistant prosecutor who asked carefully framed questions, was admitted into evidence and he was convicted of murder. The Supreme Court of Illinois affirmed.

When certiorari was granted, the lawyers involved realized, as did close students of the problem, that *Escobedo* might be a momentous case. Bernard Weisberg, author of an important article on police interrogation, *Police Interrogation of Arrested Persons: A Skeptical View,* 52 J.Crim.L. & P.S. 21 (1961), argued the case for the ACLU, as *amicus curiae.* Because he thought it "playing Hamlet without the ghost to discuss police questioning without knowing what such questioning is really like," in his article Weisberg had made very extensive use of the interrogation manuals. He did the same in his *Escobedo* brief, maintaining that these books "are invaluable because they vividly describe the kind of interrogation practices which are accepted as lawful and proper under the best current standards of professional police work." What these manuals reveal, argued Weisberg, "is that 'fair and reasonable' and 'effective interrogation' is basically unfair and inherently coercive."[f]

Former Northwestern University law professor James Thompson (who later became Governor of Illinois) argued the *Escobedo* case for the state. He warned the U.S. Supreme Court: "[A decision that the right to counsel begins at the moment of arrest] means the end of confessions as a tool of law enforcement. [For] once this petitioner's claim with Illinois is settled, the inevitable progression of the law must follow:

"*First,* if the right to counsel attaches at the moment of arrest [as the dissent in *Crooker* maintained], then it can hardly be denied that this right must be available to the poor as well as to the rich. * * *

"*Second,* if indigent criminal defendants are entitled to counsel from the moment of arrest, then already established law makes it clear that such a right does not depend upon a request. [N]ot only must the state furnish counsel to the indigent defendant at this stage of the criminal proceeding, it must make sure that he does not waive the right through ignorance of its existence. * * *"[g]

f. Weisberg's article on confessions, apparently the first to make extensive use of the interrogation manuals, and his *Escobedo* brief set the fashion for civil libertarians. The ACLU brief in *Miranda,* primarily the work of Professors Anthony Amsterdam and Paul Mishkin, reprinted a full chapter from one interrogation manual. In turn, Chief Justice Warren's opinion for the Court in *Miranda,* infra, devoted six full pages to extracts from various police manuals and texts "document[ing] procedures employed with success in the past, [and] recommend[ing] various other effective tactics." Many of the examples selected by the *Miranda* Court in 1966 were the same ones Weisberg used in his 1961 article and his 1964 *Escobedo* brief.

g. Thompson's discussion of "the inevitable progression of the law" was, of course, the statement of an advocate; Illinois deemed it advantageous to underscore the extent to which the rule espoused by its adversaries would "cripple" law enforcement. But Escobedo's lawyers were advocates, too, and they could not, or at least did not try to, minimize the impact of the rule they sought. Neither the ACLU brief nor the brief filed by Escobedo's own lawyers ever cited *Gideon, Douglas, Griffin,* or *Carnley.*

Moreover, shortly after *Escobedo* was decided, Thompson continued to view the case essentially the same way, now not as an advocate, but as assistant director of the Northwestern University Law School's Criminal Law Program. See fn. i infra.

Added Thompson: "Criminal defendants, rich as well as poor, enjoy more protection from unjust conviction today than at any time in our history. 'The terrible engine' of the criminal law has been repeatedly braked by this Court, by state courts and legislatures and by fair and honest administration of the law by prosecutors and police. We need to guard against its derailment. * * * "

A 5–4 majority of the Court, per GOLDBERG, J., struck down Escobedo's confession, but, until *Miranda* moved *Escobedo* off center stage two years later, the scope and meaning of the decision was a matter of strong and widespread disagreement. In large part this was due to the accordion-like quality of the *Escobedo* opinion. At some places the opinion launched so broad an attack on the use of confessions in general and rejected the arguments for an "effective interrogation opportunity" so forcefully that it threatened (or promised) to eliminate virtually all police interrogation. At other places, however, the language of the opinion was so narrow and confining that it arguably limited the case to its special facts:

"The interrogation here was conducted before petitioner was formally indicted. But in the context of this case, that fact should make no difference. When petitioner requested, and was denied, an opportunity to consult with his lawyer, the investigation had ceased to be a general investigation of 'an unsolved crime.' Petitioner had become the accused, and the purpose of the interrogation was to 'get him' to confess his guilt despite his constitutional right not to do so. At the time of his arrest and throughout the course of the interrogation, the police told petitioner that they had convincing evidence that he had fired the fatal shots. Without informing him of his absolute right to remain silent in the face of this accusation, the police urged him to make a statement. * * *

"Petitioner, a layman, was undoubtedly unaware that under Illinois law an admission of 'mere' complicity in the murder plot was legally as damaging as an admission of firing of the fatal shots. The 'guiding hand of counsel' was essential to advise petitioner of his rights in this delicate situation. This was the 'stage when legal aid and advice' were most critical to petitioner. *Massiah.*

"[It] is argued that if the right to counsel is afforded prior to indictment, the number of confessions obtained by the police will diminish significantly, because most confessions are obtained during the period between arrest and indictment, and 'any lawyer worth his salt will tell the suspect in no uncertain terms to make no statement to police under any circumstances.' This argument, of course, cuts two ways. The fact that many confessions are obtained during this period points up its critical nature as a 'stage when legal aid and advice' are surely needed. *Massiah.* The right to counsel would indeed be hollow if it began at a period when few confessions were obtained. * * *

"We have learned the lesson of history, ancient and modern, that a system of criminal law enforcement which comes to depend on the 'confession' will, in the long run, be less reliable and more subject to abuses than a system which depends on extrinsic evidence independently secured through skillful investigation. * * *

"We have also learned the companion lesson of history that no system of criminal justice can, or should, survive if it comes to depend for its continued effectiveness on the citizens' abdication through unawareness of their constitutional rights. No system worth preserving should have to *fear* that if an accused is permitted to consult with a lawyer, he will become aware of, and exercise, these rights. If the exercise of constitutional rights will thwart the effectiveness of a system of law enforcement, then there is something very wrong with that system.[h]

h. But consider Gerald Caplan, *Questioning Miranda,* 38 Vand.L.Rev. 1417, 1440 (1985): "This statement is misleading because the right that the Court was defending, far

"We hold, therefore, that where, as here, the investigation is no longer a general inquiry into an unsolved crime but has begun to focus on a particular suspect, the suspect has been taken into police custody, the police carry out a process of interrogations that lends itself to eliciting incriminating statements, the suspect has requested and been denied an opportunity to consult with his lawyer, and the police have not effectively warned him of his absolute constitutional right to remain silent, the accused has been denied 'the Assistance of Counsel' in violation of the Sixth Amendment to the Constitution as 'made obligatory upon the States by the Fourteenth Amendment,' *Gideon,* and that no statement elicited by the police during the interrogation may be used against him at a criminal trial. * * *

"Nothing we have said today affects the power of the police to investigate 'an unsolved crime' by gathering information from witnesses and by other 'proper investigative efforts.' We hold only that when the process shifts from investigatory to accusatory—when its focus is on the accused and its purpose is to elicit a confession—our adversary system begins to operate, and, under the circumstances here, the accused must be permitted to consult with his lawyer."[i]

Dissenting Justice STEWART protested:

"*Massiah* is not in point here. * * * Putting to one side the fact that the case now before us is not a federal case, the vital fact remains that this case does not involve the deliberate interrogation of a defendant after the initiation of judicial proceedings against him. The Court disregards this basic difference between the present case and Massiah's, with the bland assertion that "that fact should make no difference."

"It is 'that fact,' I submit, which makes all the difference. Under our system of criminal justice the institution of formal, meaningful judicial proceedings, by way of indictment, information, or arraignment, marks the point at which a criminal investigation has ended and adversary litigative proceedings have commenced. It is at this point that the constitutional guarantees attach which pertain to a criminal trial."

In a separate dissent, Justice WHITE, joined by Stewart and Clark, JJ., observed:

"[*Massiah*] held that as of the date of the indictment the prosecution is disentitled to secure admissions from the accused. The Court now moves that date back to the time when the prosecution begins to 'focus' on the accused. Although

from being of long standing, was newly discovered, indeed created, in this very opinion. What may have been 'very wrong' was not the extant 'system,' but the right the Court just announced."

i. As to whether *Escobedo* extended the constitutional role of counsel to the preindictment stage "when the process shifts from investigatory to accusatory—when its focus is on the accused and its purpose is to elicit a confession"—or when the process so shifts *and* one or some combination or all of the limiting facts in *Escobedo* are also present, see the summary of the wide disagreement over the probable meaning of the case in Kamisar Essays at 161 fn. 26.

Although many lower courts construed *Escobedo* quite narrowly, James Thompson, who had the distinction of making the losing argument in the case, read it quite broadly. He told a group of prosecuting attorneys attending a criminal law program that "in all cases where the police desire to obtain a confession from a suspect under circumstances like those in *Escobedo* [and] the suspect does not have retained counsel and does not request counsel, the police should, before interrogation, (a) inform him of his right not to say anything; and (b) inform him that anything he does say might be used against him." He also observed: "[I]n dealing with [a suspect who, unlike Danny Escobedo,] has not expressly indicated that he is aware of his right to counsel, absolute compliance with the *Escobedo* rule may well require a warning of the right to counsel along with the warning of the privilege against self-incrimination." See the extensive extracts from Thompson's analysis of *Escobedo* in Kamisar Essays, at 66–68.

the opinion purports to be limited to the facts of this case, it would be naive to think that the new constitutional right announced will depend upon whether the accused has retained his own counsel, or has asked to consult with counsel in the course of interrogation. At the very least the Court holds that once the accused becomes a suspect and, presumably, is arrested, any admission made to the police thereafter is inadmissible in evidence unless the accused has waived his right to counsel. * * *

"It is incongruous to assume that the provision for counsel in the Sixth Amendment was meant to amend or supersede the self-incrimination provision of the Fifth Amendment, which is now applicable to the States. That amendment addresses itself to the very issue of incriminating admissions of an accused and resolves it by proscribing only compelled statements.

"[The] Court chooses [to] rely on the virtues and morality of a system of criminal law enforcement which does not depend on the 'confession.' No such judgment is to be found in the Constitution. The only 'inquisitions' the Constitution forbids are those which compel incrimination. Escobedo's statements were not compelled and the Court does not hold that they were. * * *

"[The] Court may be concerned with a narrower matter: the unknowing defendant who responds to police questioning because he mistakenly believes that he must and that his admissions will not be used against him. But this worry hardly calls for the broadside the Court has now fired. [If] an accused is told he must answer and did not know better, it would be very doubtful that the resulting admissions could be used against him. When the accused has not been informed of his rights at all the Court characteristically and properly looks very closely at the surrounding circumstances. I would continue to do so. But, in this case Danny Escobedo knew full well that he need not answer and knew full well that his lawyer had advised him not to answer."[j]

ON THE MEANING OF *ESCOBEDO*

1. ***What right comes into play?*** Once the investigation has ceased to be "a general inquiry of an unsolved crime but has begun to focus on a particular suspect," what right comes into play? The right of the suspect to consult with his lawyer before resuming the interrogation or the right to enjoy his attorney's *continued presence* and *constant advice* from that point on, as a protection in the face of any further police interrogation? Cf. *Massiah.*

2. ***The role of counsel.*** Consider Gerald Caplan, *Questioning Miranda,* 38 Vand.L.Rev. 1417, 1440–41 (1985): "Danny Escobedo's lawyer had advised him not to say anything to the police. If the homicide detectives had granted Escobedo's request to see his attorney again, there would have been nothing additional for his attorney to communicate. Escobedo had already been given all the assistance his counsel could provide without actually being present to assist his client on a question-by-question basis. Was Escobedo's attorney seeking the right to be present during the interrogation? Probably not. His intent in seeking entry to the homicide bureau was most likely to bring the interrogation to a close. Given that a defense attorney's usual objective is to stop the interrogation, it is hard to understand why the Court was so certain that 'no system worth preserving should have to fear that if an accused person is permitted to consult with a lawyer, he will become aware of, and exercise [his] rights,' unless the Court simply believed that there was no social utility in police interrogation. The *Escobedo* opinion

j. In a brief separate dissent, Justice Harlan agreed with Justice White that "the rule announced today is most ill-conceived and that it seriously and unjustifiably fetters perfectly legitimate methods of criminal law enforcement."

contains no hint of anxiety that harm may accrue from a right to counsel: that there may be fewer confessions, and more crime."

3. *The "right to remain silent."* As we have seen, *Escobedo* refers to a suspect's "absolute constitutional right to remain silent." Where does this right come from? Does the privilege against self-incrimination confer (or was it intended to confer) a right to remain silent or a right to refuse to respond to incriminating questions or only the right to be free of compulsion? See Albert W. Alschuler, *A Peculiar Privilege in Historical Perspective: The Right to Remain Silent,* 94 Mich.L.Rev. 2625, 2630–32 (1996); Joseph D. Grano, *Confessions, Truth, and the Law* 141–43 (1993).

Does the Court simply mean that since the police lack legislative authorization to compel answers, a suspect is not required to provide any? Does the Court mean more—that the Constitution would prevent a legislature from investing police with the power to compel non-incriminating answers? Or does the Court mean that since a layperson cannot be expected to know what statements may be incriminating, if *in the absence of counsel,* she chooses not to incriminate herself, the only practical way she can assure that she will not do so is to remain completely silent?

F. A Late Arrival on the Scene: The Privilege Against Self-Incrimination

"[Despite] a great deal of emotional writing which elevates the privilege against self-incrimination to 'one of the great landmarks in man's struggle to make himself civilized,' [the] most abundant proof [that it does not prohibit pretrial interrogation] is to be found in the United States. There the privilege is in the Federal Constitution and in [forty-eight state constitutions]. But in none of the forty-nine jurisdictions does it apply to what happens in the police station. The police interrogate freely, sometimes for seven to eight hours on end. The statements thus extracted are given in evidence. [O]nly statements made voluntarily may be given in evidence, but that seems to be interpreted rather liberally, judged by our standards."

—Judge V.G. Hiemstra of the Supreme Court of South Africa, *Abolition of the Right Not to be Questioned,* 80 South African L.J. 187, 194–95 (1963).

As long ago as 1931, Ernest Hopkins, a member of the Wickersham Commission staff, forcefully argued that the "third degree"–indeed, all secret police interrogation as typically practiced–was fundamentally in violation of the privilege against self-incrimination. Ernest Hopkins, *Our Lawless Police* 193–95 (1931). As we have seen, however, the concurring justice in *Spano* and the majorities in *Massiah* and *Escobedo* relied primarily on the right to counsel, not the privilege against self-incrimination–the other essential mainstay of the accusatorial, adversary system. But the "prime suspect"-"focal point"-"accusatory state" test(s) of *Escobedo* threatened the admissibility of even "volunteered" statements. There was reason to think that the Court might be in the process of shaping "a novel right not to confess except knowingly and with the tactical assistance of counsel," Arnold Enker & Sheldon Elsen, *Counsel for the Suspect: Massiah v. United States and Escobedo v. Illinois,* 49 Minn.L.Rev. 47, 60–61, 69, 83 (1964). Thus *critics* of *Escobedo* turned to the privilege against self-incrimination as a less restrictive alternative. Dissenting in *Escobedo,* Justice White, joined by Clark and Stewart, JJ., observed:

"It is incongruous to assume that the provision for counsel in the Sixth Amendment was meant to amend or supersede the self-incrimination provision of the Fifth Amendment which is now applicable to the States. [*Malloy v. Hogan,* infra.] That amendment addresses itself to the very issue of incriminating admissions and resolves it by proscribing only compelled statements. [That amendment provides no support] for the idea that an accused has an absolute constitutional right not to answer even in the absence of compulsion, [no support for the view that he has] the constitutional right not to incriminate himself by making voluntary disclosures."

Even as Justice White spoke, there was reason to think that, at long last, the privilege against self-incrimination was knocking on the door of the interrogation room. Only a few months before *Escobedo* had been decided, the Court, in MALLOY v. HOGAN, 378 U.S. 1 (1964) (per Brennan, J.), had performed "what might have seemed to some a shotgun wedding of the privilege [against self-incrimination] to the confession rule," Lawrence Herman, *The Supreme Court and Restrictions on Police Interrogation,* 25 Ohio St.L.J. 449, 465 (1965), by declaring that "today the admissibility of a confession in a state criminal prosecution is tested by the same standard applied in federal prosecutions since 1897, when in *Bram v. United States,* 168 U.S. 532, the Court held that '[i]n criminal trials, in the courts of the United States, wherever a question arises whether a confession is incompetent because not voluntary, the issue is controlled by [the self-incrimination] portion of the Fifth Amendment.' "[a]

Whether or not this approach to police interrogation and confessions makes good sense it constitutes very questionable history—at least since *Brown v. Mississippi* (1936). The old *Bram* case might well have furnished a steppingstone to the standard advanced in *Malloy,* but until *Escobedo,* at any rate, it only seemed to amount to an early excursion from the prevailing multifactor or "totality of circumstances" approach. In none of the dozens of federal *or* state confession cases decided by the Court in the 1930's, 1940's and 1950's had the privilege against self-incrimination, certainly not as it applied to judicial proceedings, been the basis for judgment (although it had occasionally been mentioned in an opinion). If the privilege against self-incrimination had been the way to resolve the confession problem, then all the state courts and lower federal courts that had admitted confessions would have been reversed *per curiam.* For it was plain that law enforcement officers could, and without hesitation did, resort to methods they would never consider utilizing at the trial, that they had much greater power over a suspect or defendant away from the restraining influence of a public trial in an open courtroom.

Although certain factors, such as the length of pre-arraignment detention, had been taking on increasing significance, as Justice Frankfurter described the situation in *Culombe v. Connecticut* (1961), neither the privilege against self-incrimination nor any other "single litmus-paper test for constitutionally impermissible interrogation [had] been evolved: neither extensive cross-questioning-deprecated by the English judges; nor undue delay in arraignment-proscribed by *McNabb;* nor failure to caution a prisoner-enjoined by the [English] Judges' Rules; nor refusal to permit communication with friends and legal counsel at stages in the proceedings when the prisoner is still only a suspect-prohibited by several state statutes." That was why, as Justice Goldberg put it for a majority in *Haynes v. Washington,* 373 U.S. 503 (1963) (only a year before he wrote the opinion of the Court in *Escobedo*), "the line between proper and permissible police conduct and techniques and methods offensive to due process is, at best, a difficult one to draw,

a. Until the 1960's *Bram* had become a largely forgotten case, but in recent years it has been the subject of close analysis and spirited debate. Compare Lawrence A. Benner, *Requiem for Miranda: The Rehnquist Court's Voluntariness Doctrine in Historical Perspective,* 67 Wash.U.L.Q. 59, 107–11 (1989) and Stephen A. Saltzburg, *Miranda v. Arizona Revisited: Constitutional Law or Judicial Fiat,* 26 Washburn L.J. 1, 4–14 (1986) with Joseph D. Grano, *Confessions, Truth, and the Law* 123–31 (1993).

particularly in cases such as this where it is necessary to make fine judgments as to the effect of psychologically coercive pressures and inducements on the mind and will of an accused."

Why had the privilege against self-incrimination been excluded from the stationhouse all these years? The legal reasoning was that compulsion to testify meant *legal* compulsion. Since he is threatened neither with perjury for testifying falsely nor contempt for refusing to testify at all, it cannot be said, ran the argument, that the subject of police interrogation is being "compelled" to be "a witness against himself" within the meaning of the privilege–even though he may assume or be led to believe that there *are* legal (or extralegal) sanctions for contumacy. Since the police have no *legal right* to make a suspect answer, there is no legal obligation to answer to which a privilege in the technical sense can apply. For an appraisal of this argument, see Lewis Mayers, *Shall We Amend the Fifth Amendment?*, 82–83, 223–33 (1959); Walter Schaefer, *The Suspect and Society* 16–18 (1967); 8 John Henry Wigmore, *Evidence* 329 fn. 27 (McNaughton rev. 1961). Consider, too, Note 2, p. 839, and Note 5, p. 841.

It has been suggested that the reasoning above "had a great deal more to commend it than merely the inherent force of its 'logic' or the self-restraint and tenderness of the exempted class of interrogators," Kamisar Essays 59–60; and that among the forces at work were *"necessity"*—the conviction that police interrogation without advising the suspect of his rights was "indispensable" in law enforcement—and the *invisibility* of the process, which made it easy for society to be complacent about what was really going on and to readily accept police-prosecution "sanitized" versions of what was going on. Id. at 60–63.

How the *Malloy* opinion looked back, however, was not as important as how it looked forward. Whatever one thought of the manner in which *Malloy* had recorded the recent past, one could not treat lightly the way it anticipated the near future.

SECTION 3. THE *MIRANDA* "REVOLUTION"

ORAL ARGUMENTS IN *MIRANDA* AND COMPANION CASES[a]

* * *

MR. DUANE R. NEDRUD, on behalf of the National District Attorneys Association, *Amicus Curiae.* * * *

THE CHIEF JUSTICE: May I ask you this, please, Mr. Nedrud: if you agree on the facts that *Escobedo* should not be overruled, what would you say as to the man who did not have a lawyer, but who said he wanted a lawyer before he talked?

MR. NEDRUD: If he asked for a lawyer, and he does not waive his right to counsel, I think that he should have a lawyer. [I] would go so far as to say that I think the state should appoint a lawyer if he asks for a lawyer. I do not think, however, that we should in effect encourage him to have a lawyer.

THE CHIEF JUSTICE: Why do you say we should not encourage him to have a lawyer? Are lawyers a menace? * * *

a. These extracts from the oral arguments are not taken from an "official transcript"—no such transcript is available—but from a transcript the Institute of Criminal Law and Procedure of the Georgetown University Law Center and several private parties, including the editors of this book, arranged to have made. Substantial extracts from the oral arguments also appear in Richard J. Medalie, *From Escobedo to Miranda: The Anatomy of a Supreme Court Decision* (1966) (Inst. of Crim.L & P., Geo.U.).

MR. NEDRUD: I think [a lawyer] is not a menace at the trial level. He is not a menace, per se, but he is, in doing his duty, going to prevent a confession from being obtained. * * *

JUSTICE DOUGLAS: * * * [A lawyer] needs time to prepare for the trial, so the appointment must be at some point anterior to the trial. Our question here is how far anterior. * * *

MR. NEDRUD: The question comes down I think, Mr. Justice Douglas, to whether or not we are going to allow the trial court to determine guilt or innocence or the defense counsel. If the defense counsel comes in at the arrest stage, he will, as he should, prevent the defendant from confessing to his crime, and you will have fewer convictions. If this is what is wanted, this is what will occur.

JUSTICE BLACK: I guess there is no doubt, is there, as to the effect of the provision which provides for protection against compelling him to give testimony. Is it not fewer convictions?

MR. NEDRUD: [I believe] there is a point of diminishing returns and at some stage the police must be in a position to protect us.

JUSTICE BLACK: * * * Can you think of any time when [a person] needs a lawyer more than [at] the point of detention?

MR. NEDRUD: Mr. Justice Black, again, the question is are we interested in convicting the defendant, or are we interested in protecting or acquitting him? This is the only point that I can, in effect, make, if you say that this defendant needs counsel at this time.

For example, if I may use this illustration, I worked when I was a professor of law, which I was prior to taking this position, I worked on the defense project for the American Bar Association. In the questionnaire there was a statement, "When is the ideal time for counsel to be appointed for the defendant?"

Actually, the question is, "When is the ideal time for whom, the people or the defendant?" If it is for the defendant, then it is the earliest possible opportunity; if it is for the people, it should not be until a critical stage. * * *

JUSTICE BLACK: I have found out over many years a very critical stage is when a person is taken to the police headquarters. * * *

A person is taken to police headquarters and placed under arrest or detention. He can't leave, if he wants to, unless they let him. Would you call that voluntary for him, then, for [the police] to have him there in that situation and probe him about probable conviction of crime? Would you think of that as voluntary?

MR. NEDRUD: As being voluntarily in the police station, no. * * *

MR. VICTOR M. EARLE, III on behalf of the petitioner in VIGNERA v. NEW YORK. * * *

JUSTICE FORTAS: [Are you saying] that when the point of time comes where it appears that the police have enough information to satisfy themselves that the fellow really did the act, then the right to arrange for counsel or to give the warning attaches?

MR. EARLE: I think that is correct, although we don't have to look into the mind of the police necessarily to be able to determine that. * * * If in doubt, push it out on the other side of the warning. That is why I don't see that it should pose so much of a problem. I think the FBI Agents give warnings on this proceeding.

JUSTICE STEWART: What should this warning contain? What should this warning be?

MR. EARLE: The Chief of Police in the District of Columbia last August promulgated a warning which, I understand, is now being given by all police officials in the District. It goes something like this: You have been placed under arrest. You are not required to say anything to us any time or to answer any questions. Anything you say may be used as evidence in court. You may call a lawyer or a relative or a friend. Your lawyer may be present here, and you may talk with him. If you cannot obtain a lawyer, one will be appointed for you when your case first goes to court.

I might have a little quibble with that third point, because it suggests a little bit that you might not be able to get a lawyer now.

JUSTICE FORTAS: Much more than a little bit of quibble on the basis of what you have argued so far—that he has an absolute right for a lawyer to be appointed for him at that point, unless he waives it.

MR. EARLE: Yes, sir, unless he waives it. The question might come up of how do the police, or what do the police do when the fellow says, "Thanks. I would like a lawyer now that you mention it, but I don't happen to have any money." They have a choice. They can give him ten cents and the number of a legal aid society.

They have another alternative—just stop interrogating. That alternative was never mentioned. * * *

JUSTICE WHITE: They give him the warning, and he nods his head, yes. (laughter)

JUSTICE WHITE: What happens?

MR. EARLE: It takes a conscious relinquishing of his known rights, those rights I have been telling you about, Justice White.

JUSTICE WHITE: I thought that is what you would say. What happens then if the fellow just nods his head and just looks at him?

MR. EARLE: If we can believe he nodded his head, it is possible that he waives it. I would be very reluctant to come to that conclusion on [that] hypothesis.

JUSTICE WHITE: What else besides giving a warning and right to counsel?

MR. EARLE: I think if he writes down in his own handwriting, "I have been warned, I understand that I have a right to a lawyer now, to talk to him this minute, if I want to, or the right to say nothing if I want to. I understand that. I would like to go ahead and cooperate with the police. Signed: Michael Vignera." That would be enough.

JUSTICE WHITE: That is just barely the first stage.

MR. EARLE: That is what the police have to say.

JUSTICE WHITE: Sure, but if they want to rely on a waiver at any time, is this the only ground that you would accept for a lawyer not being present, a written waiver? Isn't that right?

MR. EARLE: I think that is right. It should be definitely recorded.

JUSTICE WHITE: It should be a written waiver?

MR. EARLE: Absolutely. It shouldn't be something he is conned into giving. * * *

JUSTICE WHITE: What if he doesn't waive? He says, "I do want counsel," and the state says, "Fine. Here is a dime, and there is the legal aid number," and the fellow calls him. He talks to the lawyer, and he comes back and sits down, and you ask him some questions, and he answers them.

MR. EARLE: Without his lawyer being present, for example?

JUSTICE WHITE: Yes.

MR. EARLE: I take it that would be a decision made by his lawyer, and the lawyer can waive rights for his client.

JUSTICE WHITE: Is that a waiver in your book? What is it, a waiver of the right to consult counsel or a waiver of the right to have counsel present?

MR. EARLE: I think it is a waiver to have a counsel in all the ways it is meant. The lawyer can make the determination of whether he should be present or not. Lawyers have waived many rights, like not filing the 30th day and the notice of appeal and the like * * *

JUSTICE WHITE: My question is really going to what you think the scope of the right is. You think the scope of the right is to have counsel present and that you must waive not only the right to consult counsel, but the right to have counsel present?

MR. EARLE: I think that is right, Mr. Justice White. I want to elaborate on it, if I might. In a deposition in a civil case, for example, customarily, the plaintiff and the defendant can have counsel present. I can certainly conceive that one lawyer will not be present. The client, through him, would, therefore, waive that right. It would seem that the only way we could distinguish this case from *Escobedo* is the fact that Vignera did not make a request. What we have been talking about is doing that.

Obviously, it wasn't the request of the individual that made the right attach. The significance of the request, I think, in *Escobedo* was that it was a subjective piece of evidence to show that a stage had been reached. * * *

JUSTICE STEWART: How can there be a waiver, if these are Constitutional rights and are important? How can anybody waive them without the consent of counsel or without the advice of counsel? Doesn't he need a lawyer before he can waive them, if you are right?

MR. EARLE: You are entitled to waive in other situations. It is true in court when they want to plead guilty, for example, the judge will decline assignment of counsel, and the judge will, typically, interrogate him to some length to realize the significance of his act, and that is a lot more advisable a situation than—and more conducive to our being receptive to the idea of a waiver than the police station. I agree that is the worst place for waiver. The party alleging waiver has control of the party alleged to have waived.

JUSTICE STEWART: It seems to follow that he needs a lawyer before he can waive his right to a lawyer.

MR. EARLE: I wouldn't be unhappy to have lawyers in the police station.

JUSTICE STEWART: It follows naturally.

MR. EARLE: It doesn't follow naturally, because a majority of the court in *Escobedo* said these rights can be waived. I think we do have to recognize some of the realities of law enforcement. They do have to investigate. They do have the public duty of—if crimes are being committed by the minute, they do have to operate out of the police station. * * *

JUSTICE HARLAN: Is there a claim that the confession was coerced?

MR. EARLE: In no sense. I don't think it was coerced at all. Mr. Justice White asked yesterday a question about compelling someone to give up his Fifth Amendment privilege. I think there is a substantial difference between that and coercing a confession. I mean, it wasn't until 1964 that the Fifth Amendment privilege applied to the states, and so * * * all through until the 1960's, really, state convictions were overturned only by looking to the generality of the totality of the circumstances under the due process clause.

Now, we have specific Constitutional guarantees that are applied in branch to the states, of both the Fifth and Sixth Amendment rights. It is true that the word "compel" is used in the Fifth Amendment with respect to the privilege, but it is quite different to say that the privilege is cut down and impaired by detention and to say a man's will has been so overborne a confession is forced from him. * * *

I hate to sound cynical, but if we go back to the totality of circumstances, that means this Court will sit all by itself as it has so many years to overturn the few confessions it can take, necessarily, by the bulk of the work. The lower courts won't do their job. We need some specific guidelines as *Escobedo* to help them along the way. * * *

MR. WILLIAM I. SIEGEL, on behalf of the respondent in VIGNERA v. NEW YORK. * * *

JUSTICE FORTAS: Mr. Siegel, [the problem presented by these cases] really affects the basic relationship of the individual and the state. It really goes beyond the administration of justice, and that has been the history of mankind. * * *

MR. SIEGEL: [T]here is an immediate objective, also, and the immediate objective is to protect society; because, if society isn't protected, it, in one degree or another, lapses into anarchy because of crime and then the opportunity to reach this beautiful ideal is gone. It is the function of the police—.

JUSTICE FORTAS: (Interrupting) * * * The problem is to reconcile a good many objectives that are not totally consonant.

I am a little troubled, I must say, when I sit here and hear so much reference to this problem as if it were merely a pragmatic problem of convicting people who did a crime, because there are many more dimensions, I suggest, to the problem than just that simple statement.

MR. SIEGEL: * * * The problem that is before this Court, it seems to me, is just how to keep the balance between the ultimate necessity of the civilized, peaceful society and the constitutional rights of a specific defendant.

JUSTICE BLACK: Don't you think that the Bill of Rights has something to do with making that balance?

MR. SIEGEL: Yes, sir.

JUSTICE BLACK: There is not any doubt, is there, that no person should be convicted on evidence he has been compelled to give? Why do we have to get into a discussion of society or the beauties of the ideal civilization when that is the issue before us?

MR. SIEGEL: Because the Bill of Rights only says that [one] shall not be compelled, but the word "compelled" is not self-defining. We, for many, many years, were told [by] a great majority of Your Honors' predecessors, that compelled meant that which couldn't make a man talk by the exercise of process.

JUSTICE BLACK: By what?

MR. SIEGEL: By the exercise of process. You couldn't subpoena him into a court and, under pain of punishment, make him talk. * * *

SOLICITOR GENERAL THURGOOD MARSHALL, on behalf of the government in WESTOVER v. UNITED STATES. * * *

JUSTICE BLACK: [As] I understand you to say, of course, any person that has a lawyer or has the money to get a lawyer could get one immediately. This man has no lawyer and has no money to get one. The only reason he doesn't have a lawyer is for that reason. Does that raise any principles as to what an indigent is entitled to? He is certainly not getting treated like a man who has the money to get a lawyer.

MR. MARSHALL: He is not being denied anything. The state is not affirmatively denying anything. The state is just not furnishing him anything. * * *

JUSTICE BLACK: I understood you to say if he had the money he would have the right to have the lawyer but the man that has no money has no chance to. That is the situation that we had in *Griffin.*

MR. MARSHALL: *Griffin* was a different point. You can't equalize the whole thing. I don't believe that we can. * * *

"I was introduced for my accomplishments primarily as being of counsel in *Miranda,* and consistently I must disabuse everyone of the accomplishment * * *. When certiorari was granted and we were asked by the ACLU to prepare and file the brief, we had a meeting in our law office in which we agreed that the briefs should be written with the entire focus on the Sixth Amendment [right to counsel] because that is where the Court was headed after *Escobedo,* and, as you are all aware, in the very first paragraph [of the *Miranda* opinion] Chief Justice Warren said, 'It is the Fifth Amendment to the Constitution that is at issue today.' That was Miranda's effective use of counsel."

—John J. Flynn, *Panel Discussion on the Exclusionary Rule,* 61 F.R.D. 259, 278 (1972).

MIRANDA v. ARIZONA (NO. 759)*

384 U.S. 436, 86 S.Ct. 1602, 16 L.Ed.2d 694 (1966).

Chief Justice WARREN delivered the opinion of the Court.

The cases before us raise questions which go to the roots of American criminal jurisprudence: the restraints society must observe [in] prosecuting individuals for crime. More specifically, we deal with the admissibility of statements obtained from an individual who is subjected to custodial police interrogation and the necessity for procedures which assure that the individual is accorded his privilege under the Fifth Amendment to the Constitution not to be compelled to incriminate himself. * * *

We start here, as we did in *Escobedo* with the premise that our holding is not an innovation in our jurisprudence, but is an application of principles long recognized and applied in other settings. We have undertaken a thorough reexamination of the *Escobedo* decision and the principles it announced, and we reaffirm it. That case was but an explication of basic rights that are enshrined in our Constitution—that "No person * * * shall be compelled in any criminal case to be a witness against himself," and that "the accused [shall] have the Assistance of Counsel"—rights which were put in jeopardy in that case through official overbearing. * * *

* Together with No. 760, *Vignera v. New York* [and] No. 761, *Westover v. United States* [and] No. 584, *California v. Stewart* * * *.

Our holding will be spelled out with some specificity in the pages which follow but briefly stated it is this: the prosecution may not use statements, whether exculpatory or inculpatory, stemming from custodial interrogation of the defendant unless it demonstrates the use of procedural safeguards effective to secure the privilege against self-incrimination. By custodial interrogation, we mean questioning initiated by law enforcement officers after a person has been taken into custody or otherwise deprived of his freedom of action in any significant way.[4] As for the procedural safeguards to be employed, unless other fully effective means are devised to inform accused persons of their right of silence and to assure a continuous opportunity to exercise it, the following measures are required. Prior to any questioning, the person must be warned that he has a right to remain silent, that any statement he does make may be used as evidence against him, and that he has a right to the presence of an attorney, either retained or appointed. The defendant may waive effectuation of these rights, provided the waiver is made voluntarily, knowingly and intelligently. If, however, he indicates in any manner and at any stage of the process that he wishes to consult with an attorney before speaking there can be no questioning. Likewise, if the individual is alone and indicates in any manner that he does not wish to be interrogated, the police may not question him. The mere fact that he may have answered some questions or volunteered some statements on his own does not deprive him of the right to refrain from answering any further inquiries until he has consulted with an attorney and thereafter consents to be questioned.

The constitutional issue we decide in each of these cases is the admissibility of statements obtained from a defendant questioned while in custody and deprived of his freedom of action in any significant way. In each, the defendant was questioned by police officers, detectives, or a prosecuting attorney in a room in which he was cut off from the outside world. In none of these cases was the defendant given a full and effective warning of his rights at the outset of the interrogation process. In all the cases, the questioning elicited oral admissions, and in three of them, signed statements as well which were admitted at their trials. They all thus share salient features—incommunicado interrogation of individuals in a police-dominated atmosphere, resulting in self-incriminating statements without full warnings of constitutional rights. * * *

Again we stress that the modern practice of in-custody interrogation is psychologically rather than physically oriented. * * * Interrogation still takes place in privacy. Privacy results in secrecy and this in turn results in a gap in our knowledge as to what in fact goes on in the interrogation rooms. A valuable source of information about present police practices, however, may be found in various police manuals and texts which document procedures employed with success in the past, and which recommend various other effective tactics. These texts are used by law enforcement agencies themselves as guides.[9]

4. This is what we meant in *Escobedo* when we spoke of an investigation which had focused on an accused.

9. The methods described in Inbau and Reid, *Criminal Interrogation and Confessions* (1962), are a revision and enlargement of material presented in three prior editions of a predecessor text, *Lie Detection and Criminal Interrogation* (3d ed. 1953). The authors and their associates are officers of the Chicago Police Scientific Crime–Detection Laboratory and have had extensive experience in writing, lecturing and speaking to law enforcement authorities over a 20–year period. They say that the techniques portrayed in their manuals reflect their experiences and are the most effective psychological stratagems to employ during interrogations. Similarly, the techniques described in O'Hara, *Fundamentals of Criminal Investigation* (1959), were gleaned from long service as observer, lecturer in police science, and work as a federal criminal investigator. All these texts have had rather extensive use among law enforcement agencies and among students of police science, with total sales and circulation of over 44,000.

It should be noted that these texts professedly present the most enlightened and effective means presently used to obtain statements through custodial interrogation. By considering these texts and other data, it is possible to describe procedures observed and noted around the country. * * *

To highlight the isolation and unfamiliar surroundings, the manuals instruct the police to display an air of confidence in the suspect's guilt and from outward appearance to maintain only an interest in confirming certain details. The guilt of the subject is to be posited as a fact. The interrogator should direct his comments toward the reasons why the subject committed the act, rather than court failure by asking the subject whether he did it. Like other men, perhaps the subject has had a bad family life, had an unhappy childhood, had too much to drink, had an unrequited desire for women. The officers are instructed to minimize the moral seriousness of the offense, to cast blame on the victim or on society. These tactics are designed to put the subject in a psychological state where his story is but an elaboration of what the police purport to know already—that he is guilty. Explanations to the contrary are dismissed and discouraged.

The texts thus stress that the major qualities an interrogator should possess are patience and perseverance. * * *

[When other techniques] prove unavailing, the texts recommend they be alternated with a show of some hostility. One ploy often used has been termed the "friendly-unfriendly" or the "Mutt and Jeff" act:

> "[In] this technique, two agents are employed. Mutt, the relentless investigator, who knows the subject is guilty and is not going to waste any time. He's sent a dozen men away for this crime and he's going to send the subject away for the full term. Jeff, on the other hand, is obviously a kindhearted man. He has a family himself. He has a brother who was involved in a little scrape like this. He disapproves of Mutt and his tactics and will arrange to get him off the case if the subject will cooperate. He can't hold Mutt off for very long. The subject would be wise to make a quick decision. The technique is applied by having both investigators present while Mutt acts out his role. Jeff may stand by quietly and demur at some of Mutt's tactics. When Jeff makes his plea for cooperation, Mutt is not present in the room."

The interrogators sometimes are instructed to induce a confession out of trickery. The technique here is quite effective in crimes which require identification or which run in series. In the identification situation, the interrogator may take a break in his questioning to place the subject among a group of men in a line-up. "The witness or complainant (previously coached, if necessary) studies the line-up and confidently points out the subject as the guilty party." Then the questioning resumes "as though there were now no doubt about the guilt of the subject." A variation on this technique is called the "reverse line-up":

> "The accused is placed in a line-up, but this time he is identified by several fictitious witnesses or victims who associated him with different offenses. It is expected that the subject will become desperate and confess to the offense under investigation in order to escape from the false accusations."

The manuals also contain instructions for police on how to handle the individual who refuses to discuss the matter entirely, or who asks for an attorney or relatives. The examiner is to concede him the right to remain silent. "This usually has a very undermining effect. First of all, he is disappointed in his expectation of an unfavorable reaction on the part of the interrogator. Secondly, a concession of this right to remain silent impresses the subject with the apparent fairness of his interrogator." After this psychological conditioning, however, the officer is told to point out the incriminating significance of the suspect's refusal to talk:

> "Joe, you have a right to remain silent. That's your privilege and I'm the last person in the world who'll try to take it away from you. If that's the way you want to leave this, O.K. But let me ask you this. Suppose you were in my shoes and I were in yours and you called me in to ask me about this and I told you, 'I don't want to answer any of your questions.' You'd think I had something to hide, and you'd probably be right in thinking that. That's exactly what I'll have to think about you, and so will everybody else. So let's sit here and talk this whole thing over."

Few will persist in their initial refusal to talk, it is said, if this monologue is employed correctly.

In the event that the subject wishes to speak to a relative or an attorney, the following advice is tendered:

> "[T]he interrogator should respond by suggesting that the subject first tell the truth to the interrogator himself rather than get anyone else involved in the matter. If the request is for an attorney, the interrogator may suggest that the subject save himself or his family the expense of any such professional service, particularly if he is innocent of the offense under investigation. The interrogator may also add, 'Joe, I'm only looking for the truth, and if you're telling the truth, that's it. You can handle this by yourself.' "

From these representative samples of interrogation techniques, the setting prescribed by the manuals and observed in practice becomes clear. In essence, it is this: To be alone with the subject is essential to prevent distraction and to deprive him of any outside support. The aura of confidence in his guilt undermines his will to resist. He merely confirms the preconceived story the police seek to have him describe. Patience and persistence, at times relentless questioning, are employed. To obtain a confession, the interrogator must "patiently maneuver himself or his quarry into a position from which the desired object may be obtained." When normal procedures fail to produce the needed result, the police may resort to deceptive stratagems such as giving false legal advice. It is important to keep the subject off balance, for example, by trading on his insecurity about himself or his surroundings. The police then persuade, trick, or cajole him out of exercising his constitutional rights.

Even without employing brutality, the "third degree" or the specific stratagems described above, the very fact of custodial interrogation exacts a heavy toll on individual liberty and trades on the weakness of individuals.

In the cases before us today, given this background, we concern ourselves primarily with this interrogation atmosphere and the evils it can bring. In *Miranda v. Arizona,* the police arrested the defendant and took him to a special interrogation room where they secured a confession. In *Vignera v. New York,* the defendant made oral admissions to the police after interrogation in the afternoon, and then signed an inculpatory statement upon being questioned by an assistant district attorney later the same evening. In *Westover v. United States,* the defendant was handed over to the Federal Bureau of Investigation by local authorities after they had detained and interrogated him for a lengthy period, both at night and the following morning. After some two hours of questioning, the federal officers had obtained signed statements from the defendant. Lastly, in *California v. Stewart,* the local police held the defendant five days in the station and interrogated him on nine separate occasions before they secured his inculpatory statement.

In these cases, we might not find the defendants' statements to have been involuntary in traditional terms. Our concern for adequate safeguards to protect precious Fifth Amendment rights is, of course, not lessened in the slightest. In each of the cases, the defendant was thrust into an unfamiliar atmosphere and run through menacing police interrogation procedures. The potentiality for compulsion is forcefully apparent, for example, in *Miranda,* where the indigent Mexican defendant was a seriously disturbed individual with pronounced sexual fantasies, and in *Stewart,* in which the defendant was an indigent Los Angeles Negro who had dropped out of school in the sixth grade. To be sure, the records do not evince overt physical coercion or patented psychological ploys. The fact remains that in none of these cases did the officers undertake to afford appropriate safeguards at the outset of the interrogation to insure that the statements were truly the product of free choice.

It is obvious that such an interrogation environment is created for no purpose other than to subjugate the individual to the will of his examiner. This atmosphere carries its own badge of intimidation. To be sure, this is not physical intimidation, but it is equally destructive of human dignity. The current practice of incommunicado interrogation is at odds with one of our Nation's most cherished principles—that the individual may not be compelled to incriminate himself. Unless adequate protective devices are employed to dispel the compulsion inherent in custodial surroundings, no statement obtained from the defendant can truly be the product of his free choice.

From the foregoing, we can readily perceive an intimate connection between the privilege against self-incrimination and police custodial questioning. It is fitting to turn to history and precedent underlying the Self–Incrimination Clause to determine its applicability in this situation.

We sometimes forget how long it has taken to establish the privilege against self-incrimination, the sources from which it came and the fervor with which it was defended. Its roots go back into ancient times.[27] * * *

[W]e may view the historical development of the privilege as one which groped for the proper scope of governmental power over the citizen. As a "noble principle often transcends its origins," the privilege has come rightfully to be recognized in part as an individual's substantive right, a "right to a private enclave where he may lead a private life. That right is the hallmark of our democracy." We have recently noted that the privilege against self-incrimination—the essential mainstay of our adversary system—is founded on a complex of values. *Murphy v. Waterfront Comm'n* [p. 840]. All these policies point to one overriding thought: the constitutional foundation underlying the privilege is the respect a government—state or federal—must accord to the dignity and integrity of its citizens. To maintain a "fair state-individual balance," to require the government "to shoulder the entire load," 8 Wigmore, *Evidence* (McNaughton rev., 1961), to respect the inviolability of the human personality, our accusatory system of criminal justice demands that the government seeking to punish an individual produce the evidence against him by its own independent labors, rather than by the cruel, simple expedient of compelling it from his own mouth. In sum, the privilege is fulfilled only when the person is guaranteed the right "to remain silent unless he chooses to speak in the unfettered exercise of his own will." *Malloy v. Hogan* [p. 569].

* * * We are satisfied that all the principles embodied in the privilege apply to informal compulsion exerted by law-enforcement officers during in-custody questioning. An individual swept from familiar surroundings into police custody, surrounded by antagonistic forces, and subjected to the techniques of persuasion described above cannot be otherwise than under compulsion to speak. As a

27. Thirteenth century commentators found an analogue to the privilege grounded in the Bible. * * * [See generally Irene Rosenberg & Yale Rosenberg, *In the Beginning: The Talmudic Rule Against Self–Incrimination,* 63 N.Y.U.L.Rev. 955 (1988) and the authorities discussed therein].

practical matter, the compulsion to speak in the isolated setting of the police station may well be greater than in courts or other official investigations, where there are often impartial observers to guard against intimidation or trickery.

This question in fact could have been taken as settled in federal courts almost seventy years ago [by] *Bram v. United States* (1897) [discussed at pp. 569, 718]. Because of the adoption by Congress of Rule 5(a) of the Federal Rules of Criminal Procedure, and this Court's effectuation of that Rule in *McNabb* and *Mallory,* we have had little occasion in the past quarter century to reach the constitutional issues in dealing with federal interrogations. These supervisory rules, requiring production of an arrested person before a commissioner "without unnecessary delay" and excluding evidence obtained in default of that statutory obligation, were nonetheless responsive to the same considerations of Fifth Amendment policy that unavoidably face us now as to the States. In [the *McNabb* and *Mallory* cases] we recognized both the dangers of interrogation and the appropriateness of prophylaxis stemming from the very fact of interrogation itself.[32]

Our decision in *Malloy v. Hogan* necessitates an examination of the scope of the privilege in state cases as well. In *Malloy,* we squarely held the privilege applicable to the States, and held that the substantive standards underlying the privilege applied with full force to state court proceedings. The implications [of *Malloy*] were elaborated in our decision in *Escobedo,* decided one week after *Malloy* applied the privilege to the States.

[In *Escobedo*], as in the cases today, we sought a protective device to dispel the compelling atmosphere of the interrogation. In *Escobedo,* however, the police did not relieve the defendant of the anxieties which they had created in the interrogation rooms. Rather, they denied his request for the assistance of counsel.[35] This heightened his dilemma, and made his later statements the product of this compulsion. [The] denial of the defendant's request for his attorney thus undermined his ability to exercise the privilege—to remain silent if he chose or to speak without any intimidation, blatant or subtle. The presence of counsel, in all the cases before us today, would be the adequate protective device necessary to make the process of police interrogation conform to the dictates of the privilege. His presence would insure that statements made in the government-established atmosphere are not the product of compulsion.

* * * Without the protections flowing from adequate warnings and the rights of counsel, "all the careful safeguards erected around the giving of testimony, whether by an accused or any other witness, would become empty formalities in a procedure where the most compelling possible evidence of guilt, a confession, would have already been obtained at the unsupervised pleasure of the police." *Mapp v. Ohio* (Harlan, J., dissenting).

Today, then, there can be no doubt that the Fifth Amendment privilege is available outside of criminal court proceedings and serves to protect persons in all settings in which their freedom of action is curtailed from being compelled to incriminate themselves. We have concluded that without proper safeguards the process of in-custody interrogation of persons suspected or accused of crime contains inherently compelling pressures which work to undermine the individual's will to resist and to compel him to speak where he would not otherwise do so

32. Our decision today does not indicate in any manner, of course, that these rules can be disregarded. When federal officials arrest an individual, they must as always comply with the dictates of the congressional legislation and cases thereunder. * * *

35. The police also prevented the attorney from consulting with his client. Independent of any other constitutional proscription, this action constitutes a violation of the Sixth Amendment right to the assistance of counsel and excludes any statement obtained in its wake. See *People v. Donovan,* 13 N.Y.2d 148, 243 N.Y.S.2d 841, 193 N.E.2d 628 (N.Y.1963) (Fuld, J.).

freely. In order to combat these pressures and to permit a full opportunity to exercise the privilege against self-incrimination, the accused must be adequately and effectively apprised of his rights and the exercise of those rights must be fully honored.

It is impossible for us to foresee the potential alternatives for protecting the privilege which might be devised by Congress or the States in the exercise of their creative rule-making capacities. Therefore we cannot say that the Constitution necessarily requires adherence to any particular solution for the inherent compulsions of the interrogation process as it is presently conducted. Our decision in no way creates a constitutional straitjacket which will handicap sound efforts at reform, nor is it intended to have this effect. We encourage Congress and the States to continue their laudable search for increasingly effective ways of protecting the rights of the individual while promoting efficient enforcement of our criminal laws. However, unless we are shown other procedures which are at least as effective in apprising accused persons of their right of silence and in assuring a continuous opportunity to exercise it, the following safeguards must be observed.[a]

At the outset, if a person in custody is to be subjected to interrogation, he must first be informed in clear and unequivocal terms that he has the right to remain silent. For those unaware of the privilege, the warning is needed simply to make them aware of it—the threshold requirement for an intelligent decision as to its exercise. More important, such a warning is an absolute prerequisite in overcoming the inherent pressures of the interrogation atmosphere. It is not just the subnormal or woefully ignorant who succumb to an interrogator's imprecations, whether implied or expressly stated, that the interrogation will continue until a confession is obtained or that silence in the face of accusation is itself damning and will bode ill when presented to a jury.[37] Further, the warning will show the individual that his interrogators are prepared to recognize his privilege should he choose to exercise it.

The Fifth Amendment privilege is so fundamental to our system of constitutional rule and the expedient of giving an adequate warning as to the availability of the privilege so simple, we will not pause to inquire in individual cases whether the defendant was aware of his rights without a warning being given. Assessments of the knowledge the defendant possessed, based on information as to his age, education, intelligence, or prior contact with authorities, can never be more than speculation;[38] a warning is a clearcut fact. More important, whatever the background of the person interrogated, a warning at the time of the interrogation is indispensable to overcome its pressures and to insure that the individual knows he is free to exercise the privilege at that point in time.

a. Ed. Note—Chief Justice Warren inserted the language in this paragraph at the suggestion of Justice Brennan, who wrote a lengthy memorandum to Warren, commenting on an early draft of the *Miranda* opinion. Brennan "agree[d] that, largely for the reasons you have stated, all four cases must be reversed for lack of any safeguards against denial of the right [against self-incrimination]. [But] should we not leave Congress and the States latitude to devise other means (if they can) which might also create an interrogation climate which has the similar effect of preventing the fettering of a person's own will?" Ironically, the language that Chief Justice Warren used at Brennan's suggestion was seized upon by Justice Rehnquist in *Michigan v. Tucker* (1974) (p. 600) as evidence that *Miranda* was not a constitutional decision.

For a discussion of, and substantial extracts from, Justice Brennan's memorandum to Chief Justice Warren, see Charles D. Weisselberg, *Saving Miranda*, 84 Cornell L.Rev. 109, 123–25 (1998).

37. [In] accord with this decision, it is impermissible to penalize an individual for exercising his Fifth Amendment privilege when he is under police custodial interrogation. The prosecution may not, therefore, use at trial the fact that he stood mute or claimed his privilege in the face of accusation.

38. Cf. *Betts v. Brady,* and the recurrent inquiry into special circumstances it necessitated. * * *

The warning of the right to remain silent must be accompanied by the explanation that anything said can and will be used against the individual in court. This warning is needed in order to make him aware not only of the privilege, but also of the consequences of forgoing it. It is only through an awareness of these consequences that there can be any assurance of real understanding and intelligent exercise of the privilege. Moreover, this warning may serve to make the individual more acutely aware that he is faced with a phase of the adversary system—that he is not in the presence of persons acting solely in his interest.

The circumstances surrounding in-custody interrogation can operate very quickly to overbear the will of one merely made aware of his privilege by his interrogators. Therefore, the right to have counsel present at the interrogation is indispensable to the protection of the Fifth Amendment privilege under the system we delineate today. Our aim is to assure that the individual's right to choose between silence and speech remains unfettered throughout the interrogation process. A once-stated warning, delivered by those who will conduct the interrogation, cannot itself suffice to that end among those who most require knowledge of their rights. A mere warning given by the interrogators is not alone sufficient to accomplish that end. Prosecutors themselves claim that the admonishment of the right to remain silent without more "will benefit only the recidivist and the professional." Brief for the National District Attorneys Association as *amicus curiae.* Even preliminary advice given to the accused by his own attorney can be swiftly overcome by the secret interrogation process. Thus, the need for counsel to protect the Fifth Amendment privilege comprehends not merely a right to consult with counsel prior to questioning but also to have counsel present during any questioning if the defendant so desires.

The presence of counsel at the interrogation may serve several significant subsidiary functions as well. If the accused decides to talk to his interrogators, the assistance of counsel can mitigate the dangers of untrustworthiness. With a lawyer present the likelihood that the police will practice coercion is reduced, and if coercion is nevertheless exercised the lawyer can testify to it in court. The presence of a lawyer can also help to guarantee that the accused gives a fully accurate statement to the police and that the statement is rightly reported by the prosecution at trial.

An individual need not make a preinterrogation request for a lawyer. While such request affirmatively secures his right to have one, his failure to ask for a lawyer does not constitute a waiver. No effective waiver of the right to counsel during interrogation can be recognized unless specifically made after the warnings we here delineate have been given. The accused who does not know his rights and therefore does not make a request may be the person who most needs counsel. * * *

Accordingly we hold that an individual held for interrogation must be clearly informed that he has the right to consult with a lawyer and to have the lawyer with him during interrogation under the system for protecting the privilege we delineate today. As with the warnings of the right to remain silent and that anything stated can be used in evidence against him, this warning is an absolute prerequisite to interrogation. No amount of circumstantial evidence that the person may have been aware of this right will suffice to stand in its stead. Only through such a warning is there ascertainable assurance that the accused was aware of this right.

If an individual indicates that he wishes the assistance of counsel before any interrogation occurs, the authorities cannot rationally ignore or deny his request on the basis that the individual does not have or cannot afford a retained attorney. The financial ability of the individual has no relationship to the scope of the rights involved here. The privilege against self-incrimination secured by the Constitution applies to all individuals. The need for counsel in order to protect the privilege exists for the indigent as well as the affluent. In fact, were we to limit these constitutional rights to those who can retain an attorney, our decisions today would be of little significance. The cases before us as well as the vast majority of confession cases with which we have dealt in the past involve those unable to retain counsel. While authorities are not required to relieve the accused of his poverty, they have the obligation not to take advantage of indigence in the administration of justice.[41] Denial of counsel to the indigent at the time of interrogation while allowing an attorney to those who can afford one would be no more supportable by reason or logic than the similar situation at trial and on appeal struck down in *Gideon* and *Douglas v. California.*

In order fully to apprise a person interrogated of the extent of his rights under this system then, it is necessary to warn him not only that he has the right to consult with an attorney, but also that if he is indigent a lawyer will be appointed to represent him. Without this additional warning, the admonition of the right to consult with counsel would often be understood as meaning only that he can consult with a lawyer if he has one or has the funds to obtain one. The warning of a right to counsel would be hollow if not couched in terms that would convey to the indigent—the person most often subjected to interrogation—the knowledge that he too has a right to have counsel present. As with the warnings of the right to remain silent and of the general right to counsel, only by effective and express explanation to the indigent of this right can there be assurance that he was truly in a position to exercise it.[43]

Once warnings have been given, the subsequent procedure is clear. If the individual indicates in any manner, at any time prior to or during questioning, that he wishes to remain silent, the interrogation must cease.[44] At this point he has shown that he intends to exercise his Fifth Amendment privilege; any statement taken after the person invokes his privilege cannot be other than the product of compulsion, subtle or otherwise. Without the right to cut off questioning, the setting of in-custody interrogation operates on the individual to overcome free choice in producing a statement after the privilege has been once invoked. If the individual states that he wants an attorney, the interrogation must cease until an attorney is present. At that time, the individual must have an opportunity to confer with the attorney and to have him present during any subsequent questioning. If the individual cannot obtain an attorney and he indicates that he wants one before speaking to police, they must respect his decision to remain silent.

This does not mean, as some have suggested, that each police station must have a "station house lawyer" present at all times to advise prisoners. It does mean, however, that if police propose to interrogate a person they must make known to him that he is entitled to a lawyer and that if he cannot afford one, a

41. See Kamisar, *Equal Justice in the Gatehouses and Mansions of American Criminal Procedure,* in Criminal Justice in Our Time (1965), 64–81; * * * Report of the Attorney General's Committee on *Poverty and the Administration of Federal Criminal Justice* (1963), p. 9 * * *.

43. While a warning that the indigent may have counsel appointed need not be given to the person who is known to have an attorney or is known to have ample funds to secure one, the expedient of giving a warning is too simple and the rights involved too important to engage in *ex post facto* inquiries into financial ability when there is any doubt at all on that score.

44. If an individual indicates his desire to remain silent, but has an attorney present, there may be some circumstances in which further questioning would be permissible. In the absence of evidence of overbearing, statements then made in the presence of counsel might be free of the compelling influence of the interrogation process and might fairly be construed as a waiver of the privilege for purposes of these statements.

lawyer will be provided for him prior to any interrogation. If authorities conclude that they will not provide counsel during a reasonable period of time in which investigation in the field is carried out, they may do so without violating the person's Fifth Amendment privilege so long as they do not question him during that time.

If the interrogation continues without the presence of an attorney and a statement is taken, a heavy burden rests on the Government to demonstrate that the defendant knowingly and intelligently waived his privilege against self-incrimination and his right to retained or appointed counsel. This Court has always set high standards of proof for the waiver of constitutional rights, *Johnson v. Zerbst,* and we reassert these standards as applied to in-custody interrogation. Since the State is responsible for establishing the isolated circumstances under which the interrogation takes place and has the only means of making available corroborated evidence of warnings given during incommunicado interrogation, the burden is rightly on its shoulders.

An express statement that the individual is willing to make a statement and does not want an attorney followed closely by a statement could constitute a waiver. But a valid waiver will not be presumed simply from the silence of the accused after warnings are given or simply from the fact that a confession was in fact eventually obtained [referring to *Carnley v. Cochran,* 369 U.S. 506 (1962)].

* * * Moreover, where in-custody interrogation is involved, there is no room for the contention that the privilege is waived if the individual answers some questions or gives some information on his own prior to invoking his right to remain silent when interrogated.[45]

Whatever the testimony of the authorities as to waiver of rights by an accused, the fact of lengthy interrogation or incommunicado incarceration before a statement is made is strong evidence that the accused did not validly waive his rights. In these circumstances the fact that the individual eventually made a statement is consistent with the conclusion that the compelling influence of the interrogation finally forced him to do so. It is inconsistent with any notion of a voluntary relinquishment of the privilege. Moreover, any evidence that the accused was threatened, tricked, or cajoled into a waiver will, of course, show that the defendant did not voluntarily waive his privilege. The requirement of warnings and waiver of rights is a fundamental with respect to the Fifth Amendment privilege and not simply a preliminary ritual to existing methods of interrogation.

The warnings required and the waiver necessary in accordance with our opinion today are, in the absence of a fully effective equivalent, prerequisites to the admissibility of any statement made by a defendant. No distinction can be drawn between statements which are direct confessions and statements which amount to "admissions" of part or all of an offense. The privilege against self-incrimination protects the individual from being compelled to incriminate himself in any manner; it does not distinguish degrees of incrimination. Similarly, for precisely the same reason, no distinction may be drawn between inculpatory statements and statements alleged to be merely "exculpatory." If a statement made were in fact truly exculpatory it would, of course, never be used by the prosecution. In fact, statements merely intended to be exculpatory by the defendant are often used to impeach his testimony at trial or to demonstrate untruths

45. Although this Court held in *Rogers v. United States,* [discussed in Note 4, p. 841] over strong dissent, that a witness before a grand jury may not in certain circumstances decide to answer some questions and then refuse to answer others that decision has no application to the interrogation situation we deal with today. No legislative or judicial fact-finding authority is involved here, nor is there a possibility that the individual might make self-serving statements of which he could make use at trial while refusing to answer incriminating statements.

in the statement given under interrogation and thus to prove guilt by implication. These statements are incriminating in any meaningful sense of the word and may not be used without the full warnings and effective waiver required for any other statement. In *Escobedo* itself, the defendant fully intended his accusation of another as the slayer to be exculpatory as to himself.

The principles announced today deal with the protection which must be given to the privilege against self-incrimination when the individual is first subjected to police interrogation while in custody at the station or otherwise deprived of his freedom of action in any significant way. It is at this point that our adversary system of criminal proceedings commences, distinguishing itself at the outset from the inquisitorial system recognized in some countries. Under the system of warnings we delineate today or under any other system which may be devised and found effective, the safeguards to be erected about the privilege must come into play at this point.

Our decision is not intended to hamper the traditional function of police officers in investigating crime. When an individual is in custody on probable cause, the police may, of course, seek out evidence in the field to be used at trial against him. Such investigation may include inquiry of persons not under restraint. General on-the-scene questioning as to facts surrounding a crime or other general questioning of citizens in the fact-finding process is not affected by our holding. It is an act of responsible citizenship for individuals to give whatever information they may have to aid in law enforcement. In such situations the compelling atmosphere inherent in the process of in-custody interrogation is not necessarily present.[46]

In dealing with statements obtained through interrogation, we do not purport to find all confessions inadmissible. Confessions remain a proper element in law enforcement. Any statement given freely and voluntarily without any compelling influences is, of course, admissible in evidence. The fundamental import of the privilege while an individual is in custody is not whether he is allowed to talk to the police without the benefit of warnings and counsel, but whether he can be interrogated. There is no requirement that police stop a person who enters a police station and states that he wishes to confess to a crime, or a person who calls the police to offer a confession or any other statement he desires to make. Volunteered statements of any kind are not barred by the Fifth Amendment and their admissibility is not affected by our holding today.

To summarize, we hold that when an individual is taken into custody or otherwise deprived of his freedom by the authorities in any significant way and is subjected to questioning, the privilege against self-incrimination is jeopardized. Procedural safeguards must be employed to protect the privilege, and unless other fully effective means are adopted to notify the person of his right of silence and to assure that the exercise of the right will be scrupulously honored, the following measures are required. He must be warned prior to any questioning that he has the right to remain silent, that anything he says can be used against him in a court of law, that he has the right to the presence of an attorney, and that if he cannot afford an attorney one will be appointed for him prior to any questioning if he so desires. Opportunity to exercise these rights must be afforded to him throughout the interrogation. After such warnings have been given, and such opportunity afforded him, the individual may knowingly and intelligently waive

46. The distinction and its significance has been aptly described in the opinion of a Scottish court:

"In former times such questioning, if undertaken, would be conducted by police officers visiting the house or place of business of the suspect and there questioning him, probably in the presence of a relation or friend. However convenient the modern practice may be, it must normally create a situation very unfavorable to the suspect." *Chalmers v. H.M. Advocate,* [1954] Sess.Cas. 66, 78 (J.C.).

these rights and agree to answer questions or make a statement. But unless and until such warnings and waiver are demonstrated by the prosecution at trial, no evidence obtained as a result of interrogation can be used against him. * * *

If the individual desires to exercise his privilege, he has the right to do so. This is not for the authorities to decide. An attorney may advise his client not to talk to police until he has had an opportunity to investigate the case, or he may wish to be present with his client during any police questioning. In doing so an attorney is merely exercising the good professional judgment he has been taught. This is not cause for considering the attorney a menace to law enforcement. He is merely carrying out what he is sworn to do under his oath—to protect to the extent of his ability the rights of his client. In fulfilling this responsibility the attorney plays a vital role in the administration of criminal justice under our Constitution.

In announcing these principles, we are not unmindful of the burdens which law enforcement officials must bear, often under trying circumstances. * * * This Court, while protecting individual rights, has always given ample latitude to law enforcement agencies in the legitimate exercise of their duties. The limits we have placed on the interrogation process should not constitute an undue interference with a proper system of law enforcement. [Although] confessions may play an important role in some convictions, the cases before us present graphic examples of the overstatement of the "need" for confessions. In each case authorities conducted interrogations ranging up to five days in duration despite the presence, through standard investigating practices, of considerable evidence against each defendant.[51] Further examples are chronicled in our prior cases.

It is also urged that an unfettered right to detention for interrogation should be allowed because it will often redound to the benefit of the person questioned. When police inquiry determines that there is no reason to believe that the person has committed any crime, it is said, he will be released without need for further formal procedures. The person who has committed no offense, however, will be better able to clear himself after warnings, with counsel present than without. It can be assumed that in such circumstances a lawyer would advise his client to talk freely to police in order to clear himself.

Custodial interrogation, by contrast, does not necessarily afford the innocent an opportunity to clear themselves. A serious consequence of the present practice of the interrogation alleged to be beneficial for the innocent is that many arrests "for investigation" subject large numbers of innocent persons to detention and interrogation. In one of the cases before us, *California v. Stewart,* police held four persons, who were in the defendant's house at the time of the arrest, in jail for five days until defendant confessed. At that time they were finally released. Police stated that there was "no evidence to connect them with any crime." Available statistics on the extent of this practice where it is condoned indicate that these four are far from alone in being subjected to arrest, prolonged detention, and interrogation without the requisite probable cause.

[The] experience in some other countries * * * suggests that the danger to law enforcement in curbs on interrogation is overplayed. The English procedure since 1912 under the Judges' Rules is significant. As recently strengthened, the Rules require that a cautionary warning be given an accused by a police officer as soon as he has evidence that affords reasonable grounds for suspicion; they also require that any statement made be given by the accused without questioning by

51. Miranda, Vignera, and Westover were identified by eyewitnesses. Marked bills from the bank robbed were found in Westover's car. Articles stolen from the victim as well as from several other robbery victims were found in Stewart's home at the outset of the investigation.

police.[57] The right of the individual to consult with an attorney during this period is expressly recognized. * * *

Because of the nature of the problem and because of its recurrent significance in numerous cases, we have to this point discussed the relationship of the Fifth Amendment privilege to police interrogation without specific concentration on the facts of the cases before us. We turn now to these facts to consider the application to these cases of the constitutional principles discussed above. In each instance, we have concluded that statements were obtained from the defendant under circumstances that did not meet constitutional standards for protection of the privilege.

57. [1964] Crim.L.Rev. 166–170. These Rules provide in part:

"II. As soon as a police officer has evidence which would afford reasonable grounds for suspecting that a person has committed an offence, he shall caution that person or cause him to be cautioned before putting to him any questions, or further questions, relating to that offence.

"The caution shall be in the following terms:

" 'You are not obliged to say anything unless you wish to do so but what you say may be put into writing and given in evidence.'

"When after being cautioned a person is being questioned, or elects to make a statement, a record shall be kept of the time and place at which any such questioning or statement began and ended and of the persons present.

* * *

"(b) It is only in exceptional cases that questions relating to the offence should be put to the accused person after he has been charged or informed that he may be prosecuted.

* * *

"IV. All written statements made after caution shall be taken in the following manner:

"(a) If a person says that he wants to make a statement he shall be told that it is intended to make a written record of what he says.

"He shall always be asked whether he wishes to write down himself what he wants to say; if he says that he cannot write or that he would like someone to write it for him, a police officer may offer to write the statement for him. * * *

"(b) Any person writing his own statement shall be allowed to do so without any prompting as distinct from indicating to him what matters are material.

* * *

"(d) Whenever a police officer writes the statement, he shall take down the exact words spoken by the person making the statement, without putting any questions other than such as may be needed to make the statement coherent, intelligible and relevant to the material matters: he shall not prompt him." * * *

Ed. Note—*England curtails the right to silence.* In the fall of 1994, the British Parliament adopted various restrictions on the right to silence, effective March 1, 1995. These restrictions were similar to those Parliament had imposed on Northern Ireland in 1988. The new law permits judges and jurors to draw adverse inferences when, during interrogation, suspects do not tell the police any fact subsequently relied upon in their defense at trial, if under the circumstances, the suspects would have "been 'reasonably expected' to mention that fact to the police. (This section corresponds to a provision of the Northern Ireland Order, which, according to the government, was designed to end terrorists' use of the 'ambush defense,' whereby terrorists would remain silent during interrogation and thus prevent the prosecution from preparing a rebuttal to subsequent defense claims.)"

[The new law also permits judges and jurors to draw adverse inferences when suspects fail to respond to police questions about any suspicious objects, substances, or marks which are found on their persons or clothing or when suspects do not explain to the police why they were present at a place at or about the time of the crime for which they were arrested. Finally, if the defendant fails to testify at trial, the new law permits the jury to draw such adverse inferences "as appear proper"—including the "common sense" inference that there is no explanation for the evidence produced against the defendant and that the defendant is guilty. See generally, Mark Berger, *Of Policy, Politics, and Parliament: The Legislative Rewriting of the British Right to Silence*, 22 Am.J.Crim.L. 391 (1995); Gregory W. O'Reilly, *England Limits the Right to Silence and Moves Toward an Inquisitional System of Justice*, 85 J.Crim.L. & C. 402 (1994).

[For the view that silence during police interrogation does not cause police to drop charges or prosecutors to dismiss cases or courts to acquit defendants; that using adverse inferences will not induce suspects to talk to the police or to reveal their defenses; that there is no indication that in the past a defendant's right to silence has been frequently invoked at trial; and that adverse inferences about a defendant's failure to testify at trial will not foster testimony by defendants, see O'Reilly, supra, at 431–42.]

No. 759. *Miranda v. Arizona.*

On March 13, 1963, petitioner, Ernesto Miranda, was arrested at his home and taken in custody to a Phoenix police station. He was there identified by the complaining witness. The police then took him to "Interrogation Room No. 2" of the detective bureau. There he was questioned by two police officers. The officers admitted at trial that Miranda was not advised that he had a right to have an attorney present. Two hours later, the officers emerged from the interrogation room with a written confession signed by Miranda. At the top of the statement was a typed paragraph stating that the confession was made voluntarily, without threats or promises of immunity and "with full knowledge of my legal rights, understanding any statement I make may be used against me."[67]

[Miranda] was found guilty of kidnapping and rape. [On] appeal, the Supreme Court of Arizona held that Miranda's constitutional rights were not violated in obtaining the confession and affirmed the conviction. In reaching its decision, the court emphasized heavily the fact that Miranda did not specifically request counsel.

We reverse. From the testimony of the officers and by the admission of respondent, it is clear that Miranda was not in any way apprised of his right to consult with an attorney and to have one present during the interrogation, nor was his right not to be compelled to incriminate himself effectively protected in any other manner. Without these warnings the statements were inadmissible. The mere fact that he signed a statement which contained a typed-in clause stating that he had "full knowledge" of his legal rights does not approach the knowing and intelligent waiver required to relinquish constitutional rights. * * *

No. 760. *Vignera v. New York.*

Petitioner, Michael Vignera, was picked up by New York police on October 14, 1960, in connection with the robbery three days earlier of a Brooklyn dress shop. They took him to the 17th Detective Squad headquarters in Manhattan. Sometime thereafter he was taken to the 66th Detective Squad. There a detective questioned Vignera with respect to the robbery. Vignera orally admitted the robbery to the detective. [T]he defense was precluded from making any showing that warnings had not been given. While at the 66th Detective Squad, Vignera was identified by the store owner and a saleslady as the man who robbed the dress shop. At about 3:00 p.m. he was formally arrested. The police then transported him to still another station, the 70th Precinct in Brooklyn, "for detention". At 11:00 p.m. Vignera was questioned by an assistant district attorney in the presence of a hearing reporter who transcribed the questions and Vignera's answers. This verbatim account of these proceedings contains no statement of any warnings given by the assistant district attorney. * * *

Vignera was [convicted of first degree robbery]. We reverse. The foregoing indicates that Vignera was not warned of any of his rights before the questioning by the detective and by the assistant district attorney. No other steps were taken to protect these rights. Thus he was not effectively apprised of his Fifth Amendment privilege or of his right to have counsel present and his statements are inadmissible.

No. 761. *Westover v. United States.*

At approximately 9:45 p.m. on March 20, 1963, petitioner, Carl Calvin Westover, was arrested by local police in Kansas City as a suspect in two Kansas City robberies. A report was also received from the FBI that he was wanted on a felony charge in California. * * * Kansas City police interrogated Westover on the

67. One of the officers testified that he read this paragraph to Miranda. Apparently, however, he did not do so until after Miranda had confessed orally.

night of his arrest. He denied any knowledge of criminal activities. The next day local officers interrogated him again throughout the morning. Shortly before noon they informed the FBI that they were through interrogating Westover and that the FBI could proceed to interrogate him. There is nothing in the record to indicate that Westover was ever given any warning as to his rights by local police. At noon, three special agents of the FBI continued the interrogation in a private interview room of the Kansas City Police Department, this time with respect to the robbery of a savings and loan association and a bank in Sacramento, California. After two or two and one-half hours, Westover signed separate confessions to each of these two robberies which had been prepared by one of the agents during the interrogation. At trial one of the agents testified, and a paragraph on each of the statements states, that the agents advised Westover that he did not have to make a statement, that any statement he made could be used against him, and that he had the right to see an attorney.

[We reverse Westover's federal conviction of the California robberies.] On the facts of this case we cannot find that Westover knowingly and intelligently waived his right to remain silent and his right to consult with counsel prior to the time he made the statement. At the time the FBI agents began questioning Westover, he had been in custody for over 14 hours and had been interrogated at length during that period. The FBI interrogation began immediately upon the conclusion of the interrogation by Kansas City police and was conducted in local police headquarters. Although the two law enforcement authorities are legally distinct and the crimes for which they interrogated Westover were different, the impact on him was that of a continuous period of questioning. There is no evidence of any warning given prior to the FBI interrogation nor is there any evidence of an articulated waiver of rights after the FBI commenced their interrogation. The record simply shows that the defendant did in fact confess a short time after being turned over to the FBI following interrogation by local police. Despite the fact that the FBI agents gave warnings at the outset of their interview, from Westover's point of view the warnings came at the end of the interrogation process. In these circumstances an intelligent waiver of constitutional rights cannot be assumed.

We do not suggest that law enforcement authorities are precluded from questioning any individual who has been held for a period of time by other authorities and interrogated by them without appropriate warnings. A different case would be presented if an accused were taken into custody by the second authority, removed both in time and place from his original surroundings, and then adequately advised of his rights and given an opportunity to exercise them. But here the FBI interrogation was conducted immediately following the state interrogation in the same police station—in the same compelling surroundings. Thus, in obtaining a confession from Westover the federal authorities were the beneficiaries of the pressure applied by the local in-custody interrogation. In these circumstances the giving of warnings alone was not sufficient to protect the privilege.

No. 584. *California v. Stewart.*

In the course of investigating a series of purse-snatch robberies in which one of the victims had died of injuries inflicted by her assailant, respondent, Roy Allen Stewart, was pointed out to Los Angeles police as the endorser of dividend checks taken in one of the robberies. At about 7:15 p.m., January 31, 1963, police officers went to Stewart's house and arrested him. One of the officers asked Stewart if they could search the house, to which he replied, "Go ahead." The search turned up various items taken from the five robbery victims. At the time of Stewart's arrest, police also arrested Stewart's wife and three other persons who were visiting him. These four were jailed along with Stewart and were interrogated. Stewart was taken to the University Station of the Los Angeles Police Department where he was placed in a cell. During the next five days, police interrogated Stewart on nine different occasions. Except during the first interrogation session, when he was confronted with an accusing witness, Stewart was isolated with his interrogators.

During the ninth interrogation session, Stewart admitted that he had robbed the deceased and stated that he had not meant to hurt her. Police then brought Stewart before a magistrate for the first time. Since there was no evidence to connect them with any crime, the police then released the other four persons arrested with him.

Nothing in the record specifically indicates whether Stewart was or was not advised of his right to remain silent or his right to counsel. In a number of instances, however, the interrogating officers were asked to recount everything that was said during the interrogations. None indicated that Stewart was ever advised of his rights.

[The] jury found Stewart guilty of robbery and first degree murder and fixed the penalty as death. On appeal, the Supreme Court of California reversed. It held that under this Court's decision in *Escobedo,* Stewart should have been advised of his right to remain silent and of his right to counsel and that it would not presume in the face of a silent record that the police advised Stewart of his rights.

We affirm. In dealing with custodial interrogation, we will not presume that a defendant has been effectively apprised of his rights and that his privilege against self-incrimination has been adequately safeguarded on a record that does not show that any warnings have been given or that any effective alternative has been employed. Nor can a knowing and intelligent waiver of these rights be assumed on a silent record. Furthermore, Stewart's steadfast denial of the alleged offenses through eight of the nine interrogations over a period of five days is subject to no other construction than that he was compelled by persistent interrogation to forgo his Fifth Amendment privilege.

Therefore, in accordance with the foregoing, [*Miranda,*[1] *Vignera,* and *Westover* are reversed and *Stewart* is affirmed].[2]

Justice CLARK, dissenting in [*Miranda, Vignera,* and *Westover,* and concurring in the result in *Stewart.*]

[I cannot] agree with the Court's characterization of the present practices of police and investigatory agencies as to custodial interrogation. The materials referred to as "police manuals" are not shown by the record here to be the official manuals of any police department, much less in universal use in crime detection. Moreover, the examples of police brutality mentioned by the Court are rare exceptions to the thousands of cases that appear every year in the law reports. * * *

[The Court's] strict constitutional specific inserted at the nerve center of crime detection may well kill the patient. Since there is at this time a paucity of information and an almost total lack of empirical knowledge on the practical operation of requirements truly comparable to those announced by the majority, I would be more restrained lest we go too far too fast. * * *

Rather than employing the arbitrary Fifth Amendment rule which the Court lays down I would follow the more pliable dictates of Due Process Clauses of the

1. On retrial, *Miranda* was again convicted of kidnapping and rape. The conviction was affirmed in *State v. Miranda,* 450 P.2d 364 (Ariz.1969). For a rich narrative of *Miranda* from arrest to reconviction, see L. Baker, *Miranda: Crime, Law & Politics* (1983).

2. A week later, the Court ruled that *Escobedo* and *Miranda* applied only to trials begun after the decisions were announced.

Fifth and Fourteenth Amendments which we are accustomed to administering and which we know from our cases are effective instruments in protecting persons in police custody. In this way we would not be acting in the dark nor in one full sweep changing the traditional rules of custodial interrogation which this Court has for so long recognized as a justifiable and proper tool in balancing individual rights against the rights of society. It will be soon enough to go further when we are able to appraise with somewhat better accuracy the effect of such a holding. * * *

Justice HARLAN, whom Justice STEWART and Justice WHITE join, dissenting. * * *

While the fine points of [the Court's new constitutional code of rules for confessions] are far less clear than the Court admits, the tenor is quite apparent. The new rules are not designed to guard against police brutality or other unmistakably banned forms of coercion. Those who use third-degree tactics and deny them in court are equally able and destined to lie as skillfully about warnings and waivers. Rather, the thrust of the new rules is to negate all pressures, to reinforce the nervous or ignorant suspect, and ultimately to discourage any confession at all. The aim in short is toward "voluntariness" in a utopian sense, or to view it from a different angle, voluntariness with a vengeance.

To incorporate this notion into the Constitution requires a strained reading of history and precedent and a disregard of the very pragmatic concerns that alone may on occasion justify such strains. I believe that reasoned examination will show that the Due Process Clauses provide an adequate tool for coping with confessions and that, even if the Fifth Amendment privilege against self-incrimination be invoked, its precedents taken as a whole do not sustain the present rules. Viewed as a choice based on pure policy, these new rules prove to be a highly debatable if not one-sided appraisal of the competing interests, imposed over wide-spread objection, at the very time when judicial restraint is most called for by the circumstances. * * *

[The] Court's asserted reliance on the Fifth Amendment [is] an approach which I frankly regard as a *trompe l'oeil*. The Court's opinion in my view reveals no adequate basis for extending the Fifth Amendment's privilege against self-incrimination to the police station. Far more important, it fails to show that the Court's new rules are well supported, let alone compelled, by Fifth Amendment precedents. Instead, the new rules actually derive from quotation and analogy drawn from precedents under the Sixth Amendment, which should properly have no bearing on police interrogation. * * *

Having decided that the Fifth Amendment privilege does apply in the police station, the Court reveals that the privilege imposes more exacting restrictions than does the Fourteenth Amendment's voluntariness test. It then emerges from a discussion of *Escobedo* that the Fifth Amendment requires for an admissible confession that it be given by one distinctly aware of his right not to speak and shielded from "the compelling atmosphere" of interrogation. From these key premises, the Court finally develops the safeguards of warning, counsel, and so forth. I do not believe these premises are sustained by precedents under the Fifth Amendment.[9]

The more important premise is that pressure on the suspect must be eliminated though it be only the subtle influence of the atmosphere and surroundings. The Fifth Amendment, however, has never been thought to forbid *all* pressure to incriminate one's self in the situations covered by it. * * *

9. I lay aside *Escobedo* itself; it contains no reasoning or even general conclusions addressed to the Fifth Amendment and indeed its citation in this regard seems surprising in view of *Escobedo's* primary reliance on the Sixth Amendment.

A closing word must be said about the Assistance of Counsel Clause of the Sixth Amendment, which is never expressly relied on by the Court but whose judicial precedents turn out to be linchpins of the confession rules announced today.

[The] only attempt in this Court to carry the right to counsel into the station house occurred in *Escobedo,* the Court repeating several times that that stage was no less "critical" than trial itself. * * * This is hardly persuasive when we consider that a grand jury inquiry, the filing of a certiorari petition, and certainly the purchase of narcotics by an undercover agent from a prospective defendant may all be equally "critical" yet provision of counsel and advice on that score have never been thought compelled by the Constitution in such cases. The sound reason why this right is so freely extended for a criminal trial is the severe injustice risked by confronting an untrained defendant with a range of technical points of law, evidence, and tactics familiar to the prosecutor but not to himself. This danger shrinks markedly in the police station where indeed the lawyer in fulfilling his professional responsibilities of necessity may become an obstacle to truthfinding. See infra, n. 12.

[The] Court's new rules aim to offset [the] minor pressures and disadvantages intrinsic to any kind of police interrogation. The rules do not serve due process interests in preventing blatant coercion since, as I noted earlier, they do nothing to contain the policeman who is prepared to lie from the start. The rules work for reliability in confessions almost only in the Pickwickian sense that they can prevent some from being given at all.[12] * * *

What the Court largely ignores is that its rules impair, if they will not eventually serve wholly to frustrate, an instrument of law enforcement that has long and quite reasonably been thought worth the price paid for it. There can be little doubt that the Court's new code would markedly decrease the number of confessions. To warn the suspect that he may remain silent and remind him that his confession may be used in court are minor obstructions. To require also an express waiver by the suspect and an end to questioning whenever he demurs must heavily handicap questioning. And to suggest or provide counsel for the suspect simply invites the end of the interrogation. See supra, n. 12. * * *

While passing over the costs and risks of its experiment, the Court portrays the evils of normal police questioning in terms which I think are exaggerated. Albeit stringently confined by the due process standards interrogation is no doubt often inconvenient and unpleasant for the suspect. However, it is no less so for a man to be arrested and jailed, to have his house searched, or to stand trial in court, yet all this may properly happen to the most innocent given probable cause, a warrant, or an indictment. Society has always paid a stiff price for law and order, and peaceful interrogation is not one of the dark moments of the law.

This brief statement of the competing considerations seems to me ample proof that the Court's preference is highly debatable at best and therefore not to be read into the Constitution. However, it may make the analysis more graphic to consider the actual facts of one of the four cases reversed by the Court. *Miranda* serves best, being neither the hardest nor easiest of the four under the Court's standards.[15]

12. The Court's vision of a lawyer "mitigat[ing] the dangers of untrustworthiness" by witnessing coercion and assisting accuracy in the confession is largely a fancy; for if counsel arrives, there is rarely going to be a police station confession. *Watts v. Indiana* (separate opinion of Jackson, J.): "[A]ny lawyer worth his salt will tell the suspect in no uncertain terms to make no statement to police under any circumstances."

15. In *Westover,* a seasoned criminal was practically given the Court's full complement of warnings and did not heed them. The *Stewart* case, on the other hand, involves long detention and successive questioning. In *Vignera,*

On March 3, 1963, an 18-year-old girl was kidnapped and forcibly raped near Phoenix, Arizona. Ten days later, on the morning of March 13, petitioner Miranda was arrested and taken to the police station. At this time Miranda was 23 years old, indigent, and educated to the extent of completing half the ninth grade. He had "an emotional illness" of the schizophrenic type, according to the doctor who eventually examined him; the doctor's report also stated that Miranda was "alert and oriented as to time, place, and person", intelligent within normal limits, competent to stand trial, and sane within the legal definition. At the police station, the victim picked Miranda out of a lineup, and two officers then took him into a separate room to interrogate him, starting about 11:30 a.m. Though at first denying his guilt, within a short time Miranda gave a detailed oral confession and then wrote out in his own hand and signed a brief statement admitting and describing the crime. All this was accomplished in two hours or less without any force, threats or promises and—I will assume this though the record is uncertain * * *—without any effective warnings at all.

Miranda's oral and written confessions are now held inadmissible under the Court's new rules. One is entitled to feel astonished that the Constitution can be read to produce this result. These confessions were obtained during brief, daytime questioning conducted by two officers and unmarked by any of the traditional indicia of coercion. They assured a conviction for a brutal and unsettling crime, for which the police had and quite possibly could obtain little evidence other than the victim's identifications, evidence which is frequently unreliable. There was, in sum, a legitimate purpose, no perceptible unfairness, and certainly little risk of injustice in the interrogation. Yet the resulting confessions, and the responsible course of police practice they represent, are to be sacrificed to the Court's own finespun conception of fairness which I seriously doubt is shared by many thinking citizens in this country.

[It is] instructive to compare the attitude in this case of those responsible for law enforcement with the official views that existed when the Court undertook three major revisions of prosecutorial practice prior to this case, *Johnson v. Zerbst*, *Mapp,* and *Gideon.* In *Johnson,* which established that appointed counsel must be offered the indigent in federal criminal trials, the Federal Government all but conceded the basic issue, which had in fact been recently fixed as Department of Justice policy. In *Mapp,* which imposed the exclusionary rule on the States for Fourth Amendment violations, more than half of the States had themselves already adopted some such rule. In *Gideon,* which extended *Johnson v. Zerbst* to the States, an *amicus* brief was filed by 22 States and Commonwealths urging that course; only two States beside the respondent came forward to protest. By contrast, in this case new restrictions on police questioning have been opposed by the United States and in an *amicus* brief signed by 27 States and Commonwealths, not including the three other States who are parties. No State in the country has urged this Court to impose the newly announced rules, nor has any State chosen to go nearly so far on its own.

[The] law of the foreign countries described by the [majority] reflects a more moderate conception of the rights of the accused as against those of society when other data is considered. Concededly, the English experience is most relevant. In that country, a caution as to silence but not counsel has long been mandated by the "Judges' Rules," which also place other somewhat imprecise limits on police cross-examination of suspects. However, in the court's discretion confessions can be and apparently quite frequently are admitted in evidence despite disregard of the Judges' Rules, so long as they are found voluntary under the common-law test. Moreover, the check that exists on the use of pretrial statements is counter-

the facts are complicated and the record somewhat incomplete.

balanced by the evident admissibility of fruits of an illegal confession and by the judge's often-used authority to comment adversely on the defendant's failure to testify. * * *

[S]ome reference must be made to [the] ironic untimeliness [of these confession rules]. There is now in progress in this country a massive re-examination of criminal law enforcement procedures on a scale never before witnessed. Participants in this undertaking include a Special Committee of the American Bar Association, under the chairmanship of Chief Judge Lumbard of the Court of Appeals for the Second Circuit; a distinguished study group of the American Law Institute, headed by Professor Vorenberg of the Harvard Law School; and the President's Commission on Law Enforcement and Administration of Justice, under the leadership of the Attorney General of the United States. Studies are also being conducted by [other groups] equipped to do practical research.

[It] is no secret that concern has been expressed lest long-range and lasting reforms be frustrated by this Court's too rapid departure from existing constitutional standards. Despite the Court's disclaimer, the practical effect of the decision made today must inevitably be to handicap seriously sound efforts at reform, not least by removing options necessary to a just compromise of competing interests. [T]he legislative reforms when they came would have the vast advantage of empirical data and comprehensive study, they would allow experimentation and use of solutions not open to the courts, and they would restore the initiative in criminal law reform to those forums where it truly belongs. * * *

Justice WHITE, with whom Justice HARLAN and Justice STEWART join, dissenting.

The proposition that the privilege against self-incrimination forbids in-custody interrogation without the warnings specified in the majority opinion and without a clear waiver of counsel has no significant support in the history of the privilege or in the language of the Fifth Amendment. As for the English authorities and the common-law history, the privilege, firmly established in the second half of the seventeenth century, was never applied except to prohibit compelled judicial interrogations. The rule excluding coerced confessions matured about 100 years later, "[b]ut there is nothing in the reports to suggest that the theory has its roots in the privilege against self-incrimination. And so far as the cases reveal, the privilege, as such, seems to have been given effect only in judicial proceedings, including the preliminary examinations by authorized magistrates." Morgan, *The Privilege Against Self–Incrimination,* 34 Minn.L.Rev. 1, 18 (1949).

[That] the Court's holding today is neither compelled nor even strongly suggested by the language of the Fifth Amendment, is at odds with American and English legal history, and involves a departure from a long line of precedent does not prove either that the Court has exceeded its powers or that the Court is wrong or unwise in its present reinterpretation of the Fifth Amendment. It does, however, underscore the obvious—that the Court has not discovered or found the law in making today's decision, nor has it derived it from some irrefutable sources; what it has done is to make new law and new public policy in much the same way that it has in the course of interpreting other great clauses of the Constitution. This is what the Court historically has done. Indeed, it is what it must do and will continue to do until and unless there is some fundamental change in the constitutional distribution of governmental powers.

But if the Court is here and now to announce new and fundamental policy to govern certain aspects of our affairs, it is wholly legitimate to examine the mode of this or any other constitutional decision in this Court and to inquire into the advisability of its end product in terms of the long-range interest of the country. At the very least the Court's text and reasoning should withstand analysis and be a fair exposition of the constitutional provision which its opinion interprets. Decisions like these cannot rest alone on syllogism, metaphysics or some ill-defined notions of natural justice, although each will perhaps play its part.

[The Court] extrapolates a picture of what it conceives to be the norm from police investigatorial manuals, published in 1959 and 1962 or earlier, without any attempt to allow for adjustments in police practices that may have occurred in the wake of more recent decisions of state appellate tribunals or this Court. But even if the relentless application of the described procedures could lead to involuntary confessions, it most assuredly does not follow that each and every case will disclose this kind of interrogation or this kind of consequence.[2]

Insofar as it appears from the Court's opinion, it has not examined a single transcript of any police interrogation, let alone the interrogation that took place in any one of these cases which it decides today. Judged by any of the standards for empirical investigation utilized in the social sciences the factual basis for the Court's premises is patently inadequate.

Although in the Court's view in-custody interrogation is inherently coercive, it says that the spontaneous product of the coercion of arrest and detention is still to be deemed voluntary. An accused, arrested on probable cause, may blurt out a confession which will be admissible despite the fact that he is alone and in custody, without any showing that he had any notion of his right to remain silent or of the consequences of his admission. Yet, under the Court's rule, if the police ask him a single question such as "Do you have anything to say?" or "Did you kill your wife?" his response, if there is one, has somehow been compelled, even if the accused has been clearly warned of his right to remain silent. Common sense informs us to the contrary. While one may say that the response was "involuntary" in the sense the question provoked or was the occasion for the response and thus the defendant was induced to speak out when he might have remained silent if not arrested and not questioned, it is patently unsound to say the response is compelled.

[If] the rule announced today were truly based on a conclusion that all confessions resulting from custodial interrogation are coerced, then it would simply have no rational foundation. * * * Even if one were to postulate that the Court's concern is not that all confessions induced by police interrogation are coerced but rather that some such confessions are coerced and present judicial procedures are believed to be inadequate to identify the confessions that are coerced and those that are not, it would still not be essential to impose the rule that the Court has now fashioned. Transcripts or observers could be required, specific time limits, tailored to fit the cause, could be imposed, or other devices could be utilized to reduce the chances that otherwise indiscernible coercion will produce an inadmissible confession.

On the other hand, even if one assumed that there was an adequate factual basis for the conclusion that all confessions obtained during in-custody interrogation are the product of compulsion, the rule propounded by the Court would still be irrational, for, apparently, it is only if the accused is also warned of his right to counsel and waives both that right and the right against self-incrimination that

2. In fact, the type of sustained interrogation described by the Court appears to be the exception rather than the rule. A survey of 399 cases in one city found that in almost half of the cases the interrogation lasted less than 30 minutes. Barrett, *Police Practices and the Law—From Arrest to Release or Charge,* 50 Calif.L.Rev. 11, 41–45 (1962). Questioning tends to be confused and sporadic and is usually concentrated on confrontations with witnesses or new items of evidence, as these are obtained by officers conducting the investigation. See generally LaFave, *Arrest: The Decision to Take a Suspect into Custody* 386 (1965); ALI, *Model Pre-Arraignment Procedure Code,* Commentary § 5.01, at 170, n. 4 (Tent.Draft No. 1, 1966).

the inherent compulsiveness of interrogation disappears. But if the defendant may not answer without a warning a question such as "Where were you last night?" without having his answer be a compelled one, how can the court ever accept his negative answer to the question of whether he wants to consult his retained counsel or counsel whom the court will appoint? And why if counsel is present and the accused nevertheless confesses, or counsel tells the accused to tell the truth, and that is what the accused does, is the situation any less coercive insofar as the accused is concerned? The court apparently realizes its dilemma of foreclosing questioning without the necessary warnings but at the same time permitting the accused, sitting in the same chair in front of the same policemen, to waive his right to consult an attorney. It expects, however, that not too many will waive the right; and if it is claimed that he has, the State faces a severe, if not impossible burden of proof.

All of this makes very little sense in terms of the compulsion which the Fifth Amendment proscribes. That amendment deals with compelling the accused himself. It is his free will that is involved. Confessions and incriminating admissions, as such, are not forbidden evidence; only those which are compelled are banned. I doubt that the Court observes these distinctions today. By considering any answers to any interrogation to be compelled regardless of the content and course of examination and by escalating the requirements to prove waiver, the Court not only prevents the use of compelled confessions but for all practical purposes forbids interrogation except in the presence of counsel. That is, instead of confining itself to protection of the right against compelled self-incrimination the Court has created a limited Fifth Amendment right to counsel—or, as the Court expresses it, a "right to counsel to protect the Fifth Amendment privilege * * *." The focus then is not on the will of the accused but on the will of counsel and how much influence he can have on the accused. Obviously there is no warrant in the Fifth Amendment for thus installing counsel as the arbiter of the privilege.

In sum, for all the Court's expounding on the menacing atmosphere of police interrogation procedures it has failed to supply any foundation for the conclusions it draws or the measures it adopts.

Criticism of the Court's opinion, however, cannot stop at a demonstration that the factual and textual bases for the rule it propounds are, at best, less than compelling. Equally relevant is an assessment of the rule's consequences measured against community values. The Court's duty to assess the consequences of its action is not satisfied by the utterance of the truth that a value of our system of criminal justice is "to respect the inviolability of the human personality" and to require government to produce the evidence against the accused by its own independent labors. More than the human dignity of the accused is involved; the human personality of others in the society must also be preserved. Thus the values reflected by the privilege are not the sole desideratum; society's interest in the general security is of equal weight.

The obvious underpinning of the Court's decision is a deep-seated distrust of all confessions. As the Court declares that the accused may not be interrogated without counsel present, absent a waiver of the right to counsel, and as the Court all but admonishes the lawyer to advise the accused to remain silent, the result adds up to a judicial judgment that evidence from the accused should not be used against him in any way, whether compelled or not. This is the not so subtle overtone of the opinion that it is inherently wrong for the police to gather evidence from the accused himself. And this is precisely the nub of this dissent. I see nothing wrong or immoral, and certainly nothing unconstitutional, with the police asking a suspect whom they have reasonable cause to arrest whether or not he killed his wife or with confronting him with the evidence on which the arrest was based, at least where he has been plainly advised that he may remain completely silent. * * * Particularly when corroborated, as where the police have confirmed the accused's disclosure of the hiding place of implements or fruits of the crime, such confessions have the highest reliability and significantly contribute to the certitude with which we may believe the accused is guilty.

[The] rule announced today [is] a deliberate calculus to prevent interrogations, to reduce the incidence of confessions and pleas of guilty and to increase the number of trials. [Under] the present law, the prosecution fails to prove its case in about 30% of the criminal cases actually tried in the federal courts. But it is something else again to remove from the ordinary criminal case all those confessions which heretofore have been held to be free and voluntary acts of the accused and to thus establish a new constitutional barrier to the ascertainment of truth by the judicial process. There is, in my view, every reason to believe that a good many criminal defendants, who otherwise would have been convicted on what this Court has previously thought to be the most satisfactory kind of evidence, will now, under this new version of the Fifth Amendment, either not be tried at all or acquitted if the State's evidence, minus the confession, is put to the test of litigation.

I have no desire whatsoever to share the responsibility for any such impact on the present criminal process. * * *

There is another aspect to the effect of the Court's rule on the person whom the police have arrested on probable cause. The fact is that he may not be guilty at all and may be able to extricate himself quickly and simply if he were told the circumstances of his arrest and were asked to explain. This effort, and his release, must now await the hiring of a lawyer or his appointment by the court, consultation with counsel and then a session with the police or the prosecutor. Similarly, where probable cause exists to arrest several suspects as where the body of the victim is discovered in a house having several residents, it will often be true that a suspect may be cleared only through the results of interrogation of other suspects. Here too the release of the innocent may be delayed by the Court's rule.

Much of the trouble with the Court's new rule is that it will operate indiscriminately in all criminal cases, regardless of the severity of the crime or the circumstances involved. It applies to every defendant whether the professional criminal or one committing a crime of momentary passion who is not part and parcel of organized crime. It will slow down the investigation and the apprehension of confederates in those cases where time is of the essence, such as kidnapping, [those] involving the national security, [and] some organized crime situations. In the latter context the lawyer who arrives may also be the lawyer for the defendants' colleagues and can be relied upon to insure that no breach of the organization's security takes place even though the accused may feel that the best thing he can do is to cooperate.

At the same time, the Court's *per se* approach may not be justified on the ground that it provides a "bright line" permitting the authorities to judge in advance whether interrogation may safely be pursued without jeopardizing the admissibility of any information obtained as a consequence. Nor can it be claimed that judicial time and effort, assuming that is a relevant consideration, will be conserved because of the ease of application of the new rule. Today's decision leaves open such questions as whether the accused was in custody, whether his statements were spontaneous or the product of interrogation, whether the accused has effectively waived his rights, and whether nontestimonial evidence introduced at trial is the fruit of statements made during a prohibited interrogation, all of which are certain to prove productive of uncertainty during investigation and litigation during prosecution. For all these reasons, if further restrictions on police interrogation are desirable at this time, a more flexible approach makes much more sense than the Court's constitutional strait-jacket which forecloses more discriminating treatment by legislative or rule-making pronouncements.

Justice Kennedy's Question About* Miranda's *Constitutional Status

During the oral arguments in *Dickerson v. United States* (p. 680), which took place 34 years after *Miranda*, U.S. Solicitor General Seth Waxman maintained that a 1968 federal statutory provision (discussed immediately below), which purported to replace *Miranda* with the pre-*Miranda* "voluntariness" test, was unconstitutional. He told the Court that Congress lacked the authority to "overrule" *Miranda* because *Miranda* was a constitutional rule. When reminded by Justice O'Connor that in the past the Department of Justice had taken the position that the *Miranda* warnings are not constitutionally required, Mr. Waxman agreed they are not. At this point Justice Kennedy interrupted: "You say the warnings are not constitutionally required, but the *Miranda* rule is constitutional.... I don't understand that."

How would you respond to Justice Kennedy?

CAN (DID) CONGRESS "REPEAL" *MIRANDA*? (and why treatment of this issue should be postponed)

A provision of Title II of the Omnibus Crime Control and Safe Streets Act of 1968, a provision usually called § 3501 (because of its designation under Title 18 of the U.S. Code), purports, in effect, to "repeal" or "overrule" *Miranda* and to reinstate the old "totality of circumstances"-"voluntariness" test.[a] At various places, the *Miranda* Court appears to say that it is interpreting the Fifth Amendment. At one point, for example, the *Miranda* Court states that application of "the constitutional principles" discussed in its opinion to the four cases before it leads to the conclusion that in each instance "the statements were obtained under circumstances that did not meet constitutional standards for protection of the privilege." (See p. 587.) Thus, it seems highly unlikely that the Court would have upheld § 3501 if it had considered its validity shortly after it was enacted.[b] But the Court did not do so. Indeed, it did not decide the fate of § 3501 until it handed down *Dickerson v. United States*—in the year 2000.[c]

In the thirty-four years between *Miranda* and *Dickerson* the Burger and Rehnquist Court's characterization of and comments about *Miranda* furnished good reason to believe that the Court's thinking about that famous case had changed dramatically since it was first decided—and therefore that § 3501's attempt to overturn *Miranda* might well succeed.

Although it was not an easy call, the editors of this book concluded that since a number of the post-*Miranda* cases seemed to downgrade and to "deconstitutionalize" that landmark decision, e.g., by referring to the *Miranda* warnings as "prophylactic" and "not themselves rights protected by the Constitution," it would be preferable to postpone discussion of § 3501 and *Dickerson* until the students had read and thought about (a) the many cases applying and explaining

a. The text of § 3501 is set forth at p. 679.

b. Indeed, in *Orozco v. Texas* (1969) (p. ___), the Court, per Black, J., told us that it was holding a confession inadmissible because obtaining it "in the absence of the required warnings was a flat violation of the Self–Incrimination Clause of the Fifth Amendment as construed in *Miranda*."

c. *Dickerson* is set forth at p. 680.

Miranda from 1966–2000 and (b) what various Justices had to say, in all that time, about the desirability, efficacy and legitimacy of *Miranda.*

Here as elsewhere, of course, reasonable people may differ. Those instructors who would rather discuss the constitutionality of § 3501 at this point in the course, not later, need only turn to pp. 679 to 695 to do so.

FOUR DECADES WITH *MIRANDA:* AN OVERVIEW

Because *Miranda* was the centerpiece of the Warren Court's "revolution in American criminal procedure" and the prime target of those who thought the courts were "soft" on criminals, almost everyone expected the so-called Burger Court to treat *Miranda* unkindly. And it did—at first. But it must also be said that the post-Warren Court interpreted *Miranda* fairly generously in some important respects.

The first blows the Burger Court dealt *Miranda* were the impeachment cases, *Harris v. New York* (1971) (p. 922) and *Oregon v. Hass* (1975) (p. 924). *Harris* held that statements preceded by defective warnings, and thus inadmissible to establish the prosecution's case-in-chief, could nevertheless be used to impeach the defendant's credibility if he chose to take the stand in his own defense. The Court noted, but seemed unperturbed by the fact, that some language in the *Miranda* opinion could be read as barring the use of statements obtained in violation of *Miranda* for *any* purpose.

The Court went a step beyond *Harris* in the *Hass* case. In this case, after being advised of his rights, the defendant *asserted* them. Nevertheless, the police refused to honor the defendant's request for a lawyer and continued to question him. The Court ruled that here, too, the resulting incriminating statements could be used for impeachment purposes. Since many suspects make incriminating statements even after the receipt of complete *Miranda* warnings, *Harris* might have been explained—and contained—on the ground that permitting impeachment use of statements acquired without complete warnings would not greatly encourage the police to violate *Miranda.* But now that *Hass* is on the books, when a suspect asserts his rights, it seems the police have virtually nothing to lose and everything to gain by continuing to question him.[a]

Although language in *Miranda* could be read as establishing a *per se* rule against any further questioning of one who has asserted his "right to silence" (as opposed to his *right to counsel,* discussed below), *Michigan v. Mosley* (1975) (p. ___) held that under certain circumstances (and what they are is unclear), if they cease questioning on the spot, the police may "try again," and succeed at a later interrogation session. At the very least, it seems, the police must promptly terminate the original interrogation, resume questioning after the passage of a significant period of time, and give the suspect a fresh set of warnings at the outset of the second session. Whether *Mosley* requires more is a matter of dispute.

The Court has read "custody" or "*custodial* interrogation" rather narrowly. *Oregon v. Mathiason* (1977) (p. 607) and *California v. Beheler* (1983) (p. 607)

a. More recently, the Court held that a defendant's prior silence could be used to impeach him when he testified in his own defense, *Jenkins v. Anderson* (1980) (Ch. 11, § 4), and that even a defendant's *post*arrest silence (so long as he was not given the *Miranda* warnings) could be used for impeachment purposes, *Fletcher v. Weir* (1982) (Ch. 11, § 4). Both *Jenkins* and *Weir* distinguished *Doyle v. Ohio* (1976) (Ch. 11, § 4), which deemed it a violation of due process to use a defendant's silence for impeachment purposes when the defendant remained silent *after* being given *Miranda* warnings.

illustrate that even *police station* questioning designed to produce incriminating statements is not necessarily "custodial interrogation." The result in *Mathiason* is more easily defensible because the suspect went down to the station house on his own after an officer had requested that he meet him there at a convenient time and he had agreed to do so. In *Beheler,* however, the suspect went to the station house in the company of the police. (He was said to have "voluntarily agreed" to accompany the police.)

In *Brown v. Illinois* (1975) (p. 908), the Court declined an invitation to do serious damage to the Fourth Amendment by making the *Miranda* warnings, in effect, a "cure-all." The Court rejected the contention that the giving of the warnings should purge the taint of any preceding illegal arrest—a view that would have permitted the admissibility at trial of any resulting incriminating statements to be considered without regard to the illegal arrest and thus would have encouraged such arrests.[b]

In the early 1980's *Miranda* seemed to enjoy a "second honeymoon." Considering the alternatives (e.g., a mechanical approach to "interrogation," one limited to situations where the police directly address a suspect), the Court gave the key term "interrogation" a fairly generous reading in *Rhode Island v. Innis* (1980) (p. 614). Although the *Innis* case itself involved police "speech," the Court's definition of "interrogation" embraces interrogation techniques that do not. The following year, in *Edwards v. Arizona* (1981) (p. 647), the Court reinvigorated *Miranda* in an important respect. In effect, it added a "bright line" test to the "bright line" *Miranda* rules. Sharply distinguishing *Mosley,* the *Edwards* Court held that when a suspect asserts his right to counsel (as opposed to his right to remain silent), the police *cannot* "try again." Under these circumstances, a suspect cannot be questioned anew "*until* counsel has been made available to him, *unless* [he] himself *initiates* further communication, exchanges or conversations with the police" (emphasis added).[c]

But then language in Supreme Court opinions which seemed to "deconstitutionalize" *Miranda*, language which first appeared in MICHIGAN v. TUCKER, 417 U.S. 433 (1974), began to reappear. Although supporters of *Miranda* were troubled by the "impeachment cases" and by decisions giving "custody" and "custodial interrogation" a narrow reading, they were troubled still more by the way the post-Warren Court characterized *Miranda* and the *Miranda* warnings.

Michigan v. Tucker was a very attractive case from the prosecutor's point of view. First of all, the police questioning occurred before *Miranda* was decided, although the defendant's trial took place afterward. Thus *Miranda* was barely applicable.[a] Second, *Tucker* dealt with the admissibility not of the defendant's own statements—they had been excluded—but only with the testimony of a witness whose identity had been discovered *as a result of* questioning the suspect without giving him a complete set of warnings.

Justice REHNQUIST's opinion for the Court in *Tucker*, holding the witness's testimony admissible, can be read very narrowly. But the opinion contains a considerable amount of broad language. The opinion seems to equate the "compulsion" barred by the privilege against self-incrimination with "coercion" or "involuntariness" under the pre-*Miranda* "totality of circumstances"-"involun-

b. *Brown* was reaffirmed and fortified in *Dunaway v. New York* (1979) and *Taylor v. Alabama* (1982), discussed at pp. 909, 910.

c. In recent years the Court has read *Edwards* expansively. See *Arizona v. Roberson* (1988) (647) and *Minnick v. Mississippi* (1990) (648). But see *Oregon v. Bradshaw* (1983) (652).

a. The Court held, a week after *Miranda*, that *Miranda* affected only those cases in which *the trial* began after that decision. *Johnson v. New Jersey* (1966) (p. 39). The Court probably should have held that *Miranda* affected only *those confessions obtained* after the date of the decision.

tariness" test. By lumping together self-incrimination "compulsion" and pre-*Miranda* "involuntariness" and then declaring that a *Miranda* violation is not necessarily a violation of the self-incrimination clause—it only is if the confession was "involuntary" under traditional standards—the *Tucker* majority seemed to reject the core premise of *Miranda*. See Geoffrey R. Stone, *The Miranda Doctrine in the Burger Court*, 1977 Sup.Ct.Rev. 99, 118–19. If *Tucker*'s view of *Miranda* were correct, it is hard to see what that landmark case would have accomplished by applying the privilege against self-incrimination to the proceedings in the police station.

Miranda supporters were troubled by other language in *Tucker* as well. The *Tucker* majority stated that the *Miranda* Court itself had "recognized that [the *Miranda* rules] were not themselves right protected by the Constitution," but only "measures to insure that the right against compulsory self-incrimination was protected," only procedures that "provid[ed] practical reinforcement for the right against compulsory self-incrimination."

A decade after *Tucker* was decided, the Court reiterated *Tucker*'s way of looking at, and thinking about, *Miranda*, in two cases: *New York v. Quarles* (1984) (p. 629) (which recognized a "public safety" exception and thus held admissible both the suspect's statement, "the gun is over there" and the gun found as a result of the statement) and *Oregon v. Elstad* (1985) (p. 701), ruling that the fact that the police had earlier obtained a statement from defendant in violation of his *Miranda* rights (when they questioned him in his home) did not bar the admissibility of a subsequent statement (obtained at the police station) when, this time, the police complied with *Miranda*.[a]

In both *Quarles* and *Elstad* the Court underscored the distinction between *actual* coercion by physical violence or threats of violence (the pre-*Miranda* "voluntariness" test) and *inherent* or *irrebuttably presumed* coercion (the basis for the *Miranda* rules) or statements obtained *merely* in violation of *Miranda*'s "procedural safeguards" or "prophylactic rules."[b]

The *Tucker–Quarles–Elstad* way of thinking about *Miranda* left defenders of that famous case somewhat in disarray. They braced themselves for the day when the Court would overturn *Miranda*, doing so either on its own initiative or by upholding § 3501, the federal statutory provision that purported, basically, to "repeal" *Miranda* and to turn the clock back to the days when the "totality of circumstances"-"voluntariness" test was the only test for the admissibility of confessions. (As it turned out, however, that day never came.) (See *Dickerson v. United States*, p. 680.)

a. In declining to apply the "fruit of the poisonous tree" doctrine to the second statement, the *Elstad* majority per O'Connor, J., observed: "If errors are made by law enforcement officers in administering the prophylactic *Miranda* procedures, they should not breed the same irremediable consequences as police infringement of the Fifth Amendment itself. [There] is a vast difference between the direct consequences from coercion of a confession by physical violence or other deliberate means [and] the uncertain consequences of disclosure of a 'guilty secret' freely given in response to an unwarned but noncoercive question, as is this case."

b. Dissenting in *Elstad*, Justice Stevens attacked "the Court's attempt to fashion a distinction between actual coercion [and] irrebuttably presumed coercion." He maintained that the presumption of coercion "is only legitimate if it is assumed that there is always a coercive aspect to custodial interrogation that is not preceded by adequate advice of the constitutional right to remain silent. [If] the presumption arises whenever the accused has been taken into custody, [it] will surely be futile to try to develop subcategories of custodial interrogation. Indeed, a major purpose of treating the presumption of coercion as irrebuttable is to avoid the kind of fact-bound inquiry that today's decision will surely engender."

APPLYING AND EXPLAINING *MIRANDA*

1. ***"Exploiting a criminal's ignorance or stupidity"; "intelligent" waivers vs. "wise" ones.*** Consider **STATE v. McKNIGHT**, 243 A.2d 240 (N.J.1968), per WEINTRAUB, C.J.:

"The Constitution is not at all offended when a guilty man stubs his toe. On the contrary, it is decent to hope that he will. [T]he Fifth Amendment does not say that a man shall not be permitted to incriminate himself, or that he shall not be persuaded to do so. It says no more than that a man shall not be 'compelled' to give evidence against himself. [It] is consonant with good morals, and the Constitution, to exploit a criminal's ignorance or stupidity in the detectional process. This must be so if Government is to succeed in its primary mission to live free from criminal attack.

"* * * Nowhere does *Miranda* suggest that the waiver of counsel at the detectional stage would not be 'knowing' or 'intelligent' if the suspect did not understand the law relating to the crime, the possible defenses, and the hazards of talking without the aid of counsel, or if the suspect was not able to protect his interests without such aid, [or] if it was not 'wise' of the prisoner to forego counsel or the right to silence. * * * However relevant to 'waiver' of the right to counsel at trial or in connection with a plea of guilty, those factors are foreign to the investigational scene where the detection of crime is the legitimate aim.

"Hence if a defendant has been given the *Miranda* warnings, if the coercion of custodial interrogation was thus dissipated, his 'waiver' was no less 'voluntary' and 'knowing' and 'intelligent' because he misconceived the inculpatory thrust of the facts he admitted, or because he thought that what he said could not be used because it was only oral or because he had his fingers crossed, or because he could well have used a lawyer. A man need not have the understanding of a lawyer to waive one."

See also *Collins v. Brierly,* 492 F.2d 735 (3d Cir.1974) (en banc): "*Miranda* speaks of 'intelligent' waiver [in the sense] that the individual must know of his available options before deciding what he thinks best suits his particular situation. In this context intelligence is not equated with wisdom." Consider, too, James J. Tomkovicz, *Standards for Invocation and Waiver of Counsel in Confession Contexts,* 71 Iowa L.Rev. 975, 1049 (1986): "The policies of the fifth amendment privilege do not demand rationality, intelligence, or knowledge, but only a voluntary choice not to remain silent." Is this (ought this be) so?

2. ***Adequacy of warnings.*** Consider DUCKWORTH v. EAGAN, 492 U.S. 195 (1989), which arose as follows: Respondent Eagan, suspected of murdering a woman, denied any involvement in the crime. He agreed to go to police headquarters for further questioning. At the stationhouse an officer read him a waiver form which provided, inter alia:

"You have a right to talk to a lawyer for advice before we ask you any questions, and to have him with you during questioning. You have the right to the advice and presence of a lawyer even if you cannot afford to hire one. *We have no way of giving you a lawyer, but one will be appointed for you, if you wish, if and when you go to court.* If you wish to answer questions now without a lawyer present, you have the right to stop answering questions at any time. You also have the right to stop answering at any time until you've talked to a lawyer." (Emphasis added.)

Eagan signed the waiver form, but again denied any involvement in the crime. He was then placed in the "lock up" at police headquarters. Some 29 hours later, the police met with Eagan again. Before questioning him, an officer read from a differently worded waiver form. Eagan signed it and then confessed to stabbing the woman. A 5–4 majority, per REHNQUIST, C.J., concluded that the initial warnings given to Eagan at police headquarters "touched all of the bases required by *Miranda*":

"*Miranda* has not been limited to station-house questioning, and the officer in the field may not always have access to printed *Miranda* warnings, or he may inadvertently depart from routine practice, particularly if a suspect requests an elaboration of the warnings. *Michigan v. Tucker.* [Reviewing courts] need not examine *Miranda* warnings as if construing a will or defining the terms of an easement. The inquiry is simply whether the warnings reasonably 'conve[y] to [a suspect] his rights as required by *Miranda.*' *California v. Prysock*, 453 U.S. 355 (1981) (per curiam) [where, in the course of upholding the challenged warnings, the Supreme Court observed: "This Court has never indicated that the 'rigidity' of *Miranda* extends to the precise formulation of the warnings given a criminal defendant."]

"[On federal habeas corpus, the U.S. Court of Appeals for the Seventh Circuit thought that the] 'if and when you go to court' language suggested that 'only those accused who can afford an attorney have the right to have one present before answering any questions,' and 'implie[d] that if the accused does not 'go to court,' i.e., the government does not file charges, the accused is not entitled to [counsel] at all.'

"In our view, the Court of Appeals misapprehended the effect of the inclusion of 'if and when you go to court' language * * *. First, this instruction accurately described the procedure for the appointment of counsel in Indiana, [where] counsel is appointed at the defendant's initial appearance in court and formal charges must be filed at or before that hearing. We think it must be relatively commonplace for a suspect, after receiving *Miranda* warnings, to ask *when* he will obtain counsel. The 'if and when you go to court' advice simply anticipates that question. Second, *Miranda* does not require that attorneys be producible on call, but only that the suspect be informed, as here, that he has the right to an attorney before and during questioning, and that an attorney would be appointed for him if he could not afford one. [If] the police cannot provide appointed counsel, *Miranda* requires only that the police not question a suspect unless he waives his right to counsel. Here, respondent did just that. * * *."

Dissenting Justice MARSHALL, joined by Brennan, Blackmun and Stevens, JJ., maintained:

"Under *Miranda,* a police warning must *'clearly infor[m]'* a suspect taken into custody 'that if he cannot afford an attorney one will be appointed for him *prior to any questioning* if he so desires.' (Emphasis added.) A warning qualified by an 'if and when you go to court' caveat does nothing of the kind; instead, it leads the suspect to believe that a lawyer will not be provided until some indeterminate time in the future *after questioning*. I refuse to acquiesce in the continuing debasement of this historic precedent * * *.

"[Upon] hearing the warnings given in this case, a suspect would likely conclude that no lawyer would be provided until trial. In common parlance, 'going to court' is synonymous with 'going to trial.' Furthermore, the negative implication of the caveat is that, if the suspect is never taken to court, he 'is not entitled to an attorney at all.' An unwitting suspect harboring uncertainty on this score is precisely the sort of person who may feel compelled to talk 'voluntarily' to the police, without the presence of counsel, in an effort to extricate himself from his predicament * * *."

Notes and Questions

(a) *Access to a Miranda card.* An officer "in the field," notes the Court, "may not always have access to printed *Miranda* warnings" or may "inadvertently depart from routine practice, particularly if a suspect requests an elaboration of the warnings." What bearing should this have on a case like *Duckworth v. Eagan,* where the suspect was questioned at police headquarters and never asked for an elaboration of the warnings? Moreover, would it be burdensome or unreasonable to require police officers always to carry a standard *Miranda* card?

(b) *Anticipating a suspect's questions.* Should it be the business of the police to "anticipate" a suspect's questions? Does this confuse the role of the police officer with that of the defense lawyer? "Anticipating" a question by Eagan, the police informed him that if he could not afford a lawyer "we have no way of giving you a lawyer" before or during questioning. What impact could that information have other than to make it *less likely* that Eagan would assert his right to appointed counsel? Should the police have "anticipated" *another* question: "If you cannot give me a lawyer now, what happens if I ask for one now?" Under *Edwards v. Arizona* (1981) (p. 647) would the truthful answer to that question have been: "Then, we would be very restricted as to how we could proceed. We would have to cease questioning on the spot. And we could not resume questioning at a later time. We could not talk to you any more about this case unless and until you yourself initiated further communication with us." What would the impact of that information be other than to make it *more likely* that Eagan would assert his right to appointed counsel?

Are the police (should the police be) free to "anticipate" those questions they would like to answer and free *not* to "anticipate" those questions they would rather not answer? Does *Duckworth* give them that freedom? See Kamisar, *Duckworth v. Eagan: A Little–Noticed Miranda Case that May Cause Much Mischief,* 25 Crim.L.Bull. 550 (1989).

(c) *Complying with Miranda.* According to *Miranda,* "if police propose to interrogate a person they must make known to him that he is entitled to a lawyer and that if he cannot afford one, a lawyer will be provided for him prior to any interrogation." Was Eagan told, in effect, that if he could not afford a lawyer, one would *not* be—and *could not* be—provided for him prior to (or during) any questioning?

(d) *"For or against you."* Suppose, instead of giving the second *Miranda* warning the way it is usually given, an officer advised a suspect: "Anything you say *can be used for or* against you." Isn't it true that sometimes something a suspect tells the police *might be* used *for* him? In light of *Duckworth v. Eagan,* would this version of the second warning constitute compliance with *Miranda*?

3. *Need for police admonitions in addition to the four Miranda warnings.*

(a) *The consequences of silence.* If, as *Miranda* points out, many suspects will assume that "silence in the face of accusation is itself damning and will bode ill when presented to a jury" (text at fn. 37), should the suspect be explicitly advised not only that any statement he makes may be used against him but that his silence may *not* be used against him? Isn't a suspect likely to ask himself most urgently: "How do I get out of this mess and avoid looking guilty?" Absent assurance on this point, are many suspects likely to stand by their *Miranda* rights? An interrogator can truthfully tell a suspect that once the police advise him of his right to remain silent the prosecution may not comment at trial on his reliance on that right, but can he truthfully tell him that his silence will not be used against him *in any way?* For example, won't the suspect's silence affect the decision to prosecute? See Sheldon Elsen & Arthur Rosett, *Protections for the Suspect under Miranda v. Arizona,* 67 Colum.L.Rev. 645, 654–55 (1967).

(b) *The right to be made aware of the subject matter of the questioning.*

In COLORADO v. SPRING, 479 U.S. 564 (1987), a 7–2 majority, per POWELL, J., held that "a suspect's awareness of all the possible subjects of questioning in advance of interrogation is not relevant to determining whether the suspect voluntarily, knowingly, and intelligently waived his Fifth Amendment privilege." The case arose as follows:

An informant told agents of the Bureau of Alcohol, Tobacco and Firearms (ATF) that Spring (a) was engaged in the interstate shipment of stolen firearms and (b) had been involved in a Colorado killing. The ATF agents set up an undercover operation to purchase firearms from Spring. On March 30, ATF agents arrested Spring in Missouri during the undercover purchase. Spring was advised of his *Miranda* rights and signed a written waiver form.

The agents first questioned Spring about the firearms transactions that led to his arrest. They then asked him if he had ever shot anyone. Spring admitted that he had "shot [a] guy once." On May 26, Colorado officers visited Spring in jail and advised him of his *Miranda* rights. He again signed a written waiver form. The officers then informed Spring that they wanted to question him about the Colorado homicide. Spring confessed to the crime and was convicted of murder.

Spring contended that his waiver of *Miranda* rights before the March 30 statement was invalid because the ATF agents had not informed him that he would be questioned about the Colorado murder and that the May 26 confession was the illegal "fruit" of the March 30 admission. The Colorado Supreme Court agreed, but the U.S. Supreme Court reversed:

"[There] is no doubt that Spring's [March 30 waiver] was knowingly and intelligently made: that is, that Spring understood that he had the right to remain silent and that anything he said could be used as evidence against him. The Constitution does not require that a criminal suspect know and understand every possible consequence of a waiver of the Fifth Amendment privilege." Nor, the Court told us, does the failure to inform a suspect of the potential subjects of interrogation constitute the police trickery and deception condemned in *Miranda:*

"Once *Miranda* warnings are given, it is difficult to see how official silence could cause a suspect to misunderstand the nature of his constitutional right—'his right to refuse to answer any question which might incriminate him.' '[W]e have never read the Constitution to require that the police supply a suspect with a flow of information to help him calibrate his self-interest in deciding whether to speak or stand by his rights.' *Moran v. Burbine* [p. 661]. Here, the additional information could affect only the wisdom of a *Miranda* waiver, not its essentially voluntary and knowing nature."

MARSHALL, joined by Brennan, J., dissented:

"Spring could not have expected questions about the [murder case] when he agreed to waive his rights, as it occurred in a different state and was a violation of state law outside the normal investigative focus of federal [ATF] agents. [If] a suspect has signed a waiver form with the intention of making a statement regarding a specifically alleged crime, the Court today would hold this waiver valid with respect to questioning about any other crime, regardless of its relation to the charges the suspect believes he will be asked to address. Yet once this waiver is given and the intended statement made, the protections afforded by *Miranda* against the 'inherently compelling pressures' of the custodial interrogation have effectively dissipated. Additional questioning about entirely separate and more serious suspicions of criminal activity can take unfair advantage of the suspect's psychological state, as the unexpected questions cause the compulsive pressures suddenly to reappear. Given this technique of interrogation, a suspect's understanding of the topics planned for questioning is, therefore, at the very least 'relevant' to assessing whether his decision to talk to the officers was voluntarily, knowingly, and intelligently made."

Notes and Questions

(i) Should the *Spring* Court have given weight to the fact that the ATF agents had deprived defendant of information regarding the *more serious charge?* Since the agents had arrested Spring in the act of selling illegal firearms, is it likely that Spring decided to talk to the agents because he felt he had nothing more to lose? See Note, 30 Ariz.L.Rev. 551, 564 (1988).

(ii) Would the Court have reached the same result if Spring had asked the ATF agents what crimes they planned to question him about and the agents (a) had remained silent or (b) had replied that the firearms transactions were the only crimes under investigation? If so, why? If not, is it sound "to fashion a confession law doctrine which turns on the fortuity of a suspect asking the right questions"? See id. at 560–61.

4. ***"Custody" vs. "focus."*** After defining "custodial interrogation" in the text, the *Miranda* Court, as one commentator put it, Kenneth W. Graham, *What Is "Custodial Interrogation"?,* 14 U.C.L.A.Rev. 59, 114 (1966), dropped an "obfuscating footnote [4]": "This is what we meant in *Escobedo* when we spoke of an investigation which has focused on an accused." This footnote led some to think that "custody" and "focus" were alternative grounds for requiring the warnings, but these are different events and they have very different consequences.[a] The likely explanation for footnote 4 was the *Miranda* Court's understandable effort to maintain some continuity with a recent precedent. Despite that footnote, however, *Miranda* actually marked a fresh start in describing the circumstances under which constitutional protections first come into play.

The "focus" test, as it had generally been understood at the time of *Escobedo* was expressly rejected in BECKWITH v. UNITED STATES, 425 U.S. 341 (1976). Agents of the Intelligence Division of the IRS did not arrest petitioner, but met with him in a private home where he occasionally stayed. Petitioner argued that the "interview," which produced incriminating statements, should have been preceded by full *Miranda* warnings (instead of the modified *Miranda* warning which petitioner received) because the taxpayer is clearly the "focus" of a criminal investigation when a case is assigned to the Intelligence Division and such a confrontation "places the taxpayer under 'psychological restraints' which are the functional, and therefore, the legal equivalent of custody." The Court per BURGER, C.J., was "not impressed with this argument in the abstract nor as applied to the particular facts of [petitioner's] interrogation":

"[Although] the 'focus' of an investigation may indeed have been on [petitioner] at the time of the interview in the sense that it was his tax liability which was under scrutiny, he hardly found himself in the custodial situation described by the *Miranda* Court as the basis for its holding. *Miranda* specifically defined 'focus,' for its purposes, as 'questioning initiated by law enforcement officers *after* a

a. *Hoffa v. United States,* p. 491, emphasized, albeit not in a *Miranda* context, that "there is no constitutional right to be arrested" and that the police "are under no constitutional duty to call a halt to a criminal investigation the moment they have the minimum evidence to establish probable cause."

person has been taken into custody or otherwise deprived of his freedom of action in any significant way.' "[b]

In *Stansbury v. California*, 511 U.S. 318 (1994) (per curiam), the Court held, "not for the first time, that an officer's subjective and undisclosed view concerning whether the person being interrogated is a suspect is irrelevant to the assessment whether the person is in custody." Unless they are communicated to the person being questioned, emphasized the Court, "an officer's evolving but unarticulated suspicions do not affect the objective circumstances of an interrogation or interview, and thus cannot affect the *Miranda* custody inquiry."

5. *What constitutes "custody" or "custodial interrogation"?* According to Israel, *Criminal Procedure, the Burger Court and the Legacy of the Warren Court,* 75 Mich.L.Rev. 1320, 1383–84 (1977), "difficulties [with *Miranda*] have arisen primarily in situations involving questioning 'on the street.' [P]olice can easily identify what constitutes 'custodial interrogation' where that concept is limited to questioning at the police station or a similar setting." In the main, the concept has been so limited. Most courts have concluded that absent special circumstances (such as arresting a suspect at gunpoint or forcibly subduing him),[a] police questioning "on the street," in a public place or in a person's home or office is not "custodial." Indeed, whether the suspect goes to the stationhouse on his own, see *Oregon v. Mathiason*, 429 U.S. 492 (1977) (per curiam), or whether he "voluntarily" agrees to accompany the police to that site, see *California v. Beheler*, 463 U.S. 1121 (1983) (per curiam), even *police station* questioning

b. See also Chief Justice Burger's plurality opinion in *United States v. Mandujano*, p. 843, rejecting the argument that a "putative" or "virtual" defendant called before the grand jury is entitled to full *Miranda* warnings and stressing that the *Miranda* warnings "were aimed at the evils seen by the Court as endemic to police interrogation of a person in custody. [*Miranda*] recognized that many official investigations, such as grand jury questioning, take place in a setting wholly different from custodial police interrogation. [To] extend [*Miranda*] concepts to questioning before a grand jury inquiring into criminal activity under the guidance of a judge is an extravagant expansion [of that case]." But see Justice Brennan's concurring opinion in *Mandujano.*

a. See *Orozco v. Texas,* 394 U.S. 324 (1969) (applying *Miranda* to a situation where defendant was questioned in his bedroom by four police officers at 4:00 a.m., circumstances that produced a "potentiality for compulsion" equivalent to police station interrogation); *New York v. Quarles* (1984) (p. 629) (defendant in "custody" when questioned in a supermarket minutes after arrested at gunpoint, surrounded by four officers, "frisked" and handcuffed, but "public safety" exception to *Miranda* applied).

The "custodial interrogation" issue arose in a unique setting in *United States v. Mesa,* 638 F.2d 582 (3d Cir.1980). After shooting and wounding both his wife and daughter, Mesa barricaded himself in a motel room. FBI agents cleared the area and repeatedly called to him, through a bullhorn, to surrender. Mesa did not respond. Believing that Mesa was armed (he was) and not knowing whether he had hostages (he did not), the FBI brought in a "hostage negotiator." Mesa agreed to take a mobile phone into his room. Before Mesa finally surrendered peacefully, the negotiator and Mesa conversed over the mobile phone for three and a half hours. The conversation consisted mainly of long narrative monologues by Mesa, but in the course of his exchange of remarks with the negotiator Mesa did make some incriminating statements about the shootings. At no time was he given the *Miranda* warnings. A 2–1 majority of the Third Circuit held that Mesa's statements were admissible, but because one judge decided the case solely on the ground that the exchange between Mesa and the negotiator did not constitute "interrogation," there was no majority opinion on the "custody" issue.

Did the judges who addressed the "custody" issue in *Mesa* make the "logical error" of assuming that exclusion of the incriminating statements would somehow *require* the police to give *Miranda* warnings in such situations? Is the best resolution of "standoff situations" for the police "simply [to] decide, as they probably did here, that it [is] better to withhold the *Miranda* warnings and do without the evidence obtained during the conversation"? See Gibbons, J., dissenting from the denial of a petition for rehearing en banc in *Mesa.* See also Note, 91 Yale L.J. 344 (1981).

How would *Miranda* and a "hostage situation" be resolved if it arose today? See Note (a), p. 633.

designed to produce incriminating statements may not be "custodial interrogation."

Consider, too, *Berkemer v. McCarty*, 468 U.S. 420 (1984), where the Court, per Marshall, J., one of *Miranda*'s strongest supporters, held (without a dissent) that the "roadside questioning" of a motorist detained pursuant to a traffic stop is quite different from questioning at the stationhouse and thus should not be considered "custodial interrogation." *Cf. Schneckloth v. Bustamonte* (p. 447) (warning requirement need not be imposed on "normal consent searches" because they occur "under informal and unstructured conditions" "immeasurably far removed from 'custodial interrogations' ")[b].

The Court has often said that "custody" for *Miranda* purposes is an objective test—how would reasonable people in the suspect's situation have perceived their circumstances? As the next case demonstrates, however, it is not always easy to apply this principle to the particular facts.

YARBOROUGH v. ALVARADO

541 U.S. 652, 124 S.Ct. 2140, 158 L.Ed.2d 938 (2004).

Justice KENNEDY delivered the opinion of the Court.

[Respondent Michael Alvaredo, 17½ years old at the time the crime occurred, helped another person (Soto) try to steal a truck, which led to the shooting of the truck's owner. Shortly thereafter Detective Cheryl Comstock, who was in charge of the investigation, left word with respondent's parents that she wanted to talk to Alvarado. Around lunchtime, Alvarado's parents brought him to the sheriff's station to be questioned. The parents waited in the lobby during the questioning session while Comstock took Alvarado to a small room where only the two of them were present.

[The questioning lasted two hours. At no time was Alvarado given the *Miranda* warnings. At first Alvarado denied any involvement in the shooting, but began to change his story and finally admitted that he had helped Soto try to steal the victim's truck and to hide the murder weapon. Toward the end of the questioning session, the detective twice asked Alvarado whether he wanted a break. When the questioning ended, she returned Alvarado to his parents, who drove him home.

[Alvarado was charged with murder and attempted robbery. The California trial court rejected his motion to exclude the incriminating statements he made to Comstock on the ground that he had not been in "custody" when questioned by the detective. The District Court of Appeal agreed. The federal district court

b. Consider *Minnesota v. Murphy,* 465 U.S. 420 (1984). Murphy, a probationer, arranged to meet with his probation officer in her office as she had requested. He then admitted, in response to her questioning, that he had committed a rape and a murder a number of years earlier. Although the terms of his probation required Murphy to report to his probation officer periodically and to respond truthfully to all her questions, and although the officer had substantial reason to believe that Murphy's answers to her questions were likely to be incriminating, a 6–3 majority, per White, J., concluded that Murphy could not claim the "in custody" exception to the general rule that the privilege against self-incrimination is not self-executing:

"Custodial arrest is said to convey to the suspect a message that he has no choice but to submit to the officers' will and to confess. It is unlikely that a probation interview, arranged by appointment at a mutually convenient time, would give rise to a similar impression. [Since] Murphy was not physically restrained and could have left the office, any compulsion he might have felt from the possibility that terminating the meeting would have led to revocation of probation was not comparable to the pressure on a suspect who is painfully aware that he literally cannot escape a persistent custodial interrogator."

denied federal habeas relief, but the U.S. Court of Appeals reversed, holding that the state courts had erred in failing to take into account Alvarado's youth and inexperience when determining whether a reasonable person in Alvarado's situation would have felt free to leave while being questioned by Comstock.

[The Ninth Circuit concluded that the state court's error warranted federal habeas relief under the Antiterrorism and Effective Death Penalty Act of 1996 (AEDPA) because, to quote the language of the Act, it "resulted in a decision [that] involved an unreasonable application [of] clearly established Federal law, as determined by [this] Court." According to the Ninth Circuit, the deference to state courts required by AEDPA did not bar relief because the relevance of juvenile status in Supreme Court law as a whole compelled the "extension of the principle that juvenile status is relevant" to the context of *Miranda* custody determinations.]

We begin by determining the relevant clearly established law. For purposes of [AEDPA], clearly established law as determined by this Court "refers to the holdings, as opposed to the dicta, of this Court's decisions as of the time of the relevant state-court decision." *Williams v. Taylor* [p. 1662]. We look for "the governing legal principle or principles set forth by the Supreme Court at the time the state court renders its decision." *Lockyer v. Andrade* [p. 1673]. * * *

After *Miranda,* the Court first applied the custody test in *Oregon v. Mathiason,* [where an officer] arranged to meet the suspect at a nearby police station. At the outset of the questioning, the officer stated his belief that the suspect was involved in the burglary but that he was not under arrest. During the 30–minute interview, the suspect admitted his guilt. He was then allowed to leave. The Court held that the questioning was not custodial because there was "no indication that the questioning took place in a context where [the suspect's] freedom to depart was restricted in any way."

In *California v. Beheler,* the Court reached the same result in a case with facts similar to those in *Mathiason*. [The] Court agreed that "the circumstances of each case must certainly influence" the custody determination, but reemphasized that "the ultimate inquiry is simply whether there is a formal arrest or restraint on freedom of movement of the degree associated with a formal arrest." [The Court] noted that how much the police knew about the suspect and how much time had elapsed after the crime occurred were irrelevant to the custody inquiry.

Our more recent cases instruct that custody must be determined based on how a reasonable person in the suspect's situation would perceive his circumstances. In *Berkemer v. McCarty,* [the] Court held the traffic stop noncustodial despite the officer's intent to arrest because he had not communicated that intent to the driver. "A policeman's unarticulated plan has no bearing on the question whether a suspect was 'in custody' at a particular time," the Court explained. "[T]he only relevant inquiry is how a reasonable man in the suspect's position would have understood his situation." * * *

[We] conclude that the state court's application of our clearly established law was reasonable. Ignoring the deferential standard of [AEDPA] for the moment, it can be said that fair-minded jurists could disagree over whether Alvarado was in custody. On one hand, certain facts weigh against a finding that Alvarado was in custody. The police did not transport Alvarado to the station or require him to appear at a particular time. They did not threaten him or suggest he would be placed under arrest. Alvarado's parents remained in the lobby during the interview, suggesting that the interview would be brief. [During] the interview, Comstock focused on Soto's crimes rather than Alvarado's. Instead of pressuring Alvarado with the threat of arrest and prosecution, she appealed to his interest in telling the truth and being helpful to a police officer. In addition, Comstock twice asked Alvarado if he wanted to take a break. At the end of the interview, Alvarado went home. All of these objective facts are consistent with an interrogation environment in which a reasonable person would have felt free to terminate the interview and leave. * * *

Other facts point in the opposite direction. Comstock interviewed Alvarado at the police station. The interview lasted two hours * * *. Alvarado was brought to the police station by his legal guardians rather than arriving on his own accord, making the extent of his control over his presence unclear. Counsel for Alvarado alleges that Alvarado's parents asked to be present at the interview but were rebuffed, a fact that—if known to Alvarado—might reasonably have led someone in Alvarado's position to feel more restricted than otherwise. These facts weigh in favor of the view that Alvarado was in custody.

These differing indications lead us to hold that the state court's application of our custody standard was reasonable. * * * We cannot grant relief under AEDPA by conducting our own independent inquiry into whether the state court was correct as a *de novo* matter. * * * Relief is [available] only if the state court's decision is objectively unreasonable. Under that standard, relief cannot be granted.

The [Ninth Circuit] reached the opposite result by placing considerable reliance on Alvarado's age and inexperience with law enforcement. Our Court has not stated that a suspect's age or experience is relevant to the *Miranda* custody analysis, and counsel for Alvarado did not press the importance of either factor on direct appeal or in habeas proceedings. According to the [Ninth Circuit], however, our Court's emphasis on juvenile status in other contexts demanded consideration of Alvarado's age and inexperience here.

* * * Our opinions applying the *Miranda* custody test have not mentioned the suspect's age, much less mandated its consideration. The only indications in the Court's opinions relevant to a suspect's experience with law enforcement have rejected reliance on such factors.

[There] is an important conceptual difference between the *Miranda* custody test and the line of cases from other contexts considering age and experience. The *Miranda* custody inquiry is an objective test. [The] objective test furthers "the clarity of [Miranda's] rule," ensuring that the police do not need "to make guesses as to [the circumstances] at issue before deciding how they may interrogate the suspect." To be sure, the line between permissible objective facts and impermissible subjective experiences can be indistinct in some cases. It is possible to subsume a subjective factor into an objective test by making the latter more specific in its formulation. Thus the [Ninth Circuit] styled its inquiry as an objective test by considering what a "reasonable 17-year-old, with no prior history of arrest or police interviews" would perceive.

At the same time, the objective *Miranda* custody inquiry could reasonably be viewed as different from doctrinal tests that depend on the actual mindset of a particular suspect, where we do consider a suspect's age and experience. For example, the voluntariness of a statement is often said to depend on whether "the defendant's will was overborne," a question that logically can depend on "the characteristics of the accused." The characteristics of the accused can include the suspect's age, education, and intelligence, see as well as a suspect's prior experience with law enforcement. [The Ninth Circuit] ignored the argument that the custody inquiry states an objective rule designed to give clear guidance to the police, while consideration of a suspect's individual characteristics—including his age—could be viewed as creating a subjective inquiry. * * *

Indeed, reliance on Alvarado's prior history with law enforcement was improper not only under the deferential standard of [AEDPA] but also as a *de novo* matter. In most cases, police officers will not know a suspect's interrogation history. Even if they do, the relationship between a suspect's past experiences and the likelihood a reasonable person with that experience would feel free to leave often will be speculative.

[The] state court considered the proper factors and reached a reasonable conclusion. * * *

Justice O'CONNOR, concurring.

I join the opinion of the Court, but write separately to express an additional reason for reversal. There may be cases in which a suspect's age will be relevant to the *Miranda* "custody" inquiry. In this case, however, Alvarado was almost 18 years old at the time of his interview. It is difficult to expect police to recognize that a suspect is a juvenile when he is so close to the age of majority. Even when police do know a suspect's age, it may be difficult for them to ascertain what bearing it has on the likelihood that the suspect would feel free to leave. That is especially true here; 17 1/2–year-olds vary widely in their reactions to police questioning, and many can be expected to behave as adults. Given these difficulties, I agree that the state court's decision in this case cannot be called an unreasonable application of federal law simply because it failed explicitly to mention Alvarado's age.

Justice BREYER, with whom Justice STEVENS, Justice SOUTER, and Justice GINSBURG join, dissenting.

In my view, Michael Alvarado clearly was "in custody" when the police questioned him (without *Miranda* warnings). [To] put the question in terms of federal law's well-established legal standards: Would a "reasonable person" in Alvarado's "position" have felt he was "at liberty to terminate the interrogation and leave"? A court must answer this question in light of "all of the circumstances surrounding the interrogation." And the obvious answer here is "no."

The law in this case asks judges to apply, not arcane or complex legal directives, but ordinary common sense. Would a reasonable person in Alvarado's position have felt free simply to get up and walk out of the small room in the station house at will during his 2–hour police interrogation? I ask the reader to put himself, or herself, in Alvarado's circumstances and then answer that question: Alvarado hears from his parents that he is needed for police questioning. His parents take him to the station. On arrival, a police officer separates him from his parents. His parents ask to come along, but the officer says they may not.

[The] police take Alvarado to a small interrogation room, away from the station's public area. A single officer begins to question him, making clear in the process that the police have evidence that he participated in an attempted carjacking connected with a murder. When he says that he never saw any shooting, the officer suggests that he is lying, while adding that she is "giving [him] the opportunity to tell the truth" and "tak[e] care of [him]self." Toward the end of the questioning, the officer gives him permission to take a bathroom or water break. After two hours, by which time he has admitted he was involved in the attempted theft, knew about the gun, and helped to hide it, the questioning ends.

What reasonable person in the circumstances—brought to a police station by his parents at police request, put in a small interrogation room, questioned for a solid two hours, and confronted with claims that there is strong evidence that he participated in a serious crime, could have thought to himself, "Well, anytime I want to leave I can just get up and walk out"? If the person harbored any doubts, would he still think he might be free to leave once he recalls that the police officer has just refused to let his parents remain with him during questioning? Would he still think that he, rather than the officer, controls the situation?

There is only one possible answer to these questions. A reasonable person would *not* have thought he was free simply to pick up and leave in the middle of the interrogation. I believe the California courts were clearly wrong to hold the contrary, and the Ninth Circuit was right in concluding that those state courts unreasonably applied clearly established federal law.

What about the majority's view that "fair-minded jurists could disagree over whether Alvarado was in custody"? Consider each of the facts it says "weigh against a finding" of custody:

(1) *"The police did not transport Alvarado to the station or require him to appear at a particular time."* True. But why does that matter? The relevant question is whether Alvarado came to the station of his own free will or submitted to questioning voluntarily. And the involvement of Alvarado's parents suggests *in*voluntary, not voluntary, behavior on Alvarado's part.

(2) *"Alvarado's parents remained in the lobby during the interview, suggesting that the interview would be brief. In fact, [Alvarado] and his parents were told that the interview 'was not going to be long.'"* Whatever was communicated to Alvarado *before* the questioning began, the fact is that the interview was not brief, nor, after the first half hour or so, would Alvarado have expected it to be brief. And those are the relevant considerations.

(3) *"At the end of the interview, Alvarado went home."* As the majority acknowledges, our recent case law makes clear that the relevant question is how a reasonable person would have gauged his freedom to leave *during,* not *after,* the interview.

(4) *"During the interview, [Officer] Comstock focused on Soto's crimes rather than Alvarado's."* In fact, the police officer characterized Soto as the ringleader, while making clear that she knew Alvarado had participated in the attempted carjacking * * *. Her questioning would have reinforced, not diminished, Alvarado's fear that he was not simply a witness, but also suspected of having been involved in a serious crime.

(5) *"[The officer did not] pressur[e] Alvarado with the threat of arrest and prosecution [but instead] appealed to his interest in telling the truth and being helpful to a police officer."* This factor might be highly significant were the question one of "coercion." But it is not. The question is whether Alvarado would have felt free to terminate the interrogation and leave. In respect to that question, police politeness, while commendable, does not significantly help the majority.

(6) *"Comstock twice asked Alvarado if he wanted to take a break."* This circumstance, emphasizing the officer's control of Alvarado's movements, makes it *less* likely, not *more* likely, that Alvarado would have thought he was free to leave at will.

The facts to which the majority points make clear what the police did *not* do, for example, come to Alvarado's house, tell him he was under arrest, handcuff him, place him in a locked cell, threaten him, or tell him explicitly that he was not free to leave. But what is important here is what the police *did* do—namely, have Alvarado's parents bring him to the station, put him with a single officer in a small room, keep his parents out, let him know that he was a suspect, and question him for two hours. These latter facts compel a single conclusion: A reasonable person in Alvarado's circumstances would *not* have felt free to terminate the interrogation and leave.

What about Alvarado's youth? The fact that Alvarado was 17 helps to show that he was unlikely to have felt free to ignore his parents' request to come to the station. And a 17–year-old is more likely than, say, a 35–year-old, to take a police officer's assertion of authority to keep parents outside the room as an assertion of authority to keep their child inside as well.

The majority suggests that the law might *prevent* a judge from taking account of the fact that Alvarado was 17. I can find nothing in the law that supports that conclusion. [T]he "reasonable person" standard does not require a court to pretend that Alvarado was a 35–year-old with aging parents whose middle-aged children do what their parents ask only out of respect. Nor does it say that a court should pretend that Alvarado was the statistically determined "average person"—a working, married, 35–year-old white female with a high school degree.

Rather, the precise legal definition of "reasonable person" may, depending on legal context, appropriately account for certain personal characteristics. In negligence suits, for example, the question is what would a "reasonable person" do " 'under the same or similar circumstances.' " In answering that question, courts enjoy "latitude" and may make "allowance not only for external facts, but sometimes for certain characteristics of the actor himself," including physical disability, youth, or advanced age. This allowance makes sense in light of the tort standard's recognized purpose: deterrence. Given that purpose, why pretend that a child is an adult or that a blind man can see?

In the present context, that of *Miranda*'s "in custody" inquiry, the law has introduced the concept of a "reasonable person" to avoid judicial inquiry into subjective states of mind, and to focus the inquiry instead upon objective circumstances that are known to both the officer and the suspect and that are likely relevant to the way a person would understand his situation. This focus helps to keep *Miranda* a workable rule.

In this case, Alvarado's youth is an objective circumstance that was known to the police. It is not a special quality, but rather a widely shared characteristic that generates commonsense conclusions about behavior and perception. To focus on the circumstance of age in a case like this does not complicate the "in custody" inquiry.

[This] Court's cases establish that, even if the police do not tell a suspect he is under arrest, do not handcuff him, do not lock him in a cell, and do not threaten him, he may nonetheless reasonably believe he is not free to leave the place of questioning—and thus be in custody for *Miranda* purposes. * * *

Common sense, and an understanding of the law's basic purpose in this area, are enough to make clear that Alvarado's age—an objective, widely shared characteristic about which the police plainly knew—is also relevant to the inquiry. Unless one is prepared to pretend that Alvarado is someone he is not, a middle-aged gentleman, well-versed in police practices, it seems to me clear that the California courts made a serious mistake. I agree with the Ninth Circuit's similar conclusions. Consequently, I dissent.

Notes and Questions

(a) If Mr. Alvarado had been confined to a wheelchair or been a non-English speaking alien, would Justice Kennedy have maintained that the trial court should have taken these factors into account? What if Mr. Alvarado had been 13½ or 14½ years old instead of 17½? Would the answer have turned on how old the suspect *looked*? On whether the police *knew* how old he was? Consider CRAIG BRADLEY, *On "Custody,"* Trial, Feb. 2005, pp. 58, 59: "The Court should have made it clear that 'in the suspect's situation' referred to obvious factors [such as those suggested above] that the police should realize would influence the suspect's sense of freedom. Instead, by labeling the test 'objective' when it clearly contains a subjective element, the Court implied that a suspect's age is irrelevant in determining whether an interrogation is custodial. And it conclusively confirmed that a suspect's past experience with the police should never be a part of the equation."

(b) Would the outcome in *Alvarado* have been different if the case had reached the Supreme Court on direct review rather than on federal habeas review? Consider Bradley, supra, at 61: "On a direct appeal, as opposed to habeas corpus petition, courts may feel free to conclude, based on *Alvarado*, that a two-hour interview of a juvenile is custodial. The younger the suspect is, the more likely courts are to reach that conclusion. Consequently, the police would be well advised to issue *Miranda* warnings for an interview of this length, especially of a juvenile. (Of course, the police can always reassure the suspect that he or she is not under arrest.) Otherwise, the appellate courts may accept *Alvarado*'s suggestion that a conclusion either way as to custody would not be unreasonable."

6. *What constitutes interrogation within the meaning of Miranda?*

RHODE ISLAND v. INNIS

446 U.S. 291, 100 S.Ct. 1682, 64 L.Ed.2d 297 (1980).

Justice STEWART delivered the opinion of the Court.

[*Miranda*] held that, once a defendant in custody asks to speak with a lawyer, all interrogation must cease until a lawyer is present. The issue in this case is whether the respondent was "interrogated" in violation [of *Miranda*].[a]

[At approximately 4:30 a.m., a patrolman arrested respondent, suspected of robbing a taxicab driver and murdering him with a shotgun blast to the back of the head. Respondent was unarmed. He was advised of his rights. Within minutes a sergeant (who advised respondent of his rights) and then a captain arrived at the scene of the arrest. The captain also gave respondent the *Miranda* warnings, whereupon respondent asked to speak with a lawyer. The captain then directed that respondent be placed in a police vehicle with a wire screen mesh between the front and rear seats and be driven to the police station. Three officers were assigned to accompany the arrestee. Although the record is somewhat unclear, it appears that Patrolman Williams was in the back seat with respondent and that Patrolmen Gleckman and McKenna were in front.]

While enroute to the central station, Patrolman Gleckman initiated a conversation with Patrolman McKenna concerning the missing shotgun.[1] As Patrolman Gleckman later testified:

> "A. At this point, I was talking back and forth with Patrolman McKenna stating that I frequent this area while on patrol and [that because a school for handicapped children is located nearby,] there's a lot of handicapped children running around in this area, and God forbid one of them might find a weapon with shells and they might hurt themselves."

Patrolman McKenna apparently shared his fellow officer's concern:

a. Why is *this* the issue? Since respondent asserted his right to counsel, why isn't the issue whether the police "scrupulously honored" the exercise of that right? Cf. *Michigan v. Mosley* (p. 646). Or why isn't the issue (a) whether the police impermissibly "prompted" respondent to change his mind after he invoked his right to counsel or (b) whether respondent "*himself initiate[d]* further communication, exchanges or conversations with the police," *Edwards v. Arizona* (p. 647) (emphasis added), after initially invoking his right to counsel?

1. Although there was conflicting testimony about the exact seating arrangements, it is clear that everyone in the vehicle heard the conversation.

"A. I more or less concurred with him [Gleckman] that it was a safety factor and that we should, you know, continue to search for the weapon and try to find it."

[Respondent then interrupted the conversation, stating that he would show the officers where the gun was located. He told the police that he understood his rights, but "wanted to get the gun out of the way because of the kids in the area in the school." He then led the police to a nearby field, where he pointed out the shotgun under some rocks.]

[Respondent was convicted of murder. The trial judge admitted the shotgun and testimony related to its discovery. On appeal, the Rhode Island Supreme Court concluded that the police had "interrogated" respondent without a valid waiver of his right to counsel; the conversation in the police vehicle had constituted "subtle coercion" that was the equivalent of *Miranda* "interrogation."]

[In determining whether respondent had been "interrogated" in violation of *Miranda*] we first define the term "interrogation" under *Miranda* before turning to a consideration of the facts of this case. [The] concern of the Court in *Miranda* was that the "interrogation environment" created by the interplay of interrogation and custody would "subjugate the individual to the will of his examiner" and thereby undermine the privilege against compulsory self-incrimination. The police practices that evoked this concern included several that did not involve express questioning [such as] the so-called "reverse lineup" in which a defendant would be identified by coached witnesses as the perpetrator of a fictitious crime, [to induce] him to confess to the actual crime of which he was suspected in order to escape the false prosecution. [It] is clear that these techniques of persuasion, no less than express questioning, were thought, in a custodial setting, to amount to interrogation.[3]

This is not to say, however, that all statements obtained by the police after a person has been taken into custody are to be considered the product of interrogation. [The *Miranda* warnings] are required not where a suspect is simply taken into custody, but rather where a suspect in custody is subjected to interrogation. "Interrogation," as conceptualized [in *Miranda*], must reflect a measure of compulsion above and beyond that inherent in custody itself.[4]

We conclude that the *Miranda* safeguards come into play whenever a person in custody is subjected to either express questioning or its functional equivalent. That is to say, the term "interrogation" under *Miranda* refers not only to express questioning, but also to any words or actions on the part of the police (other than

3. To limit the ambit of *Miranda* to express questioning would "place a premium on the ingenuity of the police to devise methods of indirect interrogation, rather than to implement the plain mandate of *Miranda*." *Commonwealth v. Hamilton,* 445 Pa. 292, 297, 285 A.2d 172, 175 [(1971)].

4. There is language in the opinion of the Rhode Island Supreme Court in this case suggesting that the definition of "interrogation" under *Miranda* is informed by this Court's decision in *Brewer v. Williams,* [p. 733, reaffirming and expansively interpreting the *Massiah* doctrine]. This suggestion is erroneous. Our decision in *Brewer* rested solely on the Sixth and Fourteenth Amendment right to counsel. That right, as we held in *Massiah,* prohibits law enforcement officers from "deliberately elicit[ing]" incriminating information from a defendant in the absence of counsel after a formal charge against the defendant has been filed. Custody in such a case is not controlling; indeed, the petitioner in *Massiah* was not in custody. By contrast, the right to counsel at issue in the present case is based not on the Sixth and Fourteenth Amendments, but rather on the Fifth and Fourteenth Amendments as interpreted in the *Miranda* opinion. The definitions of "interrogation" under the Fifth and Sixth Amendments, if indeed the term "interrogation" is even apt in the Sixth Amendment context, are not necessarily interchangeable, since the policies underlying the two constitutional protections are quite distinct. See Kamisar, *Brewer v. Williams, Massiah and Miranda: What is "Interrogation"? When Does it Matter?,* 67 Geo.L.J. 1, 41–55 (1978).

those normally attendant to arrest and custody)[a] that the police should know are reasonably likely to elicit an incriminating response from the suspect. The latter portion of this definition focuses primarily upon the perceptions of the suspect, rather than the intent of the police. This focus reflects the fact that the *Miranda* safeguards were designed to vest a suspect in custody with an added measure of protection against coercive police practices, without regard to objective proof of the underlying intent of the police. A practice that the police should know is reasonably likely to evoke an incriminating response from a suspect thus amounts to interrogation.[7] But, since the police surely cannot be held accountable for the unforeseeable results of their words or actions, the definition of interrogation can extend only to words or actions on the part of police officers that they *should have known* were reasonably likely to elicit an incriminating response.[8]

Turning to the facts of the present case, we conclude that the respondent was not "interrogated" within the meaning of *Miranda*. It is undisputed that the first prong of the definition of "interrogation" was not satisfied, for the [Gleckman–McKenna conversation] included no express questioning of the respondent. [Moreover,] it cannot be fairly concluded that the respondent was subjected to the "functional equivalent" of questioning. It cannot be said [that the officers] should have known that their conversation was reasonably likely to elicit an incriminating response from the respondent. There is nothing in the record to suggest that the officers were aware that the respondent was peculiarly susceptible to an appeal to his conscience concerning the safety of handicapped children [or that] the police knew that the respondent was unusually disoriented or upset at the time of his arrest.[9]

[The] Rhode Island Supreme Court erred, in short, in equating "subtle compulsion" with interrogation. That the officers' comments struck a responsive cord is readily apparent. Thus, it may be said, as the Rhode Island Supreme Court did say, that the respondent was subjected to "subtle compulsion." But that is not the end of the inquiry. It must also be established that a suspect's incriminating response was the product of words or actions on the part of the police that they should have known were reasonably likely to elicit an incriminating response.[10] This was not established in the present case. * * *

a. In *South Dakota v. Neville,* 459 U.S. 553 (1983), the Court noted (fn. 15) that "in the context of an arrest for driving while intoxicated, a police inquiry of whether the suspect will take a blood-alcohol test is not an interrogation within the meaning of *Miranda.*" Recalling that *Innis* had excluded "police words or actions 'normally attendant to arrest and custody' " from the definition of "interrogation," the *Neville* Court added: "The police inquiry here is highly regulated by state law, and is presented in virtually the same words to all suspects. It is similar to a police request to submit to fingerprinting or photography. Respondent's choice of refusal thus enjoys no prophylactic *Miranda* protection outside the basic Fifth Amendment protection. See generally Peter Arenella, *Schmerber and the Privilege Against Self–Incrimination: A Reappraisal,* 20 Am.Crim.L.Rev. 31, 56–58 (1982)."

7. This is not to say that the intent of the police is irrelevant, for it may well have a bearing on whether the police should have known that their words or actions were reasonably likely to evoke an incriminating response. In particular, where a police practice is designed to elicit an incriminating response from the accused, it is unlikely that the practice will not also be one which the police should have known was reasonably likely to have that effect.

8. Any knowledge the police may have had concerning the unusual susceptibility of a defendant to a particular form of persuasion might be an important factor in determining whether the police should have known that their words or actions were reasonably likely to elicit an incriminating response from the suspect.

9. The record in no way suggests that the officers' remarks were *designed* to elicit a response. It is significant that the trial judge, after hearing the officers' testimony, concluded that it was "entirely understandable that [the officers] would voice their concern [for the safety of the handicapped children] to each other."

10. By way of example, if the police had done no more than to drive past the site of the concealed weapon while taking the most direct

Chief Justice BURGER, concurring in the judgment.

Since the result is not inconsistent with *Miranda,* I concur in the judgment. The meaning of *Miranda* has become reasonably clear and law enforcement practices have adjusted to its strictures; I would neither overrule *Miranda,* disparage it, nor extend it at this late date. I fear, however, that [the Court's opinion] may introduce new elements of uncertainty; under the Court's test, a police officer, in the brief time available, apparently must evaluate the suggestibility and susceptibility of an accused. * * *

Justice MARSHALL, with whom Justice BRENNAN joins, dissenting.

I am substantially in agreement with the Court's definition of "interrogation" within the meaning of *Miranda.* In my view, the *Miranda* safeguards apply whenever police conduct is intended or likely to produce a response from a suspect in custody. As I read the Court's opinion, its definition of "interrogation" for *Miranda* purposes is equivalent, for practical purposes, to my formulation. [The] Court requires an objective inquiry into the likely effect of police conduct on a typical individual, taking into account any special susceptibility of the suspect to certain kinds of pressure of which the police know or have reason to know. I am utterly at a loss, however, to understand how this objective standard as applied to the facts before us can rationally lead to the conclusion that there was no interrogation. * * *

One can scarcely imagine a stronger appeal to the conscience of a suspect—*any* suspect—than the assertion that if the weapon is not found an innocent person will be hurt or killed. And not just any innocent person, but an innocent child—a little girl—a helpless, handicapped little girl on her way to school. [As] a matter of fact, the appeal to a suspect to confess for the sake of others, to "display some evidence of decency and honor," is a classic interrogation technique.

Gleckman's remarks would obviously have constituted interrogation if they had been explicitly directed to petitioner, and the result should not be different because they were nominally addressed to McKenna. [The officers] knew petitioner would hear and attend to their conversation, and they are chargeable with knowledge of and responsibility for the pressures to speak which they created. * * *

Justice STEVENS, dissenting.

[In] my view any statement that would normally be understood by the average listener as calling for a response is the functional equivalent of a direct question, whether or not it is punctuated by a question mark. The Court, however, takes a much narrower view. It holds that police conduct is not the "functional equivalent" of direct questioning unless the police should have known that what they were saying or doing was likely to elicit an incriminating response from the suspect. This holding represents a plain departure from the principles set forth in *Miranda.*

[In] order to give full protection to a suspect's right to be free from any interrogation at all, the definition of "interrogation" must include any police statement or conduct that has the same purpose or effect as a direct question. Statements that appear to call for a response from the suspect, as well as those that are designed to do so, should be considered interrogation. By prohibiting only those relatively few statements or actions that a police officer should know are likely to elicit an incriminating response, the Court today accords a suspect

route to the police station, and if the respondent, upon noticing for the first time the proximity of the school for handicapped children, had blurted out that he would show the officers where the gun was located, it could not seriously be argued that this "subtle compulsion" would have constituted "interrogation" within the meaning of the *Miranda* opinion.

considerably less protection. Indeed, since I suppose most suspects are unlikely to incriminate themselves even when questioned directly, this new definition will almost certainly exclude every statement that is not punctuated with a question mark from the concept of "interrogation."

The difference between the approach required by a faithful adherence to *Miranda* and the stinted test applied by the Court today can be illustrated by comparing three different ways in which Officer Gleckman could have communicated his fears about the possible dangers posed by the shotgun to handicapped children. He could have:

(1) directly asked Innis:

> Will you please tell me where the shotgun is so we can protect handicapped schoolchildren from danger?

(2) announced to the other officers in the wagon:

> If the man sitting in the back seat with me should decide to tell us where the gun is, we can protect handicapped children from danger.

or (3) stated to the other officers:

> It would be too bad if a little handicapped girl would pick up the gun that this man left in the area and maybe kill herself.

In my opinion, all three of these statements should be considered interrogation because all three appear to be designed to elicit a response from anyone who in fact knew where the gun was located. Under the Court's test, on the other hand, the form of the statements would be critical. The third statement would not be interrogation because in the Court's view there was no reason for Officer Gleckman to believe that Innis was susceptible to this type of an implied appeal; therefore, the statement would not be reasonably likely to elicit an incriminating response. Assuming that this is true, then it seems to me that the first two statements, which would be just as unlikely to elicit such a response, should also not be considered interrogation. But, because the first statement is clearly an express question, it *would* be considered interrogation under the Court's test. The second statement, although just as clearly a deliberate appeal to Innis to reveal the location of the gun, would presumably not be interrogation because (a) it was not in form a direct question and (b) it does not fit within the "reasonably likely to elicit an incriminating response" category that applies to indirect interrogation.

As this example illustrates, the Court's test creates an incentive for police to ignore a suspect's invocation of his rights in order to make continued attempts to extract information from him. If a suspect does not appear to be susceptible to a particular type of psychological pressure, the police are apparently free to exert that pressure on him despite his request for counsel, so long as they are careful not to punctuate their statements with question marks. And if, contrary to all reasonable expectations, the suspect makes an incriminating statement, that statement can be used against him at trial. The Court thus turns *Miranda*'s unequivocal rule against any interrogation at all into a trap in which unwary suspects may be caught by police deception.

* * * I think the Court is clearly wrong in holding, as a matter of law, that Officer Gleckman should not have realized that his statement was likely to elicit an incriminating response. [Moreover,] there is evidence in the record to support the view that Officer Gleckman's statement was intended to elicit a response from Innis. Officer Gleckman, who was not regularly assigned to the caged wagon, was directed by a police captain to ride with respondent to the police station. [The] record does not explain why, notwithstanding the fact that respondent was handcuffed, unarmed, and had offered no resistance when arrested by an officer acting alone, the captain ordered Officer Gleckman to ride with respondent. It is

not inconceivable that two professionally trained police officers concluded that a few well-chosen remarks might induce respondent to disclose the whereabouts of the shotgun. This conclusion becomes even more plausible in light of the emotionally charged words chosen by Officer Gleckman ("God forbid" that a "little girl" should find the gun and hurt herself). * * *

Notes and Questions

(a) If Officer Gleckman's remarks had been explicitly directed to Innis, would they have constituted "interrogation" regardless of whether they were reasonably likely—or at all likely—to elicit an incriminating response? If so, why should words or actions that are the "functional equivalent" of express questioning have to satisfy a "reasonable likelihood" or "apparent probability" of success standard? Why isn't it sufficient that the police speech or conduct—unlike "administrative questioning" (routine questions asked of all arrestees "booked" or otherwise processed) and unlike casual conversation in no way related to the case—would normally be understood as *calling for* a response about the merits of the case or be *likely to be viewed* as *having the same force and effect* as a question about the merits of the case? See Welsh White, *Interrogation without Questions,* 78 Mich. L.Rev. 1209, 1227–36 (1980); Jesse H. Choper, Yale Kamisar & Laurence H. Tribe, *The Supreme Court: Trends and Developments, 1979–80* at 88–89, 92–95 (1981) (remarks of Professor Kamisar).

(b) If Gleckman *had admitted* that his remarks to McKenna were *designed* to get Innis to make incriminating statements, would (should) they have constituted "interrogation" regardless of Gleckman's apparent likelihood of success? Why (not)? Did it (should it) matter whether the "Christian burial speech" delivered in *Brewer v. Williams,* p. 733, was reasonably likely to elicit an incriminating response from Williams? Why (not)?

(c) In ARIZONA v. MAURO, 481 U.S. 520 (1987), a 5–4 majority, per POWELL, J., held that it was not "custodial interrogation" within the meaning of *Miranda* for the police to accede to the request of defendant's wife, also a suspect in the murder of their son, to speak with defendant (being held in a room at the station house) in the presence of a police officer (Detective Manson), who placed a tape recorder in plain sight on a desk. (Defendant had been given the *Miranda* warnings and had asserted his right to counsel.) Observed the Court:

"There is no evidence that the officers sent Mrs. Mauro in to see her husband for the purpose of eliciting incriminating statements. [T]he officers tried to discourage her from talking to her husband, but finally 'yielded to her insistent demands.' Nor was Detective Manson's presence improper. [There were] a number of legitimate reasons—not related to securing incriminating statements—for having a police officer present. Finally, the weakness of Mauro's claim that he was interrogated is underscored by examining the situation from his perspective. * * * We doubt that a suspect, told by officers that his wife will be allowed to speak to him, would feel that he was being coerced to incriminate himself in any way.

"[The state supreme court] was correct to note that there was a 'possibility' that Mauro would incriminate himself while talking to his wife [and] that the officers were aware of that possibility. [But] the actions in this case were far less questionable than the 'subtle compulsion' [held] *not* to be interrogation in *Innis.* Officers do not interrogate a suspect simply by hoping that he will incriminate himself. * * *

"[In] deciding whether particular police conduct is interrogation, we must remember the purpose behind [*Miranda*]: preventing government officials from using the coercive nature of confinement to extract confessions that would not be given in an unrestrained environment. The government actions in this case do not implicate the purpose in any way."

Dissenting Justice STEVENS, joined by Brennan, Marshall and Blackmun, JJ., maintained:

"[The] facts compel the conclusion that the police took advantage of Mrs. Mauro's request to visit her husband, setting up a confrontation between them at a time when he manifestly desired to remain silent. Because they allowed [Mauro's] conversation with his wife to commence at a time when they knew it was reasonably likely to produce an incriminating statement, the police interrogated him.

"[The] intent of the detectives is clear from their own testimony. They both knew that if the conversation took place, incriminating statements were likely to be made. With that in mind, they decided to take in a tape recorder, sit near [Mauro] and his wife and allow the conversation to commence. * * *

"It is undisputed that a police decision to place two suspects in the same room and then to listen to or record their conversation may constitute a form of interrogation even if no questions are asked by any police officers.[a] That is exactly what happened here. [The Mauros] were both suspects in the murder of their son. Each of them had been interrogated separately before the officers decided to allow them to converse, an act that surely did not require a tape recorder or the presence of a police officer within hearing range. Under the circumstances, the police knew or should have known that [this encounter] was reasonably likely to produce an incriminating statement. * * *

"[Under] the circumstances, the mere fact that [Mrs. Mauro] made the initial request leading to the conversation does not alter [the fact that the police violated *Miranda*]. [They] exercised exclusive control over whether and when the suspects spoke with each other; the police knew that whatever Mauro wished to convey to his wife at that moment, he would have to say under the conditions unilaterally imposed by the officers. In brief, the police exploited the custodial situation and the understandable desire of Mrs. Mauro to speak with [her husband] to conduct an interrogation."

Notes and Questions

(i) *Likelihood of incrimination.* According to the *Mauro* majority, the meeting between Mauro and his wife did not "present a sufficient likelihood of incrimination" to satisfy the *Innis* standard [fn. 6]. What if it did? What if, as the dissenters maintained, the police did know or should have known that the meeting between Mauro and his wife was likely to produce an incriminating statement. Should this be decisive in a case like *Mauro?*

Should the *Innis* language defining police interrogation or its functional equivalent be taken literally? Did the *Innis* Court assume a basic factual setting—police conduct equivalent to direct police questioning in terms of its compulsion or pressure? Did the *Innis* Court have in mind conduct *by the police* and in *the presence of the suspect,* such as confronting the suspect with a report indicating that he "flunked" a lie detector exam or confronting him with the confession of an accomplice or bringing an effusive and accusing accomplice into the same room with the police and the suspect?[b]

a. Does Justice Stevens mean that this situation may constitute a form of interrogation within the meaning of *Miranda* even if the suspects are *unaware* that the police are listening to, or recording, their conversation? If so, why? Where is the "compulsion"? See the discussion following this case and the discussion in Note 8.

b. Although the *Innis* case involved police "speech," the Court's definition of "interroga-

(ii) *"Police blue" compulsion.* If a spouse or parent or friend meets with someone in custody, does that add significantly to the *official* compulsion, the *"police blue"* compulsion? If not, why should this conduct be considered the equivalent of "custodial *police* interrogation"?

(iii) *The purpose of the police.* The *Mauro* majority emphasizes the lack of any evidence that the police sent Mrs. Mauro to see her husband "for the purpose of eliciting incriminating statements." What if the detectives had asked Mrs. Mauro to try to get her husband to confess and she had agreed to do so? Would she have become an "agent" of the police? Why does this matter for *Miranda* purposes? If defendant *were unaware* of his wife's or the detectives' purpose, how would that purpose render defendant's environment more "compelling" or make him more likely to feel that he was being "coerced" to incriminate himself? How would the undisclosed purpose of the police alter the situation *from the defendant's perspective?*

(iv) *The suspect's awareness that the police are present.* Is the key factor in a case like *Mauro* not the intent of the police but the suspect's awareness that the police are present, or listening, when he meets with a spouse or friend? If Detective Manson had not been physically present, but the police had *secretly recorded* defendant's meeting with his wife, would *Mauro* have been a much easier case? Why (not)? See next Note.

7. ***The "jail plant" situation; "surreptitious interrogation."*** Suppose a secret government agent, posing as a fellow-prisoner, is placed in the same cell or cellblock with an incarcerated suspect and induces him to discuss the crime for which he has been arrested. Does this constitute "custodial interrogation"? No, answered the Court in ILLINOIS v. PERKINS, 496 U.S. 292 (1990): "*Miranda* warnings are not required when the suspect is unaware that he is speaking to a law enforcement officer and gives a voluntary statement."

The case arose as follows: Respondent Perkins, who was suspected of committing the Stephenson murder, was incarcerated on charges unrelated to the murder. The police placed Charlton (who had been a fellow inmate of Perkins in another prison) and Parisi (an undercover officer) in the same cellblock with Perkins. The secret government agents were instructed to engage Perkins in casual conversation and to report anything he said about the Stephenson murder. The cellblock consisted of 12 separate cells that opened onto a common room. When Charlton met Perkins in the prison he introduced Parisi by his alias. Parisi suggested that the three of them escape. There was further conversation. Parisi asked Perkins if he had ever "done" anybody. Perkins replied that he had and proceeded to describe his involvement in the Stephenson murder in detail.

In an opinion joined by six other Justices, KENNEDY, J., explained why Perkins' statements were not barred by *Miranda:*

"The essential ingredients of a 'police-dominated atmosphere' and compulsion are not present when an incarcerated person speaks freely to someone that he believes to be a fellow inmate. Coercion is determined from the perspective of the suspect. [When] a suspect considers himself in the company of cellmates and not officers, the coercive atmosphere is lacking.

tion" embraces police tactics that do not. Thus, the Court seems to have repudiated the position taken by a number of courts prior to *Innis* that *confronting* a suspect with physical or documentary evidence (e.g., a ballistics report or a bank surveillance photograph) or *arranging a meeting in the presence of the police* between an arrestee and an accomplice who has already confessed is not "interrogation" because it does not involve verbal conduct on the part of the police. For criticism of these pre-*Innis* cases, see Kamisar Essays at 156–58 n. 21.

"[It] is the premise of *Miranda* that the danger of coercion results from the interaction of custody and official interrogation. We reject the argument that *Miranda* warnings are required whenever a suspect is in custody in a technical sense and converses with someone who happens to be a government agent. [When] the suspect has no reason to think that the listeners have official power over him, it should not be assumed that his words are motivated by the reaction he expects from his listeners. '[W]hen the agent carries neither badge nor gun and wears not "police blue," but the same prison gray' as the suspect, there is no '*interplay* between police interrogation and police custody.' Kamisar, *Brewer v. Williams, Massiah and Miranda: What is 'Interrogation?' When Does it Matter?*, 67 Geo.L.J. 1, 67, 63 (1978). [The] only difference between this case and *Hoffa* is that the suspect here was incarcerated, but detention, whether or not for the crime in question, does not warrant a presumption that the use of an undercover agent to speak with an incarcerated suspect makes any confession thus obtained involuntary. * * *

"[This] Court's Sixth Amendment decisions in [the *Massiah* line of cases] also do not avail respondent. [No] charges had been filed [against him] on the subject of the interrogation, and our Sixth Amendment precedents are not applicable."[a]

Only MARSHALL, J., dissented, maintaining that "[t]he conditions that require the police to apprise a defendant of his constitutional rights—custodial interrogation conducted by an agent of the police—were present in this case. Because [respondent] received no *Miranda* warnings before he was subjected to custodial interrogation, his confession was not admissible." Continued Justice Marshall:

"Because Perkins was interrogated by police while he was in custody, *Miranda* required that the officer inform him of his rights. In rejecting that conclusion, the Court finds that 'conversations' between undercover agents and suspects are devoid of the coercion inherent in stationhouse interrogations conducted by law enforcement officials who openly represent the State. *Miranda* was not, however, concerned solely with police *coercion*. It dealt with *any* police tactics that may operate to compel a suspect in custody to make incriminating statements without full awareness of his constitutional rights. [Thus,] when a law enforcement agent structures a custodial interrogation so that a suspect feels compelled to reveal incriminating information, he must inform the suspect of his constitutional rights and give him an opportunity to decide whether or not to talk. * * *

"[The] psychological pressures inherent in confinement increase the suspect's anxiety, making him likely to seek relief by talking with others. [The] inmate is thus more susceptible to efforts by undercover agents to elicit information from him. Similarly, where the suspect is incarcerated, the constant threat of physical danger peculiar to the prison environment may make him demonstrate his toughness to other inmates by recounting or inventing past violent acts. [In] this case, the police deceptively took advantage of Perkins' psychological vulnerability by including him in a sham escape plot, a situation in which he would feel compelled to demonstrate his willingness to shoot a prison guard by revealing his past involvement in a murder.

a. Brennan, J., concurred in the judgment of the Court, "agree[ing] that when a suspect does not know that his questioner is a police agent, such questioning does not amount to 'interrogation' in an 'inherently coercive' environment so as to require application of *Miranda*"—"the only issue raised at this stage of the litigation." But he went on to say that "the deception and manipulation practiced on respondent raise a substantial claim that the confession was obtained in violation of the Due Process Clause." For "the deliberate use of deception and manipulation by the police appears to be incompatible 'with a system that presumes innocence and assures that a conviction will not be secured by inquisitional means' and raises serious concerns that respondent's will was overborne."

"[Thus,] the pressures unique to custody allow the police to use deceptive interrogation tactics to compel a suspect to make an incriminating statement. The compulsion is not eliminated by the suspect's ignorance of his interrogator's true identity. The Court therefore need not inquire past the bare facts of custody and interrogation to determine whether *Miranda* warnings are required. * * *"

Notes and Questions

(a) Is *Perkins* a case where, as dissenting Justice Marshall maintains, "a law enforcement agent structures a custodial interrogation so that a suspect feels compelled to reveal incriminating information" or is it a case where a law enforcement agent structures a situation so that a suspect feels free to reveal incriminating information?

(b) Consider Fred Cohen, *Miranda and Police Deception in Interrogation,* 26 Crim.L.Bull. 534, 543–44 (1990): "Can it be that the *Miranda* rule was intended to be responsive only to force while leaving in place and indeed encouraging the refinement of other methods for achieving an *uninformed* confession? The word *uninformed* is emphasized because I believe strongly that *Miranda* was intended to achieve some form of rough informational equivalency between the state and the accused during the interrogative phase of the investigatory stage in a criminal proceeding. [If] *Miranda* was fashioned solely to ameliorate the inherent coercion associated with a police-dominated environment, then *Perkins* was correctly decided. If *Miranda* was concerned also with informational equivalency and with giving suspects an opportunity to obtain counsel and, in effect, barter information, instead of making an uninformed gift, then *Perkins* was wrongly decided."

8. PENNSYLVANIA v. MUNIZ, 496 U.S. 582 (1990). ***What constitutes "testimonial" evidence? What questions fall within the "routine booking question" exception to Miranda? More on what amounts to "custodial interrogation" within the meaning of Miranda.*** The *Muniz* case arose as follows:

Respondent Muniz was arrested for driving while intoxicated. Without advising him of his *Miranda* rights, Officer Hosterman asked Muniz to perform three standard field sobriety tests. Muniz performed poorly and then admitted that he had been drinking. Muniz was taken to a Booking Center. Following its routine practice for receiving persons suspected of driving under the influence, the Booking Center videotaped the ensuing proceedings. Muniz was told that his action and voice were being recorded, but again he was not advised of his *Miranda* rights. Officer Hosterman first asked Muniz his name, address, height, weight, eye color, date of birth, and current age (the "first seven questions" or the seven "booking" questions). Both the delivery and content of his answers were incriminating. Next the officer asked Muniz what the Court called "the sixth birthday question": "Do you know what the date was of your sixth birthday?" Muniz responded, "No, I don't."

The officer then requested Muniz to perform the same sobriety tests that he had been asked to do earlier during the initial roadside stop. While performing the tests, Muniz made several audible and incriminating statements. Finally, Muniz was asked to submit to a breathalyzer test. He refused. At this point, for the first time, Muniz was advised of his *Miranda* rights. Both the video and audio portions of the videotape were admitted into evidence, along with the arresting officer's testimony that Muniz failed the roadside sobriety tests and made incriminating statements at the time. Muniz was convicted of driving while intoxicated.

The Court excluded only Muniz's response to the "sixth birthday question" (by a 5–4 vote). Eight members of the Court agreed that the answers to the first seven questions or "booking" questions were admissible, but they differed as to the reason. BRENNAN, J., wrote the opinion of the Court, except as to the grounds for admitting Muniz's answers to the "booking" questions.

Extracts from Justice Brennan's opinion follow (under four headings provided by the editors):

(a) Why Muniz's responses to the questions he was asked at the Booking Center were admissible even though the slurred nature of his speech was incriminating.

"The physical inability to articulate words in a clear manner due to 'the lack of muscular coordination of his tongue and mouth' is not itself a testimonial component of Muniz's responses to Officer Hosterman's introductory questions. In *Schmerber* [p. 35] we drew a distinction between 'testimonial' and 'real or physical evidence' for purposes of the privilege against self-incrimination. We noted that in *Holt v. United States*, 218 U.S. 245 (1910), Justice Holmes had written for the Court that 'the prohibition of compelling a man in a criminal court to be a witness against himself is a prohibition of the use of physical or moral compulsion to extort communications from him, not an exclusion of his body as evidence when it may be material.' * * *

"Under *Schmerber* and its progeny, * * * any slurring of speech and other evidence of lack of muscular coordination revealed by Muniz's responses to Officer Hosterman's direct questions constitute nontestimonial components of those responses. Requiring a suspect to reveal the physical manner in which he articulates words, like requiring him to reveal the physical properties of the sound produced by his voice, see *United States v. Dionisio* [p. ___], does not, without more, compel him to provide a 'testimonial' response for purposes of the privilege."

(b) More on what constitutes "testimonial" evidence. Why the response to the "sixth birthday question" was testimonial.

"[Muniz's] answer to the sixth birthday question was incriminating, not just because of his delivery, but also because of his answer's *content*; the trier of fact could infer from Muniz's answer (that he did not *know* the proper date) that his mental state was confused. [The prosecution argues] that the incriminating inference does not trigger the protections of the Fifth Amendment privilege because the inference concerns 'the physiological function of [Muniz's] brain,' which is asserted to be every bit as 'real or physical' as the physiological makeup of his blood and the timbre of his voice.

"But this characterization addresses the wrong question; that the 'fact' to be inferred might be said to concern the physical status of Muniz's brain merely describes the way in which the inference is incriminating. The correct question [is] whether the incriminating inference of mental confusion is drawn from a testimonial act or from physical evidence. In *Schmerber*, for example, we held that [compelling a suspect to provide a blood sample] was outside of the Fifth Amendment's protection, not simply because the evidence concerned the suspect's physical body, but rather because the evidence was *obtained* in a manner that did not entail any testimonial act on the part of the suspect. [In] contrast, had the police instead asked the suspect directly whether his blood contained a high concentration of alcohol, his affirmative response would have been testimonial even though it would have been used to draw the same inference concerning his physiology. [In] this case, the question is not whether a suspect's 'impaired mental faculties' can fairly be characterized as an aspect of his physiology, but rather whether Muniz's response to the sixth birthday question that gave rise to the inference of such an impairment was testimonial in nature. * * *

"At its core, the privilege reflects our fierce 'unwillingness to subject those suspected of crime to the cruel trilemma of self-accusation, perjury or contempt,' *Doe v. United States* [p. 881], that defined the operation of the Star Chamber. [Because] the privilege was designed primarily to prevent 'a recurrence of the Inquisition and the Star Chamber, even if not in their stark brutality,' [it] is evident that a suspect is 'compelled [to] be a witness against himself' at least whenever he must face the modern-day analog of the historic trilemma—either during a criminal trial where a sworn witness faces the identical three choices, or during custodial interrogation where, as we explained in *Miranda*, the choices are analogous and hence raise similar concerns. Whatever else it may include, therefore, the definition of 'testimonial' evidence articulated in *Doe* must encompass all responses to questions that, if asked of a sworn suspect during a criminal trial, could place the suspect in the 'cruel trilemma.' [Whenever] a suspect is asked for a response requiring him to communicate an express or implied assertion of fact or belief, the suspect confronts the 'trilemma' of truth, falsity, or silence, and hence the response (whether based on truth or falsity) contains a testimonial component.

[The sixth birthday question] "required a testimonial response. When Officer Hosterman asked Muniz if he knew the date of his sixth birthday and Muniz, for whatever reason, could not remember or calculate that date, he was [placed in a predicament the self-incrimination clause was designed to prevent]. By hypothesis, the inherently coercive environment created by the custodial interrogation precluded the option of remaining silent. Muniz was left with the choice of incriminating himself by admitting that he did not then know the date of his sixth birthday, or answering untruthfully by reporting a date that he did not then believe to be accurate (an incorrect guess would be incriminating as well as untruthful). [The] incriminating inference of impaired mental facilities stemmed, not just from the fact that Muniz slurred his response, but also from a testimonial aspect of that response."[a]

(c) The "routine booking question" exception to Miranda: Why Muniz's answers to the first seven questions he was asked at the Booking Center are admissible even though the questions qualify as "custodial interrogation."

"We disagree with [the prosecution's] contention that Officer Hosterman's first seven questions [regarding Muniz's name, address, height, etc.] do not qualify as custodial interrogation * * * merely because the questions were not intended

a. Justice Brennan spoke for only four Justices on this issue. Marshall, J., who concurred in the result on the issue, provided the fifth vote. Chief Justice REHNQUIST, joined by White, Blackmun and Stevens, JJ., dissented, maintaining that the answer to this question also fell into the "real or physical evidence" category:

"As an assumption about human behavior, [Justice Brennan's statement that when Muniz was asked if he knew the date of his sixth birthday he was confronted with the trilemma of truth, falsity, or silence] is wrong. Muniz would no more have felt compelled to fabricate a false date than one who cannot read the letters on an eye chart feels compelled to fabricate false letters; nor does a wrong guess call into question a speaker's veracity. The Court's statement is also a flawed predicate on which to base its conclusion that Muniz's answer to this question was 'testimonial' for purposes of the Fifth Amendment.

"[The] sixth birthday question here was an effort on the part of the police to check how well Muniz was able to do a simple mathematical exercise. Indeed, had the question related only to the date of his birth, it presumably would have come under the 'booking exception' to *Miranda*. [If] the police may require Muniz to use his body in order to demonstrate the level of his physical coordination, there is no reason why they should not be able to require him to speak or write in order to determine his mental condition. That was all that was sought here. Since it was permissible for the police to extract and examine a sample of Schmerber's blood to determine how much that part of his system had been affected by alcohol, I see no reason why they may not examine the functioning of Muniz's mental processes for the same purpose."

to elicit information for investigatory purposes. [The] *Innis* test focuses primarily upon 'the perspective of the suspect.' [But] Muniz's answers to these first seven questions are nonetheless admissible because the questions fall within a 'routine booking question' exception which exempts from *Miranda*'s coverage questions to secure the 'biographical data necessary to complete booking or pretrial services.'[b] [The] questions appear reasonably related to the police's administrative concerns. In this context, the first seven questions asked at the Booking Center fall outside the protection of *Miranda*.[c]

(d) More on what constitutes "custodial interrogation": Why Muniz's incriminating utterances during physical sobriety tests conducted by the police were admissible.

"During [the] videotaped proceedings, Officer Hosterman asked Muniz to perform the same three sobriety tests that he had earlier performed at roadside prior to his arrest [e.g., the "one leg stand" test]. While Muniz was attempting to comprehend [the officer's] instructions and then perform the requested sobriety tests, [he] made several audible and incriminating statements. * * *

"Officer Hosterman's dialogue with Muniz concerning [the] tests consisted primarily of carefully scripted instructions as to how the tests were to be performed. These instructions were not likely to be perceived as calling for any verbal responses and therefore were not "words or actions" constituting custodial interrogation * * *. Hence, Muniz's incriminating statements were 'voluntary' in the sense that they were not elicited in response to custodial interrogation. * * *

"Similarly, we conclude that *Miranda* does not require suppression of the statements Muniz made when asked to submit to a breathalyzer examination.[d] [The officer who asked Muniz to take the test] carefully limited her role to providing Muniz with relevant information about [the] test and the Implied Consent Law. She questioned Muniz only as to whether he understood her instructions and wished to submit to the test. These limited and focused inquiries were necessarily 'attendant to' the legitimate police procedure [and] not likely to be perceived as calling for any incriminating response."[e]

b. *Cf. Rhode Island v. Innis*: "[The] term 'interrogation' under *Miranda* refers not only to express questioning, but also to any words or actions on the part of the police (*other than those normally attendant to arrest and custody*) that the police should know are reasonably likely to elicit an incriminating response from the subject." (Emphasis added.)

c. On this issue Justice Brennan spoke only for four Justices. Four other members of the Court, Rehnquist, C.J., joined by White, Blackmun and Stevens, JJ., agreed that the responses to the booking questions should not be suppressed. However, because they believed that Muniz's responses to the "booking" questions were not testimonial, they deemed it unnecessary to decide whether the questions fell within the "routine booking question" exception.

Dissenting Justice MARSHALL balked at "creat[ing] yet another exception to *Miranda*," maintaining that such exceptions "undermine *Miranda*'s fundamental principle that the doctrine should be clear so that it can be easily applied by both police and courts." He continued:

"Justice Brennan's position, were it adopted by a majority of the Court, would necessitate difficult, time-consuming litigation over whether particular questions asked during booking are 'routine,' whether they are necessary to secure biographical information, whether that information is itself necessary for recordkeeping purposes, and whether the questions are—despite their routine nature—designed to elicit incriminating testimony."

Ed. Note—Both prior to and following *Muniz*, lower courts have held that routine inquiries during the booking process need not be preceded by *Miranda* warnings. See CRIMPROC § 6.7(b).

d. The Court noted that "Muniz does not and cannot challenge the introduction into evidence of his refusal to submit to the breathalyzer test." See *South Dakota v. Neville* (p. 616).

e. Dissenting Justice Marshall would have suppressed the statements made in connection with the sobriety tests and the breathalyzer examination because "the circumstances of this case—in particular, Muniz's apparent intoxication—rendered the officers' words and actions the functional equivalent' of express questioning. [For] the police should have known that their conduct was 'reasonably likely to evoke an incriminating response.' *Innes*."

9. "Physical" or "demeanor" evidence vs. evidence of silence. The fine line between "demeanor" evidence and evidence of silence is illustrated by UNITED STATES v. VELARDE–GOMEZ, 269 F.3d 1023 (9th Cir.2001) (en banc), which arose as follows: Defendant attempted to enter the United States from Mexico at a California port of entry. At an inspection site, a drug dog alerted customs officials to defendant's car's gas tank. The gas tank was found to contain 63 pounds of marijuana. Customs agents escorted defendant to an interview room. When—*before* being advised of his *Miranda* rights—Agent Salazar informed defendant that customs officials had found the marijuana in his car's gas tank, defendant did not speak or physically respond. At trial Agent Salazar testified that when defendant had been informed that the marijuana had been found "there was no response"; defendant "didn't look surprised or upset or whatever." Moreover, during her closing argument, the prosecutor emphasized how calm and relaxed defendant had been when told there was marijuana in his car: "He showed no emotion. This defendant was perfect for the job. He's the kind of guy a drug organization would want to hire because he was able to sit there and show nothing." An 8–3 majority, per WARDLAW, J., held that "the government's evidence of a lack of physical or emotional reaction was tantamount to evidence of silence" and thus the district court erred in admitting it:

"[O]nce the government places an individual in custody, that individual has a right to remain silent in the face of government questioning, regardless of whether the *Miranda* warnings are given. Moreover, the government may not burden that right by commenting on the defendant's post-arrest silence at trial.

"[Agent] Salazar's testimony about Velarde's lack of response when confronted with the sixty-three pound of marijuana in his gas tank was testimony about Velarde's silence during the pre-*Miranda* questioning. The Supreme Court has distinguished 'physical' and 'demeanor' evidence from 'testimonial' evidence, holding that evidence of the former does not engender Fifth Amendment protection. *Pennsylvania v. Muniz.* Demeanor evidence often involves the admission of evidence concerning a defendant's 'slurr[ed] speech,' *Muniz*, 'apparent nervousness,' or a defendant's demeanor during a polygraph test, even though the results may not be admissible. Here, however, [each of Agent Salazar's] comments described the same thing—that Velarde did not react at all, but remained silent in the face of confrontation.

"[When] confronted with evidence of a large quantity of drugs in his car, [defendant] was faced with a Catch 22: if he remained silent, the government could use, as it did, his silence as powerful and persuasive evidence that Velarde was the consummate drug carrier—hired for his lack of emotion, and fully knowledgeable about the drugs he carried. If, on the other hand, [defendant] denied the existence of the drugs, a response wholly consistent with innocence, the government would be able to impeach him with the physical or other evidence tending to discredit him. Thus, whatever Velarde's response, the government would now have available to it additional cumulative evidence of guilt to be argued to the jury. It is the self-incriminating nature of this evidence that the Fifth Amendment protects against."

Writing for three judges, GOULD, J. dissented on the "demeanor"/"silence" issue:

"Evidence of demeanor is different than evidence of mere silence. Demeanor evidence should normally be admissible because it is non-testimonial. * * * Asking 'what did he do,' differs from asking, 'what did he say?' The former does not relate to a communicative response and does not violate the defendant's Fifth Amendment rights. Demeanor is not a proxy for silence. For demeanor relates to a defendant's physical characteristics, says more than silence, and is something other than silence. * * *

"I agree with the majority opinion's view that Fifth Amendment rights were offended by the questions about whether Velarde–Gomez said anything or denied anything when confronted with discovery of contraband almost completely filling his gas tank. But I consider it different to inquire whether there was any response; whether Velarde–Gomez was surprised or upset; and whether he just sat there.

"* * * Demeanor, like flight, is a physical response that has probative value for a jury. As here, the demeanor of non-response may include the idea that an accused person was silent. But it is not for that reason alone a comment on silence. In fact, the demeanor inquiries here asked for and received other information that may have been relevant to a jury. Was defendant showing surprise? Did defendant look upset? Was he angry? Was he cool and collected? This information goes well beyond silence and is properly viewed in the realm of physical response. *Cf. Muniz*, (distinguishing between permissible evidence of *how* a DUI suspect spoke, his slurred speech, from impermissible testimony concerning the *content* of his speech, what he communicated). So long as there is no inquiry about silence, explicitly or implicitly as a result of context, it is for the jury to weigh demeanor evidence. This properly includes evidence of visage, composure, surprise or anger, or any other evidence of how the defendant acted except for a proscribed comment on silence. [The] Fifth Amendment should not be held to prohibit or screen out evidence of an accused person's composure, temperament, or demonstrated emotions when under pressure of events."

10. When does a response to an officer's question present a reasonable danger of incrimination? As discussed at p. 426, HIIBEL v. SIXTH JUDICIAL COURT, 124 S.Ct. 2451 (2004), sustained against a Fourth Amendment challenge Nevada's "stop and identify" statute. The Court, per KENNEDY, J., also rejected the defendant's self-incrimination challenge to the statute. The Court saw no need to decide whether, as the state argued, the privilege did not apply because a statement of identification was not "testimonial" because "even if those required actions [of self-identification] are testimonial * * * in this case disclosure of [petitioner's] name presented no reasonable danger of incrimination":

"[Petitioner's] refusal to disclose his name was not based on any articulated real and appreciable fear that his name would be used to incriminate him, or that it 'would furnish a link in the chain of evidence needed to prosecute' him. *Hoffman v. United States* [p. 839]. As best we can tell, petitioner refused to identify himself only because he thought his name was none of the officer's business. Even today, petitioner does not explain how the disclosure of his name could have been used against him in a criminal case. While we recognize petitioner's strong belief that he should not have to disclose his identity, the Fifth Amendment does not override the Nevada Legislature's judgment to the contrary absent a reasonable belief that the disclosure would tend to incriminate him.

"The narrow scope of the disclosure requirement is also important. One's identity is, by definition, unique; yet it is, in another sense, a universal characteristic. Answering a request to disclose a name is likely to be so insignificant in the scheme of things as to be incriminating only in unusual circumstances. See *Baltimore City Dept. of Social Servs. v. Bouknight*, [p. 870] (suggesting that "fact[s] the State could readily establish" may render "any testimony regarding existence or authenticity [of them] insufficiently incriminating"); Cf. *California v. Byers*, 402 U.S. 424 (1971)[a] (opinion of Burger, C.J.). In every criminal case, it is

a. *Byers* upheld a state "hit and run" statute which required the drive of a motor vehicle involved in an accident to stop at the scene and give his name and address. The Court noted

known and must be known who has been arrested and who is being tried. Cf. *Pennsylvania v. Muniz*. Even witnesses who plan to invoke the Fifth Amendment privilege answer when their names are called to take the stand. Still, a case may arise where there is a substantial allegation that furnishing identity at the time of a stop would have given the police a link in the chain of evidence needed to convict the individual of a separate offense. In that case, the court can then consider whether the privilege applies, and, if the Fifth Amendment has been violated, what remedy must follow. We need not resolve those questions here."

Justice STEVENS, dissenting on the self-incrimination issue,[b] argued that "compelled statement at issue in this case is clearly testimonial" and would be "incriminating" under the standard set forth in *Hoffman* and other cases. As to the later point, the dissent reasoned:

"The Court reasons that we should not assume that the disclosure of petitioner's name would be used to incriminate him or that it would furnish a link in a chain of evidence needed to prosecute him. But why else would an officer ask for it? And why else would the Nevada Legislature require its disclosure only when circumstances 'reasonably indicate that the person has committed, is committing, or is about to commit a crime.' [A] person's identity obviously bears informational and incriminating worth, 'even if the [name] itself is not inculpatory.' *Hubbell* [p. 871]. A name can provide the key to a broad array of information about the person, particularly in the hands of a police officer with access to a range of law enforcement databases. And that information, in turn, can be tremendously useful in a criminal prosecution. It is therefore quite wrong to suggest that a person's identity provides a link in the chain to incriminating evidence 'only in unusual circumstances.' "

Notes and Questions

(a) Is the key to the lack of incriminatory potential in the *Hiibel* setting the fact that the information supplied (the individual's name) ordinarily provides only a link to evidence already possessed? See CRIMPROC § 8.10(a) (2004 Pocket Part).

(b) Without the individual's name, it might be impossible to locate and arrest him at some subsequent time when investigation converted reasonable suspicion into probable cause. Moreover, being able to utilize a name, rather than simply a description, might be critical in obtaining from various sources further information relating to suspicious activity. However, the same law enforcement advantages might flow from the self-identification in the booking process. Does *Hiibel* say, in effect, that the advantage of attaching a name to a face, even if it eventually leads to obtaining more evidence as to the offense under investigation, does not provide a sufficient nexus to incriminating evidence to meet the *Hoffman* standard? See *id*. Cf *Byers*.

11. Questioning prompted by concern for "public safety." Consider NEW YORK v. QUARLES, 467 U.S. 649 (1984), which arose as follows:

that such statutes were regulatory measures, "not intended to facilitate criminal convictions" nor directed at all persons who drove automobiles. Moreover, there was no disclosure of inherently illegal activity as "most automobile accidents occur without creating criminal liability."

b. Justice Breyer's dissent, joined by Justices Souter and Ginsburg, concluded that the Fourth Amendment prohibited requiring responses to any police questions incident to a *Terry* stop. As to the self-incrimination issue, it did note: "There are sound reasons rooted in Fifth Amendment considerations for adhering to this Fourth Amendment legal condition circumscribing police authority * * *. See Stevens, J., dissenting."

At approximately 12:30 a.m., police apprehended respondent Quarles in the rear of a supermarket. He matched the description of the man who had just raped a woman. The woman had told the police that the rapist had just entered the supermarket and that he was carrying a gun. Apparently upon seeing Officer Kraft enter the store, respondent Quarles turned and ran toward the rear. Officer Kraft pursued him with a drawn gun and, upon regaining sight of him, ordered him to stop and put his hands over his head. Although several other officers had arrived at the scene by then, Kraft was the first to reach Quarles. He frisked him and discovered he was wearing an empty shoulder holster. After handcuffing him, the officer asked where the gun was. Quarles nodded in the direction of some empty cartons and responded, "the gun is over there." At that time, emphasized the New York Court of Appeals, Quarles was surrounded by four officers whose guns had been returned to their holsters because, as one testified, the situation was under control.

The gun was not visible, but Officer Kraft reached into one of the cartons and retrieved a loaded revolver. Quarles was then formally placed under arrest and advised of his *Miranda* rights. He waived his rights. In response to questions, he then stated that he owned the revolver and had purchased it in Miami.

In the subsequent prosecution of Quarles for criminal possession of a weapon (the record does not reveal why the state failed to pursue the rape charge), the New York courts suppressed the statement "the gun is over there" as well as the gun itself because they had been obtained in violation of Quarles's *Miranda* rights. His statements about his ownership of the gun and the place of purchase were also excluded as having been fatally tainted by the seizure of the gun and the prewarning response as to its location. A 6–3 majority per REHNQUIST, C.J., reversed:

"[We] conclude that under the circumstances involved in this case, overriding considerations of public safety justify the officer's failure to provide *Miranda* warnings before he asked questions devoted to locating the abandoned weapon.

"[We] have before us no claim that respondent's statements were actually compelled by police conduct which overcame his will to resist. Thus the only issue before us is whether Officer Kraft was justified in failing to make available to respondent the procedural safeguards associated with the privilege against compulsory self-incrimination since *Miranda*.[5]

"[We] hold that on these facts there is a 'public safety' exception to the requirement that *Miranda* warnings be given before a suspect's answers may be admitted into evidence, and that the availability of that exception does not depend upon the motivation of the individual officers involved. In a kaleidoscopic situation such as the one confronting these officers, where spontaneity rather than adherence to a police manual is necessarily the order of the day, the application of the exception which we recognize today should not be made to depend on *post hoc* findings at a suppression hearing concerning the subjective motivation of the arresting officer. Undoubtedly most police officers, if placed in Officer Kraft's position, would act out of a host of different, instinctive, and largely unverifiable motives—their own safety, the safety of others, and perhaps as well the desire to obtain incriminating evidence from the suspect.

5. The dissent curiously takes us to task for "endors[ing] the introduction of coerced self-incriminating statements in criminal prosecutions." [Of] course our decision today does nothing of the kind. [R]espondent is certainly free on remand to argue that his statement was coerced under traditional due process standards. Today we merely reject the only argument that respondent has raised to support the exclusion of his statement, that the statement must be *presumed* compelled because of Officer Kraft's failure to read him his *Miranda* warnings.

"Whatever the motivation of individual officers in such a situation, we do not believe that the doctrinal underpinnings of *Miranda* require that it be applied in all its rigor to a situation in which police officers ask questions reasonably prompted by a concern for the public safety. [The] police in this case, in the very act of apprehending a suspect, were confronted with the immediate necessity of ascertaining the whereabouts of a gun which they had every reason to believe the suspect had just removed from his empty holster and discarded in the supermarket. So long as the gun was concealed somewhere in the supermarket, with its actual whereabouts unknown, it obviously posed more than one danger to the public safety: an accomplice might make use of it, a customer or employee might later come upon it.

"In such a situation, if the police are required to recite the familiar *Miranda* warnings before asking the whereabouts of the gun, suspects in Quarles' position might well be deterred from responding. Procedural safeguards which deter a suspect from responding were deemed acceptable in *Miranda* in order to protect the Fifth Amendment privilege; when the primary social cost of those added protections is the possibility of fewer convictions, the *Miranda* majority was willing to bear that cost. Here, had *Miranda* warnings deterred Quarles from responding to Officer Kraft's question about the whereabouts of the gun, the cost would have been something more than merely the failure to obtain evidence useful in convicting Quarles. Officer Kraft needed an answer to his question not simply to make his case against Quarles but to insure that further danger to the public did not result from the concealment of the gun in a public area.

"We conclude that the need for answers to questions in a situation posing a threat to the public safety outweighs the need for the prophylactic rule protecting the Fifth Amendment's privilege against self-incrimination. We decline to place officers such as Officer Kraft in the untenable position of having to consider, often in a matter of seconds, whether it best serves society for them to ask the necessary questions without the *Miranda* warnings and render whatever probative evidence they uncover inadmissible, or for them to give the warnings in order to preserve the admissibility of evidence they might uncover but possibly damage or destroy their ability to obtain that evidence and neutralize the volatile situation confronting them.[7] * * *

"We hold that the [court below] erred in excluding the statement, 'the gun is over there,' and the gun because of the officer's failure to read respondent his *Miranda* rights before attempting to locate the weapon. Accordingly [it] also erred in excluding the subsequent statements as illegal fruits of a *Miranda* violation.[9]"

O'CONNOR J., concurred in part in the judgment and dissented in part. She would have suppressed Quarles's initial statement ("the gun is over there"), but

7. The dissent argues that a public safety exception to *Miranda* is unnecessary because in every case an officer can simply ask the necessary questions to protect himself or the public, and then the prosecution can decline to introduce any incriminating responses at a subsequent trial. But absent actual coercion by the officer, there is no constitutional imperative requiring the exclusion of the evidence that results from police inquiry of this kind; and we do not believe that the doctrinal underpinnings of *Miranda* require us to exclude the evidence, thus penalizing officers for asking the very questions which are the most crucial to their efforts to protect themselves and the public.

9. Because we hold that there is no violation of *Miranda* in this case, we have no occasion to [decide whether] the gun is admissible either because it is nontestimonial or because the police would inevitably have discovered it absent their questioning.

[A year earlier, in *Nix v. Williams (Williams II)*, p. ___, the Court had held that the "fruit of the poisonous tree" doctrine did not bar the use of evidence derived from a constitutional violation if such evidence would "ultimately" or "inevitably" have been discovered even if the police had acted lawfully. The "fruits" doctrine, formulated initially in applying the Fourth Amendment exclusionary rule, prohibits the use of evidence derived from, and thus "tainted" by, a constitutional violation.]

not the gun itself—because "nothing in *Miranda* or the privilege itself requires exclusion of nontestimonial evidence derived from informal custodial interrogation." (Twenty years later, the Supreme Court addressed this issue in *United States v. Patane*, p. 703.)

Justice O'Connor would have excluded Quarles's initial statement because "a 'public safety' exception unnecessarily blurs the edges of the clear line heretofore established and makes *Miranda's* requirements more difficult to understand. In some cases, police will benefit because a reviewing court will find that an exigency excused their failure to administer the required warnings. But in other cases, police will suffer because a reviewing court will view the 'objective' circumstances differently [than they did]. The end result will be a finespun new doctrine on public safety exigencies incident to custodial interrogation, complete with the hair-splitting distinctions that currently plague our Fourth Amendment jurisprudence." She added:

"[*Miranda*] has never been read to prohibit the police from asking questions to secure the public safety. Rather, the critical question *Miranda* addresses is who shall bear the cost of securing the public safety when such questions are asked and answered: the defendant or the State. *Miranda,* for better or worse, found the resolution of that question implicit in the prohibition against compulsory self-incrimination and placed the burden on the State. When police ask custodial questions without administering the required warnings, *Miranda* quite clearly requires that the answers received be presumed compelled and that they be excluded from evidence at trial."

MARSHALL, J.,joined by Brennan and Stevens, JJ., dissented:.

"The majority's entire analysis rests on the factual assumption that the public was at risk during Quarles' interrogation. This assumption is completely in conflict with the facts as found by New York's highest court. * * * Contrary to the majority's speculations, Quarles was not believed to have, nor did he in fact have, an accomplice to come to his rescue. When the questioning began, the arresting officers were sufficiently confident of their safety to put away their guns.

"[The] New York court's conclusion that neither Quarles nor his missing gun posed a threat to the public's safety is amply supported by the evidence presented at the suppression hearing. [Although] the supermarket was open to the public, Quarles' arrest took place during the middle of the night when the store was apparently deserted except for the clerks at the checkout counter. The police could easily have cordoned off the store and searched for the missing gun. Had they done so, they would have found the gun forthwith. The police were well aware that Quarles had discarded his weapon somewhere near the scene of the arrest.

"[Whether] society would be better off if the police warned suspects of their rights before beginning an interrogation or whether the advantages of giving such warnings would outweigh their costs did not inform the *Miranda* decision. On the contrary, the *Miranda* Court was concerned with the proscriptions of the Fifth Amendment, and, in particular, whether the Self–Incrimination Clause permits the government to prosecute individuals based on statements made in the course of custodial interrogations.

"[In] fashioning its 'public-safety' exception to *Miranda,* the majority makes no attempt to deal with the constitutional presumption established by that case. [The] majority's only contention is that police officers could more easily protect the public if *Miranda* did not apply to custodial interrogations concerning the public's safety. But *Miranda* was not a decision about public safety; it was a decision about coerced confessions. Without establishing that interrogations concerning the public's safety are less likely to be coercive than other interrogations, the majority cannot endorse the 'public-safety' exception and remain faithful to the logic of *Miranda.*

"[The] irony of the majority's decision is that the public's safety can be perfectly well protected without abridging the Fifth Amendment. If a bomb is about to explode or the public is otherwise imminently imperiled, the police are free to interrogate suspects without advising them of their constitutional rights. [If] trickery is necessary to protect the public, then the police may trick a suspect into confessing. While the Fourteenth Amendment sets limits on such behavior, nothing in the Fifth Amendment or our decision in *Miranda* proscribes this sort of emergency questioning. All the Fifth Amendment forbids is the introduction of coerced statements at trial."

Notes and Questions

(a) If a case like *Innis* or *Mesa* (the "hostage negotiator" case) arose today, would the courts quickly dispose of it by invoking the "public safety" exception to *Miranda*? For a case that does just that, see *State v. Finch*, 975 P.2d 967 (Wash.1999).

(b) *Quarles* and *Miranda*. The *Quarles* case, observes Charles Weisselberg, *Saving Miranda*, 84 Cornell L.Rev. 109, 129 (1998), "struck at the Court's original version of *Miranda* in several respects": It "reinforced the notion that the warning requirement was divorced from the Fifth Amendment"; the majority's cost-benefit analysis "represents a wholly different view of the value of the Fifth Amendment than was expressed in *Miranda*"; and "[t]hird, by creating a vague and ill-defined exception to the warning requirement, the Court reduced the efficacy of *Miranda*'s bright-line rules." However, adds Professor Weisselberg, *Quarles* "did not—as it turns out—open the door to other large exceptions to the *Miranda* rule. In the fourteen years since *Quarles* was decided, the Supreme Court has not approved any other instances of custodial interrogations in which warnings need not be given."

(c) *Asking an arrestee whether he has drugs or needles on his person.* Defendant was arrested for a drug offense and taken to a detention facility. There, before giving him any *Miranda* warnings, an officer asked the defendant whether he had any drugs or needles on his person. "No," responded the defendant, "I don't use drugs, I sell them." Is the statement admissible under the "public safety" exception to *Miranda*?

Yes, concluded *United States v. Carrillo*, 16 F.3d 1046 (9th Cir.1994). The court noted that the officer had testified that in order to avoid contact with syringes (which have poked him in the past) and toxic substances (which have caused headaches and skin irritation in the past), he now routinely asks the questions he asked defendant. Would the Supreme Court have approved of this application of *Quarles*? Should the "public safety" exception apply when no member of the public is in danger? Should it apply when the police do not come upon the scene in hot pursuit?

(d) *Miranda and the privilege against self-incrimination*, By posing the issue as "whether [the police officer] was *justified* in failing to make available to respondent the procedural safeguards associated with the privilege against compulsory self-incrimination since *Miranda*" (emphasis added), did the *Quarles* majority miss the point? Yes, maintains Steven D. Clymer, *Are Police Free to Disregard Miranda?*, 112 Yale L.J. 447, 550 (2002): "Whether there is a pressing concern for public safety or only an effort to solve a crime, neither the privilege nor *Miranda* ever dictates whether police efforts to compel a statement, by failure to give *Miranda* warnings or otherwise, are 'justified.' Instead, they leave the decision whether to use compulsion to the officer, and determine only that any compelled statements are inadmissible." See generally *Chavez v. Martinez*, p. 695.

(e) *The "rescue doctrine."* Somewhat similar to the "public safety" exception is the "rescue doctrine." Should statements obtained in violation of *Miranda* be admissible if police interrogation of a suspected kidnapper is motivated primarily by a desire to save the victim's life? Yes, answer *People v. Dean,* 114 Cal.Rptr. 555 (Cal.App.1974) and *People v. Krom,* 461 N.E.2d 276 (N.Y.1984). See generally William T. Pizzi, *The Privilege Against Self–Incrimination in a Rescue Situation,* 76 J.Crim.L. & C. (1985). It is unsound, maintains Professor Pizzi, id. at 595–603, to approach the scope of the privilege against self-incrimination "solely from the defendant's point of view while totally ignoring the threat to the lives of others and the purpose and function of the police conduct"; the privilege and its attendant rules should not control "where the police are functioning in a situation which is primarily noninvestigative and where life is at stake."

Are there (should there be) any limits on what a police officer may do to a suspected kidnapper in order to get him to reveal the location of a kidnap victim? Cf. *Leon v. State,* 410 So.2d 201 (Fla.App.1982), holding, over a forceful dissent, that the use of police threats and physical violence at the scene of arrest in order to ascertain the kidnap victim's whereabouts "did not constitutionally infect the later confessions." Consider Pizzi, supra, at 606: "[T]here are [due process] limits on the conduct of the police in their treatment of suspects even in an emergency situation where life is at stake," but "[i]n determining those limits [the] traditional scope of police conduct permitted in a purely investigative context is only a starting point."

12. When, if ever, should interrogators be allowed to use "torture" in order to obtain information from suspected terrorists? Professor Alan Dershowitz, among others, has suggested that when lives are at stake interrogators should sometimes be allowed to torture suspects to obtain information. In such circumstances, suggests Dershowitz, judges should issue "torture warrants" so that interrogators could utilize torture in extraordinary cases within our legal system rather than "outside the law." See ALAN M. DERSHOWITZ, WHY TERRORISM WORKS 131–64 (2002). Under what circumstances, if any, and pursuant to what procedures, if any, should suspected terrorists be tortured? Consider the following:

MARCY STRAUSS, *Torture*, 48 N.Y. Law Sch.L.Rev. 203, 266–68, 271–74 (2004):

If torture can be utilized to save ten lives from a bomb, why not allow it to be used to save the lives of five children hidden by a crazed neighbor? Or, why not sanction torture to reveal the name of a madman who has killed a random, innocent person almost every day for a few weeks and shows no sign of stopping?

Even if we could determine the number of lives at risk that justifies the use of torture, and the level of certainty that a crime has occurred or is about to occurr, and that the suspect in custody has critical information, how do we assess the level of exigency and the inability to obtain the information through traditional means? Must the bomb literally be ticking—what if the information pertains to a plot to plant a bomb within the month? A week? Of course, the longer the time period, the greater the chance that traditional methods of law enforcement will detect the plot. But where do we draw the line? And how do we decide that methods besides torture will not work in time?

The point is simply this: no matter how one tries to confine the use of torture to extreme, narrow circumstances, the temptation to broaden those circumstances is inevitable. Without an absolute prohibition on the use of torture, it is virtually impossible to ensure that "special cases" remain special. [As] Professor [Sanford]

Kadish so eloquently concludes, "when torture is no longer unthinkable, it will be thought about." * * *

[A] warrant requirement would do little in providing oversight to the process of torturing. It is certain, that proceedings to obtain a warrant would be conducted in secret. After all, a torture warrant would presumably be sought only in extreme circumstances dictated by national security. Even now, much of what happens to the detainees at Camp X–Ray, in Guantanamo Bay, is shrouded in secrecy. Public disclosure of a desire to obtain a "torture warrant" because of concern that a weapon of mass destruction is hidden in a major city, simply, would not happen.

[In] sum, the warrant requirement would do nothing to rectify the evils of torture, and do little to restrict its use. Indeed, having a warrant process established might encourage police officers to seek the right to torture more often than they would engage in such behavior on their own. And, in the current climate of ever-present national emergency, a judge might very well issue a warrant permitting torture in circumstances that do not begin to resemble a "ticking bomb" scenario. Put simply, a warrant procedure likely would be an invitation to the increasing use of torture.

ALAN M. DERSHOWITZ, *The Torture Warrant: A Response to Professor Strauss*, 48 N.Y. Law Sch.L.Rev. 275, 289, 291–94 (2004):

I agree [that the United States should not become a nation whose police torture a small child in order to get his terrorist parent to confess]. But I believe we are more likely to become such a nation if we leave decisions of this kind to the uncontrolled discretion of those whose only job is to protect us from terrorism and who are paid to believe that the ends always justify the means. * * *

There is a difference in principle, as Bentham noted more than 200 years ago, between torturing the guilty to save the lives of the innocent, and torturing innocent people. A system which requires an articulated justification for the use of non-lethal torture and approval by a judge is more likely to honor that principle than a system that discreetly and without open accountability relegates these decisions to law enforcement agents whose only job is to protect the public from terrorism.

[In] a democracy governed by a rule of law, we should never want our soldiers or president to take any action which we deem wrong or illegal. A good test of whether an action should or should not be done is whether we are prepared to have it disclosed—perhaps not immediately, but certainly after some time has passed. No legal system operating under the rule of law should ever tolerate an "off-the-books" approach to necessity. Even the defense of necessity must be justified lawfully. The road to tyranny has always been paved with claims of necessity made by those responsible for the security of a nation. Our system of checks and balances requires that all presidential actions, like all legislative or military actions, be consistent with governing law. If it is necessary to torture in the ticking bomb case, then our governing laws must accommodate this practice. If we refuse to change our law to accommodate any particular action then our government should not take that action. Requiring that a controversial action be made openly and with accountability is one way of minimizing resort to unjustifiable means.

SETH F. KREIMER, *Too Close to the Rack and the Screw: Constitutional Constraints on Torture in the War on Terror*, 6 U.Pa.J.Const.L. 278, 319–22, 324–25 (2003):

* * * By Professor Dershowitz's hypothesis, officials would be willing to violate a prohibition of torture to achieve antiterrorist goals; one might suspect those same officials would be inclined to "sex up" applications for torture warrants. On the judges' side, a "torture warrant" court many not be the most skeptical bench, and they, like executive officials, would be subject to public pressure to do everything possible to prevent a recurrence of September 11.

Armed with a doctrine that requires them to "balance" the rights of suspects against the needs of the public, it seems entirely plausible to predict that judges would issue warrants in cases far short of the "ticking bomb." Each warrant granted would be the starting point for an argument that a subsequent warrant should be granted in circumstances just a little short of the exigencies of the prior case. * * *

Let us grant [that] some requests for torture warrants will be turned down, and that the prospect of a skeptical judicial eye will prevent others from being presented. To carry the weight of his argument, Professor Dershowitz would still need to show that the abuse avoided by the denial of the warrants exceeds the abuse that his proposal would generate. This is a hard case to make. * * *

Faced with a threat of mass devastation that can be avoided only through torture, could an American official believe, as a matter of morality and public policy, that she should choose the path of the torturer as the lesser evil? On this question, I am prepared to concede that there is room for debate, as there is room for debate as to whether under extraordinary circumstances a public official should choose to violate any provision of the Constitution. But on the question of whether scholars or courts should announce before the fact that the Constitution permits torture, the answer seems clearer: ours is not a Constitution that condones such actions. An official who proclaims fidelity to the Constitution cannot in the same breath claim the right to use methods "too close to the rack and the screw to permit of constitutional differentiation."

ALAN M. DERSHOWITZ, *Torture Without Visibility and Accountability Is Worse Than with It*, 6 U.Pa.J.Const.L. 326 (2003):

My own normative preference would be for the courts to declare all forms of torture unconstitutional, even if its fruits are not used against the defendant and even if it is not administered as "punishment." My own normative preference would also be for law enforcement officials to refrain from using torture, but my empirical conclusion is that they will, in fact, employ it in "ticking bomb" cases. My prediction of what the current courts "will do in fact" is different from Professor Kreimer's. I hope he is right, but I think I am right.

If he is right, he should support my proposal for some kind of legal structure that promotes visibility and accountability through a "torture warrant." In the absence of some such structure, it will be difficult to get a test case before the courts, since torture will continue to be administered beneath the radar screen and with the kind of "deniability" that currently shrouds the practice. The open authorization of limited torture warrants could, on the other hand, be challenged on its face, and we would soon learn whose prediction is more accurate. If he is right, all forms of torture would be declared unconstitutional. If I am right, there would, at least, be some accountability, visibility, and limitations on a dangerous practice that is currently shrouded in secrecy and deniability. * * *

JOHN T. PARRY & WELSH S. WHITE, *Interrogating Suspected Terrorists: Should Torture Be An Option?*, 63 U.Pitt.L.Rev. 743, 763 (2002):[b]

[The] best approach is to place the decision [to resort to torture] squarely on the shoulders of the individuals who order or carry out torture. Government agents should use torture only when it provides the last remaining chance to save lives that are in imminent peril. If interrogators know that they act at their peril, because the law provides no authority for torture under any circumstances, then they are likely to be deterred from acting except when the choice—however distasteful—seems obvious.

When a government agent uses torture to gain information that would avert a future terrorist act, the necessity defense should be available in any resulting criminal prosecution. A successful necessity claim requires proof that the defendant reasonably believed his harmful actions were necessary to avert a greater, imminent harm. * * *

Allowing the necessity defense in torture cases is consistent with providing strong deterrence against torture. [Even] if interrogators know that the necessity defense is available, they will not be able to predict with certainty before they act whether the defense would be successful, and the resulting uncertainty would also foster deterrence. The primary obstacle to deterrence is prosecutorial discretion. An interrogator might assume that the government will not prosecute if torture reveals critical information. For that reason, the Department of Justice should have a clear and public policy of prosecuting without exception any law enforcement official who uses torture. * * *

13. Meeting the "heavy burden" of demonstrating waiver: should tape recordings of the warnings and police questioning be required? Five years *before* the *Miranda* case, one close student of the problem, Bernard Weisberg, *Police Interrogation of Arrested Persons: A Skeptical View*, 52 J. Crim.L. & P.S. 21, 48 (1961), attacked the secrecy surrounding police interrogation: "No other case comes to mind in which an administrative official is permitted the broad discretionary power assumed by the police interrogator, together with the power to prevent objective recordation of the facts. The absence of a record makes disputes inevitable about the conduct of the police and, sometimes, about what the prisoner has actually said. It is secrecy, not privacy, which accounts for the absence of a reliable record of interrogation proceedings in a police station. If the need for some pre-judicial questioning is assumed, privacy may be defended on grounds of necessity; secrecy cannot be defended on this or any other ground."

Recall, too, that before turning to the police manuals for valuable information about current police practices, the *Miranda* Court noted that the secrecy surrounding police questioning "results in a gap in our knowledge as to what in fact goes on in the interrogation rooms." (See p. 576.) However, as pointed out by Richard A. Leo, *Inside the Interrogation Room*, 86 J. Crim.L. & Criminology 266 (1996), three decades after *Miranda*, we knew "scant more" about actual police interrogation practices than we did at the time that famous case was decided.

At one point, the *Miranda* opinion (see p. 584) came to the very edge of requiring law enforcement officers to tape, where feasible, the warning, waiver and subsequent questioning and statements made in response: "If the interroga-

b. In the article by Professors Parry and White that follows, the authors use "torture" to refer to any coercive interrogation practice that involves the inflection of pain or extreme discomfort.

tion continues without the presence of an attorney and a statement is taken, a heavy burden rests on the Government to demonstrate that the defendant knowingly and intelligently waived his [rights]. Since the State is responsible for establishing the isolated circumstances under which the interrogation takes place and *has the only means of making available corroborated evidence* of warnings given during incommunicado interrogation, the burden is rightly on its shoulders." (Emphasis added.) However, the *Miranda* Court fell short of imposing a tape recording requirement on police interrogators—perhaps because it was well aware that such a requirement would add much fuel to the criticism that it was exercising undue control over police practices—that it was "legislating."

Despite the references to "heavy burden" and "corroborated evidence" in the *Miranda* opinion and the strong support for video, or at least audio, taping in the literature, all but two state courts have held that—even when taping the proceedings in the interrogation room is feasible—the uncorroborated testimony of an officer that he gave complete *Miranda* warnings and obtained a waiver is sufficient. The two exceptions are *Stephan v. State*, 711 P.2d 1156 (Alaska 1985) and *State v. Scales*, 518 N.W.2d 587 (Minn.1994).

Paul G. Cassell, *Miranda's Social Costs: An Empirical Assessment*, 90 Nw. U.L.Rev. 387, 486–97 (1996), has forcefully argued that a recording requirement should be viewed as an *alternative* to *Miranda*:

"[If] you were facing a police officer with a rubber hose, would you prefer a world in which he was required to mumble the *Miranda* warnings and have you waive your rights, all as reported by him in later testimony? Or a world in which the interrogation is videorecorded and the burden is on law enforcement to explain if it is not; where date and time are recorded on the videotape; where your physical appearance and demeanor during the interrogation are permanently recorded?[a]

Professor Cassell's article evoked a response from Stephen J. Schulhofer, *Miranda's Practical Effect: Substantial Benefits and Vanishingly Small Social Costs*, 90 Nw. U.L.Rev. 556–60 (1996). Professor Schulhofer agreed that videotaping is an extremely valuable tool—for both the police interrogator and the suspect—but rejected the notion that videotaping could be *a* substitute for *Miranda*. He maintained that Cassell's proposed replacement for *Miranda* would expose suspects to violations of their constitutional rights: "No doubt a videotaped record would often prevent police abuse and manipulation of the 'swearing contest.' But without clear substantive requirements against which to test the police behavior that the videotape will reveal, the objective record will lack any specific legal implications.

a. "Recent and substantial experience with a mandatory recording requirement in Britian," notes Cassell, "suggests that such a requirement would not significantly harm police efforts to obtain confessions." In 1988, a Code of Practice went into effect that generally required the police to tape record interviews with suspects. A review of this requirement five years later by the Royal Commission on Criminal Justice reported that tape recording in the stationhouse had "proved to be a strikingly successful innovation providing better safeguards for the suspect and the police officer alike." According to one survey, some 90 percent of police officers approval of the practice, with two-thirds reporting "very favorable" news about it.

If procedures relating to tape recordings are established, should the police inform the suspect that what he says is being recorded? Would such a requirement inhibit too many from talking? On the other hand, would such a requirement bring home to suspects the seriousness of their situations? See Kamisar Essays at 133 n. 22.

"The heart of the Cassell proposals is his recommendation to strip arrested suspects of their right to consult counsel during pre-arraignment interrogation, to eliminate the requirement that interrogation be preceded by an explicit waiver of rights, and to eliminate *Miranda*'s requirement that interrogation cease if a suspect makes a clear request to break off questioning or to consult with counsel. The requirements he would eliminate are not only central to the *Miranda* safeguards but have now become entrenched in the interrogation procedures of many countries around the world."[242]

The Illinois Governor's Commission on Capital Punishment (2002) (hereafter Illinois Commission) recommended (No. 4) that custodial interrogation of a homicide suspect "occurring at a public facility" should be videotaped. Such taping, the Illinois Commission made clear, "should not include merely the statement made by the suspect after interrogation, but the entire interrogation process."

In July 2003, despite substantial resistance by some law enforcement groups, who feared that a taping requirement would interfere with police work and provide another "loophole" for the guilty to escape punishment, Illinois became the first state to enact legislation requiring the electronic recording of police interrogation under certain circumstances. The new law provides that unless an electronic recording is made of the custodial interrogation of homicide suspects who are "at a police station or other place of detention," all statements made as a result of this interrogation "shall be presumed to be inadmissible against the accused."[1] Illinois police and prosecutors were given two years to fully comply with the provisions of the new law.

According to Steven A. Drizin & Beth A. Colgan, *Let the Cameras Roll: Mandatory Videotaping of Interrogations is the Solution to Illinois' Problem of False Confessions*, 32 Loyola U. Chi. L. J. 337, 339 (2001), "the push" for the Illinois legislation "arose from a spate of false confession cases and questionable interrogations that have plagued Illinois law enforcement and undermined the general public's faith in the criminal justice system." See also Steven A. Drizin & Richard A. Leo, *The Problem of False Confessions in the Post–DNA World*, 82 N.C.L.Rev. 891 (2004), analyzing 125 recent cases of proven interrogation-induced false confessions and concluding that mandatory electronic recording of police interrogations will minimize the number of false confessions.

In STATE v. COOK, 847 A.2d 530 (2004), a 5–1 majority of the New Jersey Supreme Court, per LaVECCHIA, J., rejected the argument that "modern notions

242. See Craig M. Bradley, *The Emerging International Consensus as to Criminal Procedure Rules*, 14 Mich.J.Int'l L. 171, 185 (1993) ("England's interrogation rules are *more stringent* than *Miranda*.") (emphasis added); id. at 197–98 (noting that in Canada, a suspect must be informed upon arrest of his right to counsel, and that police "must refrain from attempting to elicit evidence from the detainee until he has a reasonable opportunity to retain and instruct counsel") (quoting Martin's Annual Criminal Code CH–21 (1991)); id. at 214–15 (Germany requires warning of rights to silence and right "*at all times, even before his examination*, to consult with defense counsel of his choice") (emphasis added) (quoting German Code of Criminal Procedure § 136); id. at 217–18 (noting that Italian interrogation rules prohibit use of statements made in the absence of counsel).

1. Texas is sometimes mentioned as a state whose legislation requires the taping of police interrogations and confessions. However, Texas law only provides that in order to be admissible *oral statements* made during a custodial interrogation must be electronically recorded. The police are much more inclined to tape the "end result" of the interrogation (the confession or incriminating statement) than they are the warnings and questioning that precede the end result.

of due process require the electronic recordation of [a suspect's] custodial statements as a condition for their admissibility":

"We have rejected claimed due process violations in the past where the asserted deprivations implicated 'an area in which fair-minded men can disagree,' and 'points of view could range' over a spectrum of conclusions in respect to the alleged right involved. Because there is otherwise 'fair-minded' disagreement concerning the appropriateness of imposing a sweeping requirement of electronic recordation of custodial statements we hold that defendant's point of error 'is not of constitutional dimension.' [His] statements were not wrongfully admitted merely because they were not electronically recorded. Their admissibility can be assessed adequately under our current standards for voluntariness and trustworthiness." However, the majority went on to say:

"We acknowledge the State's concern that electronic recording may create an artificial restriction on the interrogation dynamic. However, the fact that numerous law enforcement agencies of this State have found themselves able to overcome that drawback and are using electronic recording reduces the force of the State's concern. [Indeed], we are informed that the Attorney General, acting in conjunction with the county prosecutors, has taken steps to implement an administrative policy requiring electronic recording of final statements of suspects in homicide investigations. We are told that pilot projects concerning future use of electronic recordation are contemplated. The State also has brought to our attention that there is the potential for legislative action in this area as well. [Those] steps are welcome, but this issue deserves the broad involvement of all stakeholders and, importantly, must involve the judiciary.

"The judiciary bears the responsibility to guarantee the proper administration of justice [and] particularly, the administration of criminal justice. Our courts thus have the 'independent obligation [to] take all appropriate measures to ensure the fair and proper administration of a criminal trial.' * * * Accordingly, we will establish a committee to study and make recommendations on the use of electronic recordation of custodial interrogations."

Dissenting Justice LONG exhibited less patience than her colleagues:

"[The] majority opinion falls short of what I view as necessary definitive action. I would take the lead of the Minnesota Supreme Court and declare today, pursuant to our supervisory authority, that all criminal interrogations must be recorded electronically, where feasible, when the interrogation occurs at police headquarters or at another place of detention.

"In the final analysis, a determination of the admissibility of a defendant's statement in a criminal proceeding is a purely judicial function. Why we should suffer, for one more day, the funneling of the reality of an interrogation through the lenses of partisans, with the concomitant frailty of language and recollection, when a true recording could be made, is simply beyond me. [As] the majority has acknowledged, the 'sky is falling' arguments advanced by the State are belied by the reality that police agencies throughout the nation have undertaken electronic recording with no dire consequence.[1]

1. According to a recent survey of more than 200 law enforcement agencies in 38 states, officials in police departments that electronically record interrogations of suspects have come to support the practice. They "almost uniformly said that the recordings saved time and money, created compelling evidence and were effective in resolving disputes about whether confessions were voluntary and about allegations of police misconduct." See Adam Liptak, *Taping of Interrogations Is Praised by Police*, N.Y. Times, June 13, 2004, p. A35, col. 2. The study identified 238 police departments that tape entire interrogations in serious cases. According to the Justice Department, there are 18,000 separate state and local law enforcement units nationwide. See id.

"I have no difficulty with the majority's notion of establishing a committee to study the issue further. However, it is my opinion that that committee should be charged with recommending the details and specifics of electronic recording and filling in the interstices of a procedure that we, in the first instance, should have mandated."

For the view that there are three constitutional grounds for requiring police interrogations to be taped, see CHRISTOPHER SLOBOGIN, *Toward Taping*, 1 Ohio St. J. Crim. L. 309 (2003). Professor Slobogin observes:

"The due process argument for taping is that it is the only way the government can meet its obligation to preserve evidence that is exculpatory.

"* * * Absent a tape, courts are forced to rely on the incomplete and biased accounts of the parties, which is an insufficient basis for assessing voluntariness. It was this reasoning, more or less, that proved persuasive to the Alaska Supreme Court in *Stephan*, which based its decision primarily on due process considerations (albeit derived from the Alaskan constitution rather than the federal one). To the same effect are the many lower court cases that find inadequate as a constitutional matter verbal descriptions of lineups for purposes of reconstructing the identification process. If lineups must be recorded for the defense, certainly interrogations, which involve psychological as well as physical events should be.

"As for the Fifth Amendment argument for a taping requirement, the Supreme Court has held that the state must prove by a preponderance of the evidence that police gave warnings, that the suspect understood the warnings, and that any waiver of the rights incorporated in those warnings is voluntary and intelligent. If one assumes that voluntariness cannot be assessed without taping, the tapeless prosecutor cannot meet that burden, at least where the defendant plausibly asserts he did not receive or understand warnings, was misled about them, or received improper threats, promises and the like. In such cases, at best the parties are in equipoise, and the party with the burden of proof—the government—should lose.

"[The Sixth Amendment] confrontation argument derives from a right to counsel case, *United States v. Wade* [p. 757]. In *Wade* the Supreme Court held that, under the Sixth Amendment, suspects placed in lineups after indictment are entitled to counsel. The Court's language, however, focused on confrontation concerns. [First,] the Court suggested that the right it recognized could be met not just with the provision of counsel, but also with 'substitute counsel' which presumably could include a recording of the lineup. [Second,] the Court stated that unless counsel or 'substitute counsel' is present at the lineup, 'the accused is deprived of that right of cross-examination which is an essential safeguard to his right to confront the witnesses against him.' The 'vagaries' of eyewitness identification during a lineup can only be effectively challenged, said the Court, if adequate observation of the identification process occurs. In essence, the *Wade* Court adopted in the lineup context the same two assumptions I have adopted for the interrogation context. Interrogation is subject to even more vagaries than the lineup process, and counsel, or a substitute—taping—is necessary to make sure we know about these vagaries.

"*Wade*'s right to counsel was subsequently limited to post-charging lineups, and a right to taping, so limited, would be close to useless, since most interrogations take place before charging. But, again, the Sixth Amendment argument made here is not based on the right to counsel, but on the right of confrontation.

And the Court has never limited the right of confrontation to events that occur post-charging. * * *

"[Whether] based on due process, the Fifth Amendment, or the right of confrontation, the taping requirement should not be waivable. If suspects could relinquish the right to be taped we can be assured that, just as 80% of those told of their *Miranda* rights waive them, a large percentage of those told they have a right to a recording will give up that prerogative. Some will do so because police convince them taping is a bad idea, others because they mistakenly believe untaped confessions are inadmissible even when they forfeit the right, and others because they are coerced into waiver in subtle or not so subtle ways.

"The insistence that taping occur regardless of the defendant's desires rests on more than concern for the constitutional rights of defendants, however. [The] taping requirement should be sacrosanct because government should want to know precisely what happens in the interrogation room as a means of protecting the accuracy and fairness of the criminal process."

14. *Implied waiver.* Although a waiver is not established merely by showing that a defendant was given complete *Miranda* warnings and thereafter made an incriminating statement, *Tague v. Louisiana,* 444 U.S. 469 (1980), this does not mean that a waiver of *Miranda* rights will never be recognized unless "specifically made" after the warnings are given. As the Court, per STEWART, J., observed in NORTH CAROLINA v. BUTLER, 441 U.S. 369 (1979):

"The question is not one of form, but rather whether the defendant knowingly and voluntarily waived [his *Miranda* rights]. [Although] mere silence is not enough [that] does not mean that the defendant's silence, coupled with an understanding of his rights and a course of conduct indicating waiver, may never support a conclusion that a defendant has waived his rights. The courts must presume that a defendant did not waive his rights; the prosecution's burden is great; but in at least some cases waiver can be clearly inferred from the actions and words of the person interrogated."[1]

Dissenting Justice BRENNAN, joined by Marshall and Stevens, JJ., protested: "[The Court] shrouds in half-light the question of waiver, allowing courts to construct inferences from ambiguous word and gestures. But the very premise of *Miranda* requires that ambiguity be interpreted against the interrogator. [Under the conditions inherent in custodial interrogation], only the most explicit waiver of rights can be considered knowingly and freely given. [S]ince the Court agrees that *Miranda* requires the police to obtain some kind of waiver—whether express or implied—the requirement of an express waiver would impose no burden on the police not imposed by the Court's interpretation. It would merely make that burden explicit. Had [the agent] simply elicited a clear answer to the question, 'Do you waive your right to a lawyer?' this journey through three courts would not have been necessary."

1. After reading the FBI's "Advice of Rights" form, defendant was asked whether he understood his rights. He replied that he did, but refused to sign the waiver at the bottom of the form. He was then told that he need neither speak nor sign the form, but that the agents would like him to talk to them. He replied, "I will talk to you but I am not signing any form." He then made incriminating statements. Because defendant had said nothing when advised of his right to counsel, and because the state supreme court read *Miranda* as requiring a specific waiver of each right, it concluded that defendant had not waived his right to counsel. The U.S. Supreme Court disagreed: "By creating an inflexible rule that no implicit waiver [of *Miranda* rights] can ever suffice, the [state court] has gone beyond the requirements of federal organic law."

Notes and Questions

(a) *The "intelligent and knowing" test in practice.* Consider Mark Berger, *Compromise and Continuity: Miranda Waivers, Confession Admissibility, and the Retention of Interrogation Protections,* 49 U.Pitt.L.Rev. 1007, 1063 (1988): "Current indications are that [the requirement that *Miranda* waivers meet an intelligent and knowing test] extends no further than a general awareness by the suspect that he has the right to remain silent and have the assistance of counsel, and that anything he says can be used against him. Of course, these are the elements contained in the *Miranda* warning itself, and there is no sign that the Supreme Court is likely to require anything more to meet the knowing test. In practice, it appears that as long as the warnings are given and the suspect exhibits no overt signs of a lack of capacity to understand them, his waiver will be upheld."

(b) *Should the Johnson v. Zerbst standard apply to Miranda waivers?* Under *Johnson v. Zerbst* (1938) (quoted at p. 82), the prosecution must demonstrate "an intentional relinquishment or abandonment of a known right" in order to establish a waiver of counsel *at trial.* The *Miranda* Court (p. 584) cited *Zerbst* for the proposition that "this Court has always set high standards of proof for the waiver of constitutional rights." As noted in Berger, supra, at 1031, however, the *Miranda* Court "did not specifically adopt the *Zerbst* criteria." But in the same paragraph citing *Zerbst* the Court stated that "a heavy burden rests on the Government to demonstrate that the defendant knowingly and intelligently waived" his *Miranda* rights. Was *this* an adoption of the *Zerbst* "intentional relinquishment" standard? If so, did the *Miranda* Court too hurriedly lump together *Miranda* rights and the right to counsel at trial? Should the *Zerbst* criteria and "waiver" terminology be expelled from *Miranda* law? Yes, maintains James Tomkovicz, *Standards for Invocation and Waiver of Counsel in Confession Contexts,* 71 Iowa L.Rev. 975, 1050–53 (1986):

"Elimination of the *Zerbst* formula [is] preferable not only because *Zerbst* does not accurately capture fifth amendment decisions in the abstract, but also because actual applications in fifth amendment cases prove that the formula does not describe the waivers that have been acceptable. Furthermore, those interpretations threaten to dilute the demands of the 'voluntary and knowing' standard and thereby to undermine its ability to shelter other constitutional rights for which it is appropriate. A weakened *Zerbst* waiver standard for *Miranda*'s fifth amendment counsel, for example, is easily borrowed for sixth amendment counsel waiver determinations. The vigor of that guarantee, however, depends on more stringent protection against surrender than the *Butler* dilution of *Zerbst* affords."

15. *"Qualified" waiver.* As *North Carolina v. Butler* itself illustrates (see fn. a supra), a suspect may refuse to sign a waiver but nonetheless indicate that he is willing to talk.[1] Or he may object to any notetaking by an officer but agree to talk about the case or indicate that he will talk only if a tape recorder is turned off. Are oral waivers effective in the face of such objections? A number of courts have held that they are. See, e.g., *United States v. Frazier,* 476 F.2d 891 (D.C.Cir.1973) (en banc) (*Frazier II*). But see CRIMPROC § 6.9(f) (in these situations defendant probably acted as he did "because of a mistaken impression that an oral confession which was not contemporaneously recorded could not be used against him"; therefore, police should be required to "clear up misunderstandings of this nature which are apparent to any reasonable observer").[2]

1. The *Butler* Court did not hold that this constituted a valid waiver, but only rejected the state court's view that nothing short of an express waiver would satisfy *Miranda.*

2. One study indicates that 45 percent of post-*Miranda* defendants mistakenly believed that oral statements could not be used against them. See Lawrence S. Leiken, *Police Interrogation in Colorado: The Implementation of Mi-*

The Court addressed this general problem in CONNECTICUT v. BARRETT, 479 U.S. 523 (1987). While in custody, respondent, a suspect in a sexual assault case, was thrice advised of his *Miranda* rights. On each occasion, after signing an acknowledgment that he had been informed of his rights, respondent indicated that he would not make a written statement, but that he was willing to talk about the incident that led to his arrest. On the second and third such occasions, respondent added that he would not make a written statement outside the presence of counsel, and then orally admitted his involvement in the crime. An officer reduced to writing his recollection of respondent's last such statement, and the confession was admitted into evidence at respondent's trial. The Court, per REHNQUIST, C.J., rejected the contention that respondent's expressed desire for counsel before making a written statement served as an invocation of the right for all purposes:

"[W]e know of no constitutional objective that would be served by suppression in this case. It is undisputed that Barrett desired the presence of counsel before making a written statement. [His] limited requests for counsel, however, were accompanied by affirmative announcements of his willingness to speak with the authorities. The fact that officials took [this opportunity] to obtain an oral confession is quite consistent with the Fifth Amendment. *Miranda* gives the defendant a right to choose between speech and silence, and Barrett chose to speak.

"* * * Barrett made clear his intentions and they were honored. [To] conclude that [he] invoked his right to counsel for all purposes requires not a broad interpretation of an ambiguous statement, but disregard of the ordinary meaning of respondent's statement. [The] fact that some might find Barrett's decision illogical is irrelevant, for we have never 'embraced the theory that a defendant's ignorance of the full consequences of his decisions vitiates their voluntariness.' "

BRENNAN, J., concurred in the judgment. Although "Barrett's contemporaneous waiver of his right to silence and limited invocation of his right to counsel (for the purpose of making a written statement) suggested that he did not understand that anything he *said* could be used against him," he testified that "he understood his *Miranda* rights, i.e., he knew that he need not talk to the police without a lawyer and that anything he said could be used against him. Under these circumstances, the waiver of the right to silence and the limited invocation of the right to counsel were valid."

Had the prosecution been without Barrett's trial testimony, Brennan would have dissented: "As a general matter, I believe that this odd juxtaposition (a willingness to talk and an unwillingness to have anything preserved) militates against finding a knowing or intelligent waiver of the right to silence. [But] the State has carried its 'heavy burden' of demonstrating waiver. It has shown that Barrett received the *Miranda* warnings, that he had the capacity to understand them and *in fact* understood them, and that he expressly waived his right to silence. [In] my view, each of these findings was essential to the conclusion that a voluntary, knowing, and intelligent waiver of the *Miranda* rights occurred."[1]

16. ***What constitutes an invocation of Miranda rights?*** In FARE v. MICHAEL C., 442 U.S. 707 (1979), after being fully advised of his *Miranda* rights,

randa, 47 Denver L.J. 1, 15–16, 33 (1970). If so many people do not realize the significance of an oral statement, should the warning take this form: "You have a right to remain silent and anything you say, *orally or* in writing, may (will) be used against you"? *Unif.R.Crim.P.* 212(b) and 243 so provide.

1. Stevens, J., joined by Marshall, J., dissented, deeming respondent's request for the assistance of counsel indistinguishable from the request in *Edwards*.

a juvenile, who had been taken into custody on suspicion of murder, asked, "Can I have my probation officer here?" The police officer replied that he was "not going to call [the probation officer] right now," then continued: "If you want to talk to us without an attorney present, you can. If you don't want to, you don't have to." The juvenile then agreed to talk to the police without an attorney being present and made incriminating statements. The Court, per BLACKMUN, J., held the statements admissible, deeming the request to see a probation officer not a *per se* invocation of *Miranda* rights—not the equivalent of asking for a lawyer. The admissibility of the statements on the basis of waiver turned on "the totality of the circumstance surrounding the interrogation" (e.g., evaluation of the juvenile's age, experience, background and intelligence).

"The *per se* aspect of *Miranda,*" emphasized the Court, was "based on the unique role the lawyer plays in the adversarial system of criminal justice in this country. [A] probation officer is not in the same posture with regard to either the accused or the system of justice as a whole. * * * Moreover, [he] is the employee of the State which seeks to prosecute the alleged offender. He is a peace officer, and as such is allied, to a greater or lesser extent, with his fellow peace officers. [It is the] pivotal role of legal counsel [in the administration of criminal justice] that justifies the *per se* rule established in *Miranda* and that distinguishes the request for counsel from the request for a probation officer, a clergyman, or a close friend."

Justice MARSHALL, joined by Brennan and Stevens, JJ., dissented. Noting that the California Supreme Court had "determined that probation officers have a statutory duty to represent minors' interests and, indeed, are 'trusted guardian figure[s]' to whom a juvenile would likely turn for assistance," the dissenters maintained that "*Miranda* requires that interrogation cease whenever a juvenile requests an adult who is obligated to represent his interests." Such request "constitutes both an attempt to obtain advice and a general invocation of the right to silence. For, as the California Supreme Court recognized, 'it is fatuous to assume that a minor in custody will be in a position to call an attorney for assistance,' or that he will trust the police to obtain an attorney for him. A juvenile in these circumstances will likely turn to his parents, or another adult responsible for his welfare, as the only means of securing legal counsel. Moreover, a request for such adult assistance is surely inconsistent with a present desire to speak freely."[1]

Does *Fare v. Michael C.* stand for the broad proposition that a request by any suspect (with the possible exception of a young, inexperienced juvenile; Michael C. was an "experienced" 16½ year old) to see anyone *other than an attorney,* whether it be a parent, spouse or best friend, does not *per se* constitute an assertion or invocation of *Miranda* rights? If so, is this because neither parent, spouse or best friend has the "unique ability to protect the Fifth Amendment rights" of a suspect undergoing custodial interrogation? How much weight, if any, should be given to the fact that the mother, father or husband requested by the suspect plays a "unique role" in the life of the particular suspect?

17. *The scope of "second-level" Miranda safeguards—the procedures that must be followed when suspects do assert their rights—and the distinction between invoking the right to remain silent and the right to counsel.* In most *Miranda* cases, the issue is the need for the *Miranda* warnings or the adequacy of the warnings given or the suspect's alleged waiver in response to the warnings. But different issues arise when the suspect *asserts* his rights—

1. Justice Powell wrote a separate dissent, "not satisfied that this particular 16–year-old boy, in this particular situation was subjected to a fair interrogation free from inherently coercive circumstances."

thereby triggering what have been called "second level" *Miranda* safeguards. Although this development may have surprised the *Miranda* Court, it turns out that the procedures that must be followed when a suspect invokes his rights depends on whether he asserted the right to remain silent or the right to counsel.

The Court first addressed this issue in MICHIGAN v. MOSLEY, 423 U.S. 96 (1975). Mosley was arrested in connection with certain robberies. After being given *Miranda* warnings by a robbery detective, Mosley declined to talk about the robberies (but he did not request a lawyer). The detective promptly ceased questioning and made no effort to persuade Mosley to reconsider his position. Mosley was then taken to a cell block in the building. After a two-hour interval, a homicide detective brought Mosley from the cell block to the homicide bureau for questioning about "an unrelated holdup murder." Mosley was again advised of his rights. This time he waived them and made an incriminating statement. A 7–2 majority, per STEWART, J., held the statement admissible.

After studying the *Miranda* opinion, the Court concluded that "the admissibility of statements obtained after the person in custody has decided to remain silent depends [on] whether his 'right to cut off questioning' was 'scrupulously honored.' " After examining the facts, the Court concluded that Mosley's right had been honored. The questioning by the homicide detective, emphasized the Court, had "focused exclusively on [a] crime different in nature and in time and place by occurrence from the robberies for which Mosley had been arrested and interrogated by [the robbery detective]" and the subsequent questioning by another detective about an unrelated homicide was "quite consistent with a reasonable interpretation of Mosley's earlier refusal to answer any questions about the robberies." Therefore, "this is not a case [where] the police failed to honor a decision [to] cut off questioning, either by refusing to discontinue the interrogation upon request or by persisting in repeated efforts to wear down [the suspect's] resistance and make him change his mind. [The] police here immediately ceased the interrogation, resumed questioning only after the passage of a significant period of time and the provision of a fresh set of warnings, and restricted the second interrogation to a crime that had not been a subject of the earlier interrogation."

Concurring Justice WHITE foreshadowed his opinion for the Court six years later in *Edwards v. Arizona,* below, by observing: "[The *Miranda* Court showed in its opinion] that when it wanted to create a *per se* rule against further interrogation after assertion of a right, it knew how to do so. The Court there said 'if the individual states that he wants an attorney, the interrogation must cease *until an attorney is present.*' [Emphasis added by White, J.]"

Three factors seem to be *minimal requirements* for the resumption of questioning once a suspect asserts his right to remain silent: (1) immediately ceasing the interrogation; (2) suspending questioning entirely for a significant period; (3) giving a fresh set of *Miranda* warnings at the outset of the second interrogation. May these three circumstances also be *the only* critical factors? May *Mosley* mean that these three circumstances suffice without more to eliminate the coercion inherent in the continuing custody and the renewed questioning? How significant is it that a different officer resumed the questioning? That the second interrogation occurred at another location? That the second interrogation was limited to a separate and "unrelated" crime? Compare Geoffrey Stone, *The Miranda Doctrine in the Burger Court*, 1977 Sup.Ct.Rev. 99, 134 (last factor "seems critical") with Kamisar, *The Warren Court (Was It Really So Defense–Minded?), the Burger Court*

(Is It Really So Prosecution–Oriented?) and Police Investigatory Practices, in The Burger Court: The Counter–Revolution That Wasn't 62, 83 & n. 133 (V. Blasi ed. 1983) (not at all clear that *Mosley* was meant to be or will be so limited).

Distinguishing the *Mosley* case, EDWARDS v. ARIZONA, 451 U.S. 477 (1981), held that once a suspect has invoked his right to counsel he may not be "subject[ed] to further interrogation [until] counsel has been made available to him unless [he] himself initiates further communication, exchanges or conversations with the police."

Edwards was arrested for burglary, robbery and murder and taken to the police station. He waived his rights and agreed to talk about these crimes. But some time later he asserted his right to counsel. At this point, questioning ceased and Edwards was taken to jail. The next morning, two detectives, colleagues of the officer who had questioned Edwards the previous day, came to the jail, met with Edwards and again informed him of his rights.[1] This time Edwards agreed to talk about the same crimes. He then made incriminating statements which led to his conviction for these crimes. The state supreme court held that although Edwards had asserted his right to counsel the day before, he waived this right the following day when he agreed to talk after again being given his *Miranda* warnings. The Court, per WHITE, J., disagreed:

"[H]owever sound the conclusion of the state courts as to the voluntariness of Edwards' admission may be, [neither court] undertook to focus on whether Edwards understood his right to counsel and intelligently and knowingly relinquished it. It is thus apparent that the decision below misunderstood the requirement for finding a valid waiver of the right to counsel, once invoked.

"[A]dditional safeguards [for waiver] are necessary when the accused asks for counsel; and we now hold that when an [in-custody suspect does assert this right a valid waiver of it] cannot be established by showing only that he responded to further police-initiated custodial interrogation even if he has been advised of his rights. [An] accused, such as Edwards, having expressed his desire to deal with the police only through counsel, is not subject to further interrogation by the authorities until counsel has been made available to him, unless the accused himself initiates further communication, exchanges or conversations with the police."[2]

18. *Clarification (and extension?) of the Edwards rule.* In ARIZONA v. ROBERSON, 486 U.S. 675 (1988), a 6–2 majority, per STEVENS, J., held that once a suspect effectively asserts his *Miranda–Edwards* right to counsel, the police cannot even initiate interrogation about crimes *other than* the one for which the suspect has invoked his right to counsel:

"[The] presumption raised by a suspect's request for counsel—that he considers himself unable to deal with the pressure of custodial interrogation without legal assistance—does not disappear simply because the police have approached the suspect, still in custody, still without counsel, about a separate investigation. [We] also disagree with [the] contention that fresh sets of *Miranda* warnings will 'reassure' a suspect who has been denied the counsel he has clearly requested that his rights have remained untrammeled. Especially in a case such as this, in which a period of three days elapsed between the unsatisfied request for counsel and the

1. When a guard informed Edwards that two detectives wanted to talk to him, Edwards replied that he did not want to talk to anyone. But the guard told him "he had" to talk to the detectives and then took him to meet with them. The opinion of the Court, however, seems to be written without regard to these particular facts.

2. Chief Justice Burger and Justices Powell and Rehnquist concurred in the result.

interrogation about a second offense, there is a serious risk that the mere repetition of the *Miranda* warnings would not overcome the presumption of coercion that is created by prolonged police custody."[1]

Newly appointed Justice KENNEDY, joined by Chief Justice Rehnquist, dissented, emphasizing that "*Edwards* is our rule, not a constitutional command; and it is our obligation to justify its expansion." According to Justice Kennedy the majority's approach was not "consistent with the practical realities of suspects' rights and police investigations":

"It is a frequent occurrence that [a custodial suspect] is wanted for questioning with respect to crimes unrelated to the one for which he has been apprehended. The rule announced today will bar law enforcement officials, even those from [some] other jurisdiction, from questioning a suspect about an unrelated matter if he is in custody and has requested counsel to assist in answering questions put to him about the crime for which he was arrested.

"[Having] observed that his earlier invocation of rights was effective in terminating questioning and having been advised that further questioning may not relate to that crime, [the suspect] would understand that he may invoke his rights again with respect to the new investigation, and so terminate questioning regarding that investigation as well. Indeed, the new warnings and explanations will reinforce his comprehension of a suspect's rights."[2]

When, two years later, the Court read the *Edwards* rule still more expansively in *Minnick,* set forth below, many Court watchers were surprised to learn that Justice Kennedy, the forceful dissenter in *Roberson,* had written the opinion of the Court.

MINNICK v. MISSISSIPPI

498 U.S. 146, 111 S.Ct. 486, 112 L.Ed.2d 489 (1990).

Justice KENNEDY delivered the opinion of the Court.

[Some four months after he murdered two people in Mississippi, petitioner Minnick fled to San Diego, where he was arrested by local police and placed in a San Diego jail. The next day, two FBI agents came to the jail to interview him. Minnick refused to sign a rights waiver form, but he did agree to answer some questions and he made some incriminating statements. When he declined to speak further, the agents told him he had that right. Minnick then said he would make a more complete statement when his lawyer was present.

[After the FBI interview, an appointed attorney met with Minnick. Shortly afterwards, Minnick spoke with his lawyer on two or three other occasions. However, it is not clear from the record whether all of these conversations were in person.]

[Two days after the FBI visit, a Mississippi deputy sheriff, Denham, came to the San Diego jail to interview Minnick. According to Minnick, his jailers told him

1. The Court "attach[ed] no significance to the fact that the officer who conducted the second interrogation did not know that respondent had made a request for counsel. In addition to the fact that *Edwards* focuses on the state of mind of the suspect and not of the police, custodial interrogation must be conducted pursuant to established procedures, and those procedures in turn must enable an officer who proposes to initiate an interrogation to determine whether the suspect has previously requested counsel."

2. O'Connor, J., took no part in the consideration or decision of the case.

he would "have to talk" to Denham. After being advised of his rights by the deputy sheriff, Minnick again declined to sign a rights waiver form. But once again he did agree to answer some questions. He made a number of incriminating statements. Minnick was convicted of capital murder and sentenced to death. The statements he made to Denham were admitted into evidence.]

[The] issue in the case before us is whether *Edwards'* protection ceases once the suspect has consulted with a lawyer.

[The *Edwards* rule] ensures that any statement made in subsequent interrogation is not the result of coercive pressures. *Edwards* conserves judicial resources which would otherwise be expended in making difficult determinations of voluntariness, and implements the protections of *Miranda* in practical and straightforward terms. [The] rule provides " 'clear and unequivocal' guidelines to the law enforcement profession." * * * Whatever the ambiguities of our earlier cases on this point, we now hold that when counsel is requested, interrogation must cease, and officials may not reinitiate interrogation without counsel present, whether or not the accused has consulted with his attorney.

[The] exception to *Edwards* here proposed [would] undermine the advantages flowing from *Edwards'* "clear and unequivocal" character. Respondent concedes that even after consultation with counsel, a second request for counsel should reinstate the *Edwards* protection. We are invited by this formulation to adopt a regime in which *Edwards'* protection could pass in and out of existence multiple times prior to arraignment, at which point the same protection might reattach by virtue of our Sixth Amendment jurisprudence, see *Michigan v. Jackson* [p. 658]. Vagaries of this sort spread confusion through the justice system and lead to a consequent loss of respect for the underlying constitutional principle.

In addition, adopting the rule proposed would leave far from certain the sort of consultation required to displace *Edwards.* Consultation is not a precise concept, for it may encompass variations from a telephone call to say that the attorney is in route, to a hurried interchange between the attorney and client in a detention facility corridor, to a lengthy in-person conference in which the attorney gives full and adequate advice respecting all matters that might be covered in further interrogations. * * *

Justice SCALIA, with whom The Chief Justice joins, dissenting.

The Court today establishes an irrebuttable presumption that a criminal suspect, after invoking his *Miranda* right to counsel, can *never* validly waive that right during any police-initiated encounter, even after the suspect has been provided multiple *Miranda* warnings and has actually consulted his attorney. * * * Because I see no justification for applying the *Edwards* irrebuttable presumption when a criminal suspect has actually consulted with his attorney, I respectfully dissent. * * *

Notwithstanding our acknowledgment that *Miranda* rights are "not themselves rights protected by the Constitution [but] measures to insure that the right against compulsory self-incrimination [is] protected," *Michigan v. Tucker,* we have adhered to the principle that nothing less than the *Johnson v. Zerbst* standard for the waiver of constitutional rights [see p. 584] applies to the waiver of *Miranda* rights. Until *Edwards,* however, we refrained from imposing on the States a *higher* standard for the waiver of *Miranda* rights. For example, in *Michigan v. Mosley,* we rejected a proposed irrebuttable presumption that a criminal suspect, after invoking the *Miranda* right to remain silent, could not validly waive the right during any subsequent questioning by the police. * * *

Edwards, however, broke with this approach. [The] case stands as a solitary exception to our waiver jurisprudence. [In] the narrow context in which it applies,

[it] " 'prevent[s] police from badgering a defendant' "; it "conserves judicial resources which would otherwise be expended in making difficult determinations of voluntariness"; and it provides' " 'clear and unequivocal' guidelines to the law enforcement profession." But so would a rule that simply excludes all confessions by all persons in police custody. The value of any prophylactic rule (assuming the authority to adopt a prophylactic rule) must be assessed not only on the basis of what is gained, but also on the basis of what is lost. In all other contexts we have thought the above-described consequences of abandoning *Zerbst* outweighed by " 'the need for police questioning as a tool for effective enforcement of criminal laws,' " *Moran v. Burbine* [p. 661].

[The *Edwards* rule] should not, in my view, extend beyond the circumstances present in *Edwards* itself—where the suspect in custody asked to consult an attorney, and was interrogated before that attorney had ever been provided. In those circumstances, the *Edwards* rule rests upon an assumption similar to that of *Miranda* itself: that when a suspect in police custody is first questioned he is likely to be ignorant of his rights and to feel isolated in a hostile environment. This likelihood is thought to justify special protection against unknowing or coerced waiver of rights. After a suspect has seen his request for an attorney honored, however, and has actually spoken with that attorney, the probabilities change. The suspect then knows that he has an advocate on his side, and that the police will permit him to consult that advocate. He almost certainly also has a heightened awareness (above what the *Miranda* warning itself will provide) of his right to remain silent—since at the earliest opportunity "any lawyer worth his salt will tell the suspect in no uncertain terms to make no statement to the police under any circumstances."

* * * Clear and simple rules are desirable, but only in pursuance of authority that we possess. We are authorized by the Fifth Amendment to exclude confessions that are "compelled," which we have interpreted to include confessions that the police obtain from a suspect in custody without a knowing and voluntary waiver of his right to remain silent. Undoubtedly some bright-line rules can be adopted to implement that principle. [But] a rule excluding all confessions that follow upon even the slightest police inquiry cannot conceivably be justified on this basis. It does not rest upon a reasonable prediction that all such confessions, or even most such confessions, will be unaccompanied by a knowing and voluntary waiver.

[Drawing] a distinction between police-initiated inquiry before consultation with counsel and police-initiated inquiry after consultation with counsel is assuredly more reasonable than other distinctions *Edwards* has already led us into—such as the distinction between police-initiated inquiry after assertion of the *Miranda* right to remain silent, and police-initiated inquiry after assertion of the *Miranda* right to counsel, see Kamisar, The *Edwards* and *Bradshaw* Cases: The Court Giveth and the Court Taketh Away, in 5 The Supreme Court: Trends and Developments 157 (J. Choper, Y. Kamisar, & L. Tribe eds. 1984) ("[E]ither *Mosley* was wrongly decided or *Edwards* was"); or the distinction between what is needed to prove waiver of the *Miranda* right to have counsel present and what is needed to prove waiver of rights found in the Constitution. * * *

Today's extension of the *Edwards* prohibition is the latest stage of prophylaxis built upon prophylaxis, producing a veritable fairyland castle of imagined constitutional restriction upon law enforcement. This newest tower, according to the Court, is needed to avoid "inconsisten[cy] with [the] purpose" of *Edwards'* prophylactic rule, which was needed to protect *Miranda*'s prophylactic right to have counsel present, which was needed to protect the right against *compelled self-incrimination* found (at last!) in the Constitution.

[Both *Edwards* and today's decision] are explicable, in my view, only as an effort to protect suspects against what is regarded as their own folly. The sharp-witted criminal would know better than to confess; why should the dull-witted suffer for his lack of mental endowment? Providing him an attorney at every stage where he might be induced or persuaded (though not coerced) to incriminate himself will even the odds. Apart from the fact that this protective enterprise is beyond our authority under the Fifth Amendment or any other provision of the Constitution, it is unwise. [That] some clever criminals may employ those protections to their advantage is poor reason to allow criminals who have not done so to escape justice.

[Not] only for society, but for the wrongdoer himself, "admissio[n] of guilt [if] not coerced, [is] inherently desirable," because it advances the goals of both "justice *and* rehabilitation." *Michigan v. Tucker* (emphasis added). [We should] rejoice at an honest confession, rather than pity the "poor fool" who has made it; and we should regret the attempted retraction of that good act, rather than seek to facilitate and encourage it. To design our laws on premises contrary to these is to abandon belief in either personal responsibility or the moral claim of just government to obedience. Cf. Caplan, Questioning *Miranda,* 38 Vand.L.Rev. 1417, 1471–1473 (1985). * * *

Notes and Questions

(a) *The need to prevent the police from "badgering" a suspect who has previously asserted his rights.* The *Minnick* majority reiterates that the *Edwards* rule is "designed to prevent police from badgering a defendant into waiving his previously asserted" *right to counsel* and to "ensure that any statement made in subsequent interrogation is not the result of coercive pressures." But why isn't there a comparable need for a rule designed to prevent the police from badgering or pressuring a suspect into waiving his previously asserted *right to remain silent?*

(b) Is there a "public safety" exception to *Edwards*? The Supreme Court has never addressed this question, but lower federal courts have answered in the affirmative. See *United States v. Mobley*, 40 F.3d 688 (4th Cir.1994); *United States v. DeSantis*, 870 F.2d 536 (9th Cir.1989). For a discussion of why these courts have reached the right result, see M.K.B. Darmer, *Lessons from the Lindh Case: Public Safety and the Fifth Amendment*, 68 Brooklyn L.Rev. 241, 279 (2002).

19. ***When does the "question-proof status" of a person who has asserted his right to counsel come to an end? Does a sentenced prisoner who has settled into the routine of his new life in the prison population need the extra protection of Edwards?*** Consider UNITED STATES v. GREEN, 592 A.2d 985 (D.C.App.1991), *cert. granted*, 504 U.S. 908, *vacated and cert. dismissed*, 507 U.S. 545 (1993). When arrested on a drug charge on July 18, 1989, defendant refused to answer any questions without having a lawyer present. The next day an attorney was appointed to represent him. Defendant remained incarcerated. On September 27, he pled guilty to a lesser included offense. He was then moved to a juvenile facility while a presentence report was being prepared (On Feb. 26, 1990, he was sentenced on the drug charge.) On January 4, 1990, the police obtained an arrest warrant charging defendant with an unrelated murder that had occurred six months before he had been arrested on the drug charge. The next day, January 5th, defendant was taken to the homicide division. After being advised of his rights he agreed to talk to a detective about the murder and admitted his involvement in that crime. He was then indicted for first degree murder.

Defendant contended that his confession to the murder had been obtained in violation of *Edwards* in view of his original refusal at the time of his arrest on the drug charge to answer questions without counsel being present—an event that occurred more than five months before he had been advised of his rights in connection with the murder and had agreed to talk about his involvement in that crime. The trial judge initially denied the motion to suppress. Three days after the court's initial ruling, however, the Supreme Court handed down *Minnick*. The trial judge then reversed his earlier ruling and suppressed the confession.

A 2–1 majority of the District of Columbia Court of Appeals, per FARRELL, J., affirmed. True, defendant had confessed to the murder more than three months after he had pled guilty in the drug case, the case in which he had requested, and obtained, counsel. But his plea in the drug case was "consistent with his election to communicate with the police only through counsel." Thus his guilty plea in the drug case "cannot be the pivotal break in events that *Edwards* demands before a waiver can be regarded as an initial election by the accused to deal with the authorities on his own."

When defendant died in March of 1993, the Supreme Court vacated the order granting certiorari—but not before oral arguments had been heard in the case. See 52 Crim.L.Rep. 3096. The government maintained that "a dramatic change of circumstances that changes the position of the suspect * * * makes it unreasonable to continue application of *Edwards'* irrebuttable presumption of coercion." Thus, when the suspect pleads guilty to the charge which prompted him to assert his right to counsel or a substantial period of time has elapsed between his initial invocation of rights and the second interrogation or there has been "a break in the custody of the suspect," the police may approach the suspect, in counsel's absence, to ask questions about unrelated offenses. Do you agree?

If so, does a person experience a "break in custody" when he starts serving a prison term? Yes, answers Laurie Magid, *Questioning the Question–Proof Inmate: Defining Miranda Custody for Incarcerated Suspects*, 58 Ohio State L.J. 883, 892 (1997) (one who "has settled into the routine of prison life is [no longer] in *Miranda* custody, and will return to custody for *Miranda* purposes only when he is subjected to some additional restraint beyond those of his normal life as an inmate.")

20. *What constitutes "initiating" further communication with the police?* The *Edwards* rule was deemed inapplicable in OREGON v. BRADSHAW, 462 U.S. 1039 (1983). Bradshaw, suspected of causing the death of Reynolds, a minor, by drunken driving, was arrested for furnishing liquor to Reynolds. Bradshaw agreed to talk to an officer about the fatal crash, but when the officer suggested that Bradshaw had been behind the wheel of the truck when Reynolds died, Bradshaw denied his involvement and expressed a desire to talk to a lawyer. The officers immediately terminated the conversation.

A few minutes later, either while still at the police station or enroute to the jail, Bradshaw asked the officer: "Well, what is going to happen to me now?" In response, the officer said that Bradshaw didn't have to talk to him and, because he had requested a lawyer, he didn't want Bradshaw to talk to him unless he decided to do so as a matter of his "own free will." Bradshaw said he understood. General conversation followed, in the course of which there was a discussion about where Bradshaw was being taken and the crime(s) for which he would be charged. The officer reiterated his own theory of how Bradshaw had caused Reynolds' death and then suggested that Bradshaw take a lie detector test to "clean the matter up." Bradshaw agreed.[a]

a. Should Bradshaw have been advised of his rights and a valid waiver obtained at this point (not the next day, just before Bradshaw took the lie-detector test)? Does the critical

The next day, just before he took the lie detector test, Bradshaw was given another set of *Miranda* warnings and he signed a written waiver of his rights. At the conclusion of the test, the polygraph examiner told Bradshaw that he had not been truthful in response to certain questions. Bradshaw then admitted that he had been driving the vehicle in which Reynolds was killed and that he had consumed a considerable amount of alcohol before passing out at the wheel.

The Supreme Court held that under the circumstances Bradshaw could not avail himself of the *Edwards* rule, but there was no opinion of the Court. Justice REHNQUIST, joined by Burger, C.J., and White and O'Connor, JJ., observed:

"There are some inquiries, such as a request for a drink of water or a request to use a telephone that are so routine that they cannot be fairly said to represent a desire on the part of an accused to open up a more generalized discussion relating directly or indirectly to the investigation. Such inquiries or statements, by either an accused or a police officer, relating to routine incidents of the custodial relationship, will not generally 'initiate' a conversation in the sense in which that word was used in *Edwards*.

"Although ambiguous, the respondent's question in this case as to what was going to happen to him evinced a willingness and a desire for a generalized discussion about the investigation; it was not merely a necessary inquiry arising out of the incidents of the custodial relationship. It could reasonably have been interpreted by the officer as relating generally to the investigation. That the police officer so understood it is apparent from the fact that he immediately reminded the accused that 'you do not have to talk to me,' and only after the accused told him that he 'understood' did they have a generalized conversation. On these facts we believe that there was not a violation of the *Edwards* rule.

"[The next inquiry, therefore] was 'whether a valid waiver of [Bradshaw's rights] had occurred, that is, whether the purported waiver was knowing and intelligent and found to be so under the totality of the circumstances, including

moment occur when a suspect *agrees* to take a lie detector test (or agrees to submit to further interrogation) regardless of whether the test is given (or further interrogation takes place) then or later? Compare *Bradshaw* with *Wyrick v. Fields,* 459 U.S. 42 (1982) (per curiam), which arose as follows: After discussing the matter with his private counsel and with a military attorney, Fields, a soldier charged with rape, requested a polygraph examination. Prior to undergoing the examination, Fields signed a waiver-of-rights form. He was also told: "If you are now going to discuss the offense under investigation, which is rape, with or without a lawyer present, you have a right to stop answering questions at any time or speak to a lawyer before answering further, even if you sign a waiver certificate. Do you want a lawyer at this time?" Fields answered: "No."

At the conclusion of the polygraph examination, which took less than two hours, a CID agent asked Fields if he could explain why his answers were bothering him. Fields then made some incriminating statements. On federal habeas corpus, the Eighth Circuit found that the State had failed to satisfy its burden of proving that Fields knowingly and intelligently waived his right to have counsel present at the *post*-test interrogation. The Supreme Court disagreed:

[The Eighth Circuit rule] certainly finds no support in *Edwards,* which emphasizes that the totality of the circumstances, including the fact that the suspect initiated the questioning, is controlling. Nor is the rule logical; the questions put to Fields after the examination would not have caused him to forget the rights of which he had been advised and which he had understood moments before. The rule is simply an unjustifiable restriction on reasonable police questioning.

Dissenting Justice Marshall underscored the distinction between "an agreement to submit to a polygraph examination" and "the initiation of an ordinary conversation with the authorities": "[A] polygraph examination is a discrete test. It has a readily identifiable beginning and end. An individual who submits to such an examination does not necessarily have any reason whatsoever to expect that he will be subjected to a post-examination interrogation." In any event, Justice Marshall did "not believe that this substantial constitutional question should be disposed of summarily."

the necessary fact that the accused, not the police, reopened the dialogue with the authorities.' *Edwards.*

"[The] state trial court [found that a valid waiver of defendant's rights did occur and] we have no reason to dispute these conclusions * * *."

Concurring Justice POWELL, whose vote was decisive, agreed that Bradshaw had knowingly and intelligently waived his right to counsel, but saw no need for a two-step analysis—whether the suspect "initiated" a conversation with the police, and if so, whether under the "totality of circumstances" a valid waiver of rights followed. According to Powell, J.: "Fragmenting the standard into a novel two-step analysis—if followed literally—often would frustrate justice as well as common sense. Courts should engage in more substantive inquiries than 'who said what first.' [The *Edwards* rule] cannot in my view fairly be reduced to this."

MARSHALL, J., joined by Brennan, Blackmun and Stevens, JJ., dissented, "agree[ing] with the plurality that, in order to constitute 'interrogation' under *Edwards,* an accused's inquiry must demonstrate a desire to discuss the subject matter of the criminal investigation," but expressing "baffle[ment] [at] the plurality's application of that standard to the facts of this case":

"The plurality asserts that respondent's question, 'What is going to happen to me now?', evinced both 'a willingness and a desire for a generalized discussion about the investigation.' If respondent's question had been posed by Jean–Paul Sartre before a class of philosophy students, it might well have evinced a desire for a 'generalized' discussion. But under the circumstances of this case, it is plain that respondent's only 'desire' was to find out where the police were going to take him. As the Oregon Court of Appeals stated, respondent's query came only minutes after his invocation of the right to counsel and was simply 'a normal reaction to being taken from the police station and placed in a police car, obviously for transport to some destination.'

"[To] hold that respondent's question in this case opened a dialogue with the authorities flies in the face of the basic purpose of the *Miranda* safeguards. When someone in custody asks, 'What is going to happen to me now?', he is surely responding to his custodial surroundings. The very essence of custody is the loss of control over one's freedom of movement. [To] allow the authorities to recommence an interrogation based on such a question is to permit them to capitalize on the custodial setting. Yet *Miranda's* procedural protections were adopted precisely in order 'to dispel the compulsion inherent in custodial surroundings.' "

Notes and Questions

(i) *Is the Edwards–Bradshaw test for "initiating" further communication with the police a satisfactory one?* Consider James Tomkovicz, *Standards for Invocation and Waiver of Counsel in Confession Contexts,* 74 Iowa L.Rev. 975, 1033–34 (1986), maintaining that the *Edwards-Bradshaw* test, "which at most demands evidence of a generalized desire or willingness to discuss the investigation" is too broad and too spongy because "it allows officers to recommence interrogation in many situations in which suspects may not have changed their minds [about desiring counsel]." According to Professor Tomkovicz, a definition of suspect initiation of further communication with the police "must describe conduct by the individual that revokes the earlier claim [of counsel] and conveys the message that the added support of counsel is not desired."

(ii) *The suspect's counterpart to "administrative questioning."* Should a "natural response" to arrest or transportation to a jail or police station be viewed as the suspect's counterpart to "administrative questioning"? Consider the remarks of Professor Kamisar in Choper, Kamisar & Tribe, *The Supreme Court: Trends and Developments 1982–83* (1984) at 165–66:

"When the [*Innis* Court defined 'police interrogation'] it *excluded* police words or actions 'normally attendant to arrest and custody' and properly so. Such statements, often called 'administrative questioning,' e.g., the routine questions asked of all persons 'booked' or otherwise processed, do not enhance the pressures and anxiety generated by arrest and detention. Thus, any incriminating statements in response to administrative questioning is, and should be, viewed as a 'volunteered' statement.

"The suspect's counterpart to 'administrative questioning' [is] an expression of fear, anxiety or confusion *normally attendant* to arrest, removal from the scene of arrest, or transportation to the stationhouse or jail. These expressions, such as, Where am I being taken? When can I call my lawyer? and, yes, What's going to happen to me? should not count as "initiation of dialogue" for *Edwards* purposes.

"Of course, if the officer *answers* one of the arrestee's questions about what's going to happen to him by *telling him* where he is being taken [or] when he will be able to meet with an attorney that should not count either. But when the officer's response to the suspect's expression of concern or confusion clearly goes beyond the scope of the suspect's question—when the officer exploits the situation, as he did in [*Bradshaw*]—that *should* count as 'police interrogation.' [Under] such circumstances, the suspect did not 'invite' or 'initiate' conversation about the merits of the case—the officer 'initiated' a *new* conversation."

21. *How direct, assertive and unambiguous must a suspect be in order to invoke the right to counsel?* A year before the decision in *Davis v. United States*, set forth immediately below, Professor Janet Ainsworth pointed out that sociolinguistic research indicates that certain discrete segments of the population (women and a majority of minority racial and ethnic groups) are far more likely than other groups to avoid strong, assertive means of expression and to use indirect and hedged speech patterns that give the impression of uncertainty or equivocality. See Janet E. Ainsworth, *In a Different Register: The Pragmatics of Powerlessness in Police Interrogation*, 103 Yale L.J. 259 (1993). However, observed Ainsworth, in determining whether a suspect had effectively invoked his or her right to counsel, a majority of the lower courts assumed that "direct and assertive speech—a mode of expression more characteristic of men than women—is or should be, the norm." This assumption not only manifests a "kind of gender bias"; it "does not serve the interests of the many speech communities whose discourse patterns deviate from the implicit norms in standard, 'male register' English."

Moreover, since the custodial police interrogation setting involves an imbalance of power between the suspect and his or her interrogator(s), such a setting increases the likelihood that a suspect will adopt an indirect or hedged—and thus ambiguous—means of expression. Even within speech communities whose members do not ordinarily use indirect modes of expression, one who is situationally powerless, that is, aware of the dominant power of the person he or she is addressing (and it is hard to think of a better example than a custodial suspect confronting one or more police interrogators), may also adopt a hedging or otherwise deferential speech register. According to Professor Ainsworth, only a *per se* invocation standard, a rule requiring all police questioning to cease upon any request for or reference to counsel, however equivocal or ambiguous, would provide "both assertive and deferential suspects with equivalent protection" and furnish "the powerless [the] same constitutional protections as the powerful."

However, in DAVIS v. UNITED STATES, 512 U.S. 452 (1994), Justice O'CONNOR, speaking for five members of the Court rejected the view that (a) the courts should not place a premium on suspects making direct, assertive unqualified invocations of the right to counsel and (b) all arguable references to counsel should be treated as valid invocations of the right. The *Davis* case arose as follows:

Davis, a member of the U.S. Navy, was suspected of murdering another sailor. When interviewed by agents of the Naval Investigative Service (NIS) at the NIS office, he initially waived his *Miranda* rights. About an hour and a half into the interview, he said: "Maybe I should talk to a lawyer." At this point, according to the uncontradicted testimony of one of the agents, "we made it very clear [that] we weren't going to pursue the matter unless we have it clarified is he asking for a lawyer or is he just making a comment about a lawyer" and Davis replied, "No, I'm not asking for a lawyer" and then said, "No, I don't want a lawyer."

After a short break, the agents then reminded Davis of his *Miranda* rights and the interview continued for another hour—until Davis said, "I think I want a lawyer before I say anything." At this point, questioning ceased. A military judge admitted Davis's statements and he was convicted of murder. The U.S. Court of Appeals affirmed the conviction—as did the U.S. Supreme Court:

"[To invoke the *Edwards* rule] the suspect must unambiguously request counsel. As we have observed, (a statement either is such an assertion of the right to counsel or it is not? *Smith v. Illinois*, 469 U.S. 91 (1984). [Although] a suspect need not 'speak with the discrimination of an Oxford don' (Souter, J., concurring in judgment), he must articulate his desire to have counsel present sufficiently clearly that a reasonable police officer in the circumstances would understand the statement to be a request for an attorney. If the statement fails to meet the requisite level of clarity, *Edwards* does not require that the officers stop questioning the suspect. * * *

"We decline petitioner's invitation to extend *Edwards* and require law enforcement officers to cease questioning immediately upon the making of an ambiguous or equivocal reference to an attorney. [When] the officers conducting the questioning reasonably do not know whether or not the suspect wants a lawyer, a rule requiring the immediate cessation of questioning 'would transform the *Miranda* safeguards into wholly irrational obstacles to legitimate police investigative activity,' because it would needlessly prevent the police from questioning a suspect in the absence of counsel even if the suspect did not wish to have a lawyer present. * * *

"We recognize that requiring a clear assertion of the right to counsel might disadvantage some suspects who—because of fear, intimidation, lack of linguistic skills, or a variety of other reasons—will not clearly articulate their right to counsel although they actually want to have a lawyer present. But the primary protection afforded suspects subject to custodial interrogation is the *Miranda* warnings themselves. [A] suspect who knowingly and voluntarily waives his right to counsel after having that right explained to him has indicated his willingness to deal with the police unassisted. Although *Edwards* provides an additional protection—if a suspect subsequently requests an attorney, questioning must cease—it is one that must be affirmatively invoked by the suspect.

"[If] we were to require questioning to cease if a suspect makes a statement that *might* be a request for an attorney, [the *Edwards* Rule's] clarity and ease of application would be lost. [We] therefore hold that, after a knowing and voluntary waiver of the *Miranda* rights, law enforcement officers may continue questioning until and unless the suspect clearly requests an attorney.

"[To] recapitulate: We held in *Miranda* that a suspect is entitled to the assistance of counsel during custodial interrogation even though the Constitution does not provide for such assistance. We held in *Edwards* that if the suspect invokes the right to counsel at any time, the police must immediately cease questioning him until an attorney is present. But we are unwilling to create a third layer of prophylaxis to prevent police questioning when the suspect *might* want a lawyer. Unless the suspect actually requests an attorney, questioning may continue."

Justice SOUTER, joined by Blackmun, Stevens and Ginsburg, JJ., wrote a separate opinion. Although he concurred in the judgment affirming Davis's conviction, "resting partly on evidence of statements given after agents ascertained that he did not wish to deal with them through counsel," Justice Souter could not join the majority's "further conclusion that if the investigators here had been so inclined, they were at liberty to disregard Davis's reference to a lawyer entirely, in accordance with a general rule that interrogators have no legal obligation to discover what a custodial subject meant by an ambiguous statement that could reasonably be understood to express a desire to consult a lawyer":

"[For nearly three decades], two precepts have commanded broad assent: that the *Miranda* safeguards exist 'to assure that *the individual's right to choose* between speech and silence remains unfettered throughout the interrogation process,' and that the justification for *Miranda* rules, intended to operate in the real world, 'must be consistent [with] practical realities.' *Arizona v. Roberson* (Kennedy, J., dissenting). A rule barring government agents from further interrogation until they determine whether a suspect's ambiguous statement was meant as a request for counsel fulfills both ambitions. It assures that a suspect's choice whether or not to deal with police through counsel will be 'scrupulously honored' and it faces both the real-world reasons why misunderstandings arise between suspect and interrogator and the real-world limitations on the capacity of police and trial courts to apply fine distinctions and intricate rules.

"Tested against the same two principles, the approach the Court adopts does not fare so well. First, as the majority expressly acknowledges, criminal suspects who may (in *Miranda*'s words) be 'thrust into an unfamiliar atmosphere and run through menacing police interrogation procedures,' would seem an odd group to single out for the Court's demand of heightened linguistic care. A substantial percentage of them lack anything like a confident command of the English language, many are 'woefully ignorant,' and many more will be sufficiently intimidated by the interrogation process or overwhelmed by the uncertainty of their predicament that the ability to speak assertively will abandon them.[4] Indeed, the awareness of just these realities has, in the past, dissuaded the Court from placing any burden of clarity upon individuals in custody, but has led it instead to require that requests for counsel be 'give[n] a broad, rather than a narrow, interpretation' and that courts 'indulge every reasonable presumption,' *Johnson v. Zerbst,* that a suspect has not waived his right to counsel under *Miranda.*

"[Nor] may the standard governing waivers as expressed in these statements be deflected away by drawing a distinction between initial waivers of *Miranda* rights and subsequent decisions to reinvoke them, on the theory that so long as the burden to demonstrate waiver rests on the government, it is only fair to make the suspect shoulder a burden of showing a clear subsequent assertion. *Miranda* itself discredited the legitimacy of any such distinction. The opinion described the object of the warning as being to assure 'a continuous opportunity to exercise [the right of silence].' '[C]ontinuous opportunity' suggests an unvarying one, governed by a common standard of effectiveness.

4. Social science confirms what common sense would suggest, that individuals who feel intimidated or powerless are more likely to speak in equivocal or nonstandard terms when no ambiguity or equivocation is meant. Suspects in police interrogation are strong candidates for these effects. Even while resort by the police to the "third degree" has abated since *Miranda,* the basic forms of psychological pressure applied by police appear to have changed less. * * *

"[It] is easy, amidst the discussion of layers of protection, to lose sight of a real risk in the majority's approach, going close to the core of what the Court has held that the Fifth Amendment provides. [When] a suspect understands his (expressed) wishes to have been ignored (and by hypothesis, he has said something that an objective listener could 'reasonably,' although not necessarily, take to be a request), in contravention of the 'rights' just read to him by his interrogator, he may well see further objection as futile and confession (true or not) as the only way to end his interrogation. * * *

"Our cases are best respected by a rule that when a suspect under custodial interrogation makes an ambiguous statement that might reasonably be understood as expressing a wish that a lawyer be summoned (and questioning cease), interrogators' questions should be confined to verifying whether the individual meant to ask for a lawyer. While there is reason to expect that trial courts will apply today's ruling sensibly (without requiring criminal suspects to speak with the discrimination of an Oxford don) and that interrogators will continue to follow what the Court rightly calls 'good police practice' (compelled up to now by a substantial body of state and Circuit law), I believe that the case law under *Miranda* does not allow them to do otherwise."

Ascertaining the suspect's choice vs. influencing that choice. Sometimes a police officer will respond to a suspect's ambiguous reference to a lawyer *not* by asking questions designed to clarify the suspect's wishes, but by making statements designed to *convey the message* that the suspect has no need for a lawyer or that obtaining a lawyer will not be in the suspect's best interest. See, e.g., *Mueller v. Commonwealth*, 422 S.E.2d 380 (Va.1992). Mueller waived his *Miranda* rights and agreed to talk to a detective. Two hours into the interrogation, Mueller asked the detective: "Do you think I need an attorney here?" The detective responded by shaking his head slightly, holding his arms out and his palms up in a shrug-like manner, and replying: "You're just talking to us." Several moments later, Mueller confessed to the crime (rape-murder) for which he was later sentenced to death.

The Supreme Court of Virginia held that (a) Mueller's question did not constitute the unambiguous request for counsel needed to invoke the *Edwards* rule and (b) the detective's response did not violate Mueller's *Miranda* rights. But in the brief it filed in the *Davis* case, the United States specifically disapproved of the *Mueller* ruling because the detective's response to Mueller's question conveyed the message that he did not really need a lawyer. Once a suspect has made an ambiguous reference to counsel, observed the United States, the officer's questions "must be objectively neutral and limited to ascertaining, not influencing, the choice that the suspect is entitled to make freely under *Miranda* and *Edwards*." See also *Collazo v. Estelle*, 940 F.2d 411 (9th Cir.1991) (en banc), where a 7–4 majority per Trott, J., emphasized that the police cannot attempt to discourage a suspect from speaking to a lawyer, cannot lead him to think that he can "reap some legal benefit" by excluding a defense lawyer from the process or suggest that somehow he will be "penalized" if he invokes his right to a lawyer.

22. *The Miranda–Edwards–Roberson rule and the Sixth Amendment right to counsel compared and contrasted.* In *Michigan v. Jackson,* 475 U.S. 625 (1986), defendants had waived their rights and agreed to talk to the police without counsel before their "arraignments" (in the setting of the *Jackson* case, this proceeding is often called the "first appearance"). When brought before the magistrate, however, defendants requested that counsel be appointed for them because they were indigent. After the "arraignment" and before defendants had an opportunity to consult with counsel, the police again advised them of their rights, obtained written waivers, questioned them and obtained confessions. The Court, per Stevens, J., agreed with the state supreme court that "the *Edwards* rule 'applies by analogy to those situations where an accused requests counsel before the arraigning magistrate * * *.' [The] reasons for prohibiting the interrogation of an uncounseled prisoner who has asked for the help of a lawyer are even stronger after he has been formally charged with an offense than before." Thus, because the police initiated the questioning, the post-arraignment waivers of Sixth Amendment rights were invalid.

The Court rejected the argument that defendants' requests for appointed counsel may have encompassed only representation at trial and in other formal legal proceedings, not during further questioning by the police: "[The State] has the burden of establishing a valid waiver. Doubts must be resolved in favor of protecting the constitutional claim. This settled approach to questions of waiver requires us to give a broad, rather than a narrow, interpretation to a defendant's request for counsel—we presume that the defendant requests the lawyer's services at every critical stage of the prosecution."[a]

However, in McNEIL v. WISCONSIN, 501 U.S. 171 (1991) (where a suspect asserted his Sixth Amendment right to counsel by his appearance with counsel at a bail hearing concerning an offense with which he had been charged), a 6–3 majority, per SCALIA, J., made it clear that the Sixth Amendment right to counsel provides less protection than does the *Miranda–Edwards–Roberson* rule. Unlike the latter rule, which, when invoked, protects one from police-initiated interrogation with respect to *any* crime, the Sixth Amendment right is "offense-specific." Thus, even though a defendant invokes this right, the police can initiate questioning about crimes *other than* the one with which he was charged.

The case arose as follows: After his arrest for armed robbery McNeil was represented by a public defender at a bail hearing. A short time later, a deputy sheriff visited McNeil in jail. After McNeil waived his *Miranda* rights, the deputy questioned him about a murder and attempted murder *factually unrelated* to the armed robbery with which he had been charged.[b] McNeil's statements were admitted into evidence and he was convicted of murder and attempted murder. The Court, per Scalia, J., rejected his contention that his appearance at the bail hearing for the armed robbery constituted an invocation of the *Miranda–Edwards–Roberson* right to counsel:

"[To] invoke the Sixth Amendment interest is, as a matter of *fact, not* to invoke the *Miranda-Edwards* interest. One might be quite willing to speak to the police without counsel present concerning many matters, but not the matter under prosecution. It can be said, perhaps, that it is *likely* that one who has asked for counsel's assistance in defending against a prosecution would want counsel present for all custodial interrogation, even interrogation unrelated to the charge. [But] even if [that] were true, the *likelihood* that a suspect would wish counsel to be present is not the test for applicability of *Edwards.* [That rule] requires, at a minimum, some statement that can reasonably be construed to be expression of a desire for the assistance of an attorney *in dealing with custodial interrogation by*

a. Dissenting Justice Rehnquist, joined by Powell and O'Connor, JJ., maintained that "the prophylactic rule set forth in *Edwards* makes no sense at all except when linked to the Fifth Amendment's prohibition against compelled self-incrimination." Chief Justice Burger concurred in the judgment, observing that although "stare decisis calls for my following the rule of *Edwards* in the context," "plainly the subject calls for reexamination." For forceful criticism of *Jackson,* see H. Richard Uviller, *Evidence from the Mind of the Criminal Suspect,* 87 Colum.L.Rev. 1137, 1190 (1987).

b. Once the right to counsel attaches to the offense charged, does (should) it also attach to any other offense "closely related to" or "inextricably intertwined with" the particular offense charged? See *Texas v. Cobb*, p. 749.

the police. Requesting the assistance of an attorney at a bail hearing does not bear that construction.

"[Petitioner's] proposed rule [would] seriously impede effective law enforcement. The Sixth Amendment right to counsel attaches at the first formal proceeding against an accused, and in most States, at least with respect to serious offenses, free counsel is made available at that time and ordinarily requested. Thus, if we were to adopt petitioner's rule, most persons in pretrial custody for serious offenses would be *unapproachable* by police officers suspecting them of involvement in other crimes, *even though they have never expressed any unwillingness to be questioned.* Since the ready ability to obtain uncoerced confessions is not an evil but an unmitigated good, society would be the loser."

23. *"Anticipatorily" invoking the Miranda–Edwards–Roberson right to counsel.*

Dissenting in *McNeil* (joined by Marshall and Blackmun, J.J.), Justice Stevens (author of *Michigan v. Jackson*) maintained that *McNeil* "demeans the importance of the right to counsel." But he took comfort in the fact that *McNeil* "probably will have only a slight impact on current custodial interrogation procedures":

"[If] petitioner in this case had made [a] statement indicating that he was invoking his Fifth Amendment right to counsel as well as his Sixth Amendment right to counsel, the entire offense-specific house of cards that the Court has erected today would collapse, pursuant to our holding in *Roberson,* that a defendant who invokes the right to counsel for interrogation on one offense may not be reapproached regarding any offense unless counsel is present. In future preliminary hearings, competent counsel can be expected to make sure that they, or their clients, make a statement on the record that will obviate the consequences of today's holding. That is why I think this decision will have little, if any, practical effect on police practices."

But Justice Scalia replied:

"We have in fact never held that a person can invoke his *Miranda* rights anticipatorily, in a context other than 'custodial interrogation' which a preliminary hearing will not always or even usually involve. [If] the *Miranda* right to counsel can be invoked at a preliminary hearing, it could be argued, there is no logical reason why it could not be invoked by a letter prior to arrest, or indeed even prior to identification as a suspect. Most rights must be asserted when the government seeks to take the action they protect against. The fact that we have allowed the *Miranda* right to counsel, once asserted, to be effective with respect to future custodial interrogation does not necessarily mean that we will allow it to be asserted initially outside the context of custodial interrogation, with similar future effect."

Is Justice Scalia correct? Is even a person taken in to police custody *unable* to assert his *Miranda–Edwards–Roberson* right "in a context other than 'custodial *interrogation*' "? (Emphasis added.) Consider the following *alternative* hypothetical situations:

(1) A murder suspect is arrested in his apartment and told he is being taken to police headquarters where he will be questioned by the lieutenant in charge of the case. He tells the arresting officers: "Before I leave my apartment and go with you, I want to make one thing perfectly clear. When I get to the police station, I'm not talking to the lieutenant or anybody else unless my lawyer is present."

(2) Same facts as above except that the suspect says nothing until he arrives at the police station and is ushered into the office of the lieutenant in charge of the case. At this point, the suspect tells the lieutenant: "Before you ask me

anything, I want you to know that I am well aware that I have a right to a lawyer and I want one at my side before I answer any questions."

(3) Same facts as above except that when the suspect enters the lieutenant's office, the lieutenant tells him: "I'm in charge of this case. I want you to know that I am going to treat you fairly and squarely. As soon as you take off your coat and sit down in that chair next to my desk I am going to advise you fully of your rights." The suspect, who has said nothing to any officer up to this point, remains standing and replies: "Don't bother to read me my rights. I know my rights and I want a lawyer right now. I'm not going to answer a single question without a lawyer being present."

Assume further that in each of these alternative hypothetical situations the lieutenant proceeds to give the suspect the *Miranda* warnings and in each instance the suspect *agrees* to talk to the police about his involvement in the murder when he is advised of his rights. In which instance, if any, has the suspect effectively invoked his *Miranda-Edwards* right to counsel?

The position taken by the lower courts. Relying heavily on footnote 3 to Justice Scalia's opinion in *McNeil*, most courts that have addressed the issue have balked at the notion that *Miranda-Edwards* protections can be triggered anticipatorily. However, they have left open the possibility that a suspect might be able to invoke the *Miranda-Edwards* right to counsel if custodial interrogation is about to begin or is "imminent." See, e.g., *United States v. Wyatt*, 179 F.3d 532 (7th Cir.1999); *United States v. Melgar*, 139 F.3d 1005 (4th Cir.1998); *Alston v. Redman*, 34 F.3d 1237 (3d Cir.1994).

24. *If a suspect has not requested a lawyer but, unbeknownst to him, somebody else has retained one for him, does the failure to inform the suspect that a lawyer is trying to see him vitiate the waiver of his Miranda rights? If the police mislead the attorney about whether her client will be questioned or otherwise deceive an inquiring attorney, should the confession be excluded?*

MORAN v. BURBINE

475 U.S. 412, 106 S.Ct. 1135, 89 L.Ed.2d 410 (1986).

Justice O'CONNOR delivered the opinion of the Court.

After being informed of his rights pursuant to *Miranda* and after executing a series of written waivers, respondent confessed to the murder of a young woman. At no point during the course of the interrogation, which occurred prior to arraignment, did he request an attorney. While he was in police custody, his sister attempted to retain a lawyer to represent him. The attorney telephoned the police station and received assurances that respondent would not be questioned further until the next day. In fact, the interrogation session that yielded the inculpatory statements began later that evening. The question presented is whether either the conduct of the police or respondent's ignorance of the attorney's efforts to reach him taints the validity of the waivers and therefore requires exclusion of the confessions.

[Several months after Mary Jo Hickey was beaten to death in Providence, Rhode Island, respondent Burbine and two others were arrested by Cranston, Rhode Island police for a local burglary. When the other burglary suspects implicated Burbine in Ms. Hickey's murder, a Cranston detective notified the Providence police. An hour later, early in the evening, three Providence officers arrived at Cranston police headquarters to question Burbine about the Providence murder.]

That same evening, at about 7:45 p.m., respondent's sister telephoned the Public Defender's Office to obtain legal assistance for her brother. Her sole concern was the breaking and entering charge, as she was unaware that respondent was then under suspicion for murder. [She tried to contact the attorney who was to represent her brother on the breaking and entering charge, but when unable to do so, wound up talking to another Assistant Public Defender (Ms. Munson) about her brother's situation. At 8:15 p.m. Ms. Munson phoned the Cranston police station, asked that her call be transferred to the detective division, and stated that she would act as Burbine's counsel in the event the police intended to put him in a lineup or question him. An unidentified person told her that neither act would occur and that the police were "through" with Burbine "for the night." Ms. Munson was told neither that the Providence police were at the stationhouse nor that Burbine was a suspect in Ms. Hickey's murder.]

At all relevant times, respondent was unaware of his sister's efforts to retain counsel and of the fact and contents of Ms. Munson's telephone conversation.

Less than an hour later, the police brought respondent to an interrogation room and conducted the first of a series of interviews concerning the murder. Prior to each session, respondent was informed of his *Miranda* rights, and on three separate occasions he signed a written form acknowledging that he understood his right to the presence of an attorney and explicitly indicating that he "[did] not want an attorney called or appointed for [him]" before he gave a statement. [At] least twice during the course of the evening, respondent was left in a room where he had access to a telephone, which he apparently declined to use. Eventually, respondent signed three written statements fully admitting to the murder.

[The trial judge denied respondent's motion to suppress the statements. The jury found respondent guilty of first degree murder. On federal habeas corpus, the First Circuit held that the police conduct had fatally tainted respondent's "otherwise valid" waiver. The U.S. Supreme Court reversed.]

[Applying the *Johnson v. Zerbst*] standard, we have no doubt that respondent validly waived his right to remain silent and to the presence of counsel. [Nonetheless, on federal habeas corpus, the First Circuit] believed that the "[d]eliberate or reckless" conduct of the police, in particular their failure to inform respondent of the telephone call, fatally undermined the validity of the otherwise proper waiver. We find this conclusion untenable as a matter of both logic and precedent.

Events occurring outside of the presence of the suspect and entirely unknown to him surely can have no bearing on the capacity to comprehend and knowingly relinquish a constitutional right. Under the analysis of the Court of Appeals, the same defendant, armed with the same information and confronted with precisely the same police conduct, would have knowingly waived his *Miranda* rights had a lawyer not telephoned the police station to inquire about his status. Nothing in any of our waiver decisions or in our understanding of the essential components of a valid waiver requires so incongruous a result. No doubt the additional information would have been useful to respondent; perhaps even it might have affected his decision to confess. But we have never read the Constitution to require that the police supply a suspect with a flow of information to help him calibrate his self interest in deciding whether to speak or stand by his rights. Once it is determined that a suspect's decision not to rely on his rights was uncoerced, that he at all times knew he could stand mute and request a lawyer, and that he was aware of the state's intention to use his statements to secure a conviction, the analysis is complete and the waiver is valid as a matter of law.

[Nor] do we believe that the level of the police's culpability in failing to inform respondent of the telephone call has any bearing on the validity of the waiver. [Although] highly inappropriate, even deliberate deception of an attorney could not possibly affect a suspect's decision to waive his *Miranda* rights unless he were at least aware of the incident. Nor was the failure to inform respondent of the telephone call the kind of "trick[ery]" that can vitiate the validity of a waiver. *Miranda*. [Because] respondent's voluntary decision to speak was made with full awareness and comprehension of all the information *Miranda* requires the police to convey, the waivers were valid.

* * * Regardless of any issue of waiver, [contends respondent], the Fifth Amendment requires the reversal of a conviction if the police are less than forthright in their dealings with an attorney or if they fail to tell a suspect of a lawyer's unilateral efforts to contact him. Because the proposed modification ignores the underlying purposes of the *Miranda* rules and because we think that the decision as written strikes the proper balance between society's legitimate law enforcement interests and the protection of the defendant's Fifth Amendment rights, we decline the invitation to further extend *Miranda*'s reach.

At the outset, while we share respondent's distaste for the deliberate misleading of an officer of the court, reading *Miranda* to forbid police deception of an *attorney* "would cut [the decision] completely loose from its own explicitly stated rationale."

[The] purpose of the *Miranda* warnings * * * is to dissipate the compulsion inherent in custodial interrogation and, in so doing, guard against abridgement of the suspect's Fifth Amendment rights. Clearly, a rule that focuses on how the police treat an attorney—conduct that has no relevance at all to the degree of compulsion experienced by the defendant during interrogation—would ignore both *Miranda*'s mission and its only source of legitimacy.

Nor are we prepared to adopt a rule requiring that the police inform a suspect of an attorney's efforts to reach him. While such a rule might add marginally to *Miranda*'s goal of dispelling the compulsion inherent in custodial interrogation, overriding practical considerations counsel against its adoption. [We] have little doubt that the approach urged by respondent and endorsed by the Court of Appeals would have the inevitable consequence of muddying *Miranda*'s otherwise relatively clear waters. The legal questions it would spawn are legion: To what extent should the police be held accountable for knowing that the accused has counsel? Is it enough that someone in the station house knows, or must the interrogating officer himself know of counsel's efforts to contact the suspect? Do counsel's efforts to talk to the suspect concerning one criminal investigation trigger the obligation to inform the defendant before interrogation may proceed on a wholly separate matter? We are unwilling to modify *Miranda* in a manner that would so clearly undermine the decision's central "virtue of informing police and prosecutors with specificity [what] they may do in conducting [a] custodial interrogation, and of informing courts under what circumstances statements obtained during such interrogation are not admissible."

[Moreover,] reading *Miranda* to require the police in each instance to inform a suspect of an attorney's efforts to reach him would work a substantial and, we think, inappropriate shift in the subtle balance struck in that decision. Custodial interrogations implicate two competing concerns. On the one hand, "the need for police questioning as a tool for effective enforcement of criminal laws" cannot be doubted. [On] the other hand, the Court has recognized that the interrogation process is "inherently coercive" and that, as a consequence, there exists a substantial risk that the police will inadvertently traverse the fine line between legitimate efforts to elicit admissions and constitutionally impermissible compulsion. *Miranda* attempted to reconcile these opposing concerns by giving the *defendant* the power to exert some control over the course of the interrogation.

Declining to adopt the more extreme position that the actual presence of a lawyer was necessary to dispel the coercion inherent in custodial interrogation, the Court found that the suspect's Fifth Amendment rights could be adequately protected by less intrusive means. Police questioning, often an essential part of the investigatory process, could continue in its traditional form, the Court held, but only if the suspect clearly understood that, at any time, he could bring the proceeding to a halt or, short of that, call in an attorney to give advice and monitor the conduct of his interrogators.

The position urged by respondent would upset this carefully drawn approach in a manner that is both unnecessary for the protection of the Fifth Amendment privilege and injurious to legitimate law enforcement. Because, as *Miranda* holds, full comprehension of the rights to remain silent and request an attorney are sufficient to dispel whatever coercion is inherent in the interrogation process, a rule requiring the police to inform the suspect of an attorney's efforts to contact him would contribute to the protection of the Fifth Amendment privilege only incidentally, if at all. This minimal benefit, however, would come at a substantial cost to society's legitimate and substantial interest in securing admissions of guilt.

[Respondent] also contends that the Sixth Amendment requires exclusion of his three confessions. [The] difficulty for respondent is that the interrogation sessions that yielded the inculpatory statements took place *before* the initiation of "adversary judicial proceedings." He contends, however, that [the] right to noninterference with an attorney's dealings with a [suspect] arises the moment that the relationship is formed, or, at the very least, once the defendant is placed in custodial interrogation.

We are not persuaded. At the outset, subsequent decisions foreclose any reliance on *Escobedo* and *Miranda* for the proposition that the Sixth Amendment right, in any of its manifestations, applies prior to the initiation of adversary judicial proceedings. Although *Escobedo* was originally decided as a Sixth Amendment case, "the Court in retrospect perceived that the 'prime purpose' of *Escobedo* was not to vindicate the constitutional right to counsel as such, but, like *Miranda,* 'to guarantee full effectuation of the privilege against self-incrimination....' " *Kirby v. Illinois* [p. 769]. Clearly then, *Escobedo* provides no support for respondent's argument. Nor, of course, does *Miranda,* the holding of which rested exclusively on the Fifth Amendment.

[Precedent aside,] we find respondent's understanding of the Sixth Amendment both practically and theoretically unsound. As a practical matter, it makes little sense to say that the Sixth Amendment right to counsel attaches at different times depending on the fortuity of whether the suspect or his family happens to have retained counsel prior to interrogation. More importantly, the suggestion that the existence of an attorney-client relationship itself triggers the protections of the Sixth Amendment misconceives the underlying purposes of the right to counsel. The Sixth Amendment's intended function is not to wrap a protective cloak around the attorney-client relationship for its own sake any more than it is to protect a suspect from the consequences of his own candor. [By] its very terms, [the Sixth Amendment] becomes applicable only when the government's role shifts from investigation to accusation. * * *

Finally, respondent contends that the [police treatment of Assistant Public Defender Munson] was so offensive as to deprive him of the fundamental fairness guaranteed by [due process]. We do not question that on facts more egregious than those presented here police deception might rise to a level of a due process violation. Accordingly, Justice Stevens' apocalyptic suggestion that we have approved any and all forms of police misconduct is demonstrably incorrect.[4] We hold

4. [The] dissent's misreading of *Miranda* itself is breathtaking in its scope. For example, it reads *Miranda* as creating an undifferentiated right to the presence of an attorney that is

only that, on these facts, the challenged conduct falls short of the kind of misbehavior that so shocks the sensibilities of civilized society as to warrant a federal intrusion into the criminal processes of the States. * * *

Justice STEVENS, with whom Justice BRENNAN and Justice MARSHALL join, dissenting.

[Until] today, incommunicado questioning has been viewed with the strictest scrutiny by this Court; today, incommunicado questioning is embraced as a societal goal of the highest order that justifies police deception of the shabbiest kind. * * * Police interference with communications between an attorney and his client is a recurrent problem. [The] near-consensus of state courts and the [ABA Standards of Criminal Justice] about this recurrent problem lends powerful support to the conclusion that police may not interfere with communications between an attorney and the client whom they are questioning. Indeed, at least two opinions from this Court seemed to express precisely that view.[20] The Court today flatly rejects that widely held view and [adopts] the most restrictive interpretation of the federal constitutional restraints on police deception, misinformation, and interference in attorney-client communications. * * *

Well-settled principles of law lead inexorably to the conclusion that the failure to inform Burbine of the call from his attorney makes the subsequent waiver of his constitutional rights invalid. Analysis should begin with an acknowledgment that the burden of proving the validity of a waiver of constitutional rights is always on the *government*. When such a waiver occurs in a custodial setting, that burden is an especially heavy one because custodial interrogation is inherently coercive, because disinterested witnesses are seldom available to describe what actually happened, and because history has taught us that the danger of overreaching during incommunicado interrogation is so real. * * *

[*Miranda*] clearly condemns threats or trickery that cause a suspect to make an unwise waiver of his rights even though he fully understands those rights. In my opinion there can be no constitutional distinction—as the Court appears to draw—between a deceptive misstatement and the concealment by the police of the critical fact that an attorney retained by the accused or his family has offered assistance, either by telephone or in person.

[If,] as the Court asserts, "the analysis is at an end" as soon as the suspect is provided with enough information to have the *capacity* to understand and exercise

triggered automatically by the initiation of the interrogation itself. [The] dissent condemns us for embracing "incommunicado questioning [as] a societal goal of the highest order that justifies police deception of the shabbiest kind." We, of course, do nothing of the kind. As any reading of *Miranda* reveals, the decision, rather than proceeding from the premise that the rights and needs of the defendant are paramount to all others, embodies a carefully crafted balance designed to fully protect *both* the defendant's and society's interests. The dissent may not share our view that the Fifth Amendment rights of the defendant are amply protected by application of *Miranda as written.* But the dissent is "simply wrong" in suggesting that exclusion of Burbine's three confessions follows perfunctorily from *Miranda*'s mandate. Y. Kamisar, *Police Interrogation and Confessions* 217–218, n. 94 (1980).

Quite understandably, the dissent is outraged by the very idea of police deception of a lawyer. Significantly less understandable is its willingness to misconstrue this Court's constitutional holdings in order to implement its subjective notions of sound policy.

20. See *Miranda* at n. 35 (in *Escobedo,* "[t]he police also prevented the attorney from consulting with his client. Independent of any other constitutional proscription, this action constitutes a violation of the Sixth Amendment right to the assistance of counsel and excludes any statement obtained in its wake"); *Escobedo* ("[I]t 'would be highly incongruous if our system of justice permitted the district attorney, the lawyer representing the State, to extract a confession from the accused while his own lawyer, seeking to speak with him, was kept from him by the police' ").

his rights, I see no reason why the police should not be permitted to make the same kind of misstatements to the suspect that they are apparently allowed to make to his lawyer. *Miranda,* however, clearly establishes that both kinds of deception vitiate the suspect's waiver of his right to counsel.

[In] short, settled principles about construing waivers of constitutional rights and about the need for strict presumptions in custodial interrogations, as well as a plain reading of the *Miranda* opinion itself, overwhelmingly support the conclusion reached by almost every state court that has considered the matter—a suspect's waiver of his right to counsel is invalid if police refuse to inform the suspect of his counsel's communications.

The Court makes the alternative argument that requiring police to inform a suspect of his attorney's communications to and about him is not required because it would upset the careful "balance" of *Miranda.* [The] Court's balancing approach is profoundly misguided. The cost of suppressing evidence of guilt will always make the value of a procedural safeguard appear "minimal," "marginal," or "incremental." [The] individual interest in procedural safeguards that minimize the risk of error is easily discounted when the fact of guilt appears certain beyond doubt.

What is the cost of requiring the police to inform a suspect of his attorney's call? It would decrease the likelihood that custodial interrogation will enable the police to obtain a confession. This is certainly a real cost, but it is the same cost that this Court has repeatedly found necessary to preserve the character of our free society and our rejection of an inquisitorial system. [At] the time attorney Munson made her call to the Cranston Police Station, she was acting as Burbine's attorney. Under ordinary principles of agency law the deliberate deception of Munson was tantamount to deliberate deception of her client.

[In] my view, as a matter of law, the police deception of Munson was tantamount to deception of Burbine himself. It constituted a violation of Burbine's right to have an attorney present during the questioning that began shortly thereafter.

[The] possible reach of the Court's opinion is stunning. For the majority seems to suggest that police may deny counsel all access to a client who is being held. At least since *Escobedo,* it has been widely accepted that police may not simply deny attorneys access to their clients who are in custody. This view has survived the recasting of *Escobedo* from a Sixth Amendment to a Fifth Amendment case that the majority finds so critically important. That this prevailing view is shared *by the police* can be seen in the state court opinions detailing various forms of police deception of attorneys. For, if there were no obligation to give attorneys access, there would be no need to take elaborate steps to avoid access, such as shuttling the suspect to a different location, or taking the lawyer to different locations; police could simply refuse to allow the attorneys to see the suspects. But the law enforcement profession has apparently believed, quite rightly in my view, that denying lawyers access to their clients is impermissible.

[In] my judgment, police interference in the attorney-client relationship is the type of governmental misconduct on a matter of central importance to the administration of justice that the Due Process Clause prohibits. Just as the police cannot impliedly promise a suspect that his silence will not be used against him and then proceed to break that promise, so too police cannot tell a suspect's attorney that they will not question the suspect and then proceed to question him. Just as the government cannot conceal from a suspect material and exculpatory evidence, so too the government cannot conceal from a suspect the material fact of his attorney's communication.

[This] case turns on a proper appraisal of the role of the lawyer in our society. If a lawyer is seen as a nettlesome obstacle to the pursuit of wrongdoers—as in an inquisitorial society—then the Court's decision today makes a good deal of sense. If a lawyer is seen as an aid to the understanding and protection of constitutional rights—as in an accusatorial society—then today's decision makes no sense at all. * * *

Notes and Questions

(a) *"Incommunicado questioning."* What exactly is meant by "incommunicado" or "incommunicado questioning" (terms used frequently by dissenting Justice Stevens)? These terms may mean either (1) preventing a prisoner from communicating with or meeting with counsel; or (2) not informing the outside world of the prisoner's whereabouts; or (3) denying a prisoner's friends, relatives or lawyers access to him. In which sense, if any, was Burbine held "incommunicado"?

(b) *The Miranda warnings and the need for a lawyer's advice.* Consider Note, 100 Harv.L.Rev. 125, 133 (1986): "[T]o the extent that the population at large is unaware of its fifth and sixth amendment rights, the role of the lawyer—possibly the only one capable of safeguarding these rights—must be protected." Is *a suspect advised of his rights* (as opposed to "the population at large") unaware of his rights? If a lawyer is "the only one capable of safeguarding these rights," did the *Miranda* Court commit grievous error by not requiring that a suspect first consult with a lawyer or actually have a lawyer present in order for his waiver of rights to be effective?

(c) *The Burbine dissent's reliance on fn. 35 to Miranda.* In fn. 20 to his dissenting opinion, Justice Stevens maintains that the majority opinion cannot be reconciled with fn. 35 to *Miranda,* which, discussing *Escobedo,* states that "prevent[ing] [an] attorney from consulting with his client" violates the Sixth Amendment "independent of any other constitutional proscription." Should this statement be read in light of *Escobedo*'s particular facts? Consider Kamisar, Essays 217 n. 94 (1980):

"It is hard to believe that in the course of writing a 60–page opinion *based on the premise* that police-issued warnings can adequately protect a suspect's rights the [*Miranda*] Court would say in the next breath that such warnings are insufficient when, but only when, a suspect's lawyer is not allowed to consult with him—that even though a suspect has been emphatically and unequivocally advised of his rights and insists on talking, what he says is inadmissible [when] a lawyer *whose services he has not requested* has, *unbeknown to him,* entered the picture.

"Although the police did not advise Escobedo of any of his rights, 'he repeatedly asked to speak to his lawyer.' * * * Indeed, [the *Escobedo*] opinion begins: 'The critical issue in this case is whether [the] refusal by the police to honor petitioner's request to consult with his lawyer during the course of an interrogation constitutes a denial of "the Assistance of Counsel." '[If the refusal of the police to let Escobedo's lawyer meet with him] has any relevance, it is only because Escobedo became *aware of the fact* that the police were preventing his lawyer from talking to him, and this realization may well have underscored the police domination of the situation and the gravity of his plight."

(d) *Should Burbine dishearten or encourage Miranda's defenders?* Consider Kamisar, *The "Police Practice" Phases of the Criminal Process and the Three Phases of the Burger Court,* in The Burger Years (Herman Schwartz ed. 1987) at 143, 150: "[The *Burbine* Court's view of *Miranda* as not 'proceeding from the premise that the rights and needs of the defendant are paramount to all others, [but as a case that] embodies a carefully crafted balance designed to fully protect *both* the defendant's and society's interests'] [see fn. 4 to the Court's opinion] is the way *Miranda*'s defenders—not its critics—have talked about the case for the past twenty years. [The *Burbine* Court's view of *Miranda* as a serious effort to strike a proper 'balance,' between, or to 'reconcile,' competing interests may turn out to be more important than its specific ruling." See also Kamisar, *Remembering the "Old World" of Criminal Procedure: A Reply to Professor Grano,* 23 U.Mich.J.L.Ref. 537, 575–84 (1990).

(e) *What result if, before being taken away by the police, a suspect asks a relative to contact a lawyer*? Would the result in *Burbine* have been different if, before being taken to the police station (a) the defendant had asked his sister to contact the Public Defender's Office and get somebody in the office to represent him; (b) his sister had done so; (c) the assistant public defender who had agreed to represent defendant had told the police she wanted to meet with her client immediately; but (d) the police had failed to inform defendant of this development? Why (not)? Cf. *People v. Griggs*, 604 N.E.2d 257 (Ill.1992).

(f) *Reaction of the state courts*. Can a person fully comprehend the nature of his right to counsel and the consequences of a decision to waive this right without being informed that a lawyer, who could explain the consequences of a waiver, has been retained to represent him and is immediately able to consult with him? Relying on independent state grounds, a number of state courts have answered in the negative, thereby rejecting the U.S. Supreme Court's reasoning in *Burbine*. See *State v. Stoddard*, 537 A.2d 446 (Conn.1988); *Haliburton v. State*, 514 So.2d 1088 (Fla.1987); *People v. McCauley*, 645 N.E.2d 923 (Ill.1994); *People v. Bender*, 551 N.W.2d 71 (Mich.1996); *People v. McCauley*, 645 N.E.2d 923 (Ill.1994).

25. *When U.S. law enforcement officers subject non-American citizens abroad to custodial interrogation, must they "Mirandize" them?* Consider UNITED STATES v. BIN LADEN, 132 F.Supp.2d 168 (S.D.N.Y.2001), which involved the interrogation of two defendants who were charged with participating in the bombings of American embassies in Kenya and East Africa. Judge SAND was "not dissuaded from applying *Miranda* to overseas interrogations conducted by U.S. law enforcement, even if the interrogational target is in the physical custody of foreign authorities." He thought it "uncontroversial" that American agents must tell such interrogational targets that they have the right to remain silent and that anything they say may be used against them in a court in the United States or elsewhere.

As for the right to the assistance and presence of counsel, "if the particular overseas context actually presents *no* obvious hurdle to the implementation of [that right], due care should be taken not to foreclose an opportunity that in fact exists." The court then found the advice of rights form (AOR) used by American agents abroad "facially deficient" in its failure to apprise defendants of their right to counsel under *Miranda*. (Since the deficient AOR was used to apprise defendant Al-'Owhali of his rights for the first five interrogation sessions, all statements elicited during these sessions were suppressed). The AOR contained the following three sentences:

"In the United States, you would have the right to talk to a lawyer to get advice before we ask you any questions and you could have a lawyer with you during questioning. In the United States, if you could not afford a lawyer, one would be appointed for you, if you wish, before any questioning. Because we are not in the United States, we cannot ensure that you will have a lawyer appointed for you before any questioning."

"[S]tanding alone," observed Judge Sand, "[these] three sentences * * * wrongly convey to a suspect that, due to his custodial situs outside the United States, he currently possesses no opportunity to avail himself of the services of any attorney before or during questioning by U.S. officials. The AOR as is, prematurely forecloses the significant possibility that foreign authorities themselves may, if asked, either supply counsel at public expense or permit retained counsel inside the stationhouse. [The] AOR is flawed in its message that, despite being interrogated by U.S. law enforcement, defendants only had a right to the assistance and presence of counsel if they were physically inside the United States. We find this to be an inaccurate representation of what truly was available [under] South African and (to a lesser extent) Kenyan law. [The] right to counsel was made to seem dependent on geography, when instead it actually hinged on foreign law."

For strong criticism of the *Bin Laden* court's application of *Miranda* to overseas interrogations, see Mark A. Godsey, *Miranda's Final Frontier—The International Arena: A Critical Analysis of United States v. Bin Laden and a Proposal for a New Miranda Exception Abroad*, 51 Duke L.J. 1703, 1773–76 (2002):

26. *Use of a pretrial psychiatric examination at a capital sentencing proceeding.* ESTELLE v. SMITH, 451 U.S. 454 (1981), arose as follows: Respondent was indicted for murder in Texas. The state announced its intention to seek the death penalty. Thereafter, although defense counsel had not put into issue his client's competency to stand trial or his sanity at the time of the offense, a judge informally ordered the prosecution to arrange a psychiatric examination of respondent by Dr. Grigson to determine respondent's capacity to stand trial. After respondent was convicted of murder, the doctor also testified—on the basis of his pretrial examination of respondent—as to respondent's "future dangerousness," one of the critical issues to be resolved by a Texas jury at the capital sentencing proceeding. The jury answered the "future dangerousness" question and other requisite questions in the affirmative and, thus, under Texas law, the death penalty for respondent was mandatory.

Although respondent had not been warned before the pretrial psychiatric examination that anything he said during the examination could be used against him at the sentencing proceeding, the state argued that the privilege against self-incrimination was inapplicable because (a) Dr. Grigson's testimony was used only to determine punishment after conviction, not to establish guilt; and (b) respondent's communications to Dr. Grigson were "nontestimonial" in nature. Rejecting these contentions, the Court held, per BURGER, C.J., that both respondent's Fifth and Sixth Amendment rights were violated by the use of Dr. Grigson's testimony at the penalty phase of the case:

"Just as the Fifth Amendment prevents a criminal defendant from being made 'the deluded instrument of his own conviction,' it protects him as well from being made the 'deluded instrument' of his own execution." As for the argument that respondent's communications to the examining psychiatrist were "nontestimonial" in nature, "Dr. Grigson's prognosis as to future dangerousness rested on statements respondent made and remarks he omitted in reciting the details of the crime. [Thus,] the State used as evidence against respondent the substance of his disclosures during the pretrial psychiatric examination."[a]

a. Because respondent had been indicted and assigned counsel before Dr. Grigson examined him and the examination had taken place without notice to respondent's counsel, Stewart, J., joined by Powell, J., concurred in the judgment on *Massiah* grounds without reaching the *Miranda* issue. Although he dissented, in effect, on the *Miranda* issue, Rehnquist, J., also concurred in the result of *Massiah* grounds. Thus, the Court's judgment that respondent's Sixth Amendment right to counsel had been violated was unanimous.

See also *Powell v. Texas,* 492 U.S. 680 (1989) (that defendant raised insanity defense "no basis for concluding" he waived Sixth Amendment right to counsel set out in *Estelle*).

27. *Miranda and mentally retarded suspects: The Cloud–Shepherd–Barkoff–Shur study.* The results of an empirical study, Morgan Cloud, George B. Shepherd, Alison Nodwin Barkoff and Justin V. Shur, *Words Without Meaning: The Constitution, Confessions, and Mentally Retarded Suspects*, 69 U. Chi. L.Rev. 495 (2002) (hereinafter called the Cloud study) "indicate that mentally retarded people simply do not understand the *Miranda* warnings. Virtually all of the disabled subjects failed to understand the context in which the interrogation occurs, the legal consequences embedded in the rules or the significance of confessing, the meaning of the sentences that comprise the warnings, or even the individual operative words used to construct the warnings.[a] In contrast, comparably large percentages of the non-disabled control group did understand the individual words, the complete warnings, and their legal significance."

The results of the Cloud study support two additional conclusions about the validity of confessions obtained from mentally retarded suspects:

First, "the number of people to whom the *Miranda* warnings are meaningless [appears to be] much larger than previously acknowledged within the criminal justice system. [The warnings] also are incomprehensible to people whose mental retardation is classified as mild, as well as some people whose 'intelligence quotient' (IQ) scores exceed 70, the number typically used to demarcate mental retardation."

Second, the study raises "disquieting questions" about the capacity of current doctrine to "accommodate the special problems accompanying police interrogation of mentally retarded suspects": "When confronted with challenges to the validity of a mentally retarded suspect's waiver of the *Miranda* 'rights,' courts typically revert to a 'totality of the circumstances' analysis to determine whether the suspect was capable of understanding the *Miranda* warnings." But the results of the study "suggest that the 'totalities' analysis ... is incapable of identifying suspects competent to understand the *Miranda* warnings.... Multiple regression analysis demonstrates that variations in age, education and experience with the criminal justice system or the *Miranda* warnings do not compensate for a mentally retarded person's inability to comprehend the *Miranda* warnings. If mental retardation is present, then the disabled person will not understand the warnings, regardless of the presence of the other factors."

Another serious problem posed by mentally retarded persons' confessions is that it now seems indisputable that "mentally retarded suspects are likely to confess falsely, that is confess to crimes they did not commit, far more frequently than do suspects of average and above average intelligence. Similarly, interrogation tactics generally believed to be acceptable with most suspects are more likely to produce false confessions from mentally retarded suspects."[b]

What is the solution? Should the courts take the position that *any* confession from a mentally retarded suspect is inadmissible in a criminal case? Should law enforcement officers be required to administer simplified warnings? Are the mentally retarded likely to understand warnings containing simplified synonyms

a. According to the authors of the study, "the best available data suggests that at least forty-five thousand, and perhaps more than two hundred thousand mentally retarded people currently are imprisoned in the United States. Undoubtedly, these people have been arrested. Many, probably most, have been 'Mirandized' and interrogated while in custody. Some have waived their rights and made statements to investigators."

b. "By some estimates," points out the study, "as many as 20 percent of the people on death row are mentally retarded, and death penalty opponents contend that at least three dozen mentally retarded people have been executed in the quarter century since the death penalty was reinstated."

The authors of the study ask: Should the Constitution permit a retarded person to be convicted on the basis of his confession?

for difficult words in the *Miranda* warnings much better than they do the original vocabulary of the warnings? See Part V. of the Cloud study.[c]

28. *Comparing and contrasting Miranda with (a) the prohibition against the use of involuntary or compelled statements and (b) the Fourth Amendment exclusionary rule.* In *Stone v. Powell* (p. 225), the Court held that when a state has provided a full and fair chance to litigate a Fourth Amendment claim, federal habeas review is not available to a state prisoner claiming that his conviction rests on evidence obtained through an unconstitutional search or seizure. However, in WITHROW v. WILLIAMS, 507 U.S. 680 (1993), a 5–4 majority per SOUTER, J., held that *Stone* "does not extend to a state prisoner's claim that his conviction rests on statements obtained in violation [of] *Miranda*":

"[The *Miranda* Court] acknowledged that, in barring introduction of a statement obtained without the required warnings, *Miranda* might exclude a confession that we would not condemn as 'involuntary in traditional terms,' and for this reason we have sometimes called the *Miranda* safeguards 'prophylactic' in nature. * * * Calling the *Miranda* safeguards 'prophylactic,' however, is a far cry from putting *Miranda* on all fours with *Mapp,* or from rendering *Miranda* subject to *Stone.*

"As we explained in *Stone,* the *Mapp* rule 'is not a personal constitutional right,' but serves to deter future constitutional violations; although it mitigates the juridical consequences of invading the defendant's privacy, the exclusion of evidence at trial can do nothing to remedy the completed and wholly extrajudicial Fourth Amendment violation. Nor can the *Mapp* rule be thought to enhance the soundness of the criminal process by improving the reliability of evidence introduced at trial. *Miranda* differs from *Mapp* in both respects. 'Prophylactic' though it may be, in protecting a defendant's Fifth Amendment privilege against self-incrimination *Miranda* safeguards 'a fundamental *trial* right.' [The privilege] reflects 'many of our fundamental values and most noble aspirations' [quoting *Murphy v. Waterfront Comm'n,* pp. 840, 849]. Nor does the Fifth Amendment 'trial right' protected by *Miranda* serve some value necessarily divorced from the correct ascertainment of guilt. [By] bracing against 'the possibility of unreliable statements in every instance of in-custody interrogation,' *Miranda* serves to guard against 'the use of unreliable statements at trial.'

"Finally, and most importantly, eliminating review of *Miranda* claims would not significantly benefit the federal courts in their exercise of habeas jurisdiction, or advance the cause of federalism in any substantial way. [For it] would not prevent a state prisoner from simply converting his barred *Miranda* claim into a due process claim that his conviction rested on an involuntary confession. If that is so, the federal courts would certainly not have heard the last of *Miranda* on collateral review. Under the due process approach, [courts] look to the totality of circumstances to determine whether a confession was voluntary. Those potential circumstances include [the] failure of police to advise the defendant of his rights to remain silent and to have counsel present during custodial interrogation. * * * We could lock the front door against *Miranda,* but not the back.

"We thus fail to see how abdicating *Miranda*'s bright-line (or, at least, brighter-line) rules in favor of an exhaustive totality-of-circumstances approach on

c. See also the recent report by Samuel R. Gross et al, quoted at p. 757: "[A study of exonerations of defendants convicted of serious crimes in the United States since 1989 discloses that] [f]alse confessions * * * played a large role in the murder convictions that led to exonerations, primarily among two particularly vulnerable groups of innocent defendants: juveniles, and those who are mentally retarded or mentally ill. Almost all the juvenile exonerees who falsely confessed are African American. In fact, one of our most startling findings is that 90% of all exonerated juvenile defendants are black or Hispanic, an extreme disparity that, sadly, is of a piece with racial disparities in our juvenile justice system in general."

habeas would do much of anything to lighten the burdens placed on busy federal courts."

Justice O'CONNOR, with whom The Chief Justice joined, dissented "because the principles that inform our habeas jurisprudence—finality, federalism, and fairness—counsel decisively against the result the Court reaches * * *. Like the suppression of the fruits of an illegal search or seizure, the exclusion of statements obtained in violation of *Miranda* is not constitutionally required. This Court repeatedly has held that *Miranda*'s warning requirement is not a dictate of the Fifth Amendment itself, but a prophylactic rule. [Unlike] involuntary or compelled statements—which are of dubious reliability and are therefore inadmissible for any purpose—confessions obtained in violation of *Miranda* are not necessarily untrustworthy. In fact, because *voluntary* statements are 'trustworthy' even when obtained without proper warnings, their suppression actually *impairs* the pursuit of truth by concealing probative information from the trier of fact." Justice O'Connor continued:

"[The] consideration the Court identifies as being 'most importan[t]' of all, is an entirely pragmatic one. Specifically, the Court 'project[s]' that excluding *Miranda* questions from habeas will not significantly promote efficiency or federalism because some *Miranda* issues are relevant to a statement's voluntariness. It is true that barring *Miranda* claims from habeas poses no barrier to the adjudication of voluntariness questions. But that does not make it 'reasonable to suppose that virtually all *Miranda* claims [will] simply be recast' and litigated as voluntariness claims. [A] *Miranda* claim [requires] no evidence of police overreaching whatsoever; it is enough that law enforcement officers commit a technical error. Even the forgetful failure to issue warnings to the most wary, knowledgeable, and seasoned of criminals will do. [If, as the Court maintains,] the police have truly grown in 'constitutional * * * sophistication,' then certainly it is reasonable to suppose that most technical errors in the administration of *Miranda*'s warnings are just that."

In a separate dissent, Justice SCALIA, joined by THOMAS, J., maintained:

"The issue in this case—whether the extraordinary remedy of federal habeas corpus should routinely be available for claimed violations of *Miranda* rights—involves not *jurisdiction* to issue the writ, but the *equity* of doing so. In my view, both the Court and Justice O'Connor disregard the most powerful equitable consideration: that Williams has already had full and fair opportunity to litigate this claim. [The] question at this stage is whether [a] federal habeas court should now reopen the issue and adjudicate the *Miranda* claim anew. The answer seems to me obvious: it should not. That would be the course followed by a federal habeas court reviewing a *federal* conviction; it mocks our federal system to accord state convictions less respect. * * * Prior opportunity to litigate an issue should be an important equitable consideration in *any* habeas case, and should ordinarily preclude the court from reaching the merits of a claim, unless it goes to the fairness of the trial process or to the accuracy of the ultimate result."

Notes and Questions

(a) *Does Withrow affirm that the Miranda rule contains a constitutional command?* "If the Court had viewed *Miranda* as truly non-constitutional," comments Charles D. Weisselberg, *Saving Miranda*, 84 Cornell L.Rev. 109, 130–31 (1998), "then it had little reason to refuse *Withrow*'s invitation to take mere *Miranda* violations out of federal habeas corpus. The Court in *Withrow* thus kept the universe of *Miranda* claims within the Constitution."

(b) *Do Fifth Amendment violations occur only at trial? Withrow* talks about "the Fifth Amendment 'trial right'" and about "*Miranda* safeguard[ing] 'a fundamental *trial* right.'" However, Weisselberg, supra at 180, observes that "a number of cases have found Fifth Amendment violations in circumstances in which witnesses suffered penalties for asserting the privilege against self-incrimination, even though they faced no criminal charges and had no criminal trial." [He refers to such cases as *Lefkowitz v. Cunningham*, 431 U.S. 801 (1977), holding that a grand jury witness cannot be divested of political office as a penalty for exercising his Fifth Amendment privilege; and *Gardner v. Broderick*, 392 U.S. 273 (1968), holding that a police officer cannot lose his job for asserting the privilege before a grand jury.] These cases are impossible to square with the notion that Fifth Amendment violations occur only at trial. But see *Chavez v. Martinez*, p. 695.

29. *Other Miranda problems discussed elsewhere in the book.* Is *Miranda*'s prohibition against police trickery and deception confined to their use in obtaining a waiver of rights or does it also bar such tactics *after* a person has validly waived his rights? See the next section.

If a defendant takes the stand in his own defense, may the prosecution impeach him by using statements obtained from him in violation of *Miranda*? See p. 922. May a defendant's *prior silence,* even his *post* arrest silence, be used to impeach his credibility when he chooses to testify at his trial? See 932–33.

Suppose, after a suspect is illegally arrested, he is advised of his rights, waives them, and confesses? Do the *Miranda* warnings "cure" the illegality of the arrest? See p. 908.

Suppose, an hour after the police obtain an incriminating statement from a suspect in violation of the *Miranda* rules, they give him the complete warnings and the suspect waives his rights and confesses? Is the "second confession" admissible or is it "the fruit" of the first inadmissible statement? See *Missouri v. Seibert*, p. 707. Suppose, as the result of a statement obtained in violation of the *Miranda* rules, the police find the murder weapon. Is the murder weapon admissible? Or is it the "fruit of the poisonous tree"? See *United States v. Patane*, p. 703.

THE IMPACT OF *MIRANDA* IN PRACTICE

In 1988, a special committee of the ABA's Criminal Justice Section—Special Committee on Criminal Justice in a Free Society, *Criminal Justice in Crisis* 28 (1988)—reported that "a very strong majority of those surveyed—prosecutors, judges, and police officers—agree that compliance with *Miranda* does not present serious problems for law enforcement." This report, taken together with many earlier empirical studies indicating that *Miranda* posed no significant barrier to effective law enforcement, appeared to be, as the ABA Special Committee put it, "a strong repudiation of the claim that law enforcement would be greatly improved if *Miranda* were repealed or overruled."

However, in *Miranda's Social Costs: An Empirical Reassessment*, 90 Nw. U.L.Rev. 387 (1996), Professor Paul G. Cassell attacked the general consensus, contending that despite the "conventional academic wisdom" to the contrary, "*Miranda* has significantly harmed law enforcement efforts in this country." Stephen J. Schulhofer, *Miranda's Practical Effect: Substantial Benefits and Vanishingly Small Social Costs*, 90 N.W.U.L.Rev. 500 (1996), sharply disputed Professor Cassell's statistics and emphasized that "even if we can assume that the studies [Cassell relies on] give a reliable picture of *Miranda*'s costs thirty years ago, there is strong reason to believe that such costs were transitory and that confession rates have since rebounded from any temporary decline."[a]

In his rejoinder, *All Benefits, No Costs: The Grand Illusion of Miranda's Defenders*, 90 Nw.U.L.Rev. 1084 (1996), Professor Cassell maintained that both clearance rate data and confession rate data demonstrate that "over the long haul, law enforcement never recovered from the blow inflicted by *Miranda*." Cassell relied, inter alia, on a 1994 study of police interrogation in Salt Lake City that he co-authored, Cassell & Bret Hayman, *Police Interrogation in the 1990s: An Empirical Study of the Effects of Miranda*, 43 UCLA L.Rev. 839 (1996). According to Schulhofer, supra, however the Salt Lake County study's low confession rate *includes* non-custodial interrogations (although the best reading of the pre-*Miranda* studies is that they involved only custodial interrogation) and *excludes* cases in which the suspect gave "denials with explanation" although a substantial number of such "denials" probably should have been classified as incriminating statements.

George C. Thomas III, *Plain Talk about the Miranda Empirical Debate: A "Steady–State" Theory of Confessions*, 43 U.C.L.A. L.Rev. 933 (1996), criticized the Cassell–Hayman study on grounds similar to Schulhofer's. Moreover, observed Professor Thomas: "Cassell and Hayman conclude that 12.1% of felony suspects 'who were questioned invoked their rights before police were successful in interrogation.' [If] the *Miranda* dissenters and the police in 1966 had been told that the effect of *Miranda* would be limited to 12.1% of felony suspects, they would have cheered in relief. Thus, while significant, 12.1% is hardly crippling to the law-enforcement enterprise."

Continued Thomas: "[The] available data [seems] to demonstrate that more suspects invoke their [rights] and the rate of confessions is roughly the same. This divergence supports my steady-state theory: *Miranda* encourages some suspects not to talk and encourages other to talk too much. It is possible that, in the pre-*Miranda* era, fewer suspects refused to talk but more suspects gave terse answers. Perhaps more suspects refuse to talk today, but those who do talk have a *Miranda*-created incentive to tell a fuller story."

In 1997, the Cassell–Schulhofer debate continued in the pages of another law journal. As evidence of Miranda's harmful effects, Professor Cassell noted that in 1965 the clearance rate for violent crime [stood] at nearly 60 percent—only to plunge more than twelve percentage points in the next three years. See Paul G. Cassell, *Miranda's "Negligible" Effect on Law Enforcement: Some Skeptical Observations*, 20 Harv.J.L.Pub.Pol'y 327, 333–35 (1997). Professor Schulhofer responded that clearance capacity (the number of officers and dollars available to investigate each reported crime) collapsed in the late 1960s as crime rose sharply and that the dramatic reduction in clearance *capacity* provides "the most likely explanation" for the significant decline in the clearance *rates* that occurred at the same time. See Schulhofer, *Bashing Miranda is Unjustified—and Harmful*, 20 Harv.J.L.Pub.Pol'y 347, 357–62 (1997).

At this point, another law professor joined the debate, Peter Arenella, *Miranda Stories*, 20 Harv.J.L.Pub.Pol'y 375 (1997), observing: "Neither the 'conservative' nor the 'liberal' tale provides a fully plausible account of *Miranda*'s impact on our criminal justice system because both stories commit the same fundamental error: exaggerating either *Miranda*'s costs (Cassell) or benefits (Schulhofer). Moreover, each story generates an obvious question that neither author answers persuasively. If Cassell's account is accurate, why have the police

a. Professor Cassell's article and Professor Schulhofer's response, as well as other articles on *Miranda*'s impact in the police station by Richard A. Leo, George C. Thomas III, and Cassell and Bret S. Hayman are reprinted in large part in Richard A. Leo & George C. Thomas III, *The Miranda Debate* (1998).

and a conservative Supreme Court shown no interest in eliminating the *Miranda* regime? Conversely, if Schulhofer is right (and I believe he is) that the *Miranda* regime has not impaired law enforcement's ability to secure incriminating admissions, how exactly does *Miranda*'s negligible impact demonstrate its success in eliminating the 'inherent coerciveness' of police interrogation?"

In 1998, a new critic of Cassell's work, Professor John J. Donohue III, entered the fray. He took issue with a new empirical study co-authored by Cassell and Richard Fowles, *Handcuffing the Cops? A Thirty–Year Perspective on Miranda's Harmful Effects on Law Enforcement*, 50 Stan.L.Rev. 1055 (1998), a study maintaining that *Miranda* has had a significantly adverse and long-term effect on clearance rates for both violent and property crimes. According to Donohue, *Did Miranda Diminish Police Effectiveness?*, 50 Stan.L.Rev. 1147 (1998), the Cassell–Fowles study showed no significant relationship between *Miranda* and the clearance rate for murder—the most accurately reported crime. Donohue suggests that *Miranda*'s only real impact upon clearance rates may be that it prevents the police from obtaining information from custodial suspects about crimes other than the one(s) for which the suspects have been arrested.

Finally, consider George C. Thomas III, *Stories about Miranda*, 102 Mich. L.Rev. 1959 (2004). After studying more than 200 court opinions drawn from Westlaw, Professor Thomas concludes, id. at 1998–2000:

"Suspects usually waive their rights and talk to the police, and defendants almost always lose their motions to suppress statements. Many suspects talk, not because police are skilled or calculating, but because at some level they *want* to talk to police. They *want* to tell their story because they think they can skillfully navigate the shoals of police interrogation and arrive safely on the other shore. If this is the right way to view most (not all) suspects, then the Court has for many decades had the wrong 'picture' of police interrogation....

"[The] larger implication of my study is a cautionary note for law reformers who think the law can change behavior in ways that suit the reformers. Laws can change behavior, to be sure, but only when it changes the balance of incentives and thus makes the actor choose a different course because she perceives it to be better than any other course. As long as suspects think they are better off trying to persuade police that they are not guilty, they will continue to talk to police. *Miranda* provides knowledge that it *might* not be in a suspect's best interests to talk to police. But this knowledge is meaningless as long as suspects are willing to take the chance that it *is* in their best interests to talk. As that calculation is based on a suspect's entire life telling stories, the *Miranda* Court was naïve if it thought that a set of formal warnings could change story-telling behavior. My study suggests that warnings do not change suspect behavior in any significant way."

Is it possible that Chief Justice Warren would *not* have been surprised by the result of Professor Thomas's study? Before becoming Governor of California, Warren had spent his entire professional life as a prosecuting attorney and state attorney general. He may have been the only Justice who ever interrogated murder suspects. He must have known a great deal about the dynamics of police interrogation and suspect behavior. See Kamisar, *How Earl Warren's 22 Years in Law Enforcement Affected His Work as Chief Justice* (forthcoming Ohio State J. Crim.L.).

HOW TO GET PEOPLE TO CONFESS IN THE POST-*MIRANDA* WORLD: HAVE MODERN POLICE INTERROGATORS "ADAPTED" TO *MIRANDA* OR ARE THEY VIOLATING IT?

In 1988, after persuading the Baltimore police department to grant him unlimited access to the city's homicide unit for a full year, David Simon, a *Baltimore Sun* reporter, took a leave of absence from the *Sun* and followed one shift of detectives as they traveled from interrogations to autopsies and from crime scenes to hospital emergency rooms. Simon's 1991 book, *Homicide: A Year on the Killing Streets*, was the result. In an author's note, Simon tells us that *Homicide* is a "work of journalism" and that the events he has written about "occurred in the manner described."

How, despite the seemingly formidable obstacle of *Miranda*, do the Baltimore police manage to get so many suspects to incriminate themselves? According to Simon (see pp. 194–207 of his book), the following, or something close to it, occurs:

(1) The detective produces an "Explanation of Rights" sheet, reads the warnings one at a time and when the suspect responds that he understands them, gets the suspect to initial each warning.

(2) Next, the detective gets the suspect to sign his name just below a sentence that reads: "I have read the explanation of my rights and fully understand it."

(3) At this point—and before the suspect is asked whether he wants to waive his rights and talk about the case—the detective assures the suspect that he will honor his rights if he invokes them, but in the next breath warns him that asserting his rights would make matters worse for him. For it would prevent his friend, the detective, from writing up the case as manslaughter or perhaps even self-defense, rather than first degree murder. The detective emphasizes that he is affording the suspect the opportunity to tell his side of the story (Did the man you stabbed come at you? Was it self-defense?), "but once you up and call for that lawyer, son, we can't do a damn thing for you . . . Now's the time to speak up . . . because once I walk out of this room any chance you have of telling your side of the story is gone."

(4) In a typical case, the detective also tells the suspect (falsely) that the evidence against him is overwhelming, and the only reason he is interested in hearing the suspect's version of what happened is "to make sure that there ain't nothing you can say for yourself before I write it all up" (as murder in the first degree).

(5) The suspect cautiously indicates a willingness to talk about the case or at least to consider talking about it. The suspect also indicates that he likes the suggestion that the slain man had "come at him." The detective smiles inwardly. He has given the suspect "the Out" and the suspect has taken it.

(6) The suspect is now eager to tell his story, but the detective cuts him off. Before proceeding any further, there is some "paperwork" to be completed—to do this the right way the suspect must first sign a form stating that he is willing to answer police questions without having a lawyer present and that his decision to do so has been "free and voluntary" on his part.

(7) The suspect signs the form and the detective encourages him to resume telling his story. At the same time, the detective tells himself: "End of the road, pal. It's over. It's history."

Recent articles indicate that the Baltimore detectives' tactics described by Simon are utilized by detectives in many other police departments as well. See Richard A. Leo, *Miranda's Revenge: Police Interrogation as a Confidence Game*, 30 Law & Society Rev. 259 (1996) (based on 500 hours of participant observation in three police departments); Richard A. Leo & Welsh S. White, *Adapting to Miranda: Modern Interrogators' Strategies for Dealing with the Obstacles Posed by Miranda*, 84 Minn.L.Rec. 397 (1999); Peter Carlson, *You Have the Right to Remain Silent . . .*, Washington Post Magazine, Sept. 13, 1998, pp. 6–11, 19–24 (based largely on interviews with police interrogators from Washington, D.C., and surrounding Maryland and Virginia suburbs).[a]

There is reason to believe that Mr. Simon (and many members of the Baltimore homicide unit) think that the aforementioned interrogation techniques are permitted by *Miranda*. At one point, for example, Simon observes that, forced to deal with *Miranda*, a detective "follows the requirements of the law to the letter—or close enough so as not to jeopardize his case. Just as carefully, he ignores the law's spirit and intent. He becomes a salesman, a huckster as thieving and silver-tongued as any man who ever moved used cars or aluminum siding * * *." But consider the following:

YALE KAMISAR—KILLING *MIRANDA* IN BALTIMORE: REFLECTIONS ON DAVID SIMON'S *HOMICIDE*

JURIST: Books-on-Law, Feb. 1999, vol.2, no.2 (*http://jurist.law.pitt.edu/lawbooks/*) (archived).

"[I]f the admissibility of a statement obtained as a result of the methods described [by Mr. Simon] were challenged by a defense lawyer, a Baltimore prosecutor would be in a strong position. For she would be armed with a signed waiver of rights form (and a signed explanation of rights form as well). But she would be in a strong position only if—as would hardly be surprising—the detective(s) involved in the case lied about, or conveniently failed to remember, how the suspect was induced to sign the waiver of rights form. If all the facts were known—if, for example, the entire transaction had been tape recorded—no court could or would admit the statement unless it was prepared to overrule *Miranda* itself.

Despite Mr. Simon's comments to the contrary, the Baltimore police do not follow the requirements of *Miranda* closely enough to avoid jeopardizing their cases, nor do they merely ignore *Miranda*'s spirit. Indeed, it would be more accurate to say they flout the substance of that famous case.

One of the principal purposes of the warning is, to quote from the *Miranda* opinion, "to make the individual more acutely aware that he is faced with a phase of the adversary system—that he is not in the presence of persons acting solely in his interest." But the Baltimore detectives seriously undermine this purpose by leading the suspect to believe that it is in his best interest to waive his rights and to talk to "your friends in the city homicide unit" about the case, and by

a. Thus, Professors White and Leo observe that "[o]ne of the most powerful [*Miranda*] de-emphasizing strategies involves focusing the suspect's attention on the importance of telling his story to the interrogator. The interrogators communicate to the suspect that they want to hear his 'side of the story' but they will not be able to do so until the suspect waives his *Miranda* rights." Still another common way to de-emphasize *Miranda*, report Leo and White, "is to create the appearance of a non-adversarial relationship between the interrogator and a suspect. An interrogator employing this strategy portrays himself as the suspect's friend, confidant or guardian, whose goal is not to obtain incriminating statements but rather to help the suspect improve his situation." This strategy, continue Leo and White, "not only de-emphasizes the *Miranda* warnings but also suggest to the suspect that waiving his *Miranda* warnings will be to his advantage."

pretending to be not only the suspect's friend but his protector (or at least a buffer) against the detectives' heartless superiors and the zealous prosecutor waiting outside the door, a prosecutor who has no compunctions about charging the suspect with first degree murder without bothering to hear his "side of the story."

[At one point in *Miranda*, the Court observed:] "[A]ny evidence that the accused was threatened, tricked, or cajoled into a waiver will, of course, show that the defendant did not voluntarily waive his privilege. The requirement of warnings and waiver of rights is a fundamental [and] not simply a preliminary ritual to existing methods of interrogation." Unfortunately, the very police conduct that *Miranda* tried to forbid seems to be occurring in Baltimore police stations. The police *are* threatening the suspect: they are telling him that unless he talks to them about the homicide, they will write it up as first degree murder and turn him over to a [heartless] assistant state's attorney. They *are* tricking the suspect: they are leading him to believe that it is in his best interest to tell them his side of the story; indeed, they are pretending that this is the suspect's only chance to get the homicide charge reduced (or perhaps even dismissed).

[To] quote the *Miranda* opinion again, transforming its requirements of warnings and waiver of rights into "simply a preliminary ritual to existing methods of interrogation" is also a pretty good description of what is taking place in Baltimore police stations. Indeed, to put it somewhat differently, although the police are not supposed to subject a custodial suspect to interrogation *unless and until* they obtain a waiver of his rights, what they are really doing in Baltimore (and who knows how many other places) is subjecting individuals to "interrogation" *before* they waive their rights.

At one point, Mr. Simon notes that "[t]he fraud that claims it is somehow in a suspect's interest to talk with police will forever be the catalyst in any criminal interrogation." Exactly right. This is why the methods used by the Baltimore police to get a suspect to waive his rights—methods that simultaneously manipulate him into talking about the case and, eventually, incriminating himself—should be classified as "interrogation." Whatever deception, seduction and trickery a police interrogator may be able to utilize *after* the suspect effectively waives his rights and agrees to talk (and, more than 30 years after *Miranda*, what the interrogator may do at this stage is still far from clear), the police cannot resort to any of these techniques *before* the suspect waives his rights, and they cannot use any of these techniques to *get him* to waive his rights.

Once the police have taken a suspect into custody, there is no such thing (at least there is no lawful basis for any such thing) as a "pre-interview" or "pre-waiver" interrogation. The waiver of rights transaction is supposed to take place as soon as the curtain goes up, not postponed until the second or third act.

Mr. Simon's graphic description of how the Baltimore Homicide Unit (and who knows how many other police departments?) goes about getting custodial suspects to make incriminating statements underscores the need to record on video or audio tape the entire proceedings in the police station—the reading of rights, the waiver transactions and any subsequent interrogation. Perhaps because it feared that requiring electronic recording of police questioning, whenever feasible, would have added fuel to the criticism that it was "legislating," the *Miranda* Court permitted the police to obtain waivers of a person's constitutional rights without the presence of any disinterested observer and without any objective recording of the proceedings.

[The] only startling thing about [the tape-recording] issue is that, after all these years, American law enforcement officials are still able to prevent objective recordation of all the facts of police "interviews" or "conversations" with a suspect and, of course, how the warnings are delivered and how the waiver of rights is obtained. But if you were a member of the Baltimore homicide unit (or a member of other police departments employing the same interrogation methods), would you favor tape-recording (and making available for public inspection) what really happens in the interrogation room?

David Simon describes how Baltimore interrogators manage to get custodial suspects to sign waivers of their *Miranda* rights, but what happens if a suspect *invokes* his right to remain silent or her right to counsel? There is reason to think that some detectives in some police departments continue to question the suspects in order (a) to obtain incriminating statements which will enable the prosecution to impeach the suspect if he subsequently takes the stand in his own defense or (b) to obtain evidence *derived from* statements made in violation of *Miranda*, derivative evidence such as the existence of an eyewitness or the location of the murder weapon. Discussion of these police tactics is postponed until Chapter 11, which contains materials on the "fruit of the poisonous tree" and the use of illegally obtained evidence for impeachment purposes. See pp. 934–36.

CAN (DID) CONGRESS "REPEAL" *MIRANDA*?

Consider *Title II of the Omnibus Crime Control and Safe Streets Act of 1968*,[a] which provides in relevant part:

"§ 3501. Admissibility of confessions

"(a) In any criminal prosecution brought by the United States or by the District of Columbia, a confession, as defined in subsection (e) hereof, shall be admissible in evidence if it is voluntarily given. Before such confession is received in evidence, the trial judge shall, out of the presence of the jury, determine any issue as to voluntariness. If the trial judge determines that the confession was voluntarily made it shall be admitted in evidence and the trial judge shall permit the jury to hear relevant evidence on the issue of voluntariness and shall instruct the jury to give such weight to the confession as the jury feels it deserves under all the circumstances.

"(b) The trial judge in determining the issue of voluntariness shall take into consideration all the circumstances surrounding the giving of the confession, including (1) the time elapsing between arrest and arraignment of the defendant making the confession, if it was made after arrest and before arraignment, (2) whether such defendant knew the nature of the offense with which he was charged or of which he was suspected at the time of making the confession, (3) whether or not such defendant was advised or knew that he was not required to make any statement and that any such statement could be used against him, (4) whether or not such defendant had been advised prior to questioning of his right to the assistance of counsel; and (5) whether or not such defendant was without the assistance of counsel when questioned and when giving such confession.

a. For the legislative history of Title II of the Crime Control Act, see Adam C. Breckenridge, *Congress Against the Court* (1970); Fred P. Graham, *The Self–Inflicted Wound* 305–32 (1970); Richard Harris, *The Fear of Crime* (1969); Yale Kamisar, *Can (Did) Congress "Overrule" Miranda?*, 85 Cornell L.Rev. 883, 887–906 (2000); Michael Edmund O'Neill, *Undoing Miranda*, 2000 BYU L.Rev. 185; Otis H. Stephens, Jr., *The Supreme Court and Confessions of Guilt*, 139–45, 163–66 (1973).

"The presence or absence of any of the above-mentioned factors to be taken into consideration by the judge need not be conclusive on the issue of voluntariness of the confession. * * *

"(d) Nothing contained in this section shall bar the admission in evidence of any confession made or given voluntarily by any person to any other person without interrogation by anyone, or at any time at which the person who made or gave such confession was not under arrest or other detention.

"(e) As used in this section, the term 'confession' means any confession of guilt of any criminal offense or any self-incriminating statement made or given orally or in writing."[b]

Some thirty years after § 3501 became law, *United States v. Dickerson*, 166 F.3d 667 (4th Cir.1999), held, against the express wishes of the Department of Justice, that the pre-*Miranda* due process-voluntariness test set forth in § 3501, rather than *Miranda*, governed the admissibility of confessions in the federal courts. Thus, concluded the Fourth Circuit, the district court had erred when it had excluded a voluntary confession simply because it was obtained in violation of *Miranda*. In upholding the constitutionality of § 3501, the Fourth Circuit relied heavily on the fact that the Burger and Rehnquist Courts had "consistently referred to the *Miranda* warnings as 'prophylactic' " and "not themselves rights protected by the Constitution."

When the Supreme Court granted certiorari, most experts thought the vote would be close. Most thought that Justices Stevens, Souter, Ginsburg and Breyer were almost certain to invalidate § 3501 and that the Chief Justice and Justices Scalia and Thomas were almost certain to uphold it. Most considered Justice O'Connor and Kennedy the "swing votes." But a number of *Miranda* supporters feared that, on the basis of her majority opinion in *Oregon v. Elstad* and her strong dissent in *Withrow v. Williams*, Justice O'Connor would vote to uphold § 3501. As it turned out, most experts were wide of the mark.

DICKERSON v. UNITED STATES

530 U.S. 428, 120 S.Ct. 2326, 147 L.Ed.2d 405 (2000).

Chief Justice REHNQUIST delivered the opinion of the Court.

[In] the wake of [*Miranda*], Congress enacted 18 U.S.C. § 3501, which in essence laid down a rule that the admissibility of [a custodial suspect's] state-

b. Another provision of § 3501, Part (c), is aimed squarely at a rule that law-enforcement officials strongly disliked, the *McNabb–Mallory* rule (p. 557). Part (c) provides that in any federal criminal prosecution a confession by a person under arrest or other detention "shall not be inadmissible solely because of delay in bringing such person before a commissioner * * * if such confession is found by the trial judge to have been voluntarily made [and] if such confession was made [within] six hours immediately following [the person's] arrest or other detention." Moreover, the six-hour time limitation does not apply where the delay in bringing such person before a commissioner beyond the six-hour period "is found by the trial judge to be reasonable considering the means of transportation and the distance to be traveled to the nearest available commissioner."

Since the *McNabb–Mallory* rule was fashioned "quite apart from the Constitution," *McNabb*, and in the exercise of the Supreme Court's "supervisory authority over the administration of [federal] criminal justice," id., it *is* subject to repeal by Congress. However, it is unclear whether Congress has only seriously weakened the *McNabb–Mallory* rule or whether it has completely abolished it. In *United States v. Alvarez–Sanchez*, 511 U.S. 350, 114 S.Ct. 1599, 128 L.Ed.2d 319 (1994), the government argued that § 3501 repudiated the *McNabb–Mallory* rule in its entirety and that the admissibility of a confession obtained beyond the six-hour limit is controlled by § 3501 (a), which provides that a confession is admissible so long as "it is voluntarily given." But the Court saw no need to decide the question because "the terms of § 3501 (c) were never triggered in this case."

ments should turn only on whether or not they were voluntarily made. We hold that *Miranda*, being a constitutional decision of this Court, may not be in effect overruled by an Act of Congress, and we decline to overrule *Miranda* ourselves. We therefore hold that *Miranda* and its progeny in this Court govern the admissibility of statements made during custodial interrogation in both state and federal courts.

Petitioner Dickerson was indicted for bank robbery [and] conspiracy to commit bank robbery. [Before] trial, [he] moved to suppress a statement he had made at [an FBI] field office, on the grounds that he had not received "*Miranda* warnings" before being interrogated. The District Court granted his motion to suppress, and the Government took an interlocutory appeal to the United States Court of Appeals for the Fourth Circuit. That court [reversed.] It agreed [that] petitioner had not received *Miranda* warnings before making his statement. But it went on to hold that § 3501, which in effect makes the admissibility of statements such as Dickerson's turn solely on whether they were made voluntarily, was satisfied in this case. It then concluded that our decision in *Miranda* was not a constitutional holding, and that therefore Congress could by statute have the final say on the question of admissibility.

* * * Prior to *Miranda*, we evaluated the admissibility of a suspect's confession under a voluntariness test. [Over] time, our cases recognized two constitutional bases for the requirement that a confession be voluntary to be admitted into evidence: the Fifth Amendment right against self-incrimination and the Due Process Clause of the Fourteenth Amendment. See, *e.g.*, *Bram v. United States* (1897) (stating that the voluntariness test "is controlled by that portion of the Fifth Amendment ... commanding that no person 'shall be compelled in any criminal case to be a witness against himself' "); *Brown v. Mississippi* (1936) (reversing a criminal conviction under the Due Process Clause because it was based on a confession obtained by physical coercion).

While *Bram* was decided before *Brown* and its progeny, for the middle third of the 20th century our cases based the rule against admitting coerced confessions primarily, if not exclusively, on notions of due process. We applied the due process voluntariness test in "some 30 different cases decided during the era that intervened between *Brown* and *Escobedo v. Illinois.*" Those cases refined the test into an inquiry that examines "whether a defendant's will was overborne" by the circumstances surrounding the giving of a confession. The due process test takes into consideration "the totality of all the surrounding circumstances—both the characteristics of the accused and the details of the interrogation." * * *

We have never abandoned this due process jurisprudence, and thus continue to exclude confessions that were obtained involuntarily. But our decisions in *Malloy* and *Miranda* changed the focus of much of the inquiry in determining the admissibility of suspects' incriminating statements. In *Malloy*, we held that the Fifth Amendment's Self–Incrimination Clause is incorporated in the Due Process Clause of the Fourteenth Amendment and thus applies to the States. We decided *Miranda* on the heels of *Malloy*.

In *Miranda*, [we] concluded that the coercion inherent in custodial interrogation blurs the line between voluntary and involuntary statements, and thus heightens the risk that an individual will not be "accorded his privilege under the Fifth Amendment ... not to be compelled to incriminate himself." Accordingly, we laid down "concrete constitutional guidelines for law enforcement agencies and courts to follow."

Two years after *Miranda* was decided, Congress enacted § 3501. * * *

Given § 3501's express designation of voluntariness as the touchstone of admissibility, its omission of any warning requirement, and the instruction for trial courts to consider a nonexclusive list of factors relevant to the circumstances of a confession, we agree with the Court of Appeals that Congress intended by its enactment to overrule *Miranda*. Because of the obvious conflict between our decision in *Miranda* and § 3501, we must address whether Congress has constitutional authority to thus supersede *Miranda*. If Congress has such authority, § 3501's totality-of-the-circumstances approach must prevail over *Miranda*'s requirement of warnings; if not, that section must yield to *Miranda*'s more specific requirements.

The law in this area is clear. This Court has supervisory authority over the federal courts, and we may use that authority to prescribe rules of evidence and procedure that are binding in those tribunals. However, the power to judicially create and enforce nonconstitutional "rules of procedure and evidence for the federal courts exists only in the absence of a relevant Act of Congress." Congress retains the ultimate authority to modify or set aside any judicially created rules of evidence and procedure that are not required by the Constitution.

But Congress may not legislatively supersede our decisions interpreting and applying the Constitution. This case therefore turns on whether the *Miranda* Court announced a constitutional rule or merely exercised its supervisory authority to regulate evidence in the absence of congressional direction. [Relying] on the fact that we have created several exceptions to *Miranda*'s warnings requirement and that we have repeatedly referred to the *Miranda* warnings as "prophylactic," *Quarles*, and "not themselves rights protected by the Constitution," *Tucker*, the Court of Appeals concluded that the protections announced in *Miranda* are not constitutionally required.

We disagree * * *, although we concede that there is language in some of our opinions that supports the view taken by that court. But first and foremost of the factors on the other side—that *Miranda* is a constitutional decision—is that both *Miranda* and two of its companion cases applied the rule to proceedings in state courts—to wit, Arizona, California, and New York. Since that time, we have consistently applied *Miranda*'s rule to prosecutions arising in state courts. It is beyond dispute that we do not hold a supervisory power over the courts of the several States. With respect to proceedings in state courts, our "authority is limited to enforcing the commands of the United States Constitution."

The *Miranda* opinion itself begins by stating that the Court granted certiorari "to explore some facets of the problems [of] applying the privilege against self-incrimination to in-custody interrogation, *and to give concrete constitutional guidelines for law enforcement agencies and courts to follow*." (emphasis added). In fact, the majority opinion is replete with statements indicating that the majority thought it was announcing a constitutional rule. Indeed, the Court's ultimate conclusion was that the unwarned confessions obtained in the four cases before the Court in *Miranda* "were obtained from the defendant under circumstances that did not meet constitutional standards for protection of the privilege."

Additional support for our conclusion that *Miranda* is constitutionally based is found in the *Miranda* Court's invitation for legislative action to protect the constitutional right against coerced self-incrimination. [The] Court emphasized that it could not foresee "the potential alternatives for protecting the privilege which might be devised by Congress or the States," and it accordingly opined that the Constitution would not preclude legislative solutions that differed from the prescribed *Miranda* warnings but which were "at least as effective in apprising accused persons of their right of silence and in assuring a continuous opportunity to exercise it."[6]

The Court of Appeals also relied on the fact that we have, after our *Miranda* decision, made exceptions from its rule in cases such as *Quarles* and *Harris v. New York* [p. 922]. But we have also broadened the application of the *Miranda* doctrine in cases such as *Doyle v. Ohio,* [p. 932] and *Arizona v. Roberson* [p. 647]. These decisions illustrate the principle—not that *Miranda* is not a constitutional rule—but that no constitutional rule is immutable. No court laying down a general rule can possibly foresee the various circumstances in which counsel will seek to apply it, and the sort of modifications represented by these cases are as much a normal part of constitutional law as the original decision.

The Court of Appeals also noted that in *Elstad*, we stated that " 'the *Miranda* exclusionary rule . . . serves the Fifth Amendment and sweeps more broadly than the Fifth Amendment itself.' " Our decision in that case—refusing to apply the traditional "fruits" doctrine developed in Fourth Amendment cases—does not prove that *Miranda* is a nonconstitutional decision, but simply recognizes the fact that unreasonable searches under the Fourth Amendment are different from unwarned interrogation under the Fifth Amendment.

As an alternative argument for sustaining the Court of Appeals' decision, the court-invited *amicus curiae*[7] contends that the section complies with the requirement that a legislative alternative to *Miranda* be equally as effective in preventing coerced confessions. We agree with the *amicus*' contention that there are more remedies available for abusive police conduct than there were at the time *Miranda* was decided. But we do not agree that these additional measures supplement § 3501's protections sufficiently to meet the constitutional minimum. *Miranda* requires procedures that will warn a suspect in custody of his right to remain silent and which will assure the suspect that the exercise of that right will be honored. As discussed above, § 3501 explicitly eschews a requirement of pre-interrogation warnings in favor of an approach that looks to the administration of such warnings as only one factor in determining the voluntariness of a suspect's confession. The additional remedies cited by *amicus* do not, in our view, render them, together with § 3501 an adequate substitute for the warnings required by *Miranda*.

The dissent argues that it is judicial overreaching for this Court to hold § 3501 unconstitutional unless we hold that the *Miranda* warnings are required by the Constitution, in the sense that nothing else will suffice to satisfy constitutional requirements. But we need not go farther than *Miranda* to decide this case. In *Miranda*, the Court noted that reliance on the traditional totality-of-the-circumstances test raised a risk of overlooking an involuntary custodial confession, a risk that the Court found unacceptably great when the confession is offered in the case in chief to prove guilt. The Court therefore concluded that something more than the totality test was necessary. Section 3501 reinstates the totality test as sufficient. [The statute] therefore cannot be sustained if *Miranda* is to remain the law.

6. The Court of Appeals relied in part on our statement that the *Miranda* decision in no way "creates a 'constitutional straightjacket.' " However, a review of our opinion in *Miranda* clarifies that this disclaimer was intended to indicate that the Constitution does not require police to administer the particular *Miranda* warnings, not that the Constitution does not require a procedure that is effective in securing Fifth Amendment rights.

7. Because no party to the underlying litigation argued in favor of § 3501's constitutionality in this Court, we invited Professor Paul Cassell to assist our deliberations by arguing in support of the judgment below.

Whether or not we would agree with *Miranda*'s reasoning and its resulting rule, were we addressing the issue in the first instance, the principles of *stare decisis* weigh heavily against overruling it now.

* * * *Miranda* has become embedded in routine police practice to the point where the warnings have become part of our national culture. [While] we have overruled our precedents when subsequent cases have undermined their doctrinal underpinnings, we do not believe that this has happened to the *Miranda* decision. If anything, our subsequent cases have reduced the impact of the *Miranda* rule on legitimate law enforcement while reaffirming the decision's core ruling that unwarned statements may not be used as evidence in the prosecution's case in chief.

The disadvantage of the *Miranda* rule is that statements which may be by no means involuntary, made by a defendant who is aware of his "rights," may nonetheless be excluded and a guilty defendant go free as a result. But experience suggests that the totality-of-the-circumstances test which § 3501 seeks to revive is more difficult than *Miranda* for law enforcement officers to conform to, and for courts to apply in a consistent manner. The requirement that *Miranda* warnings be given does not, of course, dispense with the voluntariness inquiry. But * * * "[c]ases in which a defendant can make a colorable argument that a self-incriminating statement was 'compelled' despite the fact that the law enforcement authorities adhered to the dictates of *Miranda* are rare."

In sum, we conclude that *Miranda* announced a constitutional rule that Congress may not supersede legislatively. Following the rule of *stare decisis*, we decline to overrule *Miranda* ourselves. * * *

Justice SCALIA, with whom Justice THOMAS joins, dissenting.

Those to whom judicial decisions are an unconnected series of judgments that produce either favored or disfavored results will doubtless greet today's decision as a paragon of moderation, since it declines to overrule *Miranda*. Those who understand the judicial process will appreciate that today's decision is not a reaffirmation of *Miranda*, but a radical revision of the most significant element of *Miranda* (as of all cases): the rationale that gives it a permanent place in our jurisprudence.

Marbury v. Madison held that an Act of Congress will not be enforced by the courts if what it prescribes violates the Constitution of the United States. That was the basis on which *Miranda* was decided. One will search today's opinion in vain, however, for a statement (surely simple enough to make) that what § 3501 prescribes—the use at trial of a voluntary confession, even when a *Miranda* warning or its equivalent has failed to be given—violates the Constitution. The reason the statement does not appear is not only (and perhaps not so much) that it would be absurd, inasmuch as § 3501 excludes from trial precisely what the Constitution excludes from trial, viz., compelled confessions; but also that Justices whose votes are needed to compose today's majority are on record as believing that a violation of *Miranda* is *not* a violation of the Constitution. And so, to justify today's agreed-upon result, the Court must adopt a significant *new*, if not entirely comprehensible, principle of constitutional law. As the Court chooses to describe that principle, statutes of Congress can be disregarded, not only when what they prescribe violates the Constitution, but when what they prescribe contradicts a decision of this Court that "announced a constitutional rule." As I shall discuss in some detail, the only thing that can possibly mean in the context of this case is that this Court has the power, not merely to apply the Constitution but to expand it, imposing what it regards as useful "prophylactic" restrictions upon Congress and the States. That is an immense and frightening antidemocratic power, and it does not exist.

It takes only a small step to bring today's opinion out of the realm of power-judging and into the mainstream of legal reasoning: The Court need only go beyond its carefully couched iterations that "*Miranda* is a constitutional decision," that "*Miranda* is constitutionally based," that *Miranda* has "constitutional underpinnings," and come out and say quite clearly: "We reaffirm today that custodial interrogation that is not preceded by *Miranda* warnings or their equivalent violates the Constitution of the United States." It cannot say that, because a majority of the Court does not believe it. The Court therefore acts in plain violation of the Constitution when it denies effect to this Act of Congress.

* * * The power we recognized in *Marbury* [will] permit us, indeed require us, to "disregard" § 3501, a duly enacted statute governing the admissibility of evidence in the federal courts, only if it "be in opposition to the Constitution"—here, assertedly, the dictates of the Fifth Amendment.

It was once possible to characterize the so-called *Miranda* rule as resting (however implausibly) upon the proposition that what the statute here before us permits—the admission at trial of un-*Mirandized* confessions—violates the Constitution. That is the fairest reading of the *Miranda* case itself. [Having] extended the privilege into the confines of the station house, the Court liberally sprinkled throughout its sprawling 60–page opinion suggestions that, because of the compulsion inherent in custodial interrogation, the privilege was violated by any statement thus obtained that did not conform to the rules set forth in *Miranda*, or some functional equivalent. [At] least one case decided shortly after *Miranda* explicitly confirmed the view. See *Orozco v. Texas* [p. 607] ("The use of these admissions obtained in the absence of the required warnings was a flat violation of the Self–Incrimination Clause of the Fifth Amendment as construed in *Miranda*").

So understood, *Miranda* was objectionable for innumerable reasons, not least the fact that cases spanning more than 70 years had rejected its core premise that, absent the warnings and an effective waiver of the right to remain silent and of the (thitherto unknown) right to have an attorney present, a statement obtained pursuant to custodial interrogation was necessarily the product of compulsion. See *Crooker v. California*. * * * Moreover, history and precedent aside, the decision in *Miranda*, if read as an explication of what the Constitution *requires*, is preposterous. There is, for example, simply no basis in reason for concluding that a response to the very first question asked, by a suspect who already *knows* all of the rights described in the *Miranda* warning, is anything other than a volitional act. And even if one assumes that the elimination of compulsion absolutely requires informing even the most knowledgeable suspect of his right to remain silent, it cannot conceivably require the right to have *counsel* present. There is a world of difference, which the Court recognized under the traditional voluntariness test but ignored in *Miranda*, between compelling a suspect to incriminate himself and preventing him from foolishly doing so of his own accord. Only the latter (which is *not* required by the Constitution) could explain the Court's inclusion of a right to counsel and the requirement that it, too, be knowingly and intelligently waived. Counsel's presence is not required to tell the suspect that he *need* not speak; the interrogators can do that. The only good reason for having counsel there is that he can be counted on to advise the suspect that he *should* not speak. * * *

Preventing foolish (rather than compelled) confessions is likewise the only conceivable basis for the rules (suggested in *Miranda*) that courts must exclude any confession elicited by questioning conducted, without interruption, after the suspect has indicated a desire to stand on his right to remain silent, or initiated by police after the suspect has expressed a desire to have counsel present. Nonthreatening attempts to persuade the suspect to reconsider that initial decision are not, without more, enough to render a change of heart the product of anything other than the suspect's free will. Thus, what is most remarkable about the *Miranda* decision—and what made it unacceptable as a matter of straightforward constitutional interpretation in the *Marbury* tradition—is its palpable hostility toward the act of confession *per se*, rather than toward what the Constitution abhors, *compelled* confession.

[For] these reasons, and others more than adequately developed in the *Miranda* dissents and in the subsequent works of the decision's many critics, any conclusion that a violation of the *Miranda* rules *necessarily* amounts to a violation of the privilege against compelled self-incrimination can claim no support in history, precedent, or common sense, and as a result would at least presumptively be worth reconsidering even at this late date. But that is unnecessary, since the Court has (thankfully) long since abandoned the notion that failure to comply with *Miranda*'s rules is itself a violation of the Constitution.

As the Court today acknowledges, since *Miranda* we have explicitly, and repeatedly, interpreted that decision as having announced, not the circumstances in which custodial interrogation runs afoul of the Fifth or Fourteenth Amendment, but rather only "prophylactic" rules that go beyond the right against compelled self-incrimination. Of course the seeds of this "prophylactic" interpretation of *Miranda* were present in the decision itself. [In] subsequent cases, the seeds have sprouted and borne fruit: The Court has squarely concluded that it is possible—indeed not uncommon—for the police to violate *Miranda* without also violating the Constitution.

In light of [such cases as *Michigan v. Tucker* (p. 600), *New York v. Quarles* (pp. 601, 629), *Oregon v. Elstad* (pp. 601, 701) and *Oregon v. Hass* (pp. 599, 924)] and our statements to the same effect in others, it is simply no longer possible for the Court to conclude, even if it wanted to, that a violation of *Miranda's* rules is a violation of the Constitution. [What] makes a decision "constitutional" in the only sense relevant here—in the sense that renders it impervious to supersession by congressional legislation such as § 3501—is the determination that the Constitution *requires* the result that the decision announces and the statute ignores. By disregarding congressional action that concededly does not violate the Constitution, the Court flagrantly offends fundamental principles of separation of powers, and arrogates to itself prerogatives reserved to the representatives of the people.

The Court seeks to avoid this conclusion in two ways: First, by misdescribing these post-*Miranda* cases as mere dicta. [But it] is not a matter of *language*; it is a matter of *holdings*. The proposition that failure to comply with *Miranda*'s rules does not establish a constitutional violation was central to the *holdings* of *Tucker*, *Hass*, *Quarles*, and *Elstad*.

The second way the Court seeks to avoid the impact of these cases is simply to disclaim responsibility for reasoned decisionmaking. It says:

> "These decisions illustrate the principle—not that *Miranda* is not a constitutional rule—but that no constitutional rule is immutable." * * *

[The] issue, however, is not whether court rules are "mutable"; they assuredly are. It is not whether, in the light of "various circumstances," they can be "modified"; they assuredly can. The issue is whether, *as mutated and modified*, they must *make sense*. The requirement that they do so is the only thing that prevents this Court from being some sort of nine-headed Caesar, giving thumbs-up or thumbs-down to whatever outcome, case by case, suits or offends its collective fancy. And if confessions procured in violation of *Miranda* are confessions "compelled" in violation of the Constitution, the post-*Miranda* decisions I have discussed do not make sense. The only reasoned basis for their outcome was that a violation of *Miranda* is *not* a violation of the Constitution. [To] say simply that "unreasonable searches under the Fourth Amendment are different from unwarned interrogation under the Fifth Amendment" is true but supremely unhelpful.

Finally, the Court asserts that *Miranda* must be a "constitutional decision" announcing a "constitutional rule," and thus immune to congressional modification, because we have since its inception applied it to the States. If this argument is meant as an invocation of *stare decisis*, it fails because, though it is true that our cases applying *Miranda* against the States must be reconsidered if *Miranda* is not required by the Constitution, it is likewise true that our cases (discussed above) based on the principle that *Miranda* is *not* required by the Constitution will have to be reconsidered if it *is*. So the *stare decisis* argument is a wash. [In] my view, our continued application of the *Miranda* code to the States despite our consistent statements that running afoul of its dictates does not necessarily—or even usually—result in an actual constitutional violation, represents not the source of *Miranda*'s salvation but rather evidence of its ultimate illegitimacy. See generally Joseph Grano, *Confessions, Truth, and the Law* 173–198 (1993); Joseph Grano, *Prophylactic Rules in Criminal Procedure: A Question of Article III Legitimacy*, 80 Nw. U. L. Rev. 100 (1985). * * *

There was available to the Court a means of reconciling the established proposition that a violation of *Miranda* does not itself offend the Fifth Amendment with the Court's assertion of a right to ignore the present statute. That means of reconciliation was argued strenuously by both petitioner and the United States, who were evidently more concerned than the Court is with maintaining the coherence of our jurisprudence. It is not mentioned in the Court's opinion because, I assume, a majority of the Justices intent on reversing believes that incoherence is the lesser evil. They may be right.

Petitioner and the United States contend that there is nothing at all exceptional, much less unconstitutional, about the Court's adopting prophylactic rules to buttress constitutional rights, and enforcing them against Congress and the States. Indeed, the United States argues that "prophylactic rules are now and have been for many years a feature of this Court's constitutional adjudication." That statement is not wholly inaccurate, if by "many years" one means since the mid–1960's. However, in their zeal to validate what is in my view a lawless practice, the United States and petitioner greatly overstate the frequency with which we have engaged in it. * * *

Petitioner and the United States are right on target [in] characterizing the Court's actions in a case decided within a few years of *Miranda*, *North Carolina v. Pearce* [p. 1584]. There, the Court concluded that due process would be offended were a judge vindictively to resentence with added severity a defendant who had successfully appealed his original conviction. Rather than simply announce that vindictive sentencing violates the Due Process Clause, the Court went on to hold that "in order to assure the absence of such a [vindictive] motivation, [the] reasons for [imposing the increased sentence] must affirmatively appear" and must "be based upon objective information concerning identifiable conduct on the part of the defendant occurring after the time of the original sentencing proceeding." The Court later explicitly acknowledged *Pearce*'s prophylactic character, see *Michigan v. Payne* [p. 1587]. It is true, therefore, that the case exhibits the same fundamental flaw as does *Miranda* when deprived (as it has been) of its original (implausible) pretension to announcement of what the Constitution itself required. That is, although the Due Process Clause may well prohibit punishment based on judicial vindictiveness, the Constitution by no means vests in the courts "any general power to prescribe particular devices 'in order to assure the absence of such a motivation' " (Black, J., dissenting). Justice Black surely had the right idea when he derided the Court's requirement as "pure legislation if there ever was legislation," although in truth *Pearce*'s rule pales as a legislative achievement when compared to the detailed code promulgated in *Miranda*.

The foregoing demonstrates that, petitioner's and the United States' suggestions to the contrary notwithstanding, what the Court did in *Miranda* (assuming, as later cases hold, that *Miranda* went beyond what the Constitution actually requires) is in fact extraordinary. That the Court has, on rare and recent occasion, repeated the mistake does not transform error into truth, but illustrates the potential for future mischief that the error entails. [The] power with which the Court would endow itself under a "prophylactic" justification for *Miranda* goes far beyond what it has permitted Congress to do under authority of [U.S. Const., Amdt. 14, § 5]. Whereas we have insisted that congressional action under § 5 of the Fourteenth Amendment must be "congruent" with, and "proportional" to, a *constitutional violation*, the *Miranda* nontextual power to embellish confers authority to prescribe preventive measures against not only constitutionally prohibited compelled confessions, but also (as discussed earlier) foolhardy ones.

I applaud, therefore, the refusal of the Justices in the majority to enunciate this boundless doctrine of judicial empowerment as a means of rendering today's decision rational. In nonetheless joining the Court's judgment, however, they overlook two truisms: that actions speak louder than silence, and that (in judge-made law at least) logic will out. Since there is in fact no other principle that can reconcile today's judgment with the post-*Miranda* cases that the Court refuses to abandon, what today's decision will stand for, whether the Justices can bring themselves to say it or not, is the power of the Supreme Court to write a prophylactic, extraconstitutional Constitution, binding on Congress and the States.[a]

Thus, while I agree with the Court that § 3501 cannot be upheld without also concluding that *Miranda* represents an illegitimate exercise of our authority to review state-court judgments, I do not share the Court's hesitation in reaching that conclusion. For while the Court is also correct that the doctrine of *stare decisis* demands some "special justification" for a departure from longstanding precedent—even precedent of the constitutional variety—that criterion is more than met here.

* * *

Neither am I persuaded by the argument for retaining *Miranda* that touts its supposed workability as compared with the totality-of-the-circumstances test it purported to replace. *Miranda*'s proponents cite *ad nauseam* the fact that the Court was called upon to make difficult and subtle distinctions in applying the "voluntariness" test in some 30–odd due process "coerced confessions" cases in the 30 years between *Brown* and *Miranda*. It is not immediately apparent, however, that the judicial burden has been eased by the "bright-line" rules adopted in *Miranda*. In fact, in the 34 years since *Miranda* was decided, this Court has been called upon to decide nearly *60* cases involving a host of *Miranda* issues * * *.

Moreover, it is not clear why the Court thinks that the "totality-of-the-circumstances test [is] more difficult than *Miranda* for law enforcement officers to conform to, and for courts to apply in a consistent manner." Indeed, I find myself persuaded by Justice O'Connor's rejection of this same argument in her opinion in

a. See the characterization of *Miranda* by Justice Thomas in his plurality opinion in *United States v. Patane*, p. 703. Justice Thomas was joined by Rehnquist, C.J., and Scalia, J. In *Patane*, did the *Dickerson* dissenters "fulfill their own prophecy" as to what *Dickerson* will come to mean? See Note, 118 Harv.L.Rev. 296, 301 (2004).

Withrow v. Williams [p. 671] (O'Connor, J., joined by Rehnquist, C.J., concurring in part and dissenting in part) * * *.

But even were I to agree that the old totality-of-the-circumstances test was more cumbersome, it is simply not true that *Miranda* has banished it from the law and replaced it with a new test. Under the current regime, which the Court today retains in its entirety, courts are frequently called upon to undertake *both* inquiries. That is [because] voluntariness remains the *constitutional* standard, and as such continues to govern the admissibility for impeachment purposes of statements taken in violation of *Miranda*, the admissibility of the "fruits" of such statements, and the admissibility of statements challenged as unconstitutionally obtained *despite* the interrogator's compliance with *Miranda*.

Finally, I am not convinced by petitioner's argument that *Miranda* should be preserved because the decision occupies a special place in the "public's consciousness." As far as I am aware, the public is not under the illusion that we are infallible. I see little harm in admitting that we made a mistake in taking away from the people the ability to decide for themselves what protections (beyond those required by the Constitution) are reasonably affordable in the criminal investigatory process. * * *

* * *

Today's judgment converts *Miranda* from a milestone of judicial overreaching into the very Cheops' Pyramid (or perhaps the Sphinx would be a better analogue) of judicial arrogance. In imposing its Court-made code upon the States, the original opinion at least *asserted* that it was demanded by the Constitution. Today's decision does not pretend that it is—and yet *still* asserts the right to impose it against the will of the people's representatives in Congress. Far from believing that *stare decisis* compels this result, I believe we cannot allow to remain on the books even a celebrated decision—*especially* a celebrated decision—that has come to stand for the proposition that the Supreme Court has power to impose extraconstitutional constraints upon Congress and the States. This is not the system that was established by the Framers, or that would be established by any sane supporter of government by the people.

I dissent from today's decision, and, until § 3501 is repealed, will continue to apply it in all cases where there has been a sustainable finding that the defendant's confession was voluntary.

Notes and Questions

1. ***Reconciling the prophylactic-rule cases with Miranda.*** Consider DONALD A. DRIPPS, *Constitutional Theory for Criminal Procedure: Miranda, Dickerson, and the Continuing Quest for Broad–But–Shallow*, 43 Wm. & Mary L.Rev. 1, 33 (2001): "Once the court granted [certiorari in *Dickerson*] court-watchers knew the hour had come. At long last the Court would have to either repudiate *Miranda*, repudiate the prophylactic-rule cases [the cases viewing *Miranda*'s requirements as not rights protected by the Constitution, but merely "prophylactic rules"] or offer some ingenious reconciliation of the two lines of precedent. The Supreme Court of the United States, however, doesn't " 'have to' do anything, as the decision in *Dickerson* again reminds us."

2. ***Foolish confessions.*** Does Miranda, as Justice Scalia maintains in his Dickerson dissent, prevent suspects from foolishly deciding to talk to the police? Don't most custodial suspects waive their Miranda rights? Are not almost all decisions by suspects to talk to the police about their cases before meeting with a lawyer foolish decisions?

3. ***Why did Chief Justice Rehnquist come to the rescue of Miranda?*** Did the Chief Justice decide to vote with the majority so that he could assign the opinion to himself rather than let it go to someone like Justice John Paul Stevens? Did the Chief Justice conclude that the best resolution of *Dickerson* would be a compromise, one that "reaffirmed" *Miranda*'s constitutional status, but preserved all the qualifications and exceptions the much-criticized case had acquired over three and a half decades? Did the Chief Justice regard *Dickerson* as an occasion for the Court to maintain its power against Congress?[a] Did he consider § 3501 "a slap at the Court"?[b] Was the Chief Justice interested in assuming an increasingly large leadership rule, as opposed to his more partisan days as Associate Justice?[c]

Was the Chief Justice concerned that the "overruling" of *Miranda* by legislation would have wiped out some 35 years of jurisprudence—nearly 60 cases? Why pay the price when, whatever their initial experience with *Miranda*, the police now seem to be living comfortably with it?[d] Did the Chief Justice know that the police obtain waiver of rights in the "overwhelming majority" of cases and that once they do "*Miranda* offers very little, if any, meaningful protection"?[e] Was the Chief Justice aware that once the police have complied with *Miranda* and a suspect has waived his rights (as suspects usually do) "it is very difficult for a defendant to establish" that any resulting confession was "involuntary" in the pre-*Miranda* due process voluntariness sense?[f]

Would overruling *Miranda* be viewed by the police as a signal that they could return to the "old days" of police interrogation?[g] Would overturning *Miranda* after all this time have caused much confusion? Would it have been easy to figure out what combination of circumstances satisfied the ever-changing voluntariness test in the twenty-first century? Would it have been easy to know exactly how the police should respond when persons *not warned* of their "rights" *asserted* what they thought were their rights on their own initiative or *asked the police* whether they had a right to a lawyer or a right to remain silent?[h]

4. ***Does Dickerson leave Miranda incoherent?*** Consider PAUL G. CASSELL, *The Paths Not Taken: The Supreme Court's Failures in Dickerson*, 99 Mich.L.Rev. 898, 901–04 (2001):

a. Consider Craig Bradley, *Behind the Dickerson Decision*, TRIAL, Oct. 2000, at 80.

b. Whether or not the Chief Justice did, some commentators did. See Michael C. Dorf & Barry Friedman, *Shared Constitutional Interpretation*, 2001 Sup.Ct.Rev. 61, 72: "[Section 3501] was a slap at the Court and if any Court was likely to slap back it was this one." See also Susan R. Klein, *Identifying and (Re)Formulating Prophylactic Rules, Safe Harbors, and Incidental Rights in Constitutional Criminal Procedure*, 99 Mich.L.Rev. 1030, 1057 (2001), calling § 3501 "an angry, disrespectful, and disingenuous attempt" to "overrule a decision [Congress] loathed."

c. Bradley, supra note a.

d. Richard A. Leo, *Questioning the Relevance of Miranda in the Twenty–First Century*, 99 Mich.L.Rev. 975, 1027 (2001), sums up the current situation as follows: "Once feared to be the equivalent of sand in the machinery of criminal justice, *Miranda* has now become a standard part of the machine."

e. Id. To be sure, suspects who agree to talk to the police may still cut off questioning or invoke their right to have counsel—but they "almost never" do. William J. Stuntz, *Miranda's Mistake*, 99 Mich.L.Rev. 975, 977 (2001).

f. See Welsh S. White, *Miranda's Failure to Restrain Pernicious Interrogation Practices*, 99 Mich.L.Rev. 1211, 1219 (2001). See also Louis Michael Seidman, *Brown and Miranda*, 80 Calif.L.Rev. 673, 743–47 (1992).

g. In a tribute to his colleague, Professor Fred E. Inbau, shortly after the latter's death, Professor Ronald Allen recalled that although Inbau was a strong critic of *Miranda* (and co-author of a famous police interrogation manual quoted at length, and never approvingly, in the *Miranda* opinion), he balked at explicitly overruling *Miranda*. As did Allen himself, Inbau "feared that [overruling *Miranda*] would be taken as a symbol by the police that, so to speak, all bets were off, and a return to the days of the third degree were acceptable." Ronald J. Allen, *Tribute to Fred Inbau*, 89 J.Crim.L. & Criminology 1271, 1273 (1999).

h. See Yale Kamisar, *Miranda Thirty–Five Years Later: A Close Look at the Majority and Dissenting Opinions in Dickerson*, 33 Ariz.St. L.J. 387, 388–90 (2001).

"[The *Dickerson* majority offers] no rationale for numerous results over the last twenty-five years. Why can the 'fruits' of *Miranda* violations be used against a defendant? The traditional rule excludes fruits of, for example, unconstitutional searches. * * * Similarly, in *New York v. Quarles* the Court carved out a 'public safety' exception to *Miranda*. The Fifth Amendment admits of no such public safety exception; the police cannot coerce an involuntary statement from a suspect and use it against him even if there are strong public safety reasons for doing so. The rationale *Quarles* gave, however, was that the *Miranda* rules were nonconstitutional rules subject to modification by the Court. * * * My thesis is that *Dickerson* could have been written coherently—that the Court could have crafted other resolutions that would have allowed it to harmonize its doctrine far more effectively than the skimpy, jerry-built opinion the Court announced. * * *

"Perhaps the simplest way for the Court to reconcile its various pronouncements was to treat *Miranda* as a form of 'constitutional common law,' to use the phrase made famous [by Henry Monaghan].[26] Under this view, the *Miranda* rules are interim remedies not required by the Constitution, but designed in the absence of legislation to assist in protecting constitutional rights. [For] present purposes, the salient feature of constitutional common law is that it is subject to change—change by the Court and, in appropriate cases, by Congress. [The] touchstone for assessing the constitutionality of Congress's remedial regime [is] not whether it matched in every respect the judicially-devised regime for which it substituted. Rather, the touchstone [is] whether the congressional regime provided 'meaningful' protection for the constitutional right at issue. If it did, then its strength compared to the judicially-devised scheme was irrelevant."

5. *Is constitutional law filled with "prophylactic rules"? On the other hand, as Justice Scalia defines "prophylactic rules," is Miranda such a rule?* Chief Justice Rehnquist did not respond directly to Justice Scalia's attack on the Court's power to promulgate "prophylactic, extraconstitutional rules." (Indeed, the *Dickerson* opinion never characterizes *Miranda* as a "prophylactic rule.") How might the Chief Justice have responded? One way would be to say that constitutional law, and constitutional-criminal procedure especially, is filled with "prophylactic rules," i.e., much constitutional law is shaped to some extent (as was *Miranda*) by institutional judgments as to how constitutional goals can best be attained and how constitutional values can best be implemented. See David A. Strauss, *The Ubiquity of Prophylactic Rules*, 55 U.Chi.L.Rev. 190 (1988); David A. Strauss, *Miranda, the Constitution, and Congress*, 99 Mich.L.Rev. 958 (2001). See also Susan R. Klein, *Identifying and (Re)Formulating Prophylactic Rules, Safe Harbors, and Incidental Rights in Constitutional Criminal Procedure*, 99 Mich.L.Rev. 1030, 1037–44 (2001). Another way to respond to Scalia is to say that *Miranda* is *not* a prophylactic rule as Justice Scalia and other critics of *Miranda* have defined such a rule (a judge-made rule that "overenforces" or "overprotects" judge-interpreted constitutional meaning).[h] Consider MITCHELL N. BERMAN, *Constitutional Decision Rules*, 90 Va.L.Rev. 1, 154 (2004):

"The *Dickerson* majority (or some member thereof) could have replied to Justice Scalia's dissent as follows: (1) the *Miranda* warnings requirement was part of a constitutional decision rule [a rule directing how courts should adjudicate claimed violations of constitutional meaning] designed to minimize errors in adjudicating whether out-of-court statements had been compelled within the meaning of the Self–Incrimination Clause (as *Miranda* interpreted that particular

26. Henry P. Monaghan, *Foreword: Constitutional Common Law*, 89 Harv.L.Rev. 1, 42 (1975).

h. As Berman, infra, points out, Justice Scalia's definition of "prophylactic rule" is similar to Professor Joseph Grano's. Grano maintained that *Miranda* was an "illegitimate" decision. His writings are cited in Justice Scalia *Dickerson* dissent.

constitutional provision); (2) constitutional decision rules are ineliminable, hence cannot be categorically illegitimate; (3) while the extent of the Court's constitutional authority to craft decision rules may be reasonably debated, the creation of decision rules to minimize adjudicating error has the strongest claim to legitimacy; (4) such a device is not a "prophylactic" rule in the Grano–Scalia sense because it does not *overenforce* constitutional meaning as measured against the appropriate baseline; rather it was adopted to *optimally* enforce constitutional meaning; (5) use of a conclusive presumption is common to constitutional decision rules * * * and is not incompatible with an interest in reducing adjudicatory error. None of this * * * is to extol *Miranda*. Like any other judicial product, it might have been wise or foolish. But, on the reading thus far developed, it is not susceptible to the charge of judicial usurpation."

6. *"The advantage of reactivism."* Consider STEPHEN F. SMITH, *Activism as Restraint: Lessons from Criminal Procedure*, 80 Texas L. Rev. 1056, 1110–12 (2002):

"Given all the Court has done in the decades since *Miranda*, in Rehnquist's wonderful, almost self-congratulatory euphemism, to 'reduce[] the impact of the *Miranda* rule on legitimate law enforcement' [*Dickerson*], it comes as no surprise that the Rehnquist Court ultimately saw no need to overrule *Miranda*. This is not to say that *Miranda* had been gutted; where it applied, *Miranda* still had teeth, and so the police had (and still have) incentives to comply with *Miranda* doctrine in interrogating suspects. Even so, the adverse impact of *Miranda* had been blunted in fairly substantial ways long before *Dickerson* came to the Court.[212]

"The end result after decades of case-by-case refinement (and frequently revisionism) was a considerable change in *Miranda* doctrine, but not a complete evisceration of *Miranda*. Neither Warren nor Rehnquist got to have his first-best preference. What they did get was a second-best approach in which the suspect must be given basic information as to his rights and has the power, by making (and sticking to) an unequivocal request for counsel, to stop all questioning. Of course, the police have ample latitude to use persuasion or clever, noncoercive means to cause suspects not to exercise that power and, ultimately, to make incriminating statements that can be used against them at trial. After *Dickerson*, it would appear that *Miranda* law is finally at an equilibrium that almost all of the Justices—including supporters and critics of *Miranda*—can accept, as shown by the fact that seven of the nine Justices signed onto without comment an opinion reaffirming *both Miranda and* all of the limitations and exceptions adopted over the ensuing three decades. This is the advantage of reactivism—it provides an efficacious means by which a Court that fundamentally disagrees with earlier precedents, but is unwilling or unable to overrule them explicitly, can move the law (and, with it, actual case outcomes) back in what it believes to be the right direction. The legal system and the public thereby gain, to varying degrees, the benefits of the overruling. At the same time, reactivism allows risk-adverse Justices and the Court as an institution to avoid the unpleasant consequences of overruling that have historically made Justices so reluctant to overrule even the most indefensible decisions.[215] Thus, the law gets 'fixed' in a way that avoids sharp doctrinal shifts."

212. In fact, so many limitations had been engrafted upon *Miranda* by the Burger Court (let alone the Rehnquist Court) that Albert Alschuler surmised back in 1987 that "a police training manual authored by Justice Holmes' 'bad man of the law'" might advise police officers, in many instances, that they should "*not* give [the suspect] the *Miranda* warnings." Albert W. Alschuler, *Failed Pragmatism: Reflections on the Burger Court*, 100 Harv. L. Rev. 1436, 1442 (1987) (emphasis added).

215. In this sense, reactivism serves the same purposes as the Warren Court's retroactivity rules did. By making controversial, law-changing rulings like *Miranda* and *Mapp* prospective only—that is, applicable only in future

7. ***Why does the "right" seek to do away with Miranda's restrictions on police questioning? Why does the "left" (or center) seek to maintain them? Does Dickerson represent an opportunity missed?*** Consider WILLIAM J. STUNTZ, *Miranda's Mistake*, 99 Mich.L.Rev. 975, 976–77 (2001):

"*Miranda* imposes only the slightest of costs on the police, and its existence may well forestall more serious, and more successful, regulation of police questioning. The right should therefore be either indifferent to *Miranda* or supportive of it. Meanwhile, *Miranda* does nothing to protect suspects against abusive police tactics. The left should therefore be its enemy, and should rejoice at the prospect of seeing it fall, since anything that took its place would likely be an improvement. Another, better answer is that *Miranda* should attract support from neither right nor left. Its effects are probably small, perhaps vanishingly so. But what effects it has are probably perverse * * *. *Dickerson* represents not a bullet dodged but an opportunity missed. As things stand now, from almost any plausible set of premises, police interrogation is badly regulated. Because of *Dickerson*, it will continue to be badly regulated for a long time to come.

"The reason has to do with *Miranda*'s regulatory strategy. The essence of that strategy was to shift, from courts to suspects, the burden of separating good police interrogation from bad. Instead of courts deciding based on all the circumstances (or at least all the circumstances disclosed during the suppression hearing) whether the suspect's confession was voluntary, *Miranda* left it for suspects to decide, by either agreeing to talk or by calling a halt to questioning and/or calling for the help of a lawyer, whether the police were behaving too coercively. A growing literature on the empirics of police questioning shows why that strategy has failed. Suspects do not, in fact, separate good questioning from bad; once suspects agree to talk to police, they almost never call a halt to questioning or invoke their right to have the assistance of counsel. Instead, suspects separate *themselves*, not the police, into two categories: talkative and quiet. The sorting says nothing at all about the police, because it happens before police questioning has begun, hence before any police coercion has begun. Rather, the sorting is a signal of the suspect's savvy and experience. Because of *Miranda*, sophisticated suspects have a right to be free from questioning altogether—not simply free from coercive questioning—while unsophisticated suspects have very nearly no protection at all. The first group receives more than it deserves, while the second receives less than it needs."

8. ***Is Congress still free to replace Miranda warnings with other procedures? Is it likely to do so?*** Consider YALE KAMISAR, *Miranda Thirty-Five Years Later: A Close Look at the Majority and Dissenting Opinions in Dickerson*, 33 Ariz.St.L.J. 387, 425 (2001): "*Miranda* left the door open for Congress to replace the warnings with other safeguards that perform the same function. Unfortunately, Congress did not walk in the door. But the door remains open.

"The alternative often mentioned is a system of audiotaping or videotaping police questioning *and* a modified set of warnings.[j] I think such a system would

prosecutions—the Warren Court was able to overrule scores of restrictive precedents in favor of vastly expanded rights of the accused yet avoid the need to reverse scores of past convictions obtained in compliance with the overruled precedents. * * *

j. See Note 13, p. 637. Consider, too judicial or judicially supervised questioning, another frequently mentioned alternative to police interrogation. Paul Kauper, *Judicial Examination of the Accused—A Remedy for the Third Degree*, 30 Mich.L.Rev. 1224 (1932), seems to be the first commentator to spell out the desirability of, and historical support, for judicial questioning. In the wake of *Miranda*, two eminent judges returned to the Kauper model and built upon it. See Walter Schaefer, *The Suspect and Society*, 76–81 (1967); Henry Friendly, *The Fifth Amendment Tomorrow: The Case for Constitutional Change*, 37 U.Cin.L.Rev. 671,

and should pass constitutional muster. (It seems clear, however, that, no matter how fool-proof, a tape recording system that dispensed with all warnings would not be upheld.[212])

"If such a system replaced the four-fold *Miranda* warnings it would make clear that 'a decision may be *both* an interpretation of the Constitution *and* a principle that Congress may modify.'[213] However, I doubt that any legislature will enact any audiotaping or videotaping system that contains some warnings of rights or any other *effective* alternative to the *Miranda* regime. For any alternative that *is* equally effective is likely to be 'politically unacceptable for precisely the reason that saves it from being constitutionally unacceptable—it would be at least as protective of the suspect (and therefore at least as burdensome to investigators) as *Miranda* itself.'[214]

"I believe Stephen Schulhofer is quite right—'politically attractive alternatives to *Miranda* can't pass constitutional muster, and constitutional alternatives cannot attract political support.'[215] That is why the *Miranda* warnings will probably be with us for a long time."

9. *Unrepentant dissenters.* Recall that, dissenting in *Dickerson*, Justice Scalia vowed that, until § 3501 was repealed by Congress, he would "continue to apply it in all cases where there had been a sustainable finding that the defendant's confession was voluntray." Is this position defensible? Consider Dripps, Note 1, supra, at 65–66:

"Whatever the theory on which the doctrine of judicial supremacy rests, no justice can consistently maintain judicial supremacy while regarding herself as unobligated by decisions of the Court. This is not to say that civil disobedience is never justified. * * * Judicial civil disobedience, however, is especially hard to

713–16 (1968). Under the "Kauper–Schaefer–Friendly" model, discussed at length in Kamisar, *Kauper's Judicial Examination of the Accused Forty Years Later—Some Comments on a Remarkable Article*, 73 Mich.L.Rev. 15 (1974), a suspect questioned either by or before a judicial officer would have the assistance of counsel and be informed that she need not answer any questions. But she would also be told that if subsequently prosecuted her refusal to answer questions at the earlier proceeding would be disclosed at trial.

Does *Griffin v. California* (1965) (set forth at p. 1453, which forbids comment on a defendant's failure to testify at trial, stand in the way of this proposal? As have many other commentators, both Judges Friendly and Schaefer assumed that their proposal could not be effectuated without a constitutional amendment. But Albert W. Alschuler, *A Peculiar Privilege in Historical Perspective: The Right to Remain Silent*, 94 Mich.L.Rev. 2625, 2670–72 (1996), and Marvin Frankel, *From Private Rights to Public Justice*, 51 N.Y.U.L.Rev. 516, 531 (1976), have forcefully argued to the contrary. They have maintained that such an alternative would probably promote accurate fact-finding (both when it would help the suspect and when it would hurt him) and sharply reduce the amount of truly compelled self-incrimination in our society.

Recently, Akhil Reed Amar & Renée B. Lettow, *Fifth Amendment First Principles: The Self-Incrimination Clause*, 93 Mich.L.Rev. 857, 858, 898, 908 (1995), revisited and revised the "Kauper–Schaefer–Friendly" proposal. Under the Amar–Lettow version, the suspect at a judicially supervised pretrial hearing who failed to answer truthfully would be held in contempt. If he did answer, he would only be entitled to "testimonial immunity," i.e., his compelled *words* could not be introduced in a criminal trial, but the evidence derived from those words—such as the whereabouts of damaging physical evidence or a potential witness for the prosecution—would be admissible. For strong criticism of the Amar–Lettow proposal see Kamisar, *On the "Fruits of Miranda Violations," Coerced Confessions, and Compelled Testimony*, 93 Mich.L.Rev. 929, 932–33 (1995).

212. As the *Dickerson* Court told us, referring to very similar language in the *Miranda* opinion, "*Miranda* requires procedures that will warn a suspect in custody of his right to remain silent and which will assure the suspect that the exercise of that right will be honored."

213. David A. Strauss, *Miranda, The Constitution and Congress*, 99 Mich.L.Rev. 958, 960 (2001).

214. Stephen J. Schulhofer, *Miranda, Dickerson and the Puzzling Persistence of Fifth Amendment Exceptionalism*, 99 Mich.L.Rev. 941, 955 (2001).

215. Id.

defend. Judges, unlike ordinary citizens, swear an oath to uphold the law. Unlike ordinary citizens, they claim the obedience of others to their decisions on the basis of a general obligation to obey the law."

SECTION 4. *MIRANDA*, THE PRIVILEGE AGAINST COMPELLED SELF-INCRIMINATION AND FOURTEENTH AMENDMENT DUE PROCESS: WHEN DOES A VIOLATION OF THESE SAFEGUARDS OCCUR?

CHAVEZ v. MARTINEZ

538 U.S. 760, 123 S.Ct. 1994, 155 L.Ed.2d 984 (2003).

Justice THOMAS announced the judgment of the Court and delivered an opinion [joined by the Chief Justice in its entirety, by Justice O'Connor with respect to Parts I and II—A, and by Justice Scalia with respect to Parts I and II].

[This case involves a § 1983 suit arising out of petitioner Ben Chavez's allegedly coercive interrogation of respondent Oliverio Martinez. The [Ninth Circuit] held that Chavez was not entitled to a defense of qualified immunity because he violated Martinez's clearly established constitutional rights. We conclude that Chavez did not deprive Martinez of a constitutional right.

I

[During an altercation with the police, an officer shot Martinez five times, causing severe injuries that left him partially blinded and paralyzed from the waist down. Chavez, a patrol supervisor who had arrived on the scene a few minutes after the shooting, accompanied Martinez to the hospital where he questioned him while he was receiving treatment from medical personnel. The questioning lasted a total of about 10 minutes over a 45–minute period, with Chavez leaving the emergency room from time to time to permit medical personnel to treat Martinez. At no point during the exchange between Martinez and Chavez was Martinez given the *Miranda* warnings.

[At first Martinez's responses to Chavez's questions about what had happened between him and the police were simply "I don't know," "I am choking" or "My leg hurts." Later, however, Martinez admitted that he had taken a pistol from an officer's holster and pointed the weapon at him. On seven different occasions, Martinez told the officer: "I am dying," "I am dying, please," or "I don't want to die, I don't want to die," but the questioning continued. At one point, Martinez told the officer: "I am not telling you anything until they [the doctors] treat me." But he continued to answer questions. According to a tape recording, toward the end of questioning, the following exchange between Chavez and Martinez occurred:

Chavez: [Do] you think you are going to die?

Martinez: Aren't you going to treat me or what?

Chavez: [That's] all I want to know, if you think you're going to die?

Martinez: My belly hurts, please treat me.

Chavez: Sir?

Martinez: If you treat me I tell you everything, if not, no.

Chavez: Sir, I want to know if you think you are going to die right now?

Martinez: I think so.

Chavez: You think so? Ok, look, the doctors are going to help you with all they can do, Ok? . . .

Martinez: Get moving, I am dying, can't you see me? Come on.

Chavez: Ah, huh, right now they are giving you medication.

[Although Martinez was never charged with a crime and his answers were never used against him in any criminal prosecution, he brought a § 1983 action, claiming that Chavez had violated both his Fifth Amendment right not to be "compelled in any criminal case to a be a witness against himself" and his Fourteenth Amendment due process right to be free from coercive questioning. The Ninth Circuit agreed with Martinez. It viewed the Fifth and Fourteenth Amendment rights asserted by Martinez clearly established by federal law, explaining that a reasonable police officer "would have known that persistent interrogation of the suspect despite repeated requests to stop violated the suspect's Fifth and Fourteenth Amendment right to be free from coercive interrogation."]

II

In deciding whether an officer is entitled to qualified immunity, we must first determine whether the officer's alleged conduct violated a constitutional right. If not, the officer is entitled to qualified immunity, and we need not consider whether the asserted right was "clearly established." We conclude that Martinez's allegations fail to state a violation of his constitutional rights.

A

The Fifth Amendment, made applicable to the States by the Fourteenth Amendment, requires that "[n]o person . . . shall be compelled *in any criminal case* to be a *witness* against himself" (emphases added). We fail to see how, based on the text of the Fifth Amendment, Martinez can allege a violation of this right, since Martinez was never prosecuted for a crime, let alone compelled to be a witness against himself in a criminal case.

Although Martinez contends that the meaning of "criminal case" should encompass the entire criminal investigatory process, including police interrogations, we disagree. In our view, a "criminal case" at the very least requires the initiation of legal proceedings. * * * Statements compelled by police interrogations of course may not be used against a defendant at trial, but it is not until their use in a criminal case that a violation of the Self-Incrimination Clause occurs. "[Although] conduct by law enforcement officials prior to trial may ultimately impair that right, *a constitutional violation occurs only at trial*" (emphases added); *Withrow v. Williams*, (describing the Fifth Amendment as a "trial right"); id. (O'Connor, J., concurring in part and dissenting in part) (describing "true Fifth Amendment claims" as "the extraction and use of compelled testimony" (emphasis altered)).

Here, Martinez was never made to be a "witness" against himself in violation of the Fifth Amendment's Self-Incrimination Clause because his statements were never admitted as testimony against him in a criminal case. Nor was he ever placed under oath and exposed to " 'the cruel trilemma of self-accusation, perjury or contempt.' " [See discussion at p. 889.] The text of the Self-Incrimination Clause simply cannot support the Ninth Circuit's view that the mere use of compulsive questioning, without more, violates the Constitution. * * *

We fail to see how Martinez was any more "compelled in any criminal case to be a witness against himself" than an immunized witness forced to testify on pain of contempt. One difference, perhaps, is that the immunized witness *knows* that his statements will not, and may not, be used against him, whereas Martinez likely did not. But this does not make the statements of the immunized witness any less "compelled" and lends no support to the Ninth Circuit's conclusion that coercive police interrogations, absent the use of the involuntary statements in a criminal case, violate the Fifth Amendment's Self-Incrimination Clause.

[In] the Fifth Amendment context, we have created prophylactic rules designed to safeguard the core constitutional right protected by the Self-Incrimination Clause. [Among] these rules is an evidentiary privilege that protects witnesses from being forced to give incriminating testimony, even in noncriminal cases, unless that testimony has been immunized from use and derivative use in a future criminal proceeding before it is compelled. [By] allowing a witness to insist on an immunity agreement *before* being compelled to give incriminating testimony in a noncriminal case, the privilege preserves the core Fifth Amendment right from invasion by the use of that compelled testimony in a subsequent criminal case. * * * Because the failure to assert the privilege will often forfeit the right to exclude the evidence in a subsequent "criminal case," [it] is necessary to allow assertion of the privilege prior to the commencement of a "criminal case" to safeguard the core Fifth Amendment trial right. If the privilege could not be asserted in such situations, testimony given in those judicial proceedings would be deemed "voluntary"; hence, insistence on a prior grant of immunity is essential to memorialize the fact that the testimony had indeed been compelled and therefore protected from use against the speaker in any "criminal case."

Rules designed to safeguard a constitutional right, however, do not extend the scope of the constitutional right itself, just as violations of judicially crafted prophylactic rules do not violate the constitutional rights of any person. * * * We have likewise established the *Miranda* exclusionary rule as a prophylactic measure to prevent violations of the right protected by the text of the Self-Incrimination Clause—the admission into evidence in criminal case of confessions obtained through coercive custodial questioning. [Accordingly,] Chavez's failure to read Miranda warnings to Martinez did not violate Martinez's constitutional rights and cannot be grounds for a § 1983 action. * * *

We are satisfied that Chavez's questioning did not violate Martinez's due process rights. Even assuming, *arguendo*, that the persistent questioning of Martinez somehow deprived him of a liberty interest, we cannot agree with Martinez's characterization of Chavez's behavior as "egregious" or "conscience shocking." [There] is no evidence that Chavez acted with a purpose to harm Martinez by intentionally interfering with his medical treatment. Medical personnel were able to treat Martinez throughout the interview and Chavez ceased his questioning to allow tests and other procedures to be performed. Nor is there evidence that Chavez's conduct exacerbated Martinez's injuries or prolonged his stay in the hospital. Moreover, the need to investigate whether there had been police misconduct constituted a justifiable government interest given the risk that key evidence would have been lost if Martinez had died without the authorities ever hearing his side of the story. * * *

Justice SOUTER, delivered an opinion, Part II of which is the opinion of the Court, and Part I of which is an opinion concurring in the judgment. [Justice Breyer joined the opinion in its entirety and Justices Stevens, Kennedy and Ginsburg joined Part II of the opinion.]

I

Respondent Martinez's claim [under] § 1983 for violation of his privilege against compelled self-incrimination should be rejected and his case remanded for further proceedings. I write separately because I believe that our decision requires a degree of discretionary judgment greater than Justice Thomas acknowledges. As he points out, the text of the Fifth Amendment * * * focuses on courtroom use of a criminal defendant's compelled, self-incriminating testimony, and the core of the guarantee against compelled self-incrimination is the exclusion of any such evidence. Justice Ginsburg makes it clear that the present case is very close to *Mincey v. Arizona* [p. 557], and Martinez's testimony would clearly be inadmissible if offered in evidence against him. But Martinez claims more than evidentiary protection in asking this Court to hold that the questioning alone was a completed violation of the Fifth and Fourteenth Amendments subject to redress by an action for damages under § 1983. * * *

I do not [believe] that Martinez can make the "powerful showing," subject to a realistic assessment of costs and risks, necessary to expand protection of the privilege against compelled self-incrimination to the point of the civil liability he asks us to recognize here. The most obvious drawback inherent in Martinez's purely Fifth Amendment claim to damages is its risk of global application in every instance of interrogation producing a statement inadmissible under Fifth and Fourteenth Amendment principles, or violating one of the complementary rules we have accepted in aid of the privilege against evidentiary use. If obtaining Martinez's statement is to be treated as a stand-alone violation of the privilege subject to compensation, why should the same not be true whenever the police obtain any involuntary self-incriminating statement, or whenever the government so much as threatens a penalty in derogation of the right to immunity, or whenever the police fail to honor *Miranda*?[1] Martinez offers no limiting principle or reason to foresee a stopping place short of liability in all such cases. * * *

II

Whether Martinez may pursue a claim of liability for a substantive due process violation is thus an issue that should be addressed on remand, along with the scope and merits of any such action that may be found open to him.[a]

Justice SCALIA, concurring in part in the judgment.

I agree with the Court's rejection of Martinez's Fifth Amendment claim, that is, his claim that Chavez violated his right not to be compelled in any criminal case to be a witness against himself. And without a violation of the right protected by the text of the Self–Incrimination Clause, (what the plurality and Justice Souter call the Fifth Amendment's "core"), Martinez's § 1983 action is doomed. Section 1983 does not provide remedies for violations of judicially created prophylactic rules, such as the rule of *Miranda*, as the Court today holds [referring to Justice Thomas's and Justice Kennedy's opinions]; nor is it concerned with "extensions" of constitutional provisions designed to safeguard actual constitutional rights [referring to Justice Souter's opinion]. Rather, a plaintiff seeking redress through § 1983 must establish the violation of a federal constitutional or statutory *right*. * * *

Justice STEVENS, concurring in part and dissenting in part.

As a matter of fact, the interrogation of respondent was the functional equivalent of an attempt to obtain an involuntary confession from a prisoner by torturous methods. As a matter of law, that type of brutal police conduct constitutes an immediate deprivation of the prisoner's constitutionally protected interest in liberty. Because these propositions are so clear, the [courts below] correctly held that petitioner is not entitled to qualified immunity.

1. The question whether the absence of *Miranda* warnings may be a basis for a § 1983 action under any circumstance is not before the Court.

a. Of the six opinions produced by *Chavez v. Martinez*, the only text that commanded a majority was Part II of Justice Souter's opinion.

I

[Most of this part of Justice Steven's opinion consists of an English translation of substantial portions of the tape-recorded questioning of Martinez in Spanish that occurred in the emergency room. This part of his opinion is omitted. However, portions of the recorded questioning are set forth at p. 695.]

The sound recording of this interrogation, which has been lodged with the Court, vividly demonstrates that respondent was suffering severe pain and mental anguish throughout petitioner's persistent questioning. * * *

Justice KENNEDY, with whom Justice Stevens joins, and with whom Justice Ginsburg joins as to Parts II and III, concurring in part and dissenting in part.

A single police interrogation now presents us with two issues: first, whether failure to give a required warning under *Miranda* was itself a completed constitutional violation actionable § 1983; and second, whether an actionable violation arose at once under the Self–Incrimination Clause [when] the police, after failing to warn, used severe compulsion or extraordinary pressure in an attempt to elicit a statement or confession.

I agree with Justice Thomas that failure to give a *Miranda* warning does not, without more, establish a completed violation when the unwarned interrogation ensues. As to the second aspect of the case, which does not involve the simple failure to give a *Miranda* warning, it is my respectful submission that Justice Souter and Justice Thomas are incorrect. They conclude that a violation of the Self–Incrimination Clause does not arise until a privileged statement is introduced at some later criminal proceeding.

A constitutional right is traduced the moment torture or its close equivalents are brought to bear. Constitutional protection for a tortured suspect is not held in abeyance until some later criminal proceeding takes place. These are the premises of this separate opinion.

II

Justice Souter and Justice Thomas are wrong, in my view, to maintain that in all instances a violation of the Self–Incrimination Clause simply does not occur unless and until a statement is introduced at trial, no matter how severe the pain or how direct and commanding the official compulsion used to extract it. * * *

[The] conclusion that the Self–Incrimination Clause is not violated until the government seeks to use a statement in some later criminal proceeding strips the Clause of an essential part of its force and meaning. This is no small matter. It should come as an unwelcome surprise to judges, attorneys, and the citizenry as a whole that if a legislative committee or a judge in a civil case demands incriminating testimony without offering immunity, and even imposes sanctions for failure to comply, that the witness and counsel cannot insist the right against compelled self-incrimination is applicable then and there. * * *

III

Had the officer inflicted the initial injuries sustained by Martinez (the gunshot wounds) for purposes of extracting a statement, there would be a clear and immediate violation of the Constitution, and no further inquiry would be needed. That is not what happened, however. The initial injuries and anguish suffered by the suspect were not inflicted to aid the interrogation.

[There] is no rule against interrogating suspects who are in anguish and pain. The police may have legitimate reasons, borne of exigency, to question a person who is suffering or in distress. Locating the victim of a kidnaping, ascertaining the whereabouts of a dangerous assailant or accomplice, or determining whether there is a rogue police officer at large are some examples. That a suspect is in fear of dying, furthermore, may not show compulsion but just the opposite. The fear may be a motivating factor to volunteer information. The words of a declarant who believes his death is imminent have a special status in the law of evidence.

[There] are, however, actions police may not take if the prohibition against the use of coercion to elicit a statement is to be respected. The police may not prolong or increase a suspect's suffering against the suspect's will. That conduct would render government officials accountable for the increased pain. The officers must not give the impression that severe pain will be alleviated only if the declarant cooperates, for that, too, uses pain to extract a statement. In a case like this one, recovery should be available under § 1983 if a complainant can demonstrate that an officer exploited his pain and suffering with the purpose and intent of securing an incriminating statement. That showing has been made here.

The transcript of the interrogation set out by Justice Stevens, and other evidence considered by the District Court demonstrate that the suspect thought his treatment would be delayed, and thus his pain and condition worsened, by refusal to answer questions.

* * * I would affirm the decision of the Court of Appeals that a cause of action under § 1983 has been stated. The other opinions filed today, however, reach different conclusions as to the correct disposition of the case. Were Justice Stevens, Justice Ginsburg, and I to adhere to our position, there would be no controlling judgment of the Court. In these circumstances, and because a ruling on substantive due process in this case could provide much of the essential protection the Self–Incrimination Clause secures, I join Part II of Justice Souter's opinion and would remand the case for further consideration.

Justice GINSBURG, concurring in part and dissenting in part.

I join Parts II and III of Justice Kennedy's opinion. For reasons well stated therein, I would hold that the Self–Incrimination Clause applies at the time and place police use severe compulsion to extract a statement from a suspect. * * * I write separately to state my view that, even if no finding were made concerning Martinez's belief that refusal to answer would delay his treatment, or Chavez's intent to create such an impression, the interrogation in this case would remain a clear instance of the kind of compulsion no reasonable officer would have thought constitutionally permissible. * * *

Convinced that Chavez's conduct violated Martinez's right to be spared from self-incriminating interrogation, I would affirm the judgment of the Court of Appeals. To assure a controlling judgment of the Court, however, * * * I join Part II of Justice Souter's opinion.

Notes and Questions

1. ***The recurring use of "prophylactic rule" terminology.*** The *Dickerson* Court called *Miranda* "a constitutional decision," "constitutionally based" and a case that "announced a constitutional rule." Although it recognized that the Court had described *Miranda* as a "prophylactic" rule *in the past*,the *Dickerson* Court itself never referred to *Miranda* as a prophylactic rule—a point underscored by the *Dickerson* dissent (Scalia, J., joined by Thomas, J.). Is it consistent with his position in *Dickerson* for Justice Thomas, speaking for four Justices in *Chavez v. Martinez*, to call *Miranda* a "prophylactic measure" established "to prevent violations of the rights protected by the text of the Self–Incrimination Clause"?

2. ***The meaning of "criminal case."*** For strong criticism of Justice Thomas's view of the meaning of "criminal case" in the text of the Fifth

Amendment, see Thomas Y. Davies, *Farther and Farther from the Original Fifth Amendment: The Recharacterization of the Right Against Self–Incrimination as a "Trial Right" in Chavez v. Martinez*, 70 Tenn.L.Rev. 987, 1009–18 (2003):

"[It] seems highly probable that the phrase 'in any criminal case' was added to the Fifth Amendment simply to clarify that the right against compelled self-incrimination did not extend to governmentally compelled interrogation, production of evidence, or oath-taking that might expose a person to only civil liability.

"[The] historical sources show that the right against self-accusation was understood to arise primarily in pretrial or preprosecution settings rather than in the context of a person's own criminal trial. Thus, a witness in the trial of another person could invoke the right to refuse to answer a potentially self-incriminating question. Again, as of the framing era, broadly applicable grants of immunity by which a person could be compelled to answer had not yet been invented."

SECTION 5. THE *PATANE* AND *SEIBERT* CASES: IS PHYSICAL EVIDENCE OR A "SECOND CONFESSION" DERIVED FROM A FAILURE TO COMPLY WITH THE *MIRANDA* RULES ADMISSIBLE? THE COURT'S ANSWERS SHED LIGHT ON DICKERSON

Background

For many years, courts have not only excluded evidence that is "direct" or "primary" in its relationship to the prior illegal arrest or search, but also "secondary" or "derivative" evidence that is tainted by the primary evidence, e.g., an otherwise "volunteered" confession obtained from an illegally arrested person or physical evidence found as the result of an illegal wiretap. To use a popular term, the courts have not only excluded the primary evidence that is illegally obtained, but the "fruit of the poisonous tree" as well. See generally pp. ___ –___.

In OREGON v. ELSTAD, 470 U.S. 298 (1985), however, the Court declined to apply the "poisoned fruit" doctrine to a "second confession" following a confession obtained without giving defendant the *Miranda* warnings. The case arose as follows: When police questioned defendant in his own home about a recent burglary, he replied, "Yes, I was there." About an hour later, after he had been taken to the sheriff's office, the defendant was advised of his rights for the first time. He waived his rights and gave the police a statement detailing his participation in the burglary. The state conceded that the statement defendant made in his own home should be excluded (a questionable concession), but argued that the second confession should be admitted. The state court ruled *both* statements inadmissible.

The U.S. Supreme Court reversed. A 6–3 majority, per O'CONNOR, J., informed us that the state court had "misconstrued" the protections afforded by *Miranda* by assuming that "a failure to administer *Miranda* warnings necessarily breeds the same consequences as police infringement of a constitutional right, so that evidence uncovered following an unwarned statement must be suppressed as 'fruit of the poisonous tree.'" There is, Justice O'Connor emphasized, "a vast difference between the direct consequences flowing from coercion of a confession by physical violence [and] the uncertain consequences of disclosure of a 'guilty secret' freely given in response to an unwarned but noncoercive question as in this case." At one point she described a person whose *Miranda* rights had been violated, but whose statements had not actually been coerced, as someone "who has suffered no identifiable constitutional harm."

The *Elstad* Court seemed to say—it certainly could plausibly be read as saying—that because a violation of *Miranda* is not a violation of a *real* constitutional right (but only a rule of evidence designed to implement the privilege against self-incrimination), it is not entitled to, or worthy of, the "fruit of the poisonous tree" doctrine. Thus, unlike evidence obtained as the result of an unreasonable search or a coerced confession (which *are* real constitutional violations), secondary evidence derived from a *Miranda* violation need not, and should not, be suppressed as the tainted fruit.

Elstad was one of the post-Warren Court cases that encouraged critics of *Miranda* to believe that some day the new Court would overrule that much-criticized case. But that day never came. Instead, as we have seen, fifteen years later, in the *Dickerson* case, the Court struck down a federal statute purporting to abolish *Miranda*, removing any doubt that "*Miranda* is a constitutional decision of this Court."

What about *Oregon v. Elstad*? As we have also seen, somewhat surprisingly, the *Dickerson* Court had nothing negative to say about that case. As for the argument that *Elstad* rested largely on the premise that *Miranda* is not a constitutional decision, Chief Justice Rehnquist commented only that *Elstad* "simply recognizes the fact that unreasonable searches under the Fourth Amendment are different from unwarned interrogation under the Fifth Amendment."

However, in *Patane*, set forth below, the U.S. Court of Appeals for the Tenth Circuit, per Ebel, J., believed, understandably, that *Dickerson* had had a greater bearing on *Elstad* than the *Dickerson* Court had been prepared to spell out. According to the Tenth Circuit, the premise upon which cases like *Elstad* relied was "fundamentally altered" in *Dickerson*; that case "undermined the logic underlying" cases like *Elstad*. (The U.S. Supreme Court was to disagree.)

Oral Arguments in the Patane case

* * *

JUSTICE SCALIA: [Is *Miranda*] a Fifth Amendment right or not a Fifth Amendment right? [It] has to be based on something in the Constitution or we would have had to respect the statute enacted by Congress in *Dickerson*. * * *

DEPUTY SOLICITOR GENERAL DREEBEN: It's a Fifth Amendment right * * *. What the Court concluded in *Miranda* and then reaffirmed in *Dickerson* is that the traditional "totality of the circumstances" test for ascertaining whether a statement is voluntary or has been compelled is not adequate when the statements are taken in the inherently pressuring environment of custodial interrogation. And to provide an extra layer of protection [in order] to avoid the violation of the defendant's Fifth Amendment rights, the Court adopted a prophylactic warnings and waiver procedure.

JUSTICE SCALIA: Whether it's prophylactic or not, it is a constitutional right, is it not? * * *

MR. DREEBEN: [It] is a constitutional right that is distinct from the right not to have one's compelled statements used against oneself. * * *

JUSTICE STEVENS: Supposing that the Government used official powers, such as a grand jury subpoena or a congressional committee subpoena [to] get a confession out of a person under the threat of contempt of court [and] the person made an answer that revealed the existence of [a] gun. [Should] the gun be admissible [in] that scenario?

MR. DREEBEN: [The] gun would not be admissible, because this Court has defined a violation of the Fifth Amendment that involves actual compulsion as entailing two different evidentiary consequences. One [is] that the statements themselves may not be used. The other evidentiary consequence is that nothing derived from the statements may be used. But the critical feature of that hypothetical, and its distinction from *Miranda*, is it involves actual compulsion. * * *

JUSTICE GINSBURG: [The *Miranda* opinion] itself said, but unless and until [the *Miranda*] warnings and waivers are demonstrated by the prosecution at trial, no evidence obtained as a result of interrogation can be used against [the defendant], no evidence as a result of interrogation. That sounds like [a] derivative evidence rule to me.

MR. DREEBEN: It does [and] there are many things in the *Miranda* opinion that have not stood the test of later litigation in this Court.

UNITED STATES v. PATANE

___ U.S. ___, 124 S.Ct. 2620, 159 L.Ed.2d 667 (2004).

Justice THOMAS announced the judgment of the Court and delivered an opinion, in which THE CHIEF JUSTICE and Justice SCALIA join.

[Defendant Patane was arrested outside his home and handcuffed. A federal agent, who had been told that defendant, a convicted felon, illegally possessed a Glock pistol, began giving him the *Miranda* warnings, but defendant interrupted the agent, stating that he knew his rights. No further *Miranda* warnings were given (which the government conceded on appeal resulted in a violation of the *Miranda* rules).

[When the federal agent told defendant he wanted to know about a Glock pistol he possessed, defendant replied: "The Glock is in my bedroom on a shelf * * *." The agent found the pistol where defendant said it would be and seized it. Defendant was convicted of being a felon in possession of a firearm in violation of federal law.]

As we explain below, the *Miranda* rule is a prophylactic employed to protect against violations of the Self–Incrimination Clause. [That clause], however, is not implicated by the admission into evidence of the physical fruit of a voluntary statement. Accordingly, there is no justification for extending the *Miranda* rule to this context. [The] *Miranda* rule is not a code of police conduct, and police do not violate the Constitution (or even the *Miranda* rules for that matter) by mere failures to warn. For this reason, the exclusionary rule articulated in various [Fourth Amendment cases] does not apply.

[The] core protection afforded by the Self–Incrimination Clause is a prohibition on compelling a criminal defendant to testify against himself at trial. See, e.g., *Chavez v. Martinez* (plurality opinion). [The] Clause cannot be violated by the introduction of nontestimonial evidence obtained as a result of voluntary statements. See, e.g., *United States v. Hubbell* [p. 871] (noting that the word "witness" in the Self–Incrimination Clause "limits the relevant category of compelled incriminating statements to those that are 'testimonial' in character").

[Because such] prophylactic rules [as the *Miranda* rule] necessarily sweep beyond the actual protections of the Self–Incrimination Clause, any further extension of these rules must be justified by its necessity for the protection of the actual right against compelled self-incrimination, *Chavez* (opinion of Souter, J.). [Furthermore,] the Self–Incrimination Clause contains its own exclusionary rule. It provides that "[n]o person [shall] be compelled in any criminal case to be a witness against himself." [We] have repeatedly explained "that those subjected to coercive interrogations have an *automatic* protection from the use of their involuntary statements (or evidence derived from their statements) in any subsequent criminal trial," *Chavez* (plurality opinion). This explicit textual protection supports a strong presumption against expanding the *Miranda* rule any further.

Finally, nothing in *Dickerson*, including its characterization of *Miranda* as announcing a constitutional rule, changes any of these observations. Indeed, [*Dickerson*] specifically noted that the Court's "subsequent cases have reduced the impact of the *Miranda* rule on legitimate law enforcement while reaffirming [*Miranda*'s] core ruling that unwarned statements may not be used as evidence in the prosecution's case in chief." [The *Dickerson* Court's] reliance on our *Miranda* precedents [including *Elstad*, which read *Miranda* narrowly] further demonstrates the continuing validity of those decisions. In short, nothing in *Dickerson* calls into question our continued insistence that the closest possible fit be maintained between the Self-Incrimination Clause and any rule designed to protect it.

Our cases also make clear the related point that a mere failure to give *Miranda* warnings does not, by itself, violate a suspect's constitutional rights or even the *Miranda* rule. See *Chavez*. [This], of course, follows from the nature of the right protected by the Self-Incrimination Clause, which the *Miranda* rule, in turn protects. "It is a fundamental *trial* right." *Withrow v. Williams* [p. 671].

[It] follows that police do not violate a suspect's constitutional rights (or the *Miranda* rule) by negligent or even deliberate failures to provide the suspect with the full panoply of warnings prescribed by *Miranda*. Potential violations occur, if at all, only upon the admission of unwarned statements into evidence at trial. And, at that point, "the exclusion of unwarned statements [is] a complete and sufficient remedy" for any perceived *Miranda* violations. *Chavez*.

Thus, unlike unreasonable searches under the Fourth Amendment or actual violations of the Due Process Clause or the Self-Incrimination Clause, there is, with respect to mere failures to warn, nothing to deter. There is therefore no reason to apply the "fruit of the poisonous tree" doctrine [utilized in Fourth Amendment cases]. It is not for this Court to impose its preferred police practices on either federal law enforcement officials or their state counterparts.

[*Dickerson*'s] characterization of *Miranda* as a constitutional rule does not lessen the need to maintain the closest possible fit between the Self-Incrimination Clause and any judge-made rule designed to protect it. And there is no such fit here. Introduction of the nontestimonial fruit of a voluntary statement, such as respondent's Glock, does not implicate the Self-Incrimination Clause. The admission of such fruit presents no risk that a defendant's coerced statements (however defined) will be used against him at a criminal trial. In any case, "[t]he exclusion of unwarned statements [is] a complete and sufficient remedy" for any perceived *Miranda* violation. *Chavez*. [There] is simply no need to extend (and therefore no justification for extending) the prophylactic rule of *Miranda* to this context.

[The Tenth Circuit] ascribed significance to the fact that, in this case, there might be "little [practical] difference between [respondent's] confessional statement" and the actual physical evidence. The distinction, the court said, "appears to make little sense as a matter of policy." But, putting policy aside, we have held that "[t]he word 'witness' in the constitutional text limits the" scope of the Self-Incrimination Clause to testimonial evidence. *Hubbell*. The Constitution itself makes the distinction.[6] And although it is true that the Court requires the exclusion of the physical fruit of actually coerced confessions, it must be remembered that statements taken without sufficient *Miranda* warnings are presumed to have been coerced only for certain purposes and then only when necessary to

6. While Fourth Amendment protections extend to "persons, houses, papers, and effects," the Self-Incrimination Clause prohibits only compelling a defendant to be a "witness against himself."

protect the privilege against self-incrimination. [We] decline to extend that presumption further. * * *

Justice KENNEDY, with whom Justice O'CONNOR joins, concurring in the judgment.

[In such cases as *Elstad* and *Quarles*], evidence obtained following an unwarned interrogation was held admissible. The result was based in large part on our recognition that the concerns underlying the [*Miranda* rule] must be accommodated to other objectives of the criminal justice system. I agree with the plurality that *Dickerson* did not undermine these precedents and, in fact, cited them in support. [Unlike] the plurality, however, I find it unnecessary to decide whether the [federal agent's] failure to give Patane the full *Miranda* warnings should be characterized as a violation of the *Miranda* rule itself, or whether there is "[any]thing to deter" so long as the unwarned statements are not later introduced at trial.

Justice SOUTER, with whom Justice STEVENS and Justice GINSBURG join, dissenting.

The majority repeatedly says that the Fifth Amendment does not address the admissibility of nontestimonial evidence, an overstatement that is beside the point. The issue actually presented today is whether courts should apply the fruit of the poisonous tree doctrine lest we create an incentive for the police to omit *Miranda* warnings before custodial interrogation. In closing their eyes to the consequences of giving an evidentiary advantage to those who ignore *Miranda*, the majority adds an important inducement for interrogators to ignore the rule in that case.

[There] is, of course, a price for excluding evidence, but the Fifth Amendment is worth a price, and in the absence of a very good reason, the logic of *Miranda* should be followed: a *Miranda* violation raises a presumption of coercion, and the Fifth Amendment privilege against compelled self-incrimination extends to the exclusion of derivative evidence, see *United States v. Hubbell* (recognizing "the Fifth Amendment's protection against the prosecutor's use of incriminating information derived directly or indirectly [from] [actually] compelled testimony"); *Kastigar v. United States* [p. 849]. That should be the end of this case.

[Of] course the premise of *Elstad* is not on point; although a failure to give *Miranda* warnings before one individual statement does not necessarily bar the admission of a subsequent statement given after adequate warnings, that rule obviously does not apply to physical evidence seized once and for all.

There is no way to read this case except as an unjustifiable invitation to law enforcement to flaunt *Miranda* when there may be physical evidence to be gained. The incentive is an odd one, coming from the Court on the same day it decides *Missouri v. Seibert* [the next main case].

Justice BREYER, dissenting.

For reasons similar to those set forth in Justice Souter's dissent and in my concurring opinion in *Seibert*, I would extend to this context the "fruit of the poisonous tree" approach, which I believe the Court has come close to adopting in *Seibert*. Under that approach, courts would exclude physical evidence derived from unwarned questioning unless the failure to provide *Miranda* warnings was in good faith. Because the courts below made no explicit finding as to good or bad faith, I would remand for such a determination.

Notes and Questions

1. ***Does the word "witness" in the text of the Self-Incrimination Clause prevent the exclusion of the pistol in a case like Patane?*** As we have

seen from the oral arguments in *Patane* (p. 702), the prosecution conceded that physical evidence derived from actually compelled testimony would be excluded. The language of the Self–Incrimination Clause does not prevent such a result in this setting. Moreover, Justice Thomas recognized that physical evidence derived from a coerced confession would also be excluded. Ever since *Malloy v. Hogan* (p. 569) (holding that the privilege against self-incrimination applies to the states and that the safeguards surrounding the admissibility of confessions in state cases have come to reflect all the policies embedded in the privilege) and *Miranda* (which applied the privilege against self-incrimination to the police station) the Self–Incrimination Clause has been widely viewed as a basis for the ban against the case of coerced confessions. Yet Justice Thomas concedes that the wording of the Self–Incrimination Clause would not prevent the exclusion of a pistol derived from an actually coerced confession. Why, then, in the circumstances that took place in *Patane*, does Justice Thomas tell us that " '[t]he word "witness" in the constitutional text limits the' scope of the Self–Incrimination Clause to testimonial evidence'?" Why does the specific language of the Self–Incrimination Clause constitute an impenetrable barrier to the exclusion of physical evidence in Mr. Patane's circumstances but become inoperative when the question presented is the admissibility of the same kind of evidence derived from statements obtained under the other circumstances discussed in this Note. In all instances we are talking about the same Self–Incrimination Clause, are we not? See Kamisar, *Postscript: Another Look at Patane and Seibert, the 2004 Miranda "Poisoned Fruit" Cases*, 2 Ohio St.J.Crim.Law 97, 102 (2004).

2. ***Are some "voluntary" statements less voluntary than others?*** Justice Thomas repeatedly asserts that "the Self–Incrimination Clause is not implicated by the admission into evidence of the physical fruit of a voluntary statement." But consider Kamisar, supra Note 1, at 99:

"The question presented in *Patane* was whether, for purposes of the Fifth Amendment's ban against the use of evidence derived from compelled statements (or, if one prefers, for purposes of the 'poisoned fruit' doctrine), a statement obtained without giving the requisite warnings should be treated as a compelled statement [or a presumptively compelled statement] or a voluntary one. Once you *assume* that statements obtained as a result of a failure to comply with the *Miranda* rules are 'voluntary'—just as voluntary for derivative evidence or tainted fruit purposes as, for example, a statement *volunteered* by someone *not* in police custody—the analysis is over. You have *assumed* the answer to the question.

"But why lump together (a) statements obtained without satisfying the *Miranda* rules and (b) what might be called purely or completely voluntary statements? Instead of putting the *Miranda*-deficient statements under the heading 'Voluntary Statements,' why not classify them under the heading 'Compelled, Coerced and Presumptively Compelled Statements'?"

3. ***The clear implication of Miranda.*** Consider Note, 118 Harv.L.Rev. 296, 302 (2004): "Although it is true that '[t]he admission of [unwarned] fruit[s] presents no risk that a defendant's *coerced* statements . . . *will be used* against him at a criminal trial' [Thomas, J., emphasis added], this focus ignores *Miranda*'s clear implication: the admission of the fruits of unwarned statements runs the constitutionally unacceptable risk that the fruits of coerced statements will be used at trial in violation of the Self–Incrimination Clause. In other words, excluding fruits is not an extension of *Miranda*'s prophylaxis; it is simply an application of it."

4. ***Patane and Dickerson.*** Consider the Harvard Note, supra, at 301: "The [*Patane*] plurality opinion characterized *Miranda* as a constitutionally based prophylactic rule. This representation is somewhat surprising because Justice

Scalia and Thomas, when dissenting in *Dickerson*, had explicitly noted that the Court failed to embrace this approach despite the strenuous arguments made for it by both the petitioner and the United States. In fact, although the dissenters recognized that this approach might have rendered *Miranda* jurisprudence coherent, they rejoiced in the Court's failure to rely on it because, believing that such prophylaxis was an 'immense and frightening antidemocratic power that does not exist,' they suggested that 'incoherence [might be] the lesser evil.' "

5. *What was the violation of the Miranda rules in the Patane case?* Justice Thomas's statement of the facts suggests that the violation occurred as follows: (a) an officer started to advise Mr. Patane of his rights, (b) Patane interrupted him, telling him he knew his *Miranda* rights, and (c) the officer did not attempt to complete the warnings. Some Court-watchers maintain, understandably, that, despite the prosecution's concession that a violation of the *Miranda* rules occurred in Patane, an officer's failure to complete the warnings when the suspect interrupts him and tells him he is aware of his rights should not be considered a failure to comply with *Miranda*. The answer is not clear. However, according to the briefs filed on behalf of Patane, this was not when the failure to comply with *Miranda* occurred. Rather, it occurred a moment later, when the officer failed to give Patane *an opportunity to assert his rights*. Even if an officer does give a suspect a complete set of *Miranda* warnings, *questioning him immediately thereafter without affording him an opportunity to assert or to waive his rights* would seem to be a clear violation of the *Miranda* rules.

MISSOURI v. SEIBERT

___ U.S. ___, 124 S.Ct. 2601, 159 L.Ed.2d 643 (2004).

Justice SOUTER announced the judgment of the Court and delivered an opinion, in which Justice STEVENS, Justice GINSBURG, and Justice BREYER join.

This case tests a police protocol for custodial interrogation that calls for giving no warnings of the rights to silence and counsel until interrogation has produced a confession. Although such a statement is generally inadmissible, since taken in violation of *Miranda*, the interrogating officer follows it with *Miranda* warnings and then leads the suspect to cover the same ground a second time. The question here is the admissibility of the repeated statement. Because this midstream recitation of warnings after interrogation and unwarned confession could not effectively comply with *Miranda*'s constitutional requirement, we hold that a statement repeated after a warning in such circumstances is inadmissible.

[Officer Hanrahan arranged for another officer to arrest Ms. Seibert, a murder suspect, specifically instructing the officer not to advise Seibert of her *Miranda* rights. After Seibert had been taken to the police station and left alone in an "interview room" for 15 to 20 minutes, Hanrahan questioned her for 30 to 40 minutes. After she made an incriminating statement, she was given a 20–minute break. Hanrahan then resumed questioning, this time advising Seibert of her *Miranda* rights. After she waived her rights, Hanrahan confronted Seibert with the incriminating statement she had made at the prewarning questioning session. As Hanrahan acknowledged, Seibert's ultimate statement was "largely a repeat of information * * * obtained" prior to the *Miranda* warnings. The trial court excluded only the statement obtained during the first questioning session. A 4–3 majority of the state supreme court reversed, holding that the statement the defendant made after she had been given the *Miranda* warnings and waived her rights had to be suppressed as well.]

* * * *Miranda* conditioned the admissibility at trial of any custodial confession on warning a suspect of his rights: failure to give the prescribed warnings and obtain a waiver of rights before custodial questioning generally requires exclusion of any statements obtained. Conversely, giving the warnings and getting a waiver has generally produced a virtual ticket of admissibility; maintaining that a statement is involuntary even though given after warnings and voluntary waiver of rights requires unusual stamina, and litigation over voluntariness tends to end with the finding of a valid waiver. * * *

[The] technique of interrogating in successive, unwarned and warned phases raises a new challenge to *Miranda.* Although we have no statistics on the frequency of this practice, it is not confined to Rolla, Missouri. An officer of that police department testified that the strategy of withholding *Miranda* warnings until after interrogating and drawing out a confession was promoted not only by his own department, but by a national police training organization and other departments in which he had worked. [The] upshot of [various training programs'] advice is a question-first practice of some popularity, as one can see from the reported cases describing its use, sometimes in obedience to departmental policy.

[*Miranda*] addressed "interrogation practices [likely] to disable [an individual] from making a free and rational choice" about speaking and held that a suspect must be "adequately and effectively" advised of the choice the Constitution guarantees. The object of question-first is to render *Miranda* warnings ineffective by waiting for a particularly opportune time to give them, after the suspect has already confessed.

[The] threshold issue when interrogators question first and warn later is thus whether it would be reasonable to find that in these circumstances the warnings could function "effectively" as *Miranda* requires. Could the warnings effectively advise the suspect that he had a real choice about giving an admissible statement at that juncture? Could they reasonably convey that he could choose to stop talking even if he had talked earlier? For unless the warnings could place a suspect who has just been interrogated in a position to make such an informed choice, there is no practical justification for accepting the formal warnings as compliance with *Miranda,* or for treating the second stage of interrogation as distinct from the first, unwarned and inadmissible segment.[1]

There is no doubt about the answer that proponents of question-first give to this question about the effectiveness of warnings given only after successful interrogation, and we think their answer is correct. By any objective measure, applied to circumstances exemplified here, it is likely that if the interrogators employ the technique of withholding warnings until after interrogation succeeds in eliciting a confession, the warnings will be ineffective in preparing the suspect

1. Respondent Seibert argues that her second confession should be excluded from evidence under the doctrine known by the metaphor of the "fruit of the poisonous tree," developed in the Fourth Amendment context in *Wong Sun v. United States*; evidence otherwise admissible but discovered as a result of an earlier violation is excluded as tainted, lest the law encourage future violations. But the Court in *Elstad* rejected the *Wong Sun* fruits doctrine for analyzing the admissibility of a subsequent warned confession following "an initial failure [to] administer the warnings required by *Miranda.*" * * * *Elstad* held that "a suspect who has once responded to unwarned yet uncoercive questioning is not thereby disabled from waiving his rights and confessing after he has been given the requisite *Miranda* warnings." In a sequential confession case, clarity is served if the later confession is approached by asking whether in the circumstances the *Miranda* warnings given could reasonably be found effective. If yes, a court can take up the standard issues of voluntary waiver and voluntary statement; if no, the subsequent statement is inadmissible for want of adequate *Miranda* warnings, because the earlier and later statements are realistically seen as parts of a single, unwarned sequence of questioning.

for successive interrogation, close in time and similar in content. After all, the reason that question-first is catching on is as obvious as its manifest purpose, which is to get a confession the suspect would not make if he understood his rights at the outset; the sensible underlying assumption is that with one confession in hand before the warnings, the interrogator can count on getting its duplicate, with trifling additional trouble. Upon hearing warnings only in the aftermath of interrogation and just after making a confession, a suspect would hardly think he had a genuine right to remain silent, let alone persist in so believing once the police began to lead him over the same ground again.[2]

A more likely reaction on a suspect's part would be perplexity about the reason for discussing rights at that point, bewilderment being an unpromising frame of mind for knowledgeable decision. What is worse, telling a suspect that "anything you say can and will be used against you," without expressly excepting the statement just given, could lead to an entirely reasonable inference that what he has just said will be used, with subsequent silence being of no avail. * * *

Missouri argues that a confession repeated at the end of an interrogation sequence envisioned in a question-first strategy is admissible on the authority of *Elstad,* but the argument disfigures that case. In *Elstad,* the police went to the young suspect's house to take him into custody on a charge of burglary. Before the arrest, one officer spoke with the suspect's mother, while the other one joined the suspect in a "brief stop in the living room," where the officer said he "felt" the young man was involved in a burglary. The suspect acknowledged he had been at the scene. [The Court] took care to mention that the officer's initial failure to warn was an "oversight" that "may have been the result of confusion as to whether the brief exchange qualified as 'custodial interrogation' * * *." [At] the outset of a later and systematic station house interrogation going well beyond the scope of the laconic prior admission, the suspect was given *Miranda* warnings and made a full confession. [On] the facts of [the] case, the Court thought any causal connection between the first and second responses to the police was "speculative and attenuated." [It] is fair to read *Elstad* as treating the living room conversation as a good-faith *Miranda* mistake, not only open to correction by careful warnings before systematic questioning in that particular case, but posing no threat to warn-first practice generally.

[The] contrast between *Elstad* and this case reveals a series of relevant facts that bear on whether *Miranda* warnings delivered midstream could be effective enough to accomplish their object: the completeness and detail of the questions and answers in the first round of interrogation, the overlapping content of the two statements, the timing and setting of the first and the second, the continuity of police personnel, and the degree to which the interrogator's questions treated the second round as continuous with the first. In *Elstad,* it was not unreasonable to see the occasion for questioning at the station house as presenting a markedly different experience from the short conversation at home; since a reasonable person in the suspect's shoes could have seen the station house questioning as a new and distinct experience, the *Miranda* warnings could have made sense as presenting a genuine choice whether to follow up on the earlier admission.

2. It bears emphasizing that the effectiveness *Miranda* assumes the warnings can have must potentially extend through the repeated interrogation, since a suspect has a right to stop at any time. It seems highly unlikely that a suspect could retain any such understanding when the interrogator leads him a second time through a line of questioning the suspect has already answered fully. The point is not that a later unknowing or involuntary confession cancels out an earlier, adequate warning; the point is that the warning is unlikely to be effective in the question-first sequence we have described.

At the opposite extreme are the facts here, which by any objective measure reveal a police strategy adapted to undermine the *Miranda* warnings.[6] The unwarned interrogation was conducted in the station house, and the questioning was systematic, exhaustive, and managed with psychological skill. When the police were finished there was little, if anything, of incriminating potential left unsaid. The warned phase of questioning proceeded after a pause of only 15 to 20 minutes, in the same place as the unwarned segment. [In] particular, the police did not advise that her prior statement could not be used.[7] Nothing was said or done to dispel the oddity of warning about legal rights to silence and counsel right after the police had led her through a systematic interrogation * * *. [The] impression that the further questioning was a mere continuation of the earlier questions and responses was fostered by references back to the confession already given. It would have been reasonable to regard the two sessions as parts of a continuum, in which it would have been unnatural to refuse to repeat at the second stage what had been said before. These circumstances must be seen as challenging the comprehensibility and efficacy of the *Miranda* warnings to the point that a reasonable person in the suspect's shoes would not have understood them to convey a message that she retained a choice about continuing to talk.

Strategists dedicated to draining the substance out of *Miranda* cannot accomplish by training instructions what *Dickerson* held Congress could not do by statute. Because the question-first tactic effectively threatens to thwart *Miranda*'s purpose of reducing the risk that a coerced confession would be admitted, and because the facts here do not reasonably support a conclusion that the warnings given could have served their purpose, Seibert's postwarning statements are inadmissible.

Justice BREYER, concurring.

In my view, the following simple rule should apply to the two-stage interrogation technique: Courts should exclude the "fruits" of the initial unwarned questioning unless the failure to warn was in good faith. I believe this is a sound and workable approach to the problem this case presents. Prosecutors and judges have long understood how to apply the "fruits" approach, which they use in other areas of law. And in the workaday world of criminal law enforcement the administrative simplicity of the familiar has significant advantages over a more complex exclusionary rule.

I believe the plurality's approach in practice will function as a "fruits" test. The truly "effective" *Miranda* warnings on which the plurality insists, will occur only when certain circumstances—a lapse in time, a change in location or interrogating officer, or a shift in the focus of the questioning—intervene between the unwarned questioning and any postwarning statement.

I consequently join the plurality's opinion in full. I also agree with Justice Kennedy's opinion insofar as it is consistent with this approach and makes clear that a good-faith exception applies.

Justice KENNEDY, concurring in the judgment.

The interrogation technique used in this case is designed to circumvent *Miranda*. It undermines the *Miranda* warning and obscures its meaning. The

6. Because the intent of the officer will rarely be as candidly admitted as it was here (even as it is likely to determine the conduct of the interrogation), the focus is on facts apart from intent that show the question-first tactic at work.

7. We do not hold that a formal addendum warning that a previous statement could not be used would be sufficient to change the character of the question-first procedure to the point of rendering an ensuing statement admissible, but its absence is clearly a factor that blunts the efficacy of the warnings and points to a continuing, not a new, interrogation.

plurality opinion is correct to conclude that statements obtained through the use of this technique are inadmissible. Although I agree with much in the careful and convincing opinion for the plurality, my approach does differ in some respects, requiring this separate statement.

The *Miranda* rule has become an important and accepted element of the criminal justice system. At the same time, not every violation of the rule requires suppression of the evidence obtained. Evidence is admissible when the central concerns of *Miranda* are not likely to be implicated and when other objectives of the criminal justice system are best served by its introduction. Thus, we have held that statements obtained in violation of the rule can be used for impeachment; [that] there is an exception to protect countervailing concerns of public safety; and that physical evidence obtained in reliance on statements taken in violation of the rule is admissible, see *Patane*. These cases, in my view, are correct. They recognize that admission of evidence is proper when it would further important objectives without compromising *Miranda*'s central concerns. Under these precedents, the scope of the *Miranda* suppression remedy depends on a consideration of those legitimate interests and on whether admission of the evidence under the circumstances would frustrate *Miranda*'s central concerns and objectives. *Elstad* reflects this approach.

[In] my view, *Elstad* was correct in its reasoning and its result. *Elstad* reflects a balanced and pragmatic approach to enforcement of the *Miranda* warning. An officer may not realize that a suspect is in custody and warnings are required. The officer may not plan to question the suspect or may be waiting for a more appropriate time. [In] light of these realities it would be extravagant to treat the presence of one statement that cannot be admitted under *Miranda* as sufficient reason to prohibit subsequent statements preceded by a proper warning.

[This] case presents different considerations. The police used a two-step questioning technique based on a deliberate violation of *Miranda*. [Further,] the interrogating officer here relied on the defendant's prewarning statement to obtain the postwarning statement used against her at trial. The postwarning interview resembled a cross-examination. The officer confronted the defendant with her inadmissible prewarning statements and pushed her to acknowledge them.

The technique used in this case distorts the meaning of *Miranda* and furthers no legitimate countervailing interest. The *Miranda* rule would be frustrated were we to allow police to undermine its meaning and effect. [When] an interrogator uses this deliberate, two-step strategy, predicated upon violating *Miranda* during an extended interview, postwarning statements that are related to the substance of prewarning statements must be excluded absent specific, curative steps.

The plurality concludes that whenever a two-stage interview occurs, admissibility of the postwarning statement should depend on "whether the *Miranda* warnings delivered midstream could have been effective enough to accomplish their object" given the specific facts of the case. This test envisions an objective inquiry from the perspective of the suspect, and applies in the case of both intentional and unintentional two-stage interrogations. In my view, this test cuts too broadly. *Miranda'* s clarity is one of its strengths, and a multifactor test that applies to every two-stage interrogation may serve to undermine that clarity. I would apply a narrower test applicable only in the infrequent case, such as we have here, in which the two-step interrogation technique was used in a calculated way to undermine the *Miranda* warning.

The admissibility of postwarning statements should continue to be governed by the principles of *Elstad* unless the deliberate two-step strategy was employed. If the deliberate two-step strategy has been used, postwarning statements that are related to the substance of prewarning statements must be excluded unless curative measures are taken before the postwarning statement is made. Curative measures should be designed to ensure that a reasonable person in the suspect's situation would understand the import and effect of the *Miranda* warning and of the *Miranda* waiver. For example, a substantial break in time and circumstances between the prewarning statement and the *Miranda* warning may suffice in most circumstances, as it allows the accused to distinguish the two contexts and appreciate that the interrogation has taken a new turn. Alternatively, an additional warning that explains the likely inadmissibility of the prewarning custodial statement may be sufficient. No curative steps were taken in this case, however, so the postwarning statements are inadmissible and the conviction cannot stand. * * *

Justice O'CONNOR, with whom THE CHIEF JUSTICE, Justice SCALIA, and JUSTICE THOMAS join, dissenting.

The plurality devours *Elstad* even as it accuses petitioner's argument of "disfigur[ing]" that decision. I believe that we are bound by *Elstad* to reach a different result, and I would vacate the judgment of the Supreme Court of Missouri.

On two preliminary questions I am in full agreement with the plurality. First, the plurality appropriately follows *Elstad* in concluding that Seibert's statement cannot be held inadmissible under a "fruit of the poisonous tree" theory. Second, the plurality correctly declines to focus its analysis on the subjective intent of the interrogating officer.

This Court has made clear that there simply is no place for a robust deterrence doctrine with regard to violations of *Miranda*. * * * Consistent with that view, the Court today refuses to apply the traditional "fruits" analysis to the physical fruit of a claimed *Miranda* violation. *Patane*. The plurality correctly refuses to apply a similar analysis to testimonial fruits.

Although the analysis the plurality ultimately espouses examines the same facts and circumstances that a "fruits" analysis would consider (such as the lapse of time between the two interrogations and change of questioner or location), it does so for entirely different reasons. The fruits analysis would examine those factors because they are relevant to the balance of deterrence value versus the "drastic and socially costly course" of excluding reliable evidence. The plurality, by contrast, looks to those factors to inform the *psychological* judgment regarding whether the suspect has been informed effectively of her right to remain silent. The analytical underpinnings of the two approaches are thus entirely distinct, and they should not be conflated just because they function similarly in practice.

The plurality's rejection of an intent-based test is also, in my view, correct. Freedom from compulsion lies at the heart of the Fifth Amendment, and requires us to assess whether a suspect's decision to speak truly was voluntary. Because voluntariness is a matter of the suspect's state of mind, we focus our analysis on the way in which suspects experience interrogation. * * *

Thoughts kept inside a police officer's head cannot affect that experience. [A] suspect who experienced the exact same interrogation as Seibert, save for a difference in the undivulged, subjective intent of the interrogating officer when he failed to give *Miranda* warnings, would not experience the interrogation any differently.

[Because] the isolated fact of Officer Hanrahan's intent could not have had any bearing on Seibert's "capacity to comprehend and knowingly relinquish" her right to remain silent, it could not by itself affect the voluntariness of her confession. Moreover, recognizing an exception to *Elstad* for intentional violations would require focusing constitutional analysis on a police officer's subjective intent, an unattractive proposition that we all but uniformly avoid. [This] case presents the uncommonly straightforward circumstance of an officer openly admitting that the violation was intentional. But the inquiry will be complicated in other situations probably more likely to occur. For example, different officers involved in an interrogation might claim different states of mind regarding the failure to give *Miranda* warnings. Even in the simple case of a single officer who claims that a failure to give *Miranda* warnings was inadvertent, the likelihood of error will be high. [These] evidentiary difficulties have led us to reject an intent-based test in several criminal procedure contexts.

[For] these reasons, I believe that the approach espoused by Justice Kennedy is ill advised. Justice Kennedy would extend *Miranda's* exclusionary rule to any case in which the use of the "two-step interrogation technique" was "deliberate" or "calculated." This approach untethers the analysis from facts knowable to, and therefore having any potential directly to affect, the suspect. Far from promoting "clarity," the approach will add a third step to the suppression inquiry. In virtually every two-stage interrogation case, in addition to addressing the standard *Miranda* and voluntariness questions, courts will be forced to conduct the kind of difficult, state-of-mind inquiry that we normally take pains to avoid.

The plurality's adherence to *Elstad,* and mine to the plurality, end there. Our decision in *Elstad* rejected two lines of argument advanced in favor of suppression. The first was based on the "fruit of the poisonous tree" doctrine. [The] second was the argument that the "lingering compulsion" inherent in a defendant's having let the "cat out of the bag" required suppression.

We rejected [the second] theory outright. We did so not because we refused to recognize the "psychological impact of the suspect's conviction that he has let the cat out of the bag," but because we refused to "endo[w]" those "psychological effects" with "constitutional implications." To do so, we said, would "effectively immuniz[e] a suspect who responds to pre-*Miranda* warning questions from the consequences of his subsequent informed waiver," an immunity that "comes at a high cost to legitimate law enforcement activity, while adding little desirable protection to the individual's interest in not being *compelled* to testify against himself."

I would analyze the two-step interrogation procedure under the voluntariness standards central to the Fifth Amendment and reiterated in *Elstad. Elstad* commands that if Seibert's first statement is shown to have been involuntary, the court must examine whether the taint dissipated through the passing of time or a change in circumstances. [In] addition, Seibert's second statement should be suppressed if she showed that it was involuntary despite the *Miranda* warnings. * * *

Because I believe that the plurality gives insufficient deference to *Elstad* and that Justice Kennedy places improper weight on subjective intent, I respectfully dissent.

Notes and Questions

1. ***Suppose a defendant had shot someone with a Glock pistol and been arrested for murder.*** Suppose further the defendant had been subjected to the same deliberate two-step questioning technique utilized in the *Seibert* case and, as a result, had revealed where she had hidden the murder weapon. Even though the interrogation technique had been "designed to circumvent Miranda" and had "undermine[d] the Miranda warning" and "obscure[d] its meaning" (Kennedy, J., concurring in Seibert), would the Glock pistol still be admissible? Why (not)?

2. Suppose, a week after Seibert was decided, a deputy district attorney told a group of officers attending a police training session the following:

"Don't write off the interrogation tactics used in *Seibert*. You can continue to use the same deliberate two-step questioning technique used in that case and still get the postwarning statements admitted into evidence. All you have to do is make one of several changes in the *Seibert* facts: (1) call for a three or four-hour break between the first and second questioning session instead of the 20–minute break that took place in *Seibert* or (2) have a different police officer resume the questioning after the break instead of using the same officer who did the questioning in the prewarning session or (3) after resuming questioning, be careful not to confront the suspect with the same incriminating statement(s) she made at the first questioning session. Making any of these changes is likely to result in the admissibility of the postwarning statement(s). Making all these changes will undoubtedly do so."

Would the deputy district attorney be right? Why (not)?

3. ***The Seibert case and the assertion of a right to counsel.*** Suppose during the first stage of a two-stage interrogation, the suspect emphatically asserts his right to counsel. Would the administration of the *Miranda* warnings during the second stage of the interrogation (after a half-hour or hour-long recess) make a "second confession" admissible? Isn't this essentially the *Edwards* case (p. 647) all over again? But what result if the officer not only gives the suspect the *Miranda* warnings during the second stage, but assures him that the incriminating statement he made during the first stage (the statement made after the police paid no attention to the request for a lawyer), is not admissible in evidence?

4. ***If the suspect is unaware of the nature of the police conduct, is the deliberate and flagrant nature of the police action relevant?*** The four *Seibert* dissenters (O'Connor, J., joined by Rehnquist, C.J., and Scalia and Thomas, JJ.) answer in the negative. But in *Oregon v. Elstad* (p. 701), the first Supreme Court case to address the question whether the "poisoned fruit" doctrine applies to *Miranda*-deficient statements, the Court, per O'Connor, J., pointed out that the failure to give the warnings in the first instance (when Elstad was in his home) "may have been the result of confusion as to whether the brief exchange [in Elstad's home] qualified as 'custodial interrogation' or it may simply have reflected [the officer's] reluctance to initiate an alarming procedure [the recitation of the *Miranda* warnings] before [a second officer] had spoken with [Elstad's] mother." But why (according to Justice O'Connor's *Seibert* dissent) was any of this relevant? Mr. Elstad had no idea what was in the officer's head. He did not know, for example, that the officer was "confused" about whether the situation called for the *Miranda* warnings. If the technical or inadvertent nature of the failure to comply with *Miranda* is relevant for derivative evidence purposes, as it seemed to be in *Elstad,* why shouldn't the deliberate and flagrant nature of the failure to comply with *Miranda* be relevant for the same purposes?

Should "something not known to the defendant" have no bearing on the coerciveness of the interrogation or the voluntariness of the defendant's decision to abandon his rights, as the *Seibert* dissenters maintain, but still be relevant when the failure to comply with *Miranda* is undisputed and *the only issue is whether the resulting evidence should be excluded*? *Cf. Brown v. Illinois* (p. 908), observing that in determining whether a confession should be excluded because it was obtained "by exploitation" of a prior illegal arrest, a number of factors are relevant—"particularly the purpose and flagrancy of the official misconduct."

Suppose the chief of police orders all officers under her command to subject all custodial suspects to the two-stage interrogation technique, promises $1,000 bonuses for every "second confession" obtained, and warns that any officer who gives the *Miranda* warnings during the first stage of the interrogation or arranges a "recess" between the first and second stages that lasts longer than 20 minutes will be suspended without pay for six months. Would (should) the police chief's communication have any bearing on the admissibility of a "second confession"? Would (should) it matter that, as would likely be the case, no custodial suspect is aware of the police chief's communication?

SECTION 6. THE "DUE PROCESS"—"VOLUNTARINESS" TEST REVISITED

Although one might say (and many commentators have) that *Miranda* displaced the due process-totality of circumstances-voluntariness test, in a number of important situations "the primary criterion of [confession] admissibility under current law is [still] the 'old' due process voluntariness test." Stephen J. Schulhofer, *Confessions and the Court*, 79 Mich.L.Rev. 865, 877 (1981). For one thing, empirical studies indicate that most suspects waive their rights and submit to police questioning. "Because the admissibility of statements given after a valid waiver of *Miranda* rights must be determined on the basis of the voluntariness test, that test remains vitally important." Welsh S. White, *What is an Involuntary Confession Now?*, 50 Rutgers L.Rev. 2001, 2004 (1998). Moreover, as Schulhofer, supra, points out, the voluntariness test is important when suspects not in custody are questioned by the police; when suspects in a custody-like situation are questioned (or threatened) by private citizens (e.g. *Commonwealth v. Mahnke*, 335 N.E.2d 660 (Mass.1975)); or when the prosecution seeks to use a confession to impeach a defendant's testimony at trial or to use the "fruits" of the confession (e.g., the murder weapon), but not the confession itself. As discussed in Ch. 12, § 2, 3, although statements obtained in violation of *Miranda* may be used for impeachment purposes, "coerced" or "involuntary" statements may not. Moreover, as we have just seen, the Court will usually permit the use of evidence derived from a *Miranda* violation but exclude the "fruits" of an "involuntary" confession.

A. *MILLER V. FENTON:* WHAT KINDS OF TRICKERY OR DECEPTION, IF ANY, MAY THE POLICE EMPLOY AFTER A SUSPECT HAS WAIVED HIS RIGHTS?

Is *Miranda*'s prohibition against police deception and trickery limited to their use in obtaining a waiver of *Miranda* rights or does it also bar such police techniques after a person has validly waived his rights? Suppose a suspect waives his rights and expresses a willingness to talk, but denies any involvement in the case. May the police then display apparent sympathy? Turn the suspect over to a friendly, gentle interrogator and then to a hostile, short-tempered one (the "Mutt and Jeff" routine)? Although such techniques seemed to have vented Chief Justice Warren's judicial ire in *Miranda*, that landmark case "did not condemn any specific techniques as such or hold that evidence obtained by use of them would be inadmissible. Reliance was placed on warning and counsel to protect the suspect." Sheldon Elsen & Arthur Rosett, *Protections for the Suspect under Miranda v. Arizona*, 67 Colum.L.Rev. 645, 667 (1967). More than three decades after *Miranda*, the issue has yet to be clearly resolved.[a]

a. Cf. *Frazier v. Cupp*, 394 U.S. 731 (1969) (admitting a confession in a pre-*Miranda* case although the police had falsely told the defendant that another had confessed and had also "sympathetically" suggested that the victim's homosexual advances may have started the fight). See also *Oregon v. Mathiason* (p. 607) (interrogator's false statement to defendant

A year after *Miranda*, Professor Fred Inbau and Mr. John Reid published a new edition of their leading interrogation manual and maintained that "all but a very few of the interrogation techniques presented in our earlier [pre-*Escobedo*, pre-*Miranda*] publication are still valid if used after the recently prescribed warnings have been given to the suspect under interrogation, and after he has waived his self-incriminating privilege and his right to counsel." See *Criminal Interrogation and Confessions*, (2d ed. 1967). See also Inbau, Reid & Buckley, *Criminal Interrogation and Confessions* 216 (3d ed. 1986), maintaining that, although the Court did not explicitly address the issue in *Frazier v. Cupp*, fn. a supra, that case "implicitly recognized" the essentiality of interrogation practices involving trickery or deceit, and approved of them. [Moreover,] there are many appellate court cases holding that a confession is admissible even when it was obtained by trickery and deceit, [provided that the trickery does not] " 'shock the conscience' [or is not] apt to induce a false confession."[b]

Welsh S. White, *Police Trickery in Inducing Confessions*, 127 U.Pa.L.Rev. 581–90, 599–600, 628–29 (1979), takes a very different view of police use of trickery in the post-*Miranda* era, maintaining that, because they are likely to render a resulting confession involuntary or because they distort the meaning or vitiate the effect of the *Miranda* warnings or because they "undermine [a] suspect's independent right to an attorney," "several widely employed interrogation tactics * * * should be absolutely prohibited." Among the techniques Professor White considers "impermissible per se" are deception that distorts the seriousness of the matter under investigation (e.g., falsely informing a murder suspect that the victim is still alive), the "assumption of non-adversary roles" by interrogating officers (e.g., assuming the role of a father figure or religious counselor), repeated assurances that the suspect is known to be guilty, and the "Mutt and Jeff" routine. See also Note, 40 Stan.L.Rev. 1593, 1612–15 (1988).

But police deception and trickery did not prevent the admissibility of the resulting confession in *Miller v. Fenton*, below. *Miller* is a dramatic illustration that the problems raised by the old "totality of the circumstances"—"due process"—"voluntariness" test have not disappeared in the post-*Miranda* era.

When he accompanied the police to a state police barracks, Miller, the prime suspect in the brutal murder of Ms. Margolin, was advised of his rights and signed "a *Miranda* card," waiving his rights.[a] Thus, the issue in MILLER v. FENTON, 796 F.2d 598 (3d Cir.1986), was the "voluntariness" of the defendant's murder confession.[b] A 2–1 majority, per BECKER, J. (joined by Seitz, J.), framed the issue

that his fingerprints were found at scene may have bearing on other issues in case, but "has nothing to do with whether [defendant] was in custody for [*Miranda*] purposes").

b. Although agreeing that a goodly number of lower courts have interpreted *Frazier* as "definitively ruling that police trickery is a mere factor to be included in a court's assessment of a confession's involuntariness under a totality of the circumstances analysis," Note, 40 Stan.L.Rev. 1593, 1607–08 (1988), maintains that "several factors make *Frazier* a particularly bad case for a definitive ruling on police trickery":

"First, the opinion does not recognize as trickery the detective's feigned sympathy in his suggestion that a homosexual advance was a reason for the fight. Also, Frazier was tried and decided before the *Miranda* decision, and so the Court's indictment of police misconduct in *Miranda* did not apply. * * * Third, apart from the one recognized and one unrecognized instances of police trickery, the interrogators' behavior was exemplary. The police gave coercive conduct a wide berth, questioning Frazier for only forty-five minutes immediately after he was brought to the police station. In addition, the interrogation was tape-recorded and the tape played for the trial judge, who subsequently concluded that the confession was voluntary. Last and most important, the police lie that [another person] had confessed, the only trickery recognized by the Court, does *not* seem to have induced Frazier's confession."

a. Several hours earlier, Miller had been questioned by the police for about 45 minutes at his place of employment, but had denied any involvement in the murder.

b. The case has a long procedural history. After a New Jersey trial court admitted his confession, Miller was convicted of murder. A

in terms of whether the tactics of Detective Boyce during the 53–minute interrogation "were sufficiently manipulative to overbear the will of a person with [defendant's] characteristics" and viewed the limits of permissible interrogation as turning on "a weighing of the circumstances of pressure [applied by the police] against the power of resistance of the person confessing." After listening to Detective Boyce's questions and defendant Miller's responses (the police had taped the interrogation), the majority concluded that "under the totality of circumstances of this case" Miller's confession was "voluntarily given":

"It is clear that Boyce made no threats and engaged in no physical coercion of Miller. To the contrary, throughout the interview, Detective Boyce assumed a friendly, understanding manner and spoke in a soft tone of voice. He repeatedly assured Miller that he was sympathetic to him and wanted to help him unburden his mind. [The detective's] statements of sympathy at times approached the maudlin. [E.g., 'This hurts me more than it hurts you because I love people * * * I'm on your side, Frank * * * I'm your brother, you and I are brothers, Frank [and] I want to help my brother.']

"Boyce also gave Miller certain factual information, some of which was untrue. At the beginning of the interrogation, for example, Boyce informed Miller that the victim was still alive; this was false. During the interview, Boyce told Miller that Ms. Margolin had just died, although in fact she had been found dead several hours earlier.

"Detective Boyce's major theme throughout the interrogation was that whoever had committed such a heinous crime had mental problems and was desperately in need of psychological treatment. [The] Detective stated several times that Miller was not a criminal who should be punished, but a sick individual who should receive help. * * *

"Boyce also appealed to Miller's conscience and described the importance of Miller's purging himself of the memories that must be haunting him. [E.g., 'First thing we have to do is let it all come out. Don't fight it because it's worse * * * It's hurting me because I feel it. I feel it wanting to come out, but it's hurting me, Frank. * * * I know how you feel inside, Frank, it's eating you up, am I right? * * * You've got to come forward. You've got to do it for yourself, for your family, for your father, this is what's important, the truth, Frank.']

"When Miller at last confessed [almost an hour after the interrogation session began], he collapsed in a state of shock. He slid off his chair and onto the floor with a blank stare on his face. The police officers sent for a first aid squad that took him to the hospital. * * *

"[Psychological] ploys may play a part in the suspect's decision to confess, but as long as that decision is a product of the suspect's own balancing of competing considerations, the confession is voluntary. The question we must answer [is] whether [the detective's] statements were so manipulative or coercive that they deprived Miller of his ability to make an unconstrained autonomous decision to confess. To that inquiry we now turn. * * *

"Miller is a mature adult, thirty-two years of age [and] has some high school education. Such a person is more resistant to interrogation than a person who is very young, uneducated or weak-minded. [Moreover,] Miller [had] served a jail

three-judge panel of an intermediate state appellate court reversed, holding Miller's confession "involuntary." But a 4–3 majority of the New Jersey Supreme Court reinstated the conviction, deeming the confession "voluntary." On federal habeas corpus, the Third Circuit, deferring to the state court's finding of "voluntariness," upheld the admissibility of the confession. The U.S. Supreme Court reversed (see p. 556), holding that on federal habeas corpus the "voluntariness" of a confession is a matter for independent federal court determination, and remanding the case for a fuller analysis under the correct standard.

sentence. Thus, he was aware of the consequences of confessing. [He had also] received Miranda warnings. Detective Boyce's interrogation of Miller lasted less than an hour. [I]t is thus distinguishable from the lengthy interrogations during incommunicado detention that have been held to result in involuntary confessions. * * *

"Boyce's supportive, encouraging manner was an interrogation tactic aimed at winning Miller's trust and making him feel comfortable about confessing. Excessive friendliness on the part of an interrogator can be deceptive. In some instances, in combination with other tactics, it might create an atmosphere in which a suspect forgets that his questioner is in an adversarial role, and thereby prompt admissions that the suspect would ordinarily make only to a friend, not to the police. [But] the 'good guy' approach is recognized as a permissible interrogation tactic.

"[While an officer's] lie [about] an important aspect of the case may affect the voluntariness of the confession, the effect of the lie must be analyzed in the context of all the circumstances of the interrogation. See, e.g., *Frazier v. Cupp*. [The] record suggests that this emotional reaction did not occur, for it appears that Miller was not affected at all by the news of the death. Indeed, he remained quite impassive. * * *

"Detective Boyce's statements that Miller was not a criminal, but rather a mentally ill individual not responsible for his actions, and Boyce's promises to help Miller raise a more serious question about the voluntariness of Miller's confession. By telling Miller that he was not responsible for anything he might have done, Boyce may have been understood to be making an implied promise to Miller that [he] would not be prosecuted, or that if he were prosecuted Boyce would aid him in presenting the insanity defense. Similarly, the promises of psychiatric help might have suggested to Miller that he would be treated, rather than prosecuted. If these promises, implicit and explicit, tricked Miller into confessing, his confession may have been involuntary. To determine whether Boyce's promises affected the voluntariness of Miller's confession, we must consider how manipulative these tactics in fact were.

"In *Bram v. United States*, (1897) [p. 569] [the Court] endorsed the view that to be voluntary a confession must not have been 'extracted by any sort of threats or violence, nor obtained by any direct or implied promises, however slight.' [Emphasis added.] Although the Bram test has been reaffirmed [it] has not been interpreted as a per se proscription against promises made during interrogation.[c] Nor does the Supreme Court even use a but-for test when promises have been made during an interrogation.

"[At] no time did Detective Boyce state that Miller would not be prosecuted or that he could successfully avail himself of the insanity defense. * * * Indeed, Boyce's statements that Miller was 'not a criminal' need not be understood as assurances of leniency at all. Since [Boyce's] strategy was to present himself as a friend to whom Miller could unburden himself, he of course attempted throughout the interview to persuade Miller to trust him and confide in him. The statement at issue can be viewed as a means of convincing Miller that Boyce was sympathetic, no matter what the state's reaction might be. 'You are not responsible' and 'You are not a criminal' thus would mean 'In my eyes, you are not responsible or a criminal and therefore you should relieve your conscience by talking to me, who understands you.' * * * Detective Boyce never stated that anyone but he thought that Miller was 'not a criminal' nor did he state that he had any authority to

c. For a discussion of the significance of a promise not to prosecute and related matters, see Note 4 following this case.

affect the charges brought against Miller. Miller's confession may have been made in the hope of leniency, but that does not mean that it was made in response to a promise of leniency. * * *

"Moreover, throughout the interview, Miller made remarks that indicate that he knew that this was an ordinary police interrogation rather than an encounter with a compassionate friend, and that he was aware that a confession would result in criminal prosecution and possibly in conviction and sentence. Throughout the session, he appears to have retained a suspicious, guarded attitude. * * *

"We have little doubt that Detective Boyce's encouraging words, perhaps in contribution with the sad announcement that the victim had just died, helped Miller to reach his decision to unburden himself. However, the test for voluntariness is not a but-for test, but a question of whether the confession was a product of free choice. * * * Many criminals experience an urge during interrogation to own up to their crimes. * * * Boyce's manner and his statements may have stirred this urge in Miller, but, in our view, they did not produce psychological pressure strong enough to overbear the will of a mature, experienced man, who was suffering from no mental or physical illness and was interrogated for less than an hour at a police station close to his home.

"Detective Boyce's method of interrogation might have overborne the will of another detainee, for example, a young, inexperienced person of lower intelligence than Miller, or a person suffering from a painful physical ailment. It might have overcome the will of Miller himself if the interrogation had been longer or if Miller had been refused food, sleep, or contact with a person he wished to see. Moreover, if Miller had made remarks that indicated that he truly believed that the state would treat him leniently because he was 'not responsible' for what he had done or that he believed that he would receive psychiatric help rather than punishment, we might not find the confession voluntary. We hold simply that, under the totality of the circumstances of this case, the confession was voluntarily given."

Dissenting Judge GIBBONS protested:

"[As] the majority well knows the state police are not in the business of acting as religious or psychiatric counselors. Boyce was not sympathetic. He was no more interested in helping Miller 'unburden his inner tensions' than he was in any other aspect of Miller's health. Instead Boyce was determined and ultimately successful in obtaining from an unwilling defendant the one thing that was his purpose—a confession. * * *

[At one point, when the interrogation was well underway, the following occurred:]

BOYCE: Now listen to me Frank. This hurts me more than it hurts you, because I love people.

MILLER: It can't hurt you anymore than it hurts me. * * *

BOYCE: Okay, listen Frank. If I promise to, you know, do all I can with the psychiatrist and everything, and we get the proper help for you, and get the proper help for you, will you talk to me about it?

MILLER: I can't talk to you about something I'm not . . .

BOYCE: Alright, listen Frank, alright, honest. I know, I know what's going on inside you, Frank. I want to help you, you know, between us right now. I know what going on inside you, Frank, you've got to come forward and tell me that you want to help yourself. You've got to talk to me about it. This is the only way we'll be able to work it out. I mean, you know, listen, I want to help you, because you are in my mind, you are not responsible. You are not responsible, Frank. Frank, what's the matter?

MILLER: I feel bad.

BOYCE: Frank, listen to me, honest to God, I'm I'm telling you, Frank (inaudible). I know, it's going to bother you, Frank, it's going to bother you. It's there, it's not going to go away, it's there. It's right in front of you, Frank. Am I right or wrong?

MILLER: Yeah.

BOYCE: You can see it Frank, you can feel it, you can feel it, but you are not responsible. This is what I'm trying to tell you, but you've got to come forward and tell me. Don't, don't, don't let it eat you up, don't, don't fight it. You've got to rectify it, Frank. We've got to get together on this thing, or I, I mean really, you need help, you need proper help and you know it, my God, you know, in God's name you, you, you know it. You are not a criminal, you are not a criminal.

MILLER: Alright. Yes, I was over there and I talked to her about the cow and left. I left in my car and I stopped up on the road where, you know, where the cow had been and she followed me in her car . . .

"Thus, approximately thirty minutes into the second interrogation, Miller made his first incriminating statement. By far the largest part of that thirty minutes is comprised of lies and promises by Boyce * * * directed to the sole purpose of obtaining a confession. There is nothing in the record from which it can be inferred that Miller's abandonment of his self-interested denials of involvement in the homicide was the product of any other influence. The majority opinion describes Boyce's conduct as if he were a confessor, offering solace under the seal of the confessional, or a psychiatrist offering relief from anxiety under the shelter of a physician-patient privilege, rather than what he was—a wily interrogator determined to break down Miller's resistance by lies and false promises. The majority's treatment of the police tactics leading to Miller's collapse is about as fair as those tactics. Confession may be good for the soul, but it was Miller's freedom, not his soul, that was at stake, and it was his freedom, not his soul, that interested Boyce. * * *

"The reason why the state had to preserve and make use of the tape-recorded interrogation appears in Boyce's testimony at the suppression hearing:

Q. I gather that [a] statement was never taken, is that right?

A. It was not.

Q. Why was that, Officer?

A. Momentarily after terminating this particular interview Mr. Miller went into as I can best define it a state of shock.

Q. What do you mean by that, sir?

A. He was sitting on a chair? . . . Mr. Miller had been sitting on a chair, had slid off the chair on the floor maintaining a blank stare on his face, staring straight ahead and we were unable to get any type of verbal response from him. * * *

"Incredibly, the only reference in the majority's opinion to Miller's collapse is the cryptic sentence [that] 'One hour into the interrogation, Miller confessed to the murder of Deborah Margolin, then passed out.' The majority does not even recognize Miller's collapse into a catatonic state and his transportation to a hospital as relevant circumstances in its totality of the circumstances analysis! This most telling of all indications as to the effect on Miller of Boyce's tactics is simply ignored. [The majority] ignores the fact that at the end of the interrogation Miller collapsed and was taken to a hospital. How can it be honestly represented that he was suffering from no mental or physical illness? And, unless the majority identifies some other reason for Miller's abrupt abandonment of his self-interested denials of guilt than the psychological coercion exercised by Boyce, what other cause is left? * * *

"Boyce's second interrogation cannot be read in pieces. Its effect was cumulative, as it was intended to be. From the moment he began it, Boyce put relentless psychological pressure on Miller. Boyce repeatedly assured Miller that he only wanted to help Miller, that Miller was not a criminal, that Miller was not responsible for his actions, and that Miller would not be punished. In addition to these express promises, Boyce confused Miller by lying to him about the time of Ms. Margolin's death and the strength of the evidence against Miller.

"The majority emphasizes that the key issue is whether, in the totality of the circumstances, Miller's will was overborne. While I agree with the majority's general focus, I disagree with the majority's method of analysis. In ascertaining the effects of Boyce's interrogation tactics on Miller, the majority attempts to place itself in Miller's position and thereby evaluate the impact of Boyce's promises and lies. Unfortunately, we cannot know what effects those promises and lies had on Miller's will. Instead what we can know is that when, as in this case, the record reveals a series of repeated promises of psychological help and assurances that the suspect will not be punished, *Bram* requires as a matter of law that we hold the resulting confession to be coerced. Any other rule leads to the kind of subjective speculation that the majority engages in. Thus applying the *Bram* rule within the totality of the circumstances of Miller's interrogation, the confession used to commit Miller must be declared inadmissible as a violation of Miller's fifth amendment right to remain silent."

Notes and Questions

1. ***Should "police trickery" in obtaining confessions be barred? What is "trickery" in the confession context?*** Consider Note, 40 Stan.L.Rev. 1593, 1594–95 (1988): "The courts have not clearly defined the term 'trickery' and 'trickery' has been used interchangeably with 'misrepresentation,' 'artifice,' 'deception,' 'fraud,' and 'subterfuge.' This note argues that the term trickery, when used in the confessions context, should be defined as police elicitation of a confession by deliberate distortion of material fact, by failure to disclose to the defendant a material fact, or by playing on a defendant's emotions or scruples. Police trickery should be viewed as a type of fraud, the use of which as an interrogation tool is inconsistent with our adversarial system of criminal justice because it allows the prosecution an unfair, indeed an unconstitutional, advantage at trial."

2. ***The relationship between Miller and Detective Boyce.*** At one point the Miller majority observes that Boyce's statements to Miller that he is "not a criminal" who should be punished, and "not responsible" for anything he might have done "need not be understood as assurances of leniency" but could be viewed as the expression of sympathy by "a friend"—"a means of convincing Miller that Boyce [personally] was sympathetic, no matter what the state's reaction might be." At another point, however, the majority opinion observes that Miller's responses indicated "he knew that this was an ordinary police interrogation, rather than an encounter with a compassionate friend." Which is it?

To avoid the prohibition against obtaining confessions by promises of leniency, one might say, as the majority does at one point, that Boyce's "interrogation strategy was to present himself as a friend to whom Miller would unburden," and that, as the majority suggests at several places, the detective's strategy succeeded. If so, however, doesn't this raise another problem? If Boyce led Miller to believe he was a sympathetic friend didn't Boyce cause Miller to forget that his questioner was in an adversarial role and thus negate the effect of the Miranda warnings?

3. ***Drawing a line between expressions of sympathy and implied promises of leniency.*** Compare the Stanford Note with Phillip Johnson, *A Statutory Replacement for the Miranda Doctrine*, 24 Am.Crim.L.Rev. 303, 305 (1987), proposing that the police be forbidden to make "any statement which is intended to imply or may reasonably be understood as implying that the suspect will not be prosecuted or punished," but approving police expressions of sympathy and compassion, whether real or feigned; police appeals to the suspect's conscience, religious or otherwise; and police appeals to the suspect's sympathy for the victim or other affected persons.

Observes Professor Johnson, id. at 310–11: "Offers of leniency can be made later in the plea bargaining process, where the accused is represented by counsel and can properly evaluate what is being offered. Promises of leniency from the police during interrogation are too likely to be deceptive, and too likely to give even an innocent suspect the impression that confession is the only way to escape conviction or mitigate the punishment. [However, police expressions of sympathy and compassion should be permitted because] a pose of sympathy is not overbearing or coercive, nor is it likely by itself to encourage an innocent person to provide a confession. A difficulty in this area is that the difference between expressions of compassionate understanding on the one hand, and implied promises of leniency on the other, is at the margin sometimes a matter of emphasis and nuance." Did Detective Boyce cross the line in the Miller case? See id. at 311.

4. ***Some courts take the position that a promise not to prosecute makes the resulting confession inadmissible, but others strongly resist "freeing a murderer" because of a promise not to prosecute.*** Although the *Miller* case suggests otherwise, according to CRIMPROC § 6.2(c), "lower courts have often held that a confession is involuntary if made in response to a promise that the result will be nonprosecution, the dropping of some charges, [or] a certain reduction in the punishment defendant may receive (although in recent years there has been a movement away from treating such promises of leniency as *per se* producing involuntariness, especially in light of [the way *Arizona v. Fulminante* (p. 725) reads the *Bram* case]). Merely promising to bring defendant's cooperation to the attention of the prosecution is not objectionable, nor is a promise that if defendant confesses the prosecutor would *discuss* leniency. [The] cases go both ways on the question of what the result should be when a confession has been obtained in response to a police assertion that cooperation would facilitate prompt release on bail or would mean that the defendant would fare better in subsequent proceedings. Especially as to the latter situation '[m]uch of the difficulty arises from failure to reconcile the voluntariness requirement with the plea bargaining process and especially the role of the police in that practice.' "

The great reluctance of some courts to "free a murderer" because of a promise not to prosecute him—without taking into account other factors such as the length of the questioning, the defendant's sophistication, and his understanding of his rights at the time of the questioning—is illustrated by UNITED STATES v. LeBRUN, 363 F.3d 715 (8th Cir.2004) (en banc). The case arose as follows: After 33 minutes of questioning, defendant LeBrun confessed to naval investigators that some thirty years earlier, when he had been in the U.S. Navy, he had killed his superior officer, Ensign Muns, after Muns caught him robbing the safe in the ship's disbursing office. On the day he confessed, LeBrun agreed to accompany naval agents to a highway patrol office where he was questioned. After they arrived, LeBrun was told he was not under arrest and that he was free to leave at any time. Moreover, according to LeBrun's testimony, he did not believe he was in custody and he felt free to leave at any time. At no time was he given any *Miranda* warnings. During the questioning session the following exchange occurred:

LeBRUN: So, I am hearing that I won't be prosecuted?

FIRST AGENT: That's what you are hearing. * * *

SECOND AGENT: If [the killing of Ensign Muns was] spontaneous, and that's the truth, you will not be prosecuted.

FIRST AGENT: That's absolutely right.

LeBRUN: I am here to tell you there was no premeditation.

SECOND AGENT: All right.

LeBRUN: It was spontaneous. * * *

SECOND AGENT: [L]et me get this clear. It was spontaneous?

LeBRUN: Correct.

Believing that the statements the agents made concerning nonprosecution rendered the confession involuntary, the district court suppressed the confession. However, the district court did not make any finding as to whether any promises were actually made, only that "LeBrun believed he would not be prosecuted if he confessed to a 'spontaneous' murder." A panel of the U.S. Court of Appeals for the Eighth Circuit affirmed, but on rehearing en banc, a 7–4 majority, per HANSEN, J., vacated the panel opinion and reversed the judgment of the district court:

"Even assuming that a reasonable person would view the Agents' statements as a promise, a promise made by law enforcement 'does not render a confession involuntary per se' [quoting an Eighth Circuit case]. [Our] polestar always must be to determine whether or not the authorities overbore the defendant's will and critically impaired his capacity for self-determination. Thus, it is not enough to show that the authorities' representations were the but-for cause of a confession. * * *

"We place substantial weight on the fact that LeBrun confessed after a mere thirty-three minutes. [We] also place significant weight on the fact that LeBrun testified that he had a subjective understanding of his *Miranda* rights at the time of the interview. [We] also place substantial weight on the fact that LeBrun was a sophisticated individual with legal training. [He] was fifty years old at the time of the interview. He [has] attended five years of college and one year of law school and worked as a manager in a real estate office.

"[The] videotape of the interview demonstrates that LeBrun was composed and aware of his surroundings and the circumstances confronting him. [After] watching the videotape, it is apparent that LeBrun is an intelligent, calculating person who erroneously perceived a substantial loophole in the prosecution's case and tried to take advantage of it by confessing to 'spontaneous' murder. Whatever his motivation, it is clear to us that LeBrun's capacity for self-determination was not impaired. Thus, the district court erred in concluding that LeBrun's confession was involuntary."

Speaking for four judges, MORRIS, ARNOLD, J., dissented:

"[The] clear purport of what the agents said in this case was that Mr. LeBrun would not be prosecuted if he said what the agents wanted him to say, and they even assured Mr. LeBrun that Mr. Muns's family approved of the deal. Indeed, they said the family would not pursue civil remedies if he confessed and apologized. What the family wanted, the interrogators said, was simply to clear Mr. Mun's name.

"In addition to the part of the interview that the court quotes in its opinion, the record reveals that, both before and after the exchange that the court isolates, the interviewers made reference to an alleged statute of limitations difficulty that would prevent prosecution for a 'spontaneous' murder; and the officers intimated, moreover, that if Mr. LeBrun would simply admit to a spontaneous killing, they would call the United States Attorney in charge of the prosecution and tell him there was no case against Mr. LeBrun.

"[We] need [to] consider the possibility that what lies at the bottom of these kinds of cases is not merely an aversion to something called coercion, but a general uneasiness about the fairness of admitting confessions that were induced by knowing, lurid falsehoods and unfulfilled promises, whether 'coercive' or not. In fact, the Supreme Court has specifically said that 'the admissibility of a confession turns as much on whether the technique for extracting the statements [are] compatible with a system that presumes innocence and assures that a conviction will not be secured by inquisitorial means as on whether the defendant's will was in fact overborne.' *Miller v. Fenton* [p. 715]."

5. ***How should the law respond to empirical data indicating that the interrogation tactics of threatening harsh punishment if the suspect does not confess and/or significant leniency if he does are likely to induce false confessions?*** According to studies of the interrogation process and of sixty known and probably false confession cases by Professors Richard J. Ofshe and Richard A. Leo, see *The Consequences of False Confessions*, 88 J.Crim.L. & C. 429 (1998) and *The Social Psychology of Police Interrogation*, 16 Studies in Law, Politics & Society 189 (1997), threatening a suspect with harsh punishment if he does not confess and/or promising him leniency if he does are "coercive" police interrogation tactics likely to induce false confessions. What follows from this? See Welsh S. White, *What Is a Voluntary Confession Now?*, 50 Rutgers L.Rev. 2001, 2052–53 (1998). After discussing *Leyra v. Denno* (1954) (p. 555) and *Lynumn v. Illinois* (1963) (p. 555), two pre-*Miranda* "voluntariness" cases "which suggest that interrogation tactics that threaten the suspect with harsh punishments if she does not confess or offer express or implied promises of significant sentencing advantages if she does may exert such unfair pressure on the suspect as to render the resulting confession involuntary," Profess White comments: "[T]he Court could establish the rule that interrogation tactics that threaten harsh consequences if the suspect does not confess or suggest that she will receive significant leniency in terms of disposition [citing Miller v. Fenton] or sentence if she does will generally be sufficient to render a resulting confession involuntary."

6. ***Distinguishing among different kinds of trickery.*** The Ofshe–Leo studies, supra Note 5, indicate that in certain situations the tactic of misrepresenting evidence of the suspect's guilt is likely to produce an untrustworthy confession and that "false evidence ploys based on scientific procedures" are more likely to produce a false confession than similar ploys based on eyewitness reports. Professor White, supra Note 5, at 2055, believes that the Leo–Ofshe data "provide a clear basis for distinguishing among different kinds of trickery. Based on [this data], a court applying the Due Process test could properly hold that certain types of misrepresentation should be strongly condemned and perhaps sufficient in themselves to render a resulting confession involuntary. Specifically, misrepresentations designed to convince the suspect that his guilt has been established by either forensic evidence or his failure to pass a lie detector test should be prohibited, or at least viewed as likely to render a resulting confession involuntary."

7. ***More on false verbal assertions by the police vs. the fabrication of scientific evidence.*** Interestingly, long before the Leo–Ofshe empirical studies had been published, one lower court drew a line between police deception generally (which does not render a confession involuntary per se) and the "manufacturing" of false documents or scientific evidence by the police (which "has no place in our criminal justice system"). *State v. Cayward*, 552 So.2d 971 (Fla.App.1989). The case arose as follows: The police suspected defendant of sexually assaulting and killing his five-year-old niece. They intentionally fabricated laboratory reports indicating that a scientific test established that the semen stains on the victim's underwear came from defendant and showed the reports to him. He confessed soon after. In upholding the trial court's suppression of the confession, the District Court of Appeal of Florida observed:

"We think [that] both the suspect's and the public's expectations concerning the built-in adversariness of police interrogations do not encompass the notion that the police will knowingly fabricate tangible documentation or physical evidence against an individual. [The] manufacturing of false documents by police officials offends our traditional notions of due process. [Moreover,] manufactured documents have the potential of indefinite life and the facial appearance of authenticity." Thus, they "might be disclosed to the media as a result of the public records law" or find their way into the courtroom.

Is there, as the Florida court believed, an "intrinsic" or "qualitative" difference between police lying, e.g., the false assertion that the suspect's fingerprints were found at the scene of the crime, and manufactured evidence? If, as the Florida court maintained, sanctioning police fabrication of documents "would greatly lessen the respect the public has for the criminal justice system and for those sworn to uphold and enforce the law," doesn't this concern apply to false verbal assertions by police interrogators as well? See Jerome H. Skolnick and Richard A. Leo, *The Ethics of Deceptive Interrogation*, Crim.Justice Ethics, Winter/Spring 1992, pp. 3, 7–9.

8. *Offering to protect a prisoner from physical harm at the hands of other inmates.* Consider ARIZONA v. FULMINANTE, 499 U.S. 279 (1991) (other aspects of which are discussed at p. 722). The case arose as follows: After defendant Fulminante's 11–year-old stepdaughter, Jeneane, was murdered, he was convicted of an unrelated federal crime and incarcerated in a federal prison. There he was befriended by another inmate, Sarivola, who was a paid informant for the FBI masquerading as an organized crime figure. Upon hearing a rumor that defendant had killed his stepdaughter, Sarivola brought up the subject several times, but defendant repeatedly denied any involvement in the murder. Then Sarivola told defendant that he knew he was "starting to get some tough treatment" from other inmates because of the rumor that he had killed his stepdaughter but that he, Sarivola, would protect defendant from his fellow inmates if he told him the truth about the murder. Defendant then confessed to Sarivola that he had sexually molested and killed Jeneane. The confession was admitted at defendant's trial and he was convicted of murder and sentenced to death. On appeal, the state supreme court held that the confession was coerced. Although it considered the question "a close one," a 5–4 majority of the Supreme Court, per WHITE, J., agreed with the state supreme court:

"In applying the totality of the circumstances test to determine that the confession to Sarivola was coerced, the Arizona Supreme Court focused on a number of relevant facts. First, the court noted that 'because [Fulminante] was an alleged child murderer, he was in physical harm at the hands of other inmates.' In addition, Sarivola was aware that Fulminante was receiving 'rough treatment from the guys.' Using his knowledge of these threats, Sarivola offered to protect Fulminante in exchange for a confession to Jeneane's murder and 'in response to Sarivola's offer of protection [Fulminante] confessed.' Agreeing with Fulminante that 'Sarivola's promise was "extremely coercive," 'the Arizona Court declared: '[T]he confession was obtained as a direct result of extreme coercion and was tendered in the belief that the defendant's life was in jeopardy if he did not confess. * * * '

"We normally give great deference to the factual findings of the state court. Nevertheless, 'the ultimate issue of "voluntariness" is a legal question requiring independent federal determination.' Although the question is a close one, we agree [that] Fulminante's confession was coerced. The Arizona Supreme Court found a credible threat of physical violence unless Fulminante confessed. [A] finding of coercion need not depend upon actual violence by a government agent; a credible threat is sufficient. [As] in *Payne v. Arkansas*, 356 U.S. 560 (1958)], where the Court found that a confession was coerced because the interrogating police officer had promised that if the accused confessed, the officer would protect the accused from an angry mob outside the jailhouse door, so too here, the Arizona Supreme Court found that it was fear of physical violence, absent protection from his friend (and Government agent) Sarivola, which motivated Fulminante to confess. Accepting the Arizona court's finding, permissible on this record, that there was a credible threat of physical violence, we agree that Fulminante's will was overborne in such a way as to render his confession the product of coercion."

Dissenting on this issue, REHNQUIST, C.J., joined by O'Connor, Kennedy and Souter, JJ., was "at a loss to see how the Supreme Court of Arizona reached the conclusion that it did":

"Fulminante offered no evidence that he believed his life was in danger or that he in fact confessed to Sarivola in order to obtain the proffered protection. Indeed, he had stipulated that '[a]t no time did the defendant indicate he was in fear of other inmates nor did he ever seek Mr. Sarivola's "protection." 'Sarivola's testimony that he told Fulminante that 'if [he] would tell the truth, he could be protected,' adds little if anything to the substance of the parties' stipulation. The decision of the Supreme Court of Arizona rests on an assumption that is squarely contrary to this stipulation, and one that is not supported by any testimony of Fulminante.

"The facts of record in the present case are quite different from those present in cases where we have found confessions to be coerced and involuntary. Since Fulminante was unaware that Sarivola was an FBI informant, there existed none of 'the danger of coercion result[ing] from the interaction of custody and official interrogation.' *Illinois v. Perkins* [p. 621]. [The] conversations between Sarivola and Fulminante were not lengthy, and the defendant was free at all times to leave Sarivola's company. Sarivola at no time threatened him or demanded that he confess; he simply requested that he speak the truth about the matter. Fulminante was an experienced habitue of prisons, and presumably able to fend for himself. In concluding on these facts that Fulminante's confession was involuntary, the Court today embraces a more expansive definition of that term than is warranted by any of our decided cases."

B. Colorado v. Connelly: Did the Court Decline to Expand the "Voluntariness" Test or Did it Revise the Test Significantly?

In COLORADO v. CONNELLY, 479 U.S. 157 (1986) (also discussed at p. 553, fns. b and c), the Court held, per REHNQUIST, C.J., that "coercive police activity is a necessary predicate to the finding that a confession is not 'voluntary' within the meaning of the Due Process Clause"; "[a]bsent police conduct causally related to the confession, there is simply no basis for concluding that any state action has deprived a criminal defendant of due process of law." The case arose as follows:

Respondent, a mentally ill person flew from Boston to Denver, approached a uniformed police officer on a downtown Denver street and, without any prompting, told the officer that "he had killed someone" and wanted to talk to the officer about it. Respondent was then handcuffed and informed of his Miranda rights. After stating that he understood his rights, respondent elaborated further on the initial statement. A homicide detective soon arrived on the scene. He readvised respondent of his rights, and asked him "what he had on his mind." Respondent then stated that he had come all the way from Boston because he wanted to confess to murdering a young girl, a crime he had committed in Denver nine months earlier. He then gave the detective the name of the victim. Next, respondent was taken to police headquarters, where records revealed that an unidentified female body had been discovered in the area respondent described. Connelly then made more incriminating statements and took the police to the place where he said the murder had occurred.

Respondent was initially found incompetent to stand trial. But he achieved competency after six months of hospitalization and treatment with antipsychotic and sedative medication. A psychiatrist, previously appointed to conduct a competency examination of respondent, testified for the defense that Connelly's statements to the police had resulted from "command auditory hallucinations," a symptom of his mental disorder. The "voice of God" had told Connelly to return to Denver to confess his crime. When he returned, the same voice became stronger and told him either to confess to the killing or to commit suicide. At that point, reluctantly following the voice's command, Connelly approached the first officer he could find and confessed. Because people suffering from command hallucinations feel they must do whatever the voice tells them, the psychiatrist was of the opinion that Connelly was unable to make a free and intelligent decision about whether to speak with, and to confess to, the police.

The trial court suppressed Connelly's statements because they were "involuntary"; respondent had not exercised "free will" in choosing to speak to the police, but had been "compelled" by his illness to confess. In upholding the trial court on this issue, the Colorado Supreme Court observed that "[o]ne's capacity for rational judgment and free choice may be overborne as much by certain forms of severe illness as by external pressure." The U.S. Supreme Court reversed:

"[The confession cases] considered by this Court over the 50 years since *Brown v. Mississippi* have focused upon the crucial element of police overreaching. [A]ll have contained a substantial element of coercive police conduct. Absent police conduct causally related to the confession, there is simply no basis for concluding that any state actor has deprived a criminal defendant of due process of law. * * *

"Respondent relies on *Blackburn v. Alabama*, 361 U.S. 199 (1960), and *Townsend v. Sain* [discussed briefly at p. 553, fn. c, a case some commentators had read as barring the use of confessions obtained from a person whose volitional power is seriously impaired, whatever the reason]. But respondent's reading of *Blackburn* and *Townsend* ignores the integral element of police overreaching present in both cases. In *Blackburn*, the Court found that [defendant] was probably insane at the time of his confession and the police learned during the interrogation that he had a history of mental problems.

"The police exploited this weakness with coercive tactics [and these] tactics supported a finding that the confession was involuntary. * * * *Townsend* presented a similar instance of police wrongdoing. In that case, a police physician had given Townsend a drug with truth-serum properties. The subsequent confession, obtained by officers who knew that Townsend had been given drugs, was held involuntary. These two cases demonstrate that while mental condition is surely relevant to an individual's susceptibility to police coercion, mere examination of the confessant's state of mind can never conclude the due process inquiry.

"[The] difficulty with the approach of the Supreme Court of Colorado is that it fails to recognize the essential link between coercive activity of the State, on the one hand, and a resulting confession by a defendant, on the other. The flaw in respondent's constitutional argument is that it would expand our previous line of 'voluntariness' cases into a far-ranging requirement that courts must divine a defendant's motivation for speaking or acting as he did even though there be no claim that governmental conduct coerced his decision.[a]

"The most outrageous behavior by a private party seeking to secure evidence against a defendant does not make that evidence inadmissible under the Due Process Clause. * * * [S]uppressing respondent's statements would serve absolutely no purpose in enforcing constitutional guarantees. The purpose of excluding confessions seized in violation of the Constitution is to substantially deter future violations of the Constitution. Only if we were to establish a brand new constitutional right—the right of a criminal defendant to confess to his crime only when totally rational and properly motivated—could respondent's present claim be sustained.

"We have previously cautioned against expanding 'currently applicable exclusionary rules by erecting additional barriers to placing truthful and probative evidence before state juries * * *.' *Lego v. Twomey* (1972) [p. 941]. We abide by that counsel now. [Respondent] would now have us require sweeping inquiries into the state of mind of a criminal defendant who has confessed, inquiries quite divorced from any coercion brought to bear on the defendant by the State. We think the Constitution rightly leaves this sort of inquiry to be resolved by state laws governing the admission of evidence and erects no standard of its own in this area. A statement rendered by one in the condition of respondent might be proved to be quite unreliable, but this is a matter to be governed by the evidentiary laws of the forum and not by the Due Process Clause * * *."

Dissenting Justice BRENNAN, joined by Marshall, J., recalled that the *Blackburn* Court had observed: "Surely in the present stage of our civilization a most basic sense of justice is affronted by the spectacle of incarcerating a human being upon the basis of a statement he made while insane * * *." "[T]he use of a mentally ill person's involuntary confession," maintained Justice Brennan, "is antithetical to the notion of fundamental fairness embodied in the Due Process Clause." He argued that "[the] holding that involuntary confessions are only those procured through police misconduct [is] inconsistent with the Court's historical insistence that only confessions reflecting an exercise of free will be admitted into evidence" and that "[u]ntil today, we have never upheld the admission of a confession that does not reflect the exercise of free will."[b]

He continued:

"Since the Court redefines voluntary confessions to include confessions by mentally ill individuals, the reliability of these confessions becomes a central concern. A concern for reliability is inherent in our criminal justice system, which relies upon accusatorial rather than inquisitorial practices. * * *

a. Consider, e.g., United States v. Erving L., 147 F.3d 1240 (10th Cir.1998), which, relying on *Connelly*, upheld the admissibility of a confession coerced by the defendant's mother.

b. The dissenters took sharp exception to the majority's reading of *Townsend*: "[Although the majority maintains that the confession in that case was obtained by officers who knew that a police doctor had given defendant a drug with truth-serum properties], in fact [as the *Townsend* Court pointed out], 'the police * * * did not know what [medications] the doctor had given [the defendant].' And the *Townsend* Court expressly states that police wrongdoing was not an essential factor:

" 'It is not significant that the drug may have been administered and the questions asked by persons unfamiliar with [the drug's] properties as a "truth serum," if these properties exist. Any questioning by police officers which *in fact* produces a confession which is not the product of a free intellect renders that confession inadmissible. The Court has usually so stated the test.' (Emphasis in original.)"

"Because the admission of a confession so strongly tips the balance against the defendant in the adversarial process, we must be especially careful about a confession's reliability. We have to date not required a finding of reliability for involuntary confessions only because all such confessions have been excluded upon a finding of involuntariness, regardless of reliability. The Court's adoption today of a restrictive definition of an 'involuntary' confession will require heightened scrutiny of a confessions' reliability.

"The instant case starkly highlights the danger of admitting a confession by a person with a severe mental illness. The trial court made no findings concerning the reliability of Mr. Connelly's involuntary confession, since it believed that the confession was excludable on the basis of involuntariness. However, the overwhelming evidence in the record points to the unreliability of Mr. Connelly's delusional mind. * * *

"Moreover, the record is barren of any corroboration of the mentally ill defendant's confession. No physical evidence links the defendant to the alleged crime. Police did not identify the alleged victim's body as the woman named by the defendant. Mr. Connelly identified the alleged scene of the crime, but it has not been verified that the unidentified body was found there or that a crime actually occurred there. There is not a shred of competent evidence in this record linking the defendant to the charged homicide. There is only Mr. Connelly's confession.

"Minimum standards of due process should require that the trial court find substantial indicia of reliability, on the basis of evidence extrinsic to the confession itself, before admitting the confession of a mentally ill person into evidence. I would require the trial court to make such a finding on remand. To hold otherwise allows the State to imprison and possibly to execute a mentally ill defendant based solely upon an inherently unreliable confession."

Notes and Questions

1. ***What if the Ku Klux Klan had kidnapped and tortured a murder suspect?*** The *Connelly* Court tells us that "the most outrageous behavior by a private party" would not make the resulting confession inadmissible under the Due Process Clause and that suppressing the confession under such circumstances "would serve absolutely no purpose in enforcing constitutional guarantees." Do you agree? Suppose the Ku Klux Klan kidnaped an African–American suspected of murder, hanged him by a rope to the limb of a tree, let him down, then hung him again, and when he was let down the second time, still protesting his innocence, tied him to a tree and severely whipped him until he confessed?[a] Suppose, further, that the state supreme court held the confession admissible, noting that it had been corroborated by extrinsic evidence. Would (should) the U.S. Supreme Court hold the confession admissible? Consider *Commonwealth v. Mahnke*, 335 N.E.2d 660 (Sup.Jud.Ct.Mass. 1975), which arose as follows: When a young woman disappeared, many suspected her boyfriend (the defendant) of foul play. After harassing the defendant for months, a group of friends and relatives of the missing woman assaulted and kidnaped defendant and drove him to an isolated, snowbound hunting cabin 128 miles away. There he was questioned by three and then five people for at least six hours. The questioning was interspersed with

a. The coercion imposed on the defendant in the hypothetical case is essentially the coercion experienced by the defendant in the first fourteenth amendment due process confession case decided by the U.S. Supreme Court, *Brown v. Mississippi* (1936) (p. 553), except that law enforcement officials were involved in extracting the confession in the *Brown* case. See generally Morgan Cloud, *Torture and Truth*, 74 Texas L.Rev. 1211, 1213–15 (1996); Michael J. Klarman, *The Racial Origins of Modern Criminal Procedure* (quoted at p. 59).

extremely rough language and threats that the defendant would never leave alive. Finally the defendant confessed. He was convicted of second-degree murder. The trial judge ruled that all statements the defendant made to his kidnappers prior to leaving the cabin were inadmissible, but ruled that, because of a "break in the stream of events," statements he made later were admissible. The Supreme Judicial Court of Massachusetts, per TAURO, C.J., agreed, but directed a verdict of a lesser degree of guilt. Massachusetts' highest court condemned the use of statements obtained at the cabin as follows:

"[The prohibition against the use of coerced confessions applies] even though the statements were extracted by private coercion unalloyed with any official government involvement. [A] statement obtained through coercion and introduced at trial is every bit as offensive to civilized standards of adjudication when the coercion flows from private hands as when official depredations elicit a confession. Statements extracted by a howling lynch mob or a lawless pack of vigilantes from a terrorized, pliable suspect are repugnant to due process mandates of fundamental fairness and protection against compulsory self-incrimination."

2. ***Is "the (exclusionary) tail wagging the (due process) dog"?*** Consider Laurence Benner, *Requiem for Miranda: The Rehnquist Court's Voluntariness Doctrine in Historical Perspective*, 67 Wash.U.L.Q. 59, 136–37 (1989):

"[The *Connelly* Court] concluded that in the absence of coercive police misconduct 'suppressing [Connelly's] statements would serve absolutely no purpose in enforcing constitutional guarantees.' From this narrow premise, the Court then leaped to the broad conclusion that the use of Connelly's deranged statements as evidence against him did not violate the due process clause.

"But surely this is the (exclusionary) tail wagging the (due process) dog, for the upshot of the Court's position is that unless exclusion will deter someone in an official capacity, there can be no due process violation no matter how unjust the result. By allowing the deterrence rationale for the exclusionary rule to control the nature of the due process inquiry, the Court thus permits the logic of deterrence to shape the actual content of due process itself. Under this formula any concern for justice is excluded from the equation. Indeed, any attempt to develop a coherent theory of justice under the due process clause is precluded."

3. ***Confessions vs. guilty pleas.*** The *Connelly* Court balked at requiring "sweeping inquiries into the state of mind of a criminal defendant who has confessed, inquiries quite divorced from any [police] coercion brought to bear on the defendant." Would such inquiries be any more burdensome than constitutionally required inquiries into a defendant's competency to stand trial, to waive her right to counsel, or to be executed? See Benner, supra, at 137. Connelly, recalls Professor Benner, "was found incompetent to stand trial immediately following the making of his custodial confession. Does it not therefore appear incongruous that Connelly could not have pled guilty in open court, on the same day he sealed his fate with a confession obtained within the precincts of the Denver police headquarters?"

4. ***Should the admissibility of a confession turn on whether in fact it is the product of a "free will" or whether in fact it is voluntary?*** What is the *Connelly* dissenters' argument? That a confession by a mentally ill (or drugged) person is inherently unreliable or at least highly suspect? Or that the use of a mentally ill (or drugged) person's confession violates due process regardless of how impressively corroborated or otherwise reliable the confession turns out to be? Or both? If a confession is not the product of police overreaching and doubts about its reliability have been dispelled, why should it matter whether it was in fact involuntarily made?

(a) Changing the facts of the *Townsend* case: In *Townsend*, the defendant was suffering from severe heroin withdrawal symptoms. A police doctor was called in to treat this condition and injected the suspect with a drug that, unknown to the doctor or the police who subsequently questioned him (according to the record), had the properties of a "truth serum." About an hour later, defendant confessed.

Suppose that Townsend's sister had visited him in his cell and given him pills to relieve his suffering and that, unknown to her, these pills had the properties of a "truth serum." Suppose further that after taking these pills Townsend had told a guard that he wanted to confess and then had proceeded to do so. Would (should) such a confession be excluded? Why (not)?

Is the confession in the hypothetical *Townsend* case any more an exercise of "free will" or any less involuntary in fact than the confession in the actual *Townsend* case? If there is a distinction, is it that in the actual case the police doctor or the police who subsequently questioned Townsend were negligent? That even if the "truth serum" were not the result of police wrongdoing, it was still the result of their doing?

(b) Changing the facts of the *Connelly* case: Suppose that Connelly had never returned to Denver, but had phoned a Denver police officer from Boston and—with the "voice of God" ringing in his ears—had made a detailed confession over the phone. Or suppose Connelly had stayed in Boston and—with the "voice of God" doing the dictation—had written out a detailed confession and mailed it to the Denver police department. Would (should) such confessions be admissible? What would Justices Brennan and Marshall say? How, if at all, are the confessions in the hypotheticals different from the statements Connelly made in the actual case?

(c) A court should care whether a confession is the product of police wrongdoing or whether it is reliable, but why should it care whether it is voluntary or involuntary in fact? If a confession is neither the product of impermissible police methods nor untrustworthy (i.e. if doubts about its reliability have been removed), why should the confession's voluntariness be a relevant constitutional question?

4. *Does "product of a free choice" talk lead anyhere? Is there an alternative approach?* Consider POSNER, J., writing for the Court in UNITED STATES v. RUTLEDGE, 900 F.2d 1127, 1129 (7th Cir.1990):

"[In] most cases in which a confession is sought to be excluded because involuntary, there is little likelihood that the inducements placed before the defendant were so overpowering as to induce an untrue confession. The courts in such cases retreat to the proposition that a confession, to be admissible, must be the product of a free choice. [As] the courts are beginning to suspect, [this approach] leads nowhere. Taken seriously it would require the exclusion of virtually all fruits of custodial interrogation, since few choices to confess can be thought truly 'free' when made by a person who in incarcerated and is being questioned by armed officers without the presence of counsel or anyone else to give him moral support. The formula is not taken seriously. *Connelly* may have driven the stake through its heart by holding that a confession which is not a product of the defendant's free choice—maybe he was so crazy, retarded, high on drugs, or intoxicated that he did not even know he was being interrogated—is admissible so long as whatever it was that destroyed the defendant's power of choice was not police conduct. In any event, very few incriminating statements, custodial or otherwise, are held to be involuntary, though few are the product of a choice that the interrogators left completely free.

"An alternative approach, which is implied by *Connelly* and may well describe the courts' actual as distinct from articulated standard, is to ask whether the government has made it impossible for the defendant to make a *rational* choice as to whether to confess—has made it in other words impossible for him to weigh the pros and cons of confessing and go with the balance as it appears at the time. This approach * * * implies, for example, that if the government feeds the defendant false information that seriously distorts his choice, by promising him that if he confesses he will be set free, or if the government drugs him so that he cannot make a conscious choice at all, then the confession must go out."[b]

5. ***Does the Connelly case mark the decline and fall of the "reliability" element?*** As we have seen (pp. 552–55), the reliability of a confession does not necessarily make it admissible. But should the unreliability of a confession (or the absence of substantial indicia of reliability) render a confession inadmissible as a matter of federal constitutional law? Compare George Dix, *Federal Constitutional Confession Law: The 1986 and 1987 Supreme Court Terms*, 67 Tex.L.Rev. 231, 272–76 (1988) with Albert Alschuler, Note 3 (d) supra, at 959–60.

Professor Dix finds "the rejection of reliability as a relevant consideration in federal constitutional law" "the most surprising aspect" of *Connelly*. The opinion, comments Dix, "misleadingly represents that the Court's prior decisions definitively settled the matter, when in fact, until *Connelly*, reliability played an important role in traditional confession law analysis." Dix concludes that "at least in the absence of more thorough consideration than *Connelly* demonstrates, a total deconstitutionalization of traditionally important reliability issues is unjustified."

"Just as the Constitution does not mandate the exclusion of unreliable eyewitness testimony," maintains Professor Alschuler, "it does not mandate the exclusion of unreliable confessions. [The] Constitution requires the exclusion of unreliable eyewitness testimony only when improper governmental conduct—for example, an impermissibly suggestive police line-up—has produced it. The rule should be no different for unreliable confessions. Unless improper governmental conduct has generated a confession, the Constitution should give the defendant only a right to present evidence of the confession's unreliability to the jury."

6. ***Confessions given by mentally handicapped suspects.*** Consider Welsh S. White, *Miranda's Waning Protections* 202–03 (2001):

"In determining whether interrogation methods employed by the police exerted unfair or coercive pressure on the suspect, the voluntariness test should take into account the suspect's special vulnerabilities, weighing the extent to which these vulnerabilities might make the suspect prone to respond to interrogation methods by providing statements sought by the interrogator regardless of his or her initial belief in the truth of those statements. In applying this approach, moreover, weight should be given to the empirical evidence indicating that for mentally handicapped suspects, 'even the average level of stress built into an interrogation can be excessive and overbearing.'

"This approach is admittedly inconsistent with *Connelly*'s dictum intimating that an interrogated suspect's mental problems are constitutionally irrelevant unless the interrogating officer is or should be aware of them. [But] *Connelly*'s dictum is inconsistent with the Court's approach in pre-*Miranda* due process cases. Moreover, determining the legitimacy of an interrogation method on the basis of what an officer knew or should have known about the suspect's mental weaknesses is not administratively feasible. Interrogating officers could often plausibly assert that they were not in fact aware and had no reason to be aware of a suspect's particular weakness, such as mental retardation. Reviving the pre-

b. See also Albert W. Alschuler, *Constraint and Confession*, 74 Denv.U.L.Rev. 957, 959 (1997).

Miranda due process test's approach of considering the individual characteristics of suspects subjected to interrogation is thus the only viable means of providing mentally handicapped suspects with protection from interrogation methods substantially likely to produce untrustworthy confessions."[b]

SECTION 7. *MASSIAH* REVISITED; *MASSIAH* AND *MIRANDA* COMPARED AND CONTRASTED

A. The Revivification of *Massiah*

"Until the Christian burial speech case [*Brewer v. Williams*, set forth below] * * * lasting fame had eluded *Massiah v. United States* [p. 561]. It was apparently lost in the shuffle of fast-moving events that reshaped constitutional-criminal procedure in the 1960s. [In] constitutional-criminal procedure circles, 1964 was the year of *Escobedo v. Illinois* [p. 563], and *Massiah* was understandably neglected in the hue and cry raised over the Illinois case. To the extent that *Massiah* was remembered at all, it was [only as a] stepping stone to *Escobedo* * * *.

"*Escobedo* may have seized the spotlight from *Massiah*, but *Escobedo* was soon shoved offstage by that blockbuster, *Miranda*, [a case that] '[did] not [enlarge] *Escobedo* as much as [it] displaced it.' Assuming that *Escobedo* had not already done so, did *Miranda* also displace *Massiah*? After Miranda, was the institution of judicial proceedings, by way of indictment or otherwise, no more constitutionally relevant than whether the investigation had 'begun to focus on a particular suspect?' [If] one searches the *Miranda* opinion for answers to these questions, [one] discovers that *Massiah* is never mentioned—not once in Chief Justice Warren's sixty-page opinion for the Court, nor in any of the three dissenting opinions, which total another forty-six pages. Yet very little else even remotely bearing on the general subject is left out."

—Kamisar, Police Interrogation and Confessions 160–64 (1980).

BREWER v. WILLIAMS (WILLIAMS I)

430 U.S. 387, 97 S.Ct. 1232, 51 L.Ed.2d 424 (1977).

Justice STEWART delivered the opinion of the Court. * * *

On the afternoon of December 24, 1968, a 10–year-old girl named Pamela Powers went with her family to the YMCA in Des Moines, Iowa. [When] she failed to return from a trip to the washroom, a search for her began. The search was unsuccessful.

Robert Williams, who had recently escaped from a mental hospital, was a resident of the YMCA. Soon after the girl's disappearance Williams was seen in the YMCA lobby carrying some clothing and a large bundle wrapped in a blanket. He obtained help from a 14–year-old boy in opening the street door of the YMCA and the door to his automobile parked outside. When Williams placed the bundle in the front seat of his car the boy "saw two legs in it and they were skinny and white." Before anyone could see what was in the bundle Williams drove away. His abandoned car was found the following day in Davenport, Iowa, roughly 160 miles east of Des Moines. A warrant was then issued in Des Moines for his arrest on a charge of abduction.

b. Consider, too, the extracts from the Cloud empirical study, Note 27, p. 670.

On the morning of December 26, a Des Moines lawyer named Henry McKnight went to the Des Moines police station and informed the officers present that he had just received a long distance call from Williams, and that he had advised Williams to turn himself in to the Davenport police. Williams did surrender that morning to the police in Davenport, and they booked him on the charge specified in the arrest warrant and gave him the [*Miranda* warnings]. The Davenport police then telephoned their counterparts in Des Moines to inform them that Williams had surrendered. McKnight, the lawyer, was still at the Des Moines police headquarters, and Williams conversed with McKnight on the telephone. In the presence of the Des Moines Chief of Police and a Police Detective named Leaming [a captain and 20–year veteran of the Des Moines police department], McKnight advised Williams that Des Moines police officers would be driving to Davenport to pick him up, that the officers would not interrogate him or mistreat him, and that Williams was not to talk to the officers about Pamela Powers until after consulting with McKnight upon his return to Des Moines. As a result of these conversations, it was agreed between McKnight and the Des Moines police officials that Detective Leaming and a fellow officer would drive to Davenport to pick up Williams, that they would bring him directly back to Des Moines, and that they would not question him during the trip.

In the meantime Williams was arraigned before a judge in Davenport on the outstanding arrest warrant.[a] The judge advised him of his *Miranda* rights and committed him to jail. Before leaving the courtroom, Williams conferred with a lawyer named Kelly, who advised him not to make any statements until consulting with McKnight back in Des Moines.

Detective Leaming and his fellow officer arrived in Davenport about noon to pick up Williams and return him to Des Moines. Soon after their arrival they met with Williams and Kelly, who, they understood, was acting as Williams' lawyer. Detective Leaming repeated the Miranda warnings, and told Williams:

> "* * * we both know that you're being represented here by Mr. Kelly and you're being represented by Mr. McKnight in Des Moines, [and] I want you to remember this because we'll be visiting between here and Des Moines."

Williams then conferred again with Kelly alone, and after this conference Kelly reiterated to Detective Leaming that Williams was not to be questioned about the disappearance of Pamela Powers until after he had consulted with McKnight back in Des Moines. When Leaming expressed some reservations, Kelly firmly stated that the agreement with McKnight was to be carried out—that there was to be no interrogation of Williams during the automobile journey to Des Moines. Kelly was denied permission to ride in the police car back to Des Moines with Williams and the two officers.

The two Detectives, with Williams in their charge, then set out on the 160–mile drive. At no time during the trip did Williams express a willingness to be interrogated in the absence of an attorney. Instead, he stated several times that "[w]hen I get to Des Moines and see Mr. McKnight, I am going to tell you the whole story." Detective Leaming knew that Williams was a former mental patient, and knew also that he was deeply religious.

The Detective and his prisoner soon embarked on a wide-ranging conversation covering a variety of topics, including the subject of religion. Then, not long after leaving Davenport and reaching the interstate highway, Detective Leaming

a. At the time *Williams* was decided, it did not seem to matter that the defendant was arraigned on the charge of abduction, not the charge of murder that grew out of the abduction. Evidently the Court assumed that when the Sixth Amendment right to counsel attached to the abduction charge it attached to the factually related crime of murder as well. But see *Texas v. Cobb*, p. 749.

delivered what has been referred to [as] the "Christian burial speech." Addressing Williams as "Reverend," the Detective said:

> "I want to give you something to think about while we're traveling down the road. * * * Number one, I want you to observe the weather conditions, it's raining, it's sleeting, it's freezing, driving is very treacherous, visibility is poor, it's going to be dark early this evening. They are predicting several inches of snow for tonight, and I feel that you yourself are the only person that knows where this little girl's body is, that you yourself have only been there once, and if you get a snow on top of it you yourself may be unable to find it. And, since we will be going right past the area on the way into Des Moines, I feel that we could stop and locate the body, that the parents of this little girl should be entitled to a Christian burial for the little girl who was snatched away from them on Christmas Eve and murdered. And I feel we should stop and locate it on the way in rather than waiting until morning and trying to come back out after a snow storm and possibly not being able to find it at all."[b]

Williams asked Detective Leaming why he thought their route to Des Moines would be taking them past the girl's body, and Leaming responded that he knew the body [was near] Mitchellville—a town they would be passing on the way to Des Moines.[1] Leaming then stated: "I do not want you to answer me. I don't want to discuss it further. Just think about it as we're riding down the road."

As the car approached Grinell, a town approximately 100 miles west of Davenport, Williams asked whether the police had found the victim's shoes. When Detective Leaming replied that he was unsure, Williams directed the officers to a service station where he said he had left the shoes; a search for them proved unsuccessful. As they continued towards Des Moines, Williams asked whether the police had found the blanket, and directed the officers to a rest area where he said he had disposed of the blanket. Nothing was found. The car continued towards Des Moines, and as it approached Mitchellville, Williams said that he would show the officers where the body was. He then directed the police to the body of Pamela Powers.

[The trial judge admitted all evidence relating to or resulting from statements Williams made in the car ride. He found that "an agreement" had been made between defense counsel and the police that Williams would not be questioned on the return trip to Des Moines, but ruled that Williams had waived his rights before giving such information. Williams was convicted of murder. The Iowa Supreme Court affirmed. On federal habeas, the District Court concluded that] the evidence in question had been wrongly admitted at Williams' trial. This conclusion was based on three alternative and independent grounds: (1) that Williams had been denied his constitutional right to the assistance of counsel; (2)

b. Although no member of the Supreme Court discussed, or even noted, this point, Captain Leaming offered two different versions of the "Christian burial speech." The captain's first version was given at a pretrial hearing to suppress evidence; his second version, the only one quoted and discussed by the Supreme Court and lower federal courts, was given four weeks later at the trial. See Kamisar, *Foreword: Brewer v. Williams—A Hard Look at a Discomfiting Record,* 66 Geo.L.J. 209, 215–18 (1977). For the view that these two versions are significantly different, see id. at 218–33.

Justice Stewart notes that the captain addressed Williams as "Reverend," and then gives the captain's *second* version of the speech and related testimony *in its entirety.* But Captain Leaming did not testify that he addressed Williams as "Reverend" in the second version, only in the first. Justice Stewart may have called attention to the "Reverend" address because the Attorney General of Iowa was sufficiently troubled by it to go outside the record to explain in his brief why Captain Leaming employed it. See Kamisar, supra, at 223. For a discussion of the significance of the " 'Reverend' ploy," see id. at 221–23.

1. The fact of the matter, of course, was that Detective Leaming possessed no such knowledge.

that he had been denied [his *Miranda* rights]; and (3) that in any event, [his] statements [had] been involuntarily made. [The] Court of Appeals appears to have affirmed the judgment on [the first two] grounds. We have concluded that only one of them need be considered here.

Specifically, there is no need to review the [*Miranda* doctrine] [or the] ruling [that] Williams' self-incriminating statements [were] involuntarily made. For it is clear that the judgment before us must in any event be affirmed upon the ground that Williams was deprived of a different constitutional right—the right to the assistance of counsel. * * * Whatever else it may mean, the right to counsel * * * means at least that a person is entitled to the help of a lawyer at or after the time that judicial proceedings have been initiated against him—"whether by way of formal charge, preliminary hearing, indictment, information, or arraignment." Kirby v. Illinois [p. 769].

There can be no doubt in the present case that judicial proceedings had been initiated against Williams before the start of the automobile ride from Davenport to Des Moines. A warrant had been issued for his arrest, he had been arraigned on that warrant before a judge in a Davenport courtroom, and he had been committed by the court to confinement in jail. The State does not contend otherwise.

There can be no serious doubt, either, that Detective Leaming deliberately and designedly set out to elicit information from Williams just as surely as—and perhaps more effectively than—if he had formally interrogated him. Detective Leaming was fully aware before departing for Des Moines that Williams was being represented in Davenport by Kelly and in Des Moines by McKnight. Yet he purposely sought during Williams' isolation from his lawyers to obtain as much incriminating information as possible. Indeed, Detective Leaming conceded as much when he testified at Williams' trial:

> "Q. In fact, Captain, whether he was a mental patient or not, you were trying to get all the information you could before he got to his lawyer, weren't you?
>
> "A. I was sure hoping to find out where that little girl was, yes, sir.
>
> "Q. Well, I'll put it this way: You [were] hoping to get all the information you could before Williams got back to McKnight, weren't you?
>
> "A. Yes, sir."[6]

[The] circumstances of this case are thus constitutionally indistinguishable from those presented in *Massiah*. [That] the incriminating statements were elicited surreptitiously in [*Massiah*], and otherwise here, is constitutionally irrelevant. Rather, the clear rule of *Massiah* is that once adversary proceedings have commenced against an individual, he has a right to legal representation when the government interrogates him.[c]

[The] Iowa courts recognized that Williams had been denied the constitutional right to the assistance of counsel. They held, however, that he had waived that right during the course of the automobile trip from Davenport to Des Moines.

[It] was incumbent upon the State to prove "an intentional relinquishment or abandonment of a known right or privilege." *Johnson v. Zerbst*. [That] strict standard applies equally to an alleged waiver of the right to counsel whether at

6. Counsel for the State, in the course of oral argument in this Court, acknowledged that the "Christian burial speech" was tantamount to interrogation * * *.

c. Isn't the clear rule of *Massiah* that once adversary proceedings have commenced against an individual, he has a right to counsel when the government *deliberately elicits* incriminating information from him (whether or not the government's efforts to obtain information constitute "interrogation" within the meaning of *Miranda*'s Fifth Amendment rights)? See Note 2 following this case.

trial or at a critical stage of pretrial proceedings. [Judged by that standard,] the record in this case falls far short of sustaining the State's burden. It is true that Williams had been informed of and appeared to understand his right to counsel. But waiver requires not merely comprehension but relinquishment, and Williams' consistent reliance upon the advice of counsel in dealing with the authorities refutes any suggestion that he waived that right. [His] statements while in the car that he would tell the whole story after seeing McKnight in Des Moines were the clearest expressions [that] he desired the presence of an attorney before any interrogation took place. But even before making these statements, Williams had effectively asserted his right to counsel by having secured attorneys at both ends of the automobile trip, both of whom, acting as his agents, had made clear to the police that no interrogation was to occur during the journey. Williams knew of that agreement and, particularly in view of his consistent reliance on counsel, there is no basis for concluding that he disavowed it.

Despite Williams' express and implicit assertions of his right to counsel, Detective Leaming proceeded to elicit incriminating statements from Williams. Leaming did not preface this effort by telling Williams that he had a right to the presence of a lawyer, and made no effort at all to ascertain whether Williams wished to relinquish that right. The circumstances of record in this case thus provide no reasonable basis for finding that Williams waived his right to the assistance of counsel.

The Court of Appeals did not hold, nor do we, that under the circumstances of this case Williams *could not*, without notice to counsel, have waived his rights under the Sixth and Fourteenth Amendments. It only held, as do we, that he did not.

* * * Although we do not lightly affirm the issuance of a writ of habeas corpus in this case, so clear a violation of the Sixth and Fourteenth Amendments as here occurred cannot be condoned.

[The] judgment of the Court of Appeals is affirmed.[12]

[The separate concurring opinions of Justices Marshall, Powell and Stevens are omitted.]

Chief Justice BURGER, dissenting.

The result in this case ought to be intolerable in any society which purports to call itself an organized society. It continues the Court—by the narrowest margin—on the much-criticized course of punishing the public for the mistakes and misdeeds of law enforcement officers, instead of punishing the officer directly, if in fact he is guilty of wrongdoing. It mechanically and blindly keeps reliable evidence from juries whether the claimed constitutional violation involves gross police misconduct or honest human error.

12. The District Court stated that its decision "does not touch upon the issue of what evidence, if any, beyond the incriminating statements themselves must be excluded as 'fruit of the poisonous tree.' " We too have no occasion to address this issue, and in the present posture of the case there is no basis for the view of our dissenting Brethren [that] any attempt to retry the respondent would probably be futile. While neither Williams' incriminating statements themselves nor any testimony describing his having led the police to the victim's body can constitutionally be admitted into evidence, evidence of where the body was found and of its condition might well be admissible on the theory that the body would have been discovered in any event, even had incriminating statements not been elicited from Williams. In the event that a retrial is instituted, it will be for the state courts in the first instance to determine whether particular items of evidence may be admitted.

[On retrial, the state court ruled that the body of Pamela Powers "would have been found in any event" and Williams was again convicted of murder. The U.S. Supreme Court upheld the state court's use of the "inevitable discovery" exception. See *Williams II,* p. 775.]

Williams is guilty of the savage murder of a small child; no member of the Court contends he is not. While in custody, and after no fewer than five warnings of his rights to silence and to counsel, he led police to the concealed body of his victim. The Court concedes Williams was not threatened or coerced and that he spoke and acted voluntarily and with full awareness of his constitutional rights. In the face of all this, the Court now holds that because Williams was prompted by the detective's statement—not interrogation but a statement—the jury must not be told how the police found the body.

[In] a variety of contexts we inquire whether application of the rule will promote its objectives sufficiently to justify the enormous cost it imposes on society. * * * Against this background, it is striking that the Court fails even to consider whether the benefits secured by application of the exclusionary rule in this case outweigh its obvious social costs. Perhaps the failure is due to the fact that this case arises not under the Fourth Amendment, but under *Miranda*, and the Sixth Amendment right to counsel. The Court apparently perceives the function of the exclusionary rule to be so different in these varying contexts that it must be mechanically and uncritically applied in all cases arising outside the Fourth Amendment. * * *

Justice WHITE, with whom Justice BLACKMUN and Justice REHNQUIST join, dissenting.

[I disagree with the majority's finding that no waiver was proved in this case.] That respondent knew of his right not to say anything to the officers without advice and presence of counsel is established on this record to a moral certainty. He was advised of the right by three officials of the State—telling at least one that he understood the right—and by two lawyers. [The] issue in this case, then, is whether respondent relinquished that right intentionally.

Respondent relinquished his right not to talk to the police about his crime when the car approached the place where he had hidden the victim's clothes. Men usually intend to do what they do and there is nothing in the record to support the proposition that respondent's decision to talk was anything but an exercise of his own free will. Apparently, without any prodding from the officers, respondent—who had earlier said that he would tell the whole story when he arrived in Des Moines—spontaneously changed his mind about the timing of his disclosures when the car approached the places where he had hidden the evidence. However, even if his statements were influenced by Detective Leaming's above-quoted statement, respondent's decision to talk in the absence of counsel can hardly be viewed as the product of an overborne will. The statement by Leaming was not coercive; it was accompanied by a request that respondent not respond to it; and it was delivered hours before respondent decided to make any statement. Respondent's waiver was thus knowing and intentional. * * *

Justice BLACKMUN, with whom Justice WHITE and Justice REHNQUIST join, dissenting. * * *

The Court rules that the Sixth Amendment was violated because Detective Leaming "purposely sought during Williams' isolation from his lawyers to obtain as much incriminating information as possible." I cannot regard that as unconstitutional per se.

First, the police did not deliberately seek to isolate Williams from his lawyers so as to deprive him of the assistance of counsel. Cf. Escobedo. The isolation in this case was a necessary incident of transporting Williams to the county where the crime was committed.

Second, Leaming's purpose was not solely to obtain incriminating evidence. The victim had been missing for only two days, and the police could not be certain that she was dead. Leaming, of course, and in accord with his duty, was "hoping to find out where that little girl was," but such motivation does not equate with an intention to evade the Sixth Amendment.[d] * * *

Third, not every attempt to elicit information should be regarded as "tantamount to interrogation." I am not persuaded that Leaming's observations and comments, made as the police car traversed the snowy and slippery miles between Davenport and Des Moines that winter afternoon, were an interrogation, direct or subtle, of Williams. Williams, after all, was counseled by lawyers, and warned by the arraigning judge in Davenport and by the police, and yet it was he who started the travel conversations and brought up the subject of the criminal investigation.

[In] summary, it seems to me that the Court is holding that *Massiah* is violated whenever police engage in any conduct, in the absence of counsel, with the subjective desire to obtain information from a suspect after arraignment. Such a rule is far too broad. Persons in custody frequently volunteer statements in response to stimuli other than interrogation. * * *

Notes and Questions

1. ***Was it constitutionally irrelevant whether the "Christian burial speech" constituted "interrogation"?*** Did the Court deem it necessary (or at least important) to classify Leaming's speech as a "form of interrogation" or "tantamount to interrogation"? If so, why? Once the Court chose the "Sixth Amendment—*Massiah*" route over a "Fifth Amendment—*Miranda*" approach, did the question whether Leaming engaged in "interrogation" become, or should it have become, constitutionally irrelevant? Did the secret government agent engage in "interrogation" in *Massiah*?

2. ***More on "interrogation" vs. "deliberate elicitation."*** Although Justice Stewart misspoke in *Brewer v. Williams* when he talked about "interrogation" in the context of *Massiah* [see the text of his *Williams* opinion at fn. c], he, in effect, corrected himself when, three years later, he wrote footnote 4 to his opinion of the Court in *Rhode Island v. Innis* [p. 614]. In that footnote, Stewart pointed out that any suggestion in *Brewer v. Williams* that the terms "interrogation" and "deliberate elicitation" are interchangeable was erroneous. Justice Stewart then cited a law review article criticizing his use of the term "interrogation" in *Brewer v. Williams*.

Unfortunately, confusion over these terms has persisted in the lower courts. Hopefully, the Court put an end to this in *Fellers v. United States*, 540 U.S. 519 (2004). In the course of ruling that the Court of Appeals had committed reversible error in ruling that the absence of an "interrogation" foreclosed petitioner's *Massiah* claim, the Supreme Court, per O'Connor, J., underscored the distinction between "interrogation" within the meaning of *Miranda* and "deliberate elicitation" within the meaning of *Massiah*. The *Fellers* Court recalled that *Massiah* [p. 561] had held that "an accused is denied 'the basic protection' of the Sixth Amendment 'when there [is] used against him at his trial evidence of his own incriminating words, which [the police have] deliberately elicited from him after he has been indicted and in absence of his counsel.' "

d. But see Kamisar, *Police Interrogation and Confessions* 146–47 (1980), maintaining that although at one point Leaming did testify that he was "hoping to find out where that little *girl* was," in light of the entire record he apparently meant the girl's *body*. Leaming testified that he heard Williams' lawyer say to him over the phone that he would have to tell the police "where *the body* is" when he got back. Leaming also testified that before he drove to Davenport to pick up Williams, Williams' lawyer told him that the girl "was dead when [Williams] left the YMCA with her."

The "interrogtaion"/"deliberate elicitation" distinction is especially important in the "jail plant" situation. *Miranda* is not implicated when the suspect is *unaware* that he is speaking to a law enforcement officer or his agent because a "police-dominated atmosphere" and "compulsion" are not present. Recall *Illinois v. Perkins*. However, *Massiah* can be implicated if a suspect has already been indicted even though he is speaking freely with someone he believes to be a fellow inmate. See *United States v. Henry*. A person cannot be "interrogated" within the meaning of *Miranda* unless he is aware of it, but he can be subjected to police efforts to "deliberately elicit"statements from him without being aware of it.

3. *Even if Brewer v. Williams were deemed a "Miranda case," would whether Leaming engaged in "interrogation" still be the wrong question?* Since Williams had asserted both his right to remain silent and his right to counsel several times before he was driven back to Des Moines, should the relevant question have been whether Leaming "fully respected" or "scrupulously honored" Williams' *Miranda* rights? Cf. *Michigan v. Mosley*, p. 647. How could it be said that Leaming did, when he "deliberately and designedly set out to elicit information" from Williams?

Brewer v. Williams was decided four years before *Edwards v. Arizona*, p. 647. Looking back at *Williams* in light of *Edwards*, if *Williams* were a "*Miranda* case," should the relevant question have been whether, after expressing his unwillingness to talk to the police without his lawyer, *Williams* changed his mind on his own initiative or whether Leaming "persuaded" or "prompted" him to change his mind?

4. *Does the "poisoned fruit" doctrine apply to Massiah violations?* As we have seen, the Court has balked at applying the "poisoned fruit" doctrine to violations of the *Miranda* rules, except for the most extraordinary circumstances. See *Elstad* (p. 701), *Patane* (p. 703) and *Seibert* (p. 707). What about *Massiah* violations? In *Nix v. Williams* (p. 916) (the *Williams* case on retrial), the Supreme Court *assumed* that the "poisoned fruit" doctrine did apply to *Massiah* violations. But in *Fellers*, Note 2, supra, the Court remanded the case to the Court of Appeals to address this issue in the first instance.

5. *What constitutes a valid waiver of the "Sixth Amendment—Massiah" right?* PATTERSON v. ILLINOIS, 487 U.S. 285 (1988), per WHITE, J., rejected "petitioner's argument, which has some acceptance from courts and commentators, that since 'the sixth amendment right [to counsel] is far superior to that of the fifth amendment right' and since '[t]he greater the right the greater the loss from a waiver of that right,' waiver of an accused's Sixth Amendment right to counsel should be 'more difficult' to effectuate than waiver of a suspect's Fifth Amendment rights." The Court ruled instead that "[a]s a general matter [an] accused who is [given the *Miranda* warnings] has been sufficiently apprised of the nature of the Sixth Amendment rights, and of the consequences of abandoning those rights, so that his waiver on this basis will be considered a knowing and intelligent one."

The case arose as follows: Patterson and other members of a street gang were arrested in the course of investigating the murder of Jackson. Patterson was advised of his *Miranda* rights and agreed to answer questions, but denied knowing anything about Jackson's death. He was held in custody while the investigation continued. Two days later, Patterson and two other gang members were indicted for the murder of Jackson. The same officer who had questioned him earlier told him that because he had been indicted he was being transferred from the lockup, where he was being held, to the county jail. Patterson asked the officer which of the gang members had been indicted for Jackson's murder, and upon learning that one particular gang member had not been indicted, responded: "[W]hy wasn't he indicted, he did everything."

Patterson then began to explain that a witness would support his account of the crime. At this point, the officer handed Patterson a *Miranda* waiver form and read the warnings aloud. Patterson initialed each of the warnings, signed the form and made a lengthy incriminating statement. He subsequently made additional statements. He was found guilty of murder, but maintained that the warnings he received, although they protected his *Miranda* rights, did not adequately inform him of his Sixth Amendment right to counsel during postindictment questioning. A 5–4 majority disagreed:

"[The] key inquiry in a case such as this one must be: Was the accused, who waived his Sixth Amendment rights during postindictment questioning, made sufficiently aware of his right to have counsel present during the questioning, and of the possible consequences of a decision to forgo the aid of counsel? In this case, we are convinced that by admonishing petitioner with the *Miranda* warnings, [the State] has met this burden and that petitioner's waiver of his right to counsel at questioning was valid. * * *

"Our conclusion is supported by petitioner's inability, in the proceedings before this Court, to articulate with precision what additional information should have been provided to him before he would have been competent to waive his right to counsel. * * *[8]"

As a general matter, then, an accused who is admonished with the [*Miranda* warnings] has been sufficiently apprised of the nature of his Sixth Amendment rights, and of the consequences of abandoning these rights, so that his waiver on this basis will be considered a knowing and intelligent one.[9]

"[While] our cases have recognized a 'difference' between the Fifth Amendment and Sixth Amendment rights to counsel, and the 'policies' behind these Constitutional guarantees, we have never suggested that one right is 'superior' or 'greater' than the other, nor is there any support in our cases for the notion that because a Sixth Amendment right may be involved, it is more difficult to waive than the Fifth Amendment counterpart.

"[W]e require a more searching or formal inquiry before permitting an accused to waive his right to counsel at trial [see *Faretta v. California*, p. 119]

8. [Some courts have suggested] that, in addition to the *Miranda* warnings, an accused should be informed that he has been indicted before a postindictment waiver is sought. Because, in this case, petitioner concedes that he was so informed, we do not address [this issue].

Beyond this, only one Court of Appeals—the Second Circuit—has adopted substantive or procedural requirements (in addition to *Miranda*) that must be completed before a Sixth Amendment waiver can be effectuated for postindictment questioning. See *United States v. Mohabir,* 624 F.2d 1140 (1980). [Stressing that the "strict standard" governing waiver of counsel at trial should apply to an alleged waiver of the *Massiah* right to counsel as well, the *Mohabir* court exercised its supervisory power over federal criminal justice to hold that a valid waiver of the "Sixth Amendment—*Massiah*" right "must be preceded by a federal judicial officer's explanation of the content and significance of this right."] As have a majority of the Court of Appeals, we reject *Mohabir's* holding that some "additional" warnings or discussions with an accused are required in this situation or that any waiver in this context can only properly be made before a "neutral * * * judicial officer."

9. This does not mean, of course, that all Sixth Amendment challenges to the conduct of postindictment questioning will fail whenever the challenged practice would pass constitutional muster under *Miranda.* For example, we have permitted a *Miranda* waiver to stand where a suspect was not told that his lawyer was trying to reach him during questioning; in the Sixth Amendment context, this waiver would not be valid. See *Moran v. Burbine* * * *.

Thus, because the Sixth Amendment's protection of the attorney-client relationship—"the right to rely on counsel as a 'medium' between [the accused] and the State"—extends beyond *Miranda*'s protection of the Fifth Amendment right to counsel, there will be cases where a waiver which would be valid under *Miranda* will not suffice for Sixth Amendment purposes.

than we require for a Sixth Amendment waiver during postindictment questioning—not because postindictment questioning is 'less important' than a trial [but] because the full 'dangers and disadvantages of self-representation,' *Faretta*, during questioning are less substantial and more obvious to an accused than they are at trial. Because the role of counsel at questioning is relatively simple and limited, we see no problem in having a waiver procedure at that stage which is likewise simple and limited."

Justice STEVENS, joined by Brennan and Marshall, JJ., dissented:

"Given the significance of the initiation of formal proceedings and the concomitant shift in the relationship between the state and the accused, I think it quite wrong to suggest that *Miranda* warnings—or for that matter, any warnings offered by an adverse party—provide a sufficient basis for permitting the undoubtedly prejudicial—and, in my view, unfair—practice of permitting trained law enforcement personnel and prosecuting attorneys to communicate with as-of-yet unrepresented criminal defendants.

"[The] majority premises its conclusions that *Miranda* warnings lay a sufficient basis for accepting a waiver of the right to counsel on the assumption that those warnings make clear to an accused 'what a lawyer could "do for him" during the postindictment questioning: namely, advise [him] to refrain from making any [incriminating] statements.' Yet, this is surely a gross understatement of the disadvantage of proceeding without a lawyer and an understatement of what a defendant must understand to make a knowing waiver. The *Miranda* warnings do not, for example, inform the accused that a lawyer might examine the indictment for legal sufficiency before submitting his or her client to interrogation or that a lawyer is likely to be considerably more skillful at negotiating a plea bargain and that such negotiations may be most fruitful if initiated prior to any interrogation. Rather, the warnings do not even go so far as to explain to the accused the nature of the charges pending against him—advice that a court would insist upon before allowing a defendant to enter a guilty plea with or without the presence of an attorney."[a]

Notes and Questions

(a) In addition to his principal contention, Patterson also argued (unsuccessfully) that someone in his situation should be equated with a preindictment suspect who asserts his right to counsel, thereby triggering *Edwards*. Even if this is so, didn't Patterson, when being transferred to the county jail, "initiate" further communication with the police within the meaning of *Edwards*?

(b) Reconsider fn. 9 to the majority opinion in *Patterson*. Is the Court saying that even if a postindictment interrogatee were unaware that a friend or relative had retained a lawyer on his behalf, a waiver of his Sixth Amendment right to counsel would not be valid unless the police informed him that he had a lawyer and that that lawyer was trying to reach him? If so, why? Does this view make the Sixth Amendment right to counsel "superior" to the Fifth when somebody happens to retain a lawyer for the defendant, but not when the defendant is too unlucky or friendless for this to occur? Should the test for waiver of the Sixth Amendment right to counsel vary at different times "depending on the fortuity of whether [the suspect's family] happens to have retained counsel [for him] prior to interrogation"? Cf. *Moran v. Burbine*.

a. Blackmun, J., wrote a separate dissent, "agree[ing] with most of what Justice Stevens said." He would equate someone in Patterson's situation with a suspect who asserted his Fifth Amendment right to counsel, thus invoking the protection of *Edwards*.

6. ***The "no-contact" rule: Should prosecutors be bound by the ethical rule prohibiting a lawyer from communicating with an opposing party represented by counsel without the consent of the other lawyer?*** The "no-contact" or "anti-contact" ethical rule has a long history in legal ethics: The rule is designed to protect laypersons from overreaching by those who have superior legal skills and knowledge and to protect the attorney-client relationship. The most common version of the ethical rule is Rule 4.2 of the *ABA Model Rules of Professional Conduct*, which provides: "In representing a client, a lawyer shall not communicate about the subject of the representation with a party the lawyer knows to be represented by another lawyer in the matter, unless the lawyer has the consent of the other lawyer or is authorized by law to do so." Disciplinary Rule 7–104(A)(1) of the *Model Code of Professional Responsibility* is a virtually identical provision. Every state and the District of Columbia has adopted a version of the Model Code or Model Rules to govern the conduct of lawyers admitted to practice in that jurisdiction.

Should this rule apply in criminal, as well as civil, proceedings or should communications between a prosecutor and a suspect or defendant be judged by the special body of law developed by *Massiah* and its progeny? Do disciplinary rules such as Rule 4.2 take into account the full range of interests governing the balance between effective law enforcement and defendants' rights? Are the interests protected by Rule 4.2 adequately protected in the criminal context by the Sixth Amendment and the Federal Rules of Criminal Procedure? See Roger Cramton & Lisa Udel, *State Ethics Rules and Federal Prosecutors*, 53 U.Pitt.L.Rev. 291, 332–33 (1992); F. Dennis Saylor & J. Douglas Wilson, *Putting a Square Peg in a Round Hole: The Application of Model Rule 4.2 to Federal Prosecutors*, 53 U.Pitt.L.Rev. 459, 464–65 (1992).

Vindicating the views of the American Bar Association and state ethics authorities who have long maintained that federal prosecutors should be held to the same standards as other lawyers, the Citizens Protection Act, 28 U.S.C. § 530B, often called the "McDade Amendment," went into effect on April 19, 1999. The Act requires federal prosecutors to comply with state laws and rules, as well as local federal court rules, that govern lawyer conduct in the states where the federal prosecutors work.

The Act went into effect over the strong objections of Sen. Orrin Hatch, who argued that it "would cripple the ability of the Department of Justice to enforce federal law and cede authority to regulate the conduct of federal criminal investigations and prosecutors to more than 50 state bar associations," 64 Crim.L.Rep. 319, 337–38 (Feb. 3, 1999). Moreover, at a March 24 hearing before the U.S. Senate Judiciary Committee's Subcommittee on Criminal Justice Oversight, current and former prosecutors warned that the ability of federal prosecutors to supervise multistate investigations would be seriously hindered by state ethics rules restricting lawyers' direct contacts with persons represented by counsel. However, other witnesses testified that federal government lawyers should be governed by the same rules of ethics that apply to lawyers generally and maintained that the Department of Justice (DOJ) had not substantiated its claim that it needed an exemption from these rules. See 65 Crim.L.Rep. 1, 19 (April 7, 1999).

The same day the Citizens' Protection Act went into effect, the DOJ issued an interim final regulation implementing the new statute. The interim rule, *Ethical Standards for Attorneys for the Government*, 28 CFR 77.1–77.5 (set forth in full in 65 Crim.L.Rep. 77, 110 (April 28, 1999)), requires DOJ attorneys and lawyers acting pursuant to DOJ authorization to comply only with state rules of ethical conduct, such as codes of professional responsibility—not with state evidentiary and procedural rules or substantive state law.

The DOJ's interim rule supersedes the much-criticized 1994 Justice regulation, 28 CFR 77.10(a), which purported to exempt federal government lawyers from state ethical rules prohibiting ex parte communications with persons represented by counsel if the communication occurred prior to the initiation of formal proceedings against the person. As indicated by the discussion in 9th ed. at 632–33, the 1994 regulation received a rocky reception in the federal courts.

United States v. Lowery, 166 F.3d 1119 (11th Cir.1999) held, per Carnes, J., that even though the Citizens Protection Act requires federal prosecutors to comply with state or local rules of professional conduct, it does not follow that evidence obtained in violation of such rules has to be excluded:

"Assuming for present purposes that the [Florida Bar Rules of Professional Conduct are] violated when a prosecutor promises a witness some consideration regarding charges or sentencing in return for testimony, a state rule of professional conduct cannot provide an adequate basis for a federal court to suppress evidence that is otherwise admissible. [When] it comes to the admissibility of evidence in federal court, the federal interest in enforcement of federal law, including federal evidentiary rules, is paramount. [Did] Congress intend by the enactment to turn over to state supreme courts in every state—and state legislatures, too, assuming they can also enact codes of professional conduct for attorneys—the authority to decide that otherwise admissible evidence cannot be used in federal court? We think not."

7. ***If the government obtains incriminating statements from a defendant after her right to counsel has attached, but the government does so for legitimate reasons unrelated to the gathering of evidence concerning charges to which the right to counsel has attached (e.g. to investigate a report that defendant plans to harm a witness), are the statements admissible at the trial of the crimes for which formal charges had already been filed?*** No, answered the Court, per BRENNAN, J., in MAINE v. MOULTON, 474 U.S. 159 (1985):

"In *Massiah*, the Government also contended that incriminating statements obtained as a result of its deliberate efforts should not be excluded because law enforcement agents had 'the right, if not indeed the duty, to continue their investigation of [*Massiah*] and his alleged criminal associates.' [We] rejected this argument, and held:

" 'We do not question [that] it was entirely proper to continue an investigation of the suspected criminal activities of the defendant and his alleged confederates, even though the defendant had already been indicted. [But] the defendant's own incriminating statements, obtained by federal agents under the circumstances here disclosed, could not constitutionally be used by the prosecution as evidence against him at his trial.' (Emphasis omitted.)

"We reaffirm this holding, which states a sensible solution to a difficult problem. The police have an interest in the thorough investigation of crimes for which formal charges have already been filed. They also have an interest in investigating new or additional crimes. Investigations of either type of crime may require surveillance of individuals already under indictment. Moreover, law enforcement officials investigating an individual suspected of committing one crime and formally charged with having committed another crime obviously seek to discover evidence useful at a trial of either crime. In seeking evidence pertaining to pending charges, however, the Government's investigative powers are limited by the Sixth Amendment rights of the accused. To allow the admission of evidence obtained from the accused in violation of his Sixth Amendment rights whenever the police assert an alternative, legitimate reason for their surveillance [in this case, to insure the safety of their secret agent and to gather information concerning a report that defendant was planning to kill a witness] invites abuse by law enforcement personnel in the form of fabricated investigations and risks the evisceration of the Sixth Amendment right recognized in *Massiah*. On the other hand, to exclude evidence pertaining to charges as to which the Sixth Amendment right to counsel had not attached at the time the evidence was obtained, simply because other charges were pending at that time, would unnecessarily frustrate the public's interest in the investigation of criminal activities. Consequently, incriminating statements pertaining to pending charges are inadmissible at the trial of those charges, notwithstanding the fact that the police were also investigating other crimes, if, in obtaining this evidence, the State violated the Sixth Amendment by knowingly circumventing the accused's right to the assistance of counsel."

Chief Justice BURGER, joined by White, Rehnquist and O'Connor, JJ., dissented, maintaining that "application of the exclusionary rule here makes little sense."

"We have explained, [that] 'the deterrent purpose of the exclusionary rule necessarily assumes that the police have engaged in willful, or at the very least negligent, conduct which has deprived the defendant of some right.' Here the trial court found that the State obtained statements from respondent 'for legitimate purposes not related to the gathering of evidence concerning the crime for which [respondent] had been indicted.' Since the State was not trying to build its theft case against respondent in obtaining the evidence, excluding the evidence from the theft trial will not affect police behavior at all. The exclusion of evidence 'cannot be expected, and should not be applied, to deter objectively reasonable law enforcement activity.' *Leon*. Indeed, [it] is impossible to identify any police 'misconduct' to deter in this case. In fact, if anything, actions by the police of the type at issue here should be encouraged. The diligent investigation of the police in this case may have saved the lives of several potential witnesses and certainly led to the prosecution and conviction of respondent for additional serious crimes."

B. "PASSIVE" VS. "ACTIVE" SECRET AGENTS

The *Massiah* doctrine probably reached its high point in UNITED STATES v. HENRY, 447 U.S. 264 (1980), which applied the doctrine to a situation where the FBI had instructed its paid government informant, ostensibly defendant's "cellmate," not to question defendant about the crime, and there had been no showing that he had. Nevertheless, a 6–3 majority, per BURGER, C.J., rejected the argument that the incriminating statements were not the result of any "affirmative conduct" on the part of the government agent to solicit evidence. The informant "was not a passive listener; rather he had 'some conversations with Mr. Henry' while he was in jail and Henry's incriminating statements were 'the product of this conversation.' " Moreover, and more generally—

"[Even if we accept the FBI agent's statement that] he did not intend that [the informant] would take affirmative steps to secure incriminating information, he must have known that such propinquity likely would lead to that result. [By] intentionally creating a situation likely to induce Henry to make incriminating statements without the assistance of counsel [after Henry had been indicted and counsel had been appointed for him], the government violated [his] Sixth Amendment right to counsel."

This broad language would seem to prohibit the government from "planting" even a completely "passive" secret agent in a person's cell once adversary proceedings have commenced against him. But the Henry Court cautioned that it was not "called upon to pass on the situation where an informant is placed in [close] proximity [to a prisoner] but makes no effort to stimulate conversations about the crime charged."

Moreover, concurring Justice POWELL made it plain that he could not join the majority opinion if it held that "the mere presence or incidental conversation of an informant in a jail cell would violate *Massiah*." The *Massiah* doctrine, emphasized Powell, "does not prohibit the introduction of spontaneous statements that are not elicited by governmental action. Thus, the Sixth Amendment is not violated when a passive listening device collects, but does not induce, incriminating comments."[a]

As *Kuhlmann v. Wilson* (discussed below), well illustrates, the line between "active" and "passive" secret agents—between "stimulating" conversations with a defendant in order to "elicit" incriminating statements and taking no action "beyond merely listening"—is an exceedingly difficult one to draw.

KUHLMANN v. WILSON, 477 U.S. 436 (1986), arose as follows: Respondent Wilson and two confederates robbed a garage and fatally shot a dispatcher. He admitted that he had witnessed the robbery and murder, but denied any involvement in the crimes and denied knowing who the robbers were. After his arraignment for robbery and murder, Wilson was placed in a cell with a prisoner (Lee) who was a secret police informant. According to his arrangement with the police, Lee was not to ask any questions, but simply to "keep his ears open." Without any prompting, Wilson told Lee the same story he had told the police. Lee advised Wilson that his story "didn't sound too good" and that "things didn't look too good for him," but Wilson did not alter his story at that time. However, several days later, after a visit from his brother, who mentioned that members of the family were upset because they believed he had killed the dispatcher, Wilson changed his story. He admitted to Lee that he and two other men had planned and carried out the robbery and killed the dispatcher. Lee reported these incriminating statements to the police.

The trial court denied Wilson's motion to suppress his statements. Wilson was convicted of murder. The conviction was affirmed and he was denied federal habeas relief. However, following the decision in *Henry*, Wilson relitigated his claim. This time the Court of Appeals for the Second Circuit granted federal habeas relief, viewing the circumstances of his case indistinguishable from the facts of *Henry*. The Supreme Court, per POWELL, J., reversed:

"[Since]" the Sixth Amendment is not violated whenever—by luck or happenstance—the State obtains incriminating statements from the accused after the right to counsel has attached, *Moulton*, a defendant does not make out a violation of that right simply by showing that an informant, [reported] his incriminating statements to the police. Rather, the defendant must demonstrate that the police and their informant took some action, beyond merely listening, that was designed deliberately to elicit incriminating remarks. It is thus apparent that the Court of Appeals erred in concluding that respondent's right to counsel was violated under

a. Dissenting Justice Blackmun, joined by White, J., contended that "the Court not only missteps in forging a new *Massiah* test; it proceeds to misapply the very test it has created. The new test requires a showing that the agent created a situation 'likely to induce' the production of incriminating remarks, and that the informant in fact 'prompted' the defendant. Even accepting the most capacious reading of both this language and the facts, I believe that neither prong of the Court's test is satisfied."

In a separate dissent, Justice Rehnquist maintained "that *Massiah* constitutes such a substantial departure from the traditional concerns that underlie the Sixth Amendment guarantee that its language, if not its actual holding, should be re-examined."

the circumstances of this case. [It failed] to accord to the state trial court's factual findings the presumption of correctness expressly required by 28 U.S.C. § 2254(d).

"The state court found that, [following police instructions, Lee] 'at no time asked any questions' of respondent concerning the pending charges * * *. The only remark made by Lee that has any support in this record was his comment that respondent's initial version of his participation in the crimes 'didn't sound too good.' [The] Court of Appeals focused on that one remark and gave a description of Lee's interaction with respondent that is completely at odds with the facts found by the trial court. [The Court of Appeals' conclusion] that the police 'deliberately elicited' respondent's [statements] conflicts with the decision of every other state and federal judge who reviewed this record, and is clear error in light of the provisions and intent of § 2254(d)."[b]

Dissenting Justice BRENNAN, joined by Marshall, J., maintained that "the state trial court simply found that Lee did not ask respondent any direct questions about the crime for which respondent was incarcerated. [The Court of Appeals] expressly accepted that finding, but concluded that, as a matter of law, the deliberate elicitation standard of *Henry* and *Massiah*, encompasses other, more subtle forms of stimulating incriminating admissions than overt questioning. [The court] observed that, while Lee asked respondent no questions, Lee nonetheless stimulated conversation concerning respondents' role in [the] robbery and murder by remarking that respondent's exculpatory story did not "sound too good" and that he had better come up with a better one. Thus,[it] concluded that the respondent's case [was] virtually indistinguishable from *Henry*.

"[Like the police informant in *Henry*,] Lee encouraged respondent to talk about his crime by conversing with him on the subject over the course of several days and by telling respondent that his exculpatory story would not convince anyone without more work. However, unlike the situation in *Henry*, a disturbing visit from respondent's brother, rather than a conversation with the informant, seems to have been the immediate catalyst for respondent's confession to Lee. While it might appear from this sequence of events that Lee's comment regarding respondent's story and his general willingness to converse with respondent about the crime were not the immediate causes of respondent's admission, I think that the deliberate elicitation standard requires consideration of the entire course of government behavior.

"The State intentionally created a situation in which it was foreseeable that respondent would make incriminating statements without the assistance of counsel. [While] the coup de grace was delivered by respondent's brother, the groundwork for respondent's confession was laid by the State. Clearly the State's actions had a sufficient nexus with respondent's admission of guilt to constitute deliberate elicitation within the meaning of *Henry*."[c]

Notes and Questions

1. ***The distinction between placing an "ear" in the defendant's cell and placing a "voice" there to encourage conversations.*** As a practical matter, is there any difference, let alone "a vast difference" (see fn. b, supra), between placing an "ear" in the cell and placing a "voice" there? Doesn't the "voice" go with the "ear"?

b. Chief Justice Burger, the author of *Henry,* joined the opinion of the Court, but also wrote a brief concurring opinion noting "a vast difference between placing an 'ear' in the suspect's cell and placing a voice in the cell to encourage conversation for the 'ear' to record."

c. Stevens, J., filed a separate dissent, agreeing with Justice Brennan's analysis of the merits of respondent's habeas petition.

Is a defendant likely to make incriminating statements to a "cellmate" unless the latter has developed a relationship of trust and confidence with the defendant? Doesn't a police informant have to exchange remarks with the defendant if only to avoid "alerting" the defendant that something is amiss? If two people share the same cell for days or even weeks, don't they both talk—and talk back and forth? How likely is it that the flow of conversation and the progression of various conversations can be accurately reconstructed? How much incentive does the informant have to do so? Once formal proceedings have been initiated, is the only effective way to prevent police interference with the attorney-client relationship to prohibit any government agent from approaching a defendant in the absence of counsel? See the remarks of Professor Kamisar in Choper, Kamisar & Tribe, *The Supreme Court: Trends and Development*, 1979–80 (1981) at 107–08.

2. *Are the courts asking the wrong questions in cases like Henry and Wilson? Is the true issue in these cases "privacy"?* Yes, maintains H. Richard Uviller, *Evidence from the Mind of the Criminal Suspect*, 87 Colum.L.Rev. 1137, 1191, 1195 (1987):

"The fourth amendment is the guardian of privacy and the questions the courts should be asking are: Did the defendant enjoy a protected expectation of privacy in the circumstances, and if so did the state have a properly predicated warrant to encroach, or some good basis for the lack of it? * * *

"[W]hile a defendant may be required to bear the risk of ordinary disloyalty among trusted associates, it does not follow that he must also bear the risk that the government is engaging in surreptitious invasions. The fact that informers are commonplace in the councils of criminals does not deprive the criminals of reasonable expectations of privacy for fourth amendment purposes any more than the frequency of wiretaps in Mafia investigations excuses the government from the duty to take its case to a judge for advance authorization of an electronic surveillance. [The *Hoffa* Court, see p. 491] should have regarded Partin as the human bug he was and treated his intrusion as a search and seizure (unless, of course, the government was right in the claim that they had not 'placed' him in Hoffa's company).

"Thus, Stewart [, who wrote the opinion of the Court in both *Hoffa* and *Massiah*,] unnaturally distorted the sixth amendment's promise of a skilled advocate in order to narrow the interval in which the suspect's mind could be probed and unwisely shortened the reach of the fourth amendment's guarantee of security by permitting the government deliberately to insert a human spy into the suspect's private space to report on declarations and behavior that might betray a guilty mind."

3. But consider James Tomkovicz, *An Adversary System Defense of the Right to Counsel Against Informants: Truth, Fair Play, and the Massiah Doctrine*, 22 U.C.Davis L.Rev. 1, 36–38 (1988):

"[If the fourth amendment] were the real basis for protection against government informants, the resulting doctrine would have to be considerably different than the current *Massiah* doctrine. For example, fourth amendment protection would not depend either on the initiation of adversarial proceedings or on active elicitation.

"More important, *Massiah*'s substantive sixth amendment protection is radically different than the substance of prospective fourth amendment shelter. The prohibition against 'unreasonable' searches would provide a limited safeguard against the informant surveillance itself. The *Massiah* right, on the other hand, raises an absolute barrier not to the surveillance, but to the use of its products at trial. Consequently, one cannot rationalize the current *Massiah* entitlement upon a fourth amendment foundation. Both the doctrine and the right belie any fourth amendment roots.[175]"

4. ***Private citizens vs. state agents.*** As pointed out in Tomkovicz, supra, at 72 n. 283, "lower courts have struggled to discern standards for determining when private citizens become state agents for *Massiah* purposes," relying upon several interrelated criteria: the existence of an explicit agreement or prearrangement between law enforcement and an informant; the source of an informant's motivation; the benefits accruing to the informant; and the governmental involvement in placing the informant near the defendant. Should the *Massiah* doctrine govern an informant's conduct "if a reasonable person would conclude that the informant has secured and reported inculpatory remarks at least in part because of affirmative governmental encouragement"? See id. at 74.

ONCE THE SIXTH AMENDMENT RIGHT TO COUNSEL ARISES, DOES IT ATTACH TO ALL OTHER OFFENSES CLOSELY RELATED TO THE PARTICULAR OFFENSE CHARGED?

TEXAS v. COBB

532 U.S. 162, 121 S.Ct. 1335, 149 L.Ed.2d 321 (2001).

Chief Justice REHNQUIST delivered the opinion of the Court.

[Respondent confessed to the burglary of a home, but denied knowing anything about the disappearance of a woman and child from the home. He was indicted for the burglary and counsel was appointed to represent him. While in police custody, he waived his *Miranda* rights and confessed to the murders of the woman and child who had disappeared from the home. (After the woman had confronted him during the burglary, he had killed her and buried her and her baby.) He was convicted of capital murder and sentenced to death. The Texas Court of Appeals reversed respondent's conviction, concluding that his Sixth Amendment right to counsel had attached on the capital murder charge even though he had not yet been charged with that offense: "Once the right to counsel attaches to the offense charged, it also attaches to any other offense that is very closely related factually to the offense charged." But the U.S. Supreme Court disagreed.]

In *McNeil v. Wisconsin* [p. 659], we explained [that when the Sixth Amendment right to counsel] arises "[it] is offense specific. It cannot be invoked once for all future prosecutions, for it does not attach until a prosecution is commenced * * *." Accordingly, we held that a defendant's statements regarding offenses for which he had not been charged were admissible notwithstanding the attachment of the Sixth Amendment right to counsel on other charged offenses.

Some [lower courts], however, have read into *McNeil*'s offense-specific definition an exception for crimes that are "factually related" to a charged offense. * * * We decline to do so.

175. This statement is not meant to imply that the Court's unease with its repeated refusals to accord any fourth amendment protection against informant surveillance [has] not contributed to the birth and perpetuation of the *Massiah* doctrine. Although not a principled basis, the Court's discomfort cannot be discounted entirely as an actual influence upon the law in this area.

In addition, the textual discussion is not meant to imply that the fourth amendment should not have a role in informant contexts. [Rather,] the point [is] that the *Massiah* doctrine is not fourth amendment law in disguise.

[Respondent] predicts that the offense-specific rule will prove "disastrous" to suspects' constitutional rights and will "permit law enforcement officers almost complete and total license to conduct unwanted and uncounseled interrogations." Besides offering no evidence that such a parade of horribles has occurred in those jurisdictions that have not enlarged upon *McNeil,* he fails to appreciate the significance of two critical considerations. First, there can be no doubt that a suspect must be apprised of his rights against compulsory self-incrimination and to consult with an attorney before authorities may conduct custodial interrogation. In the present case, police scrupulously followed *Miranda*'s dictates when questioning respondent.[2] Second, it is critical to recognize that the Constitution does not negate society's interest in the ability of police to talk to witnesses and suspects, even those who have been charged with other offenses.

[Although] it is clear that the Sixth Amendment right to counsel attaches only to charged offenses, we have recognized in other contexts that the definition of an "offense" is not necessarily limited to the four corners of a charging instrument. In *Blockburger v. United States,* [discussed in *United States v. Dixon,* p. 1162], we explained that "where the same act or transaction constitutes a violation of two distinct statutory provisions, the test to be applied to determine whether there are two offenses or only one, is whether each provision requires proof of a fact which the other does not." We have since applied the *Blockburger* test to delineate the scope of the Fifth Amendment's Double Jeopardy Clause, which prevents multiple or successive prosecutions for the "same offence." We see no constitutional difference between the meaning of the term "offense" in the contexts of double jeopardy and of the right to counsel. Accordingly, we hold that when the Sixth Amendment right to counsel attaches, it does encompass offenses that, even if not formally charged, would be considered the same offense under the *Blockburger* test.[3]

While simultaneously conceding that its own test "lacks the precision for which police officers may hope," the dissent suggests that adopting *Blockburger*'s definition of "offense" will prove difficult to administer. But it is the dissent's vague iterations of the " 'closely related to' " or " 'inextricably intertwined with' " test that would defy simple application. The dissent seems to presuppose that officers will possess complete knowledge of the circumstances surrounding an incident, such that the officers will be able to tailor their investigation to avoid addressing factually related offenses. Such an assumption, however, ignores the reality that police often are not yet aware of the exact sequence and scope of events they are investigating—indeed, that is why police must investigate in the first place. Deterred by the possibility of violating the Sixth Amendment, police likely would refrain from questioning certain defendants altogether.

It remains only to apply these principles to the facts at hand. [As] defined by Texas law, burglary and capital murder are not the same offense under *Blockburger.* [Accordingly,] the Sixth Amendment right to counsel did not bar police from

2. Curiously, while predicting disastrous consequences for the core values underlying the Sixth Amendment, the dissenters give short shrift to the Fifth Amendment's role (as expressed in *Miranda* and *Dickerson*) in protecting a defendant's right to consult with counsel before talking to police. Even though the Sixth Amendment right to counsel has not attached to uncharged offenses, defendants retain the ability under *Miranda* to refuse any police questioning, and, indeed, charged defendants presumably have met with counsel and have had the opportunity to discuss whether it is advisable to invoke those Fifth Amendment rights. Thus, in all but the rarest of cases, the Court's decision today will have no impact whatsoever upon a defendant's ability to protect his Sixth Amendment right. * * *

3. In this sense, we could just as easily describe the Sixth Amendment as "prosecution specific," insofar as it prevents discussion of charged offenses as well as offenses that, under *Blockburger,* could not be the subject of a later prosecution. And, indeed, the text of the Sixth Amendment confines its scope to "all criminal *prosecutions.*"

interrogating respondent regarding the murders, and respondent's confession was therefore admissible. * * *

Justice KENNEDY, with whom Justice SCALIA and Justice THOMAS join, concurring. * * *

As the facts of the instant case well illustrate, it is difficult to understand the utility of a Sixth Amendment rule that operates to invalidate a confession given by the free choice of suspects who have received proper advice of their *Miranda* rights but waived them nonetheless. The *Miranda* rule, and the related preventative rule of *Edwards v. Arizona*, serve to protect a suspect's voluntary choice not to speak outside his lawyer's presence. The parallel rule announced in Jackson, however, supersedes the suspect's voluntary choice to speak with investigators. [While] the *Edwards* rule operates to preserve the free choice of a suspect to remain silent, if Jackson were to apply it would override that choice. [The] Sixth Amendment right to counsel attaches quite without reference to the suspect's choice to speak with investigators after a *Miranda* warning. It is the commencement of a formal prosecution, indicated by the initiation of adversary judicial proceedings, that marks the beginning of the Sixth Amendment right. These events may be quite independent of the suspect's election to remain silent, the interest which the *Edwards* rule serves to protect with respect to *Miranda* and the Fifth Amendment, and it thus makes little sense for a protective rule to attach absent such an election by the suspect. We ought to question the wisdom of a judge-made preventative rule to protect a suspect's desire not to speak when it cannot be shown that he had that intent.

Even if *Jackson* is to remain good law, its protections should apply only where a suspect has made a clear and unambiguous assertion of the right not to speak outside the presence of counsel, the same clear election required under *Edwards*. Cobb made no such assertion here, yet Justice Breyer's dissent rests upon the assumption that the *Jackson* rule should operate to exclude the confession no matter. * * *

Justice Breyer defends *Jackson* by arguing that, once a suspect has accepted counsel at the commencement of adversarial proceedings, he should not be forced to confront the police during interrogation without the assistance of counsel. But the acceptance of counsel at an arraignment or similar proceeding only begs the question: acceptance of counsel for what? It is quite unremarkable that a suspect might want the assistance of an expert in the law to guide him through hearings and trial, and the attendant complex legal matters that might arise, but nonetheless might choose to give on his own a forthright account of the events that occurred. A court-made rule that prevents a suspect from even making this choice serves little purpose, especially given the regime of *Miranda* and *Edwards*.

Justice BREYER, with whom Justice STEVENS, Justice SOUTER, and Justice GINSBURG join, dissenting. * * *

This case focuses [upon] the meaning of the words "offense specific." These words appear in this Court's Sixth Amendment case law, not in the Sixth Amendment's text. See U.S. Const., Amdt. 6 (guaranteeing right to counsel "[i]n all criminal prosecutions"). The definition of these words is not self-evident. [This] case requires us to determine whether an "offense"—for Sixth Amendment purposes—includes factually related aspects of a single course of conduct other than those few acts that make up the essential elements of the crime charged.

We should answer this question in light of the Sixth Amendment's basic objectives as set forth in this Court's case law. At the very least, we should answer it in a way that does not undermine those objectives. But the Court today decides that "offense" means the crime set forth within "the four corners of a charging instrument," along with other crimes that "would be considered the same offense" under the test established by *Blockburger*. In my view, this unnecessarily technical definition undermines Sixth Amendment protections while doing nothing to further effective law enforcement. * * *

Jackson focuses upon a suspect—perhaps a frightened or uneducated suspect—who, hesitant to rely upon his own unaided judgment in his dealings with the police, has invoked his constitutional right to legal assistance in such matters. * * * *Jackson* says that, once such a request has been made, the police may not simply throw that suspect—who does not trust his own unaided judgment—back upon his own devices by requiring him to rely for protection upon that same unaided judgment that he previously rejected as inadequate. In a word, the police may not force a suspect who has asked for legal counsel to make a critical legal choice without the legal assistance that he has requested and that the Constitution guarantees. [The] Constitution does not take away with one hand what it gives with the other. * * *

Justice Kennedy [criticizes] *Jackson* on the ground that it prevents a suspect "[from] making th[e] choice" to "give [a] forthright account of the events that occurred." But that is not so. A suspect may initiate communication with the police, thereby avoiding the risk that the police induced him to make, unaided, the kind of critical legal decision best made with the help of counsel, whom he has requested.

Unlike Justice Kennedy, the majority does not call *Jackson* itself into question. But the majority would undermine that case by significantly diminishing the Sixth Amendment protections that the case provides. That is because criminal codes are lengthy and highly detailed, often proliferating "overlapping and related statutory offenses" to the point where prosecutors can easily "spin out a startlingly numerous series of offenses from a single * * * criminal transaction." Thus, an armed robber who reaches across a store counter, grabs the cashier, and demands "your money or your life," may through that single instance of conduct have committed several "offenses," in the majority's sense of the term, including armed robbery, assault, battery, trespass, use of a firearm to commit a felony, and perhaps possession of a firearm by a felon, as well. A person who is using and selling drugs on a single occasion might be guilty of possessing various drugs, conspiring to sell drugs, being under the influence of illegal drugs, possessing drug paraphernalia, possessing a gun in relation to the drug sale, and, depending upon circumstances, violating various gun laws as well. A protester blocking an entrance to a federal building might also be trespassing, failing to disperse, unlawfully assembling, and obstructing Government administration all at one and the same time.

The majority's rule permits law enforcement officials to question those charged with a crime without first approaching counsel, through the simple device of asking questions about any other related crime not actually charged in the indictment. Thus, the police could ask the individual charged with robbery about, say, the assault of the cashier not yet charged, or about any other uncharged offense (unless under *Blockburger*'s definition it counts as the "same crime"), all *without notifying counsel*. Indeed, the majority's rule would permit law enforcement officials to question anyone charged with any crime in any one of the examples just given about his or her conduct on the single relevant occasion without notifying counsel unless the prosecutor has charged every possible crime arising out of that same brief course of conduct. What Sixth Amendment sense—what common sense—does such a rule make? The majority's approach [will] undermine the lawyer's role as " 'medium' " between the defendant and the government. And it will, on a random basis, remove a significant portion of the protection that this Court has found inherent in the Sixth Amendment.

[In] *Brewer v. Williams*, the effect of the majority's rule would have been even more dramatic. Because first-degree murder and child abduction each required proof of a fact not required by the other, and because at the time of the impermissible interrogation Williams had been charged only with abduction of a child, Williams' murder conviction should have remained undisturbed.[a] [This] is not to suggest that this Court has previously addressed and decided the question presented by this case. Rather, it is to point out that the Court's conception of the Sixth Amendment right at the time [that] *Brewer* [was] decided naturally presumed that it extended to factually related but uncharged offenses.

At the same time, the majority's rule threatens the legal clarity necessary for effective law enforcement. That is because the majority, aware that the word "offense" ought to encompass something beyond "the four corners of the charging instrument," imports into Sixth Amendment law the definition of "offense" set forth in *Blockburger*, a case interpreting the Double Jeopardy Clause of the Fifth Amendment, which Clause uses the word "offence" but otherwise has no relevance here. Whatever Fifth Amendment virtues *Blockburger* may have, to import it into this Sixth Amendment context will work havoc.

[The] simple-sounding *Blockburger* test has proved extraordinarily difficult to administer in practice. Judges, lawyers, and law professors often disagree about how to apply it. [The] test has emerged as a tool in an area of our jurisprudence that The Chief Justice has described as "a veritable Sargasso Sea which could not fail to challenge the most intrepid judicial navigator." Yet the Court now asks, not the lawyers and judges who ordinarily work with double jeopardy law, but police officers in the field, to navigate *Blockburger* when they question suspects. Some will apply the test successfully; some will not. Legal challenges are inevitable. The result, I believe, will resemble not so much the Sargasso Sea as the criminal law equivalent of Milton's "Serbonian Bog ... Where Armies whole have sunk."

There is, of course, an alternative. We can, and should, define "offense" in terms of the conduct that constitutes the crime that the offender committed on a particular occasion, including criminal acts that are "closely related to" or "inextricably intertwined with" the particular crime set forth in the charging instrument. This alternative is not perfect. The language used lacks the precision for which police officers may hope; and it requires lower courts to specify its meaning further as they apply it in individual cases. Yet virtually every lower court in the United States to consider the issue has defined "offense" in the Sixth Amendment context to encompass such closely related acts. * * *

One cannot say in favor of this commonly followed approach that it is perfectly clear—only that, because it comports with common sense, it is far easier to apply than that of the majority. One might add that, unlike the majority's test, it is consistent with this Court's assumptions in previous cases [citing *Maine v. Moulton* and *Brewer v. Williams*]. And, most importantly, the "closely related" test furthers, rather than undermines, the Sixth Amendment's "right to counsel," a right so necessary to the realization in practice of that most "noble ideal," a fair trial.

a. But see Craig M. Bradley, *Seas, Bogs and Police Interrogation*, Trial, Oct. 2001, pp. 71, 73: "It is true that under *Cobb*, the fact that Williams had a right to counsel as to the kidnapping charge would not protect him from interrogation on the murder charge. But there are several reasons why *Williams* would still come out the same way even after *Cobb*. The first is that, unlike Cobb, Williams was not given his *Miranda* warnings before the interrogation in the police car. Second, Williams had been given *Miranda* warnings earlier and had indicated that he didn't want to speak to the police without counsel. Thus, although Williams might not have a *Sixth* Amendment right to counsel, his *Fifth* Amendment rights would still have been violated. Third, the police had promised counsel that they would not interrogate him during the car trip, so they may have violated William's due process rights when they broke that promise."

The Texas Court of Criminal Appeals, following this commonly accepted approach, found that the charged burglary and the uncharged murders were "closely related." All occurred during a short period of time on the same day in the same basic location. The victims of the murders were also victims of the burglary. Cobb committed one of the murders in furtherance of the [burglary,] the other to cover up the crimes. The police, when questioning Cobb, knew that he already had a lawyer representing him on the burglary charges and had demonstrated their belief that this lawyer also represented Cobb in respect to the murders by asking his permission to question Cobb about the murders on previous occasions. The relatedness of the crimes is well illustrated by the impossibility of questioning Cobb about the murders without eliciting admissions about the burglary. [Nor,] in my view, did Cobb waive his right to counsel. These considerations are sufficient. The police officers ought to have spoken to Cobb's counsel before questioning Cobb. * * *

SHOULD MASSIAH BE OVERRULED?

Should the Cobb Court have abolished Massiah altogether? Consider SHERRY F. COLB, *Why the Supreme Court Should Overrule the Massiah Doctrine and Permit Miranda Alone to Govern Interrogations*, <http://writ.news.findlaw.com/colb/20010509.html> (May 9, 2001):

"[When the Court handed down its decision in *Miranda*], [m]any of us expected *Massiah* eventually to disappear. After all, once *Miranda* was decided, it seemed no longer necessary and even counterproductive to apply different legal standards to interrogations, depending on whether a suspect had been indicted.

"[In] defense of *Massiah*'s 'indictment' distinction, the Court has claimed that indictment is 'a critical stage' in prosecuting a defendant, for then the defendant can harm himself irreparably by statements he makes before a lawyer arrives on the scene, before the trial even begins. Fair enough. But that argument simply suggests that *Massiah* rights should be triggered long before trial—without explaining why they should not be triggered long before indictment, too.

"There is nothing to stop a pre-indictment suspect from doing exactly the same self-inflicted harm as his post-indictment counterpart. Indeed, a suspect may do even greater harm prior to indictment, since an indictment can serve to put a suspect on notice that a prosecutor has made the decision to target him in particular and that he therefore ought to exercise discretion.

"*Massiah* rights will thus often come into being too late to be of any use to the defendant. The fortuity of when the prosecution decides to charge him with a particular crime, a matter over which the defendant has no control, can therefore be decisive.

"The *Cobb* Court could—and should—have gotten rid of *Massiah*'s distinction, and let *Miranda* alone protect suspects. But it did not.

"[The] *Cobb* dissenters argued [that] *Miranda* does not sufficiently protect suspects from interrogation they feel ill-equipped to handle on their own. The dissenters may be right. [But] whether one agrees with the majority or with the dissent, it should be *Miranda*—not *Massiah*—that is at issue.

"The dissent's arguments are really arguments for expanding *Miranda*, either by defining *Miranda* 'interrogation' more broadly, by extending its protections beyond the custodial setting, or by making a waiver of *Miranda* rights more difficult. These arguments are not, however, arguments for preserving *Massiah*'s groundless distinction between those who have, and those who have not, been indicted.

"The Court should abandon the separate *Massiah* doctrine, and conduct the important debate that is waiting in the wings, about the scope of *Miranda*. That debate will probably turn largely on the perceived desirability of obtaining voluntary (but ill-advised) confessions from criminal suspects. The Court could have hashed out that debate more fully in *Cobb*; let us hope that it will take the chance to do so in the next *Massiah* case it hears."

Chapter 10

LINEUPS, SHOWUPS AND OTHER PRE–TRIAL IDENTIFICATION PROCEDURES

"[N]umerous analyses over several decades have consistently shown that mistaken eyewitness identification is the single largest source of wrongful convictions. [A 1988] review of 205 cases of proven wrongful conviction, for example, showed that 52% were associated with mistaken eyewitness identification."

—Gary L. Wells & Eric P. Seelau, *Eyewitness Identification and Legal Policy on Lineups*, 1 Psychology, Pub. Pol'y. & L. 765 (1995).

"[A recent study by the American Psychology/Law Society] of forty cases of innocent people who were convicted of serious crimes and served time in prison, five on death row, [found] that 90% involved eyewitness identification evidence in which one or more eyewitnesses falsely identified the person."

—Margaret Malkin Koosed, *The Proposed Innocence Protection Act Won't–Unless it Also Curbs Mistaken Eyewitness Identifications*, 63 Ohio St.L.J. 263, 307 (2002).

"Who hasn't seen the sensational news reports of cases in which DNA evidence has been used to exonerate individuals previously convicted of crimes? What evidence, then, was used to obtain these convictions in the first place? And how could justice have repeatedly gone so awry?

"When researchers and criminal justice practitioners began to ask these and corollary questions, they uncovered some startling results. Of the first 60 wrongful convictions revealed by DNA technology, 53 had relied to some extent on confident, but mistaken, eyewitnesses."

—James M. Doyle, Mark R. Larson, & Caterina M. DiTraglia, *The Eyes Have It–Or Do They?*, Criminal Justice (ABA Criminal Justice Section), Fall, 2001, p. 12.

"We can't come close to estimating the number of false convictions that occur in the United States, but the accumulating mass of exonerations gives us a glimpse of what we're missing. We have located 328 exonerations since 1989, not counting at least 135 defendants in the Tulia and Rampart mass exonerations, or more than 70 convicted childcare sex abuse defendants. Almost all the individual exonerations that we know about are clustered in two crimes, rape and murder. They are surrounded by widening circles of categories of cases with false convictions that have not been detected: rape convictions that have not been reexamined with DNA evidence; robberies, for which DNA identification is useless; murder cases that are ignored because the defendants were not sentenced to death; assault and drug convictions that are forgotten entirely. Any plausible guess at the total number of miscarriages of justice in America in the last fifteen years must be in the thousands, perhaps tens of thousands.

"We can see some clear patterns in those false convictions that have come to light: who was convicted, and why. For rape the dominant problem is eyewitness misidentification–and cross-racial misidentification in particular, which accounts for the extraordinary number of the false rape convictions with black defendants and white victims. * * * "

—Samuel R. Gross, Kristen Jacoby, Daniel J. Matheson, Nicholas Montgomery & Sujata Patil, *Exonerations in the United States 1989 Through 2003* (2004).[a]

SECTION 1. *WADE* AND *GILBERT*: CONSTITUTIONAL CONCERN ABOUT THE DANGERS INVOLVED IN EYEWITNESS IDENTIFICATIONS

UNITED STATES v. WADE*

388 U.S. 218, 87 S.Ct. 1926, 18 L.Ed.2d 1149 (1967).

Justice BRENNAN delivered the opinion of the Court.

The question here is whether courtroom identifications of an accused at trial are to be excluded from evidence because the accused was exhibited to the witnesses before trial at a post-indictment lineup conducted for identification purposes without notice to and in the absence of the accused's appointed counsel.

The federally insured bank in Eustace, Texas, was robbed on September 21, 1964. A man with a small strip of tape on each side of his face entered the bank, pointed a pistol at the female cashier and the vice president, the only persons in the bank at the time, and forced them to fill a pillowcase with the bank's money. The man then drove away with an accomplice who had been waiting in a stolen car outside the bank. On March 23, 1965, an indictment was returned against respondent, Wade, and two others for conspiring to rob the bank, and against Wade and the accomplice for the robbery itself. Wade was arrested on April 2, and counsel was appointed to represent him on April 26. Fifteen days later [after counsel was appointed] an FBI agent, without notice to Wade's lawyer, arranged to have the two bank employees observe a lineup made up of Wade and five or six other prisoners and conducted in a courtroom of the local county courthouse. Each person in the line wore strips of tape such as allegedly worn by the robber and upon direction each said something like "put the money in the bag," the words allegedly uttered by the robber. Both bank employees identified Wade in the lineup as the bank robber.

a. See http://www.law.umich.edu/newsandinfo/exonerations-in-us.pdf. A revised version of this Report will appear in a forthcoming issue of the *Journal of Criminal Law & Criminology*.

* The Court decided two other pretrial identification cases the same day: *Gilbert v. California*, 388 U.S. 263 (1967) and *Stovall v. Denno*, 388 U.S. 293 (1967), both discussed infra.

At trial the two employees, when asked on direct examination if the robber was in the courtroom, pointed to Wade. The prior lineup identification was then elicited from both employees on cross-examination.

[The] fact that the lineup involved no violation of Wade's privilege against self-incrimination[a] does not [dispose] of his contention that the courtroom identifications should have been excluded because the lineup was conducted without notice to and in the absence of his counsel. [In] this case it is urged that the assistance of counsel at the lineup was indispensable to protect Wade's most basic right as a criminal defendant—his right to a fair trial at which the witnesses against him might be meaningfully cross-examined.

[The] Government characterizes the lineup as a mere preparatory step in the gathering of the prosecution's evidence, not different—for Sixth Amendment purposes—from various other preparatory steps, such as systematized or scientific analyzing of the accused's fingerprints, blood sample, clothing, hair, and the like. We think there are differences which preclude such stages being characterized as critical stages at which the accused has the right to the presence of his counsel. Knowledge of the techniques of science and technology is sufficiently available, and the variables in techniques few enough, that the accused has the opportunity for a meaningful confrontation of the Government's case at trial through the ordinary processes of cross-examination of the Government's expert witnesses and the presentation of the evidence of his own experts. The denial of a right to have his counsel present at such analyses does not therefore violate the Sixth Amendment; they are not critical stages since there is minimal risk that his counsel's absence at such stages might derogate from his right to a fair trial.[b]

But the confrontation compelled by the State between the accused and the victim or witnesses to a crime to elicit identification evidence is peculiarly riddled with innumerable dangers and variable factors which might seriously, even

a. On this issue, relying on *Schmerber v. California* (p. 35), a 5–4 majority ruled that neither requiring a person to appear in a lineup and to speak for identification (*Wade*) nor requiring a person to provide handwriting exemplars (*Gilbert*) violated the privilege. *Schmerber,* which involved the taking of a blood sample, over his objection, from a person arrested for drunken driving, rejected the contention that the defendant had been "compelled [to] be a witness against himself" in violation of the Fifth Amendment. The self-incrimination clause, observed the Court, "protects an accused only from being compelled to testify against himself, or otherwise provide the State with evidence of a testimonial or communicative nature." See also the discussion of these rulings in *Doe v. United States,* p. 881, and Note 8, p. 889.

A self-incrimination issue recently arose in a most unusual setting: *People v. Slavin,* 807 N.E.2d 259 (N.Y.Ct. App. 2004) held that none of defendant's rights were violated by the introduction into evidence of photographs of defendant's upper body tattoos to show his motive for committing a hate crime. (The tattoos included a Nazi swastika; two lightning bolts, the symbol for the Nazi "SS"; and anti-Semitic cartoonish figures.) In upholding defendant's conviction of attempted murder and assault in the first degree, the court, per Read, J., observed:

"The tattoos were physical characteristics, not testimony forced from his mouth * * *. However much the tattoos may have reflected defendant's inner thoughts, the [State] did not compel him to create them in the first place (compare *United States v. Hubbell* [p. 871]).

"The privilege does not necessarily bar compelling the disclosure of evidence that a criminal defendant created voluntarily in the past, even if the evidence betrays 'incriminating assertions of fact or belief' * * *. The [State] did not force defendant to reveal his thoughts and beliefs; [it] presented an expert witness who testified about the customary meaning of the images depicted by defendant's tattoos."

b. Consider, too, the companion case of *Gilbert,* where the Court held, 5–4 on this issue, that the taking of handwriting exemplars from petitioner "was not a 'critical' stage of the criminal proceedings entitling petitioner to the assistance of counsel" for "there is minimal risk that the absence of counsel might derogate from his right to a fair trial. [If,] for some reason, an unrepresentative exemplar is taken, this can be brought out and corrected through the adversary process at trial since the accused can make an unlimited number of additional exemplars for analysis and comparison by government and defense handwriting experts."

crucially, derogate from a fair trial. The vagaries of eyewitness identification are well-known; the annals of criminal law are rife with instances of mistaken identification. [A] major factor contributing to the high incidence of miscarriage of justice from mistaken identification has been the degree of suggestion inherent in the manner in which the prosecution presents the suspect to witnesses for pretrial identification. A commentator has observed that "[t]he influence of improper suggestion upon identifying witnesses probably accounts for more miscarriages of justice than any other single factor—perhaps it is responsible for more such errors than all other factors combined." Wall, *Eye-Witness Identification in Criminal Cases* 26 [1965]. Suggestion can be created intentionally or unintentionally in many subtle ways. And the dangers for the suspect are particularly grave when the witness' opportunity for observation was insubstantial, and thus his susceptibility to suggestion the greatest.

Moreover, "[i]t is a matter of common experience that, once a witness has picked out the accused at the line-up, he is not likely to go back on his word later on, so that in practice the issue of identity may (in the absence of other relevant evidence) for all practical purposes be determined there and then, before the trial."

The pretrial confrontation for purpose of identification may take the form of a lineup, also known as an "identification parade" or "showup," as in the present case, or presentation of the suspect alone to the witness, as in *Stovall v. Denno.*[c] It is obvious that risks of suggestion attend either form of confrontation and increase the dangers inhering in eyewitness identification. But as is the case with secret interrogations, there is serious difficulty in depicting what transpires at lineups and other forms of identification confrontations. [The] defense can seldom reconstruct the manner and mode of lineup identification for judge or jury at trial. [The] impediments to an objective observation are increased when the victim is the witness. Lineups are prevalent in rape and robbery prosecutions and present a particular hazard that a victim's understandable outrage may excite vengeful or spiteful motives. In any event, neither witnesses nor lineup participants are apt to be alert for conditions prejudicial to the suspect. And if they were, it would likely be of scant benefit to the suspect since neither witnesses nor lineup participants are likely to be schooled in the detection of suggestive influences.[13] Improper influences may go undetected by a suspect, guilty or not, who experiences the emotional tension which we might expect in one being confronted with potential accusers. Even when he does observe abuse, if he has a criminal record he may be reluctant to take the stand and open up the admission of prior convictions. Moreover any protestations by the suspect of the fairness of the lineup made at trial are likely to be in vain; the jury's choice is between the accused's unsupported version and that of the police officers present. In short, the accused's inability effectively to reconstruct at trial any unfairness that occurred at the lineup may deprive him of his only opportunity meaningfully to attack the credibility of the witness' courtroom identification.

[The] potential for improper influence is illustrated by the circumstances, insofar as they appear, surrounding the prior identifications in the three cases we decide today. In the present case, the testimony of the identifying witnesses elicited on cross-examination revealed that those witnesses were taken to the courthouse and seated in the courtroom to await assembly of the lineup. The courtroom faced on a hallway observable to the witnesses through an open door.

c. See pp. 768 and 776.

13. An additional impediment to the detection of such influences by participants, including the suspect, is the physical conditions often surrounding the conduct of the lineup. In many, lights shine on the stage in such a way that the suspect cannot see the witness. [In] some a one-way mirror is used and what is said on the witness' side cannot be heard. * * *

The cashier testified that she saw Wade "standing in the hall" within sight of an FBI agent. Five or six other prisoners later appeared in the hall. The vice president testified that he saw a person in the hall in the custody of the agent who "resembled the person that we identified as the one that had entered the bank."

The lineup in *Gilbert* was conducted in an auditorium in which some 100 witnesses to several alleged state and federal robberies charged to Gilbert made wholesale identifications of Gilbert as the robber in each other's presence, a procedure said to be fraught with dangers of suggestion. And the vice of suggestion created by the identification in *Stovall* was the presentation to the witness of the suspect alone handcuffed to police officers. It is hard to imagine a situation more clearly conveying the suggestion to the witness that the one presented is believed guilty by the police. * * *

Insofar as the accused's conviction may rest on a courtroom identification in fact the fruit of a suspect pretrial identification which the accused is helpless to subject to effective scrutiny at trial, the accused is deprived of that right of cross-examination which is an essential safeguard to his right to confront the witnesses against him. And even though cross-examination is a precious safeguard to a fair trial, it cannot be viewed as an absolute assurance of accuracy and reliability. Thus in the present context, where so many variables and pitfalls exist, the first line of defense must be the prevention of unfairness and the lessening of the hazards of eyewitness identification at the lineup itself. The trial which might determine the accused's fate may well not be that in the courtroom but that at the pretrial confrontation, with the State aligned against the accused, the witness the sole jury, and the accused unprotected against the overreaching, intentional or unintentional, and with little or no effective appeal from the judgment there rendered by the witness—"that's the man."

Since it appears that there is grave potential for prejudice, intentional or not, in the pretrial lineup, which may not be capable of reconstruction at trial, and since presence of counsel itself can often avert prejudice and assure a meaningful confrontation at trial,[d] there can be little doubt that for Wade the post-indictment lineup was a critical stage of the prosecution at which he was "as much entitled to such aid [of counsel as] at the trial itself." *Powell v. Alabama.* Thus both Wade and his counsel should have been notified of the impending lineup, and counsel's presence should have been a requisite to conduct of the lineup, absent an "intelligent waiver." No substantial countervailing policy considerations have been advanced against the requirement of the presence of counsel. Concern is expressed that the requirement will forestall prompt identifications and result in obstruction of the confrontations. As for the first, we note that in the two cases in which the right to counsel is today held to apply, counsel had already been appointed and no argument is made in either case that notice to counsel would have prejudicially delayed the confrontations. Moreover, we leave open the question whether the presence of substitute counsel might not suffice where notification and presence of the suspect's own counsel would result in prejudicial delay. And to refuse to recognize the right to counsel for fear that counsel will obstruct the course of justice is contrary to the basic assumptions upon which this Court has operated in Sixth Amendment cases. We rejected similar logic in *Miranda,* concerning presence of counsel during custodial interrogation.

[In] our view counsel can hardly impede legitimate law enforcement; on the contrary, for the reasons expressed, law enforcement may be assisted by preventing the infiltration of taint in the prosecution's identification evidence. That result

d. At this point, the Court refers to and describes a model statute proposed in Daniel E. Murray, *The Criminal Lineup at Home and Abroad,* 1966 Utah L.Rev. 610, 627–28, a statute providing not only for counsel, but other safeguards as well.

cannot help the guilty avoid conviction but can only help assure that the right man has been brought to justice.[29]

Legislative or other regulations, such as those of local police departments, which eliminate the risks of abuse and unintentional suggestion at lineup proceedings and the impediments to meaningful confrontation at trial may also remove the basis for regarding the stage as "critical." But neither Congress nor the federal authorities have seen fit to provide a solution. What we hold today "in no way creates a constitutional strait-jacket which will handicap sound efforts at reform, nor is it intended to have this effect." *Miranda.*

We come now to the question whether the denial of Wade's motion to strike the courtroom identification by the bank witnesses at trial because of the absence of his counsel at the lineup required, as the Court of Appeals held, the grant of a new trial at which such evidence is to be excluded. We do not think this disposition can be justified without first giving the Government the opportunity to establish by clear and convincing evidence that the in-court identifications were based upon observations of the suspect other than the lineup identification. * * * Where, as here, the admissibility of evidence of the lineup identification itself is not involved, a *per se* rule of exclusion of courtroom identification would be unjustified.[e] [A] rule limited solely to the exclusion of testimony concerning identification at the lineup itself, without regard to admissibility of the courtroom identification, would render the right to counsel an empty one. The lineup is most often used, as in the present case, to crystallize the witnesses' identification of the defendant for future reference. We have already noted that the lineup identification will have that effect. The State may then rest upon the witnesses' unequivocal courtroom identification, and not mention the pretrial identification as part of the State's case at trial. Counsel is then in the predicament in which Wade's counsel found himself—realizing that possible unfairness at the lineup may be the sole means of attack upon the unequivocal courtroom identification, and having to probe in the dark in an attempt to discover and reveal unfairness, while bolstering the government witness' courtroom identification by bringing out and dwelling upon his prior identification. Since counsel's presence at the lineup would equip him to attack not only the lineup identification but the courtroom identification as well, limiting the impact of violation of the right to counsel to exclusion of evidence only of identification at the lineup itself disregards a critical element of that right.

We think it follows that the proper test to be applied in these situations is that quoted in *Wong Sun v. United States* [p. 907], " '[W]hether, granting establishment of the primary illegality the evidence to which instant objection is made has been come at by exploitation of that illegality or instead by means sufficiently distinguishable to be purged of the primary taint.' Maguire, *Evidence of Guilt* 221 (1959)." Application of this test in the present context requires consideration of various factors; for example, the prior opportunity to observe the alleged criminal act, the existence of any discrepancy between any pre-lineup description and the defendant's actual description, any identification prior to lineup of another person, the identification by picture of the defendant prior to

29. Many other nations surround the lineup with safeguards against prejudice to the suspect. In England the suspect must be allowed the presence of his solicitor or a friend; Germany requires the presence of retained counsel; France forbids the confrontation of the suspect in the absence of his counsel; Spain, Mexico, and Italy provide detailed procedures prescribing the conditions under which confrontation must occur under the supervision of a judicial officer who sees to it that the proceedings are officially recorded to assure adequate scrutiny at trial. Murray, [fn. d supra, at 621–27].

e. In *Gilbert,* however, the Court did apply a *per se* exclusionary rule to the testimony of various prosecution witnesses that they had also identified petitioner at a pretrial lineup. See fn. f infra.

the lineup, failure to identify the defendant on a prior occasion, and the lapse of time between the alleged act and the lineup identification. It is also relevant to consider those facts which, despite the absence of counsel, are disclosed concerning the conduct of the lineup.[33]

Jgmt.

On the record now before us we cannot make the determination whether the in-court identifications had an independent origin. [T]he appropriate procedure to be followed is to vacate the conviction pending a hearing to determine whether the in-court identifications had an independent source, or whether, in any event, the introduction of the evidence was harmless error, *Chapman v. California* [Ch. 27, § 5], and for the District Court to reinstate the conviction or order a new trial, as may be proper.[f] * * *

Justice BLACK, dissenting in part and concurring in part. * * *

I would reverse Wade's conviction without further ado had the prosecution at trial made use of his lineup identification either in place of courtroom identification or [as it did in *Gilbert*] to bolster in a harmful manner crucial courtroom identification. But the prosecution here did neither of these things. After prosecution witnesses under oath identified Wade in the courtroom, it was the defense, and not the prosecution, which brought out the prior lineup identification. While stating that "a *per se* rule of exclusion of courtroom identification would be unjustified," the Court, nevertheless remands this case for "a hearing to determine whether the in-court identifications had an independent source," or were the tainted fruits of the invalidly conducted lineup. From this holding I dissent.

In the first place, even if this Court has power to establish such a rule of evidence, I think the rule fashioned by the Court is unsound. The "tainted fruit" determination required by the Court involves more than considerable difficulty. I think it is practically impossible. How is a witness capable of probing the recesses of his mind to draw a sharp line between a courtroom identification due exclusively to an earlier lineup and a courtroom identification due to memory not based on the lineup? [In] my view, the Fifth and Sixth Amendments are satisfied if the prosecution is precluded from using lineup identification as either an alternative to or corroboration of courtroom identification. If the prosecution does neither and its witnesses under oath identify the defendant in the courtroom, then I can find no justification for stopping the trial in midstream to hold a lengthy "tainted fruit" hearing. * * *

Justice WHITE whom Justice HARLAN and Justice STEWART join, dissenting in part and concurring in part.

33. Thus it is not the case that "[i]t matters not how well the witness knows the suspect, whether the witness is the suspect's mother, brother, or long-time associate, and no matter how long or well the witness observed the perpetrator at the scene of the crime" [quoting from Justice White's opinion in *Wade*]. Such factors will have an important bearing upon the true basis of the witness' in-court identification. * * *

f. Compare *Gilbert,* where various witnesses who identified petitioner in the courtroom also testified, on direct examination by the prosecution, that they had identified petitioner at a prior lineup. "That [pretrial lineup] testimony," ruled the Court, "is the direct result of the illegal lineup 'come at by exploitation of [the primary] illegality.' *Wong Sun.* The State is therefore not entitled to an opportunity to show that that testimony had an independent source. Only a *per se* exclusionary rule as to such testimony can be an effective sanction to assure that law enforcement authorities will respect the accused's constitutional right to the presence of his counsel at the critical lineup. [That] conclusion is buttressed by the consideration that the witness' testimony of his lineup identification will enhance the impact of his in-court identification on the jury and seriously aggravate whatever derogation exists of the accused's right to a fair trial. Therefore, unless the [state supreme court] is 'able to declare a belief that it was harmless beyond a reasonable doubt,' *Chapman,* Gilbert will be entitled on remand to a new trial * * *."

The Court has again propounded a broad constitutional rule barring the use of a wide spectrum of relevant and probative evidence, solely because a step in its ascertainment or discovery occurs outside the presence of defense counsel.

[The] Court's opinion is far-reaching. It proceeds first by creating a new *per se* rule of constitutional law: a criminal suspect cannot be subjected to a pretrial identification process in the absence of his counsel without violating the Sixth Amendment. If he is, the State may not buttress a later courtroom identification of the witness by any reference to the previous identification. Furthermore, the courtroom identification is not admissible at all unless the State can establish by clear and convincing proof that the testimony is not the fruit of the earlier identification made in the absence of defendant's counsel—admittedly a heavy burden for the State and probably an impossible one. To all intents and purposes, courtroom identifications are barred if pretrial identifications have occurred without counsel being present.

The rule applies to any lineup, to any other techniques employed to produce an identification and *a fortiori* to a face-to-face encounter between the witness and the suspect alone, regardless of when the identification occurs, in time or place, and whether before or after indictment or information. It matters not how well the witness knows the suspect, whether the witness is the suspect's mother, brother, or long-time associate, and no matter how long or well the witness observed the perpetrator at the scene of the crime. The kidnap victim who has lived for days with his abductor is in the same category as the witness who has had only a fleeting glimpse of the criminal. Neither may identify the suspect without defendant's counsel being present. The same strictures apply regardless of the number of other witnesses who positively identify the defendant and regardless of the corroborative evidence showing that it was the defendant who had committed the crime.

[The] Court apparently believes that improper police procedures are so widespread that a broad prophylactic rule must be laid down, requiring the presence of counsel at all pretrial identifications, in order to detect recurring instances of police misconduct.[1] I do not share this pervasive distrust of all official investigations. None of the materials the Court relies upon supports it. Certainly, I would bow to solid fact, but the Court quite obviously does not have before it any reliable, comprehensive survey of current police practices on which to base its new rule. Until it does, the Court should avoid excluding relevant evidence from state criminal trials.

[There] are several striking aspects to the Court's holding. First, the rule does not bar courtroom identifications where there have been no previous identifications in the presence of the police, although when identified in the courtroom, the defendant is known to be in custody and charged with the commission of a crime.[g] Second, the Court seems to say that if suitable legislative standards were adopted for the conduct of pretrial identifications, thereby lessening the hazards in such confrontations, it would not insist on the presence of counsel. But if this is true,

1. Yet in *Stovall v. Denno* [p. 768] the Court recognizes that improper police conduct in the identification process has not been so widespread as to justify full retroactivity for its new rule.

g. Consider Joseph D. Grano, *Kirby, Biggers, and Ash: Do Any Constitutional Safeguards Remain Against the Danger of Convicting the Innocent?*, 72 Mich.L.Rev. 717, 785 (1974): "[A]n identification more unreliable than the witness's familiar selection of the conspicuous defendant, frequently after scanning the courtroom for dramatic effect, is difficult to imagine. In effect, [these identifications are] one-man showups, albeit in the courtroom." Consider, too, H. Richard Uviller, *The Role of the Defense Lawyer at a Lineup in Light of the Wade, Gilbert and Stovall Decisions,* 4 Crim.L.Bull. 273, 284 (1968).

How can defense counsel avoid or minimize the impact of a suggestive confrontation between a witness and defendant in the courtroom? See Note 6 following this case.

why does not the Court simply fashion what it deems to be constitutionally acceptable procedures for the authorities to follow? Certainly the Court is correct in suggesting that the new rule will be wholly inapplicable where police departments themselves have established suitable safeguards.

Third, courtroom identification may be barred, absent counsel at a prior identification, regardless of the extent of counsel's information concerning the circumstances of the previous confrontation between witness and defendant—apparently even if there were recordings or sound-movies of the events as they occurred. But if the rule is premised on the defendant's right to have his counsel know, there seems little basis for not accepting other means to inform. A disinterested observer, recordings, photographs—any one of them would seem adequate to furnish the basis for a meaningful cross-examination of the eyewitness who identifies the defendant in the courtroom. * * *

I would not extend [the adversary] system, at least as it presently operates, to police investigations and would not require counsel's presence at pretrial identification procedures. Counsel's interest is in not having his client placed at the scene of the crime, regardless of his whereabouts. Some counsel may advise their clients to refuse to make any movements or to speak any words in a lineup or even to appear in one. [Others] will hover over witnesses and begin their cross-examination then, menacing truthful factfinding as thoroughly as the Court fears the police now do. Certainly there is an implicit invitation to counsel to suggest rules for the lineup and to manage and produce it as best he can.[h] I therefore doubt that the Court's new rule, at least absent some clearly defined limits on counsel's role, will measurably contribute to more reliable pretrial identifications. My fears are that it will have precisely the opposite result. * * *

ON THE MEANING OF THE LINEUP DECISIONS

1. ***Waiver.*** If *Wade* seeks to protect the reliability of the identification process and to make available testimony about the conditions under which such process is carried out, why should the right to counsel at the lineup be subject to waiver? Permitting waiver of *Miranda* rights may be defended on the ground that an important, legitimate object is served by permitting suspects to bear witness to the truth under conditions which safeguard the exercise of responsible choice, but what comparable value is served by allowing suspects to waive counsel at the identification process?

2. ***The role of counsel.*** What is the role of defense counsel at the lineup? Consider Commentary to the *Model Pre–Arraignment Code* at 429–33:

"The two extreme positions might be stated thus:

"(1) Counsel is to be present merely as an observer to assure against abuse and bad faith by law enforcement officers, and to provide the basis for any attack he might wish to make on the identification at trial.

"(2) The lineup procedure is to be a fully adversary proceeding in which the counsel for the suspect may make objections and proposals, which if they are proper or even reasonable must be respected.

"The cases and commentaries, as well as the practice since *Wade* would indicate that the first interpretation of the counsel's role comes closer to describing the general interpretation of the constitutional requirement and to describing the practice under it. The major difficulty with this interpretation is that by forcing counsel into the role of a merely passive observer it gives him a job which

h. But see Note 2 following this case.

at best can be accomplished in a large variety of ways including video recording and at worst is uncomfortable or demeaning.

"[On] the other hand, any attempt to give counsel at identification a more active role is fraught with difficulties not only for the police but for counsel himself. For the police the difficulty is that a procedure which is often under the supervision not of lawyers but of police officers will be subject to manipulation and objection by a trained legal counsel for one side only.

"[The] assigning of a more active role to counsel has perils for counsel as well. If he is entitled to make objections at the lineup procedure, will he be held to have waived these objections if he does not make them at the procedure and he wishes later to question the fairness or accuracy of the identification at trial? If such a possibility of waiver exists will he not almost be under an obligation to raise every conceivable objection? Moreover, this hard choice would be imposed on a lawyer at a very early stage of his contact with the case. Indeed the lawyer who did this work is often likely to be a junior member of the public defender's staff assigned on rotation to do 'lineup work,' and thus would not likely be the lawyer to handle the case at trial."

3. ***Refusals to cooperate; obstructionist efforts.*** Since the lineup or the taking of exemplars is not protected by the privilege against self-incrimination, the prosecution may comment on the suspect's refusal to cooperate. The refusal is considered circumstantial evidence of consciousness of guilt. On occasion, courts have utilized civil or criminal contempt to coerce or punish the suspect who refuses to comply with a court order to participate in some identification proceeding. Still another possibility is for the police to proceed to conduct the identification proceeding over the suspect's objection. See CRIMPROC § 7.2(c).

What may be done in response to a suspect's drastic alteration of his appearance between the time of arrest (or the occurrence of the crime) and his appearance in a lineup?[a] One possibility is to bring this alteration to the attention of the jury for consideration as evidence of defendant's consciousness of guilt. Another possibility is to conduct the identification procedure in such a way as to simulate the defendant's prior appearance. See CRIMPROC § 7.2(d).

4. ***Invalid pre-trial identification procedures and the "independent origin" of in-court identifications.*** Reconsider Justice Black's complaint in *Wade* about the difficulties involved in determining whether or not an in-court identification is the "tainted fruit" of an improperly conducted lineup. Does it follow, as Justice Black maintained, that therefore *every* courtroom identification made subsequent to an illegal police lineup (so long as not supplemented or corroborated by the earlier lineup) should be admitted? Or do the very reasons advanced by Justice Black—the great difficulties, if not impossibility of ascertaining the "taint" or lack of it—suggest that *no* courtroom identification preceded by an illegal police lineup should be allowed?[b]

a. What ethical questions, if any, are raised by a defense lawyer who encourages his client to "disguise himself" prior to a lineup?

b. The difficulties of determining whether there is an "independent source" for in-court identifications following invalid pre-trial lineups are illustrated by *Clemons v. United States,* 408 F.2d 1230 (D.C.Cir.1968) and explored in Robert Pitler, "*The Fruit of the Poisonous Tree*" *Revisited and Shepardized,* 56 Calif.L.Rev. 579, 636–41 (1968); Note 45 Wash.L.Rev. 202 (1970). See generally Felice J. Levine & June L. Tapp, *The Psychology of Criminal Identification: The Gap from Wade to Kirby,* 121 U.Pa.L.Rev. 1079 (1973). The difficulties are compounded when a courtroom identification is preceded by a corporeal identification which, in turn, is preceded by a photographic identification. For the corporeal identification "may be based not upon the witness's recollection of the features of the guilty party, but upon his recollection of the photograph. Thus, although a witness who is asked to attempt a corporeal identification of a person whose photograph he has previously identified may say, 'That's the man that did it,' what he may actually mean is, 'That's the

Is the requirement that the prosecution establish by clear and convincing proof that the courtroom testimony is untainted by the earlier illegal identification a "heavy" and "probably an impossible" burden, as Justice White maintained in *Wade*? If pre-trial identifications are held in violation of the suspect's right to counsel, does the *Wade-Gilbert* rule, as Justice White claimed, bar all courtroom identifications "to all intents and purposes"? Consider the remarks of A.J. Davis, *The Role of the Defense Lawyer at a Lineup in Light of the Wade, Gilbert and Stovall Decisions,* 4 Crim.L.Bull. 273, 294–95 (1968) (panel discussion), a year after the lineup cases were decided:

"How [is the defense lawyer] going to prove that the in-court identification that the victim is about to make is the fruit of [the invalid police lineup]? The Supreme Court may say the burden of proof is on the prosecution, but you know and I know that the attitude of the trial judge is going to be that the burden of proof is on [the defense lawyer] as a practical matter to convince that judge. He is not going to be terribly sympathetic to these cases.

"What is the prosecution going to do? The prosecution is going to put the victim on the stand and the victim is going to say, 'When this robber came to me and put that gun in my face, I looked at him and I formed a mental picture. [Then,] I had this lineup and I compared this portrait in my mind with the people in the lineup and I picked out that defendant. Now I am in court and what am I doing? I am not paying any attention to the lineup. I am again conjuring up that [mental picture] which I evolved in my mind at the time of the robbery, and I am taking that [picture] and putting it next to this defendant at the counsel table and I am saying that they are precisely the same,' and the judge is going to say, 'Whoopie, there's an independent origin,' and you can attempt to prove from today to tomorrow that the pre-trial identification was unfair, but the trial court has a finding of fact to make here, and nine times out of ten, unless you have a very exceptional trial court, he is going to find against you on this issue."

Mr. Davis has turned out to be a better prognosticator than Justice White. The cases support the conclusions of commentators that when confronted with invalid pre-trial identifications the lower courts have "easily found an 'independent source' for an in-court identification," Note, 55 Minn.L.Rev. 779, 818 (1971), and have "readily avoided reversing convictions by stretching, often beyond reason and logic, the doctrines of independent source and harmless error," Grano, p. 625, fn. g supra, at 722.

5. *Defendant's right to a lineup or other identification procedure.* Reconsider fn. g, p. 763. Should a defendant be allowed to sit among spectators or with nonsuspects at counsel table? Should he be entitled to an in-court lineup, or a pretrial lineup, before being required to confront witnesses in the courtroom?

Consider *Moore v. Illinois,* 434 U.S. 220 (1977) (also discussed at p. 772). In rejecting the contention that because the corporeal identification occurred "in the course of a judicial proceeding" (a preliminary hearing to determine whether petitioner should be bound over to the grand jury and to set bail) petitioner had no *Wade-Gilbert* right to counsel at the identification procedure, the Court, per Powell, J., pointed out that the identification, "a one-on-one confrontation," had been made under highly suggestive circumstances and that "[h]ad petitioner been represented by counsel, some or all of this suggestiveness could have been avoided." It then noted:

"For example, counsel could have requested that the hearing be postponed until a lineup could be arranged at which the victim would view petitioner in a

man whose photograph I identified.' "Patrick E. Wall, *Eye-Witness Identification in Criminal Cases* 68 (1965).

less suggestive setting. Short of that, counsel could have asked that the victim be excused from the courtroom while the charges were read and the evidence against petitioner was recited, and that petitioner be seated with other people in the audience when the victim attempted an identification. * * * Because it is in the prosecution's interest as well as the accused's that witnesses' identifications remain untainted, we cannot assume that such requests would have been in vain. Such requests are usually addressed to the sound discretion of the court; we express no opinion as to whether the preliminary hearing court would have been required to grant any such requests."

Although such requests are occasionally granted, trial judges, in their discretion, often deny them. See generally CRIMPROC § 7.4(f). A leading case on this point is *Evans v. Superior Court,* 522 P.2d 681 (Cal.1974), holding that due process requires that in an appropriate case defendant should be afforded a pretrial lineup, but that such a right arises "only when eyewitness identification is shown to be in material issue and there exists a reasonable likelihood of a mistaken identification which a lineup would tend to resolve." See also *United States v. Archibald,* 734 F.2d 938 (2d Cir.1984), per Oakes, J., pointing out that defendant's request that he be seated away from the defense table and that other black men be seated in the courtroom "should not have been dismissed so quickly or so absolutely by the trial court. [While] it was not necessary for the court to conduct a true *Wade*-type lineup, these relatively minor steps were required to ensure that the identification was not unfair. The in-court identification procedure utilized here was so clearly suggestive as to be impermissible, however traditional it may be."[c]

Model Pre–Arraignment Code § 170.2 permits a person "arrested for or charged with an offense or a person who shows a reasonable basis for believing he may be so charged" to request a nontestimonial identification order requiring persons *other than himself* to appear (presumably to "clear" himself by shifting suspicion to another) or to request an identification procedure involving himself.[d]

6. *On the use of cautionary instructions.* Edith Greene, *Eyewitness Testimony and the Use of Cautionary Instructions,* 8 U.Bridgeport L.Rev. 15 (1987), casts serious doubt about the effectiveness of the most widely used cautionary instruction on eyewitness testimony. Jurors given this instruction seem to be no better informed about the governing legal standards and the factors that affect the reliability of eyewitness testimony than jurors who received no cautionary instruction. Thus, concludes Greene, the many judges who refuse to admit expert testimony about the factors that influence witness reliability because they believe a cautionary instruction will be effective at conveying the information to jurors are acting on an unwarranted assumption. This is not surprising, since other research shows that most jurors fail to understand most of the instructions they receive. See R. Charrow & V. Charrow, *Making Legal Language Understandable: A Psycholinguistic Study of Jury Instructions,* 79 Colum.L.Rev. 1306 (1979).

c. On petition for rehearing, 756 F.2d 223 (2d Cir.1984), *Archibald* was modified to make it clear that special in-court identification procedures are necessary "only when (1) identification is a contested issue; (2) the defendant has moved in a timely manner prior to trial for a lineup; and (3) despite that defense request, the witness has not had an opportunity to view a fair out-of-court lineup prior to his trial testimony."

d. Perhaps because trial judges frequently deny requests, to hold an in-court lineup or to seat the defendant in the courtroom audience before and during the testimony of the prosecution's identification witnesses, defense attorneys have sometimes resorted to "self-help," i.e., substituted another person for the defendant at counsel table without the court's permission or knowledge. This "has been viewed as a violation of ethical standards and an obstruction of justice punishable by criminal contempt." CRIMPROC, § 7.5(g).

7. ***The use of expert psychological testimony.*** Increasingly, defendants are attempting to use experts to explain to the jury the frailty and fallibility of eyewitness testimony. But the admissibility of expert testimony is largely a matter of trial court discretion. And in the main the judicial response to such defense efforts has been very cool. For a discussion—and strong criticism—of the arguments against the use of expert testimony on eyewitness identification, see James Murphy, *An Evaluation of the Arguments Against the Use of Expert Testimony on Eyewitness Identification,* 8 U.Bridgeport L.Rev. 21 (1987). Professor Murphy maintains that "eyewitness testimony not sufficiently understood by the jury is dangerous evidence which may easily result in miscarriages of justice," and that trial court discretion "is not a license for a court to shut its eyes to advancements in knowledge in other fields." For recent articles evaluating the arguments for and against the admissibility of expert testimony concerning eyewitness identification, see Thomas Dillickrath, *Expert Testimony on Eyewitness Identification: Admissibility and Alternatives,* 55 U. Miami L.Rev. 1059 (2001); Edward Stein, *The Admissibility of Expert Testimony About Cognitive Science Research on Eyewitness Identification,* 2 Law, Probability & Risk 295 (2003).

THE DUE PROCESS "BACK–UP" TEST

STOVALL v. DENNO, 388 U.S. 293 (1967) (a federal habeas corpus proceeding collaterally attacking a state criminal conviction) (discussed more extensively in § 3, infra), held that the newly announced *Wade-Gilbert* principles would not be applied retroactively but would affect only those identification procedures conducted in the absence of counsel after the date the *Wade* and *Gilbert* decisions were handed down.[a] The court did consider, however, whether "the confrontation conducted in this case was so unnecessarily suggestive and conducive to irreparable mistaken identification" that petitioner was denied due process of law—"a recognized ground of attack upon a conviction independent of any right to counsel claim," but one that must be evaluated in light of the totality of surrounding circumstances. Since the record revealed that the showing of petitioner to a victim of the assault "in an immediate hospital confrontation was imperative," the due process claim was denied. As *Stovall* illustrates, and as the Court later articulated the due process test when it applied it to a pretrial identification by photograph, the question is whether the identification procedure "was so *impermissibly* suggestive as to give rise to a very substantial likelihood of irreparable misidentification." *Simmons v. United States,* 390 U.S. 377 (1968). (Emphasis added.)

THE EYE–WITNESS TESTIMONY PROVISIONS OF THE 1968 CRIME CONTROL ACT

Consider the constitutionality of Title II of the Omnibus Crime Control and Safe Streets Act of 1968, 18 U.S.C. § 3502, designed to "repeal" the *Wade-Gilbert* rule in federal prosecutions: "The testimony of a witness that he saw the accused commit or participate in the commission of the crime for which the accused is being tried shall be admissible in evidence in a criminal prosecution in any trial court ordained and established under article III of the Constitution of the United States."

Consider Judge Carl McGowan, *Constitutional Interpretation and Criminal Identification,* 12 Wm. & Mary L.Rev. 235, 249–50 (1970): "As a practical matter,

a. For a general discussion of the retroactive effect of a new constitutional decision in the criminal procedure field, see pp. 38–44.

the Congressional [response to *Wade–Gilbert–Stovall*] has proved to be meaningless. The inferior federal courts have considered themselves bound by the Supreme Court's reading of the Constitution rather than that of the Congress and have appeared to ignore the new statute. [Congress] appeared to overlook completely the threat to the conviction rate inherent in the impatience of juries with prosecution cases limited to in-court identification. It showed no awareness of the values that may reside, for the prosecution as well as the defense, in tightening up pretrial identification procedures so that impressively credible identification evidence can be adduced." See also Commentary to *Model Pre–Arraignment Code* at 427 & n. 15.

In light of its sparse legislative history, may § 3502 be read as excepting from its language lineups conducted in violation of due process, which *Stovall* recognized as a basis for attacking identification testimony independent of any right to counsel claim?

SECTION 2. THE COURT RETREATS: *KIRBY* AND *ASH*

KIRBY v. ILLINOIS

406 U.S. 682, 92 S.Ct. 1877, 32 L.Ed.2d 411 (1972).

Justice STEWART announced the judgment of the Court in an opinion in which The Chief Justice, Justice BLACKMUN, and Justice REHNQUIST join.

[In] the present case we are asked to extend the *Wade-Gilbert* per se exclusionary rule to identification testimony based upon a police station show-up that took place *before* the defendant had been indicted or otherwise formally charged with any criminal offense.

[Kirby and a companion, Bean, were arrested for a robbery that had occurred two days earlier and taken to the police station. The police then brought the robbery victim to the stationhouse. As soon as he entered the room where Kirby and his companion were seated, the victim identified them as the men who had robbed him. Neither of the two suspects had asked for, or been advised of, counsel. At the trial, the victim described his identification of the two men at the police station. He also identified them again in the courtroom.]

[In] a line of constitutional cases in this Court stemming back to the Court's landmark opinion in *Powell v. Alabama,* it has been firmly established that a person's Sixth and Fourteenth Amendment right to counsel attaches only at or after the time that adversary judicial proceedings have been initiated against him.

This is not to say that a defendant in a criminal case has a constitutional right to counsel only at the trial itself. [But] the point is [that] *all* of [the right to counsel cases] have involved points of time at or after the initiation of adversary judicial criminal proceedings—whether by way of formal charge, preliminary hearing, indictment, information, or arraignment.

The only seeming deviation from this long line of constitutional decisions was *Escobedo* [which] is not apposite here for two distinct reasons. First, the Court in retrospect perceived that the "prime purpose" of *Escobedo* was not to vindicate the constitutional right to counsel as such, but, like *Miranda,* "to guarantee full effectuation of the privilege against self-incrimination. * * * " Secondly, and perhaps even more important for purely practical purposes, the Court has limited the holding of *Escobedo* to its own facts, and those facts are not remotely akin to the facts of the case before us.

The initiation of judicial criminal proceedings is far from a mere formalism. It is the starting point of our whole system of adversary criminal justice. For it is only then that the Government has committed itself to prosecute, and only then that the adverse positions of Government and defendant have solidified. It is then that a defendant finds himself faced with the prosecutorial forces of organized society, and immersed in the intricacies of substantive and procedural criminal law. It is this point, therefore, that marks the commencement of the "criminal prosecutions" to which alone the explicit guarantees of the Sixth Amendment are applicable.

In this case we are asked to import into a routine police investigation an absolute constitutional guarantee historically and rationally applicable only after the onset of formal prosecutorial proceedings. We decline to do so. We decline to [impose] a *per se* exclusionary rule upon testimony concerning an identification that took place long before the commencement of any prosecution whatever.

What has been said is not to suggest that there may not be occasions during the course of a criminal investigation when the police do abuse identification procedures. Such abuses are not beyond the reach of the Constitution. [The] Due Process Clause of the Fifth and Fourteenth Amendments forbids a lineup that is unnecessarily suggestive and conducive to irreparable mistaken identification.[8] When a person has not been formally charged with a criminal offense, *Stovall* strikes the appropriate constitutional balance between the right of a suspect to be protected from prejudicial procedures and the interest of society in the prompt and purposeful investigation of an unsolved crime.[a]

The judgment is affirmed.

Justice BRENNAN, with whom Justice DOUGLAS and Justice MARSHALL join, dissenting. * * *

While it should go without saying, it appears necessary, in view of the plurality opinion today, to re-emphasize that *Wade* did not require the presence of counsel at pretrial confrontations for identification purposes simply on the basis of an abstract consideration of the words "criminal prosecutions" in the Sixth Amendment, [but] in order to safeguard the accused's constitutional rights to confrontation and the effective assistance of counsel at his trial.

In view of *Wade,* it is plain, and the plurality today does not attempt to dispute it, that there inhere in a confrontation for identification conducted after arrest[5] the identical hazards to a fair trial that inhere in such a confrontation conducted "after the onset of formal prosecutorial proceedings." [The] plurality offers no reason, and I can think of none, for concluding that a post-arrest confrontation for identification, unlike a post-charge confrontation, is not among those "critical confrontations of the accused by the prosecution at pretrial proceedings where the results might well settle the accused's fate and reduce the trial itself to a mere formality."

8. In view of our limited grant of certiorari, we do not consider whether there might have been a deprivation of due process in the particularized circumstances of this case. That question remains open for inquiry in a federal habeas corpus proceeding.

[Following the U.S. Supreme Court's decision, the denial of Kirby's petition for federal habeas corpus relief was affirmed by the Seventh Circuit in *United States ex rel. Kirby v. Sturges,* 510 F.2d 397 (1975).]

a. As he "would not extend the *Wade-Gilbert* exclusionary rule," Powell, J., concurred in the result.

5. This case does not require me to consider confrontations that take place before custody, nor accidental confrontations not arranged by the police, nor on-the-scene encounters shortly after the crime.

The highly suggestive form of confrontation employed in this case underscores the point. This showup was particularly fraught with the peril of mistaken identification. In the setting of a police station squad room where all present except petitioner and Bean were police officers, the danger was quite real that [the victim's] understandable resentment might lead him too readily to agree with the police that the pair under arrest, and the only persons exhibited to him, were indeed the robbers. [On] direct examination, Shard identified petitioner and Bean not as the alleged robbers on trial in the courtroom, but as the pair he saw at the police station. * * *

Wade and *Gilbert,* of course, happened to involve post-indictment confrontations. Yet even a cursory perusal of the opinions in those cases reveals that nothing at all turned upon that particular circumstance." * * *

Justice WHITE, dissenting.

Wade and *Gilbert* govern this case and compel reversal of the judgment below.

Notes and Questions

1. ***Wade and Escobedo.*** Does the "reinterpretation" of *Escobedo* (as designed not to vindicate the right to counsel as such but to effectuate the privilege against self-incrimination) support Justice Stewart's holding in *Kirby?* Consider Grano at 728: "*Wade,* like *Escobedo* in its new guise, did not vindicate the right to counsel as such, but rather vindicated the rights of cross-examination, confrontation, and fair trial. *Escobedo* still suggests that counsel must be provided at *any* pretrial stage when necessary to protect other constitutional rights."

2. ***Wade and Powell.*** Did the early right to counsel precedents, as Justice Stewart indicates, mandate the result in *Kirby?* Consider Grano at 727: "*Powell v. Alabama* [and its pre-*Gideon* progeny] relied on the fourteenth amendment due process clause rather than on the sixth amendment. Since the protections under the fourteenth amendment are not limited to any particular stage of a criminal proceeding, the fact that the defendants in these cases had already been charged is irrelevant."

3. ***"Custody" vs. "the initiation of adversary judicial criminal proceedings."*** Is it sound to view (as does Justice Stewart for the plurality in *Kirby*) the "initiation of judicial criminal proceedings [as] the starting point of our whole system of adversary criminal justice"? Is it realistic to say, (as Justice Stewart does for the *Kirby* plurality) that "it is only then [that] the adverse positions of Government and defendant have solidified"? Is the postcustody police attitude supposed to be "neutral" or merely "investigative" rather than "accusatory"? Didn't the Court explicitly recognize in *Miranda* that the accusatory function begins very soon after the defendant is taken into custody? Again, see Grano at 726–27. Recall the statement in *Escobedo*—over Justice Stewart's strong dissent—that "it would exalt form over substance to make the right to counsel, under these circumstances, depend on whether at the time of the interrogation the authorities had secured a formal indictment. Petitioner had, for all practical purposes, already been charged * * *."

4. ***Alley confrontations.*** To what extent did *Kirby* reject the "custody" approach because such an approach would pose a serious threat to the common police practice of conducting "alley confrontations," i.e., prompt confrontations with the victim or an eyewitness at the scene of the crime? See Grano at 731. Prior to *Kirby* most courts exempted these identifications from the right to counsel requirement. See, e.g., *Russell v. United States,* 408 F.2d 1280 (D.C.Cir. 1969) (Bazelon, C.J.).

For the view that all the psychological assumptions on which *Russell* and similar cases are premised—(a) the victim or witness to a crime can be counted on to form an accurate mental image of the offender; (b) this image will be more accurate on the scene immediately after the crime than at the police station some hours later; and (c) the suggestion inherent in one-man confrontations is insignificant in light of the other factors—are speculative and questionable, see Grano at 734–38.

5. *When are adversary judicial criminal proceedings "initiated"?* In MOORE v. ILLINOIS, 434 U.S. 220 (1977), a police officer accompanied the victim to a courtroom where petitioner, a rape suspect, was to appear for his preliminary hearing to determine whether he should be bound over to the grand jury and to set bail. Petitioner was not represented by counsel at this hearing, nor offered appointed counsel. After petitioner's name was called and he was led before the bench, and after the prosecutor had recited evidence believed to implicate petitioner, the victim was asked by the prosecutor where she saw her assailant in the courtroom and she pointed at petitioner. At trial, the victim testified on direct that she had identified petitioner at the preliminary hearing. In reversing the judgment of the federal court of appeals denying habeas corpus relief, the Court, per POWELL, J., rejected, inter alia, the contention that evidence of a corporeal identification conducted in the absence of defense counsel must be excluded only if the identification is made after the defendant is indicted:

"The prosecution in this case was commenced under Illinois law when the victim's complaint was filed in court. The purpose of the preliminary hearing was to determine whether there was probable cause to bind petitioner over to the grand jury and to set bail. Petitioner had the right to oppose the prosecution at that hearing by moving to dismiss the charges and to suppress the evidence against him. He faced counsel for the State * * *. It is plain that '[t]he government ha[d] committed itself to prosecute,' and that petitioner found 'himself faced with the prosecutorial forces of organized society, and immersed in the intricacies of substantive and procedural criminal law.' *Kirby*. The State candidly concedes that the preliminary hearing marked the 'initiation of adversary judicial criminal proceedings' against petitioner, and it hardly could contend otherwise."[a]

Section 160.3(2) of the *Model Code* "codifies" *Kirby* by granting a suspect a right to counsel at corporeal identification procedures "if a complaint has been filed charging a person with crime, or a person has been indicted for crime." Rule 403 of the *Model Rules* reads *Kirby* as giving a suspect "the right to a lawyer for any lineup connected with an arrest for which he was arrested or charged—and to have a lawyer appointed for this purpose if he cannot afford one—if the lineup is held following the start of criminal proceedings against him" (emphasis in the original) and provides further: "Criminal proceedings may be begun by any one of the following: a formal charge (sworn complaint); a preliminary hearing; an indictment; an arraignment; an initial appearance for a magistrate." See also Grano at 788–89.

UNITED STATES v. ASH

413 U.S. 300, 93 S.Ct. 2568, 37 L.Ed.2d 619 (1973).

Justice BLACKMUN delivered the opinion of the Court.

[Shortly before trial, almost three years after the crime, and long after defendant had been incarcerated and appointed counsel, the government conduct-

a. The Court also rejected the view that petitioner had no right to counsel at this identification procedure because "it was conducted in the course of a judicial proceeding": "The reasons supporting *Wade's* holding that a corporeal identification is a critical stage of a criminal prosecution for Sixth Amendment purposes apply with equal force to this identification. It is difficult to imagine a more suggestive manner in which to present a suspect to a witness for their critical first confrontation than was employed in this case. * * * Had petitioner been represented by counsel, some or all of this suggestiveness could have been avoided."

ed a photographic display without notifying counsel. The prosecutor showed five color photographs to four witnesses who previously had tentatively identified the black-and-white photograph of defendant. Three witnesses selected defendant's photo, but one was unable to make any selection. The U.S. Court of Appeals for the D.C. Circuit ruled that defendant's right to counsel had been violated when his attorney was not afforded the opportunity to be present at the photographic display. The Supreme Court reversed.]

[Although the right to counsel guarantee has been expanded beyond the formal trial itself], the function of the lawyer has remained essentially the same as his function at trial. In all cases considered by the Court, counsel has continued to act as a spokesman for, or advisor to, the accused. The accused's right to the "Assistance of Counsel" has meant just that, namely, the right of the accused to have counsel acting as his assistant. [In] *Massiah* counsel could have advised his client on the benefits of the Fifth Amendment and could have sheltered him from the overreaching of the prosecution.

[The] function of counsel in rendering "Assistance" continued at the lineup under consideration in *Wade* and its companion cases. Although the accused was not confronted there with legal questions, the lineup offered opportunities for prosecuting authorities to take advantage of the accused.

[A] substantial departure from the historical test would be necessary if the Sixth Amendment were interpreted to give Ash a right to counsel at the photographic identification in this case. Since the accused himself is not present at the time of the photographic display, and asserts no right to be present, no possibility arises that the accused might be misled by his lack of familiarity with the law or overpowered by his professional adversary. Similarly, the counsel guarantee would not be used to produce equality in a trial-like adversary confrontation. Rather, the guarantee was used by the Court of Appeals to produce confrontation at an event that previously was not analogous to an adversary trial.

Even if we were willing to view the counsel guarantee in broad terms as a generalized protection of the adversary process, we would be unwilling to go so far as to extend the right to a portion of the prosecutor's trial-preparation interviews with witnesses. Although photography is relatively new, the interviewing of witnesses before trial is a procedure that predates the Sixth Amendment. [The] traditional counterbalance in the American adversary system for these interviews arises from the equal ability of defense counsel to seek and interview witnesses himself.

That adversary mechanism remains as effective for a photographic display as for other parts of pretrial interviews. No greater limitations are placed on defense counsel in constructing displays, seeking witnesses, and conducting photographic identifications than those applicable to the prosecution. Selection of the picture of a person other than the accused, or the inability of a witness to make any selection, will be useful to the defense in precisely the same manner that the selection of a picture of the defendant would be useful to the prosecution.

[Pretrial] photographic identifications, [are] hardly unique in offering possibilities for the actions of the prosecutor unfairly to prejudice the accused. Evidence favorable to the accused may be withheld; testimony of witnesses may be manipulated; the results of laboratory tests may be contrived. In many ways the prosecutor, by accident or by design, may improperly subvert the trial. The primary safeguard against abuses of this kind is the ethical responsibility of the prosecutor, who, as so often has been said, may "strike hard blows" but not "foul ones." If that safeguard fails, review remains available under due process standards. These same safeguards apply to misuse of photographs. * * *

We are not persuaded that the risks inherent in the use of photographic displays are so pernicious that an extraordinary system of safeguards is required. * * *

Reversed and remanded.

Justice STEWART, concurring in the judgment. * * *

[The *Wade* Court held] that counsel was required at a lineup, primarily as an observer, to ensure that defense counsel could effectively confront the prosecution's evidence at trial. Attuned to the possibilities of suggestive influences, a lawyer could see any unfairness at a lineup, question the witnesses about it at trial, and effectively reconstruct what had gone on for the benefit of the jury or trial judge.*

A photographic identification is quite different from a lineup, for there are substantially fewer possibilities of impermissible suggestion when photographs are used, and those unfair influences can be readily reconstructed at trial. It is true that the defendant's photograph may be markedly different from the others displayed, but this unfairness can be demonstrated at trial from an actual comparison of the photographs used or from the witness' description of the display. Similarly, it is possible that the photographs could be arranged in a suggestive manner, or that by comment or gesture the prosecuting authorities might single out the defendant's picture. But these are the kinds of overt influence that a witness can easily recount and that would serve to impeach the identification testimony. In short, there are few possibilities for unfair suggestiveness—and those rather blatant and easily reconstructed. Accordingly, an accused would not be foreclosed from an effective cross-examination of an identification witness simply because his counsel was not present at the photographic display. For this reason, a photographic display cannot fairly be considered a "critical stage" of the prosecution.[a] * * *

Justice BRENNAN, with whom Justice DOUGLAS and Justice MARSHALL join, dissenting.

[T]oday's decision marks simply another step towards the complete evisceration of the fundamental constitutional principles established by this Court, only six years ago, in *Wade*, *Gilbert* and *Stovall.*

[To] the extent that misidentification may be attributable to a witness' faulty memory or perception, or inadequate opportunity for detailed observation during the crime, the risks are obviously as great at a photographic display as at a lineup. But "[b]ecause of the inherent limitations of photography, which presents its subject in two dimensions rather than the three dimensions of reality, [a] photographic identification, even when properly obtained, is clearly inferior to a properly obtained corporeal identification." P. Wall, *Eye-Witness Identification in Criminal Cases* 70 (1965). * * *

* I do not read *Wade* as requiring counsel because a lineup is a "trial-type" situation, nor do I understand that the Court required the presence of an attorney because of the advice or assistance he could give to his client at the lineup itself. Rather, I had thought the reasoning of *Wade* was that the right to counsel is essentially a protection for the defendant at trial, and that counsel is necessary at a lineup in order to ensure a meaningful confrontation and the effective assistance of counsel at trial.

a. Is a post-indictment corporeal lineup recorded on video tape and played for the trial court at the suppression hearing a "critical stage" within the meaning of *Wade?*

Moreover, as in the lineup situation, the possibilities for impermissible suggestion in the context of a photographic display are manifold.

[A]s with lineups, the defense can "seldom reconstruct" at trial the mode and manner of photographic identification. It is true, of course, that the photographs used at the pretrial display might be preserved for examination at trial. But "it may also be said that a photograph can preserve the record of a lineup; yet this does not justify a lineup without counsel."[b] Indeed, in reality, preservation of the photographs affords little protection to the unrepresented accused. [For] retention of the photographs [cannot] in any sense reveal to defense counsel the more subtle, and therefore more dangerous, suggestiveness that might derive from the manner in which the photographs were displayed or any accompanying comments or gestures.

[The] fundamental premise underlying *all* of this Court's decisions holding the right to counsel applicable at "critical" pretrial proceedings, is that a "stage" of the prosecution must be deemed "critical" for the purposes of the Sixth Amendment if it is one at which the presence of counsel is necessary "to protect the fairness of *the trial itself.*" *Schneckloth v. Bustamonte* (emphasis added). [This] established conception of the Sixth Amendment guarantee is, of course, in no sense dependent upon the physical "presence of the accused," at a "trial-like confrontation" with the Government, at which the accused requires the "guiding hand of counsel." * * *

[C]ontrary to the suggestion of the Court, the conclusion in *Wade* that a pretrial lineup is a "critical stage" of the prosecution did not in any sense turn on the fact that a lineup involves the physical "presence of the accused" at a "trial-like confrontation" with the Government. And that conclusion most certainly did not turn on the notion that presence of counsel was necessary so that counsel could offer legal advice or "guidance" to the accused at the lineup. On the contrary, *Wade* envisioned counsel's function at the lineup to be primarily that of a trained observer, able to detect the existence of any suggestive influences and capable of understanding the legal implications of the events that transpire. Having witnessed the proceedings, counsel would then be in a position effectively to reconstruct at trial any unfairness that occurred at the lineup, thereby preserving the accused's fundamental right to a fair trial on the issue of identification.

There is something ironic about the Court's conclusion today that a pretrial lineup identification is a "critical stage" of the prosecution because counsel's presence can help to compensate for the accused's deficiencies as an observer, but that a pretrial photographic identification is not a "critical stage" of the prosecution because the accused is not able to observe at all. * * *

b. Doesn't it, at least after *Ash?* Suppose defense counsel was not notified of or in attendance at either a post-indictment lineup viewed by witness A or at the subsequent exhibition of a photograph of the lineup viewed by witness B. Would *Wade* prevent witness A from testifying that he had identified the accused at the uncounselled lineup or would the fact that the lineup was photographed and thus "preserved" for the trial court mean that it was not a "critical stage"? Assuming arguendo that *Wade* would bar witness A from testifying that he had identified the accused at the uncounselled lineup, wouldn't *Ash* allow witness B to testify that he had identified the accused at the subsequent showing of the photograph of the lineup?

See *United States v. Barker*, 988 F.2d 77 (9th Cir.1993) holding that when the defendant is identified in a photograph of a lineup *Ash* applies, not *Wade* because, inter alia, the defendant's absence at the time the photo of the lineup is shown means that he cannot be "misled" or "overpowered."

Notes and Questions

1. ***Wade, Kirby and Ash.*** The *Ash* majority, per Blackmun, J., looks back on *Wade* as concluding that "the lineup constituted a trial-like confrontation" requiring counsel in order "to render 'Assistance' [to a suspect] in counterbalancing any 'overreaching' by the prosecution," implying that counsel is to be an active adversary at this stage. Was the *Ash* majority compelled to so interpret *Wade* because its historical analysis led it to the conclusion that the lawyer's assistance is limited to the *immediate* aid he can give his client? See Note, 64 J.Crim.L.C. & P.S. 428 (1973). Does concurring Justice Stewart disclaim this reading of *Wade?* If so, which interpretation is more consistent with the cases, commentaries and practice since *Wade?* Reconsider Note 2, p. 764. Consider, too, 64 J.Crim.L.C. & P.S. at 433 & n. 40.

2. ***Massiah and Ash.*** According to the *Ash* majority, "in *Massiah* counsel could have advised his client on the benefits of the Fifth Amendment and could have sheltered him from the overreaching of the prosecution." Was the defendant in *Massiah* entitled to Fifth Amendment protection? Was he compelled to speak? How would the presence of counsel in *Massiah* have provided "assistance" at the "confrontation" unless counsel were aware the meeting was a confrontation? And if counsel were so aware, wouldn't he have *prevented* the confrontation from occurring? See Grano at 762 & n. 285.

3. ***The significance of defendant's right to be personally present.*** As noted by the Court, the defendant in *Ash* did not claim the right to be personally present at the photographic display. But does the right to counsel *only* exist when the defendant is entitled to be personally present? Voluntary absence or contumacious conduct (see *Illinois v. Allen,* Ch. 25, § 3) may cause a defendant to lose his right to be present at trial, but does it follow that he also loses his right to counsel? Defendants on appeal have the right to counsel, but do they have the right to be personally present? See generally Grano at 764–67.

4. ***Justice Stewart's concurring opinion.*** All of the distinctions Justice Stewart made between photographic displays and lineups—photographic displays are less vulnerable to improper suggestion, are easier to reconstruct at trial and are less indelible in their effect upon a witness—are sharply challenged in Grano at 767–70.

5. ***Photographic displays and other pretrial interviews of prospective witnesses.*** Both the majority and concurring opinions in *Ash* indicated concern that granting a right to counsel at photographic displays might lead to the extension of the right to counsel to all pretrial interviews of prospective witnesses. But consider Note, 26 Stan.L.Rev. 399, 416–17 (1974): "[The] basis for extending the right to counsel to the identification context was that identifications by eyewitnesses—like confessions—are such damning evidence that they may completely decide the guilt or innocence of the accused. Photographic identifications can be just as critical to the future outcome of a trial as can corporeal identifications. Routine interviews between the prosecutor and his witnesses, on the other hand, do not have the potential for such damaging results, at least assuming good faith on the part of the prosecutor."

SECTION 3. DUE PROCESS AND OTHER LIMITATIONS

As already pointed out, see p. 768, one unable to make a *Wade-Gilbert* right to counsel argument may still establish that the identification procedure conducted in his case "was so unnecessarily suggestive and conducive to irreparable mistaken identification that he was denied due process of law." STOVALL v. DENNO, 388 U.S. 293 (1967). In this case, the stabbing victim (Mrs. Behrendt), was hospitalized for major surgery. Without affording petitioner time to retain counsel (an arraignment had been promptly held but then postponed until petitioner could retain counsel), the police, with the cooperation of the victim's surgeon, arranged a confrontation between petitioner and the victim in her hospital room. Petitioner was handcuffed to one of the seven law enforcement officials who brought him to the hospital room. He was the only black person in the room. After being asked by an officer whether petitioner "was the man," the victim identified him from her hospital bed. Both Mrs. Behrendt and the police then testified at the trial to her identification in the hospital. Despite the suggestiveness of the confrontation, the Court, per BRENNAN, J., affirmed the Second Circuit's denial of federal habeas corpus relief, observing:

"The practice of showing suspects singly to persons for the purpose of identification, and not as part of a lineup has been widely condemned. However, a claimed violation of due process of law in the conduct of a confrontation depends on the totality of the circumstances surrounding it, and the record in the present case reveals that the showing of Stovall to Mrs. Behrendt in an immediate hospital confrontation was imperative. The Court of Appeals en banc, stated [355 F.2d 731, 735 (2d Cir.1966) (per Moore, J.)]:

" 'Here was the only person in the world who could possibly exonerate Stovall. Her words, and only her words, "He is not the man" could have resulted in freedom for Stovall. The hospital was not far distant from the courthouse and jail. No one knew how long Mrs. Behrendt might live. Faced with the responsibility of identifying the attacker, with the need for immediate action and with the knowledge that Mrs. Behrendt could not visit the jail, the police followed the only feasible procedure and took Stovall to the hospital room. Under these circumstances, the usual police station line-up, which Stovall now argues he should have had, was out of the question.' "[a]

MANSON v. BRATHWAITE

432 U.S. 98, 97 S.Ct. 2243, 53 L.Ed.2d 140 (1977).

Justice BLACKMUN delivered the opinion of the Court. * * *

[Several minutes before sunset, Glover, a black undercover police officer, purchased heroin from a seller through the open doorway of an apartment while standing for two or three minutes within two feet of the seller in a hallway

a. But consider Judge Friendly, joined by Waterman, J., dissenting below, 355 F.2d at 744–45:

"[The argument that law enforcement officials were confronted with an emergency] ignores the huge amount of circumstantial identification the excellent police investigation had produced; moreover, if the state officials were motivated [by] solicitude [for Stovall], the natural course would have been to ask Stovall whether he wanted to go. The emergency argument fails both on the facts and on the law. [If] Mrs. Behrendt's condition had been as serious as my brothers suppose, nothing prevented the prosecutor from informing the state district judge at the preliminary hearing that Stovall had to be taken immediately before her, and suggesting that counsel be assigned forthwith for the limited purpose of advising him in that regard—rather than standing silent when Stovall told the judge of his desire to have counsel and then carting him off to a confrontation by the victim which counsel might have done something to mitigate."

Lower courts have not only followed *Stovall* in similar cases of serious injury to the victim or a witness but have applied it to situations where the *suspect* is seriously injured. See Commentary to § 160.5 of the *Model Pre–Arraignment Code* at 451–52. Is a "showup" in such cases necessary? Could a photographic array be utilized? If the suspect is hospitalized for an extended period, could the witness be taken to several hospital rooms? See *Model Code* at 452.

illuminated by natural light. A few minutes later, Glover described the seller to a back-up officer, D'Onofrio, as being "a colored man, approximately five feet eleven inches tall, dark complexion, black hair, short Afro style, and having high cheekbones, and of heavy build. He was wearing at the time blue pants and a plaid shirt."

[On the basis of the description, D'Onofrio thought that respondent might be the heroin seller. He obtained a single photograph of respondent from police files and left it at Glover's office. Two days later, while alone, Glover viewed the photograph and identified it as that of the seller. At respondent's trial, Glover testified that there was "no doubt whatsoever" that the person shown in the photograph was respondent. Glover also made a positive in-court identification. No explanation was offered by the prosecution for the failure to utilize a photographic array or to conduct a lineup.

[After the Connecticut Supreme Court affirmed respondent's conviction, he sought federal habeas corpus relief. The Second Circuit, per Friendly, J., held that because the showing of the single photograph was "suggestive" and concededly "unnecessarily so," evidence pertaining to it was subject to a *per se* rule of exclusion.]

Neil v. Biggers, 409 U.S. 188 (1972) concerned a respondent who had been convicted [of] rape, on evidence consisting in part of the victim's visual and voice identification of Biggers at a [one-person] station-house showup seven months after the crime. [The] Court expressed concern about the lapse of seven months between the crime and the confrontation, [but pointed out that the] "central question" [was] "whether under the 'totality of the circumstances' the identification was reliable even though the confrontation procedure was suggestive." Applying that test, the Court found "no substantial likelihood of misidentification. The evidence was properly allowed to go to the jury."[a]

Biggers well might be seen to provide an unambiguous answer to the question before us: The admission of testimony concerning a suggestive and unnecessary identification procedure does not violate due process so long as the identification possesses sufficient aspects of reliability.[9] In one passage, however, the Court

a. The *Biggers* Court, per Powell, J., observed:

"The victim spent a considerable period of time with her assailant, up to half an hour. She was with him under adequate artificial light in her house and under a full moon outdoors, and at least twice, once in the house and later in the woods, faced him directly and intimately. [Her] description to the police, which included the assailant's approximate age, height, weight, complexion, skin texture, build, and voice [was] more than ordinarily thorough. She had 'no doubt' that respondent was the person who raped her. [The] victim here, a practical nurse by profession, had an unusual opportunity to observe and identify her assailant. She testified at the habeas corpus hearing that there was something about his face 'I don't think I could ever forget.'

"There was, to be sure, a lapse of seven months between the rape and the confrontation. This would be a seriously negative factor in most cases. Here, however, the testimony is undisputed that the victim made no previous identification at any of the showups, lineups, or photographic showings. Her record for reliability was thus a good one, as she had previously resisted whatever suggestiveness inheres in a showup. Weighing all the factors, we find no substantial likelihood of misidentification."

9. Justice Marshall argues in dissent that our cases have "established two different due process tests for two very different situations." Pretrial identifications are to be covered by *Stovall,* which is said to require exclusion of evidence concerning unnecessarily suggestive pretrial identifications without regard to reliability. In-court identifications, on the other hand, are to be governed by *Simmons v. United States,* 390 U.S. (1968) and admissibility turns on reliability. The Court's cases are sorted into one category or the other. *Biggers,* which clearly adopts the reliability of the identification as the guiding factor in the admissibility of both pre-trial and in-court identifications, is condemned for mixing the two lines and for adopting a uniform rule.

[Our cases] hardly suggest the formal structure the dissent would impose on them. If our cases truly established two different rules, one might expect at some point at least passing

observed that the challenged procedure occurred pre-*Stovall* and that a strict rule would make little sense with regard to a confrontation that preceded the Court's first indication that a suggestive procedure might lead to the exclusion of evidence. One perhaps might argue that, by implication, the Court suggested that a different rule could apply post-*Stovall*. The question before us, then, is simply whether the *Biggers* analysis applies to post-*Stovall* confrontations as well to those pre-*Stovall*. * * *

Petitioner at the outset acknowledges that "the procedure in the instant case was suggestive [because only one photograph was used] and unnecessary" [because there was no emergency or exigent circumstance]. The respondent, in agreement with the Court of Appeals, proposes a *per se* rule of exclusion that he claims is dictated by the demands of the Fourteenth Amendment's guarantee of due process. He rightly observes that this is the first case in which this Court has had occasion to rule upon strictly post-*Stovall* out-of-court identification evidence of the challenged kind.

Since the decision in *Biggers*, the Courts of Appeals appear to have developed at least two approaches to such evidence. See Pulaski, *Neil v. Biggers: The Supreme Court Dismantles the Wade Trilogy's Due Process Protection*, 26 Stan. L.Rev. 1097, 1111–1114 (1974). The first, or *per se* approach, employed by the Second Circuit in the present case, focuses on the procedures employed and requires exclusion of the out-of-court identification evidence, without regard to reliability, whenever it has been obtained through unnecessarily suggested confrontation procedures.[10] The justifications advanced are the elimination of evidence of uncertain reliability, deterrence of the police and prosecutors, and the stated "fair assurance against the awful risks of misidentification."

The second, or more lenient, approach is one that continues to rely on the totality of the circumstances. It permits the admission of the confrontation evidence if, despite the suggestive aspect, the out-of-court identification possesses certain features of reliability. This second approach, in contrast to the other, is ad hoc and serves to limit the societal costs imposed by a sanction that excludes relevant evidence from consideration and evaluation by the trier of fact. * * *

There are, of course, several interests to be considered and taken into account. The driving force behind [*Wade, Gilbert* and *Stovall*] was the Court's concern with the problems of eyewitness identification. Usually the witness must testify about an encounter with a total stranger under circumstances of emergency or emotional stress. The witness' recollection of the stranger can be distorted easily by the circumstances or by later actions of the police. Thus, *Wade* and its companion cases reflect the concern that the jury not hear eyewitness testimony unless that evidence has aspects of reliability. It must be observed that both approaches before us are responsive to this concern. The *per se* rule, however, goes too far since its application automatically and peremptorily, and without consideration of alleviating factors, keeps evidence from the jury that is reliable and relevant.

reference to the fact. There is none. And if *Biggers* departed so grievously from the past cases, it is surprising that there was not at least some mention of the point in Justice Brennan's dissent. * * * *Biggers* is not properly seen as a departure from the past cases, but as a synthesis of them.

10. Although the *per se* approach demands the exclusion of testimony concerning unnecessarily suggestive identifications, it does permit the admission of testimony concerning a subsequent identification, including an in-court identification, if the subsequent identification is determined to be reliable. The totality approach, in contrast, is simpler: if the challenged identification is reliable, then testimony as to it and any identification in its wake is admissible.

The second factor is deterrence. Although the *per se* approach has the more significant deterrent effect, the totality approach also has an influence on police behavior. The police will guard against unnecessarily suggestive procedures under the totality rule, as well as the *per se* one, for fear that their actions will lead to the exclusion of identifications as unreliable.

The third factor is the effect on the administration of justice. Here the *per se* approach suffers serious drawbacks. Since it denies the trier reliable evidence, it may result, on occasion, in the guilty going free. Also, because of its rigidity, the *per se* approach may make error by the trial judge more likely than the totality approach. And in those cases in which the admission of identification evidence is error under the *per se* approach but not under the totality approach—cases in which the identification is reliable despite an unnecessarily suggestive identification procedure—reversal is a Draconian sanction. Certainly, inflexible rules of exclusion that may frustrate rather than promote justice have not been viewed recently by this Court with unlimited enthusiasm. * * *

We therefore conclude that reliability is the linchpin in determining the admissibility of identification testimony for both pre-and post-*Stovall* confrontations. The factors to be considered are set out in *Biggers*. These include the opportunity of the witness to view the criminal at the time of the crime, the witness' degree of attention, the accuracy of his prior description of the criminal, the level of certainty demonstrated at the confrontation, and the time between the crime and the confrontation. Against these factors is to be weighed the corrupting effect of the suggestive identification itself.

We turn, then, to the facts of this case and apply the analysis:

1. *The opportunity to view.* Glover testified that for two to three minutes he stood at the apartment door, within two feet of the respondent. The door opened twice, and each time the man stood at the door. * * * Natural light from outside entered the hallway through a window. There was natural light, as well, from inside the apartment.

2. *The degree of attention.* Glover was not a casual or passing observer, [but] a trained police officer on duty—and specialized and dangerous duty—when he [made the heroin purchase]. Glover himself was a Negro and unlikely to perceive only general features of [black males].

3. *The accuracy of the description.* Glover's description was given to D'Onofrio within minutes after the transaction. It included the vendor's race, his height, his build, the color and style of his hair, and the high cheekbone facial feature. It also included clothing the vendor wore. No claim has been made that respondent did not possess the physical characteristics so described. * * *

4. *The witness' level of certainty.* There is no dispute that the photograph in question was that of respondent. Glover, in response to a question whether the photograph was that of the person from whom he made the purchase, testified: "There is no question whatsoever." This positive assurance was repeated.

5. *The time between the crime and the confrontation.* Glover's description of his vendor was given to D'Onofrio within minutes of the crime. The photographic identification took place only two days later. We do not have here the passage of weeks or months between the crime and the viewing of the photograph.

These indicators of Glover's ability to make an accurate identification are hardly outweighed by the corrupting effect of the challenged identification itself. Although identifications arising from single-photograph displays may be viewed in general with suspicion, we find in the instant case little pressure on the witness to acquiesce in the suggestion that such a display entails. D'Onofrio had left the photograph at Glover's office and was not present when Glover first viewed it two days after the event. There thus was little urgency and Glover could view the photograph at his leisure. And since Glover examined the photograph alone, there was no coercive pressure to make an identification arising from the presence of another. The identification was made in circumstances allowing care and reflection. * * *

Surely, we cannot say that under all the circumstances of this case there is "a very substantial likelihood of irreparable misidentification." Short of that point, such evidence is for the jury to weigh. We are content to rely upon the good sense and judgment of American juries, for evidence with some element of untrustworthiness is customary grist for the jury mill. Juries are not so susceptible that they cannot measure intelligently the weight of identification testimony that has some questionable feature. * * *

We conclude that the criteria laid down in *Biggers* are to be applied in determining the admissibility of evidence offered by the prosecution concerning a post-*Stovall* identification, and that those criteria are satisfactorily met and complied with here.[b] * * *

Justice MARSHALL, with whom Justice BRENNAN joins, dissenting.

Today's decision can come as no surprise to those who have been watching the Court dismantle the protections against mistaken eyewitness testimony erected a decade ago in [*Wade*, *Gilbert* and *Stovall*]. But it is still distressing to see the Court virtually ignore the teaching of experience embodied in those decisions and blindly uphold the conviction of a defendant who may well be innocent.

[In] determining the admissibility of the *post-Stovall* identification in this case, the Court considers two alternatives, a *per se* exclusionary rule and a totality-of-the-circumstances approach. The Court weighs three factors in deciding that the totality approach, which is essentially the test used in *Biggers,* should be applied. In my view, the Court wrongly evaluates the impact of these factors.

First, the Court acknowledges that one of the factors, deterrence of police use of unnecessarily suggestive identification procedures, favors the *per se* rule. Indeed, it does so heavily, for such a rule would make it unquestionably clear to the police they must never use a suggestive procedure when a fairer alternative is available. I have no doubt that conduct would quickly conform to the rule.

Second, the Court gives passing consideration to the dangers of eyewitness identification recognized in the *Wade* trilogy. It concludes, however, that the grave risk of error does not justify adoption of the *per se* approach because that would too often result in exclusion of relevant evidence. In my view, this conclusion totally ignores the lessons of *Wade.* The dangers of mistaken identification are, as *Stovall* held, simply too great to permit unnecessarily suggestive identifications. * * *

Finally, the Court errs in its assessment of the relative impact of the two approaches on the administration of justice. The Court relies most heavily on this factor * * *.

First, the *per se* rule here is not "inflexible." Where evidence is suppressed, for example, as the fruit of an unlawful search, it may well be forever lost to the prosecution. Identification evidence, however, can by its very nature be readily and effectively reproduced. The in-court identification, permitted under *Wade* [if]

b. Stevens, J., concurring, joined the Court's opinion, but emphasized that although "the arguments in favor of fashioning new rules to minimize the danger of convicting the innocent on the basis of unreliable eyewitness testimony carry substantial force, [this] rule-making function can be performed 'more effectively by the legislative process than by somewhat clumsy judicial fiat,' and that the Federal Constitution does not foreclose experimentation by the States in the development of such rules."

it has a source independent of an uncounseled or suggestive procedure, is one example. Similarly, when a prosecuting attorney learns that there has been a suggestive confrontation, he can easily arrange another lineup conducted under scrupulously fair conditions. * * *

Second, other exclusionary rules have been criticized for preventing jury consideration of relevant and usually reliable evidence in order to serve interest unrelated to guilt or innocence, such as discouraging illegal searches or denial of counsel. Suggestively obtained eyewitness testimony is excluded, in contrast, precisely because of its unreliability and concomitant irrelevance. Its exclusion both protects the integrity of the truth-seeking function of the trial and discourages police use of needlessly inaccurate and ineffective investigatory methods.

[For] these reasons, I conclude that adoption of the *per se* rule would enhance, rather than detract from, the effective administration of justice. In my view, the Court's totality test will allow seriously unreliable and misleading evidence to be put before juries. * * *

Even more disturbing than the Court's reliance on the totality test, however, is the analysis it uses. [The] decision suggests that due process violations in identification procedures may not be measured by whether the government employed procedures violating standards of fundamental fairness. By relying on the probable accuracy of a challenged identification, instead of the necessity for its use, the Court seems to be ascertaining whether the defendant was probably guilty. * * *

Despite my strong disagreement with the Court over the proper standards to be applied in this case, I am pleased that its application of the totality test does recognize the continuing vitality of *Stovall*. In assessing the reliability of the identification, the Court mandates weighing "the corrupting effect of the suggestive identification itself" against the "indicators of [a witness'] ability to make an accurate identification." The Court holds, as *Biggers* failed to, that a due process identification inquiry must take account of the suggestiveness of a confrontation and the likelihood that it led to mis-identification, as recognized in *Stovall* and *Wade*. Thus, even if a witness did have an otherwise adequate opportunity to view a criminal, the later use of a highly suggestive identification procedure can render his testimony inadmissible. Indeed, it is my view that, assuming applicability of the totality test enunciated by the Court, the facts of the present case require that result.

I consider first the opportunity that Officer Glover had to view the suspect. Careful review of the record shows that he could see the heroin seller only for the time it took to speak three sentences of four or five short words, to hand over some money, and later after the door reopened, to receive the drugs in return. The entire face-to-face transaction could have taken as little as 15 or 20 seconds. But during this time, Glover's attention was not focused exclusively on the seller's face. He observed that the door was opened 12 to 18 inches, that there was a window in the room behind the door, and, most importantly, that there was a woman standing behind the man. Glover was, of course, also concentrating on the details of the transaction—he must have looked away from the seller's face to hand him the money and receive the drugs. The observation during the conversation thus may have been as brief as 5 or 10 seconds.

As the Court notes, Glover was a police officer trained in and attentive to the need for making accurate identifications. [But] the mere fact that he has been so trained is no guarantee that he is correct in a specific case. * * * Moreover, "identifications made by policemen in highly competitive activities, such as undercover narcotic [work], should be scrutinized with special care." P. Wall, *Eye-*

Witness Identification in Criminal Cases 14 (1965). Yet it is just such a searching inquiry that the Court fails to make here.

Another factor on which the Court relies—the witness' degree of certainty in making the identification—is worthless as an indicator that he is correct. Even if Glover had been unsure initially about his identification of respondent's picture, by the time he was called at trial to present a key piece of evidence for the State that paid his salary, it is impossible to imagine his responding negatively to such questions as "is there any doubt in your mind whatsoever" that the identification was correct. * * *

Next, the Court finds that because the identification procedure took place two days after the crime, its reliability is enhanced. While such temporal proximity makes the identification more reliable than one occurring months later, the fact is that the greatest memory loss occurs within hours after an event. After that, the dropoff continues much more slowly. * * *

Finally, the Court makes much of the fact that Glover gave a description of the seller to D'Onofrio shortly after the incident. [But the description was only] a general summary of the seller's appearance. We may discount entirely the seller's clothing, for that was of no significance later in the proceeding. Indeed, to the extent that Glover noticed clothes, his attention was diverted from the seller's face. * * * Conspicuously absent is any indication that the seller was a native of the West Indies, certainly something which a member of the black community could immediately recognize from both appearance and accent.[12]

From all of this, I must conclude that the evidence of Glover's ability to make an accurate identification is far weaker than the Court finds it. In contrast, the procedure used to identify respondent was both extraordinarily suggestive and strongly conducive to error. [By] displaying a single photograph of respondent to the witness Glover under the circumstances in this record almost everything that could have been done wrong was done wrong.

In this case, [the] pressure [to identify respondent] was not limited to that inherent in the display of a single photograph. Glover, the identifying witness, was a state police officer on special assignment. He knew that D'Onofrio, an [experienced] narcotics detective, presumably familiar with local drug operations, believed respondent to be the seller. There was at work, then, both loyalty to another police officer and deference to a better-informed colleague. * * *

Notes and Questions

1. ***Deterrence.*** Will the *Manson* approach significantly deter the use of suggestive identification procedures? Consider Randolph Jonakait, *Reliable Identification: Could the Supreme Court Tell in Manson v. Brathwaite?,* 52 U.Colo. L.Rev. 511, 515 n. 15 (1981): "[R]egardless of how specifically opinions define what is unnecessarily suggestive, a police officer can never know whether he is violating a suspect's constitutional rights when he is conducting an identification procedure. That can be determined only when the indicia of reliability are examined. These factors may not be known to the officer and certainly cannot be controlled by him. The Court's approach leaves the officer without any firm rules as to what conduct violates the Constitution. If the officer has no way of knowing what actions are forbidden, he can hardly be deterred from those actions."

12. Brathwaite had come to the United States from his native Barbados as an adult. It is also noteworthy that the informant who witnessed the transaction and was described by Glover as "trustworthy," disagreed with Glover's recollection of the event. The informant testified that it was a woman in the apartment who took the money from Glover and gave him the drugs in return.

See also Steven Grossman, *Suggestive Identifications: The Supreme Court's Due Process Test Fails to Meet Its Own Criteria,* 11 Balt.L.Rev. 53, 59–60 (1981) (rather than deterring show-ups and the showing of single photographs, "the effect of *Biggers* and *Manson* has been to provide the police with a fairly clear signal that absent extremely aggravating circumstances, the one-on-one presentation of suspects to witnesses will result in no suppression"); Wallace Sherwood, *The Erosion of Constitutional Safeguards in the Area of Eyewitness Identification,* 30 How.L.J. 731, 770 (1987) (the "totality of circumstances" test, "which places a premium on the probable guilt of the accused, will not serve as a deterrent to police use of suggestive procedures but will have the opposite result").

2. *"The other side of the scale": suggestiveness.* Although the *Manson* Court offered guidelines to determine reliability, "it failed," comments Grossman, supra, at 80, 96–97, "to articulate such criteria in evaluating the other side of the scale, suggestiveness. Police and lower courts were not given examples of what types of identification procedures were objectionable and, perhaps more important in a weighing process, what forms of suggestive behavior were more likely than others to result in an unreliable identification. [As] a result, many courts have come to regard suggestion as a monolithic concept devoid of gradations or merely as a prerequisite to be met prior to analyzing the [*Biggers-Manson*] reliability factors. [The] Supreme Court can [provide guidance] by indicating what types of suggestive conduct are more likely to result in unreliable identification testimony. As to these extreme forms of suggestive procedures [e.g., informing a witness that the suspect has confessed, having several witnesses view a display at the same time, presenting the suspect with a distinguishing trait or item also possessed by the perpetrator], a higher degree of reliability need be shown than that necessary to overcome nominal or less severe types of suggestive practices."

3. *Do the assumptions of the Manson majority find support in psychological research?* Drawing upon studies by Elizabeth Loftus and others, Jonakait, Note 1 supra, at 519–22, maintains that many of the assumptions made by the *Manson* majority are unwarranted. E.g., "studies do not support the idea that police make more reliable witnesses than civilians or that their training in any way improves their ability to make identifications"; dangerous police work generates great stress and, although the Court may think that danger heightens awareness, "psychologists have known for some time that stress does not aid perception and learning, but inhibits them"; research indicates no relationship between the expressed confidence of an eyewitness and the accuracy of his or her identification. See also Grossman, supra, at 72–79.

4. *Should we bar the state from seeking death when suggestive identification procedures have been used?* Consider Margery Malkin Koosed, *The Proposed Innocence Protection Act Won't–Unless It Also Curbs Mistaken Eyewitness Identifications*, 63 Ohio St.L.J. 263, 265 (2002): "While cautionary instructions and expert testimony may be helpful, these have not proved strong enough in our battle to assure against mistaken identification. Altering the *Manson* standard for admission of the in-court identification and returning to the *Stovall* inquiry of whether the pretrial procedure was 'conducive to irreparable mistaken identification' (or an analogous 'any likelihood of misidentification will exclude the in-court testimony' standard) may further improve our arsenal. But the better approach would be for legislatures to simply bar the State from seeking death when suggestive procedures have been used."

How to Increase the Accuracy of Eyewitness Identifications: Gary Wells' Writings and the National Institute of Justice's (NIJ's) *Eyewitness Evidence: A Guide for Law Enforcement*

Gary L. Wells & Eric P. Seelau, *Eyewitness Identification: Psychological Research and Legal Policy on Lineups*, 1 Psychology, Pub. Pol'y. & L. 765 (1995), maintain that there is a need to articulate some simple and minimal requirements for lineups and photospreads in the average case because: (1) there is little evidence to support the idea that jurors can understand and appreciate the influence of suggestive identification procedures; (2) many of the suggestive influences that can be handled by rules are *hidden* influences, such as nonverbal suggestions by the officer conducting the lineup or photospread not known to the jurors; and (3) rules serve to prevent the risky practices whereas the Supreme Court's current approach is to try to assess or to diagnose the risky practices. Professors Wells and Seelau and the American Psychology/Law Society propose the following four rules:

1. *The person conducting the lineup or photospread should not be aware of which member of the lineup or photospread is the suspect.* (It is current common practice for a police officer involved closely in the case, who knows where the suspect is placed, to conduct the lineup or to administer the photospread.)[a]

2. *Eyewitnesses should be told explicitly that the suspected offender might not be in the lineup or photospread, and, therefore that they should not feel they have to make an identification.* (The danger of false identification arises from a tendency for eyewitnesses to identify the person who most closely resembles the offender relative to the other in the lineup.)[b]

3. *The suspect should not stand out in the lineup or photospread as being different from the distractors on the basis of the witness's previous description of the offender or other factors that would draw special attention to the suspect.* E.g., the suspect should not be the only one dressed in the type of clothes the victim said was worn by the offender or the suspect's photo should not be taken from a different angle than the other photos.

4. *At the time the identification is made, and prior to any feedback, a clear statement should be taken from the eyewitness regarding his degree of confidence that the person identified is the actual offender.* Confidence statements from eyewitnesses can be greatly affected by postidentification events that have nothing to do with the witness's memory. E.g., an eyewitness might learn, after his identification, that another witness has identified the same person or that the person he has identified has a prior record for offenses of the same type.

The many articles that Professor Gary Wells and various co-authors have written greatly influenced the law enforcement, legal, and research professionals convened by the National Institute of Justice (NIJ) in 1998. This group produced *Eyewitness Evidence: A Guide for Law Enforcement* (1999), a compilation of

a. Administering the lineup "blind"—i.e., using the technique of assigning the lineup procedure to an officer who does not know which lineup member is the suspect—has been adopted in the New Jersey Attorney General's *Guidelines for Preparing and Conducting Photo and Lineup Identification Procedures*, the first set of state eyewitness evidence procedures based on the recommendations in National Institute of Justice: *A Guide for Law Enforcement* (1999).

b. Cf. Randolph N. Jonakait, *Reliable Identificaion; Could the Supreme Court Tell in Manson v. Brathwaite?*, 52 U.Colo.L.Rev. 511, 525 (1981); Gerald Lefcourt, *The Blank Lineup: An Aid to the Defense*, 14 Crim.L.Bull. 428 (1978), advocating the use of "blank" lineups. This entails the viewing of two separate lineups. The witness should be told the suspect may or may not be in the first lineup. Thereafter, the suspect is presented in the second lineup.

Consider, too, one of the techniques discussed in the *Guide for Law Enforcement*, fn. a supra, displaying people in a lineup one at a time—sequentially—rather than in a line at the same time, thereby reducing the chance that the witness will simply pick the person who looks most like the perpetrator of the crime.

refined investigative techniques that can be used by various jurisdictions in handling eyewitness evidence. The *Guide* provides recommendations to law enforcement officials that incorporate some, but not all of the recommendations of the American Psychology/Law Society. See generally Donald P. Judges, *Two Cheers for the Department of Justice's Eyewitness Evidence: A Guide for Law Enforcement*, 53 Ark.L.Rev. 231 (2000). James M. Doyle, Mark R. Larson & Caterina M. DiTraglia, *The Eyes Have It—or Do They?*, Criminal Justice (ABA Criminal Justice Section), Fall 2001, pp. 12, 19, report:

"The New Jersey Office of the Attorney General has integrated many of the *Guide*'s findings—as well as additional findings not embodied in the *Guide*—into that state's practice. Ideas and training are currently being exchanged freely, with none of the acrimony that often pervades the debate surrounding cases headed for court. [The] NIJ has remained involved and developed training materials for law enforcement based on the *Guide*."

Detention for Identification Procedures in the Absence of Probably Cause

In *Davis v. Mississippi* (1969) (p. 436), petitioner and 24 other black youths were detained for questioning and fingerprinting in connection with a rape for which the only leads were a general description given by the victim and a set of fingerprints around the window through which the assailant entered. Petitioner's prints were found to match those at the scene of the crime, and this evidence was admitted at his trial. The Court, per Brennan, J., held that the prints should have been excluded as the fruits of a seizure of petitioner in violation of the Fourth Amendment, but intimated that a detention for such a purpose might sometimes be permissible on evidence falling short of the traditional probable cause needed for an arrest.

See also *Hayes v. Florida*, 470 U.S. 811 (1985). Although the Court, per White, J., held that *transporting a suspect to the police station* without probable cause or prior judicial authorization violated his Fourth Amendment right, it reserved the possibility, as it had in *Davis*, that "a brief detention *in the field* for the purpose of fingerprinting, where there is only reasonable suspicion not amounting to probable cause" (emphasis added), might pass constitutional muster. *Hayes* also left open the possibility that "under circumscribed procedures, the Fourth Amendment might permit *the judiciary to authorize* the seizure of a person on less than probable cause and his removal to the police station for the purpose of fingerprinting." (Emphasis added.)

As noted in Charles H. Whitebread & Christopher Slobogin, *Criminal Procedure* 482 (4th ed. 2000), "the reasoning of the dictum in *Hayes* would also justify seizures from the home for the purpose of a lineup or showup, based solely on a judicial finding of reasonable suspicion. Further, again assuming reasonable suspicion, *Hayes* would allow police to act on their own in arranging on-the-scene lineups or showups. On the other hand, suspicionless or random seizures of a person for such identification procedures would be impermissible."

On the basis of the *Davis* dictum, Art. 170 of the *Model Pre–Arraignment Code* delineates a court order procedure for detaining persons for nontestimonial identification purposes on less than "probable cause" and a number of states have passed similar legislation. See Commentary to Art. 170 at 475–77; SEARCHSZR § 9.7(b); Note, 45 Fordham L.Rev. (1976) (hereafter referred to as "Fordham Note"). The Model Code article covers many "identification procedures," e.g., procedures to obtain identification by fingerprints, footprints, dental impressions, specimens or samples of blood, urine or hair, and procedures to obtain witness identification through lineups and handwriting exemplars. To what extent should the requisite basis for the detention vary with the kind of identification involved? For example, since eyewitness identifications are a less reliable form of evidence than fingerprints, should Fourth Amendment requirements for detentions for lineup purposes be significantly more stringent? Or should the basis for detention for lineup purposes be the same, but the suspect afforded the right to counsel at the lineup? See Fordham Note at 128–29.

Although the most serious Fourth Amendment question would seem to be whether, when the police lack "probable cause" to arrest a person *for any offense*, they may detain him for identification purposes (with or without a court order), Fourth Amendment problems also arise in other contexts. Courts have generally found no Fourth Amendment violation when a person *lawfully in custody for one crime* is ordered into a lineup for other crimes for which there is no probable cause to arrest him. But some courts have indicated that even under these circumstances there must be a "reasonable suspicion" that the person committed the crimes. See generally Fordham Note at 125–32. However, why should *the viewing* of suspects by witnesses—as opposed to *the basis for detaining* them in order to permit the viewing—raise any Fourth Amendment problems? Cf. *United States v. Dionisio* (1973) (p. 816).

When a defendant has been released on bail, he is generally subject to the control of the court, which is empowered to order his appearance. A number of courts have exercised this power to order defendants to appear in a lineup for an unrelated crime, but again it is unclear whether this may be done indiscriminately or only when there is at least "reasonable suspicion" that the defendant has committed the unrelated crime under investigation. See Fordham Note at 127.

Chapter 11
GRAND JURY INVESTIGATIONS[aa]

SECTION 1. THE ROLE OF THE INVESTIGATIVE GRAND JURY

A. The Investigative Authority of the Grand Jury

1. ***Dual functions***. The grand jury is often described as providing both a "shield" and a "sword" to the criminal justice process. A "shield" against mistaken and vindictive prosecutions is provided by granting to the grand jury the decision as to whether or not to issue an indictment. In making that determination, the grand jury's role is to "screen" the prosecution's decision to charge, ensuring that no person is charged on evidence insufficient to justify a prosecution. On the other side, the grand jury is said to act as a "sword," combating crime, in the use of its investigative authority. Here, the grand jury's role is to uncover evidence not previously available to the government and thereby secure convictions that might otherwise not be obtained. The shielding function of the grand jury will be discussed in Chapter Sixteen.[a] In this Chapter we will concentrate upon the operation of the grand jury in its investigatory role. It should be kept in mind, however, that the two functions of the grand jury commonly are performed by the same grand jury. In particular, once a grand jury investigation is complete, the same group of grand jurors ordinarily will then be called upon to determine whether the evidence produced is sufficient to issue an indictment.

2. ***Historical Developments***. At the time of the adoption of the Constitution, the grand jury was an institution revered not only for its independence in screening, but also for its service as a "public watchdog," uncovering and proceeding against criminal activity that government officials chose to ignore. The colonial grand juries not only refused to issue indictments in infamous prosecutions sought by the Crown (e.g., in the Peter Zenger case), but also brought charges (to which the Crown was opposed) against various royal officials (including British soldiers). It was the screening function of the grand jury that was guaranteed as a constitutional safeguard for the accused in the grand jury clauses of various state constitutions and in the Fifth Amendment of the federal constitution. These provisions also recognized, however, in an indirect way, the investiga-

aa. For citations to relevant source materials, as well as a much more detailed and comprehensive discussion of grand jury investigations, see Sara Sun Beale, William C. Bryson, James E. Felman, & Michael J. Elston, *Grand Jury Law and Practice* (2d Ed. 1998) (hereafter cited as Beale et al.); Susan W. Brenner & Gregory G. Lockhart, *Federal Grand Jury* (1996) (hereafter cited as Brenner & Lockhart); CRIMPROC §§ 8.1–8.15.

a. Various aspects of the grand jury's procedure and structure relate both to its screening and investigatory functions. Those aspects that have a major impact upon its investigatory performance are discussed in this Chapter. Others that have a less significant bearing on investigations are discussed in Chapter 16. The composition of the grand jury, because it arguably has a greater impact on the screening function, is discussed in Chapter 16. See also Ch. 1, § 2, step (11).

tive authority of the grand jury. The grand jury clauses required that prosecutions for felonies be brought by a grand jury's "indictment" or "presentment." The indictment was the charging instrument issued by a grand jury on finding that the evidence presented to it by a prosecuting official was sufficient to justify forcing the accused to trial. The presentment was the charging instrument issued by the grand jury on its own initiative (i.e., not at the request of prosecuting officials). Presentments often were based on information provided initially by citizen complainants (or by a grand juror), which then was supplemented through the use of the grand jury's investigative authority. Thus, in recognizing the presentment, the grand jury clauses arguably assumed the continued use of the grand jury's investigative authority.

Over the first half of the nineteenth century, grand juries, particularly in the western states, actively reviewed a wide range of grievances presented by citizens, and achieved a reputation as the foremost "public watchdog" as a result of their investigations into governmental corruption and widespread evasions of the law. Over that last half of that century, however, several developments combined to alter the character and significance of grand jury investigations.

As local police departments became a major element of law enforcement administration, and expanded their investigative capabilities, there was less need for grand juries to be involved in the investigation of many types of offenses that had previously attracted their attention. At the same time, local prosecutors came to exercise a virtual monopoly over the decision to prosecute, and private parties were no longer able to institute prosecutions after first having received the investigative and charging assistance of the grand jury. As a result, the grand jury came to be called upon to investigate only where the prosecutor requested its assistance, and then did so under the leadership of the prosecutor.

Moreover, in a growing number of states, the grand jury was no longer a continuously functioning body, and that development restricted its investigative role even in assisting the prosecutor. Many states, as part of a sweeping reform movement, eliminated the requirement that all felony charges be screened and approved by a grand jury. They granted prosecutors the option of proceeding either by grand jury indictment or by a prosecutor's information. With indictments no longer required, many counties in such states discontinued the practice of having standing grand juries. A prosecutor seeking the investigatory assistance of a grand jury would have to petition the court for impanelment of a special grand jury, and that imposed administrative and political costs that caused prosecutors to act only in exceptional cases.

Over the twentieth century, the investigative role of the grand jury varied considerably among the states (and sometimes among counties within a state). Where grand juries continued to be used for screening, the common pattern was to also continue to make use of their investigative authority, but only for a select group of crimes. Use of the grand jury for investigations tended to be less frequent in those states that commonly prosecuted by information and therefore did not have standing grand juries. In some, prosecutors regularly sought the assistance of specially impaneled grand juries, but did so for an even narrower band of offenses than prosecutors in indictment jurisdictions. The two groups of offenses most often calling for the grand jury's investigative assistance were offenses involving complex financial transactions and offenses involving the widespread distribution of illegal services. The latter investigations led to the popular description of the grand jury as the nation's "number one instrument of discovery against organized crime." In other information jurisdictions, prosecutors rarely, if ever, sought the impanelment of grand juries (in part, because these prosecutors simply did not deal with the offenses that most clearly required the investigative tools of the grand jury).

Perhaps the most prominent state grand jury investigations of the twentieth century were the investigations of public corruption.[b] As in the nineteenth century, although with less frequency, those investigations were at times largely the product of the initiative of the grand jurors. While some states now restricted the grand jury to investigating matters put before it by the prosecutor, and others adopted procedural barriers to grand jury initiated investigations (e.g., prohibiting citizens from conveying their complaints directly to the grand jury), most states retained what was described at common law as the "independent inquisitorial authority" of the grand jury. Of course, that authority was subject to severe practical restraints if the grand jury could not commandeer the resources available to the prosecutor, but in some instances, reluctant prosecutors acceded to the grand jurors' wishes when they threatened otherwise to become a "runaway grand jury," and in other instances, the grand jury successfully petitioned the court for the appointment of a special prosecutor.

The federal criminal justice system undoubtedly made the most extensive use of the grand jury's investigative authority through most of the twentieth century. The federal system dealt far more frequently than the states with offenses that could be uncovered only by unraveling a complex criminal structure or obtaining and analyzing extensive business records. Federal investigations of white collar crime, regulatory offenses, and the various transactions of criminal "gangs" and "families" naturally called for use of the investigative powers available to the grand jury. Federal success in the prosecution of these crimes added luster to government's use of the grand jury's investigative authority, but the potential for misuse of that authority was highlighted by other federal grand jury investigations (in particular, the investigations of alleged criminal activities of radical groups—primarily during the Viet Nam War era—that were characterized by some observers as directed more at harassment than developing supportable indictments). That potential led to a series of proposed reforms aimed at restricting the investigative authority of grand juries and expanding the rights of grand jury witnesses. These proposals met with some success at the state level, where, for example, over twenty states adopted legislation allowing grand jury witnesses to be accompanied by counsel (see Note 10, p. 847). Congress, however, consistently rejected the proposed reform legislation. It left the regulation of federal grand jury investigations to the federal judiciary (which largely continued with the standards of the common law) and to internal regulations of the Department of Justice (which did direct federal prosecutors to adhere to certain procedural protections that had been part of the reform proposals).

3. *Current status.* Only eighteen states still require prosecution by indictment in all felony cases, and most of these states continue to utilize the investigative authority of the grand jury on a fairly regular basis. While the vast majority of the cases brought before the grand jury have been fully investigated by the police, in a small percentage, the grand jury's investigative authority will be used to "finish off" the investigation, and in a still smaller percentage, the primary investigation will be conducted by the prosecution through the grand jury. This latter group will involve crimes in which the grand jury's investigative

b. The grand jury's "public watchdog" image rested historically on two quite different aspects of its investigative authority: (1) the investigation of criminal activity of public officials, leading to indictments and presentments; and (2) the investigation of inefficiency, negligence, and malfeasance in public administration, leading to grand jury reports, issued to the community. While the grand jury's reporting authority has been restricted or eliminated in many jurisdictions, it had been retained in many others, with grand juries even assigned by statute the duty of periodically investigating and reporting on certain aspects of public administration (e.g., conditions in jails). The discussion in this chapter is limited to the investigation of potentially criminal behavior. As for grand jury reports and investigations conducted in connection with those reports, see CRIMPROC § 8.3(h).

authority offers one or more of the advantages over police investigative authority that are discussed in subsection B infra. In states in which prosecutions are traditionally brought by information, grand juries tend to be used only in the investigation of the most pressing of such offenses. In some counties in such states, as a result of prosecutors not encountering such crimes or lacking adequate resources, grand jury investigations are not simply rare, but nonexistent.

In the federal system, on the other hand, use of the grand jury's investigative authority continues to be ubiquitous (although not a feature found in the majority of federal prosecutions). Indeed, in the more heavily populated federal districts, where several grand juries will be sitting at the same time, one or more of these grand juries will be assigned to investigations that are likely to run at least several months. Such grand juries are likely to be impaneled not under Federal Rule 6(a), but under the Organized Crime Control Act (18 U.S.C.A. §§ 3322–34), which provides for an 18 month grand jury term that can be extended to 36 months.

B. Investigative Advantages

Compared to police investigations, grand jury investigations are expensive, time consuming, and logistically cumbersome. Accordingly, the grand jury ordinarily is used to investigate only when it has a distinct investigative advantage over the police. The grand jury's advantages in investigating criminal activity stem primarily from the six elements of its investigatory processes discussed below—(1) the use of the subpoena ad testificandum, (2) the psychological pressure imposed by the grand jury setting, (3) the use of immunity grants, (4) the use of the subpoena duces tecum (5) grand jury secrecy requirements, and (6) public confidence attributable to lay participation. These advantages become significant where criminal investigators must gain the assistance of victims or witnesses who are reluctant to cooperate, unravel a complex criminal structure, obtain information contained in extensive business records, or keep a continuing investigative effort from the public gaze. Criminal activities that often present one or more of these difficulties include public corruption (e.g., bribery), misuse of economic power (e.g., price-fixing), the widespread distribution of illegal services and goods (e.g., gambling and narcotics distribution), complex fraudulent schemes, and various regulatory violations. Most grand jury investigations are directed at such offenses, but a particular advantage of the grand jury's investigative authority also may come into play in the course of an investigation of the type of crime that ordinarily can be successfully resolved by the police alone (e.g., where a key witness to an assault refuses to give testimony and must be compelled to do so through a grant of immunity).

1. *Subpoena ad testificandum*. The basic investigative advantage provided by the grand jury is its authority to compel the production of evidence through the subpoena authority of the court that impaneled it. The subpoena duces tecum (discussed in Note 4 infra) is available to compel the production of tangible evidence, while the subpoena ad testificandum is available to compel persons to appear before the grand jury and give testimony. Both subpoenas are supported by the court's authority to hold in contempt any person who willfully refuses, without legal justification, to comply with a subpoena's directive.[c]

c. The contemnor may be held in either civil or criminal contempt. Civil contempt is used to coerce the contemnor into complying with the subpoena. The contemnor is sentenced to imprisonment or to a fine (which may increase daily), but he may purge himself of the sentence by complying with the subpoena. As courts have frequently noted, he "carries the keys to the prison in his pocket." The civil contemnor who refuses to purge himself will remain under sentence until the grand jury completes its term and is discharged. Moreover, if the information the contemnor possesses is still needed, he may be subpoenaed

The contempt sanction makes the subpoena ad testificandum particularly useful in obtaining statements from persons who will not voluntarily furnish information to the police. While those persons have the right to refuse to cooperate with the police, their refusal to comply with a grand jury subpoena invokes the threat of a possible jail sentence. Faced with that threat, a recalcitrant witness often will have a change of heart and will give to the grand jury information that he previously refused to give to the police. Of course, if the information sought could be incriminating, the witness (unless granted immunity) may still refuse to cooperate by relying on his privilege against self-incrimination. However, many persons unwilling to furnish information to the police, will willingly testify before the grand jury without regard to whether the self-incrimination privilege might offer an avenue for refusing to do so. Thus, the victim of a fraudulent gambling operation or a loansharking operation may be either too embarrassed or too fearful to voluntarily furnish information to the police, yet be willing to furnish that information to the grand jury when faced with the threat of contempt. Similarly, an employee may wish to avoid the appearance of voluntarily assisting officials investigating his employer, yet testify freely under the compulsion of a subpoena.

The grand jury subpoena ad testificandum also has the advantage of requiring witnesses to testify under oath. If a witness fails to tell the truth, he may be prosecuted for perjury. Generally, a person who gives false information to a police officer will not have committed a crime (though there is such a crime as to federal investigators). Accordingly, where a witness might be willing to talk to the police, but also is likely to "shade his story," requiring him to testify before a grand jury may produce more complete and truthful statements. Even where a witness is willing to give an entirely truthful statement to the police, there may be value in requiring him to testify before the grand jury. Arguably, a person who has testified under oath before the grand jury will be somewhat more hesitant to "change his story" when he testifies at trial. Also, if the witness does change his story and his prior statement is used to impeach him, the petit jurors may give greater weight to his prior grand jury testimony than they would to a prior statement he made to the police.

2. *Psychological pressure.* In addition to the compulsion of the subpoena, the psychological pressure of grand jury interrogation also is cited as a factor that frequently enables the grand jury to obtain statements from witnesses unwilling to cooperate with the police. Of course the pressure accompanying police custodial interrogation may be greater, but a prerequisite for such interrogation is the probable cause needed to take a person into custody. Persons can be called to testify before the grand jury without probable cause (or even reasonable suspicion).

Proponents of grand jury investigations claim that the psychological pressure of grand jury interrogation stems from the moral force exerted by the grand jury. Thus, two prosecuting attorneys note:

> "Most witnesses before grand juries feel a moral compulsion to be honest and forthright in discharging their duties as citizens, because their peers, the members of the grand jury, have also been taken away from their jobs, businesses, and private pursuits, and have accepted the inconvenience of becoming involved. The grand jurors manifest a serious purpose and are persons with whom witnesses can identify. Thus, even though their associates may be determined not to cooperate, certain witnesses may be ashamed to

by a successor grand jury and held in contempt again if he continues to refuse to supply that information.

engage or persist in deceitful or obstreperous conduct to deny the grand jury the information it needs." John Keeney & Paul Walsh, *The American Bar Association's Grand Jury Principles: A Critique From A Federal Criminal Justice Perspective,* 14 Idaho L.Rev. 545, 579 (1978).

On the other side, critics of grand jury investigations claim that the psychological pressure stems primarily from what they describe as the "star chamber setting" of grand jury interrogation. "In all of the United States legal system," they note, "no person stands more alone than a witness before a grand jury; in a secret hearing he faces an often hostile prosecutor and 23 strangers with no judge present to guard his rights, no lawyer present to counsel him, and sometimes no indication of why he is being questioned." As to many jurisdictions, this description of the pressure presented by the witness' predicament is clearly overstated, as the witness may consult with counsel (located within the grand jury room in some jurisdictions, and in an outside anteroom in others) prior to answering a troubling question. See Notes 9-10, pp. 847–48. However, even here, the witness faces the pressures of being subjected to a far ranging inquiry, without knowing in advance what will be asked (or sometimes, even the subject matter under inquiry), while aware that answers deemed false could well lead to a perjury prosecution. At the same time, the witness may fear that repeated consultations with counsel will be viewed by the grand jury as an attempt at evasion.

3. ***Immunity grants.*** An immunity grant is a court order granting a witness sufficient immunity from future prosecution to supplant the witness' self-incrimination privilege. Once the recalcitrant witness has been granted immunity, he may no longer rely upon the privilege. Since immunity grants are tied to the exercise of the privilege by a person under a legal obligation to testify, they are not available to persons who simply refuse to give a statement to the police. At the investigatory stage, almost the only way the prosecution can make use of an immunity grant is in conjunction with a subpoena directing the uncooperative witness to testify before the grand jury. The immunity grant may be needed to gain information from various types of recalcitrant witnesses. For example, immunity quite frequently is given to a lower-level participant in organized crime in order to obtain testimony against higher-level participants. It also often is used to force testimony from witnesses who are not themselves involved in criminal activities, but desire not to give testimony that may hurt others. Although the privilege is not available simply to protect others (see Note 2, p. 839), witnesses who do not actually fear personal incrimination have been known to falsely claim that they do in order to avoid testifying against their friends. Since such claims are difficult to dispute, the prosecutor may simply prefer to grant the witness immunity.

4. ***Subpoena duces tecum.*** The grand jury subpoena duces tecum offers several advantages over the primary device available to the police for obtaining documents and other physical evidence—the search pursuant to a warrant. Unlike the search warrant, the subpoena duces tecum can issue without a showing of probable cause. Moreover, even where probable cause can be established, there are times when the subpoena duces tecum will offer administrative advantages. These advantages are less likely to prevail where documents are sought from the target of the investigation, as there is often a concern that the target will destroy, conceal, or alter the documents rather than properly comply with the subpoena. However, there are instances in which the target would find it too risky to take such actions (typically the case as to records that have been shared with employees or advisors), and here the subpoena might be used even though a search warrant alternative is available. For example, there may be a need to seize so many records from various locations that a search would be impractical. With a subpoena duces tecum, the recipient of the subpoena is required to undertake the

extensive task of bringing together the records from several different locations and sorting through them to collect those covered by the subpoena. Also, the subpoena may broadly describe the documents sought, thereby ensuring that no relevant documents are missed (a risk not so readily avoided in meeting the "particularity of description" requirement of a search warrant). A subpoena also has the advantage of keeping the grounding of the investigation from the target, as it will include only a brief statement of the subject of the grand jury's inquiry. A search warrant, on the other hand, requires an affidavit setting forth the specifics of the probable cause supporting the search, and that affidavit is available to the target (absent a not-readily-obtainable sealing order).[d]

Although the Supreme Court has held that the Fourth Amendment does not preclude use of a search to obtain documents from a disinterested third party (e.g., a bank) (see Note 2, p. 274), the subpoena duces tecum remains the standard vehicle for obtaining documents from such third parties, both where the government has and does not have probable cause to seize the documents.[e] The primary concerns here are to avoid the disruptive impact of a search upon the third party (typically a commercial entity) and to gain the party's cooperation and expertise in identifying and locating the records sought.

Finally, the subpoena avoids the risk of a complete loss of evidence. Where the search was made pursuant to a warrant so deficient as preclude police reliance upon the "good faith" exception to the exclusionary rule (see Note 7, p. 237), or the execution of the search was unconstitutional (see Pt. B, pp. 308–16), the government loses the use of unconstitutionally seized documents and any additional evidence that falls within the "fruit of the poisonous tree doctrine". On the other hand, where a subpoena duces tecum is impermissible in scope or issuance, the challenge must be raised prior to the response and the consequence of a successful challenge is a quashing of the subpoena. This allows the government to refashion the subpoena to meet the sustained objections, so there is no loss of evidence that could have been obtained through a curable illegality.

5. ***Secrecy.*** Grand jury secrecy requirements vary somewhat from one jurisdiction to another, but even the weakest of secrecy requirements is thought to add to the grand jury's effectiveness as an investigative agency. All jurisdictions

d. These potential advantages of the grand jury subpoena may, in turn, be offset by certain administrative advantages presented by the search warrant process, even where there is no serious concern that the target would conceal, destroy, or alter the documents identified in the subpoena (a risk avoided by the search process, as it comes without advance notice). Those administrative advantages of the search warrant include: (1) the search gives the government immediate access to the documents (the subpoena must provide a reasonable time for delivery and delivery may be further delayed by a motion challenging the subpoena); (2) the search places an officer in a position to examine a larger body of documents in seeking to identify these specified in the warrant, and should the officer find in plain view any incriminating documents beyond those the government had anticipated, the officer can seize those documents; (3) the officer executing the warrant may gain valuable information from discussions with the target or the target's employees in the course of executing the search; (4) the disruptive impact of the search may convey to the target the message that the government is taking a tough, aggressive stance; (5) the use of a search may be publicized and convey a similar message to the public, whereas the issuance of a grand jury subpoena cannot be made public by the government, and (6) an individual (though not an entity) may raise a self-incrimination objection to the required production of documents under a subpoena, but that objection is not available where the documents are seized by the government (see Note 7, p. 857).

e. In the federal system, the Privacy Protection Act, 42 U.S.C.A. § 2000–a–11, restricts the use of search warrants to obtain documentary materials in the possession of a "disinterested third party." The guidelines adopted pursuant to the directive of that Act, found in 28 CFR § 59.4, require that applications for such search warrants receive the prior authorization of an "attorney for the government" (except in cases of an emergency), and conditions such authorization on a determination that use of a subpoena (rather than a search) "would substantially jeopardize the availability or usefulness of the material sought."

prohibit the prosecutor, the prosecutor's staff (including investigative agents), the grand jurors, and the grand jury stenographer from disclosing grand jury testimony and other information relating directly to grand jury proceedings (e.g., what persons have been subpoenaed), unless such disclosure is authorized by the court upon a special showing of need.[f] Although several jurisdictions extend this obligation of secrecy to grand jury witnesses (who thereby are prohibited from disclosing their participation and their testimony to persons other than counsel), the vast majority (including the federal system) do not attempt to hold a witness to a secrecy obligation. Here, witnesses are free to disclose publicly or privately both their own testimony and whatever information was revealed to them in the course of giving that testimony.

In *United States v. Procter & Gamble Co.,* 356 U.S. 677 (1958), the Supreme Court noted five objectives of grand jury secrecy requirements imposed in the federal system:

> "(1) to prevent the escape of those whose indictment may be contemplated; (2) to insure the utmost freedom to the grand jury in its deliberations, and to prevent persons subject to indictment or their friends from importuning the grand jurors; (3) to prevent subornation of perjury or tampering with the witnesses who may testify before grand jury and later appear at the trial of those indicted by it; (4) to encourage free and untrammeled disclosures by persons who have information with respect to the commission of crimes; (5) to protect the innocent accused who is exonerated from disclosure of the fact that he has been under investigation, and from the expense of standing trial where there was no probability of guilt."

While the second objective cited by the Court relates primarily to the screening function of the grand jury, the remaining four promote the grand jury's effectiveness as an investigative agency. The first objective—preventing the flight of the person being investigated—depends initially upon the grand jury having no need to subpoena the target as that would clearly put the target on notice (indeed, in the federal system and many states, a subpoenaed party will be informed if he, she, or it is a target of the investigation). Assuming information is sought only from witnesses, there remains the need to ensure that the witnesses do not inform the target of the inquiry. In the vast majority of jurisdictions, since the witnesses are not sworn to secrecy, this depends upon the inclination of the witnesses (although court orders prohibiting disclosure during an ongoing investigation may be possible). It is debatable whether a witness is more likely to be inclined not to inform the target where the investigation is being conducted by the grand jury, as opposed to the police, although grand jury witnesses do have the added assurance that the people conducting a grand jury investigation are prohibited by law from "going public" with the investigation.

Grand jury secrecy arguably makes a more substantial contribution to the third objective noted in *Procter & Gamble*—precluding subornation of perjury and witness tampering. Even should some of the initial witnesses inform the target of the ongoing investigation, that information may not be sufficiently detailed to allow the target to anticipate who else will be called before the grand jury, and

f. As a result, neither the prosecutor nor the prosecutor's investigative staff may make a public disclosure as to what the grand jury is investigating, who has been subpoenaed, or what evidence has been uncovered by the grand jury. Neither state nor federal law, similarly restricts the police or prosecutor from making public statements relating to the character, status, and elements of their ongoing investigations (although individual units may impose internal controls). See Daniel C. Richman, *Grand Jury Secrecy: Plugging the Leaks in an Empty Bucket*, 36 Am.Crim.L.Rev. 399 (1999) (suggesting that several of the justifications supporting grand jury secrecy are equally applicable to police investigations); United States Attorneys' Manual § 1–7.530 (internal D.O.J. standard as to public disclosure of information concerning ongoing investigations).

once the witnesses have testified under oath, a major shift in their later testimony is likely to raise suspicions of witness tampering. Where the target does anticipate in advance who will testify, there remains the obstacle of having no means to be certain that the witness testified as the target demanded. The witness has the protection of testifying in a closed proceeding (even counsel, who may have been provided by the target, is excluded in the federal system and many states). Thus, what the target learns of a witness' testimony is only what the witness chooses to tell the target (subject to the possibility of post-indictment discovery as discussed below).

The fourth objective noted in *Procter & Gamble* probably is the most significant for investigatory success. Witnesses often are much more willing to testify if they know that their identity will be kept from the target and the public (typically because they fear attempts at intimidation, fear economic or social repercussions, or simply seek to avoid notoriety). Though the jurisdiction does not swear witnesses to secrecy, witnesses know that, if they decide not to reveal their participation and testimony, the obligation of secrecy imposed on the grand jurors and prosecution personnel provides assurance that those persons will not reveal that information.

Of course, if an indictment is issued and the grand jury witness is called as a trial witness (indeed, in some jurisdictions, if the prosecution simply anticipates possibly calling him as a trial witness), his participation (and his grand jury testimony) will become known to the defendant (and probably the public).[g] However, even if an indictment is issued, the grand jury witness may not be needed as a prospective trial witness (the witness' testimony may be unnecessary in light of leads he and others provide to more incriminating evidence) or a trial may not occur (e.g., the defendant may plead guilty). Moreover, if the grand jury witness can be assured that his identity will be revealed only in connection with the issuance of an indictment,[h] he may have fewer qualms about testifying fully and truthfully. He may be less wary of being criticized as an "informer" if he knows that his role will be revealed only after a grand jury has supported his judgment and veracity by issuing an indictment.

g. Where a witness testifies at trial, all jurisdictions will make his prior grand jury testimony available to the defense for impeachment purposes. See CRIMPROC § 24.3(c). In many jurisdictions, the prosecution must disclose in pretrial discovery the names of its intended witnesses and their prior recorded statements (which includes grand jury testimony). In others, including the federal system, pretrial disclosure of the names of prospective witnesses is not required. See CRIMPROC §§ 8.5(f), 20.3(i).

Documents disclosed to the defendant as part of pretrial discovery generally are viewed as outside of public record provisions, and therefore are not automatically accessible to the media. See CRIMPROC § 23.1(d). However, should the prior testimony be used at trial, it clearly becomes a public document.

h. Whether or not an indictment is issued, disclosure is still a possibility should a court permit disclosure of grand jury testimony to participants in a civil litigation involving the same subject matter. However, courts considering requests that they order such disclosure give great weight to the grand jury witness' interest in keeping his testimony secret. Consider, e.g., *Douglas Oil Co. of California v. Petrol Stops Northwest,* 441 U.S. 211 (1979), where the Supreme Court (in discussing the "particularized need" standard that must be met by the civil litigant to gain disclosure) noted: "[I]n considering the effects of disclosure on grand jury proceedings, the courts must consider not only the immediate effects upon a particular grand jury, but also the possible effect upon the functioning of future grand juries. Persons called upon to testify will consider the likelihood that their testimony may one day be disclosed to outside parties. Fear of future retribution or social stigma may act as powerful deterrents to those who would come forward and aid the grand jury in the performance of its duties. Concern as to the future consequences of frank and full testimony is heightened where the witness is an employee of a company under investigation. Thus, the interests in grand jury secrecy, although reduced, are not eliminated merely because the grand jury has ended its activities."

The fifth objective noted in *Procter & Gamble* serves, in part, to justify the sweeping investigative power granted to the grand jury. Where an investigation can be based on "tips" and "rumors" (see *Dionisio*, p. 818), there is special need to protect the reputation of the target of the investigation (who may well be innocent). That protection is provided by secrecy requirements that prohibit those involved in the grand jury investigation from disclosing to the media and others the identity of those under investigation. This shield of secrecy is thought to be especially important in the investigation of public figures, and, indeed, needed to overcome a natural hesitancy to pursue investigations of such persons in the absence of strong evidence of criminality.

Critics contend, however, that grand jury secrecy requirements are practically worthless in the investigation of high profile targets. They note that, in the vast majority of jurisdictions, the secrecy requirements do not extend to grand jury witnesses, and a witness hostile to the target may be eager to inform a curious media of questioning relating to the target.[i] In many jurisdictions, those secrecy requirements also do not bar a prosecutor from releasing to the media a carefully worded description of the investigation and its targets that simply avoids reference to the activities of the grand jury itself. Where the target is aware of the investigation and is a corporate enterprise, it will have an obligation to investors to reveal that it is being investigated by a grand jury investigation. Above all critics argue, even where the target, the witnesses, and the prosecutor all desire to keep "under wraps" the investigation of a high profile target, there remains a distinct possibility of an "unauthorized leak" by investigators or other prosecution personnel. Here, it is claimed, the potential sanctions for violating grand jury secrecy through improper leaking of grand jury testimony lose their effectiveness as a deterrent as the person leaking that information generally can do so through a reporter who will not only publish the information but also protect the identity of her source (even if that means risking a contempt sanction for refusing to provide that information, generally not privileged, in a subsequent judicial inquiry regarding the leak). The strength of this contention cannot be determined as an empirical matter. Admittedly, the media not infrequently reports on grand jury investigations of high profile targets, attributing its information to an anonymous source, but courts conducting inquiries directed at determining whether the anonymous source was a person bound by grand jury secrecy requirements or some other person familiar with the investigation (e.g., a witness or an agent of the target) have almost uniformly been unable to identify that source.

i. Even in those jurisdictions which extend grand jury secrecy to witnesses, it is not certain that the state may prohibit the witness from "going public" after the investigation has ended. *Butterworth v. Smith*, 494 U.S. 624 (1990), sustained a First Amendment challenge to a state secrecy requirement so broad as to prohibit the witness from disclosing the "content, gist, or import" of his testimony notwithstanding the discharge of the grand jury. The Court emphasized, however, that ruling was based on the secrecy requirement having prohibited the disclosure of information that the witness "had acquired on his own" (i.e., apart from his grand jury testimony). Thus, *Hoffmann-Pugh v. Keenan*, 338 F.3d 1136 (10th Cir.2003), distinguished *Butterworth* in sustaining a secrecy rule that prohibited the witness from disclosing in a forthcoming publication her experience in testifying before a now-discharged grand jury that had investigated a famous unsolved murder (of Jon Benet Ramsey). Although the investigation there was potentially ongoing (through a new grand jury), the Tenth Circuit also emphasized that the secrecy requirement here was limited to what had transpired before the grand (and thus "did not prohibit disclosure of information the witness already had independently of the grand jury process") and that the state secrecy rule permitted a witness to apply to the court for a determination that secrecy was no longer needed, which would "free he[r] of the [secrecy] restriction * * * at such time as the investigation is truly closed and the state no longer has a legitimate interest in preserving the secrecy of the testimony." The court did not discuss whether the state would have such a legitimate interest in preserving secrecy as to the identity of non-indicted grand jury targets even after an investigation is "truly closed".

6. ***Maintaining public confidence.*** Where the subject to be investigated is a matter of public knowledge (as in the case of investigations into matters already given considerable media coverage), grand jury participation often helps in maintaining community confidence in the integrity of the investigatory process. This is especially important where the person under investigation is a public official. The community tends to be suspicious of partisan influences in such investigations, especially where the investigation results in a decision not to prosecute. As one court noted: "Where corruption is charged, it is desirable to have someone outside the administration [i.e., the grand jury] act, so that the image, as well as the fact of impartiality in the investigation can be preserved and allegations of cover-up or white-wash can be avoided." *Losavio v. Kikel,* 529 P.2d 306 (Colo.1974). The prosecutor may also look to the grand jury to help allay other public concerns, as in cases in which investigated parties are almost certain to claim police and prosecutor harassment.

C. Alternative Routes to Investigation by Subpoena

The primary investigative tool of the grand jury is the subpoena, and many jurisdictions grant the subpoena power to other agencies for either criminal investigations or civil investigations that may uncover evidence of criminal activities. As discussed below, to some extent, the law governing grand jury investigations also bears on these agencies as well.

1. ***Alternative criminal investigative authority.*** A small number of states have created investigate authorities which are roughly similar to the grand jury, except that they utilize judges or other officials rather than lay grand juries. These investigative alternatives include the "one man grand jury" (a judge acting, in effect, as a grand jury, assisted by a specially appointed prosecutor), the "John Doe" proceeding (a prosecutorial inquiry into the commission of specified criminal activity, conducted before a judge), and the special crime commission (typically a specially created state commission assigned to investigating and reporting on a particular type of crime). In some instances, these investigative authorities can actually bring criminal charges, while in others the prosecutor must decide whether to proceed on the results of the investigation.

Several states authorize the local prosecutor to use subpoenas in the investigation of some or all offenses. Some condition such authority on the prior approval of the court in the individual case (requiring a showing of need), while others allow the prosecution to issue the subpoenas on its own initiative (although they are then subject to challenge in court). Still other states grant investigative subpoena authority to the state's Attorney General as to certain types of offenses.

In the federal system, Congress has granted to U.S. Attorneys and other Justice Department attorneys the authority to issue administrative subpoenas in the investigation of specific areas of potential criminal liability, including: health care offenses and offenses involving the sexual exploitation of children, 18 U.S.C.A. § 3486 (limited to the production of records or other tangible); offenses relating to controlled substances, 21 U.S.C.A. § 876 (subpoena may compel production of records and attendance and testimony of witnesses); racketeering offenses, 18 U.S.C.A. § 1968 (civil investigative demand, which operates as an administrative subpoena duces tecum); and fraud on government contracts, 31 U.S.C.A. § 3733 (also a civil investigative demand). These subpoenas, or subpoena-counterparts, operate in the same fashion as the administrative agency subpoenas discussed in Note 2 infra. See *In re Administrative Subpoena*, 253 F.3d 256 (6th Cir.2001). In dealing with possible terrorism, Congress has taken a further step and authorized the F.B.I. to obtain a court order "requiring the production of any tangible things (including books, records, papers, documents and other items) for an investigation to obtain foreign intelligence information not concerning a United States person or to protect against international terrorism or clandestine intelligence activities, provided that such investigation of a United States person is not conducted solely upon the basis of activities protected by the first amendment to the Constitution." 50 U.S.C.A. § 1861[j]

2. ***Civil administrative subpoenas.*** Most federal administrative agencies and many state administrative agencies are given administrative subpoena authority, to be used in the investigation of possible regulatory provisions (which may often constitute criminal as well as civil violations, as on the case of S.E.C. violations). The administrative subpoenas (also called "summonses") may compel the production of documents or the appearance and giving of testimony. Administrative subpoenas, unlike grand jury subpoenas, do not utilize the process of the court (which use, in the grand jury context, places on the recipient the legal obligation of either complying or challenging the subpoena by a motion to quash). To enforce an administrative subpoena, the agency must bring an independent civil action. Should the administrative investigatory process produce evidence of a criminal violation, that evidence may be turned over to the prosecutor with a request for prosecution.

3. ***Legal similarities and differences.*** The alternative routes to investigation by subpoena tend to differ in several important respects from the grand jury subpoena. Apart from the grand jury counterparts (e.g., the one-man grand jury), they do not ask that testimony be given (or documents produced) in a closed proceeding. Where a witness is required to appear to give testimony, that witness may be accompanied by counsel. Since the enforcement of administrative subpoenas is by a civil suit, the judicial enforcement of the subpoena presents a final judgment and may be appealed in the same manner as an civil judgment (in contrast to the enforcement of a grand jury subpoena, where the party directed to comply ordinarily can gain review only by being held in contempt). Since the administrative subpoena is commonly tied to the investigation of a limited class of offenses and often subject to other statutory limits as well, the standard of judicial review may be somewhat more rigorous than the very limited Rule 17(c) standard applied to grand jury subpoenas (see e.g., *R. Enterprises, Inc.*, p. 824).

On the other hand, the Fourth Amendment standard applied to subpoenas duces tecum are similar for grand juries, grand jury counterparts, and administrative subpoenas. The application of the self-incrimination privilege is identical, and thus one of the leading case on the application of the privilege to the production of documents (see *Fisher*, p. 857) involves an Internal Revenue Service summons rather than a grand jury subpoena. Similarly, where the applicable state or federal law allows the prosecutor or agency given subpoena authority to replace the self-incrimination privilege with an immunity order, the same constitutional standards

j. This provision states that the court "shall enter an ex parte order as requested, or as modified, approving the release of records if the judge finds that application meets the requirement of this section." Whether that language allows judicial review of the type applied to administrative subpoenas (see Note 3 infra) is debatable. Compare Christopher Slobogin, *Transaction Surveillance by the Government*, ___ U.Miss.L.Rev. ___ (2005), with Paul Rosenzweig, *Civil Liberty and the Response to Terrorism*, 42 Duq.L.Rev. 663, 694–96 (2004). Consider also *Doe v. Ashcroft*, 334 F.Supp.2d 471 (S.D.N.Y.2004) (discussing a similar question as to the role of judicial review under the National Security Letter procedure, 18 U.S.C.A. § 2709, which allows the F.B.I. to itself issue a directive to an internet service provider or telephone company to compel production of subscriber information, including certain transactional records).

50 U.S.C.A. § 1861 also provides that "no person shall disclose to any other person (other than those persons necessary to produce the tangible things under this section) that the Federal Bureau of Investigation has sought or obtained tangible things under this section." As to prohibitions against disclosure by grand jury witnesses subpoenaed to produce tangible things (primarily documents), see Notes 2–3, pp. 836–38.

apply to immunity granted in that setting as immunity granted in the grand jury setting (see Pt. B, pp. 848–52).

D. Judicial Regulation: Some Differing Perspectives

1. ***CRIMPROC § 8.2(c).*** "The grand jury investigation is frequently described as introducing an 'inquisitorial element' into a criminal justice system that is basically accusatorial. Critics argue that the grand jury's investigative authority should therefore be viewed as an anomaly and kept within narrow confines by close judicial supervision. They recognize that this position faces difficulties if history reveals that the grand jury inquest was accepted from the outset as an institution that coexisted with the accusatorial elements of the Anglo–American criminal justice process. The critics argue, however, that a careful reading of the history of the grand jury reveals no such accommodation. First, they note, the early grand juries did not frequently exercise the basic element of its modern investigative authority—its power to compel testimony—but instead relied primarily upon information known to the jurors or the voluntary testimony of aggrieved persons. Secondly, they argue, the investigative role of the grand jury was not critical to its initial acceptance in this country. It was the shielding role of the grand jury that earned it a place in the Bill of Rights and the early state constitutions. The grand jury's investigatory role was then viewed as entirely secondary and not necessarily distinct from its screening role. Today, it is argued, the significance of the two roles has been reversed.

"Supporters of the grand jury respond that the early history of the grand jury clearly establishes the legitimacy of its extensive investigative authority. The power of the grand jury to compel testimony was recognized well before the adoption of the Constitution and was used in some of the most notable grand jury inquests. At the time of the Constitution's adoption, the grand jury was a revered institution not simply because it served as a buffer between the state and the individual, but equally for its service as a watchdog against public corruption and its capacity to ferret out criminal activity that local officials either chose to ignore or were unable to investigate. The importance of this investigative authority was implicitly recognized, it is argued, in constitutional and statutory provisions authorizing the institution of prosecution by presentment as well as indictment.

"With few exceptions, American courts have accepted the position that the history of the grand jury provides a solid foundation for its broad investigative authority. The Supreme Court's discussion of that authority in *Blair v. United States* [see Note 2 infra] is typical.[k] The Court there noted that the grand jury's authority to resort to compulsory process had been recognized in England as early as 1612, and the inquisitorial function of the grand jury was well established at the time of the Constitution's adoption. Both the Fifth Amendment and the earliest federal statutes recognized an investigative authority of the grand jury that included the 'same powers that pertained to its British prototype.' The Supreme Court would not view that authority with suspicion and subject it to new limitations. * * *

k. Consider, however, Niki Kuckes, *The Useful Dangerous Fiction of Grand Jury Independence*, 41 Amer.Crim.L.Rev. 1 (2004), arguing that the Supreme Court opinions have as frequently sustained the broad investigative authority of the grand jury not because of the grand jury's role as a law enforcement agency (highlighted in *Blair*), but because of its role as a "protective bulwark," reasoning that such investigative powers are needed to ensure that it properly exercises its screening function (i.e., "the Supreme Court has broadly claimed that the grand jury is given broad investigative powers for the putative defendant's benefit"). The author cites as illustrative the last paragraph of the Dionisio opinion, quoted at p. 819.

"Critics of the grand jury also contend that even if a broad investigative authority is sanctioned by history, the same historical sources also indicate that authority was tied to an assumption of substantial grand jury independence. * * * Today, the critics argue, the sweeping powers of the grand jury are exercised in reality by the prosecutor alone. Working with the police, the prosecutor determines what witnesses will be called and when they will appear. He examines the witnesses and advises the grand jury on the validity of any legal objections the witnesses might present. If a witness refuses to comply with a subpoena, it is the prosecutor who seeks a contempt citation. If a witness refuses to testify on grounds of self-incrimination, it is the prosecutor who determines whether an immunity grant will be obtained. The grand jury must, almost of necessity, rely upon the prosecutor's leadership. Few investigations can succeed without the investigative work, skillful interrogation, legal advice, and even the secretarial assistance, provided by the prosecutor and his staff. So too, grand jurors are neophytes in the field of criminal investigation and are participating only on a part-time basis; it is only natural that they are disposed to rely upon the prosecutor—the 'professional' who commands the expertise necessary to their venture.

"Critics argue that this change in the nature of the investigative grand jury, which [they say] has converted it into the 'prosecutor's puppet,' requires a corresponding change in judicial attitudes. The courts should not, they argue, feel bound by precedent that was developed during an era when grand juries were independent bodies. Instead, they should 'pull back the veil of history and view the investigating grand jury as one would view any other investigatory instrument of government.' The power of the grand jury should be subject to the same kinds of limitations as are imposed upon other weapons in the prosecutor's investigative arsenal.[l]

"Supporters of the grand jury readily acknowledge that the prosecutor plays a substantial role in directing today's grand jury investigations. They suggest that this is a beneficial development that makes the investigatory authority more effective and helps to ensure that it is not misused. Moreover, it is noted, this development dates back over one hundred years, preceding many of the decisions that speak most eloquently of the necessary breadth of the grand jury's investigative authority. The key to the historical grant of that authority, they argue, was a legal structure that rendered the government's use of the grand jury's investigative powers subject to the veto of the jurors, who sat as community representatives. That structure has not been substantially altered, and its very presence, the argument continues, serves to hold the prosecutor in check and to distinguish grand jury investigations from investigatory tools granted directly to the prosecutor or the police.[m] The fact that the grand jury only occasionally exercises its

l. See also Kuckes, supra note k, arguing that few courts have taken note of this obvious reality (*In re Grand Jury*, Note 3 infra, being the most prominent exception) because the "fiction" of grand jury independence has allowed the courts to reach several results "important to the functioning of the criminal justice system, and which it would be difficult or impossible to reach if one were to acknowledge that the grand jury is the captive of the prosecutor." Thus, "the fiction of grand jury independence enables the Court to expand the powers of the prosecutor, who would otherwise have virtually no ability to demand the production of evidence in a criminal investigation * * * [and] enables the Court to limit judicial oversight of prosecutors engaged in investigative activities by hypothesizing that the grand jury is a separate and 'independent' institution." The end result, it is argued, is to "impede honest debate" and preclude the "thoughtful discussion that should accompany the expansion of prosecutorial authority," making grand jury independence a "dangerous" legal fiction.

m. See e.g., Justice Black's oft-quoted dissent in *In re Groban,* 352 U.S. 330 (1957). Commenting on the distinction between a grand jury proceeding (where Justice Black agreed that "a witness cannot insist, as a matter of constitutional right, on being represented by counsel") and a fire marshall's closed

power to override the prosecutor does not detract from the significance of that power. The prosecutor must respect the existence of that power and act in a way that he knows, from past experience, will be acceptable to the jurors."

2. **BLAIR v. UNITED STATES**, 250 U.S. 273 (1919). Responding to a grand jury witness' challenge to a subpoena on the ground that the federal government lacked constitutional authority to regulate, and the federal grand jury therefore lacked jurisdiction to investigate, the campaign practices of a candidate in a state primary election for U.S. Senator, PITNEY, J., speaking for a unanimous Court, noted:

"[T]he giving of testimony and the attendance upon court or grand jury in order to testify are public duties which every person within the jurisdiction of the Government is bound to perform upon being properly summoned, and for performance of which he is entitled to no further compensation than that which the statutes provide. The personal sacrifice involved is a part of the necessary contribution of the individual to the welfare of the public. The duty, so onerous at times, yet so necessary to the administration of justice according to the forms and modes established in our system of government is subject to mitigation in exceptional circumstances; there is a constitutional exemption from being compelled in any criminal case to be a witness against oneself, entitling the witness to be excused from answering anything that will tend to incriminate him; some confidential matters are shielded from considerations of policy, and perhaps in other cases for special reasons a witness may be excused from telling all that he knows.

"But, aside from exceptions and qualifications—and none such is asserted in the present case—the witness is bound not only to attend but to tell what he knows in answer to questions framed for the purpose of bringing out the truth of the matter under inquiry. He is not entitled to urge objections of incompetency or irrelevancy, such as a party might raise, for this is no concern of his. On familiar principles, he is not entitled to challenge the authority of the court or of the grand jury, provided they have a *de facto* existence and organization. He is not entitled to set limits to the investigation that the grand jury may conduct. * * * It is a grand inquest, a body with powers of investigation and inquisition, the scope of whose inquiries is not to be limited narrowly by questions of propriety or forecasts of the probable result of the investigation, or by doubts whether any particular individual will be found properly subject to an accusation of crime."

3. **IN RE GRAND JURY PROCEEDINGS (SCHOFIELD I)**, 486 F.2d 85 (3d Cir.1973). Rejecting the government's claim that a grand jury witness should be held in contempt for failing to respond to a grand jury subpoena with no more showing as to the grounding of the subpoena than "what appears on the face of the subpoena", the Third Circuit (per GIBBONS, J.) noted:

"[I]t is well to start with some fundamental propositions. First, although federal grand juries are called into existence by order of the district court, Fed.R.Crim.P. 6(a), they are 'basically . . . a law enforcement agency.' They are for all practical purposes an investigative and prosecutorial arm of the executive

inquiry (where Justice Black, disagreeing with the *Groban* majority, argued that the witness had a constitutional right to be accompanied by counsel), Justice Black emphasized the special role of the grand jurors: "They bring into the grand jury room the experience, knowledge and viewpoint of all sections of the community. They have no axes to grind and are not charged personally with the administration of the law. No one of them is a prosecuting attorney or law-enforcement officer ferreting out crime. It would be very difficult for officers of the state seriously to abuse or deceive a witness in the presence of the grand jury. Similarly the presence of the jurors offers a substantial safeguard against the officers' misrepresentation, unintentional or otherwise, of the witness statements and conduct before the grand jury."

branch of government. Second, although like all federal court subpoenas grand jury subpoenas are issued in the name of the district court over the signature of the clerk, they are issued pro forma and in blank to anyone requesting them. Fed.R.Crim.P. 17(a). The court exercises no prior control whatsoever upon their use. Third, although grand jury subpoenas are occasionally discussed as if they were the instrumentalities of the grand jury, they are in fact almost universally instrumentalities of the United States Attorney's office or of some other investigative or prosecutorial department of the executive branch. Grand jury subpoenas then, when they are brought before the federal courts for enforcement, for all practical purposes are exactly analogous to subpoenas issued by a federal administrative agency on the authority of a statute * * *. [A] court's determination under 28 U.S.C. § 1826(a) [the civil contempt enforcement provision] of the existence or nonexistence of just cause for refusing to obey a subpoena entails the same full judicial consideration as in the administrative subpoena cases."

4. **UNITED STATES v. WILLIAMS**, 504 U.S. 36 (1992). The *Williams* majority opinion held that a federal court could not on its own initiative impose a duty on the government to present to the grand jury material exculpatory evidence within its possession, and the court accordingly could not dismiss an indictment because the prosecutor failed to present such evidence. Explaining the limited authority of federal courts to mandate grand jury procedures beyond those "specifically required by the Constitution or Congress," SCALIA, J., noted:

" '[R]ooted in long centuries of Anglo–American history,' the grand jury is mentioned in the Bill of Rights, but not in the body of the Constitution. It has not been textually assigned, therefore, to any of the branches described in the first three Articles. It 'is a constitutional fixture in its own right.' In fact the whole theory of its function is that it belongs to no branch of the institutional government, serving as a kind of buffer or referee between the Government and the people. * * * Although the grand jury normally operates, of course, in the courthouse and under judicial auspices, its institutional relationship with the judicial branch has traditionally been, so to speak, at arm's length. Judges' direct involvement in the functioning of the grand jury has generally been confined to the constitutive one of calling the grand jurors together and administering their oaths of office. * * * The grand jury requires no authorization from its constituting court to initiate an investigation, nor does the prosecutor require leave of court to seek a grand jury indictment. And in its day-to-day functioning, the grand jury generally operates without the interference of a presiding judge. It swears in its own witnesses, Fed.Rule 6(c), and deliberates in total secrecy.

"True, the grand jury cannot compel the appearance of witnesses and the production of evidence, and must appeal to the court when such compulsion is required. And the court will refuse to lend its assistance when the compulsion the grand jury seeks would override rights accorded by the Constitution * * *. Even in this setting, however, we have insisted that the grand jury remain 'free to pursue its investigations unhindered by external influence or supervision so long as it does not trench upon the legitimate rights of any witness called before it.' *United States v. Dionisio* [p. 819]. Recognizing this tradition of independence, we have said that the Fifth Amendment's 'constitutional guarantee *presupposes* an investigative body "acting independently of either prosecuting attorney *or judge*". . . .' *Dionisio*.

"Given the grand jury's operational separateness from its constituting court, it should come as no surprise that we have been reluctant to invoke the judicial supervisory power as a basis for prescribing modes of grand jury procedure. Over the years, we have received many requests to exercise supervision over the grand jury's evidence-taking process, but we have refused them all, including some more appealing than the one presented today. [Citing *Calandra,* Note 4, p. 823]. * * *

These authorities suggest that any power federal courts may have to fashion, on their own initiative, rules of grand jury procedure is a very limited one, not remotely comparable to the power they maintain over their own proceedings."

SECTION 2. FOURTH AMENDMENT CHALLENGES TO THE INVESTIGATION

A. The Initial Approach

BOYD v. UNITED STATES

116 U.S. 616, 6 S.Ct. 524, 29 L.Ed. 746 (1886).

[Customs officials seized 35 cases of glass, imported by the partnership of Boyd and Sons, and instituted a forfeiture proceeding. That proceeding was brought under a statute providing that any importer who defrauded the government and thereby avoided payment of customs revenue was subject to fine, incarceration, and forfeiture of the imported merchandise. Utilizing an 1874 statute, the government's attorney obtained a court "notice" directing Boyd to produce an invoice covering 29 of the cases of glass. That statute authorized the trial judge, on motion of the prosecutor describing a particular document and indicating what it might prove, to issue a notice directing the importer to produce the document. The importer could refuse to produce without being held in contempt (which distinguished the "notice" from a subpoena), but the consequence of a failure to produce was that the allegation of the prosecutor as to what the document stated was "taken as confessed." The defendants produced the invoice in compliance with the notice, but objected to the validity of the court's order, and objected again when the invoice was offered as evidence. The jury subsequently found for the United States, and a judgment of forfeiture against the 35 cases was granted.]

BRADLEY, J.

The clauses of the Constitution, to which it is contended that these laws are repugnant, are the Fourth and Fifth Amendments. * * * [I]n regard to Fourth Amendment, it is contended that * * * [the Act of 1874], under which the order in the present case was made, is free from constitutional objection, because it does not authorize the search and seizure of books and papers, but only requires the defendant or claimant to produce them. That is so; but it declares that if he does not produce them, the allegations which it is affirmed they will prove shall be taken as confessed. This is tantamount to compelling their production; for the prosecuting attorney will always be sure to state the evidence expected to be derived from them as strongly as the case will admit of. It is true that certain aggravating incidents of actual search and seizure, such as forcible entry into a man's house and searching amongst his papers, are wanting, and to this extent the proceeding under the act of 1874 is a mitigation of that which was authorized by the former acts; but it accomplishes the substantial object of those acts in forcing from a party evidence against himself. It is our opinion, therefore, that a compulsory production of a man's private papers to establish a criminal charge against him, or to forfeit his property, is within the scope of the Fourth Amendment to the Constitution, in all cases in which a search and seizure would be; because it is a material ingredient, and effects the sole object and purpose of search and seizure.

The principal question, however, remains to be considered. Is a search and seizure, or, what is equivalent thereto, a compulsory production of a man's private papers, to be used in evidence against him in a proceeding to forfeit his property for alleged fraud against the revenue laws—is such a proceeding for such a purpose an "*unreasonable* search and seizure" within the meaning of the Fourth Amendment of the Constitution? or, is it a legitimate proceeding? * * *

As before stated, the [predecessor] act of 1863 was the first act in this country, and, we might say, either in this country or in England, so far as we have been able to ascertain, which authorized the search and seizure of a man's private papers, or the compulsory production of them, for the purpose of using them in evidence against him in a criminal case, or in a proceeding to enforce the forfeiture of his property. Even the act under which the obnoxious writs of assistance were issued did not go as far as this, but only authorized the examination of ships and vessels, and persons found therein, for the purpose of finding goods prohibited to be imported or exported, or on which the duties were not paid, and to enter into and search any suspected vaults, cellars, or warehouses for such goods. The search for and seizure of stolen or forfeited goods, or goods liable to duties and concealed to avoid the payment thereof, are totally different things from a search for and seizure of a man's private books and papers for the purpose of obtaining information therein contained, or of using them as evidence against him. The two things differ *toto coelo*. In the one case, the government is entitled to the possession of the property; in the other it is not. * * *

In order to ascertain the nature of the proceedings intended by the Fourth Amendment to the Constitution under the terms "unreasonable searches and seizures," it is only necessary to recall the contemporary or then recent history of the controversies on the subject, both in this country and in England. * * * Prominent and principal among these was the practice of issuing general warrants by the Secretary of State, for searching private houses for the discovery and seizure of books and papers that might be used to convict their owner of the charge of libel. * * * The case [which] will always be celebrated as being the occasion of Lord Camden's memorable discussion of the subject, was that of *Entick v. Carrington and Three Other King's Messengers,* reported at length in 19 Howell's State Trials, 1029. The action was trespass for entering the plaintiff's dwelling-house in November, 1762, and breaking open his desks, boxes, & c., and searching and examining his papers. The jury rendered a special verdict, and the case was twice solemnly argued at the bar. Lord Camden pronounced the judgment of the court in Michaelmas Term, 1765, and the law as expounded by him has been regarded as settled from that time to this, and his great judgment on that occasion is considered as one of the landmarks of English liberty. * * * As every American statesmen, during our revolutionary and formative period as a nation, was undoubtedly familiar with this monument of English freedom, and considered it as the true and ultimate expression of constitutional law, it may be confidently asserted that its propositions were in the minds of those who framed the Fourth Amendment to the Constitution, and were considered as sufficiently explanatory of what was meant by unreasonable searches and seizures. * * *

After describing the power claimed by the Secretary of State for issuing general search warrants, and the manner in which they were executed, Lord Camden says [in *Entick*]:

> * * * Papers are the owner's goods and chattels; they are his dearest property; and are so far from enduring a seizure, that they will hardly bear an inspection; and though the eye cannot by the laws of England be guilty of a trespass, yet where private papers are removed and carried away the secret nature of those goods will be an aggravation of the trespass, and demand more considerable damages in that respect. Where is the written law that gives any magistrate such a power? I can safely answer, there is none; and

therefore, it is too much for us, without such authority, to pronounce a practice legal which would be subversive of all the comforts of society. * * *

Lastly, it is urged as an argument of utility, that such a search is a means of detecting offenders by discovering evidence. I wish some cases had been shown, where the law forceth evidence out of the owner's custody by process. There is no process against papers in civil causes. It has been often tried, but never prevailed. Nay, where the adversary has by force or fraud got possession of your own proper evidence, there is no way to get it back but by action. In the criminal law such a proceeding was never heard of; and yet there are some crimes, such, for instance, as murder, rape, robbery, and house-breaking, to say nothing of forgery and perjury, that are more atrocious than libeling. But our law has provided no paper-search in these cases to help forward the conviction. Whether this proceedeth from the gentleness of the law towards criminals, or from a consideration that such a power would be more pernicious to the innocent than useful to the public, I will not say. It is very certain that the law obligeth no man to accuse himself; because the necessary means of compelling self-accusation, falling upon the innocent as well as the guilty, would be both cruel and unjust; and it would seem, that search for evidence is disallowed upon the same principle. Then, too, the innocent would be confounded with the guilty.

* * * The principles laid down in this opinion affect the very essence of constitutional liberty and security. They reach farther than the concrete form of the case then before the court, with its adventitious circumstances; they apply to all invasions on the part of the government and its employees of the sanctity of a man's home and the privacies of life. It is not the breaking of his doors, and the rummaging of his drawers, that constitutes the essence of the offence; but it is the invasion of his indefeasible right of personal security, personal liberty and private property, where that right has never been forfeited by his conviction of some public offence,—it is the invasion of this sacred right which underlies and constitutes the essence of Lord Camden's judgment. Breaking into a house and opening boxes and drawers are circumstances of aggravation; but any forcible and compulsory extortion of a man's own testimony or of his private papers to be used as evidence to convict him of crime or to forfeit his goods, is within the condemnation of that judgment. In this regard the Fourth and Fifth Amendments run almost into each other. * * *

Reverting then to the peculiar phraseology of this act, and to the information in the present case, which is founded on it, we have to deal with an act which expressly excludes criminal proceedings from its operation (though embracing civil suits for penalties and forfeitures), and with an information not technically a criminal proceeding, and neither, therefore, within the literal terms of the Fifth Amendment to the Constitution any more than it is within the literal terms of the Fourth. Does this relieve the proceedings or the law from being obnoxious to the prohibitions of either? We think not; we think they are within the spirit of both.

We have already noticed the intimate relation between the two amendments. They throw great light on each other. For the "unreasonable searches and seizures" condemned in the Fourth Amendment are almost always made for the purpose of compelling a man to give evidence against himself, which in criminal cases is condemned in the Fifth Amendment; and compelling a man "in a criminal case to be a witness against himself," which is condemned in the Fifth Amendment, throws light on the question as to what is an "unreasonable search and seizure" within the meaning of the Fourth Amendment. And we have been unable to perceive that the seizure of a man's private books and papers to be used in evidence against him is substantially different from compelling him to be a witness against himself. * * * We are also clearly of opinion that proceedings instituted for the purpose of declaring the forfeiture of a man's property by reason of offences committed by him, though they may be civil in form, are in their nature criminal. In this very case, the ground of forfeiture * * * consists of certain acts of fraud committed against the public revenue in relation to imported merchandise, which are made criminal by the statute * * *. As, therefore, suits for penalties and forfeitures incurred by the commission of offences against the law, are of this quasi-criminal nature, we think that they are within the reason of criminal proceedings for all the purposes of the Fourth Amendment of the Constitution, and of that portion of the Fifth Amendment which declares that no person shall be compelled in any criminal case to be a witness against himself; and we are further of opinion that a compulsory production of the private books and papers of the owner of goods sought to be forfeited in such a suit is compelling him to be a witness against himself, within the meaning of the Fifth Amendment to the Constitution, and is the equivalent of a search and seizure—and an unreasonable search and seizure—within the meaning of the Fourth Amendment.

Though the proceeding in question is divested of many of the aggravating incidents of actual search and seizure, yet, as before said, it contains their substance and essence, and effects their substantial purpose. It may be that it is the obnoxious thing in its mildest and least repulsive form; but illegitimate and unconstitutional practices get their first footing in that way, namely, by silent approaches and slight deviations from legal modes of procedure. This can only be obviated by adhering to the rule that constitutional provisions for the security of person and property should be liberally construed. A close and literal construction deprives them of half their efficacy, and leads to gradual depreciation of the right, as if it consisted more in sound than in substance. It is the duty of courts to be watchful for the constitutional rights of the citizen, and against any stealthy encroachments thereon. Their motto should be *obsta principiis.* * * *

Justice MILLER, with whom was The Chief Justice concurring:

I concur in the judgment of the court * * * and in so much of the opinion of this court as holds the 5th section of the act of 1874 void as applicable to the present case. * * * The order of the court under the statute is in effect a subpoena duces tecum, and, though the penalty for the witness's failure to appear in court with the criminating papers is not fine and imprisonment, it is one which may be made more severe, namely, to have charges against him of a criminal nature, taken for confessed, and made the foundation of the judgment of the court. That this is within the protection which the Constitution intended against compelling a person to be a witness against himself, is, I think, quite clear.

But this being so, there is no reason why this court should assume that the action of the court below, in requiring a party to produce certain papers as evidence on the trial, authorizes an unreasonable search or seizure of the house, papers, or effects of that party. There is in fact no search and no seizure authorized by the statute. No order can be made by the court under it which requires or permits anything more than service of notice on a party to the suit. * * *

Nothing in the nature of a search is here hinted at. Nor is there any seizure, because the party is not required at any time to part with the custody of the papers. They are to be produced in court, and, when produced, the United States attorney is permitted, under the direction of the court, to make examination in presence of the claimant, and may offer in evidence such entries in the books, invoices, or papers as relate to the issue. The act is careful to say that "the owner of said books and papers, his agent or attorney, shall have, subject to the order of the court, the custody of them, except pending their examination in court as aforesaid." . . .

The things . . . forbidden [by the Fourth Amendment] are two—search and seizure. * * * But what search does this statute authorize? If the mere service of a notice to produce a paper to be used as evidence, which the party can obey or not as he chooses is a search, then a change has taken place in the meaning of words, which has not come within my reading, and which I think was unknown at the time the Constitution was made. The searches meant by the Constitution were such as led to seizure when the search was successful. But the statute in this case uses language carefully framed to forbid any seizure under it, as I have already pointed out. * * *

Notes and Questions

1. ***A civil liberties icon.*** *Boyd* has been praised by commentators and courts as a landmark civil liberties case. Dissenting in *Olmstead v. United States*, 277 U.S. 438 (1928), Justice Brandeis noted: "*Boyd v. United States* [is] a case that will be remembered as long as civil liberty lives in the United States." See also William J. Stuntz, *Privacy's Problem and the Law of Criminal Procedure*, 93 Mich.L.Rev. 1016 (1995) ("*Boyd* is conventionally seen as the *Miranda* of its day, a criminal procedure case that courageously protected the rights (particularly the privacy rights) of individuals against the government. Its passing—essentially nothing in *Boyd's* holding is good law anymore—is mourned as a sign of citizens' diminished protection against an overly aggressive criminal justice system").

What made *Boyd* a civil liberties icon? Was it the statement in last paragraph of the majority's opinion on the need for liberal construction of constitutional safeguards—a statement quoted with approval in numerous Supreme Court opinions? Was it the Court's attempt to bring together the Fourth and Fifth Amendment guarantees—its linking of the constitutional protection of "the privacies of life" not only to the restrictions on search and seizure but also to the privilege against self-incrimination? See Stuntz, supra. Was it the Court's focus on consequence rather than procedural form—its treatment of the court order to produce a document as the functional equivalent of a search and the production of an incriminating document through a search as the functional equivalent of being compelled to testify as to the incriminating contents of that document? See Note 1, p. 853.

2. Commentators have suggested that many aspects of the reasoning of *Boyd* do not "ring true" for a civil liberties icon. Thus, *Boyd* has been described as a product of "nineteenth century legal formalism" that was founded "on the view that adjudication proceeds by deduction from virtually absolute principles rooted in natural law and enshrined in both the common law and the Constitution." Note, 90 Harv.L.Rev. 943 (1977). See also William J. Stuntz, *The Substantive Origins of Criminal Procedure*, 105 Yale L.J. 393 (1995) (comparing *Boyd* to the Supreme Court's pre–1930's substantive due process cases). Also, *Boyd* is characterized as a ruling grounded more on the protection of private property than the protection of privacy. See e.g., Stanton D. Krauss, *The Life and Times of Boyd v. United States (1886–1976)*, 76 Mich.L.Rev. 184 (1977) ("[C]onfidentiality was not the interest the Court sought to protect. Whether the Boyds had kept the invoice a secret to the world or whether they had made its contents a matter of public knowledge was irrelevant; either way the government's action was illegal"). The key to *Boyd*, under this view, was that the invoice was properly possessed private property—i.e., not contraband or the fruits of a crime.

Boyd, unlike most other civil liberties icons in the criminal procedure field, dealt with investigative techniques "far removed from ordinary criminal law." Stuntz, supra. As noted in Stuntz, Note 1 supra: "In the decades following the Court's decision, few ordinary criminal investigations led to *Boyd*-type claims, either in the form of challenges to subpoenas or as trespass actions against officers. On the other hand, regulatory cases were common. In a number of bankruptcy cases, the debtor sought to avoid certain kinds of compelled disclosure. Antitrust cases began to crop up following the Sherman Act in 1890, with defendants raising Fifth Amendment objections to subpoenas or questioning. Railroad regulation disputes were especially numerous and especially high-profile, with corporate officials striving to avoid testifying or producing documents in ICC proceedings." Indeed, Professor Stuntz argues, it was concern for the barriers *Boyd* posed to economic regulation that led to the first step in the dismantling of *Boyd* in *Hale v. Henkel*. Note 2, p. 810.

3. ***The dismantling of Boyd.*** *Boyd* and its reasoning survived intact for less than two decades. Yet its dismantling took almost a century, and some would argue that at least a small remnant of the *Boyd* analysis has current vitality. See Note 1, p. 863. But see *Krause*, Note 2 supra ("*Boyd* is dead").

Initially, the Court in *Hale* (Note 1, p. 809) separated *Boyd's* Fifth Amendment and Fourth Amendment analyses, concluded that corporations had no self-incrimination privilege, and announced a separate (and more lenient) Fourth Amendment standard for the subpoena of documents. In later cases dealing with *Boyd's* commentary on the Fourth Amendment and searches, the Court first held that a search and seizure could extend to private property that constituted the instrumentality of the crime, *Marron v. United States*, 275 U.S. 192 (1927), then in 1967 rejected the reading of *Boyd* as prohibiting a search for property that constituted no more than "mere evidence" of a crime, *Warden v. Hayden* (p. 271), and finally in 1976 held that Fourth Amendment did not prohibit a search for documents, *Andresen v. Maryland* (p. 272). The major developments in the Court's dismantling of *Boyd's* Fifth Amendment analysis and ruling are discussed in section 5 of this chapter.

B. The Overbreadth Doctrine

1. ***Hale v. Henkel (the introduction of the overbreadth doctrine).*** In HALE v. HENKEL, 201 U.S. 43 (1906), the Court had before it a challenge to a subpoena directing the petitioner to produce before a grand jury (which was conducting an investigation into possible violations of the antitrust laws) various corporate documents. Petitioner's challenge was based on the combined impact of the Fourth and Fifth Amendments, but the Court initially separated those claims. Cases subsequent to *Boyd,* it noted, had "treated the Fourth and Fifth Amendments as quite distinct, having different histories, and performing separate functions." Turning first to the petitioner's self-incrimination claim, the Court found that claim clearly unsupportable since the statute authorizing the subpoena granted petitioner immunity from prosecution (see Note 1, p. 848) and the corporation itself had no self-incrimination privilege (see Note 2, p. 854). The petitioner's Fourth Amendment claim did have merit, but for reasons other than that which might have been assumed from *Boyd.* Speaking for the Court, BROWN, J., noted:

"Although * * * we are of the opinion that an officer of a corporation * * * cannot refuse to produce the books and papers of such corporation, we do not wish to be understood as holding that a corporation is not entitled to immunity, under the Fourth Amendment, against *unreasonable* searches and seizures. A corporation is, after all, but an association of individuals under an assumed name and with a distinct legal entity. In organizing itself as a collective body it waives no constitutional immunities appropriate to such body. * * * We are also of opinion that an order for the production of books and papers may constitute an unreasonable search and seizure within the Fourth Amendment. While a search ordinarily implies a quest by an officer of the law, and a seizure contemplates a forcible dispossession of the owner, still, as was held in the *Boyd* case, the substance of the offense is the compulsory production of private papers, whether under a search warrant or a subpoena duces tecum, against which the person, be he individual or corporation, is entitled to protection. Applying the test of reasonableness to the present case, we think the subpoena duces tecum is far too sweeping in its terms to be regarded as reasonable. It does not require the production of a single contract, or of contracts with a particular corporation, or a limited number of documents, but all understandings, contracts, or correspondence between the MacAndrews & Forbes Company, and no less than six different companies, as well as all reports made, and accounts rendered by such companies from the date of the organization of the MacAndrews & Forbes Company, as well as all letters received by that company since its organization from more than a dozen different companies, situated in seven different States in the Union.

"If the writ had required the production of all the books, papers and documents found in the office of the MacAndrews & Forbes Company, it would scarcely be more universal in its operation, or more completely put a stop to the business of that company. Indeed, it is difficult to say how its business could be carried on after it had been denuded of this mass of material, which is not shown to be necessary in the prosecution of this case, and is clearly in violation of the general principle of law with regard to the particularity required in the description of documents necessary to a search warrant or subpoena. Doubtless many, if not all, of these documents may ultimately be required, but some necessity should be shown, either from an examination of the witnesses orally, or from the known transactions of these companies with the other companies implicated, or some evidence of their materiality produced, to justify an order for the production of such a mass of papers. A general subpoena of this description is equally indefensible as a search warrant would be if couched in similar terms."

McKENNA, J., concurring separately in *Hale,* questioned the Court's Fourth Amendment analysis: "It is said 'a search implies a quest by an officer of the law; a seizure contemplates a forcible dispossession of the owner.' Nothing can be more direct and plain; nothing more expressive to distinguish a subpoena from a search warrant. Can a subpoena lose this essential distinction from a search warrant by the generality or speciality of its terms? I think not. The distinction is based upon what is authorized or directed to be done—not upon the form of words by which the authority or command is given. 'The quest of an officer' acts upon the things themselves—may be secret, intrusive, accompanied by force. The service of a subpoena is but the delivery of a paper to a party—is open and aboveboard. There is no element of trespass or force in it. It does not disturb the possession of property. It cannot be finally enforced except after challenge, and a judgment of the court upon the challenge. This is a safeguard against abuse the same as it is of other processes of the law, and it is all that can be allowed without serious embarrassment to the administration of justice."

2. *Explaining the overbreadth doctrine.* As Judge Friendly noted in *In re Horowitz,* 482 F.2d 72 (2d Cir.1973), "the Fourth Amendment portion of the *Boyd* decision was surely not based on the overbreadth of the Government's demand; the Government [there] sought only a single invoice of unquestionable relevance." Although relying on *Boyd, Hale v. Henkel*

> left the applicability of the Fourth Amendment to subpoena duces tecum in a most confusing state. None of the Justices seemed to think that such a subpoena could be issued only "upon probable cause, supported by oath or affirmation," as would be required for a search warrant. Nevertheless, except for Mr. Justice McKenna, all were of the view that an overbroad subpoena duces tecum against an individual would be an unreasonable search and seizure.

Judge Friendly suggested in *Horowitz* that the overbreadth doctrine of *Hale* might find firmer support in the due process clause than in the Fourth Amendment. Although a due process grounding for the doctrine is suggested in *Oklahoma Press Publishing Co. v. Walling,* 327 U.S. 186 (1946) (a leading case on the application of the overbreadth doctrine to an administrative agency subpoena[a]), more recent cases have referred to the doctrine as based on the Fourth Amendment.

Accepting the Court's premise that the Fourth Amendment does apply to the subpoena duces tecum, why should the overbreadth doctrine be the sole Fourth Amendment limitation as to the subpoena duces tecum? One explanation is that the requirements of the Fourth Amendment's warrant clause are inapplicable in light of (1) the long history of subpoenas issued without regard to probable cause (particularly in the trial context, see Fed.R.Crim.P. 17), and (2) the lesser intrusion upon privacy resulting from a subpoena (as compared to the traditional search). This leaves applicable only the Fourth Amendment's general mandate of "reasonableness," which is reflected in the overbreadth doctrine. See Wayne R. LaFave, *Search and Seizure* § 4.13(e) (3d ed. 1996). This explanation makes *Hale* the forerunner of the Supreme Court's later line of cases which looked to similar factors in concluding that the Fourth Amendment permits administrative searches (e.g., health inspections) without a case-specific showing akin to probable cause or reasonable suspicion. See Ch. 6, § 9. But consider CRIMPROC § 8.7(a), responding that this explanation would seem to call for a standard of reasonableness that is more rigorous where there is a greater invasion of privacy due to the heightened confidentiality of the particular document (distinguishing for example between the subpoena of business documents and diaries), a position not suggested in *Hale*. "Also, such an analysis does not lead to protection conditioned on the subpoena compelling production of a substantial body of documents (as *Hale* seemed to suggest) and would not test overbreadth by reference to the economic burden imposed upon the individual or entity by being forced to relinquish those documents (as *Hale* clearly did)." Ibid.

A second explanation of *Hale* builds upon Justice McKenna's suggestion that the *Hale* majority found the Fourth Amendment applicable only when the subpoena was overly broad. The theory here is that the subpoena is not comparable to search, except where it potentially is too sweeping. Calling for a mass of documents without regard to what is relevant, necessarily requires a sifting through those documents to identify those that are relevant. Whether that sifting takes place on the premises of the owner or in the offices of the prosecutor assisting the grand jury, it would constitute a search, and therefore the Fourth prohibits a subpoena where it clearly is so sweeping as to include the relevant and the irrelevant. This explanation, although it arguably fits the subpoena in the *Hale*

a. Speaking to petitioners' claim that enforcement of the subpoena duces tecum would violate rights secured by the Fourth Amendment, Justice Rutledge noted that the "short answer" to this contention was that "these cases present no question of actual search and seizure" as they involved no attempt by government officials "to enter petitioners' premises against their will, to search them, or to seize or examine their books." He later added: "The primary source of misconception concerning the Fourth Amendment's function lies perhaps in the identification of cases involving so-called 'figurative' or 'constructive' search with cases of actual search and seizure. Only in this analogical sense can any question related to search and seizure be thought to arise in situations which, like the present ones, involve only the validity of authorized judicial orders."

Oklahoma Press set forth three prerequisites for administrative agency subpoenas: (1) the investigation must be for a "lawfully authorized purpose within the power of Congress"; (2) the documents sought must be "relevant to the inquiry"; (3) the element of "particularity" must be satisfied by a "specification of the documents to be produced adequate, but not excessive for the purpose of reasonable inquiry." Lower courts have described this standard as lenient, but not as lenient as "the lowest standard [which] is reserved for federal grand jury subpoenas." *Oman v. State*, 737 N.E.2d 1131 (Ind. 2000).

case, does not explain the emphasis in *Hale* upon the burden that the subpoena imposed upon the MacAndrew & Forbes Co.

A third explanation, stresses the different investigative focus of searches and grand jury subpoenas. The underlying premise of this explanation is that a Fourth Amendment that looks to the invasion of privacy would not on that ground draw a distinction between searches and subpoenas to produce documents.[b] Rather, the key to that distinction is "substantive necessity," as reflected in the character of the crime typically investigated by documentary subpoena as opposed to the crimes typically investigated through physical searches. See William J. Stuntz, *O.J. Simpson, Bill Clinton, and the Transsubstantive Fourth Amendment*, 114 Harv.L.Rev. 842 (2001): "[I]f the government is to regulate business and political affairs—the usual stuff of white-collar criminal law—it must have the power to subpoena witnesses and documents before it knows whether those witnesses and documents will yield incriminating evidence." Though *Hale* did not point to this reality in explaining its "lax" Fourth Amendment standard, the Court did so in another portion of the opinion (see Note 2, p. 854), where it rejected *Hale's* Fifth Amendment argument "in a pair of dismissive sentences," noting: "[T]he privilege claimed would practically nullify the whole [Sherman Act]. Of what use would it be for the legislature to declare these combinations unlawful if the judicial power may close the door of access to every available source of information upon the subject?" Here, it is argued, "[t]he Court did not deny that subpoenas infringe privacy, nor did it scoff at the degree of the infringement. Instead, the Court said that regardless of how serious it was, the infringement had to be tolerated: we need antitrust regulation, and we need a broad subpoena power in order to have antitrust regulation." Stuntz, supra.

3. ***Applying the overbreadth doctrine.*** Lower courts applying the overbreadth doctrine in the grand jury setting frequently note that the doctrine requires a fact-specific judgment, with each ruling tied to the circumstances of the individual case. At the same time, they have sought to develop some general criteria to guide that judgment. Initially, the subpoena carries with it a presumption of regularity that will be called into question only if the subpoena has "sufficient breadth to suggest either that compliance will be burdensome or that the subpoena's scope may not have been shaped to the purposes of the inquiry." CRIMPROC § 8.7(c). If the subpoena has such breadth, the courts will then examine its scope in light of three criteria: (1) whether it "commands only the production of documents relevant to the investigation being pursued"; (2) whether the specification of the documents is made with "reasonable particularity" (measured by reference to both the subpoenaed party's ability to identify what "he is being asked to produce" and any "unreasonable business detriment" flowing from

b. See William J. Stuntz, *Privacy's Problem and the Law of Criminal Procedure*, 93 Mich. L.Rev. 1016 (1995): "When the police search a car, they see anything that happens to be in the car, not just guns or drugs. A subpoena, on the other hand, asks only for the evidence being sought; nothing else need be disclosed. This difference could suggest that searches by their very nature invade privacy more than subpoenas do * * * [but] the line is incoherent in privacy terms. * * * The relevant privacy interest is the interest in keeping secret whatever the government is examining."

Consider also, Christopher Slobogin, *Subpoenas and Privacy*, 54 DePaul L.Rev. ___ (2005): "The fact that it is the target * * * rather than the police who locates the documents obviously does not change the nature of the revelations [the documents] contain, which can include information about medical treatment, finances, education, the identity of one's communicants, and even the contents of one's communications. The target's ability to challenge a subpoena, while it may inhibit some fishing expeditions, at most will only delay government access to the records, unless something beyond the current relevance standard is applicable [to subpoenas]. * * * And if the notion that searches only occur when government engages in physical invasion of private space were correct, then electronic surveillance and technologically-assisted physical surveillance of the home would not be a search, since neither usually requires a trespass or use of force."

collecting and relinquishing the quantity and range of the documents requested); and (3) whether the documents to be produced cover "only a reasonable period of time." Ibid. Applying these criteria, courts have upheld subpoenas requiring production of as much as 50 tons of documents, see *Petition of Borden,* 75 F.Supp. 857 (N.D.Ill.1948); yet they also have rejected requests for records that presumably would have occupied no more than a single filing cabinet. See e.g., *In re Certain Chinese Family Benevolent Ass'n,* 19 F.R.D. 97 (N.D.Cal.1956) (rejecting subpoenas requiring various Chinese family associations to produce available membership lists, income records, and membership photographs, dating back to the association's origin, for use in an investigation of immigration fraud).

Critical to the permissible scope of the subpoena is the nature of the investigation, as courts recognize that certain types of investigations, such as antitrust, necessarily demand a broader range of documents since the violation may be reflected in many aspects of a company's business. See also *In re Corrado Brothers,* 367 F.Supp. 1126 (D.Del.1973) (where the grand jury was investigating a kickback scheme involving the government highway department, all financial records were relevant since "cash for kickbacks can be readily generated by padding the * * * accounting records relating to a totally unrelated party"). Courts recognize also that "some exploration or fishing necessarily is inherent" since the grand jury will not ordinarily have a "catalogue of what books or papers exist nor any basis for knowing what their character or contents immediately are." *Schwimmer v. United States,* 232 F.2d 855 (8th Cir.1956). Even so, they will resist a subpoena category so broad as to possibly suggest no "stopping point." See e.g., *In re Corrado Brothers*, supra (where investigation related to kickbacks only as to government highway projects, subpoena requiring production of written communications with contractors, subcontractors, and other business associates was overly broad insofar as it included communications which did not relate to the highway department projects: while "it is possible these communications might contain an important scrap of information needed to tie a public official to a kickback," that "reasoning carried to its logical extreme, places no limits on the scope of materials subject to grand jury investigation," as every document, "no matter how remote from the nature of the investigation * * * *might* possibly contain important information"); In re Horowitz, 482 F.2d 72 (2d Cir.1973) (subpoena of a grand jury investigating target's possible fraud in former business enterprise demanded complete contents of three filing cabinets in which accountant had stored the records of the enterprise along with various personal documents of target; subpoena held overly broad in its failure to distinguish documents according to content or time frame, thereby including such personal documents as wills and trust agreements).

Although the overbreadth doctrine is a separate ground for challenging a subpoena duces tecum, as to federal courts, it may largely overlap with the Rule 17(c) objection discussed in *R. Enterprises* (p. 824), which imposes a similar limitation. See e.g., *In re Grand Jury Subpoena Duces Tecum Dated November 15, 1993,* 846 F.Supp. 11 (S.D.N.Y. 1994) (Rule 17(c) objection sustained, looking to reasoning of *Horowitz*, supra, as to a subpoena which demanded all computer hard drives and floppy diskettes, ignoring the possibility of identifying relevant materials by key words or particular categories of documents; although extension of investigation to obstruction of justice in incomplete responses to prior subpoenas justified a broader subpoena, it did not justify a subpoena which encompassed all files and therefore some "completely irrelevant" documents).

4. *Third-party objections.* In UNITED STATES v. MILLER, 425 U.S. 435 (1976), respondent Miller sought to raise a Fourth Amendment challenge to the government's acquisition of bank records through a grand jury subpoena. In the course of an investigation of Miller's alleged involvement in a bootlegging conspiracy, the federal agents served upon two banks grand jury subpoenas directing production of "all records of accounts, i.e., savings, checking loan or otherwise, in the name of Mitch Miller." Without informing Miller of the subpoena, the banks complied by making the records available to the agents for inspection and allowing the agents to make copies. After *Miller* was indicted, he moved to suppress all evidence derived from the information contained in the bank records. Upon appeal following his conviction, the Court of Appeals concluded that suppression should have been granted because "the Government had improperly circumvented *Boyd's* protection of respondent's Fourth Amendment right against 'unreasonable searches and seizures' by 'first requiring a third party bank to copy all of its depositors' personal checks [a requirement of the Bank Secrecy Act] and then, with an improper invocation of legal process [relating to defects in the issuance of the subpoena], calling upon the bank to allow inspection and reproduction of those copies." The Supreme Court majority, per POWELL, J., found no need to consider whether the grand jury process was defective, as the respondent had no protected Fourth Amendment interest in the bank records. The Court reasoned:

"Even if we direct our attention to the original checks and deposit slips, rather than to the microfilm copies actually viewed and obtained by means of the subpoena, we perceive no legitimate 'expectation of privacy' in their contents. The checks are not confidential communications but negotiable instruments to be used in commercial transactions. All of the documents obtained, including financial statements and deposit slips, contain only information voluntarily conveyed to the banks and exposed to their employees in the ordinary course of business. The lack of any legitimate expectation of privacy concerning the information kept in bank records was assumed by Congress in enacting the Bank Secrecy Act, the expressed purpose of which is to require records to be maintained because they 'have a high degree of usefulness in criminal tax, and regulatory investigations and proceedings.' 12 U.S.C. § 1829b(a)(1). * * *

"The depositor takes the risk, in revealing his affairs to another, that the information will be conveyed by that person to the Government. *United States v. White*. [p. 496]. This Court has held repeatedly that the Fourth Amendment does not prohibit the obtaining of information revealed to a third party and conveyed by him to Government authorities, even if the information is revealed on the assumption that it will be used only for a limited purpose and the confidence placed in the third party will not be betrayed. Id., *Hoffa v. United States* [p. 491]. * * * This analysis is not changed by the mandate of the Bank Secrecy Act that records of depositors' transactions be maintained by banks. In *California Bankers Assn. v. Shultz*, 416 U.S. 21 (1974), we rejected the contention that banks, when keeping records of their depositors' transactions pursuant to the Act, are acting solely as agents of the Government. But, even if the banks could be said to have been acting solely as Government agents in transcribing the necessary information and complying without protest with the requirements of the subpoenas, there would be no intrusion upon the depositors' Fourth Amendment rights. * * * Since no Fourth Amendment interests of the depositor are implicated here, this case is governed by the general rule that the issuance of a subpoena to a third party to obtain the records of that party does not violate the rights of a defendant, even if a criminal prosecution is contemplated at the time * * * the subpoena is issued."

Justices BRENNAN and MARSHALL each issued a separate dissent in *Miller*. Justice Brennan relied on the contrary reasoning in *Burrows v. Superior Court*, 529 P.2d 590 (Cal.1974), which concluded that the customer should be recognized as having a reasonable expectation of privacy in records of bank transactions, as the "totality of bank records provides a virtual current biography" which is given to the bank only because "it is impossible to participate in the economic life of contemporary society without maintaining a bank account." Justice Marshall's dissent stressed the recordkeeping requirements of the Bank Secrecy Act, which he viewed as unconstitutional.

Congress responded to the *Miller* decision with the adoption of the Right to Financial Privacy Act, discussed in Note 3, at p. 836.

5. As noted in Christopher Slobogin, *Subpoenas and Privacy*, 54 DePaul L.Rev. ___ (2005), "the Supreme Court has applied *Miller's* rationale to phone company records and loan applications, and lower courts have used it to uphold subpoenas for personal records from medical institutions, auditors and accountants, trustees in bankruptcy, and government institutions." Professor Slobogin urges reconsideration of both *Miller* and *Hale* as applied to subpoenas for personal documents. He points, in particular, to the special context in which the governing doctrine was developed and the changed circumstances that have dramatically altered the impact of that doctrine:[c]

"[T]he Court's de-regulation of subpoenas came in cases [like *Hale*] involving government attempts to regulate *businesses*; not a single one of them involved searches of personal papers. Because, as far as the Court was concerned, personal records held by the person himself or herself—i.e., most personal records—remained protected by the Fifth Amendment's prohibition on compelling persons to give testimony, the virtual elimination of Fourth Amendment protection against subpoenas [in *Hale* and related cases] had no impact in that area. Two developments * * * have changed all that. First, within the past three decades, the Supreme Court has radically altered its approach to the Fifth Amendment privilege, so that now personal records held by the target are almost as unprotected as corporate records as far as that constitutional provision is concerned. Far more importantly, the modernization of society has rendered the Fifth Amendment's application to personal records largely irrelevant in any event. That is because, in contrast to nineteenth century culture, so much more of our personal information is now recorded and held by third parties. When third parties are ordered to produce information via a subpoena, they cannot, under any plausible interpretation, be said to be incriminating themselves. * * * Since today most subpoenas for personal documents are aimed at third party recordholders, the upshot of these developments is that government is almost entirely unrestricted, by either the Fifth Amendment or the Fourth Amendment, in its efforts to obtain documentary evidence of non-business crime."

6. Does *Miller* preclude a customer's Fourth Amendment challenge to a subpoena directing an Internet Service Provider (e.g., AOL) to produce e-mails and drafts of documents that are being stored by the ISP for the customer. As discussed in Note 3, p. 836, Title II of the Electronic Communications Privacy Act

c. Professor Slobogin also finds flawed the rationales that have been advanced in support of the current "regulatory regime," insofar as it permits subpoenas of personal records without probable cause and without giving the target any opportunity to object where those records are in the possession of a third party. He identifies (and rejects) six justifications for that regime ("the first and last of which apply to all subpoenas and the rest of which are relevant only to third party subpoenas"): "The first justification, offered over a century ago, is that subpoenas are not 'searches' under the Fourth Amendment because they do not involve physical intrusion. The second, put forward by the modern Court, is that third party subpoenas are not searches because the information they seek is already exposed to others. The next three reasons are not as clearly stated in Supreme Court opinions but are implicit in the language of some of its cases or are found in lower court decisions: the records obtained through third-party subpoenas belong to the third party, not the target; third party recordholders are not different from third party witnesses who have information about a suspect; and third parties have an obligation to provide information to the government. The final reason given for leaving subpoenas essentially unregulated is the one most commonly seen in Supreme Court and lower court opinions: imposition of rigorous Fourth Amendment requirements on subpoenas would stultify important government investigations."

governs such subpoenas, but in some situations, the Fourth Amendment arguably could provide greater protection for the customer. *Miller* has been held applicable to basic subscriber information, see e.g., *Guest v. Leis*, 255 F.3d 325 (6th Cir.2001), but would the content of stored communication be different? See LaFave, Note 2 supra, at § 2.6(f) (in *Miller*, the information was given to a third party for the party's use, as it was "needed to provide the requested service," but computer operators have no legitimate purpose in reading records unrelated to the computer operator's function, and thus the "user does have a legitimate expectation of privacy as to the contents of electronic mail messages or personal files"); Deidre Mulligan, *Reasonable Expectations in Electronic Communications: A Critical Perspective in the Electronics Communications Privacy Act*, 72 Geo.Wash. L.Rev. 1557 (2004) (rejecting the contention that electronic mail should be treated less favorably than telephone communications because the process of transmission leaves replicas of the communication in the hands of third-party servers; the creation of the replicas is not a product of an intentional disclosure to the third party for its use; unlike checks and bank deposits that were the subjects of the records involved in *Miller*, electronic mail is transmitted by the sender as a private communication). *Doe v. Ashcroft*, 334 F.Supp.2d 471 (S.D.N.Y.2004) (refusing to extend *Miller*, and holding that a customer has a First Amendment interest in challenging a subpoena that would require an internet service provider to reveal customer identity information; the "unique features of internet communications" requires a challenge process which ensures that the internet subscriber's "right to engage in anonymous speech" is adequately protected).

C. Compelling Testimony (and Identification Exemplars)

UNITED STATES v. DIONISIO

410 U.S. 1, 93 S.Ct. 764, 35 L.Ed.2d 67 (1973).

Justice STEWART delivered the opinion of the Court.

A special grand jury was convened in the Northern District of Illinois in February 1971, to investigate possible violations of federal criminal statutes relating to gambling. In the course of its investigation the grand jury received in evidence certain voice recordings that had been obtained pursuant to court orders. The grand jury subpoenaed approximately 20 persons, including the respondent Dionisio, seeking to obtain from them voice exemplars for comparison with the recorded conversations that had been received in evidence. Each witness was advised that he was a potential defendant in a criminal prosecution. Each was asked to examine a transcript of an intercepted conversation, and to go to a nearby office of the United States Attorney to read the transcript into a recording device. The witnesses were advised that they would be allowed to have their attorneys present when they read the transcripts. Dionisio and other witnesses refused to furnish the voice exemplars, asserting that these disclosures would violate their rights under the Fourth [Amendment]. * * * Following a hearing, the district judge rejected the witnesses' constitutional arguments and ordered them to comply with the grand jury's request. * * * When Dionisio persisted in his refusal to respond to the grand jury's directive, the District Court adjudged him in civil contempt and ordered him committed to custody. * * *

The Court of Appeals for the Seventh Circuit reversed. * * * The court found that the Fourth Amendment applied to the grand jury process * * *. Equating the procedures followed by the grand jury in the present case to the fingerprint detentions in *Davis v. Mississippi* [Note 1, p. 436], the Court of Appeals reasoned that "[t]he dragnet effect here, where approximately 30 persons were subpoenaed for purposes of identification, has the same invidious effect on fourth amendment rights as the practice condemned in *Davis*."[a] The Court of Appeals held that the Fourth Amendment required a preliminary showing of reasonableness before a grand jury witness could be compelled to furnish a voice exemplar, and that in this case the proposed "seizures" of the voice exemplars would be unreasonable because of the large number of witnesses summoned by the grand jury and directed to produce such exemplars. We disagree. * * *

As [this] Court made clear in *Schmerber v. California* [p. 35], the obtaining of physical evidence from a person involves a potential Fourth Amendment violation at two different levels—the "seizure" of the "person" necessary to bring him into contact with government agents, see *Davis v. Mississippi,* and the subsequent search for and seizure of the evidence. * * * The constitutionality of the compulsory production of exemplars from a grand jury witness necessarily turns on the same dual inquiry—whether either the initial compulsion of the person to appear before the grand jury, or the subsequent directive to make a voice recording is an unreasonable "seizure" within the meaning of the Fourth Amendment.

It is clear that a subpoena to appear before a grand jury is not a "seizure" in the Fourth Amendment sense, even though that summons may be inconvenient or burdensome. Last Term we again acknowledged what has long been recognized, that "[c]itizens generally are not constitutionally immune from grand jury subpoenas...." *Branzburg v. Hayes* [Note 4, p. 829]. * * * [*Branzburg* and other decisions] are recent reaffirmations of the historically grounded obligations of every person to appear and give his evidence before the grand jury. "The personal sacrifice involved is a part of the necessary contribution of the individual to the welfare of the public." *Blair v. United States* [Note 2, p. 802].

The compulsion exerted by a grand jury subpoena differs from the seizure effected by an arrest or even an investigative "stop" in more than civic obligation. For, as Judge Friendly wrote for the Court of Appeals for the Second Circuit:

> "The latter is abrupt, is effected with force or the threat of it and often in demeaning circumstances, and, in the case of arrest, results in a record involving social stigma. A subpoena is served in the same manner as other legal process; it involves no stigma whatever; if the time for appearance is inconvenient, this can generally be altered; and it remains at all times under the control and supervision of a court."

Thus, the Court of Appeals for the Seventh Circuit correctly recognized in a case subsequent to the one now before us, that a "grand jury subpoena to testify is not that kind of governmental intrusion on privacy against which the Fourth Amendment affords protection, once the Fifth Amendment is satisfied." * * *

This case is thus quite different from *Davis v. Mississippi,* on which the Court of Appeals primarily relied. For in *Davis* it was the initial seizure—the lawless dragnet detention—that violated the Fourth and Fourteenth Amendments—not the taking of the fingerprints. * * * *Davis* is plainly inapposite to a case where the initial restraint does not itself infringe the Fourth Amendment.

This is not to say that a grand jury subpoena is some talisman that dissolves all constitutional protections. The grand jury cannot require a witness to testify

a. In *Davis*, petitioner and 24 other black youths were taken into custody, and questioned and fingerprinted, in connection with a rape for which the only leads were the victim's general description of the assailant and fingerprints around a window. The Supreme Court subsequently held that petitioner's prints should have been excluded from trial because they were obtained in violation of the Fourth Amendment. The Court left open the possibility that a court order directing that a person be detained briefly only for the purpose of obtaining his fingerprints could be sustained under the Fourth Amendment even though the individualized suspicion fell short of "probable cause in the traditional sense."

against himself. It cannot require the production by a person of private books and records that would incriminate him. See *Boyd v. United States.* The Fourth Amendment provides protection against a grand jury subpoena *duces tecum* too sweeping in its terms "to be regarded as reasonable." *Hale v. Henkel.* And last Term, in the context of a First Amendment claim, we indicated that the Constitution could not tolerate the transformation of the grand jury into an instrument of oppression: "Official harassment of the press undertaken not for purposes of law enforcement but to disrupt a reporter's relationship with his news sources would have no justification. Grand juries are subject to judicial control and subpoenas to motions to quash. We do not expect courts will forget that grand juries must operate within the limits of the First Amendment as well as the Fifth." *Branzburg v. Hayes.*

But we are here faced with no such constitutional infirmities in the subpoena to appear before the grand jury or in the order to make the voice recordings. There is * * * no valid Fifth Amendment claim. There was no order to produce private books and papers, and no sweeping subpoena *duces tecum.* And even if *Branzburg* be extended beyond its First Amendment moorings and tied to a more generalized due process concept, there is still no indication in this case of the kind of harassment that was of concern there.

The Court of Appeals found critical significance in the fact that the grand jury had summoned approximately 20 witnesses to furnish voice exemplars. We think that fact is basically irrelevant to the constitutional issues here. The grand jury may have been attempting to identify a number of voices on the tapes in evidence, or it might have summoned the 20 witnesses in an effort to identify one voice. But whatever the case, "[a] grand jury's investigation is not fully carried out until every available clue has been run down and all witnesses examined in every proper way to find if a crime has been committed." * * * The grand jury may well find it desirable to call numerous witnesses in the course of an investigation. It does not follow that each witness may resist a subpoena on the ground that too many witnesses have been called. Neither the order to Dionisio to appear, nor the order to make a voice recording was rendered unreasonable by the fact that many others were subjected to the same compulsion.

But the conclusion that Dionisio's compulsory appearance before the grand jury was not an unreasonable "seizure" is the answer to only the first part of the Fourth Amendment inquiry here. Dionisio argues that the grand jury's subsequent directive to make the voice recording was itself an infringement of his rights under the Fourth Amendment. We cannot accept that argument. In *Katz v. United States* [p. 247], we said that the Fourth Amendment provides no protection for what "a person knowingly exposes to the public, even in his home or office...." The physical characteristics of a person's voice, its tone and manner, as opposed to the content of a specific conversation, are constantly exposed to the public. Like a man's facial characteristics, or handwriting, his voice is repeatedly produced for others to hear. No person can have a reasonable expectation that others will not know the sound of his voice, any more than he can reasonably expect that his face will be a mystery to the world. * * *

Since neither the summons to appear before the grand jury, nor its directive to make a voice recording infringed upon any interest protected by the Fourth Amendment, there was no justification for requiring the grand jury to satisfy even the minimal requirement of "reasonableness" imposed by the Court of Appeals. A grand jury has broad investigative powers to determine whether a crime has been committed and who has committed it. The jurors may act on tips, rumors, evidence offered by the prosecutor, or their own personal knowledge. *Branzburg v. Hayes.* No grand jury witness is "entitled to set limits to the investigation that the grand jury may conduct." *Blair v. United States.* And a sufficient basis for an indictment may only emerge at the end of the investigation when all the evidence has been received. * * * Since Dionisio raised no valid Fourth Amendment claim, there is no more reason to require a preliminary showing of reasonableness here than there would be in the case of any witness who, despite the lack of any constitutional or statutory privilege, declined to answer a question or comply with a grand jury request. Neither the Constitution nor our prior cases justify any such interference with grand jury proceedings.[14]

The Fifth Amendment guarantees that no civilian may be brought to trial for an infamous crime "unless on a presentment or indictment of a Grand Jury." This constitutional guarantee presupposes an investigative body "acting independently of either prosecuting attorney or judge," whose mission is to clear the innocent, no less than to bring to trial those who may be guilty. Any holding that would saddle a grand jury with mini trials and preliminary showing would assuredly impede its investigation and frustrate the public's interest in the fair and expeditious administration of the criminal laws. The grand jury may not always serve its historic role as a protective bulwark standing solidly between the ordinary citizen and an overzealous prosecutor, but if it is even to approach the proper performance of its constitutional mission, it must be free to pursue its investigations unhindered by external influence or supervision so long as it does not trench upon the legitimate rights of any witness called before it. * * *

Justice MARSHALL, dissenting.[b]

* * * There can be no question that investigatory seizures effected by the police are subject to the constraints of the Fourth and Fourteenth Amendments. *Davis v. Mississippi.* * * * Like *Davis,* the present cases involve official investigatory seizures which interfere with personal liberty. The Court considers dispositive, however, the fact that the seizures were effected by the grand jury, rather than the police. I cannot agree. * * * [I]n *Hale v. Henkel,* the Court held that a subpoena *duces tecum* ordering "the production of books and papers [before a grand jury] may constitute an unreasonable search and seizure within the Fourth Amendment," and on the particular facts of the case, it concluded that the subpoena was "far too sweeping in its terms to be regarded as reasonable." Considered alone, *Hale* would certainly seem to carry a strong implication that a subpoena compelling an individual's personal appearance before a grand jury, like a subpoena ordering the production of private papers, is subject to the Fourth Amendment standard of reasonableness. The protection of the Fourth Amendment is not, after all, limited to personal "papers," but extends also to "persons," "houses," and "effects." It would seem a strange hierarchy of constitutional values that would afford papers more protection from arbitrary governmental intrusion than people.

14. Mr. Justice Marshall in dissent suggests that a preliminary showing of "reasonableness" is required where the grand jury subpoenas a witness to appear and produce handwriting or voice exemplars, but not when it subpoenas him to appear and testify. Such a distinction finds no support in the Constitution. The dissent argues that there is a potential Fourth Amendment violation in the case of a subpoenaed grand jury witness because of the asserted intrusiveness of the initial subpoena to appear—the possible stigma from a grand jury appearance and the inconvenience of the official restraint. But the initial directive to appear is as intrusive if the witness is called simply to testify as it is if he is summoned to produce physical evidence.

b. In the companion case of *United States v. Mara,* 410 U.S. 19 (1973), the Court applied *Dionisio* to reject a lower court ruling that a preliminary showing of reasonableness was needed to justify a grand jury subpoena directing a witness to produce handwriting exemplars for the purpose of determining whether he was the author of certain writings. Justice Marshall's dissent was to both rulings. The separate dissents of Justices Douglas and Brennan are omitted. Justice Douglas' dissent proceeded from the premise, described as now being "common knowledge," that "the grand jury, having been conceived as a bulwark between the citizen and the Government, is now a tool of the Executive."

The Court, however, offers two interrelated justifications for excepting grand jury subpoenas directed at "persons," rather than "papers," from the constraints of the Fourth Amendment. These are an "historically grounded obligation of every person to appear and give his evidence before the grand jury" [p. 817], and the relative unintrusiveness of the grand jury subpoena on an individual's liberty.

In my view, the Court makes more of history than is justified. The Court treats the "historically grounded obligation" * * * as extending to all "evidence," whatever its character. Yet, so far as I am aware, the obligation "to appear and give evidence" has heretofore been applied by this Court only in the context of testimonial evidence, either oral or documentary. * * * In the present case, * * * it was not testimony that the grand jury sought from respondents, but physical evidence. * * *

The Court seems to reason that the exception to the Fourth Amendment for grand jury subpoenas directed at persons is justified by the relative unintrusiveness of the grand jury process on an individual's liberty. * * * It may be that service of a grand jury subpoena does not involve the same potential for momentary embarrassment as does an arrest or investigatory "stop." But this difference seems inconsequential in comparison to the substantial stigma which—contrary to the Court's assertion—may result from a grand jury appearance as well as from an arrest or investigatory seizure. Public knowledge that a man has been summoned by a federal grand jury investigating, for instance, organized criminal activity can mean loss of friends, irreparable injury to business, and tremendous pressures on one's family life. Whatever nice legal distinctions may be drawn between police and prosecutor, on the one hand, and the grand jury, on the other, the public often treats an appearance before a grand jury as tantamount to a visit to the station house. Indeed, the former is frequently more damaging than the latter, for a grand jury appearance has an air of far greater gravity than a brief visit "downtown" for a "talk." The Fourth Amendment was placed in our Bill of Rights to protect the individual citizen from such potentially disruptive governmental intrusion into his private life unless conducted reasonably and with sufficient cause.

Nor do I believe that the constitutional problems inherent in such governmental interference with an individual's person are substantially alleviated because one may seek to appear at a "convenient time." In *Davis v. Mississippi,* it was recognized that an investigatory detention effected by the police "need not come unexpectedly or at an inconvenient time." But this fact did not suggest to the Court that the Fourth Amendment was inapplicable * * *. No matter how considerate a grand jury may be in arranging for an individual's appearance, the basic fact remains that his liberty has been officially restrained for some period of time. In terms of its effect on the individual, this restraint does not differ meaningfully from the restraint imposed on a suspect compelled to visit the police station house. Thus, the nature of the intrusion on personal liberty caused by a grand jury subpoena cannot, without more, be considered sufficient basis for denying respondents the protection of the Fourth Amendment. * * *

Whatever the present day validity of the historical assumption of neutrality which underlies the grand jury process, it must at least be recognized that if a grand jury is deprived of the independence essential to the assumption of neutrality—if it effectively surrenders that independence to a prosecutor—the dangers of excessive and unreasonable official interference with personal liberty are exactly those which the Fourth Amendment was intended to prevent. So long as the grand jury carries on its investigatory activities only through the mechanism of testimonial inquiries, the danger of such official usurpation of the grand jury process may not be unreasonably great. Individuals called to testify before the grand jury will have available their Fifth Amendment privilege against self-incrimination. Thus, at least insofar as incriminating information is sought directly from a particular criminal suspect, the grand jury process would not appear to offer law enforcement officials a substantial advantage over ordinary investigative techniques.

But when we move beyond the realm of grand jury investigations limited to testimonial inquiries, as the Court does today, the danger increases that law enforcement officials may seek to usurp the grand jury process for the purpose of securing incriminating evidence from a particular suspect through the simple expedient of a subpoena. * * * Thus, if the grand jury may summon criminal suspects [to obtain handwriting and voice exemplars] without complying with the Fourth Amendment, it will obviously present an attractive investigative tool to prosecutor and police. For what law enforcement officers could not accomplish directly themselves after our decision in *Davis v. Mississippi,* they may now accomplish indirectly through the grand jury process.

Thus, the Court's decisions today can serve only to encourage prosecutorial exploitation of the grand jury process, at the expense of both individual liberty and the traditional neutrality of the grand jury. * * * [B]y holding that the grand jury's power to subpoena these respondents for the purpose of obtaining exemplars is completely outside the purview of the Fourth Amendment, the Court fails to appreciate the essential difference between real and testimonial evidence in the context of these cases, and thereby hastens the reduction of the grand jury into simply another investigative device of law enforcement officials. By contrast, the Court of Appeals, in proper recognition of these dangers, imposed narrow limitations on the subpoena power of the grand jury which are necessary to guard against unreasonable official interference with individual liberty but which would not impair significantly the traditional investigatory powers of that body. * * *

Notes and Questions

1. ***Subpoenas and "seizures."*** Are there any circumstances under which a grand jury subpoena might be viewed as producing "a 'seizure' in the Fourth Amendment sense" (see *Dionisio* at p. 817)? What if the subpoena calls for "forthwith" compliance, i.e., the immediate production of evidence for presentation to the grand jury or the immediate appearance of the witness before the grand jury? See CRIMPROC § 8.7(e) ("federal courts have refused to hold forthwith subpoenas per se invalid by concluding that the forthwith subpoena cannot be used like a search or arrest warrant" to allow agents to engage in an immediate search or seizure of the person over the opposition of a subpoenaed party who desires to contest the subpoena in court; but they also have "rejected the contention that * * * [immediate] compliance [by the party subpoenaed] is so suspect as to assume an involuntary relinquishment of rights," determining voluntariness instead by reference to "the [particular] circumstances of the case"). See also Brenner & Lockhart, § 14.5: "Because of the potential for abuse and the unfairness that can result from requiring an immediate response from a witness, a Department of Justice internal policy limits the use of forthwith subpoenas. The policy requires prosecutors to consider the following in deciding if a forthwith subpoena is warranted: (i) the risk of flight; (ii) the risk that evidence will be destroyed or fabricated; (iii) the need for the orderly presentation of evidence to the grand jury; and (iv) the degree of inconvenience to the witness. A forthwith subpoena must be approved in advance by the U.S. Attorney. Like other Department of Justice policies, this policy does not create any rights that can be enforced against the government."

2. ***Other subpoena authority.*** Where a subpoena to testify is used in a criminal investigation, but the grand jury plays no role, does it still follow that

Fourth Amendment plays no role in regulating the issuance of such a subpoena? Although some of the states granting the prosecutor investigative subpoena authority (see Note 1, p. 798) condition that authority on a showing that the person to be subpoenaed is likely to have relevant information, others require no such showing. CRIMPROC § 8.1(c). They view requiring testimony pursuant to such a subpoena as not substantially different from requiring a person to give testimony in a discovery deposition (in both instances the witness may be accompanied by counsel and testifies outside the presence of the judge), and parties to a litigation need make no showing in support of their selection of persons to be deposed.

3. *Other identification procedures.* Does the reasoning of *Dionisio* extend to a grand jury subpoena directing the subpoenaed party to appear in a lineup? Several courts have held that it does, although some (to preclude the use of such orders simply to assist a police investigation, see Note 4, p. 834) have required that such a subpoena be approved by the grand jury itself. See *In re Melvin,* 546 F.2d 1 (1st Cir.1976). Consider also *In re Kelley*, 433 A.2d 704 (D.C.App.1981) (suggesting that a lineup is distinguishable from the identification procedures presented in *Dionisio* and *Mara* because "it entails the humiliation of standing on a stage, under floodlights, removed from counsel, subject to being compelled to speak certain words and perform actions directed by the police, all at considerably more risk of mistake and misidentification"; in any event, to prevent the prosecutor from utilizing a "grand jury pass through" to avoid the "reasonable suspicion" standard that must be met to obtain a court order directing a non-arrested suspect to appear in a lineup, court will exercise its supervisory power to mandate that "a grand jury subpoena to appear in a lineup [be supported] by an affidavit * * * mak[ing] a minimal factual showing sufficient to permit the judge to conclude that there is a reason for the lineup which is consistent with the legitimate function of the grand jury").

Courts have agreed that a special showing is needed as to the taking of blood, which has long been held to constitute a search when performed at the direction of the police (see p. 35), but have divided as to whether the presence of a grand jury subpoena alters the character of the required showing. Compare In re Grand Jury Proceedings (T.S.), 816 F.Supp. 1196 (W.D.Ky.1993) (grand jury subpoena is not available; search warrant must be obtained); *Woolverton v. Multi–County Grand Jury, Oklahoma County*, 859 P.2d 1112 (Okla.Crim.App.1993) (subpoena may be used if supported by probable cause); *Henry v. Ryan*, 775 F.Supp. 247 (N.D.Ill.1991) ("individualized suspicion" sufficient, since grand jury subpoena affords an opportunity to challenge prior to taking blood, and as Supreme Court noted in *R. Enterprise* (p. 824), at the investigatory stage of a grand jury proceeding, "the government cannot be required to justify * * * a grand jury subpoena by * * * probable cause"). As to other identification procedures, consider: *In re May 1991 Will County Grand Jury*, 604 N.E.2d 929 (Ill.1992) (*Dionisio* must be read in light of cases like *Winston v. Lee*, (Note 6, p. 349) and *Schmerber* (p. 35), so a grand jury subpoena for pubic hair samples will require a showing of probable cause); *In re Grand Jury Proceedings* (*Mills*), 686 F.2d 135 (3d Cir.1982) (*Dionisio* governs as to grand jury subpoena for scalp and facial hair; finding no need to decide whether the taking of a hair root would implicate the Fourth Amendment); In re Grand Jury Proceeding Involving Vickers, 38 F.Supp.2d 159 (D.N.H.1998) (subpoena requiring witness to furnish saliva falls "toward the middle of the continuum extending from the procedures involved in *Dionisio* and *Mara* and the taking of a blood sample; reasonableness for a grand jury subpoena established where: "the government has demonstrated that the evidence sought: (1) is plainly relevant to a legitimate and ongoing investigation being conducted by the grand jury; (2) is described with sufficient particularity to notify respondents of precisely what is sought; (3) is not sought to harass respondents or to impose some burden because of their social or political views; (4) could be probative in identifying or eliminating persons who may have participated in, or may have knowledge of or evidence relating to, the crimes under investigation; (5) can be obtained from respondents with very minimal invasion of their bodily integrity (i.e., by simply swabbing the inside of the mouth); and (6) can be obtained with no risk of physical pain, injury, or embarrassment to respondents, and with the most minimal personal inconvenience."); *In re Shabazz*; 200 F.Supp.2d 578 (D.S.C. 2002) (by analogy to cases treating breathalyzer tests and urine samples as "searches", see *Skinner v. Railway Labor Executives' Ass'n.* [Note 6, p. 442], commanding production of a saliva sample constitutes a "search" within the meaning of the Fourth Amendment; however, because a saliva swab is not as intrusive as a blood test or a surgical bullet-removal, and because the production is here ordered by a grand jury subpoena, applicable standard is "reasonable individualized suspicion" rather than probable cause).

4. ***Underlying Fourth Amendment violations.*** In UNITED STATES v. CALANDRA, 414 U.S. 338 (1974), grand jury witness Calandra was asked questions about certain records (evidencing "loan-sharking" activities) that had been seized by federal agents in connection with a search of Calandra's office. Calandra initially invoked his privilege against self-incrimination, but subsequently was granted immunity. He then requested and received a postponement of the grand jury proceedings so that he could present a pre-charge motion for return and suppression of the seized evidence under Federal Rule 41(e). The district court granted the motion, holding that the search had been unconstitutional. The district court also held that "Calandra need not answer any of the grand jury's questions based on suppressed evidence," since such questions constituted the fruit of the poisonous tree. A divided Supreme Court (6–3), per POWELL, J., reversed.

"In deciding whether to extend the exclusionary rule to grand jury proceedings, we must weigh the potential injury to the historic role and functions of the grand jury against the potential benefits of the rule as applied in this context. It is evident that this extension of the exclusionary rule would seriously impede the grand jury. Because the grand jury does not finally adjudicate guilt or innocence, it has traditionally been allowed to pursue its investigative and accusatorial functions unimpeded by the evidentiary and procedural restrictions applicable to a criminal trial. Permitting witnesses to invoke the exclusionary rule before a grand jury would precipitate adjudication of issues hitherto reserved for the trial on the merits and would delay and disrupt grand jury proceedings. Suppression hearings would halt the orderly progress of an investigation and might necessitate extended litigation of issues only tangentially related to the grand jury's primary objective. The probable result would be 'protracted interruptions of grand jury proceedings,' effectively transforming them into preliminary trials on the merits. In some cases the delay might be fatal to the enforcement of the criminal law. Just last Term we reaffirmed our disinclination to allow litigious interference with grand jury proceedings. *United States v. Dionisio.*

"Against this potential damage to the role and functions of the grand jury, we must weigh the benefits to be derived from this proposed extension of the exclusionary rule. * * * [The Court here considered the "incremental deterrent effect which might be achieved by extending the exclusionary rule to grand jury proceedings," and for reasons discussed in Note 1, p. 241, found "unrealistic" the assumption that such an extension would significantly further deterrence of illegal searches.] We decline to embrace a view that would achieve a speculative and undoubtedly minimal advance in the deterrence of police misconduct at the expense of substantially impeding the role of the grand jury."[c]

SECTION 3. OTHER OBJECTIONS TO THE INVESTIGATION

UNITED STATES v. R. ENTERPRISES, INC.

498 U.S. 292, 111 S.Ct. 722, 112 L.Ed.2d 795 (1991).

Justice O'CONNOR delivered the opinion of the Court.

This case requires the Court to decide what standards apply when a party seeks to avoid compliance with a subpoena *duces tecum* issued in connection with a grand jury investigation.

Since 1986, a federal grand jury sitting in the Eastern District of Virginia has been investigating allegations of interstate transportation of obscene materials. In early 1988, the grand jury issued a series of subpoenas to three companies—Model Magazine Distributors, Inc. (Model), R. Enterprises, Inc., and MFR Court Street Books, Inc. (MFR). Model is a New York distributor of sexually oriented paperback books, magazines, and videotapes. R. Enterprises, which distributes adult materials, and MFR, which sells books, magazines, and videotapes, are also based in New York. All three companies are wholly owned by Martin Rothstein. The grand jury subpoenas sought a variety of corporate books and records and, in Model's case, copies of 193 videotapes that Model had shipped to retailers in the Eastern District of Virginia. All three companies moved to quash the subpoenas, arguing that the subpoenas called for production of materials irrelevant to the grand jury's investigation and that the enforcement of the subpoenas would likely infringe their First Amendment rights.

The District Court, after extensive hearings, denied the motions to quash. As to Model, the court found that the subpoenas for business records were sufficiently specific and that production of the videotapes would not constitute a prior restraint. As to R. Enterprises, the court found a "sufficient connection with Virginia for further investigation by the grand jury." The court relied in large part on the statement attributed to Rothstein that the three companies were "all the same thing, I'm president of all three." Additionally, the court explained in denying MFR's motion to quash that it was "inclined to agree" with "the majority of the jurisdictions," which do not require the Government to make a "threshold showing" before a grand jury subpoena will be enforced. Even assuming that a preliminary showing of relevance was required, the court determined that the Government had made such a showing. It found sufficient evidence that the companies were "related entities," at least one of which "certainly did ship sexually explicit material into the Commonwealth of Virginia." * * * Notwithstanding these findings, the companies refused to comply with the subpoenas. The District Court found each in contempt and fined them $500 per day, but stayed imposition of the fine pending appeal.

The Court of Appeals for the Fourth Circuit upheld the business records subpoenas issued to Model, but remanded the motion to quash the subpoena for Model's videotapes. Of particular relevance here, the Court of Appeals quashed the business records subpoenas issued to R. Enterprises and MFR. In doing so, it applied the standards set out by this Court in *United States v. Nixon,* 418 U.S. 683

c. In *Gelbard v. United States,* 408 U.S. 41 (1972), the Court held that the broad exclusionary remedy of the federal wiretap Act (see fn. a, p. 474) gave grand jury witnesses the right to object to the grand jury's use of information derived from illegal electronic surveillance.

(1974). The court recognized that *Nixon* dealt with a trial subpoena, not a grand jury subpoena, but determined that the rule was "equally applicable" in the grand jury context. Accordingly, it required the Government to clear the three hurdles that *Nixon* established in the trial context—relevancy, admissibility, and specificity—in order to enforce the grand jury subpoenas. The court concluded that the challenged subpoenas did not satisfy the *Nixon* standards, finding no evidence in the record that either company had ever shipped materials into, or otherwise conducted business in, the Eastern District of Virginia. The Court of Appeals specifically criticized the District Court for drawing an inference that, because Rothstein owned all three businesses and one of them had undoubtedly shipped sexually explicit materials into the Eastern District of Virginia, there might be some link between the Eastern District of Virginia and R. Enterprises or MFR. It then noted that "any evidence concerning Mr. Rothstein's alleged business activities outside of Virginia, or his ownership of companies which distribute allegedly obscene materials outside of Virginia, would most likely be inadmissible on relevancy grounds at any trial that might occur," and that the subpoenas therefore failed "to meet the requirements [*sic*] that any documents subpoenaed under [Federal] Rule [of Criminal Procedure] 17(c) must be admissible as evidence at trial," citing *Nixon*. * * * We granted certiorari to determine whether the Court of Appeals applied the proper standard in evaluating the grand jury subpoenas issued to respondents. We now reverse.

The grand jury occupies a unique role in our criminal justice system. * * * [It] "can investigate merely on suspicion that the law is being violated, or even just because it wants assurance that it is not." *United States v. Morton Salt*, 338 U.S. 632 (1950). The function of the grand jury is to inquire into all information that might possibly bear on its investigation until it has identified the offense or has satisfied itself that none occurred. As a necessary consequence of its investigatory function, the grand jury paints with a broad brush. * * * A grand jury subpoena is thus much different from a subpoena issued in the context of a prospective criminal trial, where a specific offense has been identified and a particular defendant charged. * * *

This Court has emphasized on numerous occasions that many of the rules and restrictions that apply at a trial do not apply in grand jury proceedings. This is especially true of evidentiary restrictions. The same rules that, in an adversary hearing on the merits may increase the likelihood of accurate determinations of guilt or innocence do not necessarily advance the mission of a grand jury, whose task is to conduct an *ex parte* investigation to determine whether or not there is probable cause to prosecute a particular defendant. * * * The teaching of the Court's decisions is clear: A grand jury "may compel the production of evidence or the testimony of witnesses as it considers appropriate, and its operation generally is unrestrained by the technical procedural and evidentiary rules governing the conduct of criminal trials." *United States v. Calandra* [Note 4, p. 823].

This guiding principle renders suspect the Court of Appeals' holding that the standards announced in *Nixon* as to subpoenas issued in anticipation of trial apply equally in the grand jury context. The multifactor test announced in *Nixon* would invite procedural delays and detours while courts evaluate the relevancy and admissibility of documents sought by a particular subpoena. We have expressly stated that grand jury proceedings should be free of such delays. * * * *United States v. Dionisio*. Additionally, application of the *Nixon* test in this context ignores that grand jury proceedings are subject to strict secrecy requirements. See Fed. Rule Crim.Proc. 6(e). Requiring the Government to explain in too much detail the particular reasons underlying a subpoena threatens to compromise "the indispensable secrecy of grand jury proceedings." Broad disclosure also affords the targets of investigation far more information about the grand jury's internal workings than the Federal Rules of Criminal Procedure appear to contemplate.

The investigatory powers of the grand jury are nevertheless not unlimited. Grand juries are not licensed to engage in arbitrary fishing expeditions, nor may they select targets of investigation out of malice or an intent to harass. In this case, the focus of our inquiry is the limit imposed on a grand jury by Federal Rule of Criminal Procedure 17(c), which governs the issuance of subpoenas *duces tecum* in federal criminal proceedings. The Rule provides that "the court on motion made promptly may quash or modify the subpoena if compliance would be unreasonable or oppressive." * * * This standard is not self-explanatory. As we have observed, "what is reasonable depends on the context." In *Nixon,* this Court defined what is reasonable in the context of a jury trial. * * * But, for the reasons we have explained above, the *Nixon* standard does not apply in the context of grand jury proceedings. In the grand jury context, the decision as to what offense will be charged is routinely not made until after the grand jury has concluded its investigation. One simply cannot know in advance whether information sought during the investigation will be relevant and admissible in a prosecution for a particular offense.

To the extent that Rule 17(c) imposes some reasonableness limitation on grand jury subpoenas, however, our task is to define it. In doing so, we recognize that a party to whom a grand jury subpoena is issued faces a difficult situation. As a rule, grand juries do not announce publicly the subjects of their investigations. A party who desires to challenge a grand jury subpoena thus may have no conception of the Government's purpose in seeking production of the requested information. Indeed, the party will often not know whether he or she is a primary target of the investigation or merely a peripheral witness. Absent even minimal information, the subpoena recipient is likely to find it exceedingly difficult to persuade a court that "compliance would be unreasonable." As one pair of commentators has summarized it, the challenging party's "unenviable task is to seek to persuade the court that the subpoena that has been served on [him or her] could not possibly serve any investigative purpose that the grand jury could legitimately be pursuing." S. Beale & W. Bryson, *Grand Jury Law and Practice* § 6:28 (1986).

Our task is to fashion an appropriate standard of reasonableness, one that gives due weight to the difficult position of subpoena recipients but does not impair the strong governmental interests in affording grand juries wide latitude, avoiding minitrials on peripheral matters, and preserving a necessary level of secrecy. We begin by reiterating that the law presumes, absent a strong showing to the contrary, that a grand jury acts within the legitimate scope of its authority. * * * Consequently, a grand jury subpoena issued through normal channels is presumed to be reasonable, and the burden of showing unreasonableness must be on the recipient who seeks to avoid compliance. Indeed, this result is indicated by the language of Rule 17(c), which permits a subpoena to be quashed only "on motion" and "if *compliance* would be unreasonable" (emphasis added). To the extent that the Court of Appeals placed an initial burden on the Government, it committed error. Drawing on the principles articulated above, we conclude that where, as here, a subpoena is challenged on relevancy grounds, the motion to quash must be denied unless the district court determines that there is no reasonable possibility that the category of materials the Government seeks will produce information relevant to the general subject of the grand jury's investigation. Respondents did not challenge the subpoenas as being too indefinite nor did they claim that compliance would be overly burdensome. The Court of Appeals accordingly did not consider these aspects of the subpoenas, nor do we.

It seems unlikely, of course, that a challenging party who does not know the general subject matter of the grand jury's investigation, no matter how valid that party's claim, will be able to make the necessary showing that compliance would be unreasonable. After all, a subpoena recipient "cannot put his whole life before the court in order to show that there is no crime to be investigated." Consequently, a court may be justified in a case where unreasonableness is alleged in requiring the Government to reveal the general subject of the grand jury's investigation before requiring the challenging party to carry its burden of persuasion.[a] We need not resolve this question in the present case, however, as there is no doubt that respondents knew the subject of the grand jury investigation pursuant to which the business records subpoenas were issued. In cases where the recipient of the subpoena does not know the nature of the investigation, we are confident that district courts will be able to craft appropriate procedures that balance the interests of the subpoena recipient against the strong governmental interests in maintaining secrecy, preserving investigatory flexibility, and avoiding procedural delays. For example, to ensure that subpoenas are not routinely challenged as a form of discovery, a district court may require that the Government reveal the subject of the investigation to the trial court *in camera,* so that the court may determine whether the motion to quash has a reasonable prospect for success before it discloses the subject matter to the challenging party.[b]

Applying these principles in this case demonstrates that the District Court correctly denied respondents' motions to quash. It is undisputed that all three companies—Model, R. Enterprises, and MFR—are owned by the same person, that all do business in the same area, and that one of the three, Model, has shipped sexually explicit materials into the Eastern District of Virginia. The District Court could have concluded from these facts that there was a reasonable possibility that the business records of R. Enterprises and MFR would produce information relevant to the grand jury's investigation into the interstate transportation of obscene materials. Respondents' blanket denial of any connection to Virginia did not suffice to render the District Court's conclusion invalid. A grand jury need not accept on faith the self-serving assertions of those who may have committed criminal acts. Rather, it is entitled to determine for itself whether a crime has been committed.

Both in the District Court and in the Court of Appeals, respondents contended that these subpoenas sought records relating to First Amendment activities, and that this required the Government to demonstrate that the records were particularly relevant to its investigation. The Court of Appeals determined that the subpoenas did not satisfy Rule 17(c) and thus did not pass on the First Amendment issue. We express no view on this issue and leave it to be resolved by the Court of Appeals. * * *

Justice STEVENS, with whom Justices MARSHALL and BLACKMUN join, concurring in part and concurring in the judgment.

Federal Rule of Criminal Procedure 17(c) * * * requires the district court to balance the burden of compliance, on the one hand, against the governmental interest in obtaining the documents on the other. A more burdensome subpoena should be justified by a somewhat higher degree of probable relevance than a subpoena that imposes a minimal or nonexistent burden. Against the procedural history of this case, the Court has attempted to define the term "reasonable" in the abstract, looking only at the relevance side of the balance. Because I believe that this truncated approach to the Rule will neither provide adequate guidance to

a. The United States Attorneys' Manual directs that subpoenas contain an "advice of rights" statement (see Note 6, p. 845), which includes the following: "The grand jury is conducting an investigation of possible violations of Federal criminal laws involving: (state here the general subject matter of inquiry, e.g., conducting an illegal gambling business in violation of 18 U.S.C. § 1955)." U.S.A.M. 9–11.151.

b. Justice Scalia did not join this paragraph of the Court's opinion.

the district court nor place any meaningful constraint on the overzealous prosecutor, I add these comments. * * *

The moving party has the initial task of demonstrating to the Court that he has some valid objection to compliance. This showing might be made in various ways. Depending on the volume and location of the requested materials, the mere cost in terms of time, money, and effort of responding to a dragnet subpoena could satisfy the initial hurdle. Similarly, if a witness showed that compliance with the subpoena would intrude significantly on his privacy interests, or call for the disclosure of trade secrets or other confidential information, further inquiry would be required. Or, as in this case, the movant might demonstrate that compliance would have First Amendment implications.

The trial court need inquire into the relevance of subpoenaed materials only after the moving party has made this initial showing. And, as is true in the parallel context of pretrial civil discovery, a matter also committed to the sound discretion of the trial judge, the degree of need sufficient to justify denial of the motion to quash will vary to some extent with the burden of producing the requested information. For the reasons stated by the Court, in the grand jury context the law enforcement interest will almost always prevail, and the documents must be produced. I stress, however, that the Court's opinion should not be read to suggest that the deferential relevance standard the Court has formulated will govern decision in every case, no matter how intrusive or burdensome the request. * * *

Notes and Questions

1. ***The Schofield Approach.*** As noted by the district court in *R. Enterprises*, the "majority of jurisdictions" (indeed the vast majority) do not require the government to make a "threshold showing" as a prerequisite for enforcing a grand jury subpoena. One federal circuit does require such a showing, however. In IN RE GRAND JURY PROCEEDINGS (*Schofield*), 486 F.2d 85 (3d Cir.1973), a pre-*R. Enterprises* ruling, the Third Circuit adopted such a requirement, which it continues to apply. The petitioner in *Schofield* had refused to comply with a subpoena directing her to provide handwriting samples, photographs, and fingerprints to the grand jury, and the government had sought to have her held in civil contempt. The Third Circuit concluded that the petitioner could not be found in contempt since the government had failed to show that the items sought were "relevant to the grand jury's investigation of an offense falling within its jurisdiction." The Court (per GIBBONS, J.) reasoned:

"In view of the fact that information which would justify obtaining the handwriting exemplars, fingerprints, and a mug shot, is in the Government's sole possession, we think it reasonable that the Government be required to make some preliminary showing by affidavit that each item is at least relevant to an investigation being conducted by the grand jury and properly within its jurisdiction, and is not sought primarily for another purpose. We impose this requirement both pursuant to the federal courts' supervisory power over grand juries and pursuant to our supervisory power over civil [contempt] proceedings brought in the district court pursuant to 28 U.S.C. § 1826(a). We do not rule out the possibility that the Government's affidavit may be presented to the court *in camera,* but we do hold that Rule 6(e) does not require *in camera* presentation. * * * [U]nless extraordinary circumstances appear, the nature of which we cannot anticipate, the Government's supporting affidavit should be disclosed to the witness in the enforcement proceeding. If after such disclosure the witness makes application to the district court for additional discovery in the enforcement proceeding, the court must in deciding that request weigh the quite limited scope of an inquiry into abuse of the subpoena process, and the potential for delay, against any need for additional information which might cast doubt upon the accuracy of the Government's representations."

As noted in Beale et al., § 6.21, the Third Circuit has "generally deferred to the district courts' judgments about the sufficiency of particular '*Schofield* affidavits' in the circumstances of each case," and it accordingly has affirmed rulings holding "adequate even 'scanty' affidavits which describe the relevance of the subpoenaed material and the purpose of the grand jury investigation in only general terms." See e.g., *In re Grand Jury, Schmidt,* 619 F.2d 1022 (3d Cir.1980) (affidavit identified particular manufacturing practice under investigation, noted possible statutes violated, and identified witnesses as employees likely to be familiar with the practice and the whereabouts of relevant records). Even so interpreted, is the *Schofield* requirement consistent with the discussion in *R. Enterprises* of the applicable standard of reasonableness and the district court's authority in crafting appropriate procedures for relevancy challenges?

2. The Third Circuit applies its *Schofield* requirement to witness refusals to testify as well as refusals to comply with a subpoena *duces tecum.* However, where the witness cited for contempt had refused to give testimony, *Schofield*'s relevancy element is held to require a government showing of relevancy only as to the general subject matter of the total group of questions rather than as to specific questions. See *In re Grand Jury Investigation (Bruno),* 545 F.2d 385 (3d Cir.1976). Since *R. Enterprises* was based on Rule 17(c), which refers only to a subpoena duces tecum, does it allow for application of a similar standard of relevancy (either as to a general group of questions or as to specific questions) with respect to witness testimony? Consider also the statement of *Blair,* Note 2, p. 802, as to witness objections to relevancy.

3. ***Balancing.*** Would the balancing approach discussed in Justice Stevens concurring opinion in *R. Enterprises* permit consideration of such factors as: (1) the seriousness of the crime being investigated (see Stuntz, Note 2, p. 812); (2) the likelihood that the evidence subpoenaed would only duplicate evidence previously received (e.g., where the grand jury has previously received from a bank an individual's checking account records and now subpoenas those records from the individual); (3) the breadth of information likely to be disclosed by compliance (e.g., where the subpoena requires all financial records), and (4) the likelihood that the documents will disclose "personal" (as opposed to "organizational") information (see Slobogin, Note 5, p. 815)? Lower courts have not read the *R. Enterprises* opinions as authorizing a general case-by-case balancing in applying Rule 17(c) to subpoenas duces tecum, but they have been open to requiring something more than the *R. Enterprises* standard of relevance under special circumstances, as illustrated by Notes 4, 5, and 6 below.

4. ***"Chilling effect": First Amendment objections.*** Lower courts have divided as to the standard to be applied where the subpoenaed party claims that compliance would have a chilling impact upon the exercise of a First Amendment right. In *Branzburg v. Hayes,* 408 U.S. 665 (1972), the Supreme Court rejected the contention that the First Amendment prohibited a subpoena compelling reporters to testify before the grand jury as to information received in confidence (including the identity of their confidential sources) absent a government showing of "compelling need." The Court concluded that even if requiring reporters to appear and testify might have a negative impact upon news gathering by deterring future confidential sources, that impact did not outweigh the interest of the public in the grand jury's investigation of crime. The majority noted (and Justice Powell's concurring opinion stressed in particular) that judicial control of the grand jury process was always available to provide an appropriate remedy if the grand jury process was used to "harass the press."[c]

Relying on *Branzburg*, the Fourth Circuit, on remand in *R. Enterprises*, rejected the First Amendment claim that had not been considered by the Supreme Court. See *In re Grand Jury 87–3 Subpoena Duces Tecum*, 955 F.2d 229 (4th Cir.1992). The Fourth Circuit found unpersuasive the reasoning of the Ninth Circuit in *Bursey v. United States*, 466 F.2d 1059 (9th Cir.1972). *Bursey* had distinguished *Branzburg* as a case involving only a peripheral First Amendment concern. It had insisted upon the government showing a "substantial connection" between the information sought by the grand jury and an overriding government interest in the subject matter under investigation where disclosure of that information would bear directly on the exercise of First Amendment rights (applicable there, where the grand jury sought information relating to the activities of the Black Panthers and their publication of a newspaper, which had reported a threat against the president). The Fourth Circuit read *Branzburg* as having rejected requiring such a special showing of need, and having instead relied upon the district court's capacity to prevent the "bad faith" use of the subpoena authority to "harass" as "striking a proper balance" between the "obligation of all citizens to give relevant testimony with respect to criminal conduct" and the possible chilling impact on the exercise of First Amendment rights.

Other courts have also refused to require a special showing of need, but some have been divided in doing so. See *In re Grand Jury Matter (Gronowicz),* 764 F.2d 983 (3d Cir.1985) (en banc) (where grand jury was investigating author's possible fraud in representing to the publisher that the book was based on interviews with high church officials, and it subpoenaed materials concerning the alleged interviews, no special First Amendment limitations would be imposed even though grand jury inquiry necessarily would be examining the truthfulness of the book's description of those interviews; two dissenters argued that the government lacked a sufficiently compelling interest for such an investigation, which would undermine First Amendment values, and it therefore could not justify the subpoena); *In re Grand Jury Subpoenas for Locals 17, 135, 257 and 608,* 528 N.E.2d 1195 (N.Y.1988) (where grand jury was investigating union corruption, possibly extending to rank and file members as well as officials, subpoena requesting names, addresses, telephone numbers and social security numbers of all 10,000 members is supported by a "legitimate and compelling" need as it will enable the grand jury to locate and identify potential witnesses "without unduly burdening or delaying the search and without having to proceed through the traditional channels of first notifying the union leaders and exposing witnesses to possible intimidation"; dissent concluded that disclosure would infringe "on associational and privacy rights by chilling members' participation in the full range of union activities," particularly with fear of newspaper leaks regarding the investigation, and the grand jury therefore should be required to show the inadequacy of seemingly viable alternatives, such as disclosure of a percentage of the membership, or protecting against the union learning of the key target groups by having it deliver

c. A subsequently adopted Department of Justice policy statement relating to "subpoenas to members of the news media" and "subpoenas for telephone toll records of members of the news media" (a helpful vehicle in determining a reporter's contacts) includes the following directives: (1) "all reasonable attempts should first be made to obtain information from alternative sources"; (2) negotiations with the media should be pursued, seeking to "accommodate the interests * * * of the grand jury with the interests of the media"; (3) no subpoena shall be issued without the express authorization of the Attorney General; and (4) "in criminal cases, there should be reasonable grounds to believe, based on information obtained from nonmedia sources, that a crime has occurred, and that the information sought is essential to a successful investigation—particularly with reference to directly establishing guilt or innocence, * * * [with the subpoena] not be used to obtain peripheral, nonessential, or speculative information." 28 CFR § 50.10.

the complete list to a neutral third party, with the government then obtaining from that custodian the needed information as to those groups).

Library records. By amending 50 U.S.C.A. § 1861 (see Note 1, p. 798) to encompass all business records, the USA PATRIOT ACT of 2001 opened up the possibility that the F.B.I., in a terrorism investigation, could obtain a court order directing a library to disclose the borrowing records of its patrons (and prohibiting the library from informing the patrons of that disclosure, see fn. j, p. 799). That potential (the Department of Justice subsequently announced in 2003 that such authority had never been used) has led to proposed legislation that would provide special protection for library patron records. See Ann Klinefelter, *The Role of Librarians in Challenges to the USA PATRIOT ACT*, 5 N.C.J. L. & Tech. 219 (2004), Note 6, p. 277. The proposed legislation focuses on § 1861 and does not impact grand jury subpoenas. As noted in Paul Rosenzweig, *Civil Liberty and the Response to Terrorism*, 42 Duq.L.Rev. 663 (2004), "ordinary grand juries" have subpoenaed patron records from libraries and bookstores in various investigations, including several that were quite prominent: "[I]n the 1997 Gianni Versace murder case, a Florida grand jury subpoenaed records from public libraries in Miami Beach, and in the 1990 Zodiac gunmen investigation, a New York grand jury subpoenaed records from a public library in Manhattan. Investigators believed that the gunman was inspired by a Scottish occult poet, and wanted to learn who had checked out his books. In the Unibomber investigation, law enforcement officials sought the records of various libraries, hoping to identify the Unibomber as a former student with particular reading interests."

5. *"Chilling effect": Attorney subpoenas.* Assume that a grand jury subpoenas the attorney representing one of several targets in an organized crime investigation and asks that attorney for information of possible relevancy to the investigation that is not protected by the attorney-client privilege (e.g., whether that target arranged for the legal representation of certain persons thought to be a member of the same organized crime "family"). Should a special showing of need, similar to that imposed in *Bursey,* Note 4 supra, be required to overcome the "chilling impact" that such questioning may have upon the lawyer-client relationship?[d] The several circuit courts considering the issue have all refused to impose such a requirement as a general rule (although some dissenting judges would have done so). See CRIMPROC § 8.8. They have noted that: (1) the target has no constitutional right to counsel with respect to the grand jury proceeding (see Note 8, p. 846); (2) the attorney-client privilege provides adequate protection of the attorney-client relationship; (3) it is at most a "speculative" and "abstract possibility" that the attorney's testimony before the grand jury will lead to his or her disqualification as defense counsel should the target eventually be indicted; and (4) the target is asking, in effect, for the "same kind of preliminary showing which the Supreme Court had disapproved [in *Dionisio* and *Branzburg*] as causing indeterminate delays in grand jury investigations." At the same time, the district court has been held to have authority to quash such a subpoena under "compel-

d. As a matter of internal policy, the Department of Justice does impose special prerequisites for subpoenaing an attorney to furnish information before a grand jury regarding a past or current client. U.S. Attorneys' Manual 9–13.410 authorizes use of attorney subpoenas (upon approval of an Assistant Attorney General) where (i) there exists "reasonable grounds to believe that a crime has been or is being committed and that the information sought is reasonably needed for the successful completion of the investigation," (ii) "all reasonable attempts to obtain the information from alternative sources shall have proved to be unsuccessful," (iii) the information is not "protected by a valid claim of privilege," and is not "peripheral or speculative," and (iv) "the need for the information * * * outweigh[s] the potential adverse effects upon the attorney-client relationship" (in particular, "the risk that the attorney will be disqualified from representation of the client as a result of having to testify against the client").

ling circumstances''. See *In re Grand Jury Matters,* 751 F.2d 13 (1st Cir.1984) (attorneys were currently representing same client in a state criminal proceeding).

In 1990, the ABA amended Rule 3.8 of the Model Rules of Professional Responsibility to deal specifically with attorney subpoenas. Subsection (f) provided that a "prosecutor in a criminal case * * * shall not subpoena a lawyer in a grand jury or other criminal proceeding to present evidence about a past or current client unless (1) the prosecutor reasonably believes: (i) the information sought is not protected from disclosure by any applicable privilege; (ii) the evidence sought is essential to the successful completion of an ongoing investigation or prosecution; (iii) there is no other feasible alternative to obtain the information; and (2) the prosecutor obtains prior judicial approval after an opportunity for an adversarial proceeding." In 1995, the subparagraph (2) requirement of prior judicial approval was deleted from Rule 3.8(f). However several states had already adopted Rule 3.8 with that provision. When federal district courts sought to make those ethical rules applicable to United States Attorneys, two circuits divided on whether they had the authority to do so. See *United States v. Colorado Supreme Court,* 87 F.3d 1161 (10th Cir.1996) (collecting citations and also recognizing the standing of the U.S. Attorney to challenge the state high court's application of those rules to lawyers in that office).

In 1998, Congress adopted the Citizen Protection Act, 28 U.S.C.A § 530B, which provides that an "attorney for 'the Government' shall be subject to State laws and rules and local Federal court rules governing attorneys * * * to the same extent and in the same manner as other attorneys in that State." Where states have adopted the original version of Rule 3.8(f), does the Citizens Protection Act create federal district court jurisdiction to review under the standards of Rule 3.8(f) federal grand jury subpoenas directed to attorneys? In *Stern v. United States District Court,* 214 F.3d 4 (1st Cir.2000), the First Circuit held that the CPA did not encompass the 1991 version of ABA Model Rule 3.8, because the CPA extended only to "ethical standards," and Rule 3.8, though "doubtless motivated by ethical concerns," is "more than an ethical standard"; "it adds a novel procedural step—the opportunity for a pre-service adversarial hearing—and to compound the matter, ordains that the hearing be conducted with new substantive standards in mind."

United States v. Colorado Supreme Court, 189 F.3d 1281 (10th Cir.1999), considered the application in a non-grand jury setting of a state rule incorporating the amended ABA Rule 3.8. The Tenth Circuit concluded that the CPA did encompass such a rule, but the remedy for violation could only be a disciplinary proceeding, not quashing the subpoena, as there was no indication that Congress intended through the CPA to alter Federal Rule 17(c) and the substantive standards for issuing subpoenas developed under that rule. Cf. United States v. Lowery, Note 6, p. 744 (no exclusionary rule for evidentiary fruits of a CPA violation). Does limiting the remedy for violating the CPA to disciplinary proceedings provide sufficient implementation of the court's conclusion that Congress decided not to grant to the states authority to modify federal "substantive law" governing subpoenas? Consider Jesselyn Radack, *The Big Chill: Negative Effects of the McDade Amendment and Conflict Between Federal Statutes*, 14 Geo.J. Legal Ethics 707 (2001) (citing instances in which Federal prosecutors, fearing possible disciplinary sanctions, have not exercised authority seemingly authorized under federal law).

6. *Oppressive burdens.* Rule 17(c) and similar state provisions authorize quashing subpoenas where compliance would be "unreasonable or oppressive." Does oppressiveness constitute an alternative and distinct ground for quashing a grand jury subpoena? Consider in *In re Grand Jury Proceedings (Danbom),* 827 F.2d 301 (8th Cir.1987). The Eighth Circuit acknowledged that a subpoena seeking records of all wire transfers of $1,000 or more over a 2 year period from Western Union's major Kansas City office met relevancy requirements for a grand jury investigating drug trafficking, but concluded that, under Rule 17(c), consideration could be given to Western Union's concern that the publicity resulting from its production of the records of many innocent persons would lead such persons to stop transmitting funds through Western Union.

7. ***Subject matter challenges.*** After commenting generally upon the scope of the grand jury's investigative authority and the corresponding obligations and rights of grand jury witnesses [see Note 2, p. 802], the Court in *Blair v. United States,* 250 U.S. 273 (1919), quickly disposed of the petitioners' claim that their refusal to testify was justified because the subject under investigation (possible violations of the Federal Corrupt Practices Act in the course of a primary election) was beyond the regulatory authority of the federal government. Justice Pitney noted for the Court: "And for the same reasons, witnesses are not entitled to take exception to the jurisdiction of the grand jury or the court over the particular subject-matter that is under investigation. In truth it is in the ordinary case no concern of one summoned as a witness whether the offense is within the jurisdiction of the court or not. At least, the court and grand jury have authority and jurisdiction to investigate the facts in order to determine the question whether the facts show a case within their jurisdiction. The present cases are not exceptional, and for the reasons that have been outlined we are of opinion that appellants were not entitled to raise any question about the constitutionality of the statutes under which the grand jury's investigation was conducted."

Prior to *R. Enterprises,* lower courts had divided as to whether *Blair* precluded consideration of a witness' objection that a grand jury inquiry concerns alleged criminal activity having no bearing upon the district in which the grand jury sits (and therefore activity for which the grand jury may not indict). Does *R. Enterprises* now make that a cognizable objection (albeit one difficult to sustain)? What of the challenge raised in *In re Sealed Case,* 827 F.2d 776 (D.C.Cir.1987)—that the grand jury subpoena was issued upon application of the office Independent Counsel and "that office violated constitutional principles of separation of powers"? In *Morrison v. Olson,* 487 U.S. 654 (1988), the Court reached the merits of that claim (and rejected it), but noted that the Independent Counsel had failed to object in the district court to consideration of the merits of the challenge to her office, and such an objection, "is not 'jurisdictional' in the sense that it cannot be waived by failing to raise it at the proper time and place." As discussed in the notes below, federal courts have long held cognizable challenges to alleged prosecutorial misuse of grand jury subpoenas.

NOTES ON MISUSE OBJECTIONS

1. Both federal and state courts traditionally have recognized witness objections to alleged prosecutorial misuse of the grand jury process (i.e., using the process for purposes other than furthering the grand jury's investigation). Such instances of misuse include: (1) employment of the grand jury process "primarily" to elicit evidence for use in a pending or future civil action; (2) employment of the grand jury process "for the sole or dominating purpose of preparing an already pending indictment for trial"; (3) employment of the grand jury process to further independent investigations by police or prosecutor rather than to produce evidence for grand jury use; and (4) calling a witness for the purpose of "harassment," with "harassment" described as encompassing various objectives other than producing relevant evidence, such as burdening the witness with repeated appearances or seeking to punish the witness by forcing him into a situation where he will refuse to answer (or lie) and be held for contempt (or perjury). See CRIMPROC § 8.8.

2. As noted in CRIMPROC § 8.8, a common thread running through the judicial treatment of misuse objections is that "a presumption of regularity" attaches to the grand jury proceeding and the objecting party bears a substantial burden in seeking to overcome that presumption. It clearly is not sufficient simply to show that the use of the process has (or will) benefit the government with respect to civil discovery, criminal discovery on a pending indictment, or some other alleged improper purpose. Courts have stressed that misuse exists only if the "sole or dominant" prosecutorial purpose is improper, and that the prosecutor will not be enjoined from carrying forward a legitimate grand jury investigation simply because one byproduct may be the production of evidence useful in other proceedings in which the government has some interest. To gain an evidentiary hearing on a claim of alleged misuse, the objecting party ordinarily must at least point to surrounding circumstances "highly suggestive" of improper purpose.

What should constitute such a showing? Where a grand jury investigation was instituted shortly after the target's legal challenges stymied the government's civil investigation, does that suggest misuse notwithstanding a substantial overlap in the applicable civil and criminal law governing the activities in question? Cf. *In re Grand Jury Subpoenas, April, 1978,* 581 F.2d 1103 (4th Cir.1978). Where a grand jury is investigating the same basic activities that led to indictment of the objecting party, and that party alleges that some of the witnesses to be called before that grand jury may be defense witnesses, does that establish a sufficient grounding for an evidentiary hearing notwithstanding a government response that the grand jury investigation is aimed at determining whether others had also been involved in the offense? Cf. *United States v. Doe (Ellsberg),* 455 F.2d 1270 (1st Cir.1972).

3. Even where the surrounding circumstances strongly suggest improper use to obtain civil discovery or discovery on a pending criminal indictment, courts have expressed a reluctance to judge the dominant purpose of the investigation while it is still ongoing. The objecting party, it is noted, should not be allowed to "break up the play before it was started and then claim the government was offsides." *United States v. Doe (Ellsberg),* supra. A preferable remedy, courts note, is to allow the investigation to continue to its completion and then judge its purpose if the government should attempt to utilize the fruits of its alleged misuse in another proceeding. Where the alleged improper purpose is the development of evidence for a civil proceeding, the Rule 6(e) motion needed to disclose the grand jury material to civil attorneys (see fn. h, p. 796) ordinarily will provide the objecting party with an opportunity to challenge the purpose of the investigation after it has been completed. See *In re Grand Jury Subpoenas, April, 1978,* Note 2 supra. Where the alleged improper purpose is gaining additional information for use in the trial on a pending indictment, the judge presiding at that trial can determine whether to require an inquiry into the dominant purpose of the post-indictment grand jury investigation when (and if) the government makes use in its prosecution of the fruits of that allegedly tainted investigation. See *United States v. Doe (Ellsberg).*

4. Claims that the grand jury process was used to further independent police investigations commonly are presented where the individual subpoenaed to appear before the grand jury was offered the opportunity to avoid the grand jury appearance by giving a statement to the police or prosecutor. Although noting that it is improper to use the grand jury subpoena "as a ploy to secure the attendance of a witness at the prosecutor's office," courts have held that offering the witness the option of presenting information informally is not misuse where the prosecutor intends (after screening) to present that information to the grand jury. CRIMPROC § 8.8. So too, where the witness was first approached by the police and refused to provide information, the prosecutor may convert the investigation into a grand jury inquiry and seek the same information by subpoena. Ibid.

NOTES ON THIRD PARTY SUBPOENAS

1. ***Target standing.*** As discussed in Note 4, p. 813, *Miller v. United States* concluded that a target of an investigation lacks standing to raise a Fourth Amendment challenge to a subpoena demanding from a third party its records relating to the target, even where those records were originally created by the target. Lower courts have held, however, that where a challenge to a third party subpoena is based on a grand jury misuse that impacts the rights of the target, then the target may challenge that subpoena. Thus, *In re Grand Jury Proceedings (Fernandez Diamante)*, 814 F.2d 61 (1st Cir.1987), held that an indicted defendant could move to quash a subpoena directing a travel agency to produce records relating to defendant's airline travel where the defendant alleged that government was misusing the grand jury subpoena for discovery in the criminal case against him. The First Circuit acknowledged that, unlike certain cases recognizing victim standing in other contexts, the defendant here did not have any property interest in the travel agency's records and could not allege that production of those records would violate some privilege of non-disclosure to which he was entitled. However, standing to challenge the subpoena could also be based on "the harm to [petitioner's] interest as a defendant in a criminal trial and as a victim of a systematic abuse of the powers of the grand jury." The court found support for such standing in Supreme Court precedent recognizing a civil defendant's right to challenge the governments improper disclosure of grand jury material for possible use against it in a civil suit. *See United States v. Sells Engineering, Inc.*, 463 U.S. 418 (1983). The court further noted that it was not carrying standing as far as suggested in a Third Circuit decision, *In re Grand Jury (Schmidt)*, 619 F.2d 1022 (3rd Cir.1980) which could conceivably be read as allowing a corporate employer to challenge subpoenas aimed at the harassment of its witness-employees.

In re Grand Jury, 111 F.3d 1066 (3rd Cir.1997), recognized the standing of victims of a privately executed wiretap to quash a subpoena duces tecum directing the perpetrator of the wiretap to convey recordings of the unlawful intercepted communications to the grand jury. The court majority noted that, in light of the statutory prohibition against use of illegally intercepted wire communication in grand jury proceedings (see fn.c, p. 824), the interests asserted by the wiretap victims (the target of the grand jury investigation and her husband) could "fairly be said to resemble a privilege," but in light of the reasoning of *Schmidt*, supra, it "need not characterize their interests as such in order to find standing." At stake here was a privacy interest, given "maximum protection" by a federal statute, which would be further violated by any unlawful disclosure to the grand jury. The petitioners here met the "jurisprudential concerns" of standing doctrine: they presented a claim based on their own statutory right, rather than that of the witness; that claim presented "a precise question arising from a specific grievance," rather than an "abstract question"; and since the subpoena recipient was the alleged perpetrator of the unlawful recordings, it was "the interveners and not the witness herself who are best suited to assert [the statutory] claim." While "recognition of standing in situations such as this one will undoubtedly result in delays in grand jury investigations," a motion to quash "had not traditionally been regarded an unreasonable burden on grand jury proceedings" where filed by the subpoena recipient, and should not be so viewed where filed by "a third party with an important interest as stake." The dissenting opinion disagreed, in particular, with this last prong of the majority's analysis. It concluded that "the majority's holding that a third party, such as a target * * *, may move to quash the subpoena issued to a witness during the grand jury investigation * * * runs counter to well-established precedent [e.g., *Dionisio*] disallowing procedures that would delay and disrupt grand jury proceedings."

2. *Target notification.* To make effective use of any standing to quash a subpoena issued to a third party, the target needs notification of the issuance of the subpoena in time to intervene before the third party complies. In *Securities and Exchange Commission v. Jerry T. O'Brien, Inc.*, 467 U.S. 735 (1984), in the context of an administrative agency subpoena (see Note 2, p. 799), the Supreme Court concluded that, assuming arguendo that the target of an investigation had standing to challenge a subpoena requiring a third party (here a brokerage firm) to produce records relating to the target's activities, the administrative agency had no obligation to notify the target of the issuance of the subpoena. Requiring such notice, the Court noted, would be highly burdensome for the agency and would "substantially increase the ability of persons who have something to hide to impede legitimate investigations" by informing them that they are being investigated. The Court would not impose such a notification requirement where Congress had failed to do so.

In the grand jury setting, the secrecy obligation imposed on the prosecution precludes it from informing a target that the grand jury has issued a subpoena to a third party. Where the secrecy obligation is also imposed on witnesses (see fn. i, p. 797), that obligation would also bar the third party witness from informing the target of the subpoena. In the vast majority of jurisdictions, including the federal system, the witness is not subject to a secrecy obligation. Thus, the witness is free to inform the target, and is likely to do so where the target is a customer of the third party witness (as in *Fernandez Diamante*, Note 1 supra). Several federal courts have recognized an inherent judicial authority to issue a protective order prohibiting witness disclosures during an ongoing investigation upon a prosecution showing of "compelling need" (e.g., that an informed target will seek to obstruct justice). Others suggest, however, that such authority is preempted by the Rule 6(e) directive that "no obligation of secrecy may be imposed except in accordance with Rule 6(e)(2)(B)" (which lists the persons subject to secrecy and does not include witnesses). See CRIMPROC § 8.5(d).

3. *Legislative grants of standing and notification.* In several instances, Congress has granted to potential targets standing to challenge third party subpoenas on specific grounds, and has implemented that right by generally requiring notification. The most prominent of such statutes are the Right to Financial Privacy Act (RFPA), 12 U.S.C.A. §§ 3401–3420, and Title II of the Electronic Communication Privacy Act (ECPA), 18 U.S.C. §§ 2701–2711 (also known as the "Stored Communications Act"). Although similar in some respects, these Act take quite different approaches as to grand jury subpoenas.

(a) *The RFPA.* The RFPA, in general, places conditions on the use of federal process to obtain from financial institutions (which include not only the usual variety of banks, but also "consumer finance institutions" and issuers of "credit cards") the financial account records of a limited class of their customers (basically individuals and small partnerships). As to both "administrative" and "judicial" subpoenas, the RFPA generally requires: (1) customer notification, (2) a waiting period prior to actual disclosure by the financial institution, and (3) a right of the customer to challenge the subpoena during the waiting period on the grounds that "the financial records are not relevant to the legitimate law enforcement inquiry stated by the Government authority in its notice [to the customer]" or that "there has not been substantial compliance with this chapter" (although the notice provision speaks generally of challenging relevancy or advancing "any other legal basis for objecting to the release of the records"). See 12 U.S.C.A. §§ 3405, 3407, 3410. The RFPA also provides, however, that the notice required under the administrative subpoena and judicial subpoena provisions may be delayed by court order upon a finding that: (1) the investigation being conducted is "within the lawful jurisdiction of the Government authority seeking the financial records," (2) there is reason to believe that the records are "relevant" to that investigation, and (3) notification will result in either (i) endangering the life or safety of any person, (ii) flight from prosecution, (iii) "destruction of or tampering with evidence," (iv) intimidation of a potential witness, or (iv) "otherwise seriously jeopardizing the investigation." 12 U.S.C.A. § 3409. The mandated delay ordinarily is limited to 90 days, with the customer thereafter receiving notice that the subpoena was issued and the identified documents were delivered to the government by the financial institution.

The basic RFPA provisions do not apply to grand jury subpoenas, as RFPA's exemption provision excludes disclosures to the grand jury (as well to the IRS and intelligence agencies). The grand jury exemption provision means that the RFPA does not create customer standing to challenge the subpoena and does not require customer notification as to a grand jury subpoena. In general, the RFPA leaves disclosure of a grand jury subpoena to the secrecy provisions of Federal Rule 6 (see Note 5, p. 794), which would permit the subpoenaed financial institution, at its option, to notify the customer. However, the RFPA does authorize the grand jury to obtain a judicial order that bars the financial institution from notifying the customer as to the "existence of the subpoena or the information furnished." That order is to be issued by the court for the period specified, and under the procedures established, in the § 3409 delayed-notice provision described above. In addition, § 3420 contains a seemingly permanent prohibition against disclosure to the target where the investigation relates to drug offenses and crimes against a financial institution. But cf. *Doe v. Ashcroft*, 334 F.Supp.2d 471 (S.D.N.Y.2004) (distinguishing the grand jury cases discussed in fn. i, p. 797, the court holds unconstitutional a provision permanently barring an internet service provider from notifying its customer of receipt of a National Security Letter from the F.B.I. that required the provider to furnish customer records; the permanent disclosure prohibition is not sufficiently "narrowly tailored" to be an acceptable restriction on speech, as it is not subject to judicial review and modification).

(b) *The ECPA*. The ECPA governs the use of federal or state process to obtain a variety of stored account information from different types of interstate network service providers. The ECPA allows only certain classes of information to be obtained by subpoena, and where that is allowed, no distinction is drawn between a grand jury subpoena and an administrative subpoena. See e.g., 18 U.S.C.A. § 2703(b)(B)(i). Initially, compelled disclosure of an unretrieved (i.e., unopened) communication (e.g., voice mail or e-mail) held in storage less than 180 days is treated as the equivalent of a search and requires a search warrant (i.e., it cannot be reached by a grand jury subpoena). Secondly, certain transactional and account records also cannot be reached by subpoena, as compelled disclosure here requires either a search warrant or special court order. Under § 2703(d) issuance of that order requires a "specific and articulable facts showing that there are reasonable grounds to believe * * * that the records * * * sought are relevant and material to an ongoing investigation." Third, unretrieved communications left in electronic storage for 180 days (or more) can be obtained by subpoena, but generally only with "prior notice from the government entity to the subscriber or customer." 18 U.S.C.A. § 2703(b)(B). A court order that permits the subpoena to issue with notice delayed for 90 days is available under standards roughly identical to RFPA's delayed notice provision. Fourth, accessed (i.e., opened) communications left with the provider in storage also can be obtained by subpoena only with customer notification (or a court order delaying notice) where obtained from providers making services available to the public (e.g., AOL). However, where accessed communications are left in storage with a non-public provider (e.g., an employer), the FCPA does not apply, thereby permitting use of a grand jury subpoena without notice. Finally, basic subscriber information is available by subpoena without any required notification. However, a court order prohibiting the service provider from notifying the customer for 90 days is available upon a showing as to any of the five adverse results noted in the delayed-notification provision.

The ECPA permits a "subscriber" to bring a civil action for a "violation of this chapter in which the conduct constituting the violation is engaged in with a knowing or intentional state of mind." That grounding for relief is restricted both by its mens rea prerequisite and its limitation to violations of the requirements of the chapter, which do not include any requirement as to the specific grounding for issuance of a grand jury subpoena. If the Act itself was violated with the necessary mens rea, and the subscriber is able to bring the civil action prior to compliance, enforcement of a subpoena could be enjoined as the available relief includes such "equitable or declaratory relief as may be appropriate." However, if the government has already obtained the records in question, exclusion will not be available as the listed remedies do not include exclusion and the ECPA specifically provides that those remedies "are the only judicial remedies * * * for nonconstitutional violations of this chapter." See also U.S. Department of Justice, *Searching and Seizing Computers and Obtaining Electronic Evidence in Criminal Investigations* (July 2002) (providing a much more detailed analysis of the various complexities of the ECPA); Orin G. Kerr, *A User's Guide to the Stored Communications Act—And a Legislator's Guide to Amending It*, 72 Geo.Wash.L.Rev. 1208 (2004).

SECTION 4. GRAND JURY TESTIMONY AND THE PRIVILEGE AGAINST SELF-INCRIMINATION[a]

A. GRAND JURY TESTIMONY

1. ***Application of the privilege.*** *Counselman v. Hitchcock,* 142 U.S. 547 (1892), put to rest any doubts as to whether the privilege against self-incrimination was available to a grand jury witness. The grand jury witness testifies pursuant to a subpoena so the requisite element of "compulsion" clearly is present. However, the Amendment states only that a person shall not be compelled to be a witness against himself "in a criminal case." The *Counselman* Court reasoned that the grand jury inquiry into criminal liability was itself a "criminal case," but that characterization was not, in any event, a prerequisite to the availability of the privilege. The Fifth Amendment's "criminal case" requirement, it noted, refers to the eventual use of the testimony, not the nature of the proceeding in which it is compelled. Accordingly, the Fifth Amendment applies to a witness "in any proceeding" who is being compelled to give testimony that might incriminate him in a subsequent criminal case.[b]

a. The grand jury witness may also utilize any other testimonial privileges recognized in the particular jurisdiction. Thus, the privileges applicable before federal grand juries are those generally recognized in federal courts. See Fed. R.Evid. 1101(d)(2), 501. We have focused here on the privilege against self-incrimination because it provides "what is undoubtedly [the witness'] most significant safeguard in responding to a subpoena ad testificandum." CRIMPROC § 8.10(a).

b. *Counselman's* analysis of the function of the "criminal case" phrasing in the Fifth Amendment had significance far beyond the grand jury. It led to a long line of cases holding the self-incrimination privilege available to witnesses in various non-criminal proceedings, including civil cases and administrative agency hearings. These rulings traditionally were viewed, consistent with *Counselman's* analysis, as reflecting the command of the Fifth Amendment itself; but that position seemingly was rejected by a majority of the Court in *Chavez v. Martinez* [p. 695]. In *Chavez*, the opinions of both Justice Thomas and Justice Souter considered the grounding of the various rulings allowing witnesses in civil cases and other noncriminal proceedings to exercise the privilege. The Thomas opinion described those cases as establishing a "prophylactic rule" (see p. 697), and the Souter opinion described those opin-

2. ***The nature of "incriminating" testimony.*** As *Counselman* noted, the privilege only applies to testimony which is "incriminating"—i.e., to testimony which may "tend to show" that the witness himself "had committed a crime." What standard is applied in determining whether particular testimony has that tendency and who makes that determination? The leading case on both questions is HOFFMAN v. UNITED STATES, 341 U.S. 479 (1951). In that case, a witness subpoenaed before a federal grand jury relied on the privilege in refusing to answer questions as to his current occupation and his contacts with a fugitive witness. The district court found that there was "no real and substantial danger of incrimination" and the privilege therefore was inapplicable. When the witness persisted in his claim, he was held in contempt. In reversing that conviction, the Supreme Court (per CLARK, J.) set forth the following guidelines for the district courts:

"The privilege afforded not only extends to answers that would in themselves support a conviction under a federal criminal statute but likewise embraces those which would furnish a link in the chain of evidence needed to prosecute the claimant for a federal crime. But this protection must be confined to instances where the witness has reasonable cause to apprehend danger from a direct answer. The witness is not exonerated from answering merely because he declares that in so doing he would incriminate himself—his say-so does not of itself establish the hazard of incrimination. It is for the court to say whether his silence is justified, and to require him to answer if 'it clearly appears to the court that he is mistaken.' However, if the witness, upon interposing his claim, were required to prove the hazard in the sense in which a claim is usually required to be established in court, he would be compelled to surrender the very protection which the privilege is designed to guarantee. To sustain the privilege, it need only be evident from the implications of the question, in the setting in which it is asked, that a responsive answer to the question or an explanation of why it cannot be answered might be dangerous because injurious disclosure could result."

It has been suggested that under the *Hoffman* guidelines, it will be a "rare case" in which a court can reject a grand jury witness' assertion of the privilege. See CRIMPROC § 8.10(a).[c] Consider in this connection the *Hoffman* case itself, where the Court had no difficulty in concluding that the district court erred in denying petitioner's claim of the privilege. The Court reasoned that, since the district court was aware that the grand jury was investigating racketeering, it should have recognized that questions concerning Hoffman's current occupation might require answers relating to violations of federal gambling laws. It also should have recognized that information concerning Hoffman's contacts with the fugitive witness might tie him to efforts to hide that witness. See also *Ohio v. Reiner*. 532 U.S. 17 (2001) (state court erred in holding that privilege would not have been available to babysitter who later testified, under an immunity grant, that she had never shaken deceased infant or his twin brother and "she was unaware of and had nothing to do with the * * * injuries" to the two infants, as her testimony also acknowledged that she "spent extended periods of time alone with the children in the weeks immediately preceding discovery of their injuries" and "was with [the deceased infant] within the potential time frame of [his] fatal

ions as resting on "law * * * outside the Fifth Amendment's core," which provided "complimentary protection" to the core's prohibition of "courtroom use of a criminal defendant's compelled self-incriminatory testimony." As for the potential significance of this characterization of the progeny of *Counselman*, consider CRIMPROC § 8.10 ("it may well be that the only practical consequence will be the absence of a damage remedy" should a witness be denied the exercise of the privilege in a civil or administrative proceeding).

c. The reference here is an assertion of the privilege as to a question other than self-identification. As to the exercise of the privilege to refuse to reveal one's name, see Note 10, p. 628.

trauma"; the standard of "reasonable cause to apprehend danger" by providing a "link in the chain of evidence" recognizes that "truthful responses of an innocent witness, as well as those of a wrongdoer may provide the government with incriminating evidence").

3. *Incrimination under the laws of another sovereign.* For many years, American courts took the position that the privilege protected only against incrimination under the laws of that sovereign which was attempting to compel the incriminating testimony. In applying this rule, said to be derived from the English common law, the Supreme Court treated as separate sovereigns not only separate nations but also each state and the federal government. Thus, if a witness appearing before a federal grand jury did not face potential incrimination in the federal system (e.g., he had been granted immunity from federal prosecution), he could not refuse to testify on the ground that he risked incrimination under state law. However, the Warren Court, in one of its seminal rulings, *Murphy v. Waterfront Comm.*, 378 U.S. 52 (1964), rejected this "separate sovereign" precedent as applied to state and federal inquiries. Noting that a "separate sovereign" limitation would permit a witness to be "whipsawed into incriminating himself under both state and federal law," the Court concluded that the "policies and purposes" of the Fifth Amendment required that the privilege protect "a state witness against incrimination under federal as well as state law and a federal witness against incrimination under state as well as federal law." *Murphy* left open the question of whether the privilege would also be available where a witness in a state or federal proceeding feared incrimination only in a foreign country.

In United States v. Balsys, 524 U.S. 666 (1998), the Court majority (7–2) held that the separate sovereign doctrine continued to apply as to incrimination under the laws of a foreign country. Thus, respondent Balsys, a resident alien subpoenaed to testify about his possible participation in Nazi persecution during World War II, could not utilize the privilege to refuse to provide testimony that could subject him to a "real and substantial danger of prosecution of Lithuania and Israel." (The only consequence of his testimony in this country was deportation, long established as having a "civil character"). The Court majority acknowledged that *Murphy* included reasoning that supported a complete rejection of the separate sovereign limitation. Thus, the two dissenting justices (Ginsberg, J. and Breyer, J.) relied in part on *Murphy's* reading of the history of the privilege (including its application under English common law), and on *Murphy's* analysis of the purposes of the privilege as inconsistent with a separate sovereign limitation. As to legal history, the *Balsys* majority rejected *Murphy's* conclusion that pre-*Murphy* Supreme Court precedent had misread the English common law (*Murphy* having concluded that the English common law actually had rejected the separate sovereign limitation). As to policy,[d] the Court noted that, while *Murphy* catalogued multiple "aspirations" of the self-incrimination clause (see p. 882), some of which might support the privilege's extension to the fear of foreign prosecution, *Murphy* had failed "to weigh the host of competing policy concerns that would be raised in a legitimate reconsideration of the Clause's scope." Those costs included the loss of evidence in domestic law enforcement, due to the government's inability to grant immunity that would extend to foreign prosecution.

The *Balsys* majority concluded that *Murphy* was better read as resting on an "alternative rationale," which tied its rejection of the separate sovereign limitation to the applicability of the self-incrimination privilege to both the federal and state governments. The Court explained that *Murphy* was a product of the

d. Justices Scalia and Thomas did not join Part IV of the opinion for the Court, which considered relevant both *Murphy's* discussion of self-incrimination policies and competing policy concerns not presented in *Murphy*.

application of the self-incrimination clause to the states (via the Fourteenth Amendment) in *Malloy v. Hogan* (p. 30), decided on the same day as *Murphy*. Once the states become bound by the Fifth Amendment guarantee, the self-incrimination clause "could no longer be seen as framed for one jurisdiction (i.e., state or federal government) alone, each jurisdiction having instead become subject to the same claim of privilege flowing from the one limitation." The concept of a single guarantee, moreover, was consistent with a "feature unique to the [self-incrimination] guarantee," an "option to exchange the privilege for an immunity to prosecutorial use of any compelled testimony." That option remained available by viewing the state and federal governments as extending their immunity to prosecutions by the other (a step taken in *Murphy*, see Note 2, p. 849). Neither state nor federal government, however, could grant immunity as to a prosecution by a foreign nation.

4. ***Waiver.*** Once a grand jury witness begins to provide incriminating information on a particular subject, does that action bar raising the privilege as to subsequent questions dealing with the same subject? If the answer might be incriminating as to a different offense, the privilege clearly is available, but that may not be the case where the only potential for incrimination is to the same offense suggested by the earlier testimony. Here the applicable standard is that set forth in *Rogers v. United States,* 340 U.S. 367 (1951). The Court there noted that "disclosure of [an incriminating] fact waives the privilege as to details," as the further disclosure does not then present "a reasonable danger of further incrimination in light of all the circumstances, including [the] previous disclosures." To allow a claim of the privilege as to details "would [only] open the way to distortion of facts by permitting a witness to select any stopping point in the testimony."

Application of the *Rogers* standard is not always easy, as the division of the Court in *Rogers* itself suggests. In that case, a grand jury was seeking various records of the Communist Party branch in Denver. The witness Rogers admitted that she had been treasurer of the branch, but stated that she had turned the records over to another person. When asked to name that person, she initially refused to do so on the ground that she would not subject other persons to "the same thing that I'm going through." After consulting with counsel, she shifted to reliance on her privilege against self-incrimination. A divided Supreme Court (5–3) rejected that claim (described by the Court majority as a "pure afterthought"). The majority noted that the privilege was "purely personal" and could not be utilized to protect others. Rogers had already incriminated herself by admitting her party membership and her prior possession and transfer of the records; the "mere disclosure of the name of the recipient of the books" presented no more than an "imaginary possibility" of "increasing the danger of her prosecution" for a possible conspiracy to violate the Smith Act. While it was true that "at least two persons are required to constitute a conspiracy, * * * the identity of the other members [is] not needed inasmuch as one person can be convicted of conspiring with persons whose names are unknown." The dissenters saw the matter quite differently. There was a clear potential for additional incrimination, they noted, since petitioner's conviction could well "depend on testimony of the witnesses she was * * * asked to identify." The Court's analysis, they contended, made the "protection [of the privilege] dependent on timing that was so refined that lawyers, let alone laymen, will have difficulty in knowing when to claim it."

5. ***Exercise of the privilege by the target.*** The self-incrimination privilege has long been held to prohibit the prosecution from forcing a defendant to appear as a witness at his own trial. Should the prosecutor similarly be prohibited from forcing the target of an investigation who desires to exercise the privilege to appear before the grand jury, or is the Fifth Amendment satisfied by simply

allowing the target-witness, like any other witness, to refuse to respond to individual questions where his answer might be incriminating? A few state courts have argued that the target of an investigation is, in effect, a "putative" or "de facto" defendant, and he therefore should be allowed to exercise his privilege in much the same manner as a "de jure defendant" at trial. They suggest that, unless the target expressly waives his self-incrimination privilege, the prosecution cannot use the grand jury's subpoena authority to force him to appear. See CRIMPROC § 8.10(c). Consider also Justice Brennan's opinion in *United States v. Mandujano*, discussed in Note 6 infra. On the other side, the federal courts and most state courts have taken the position that the Fifth Amendment, as to the target as well as any other grand jury witness, presents only an "option of refusal and not a prohibition of inquiry." *O'Connell v. United States,* 40 F.2d 201 (2d Cir.1930).[e] The "obligation to appear," the Supreme Court stated in a *Dionisio*, (p. 816) footnote, is "no different for a person who may himself be the subject of the grand jury inquiry."

What justifies the different treatment of the trial defendant and the grand jury target, even when that target is so close to indictment that a court will refer to him as a "putative" defendant? Consider the following arguments: (1) the defendant's right of silence grew out of the early common law rule on the incompetency of parties to testify, which had a bearing only on the trial; (2) the defendant's right not to take the stand at trial is aimed, in part, at protecting the defendant from being placed in a position where he may be forced to refuse to answer questions on self-incrimination grounds in the presence of the jury (who may conclude that he therefore has something to hide), but that protective feature has less significance in the grand jury setting since that body simply decides whether to charge and its proceedings therefore need not be conducted "with the assiduous regard for the preservation of procedural safeguards which normally attends the ultimate trial of the issues"; (3) the grand jury, having an obligation to "run down every clue," cannot ignore the possibility that the target's testimony may lead to the identification of others who also participated in the criminal enterprise; (4) the grand jury, having an obligation to "shield the innocent," must be able to seek the target's own testimony to determine whether it might not "explain away" the evidence against him; and (5) determining whether a witness is a "target" is not easy under any standard for establishing that status, so that a prohibition against compelling a target to appear invariably would lead to after-the-fact disputes as to whether a later-indicted witness actually had been a target.[f]

e. Internal Justice Department guidelines provide that, to avoid the possible "appearance of unfairness," where the testimony of a grand jury "target" (see fn. f infra) might be helpful, an effort should first be made to secure the voluntary appearance of the target. However, the grand jury and U.S. Attorney may jointly agree to subpoena the target in exceptional cases. In making that determination, the grand jury and U.S. Attorney are directed to give "careful attention" to the importance of the testimony sought from the target, whether the substance of that testimony could be provided by other witnesses, and whether the "questions the prosecutor and the grand jurors intend to ask * * * would be protected by a valid claim of the privilege." United States Attorneys' Manual 9–11.150. Should the subpoenaed "target * * * and his or her attorney state in writing, signed by both, that the 'target' will refuse to testify on Fifth Amendment grounds, the witness ordinarily should be excused," but the "grand jury and United States Attorney [may] agree to insist on appearance" based on the considerations "which justified the subpoena in the first place." U.S.A.M. 9–11.154.

f. The United States Attorneys' Manual, in its provisions on target subpoenas (see fn. e supra) and target notification (see Note 7 infra), uses the following definition of a target: "[A] person as to whom the prosecutor or the grand jury has substantial evidence linking him or her to the commission of a crime and who, in the judgment of the prosecutor, is a putative defendant." The target is distinguished from a "subject of an investigation," who is "a person whose conduct is within the scope of the grand jury's investigation." U.S.A.M. 9–11.151.

Concurring in *United States v. Mandujano*, discussed in Note 6 infra, Justice Brennan described the "target" as "one against whom

6. ***Self-incrimination warnings.*** To what extent, if any, does the Fifth Amendment require that grand jury witnesses be advised prior to testifying of their right to exercise the privilege against self-incrimination? In UNITED STATES v. MANDUJANO, 425 U.S. 564 (1976), there was considerable discussion bearing on that question although the Court found it unnecessary to resolve the issue. The defendant Mandujano, known by the prosecutor to be a narcotics user, was called before the grand jury in the hope that he would furnish information about significant dealers. Instead, he steadfastly denied any involvement in the sale of narcotics and specifically disclaimed having sought within the year to make a purchase for a third-party for $650.00. The latter statement was a lie since (as the prosecutor already knew) Mandujano had recently tried to make such a purchase for a person who was actually an undercover agent. Subsequently prosecuted for perjury, Mandujano moved to suppress the grand jury testimony that was the basis of the charge. The trial court granted the motion on the ground that Mandujano had not been given full *Miranda* warnings prior to testifying. He had been informed of his privilege against self-incrimination and had been advised that he could have a retained lawyer located outside the grand jury room for the purpose of consultation. However, when Mandujano responded that he could not afford a lawyer, the prosecutor did not state that an indigent could obtain appointed counsel (the last portion of the *Miranda* warnings).

The Supreme Court unanimously concluded that even if adequate warnings had not been provided, that would not constitute a defense to a perjury charge. The Court had previously held that sanctions could be imposed for perjury "even in instances where the perjurer complained the Government exceeded its constitutional powers in making the inquiry." Six of the justices also went on to speak to the adequacy of the warnings.

Speaking for four justices, Chief Justice BURGER's plurality opinion concluded that the warnings here were clearly adequate, as *Miranda* certainly did not apply to the grand jury witness. The *Miranda* Court itself, in distinguishing custodial interrogation in a police station from interrogation "in courts or other official investigations where there are often impartial observers to guard against intimidation or trickery," had recognized that investigations "such as grand jury questioning take place in a setting wholly different from custodial interrogation." "Indeed," it was noted, "the Court's opinion in *Miranda* reveals a focus on what was seen by the Court as police coercion derived from 'factual studies' [relating to] police violence and the third degree * * *—beating, hanging, whipping—and to sustained and protracted questioning incommunicado in order to extort confessions. * * * To extend these concepts to questioning before a grand jury inquiring into criminal activity under the guidance of a judge is an extravagant expansion never remotely contemplated by this Court in *Miranda*; the dynamics of constitutional interpretation do not compel constant extension of every doctrine announced by the Court."

[the government] has probable cause—as measured by an objective standard." Justice Brennan noted that "others have argued for a rule which would combine objective elements with the prosecutor's subjective intent subsequently to charge the individual by indictment * * * but this subjective intent requirement may pose grave administrative difficulties." But compare Arnold Enker and Sheldon Elson, *Counsel for the Suspect,* 49 Minn.L.Rev. 47, 74 (1964) (critical of a solely objective standard that asks only whether probable cause existed, as prosecutors, "having not yet analyzed the complete record of the investigation, or hav[ing] done so only tentatively or hastily, or hav[ing] made an error—as happens in any large human enterprise—may not realize that probable cause exists" as to witnesses they do not view as targets). As noted in Beale et al., § 6.23, "most of the court decisions and statutes addressing grand jury procedures do not address [the definitional] issue, but simply use terms such as 'suspect,' 'target,' 'subject' and 'prospective defendant' interchangeably."

Chief Justice Burger added in a footnote that, since "warnings were provided in this case to advise respondent of his Fifth Amendment privilege," it was "unnecessary to consider whether any warning is required." However, in discussing the availability of the privilege, the Chief Justice suggested that grand jury witnesses, like witnesses in trial and administrative proceedings, were not constitutionally entitled to a warning even where the question posed had obvious potential for incrimination. The plurality opinion noted: "The very availability of the Fifth Amendment privilege to grand jury witnesses suggests that occasions will often arise when potentially incriminating questions will be asked in the ordinary course of the jury's investigation. * * * [T]he witness can, of course, stand on the privilege, assured that its protection 'is as broad as the mischief against which it seeks to guard.' *Counselman v. Hitchcock* [Note 1 supra]. The witness must invoke the privilege however, as the 'Constitution does not forbid the asking of criminative questions.' *United States v. Monia*, 317 U.S., at 433 [1943] (Frankfurter, J., dissenting):

> The [Fifth] Amendment speaks of compulsion. It does not preclude a witness from testifying voluntarily in matters which may incriminate him. If, therefore, he desires the protection of the privilege, he must claim it or he will not be considered to have been "compelled" within the meaning of the Amendment.

Absent a claim of the privilege, the duty to give testimony remains absolute."

BRENNAN, J., joined by Marshall, J., responded to what he viewed as a "denigration of the privilege against self-incrimination" in the Chief Justice's opinion. Justice Brennan did not challenge the Chief Justice's efforts to distinguish *Miranda*, but criticized instead the Chief Justice's "mechanical" reliance upon *United States v. Monia*. Justice Brennan argued *Monia* involved a deportation proceeding, and the Court had noted that the tribunal there had no notice of the likely incriminating quality of the witness' answer unless that potential was brought to its attention by the witness. But where the government is "acutely aware of the potentially incriminating nature of the disclosures sought," a knowing and completely voluntary waiver should be required. Just as grand jury could not call an indicted defendant before it and interrogate him concerning the subject matter of the charged crime, absent an intelligent and voluntary waiver, the same should be true of a *de facto* defendant. Accordingly, Justice Brennan noted: "I would hold that, in the absence of an intentional and intelligent waiver by the individual of his known right to be free from compulsory self-incrimination, the Government may not call before a grand jury one whom it has probable cause—as measured by an objective standard—to suspect committed a crime and by use of judicial compulsion compel him to testify with regard to that crime. In the absence of such a waiver, the Fifth Amendment requires that any testimony obtained in this fashion be unavailable to the Government for use at trial. Such a waiver could readily be demonstrated by proof that the individual was warned prior to questioning that he is currently subject to possible criminal prosecution for the commission of a stated crime, that he has a constitutional right to refuse to answer any and all questions that may tend to incriminate him, and by record evidence that the individual understood the nature of his situation and privilege prior to giving testimony."

Relying on the *Mandujano* plurality opinion, the lower federal courts generally have assumed that self-incrimination "warnings" are not constitutionally mandated even as to targets.[g] Several state courts, however, viewing the target

g. In *Minnesota v. Murphy*, fn. b, p. 608, the Supreme Court drew an analogy to the grand jury setting in holding that a probationer questioned by his probation officer was not entitled to *Miranda* warnings. The interview setting in *Murphy*, the Court noted, subjected

grand jury witness as distinct from witnesses in other proceedings, have held that self-incrimination warnings for target witnesses are constitutionally required. See CRIMPROC § 8.10(d). In the federal system, internal prosecutorial guidelines require that both subpoenaed "targets" and "subjects" (see fn. f supra) be informed of the self-incrimination privilege, both by an "advice of rights" statement appended to the subpoena and a statement of the prosecutor on record when the witness appears before the grand jury. The prescribed statement includes notification to the subpoenaed witness that "you may refuse to answer any question if a truthful answer to the question would tend to incriminate you" and that "anything that you do say may be used against you by the grand jury or in a subsequent legal proceeding." United States Attorneys' Manual 9–11.151. Warnings on the record also are common in state practice, at least as to targets, and are required by statute in roughly 10 jurisdictions. See Beale et al., § 6.24.

7. *Target warnings.* In UNITED STATES v. WASHINGTON, 431 U.S. 181 (1977), the Court answered one of the issues left open in *Mandujano:* a witness need not be warned that he is a target of the grand jury investigation. Noted the Court (per BURGER, C.J.):

"After being sworn, respondent was explicitly advised that he had a right to remain silent and that any statements he did make could be used to convict him of crime. It is inconceivable that such a warning would fail to alert him to his right to refuse to answer any questions which might incriminate him. * * * Even in the presumed psychologically coercive atmosphere of police custodial interrogation, *Miranda* does not require that any additional warnings be given simply because the suspect is a potential defendant; indeed, such suspects are potential defendants more often than not. Respondent points out that unlike one subject to custodial interrogation, whose arrest should inform him only too clearly that he is a potential criminal defendant, a grand jury witness may well be unaware that he is targeted for possible prosecution. While this may be so in some situations, it is an overdrawn generalization. In any case, events here [which included prior questioning by the prosecutor] clearly put respondent on notice that he was a suspect in the motorcycle theft. * * * However, all of this is largely irrelevant, since we do not understand what constitutional disadvantage a failure to give potential defendant warnings could possibly inflict on a grand jury witness, whether or not he has received other warnings. * * * Because target witness status neither enlarges nor diminishes the constitutional protection against compelled self-incrimination, potential defendant warnings add nothing of value to protection of Fifth Amendment rights."

Justice Brennan, joined by Justice Marshall, dissented, relying in substantial part on his discussion of the need for warnings in *Mandujano.* Several state courts, relying on a state statute or state constitutional provision, have held that target witnesses must be warned of their target status. United States Attorneys' Manual 9–11.151 states that the prosecutor should "advise witnesses who are known 'targets' that their conduct is being investigated for possible violation of federal criminal law." As to targets who are not witnesses, prosecutors are encouraged to provide notification of target status in "appropriate cases" (not the "routine clear case" or the case presenting a potential for flight or evidence

the probationer to "less intimidating pressure than is imposed upon a grand jury witness." Accordingly, since the Court had "never held that [warnings] must be given to the grand jury witness," it would "decline to require them here." Federal lower courts have viewed *Murphy* as reaffirming the strong suggestion of *Mandujano* that the Constitution does not demand any warning, but the lower court cases have not squarely presented the issue, as they have involved target/witnesses who received some form of notification of the self-incrimination privilege. See e.g., *United States v. Gillespie*, 974 F.2d 796 (7th Cir.1992).

tampering) in order to permit that person to request the opportunity to testify voluntarily. U.S.A.M. 9–11. 153

8. ***Constitutional right to counsel.*** In UNITED STATES v. MANDUJANO (described in Note 6 supra), Chief Justice BURGER'S plurality opinion also spoke to the grand jury witness' right to counsel. Initially, in rejecting the lower court's extension of *Miranda*, the plurality opinion also rejected the contention that the "*Miranda* right to counsel, fashioned to secure the suspect's Fifth Amendment privilege," should apply to grand jury questioning. Turning to other possible sources of a constitutional right to counsel, the plurality added: "Respondent was also informed that if he desired he could have the assistance of counsel, but that counsel could not be inside the grand jury room. That statement was plainly a correct recital of the law. No criminal proceedings had been instituted against respondent, hence the Sixth Amendment right to counsel had not come into play. *Kirby v. Illinois* [p. 769]. A witness 'before a grand jury cannot insist, as a matter of constitutional right, on being represented by his counsel. . . .' *In re Groban*, 352 U.S. 330 (1957). Under settled principles the witness may not insist upon the presence of his attorney in the grand jury room. Fed. Rule Crim. Proc. 6(d)."

Justice BRENNAN's separate opinion in *Mandujano* also challenged this portion of the plurality opinion. The statement from *Groban* quoted by the plurality was dictum that should be reexamined in light of *Miranda* and *Escobedo v. Illinois* [p. 563] and their "recognit[ion] of the 'substantive affinity' and therefore the 'coextensiveness' in certain circumstance of the right to counsel and the privilege against self-incrimination," and their rejection of the regime of "squalid discrimination" that distinguished between those "wealthy enough to hire a lawyer" and the indigent. Similarly, relying on *Kirby* was inappropriate because the line drawn there as to when "criminal proceedings had been instituted" (the "initiation of adversary judicial proceedings") assumed that the self-incrimination privilege was not "implicated." Where "the putative defendant is called and interrogated before the grand jury," as in the case of a person subjected to adversary judicial proceedings, he was "faced with the prosecutorial forces of organized society and immersed in the intricacies of substantive and procedural law."

Justice Brennan argued that, at a minimum, the putative defendant was entitled constitutionally to be told "that he has a right to consult with an attorney prior to questioning, that if he cannot afford an attorney one will be appointed for him, that during the questioning he may have that attorney wait outside the grand jury room, and that he may at any and all times during questioning consult with the attorney prior to answering any question posed." Justice Brennan also opened the door to a possibly broader constitutional protection: he noted that several commentators had argued that "the presence of counsel inside the grand jury room is required," and added that there "certainly * * * is no viable argument that allowing counsel to be present in the grand jury room for the purposes of consultation regarding testimonial privileges would subvert the nature or functioning of the grand jury proceeding."

The *Mandujano* plurality opinion generally is viewed as having put to rest any possible Sixth Amendment grounding for a constitutional right to counsel. See also Pt. B, p. 95. Several lower courts, however, following an analysis similar to that advanced by Justice Brennan, have suggested a Fifth Amendment grounding for the right to counsel. Beale et al. § 6.26, suggest that this grounding has "broad implications that some courts may be hesitant to accept"—such as applicability to witnesses in other settings (e.g., administrative and civil proceedings relating to transactions that could conceivably involve criminality), recognizing a right to appointed counsel as well as a right to retained counsel, and creating a right to the effective assistance of counsel (at least as to advice relating to the exercise of the privilege).

A due process grounding for a right to counsel has also been suggested. Here, the right would flow from a general liberty interest of the individual to expend his resources to seek counsel's assistance whenever that assistance would not disrupt or alter the basic character of the proceeding involved. See Beale et al., § 6.26 (noting the statement in *Powell v. Alabama,* p. 82, that an "arbitrary" denial of a right to be represented by retained counsel even in a civil case would be viewed as a "denial of a hearing" and therefore a due process violation). In treating the issues discussed in Notes 9 and 10 below, several courts appear to have assumed the existence of such a due process right to retain and consult with counsel.

9. *Availability of counsel.* Pursuant to internal guidelines, all federal grand jury witnesses are advised that they may retain counsel (who may be located in the anteroom) and that "the grand jury will permit you a reasonable opportunity to step outside the grand jury room to consult with counsel if you so desire." United States Attorneys' Manual, 9–11.151. Where the witness requests the assistance of counsel, but notes that he is indigent, that request is often conveyed to the federal district judge, who may then request that the federal defender or private counsel (in districts without defenders) assume representation. However, the Criminal Justice Act does not provide for appointment of counsel for grand jury witnesses. See 18 U.S.C. § 3006A(a)(1).

Lawyers representing federal grand jury witnesses commonly urge their clients to take full advantage of the opportunity to leave the grand jury room and consult with counsel. Indeed, some lawyers insist that their clients consult after each question, which allows the lawyer to construct a complete record of the questions asked. Although federal prosecutors contend that this practice demands more than a "reasonable opportunity" to consult, it usually has not been contested. A few federal courts have stated that, at least where the witness has been granted immunity (and therefore does not need self-incrimination advice), the witness can be limited to consultations on a less regular basis (e.g., after every few questions). CRIMPROC § 8.15(c).

Most states follow a practice similar to the federal practice as to notification of the right to consult with retained counsel and providing through an informal arrangement public defender assistance for the indigent witness who requests counsel (although several states provide by statute for the appointment of counsel for indigent witnesses). State courts may be somewhat less liberal, however, in allowing the witness to leave the grand jury for consultations. Those states that are less liberal commonly justify that position on two grounds—avoidance of "undue delay" and restricting counsel to his proper role. If witnesses are allowed to consult after each question, no matter what its nature, they may, it is argued, simply "wear down the grand jury." Moreover, if the attorney's advice properly is limited to counseling the witnesses on the exercise of testimonial privileges, there simply is no reason to allow consultation when the question clearly poses no such difficulty. See e.g., *People v. Ianniello,* 235 N.E.2d 439 (N.Y.1968) (where witness had been immunized and had previous opportunity to consult with counsel on the same line of questioning, grand jury appropriately refused to allow him to leave for the obvious purpose of obtaining "strategic advice" rather than counseling as to any legal right that would allow him to refuse to answer).

10. *The location of counsel.* Roughly twenty states now have statutes permitting at least certain witnesses to be assisted by counsel located within the grand jury room. See CRIMPROC § 8.15(b). Most of these provisions apply to all witnesses, but several are limited to targets or to witnesses who have not been immunized. The statutes commonly contain provisions limiting the role of counsel while before the grand jury. Several state that the lawyer may "advise the witness," but "may not otherwise take any part in the proceeding." One jurisdiction also allows counsel to "interpose objections on behalf of the witness." See Kan.Stat.Ann. § 22–3009 (2).

Proponents of such statutes argue that they are needed to adequately protect the rights of the grand jury witness. They contend that even the most liberal right to leave the grand jury room to consult with counsel imposes substantial burdens upon the client's access to counsel and counsel's ability to advise the client. Those opposing the presence of counsel in the grand jury room acknowledge that the location of counsel outside the grand jury room poses certain difficulties for the witness and counsel, but claim that those difficulties are not so great as to undermine the witness' ability to exercise his rights, particularly as to the privilege against self-incrimination. They see any additional protection of witness rights as clearly outweighed by the detrimental effect that counsel's presence would have upon the grand jury's capacity to conduct effective investigations. They argue that, notwithstanding statutory prohibitions, counsel accompanying witnesses would find techniques, such as stage whispers and objections presented through the witness, for challenging the prosecutor's questions, and conveying their arguments to the jurors. With no judge present to put an immediate stop to such tactics, the end result would be disruption and delay of the investigation. They further argue that with counsel at the witness' side, more witnesses will reply to questions by merely parroting responses formulated by counsel—responses that too often furnish as little information as possible or are purposely ambiguous so as to avoid potential perjury charges. The critics draw an analogy to the trial, where the defendant, once taking the stand, is not allowed to interrupt his testimony for further discussions with counsel. Finally, it is noted that, in some instances, the witness may be wary of counsel's loyalty and therefore prefer not to have counsel present. The witness may be forced to accept counsel provided by others (e.g., his employer) and fear retaliation if the full scope of his testimony is carried back to such persons. Once the law permits counsel to be present, the witness will be under pressure to allow counsel to accompany him, and will lose the capacity to be selective in the disclosure of his testimony to counsel.

B. Immunity Grants

1. *Constitutionality.* The use of an immunity grant to preclude reliance upon the self-incrimination privilege dates back to the English practice known as providing "indemnity" against prosecution. See *Kastigar v. United States,* Note 2 infra (also noting the use of immunity grants in the American Colonies). Immunity grants were first upheld under the federal constitution in *Brown v. Walker,* 161 U.S. 591 (1896). A divided Court there concluded that the Fifth Amendment could not be "construed literally as authorizing the witness to refuse to disclose any fact which might tend to incriminate, disgrace, or expose him to unfavorable comments." The history of the Amendment, the majority noted, indicated that its object was only to "secure the witness against criminal prosecution." Thus, the self-incrimination privilege had been held inapplicable where the witness' compelled testimony would relate only to an offense as to which he had been pardoned or as to which the statute of limitations had run. So too, the privilege did not apply where the witness' response might tend to "disgrace him or bring him into disrepute" but would furnish no information relating to a criminal offense. The majority reasoned that, once it is accepted that the object of the privilege is limited to protecting the witness against criminal prosecution, the constitutionality of the immunity grant necessarily follows. Since the grant removes the danger against which the privilege protects, the witness can no longer rely upon the privilege.

2. ***Scope of the Immunity.*** *Counselman v. Hitchcock,* 142 U.S. 547 (1892), struck down a federal immunity statute that granted the witness protection only against the use of his immunized testimony as evidence in any subsequent prosecution. The Supreme Court concluded that such limited protection immunity was not sufficient to replace the Fifth Amendment privilege. The Court stressed that there was no protection against derivative use of the witness' testimony. Thus, the statute "could not, and would not, prevent the use of his testimony to search out other testimony to be used in evidence against him." At the conclusion of its opinion, however, the Court spoke in terms of even broader protection. "To be valid," it noted, an immunity grant "must afford absolute immunity against future prosecution for the offense to which the question relates." This statement was read as indicating that the immunity grant must absolutely bar prosecution for any transaction noted in the witness' testimony. Accordingly, Congress adopted a new immunity statute providing for "transactional immunity." It provided that a witness directed to testify or produce documentary evidence pursuant to an immunity order could not be prosecuted "for or on account of any transaction, matter, or thing concerning which he may testify or produce evidence." The constitutionality of this provision was upheld in *Brown v. Walker,* supra, and subsequent state and federal immunity statutes were largely patterned upon the *Brown* statute.

Subsequent decisions—and the language of later statutes—recognized two limitations on the scope of transactional immunity. First, transactional immunity does not preclude a prosecution for perjury based on the immunized testimony. Second, transactional immunity does not extend to an event described in an answer totally unresponsive to the question asked. Thus, the witness cannot gain immunity from prosecution for all previous criminal acts by simply including a reference to those acts in his testimony without regard to the subject on which he was asked to testify.

In *Murphy v. Waterfront Commission,* Note 3, p. 840, the Court first upheld immunity that was not as broad in scope as the traditional transactional immunity. After rejecting the separate sovereign doctrine as a limitation on the privilege's availability where incrimination remains possible under either federal or state law, *Murphy* turned to the scope of the immunity that must be granted to supplant the privilege as it related to prosecution in that other jurisdiction. It concluded that the immunity granted in one jurisdiction (federal or state) need not absolutely bar prosecution in the other; it was sufficient to bar both use and derivative use of the witness' testimony in the other jurisdiction. This ruling allowed the Court to fashion an immunity for state witnesses that would be sufficiently broad to replace the privilege. Congress' preemptive legislative authority permitted it to grant an immunity that extended to state proceedings, but the states lacked authority to legislate as to federal proceedings. However, to accommodate "the interests of State and Federal governments in investigating and prosecuting crime," the Court could (and would) exercise its supervisory power to prohibit the federal government from using in federal courts state immunized testimony or the fruits thereof.

Following *Murphy,* Congress adopted a general immunity provision that granted federal witnesses protection only against use and derivative use as to federal as well as state prosecutions. The statute provided that "no testimony or other information compelled under the [immunity] order (or any information directly or indirectly derived from such testimony or other information) may be used against the witness in any criminal case, except a prosecution for perjury, giving a false statement, or otherwise failing to comply with the order." 18 U.S.C. § 6002. In KASTIGAR v. UNITED STATES, 406 U.S. 441 (1972), a divided Court (5–2) upheld the new federal provision.

Justice POWELL's opinion for the *Kastigar* majority discounted the "broad language in *Counselman,*" which suggested the need for transactional immunity, as inconsistent with the "conceptual basis" of the *Counselman* ruling. The crucial question, as *Counselman* noted, was whether the immunity granted was "coextensive with the scope of the privilege against self-incrimination." Both *Murphy* and the cases applying the exclusionary rule to confessions obtained through Fifth Amendment violations indicated that the constitutional privilege required no more than a prohibition against use and derivative use. The new federal statute clearly met that standard: "The statute provides a sweeping proscription of any use, direct or indirect, of the compelled testimony and any information derived therefrom. This total prohibition on use provides a comprehensive safeguard, barring the use of compelled testimony as an 'investigatory lead,' and also barring the use of any evidence obtained by focusing investigation on a witness as a result of his compelled disclosures."

The *Kastigar* majority rejected the argument, relied on by the dissenters, that the bar against derivative use could not be enforced effectively. Appropriate procedures for "taint hearings" could ensure that derivative use was not made of immunized testimony. Those procedural safeguards were described as follows: "As stated in *Murphy:* 'Once a defendant demonstrates that he has testified, under a state grant of immunity to matters related to the federal prosecution, the federal authorities have the burden of showing that their evidence is not tainted by establishing that they had an independent, legitimate source for the disputed evidence.' This burden of proof, which we reaffirm as appropriate, is not limited to a negation of taint; rather, it imposes on the prosecution the affirmative duty to prove that the evidence it proposes to use is derived from a legitimate source wholly independent of the compelled testimony. This is very substantial protection, commensurate with that resulting from invoking the privilege itself. * * * [Indeed], a defendant against whom incriminating evidence has been obtained through a grant of immunity may be in a stronger position at trial than a defendant who asserts a Fifth Amendment coerced-confession claim. One raising a claim under this statute need only show that he testified under a grant of immunity in order to shift to the government the heavy burden of proving that all of the evidence it proposes to use was derived from legitimate independent sources. On the other hand, a defendant raising a coerced-confession claim under the Fifth Amendment must first prevail in a voluntariness hearing before his confession and evidence derived from it become inadmissible."

3. In a companion case to *Kastigar, Zicarelli v. New Jersey State Comm. of Investigation,* 406 U.S. 472 (1972), the Court upheld a state counterpart of 18 U.S.C. § 6002, providing for use/derivative-use immunity in state proceedings. Since *Zicarelli* was decided, a substantial number of states have moved from transactional to use/derivative-use immunity. The A.B.A. and N.C.C.U.S.L. have urged retention of transactional immunity, however, and roughly twenty states continue to provide the broader immunity, see Beale et al., § 7.8. Those opposing a shift to use/derivative use immunity have argued that the opportunity it offers to prosecute based on independently obtained evidence is too insignificant as a practical matter to offset the risk that derivative use will not be detected by a taint hearing. Those supporting use/derivative use immunity contend that taint hearings are effective and that instances allowing permissible prosecutions of immunized witnesses, though small in number, should not be cut off where that is not constitutionally required. They also argue that use/derivative use immunity affords substantial advantages apart from the possibility of a subsequent prosecution. They maintain that such immunity encourages the immunized witness to provide as much detail as possible so as to make it more difficult for the government to survive a taint hearing should it subsequently decide to prosecute.

They also contend that the absence of an absolute protection against subsequent prosecution makes the immunized witness' testimony more credible to the jury.

4. ***Subsequent prosecutions and the problem of taint.*** While use/derivative use immunity leaves open the possibility of prosecuting an immunized witness, the prosecution must meet the prerequisite of establishing that its evidence is independently derived, as described in *Kastigar*. Lower courts have read *Kastigar* to be satisfied by application of a preponderance of the evidence standard to this burden. See CRIMPROC § 8.11. Also, some courts have been willing to hold the *Kastigar* taint hearing after trial, thereby allowing the government to proceed to trial without providing the broad pretrial disclosure that is inherent in a pretrial taint hearing. Ibid. Nonetheless, prosecuting an immunized witness is not lightly undertaken, and commonly requires advance planning at the time the witness gives the immunized testimony.

The *Kastigar* burden is most readily met when the prosecution has completed or substantially completed its investigation before the witness is immunized. Thus, a prosecutor can readily meet the *Kastigar* burden where immunity was granted to force the testimony of a defendant who had already been convicted, but who had claimed the privilege because his appeal was still pending, and the prosecutor now seeks to reprosecute after an appellate reversal of that earlier conviction; the prosecution here can simply restrict itself to the evidence introduced at the earlier trial, which obviously was uncovered without the aid of the subsequent grant of immunity. The *Kastigar* burden can also be met, although not as easily, in cases in which the prosecution had sufficient evidence to prosecute, and had intended to prosecute, but had a need to first gain the prospective defendant's testimony in a prosecution against another participant in the same general criminal enterprise. A similar possibility is presented where the prosecution was well on its way to obtaining an indictment when another governmental agency (a prosecutor in another jurisdiction or a legislative body) required the prospective defendant to testify under a grant of immunity. The preferred practice in such cases is for the prosecutor to make a record of all of the evidence collected prior to the grant of immunity, to file that record with the court, and then at the taint hearing, note its intent to utilize only that previously acquired evidence and further evidence directly acquired from that evidence. See Beale et al., § 7.20. That procedure may not be foolproof, however.

In *United States v. North,* 910 F.2d 843 (D.C.Cir.1990), the Independent Counsel conducting a grand jury investigation of the Iran–Contra affair followed such a procedure when Congress proceeded to hold public hearings and grant witness immunity to the target. Although the government's criminal prosecution rested on the testimony of witnesses who had testified before the grand jury before the target gave immunized testimony to Congress, and the Independent Counsel had established a "Chinese Wall" to ensure that its staff was not exposed to that immunized testimony, that was held insufficient to met the *Kastigar* burden. The district court had found that the "witnesses had their memories refreshed with [the] immunized testimony by 'hearing the testimony, reading about it, being questioned about aspects of it before the Select Committees and, to some extent, by exposure to it in the course of responding to inquiries within their respective agencies.' " Insofar as the testimony of the witnesses was shaped by their memories having been refreshed, the government was making "use" of the immunized testimony contrary to *Kastigar*. Accordingly the case was remanded for further proceedings to see if "it is possible * * * to separate the wheat of the witness' unspoiled memory from the chaff of North's immunized testimony."[a]

a. The lower court was directed to engage in a "line-by-line" inquiry into "the content as well as the sources" of each witness' testimony. On the denial of an application for rehear-

Assuming the prosecution can establish that the evidence it will use at trial is independently derived, some courts have found that mere prosecutorial familiarity with the immunized testimony poses difficulties because of the possibility of "nonevidentiary use." Indeed, *United States v. McDaniel,* 482 F.2d 305 (8th Cir.1973), characterized as "insurmountable" the government's burden in such a case, as the court could not "escape the conclusion that the testimony could not be wholly obliterated from the prosecutor's mind in his preparation and trial of the case." The *McDaniel* court reasoned that "if the immunity protection is to be coextensive with the Fifth Amendment privilege, as it must to be constitutionally sufficient, then it must forbid all prosecutorial use of the testimony, not merely that which results in the presentation of evidence before the jury." Other courts have disagreed, arguing that the Fifth Amendment privilege is concerned only with direct and indirect use of evidence and not such matters as "deciding to initiate prosecution, refusing to plea bargain, interpreting evidence, planning cross-examination, and otherwise generally planning trial strategy." *United States v. Serrano,* 870 F.2d 1 (1st Cir.1989).

5. *Prosecutorial discretion.* Although immunity statutes commonly require that the immunity order be issued by the court, the judge's role in ruling on a request for such an order often is limited to ensuring that the procedural requirements of the statute are met (e.g., under the federal statute, that the application was approved by one of the statutorily designated higher echelon Justice Department officials and that the order properly states the scope of the immunity[b]). Under such provisions, the judge may not refuse to grant the order because it disagrees with the prosecutor's judgment that a grant of immunity is in the public interest. United States Attorneys' Manual 9–23.21 directs the appropriate Justice Department official, in making that judgment, to consider a wide range of factors, including the following: (1) the importance of the investigation; (2) the value of the person's testimony; (3) the likelihood of prompt and full compliance, and the effectiveness of available sanctions if there is no compliance; (4) the person's relative culpability; (5) the possibility of successfully prosecuting the person prior to compelling testimony through immunization; and (6) the likelihood of adverse collateral consequences to the person if compelled to testify.

SECTION 5. SELF–INCRIMINATION AND THE COMPELLED PRODUCTION OF DOCUMENTS

A. The Dismantling of Boyd

ing, the Court of Appeals rejected the Independent Counsel's argument that *Kastigar* did not apply because its own activities were free from taint. The Court noted: "*Kastigar* is * * * violated whenever the prosecution puts on a witness whose testimony is shaped, directly or indirectly, by compelled testimony, regardless of *how or by whom* he was exposed to that compelled testimony." 920 F.2d 940 (D.C.Cir. 1990). The government subsequently was unable to meet its burden, and the target's conviction was reversed and the charges against him dismissed.

b. Does it follow from the legislative authorization of immunity grants under specific procedures that the prosecutor should not be allowed to employ informal grants of immunity (i.e., an agreement not to exercise prosecutorial authority in exchange for the witness' testimony)? Very often, the informal grants not only will bypass the statutory procedures for immunity grants, but also will contain prosecutorial promises that are substantially narrower than the immunity provided by statute. While such informal grants are dependent upon witness acceptance (i.e., the court will not force a witness to testify in response to such a nonstatutory promise), if the witness does accept and does testify, the court will require the prosecution to live up to its promise. See Hughes, *Agreements for Cooperation in Criminal Cases,* 45 Vand.L.Rev. 1 (1992). Federal prosecutors regularly utilize such informal grants as simply another exercise of the prosecutor's discretion over the decision to charge. See United States Attorneys' Manual 9–27.00, Beale et al., § 7.12.

1. ***Self–Incrimination and Boyd.*** In sustaining the petitioner's challenge to the compelled production of a document, Boyd v. United States, set forth at p. 804, relied upon the Fifth Amendment's prohibition against "compelling a man 'in a criminal case to be a witness against himself,' " as well as the Fourth Amendment prohibition against unreasonable searches. Commentators and courts have offered various explanations of the self-incrimination grounding of *Boyd*. Consider, for example, the following:

(a) *Boyd* rested on a "personal property" rationale. *Boyd,* under this view, simply utilized the privilege to characterize as "unreasonable" all "searches" (which included a subpoena-mandated production) aimed at obtaining a person's personal property for possible use against him in a "criminal case" (which included a forfeiture proceeding). Robert S. Gerstein, *The Demise of Boyd: Self–Incrimination and Private Papers in the Burger Court,* 27 U.C.L.A.L.Rev. 265 (1979). Thus, *Boyd* was largely a Fourth Amendment case, not a direct application of the self-incrimination clause, and lost its grounding when the Supreme Court held that searches could extend to all evidence of a crime (including personal property). See Note 3, p. 809. Unlike the other explanations offered below, this explanation finds no support in judicial discussions of *Boyd's* self-incrimination analysis, and is contrary to the many post-*Boyd* rulings recognizing challenges to the compelled production of documents that rested entirely on the self-incrimination privilege.

(b) *Boyd* recognizes that the self-incrimination clause prohibits compelling a person to produce physical evidence that would be incriminating. Thus, *Boyd* was not limited to the production of documents, as recognized in *United States v. White* 322 U.S. 694 (1944), where the Court spoke of the privilege as protecting the individual "from any disclosure, in the form of oral testimony, documents, or *chattels*, sought by legal process against him as a witness." (emphasis added). See Richard A. Nagareda, *Compulsion "To Be a Witness" and the Resurrection of Boyd*, 74 N.Y.U.L.Rev. 1575 (1999), noting also that this interpretation of the self-incrimination clause finds support in the text of the Fifth Amendment, the content of related constitutional guarantees, and the history of the privilege against self incrimination.

(c) *Boyd* recognized that the self-incrimination privilege serves to protect "a private inner sanctum of individual feeling and thought," *Bellis v. United States*, 417 U.S. 85 (1974), and that this area of privacy is invaded not only in compelling a witness to testify but also in compelling him to disclose his writings. See Brennan, J., in *Fisher v. United States* (p. 857) ("Many of the matters within an individual's knowledge may as easily be retained within his head as set down on a scrap of paper. I perceive of no principle which does not permit compelling the disclosure of the contents of one's mind but does permit compelling the disclosure of the contents of that scrap of paper by compelling its production.") *Boyd*, of course, did not involve a document authored by anyone associated with Boyd and Sons, but in looking to *Entick's* characterization of the individual's papers as his "dearest property," the *Boyd* opinion recognized that the compelled disclosure of certain documents written by others (e.g., letters) also could bear upon the individual's personal privacy of thought by revealing his knowledge of the often-personal contents of these documents. Cf. Brennan J., concurring in Fisher (p. 862).

(d) *Boyd*, in merging Fourth and Fifth Amendment, advanced a much larger privacy protection, which extended to all documents, as the compelled production of documents necessarily spells out the "private information" of the person who possesses those documents. See Stuntz, fn. b, p. 812.

(e) *Boyd* simply viewed the person compelled to produce a document as compelled, in effect, to recite the contents of the documents (and thereby to give testimony). See CRIMPROC. § 8.12(a) (describing one possible reading).

2. *The entity exception.* HALE v. HENKEL, 201 U.S. 43 (1906), decided only two decades after *Boyd*, not only reconstructed *Boyd's* Fourth Amendment analysis (see Note 1, p. 809), but also added a major exception to its Fifth Amendment rationale. *Hale* held that the self-incrimination privilege was not available to a corporation and therefore *Boyd*'s self-incrimination analysis did not bar a grand jury subpoena duces tecum requiring production of corporate documents. *Hale* reasoned that the privilege against self-incrimination was a personal right, and therefore was not available to the corporation. The corporation, unlike the individual was a "creature of the state," subject to the "reserved right" of the state to compel its assistance in assuring that it had not "exceeded its powers."[a] The Court also stressed the enforcement needs of the government in compelling, the production of corporate documents: if such production were precluded by a self-incrimination on behalf of the corporation, "it would result in a failure of a large number of cases where the illegal combination was determinable only upon such papers."[b]

3. In UNITED STATES v. WHITE, 322 U.S. 694 (1944), the Court (per MURPHY, J.) extended the *Hale* exception to other entities. *White* held that the president of an unincorporated labor union could not invoke his personal privilege to a subpoena demanding union records. Characterizing the Court's previous reliance on the State's visitorial power as "merely a convenient vehicle for justification of governmental investigation of corporate books and records," the *White* Court concluded that the exception recognized in *Hale* was derived from the inappropriateness of affording the privilege to an impersonal collective entity, whether or not that entity took the corporate form. The privilege against self-incrimination, the Court noted, "was essentially a personal [privilege], applying only to natural individuals," as evidenced by its underlying functions. The privilege grew out of "the high sentiment and regard of our jurisprudence for conducting criminal trials, and investigatory proceedings upon a plane of dignity, humanity, and impartiality." It was "designed to prevent the use of legal process to force from the lips of the accused the evidence necessary to convict him or force him to produce and authenticate any personal documents that might incriminate

a. This reserved right was not seen as depriving the corporation of the protection of the Fourth Amendment, and the subpoena was quashed on that ground. See Note 1, p. 809. Consider also the availability (and unavailability) to the collective entity of other constitutional rights, such as: the Fifth Amendment protection against being placed twice in jeopardy (assumed to apply); the Fifth Amendment right to prosecution by grand jury indictment (not applicable, according to the Ninth Circuit, since potential punishment, imposed on corporations does not include imprisonment, and therefore is not "infamous"); and the Sixth Amendment right to a jury trial (applicable). See Peter Henning, *The Conundrum of Corporate Criminal Liability: Seeking A Consistent Approach to the Constitutional Rights of Corporations in Criminal Prosecutions*, 63 Tenn. L.Rev. 783, (1996).

b. In *Hale*, the corporate official called upon to produce the documents had been immunized, so he could not claim that production of the records posed a self-incrimination risk as to himself. *Wilson v. United States*, 221 U.S. 361 (1911), subsequently rejected such a claim by a corporate official who had not been immunized. The State's "reserved power of visitation," the Court noted, "would seriously be embarrassed, if not wholly defeated in its effected exercise, if guilty officers could refuse inspection of the records and papers of the corporation." As the records were those of the corporation, not personal records, and were held "subject to the corporate duty," the official could "assert no personal right * * * against any demand of the government which the corporation was bound to recognize." The subpoena in *Wilson* was directed to the corporation, but *Dreier v. United States*, 221 U.S. 394 (1911), held that the result was the same where the subpoena was directed to a specific individual in his capacity as corporate custodian. See Note 6, p. 867 as to the reconsideration of this issue under the act-of-production doctrine.

him," and "thereby avoided * * * physical torture and other less violent but equally reprehensible modes of compelling the production of incriminating evidence." These concerns did not apply to the entity, which lacked the qualities of human personality and therefore could not suffer the "immediate and potential evils of compulsory self-disclosure".

The *White* majority also spoke to regulatory considerations "underlying the restriction of the constitutional privilege to natural individuals acting in their own private capacity." It noted: "The scope and nature of the economic activities of incorporated and unincorporated organizations and their representatives demand that the constitutional power of the federal and state governments to regulate those activities be correspondingly effective. The greater portion of evidence of wrongdoing by an organization or its representatives is usually to be found in the official records and documents of that organization. Were the cloak of the privilege to be thrown around these impersonal records and documents, effective enforcement of many federal and state laws would be impossible. The framers of the constitutional guarantee against compulsory self-disclosure, who were interested primarily in protecting individual civil liberties, cannot be said to have intended the privilege to be available to protect economic or other interests of such organizations so as to nullify appropriate governmental regulations."[c]

4. The *White* opinion characterized the labor union as an organization with "a character so impersonal in the scope of its membership and activities that it cannot be said to embody or represent the purely private or personal interests of its constituents, but rather to embody their common or group interests only." In *Bellis v. United States*, 417 U.S. 85 (1974), however, the Court concluded that the entity exception remained applicable even though the entity embodied personal as well as group interests. The functional key was that the organization "be recognized as an independent entity apart from its individual members." Thus, a small law firm, organized as a partnership, was an entity for this purpose even though it "embodie[d] little more than the personal legal practice of the individual partners." The partnership was not an "informal association or a temporary arrangement for the undertaking of a few projects of short-lived duration," but a "formal institutional arrangement organized for the continuing conduct of the firm's legal practice." State law, through the Uniform Partnership Act, imposed a "certain organizational structure"; the firm maintained a bank account in the partnership name; it had employees who worked for the firm as such; and, the firm "held itself out to third parties as an entity with an independent institutional identity."[d]

c. Various commentators have found fault in both elements of the *White* reasoning. They argue that several of the values traditionally cited as supporting the privilege (see fn. a, p. 854) (e.g., a privacy interest) are clearly applicable to entities as well as individuals. See e.g., Stuntz, fn. b, p. 812 (privacy "is something that individuals possess within institutions not just outside them"). Also, insofar as the application of the privilege was restricted in *White* and other cases because of the difficulties that a prohibition against compelled production of documents would present to "legitimate government regulation," the same difficulties arise as to businesses run as individual proprietorships, where *White* would recognize the application of the privilege. They further note, in this regard, that the required records doctrine, which reflects similar concerns, does not distinguish between entities and sole proprietors. See Gerstein, Note 1, p. 853; Mosteller, Note 3, p. 866.

d. *Bellis* left open the possibility that a "small family partnership" might be treated differently, as might a temporary arrangement for undertaking a short-lived project, or an association based on some "pre-existing relationship of confidentiality among the partners." Lower courts view any such exception as quite narrow. A corporation, even a one-person corporation or a closely held family corporation, will be viewed as an entity no matter how closely it would otherwise resemble the possible "small-family-partnership" exception noted in *Bellis*. See CRIMPROC § 8.12(b). Consider also Note 6, p. 855.

5. *The "required records" exception.* *Shapiro v. United States*, 335 U.S. 1 (1948), expanding upon some dictum in *Wilson* (fn. b, p. 854), held that the self-incrimination clause is not violated by requiring a person to keep records of certain business activities and to make those records available for government inspection. Accordingly, a grand jury subpoena requiring the production of required records could not be successfully challenged on self-incrimination grounds even though the records were those of a business conducted as an individual proprietorship rather than an entity. See *Grand Jury Subpoena Duces Tecum (Underhill),* 781 F.2d 64 (1986). Business records will not be classified as required records under *Shapiro* unless three prerequisites are met: (1) the governmental requirement that records be kept must be "essentially regulatory" in nature; (3) the records must be "of a kind which the regulated party has customarily kept," and (3) the records "must have assumed some 'public aspects' which render them at least analogous to public documents." *Grosso v. United States,* 390 U.S. 62 (1968).

6. *The "testimonial" limitation.* A series of cases dealing with production of identification evidence (see fn. a, p. 758) made clear that the *Boyd* analysis was limited to the production of documents. *Schmerber v. California*, 384 U.S. 757 (1966), was the most prominent of those rulings. *Schmerber* held that the privilege did not prohibit the compelled extraction of a blood sample from an accused and the subsequent admission of that sample as incriminatory evidence at his trial. The Court reasoned that the history of the privilege limited its application to compelled production of an accused's "communications" or "testimony." While this protection extended beyond words compelled from "a person's own lips" and extended to "communications * * * in whatever form they may take," it did not encompass "compulsion which makes a suspect or accused the source of 'real or physical' evidence." Citing *Boyd*, the *Schmerber* opinion distinguished the non-testimonial compulsion in identification procedures from the "compulsion of responses which are also communications, for example, compliance with a subpoena to produce one's papers."

Schmerber's analysis was carried over to the compelled writing of a document in *Doe v. United States*, p. 881 (commonly cited as *Doe II*, to distinguish the earlier *United States v. Doe,* Note 1, p. 863). The Court there held that a judicial order requiring an individual to sign a form directing any foreign bank to release the records of any account he might have at that bank did not compel "testimony" for Fifth Amendment purposes. This was so since the government did not seek to use the signed form itself as a factual assertion of the individual. Indeed, the form was carefully drafted so that the signing party noted that he was acting under court order and did not acknowledge the existence of any account in any particular bank. The compelled writing did not indicate whether the requested documents existed, and offered no assistance to the government in later establishing the authenticity of any records produced by the bank. Thus, while the signed form did constitute a communication, it did not constitute "testimony." The individual in signing a directive fully prescribed as to content was not revealing the "content of his mind" and the government was "not relying on the 'truthtelling' of Doe's directive to show the existence of, or his control over foreign bank account records."[e]

e. The Court acknowledged that the directive could result in the production of evidence, but that was not because of any information that the petitioner Doe was required to provide, but the response (if any) of the recipient of the directive. While Justice Stevens, in dissent, argued that requiring the petitioner to provide the directive was no different than compelling a person to reveal the combination to his safe, the majority characterized it as more like "requiring the individual to surrender a key to a strong box containing incriminatory documents."

7. ***The "personal compulsion" limitation.*** In *Andresen v. Maryland* [p. 272], in the course of sustaining a search for documents, the Court rejected the claim that the seizure was prohibited by the Fifth Amendment. The Court noted that the broad language of *Boyd* no longer governed, as later cases had emphasized that application of privilege required the "compulsion of the accused." Thus, *Couch v. United States*, 409 U.S. 322 (1973), held that a taxpayer could not assert the privilege as to a summons served on the taxpayer's accountant requiring the accountant to produce the taxpayer's personal business records. The records were not in the possession of the taxpayer and the taxpayer was "not asked to say or do anything."[f] The same was true where it was law enforcement officers who searched for and seized the target's documents.

8. ***The act-of-production analysis.*** The most far reaching development in the dismantling of the *Boyd* analysis, was the adoption of act-of-production doctrine discussed. That is the doctrine to which the courts now look on determining the application of the privilege to a subpoena requiring an individual to himself produce non-entity documents in his possession (assuming these documents are not required records).

B. The Act-of-Production Doctrine

FISHER v. UNITED STATES

425 U.S. 391, 96 S.Ct. 1569, 48 L.Ed.2d 39 (1976).

Justice WHITE delivered the opinion of the Court.

In these two cases we are called upon to decide whether a summons directing an attorney to produce documents delivered to him by his client in connection with the attorney-client relationship is enforceable over claims that the documents were constitutionally immune from summons in the hands of the client and retained that immunity in the hands of the attorney. In each case, an Internal Revenue agent visited the taxpayer or taxpayers and interviewed them in connection with an investigation of possible civil or criminal liability under the federal income tax laws. Shortly after the interviews * * *, the taxpayers obtained from their respective accountants certain documents relating to the preparation by the accountant of their tax returns. Shortly after obtaining the documents * * *, the taxpayers transferred the documents to their lawyers—each of whom was retained to assist the taxpayer in connection with the investigation. Upon learning of the whereabouts of the documents, the Internal Revenue Service served summonses on the attorneys directing them to produce documents listed therein. [Those documents were accountants' work sheets, retained copies of income tax returns, and the accountants' copies of correspondence between the accounting firm and the taxpayer]. * * * In each case, the lawyer declined to comply with the

f. *Couch* noted that "situations may well arise where constructive possession is so clear or the relinquishment of possession is so temporary and insignificant to leave the personal compulsions upon the accused [who is not in actual possession] substantially intact," and therefore allow that person to assert the privilege. In large part, this exception has been limited to settings in which an office employee has been subpoenaed to produce documents of an employer who has equal access to the records. See e.g., *In re Grand Jury Subpoena (Kent)*, 646 F.2d 963 (5th Cir.1981) (where proprietor actively participated in management of a small office, and the subpoenaed employee was "never delegated the exclusive responsibility for the preparation and custody of the subpoenaed records," proprietor could assert the privilege). But compare *In re Grand Jury Investigation (Heller)*, 921 F.2d 1184 (11th Cir. 1991) (where subpoenaed legal secretary had "intimate involvement" in the preparation and maintenance of trust account records of the attorney, the attorney could not assert the privilege even though he was actively involved in the use of the records and maintained a "degree of control over them").

summons directing production of the documents, and enforcement actions were commenced by the Government. * * *

All of the parties in these cases and the Court of Appeals have concurred in the proposition that if the Fifth Amendment would have excused a *taxpayer* from turning over the accountant's papers had he possessed them, the *attorney* to whom they are delivered for the purpose of obtaining legal advice should also be immune from subpoena. Although we agree with this proposition for the reasons set forth * * * infra, we are convinced that, under our decision in *Couch v. United States,* [Note 7, p. 857], it is not the taxpayer's Fifth Amendment privilege that would excuse the *attorney* from production.

The relevant part of that Amendment provides:

> "No person . . . shall be *compelled* in any criminal case to be a *witness against himself.*" (Emphasis added.)

The taxpayer's privilege under this Amendment is not violated by enforcement of the summonses involved in these cases because enforcement against a taxpayer's lawyer would not "compel" the taxpayer to do anything—and certainly would not compel him to be a "witness" against himself. The Court has held repeatedly that the Fifth Amendment is limited to prohibiting the use of "physical or moral compulsion" exerted on the person asserting the privilege. In *Couch v. United States,* supra, we recently ruled that the Fifth Amendment rights of a taxpayer were not violated by the enforcement of a documentary summons directed to her accountant and requiring production of the taxpayer's own records in the possession of the accountant. We did so on the ground that in such a case "the ingredient of personal compulsion against an accused is lacking." Here, the taxpayers are compelled to do no more than was the taxpayer in *Couch.* The taxpayers' Fifth Amendment privilege is therefore not violated by enforcement of the summonses directed toward their attorneys. This is true whether or not the Amendment would have barred a subpoena directing the taxpayer to produce the documents while they were in his hands. * * *

The Court of Appeals suggested that because legally and ethically the attorney was required to respect the confidences of his client, the latter had a reasonable expectation of privacy for the records in the hands of the attorney and therefore did not forfeit his Fifth Amendment privilege with respect to the records by transferring them in order to obtain legal advice. It is true that the Court has often stated that one of the several purposes served by the constitutional privilege against compelled testimonial self-incrimination is that of protecting personal privacy. See e.g., *Murphy v. Waterfront Comm'n* [p. 882]. But the Court has never suggested that every invasion of privacy violates the privilege. Within the limits imposed by the language of the Fifth Amendment, which we necessarily observe, the privilege truly serves privacy interests; but the Court has never on any ground, personal privacy included, applied the Fifth Amendment to prevent the otherwise proper acquisition or use of evidence which, in the Court's view, did not involve compelled testimonial self-incrimination of some sort.

The proposition that the Fifth Amendment protects private information obtained without compelling self-incriminating testimony is contrary to the clear statements of this Court that under appropriate safeguards private incriminating statements of an accused may be overheard and used in evidence, if they are not compelled at the time they were uttered, *Katz v. United States* [p. 247], and that disclosure of private information may be compelled if immunity removes the risk of incrimination. *Kastigar v. United States* [Note 2, p. 849]. If the Fifth Amendment protected generally against the obtaining of private information from a man's mouth or pen or house, its protections would presumably not be lifted by probable cause and a warrant or by immunity. The privacy invasion is not mitigated by immunity; and the Fifth Amendment's strictures, unlike the Fourth's are not removed by showing reasonableness. The Framers addressed the subject of personal privacy directly in the Fourth Amendment. * * * They did not seek in still another Amendment—the Fifth—to achieve a general protection of privacy but to deal with the more specific issue of compelled self-incrimination.

We cannot cut the Fifth Amendment completely loose from the moorings of its language, and make it serve as a general protector of privacy—a word not mentioned in its text and a concept directly addressed in the Fourth Amendment. We adhere to the view that the Fifth Amendment protects against "compelled self-incrimination, not [the disclosure of] private information." * * * Insofar as private information not obtained through compelled self-incriminating testimony is legally protected, its protection stems from other sources—the Fourth Amendment's protection against seizures without warrant or probable cause and against subpoenas which suffer from "too much indefiniteness or breadth in the things required to be 'particularly described,'" the First Amendment, or evidentiary privileges such as the attorney-client privilege.[7]

* * * [While the] taxpayers have erroneously relied on the Fifth Amendment without urging the attorney-client privilege in so many words, they have nevertheless invoked the relevant body of law and policies that govern the attorney-client privilege. In this posture of the case, we feel obliged to inquire whether the attorney-client privilege applies to documents in the hands of an attorney which would have been privileged in the hands of the client by reason of the Fifth Amendment. * * * This Court and the lower courts have * * * uniformly held that pre-existing documents which could have been obtained by court process from the client when he was in possession may also be obtained from the attorney by similar process following transfer by the client in order to obtain more informed legal advice. * * * It is otherwise if the documents are not obtainable by subpoena duces tecum or summons while in the exclusive possession of the client, for the client will then be reluctant to transfer possession to the lawyer unless the documents are also privileged in the latter's hands. Where the transfer is made for the purpose of obtaining legal advice, the purposes of the attorney-client privilege would be defeated unless the privilege is applicable. * * *

Since each taxpayer [here] transferred possession of the documents in question from himself to his attorney in order to obtain legal assistance in the tax investigations in question, the papers, if unobtainable by summons from the client, are unobtainable by summons directed to the attorney by reason of the attorney-client privilege. We accordingly proceed to the question whether the documents could have been obtained by summons addressed to the taxpayer while the documents were in his possession. The only bar to enforcement of such summons asserted by the parties or the courts below is the Fifth Amendment's privilege against self-incrimination. * * *

The proposition that the Fifth Amendment prevents compelled production of documents over objection that such production might incriminate stems from *Boyd v. United States* * * *. Several of *Boyd's* express or implicit declarations have not stood the test of time. The application of the Fourth Amendment to subpoenas was limited by *Hale v. Henkel* [Note 1, p. 810] and more recent cases. Purely evidentiary (but "nontestimonial") materials, as well as contraband and fruits and instrumentalities of crime, may now be searched for and seized under

7. The taxpayers and their attorneys have not raised arguments of a Fourth Amendment nature before this Court and could not be successful if they had. The summonses are narrowly drawn and seek only documents of unquestionable relevance to the tax investigation. Special problems of privacy which might be presented by subpoena of a personal diary, *United States v. Bennett,* 409 F.2d 888, 897 (C.A.2 1969) (Friendly, J.), are not involved here. First Amendment values are also plainly not implicated in these cases.

proper circumstances, *Warden v. Hayden* [p. 271]. Also, any notion that "testimonial" evidence may never be seized and used in evidence is inconsistent with [various cases] approving the seizure under appropriate circumstances of conversations of a person suspected of crime. See *Katz v. United States* [p. 247]. It is also clear that the Fifth Amendment does not independently proscribe the compelled production of every sort of incriminating evidence but applies only when the accused is compelled to make a *testimonial* communication that is incriminating. See *Schmerber v. California* [Note 6, p. 856]. * * * Furthermore, despite *Boyd,* neither a partnership nor the individual partners are shielded from compelled production of partnership records on self-incrimination grounds. *Bellis v. United States* [Note 4, p. 855]. It would appear that under that case the precise claim sustained in *Boyd* would now be rejected for reasons not there considered.

The pronouncement in *Boyd* that a person may not be forced to produce his private papers has nonetheless often appeared as dictum in later opinions of this Court. * * * To the extent, however, that the rule against compelling production of private papers rested on the proposition that seizures of or subpoenas for "mere evidence," including documents, violated the Fourth Amendment and therefore also transgressed the Fifth, the foundations for the rule have been washed away. In consequence, the prohibition against forcing the production of private papers has long been a rule searching for a rationale consistent with the proscriptions of the Fifth Amendment against compelling a person to give "testimony" that incriminates him. Accordingly, we turn to the question of what, if any, incriminating testimony within the Fifth Amendment's protection, is compelled by a documentary summons.

A subpoena served on a taxpayer requiring him to produce an accountant's workpapers in his possession without doubt involves substantial compulsion. But it does not compel oral testimony; nor would it ordinarily compel the taxpayer to restate, repeat, or affirm the truth of the contents of the documents sought. Therefore, the Fifth Amendment would not be violated by the fact alone that the papers on their face might incriminate the taxpayer, for the privilege protects a person only against being incriminated by his own compelled testimonial communications. *Schmerber v. California,* supra. The accountant's workpapers are not the taxpayer's. They were not prepared by the taxpayer, and they contain no testimonial declarations by him. Furthermore, as far as this record demonstrates, the preparation of all of the papers sought in these cases was wholly voluntary, and they cannot be said to contain compelled testimonial evidence, either of the taxpayers or of anyone else. The taxpayer cannot avoid compliance with the subpoena merely by asserting that the item of evidence which he is required to produce contains incriminating writing, whether his own or that of someone else.[11]

The act of producing evidence in response to a subpoena nevertheless has communicative aspects of its own, wholly aside from the contents of the papers produced. Compliance with the subpoena tacitly concedes the existence of the papers demanded and their possession or control by the taxpayer. It also would indicate the taxpayer's belief that the papers are those described in the subpoena. The elements of compulsion are clearly present, but the more difficult issues are whether the tacit averments of the taxpayer are both "testimonial" and "incrimi-

11. The fact that the documents may have been written by the person asserting the privilege is insufficient to trigger the privilege. *Wilson v. United States* [fn. b, p. 854]. And, unless the government has compelled the subpoena person to write the document, the fact that it was written by him is not controlling with respect to the Fifth Amendment. Conversations may be seized and introduced in evidence under proper safeguards * * * if not compelled. In the case of a documentary subpoena the only thing compelled is the act of producing the document and the compelled act is the same as one performed when a chattel or document not authored by the producer is demanded.

nating" for purposes of applying the Fifth Amendment. These questions perhaps do not lend themselves to categorical answers; their resolution may instead depend on the facts and circumstances of particular cases or classes thereof. In light of the records now before us, we are confident that however incriminating the contents of the accountant's workpapers might be, the act of producing them—the only thing which the taxpayer is compelled to do—would not itself involve testimonial self-incrimination.

It is doubtful that implicitly admitting the existence and possession of the papers rises to the level of testimony within the protection of the Fifth Amendment. The papers belong to the accountant, were prepared by him, and are the kind usually prepared by an accountant working on the tax returns of his client. Surely the Government is in no way relying on the "truth telling" of the taxpayer to prove the existence of or his access to the documents. The existence and location of the papers are a foregone conclusion and the taxpayer adds little or nothing to the sum total of the Government's information by conceding that he in fact has the papers. Under these circumstances by enforcement of the summons "no constitutional rights are touched. The question is not of testimony but of surrender."

When an accused is required to submit a handwriting exemplar he admits his ability to write and impliedly asserts that the exemplar is his writing. But in common experience, the first would be a near truism and the latter self-evident. In any event, although the exemplar may be incriminating to the accused and although he is compelled to furnish it, his Fifth Amendment privilege is not violated because nothing he has said or done is deemed to be sufficiently testimonial for purposes of the privilege. This Court has also time and again allowed subpoenas against the custodian of corporate documents or those belonging to other collective entities such as unions and partnerships and those of bankrupt businesses over claims that the documents will incriminate the custodian despite the fact that producing the documents tacitly admits their existence and their location in the hands of their possessor. The existence and possession or control of the subpoenaed documents being no more in issue here than in the above cases, the summons is equally enforceable.

Moreover, assuming that these aspects of producing the accountant's papers have some minimal testimonial significance, surely it is not illegal to seek accounting help in connection with one's tax returns or for the accountant to prepare workpapers and deliver them to the taxpayer. At this juncture, we are quite unprepared to hold that either the fact of existence of the papers or of their possession by the taxpayer poses any realistic threat of incrimination to the taxpayer.

As for the possibility that responding to the subpoena would authenticate the workpapers, production would express nothing more than the taxpayer's belief that the papers are those described in the subpoena. The taxpayer would be no more competent to authenticate the accountant's workpapers or reports by producing them than he would be to authenticate them if testifying orally. The taxpayer did not prepare the papers and could not vouch for their accuracy. The documents would not be admissible in evidence against the taxpayer without authenticating testimony. Without more, responding to the subpoena in the circumstances before us would not appear to represent a substantial threat of self-incrimination. * * *

Whether the Fifth Amendment would shield the taxpayer from producing his own tax records in his possession is a question not involved here; for the papers demanded here are not his "private papers," see *Boyd v. United States,* supra. We do hold that compliance with a summons directing the taxpayer to produce the accountant's documents involved in this case would involve no incriminating testimony within the protection of the Fifth Amendment.

Justice STEVENS took no part in the consideration or disposition of these cases.

Justice BRENNAN, concurring in the judgment.

Given the prior access by accountants retained by the taxpayers to the papers involved in these cases and the wholly business rather than personal nature of the papers, I agree that the privilege against compelled self-incrimination did not in either of these cases protect the papers from production in response to the summonses. See *Couch v. United States.* I do not join the Court's opinion, however, because of the portent of much of what is said of a serious crippling of the protection secured by the privilege against compelled production of one's private books and papers. * * * [I]t is but another step in the denigration of privacy principles settled nearly 100 years ago in *Boyd v. United States.* * * *

Expressions are legion in opinions of this Court that the protection of personal privacy is a central purpose of the privilege against compelled self-incrimination. * * * The Court pays lip-service to this bedrock premise of privacy in the statement that "[w]ithin the limits imposed by the language of the Fifth Amendment, which we necessarily observe, the privilege truly serves privacy interests." But this only makes explicit what elsewhere highlights the opinion, namely, the view that protection of personal privacy is merely a byproduct and not, as our precedents and history teach, a factor controlling in part the determination of the scope of the privilege. This cart-before-the-horse approach is fundamentally at odds with the settled principle that the scope of the privilege is not constrained by the limits of the wording of the Fifth Amendment but has the reach necessary to protect the cherished value of privacy which it safeguards. * * *

* * * [The Court's] analysis is patently incomplete: the threshold inquiry is whether the taxpayer is compelled to produce incriminating papers. That inquiry is not answered in favor of production merely because the subpoena requires neither oral testimony from nor affirmation of the papers' contents by the taxpayer.[a] To be sure, the Court correctly observes that "[t]he taxpayer cannot avoid compliance with the subpoena *merely* by asserting that the item of evidence which he is required to produce contains incriminating writing, whether his own or that of someone else." For it is not enough that the production of a writing, or books and papers, is compelled. Unless those materials are such as to come within the zone of privacy recognized by the Amendment, the privilege against compulsory self-incrimination does not protect against their production.

We are not without guideposts for determining what books, papers, and writings come within the zone of privacy recognized by the Amendment. * * * *Couch v. United States* expressly held that the Fifth Amendment protected against the compelled production of testimonial evidence only if the individual resisting production had a reasonable expectation of privacy with respect to the evidence.

a. Justice Brennan's opinion also questioned whether the Court's reasoning was consistent with its own analysis: "I also question the Court's treatment of the question whether the act of producing evidence is 'testimonial.' I agree that the act of production implicitly admits the existence of the evidence requested and possession or control of that evidence by the party producing it. It also implicitly authenticates the evidence as that identified in the order to compel. I disagree, however, that implicit admission of the existence and possession or control of the papers in this case is not 'testimonial' merely because the Government could readily have otherwise proved existence and possession or control in these cases. I know of no Fifth Amendment principle which makes the testimonial nature of evidence and, therefore, one's protection against incriminating himself, turn on the strength of the Government's case against him."

* * * A precise cataloguing of private papers within the ambit of the privacy protected by the privilege is probably impossible. Some papers, however, do lend themselves to classification. Production of documentary materials created or authenticated by a State or the Federal Government, such as automobile registrations or property deeds, would seem ordinarily to fall outside the protection of the privilege. They hardly reflect an extension of the person. Economic and business records may present difficulty in particular cases. The records of business entities generally fall without the scope of the privilege. But, as noted, the Court has recognized that the privilege extends to the business records of the sole proprietor or practitioner. Such records are at least an extension of an aspect of a person's activities, though concededly not the more intimate aspects of one's life. Where the privilege would have protected one's mental notes of his business affairs in a less complicated day and age, it would seem that protection should not fall away because the complexities of another time compel one to keep business records.

Nonbusiness economic records in the possession of an individual, such as canceled checks or tax records, would also seem to be protected. They may provide clear insights into a person's total lifestyle. They are, however, like business records and the papers involved in these cases, frequently, though not always, disclosed to other parties; and disclosure, in proper cases, may foreclose reliance upon the privilege. Personal letters constitute an integral aspect of a person's private enclave. And while letters, being necessarily interpersonal, are not wholly private, their peculiarly private nature and the generally narrow extent of their disclosure would seem to render them within the scope of the privilege. Papers in the nature of a personal diary are *a fortiori* protected under the privilege. * * *

Justice MARSHALL, concurring in the judgment.

* * * I would have preferred it had the Court found some room in its theory for recognition of the import of the contents of the documents themselves. * * * Nonetheless, I am hopeful that the Court's new theory, properly understood and applied, will provide substantially the same protection as our prior focus on the contents of the documents. * * * Indeed, there would appear to be a precise inverse relationship between the private nature of the document and the permissibility of assuming its existence. Therefore, under the Court's theory, the admission through production that one's diary, letters, prior tax returns, personally maintained financial records, or canceled checks exist would ordinarily provide substantial testimony. The incriminating nature of such an admission is clear, for while it may not be criminal to keep a diary, or write letters or checks, the admission that one does and that those documents are still available may quickly—or simultaneously—lead to incriminating evidence. If there is a "real danger" of such a result, that is enough under our cases to make such testimony subject to the claim of privilege. Thus, in practice, the Court's approach should still focus upon the private nature of the papers subpoenaed and protect those about which *Boyd* and its progeny were most concerned. * * *

Notes and Questions

1. ***The demise of Boyd?*** In UNITED STATES v. DOE, 465 U.S. 605 (1984) (commonly described as *Doe I*, to distinguish it from *Doe II*, see Note 6, p. 856), the subpoena at issue directed a sole proprietor to produce for grand jury use a broad range of records, including billings, ledgers, canceled checks, telephone records, contracts and paid bills. The district court sustained the proprietor's claim of privilege, applying *Fisher's* act-of-production analysis. It concluded that compliance with the subpoena would require the proprietor to "admit that the records exist, that they are in his possession, and that they are authentic" and that each of these testimonial elements of production was potentially incrimina-

tory. The Third Circuit agreed with this reasoning, but also added that the privilege applied because compelled disclosure of the contents of the documents violated the Fifth Amendment. Relying upon a privacy analysis of *Boyd*, it reasoned that the contents of personal records were privileged under the Fifth Amendment and that "business records of a sole proprietorship are no different from the individual's personal records." Justice POWELL's opinion for the *Doe I* Court affirmed the rulings below insofar as they relied on the act-of-production doctrine of *Fisher*, but rejected the Third's Circuit conclusion that the self-incrimination privilege also applied because it protected the contents of the papers.

Justice Powell initially acknowledged that the Court in *Fisher* had "declined to reach the question whether the Fifth Amendment privilege protects the contents of an individual's tax records in his possession" (see p. 861). The "rationale" underlying *Fisher's* holding, however, was equally persuasive as to such records and the records here. *Fisher* had emphasized that "the Fifth Amendment protects the person asserting the privilege only from compelled self-incrimination." That a record was prepared by a subpoenaed party and is in his possession is "irrelevant to the determination of whether its creation * * * was compelled." The business records here, like the accountant's workpapers in *Fisher*, had been prepared voluntarily, and therefore only their production, and not their creation, was compelled. The contention that the Fifth Amendment created a "zone of privacy" that protected the content of such papers had been rejected in *Fisher* and that rejection had been reinforced by the *Andresen v. Maryland* (p. 272) sustaining a search for personal business records. The respondent could not avoid compliance with a subpoena "merely by asserting that the item of evidence which he is required to produce contains incriminating writing, whether his own or that of someone else."

Although *Doe I* dealt with business records, the opinion did not suggest any opening for separate treatment of diaries (see fn. 7 of *Fisher*) or other documents of a more intimate nature. Justice O'CONNOR, in a separate concurring opinion, sought to shut the door on any such exception. She noted: "I write separately * * * to make explicit what is implicit in the analysis of [Justice Powell's] opinion: that the Fifth Amendment provides absolutely no protection for the contents of private papers of any kind. The notion that the Fifth Amendment protects the privacy of papers originated in *Boyd v. United States*, but our decision in *Fisher v. United States*, sounded the death-knell for *Boyd*. 'Several of *Boyd's* express or implicit declarations [had] not stood the test of time * * * and its privacy of papers concept ha[d] long been a rule searching for a rationale.' *Fisher*. Today's decision puts a long overdue end to that fruitless search."

Justice O'Connor's opinion brought forth a response from Justice MARSHALL, joined by Justice Brennan. "This case," Justice Marshall noted, "presented nothing remotely close to the question that Justice O'Connor eagerly poses and answers." The documents in question here were business records, "which implicate a lesser degree of concern for privacy interests than, for example, personal diaries." It accordingly could not be said that the Court had "reconsidered the question of whether the Fifth Amendment provides protection for the content of 'private papers of any kind.' "

As to the post *Doe I* lower court treatment of this issue, see CRIMPROC § 8.12(f): "In the years since *Doe I*, lower courts usually have found it unnecessary to decide whether anything remains of *Boyd*. 'If the contents of papers are protected at all,' they note, 'it is only in rare situations, where compelled disclosure would break the heart of our sense of privacy.' That might be the case as to subpoena compelling production of 'intimate papers such as private diaries and drafts of letters or essays,' but it certainly would not cover the business and other financial records that typically are in issue. * * * A growing number of courts, however, have come to the conclusion that the rationale of *Doe* and *Fisher* precludes self-incrimination protection of the contents of a voluntarily prepared document, no matter how personal the document. Thus, courts have held that the act-of-production doctrine provides the only protection for such personal records as diaries and pocket calendars. In all of those cases, however, once the concept of a *Boyd*-based content protection was rejected, the government was able to overcome an act-of-production objection because the documents had been shared with others and their existence, possession, and authentication were established as foregone conclusions. Ordinarily such documents are kept more privately and the individual required to produce them would implicitly be giving testimony as to those elements and therefore be entitled to the protection of the privilege."

Consider also Robert Heidt, *The Fifth Amendment Privilege and Documents–Cutting Fisher's Tangled Line*, 49 Mo.L.Rev. 440 (1984) (arguing that the protection of the most private documents from forced disclosure is more appropriately considered as a First Amendment issue, as procedural requirements applicable to Fifth Amendment claims, as prescribed in *Hoffman,* Note 2, p. 839, would restrict judicial inquiry into elements relevant to a privacy claim, such as whether the party actually authored the subpoenaed documents).

2. *Authentication and the foregone conclusion doctrine.* *Fisher's* reasoning as to why the implicit admission of the existence and possession of accountant's workpapers did not "rise to the level of testimony under the protection of the Fifth Amendment" (p. 861) came to be known as the "foregone conclusion" doctrine. In *Doe I*, the Court described that doctrine as extending also to implicit admissions of authentication. The lower courts there had sustained Doe's claim that the act of producing the documents subpoenaed would "tacitly admit their existence and his possession" and would "reliev[e] the government of the need for authentication" under Fed. R. Evid. 901.[a] The Supreme Court, in turn, also accepted that claim, based upon its traditional "reluctan[ce] to disturb findings of fact in which two courts below concurred." The Court noted that findings of the lower court as to the testimonial components of production were "sufficient to establish a valid claim of the privilege against self-incrimination," but it then added: "This is not to say that the government was foreclosed from rebutting respondents claim by producing evidence that possession existence, *and authentication* were a 'foregone conclusion.' *Fisher*. In this case, however, the Government failed to make such a showing." 465 U.S. at 614, fn. 13. (emphasis added)

3. *The rationale of the foregone conclusion doctrine.* As Justice Brennan noted in *Fisher* (see fn. a, p. 862), in determining whether a witness' testimony is protected by the privilege, courts look solely to whether the facts acknowledged in the testimony carry a potential for incrimination; they do not further inquire as to whether the prosecution might establish those same incriminatory facts without relying on the witness' testimony. Does the *Fisher* ruling that the privilege does not apply when "possession, existence, and authentication" are

a. Fed. R. Evid. 901 provides that authentication "is satisfied by evidence sufficient to support a finding that the matter in question is what its proponent claims." Subdivisions (1)–(10) of Fed. R. Evid. 901 offer illustrations of evidence that may support such a finding, including testimony of a witness with knowledge (subdivision 1), expert and nonexpert testimony as to the genuineness of handwriting (subdivisions 2 and 3), and distinctive characteristics of the document as contained in its "appearance, contents, substance, internal patterns, or other distinctive characteristics, taken in conjunction with circumstances" (subdivision 4). Doe's claim apparently was that his act of production would have provided authentication under subdivision (1). Some of the documents may have been capable of authentication under subdivision (4), without reliance on Doe having produced the documents, but there was no discussion of this possibility.

a "foregone conclusion" require precisely that inquiry in determining whether the act of production is testimonial (and therefore subject to protection by the privilege)? If so, why this different treatment of the act of production (as opposed to traditional testimony)? Consider in this connection, Robert Mosteller, *Simplifying Subpoena Law: Taking the Fifth Amendment Seriously,* 73 Va.L.Rev. 1, 32–33 (1987):

"More plausibly, the Court is suggesting [in its 'foregone conclusion' analysis] that when an implicit as opposed to an explicit communication is involved, it is necessary to consider whether the government is really asking a 'question' through the subpoena. Granted, the defendant's response to a documentary subpoena always reveals that the item does or does not exist; the government cannot eliminate the implicit question about the document's existence no matter how it phrases the subpoena's demand. But if the government already knows the answer to that question and is truly uninterested in the implicit answer provided by production, the witness' gratuitous communication of it should not violate the fifth amendment. In short, the *Fisher* decision suggests that constitutional rights are not violated by implicit communications that are inherent in a response to a documentary subpoena where those communications are unwanted because, though technically admissible, they are not substantially relevant to the prosecution's case given its other evidence."

4. *Potential incrimination.* Assuming that the government does not establish that possession, authentication, and existence are a foregone conclusion, under what circumstances will the privilege nonetheless not be applicable because the likelihood of incrimination is not "substantial and real" (see *Doe I*, 465 U.S. at 614, fn. 13)? Note in this regard *Fisher*'s comments on the incriminatory aspects of producing records that were authored by another and clearly could be lawfully possessed. What did the Court mean when it said that, "at this juncture," it was unwilling to hold that either the existence of the papers or their possession posed a realistic threat of incrimination (see p. 861)? Are the possible contents of the papers irrelevant to the determination of potential incrimination since the privilege does not protect the contents but the act of production? Assuming that the contents of the tax work papers were incriminatory, wouldn't possession suggest knowledge of that content and thereby pose a realistic threat?

One answer is that the Court in *Fisher* may simply not have been willing to conclude, on the record before it, that a realistic threat existed that the contents were incriminatory. *Fisher* involved an IRS investigation, with no criminal overtones, and in that context, lower courts have commonly required more than a "blanket claim" (encompassing all records subpoenaed and offering no explanation) to establish a realistic threat of incrimination. See CRIMPROC § 8.13(b).

In *Doe I*, the Court returned to the issue of incrimination in a footnote that responded to the government's contention that, even if the act of production there did have "testimonial aspects," any incrimination would be "so trivial" that the Fifth Amendment would not be implicated. The risk of incrimination here, the Court noted, was "substantial and real," meeting the *Hoffman* standard (Note 2, p. 839), since the act of production established the existence and possession of the business records in question (points "not conceded" by Doe) and relieved the government of the need to otherwise establish "authenticity" under Fed. R. Evid. 901. 465 U.S. at 614, fn. 13. No reference was made to the general character of the documents, although, as in *Fisher*, they certainly were documents that could be "lawfully possessed," and in some instances, may have been authored by others. *Doe I*, in contrast to *Fisher*, involved a grand jury investigation.

5. *Act of production immunity.* The government in *Doe I* maintained that, accepting arguendo the lower court's finding of testimonial self-incrimination, the district court should nevertheless have enforced the subpoena and granted to Doe immunity as to his act of production. The government argued that it had, in effect, offered such immunity by telling the district court that it would not use the act of production against Doe. The Court responded that the government, if it wanted to grant act-of-production immunity, must make a proper application pursuant to the immunity statute. (see Note 5, p. 852). It did, however, reject Doe's contention that the immunity granted under the statute must extend to the contents of the documents subpoenaed. The Court reasoned: "Respondent argues that any grant of use immunity must cover the contents of the documents as well as the act of production. We find this contention unfounded. To satisfy the requirements of the Fifth Amendment, a grant of immunity need be only as broad as the privilege against self-incrimination. *Murphy v. Waterfront Commission* [Note 2, p. 849]. * * * [T]he privilege in this case extends only to the act of production. Therefore, any grant of use immunity need only protect respondent from the self-incrimination that might accompany the act of producing his business records." 465 at 617, fn. 17.

6. *Production by an entity agent.* In BRASWELL v. UNITED STATES, 487 U.S. 99 (1988), the petitioner, a corporate president and sole shareholder, was subpoenaed to produce various corporate records. Raising the privilege against self-incrimination, petitioner sought to distinguish earlier precedent holding a corporate agent could not raise the privilege in such a situation (see fn. b, p. 854). He argued that: (1) the earlier rulings had assumed that the availability of the privilege flowed from the privacy rationale of *Boyd* and protected the contents of the records to be produced (which did not include entity records); (2) *Fisher*, however, had shifted the focus to the incrimination of the act of production, and (3) such testimonial incrimination also occurred where a corporate agent was required to produce corporate documents which that agent had created or used. A closely divided Supreme Court rejected that contention, although it did provide the custodian with a layer of protection that went beyond the earlier precedent. Speaking for the majority, Chief Justice REHNQUIST reasoned:

"To be sure, the holding in *Fisher*—later reaffirmed in *Doe*—embarked upon a new course of Fifth Amendment analysis. We cannot agree, however, that it rendered the collective entity rule obsolete. * * * From *Wilson* forward, the Court has consistently recognized that the custodian of corporate or entity records holds those documents in a representative rather than a personal capacity. Artificial entities such as corporations may act only through their agents, and, a custodian's assumption of his representative capacity leads to certain obligations, including the duty to produce corporate records on proper demand by the Government. Under those circumstances, the custodian's act of production is not deemed a personal act, but rather an act of the corporation. Any claim of Fifth Amendment privilege asserted by the agent would be tantamount to a claim of privilege by the corporation—which of course possesses no such privilege. * * *

"The *Fisher* court cited the collective entity decisions with approval and offered those decisions to support the conclusion that the production of the accountant's workpapers would "not * * * involve testimonial self-incrimination." * * * In a footnote, the Court explained: "In these [collective entity] cases compliance with the subpoena is required even though the books have been kept by the person subpoenaed and his producing them would itself be sufficient authentication to permit their introduction against him." n. 14. The Court thus reaffirmed the obligation of a corporate custodian to comply with a subpoena addressed to him.

"That point was reiterated by Justice Brennan in his concurrence in *Fisher*. Although Justice Brennan disagreed with the majority as to its use of the collective entity cases to support the proposition that the act of production is not testimonial, he nonetheless acknowledged that a custodian may not resist a subpoena on the ground that the act of production would be incriminating. * * * [For] "one in control of the records of an artificial organization undertakes an obligation with respect to those records foreclosing any exercise of his privilege." Thus, whether one concludes—as did the Court—that a custodian's production of corporate records is deemed not to constitute testimonial self-incrimination, or instead that a custodian waives the right to exercise the privilege, the lesson of *Fisher* is clear: A custodian may not resist a subpoena for corporate records on Fifth Amendment grounds. * * *

"We note further that recognizing a Fifth Amendment privilege on behalf of the records custodians of collective entities would have a detrimental impact on the Government's efforts to prosecute 'white-collar crime,' one of the most serious problems confronting law enforcement authorities. 'The greater portion of evidence of wrongdoing by an organization or its representatives is usually found in the official records and documents of that organization. Were the cloak of the privilege to be thrown around these impersonal records and documents, effective enforcement of many federal and state laws would be impossible.' *White* [Note 3, p. 855]. If custodians could assert a privilege, authorities would be stymied not only in their enforcement efforts against those individuals but also in their prosecutions or organizations. * * *[b]

"Petitioner suggests, however, that these concerns can be minimized by the simple expedient of either granting the custodian statutory immunity as to the act of production, 18 U.S.C. §§ 6002–6003, or addressing the subpoena to the corporation and allowing it to choose an agent to produce the records who can do so without incriminating himself. We think neither proposal satisfactorily addresses these concerns. Taking the last first, it is no doubt true that if a subpoena is addressed to a corporation, the corporation "must find some means by which to comply because no Fifth Amendment defense is available to it." The means most commonly used to comply is the appointment of an alternate custodian. But petitioner insists he cannot be required to aid the appointed custodian in his search for the demanded records, for any statement to the surrogate would itself be testimonial and incriminating. If this is correct, then petitioner's 'solution' is a chimera. In situations such as this—where the corporate custodian is likely the only person with knowledge about the demanded documents—the appointment of a surrogate will simply not ensure that the documents sought will ever reach the grand jury room; the appointed custodian will essentially be sent on an unguided search.

"This problem is eliminated if the Government grants the subpoenaed custodian statutory immunity for the testimonial aspects of his act of production. But that 'solution' also entails a significant drawback. All of the evidence obtained under a grant of immunity to the custodian may of course be used freely against the corporation, but if the Government has any thought of prosecuting the custodian, a grant of act of production immunity can have serious consequences. Testimony obtained pursuant to a grant of statutory use immunity may be used neither directly nor derivatively. 18 U.S.C. § 6002. And '[o]ne raising a claim under [the federal immunity] statute need only show that he testified under a grant of immunity in order to shift to the government the heavy burden of

b. Responding to this contention, the dissent (per Kennedy J.) noted: "The majority's abiding concern is that if a corporate officer who is the target of a subpoena is allowed to assert the privilege, it will impede the Government's power to investigate corporations, unions, and partnerships, to uncover and prosecute white collar crimes, and otherwise to enforce its visitatorial powers. There are at least two answers to this. The first, and most fundamental, is that the text of the Fifth Amendment does not authorize exceptions premised on such rationales. Second, even if it were proper to invent such exceptions, the dangers prophesied by the majority are overstated."

proving that all of the evidence it proposes to use was derived from legitimate independent sources.' *Kastigar* [Note 2, p. 849]. Even in cases where the Government does not employ the immunized testimony for any purpose—direct or derivative—against the witness, the Government's inability to meet the 'heavy burden' it bears may result in the preclusion of crucial evidence that was obtained legitimately.

"Although a corporate custodian is not entitled to resist a subpoena on the ground that his act of production will be personally incriminating, we do think certain consequences flow from the fact that the custodian's act of production is one in his representative rather than personal capacity. Because the custodian acts as a representative, the act is deemed one of the corporation and not the individual. Therefore, the Government concedes, as it must, that it may make no evidentiary use of the 'individual act' against the individual. For example, in a criminal prosecution against the custodian, the Government may not introduce into evidence before the jury the fact that the subpoena was served upon and the corporation's documents were delivered by one particular individual, the custodian.[c] The Government has the right, however, to use the corporation's act of production against the custodian. The Government may offer testimony—for example, from the process server who delivered the subpoena and from the individual who received the records—establishing that the corporation produced the records subpoenaed. The jury may draw from the corporation's act of production the conclusion that the records in question are authentic corporate records, which the corporation possessed, and which it produced in response to the subpoena. And if the defendant held a prominent position within the corporation that produced the records, the jury may, just as it would had someone else produced the documents, reasonably infer that he had possession of the documents or knowledge of their contents. Because the jury is not told that the defendant produced the records, any nexus between the defendant and the documents results solely from the corporation's act of production and other evidence in the case.[11]"

c. The dissent characterized this ruling as revealing the inherent flaw in the majority's reasoning. It noted: "Beginning from ordinary principles of agency, the majority proceeds to the conclusion that when a corporate employee, or an employee of a labor union or partnership, complies with a subpoena for production of documents, his act is necessarily and solely the act of the entity. * * * [But] the heart of the matter, as everyone knows, is that the Government does not see Braswell as a mere agent at all; and the majority's theory is difficult to square with what will often be the Government's actual practice. The subpoena in this case was not directed to Worldwide Machinery Sales, Inc., or Worldwide Purchasing, Inc. It was directed to 'Randy Braswell, President, Worldwide Machinery Sales, Inc., Worldwide Purchasing, Inc.' and informed him that '[y]ou are hereby commanded' to provide the specified documents. The Government explained at oral argument that it often chooses to designate an individual recipient, rather than the corporation generally, when it serves a subpoena because '[we] want the right to make that individual comply with the subpoena.' This is not the language of agency. By issuing a subpoena which the Government insists is directed to petitioner personally, it has forfeited any claim that it is simply making a demand on a corporation that, in turn, will have to find a physical agent to perform its duty. What the Government seeks instead is the right to choose any corporate agent as a target of its subpoena and compel that individual to disclose certain information by his own actions. * * * The majority gives the corporate agent fiction a weight it simply cannot bear. In a peculiar attempt to mitigate the force of its own holdings, it impinges upon its own analysis by concluding that, while the Government may compel a named individual to produce records, in any later proceeding against the person it cannot divulge that he performed the act. But if that is so, it is because the Fifth Amendment protects the person without regard to his status as a corporate employee; and once this be admitted, the necessary support for the majority's case has collapsed."

11. We reject the suggestion that the limitation on the evidentiary use of the custodian's act of production is the equivalent of constructive use immunity barred under our decision in *Doe* [see Note 5, p. 866]. Rather, the limitation is a necessary concomitant of the notion that a corporate custodian acts as an agent and not an individual when he produces corporate rec-

7. What is the grounding of the evidentiary-use prohibition imposed by *Braswell*? See Peter Henning, *Finding What Was Lost: Sorting Out the Custodian's Privilege Against Self-Incrimination From the Compelled Production of Records*, 77 Neb.L.Rev. 34 (1998) (asking whether the Court here has established a "quasi-constitutional" prohibition or a standard based upon its "supervisory power.")

The prohibition of evidentiary use of the act of production does not bar use of the contents of the documents against the custodian. But would a bar against such use be required in the situation described in the second paragraph of footnote 11 of *Braswell* ? *In re Grand Jury 89–4 Subpoena Duces Tecum,* 727 F.Supp. 265 (E.D.Va.1989), suggests that the issue left open in that footnote could bear upon not only upon a one-person corporation, but also upon a small family corporation in which one member (Doe) was the dominant actor. The court noted that a two step inquiry was required: "(1) would a jury, told that the corporation produced the documents, nonetheless inevitably conclude that it was Doe who had possession of the documents and produced them, and if so (2) would this give rise to any incriminating inferences concerning a document's (i) existence, (ii) authenticity, or (iii) custody." Finding that an insufficient showing had been made as to the second element, the court found it unnecessary to consider the consequences if both inquiries produced affirmative responses.

8. ***The non-documentary act-of-production.*** The implications of the several doctrines discussed in this section were brought together in an unusual setting in *Baltimore City Department of Social Services v. Bouknight,* 493 U.S. 549 (1990). The Supreme Court there rejected a self-incrimination objection to a subpoena directing respondent Bouknight to produce her infant son, an abused child who had previously been declared a ward of the court. The Court noted that the respondent could not claim the privilege based upon "anything an examination of the [child] might reveal," as that would be a claim based upon "the contents or nature of the thing demanded." However, the mother could conceivably claim the privilege because "the act of production would amount to testimony regarding her control over and possession of [the child]." While the state could "readily introduce [other] evidence of Bouknight's continuing control over the child" (including the court order giving her limited custody and her previous statements reflecting control), her "implicit communication of control over [the child] at the moment of production might aid the state in prosecuting Bouknight [for child abuse]." The Court had no need to decide, however, whether "this limited testimonial assertion is sufficiently incriminating and sufficiently testimonial for purposes of the privilege." In receiving conditional custody from the juvenile court, the mother had "assumed custodial duties related to production" (analogous to that of an entity agent) and had done so as part of noncriminal regulatory scheme which included a production component (analogous to regulations sustained under the required records doctrine). The Court added that it had no need in the case before it "to define the precise limitations that may exist upon the State's ability to use the testimonial aspects of Bouknight's act of production [against her] in subsequent criminal proceedings," but the "imposition of such limitations," as done in *Braswell,* was not "foreclosed."

9. ***Hubbell.*** The Court's latest ruling applying the act-of-production doctrine, *United States v. Hubbell*, set forth below, addressed several of the issues that the lower courts had found most troubling in that doctrine's application.

ords in response to a subpoena addressed to him in his representative capacity.

We leave open the question whether the agency rationale supports compelling a custodian to produce corporate records when the custodian is able to establish, by showing for example that he is the sole employee and officer of the corporation, that the jury would inevitably conclude that he produced the records.

UNITED STATES v. HUBBELL

530 U.S. 27, 120 S.C. 2037, 147 L.Ed.2d 24 (2000).

Justice STEVENS delivered the opinion of the Court. The two questions presented concern the scope of a witness' protection against compelled self-incrimination: (1) whether the Fifth Amendment privilege protects a witness from being compelled to disclose the existence of incriminating documents that the Government is unable to describe with reasonable particularity; and (2) if the witness produces such documents pursuant to a grant of immunity, whether 18 U.S.C. § 6002 prevents the Government from using them to prepare criminal charges against him.

This proceeding arises out of the second prosecution of respondent, Webster Hubbell, commenced by the Independent Counsel appointed in August 1994 to investigate possible violations of federal law relating to the Whitewater Development Corporation. The first prosecution was terminated pursuant to a plea bargain. In December 1994, respondent pleaded guilty to charges of mail fraud and tax evasion arising out of his billing practices as a member of an Arkansas law firm from 1989 to 1992, and was sentenced to 21 months in prison. In the plea agreement, respondent promised to provide the Independent Counsel with "full, complete, accurate, and truthful information" about matters relating to the Whitewater investigation.

The second prosecution resulted from the Independent Counsel's attempt to determine whether respondent had violated that promise. In October 1996, while respondent was incarcerated, the Independent Counsel served him with a subpoena duces tecum calling for the production of 11 categories of documents before a grand jury sitting in Little Rock, Arkansas. See Appendix, infra.[a] On November 19, he appeared before the grand jury and invoked his Fifth Amendment privilege

a. The Appendix to Justice Stevens' opinion set forth verbatim the "subpoena rider," which identified the 11 categories of documents in paragraphs (A)-(K). In essence, the 11 categories (each subject to a time frame limit of "January 1, 1993 to the present") were: (1) all documents "reflecting, referring, or relating to any direct or indirect sources of money or other things of value received by Webster Hubbell, his wife or children [collectively, the 'Hubbell family'] * * *, 'including but not limited to the identity of employers or clients of legal or any other type of work'; (3) all documents 'reflecting, referring, or related to' any 'direct or indirect sources of money or other things of value' received by the Hubbell family, including 'billing memoranda, draft statements, bills, final statements and/or bills for work performed or time billed'; (3) copies of all bank records of the Hubbell family, including 'statements, registers, ledgers, canceled checks, deposit items and wire transfers'; (4) all documents reflecting, referring, or related to 'time worked or billed by Webster Hubbell,' including 'original time sheets, books, notes, papers, and/or computer records'; (5) all documents reflecting 'expenses incurred by and/or disbursements of money by Webster Hubbell for work performed or to be performed'; (6) all documents 'reflecting, referring, or relating to Webster Hubbell's schedule of activities,' including 'all calendars, daytimers, time books, appointment books, diaries, records of reverse telephone toll charges, credit card calls, telephone message slips, logs, other telephone records, minutes databases, electronic mail messages, travel records, itineraries, tickets for transportation of any kind, payments, bills, expense backup documentation, schedules, and/or any other document or database that would disclose Webster Hubbell's activities'; (7) all documents 'reflecting, referring, or relating to any retainer agreements or contracts for employment' of the Hubbell family; (8) all 'tax returns, tax return information, including but not limited to all W–2s, form 1099s, schedules, draft returns, work papers, and backup documents filed, created or held by or on behalf of [the Hubbell family], and/or any business in which [the Hubbell family] holds or has held an interest'; (9) all documents 'reflecting, referring, or relating to work performed or to be performed for the City of Los Angeles, the Los Angeles Department of Airports or any other Los Angeles municipal or governmental entity, Mary Leslie, and/or Alan Arkatov'; (10) all documents 'reflecting, referring, or related to work performed by [the Hubbell family] on the recommendation, counsel, or other influence of Mary Leslie and/or Alan Arkatov'; and (11) all documents related to work performed for or on behalf of specified entities (e.g., Lippo Ltd.) and specified individuals (e.g., James Ria-

against self-incrimination. In response to questioning by the prosecutor, respondent initially refused "to state whether there are documents within my possession, custody, or control responsive to the Subpoena." Thereafter, the prosecutor produced an order, which had previously been obtained from the District Court pursuant to 18 U.S.C. § 6003(a), directing him to respond to the subpoena and granting him immunity "to the extent allowed by law." Respondent then produced 13,120 pages of documents and records and responded to a series of questions that established that those were all of the documents in his custody or control that were responsive to the commands in the subpoena, with the exception of a few documents he claimed were shielded by the attorney-client and attorney work-product privileges.

The contents of the documents produced by respondent provided the Independent Counsel with the information that led to this second prosecution. On April 30, 1998, a grand jury in the District of Columbia returned a 10–count indictment charging respondent with various tax-related crimes and mail and wire fraud. The District Court dismissed the indictment relying, in part, on the ground that the Independent Counsel's use of the subpoenaed documents violated § 6002 because all of the evidence he would offer against respondent at trial derived either directly or indirectly from the testimonial aspects of respondent's immunized act of producing those documents. Noting that the Independent Counsel had admitted that he was not investigating tax-related issues when he issued the subpoena, and that he had "learned about the unreported income and other crimes from studying the records' contents," the District Court characterized the subpoena as "the quintessential fishing expedition." * * *

The Court of Appeals vacated the judgment and remanded for further proceedings. The majority concluded that the District Court had incorrectly relied on the fact that the Independent Counsel did not have prior knowledge of the contents of the subpoenaed documents. The question the District Court should have addressed was the extent of the Government's independent knowledge of the documents' existence and authenticity, and of respondent's possession or control of them. It explained: "On remand, the district court should hold a hearing in which it seeks to establish the extent and detail of the [G]overnment's knowledge of Hubbell's financial affairs (or of the paperwork documenting it) on the day the subpoena issued. It is only then that the court will be in a position to assess the testimonial value of Hubbell's response to the subpoena. Should the Independent Counsel prove capable of demonstrating with reasonable particularity a prior awareness that the exhaustive litany of documents sought in the subpoena existed and were in Hubbell's possession, then the wide distance evidently traveled from the subpoena to the substantive allegations contained in the indictment would be based upon legitimate intermediate steps. To the extent that the information conveyed through Hubbell's compelled act of production provides the necessary linkage, however, the indictment deriving therefrom is tainted."

In the opinion of the dissenting judge, the majority failed to give full effect to the distinction between the contents of the documents and the limited testimonial significance of the act of producing them. In his view, as long as the prosecutor could make use of information contained in the documents or derived therefrom without any reference to the fact that respondent had produced them in response to a subpoena, there would be no improper use of the testimonial aspect of the immunized act of production. In other words, the constitutional privilege and the statute conferring use immunity would only shield the witness from the use of any information resulting from his subpoena response "beyond what the prosecutor

dy) 'or any affiliate, subsidiary, or corporation owned or controlled by or related to the aforementioned entities or individuals.' "

would receive if the documents appeared in the grand jury room or in his office unsolicited and unmarked, like manna from heaven."

On remand, the Independent Counsel acknowledged that he could not satisfy the "reasonable particularity" standard prescribed by the Court of Appeals and entered into a conditional plea agreement with respondent. In essence, the agreement provides for the dismissal of the charges unless this Court's disposition of the case makes it reasonably likely that respondent's "act of production immunity" would not pose a significant bar to his prosecution. The case is not moot, however, because the agreement also provides for the entry of a guilty plea and a sentence that will not include incarceration if we should reverse and issue an opinion that is sufficiently favorable to the Government to satisfy that condition. Despite that agreement, we granted the Independent Counsel's petition for a writ of certiorari in order to determine the precise scope of a grant of immunity with respect to the production of documents in response to a subpoena. We now affirm.

It is useful to preface our analysis of the constitutional issue with a restatement of certain propositions that are not in dispute. The term "privilege against self-incrimination" is not an entirely accurate description of a person's constitutional protection against being "compelled in any criminal case to be a witness against himself." The word "witness" in the constitutional text limits the relevant category of compelled incriminating communications to those that are "testimonial" in character. As Justice Holmes observed, there is a significant difference between the use of compulsion to extort communications from a defendant and compelling a person to engage in conduct that may be incriminating. Thus, even though the act may provide incriminating evidence, a criminal suspect may be compelled to put on a shirt, to provide a blood sample or handwriting exemplar, or to make a recording of his voice. The act of exhibiting such physical characteristics is not the same as a sworn communication by a witness that relates either express or implied assertions of fact or belief. * * *

More relevant to this case is the settled proposition that a person may be required to produce specific documents even though they contain incriminating assertions of fact or belief because the creation of those documents was not "compelled" within the meaning of the privilege. [*Fisher v. United States*]. * * * It is clear, therefore, that respondent Hubbell could not avoid compliance with the subpoena served on him merely because the demanded documents contained incriminating evidence, whether written by others or voluntarily prepared by himself. * * * On the other hand, we have also made it clear that the act of producing documents in response to a subpoena may have a compelled testimonial aspect. We have held that "the act of production" itself may implicitly communicate "statements of fact" * * *. By "producing documents in compliance with a subpoena, the witness would admit that the papers existed, were in his possession or control, and were authentic." Moreover, as was true in this case, when the custodian of documents responds to a subpoena, he may be compelled to take the witness stand and answer questions designed to determine whether he has produced everything demanded by the subpoena. The answers to those questions, as well as the act of production itself, may certainly communicate information about the existence, custody, and authenticity of the documents. Whether the constitutional privilege protects the answers to such questions, or protects the act of production itself, is a question that is distinct from the question whether the unprotected contents of the documents themselves are incriminating.

Finally, the phrase "in any criminal case" in the text of the Fifth Amendment might have been read to limit its coverage to compelled testimony that is used against the defendant in the trial itself. It has, however, long been settled that its protection encompasses compelled statements that lead to the discovery of incriminating evidence even though the statements themselves are not incriminating and are not introduced into evidence. * * * Compelled testimony that communicates information that may "lead to incriminating evidence" is privileged even if the information itself is not inculpatory. * * * It is the Fifth Amendment's protection against the prosecutor's use of incriminating information derived directly or indirectly from the compelled testimony of the respondent that is of primary relevance in this case.

Acting pursuant to 18 U.S.C. § 6002, the District Court entered an order compelling respondent to produce "any and all documents" described in the grand jury subpoena and granting him "immunity to the extent allowed by law." In *Kastigar v. United States* [Note 2, p. 849], we upheld the constitutionality of § 6002 because the scope of the "use and derivative-use" immunity that it provides is coextensive with the scope of the constitutional privilege against self-incrimination. * * * We particularly emphasized the critical importance of protection against a future prosecution" 'based on knowledge and sources of information obtained from the compelled testimony.' " * * * [W]e held that the statute imposes an affirmative duty on the prosecution, not merely to show that its evidence is not tainted by the prior testimony, but "to prove that the evidence it proposes to use is derived from a legitimate source wholly independent of the compelled testimony." * * * The "compelled testimony" that is relevant in this case is not to be found in the contents of the documents produced in response to the subpoena. It is, rather, the testimony inherent in the act of producing those documents. The disagreement between the parties focuses entirely on the significance of that testimonial aspect.

The Government correctly emphasizes that the testimonial aspect of a response to a subpoena duces tecum does nothing more than establish the existence, authenticity, and custody of items that are produced. We assume that the Government is also entirely correct in its submission that it would not have to advert to respondent's act of production in order to prove the existence, authenticity, or custody of any documents that it might offer in evidence at a criminal trial; indeed, the Government disclaims any need to introduce any of the documents produced by respondent into evidence in order to prove the charges against him. It follows, according to the Government, that it has no intention of making improper "use" of respondent's compelled testimony. The question, however, is not whether the response to the subpoena may be introduced into evidence at his criminal trial. That would surely be a prohibited "use" of the immunized act of production. But the fact that the Government intends no such use of the act of production leaves open the separate question whether it has already made "derivative use" of the testimonial aspect of that act in obtaining the indictment against respondent and in preparing its case for trial. It clearly has.

It is apparent from the text of the subpoena itself that the prosecutor needed respondent's assistance both to identify potential sources of information and to produce those sources. See Appendix [fn. a supra]. Given the breadth of the description of the 11 categories of documents called for by the subpoena, the collection and production of the materials demanded was tantamount to answering a series of interrogatories asking a witness to disclose the existence and location of particular documents fitting certain broad descriptions. The assembly of literally hundreds of pages of material in response to a request for "any and all documents reflecting, referring, or relating to any direct or indirect sources of money or other things of value received by or provided to" an individual or members of his family during a 3-year period, is the functional equivalent of the preparation of an answer to either a detailed written interrogatory or a series of oral questions at a discovery deposition. Entirely apart from the contents of the 13,120 pages of materials that respondent produced in this case, it is undeniable that providing a catalog of existing documents fitting within any of the 11 broadly worded subpoena categories could provide a prosecutor with a "lead to incriminating evidence," or "a link in the chain of evidence needed to prosecute."

Indeed, the record makes it clear that is what happened in this case. The documents were produced before a grand jury sitting in the Eastern District of Arkansas in aid of the Independent Counsel's attempt to determine whether respondent had violated a commitment in his first plea agreement. The use of those sources of information eventually led to the return of an indictment by a grand jury sitting in the District of Columbia for offenses that apparently are unrelated to that plea agreement. What the District Court characterized as a "fishing expedition" did produce a fish, but not the one that the Independent Counsel expected to hook. It is abundantly clear that the testimonial aspect of respondent's act of producing subpoenaed documents was the first step in a chain of evidence that led to this prosecution. The documents did not magically appear in the prosecutor's office like "manna from heaven." They arrived there only after respondent asserted his constitutional privilege, received a grant of immunity, and—under the compulsion of the District Court's order—took the mental and physical steps necessary to provide the prosecutor with an accurate inventory of the many sources of potentially incriminating evidence sought by the subpoena. It was only through respondent's truthful reply to the subpoena that the Government received the incriminating documents of which it made "substantial use ... in the investigation that led to the indictment." Brief for United States 3.

For these reasons, we cannot accept the Government's submission that respondent's immunity did not preclude its derivative use of the produced documents because its "possession of the documents [was] the fruit only of a simple physical act—the act of producing the documents." Brief, at 29. It was unquestionably necessary for respondent to make extensive use of "the contents of his own mind" in identifying the hundreds of documents responsive to the requests in the subpoena. The assembly of those documents was like telling an inquisitor the combination to a wall safe, not like being forced to surrender the key to a strongbox. *Doe II* [fn. e, p. 856]. The Government's anemic view of respondent's act of production as a mere physical act that is principally non-testimonial in character and can be entirely divorced from its "implicit" testimonial aspect so as to constitute a "legitimate, wholly independent source" (as required by *Kastigar*) for the documents produced simply fails to account for these realities.

In sum, we have no doubt that the constitutional privilege against self-incrimination protects the target of a grand jury investigation from being compelled to answer questions designed to elicit information about the existence of sources of potentially incriminating evidence. That constitutional privilege has the same application to the testimonial aspect of a response to a subpoena seeking discovery of those sources. Before the District Court, the Government arguably conceded that respondent's act of production in this case had a testimonial aspect that entitled him to respond to the subpoena by asserting his privilege against self-incrimination. * * * On appeal and again before this Court, however, the Government has argued that the communicative aspect of respondent's act of producing ordinary business records is insufficiently "testimonial" to support a claim of privilege because the existence and possession of such records by any businessman is a "foregone conclusion" under our decision in *Fisher v. United States*. This argument both misreads *Fisher* and ignores our subsequent decision in *Doe I* [Note 1, p. 863]. * * * Whatever the scope of this "foregone conclusion" rationale, the facts of this case plainly fall outside of it. While in *Fisher* the Government already knew that the documents were in the attorneys' possession and could independently confirm their existence and authenticity through the accountants who created them, here the Government has not shown that it had any prior knowledge of either the existence or the whereabouts of the 13,120 pages of documents ultimately produced by respondent. The Government cannot cure this deficiency through the overbroad argument that a businessman such as respondent will always possess general business and tax records that fall within the broad categories described in this subpoena. The *Doe I* subpoenas also sought several broad categories of general business records, yet we upheld the District Court's finding that the act of producing those records would involve testimonial self-incrimination.

Given our conclusion that respondent's act of production had a testimonial aspect, at least with respect to the existence and location of the documents sought by the Government's subpoena, respondent could not be compelled to produce those documents without first receiving a grant of immunity under § 6003. As we construed § 6002 in *Kastigar*, such immunity is co-extensive with the constitutional privilege. *Kastigar* requires that respondent's motion to dismiss the indictment on immunity grounds be granted unless the Government proves that the evidence it used in obtaining the indictment and proposed to use at trial was derived from legitimate sources "wholly independent" of the testimonial aspect of respondent's immunized conduct in assembling and producing the documents described in the subpoena. The Government, however, does not claim that it could make such a showing. Rather, it contends that its prosecution of respondent must be considered proper unless someone—presumably respondent—shows that "there is some substantial relation between the compelled testimonial communications implicit in the act of production (as opposed to the act of production standing alone) and some aspect of the information used in the investigation or the evidence presented at trial." Brief for United States 9. We could not accept this submission without repudiating the basis for our conclusion in *Kastigar* that the statutory guarantee of use and derivative-use immunity is as broad as the constitutional privilege itself. This we are not prepared to do. Accordingly, the indictment against respondent must be dismissed. The judgment of the Court of Appeals is affirmed. * * *

Chief Justice REHNQUIST dissents and would reverse the judgment of the Court of Appeals in part, for the reasons given by Judge Williams in his dissenting opinion in that court, 167 F.3d 552, 597 (C.A.D.C.1999).[b]

Justice THOMAS, with whom Justice SCALIA joins, concurring.

Our decision today involves the application of the act-of-production doctrine, which provides that persons compelled to turn over incriminating papers or other physical evidence pursuant to a subpoena duces tecum or a summons may invoke the Fifth Amendment privilege against self-incrimination as a bar to production only where the act of producing the evidence would contain "testimonial" features. I join the opinion of the Court because it properly applies this doctrine, but

b. Judge Williams reasoned that, since the prosecution had "relied on the documents only for the information they contained," it had not made use of any testimonial elements of the act of production with respect to Hubbell's possession or authentication. As to "existence," the *Fisher* reasoning should appropriately limit the testimonial element of the act of production to the act's acknowledging "responsiveness of the documents to the subpoena." That would prohibit the government from "referring back to the subpoena to identify the documents and to clarify relationships that were not clear on their face." But it would not extend to "existence in a quite different sense—the fact that these particular pieces of paper are in being," for that "is quite easily confirmed by these papers own physical existence." Whether or not the government could previously establish that physical existence as a foregone conclusion, the act of production was not testimonial in establishing that existence, just as the act of providing a blood sample or a handwriting exemplar is not testimonial in establishing what third persons observe—that blood or handwriting come from the particular person. Thus, just as the prosecutor could make use of data drawn from the blood and handwriting (blood type, DNA, or handwriting idiosyncracies), the prosecutor could use the contents of the documents.

I write separately to note that this doctrine may be inconsistent with the original meaning of the Fifth Amendment's Self–Incrimination Clause. A substantial body of evidence suggests that the Fifth Amendment privilege protects against the compelled production not just of incriminating testimony, but of any incriminating evidence. In a future case, I would be willing to reconsider the scope and meaning of the Self–Incrimination Clause.

The Fifth Amendment provides that "[n]o person ... shall be compelled in any criminal case to be a witness against himself." The key word at issue in this case is "witness." The Court's opinion, relying on prior cases, essentially defines "witness" as a person who provides testimony, and thus restricts the Fifth Amendment's ban to only those communications "that are 'testimonial' in character." None of this Court's cases, however, has undertaken an analysis of the meaning of the term at the time of the founding. A review of that period reveals substantial support for the view that the term "witness" meant a person who gives or furnishes evidence, a broader meaning than that which our case law currently ascribes to the term.[c] If this is so, a person who responds to a subpoena duces tecum would be just as much a "witness" as a person who responds to a subpoena ad testificandum.[1] * * *

This Court has not always taken the approach to the Fifth Amendment that we follow today. The first case interpreting the Self–Incrimination Clause—*Boyd v. United States*—was decided, though not explicitly, in accordance with the understanding that "witness" means one who gives evidence. * * * But this Court's decision in *Fisher v. United States*, rejected this understanding, permitting the Government to force a person to furnish incriminating physical evidence and protecting only the "testimonial" aspects of that transfer. In so doing, *Fisher* not only failed to examine the historical backdrop to the Fifth Amendment, it also required—as illustrated by extended discussion in the opinions below in this case—a difficult parsing of the act of responding to a subpoena duces tecum. None of the parties in this case has asked us to depart from *Fisher*, but in light of the historical evidence that the Self–Incrimination Clause may have a broader reach than *Fisher* holds, I remain open to a reconsideration of that decision and its progeny in a proper case.

Notes and Questions

1. ***Establishing a foregone conclusion.*** Does *Hubbell* in its discussion of the lack of a sufficient "foregone-conclusion" showing in that case, and the presence of a sufficient showing in *Fisher*, adopt, in effect, the "reasonable particularity" standard advanced by the Court of Appeals (see p. 872)? See In re Grand Jury Subpoena, Dated April 18, 2003, 383 F.3d 905 (9th Cir.2004) (applying

c. Justice Thomas cited the following sources from that period: (1) dictionary definitions of the term "witness"; (3) state constitutional provisions that granted a right against compulsion "to give evidence" or to "furnish evidence"; (3) the use of similar wording by the four states that proposed inclusion of a self-incrimination provision in the Bill of Rights, and the lack of any indication that Madison's "unique phrasing" in the proposal he offered to Congress was designed to narrow those state proposals; and (4) the Sixth Amendment's compulsory process clause, which the Court had long held to encompass the right to secure papers as well as testimony. For a more extensive review of this historical material, see Richard A. Nagareda, *Compulsion "To Be A Witness" and the Resurrection of Boyd*, 74 N.Y.U.L.Rev. 1575 (1999), also cited by Justice Thomas.

1. Even if the term "witness" in the Fifth Amendment referred to someone who provides testimony, as this Court's recent cases suggest without historical analysis, it may well be that at the time of the founding a person who turned over documents would be described as providing testimony. See Amey v. Long, 9 East. 472, 484, 103 Eng. Rep. 653, 658 (K.B.1808) (referring to documents requested by subpoenas duces tecum as "written ... testimony"). * * *

a "reasonable particularity" standard and citing *Hubbell* as supporting that standard); Robert Mosteller, *Cowboy Prosecutors and Subpoenas for Incriminating Evidence: The Consequences and Corrections of Excess*, 58 Wash. & Lee L.Rev. 487 (2001) (questioning significance of Court's failure to adopt the lower court's standard).

2. To what extent must the preexisting knowledge establishing a forgone conclusion relate to a specific document? Consider CRIMPROC. § 8.13(a), asking what the government would have needed to meet the foregone conclusion standard as to its demand for "tickets of transportation": "Must [the government] identify the specific [travel] document as one known to be in the party's possession (e.g., an airline ticket for a known trip on a particular day) or may it refer to a somewhat broader grouping of documents upon showing that the party engaged in a particular type of activity which involved receipt of such documents (e.g., airline tickets from a specific airline which the subpoena party regularly used)?" Is it significant in this regard that *Hubbell* described the government's prior knowledge in *Fisher* "as relating to [the accountant's] workpapers as a group, not as relating to the specific documents within that grouping." Ibid

3. In *Grand Jury Subpoena, April 18*, Note 1 supra, the Court held that the government had failed to meet the foregone conclusion standard as to its subpoena to Doe (a former salesman for the target corporation) for the production of all documents "relating to the production or sale of * * * DRAM [a computer memory chip], including * * * handwritten notes, calendars, diaries, daybooks, appointment calendars, or notepads, or any similar documents." The government had established a prior knowledge of specific conversations between Doe and a competitor's employee regarding the pricing of DRAM (indeed, Doe acknowledged those meetings), and (2) the types of materials sought from Doe "were found in the employee records of other DRAM salesmen (including Doe's successor)." The Ninth Circuit reasoned that the government was not required "to have actual knowledge of each and every responsive document," but the "reasonable particularity" standard required more than it had here. The "government probably could identify * * * phone records corroborating that Doe spoke to his competitors, and records establishing the meetings with certain competitors because Doe made substantial admissions * * * [in his] interview regarding these documents" but the government had "failed to draft the subpoena narrowly" so as to limit it to such documents. Its "argument that a salesman such as Doe will always possess business records describing or memorializing meetings or prices" failed, in light of *Hubbell*, to "establish the reasonably particular knowledge required."

4. *Hubbell* describes *Fisher* as a case in which the "Government already knew the documents were in the attorney's possession (p. 875)." Since the attorneys there raised the attorney-client privilege in response to the subpoena, they had to acknowledge that they currently possessed the documents. To establish existence and possession as foregone conclusions, must the government show that it not only has knowledge that the documents were created and placed in the possession of the subpoenaed party, but also knowledge that documents remain in the possession of the subpoenaed party on the day of the issuance of the subpoena? If so, can the government rely on the documents being records of a type ordinarily preserved for at least a few years, or must it show that this particular party has a practice of retaining such records. See Mosteller, supra Note 1 (a strict requirement of proof as to current possession would present a substantial "practical problem for prosecutors" as to "readily destructible items, such as specific documents").

5. Assuming that the government has prior knowledge as the existence and possession of particular types of documents relating to specific events, does *Hubbell* also require that the description of the documents permit the subpoenaed party to identify the documents without using the "contents of his own mind" (p. 875)? Must the documents be identified "by reference to such features as letterhead, signature, or location," rather by a relationship that will require the subpoenaed party to utilize "his or her special knowledge of historical fact" CRIMPROC. § 8.13(a). Consider Richard Uviller, *Fisher Goes On The Quintessential Fishing Expedition and Hubbell is Off the Hook*, 91 J.Crim.L. & Criminology 311 (2001) (such a restriction "goes too far" as "virtually every custodian * * * must use his or her own mind to sort out the files and to cull and organize documents * * * [and] the process of recognition and implicit voucher of authenticity * * * are, of course, the predicates of *Fisher*"). See also *United States v. Ponds*, 290 F.Supp.2d 71 (D.D.C.2003) (in distinguishing *Hubbell*, the court notes: "The degree of interpretation, locating, cataloging and assembling of documents so important in *Hubbell* was simply not demanded by the narrow subpoena at issue here"—which required the production of documents (which the government already knew to exist) "relating to" such subjects as "the use, ownership, possession, custody, or control of the 1991 Mercedes Benz," and "the payment of legal fees by Harris to defendant,").

6. Would the combination of requiring "reasonable particularity" in the government's prior awareness of the subpoenaed party's possession of the document and "reasonable particularity" in the subpoena's description of the document be equivalent to requiring the probable cause needed to obtain a search warrant? See William J. Stuntz, *O.J. Simpson, Bill Clinton, and the Transsubstantive Fourth Amendment*, 114 Harv. L. Rev. 842 (2001): "Last Term, in *United States v. Hubbell*, the Supreme Court appeared to conclude that unless the government knows—really knows—of a particular document's existence, a subpoena's target is free to refuse to turn the document over, because the act of producing the document would testify to the fact that it does indeed exist. Of course, if the government really does know that the document exists, and hence knows what is in it (knowledge of content tends to track knowledge of existence), the government can probably get a warrant to search for and seize the document." See also Lance Cole, *The Fifth Amendment and Compelled Protection of Personal Documents. After United States v. Hubbell—New Protection for Private Papers*, 29 Am.J.Crim.L. 123 (2002) ("After Hubbell * * * prosecutors who take the subpoena approach may face a burden comparable to that presented by the probable cause and particularity requirements for obtaining a search warrant").

Compare, however, CRIMPROC § 8.13(a), noting that the *Hubbell*, opinion in distinguishing *Fisher*, did not necessarily indicate that a foregone conclusion showing must be as strong as that in *Fisher*, and even such a showing is hardly the equivalent of probable cause: "For example, the government may learn from an employee that a particular document exists and that it is the most likely of all documents to contain information relating to a particular criminal activity (e.g., price-fixing), but have only a mere suspicion that the crime was actually committed—and thus be short of probable cause, but have a proper basis for a grand jury investigation."

7. ***Act-of-production immunity.*** In *Fisher*, Justice Marshall suggested in his concurring opinion that act-of-production immunity, though it did not directly immunize the contents of the document, would preclude use of the content except for the rare situation where the government had previous knowledge of the existence and whereabouts of the document, but utilized immunity because it could not authenticate without the act of production. Does *Hubbell* establish that position, and thereby preclude use of the contents of the document produced under act-of-production immunity except in rare cases? Consider *United States v. Ponds*, Note 5 supra. The court there rejected the view that act-of-production-immunity "routinely extends to the contents of the document." In holding that the contents could be used to obtain other evidence, the court emphasized that the subpoena before it, unlike that in *Hubbell*, did not lead the government to the documents through the "mental statements" inherent in the witness' "interpretation and response to a broad subpoena through the assembly and production of documents." See Note 5 supra. Speaking to the defendant's contention that the government had used the content of the document to identify an employee who became a government key witness, the court noted (1) it had been a "foregone conclusion * * * [that] defendant would possess documents identifying someone who worked for him in his practice," and (2) excluding the witness as derivative evidence would "eliminate any distinction between content and the act of production, a result squarely at odds with the careful differentiation explained in *Hubbell*."

8. ***Compelled-to-give-evidence.*** Does the position for which Justice Thomas urges reconsideration find support in any aspect of *Boyd* other than its precise holding? See Note 1(b), p. 853. Would the replacement of *Fisher* with a "compelled-to-give-evidence" standard also require reconsideration of the Court's modification of other aspect of *Boyd's* analysis (e.g., the recognition of a "collective entity exception")? Would adoption of that standard require that the Court also reject the line of identification-procedure cases cited in *Hubbell* as illustrating the limitation of the privilege to "compelled incriminating communications" that are "testimonial in character" (p. 873)? Nagareda, Note 1(b), p. 853, notes that, while the concept of "giving evidence" is hardly limited to documentary evidence, in the identification-procedure cases, a distinction can be drawn where the government is not requiring the affirmative act of production, but simply is "taking the evidence" from the body of the person.

SECTION 6. FIFTH AMENDMENT HISTORY AND VALUES

The Supreme Court has considered self-incrimination issues in a variety of contexts, including many that did not directly involve the criminal justice process (e.g., the exercise of the privilege in civil, legislative, and administrative proceedings). Within the criminal justice process, self-incrimination issues have been considered in connection with searches for documents, police interrogation of suspects, compelled arrestee participation in identification procedures, grand jury subpoenas (both ad testificandum and duces tecum), witness testimony (in both pretrial and trial proceedings), grants of immunity, court-ordered defense discovery to the prosecution, evidentiary and other uses of compelled confessions, the defendant's silence (at trial and during interrogations), and sentencing procedures. The issues presented in these contexts include: who may exercise the privilege; what constitutes "compulsion"; what constitutes "incrimination"; what constitutes "being a witness"; what constitutes a "criminal case"; the scope of the prohibition against government use of evidence obtained in violation of the privilege; what governmentally imposed burdens so impair the exercise of the privilege as to be unconstitutional; and what should be required for waiver of the privilege.

The end product of the Court's consideration of such diverse issues in equally diverse contexts has been a variety of different doctrinal standards, each shaped to fit the particular issue in the particular context in which it is presented. Those standards are discussed in decisions that are spread throughout this book. Treated here are two common threads that run through the Supreme Court opinions dealing with self-incrimination issues—references to the history of the privilege and to the basic policies that underlie the privilege. Supreme Court decisions resolving self-incrimination issues most frequently discuss precedent, but discussions of the history and policies of the privilege probably rank next in order. See CRIMPROC § 8.14.

References to self-incrimination history and values are found in opinions dealing with all of the different contexts in which self-incrimination issues are presented, but many of the most prominent discussions are found in cases involving grand jury investigations. Among these is the discussion in *Doe v. United States*, (often referred to as *Doe II*, see Note 6, p. 856).

EXCERPTS FROM DOE v. UNITED STATES—OPINION OF THE COURT

487 U.S. 201, 108 S.Ct. 2341, 101 L.Ed.2d 184 (1988).

(PER BLACKMUN J.)

[At issue here was a self-incrimination objection to a court order directing the petitioner Doe (the target of a grand jury investigation to sign forms stating that he was "directing any bank * * * at which I may have a bank account of any kind or at which a corporation has a bank account of any kind upon which I am authorized to draw" to deliver records of those accounts to the grand jury). The form specifically noted that petitioner's directive was being made pursuant to court order, and that the directive was intended to provide compliance with the bank secrecy laws of the Cayman Islands and Bermuda. Both the petitioner and the government agreed that "this case turns on whether the act of executing the form is a 'testimonial communication.' " Petitioner contended that "a compelled statement is testimonial if the Government could use the content of the [compelled] speech or writing, as opposed to its physical characteristics, to further a criminal investigation of the witness." The prosecution argued that "a compelled statement is not testimonial for purposes of the privilege, unless it implicitly or explicitly relates a factual assertion or otherwise conveys information to the Government." The prosecution pointed to *Fisher* (p. 857) and *Doe I* (Note 1, p. 863) as supporting its contention. As the Court noted, those cases "made clear that the Fifth Amendment privilege against self-incrimination applies to acts that imply assertions of fact." Petitioner argued, however, that these precedents did not apply to a compelled statement. The excerpts that follow responded to that argument.]

We reject petitioner's argument that this test [requiring an implicit assertion of fact] does not control the determination as to when the privilege applies to oral or written statements. While the Court in *Fisher* and *Doe* did not purport to announce a universal test for determining the scope of the privilege, it also did not purport to establish a more narrow boundary applicable to acts alone. To the contrary, the Court applied basic Fifth Amendment principles. An examination of the Court's application of these principles in other cases indicates the Court's recognition that, in order to be testimonial, an accused's communication must itself, explicitly or implicitly, relate a factual assertion or disclose information. Only then is a person compelled to be a "witness" against himself.

This understanding is perhaps most clearly revealed in those cases in which the Court has held that certain acts, though incriminating, are not within the privilege. Thus, a suspect may be compelled to furnish a blood sample, to provide a handwriting exemplar or a voice exemplar, to stand in a lineup, and to wear particular clothing. * * * These decisions are grounded on the proposition that "the privilege protects an accused only from being compelled to testify against himself, or otherwise provide the State with evidence of a testimonial or communicative nature." *Schmerber v. California* [Note 6, p. 856]. * * * It is the "extortion of information from the accused," the attempt to force him "to disclose the contents of his own mind," that implicates the Self–Incrimination Clause. * * * "Unless some attempt is made to secure a communication—written, oral or otherwise—upon which reliance is to be placed as involving [the accused's] consciousness of the facts and the operations of his mind in expressing it, the demand made upon him is not a testimonial one." 8 J. Wigmore, Evidence § 2265 (McNaughton rev. 1961).

It is consistent with the history of and the policies underlying the Self–Incrimination Clause to hold that the privilege may be asserted only to resist compelled explicit or implicit disclosures of incriminating information. Historically, the privilege was intended to prevent the use of legal compulsion to extract from the accused a sworn communication of facts which would incriminate him. Such was the process of the ecclesiastical courts and the Star Chamber—the inquisitorial method of putting the accused upon his oath and compelling him to answer questions designed to uncover uncharged offenses, without evidence from another source. The major thrust of the policies undergirding the privilege is to prevent such compulsion. * * *

The Court in *Murphy v. Waterfront Comm'n*, 378 U.S. 52, 84 (1964), explained that the privilege is founded on

> "[1] our unwillingness to subject those suspected of crime to the cruel trilemma of self-accusation, perjury or contempt; [2] our preference for an accusatorial rather than an inquisitorial system of criminal justice; [3] our fear that self-incriminating statements will be elicited by inhumane treatment and abuses; [4] our sense of fair play which dictates 'a fair state-individual balance by requiring the government to leave the individual alone until good cause is shown for disturbing him and by requiring the government in its contest with the individual to shoulder the entire load,' . . .; [5] our respect for the inviolability of the human personality and of the right of each individual 'to a private enclave where he may lead a private life,' . . .; [6] our distrust of self-deprecatory statements; and [7] our realization that the privilege, while sometimes 'a shelter to the guilty,' is often 'a protection to the innocent.' "[a]

These policies are served when the privilege is asserted to spare the accused from having to reveal, directly or indirectly, his knowledge of facts relating him to the offense or from having to share his thoughts and beliefs with the Government.[11]

a. Justice Goldberg's listing of values in *Murphy* is the most frequently cited description of the values underlying the self-incrimination clause. Bracketed numbers are added here to facilitate reference to particular values in the Notes and Questions that follow.

The *Murphy* opinion added in fn. 5: "As noted in the text, * * * the privilege against self-incrimination represents many fundamental values and aspirations. It is an expression of the moral striving of the community. * * * a reflection of our common conscience * * *. That is why it is regarded as so fundamental a part of our constitutional fabric, despite the fact that 'the law and the lawyers * * * have never made up their minds just what it is supposed to do or just whom it is intended to protect.' Kalven, *Invoking the Fifth Amendment—Some Legal and Impractical Considerations*, 9 Bull.Atomic Sci. 181, 182. It will not do, therefore, to assign one isolated policy to the privilege, and then to argue that since 'the' policy may not be furthered measurably by applying the privilege across state-federal lines, it follows that the privilege should not be so applied."

11. Petitioner argues that at least some of these policies would be undermined unless the Government is required to obtain evidence against an accused from sources other than his compelled statements, whether or not the statements make a factual assertion or convey information. Petitioner accordingly maintains that the policy of striking an appropriate balance between the power of the Government and the sovereignty of the individual precludes the Government from compelling an individual to utter or write words that lead to incriminating evidence. Even if some of the policies underlying the privilege might support petitioner's interpretation of the privilege, "it is clear that the scope of the privilege does not coincide with the complex of values it helps to protect. Despite the impact upon the inviolabil-

We are not persuaded by petitioner's arguments that our articulation of the privilege fundamentally alters the power of the Government to compel an accused to assist in his prosecution. There are very few instances in which a verbal statement, either oral or written, will not convey information or assert facts. The vast majority of verbal statements thus will be testimonial and, to that extent at least, will fall within the privilege. Furthermore, it should be remembered that there are many restrictions on the Government's prosecutorial practices in addition to the Self–Incrimination Clause. Indeed, there are other protections against governmental efforts to compel an unwilling suspect to cooperate in an investigation, including efforts to obtain information from him.[12] We are confident that these provisions, together with the Self–Incrimination Clause, will continue to prevent abusive investigative techniques.

Notes and Questions

1. ***What history is relevant?*** The Supreme Court has noted that the Fifth Amendment itself provides no "helpful legislative history." *United States v. Balsys*, Note 3, p. 840. As a result, the Court looks to the common law history of the privilege on the assumption that the framers adopted the privilege as it existed at common law and were familiar with the events which shaped that common law privilege. But see Katharine B. Hazlett, The *Nineteenth Century Origins of the Fifth Amendment Privilege Against Self–Incrimination*, 42 Am.J.Legal Hist. 235 (1998) (arguing that it was not until the mid–19th Century that the Fifth Amendment's self-incrimination clause was viewed as incorporating the full scope of the common law privilege). An extensive body of literature explores the scope of the common law privilege and the events that shaped its development. See CRIMPROC § 8.14(b) (collecting citations).

In *Doe II*, in determining that the privilege is limited to compelled disclosures of the "contents of the mind" (i.e., testimonial disclosures), the Court looks to the notorious "inquisitorial" practices of the 17th Century ecclesiastical courts and Star Chamber (often cited as the evil that led to the creation of the privilege). On the other hand, in suggesting that limiting the privilege to "testimonial" disclosures may be "inconsistent with the original meaning of the Fifth Amendment's Self–Incrimination Clause," Justice Thomas, in his concurring opinion in *Hubbell*, looked to other sources. See fn. c at p. 877. To what extent should the focus be on (1) the English common law developments that developed the core privilege, (2) subsequent developments in England prior to the adoption of the Constitution (3) the privilege as shaped in the law of the various states at the time of the adoption of the Fifth Amendment?

2. ***The significance of history.*** Consider CRIMPROC § 8.14(b): "The significance [of history in the interpretation self-incrimination clause], * * * has

ity of the human personality, and upon our belief in an adversary system of criminal justice in which the Government must produce the evidence against an accused through its own independent labors, the prosecution is allowed to obtain and use ... evidence which although compelled is generally speaking not 'testimonial,' *Schmerber v. California.*" *Grosso v. United States,* 390 U.S. 62 (1968) (Brennan, J., concurring). If the societal interests in privacy, fairness, and restraint of governmental power are not unconstitutionally offended by compelling the accused to have his body serve as evidence that leads to the development of highly incriminating testimony, as *Schmerber* and its progeny make clear, it is difficult to understand how compelling a suspect to make a nonfactual statement that facilitates the production of evidence by someone else offends the privilege.

12. For example, the Fourth Amendment generally prevents the Government from compelling a suspect to consent to a search of his home; the attorney-client privilege prevents the Government from compelling a suspect to direct his attorney to disclose confidential communications; and the Due Process Clause imposes limitations on the Government's ability to coerce individuals into participating in criminal prosecutions, see generally *Rochin v. California* [p. 33].

varied with the setting. Justice Frankfurter once described the privilege as 'a specific provision of which it is particularly true that "a page of history is worth a volume of logic.' " *Ullman v. United States*, 350 U.S. 422 (1956). That statement was made, however, in a case presenting a self-incrimination issue on which the historical practice was quite clear—the use of immunity grants to displace the witness' right to claim the privilege. But changed circumstances make rare such a square fit. Most often, the Court has noted that it is looking to the general 'lessons of history' as they point to the need for a 'liberal construction' of the privilege. Those lessons, in turn, repeatedly bring the Court back to the evils of 'ecclesiastical inquisitions and Star Chamber proceedings' and the need to avoid a system that 'creates a temptation on the part of the State to resort to the expedient of compelling incriminating evidence from one's own mouth.' *Couch v. United States* [Note 7, p. 857]. Very often, however, that historical experience 'sheds no light whatever on the subject [before the Court], unless indeed that which is adverse, resulting from the contrast between the dilemma of which petitioner complains and the historical excesses which gave rise to the privilege.' *McGautha v. California*, 402 U.S. 183 (1971) ('unitary trial,' deciding both guilt and capital sentence did not impose impermissible burden on defendant's right of silence). * * * [Moreover,] where the historical confines of the privilege seem not to fit its general lessons of history [e.g., where the common law accepted a practice that ran counter to the general thrust of the privilege], the Court has not hesitated to note, as it did in *Miranda* [p. 579], that 'a noble principle often transcends its origins.' "

3. *The role of the underlying values.* While the Court has frequently referred to the "complex of values" underlying the Fifth Amendment privilege (*Murphy*) as an important source in the shaping of Fifth Amendment doctrine, it has also noted, as in footnote 11 of *Doe II*, that there will be instances in which "the scope of the privilege does not coincide with the complex of values it helps to protect." What justifies adopting a more limited view of the privilege than a logical extension of those values might suggest, particularly in light of the admonition of *Counselman v. Hitchcock* (Note 1, p. 838) that the privilege be construed "as broad as the mischief against which it seeks to guard"?

Does the language of the self-incrimination clause impose limits upon conclusions drawn strictly from a values analysis? Consider e.g., Justice White's response in *Fisher* to the taxpayer's reliance there upon a "privacy" analysis [p. 859].

As previously noted (see Note 2 supra), the implementation of the values underlying the privilege has sometimes prevailed over the limitations found in the common law privilege. See also Albert w. Alschuler, *A Peculiar Privilege in Historical Perspective; The Right to Romain Silent*, 94 Mich.L.Rev. 2625 (1996) (common law privilege focused on the oath, the "Christian world's favored instrument of spiritual coercion," but with "oaths having lost their terror and even their meaning" in the modern world, *Miranda* extended the privilege to compelled unsworn statements) (see fn. f infra). Certain justices, however, have argued that a clear answer under historical practice should render irrelevant a values analysis. See e.g., the position taken by Justices Thomas and Scalia in *Balsys*, fn. d, p. 840, and *Hubbell*, p. 876. Should history at least prevail where it appears to give the privilege a broader reach than a values analysis? See e.g., the concurring opinion in *Hubbell*, (p. 876), and Note 8, p. 880.

Commentators have characterized the coverage distinction drawn in *Doe II* and the identification cases on which it relies—i.e., the distinction between compelled communicative and non-communicative writings and acts—as one that "cannot be reconciled with the purposes served by the right against self-incrimination," finding its justification, instead, in "pragmatic compromise." Charles

Geyh, *The Testimonial Component of The Right Against Self–Incrimination*, 36 Catholic U.LRev. 611 (1987) (characterizing that compromise as one that preserves "the individual right to resist more egregious forms of self-incrimination" by allowing the state to obtain "vital nontestimonial physical evidence"). The "collective entity" exception has also been characterized as a doctrine inconsistent with self-incrimination values but reflective of enforcement needs. See Notes 2 and 3, pp. 854–55, and fn. b., p. 868. Are those characterizations misguided in their view of Fifth Amendment values, or have enforcement needs played a significant role in limiting the logical extension of self-incrimination values? Cf. Harlan, J., dissenting in *Spevack v. Klein,* 385 U.S. 511 (1967) (the Court "has chiefly derived its [Fifth Amendment] standards from consideration of two factors: the history and purposes of the privilege and the character and urgency of the other public interests involved").

4. *Distinguishing values.* The "complex of values" underlying the Fifth Amendment has been the subject of extensive commentary, and the commentators are virtually unanimous in concluding that at least some of the values cited in *Murphy* simply do not assist in explaining the privilege. See David Dolinko, *Is There a Rationale for the Privilege Against Self–Incrimination?,* 33 U.C.L.A.L.Rev. 1063 (1986).[b] The commentators have noted that while the privilege may incidentally serve the various values cited in *Murphy,* certain of those values (and for some commentators, all of those values) fail to provide a logical conceptual foundation for the existence of the privilege. Whether the Court has gone so far as to flatly reject the relevancy to Fifth Amendment interpretations of any of the values cited in *Murphy* is open to debate. Consider e.g., the comments regarding a privacy justification in *Fisher*, p. 859, and *Balsys*, fn. g, p. 890. Nobody disputes however that the Court has at least reached the conclusion that "some Fifth Amendment purposes are more important than others." Peter Arenella, *Schmerber and the Privilege Against Self–Incrimination: A Reappraisal*, 20 Am. Crim. L. Rev. 31 (1982). Interestingly, that determination has been explained as a reflection of the fact that certain values are more in line with the language and history of the privilege than others, rather than as a reflection of particular values being more important than others in achieving a fair criminal justice process. See e.g., *Doe II* (pp. 881–82), *Fisher* (pp. 858–59), and *Balsys*, fn g, p. 890.

5. *Systemic rationales.* Commentators have most frequently discounted those values listed in *Murphy* that provide a "systemic rationale" for the privilege—i.e., the values that see the privilege as designed to further other procedural objectives of the criminal justice process, rather than as an end in itself, directed at safeguarding "human dignity and individuality". See Dolinko, Note 4 supra. The values most frequently characterized as systemic, and criticized as failing to explain the privilege, are the 3rd, 6th, and 7th values cited in *Murphy*.

Murphy's sixth listed value sees the privilege as a reflection of the concern that incriminatory admissions are inherently unreliable. Admittedly, that concern has a rough historical counterpart in the common law rule that excluded all testimony by parties to a case because their inherent self-interest might lead them to lie. But it certainly was not reflected, at least as an absolute prohibition, in other aspects of the common law viewed at the time as consistent with the self-incrimination privilege. Magistrates could sharply interrogate the unsworn accused and recount any incriminatory admissions in their testimony before the trial

b. The questioning of the conceptual foundation of the privilege dates back at least to Jeremy Bentham's classic critique of the privilege in 1827. See Jeremy Bentham, *A Rationale of Judicial Evidence* (1827). It has continued with each new generation of commentary. Professor Dolinko's article is the most widely cited and thorough critique of the current generation. For an extensive collection of additional commentary, both critical and supportive of the privilege, see CRIMPROC § 8.14(c).

court; confessions could be admitted into evidence if corroborated by other evidence; and convictions could be based solely on guilty pleas. Thus, not surprisingly, when arguments for applying the privilege have been based entirely on *Murphy's* sixth value, they have not been successful. The "privilege against self-incrimination," the Court has noted "is not designed to enhance the reliability of the fact-finding determination: it stands in the constitution for entirely independent reasons." *Allen v. Illinois*, 478 U.S. 364 (1986) (self-incrimination was not a safeguard that had to be applied in a non-criminal proceeding as part of due process reliability concerns). More significantly, the Court has not shaped the privilege to focus primarily on reliability concerns, as it has, for example, held that the privilege bars the use of reliable physical evidence uncovered through the use of a compelled statement of the accused, and applied the privilege to the compelled production of documents. See Akhil Amar and Renee Lettow, *Fifth Amendment First Principles: The Self Incrimination Clause*, 83 Mich.L.Rev. 857 (1995) (reviewing such rulings and arguing for their reconsideration in light of the reliability focus which the authors find inherent in the language of the self-incrimination clause; that clause, they argue, simply prohibits the use of the defendant's "compelled testimony" * * * "at trial *in* [his own] *criminal case*," reflecting the conclusion that "compelled testimony may be partly or wholly misleading and unreliable").

Murphy's seventh value—protecting the innocent—is seen by many as primarily related to the previously mentioned concern as to the reliability of self-deprecatory statements.[c] Some commentators have suggested, however, that the privilege may also protect the innocent where an innocent accused, if forced to testify, would leave the jury with a false impression as to his guilt (due to poor demeanor on the stand or an extensive criminal record used by the prosecution to impeach his credibility). See Stephen Schulhofer, *Some Kind Words for the Privilege Against Self-Incrimination*, 26 Val. U. L. Rev. 311 (1991). But this would explain only one aspect of the privilege (the defendant's right to refuse to testify), not the privilege as a whole. Moreover, the Supreme Court itself has noted that "the basic purposes that lie behind the privilege against self-incrimination do not relate to protecting the innocent from conviction." *Tehan v. United States ex rel. Shott,* 382 U.S. 406 (1966), although it has also described its *Miranda* ruling as serving exactly that purpose, *Withrow v. Williams* (p. 671).

c. Dean Wigmore, in particular, advanced a variation on the reliability argument that looked to protecting the innocent. His rationale, sometimes described as the "lazy prosecutor rationale," was that the self-incrimination privilege was adopted to discourage overreliance on obtaining incriminatory statements of the accused (as illustrated by the historical use of the ex officio oath) and to thereby encourage more thorough investigations that would protect the innocent by having a better chance of uncovering exculpatory evidence and ensuring that guilt was based on more reliable evidence than compelled admissions. John Henry Wigmore, *Evidence* § 2251 (3d ed. 1940). Commentators critical of this rationale have pointed to the same historical arguments that are advanced against *Murphy's* sixth value. See CRIMPROC § 8.14(d) (also noting that a major eighteenth century development of the privilege—its availability to witnesses in both civil and criminal cases—gave it an impact in proceedings that did not involve the government's gathering of evidence, and could work to preclude an innocent defendant from producing evidence in his favor). While the Court has suggested that the privilege was a product of the concerns expressed by the lazy prosecutor rationale, see e.g. *Couch v. United States*, 409 U.S. 322, 327 (1973), its interpretation of the privilege has been criticized as being inconsistent with encouraging the prosecutor to seek out more reliable evidence (as in the case of documents and derivative physical evidence). Consider also Donald Dripps, *Against Police Interrogation—And the Privilege Against Self-Incrimination*, 78 J. Crm. L. & Criminology 699 (1988) (privilege poses such barriers to acquiring reliable evidence, including open court interrogation under oath, that it has operated to create "tolerance and even encouragement" for reliance upon the less reliable vehicle of police interrogation).

The second and fourth values cited in *Murphy* have garnered the most commentator support among the systemic justifications for the privilege, but they too have fallen short for many commentators. In part, these two values simply state in different terms the same basic objective of the process. The second value notes a preference for an "accusatorial process," but as the Court has noted in several opinions, an accusatorial process is basically one in which the government "shoulders the entire load" (part of *Murphy*'s fourth value). The imposition of this "entire load" obligation upon the prosecution may be seen as an aspect of neutralizing certain basic resource advantages of the state so as to achieve a "fair state-individual balance" (disparaged by Bentham as the "fox hunters' reason," designed to give the defendant a "sporting chance"), or it may be viewed as simply an additional safeguard to ensure against the conviction of the innocent. The end requirement, however, remains the same—that the state bear the full responsibility for establishing guilt, as contrasted to a system in which the defendant must establish his innocence.

Although frequently cited by the Court (perhaps more than any other justification for the privilege), the requirement that the state "bear the full responsibility for establishing guilt" fails to fully explain the self-incrimination doctrine. It fails to explain, for example, the availability of the privilege to witnesses in contexts in which the government is not seeking evidence, such as civil suits brought by private parties. Yet even where the government is seeking to establish its criminal case, the accusatorial structure of the process falls short of justifying distinctions drawn in applying the privilege. While the accusatorial structure commonly is described as mandating that the prosecution establish its case through its "own independent labors," the Fourth Amendment makes clear that this does not preclude the use of defendant as a source of evidence. The questions therefore arise as to why compelling the defendant to disclose evidence is distinguished from "taking evidence" from the accused (through a search), and why even that direct compulsion is limited to testimonial evidence and thereby fails to encompass all compelled acts of the defendant that produce evidence for the prosecution (e.g., the acts compelled in *Doe II*). The answers apparently lie in the special qualities of testimonial compulsion, but what gives those qualities particular significance is not the procedural structure produced by a preference for an accusatorial over an inquisitorial process,[d] but values that exist independent of that structure. They apparently stem, as the Court has recognized, from dignitary values. Thus, *Schmerber* [Note 6, p. 856] acknowledged that "the compulsion [through forced participation in an identification procedure] violates at least one

d. *Murphy*'s description of the accusatorial process as one contrasted with an "inquisitorial process" might also be seen as seeking primarily to distinguish the non-adversarial aspect of an inquisitorial process. Thus, the privilege has been characterized as a natural attribute of the adversarial element of the criminal justice process. See Abe Fortas, *The Fifth Amendment: Nemo Tenetur Prodere Seipsum,* 25 Cleve.B.A.J. 95 (1954): "[T]he principle that man is not obliged to furnish the state with ammunition to use against him is basic to this conception. Equals meeting in battle, owe no duty to one another, regardless of the obligations they may be under prior to battle."

Here too, however, critics have responded that, in light of the state's capacity to use the defendant as a source of evidence in other ways, the restriction imposed by the privilege can no more be said to flow from the basic tenets of an adversarial system than from the basic tenets of an accusatorial system. The adversary process does not have as its objective the structuring of a "battle between equally meritorious combatants to see which of two inconsistent but equally weighty goals" will prevail, but rather the achievement of "accurate determinations" that "clear the innocent and convict the guilty." Kent Greenawalt, *Silence as a Moral and Constitutional Right,* 23 Wm. & Mary L.Rev. 15, 38–39 (1981). Thus, as evidenced by the prosecutor's obligation to disclose exculpatory evidence, it is not inconsistent with an adversary process to impose upon the litigants an obligation to produce evidence that contributes to an accurate fact-finding determination (just as it is appropriate to bar litigant concealment or destruction of relevant evidence), though that obligation obviously is contrary to their interests as adversaries.

meaning of the requirement that the State procure the evidence against an accused 'by its own independent labors,' " but concluded that the "independent-labors" concept, taken in light of other privilege values, was basically limited to precluding the state from producing evidence through "the cruel, simple expedient of compelling it through [defendant's] own mouth." See fn. 11, p. 882. So too, the entity cases implicitly recognize that the privilege rests on values that go beyond implementing an accusatorial process, since a collective entity, no less than an individual, is entitled to the safeguards traditionally found in an accusatory process (e.g., the presumption of innocence). See fn. a, p. 854.

Murphy's fourth listed value also refers to requiring the "government to leave the individual alone until good cause is shown for disturbing him." The privilege obviously assists in this regard by restricting what the state can expect to gain through a prosecution that is a mere fishing expedition. It cannot "charge first" and then hope to make its case by forcing the defendant to explain his actions. Also, while the privilege does not bar prosecutorial attempts to harass by subjecting targets to grand jury questioning without any substantial basis for believing they are guilty of wrongdoing, it places in the hands of those targets a means of limiting their disclosures in response to such questioning. However, the protection against fishing expeditions hardly explains the availability of the privilege at trial, after the prosecution has produced enough evidence to justify a charge. In an early stage of its evolution, the privilege arose out of efforts to protect against persons being forced to submit to the oath without any properly supported accusation (see *Doe II*, p. 882), but the self-incrimination privilege subsequently was extended to proceedings (e.g., the trial) that followed a formal independent determination by the grand jury that there existed sufficient evidence to charge the individual. So too, it had been made available to witnesses in civil proceedings, including those in no way connected to criminal investigations.

6. *Dignitary values.* Commentary explaining the policies underlying the privilege have most frequently looked to one or more "dignitary values"—that is, values that recognize the privilege as a means of preserving human dignity and individuality. The first, third, and fifth values of the *Murphy* listing fall in this category. Of these, the third value—"the fear that self-incriminating statements will be elicited by inhumane treatment and abuses"—tends to be seen as presenting the greatest difficulties in justifying the privilege in its current and its original scope.

Concern about inhumane treatment was certainly expressed in the earliest commentary on the privilege. Though, it is sometimes suggested that the origins of the common law privilege were tied to prohibiting torture, the official use of torture had been discontinued long before the abolishment of the oath *ex officio*, which gave rise to the recognition of the privilege. However, the *ex officio* oath procedure clearly was viewed by its opponents as an inhumane procedure (indeed, it was characterized by some as a species of torture). This might suggest a general understanding that it was inhumane and abusive to use any governmental power to force a person to present evidence against himself, leading to a privilege designed to ensure that would not occur through some new device, replacing the oath *ex officio*. Cf. Erwin Griswold, *The Fifth Amendment Today* 7 (1955) (drawing a parallel between compelled self-incrimination and requiring a condemned murderer to "sign his own death warrant or dig his grave"). Of course, such a reading of the privilege brings into question some of the limitations placed upon the privilege—see e.g., the testimonial distinction noted in *Doe II*, and the required records cases. But more significantly, it does not appear to explain the common law privilege as it stood at the time of the adoption of the Fifth Amendment. At that time, the privilege was not viewed as precluding magistrates from pressuring, and even browbeating, an accused into offering an explanation of his actions (often incriminating) in an unsworn statement, with that statement (or the failure to respond) duly noted at trial. See CRIMPROC § 8.14(b) (also noting that the defendant at trial typically was not represented by counsel and therefore "had almost no choice but to take advantage of his right to make an unsworn presentation of his side of the case and respond to any questions of judge or jury"). Moreover, the critical practical significance of the privilege at that point had nothing to do with threatening or bullying a defendant. It was the availability of the privilege to *witnesses* being examined in open court in criminal and civil cases (defendants in criminal cases could not be called to testify, apart from any ramifications of the privilege, because of the prohibitions against parties to the action giving sworn testimony).

7. ***The cruel trilemma.*** Although many commentators quarrel with the underlying moral judgment, almost all acknowledge that the privilege arose originally from a belief that it was uniquely cruel and inhumane to subject a person to what *Murphy* described as the "the cruel trilemma of self-accusation, perjury, or contempt."[e] Under this view, the privilege is appropriately limited to testimonial communications because if the compulsion does not "convey information or assert facts," it does not present as one of the forced alternatives the possibility of lying under oath, an act considered historically to be an "unpardonable and cardinal sin * * * simply not an option for a religious man." Leonard Levy, *The Origins of the Fifth Amendment: The Right Against Self-Incrimination* 133–34 (2d.ed. 1986).

The cruel trilemma rationale also explains why the privilege was extended to witnesses and denied collective entities (which have no soul to damn), although denial of privilege to the entity agent arguably becomes more troublesome (even with the *Braswell* safeguard), as does the required records doctrine. Of course, *Miranda* also presents difficulties since neither perjury nor damnation follow from lying to the police. On the other hand, tying the privilege to the oath and the potential for a perjury conviction appears highly ritualistic (and outdated) when one recognizes the wide range of pressures that can be placed upon an individual to force him to reveal the contents of his mind.[f]

8. ***Protection of privacy.*** The fifth value cited in *Murphy*—"respect for the inviolability of the human personality" and the need for a "private enclave"—has commonly been characterized as the "privacy" justification for the privilege. Both critics and supporters of this rationale acknowledge that it remains unpersuasive unless there exists a satisfactory answer to a critical question—why the particular element of privacy that falls within the privilege is given absolute protection, as compared to the relative protection given other privacy interests under the Fourth and First Amendments. The answer usually offered is that the privilege protects the most significant element of individual privacy, the privacy "of the mind"; it "respects a private inner sanctum of individual feeling and thought." *Couch v.*

e. See p. 882. The assumption that forcing such a choice upon a defendant is uniquely cruel was challenged by Bentham, supra fn. b (who characterized it as the "old woman's reason" for the privilege) and modern critics have built upon his analysis. They argue that the choice imposed here is no more cruel than that imposed in other settings (e.g., where a parent is forced to testify against a child); that it assumes a moral justification in refusing to confess to criminality which is contrary to commonly accepted moral and social standards in most other settings; and that forcing that choice upon the individual is justified by a legitimate state objective (determining the truth) no less significant than other interests thought to justify requiring a person to act against his natural instinct of self-preservation.

f. Thus, *Miranda* noted that the policies cited in *Murphy* "point to one overriding thought"—that the government must respect "the dignity and integrity of its citizens." That respect was missing where the compulsion of custodial interrogation, which "may well be greater" than that imposed by judicial process, is used to force the individual to furnish incriminatory evidence "from his own mouth."

United States (Note 7, p. 857). But this response only raises the further question as to why the privilege, if it is designed to protect mental privacy from state intrusion, affords such protection only as to thoughts, feelings, and beliefs that would furnish a link in the chain of evidence needed to establish criminal liability. See *United States v. Balsys*, Note 3, p. 840.[g] One explanation for this limitation is that privilege seeks to protect only a "particular corner of the private enclave" that is especially significant in the development of "moral autonomy"—the "integrity of conscience." See Robert Gerstein, *The Demise of Boyd: Self–Incrimination and Private Papers in the Burger Court,* 27 U.C.L.A.L.Rev. 343 (1979). The critical element of the privilege, from this perspective, is that it preserves to the individual alone the essential right of determining whether and when to acknowledge responsibility for his actions. See Fortas, fn. d supra ("*Mea culpa* belongs to a man and his God. It is a plea that cannot be extracted from free men by human authority.") Accepting this view, should the privilege be even narrower than suggested in *Doe II?* Is there a sufficient element of compulsory "self-condemnation" present to render the privilege applicable when a person is required to furnish only factual information, especially where that information is not incriminatory on its face (as in the compelled disclosure of the combination to one's safe, see fn. e, p. 856)?

g. The *Balsys* majority sharply questioned *Murphy's* suggestion that the self-incrimination clause reflects the "the inviolability of the human personality and the right of each individual to a private enclave where he may lead a private life". It noted initially that " 'inviolability' is, after all, an uncompromising term, and we know as well from Fourth Amendment law * * * that breaches of privacy are complete at the moment of illicit intrusion, whatever use may or may not later be made of such fruits." "Inviolability", it pointed out, hardly describes a regime which allows the government to compel testimony provided it was willing to pay the price of "use and derivative use immunity." The Court then added: "One might reply that the choice of the word 'inviolability' was just unfortunate; while testimonial integrity may not be inviolable, it is sufficiently served by requiring the Government to pay a price in the form of use (and derivative use) immunity before a refusal to testify will be overruled. But that answer overlooks the fact that when a witness's response will raise no fear of criminal penalty, there is no protection for testimonial privacy at all. Thus, what we find in practice is not the protection of personal testimonial inviolability, but a conditional protection of testimonial privacy subject to basic limits recognized before the framing and refined through immunity doctrine in the intervening years."

Chapter 12

THE SCOPE OF THE EXCLUSIONARY RULES*

SECTION 1. "STANDING" TO OBJECT TO THE ADMISSION OF EVIDENCE (OR "THE EXTENT OF A PARTICULAR DEFENDANT'S RIGHTS UNDER THE FOURTH AMENDMENT")**

A. HISTORICAL BACKGROUND AND OVERVIEW

1. ***Must the person asserting a Fourth Amendment claim have been the victim of the challenged search or seizure?*** Long before the Supreme Court authoritatively resolved the issue, the lower courts had developed the doctrine that a defendant lacked "standing" to challenge evidence seized in violation of a third party's constitutional rights. The early basis for this doctrine seems to have been "the joint foundation of the Fourth Amendment and the self-incrimination clause of the Fifth," Comment, 58 Yale L.J. 144, 156 (1948). The rule was also "based on the theory that the evidence is excluded to provide a remedy for a wrong done to the defendant, and that accordingly, if the defendant has not been wronged he is entitled to no remedy." *People v. Martin,* 290 P.2d 855, 857 (Cal.1955) (Traynor, J.).

Six years before *Mapp,* the California Supreme Court's emphasis on the deterrence rationale for the exclusionary rule led it to abolish the "standing" requirement. *People v. Martin,* supra. "Such a limitation," observed the California court, "virtually invites law enforcement officers to violate the rights of third parties and to trade the escape of a criminal whose rights are violated for the conviction of others by the use of the evidence illegally obtained against them." Id.[a]

* Harmless error is treated elsewhere; see p. 1613.

** *Rakas v. Illinois* (1978) (discussed at p. 896).

a. *In re Lance W.,* 694 P.2d 744 (Cal.1985) (discussed at p. 50), held that Proposition 8, an initiative approved by California voters in 1982, had abolished *Martin's* "vicarious exclusionary rule."

The California Supreme Court had ruled earlier, *People v. Varnum,* 427 P.2d 772 (Cal. 1967), that *Martin* did not apply to *Escobedo-Miranda* violations. The majority, per Traynor, J., reasoned: "Noncoercive questioning is not in itself unlawful [and the rights] protected by *Escobedo* [and] *Miranda* are violated only when evidence obtained without the required warnings and waiver is introduced against the person whose questioning produced the evidence. The basis for the [*Miranda* warnings] is the privilege against self-incrimination [which] is not violated when the information elicited from an unwarned suspect is not used against him. [Unlike unreasonable searches and seizures], there is nothing unlawful in questioning an unwarned suspect so long as the police refrain [from tactics] condemned by due process and do not use against the suspect any evidence obtained."

For criticism of *Varnum,* see Notes, 37 U.Cin.L.Rev. 234 (1968); 15 U.C.L.A.L.Rev. 1060 (1968).

California's abolition of the "standing" requirement was "enthusiastically endorsed by most commentators," SEARCHSZR § 11.3 (j) (citing thirteen commentators), and when, in *Linkletter v. Walker* (1965) (p. 1636), the U.S. Supreme Court seemed to explain and to justify the Fourth Amendment exclusionary rule as "the only effective deterrent to lawless police action," there was reason to think that the High Court, too, might scrap the "standing" requirement. Thus, two years after *Linkletter* and two years before *Alderman* infra, one commentator pointed out that "a system of classification based on 'victimness' provides no deterrence" against "searches that turn up evidence against persons other than the victim" and concluded that "the standing requirement is inconsistent with the presently accepted general deterrence theory of the exclusionary rule." Note, 34 U.Chi.L.Rev. 342, 358 (1967).

However, in ALDERMAN v. UNITED STATES, 394 U.S. 165 (1969), the Court, per WHITE, J., reaffirmed "the established principle [that] suppression of the product of a Fourth Amendment violation can be successfully urged only by those whose rights were violated by the search itself, not by those who are aggrieved solely by the introduction of damaging evidence. Coconspirators and codefendants have been accorded no special standing."[b] The Court was unmoved by the ascendancy of the deterrence rationale: "[We] are not convinced that the additional benefits of extending the exclusionary rule to other defendants would justify further encroachment upon the public interest in prosecuting those accused of crime and having them acquitted or convicted on the basis of all the evidence which exposes the truth."

Concurring in part and dissenting in part, FORTAS, J., argued that there was much to be said for abolishing the "standing" requirement: "The Fourth Amendment, unlike the Fifth, is couched in terms of a guarantee that the Government will not engage in unreasonable searches and seizures. It is a general prohibition[,] * * * not merely a privilege accorded to him whose domain has been lawlessly invaded. [It] is an assurance to all that the Government will exercise its formidable powers to arrest and to investigate only subject to the rule of law."[c]

2. *Does Alderman represent a genuine effort to strike a balance between the costs of exclusion and the need for deterrence?* Daniel Meltzer, *Deterring Constitutional Violations by Law Enforcement Officials: Plaintiffs and Defendants as Private Attorneys General,* 88 Colum.L.Rev. 247, 275 (1988) finds it hard to so understand the Court's standing doctrine: "It is possible, of course, that an effort to strike a desirable balance would result in a standing doctrine limited to those whose rights were violated by the illegal search. But such a result would be extremely surprising, as there are factors more relevant to the need for and benefits of deterrent remedies. These include the seriousness of the harm caused by the search; the likelihood of detection; the perception of the sanction's severity; whether the violation was obvious or intentional; how susceptible to

b. A quarter-century later, in *United States v. Padilla,* 508 U.S. 77 (1993) (per curiam), a unanimous Court quoted this language from *Alderman* in rejecting a so-called "coconspirator exception" to the standing doctrine. Under this exception, developed by the U.S. Court of Appeals for the Ninth Circuit, a coconspirator obtained a legitimate expectation of privacy for Fourth Amendment purposes if she had either a supervisory role in the conspiracy or joint control over the place of property involved in the challenged search or seizure. Such an exception, observed the *Padilla* Court is "not only contrary to the holding of *Alderman,* but at odds with [the expectation of privacy approach taken in *Rakas,* p. 896, that now] govern[s] the analysis of Fourth Amendment search and seizure claims. Participants in a criminal conspiracy may have [exceptions of privacy and property interests], but the conspiracy itself neither adds to or detracts from them."

c. Justice Fortas' view is supported in Donald Doernberg, *"The Right of the People": Reconciling Collective and Individual Interests under the Fourth Amendment,* 58 N.Y.U.L.Rev. 259 (1983); Richard B. Kuhns, *The Concept of Personal Aggrievement in Fourth Amendment Standing Cases,* 65 Iowa L.Rev. 493 (1980).

deterrence the search is; and how easily the resulting rules can be administered. A truly deterrence-focused standing doctrine would at least consider such factors, rather than simply assume that the optimal result is reached when only those who were victims of the search are empowered to suppress evidence."

3. ***The tension between the standing requirement and the exclusionary rule***. Consider JOSHUA DRESSLER, *Understanding Criminal Procedure* 358 (3d ed.2002): "Professor Anthony Amsterdam once noted that there are two competing perspectives on the Fourth Amendment. One view, the 'atomistic' perspective, is that the Fourth Amendment is 'a collection of protections of atomistic spheres of interest of individual citizens.' That is, the Fourth Amendment protects isolated individuals ('atoms'), in the sense that the amendment 'safeguard[s]' *my* person and *your* house and *her* papers and *his* effects against unreasonable searches and seizures.'[12] The second view, the 'regulatory' perspective, is that the Fourth Amendment functions 'as a regulation of governmental conduct.' In other words, the amendment is intended to safeguard the collective 'people,' as in 'we, the people,' from governmental overreaching."

"As Fourth Amendment jurisprudence has developed, standing—based as it is on the premise that a person may raise a Fourth Amendment challenge only if he *personally* was a victim of unreasonable police activity—is based on the atomistic philosophy. In contrast, the exclusionary rule is regulatory in nature, in that its purpose is to deter police misconduct, in order to safeguard society as a whole."

"Understood in this way, the standing requirement and the exclusionary rule act, at least in part, in opposition to each other. This is because evidence seized in violation of the Fourth Amendment is excluded at trial in order to deter police misconduct; but, the requirement of standing to raise a Fourth Amendment claim often undercuts this deterrence goal, as it limits the number of people ('atoms') who can bring the misconduct to the attention of the courts so that the exclusionary rule can be applied."

As an example, Professor Dressler cites the *Payner* case, discussed in the next Note.

4. ***The use of the federal courts' "supervisory power" to overcome the standing requirement.*** If there has ever been a case that called for the exercise of the federal courts' supervisory power to break out of the standing restriction it was UNITED STATES v. PAYNER, 447 U.S. 727 (1980) (also discussed at p. 46). Nevertheless, a 6–3 majority, per POWELL, J., was unmoved.

Payner arose as follows: An IRS investigation into the financial activities of American citizens in the Bahamas focused on a certain Bahamian bank. When an official of that bank visited the United States, IRS agents stole his briefcase for a time, removed hundreds of documents from the briefcase, and photographed them. As a result of this "briefcase caper," Payner—precisely the kind of offender the IRS agents were seeking when they violated the bank official's rights—was convicted of federal income tax violations. Hemmed in by the standing requirement, but outraged by the government's "purposefully" illegal tactics, the federal district court invoked its supervisory power to exclude the tainted evidence.

But the Supreme Court rejected the federal court's "substitution of individual judgment for the controlling decisions of this Court." "The values assigned to the competing interests do not change," pointed out Justice Powell, "because a court has elected to analyze the question under the supervisory power instead of the

12. Anthony G. Amsterdam, *Perspectives on the Fourth Amendment*, 58 Minn.L.Rev. 349, 367 (1974).

Fourth Amendment. In either case, the need to deter the underlying conduct and the detrimental impact of excluding the evidence remain precisely the same."[d]

The *Payner* Court cautioned that exclusion of evidence in every case of illegality must be "weighed against the considerable harm that would flow from *indiscriminate application* of an exclusionary rule" (emphasis added), and that "*unbending application* of the exclusionary sanction * * * would impede unacceptably the truthfinding functions of judge and jury" (emphasis added). But consider Kamisar, *Does (Did) (Should) the Exclusionary Rule Rest on a "Principled Basis" Rather than an "Empirical Proposition"?*, 16 Creighton L.Rev. 565, 638 (1983):

"The relevant question in *Payner* [was] not whether the exclusionary rule should *always* be applied when police illegality is somewhere in the picture, but whether it should *ever* be applied—taking into account the seriousness or flagrancy of the illegality—when the defendant lacks 'standing.' The question was not whether the exclusionary rule should be given 'unbending application,' but whether *the 'standing' requirement* should be. By deciding that even in a case like *Payner* a federal court is *unable* to exercise its supervisory powers to bar the evidence—by holding that 'judicial impotency is *compelled* in the face of such scandalous conduct' [SEARCHSZR § 11.3(h)]—the Court gave us its answer."

"[The] *Payner* Court seemed content [to rely on] the balance it had struck in the early standing cases. But because it grew out of special and outrageous circumstances, the interests to be balanced in *Payner* were different. The question presented was[:] When the government has *intentionally manipulated* the standing requirement of the fourth amendment—when it has *deliberately and patently* violated the constitutional rights of a third party in order to obtain evidence against its real targets, and defendant is one of those targets—does the interest in discouraging (or reducing) the incentive to make *such* searches justify the exclusion of tainted evidence at the instance of a party who was not the [direct] victim of the challenged practice? The *Payner* Court never really spoke to this issue because it never really asked this question."

5. *"Automatic" standing.* In *Jones v. United States,* 362 U.S. 257 (1960), the defendant was charged with selling and distributing narcotics and facilitating the concealment and sale of the same narcotics, which permitted conviction largely on proof of unexplained possession of narcotics. The lower court denied standing because defendant had failed either to assert a sufficient interest in the apartment where the search occurred[e] or to allege ownership or possession of the narcotics, although doing so would have "forced" him to allege facts that would tend to convict him. The Supreme Court reversed: The "same element in this prosecution which has caused a dilemma, i.e., that possession both convicts and confers standing, eliminates any necessity for a preliminary showing of an interest in the premises searched or the property seized, which ordinarily is required when standing is challenged." To hold otherwise "would be to permit the Government to have the advantage of contradictory positions as a basis of conviction."

However, the Court subsequently held, in *Simmons v. United States,* 390 U.S. 377 (1968), that testimony given by a defendant in order to establish his "standing" "may not thereafter be used against him at trial on the issue of guilt."

d. "The Court's decision to engraft the standing limitations of the Fourth Amendment onto the exercise of supervisory powers," protested dissenting Justice Marshall, joined by Brennan and Blackmun, JJ., "appears to render the supervisory powers superfluous. In order to establish that suppression of evidence under the supervisory powers would be proper, the Court would also require Payner to establish a violation of his [constitutional rights]. This approach is totally unfaithful to our prior supervisory power cases [see generally pp. 44–48], which, contrary to the Court's suggestion, are not constitutional cases in disguise."

e. For this aspect of *Jones,* see Note 6 infra.

Were it otherwise, "a defendant who wishes to establish standing must do so at the risk that the words which he utters may later be used to incriminate him."

On the basis of *Simmons,* the Court subsequently abolished the *Jones* "automatic standing" rule and held that "defendants charged with crimes of possession may only claim the benefits of the exclusionary rule if their own Fourth Amendment rights have in fact been violated." UNITED STATES v. SALVUCCI, 448 U.S. 83 (1980). Observed the Court, per REHNQUIST, J.: "The 'dilemma' identified in *Jones* * * * was eliminated [by] *Simmons,* [which] not only extends protection against [the] risk of self-incrimination in all of the cases covered by *Jones,* but also grants a form of 'use' immunity to those defendants charged with nonpossessory crimes."[f]

As for the vice of prosecutorial contradiction, the Court stated it need not decide whether that "could alone support a rule countenancing the exclusion of probative evidence on the grounds that someone other than the defendant was denied a Fourth Amendment right," for at least after *Rakas* [p. 895] it is clear that "a prosecutor may simultaneously maintain that a defendant criminally possessed the seized good, but was not subject to a Fourth Amendment deprivation, without legal contradiction." For a "person in legal possession of a good seized during an illegal search has not necessarily been subject to a Fourth Amendment deprivation. * * * We simply decline to use possession of a seized good as a substitute for a factual finding that the owner of the good has a legitimate expectation of privacy in the area searched."[g]

6. *Residential premises.* It has long been true, and is still so under the current expectation-of-privacy approach discussed in the next subsection, that one with a present possessory interest in the premises searched, e.g., a member of the family regularly residing in a home, may challenge that search even though not present when the search was conducted. As the *Alderman* Court explained: "If the police make an unwarranted search of a house and seize tangible property belonging to third parties [the] home owner may object to its use against him, not because he had any interest in the seized items [but] because they were the fruits of an unauthorized search of his house, which is itself expressly protected by the Fourth Amendment." The *Alderman* majority thus concluded that a person should have standing to challenge the legality of electronically overheard conversations in which he participated "or *conversations occurring on his premises,*

f. Dissenting Justice Marshall, joined by Brennan, J., disagreed that "*Simmons* provides complete protection against the 'self-incriminating dilemma,'" for "the prosecutor may still be permitted to use the defendant's testimony [at the suppression hearing] to impeach him at trial." The *Salvucci* majority managed to sidestep this argument, but somewhat misleadingly it asserted that "the Court has held that 'the protective shield of *Simmons* is not to be converted into a license for false representations,'" quoting from *United States v. Kahan,* 415 U.S. 239 (1974). But *Kahan* involved the impeachment use of false testimony given at a pretrial hearing to establish defendant's eligibility for appointed counsel and the *Kahan* Court pointed out: "We are not dealing, as was the Court in *Simmons,* with what was 'believed' by the claimant to be a 'valid' constitutional claim. Respondent was not, therefore, faced with the type of intolerable choice *Simmons* sought to relieve. The protective shield of *Simmons* is not to be converted into a license for false representations *on the issue of indigency* free from the risk that the claimant will be held accountable for his falsehood." (Emphasis added.)

Consider CRIMPROC § 9.2(a): "The best analogy [is] *New Jersey v. Portash* [440 U.S. 450 (1979)], holding that testimony given before a grand jury following a grant of use testimony could not be used for impeachment purposes at the subsequent criminal trial. [It] would seem that defendant's testimony at a suppression hearing [is] 'compelled' in the *Portash* sense, for, as *Simmons* teaches, the defendant is confronted with the choice 'either to give up what he believed, with advice of counsel, to be a valid Fourth Amendment claim or, in effect, to waive his Fifth Amendment privilege against self-incrimination.'"

g. See also *Rawlings v. Kentucky,* p. 898.

whether or not he was present or participated in those conversations" (emphasis added).[h]

In *Jones v. United States,* Note 5, the Court held that "anyone legitimately on premises where a search occurs may challenge its legality." The defendant not only had permission to use the apartment of his friend, but had a key to the apartment with which he admitted himself on the day of the search. He also kept some possessions in the apartment. In the more recent *Rakas* case (below), the Court rejected the *Jones* "legitimately on premises" *formulation*—this phrase "creates too broad a gauge for measurement of Fourth Amendment rights"—but it did not question *the result* in that case. The *Jones* holding "can best be explained," observed the *Rakas* Court, "by the fact that Jones had a legitimate expectation of privacy in the premises he was using [even] though his 'interest' in those premises might not have been a recognized property interest at common law."

Thirty years after *Jones* was decided, the Court held in *Minnesota v. Olson,* 495 U.S. 91 (1990), that defendant's "status as an overnight guest" showed that he had "an expectation of privacy in the home that society is prepared to recognize as reasonable." Thus he had a sufficient interest in the home to challenge the legality of the warrantless entry there.

7. *Business premises.* In *Mancusi v. DeForte,* 392 U.S. 364 (1968), where state police seized records belonging to a union local from an office defendant shared with several other union officials, the Court viewed the "crucial issue" as "whether the area was one in which there was a reasonable expectation of freedom from governmental intrusion." The Court answered in the affirmative. Even though defendant shared an office with others, he "still could reasonably have expected that only those persons and [their guests] would ever enter the office, and that records would not be touched except with their permission or that of union higherups."

"Consistent with *Mancusi,* courts have held that a corporate or individual defendant in possession of the business premises searched has standing, and that an officer or employee of the business enterprise has standing if 'there was a demonstrated nexus between the area searched and the work space of the defendant.' Exclusive use would seem clearly to establish standing, but (as *Mancusi* teaches) there can be a justified expectation of privacy even absent exclusivity." CRIMPROC § 9.1(c).

B. The Current Approach

In RAKAS v. ILLINOIS, 439 U.S. 128 (1978), as Charles H. Whitebread & Christopher Slobogin, *Criminal Procedure* 130 (4th ed. 2000), observe, "the Court explicitly recognized the connection between search and standing analysis. That is, the Court held that standing should depend on whether the police action sought to be challenged is a search (i.e., a violation of legitimate expectations of privacy) *with respect to the person challenging the intrusion.*"

In *Rakas*, in the course of affirming a ruling that when the police stopped and searched a car, which petitioners neither owned nor leased but were occupying as passengers, the police violated none of *their* rights,[a] REHNQUIST, J., speaking for

h. Justice Harlan, joined by Stewart, J., argued that this should not be so when the eavesdropped occurred without physical penetration, for then the absent householder's property interest has not been disturbed, and he can claim no privacy interest in conversations in which he did not participate.

a. Suspecting that the vehicle might have been the "getaway car" in a recent robbery, police stopped the car in which petitioners

a 5–4 majority, asked "whether it serves any useful analytical purpose to consider [the principle that Fourth Amendment rights are personal rights] a matter of standing, distinct from the merits of a defendant's Fourth Amendment claim." He answered that inquiry in the negative: "[W]e think the better analysis forthrightly focuses on the extent of a particular defendant's rights under the Fourth Amendment, rather than on any theoretically separate, but invariably intertwined concept of standing. * * * Analyzed in these terms, the question is whether the challenged search or seizure violated the Fourth Amendment rights of a criminal defendant who seeks to exclude the evidence obtained during it. That inquiry in turn requires a determination of whether the disputed search and seizure has infringed an interest of the defendant which the Fourth Amendment was designed to protect."

Is there still something to be said for treating "standing" and the issue whether a Fourth Amendment violation has occurred at all as distinct inquiries? Consider SEARCHSZR, § 11.3 at 121: "[It] is important to keep in mind that the question traditionally labeled as standing (did the police intrude upon *this defendant's* justified expectation of privacy?) is not identical to, for example, the question of whether any Fourth Amendment search has occurred (did the police intrude upon *anyone's* justified expectation of privacy?), and that therefore the [issues traditionally called "standing" issues] are still rather discrete and deserving of separate attention, no matter what label is put on them."[b]

In *Rakas*, it should be noted, Justice Rehnquist could "think of no decided cases of this Court that would have come out differently had we concluded, as we do now, that [the standing requirement] is more properly subsumed under substantive Fourth Amendment doctrine." He also told us that although he believed that the traditional standing requirement "belongs more properly under the heading of substantive Fourth Amendment doctrine," he was "under no illusion that by dispensing with the rubric of standing * * * we have rendered any

were riding. After the occupants of the car (petitioners and two female companions) were ordered out, the police searched the interior of the vehicle and discovered a sawed-off rifle under the front passenger seat and a box of rifle shells in the glove compartment (which had been locked). Because petitioners did not assert ownership of the rifle or the shells and because they conceded that they did not own the automobile, but were simply passengers (the owner of the vehicle had been driving it at the time of the search), the trial court ruled that they lacked "standing" to contest the search and seizure. Thus the judge denied their motions to suppress the evidence, without ever reaching the question whether the police conduct involved was lawful.

Applying its new approach to what had traditionally been called "standing" problems, the U.S. Supreme Court agreed that "petitioners' claims must fail": "They asserted neither a property nor a possessory interest in the automobile, nor an interest in the property seized. And [the] fact that they were "legitimately on [the] premises" in the sense that they were in the car with the permission of its owner is not determinative of whether they had a legitimate expectation of privacy in the particular areas of the automobile searched. It is unnecessary for us to decide here whether the same expectations of privacy are warranted in a car as would be justified in a dwelling place in analogous circumstances. [But] here petitioners' claim is one which would fail even in an analogous situation in a dwelling place, since they made no showing that they had any legitimate expectation of privacy in the glove compartment or area under the seat of the car in which they were merely passengers. Like the trunk of an automobile, these are areas in which a passenger *qua* passenger simply would not normally have a legitimate expectation of privacy."

"[*Jones v. United States* (1960)] involved significantly different factual circumstances. Jones not only had permission to use the apartment of his friend, but had a key to the apartment with which he admitted himself on the day of the search and kept possessions in the apartment. Except with respect to his friend, Jones had complete dominion and control over the apartment and could exclude others from it. [Jones] could legitimately expect privacy in the areas which were the subject of the search and seizure [he] sought to contest. No such showing was made by these petitioners with respect to those portions of the automobile which were searched and from which incriminating evidence was seized."

b. See also Joshua Dressler, *Understanding Criminal Procedure* 356–58 (3d ed. 2002).

simpler the determination of whether the proponent of a motion to suppress is entitled to contest the legality of a search and seizure."

In *Rakas*, as pointed out earlier, neither passenger asserted ownership in the items taken from the car. The Court seemed to imply that if the passengers had done so, they could have challenged the police conduct. But RAWLINGS v. KENTUCKY, 448 U.S. 98 (1980), rejected the argument that one could challenge a search of an area (in this instance another person's purse) simply because he claimed ownership of the property seized during the search. The case arose as follows:

On the day of the challenged police conduct, petitioner and Ms. Cox, who had been his companion for several days, were visitors at the house of one Marquess. Shortly before six police officers arrived, armed with a warrant for the arrest of Marquess, petitioner, who had been carrying a large quantity of illegal drugs, dumped them into the purse of Ms. Cox. Although there was a dispute about their discussion, petitioner testified that he had asked Ms. Cox "if she would carry this for me, and she said 'yes.' "(Although unclear, one plausible inference is that petitioner had put the contraband in the purse because he had seen police approaching the house.)

While unsuccessfully searching for Marquess in his house, the police came upon evidence of drug violations. Two of the officers then left to obtain a warrant to search the house, while the remaining officers detained the occupants, including petitioner and Cox, allowing them to leave only if they consented to a body search. Upon returning with the search warrant some 45 minutes later, the officers ordered Cox to empty her purse onto a table. As she poured out the contents of her purse, Cox told petitioner "to take what was his" and petitioner immediately claimed ownership of the drugs. Considering the "totality of the circumstances," including petitioner's admission at the suppression hearing that he did not believe that Cox's purse would be free from governmental intrusion, the state supreme court concluded that petitioner had no "standing" because he had failed to make "a sufficient showing that his legitimate or reasonable expectations of privacy were violated by the search of the purse." A 7–2 majority, again per REHNQUIST, J., found no reason to overturn that conclusion:

"[1] At the time petitioner dumped thousands of dollars worth of illegal drugs into Cox's purse, he had known her only a few days. [2] According to Cox's uncontested testimony, petitioner had never sought or received access to her purse prior to that sudden bailment. [3] Nor did petitioner have any right to exclude other persons access to Cox's purse. [4] In fact, [a third person] a longtime acquaintance and frequent companion of Cox's had free access to her purse. [5] [Moreover,] even assuming that petitioner's version of the bailment is correct [,the] precipitous nature of the transaction hardly supports a reasonable inference that petitioner took normal precautions to maintain his privacy. [6] [Finally] the record also contains a frank admission by petitioner that he had no subjective expectation that Cox's purse would remain free from governmental intrusion * * *.[c]

c. According to SEARCHSZR § 11.3(c) at 154, none of the points made by Justice Rehnquist "can withstand close scrutiny." He then responds to Justice Rehnquist's points as follows (id. At 154–58):

(1) The fact that Rawlings had only known Ms. Cox for a few days "hardly establishes the absence of a justified expectation of privacy."

(2) Rawlings' expectation of privacy was not diminished because this was the first time he had used Ms. Cox's purse. Otherwise, "we would be left with the curious notion that a first-time bailment [would] not carry with it a justified expectation that one's goods are secure in the hands of the bailee."

As for (3), "while a 'right to exclude' may be an easy way to establish the requisite legitimate expectation of privacy, it hardly follows that it is the *only* way * * *. Reliance on this 'right to exclude' factor is also inconsistent

"Petitioner contends nevertheless that, because he claimed ownership of the drugs in Cox's purse, he should be entitled to challenge the search regardless of his expectation of privacy. We disagree. While petitioner's ownership of the drugs is undoubtedly one fact to be considered in this case, *Rakas* emphatically rejected the notion that 'arcane' concepts of property law ought to control the ability to claim the protections of the Fourth Amendment. Had petitioner placed his drugs in plain view, he would still have owned them, but he could not claim any legitimate expectation of privacy. Prior to *Rakas*, petitioner might have been given 'standing' in such a case to challenge a 'search' that netted those drugs but probably would have lost his claim on the merits. After *Rakas*, the two inquiries merge into one: whether governmental officials violated any legitimate expectation of privacy held by petitioner."

BLACKMUN, J., joined the Court's opinion, but also wrote separately. He agreed with the majority that determining (1) whether the defendant has a "legitimate expectation of privacy" that has been invaded by the police and (2) whether "applicable cause and warrant requirements have been properly observed" " 'merge into one' in the sense that both are to be addressed under the principles of Fourth Amendment analysis developed in *Katz* and its progeny." But he did not read *Rawlings*, or *Rakas*, "as holding that it is improper for lower courts to treat these inquiries as distinct components of a Fourth Amendment claim." "Indeed," he added, "I am convinced that it would invite confusion to hold otherwise. It remains possible for a defendant to prove that his legitimate interest of privacy was invaded, and yet fail to prove that the police acted illegally in doing so. And it is equally possible for a defendant to prove that the police acted illegally, and yet fail to prove that his own privacy interest was affected."

---

with the later [holding] of *Minnesota v. Olson*, (1990) [p. 896], [that] an overnight guest had [a legitimate expectation of privacy in the premises] without regard to whether the guest 'had complete dominion and control over the apartment and could exclude others from it.' "

(4) The fact that a third party had access to Ms Cox's purse should not matter. The issue was not whether Rawlings "reasonably believed he was free from intrusion by *anyone*," but " 'whether the area [searched] was one in which there was a reasonable expectation of privacy from *governmental* intrusion.' "

As for (5), the argument that Rawlings did not take adequate precautions to maintain his privacy, "a container does not have to be locked to give rise to that especially strong expectation of privacy which makes the warrant clause of the Fourth Amendment applicable and thus it can hardly be said that an unlocked container carries with it no justified privacy expectation at all." Furthermore, if it can be said that Rawlings did not take adequate precautions in putting his effects into a closed container with the owner's consent, "then surely Ms. Cox likewise had no justified expectation of privacy in the same purse because she did not better safeguard her effects in that purse."

(6) The "frank admission" by Rawlings that "he had no subjective expectation that Cox's purse would remain free from governmental intrusion" turns out to be a "No, sir" answer when asked at the suppression hearing whether he thought the purse would be free from police intrusion. Rawlings was being asked "what he thought was going to happen *after* the police were on the scene and *after* they told him and others that a warrant was being sought and they could leave prior to the warrant execution only by submitting to a personal search. [But] if one can be deprived of Fourth Amendment standing by being informed in advance by the police of the intrusion they intend to make, [then] Rawlings likewise had no standing with respect to his own person, which he also expected would be intruded upon by the police."

According to Professor LaFave, id., "*Rawlings* is best viewed as an unusual case in which the result is more attributable to certain undercurrents in the case than to the reasoning offered by the Court." LaFave notes at this point that although none of the lower courts specifically found that Ms. Cox had not consented to the bailment, "the trial court was somewhat 'skeptical about [Rawlings'] version of events' and seemed to think that [he] probably saw the police approaching the premises and then thrust the controlled substances onto Cox over her objection. The thrust of the majority opinion in *Rawlings* strongly suggests the Court was influenced by an assumption that this latter version was correct."

It is interesting to note that in the very recent case of *Minnesota v. Carter*, set forth immediately below, "the parties' briefs to the U.S. Supreme Court, as well as the state supreme court's opinion, analyze[d] the case in terms of the defendants' 'standing' to assert a Fourth Amendment violation." 64 Crim.L.Rep. 2033, 2037 (Oct. 14, 1998). At one point during the oral arguments before the U.S. Supreme Court, the lawyer for the state referred to the defendants' "standing" to raise a search and seizure claim. This led Justice Kennedy to point out that in *Rakas* the Court had "abandoned the idea of 'standing' in the Fourth Amendment context." Id. Nevertheless, "throughout the oral arguments, the idea of Fourth Amendment 'standing' continued to be employed by the parties and the justices to describe the concepts at issue." *Id.*

MINNESOTA v. CARTER

525 U.S. 83, 119 S.Ct. 469, 142 L.Ed.2d, 373 (1998).

Chief Justice REHNQUIST delivered the opinion of the Court.

[A confidential informant told a Minnesota police officer (Thielen) that he had walked by the window of a ground-floor apartment and had seen people putting a white powder into bags. After looking in the same window through a gap in the closed blind and observing three men engaged in the bagging operation (respondents Carter and Johns and the apartment's lessee, Ms. Thompson), the officer notified headquarters, which began preparing affidavits for a search warrant. When respondents left the building in a previously identified vehicle, they were stopped and arrested. A later police search of the vehicle turned up cocaine. After seizing the vehicle, the police returned to the apartment and arrested the occupant, Ms. Thompson. A search of the apartment pursuant to a warrant revealed more evidence of cocaine.]

[The police later learned that Carter and Johns had never been in Thompson's apartment before and were only in it for 2 ½ hours, and that they had come to the apartment for the sole purpose of packaging the cocaine. In return for the use of the apartment, Carter and Johns had given Thompson one-eighth of an ounce of the cocaine.]

[Respondents were convicted of state drug offenses. The trial court held that (a) since they were only temporary out-of-state visitors, respondents could not challenge the legality of the government intrusion into Ms. Thompson's apartment; (b) Officer Thielen's observations through a gap in the closed blind was not a "search" within the meaning of the Fourth Amendment. The state supreme court reversed, holding that respondents did have "standing" because they had a " 'legitimate expectation of privacy in the invaded place' "(quoting *Rakas*). Even though "society does not recognize as valuable the task of bagging cocaine," observed the court, "society does recognize as valuable the rights of property owners or leaseholders to invite persons into the privacy of their homes to conduct a common task, be it legal or illegal activity." The court went on to hold that the officer's observation constituted an unreasonable "search" of the apartment. The U.S. Supreme Court reversed without reaching the question whether the officer's observation was a "search."]

The Minnesota courts analyzed whether respondents had a legitimate expectation of privacy under the rubric of "standing" doctrine, an analysis which this Court expressly rejected 20 years ago in *Rakas*. In that case, we held that automobile passengers could not assert the protection of the Fourth Amendment against the seizure of incriminating evidence from a vehicle where they owned neither the vehicle nor the evidence. Central to our analysis was the idea that in determining whether a defendant is able to show the violation of his (and not someone else's) Fourth Amendment rights, the "definition of those rights is more properly placed within the purview of substantive Fourth Amendment law than within that of standing." Thus, we held that in order to claim the protection of the Fourth Amendment, a defendant must demonstrate that he personally has an expectation of privacy in the place searched, and that his expectation is reasonable; *i.e.*, one which has a "source outside of the Fourth Amendment, either by reference to concepts of real or personal property law or to understandings that are recognized and permitted by society."

[The Fourth] Amendment protects persons against unreasonable searches of "their persons [and] houses" and thus indicates that the Fourth Amendment is a personal right that must be invoked by an individual. See *Katz.* ("[T]he Fourth Amendment protects people, not places"). But the extent to which the Fourth Amendment protects people may depend upon where those people are. We have held that "capacity to claim the protection of the Fourth Amendment depends [upon] whether the person who claims the protection of the Amendment has a legitimate expectation of privacy in the invaded place." *Rakas.*

The text of the Amendment suggests that its protections extend only to people in "their" houses. But we have held that in some circumstances a person may have a legitimate expectation of privacy in the house of someone else. In *Minnesota v. Olson* (1990), for example, we decided that an overnight guest in a house had the sort of expectation of privacy that the Fourth Amendment protects. We said:

> "To hold that an overnight guest has a legitimate expectation of privacy in his host's home merely recognizes the every day expectations of privacy that we all share. Staying overnight in another's home is a longstanding social custom that serves functions recognized as valuable by society. We stay in others' home when we travel to a strange city for business or pleasure, we visit our parents, children, or more distant relatives out of town, when we are in between jobs or homes, or when we house-sit for a friend."
>
> "[From] the overnight guest's perspective, he seeks shelter in another's home precisely because it provides him with privacy, a place where he and his possessions will not be disturbed by anyone but his host and those his host allows inside. * * * "

In *Jones v. United States* (1960), the defendant seeking to exclude evidence resulting from a search of an apartment had been given the use of the apartment by a friend. He had clothing in the apartment, had slept there "maybe a night," and at the time was the sole occupant of the apartment. But while the holding of *Jones*—that a search of the apartment violated the defendant's Fourth Amendment rights—is still valid, its statement that "anyone legitimately on the premises where a search occurs may challenge its legality" was expressly repudiated in *Rakas.* Thus an overnight guest in a home may claim the protection of the Fourth Amendment, but one who is merely present with the consent of the householder may not.

Respondents here were obviously not overnight guests, but were essentially present for a business transaction and were only in the home a matter of hours. There is no suggestion that they had a previous relationship with Thompson, or that there was any other purpose to their visit. Nor was there anything similar to the overnight guest relationship in *Olson* to suggest a degree of acceptance into the household.[1] * * *.

Property used for commercial purposes is treated differently for Fourth Amendment purposes than residential property. [And] while it was a "home" in which respondents were present, it was not their home. Similarly, the Court has held that in some circumstances a worker can claim Fourth Amendment protection over his own workplace. See, *e.g. O'Connor v. Ortega*, 480 U.S. 709 (1987). But there is no indication that respondents in this case had nearly as significant a connection to Thompson's apartment as the worker in *O'Connor* had to his own private office.

If we regard the overnight guest in *Minnesota v. Olson* as typifying those who may claim the protection of the Fourth Amendment in the home of another, and one merely "legitimately on the premises" as typifying those who may not do so, the present case is obviously somewhere in between. But the purely commercial nature of the transaction engaged in here, the relatively short period of time on the premises, and the lack of any previous connection between respondents and the householder, all lead us to conclude that respondents' situation is closer to that of one simply permitted on the premises. We therefore hold that any search which may have occurred did not violate their Fourth Amendment rights. [Thus] we need not decide whether the police officer's observation constituted a "search." * * *

JUSTICE SCALIA, with whom JUSTICE THOMAS joins, concurring.

I join the opinion of the Court because I believe it accurately applies our recent case law, including *Minnesota v. Olson*. I write separately to express my view that that case law—like the submissions of the parties in this case—gives short shrift to the text of the Fourth Amendment, and to the well and long understood meaning of that text. Specifically, it leaps to apply the fuzzy standard of "legitimate expectation of privacy"—a consideration that is often relevant to whether a search or seizure covered by the Fourth Amendment is "unreasonable"—to the threshold question whether a search or seizure covered by the Fourth Amendment *has occurred*. If that latter question is addressed first and analyzed under the text of the Constitution as traditionally understood, the present case is not remotely difficult.

The Fourth Amendment protects "[t]he right of the people to be secure in *their* persons, houses, papers, and effects, against unreasonable searches and seizures...." U.S. Const., Amdt. 4 (emphasis added). [The] obvious meaning of the provision is that *each* person has the right to be secure against unreasonable searches and seizures in *his own* person, house, papers, and effects.

The Founding-era materials that I have examined confirm that this was the understood meaning. [Justice Scalia then discusses various historical materials.]

[Thus,] in deciding the question presented today we write upon a slate that is far from clean. The text of the Fourth Amendment, the common-law background against which it was adopted, and the understandings consistently displayed after its adoption make the answer clear. We were right to hold in *Chapman v. United States* [p. 460] that the Fourth Amendment protects an apartment tenant against

1. Justice Ginsburg's dissent would render the operative language in *Minnesota v. Olson*, 495 U.S. 91 (1990), almost entirely superfluous. There, we explained the justification for extending Fourth Amendment protection to the overnight visitor: "Staying overnight in another's home is a longstanding social custom that serves functions recognized as valuable by society ... We are at our most vulnerable when we are asleep because we cannot monitor our own safety or the security of our belongings." If any short-term business visit by a stranger entitles the visitor to share the Fourth Amendment protection of the lease holder's home, the Court's explanation of its holding in *Olson* was quite unnecessary.

an unreasonable search of his dwelling, even though he is only a leaseholder. And we were right to hold in *Bumper v. North Carolina* [p. 453] that an unreasonable search of a grandmother's house violated her resident grandson's Fourth Amendment rights because the area searched "was *his* home" (emphasis added). We went to the absolute limit of what text and tradition permit in *Minnesota v. Olson*, when we protected a mere overnight guest against an unreasonable search of his hosts' apartment. But whereas it is plausible to regard a person's overnight lodging as at least his "temporary" residence, it is entirely impossible to give that characterization to an apartment that he uses to package cocaine.

[The] dissent believes that "[o]ur obligation to produce coherent results" requires that we ignore this clear text and four-century-old tradition, and apply instead the notoriously unhelpful test adopted in a "benchmar[k]" decision that is 31 years old, citing *Katz*. In my view, the only thing the past three decades have established about the *Katz* test (which has come to mean the test enunciated by Justice Harlan's separate concurrence in *Katz*) is that, unsurprisingly, those "actual (subjective) expectation[s] of privacy" that society is prepared to recognize as "reasonable" "bear an uncanny resemblance to those expectations of privacy that this Court considers reasonable. When that self-indulgent test is employed (as the dissent would employ it here) to determine whether a "search or seizure" within the meaning of the Constitution has *occurred* (as opposed to whether that "search or seizure" is an "unreasonable" one), it has no plausible foundation in the text of the Fourth Amendment. That provision did not guarantee some generalized "right of privacy" and leave it to this Court to determine which particular manifestations of the value of privacy "society is prepared to recognize as 'reasonable.' "

[The] dissent may be correct that a person invited into someone else's house to engage in a common business (even common monkey-business, so to speak) *ought* to be protected against government searches of the room in which that business is conducted; and that persons invited in to deliver milk or pizza (whom the dissent dismisses as "classroom hypotheticals," as opposed, presumably, to flesh-and-blood hypotheticals) ought *not* to be protected against government searches of the rooms that they occupy. I am not sure of the answer to those policy questions. But I am sure that the answer is not remotely contained in the Constitution, which means that it is left—as *many*, indeed *most*, important questions are left—to the judgment of state and federal legislators. * * *

JUSTICE KENNEDY, concurring.

I join the Court's opinion, for its reasoning is consistent with my view that almost all social guests have a legitimate expectation of privacy, and hence protection against unreasonable searches, in their host's home.

[The] homeowner's right to privacy is not an issue in this case. The Court does not reach the question whether the officer's unaided observations of Thompson's apartment constituted a search. If there was in fact a search, however, then Thompson had the right to object to the unlawful police surveillance of her apartment and the right to suppress any evidence disclosed by the search. [Our] cases establish, however, that respondents have no independent privacy right, the violation of which results in exclusion of evidence against them, unless they can establish a meaningful connection to Thompson's apartment.

[In] this case respondents have established nothing more than a fleeting and insubstantial connection with Thompson's home. For all that appears in the record, respondents used Thompson's house simply as a convenient processing station, their purpose involving nothing more than the mechanical act of chopping and packing a substance for distribution.

[If] respondents here had been visiting twenty homes, each for a minute or two, to drop off a bag of cocaine and were apprehended by a policeman wrongfully present in the nineteenth home; or if they had left the goods at a home where they were not staying and the police had seized the goods in their absence, we would have said that *Rakas* compels rejection of any privacy interest respondents might assert. So it does here, given that respondents have established no meaningful tie or connection to the owner, the owner's home, or the owner's expectation of privacy.

We cannot remain faithful to the underlying principle in *Rakas* without reversing in this case, and I am not persuaded that we need depart from it to protect the homeowner's own privacy interests. * * *

JUSTICE GINSBURG, with whom JUSTICE STEVENS and JUSTICE SOUTER join, dissenting.

The Court's decision undermines not only the security of short-term guests, but also the security of the home resident herself. In my view, when a homeowner or lessor personally invites a guest into her home to share in a common endeavor, whether it be for conversation, to engage in leisure activities, or for business purposes licit or illicit, that guest should share his host's shelter against unreasonable searches and seizures.

I do not here propose restoration of the "legitimately on the premises" criterion stated in *Jones*, for the Court rejected that formulation in *Rakas* * * *. First, the disposition I would reach in this case responds to the unique importance of the home—the most essential bastion of privacy recognized by the law. See *United States v. Karo*, [p. 265]. * * * Second, even within the home itself, the position to which I would adhere would not permit "a casual visitor who has never seen, or been permitted to visit, the basement of another's house to object to a search of the basement if the visitor happened to be in the kitchen of the house at the time of the search." *Rakas*. Further, I would here decide only the case of the homeowner who chooses to share the privacy of her home and her company with a guest, and would not reach classroom hypotheticals like the milkman or pizza deliverer.

My concern centers on an individual's choice to share her home and her associations there with persons she selects. Our decisions indicate that people have a reasonable expectation of privacy in their homes in part because they have the prerogative to exclude others. [The] power to exclude implies the power to include. See, e.g., Mary Irene Coombs, *Shared Privacy and the Fourth Amendment*, or the *Rights of Relationships*, 75 Calif.L.Rev. 1593, 1618 (1987); Albert W. Alschuler, *Interpersonal Privacy and the Fourth Amendment* 4 N.Ill.U.L.Rev. 1, 13 (1983). Our Fourth Amendment decisions should reflect those complementary prerogatives.

A home dweller places her own privacy at risk, the Court's approach indicates, when she opens her home to others, uncertain whether the duration of their stay, their purpose, and their "acceptance into the household" will earn protection. * * * Human frailty suggests that today's decision will tempt police to pry into private dwellings without warrant, to find evidence incriminating guests who do not rest there through the night. * * * *Rakas* tolerates that temptation with respect to automobile searches. See Gerald D. Ashdown, *The Fourth Amendment and the "Legitimate Expectation of Privacy,"* 34 Vand.L.Rev. 1289, 1321 (1981). * * * I see no impelling reason to extend this risk into the home.

[Through] the host's invitation, the guest gains a reasonable expectation of privacy in the home. *Minnesota v. Olson*, so held with respect to an overnight guest. The logic of that decision extends to shorter term guests as well. See SEARCHSZR § 11.3(b). [In] sum, when a homeowner chooses to share the privacy of her home and her company with a short-term guest, the twofold requirement "emerg[ing] from prior decisions" has been satisfied: Both host and guest "have exhibited an actual (subjective) expectation of privacy"; that "expectation [is] one [our] society is prepared to recognize as 'reasonable.' " *Katz* (Harlan, J., concurring).[2] * * *

Our leading decision in *Katz* is key to my view of this case. There, we ruled that the Government violated the petitioner's Fourth Amendment rights when it electronically recorded him transmitting wagering information while he was inside a public telephone booth. We were mindful that "the Fourth Amendment protects people, not places," and held that this electronic monitoring of a business call "violated the privacy upon which [the caller] justifiably relied while using the telephone booth." Our obligation to produce coherent results in this often visited area of the law requires us to inform our current expositions by benchmarks already established.

[The] Court's decision in this case veers sharply from the path marked in *Katz*. I do not agree that we have a more reasonable expectation of privacy when we place a business call to a person's home from a public telephone booth on the side of the street, see *Katz*, than when we actually enter that person's premises to engage in a common endeavor. * * *[a]

Note on Carter

Consider Craig Bradley, *The Fourth Amendment's Iron Triangle: Standing, Consent and Searchability,* Trial, Aug. 1999, p. 75: "Who may be searched? Who may consent to a search? Who has standing to protest a search? These three, seemingly unrelated, questions frequently arise in criminal cases. But though these issues have always appeared to the Sumpreme Court to be unconnected, consideration of two recent cases, *Wyoming v. Houghton* [p. 384] and *Minnesota v. Carter*, has led me to the conclusion that these three questions hinge on exactly the same issue: *What is the subject's interest in or connection to the place to be searched?* Further, they should all have the same answer. That is, if a person has authority to consent to a search, he also has standing to protest it, and is searchable if found at the scene of the search, and vice versa. Recognition that the answer to these questions is the same means that once the Court has put one side of this equilateral triangle into position, the position of the other two sides has been resolved as well. Moreover, it may cause decision makers to think more

2. In his concurring opinion, Justice Kennedy maintains that respondents here lacked "an expectation of privacy that society recognizes as reasonable" because they "established nothing more than a fleeting and insubstantial connection" with the host's home. As the Minnesota Supreme Court reported, however, the stipulated facts showed that respondents were inside the apartment with the host's permission, remained inside for at least 2 1/2 hours, and, during that time, engaged in concert with the host in a collaborative venture. These stipulated facts—which scarcely resemble a stop of a minute or two at the 19th of 20 homes to drop off a packet—securely demonstrate that the host intended to share her privacy with respondents, and that respondents, therefore, had entered into the homeland of Fourth Amendment protection. While I agree with the Minnesota Supreme Court that, under the rule settled since *Katz*, the reasonableness of the expectation of privacy controls, not the visitor's status as social guest, invitee, licensee, or business partner, I think it noteworthy that five Members of the Court would place under the Fourth Amendment's shield, at least, "almost all social guests."

a. Although Justice Breyer concurred in the judgment because he did not believe that Officer Thielen's observation of the apartment, "made from a public area outside the curtilage," constituted an "unreasonable search," he "agree[d] with Justice Ginsburg that respondents can claim the Fourth Amendment's protection."

carefully about finding no standing for passengers in a car, for example, if they realize that will lead to a reduction in authority of such passengers to consent to a search and their 'searchability' by virtue of their presence in that car."

SECTION 2. THE "FRUIT OF THE POISONOUS TREE"

A. Historical Background and Overview

"In the simplest of exclusionary rule cases," observes CRIMPROC, § 9.3(a), "the challenged evidence is quite clearly 'direct' or 'primary' in its relationship to the prior arrest, search, interrogation [or lineup] [e.g., a confession made in response to impermissible interrogation or physical evidence obtained by an illegal search]." Not infrequently, however, points out CRIMPROC, "challenged evidence is 'secondary' or 'derivative' in character. This occurs when, for example, a confession is obtained after an illegal arrest[a] [or] physical evidence is located after an illegally obtained confession.[b] [In] these situations, it is necessary to determine whether the derivative evidence is 'tainted' by the prior constitutional or other violation. To use the phrase coined by Justice Frankfurter, it must be decided whether that evidence is 'the fruit of the poisonous tree.' "[c]

1. ***Genesis of the rule; the doctrine of "attenuation."*** (a) The genesis of the "taint" or "fruit of the poisonous tree" doctrine, as it came to be called, appears in *Silverthorne Lumber Co. v. United States,* 251 U.S. 385 (1920), where, in holding that the government could not use information obtained during an illegal search to subpoena the very documents illegally viewed, the Court, per Holmes, J., pointed out: "The essence of a provision forbidding the acquisition of evidence in a certain way is that not merely evidence so acquired shall not be used before the Court but that it shall not be used at all. Of course this does not mean that the facts thus obtained become sacred and inaccessible. If knowledge of them is gained from an independent source they may be proved like any others, but the knowledge gained by the Government's own wrong cannot be used by it in the way proposed."

Did *Silverthorne* mean that illegally seized *evidence* may never be used by the government although the *facts* revealed by that evidence may be obtained from an independent source? See Robert M. Pitler, *"The Fruit of the Poisonous Tree" Revisited and Shepardized,* 56 Calif.L.Rev. 579, 589 (1968).

(b) In *Nardone v. United States,* 308 U.S. 338 (1939), which first used the phrase "fruit of the poisonous tree," the Court, per Frankfurter, J., refused to permit the prosecution to avoid an inquiry into its use of information gained by illegal wiretapping, observing that "to forbid the direct use of methods [but] to put no curb on their full indirect use would only invite the very methods deemed 'inconsistent with ethical standards and destructive of personal liberty.' "[a] The case also established the "attenuation" doctrine, being the first to authoritatively recognize that even where the challenged evidence did not have an "independent source" it might still be admissible: "Sophisticated argument may prove a causal connection between information obtained through illicit wire-tapping and the Government's proof. As a matter of good sense, however, such connection may have become so attenuated as to dissipate the taint."

a. See, e.g., *Brown v. Illinois,* p. 908.

b. See, e.g., *New York v. Quarles,* p. 629.

c. *Nardone v. United States,* Note 1(b).

a. But cf. *United States v. Calandra,* p. 241, holding that a witness may not refuse to answer grand jury questions on the ground that they are based on evidence obtained from him in an earlier unlawful search.

2. *Verbal evidence as the "fruit" of illegal search and seizure.* In WONG SUN v. UNITED STATES, 371 U.S. 471 (1963) (other aspects of which are discussed at pp. 206, 655), six federal narcotics agents illegally broke into Toy's laundry, chased him into the living quarters at the back of his shop, where Toy's wife and child were sleeping, and handcuffed him. Toy then told the agents that Yee had been selling narcotics. The agents immediately went to Yee, who surrendered heroin to them and implicated Toy and a third party, Wong Sun. A 5–4 majority, per BRENNAN, J., held that both Toy's declarations, upon being handcuffed in his bedroom, *and* "the narcotics taken from Yee, to which [Toy's] declarations led the police" had to be excluded as the "fruits" of the agents' unlawful entry into Toy's bedroom and the "bedroom arrest."

The Court recognized that "traditionally" the exclusionary rule had barred only "physical, tangible materials," but concluded that "verbal evidence which derives so immediately from an unlawful entry and an unauthorized arrest [as here] is no less the 'fruit' of official illegality than the more common tangible fruits of the unwarranted intrusion."[b] Not "all evidence is 'fruit of the poisonous tree' simply because it would not have come to light but for the illegal actions of the police. Rather, the more apt question in such a case is 'whether, granting establishment of the primary illegality [the evidence] has been come at by exploitation of that illegality or instead by means sufficiently distinguishable to be purged of the primary taint.' J. Maguire, *Evidence of Guilt* 221 (1959). We think it clear that the narcotics [taken from Yee] were 'come at by the exploitation of that illegality [the lawless search and seizure of Toy]' and hence that they may not be used against Toy."

On the other hand, although Wong Sun had also been unlawfully arrested, his confession was not the "fruit" of his illegal arrest. Since he had been released on his own recognizance after a lawful arraignment and had returned voluntarily several days later to make the statement, "the connection between [Wong Sun's] arrest and [his] statement had 'become so attenuated as to dissipate the taint.' "

Notes and Questions

(a) *The relevant question.* Does the *Wong Sun* Court's talk of "purging the primary taint" obfuscate the relevant question—whether the admission of the secondary evidence will significantly encourage police misconduct in the future? See Pitler, supra, at 588–89; Note, 115 U.Pa.L.Rev. 1136, 1147 (1967).

(b) *"Purging the taint" of Fourth Amendment violations.* Are there events short of release from custody (which occurred in *Wong Sun*) which operate to "purge the taint" of an illegal arrest or search? Can the mere passage of time suffice? Or would such a rule only "postpone the testing" of the fruit but "not diminish its temptation"? See *Collins v. Beto,* 348 F.2d 823, 828 (5th Cir.1965). Would *Miranda* warnings purge the taint of an illegal arrest? See *Brown v. Illinois,* below.

3. *"Independent source"; "inevitable discovery."* The *Wong Sun* Court quoted from *Silverthorne,* supra, the proposition that the exclusionary rule has no application when "the Government learned of the evidence 'from an independent source.' "This means that if not even a "but for" test can be satisfied, the challenged evidence is not a fruit of the prior violation—a violation of a person's rights should not put him beyond the law's reach if his guilt can be established by evidence unconnected with or "untainted" by the violation.

b. The dissenters, Clark, J., joined by Harlan, Stewart and White, JJ., did not challenge the manner in which the Court applied the "fruits" doctrine, but maintained that Toy's arrest was lawful and thus provided "no 'poisonous tree' whose fruits we must evaluate."

A variation of the "independent source" exception is the "inevitable discovery" or "hypothetical independent source" rule, a doctrine long utilized by many lower courts and recently accepted by the U.S. Supreme Court.[a] This doctrine differs from the "independent source" exception in that the question is not whether the police *actually* acquired certain evidence by reliance upon an untainted source, but whether evidence in fact obtained illegally would inevitably or eventually or probably have been discovered lawfully.

The doctrine is most palatable, and has been most frequently applied, when the police misconduct occurred "while an investigation was already in progress and resulted in the discovery of evidence that would have eventually have been obtained through routine police investigatory procedure. The illegalities in such cases, therefore, had the effect of simply accelerating the discovery." Note, 74 Colum.L.Rev. 88, 90 (1974).

Because mechanical application of the "inevitable discovery" doctrine would seem to encourage unconstitutional shortcuts, and one purpose of the exclusionary rule is to discourage such shortcuts, it has been argued that the doctrine should be permitted only when the police have not acted in "bad faith" to accelerate the discovery of the challenged evidence. See, e.g., SEARCHSZR, § 11.4(a) at 382. But the Court rejected such a limitation in *Nix v. Williams,* p. 916.

4. *Confession as the "fruit" of an illegal arrest.* BROWN v. ILLINOIS, 422 U.S. 590 (1975), arose as follows: Following his illegal arrest, petitioner, a murder suspect, was taken to a police station where, after being given the *Miranda* warnings and waiving his rights, he made incriminating statements within two hours of the arrest. The state supreme court affirmed the murder conviction, taking the view that "the *Miranda* warnings in and of themselves" purged the taint of the prior illegal arrest. The Court, per BLACKMUN, J., reversed:

"The exclusionary rule, [when] utilized to effectuate the Fourth Amendment, serves interests and policies that are distinct from those it serves under the Fifth. [E]xclusion of a confession made without *Miranda* warnings might be regarded as necessary to effectuate the Fifth Amendment, but it would not be sufficient fully to protect the Fourth. *Miranda* warnings, and the exclusion of a confession made without them, do not alone sufficiently deter a Fourth Amendment violation."

"[If] *Miranda* warnings, by themselves, were held to attenuate the taint of an unconstitutional arrest, regardless of how wanton and purposeful the Fourth Amendment violation, the effect of the exclusionary rule would be substantially diluted. [Illegal arrests] would be encouraged by the knowledge that evidence derived therefrom hopefully could be made admissible at trial by the simple expedient of giving *Miranda* warnings. Any incentive to avoid Fourth Amendment violations would be eviscerated by making the warnings, in effect, a 'cure-all' * * *."

Although the Court rejected the *per se* rule of the Illinois court whereunder the *Miranda* warnings were deemed to break the causal connection between the arrest and confession, it declined to adopt a *per se* or "but for" rule running in the other direction. It concluded instead that such taint issues "must be answered on the facts of each case. No single fact is dispositive. [The] *Miranda* warnings are an important factor, to be sure, in determining whether the confession is obtained by exploitation of an illegal arrest. But they are not the only factor to be considered. The temporal proximity of the arrest and the confession, the presence of intervening circumstances and, particularly, the purpose and flagrancy of the official misconduct, are all relevant. The voluntariness of the statement is a threshold

a. See *Nix v. Williams,* p. 916.

requirement. And the burden of showing admissibility rests, of course, on the prosecution."

The Court then concluded that the prosecution had failed to sustain its burden: "[Petitioner's] first statement was separated from his illegal arrest by less than two hours, and there was no intervening event of significance whatsoever. * * * We could hold [petitioner's] first statement admissible only if we overrule *Wong Sun*. We decline to do so. [The] illegality here, moreover, had a quality of purposefulness. The impropriety of the arrest was obvious. [The] detectives embarked upon this expedition for evidence in the hope that something might turn up."

Justice WHITE expressed agreement with the Court insofar as it "holds (1) that despite *Miranda* warnings the Fourth and Fourteenth Amendments require the exclusion from evidence of statements obtained as the fruit of an arrest which the arresting officers *knew or should have known* was without probable cause and unconstitutional, and (2) that the statements obtained in this case were in this category" (emphasis added), and therefore concurred in the judgment.

Justice POWELL, joined by Rehnquist, J., joined the Court insofar as it rejected the Illinois courts' *per se* rule, but "would remand the case for reconsideration under the general standards articulated in the Court's opinion." In Justice Powell's view, "the flagrantly abusive violations of Fourth Amendment rights, on the one hand, and 'technical' Fourth Amendment violations, [on the other] call for significantly different judicial responses":

"I would require the clearest indication of attenuation in cases in which official conduct was flagrantly abusive of Fourth Amendment rights. [In such cases] I would consider the equalizing potential of *Miranda* warnings rarely sufficient to dissipate the taint. [At] the opposite end of the spectrum lie 'technical' violations of Fourth Amendment rights where, for example, officers in good faith arrest an individual in reliance on a warrant later invalidated or pursuant to a statute that subsequently is declared unconstitutional. [In such cases] the deterrence rationale of the exclusionary rule does not obtain, and I can see no legitimate justification for depriving the prosecution of reliable and probative evidence. Thus, with the exception of statements given in the immediate circumstances of the illegal arrest—a constraint I think is imposed by existing exclusionary rule law—I would not require more than proof that effective *Miranda* warnings were given and that the ensuing statement was voluntary in the Fifth Amendment sense."

In *Dunaway v. New York,* other aspects of which are discussed at p. 438, the Court, per Brennan, J., reaffirmed the view that *Miranda* warnings, by themselves, are not necessarily sufficient to attenuate the taint of an unconstitutional arrest: "The situation in this case is virtually a replica of the situation in *Brown*. Petitioner was also admittedly seized without probable cause in the hope that something might turn up, and confessed without any intervening event of significance. [To] admit petitioner's confession in such a case would allow 'law enforcement officers to violate the Fourth Amendment with impunity, safe in the knowledge that they could wash their hands in the "procedural safeguards" of the Fifth' [Comment, 25 Emory L.J. 227, 238 (1976)]."

Justice Stevens joined the Court's opinion but added a comment on "the significance of two factors that may be considered when determining whether a confession has been obtained by exploitation of an illegal arrest":

"The temporal relationship between the arrest and the confession may be an ambiguous factor. If there are no relevant intervening circumstances, a prolonged detention may well be a more serious exploitation of an illegal arrest than a short one. Conversely, even an immediate confession may have been motivated by a prearrest event such as a visit with a minister. The flagrancy of the official misconduct is relevant, in my judgment, only insofar as it has a tendency to motivate the defendant. A midnight arrest with drawn guns will be equally frightening whether the police acted recklessly or in good faith. Conversely, a courteous command has the same effect on the arrestee whether the officer thinks he has probable cause or knows that he does not. In either event, if the Fourth Amendment is violated, the admissibility question will turn on the causal relationship between that violation and the defendant's subsequent confession."[a]

The *Brown-Dunaway* rule was applied (extended?) to a complicated set of facts in *Taylor v. Alabama,* 457 U.S. 687 (1982). A 5–4 majority, per Marshall, J., held that petitioner's confession was the impermissible fruit of his illegal arrest even though (a) six hours had elapsed between the illegal arrest and the time petitioner confessed; (b) petitioner was advised of his rights three times; and (c) he was allowed to visit briefly with his girlfriend and his neighbor shortly before he confessed.

Dissenting Justice O'Connor joined by the Chief Justice, and Powell and Rehnquist, JJ., maintained that *Brown* and *Dunaway* required a contrary result. As the dissent saw it, "[t]he petitioner's confession was not proximately caused by his illegal arrest, but was the product of a decision based both on knowledge of his constitutional rights and on the discussion with his friends."

Compare the *Brown–Dunaway–Taylor* line of cases with *Rawlings v. Kentucky* (1980), discussed at p. 898. Petitioner argued that his admission of the ownership of drugs which had been found in Ms. Cox's purse (after the contents of the purse had been emptied, pursuant to a police order) was the fruit of an illegal detention. The Court, per Rehnquist, J., disagreed. Assuming that Rawlings and others were illegally detained in a house while the police obtained a search warrant for the premises, the Court noted, inter alia, that the detention was in a "congenial atmosphere"; that petitioner's admissions were "apparently spontaneous reactions to the discovery of his drugs in Cox's purse" and not the product of the initial illegality, and the police action "does not rise to the level of conscious or flagrant misconduct requiring prophylactic exclusion of petitioner's statements. Contrast *Brown.*"[b]

5. *Identification of a person as a "fruit" of an illegal arrest.* UNITED STATES v. CREWS, 445 U.S. 463 (1980), arose as follows: Immediately after being assaulted and robbed in a public restroom, the victim gave the police a full description of her assailant. Crews, who matched the suspect's description, was illegally taken into custody, photographed, and then released. Thereafter, when shown an array of eight photographs, the victim selected Crews' photograph as that of the man who had robbed her. At a court-ordered lineup, Crews was again positively identified. Finally, Crews was identified at the trial. Crews was convicted of robbery, but the District of Columbia Court of Appeals held the victim's in-court identification inadmissible, viewing it as obtained by official "exploitation" of the "primary illegality"—Crews' unlawful arrest.[a] The Court, per BRENNAN, J., disagreed:

a. Rehnquist, J., joined by Burger, C.J., dissented, maintaining that the police had acted in "good faith and not in a flagrant manner" and that in such cases "no more [should be required] than that proper *Miranda* warnings [be] given and that the statement be voluntary within the meaning of the Fifth Amendment."

b. Dissenting Justice Marshall, joined by Brennan, J., maintained that "petitioner's admissions were obviously the fruit of the illegal detention."

a. The trial court had excluded both the photographic and lineup identifications as the "fruits" of Crews' illegal arrest and on appeal

A victim's in-court identification has "three distinct elements": "[1], the victim is present at trial to testify as to what transpired between her and the offender, and to identify the defendant as the culprit. [2], the victim possesses knowledge of and the ability to reconstruct the prior [crime] and to identify the defendant from her observations of him at the time of the crime. And [3], the defendant is also physically present in the courtroom, so that the victim can observe him and compare his appearance to that of the offender. In the present case, none of these three elements 'has been come at by exploitation' of the defendant's Fourth Amendment rights."

As for (1), the victim's presence and cooperation were "surely not the product of any police misconduct"; as for (3), because an "illegal arrest, without more, has never been viewed as a bar to subsequent prosecution," the defendant was "not himself a suppressible 'fruit,' and the illegality of his detention cannot deprive the Government of the opportunity to prove his guilt through the introduction of evidence wholly untainted by the police misconduct."

As for (2): "Nor did the illegal arrest infect the victim's ability to give accurate identification testimony. Based upon her observations at the time of the robbery, [she] constructed a mental image of her assailant. At trial, she retrieved this mnemonic representation, compared it [to] defendant, and positively identified him as the robber. No part of this process was affected by [the] illegal arrest."

Because it was clear that prior to his illegal arrest, the police both knew defendant's identity and had some reason to believe he was involved in the robbery, Justice Brennan would have reserved judgment as to whether a defendant's face could ever be considered a suppressible "fruit" of an illegal arrest.[b] But a majority of the Court, in two separate concurring opinions, explicitly rejected this possibility.

6. *Confession as the "fruit" of a Payton violation.* *Payton v. New York* (p. 364) holds that the Fourth Amendment prohibits the police from effecting a warrantless entry into a suspect's home in order to make a routine felony arrest. In NEW YORK v. HARRIS, 495 U.S. 14 (1990), a 5–4 majority, per WHITE, J., held that where the police have probable cause to arrest a suspect, the exclusionary rule does not bar the use of a statement made by the suspect *outside* his home even though the statement is obtained after an *in-house* arrest in violation of *Payton*.

The police had probable cause to believe Harris had killed a woman. They went to his apartment to take him into custody, but did not first obtain an arrest warrant. After being advised of his *Miranda* rights and waiving them, Harris reportedly admitted that he had committed the homicide. He was then taken to the station house, where, after again being advised of his rights and again waiving them, he signed a written inculpatory statement. Since the state did not challenge the trial court's suppression of Harris' statement to the police while still inside his home, the sole issue was the admissibility of the statement he made at the station house. The New York Court of Appeals ruled that it was the inadmissible fruit of the *Payton* violation, but the Supreme Court reversed:

"Nothing in the reasoning of [*Payton*] suggests that an arrest in a home without a warrant but with probable cause somehow renders unlawful continued custody of the suspect once he is removed from the house. [Because] the officers had probable cause to arrest Harris for a crime, Harris was not unlawfully in custody when he was removed to the station house. [For] Fourth Amendment

the government conceded that both were inadmissible. Why? Wasn't *the lineup identification* admissible for the same reasons the Supreme Court held that the in-court identification was?

b. As Justice Brennan noted, this part of his opinion was joined only by Stewart and Stevens, JJ.

purposes, the legal issue is the same as it would be had the police arrested Harris on his door step, illegally entered his home to search for evidence, and later interrogated Harris at the station house. Similarly, if the police had made a warrantless entry into Harris' home, not found him there, but arrested him on the street when he returned, a later statement made by him after proper warnings would no doubt be admissible. * * *"

"Harris's statement taken at the police station was not the product of being in unlawful custody. Neither was it the fruit of having been arrested in the home rather than someplace else. The case is analogous to *Crews*. In that case, we refused to suppress a victim's in-court identification despite the defendant's illegal arrest. The Court found that the evidence was not 'come at by exploitation [of] the defendant's Fourth Amendment rights,' and that it was not necessary to inquire whether the 'taint' of the Fourth Amendment violation was sufficiently attenuated to permit the introduction of the evidence. Here, likewise, the police had a justification to question Harris prior to his arrest; therefore, his subsequent statement was not an exploitation of the illegal entry into Harris's home. * * *"

"[S]uppressing the statement taken outside the house would not serve the purpose of the rule that made Harris's in-house arrest illegal. The warrant requirement for an arrest in the home is imposed to protect the home, and anything incriminating the police gathered from arresting Harris in his home, rather than elsewhere, has been excluded, as it should have been; the purpose of the rule has thereby been vindicated. [The] principal incentive to obey *Payton* still obtains: the police know that a warrantless entry will lead to the suppression of any evidence found or statements taken inside the home. If we did suppress statements like Harris's, moreover, the incremental deterrent value would be minimal. Given that the police have probable cause to arrest a suspect in Harris's position, they need not violate *Payton* in order to interrogate the suspect."

Dissenting Justice MARSHALL, joined by Brennan, Blackmun and Stevens, JJ., deemed *Brown v. Illinois* controlling:

"An application of the *Brown* factors to this case compels the conclusion that Harris' statement at the station house must be suppressed. About an hour elapsed between the illegal arrest and Harris' confession, without any intervening factor other than the warnings required by *Miranda*. This Court has held, however, that '*Miranda* warnings, *alone* and *per se*, ... cannot assure in every case that the Fourth Amendment violation has not been unduly exploited.' *Brown*. Indeed, in *Brown*, we held that a statement made almost *two* hours after an illegal arrest, and after *Miranda* warnings had been given, was not sufficiently removed from the violation so as to dissipate the taint."

"[The] officers decided, apparently consistent with a 'departmental policy,' to violate Harris' Fourth Amendment rights so they could get evidence that they could not otherwise obtain. As the trial court held, 'No more clear violation of [*Payton*], in my view, could be established.' Where, as here, there is a particularly flagrant constitutional violation and little in the way of elapsed time or intervening circumstances, the statement in the police station must be suppressed. * * *

"Perhaps the most alarming aspect of the Court's ruling is its practical consequences for the deterrence of *Payton* violations. Imagine a police officer who has probable cause to arrest a suspect but lacks a warrant. [The] officer knows that if he breaks into the house without a warrant and drags the suspect outside, the suspect, shaken by the enormous invasion of privacy he has just undergone, may say something incriminating. Before today's decision, the government would only be able to use that evidence if the Court found that the taint of the arrest had been attenuated; after the decision, the evidence will be admissible regardless of whether it was the product of the unconstitutional arrest. Thus, the officer envisions the following best-case scenario if he chooses to violate the Constitution: he avoids a major expenditure of time and effort, ensures that the suspect will not escape, and procures the most damaging evidence of all, a confession. His worst-case scenario is that he will avoid a major expenditure of effort, ensure that the suspect will not escape, and will see evidence in the house (which would have remained unknown absent the constitutional violation) that cannot be used in the prosecution's case-in-chief. The Court thus creates powerful incentives for police officers to violate the Fourth Amendment. In the context of our constitutional rights and the sanctity of our homes, we cannot afford to presume that officers will be entirely impervious to those incentives."

7. ***A warrant search as the fruit of an illegal entry and occupation of the premises.*** SEGURA v. UNITED STATES (1984) (also discussed at p. 361) arose as follows: When Segura, a suspected narcotics violator, entered his apartment building one evening, he was immediately arrested and taken to his apartment. The agents entered the apartment without requesting or obtaining permission. Four other people were there. The agents told them that Segura was under arrest and that a search warrant for the premises was being obtained.

The agents then conducted a limited security check of the apartment, in the process observing drug paraphernalia. They then took Segura and the other occupants of the apartment to headquarters. Two agents remained in the apartment awaiting the warrant. Because of "administrative delay," the search warrant was not issued until some 19 hours after the initial entry. When the agents executed the warrant they discovered narcotics and records of narcotics transactions.

Since the government did not dispute the rulings below that the initial entry and security search were unlawful, "the only issue" before the Court was whether items "not observed during the illegal entry and first discovered by the agents the day after the entry, under an admittedly valid search warrant, should have been suppressed."[a] A 5–4 majority, per BURGER, C.J., answered in the negative. The legality of the initial entry had no bearing on the admissibility of the challenged evidence "because there was an independent source for the warrant under which that evidence was seized": "No information obtained during the initial entry or occupation of the apartment was needed or used by the agents to secure the warrant. [The] valid warrant search was a 'means sufficiently distinguishable' to purge the evidence of any 'taint' arising from the entry."

Dissenting Justice STEVENS, joined by Brennan, Marshall and Blackmun, JJ., maintained that "the controlling question" was "whether the deterrent purposes of the exclusionary rule would be served or undermined by the suppression of this evidence." He thought the deterrence rationale "plainly applicable": "The agents impounded the apartment precisely because they wished to avoid risking a loss of access to the evidence within it. Thus, the unlawful benefit they [obtained] was exactly the benefit [that] motivated [them] in the case to violate the Constitution."

In MURRAY v. UNITED STATES, 487 U.S. 533 (1988), the Court, by a 4–3 vote (Brennan and Kennedy, JJ., not participating), declined to read *Segura* narrowly and held that evidence observed by the police during an illegal entry of premises need not be excluded if such evidence is subsequently discovered during the execution of an otherwise valid search warrant sought and issued on the basis

a. Such illegal entries, observed the Court, are sufficiently deterred by the officers' realization that "whatever evidence they discover as a direct result of the entry may be suppressed." The four dissenters found the suggested distinction a puzzling one: "If the execution of a valid warrant takes the poison out of the hidden fruit, I should think that it would also remove the taint from the fruit in plain view."

of information wholly unconnected to the prior entry. After receiving information that a warehouse was being used for illegal drug activities, federal agents forced their way into the warehouse and observed in plain view bales of marijuana. The agents then left without disturbing the bales and applied for a search warrant. In their application, they did not mention the prior entry or include any recitations of their observations during that entry. Upon issuance of the warrant, the agents reentered the warehouse and seized the bales and other evidence of crime. In upholding the admissibility of the evidence, the Court, per SCALIA, J., observed:

"Knowledge that the marijuana was in the warehouse was assuredly acquired at the time of the unlawful entry. But it was also acquired at the time of entry pursuant to the warrant, and if that later acquisition was not the result of the earlier entry there is no reason why the independent source doctrine should not apply. Invoking the exclusionary rule would put the police (and society) not in the *same* position they would have occupied if no violation occurred, but in a *worse* one. See *Nix v. Williams* [p. 916]. We think this is also true with respect to the tangible evidence, the bales of marijuana. [S]o long as a later, lawful seizure is genuinely independent of an earlier, tainted one (which may well be difficult to establish where the seized goods are kept in the police's possession) there is no reason why the independent source doctrine should not apply."

"The ultimate question, therefore, is whether the search pursuant to warrant was in fact a genuinely independent source of the information and tangible evidence at issue here. This would not have been the case if the agents' decision to seek the warrant was prompted by what they had seen during the initial entry, or if information obtained during that entry was presented to the Magistrate and affected his decision to issue the warrant. [The] District Court found that the agents did not reveal their warrantless entry to the Magistrate and that they did not include in their application for a warrant any recitation of their observations in the warehouse. It did not, however, explicitly find that the agents would have sought a warrant if they had not earlier entered the warehouse. [Thus], we vacate the judgments and remand these cases [for] determination whether the warrant-authorized search of the warehouse was an independent source of the challenged evidence in the sense we have described."

Dissenting Justice MARSHALL, joined by Stevens and O'Connor, JJ., maintained that "the Court's decision, by failing to provide sufficient guarantees that the subsequent search was, in fact, independent of the illegal search, emasculates the Warrant Clause and undermines the deterrence function of the exclusionary rule":

"[When], as here, the same team of investigators is involved in both the first and second search, there is a significant danger that the 'independence' of the source will in fact be illusory, and that the initial search will have affected the decision to obtain a warrant notwithstanding the officers' subsequent assertions to the contrary. It is therefore crucial that the factual premise of the exception—complete independence—be clearly established before the exception can [apply]. I believe the Court's reliance on the intent of the law enforcement officers who conducted the warrantless search provides insufficient guarantees that the subsequent legal search was unaffected by the prior illegal search. * * *

"*Segura* is readily distinguished from the present case. The admission of evidence first discovered during a legal search does not significantly lessen the deterrence facing the law enforcement officers contemplating an illegal entry *so long as* the evidence that is seen is excluded. This was clearly the view of [the *Segura* majority]. [E]xtending *Segura* to cover evidence discovered during an initial illegal search will eradicate this remaining deterrence to illegal entry. Moreover, there is less reason to believe that an initial illegal entry was prompted by a desire to determine whether to bother to get a warrant in the first place, and thus was not wholly independent of the second search, if officers understand that evidence they discover during the illegal search will be excluded even if they subsequently return with a warrant."[a]

Consider Craig M. Bradley, *Murray v. United States: The Bell Tolls for the Search Warrant Requirement*, 64 Ind.L.J. 907, 920 (1989):

"While I agree with the dissent in *Murray* that the decision 'emasculates the Warrant Clause,' I don't necessarily disagree with the result. This is [because] nothing in the amendment itself or, apparently, in the minds of its framers, requires a warrant as a prerequisite for a reasonable search; it only requires probable cause as a prerequisite for a warrant. [I]nstead of claiming that there is a warrant requirement and then, as recently illustrated in *Murray*, repeatedly finding ways to ignore it, the Court ought to adopt one of two models of the fourth amendment * * *.

[Professor Bradley then discusses the 'no lines' or 'general reasonableness' model, under which obtaining a warrant is only one of a number of relevant factors; and the 'bright line' approach, under which a warrant is *always* required for *every* search and seizure when it is practicable to obtain one.] With *Murray*, the Court clearly shows its preference for [a] reasonableness approach to fourth amendment law. *Murray* reeks of 'reasonableness' analysis and cannot be reconciled with the proposition that a search warrant is, in any meaningful sense, required."

8. *The "tainted" witness*. UNITED STATES v. CECCOLINI, 435 U.S. 268 (1978), grew out of the following facts: An officer in a flower shop on a social visit illegally picked up an envelope and found it to contain money and policy slips. He then learned from his friend, Ms. Hennessey, an employee of the shop (who did not notice his discovery), that the envelope belonged to the defendant, the owner of the shop. The information reached the FBI four months later. An agent questioned Hennessey about defendant, without specifically mentioning the illegally discovered policy slips. She said she was willing to help, and she testified against defendant both before the grand jury and at his trial for perjury.

A 6–2 majority of the Court (Blackmun, J., not participating) held Hennessey's testimony admissible. Although it declined to adopt a *per se* rule that the testimony of a live witness should always be admissible,[a] the Court, per REHNQUIST, J., pointed out that various factors indicate that "the exclusionary rule should be invoked with much greater reluctance where the claim is based on a causal relationship between a constitutional violation and the discovery of a live witness than when a similar claim is advanced to support suppression of an inanimate object":

"The greater the willingness of the witness to freely testify, the greater the likelihood that he or she will be discovered by legal means and, concomitantly, the smaller the incentive to conduct an illegal search to discover the witness. Witnesses are not like guns or documents which remain hidden from view until one turns over a sofa or opens a filing cabinet. Witnesses can, and often do, come forward and offer evidence entirely of their own volition. And evaluated properly,

a. While Stevens, J., joined Justice Marshall's dissent, he noted in a separate dissent that he "remain[ed] convinced that the *Segura* decision itself was unacceptable" because it provided government agents with an "affirmative incentive" to conduct illegal searches.

a. Concurring Chief Justice Burger would adopt such a rule.

the degree of free will necessary to dissipate the taint will very likely be found more often in the case of live-witness testimony than other kinds of evidence."

"Moreover, exclusion of testimony" would perpetually disable a witness from testifying about relevant and material facts, regardless of how unrelated such testimony might be to the purpose of the originally illegal search or the evidence discovered thereby. [S]ince the cost of excluding live-witness testimony often will be greater, a closer, more direct link between the illegality and that kind of testimony is required."

Dissenting Justice MARSHALL, joined by Brennan, J., did not see how "the same tree, having its roots in an unconstitutional search or seizure, can bear two different kinds of fruit, with one kind less susceptible than the other to exclusion on Fourth Amendment grounds." The dissent charged the majority with "judicial 'double counting' ": "The majority allows a court to consider whether the witness came forward and then, if he did not, to consider that generally (but not in this case) witnesses come forward." As for the majority's argument that often the exclusion of live-witness testimony will be very costly to society, "at least as often the exclusion of physical evidence [will be equally] costly * * *."

B. The "Inevitable Discovery" Doctrine: The Sequel to *Brewer v. Williams*

Consider NIX v. WILLIAMS (WILLIAMS II), 467 U.S. 431 (1984), which arose as follows: After his conviction was overturned (see *Brewer v. Williams*, p. 733), Williams was retried and again found guilty of first-degree murder. At Williams's second trial, the prosecution did not offer Williams's statements into evidence. Nor did it seek to show that Williams had directed the police to the child's body. The only evidence admitted was the condition of the victim's body as it was found, articles of the victim's clothing, and the results of post mortem medical and chemical tests on her body. The trial court concluded that the State had proved by a preponderance of the evidence that, if the search had not been suspended and Williams had not led the police to the victim, the searching party would have discovered the body in essentially the same condition as it was actually found. The trial court also ruled that if the police had not located the body, "the search would clearly have been taken up again where it left off, given the extreme circumstances of this case, and the body would [have] been found *in short order*" (emphasis added).

Both the Supreme Court of Iowa, which affirmed the conviction, and the U.S. District Court, which denied habeas relief, adopted the "inevitable discovery" exception to the exclusionary rule and upheld the conviction on that basis. However, the U.S. Court of Appeals for the Eighth Circuit reversed the district court's denial of habeas relief, maintaining that an "inevitable discovery" exception requires proof that the police did not act in "bad faith" and the record could not support such a finding. A 6–3 majority, per BURGER, C.J., reversed:

"[The] core rationale consistently advanced by this Court for extending the Exclusionary Rule to evidence that is the fruit of unlawful police conduct has been that this admittedly drastic and socially costly course is needed to deter police from violations of constitutional and statutory protections. [On] this rationale, the prosecution is not to be put in a better position than it would have been in if no illegality had transpired.

"By contrast, the derivative evidence analysis ensures that the prosecution is not put in a *worse* position simply because of some earlier police error or misconduct. The independent source doctrine allows admission of evidence that has been discovered by means wholly independent of any constitutional violation.

[The] independent source doctrine teaches us that the interest of society in deterring unlawful police conduct and the public interest in having juries receive all probative evidence of a crime are properly balanced by putting the police in the same, not a *worse,* position than they would have been in if no police error or misconduct had occurred. [There] is a functional similarity between [the independent source and inevitable discovery doctrines] in that exclusion of evidence that would inevitably have been discovered would also put the government in a worse position, because the police would have obtained that evidence if no misconduct had taken place. Thus, while the independent source exception would not justify admission of evidence in this case, its rationale is wholly consistent with and justifies our adoption of the ultimate or inevitable discovery exception to the Exclusionary Rule."

"[If] the prosecution can establish by a preponderance of the evidence that the information ultimately or inevitably would have been discovered by lawful means—here the volunteers' search—then the deterrence rationale has so little basis that the evidence should be received. Anything less would reject logic, experience, and common sense.

"The requirement that the prosecution must prove the absence of bad faith, [would] place courts in the position of withholding from juries relevant and undoubted truth that would have been available to police absent any unlawful police activity. Of course, that view would put the police in a *worse* position than they would have been in if no unlawful conduct had transpired. And, of equal importance, it wholly fails to take into account the enormous societal cost of excluding truth in the search for truth in the administration of justice. Nothing in this Court's prior holdings supports any such formalistic, pointless, and punitive approach.

"The Court of Appeals concluded [that] if an absence of bad faith requirement were not imposed, 'the temptation to risk deliberate violations of the Sixth Amendment would be too great, and the deterrent effect of the Exclusionary Rule reduced too far.' We reject that view. A police officer who is faced with the opportunity to obtain evidence illegally will rarely, if ever, be in a position to calculate whether the evidence sought would inevitably be discovered.

"[On] the other hand, when an officer is aware that the evidence will inevitably be discovered, he will try to avoid engaging in any questionable practice. In that situation, there will be little to gain from taking any dubious 'shortcuts' to obtain the evidence. Significant disincentives to obtaining evidence illegally—including the possibility of departmental discipline and civil liability—also lessen the likelihood that the ultimate or inevitable discovery exception will promote police misconduct. In these circumstances, the societal costs of the Exclusionary Rule far outweigh any possible benefits to deterrence that a good-faith requirement might produce.

"[On] this record it is clear that the search parties were approaching the actual location of the body and we are satisfied, along with three courts earlier, that the volunteer search teams would have resumed the search had Williams not earlier led the police to the body and the body inevitably would have been found."

Justice STEVENS, concurring in the judgment, observed:

"[The] majority is correct to insist that any rule of exclusion not provide the authorities with an incentive to commit violations of the Constitution. [But] when the burden of proof on the inevitable discovery question is placed on the prosecution, *it* must bear the risk of error in the determination made necessary by its constitutional violation. The uncertainty as to whether the body would have been discovered can be resolved in its favor here only because, as the Court explains, petitioner adduced evidence demonstrating that at the time of the constitutional violation an investigation was already under way which, in the natural and probable course of events, would have soon discovered the body. This is not a case in which the prosecution can escape responsibility for a constitutional violation through speculation; to the extent uncertainty was created by the constitutional violation the prosecution was required to resolve that uncertainty through proof.[8]"

Dissenting Justice BRENNAN, joined by Marshall, J., underscored the distinction between the inevitable discovery and the independent source doctrines:

"The inevitable discovery exception necessarily implicates a hypothetical finding that differs in kind from the factual finding that precedes application of the independent source rule. To ensure that this hypothetical finding is narrowly confined to circumstances that are functionally equivalent to an independent source, and to protect fully the fundamental rights served by the exclusionary rule, I would require clear and convincing evidence before concluding that the government had met its burden of proof on this issue."[a]

Notes and Questions

1. ***Must the independent line of investigation be underway?*** In his dissent, Justice Brennan describes the *Williams II* majority as "conclud[ing] that unconstitutionally obtained evidence may be admitted at trial if it inevitably would have been discovered in the same condition by an independent line of investigation *that was already being pursued* when the constitutional violation occurred." (Emphasis added.) Consider also concurring Justice Stevens' observation that "[t]he uncertainty as to whether the body would have been discovered can be resolved in [the prosecution's] favor here *only because* [the prosecution demonstrated] that at the time of the constitutional violation an investigation *was already under way which, in the natural and probable course of events, would have soon discovered the body.*" (Emphasis added.) Is *Williams II* limited along the lines indicated by Justices Brennan and Stevens? Should it be? See generally, Stephen E. Hessler, *Establishing Inevitability Without Active Pursuit: Defining the Inevitable Discovery Exception to the Fourth Amendment Exclusionary Rule,* 99 Mich.L.Rev. 238 (2000).

2. ***Primary evidence vs. secondary evidence.*** *Nix* applied the inevitable discovery exception to secondary or derivative evidence, but most federal courts of appeals have also applied the exception to primary evidence (evidence acquired during the course of the search itself). See Robert M. Bloom, *Inevitable Discovery: An Exception beyond the Fruits,* 20 Am.J.Crim.L. 79, 87 (1992). Should a distinction between primary and secondary evidence be drawn on the ground that application of the inevitable discovery rule to secondary evidence does not excuse the unlawful police action by admitting what was obtained as a direct result of the

8. I agree with the majority's holding that the prosecution must prove that the evidence would have been inevitably discovered by a preponderance of the evidence rather than by clear and convincing evidence. An inevitable discovery finding is based on objective evidence concerning the scope of the ongoing investigation which can be objectively verified or impeached. Hence an extraordinary burden of proof is not needed in order to preserve the defendant's ability to subject the prosecution's case to the meaningful adversarial testing required by the Sixth Amendment.

a. For an in-depth analysis of the Supreme Court's opinion in *Williams II,* see Silas J. Wasserstrom & William J. Mertens, *The Exclusionary Rule on the Scaffold: But Was it a Fair Trial?* 22 Am.Crim.L.Rev. 85, 130–79 (1984). For an incisive treatment of the "fruit of the poisonous tree" problems raised by the second *Williams* case, or Williams II, prior to the Supreme Court's decision in that case, see Phillip E. Johnson, *The Return of the "Christian Burial Speech" Case,* 32 Emory L.J. 349 (1983).

initial misconduct, but that application of the rule to primary evidence constitutes an after the fact purging of initial wrongful conduct? See id. at 87–94.

3. ***The significance of Murray v. United States.*** Recall that in *Murray,* an *independent source* case, bales of marijuana (primary evidence) were discovered as the result of an illegal entry. Nevertheless, the Court allowed for the introduction of the bales, provided that the subsequent lawful entry with a warrant was not based on information related to the initial illegal entry. Does *Murray* support the use of the *inevitable discovery exception* to avoid suppression of primary evidence? See Bloom, supra, at 92–94.

4. ***The relatively easy case.*** As pointed out in CRIMPROC § 9.3(e), "lower courts have had the least difficulty in applying the inevitable discovery doctrine where that discovery would have come about through a routine procedure invariably applied under the particular circumstances. That commonly is the case where the government argues that the evidence discovered through an illegal warrantless search would have been uncovered in an inventory search. The inventory search ordinarily will have been performed even after the discovery through the illegal search, thereby lending support to the contention that it was an inevitable procedure."

5. ***Inevitable discovery and the warrant requirement; "could have" or "might have" vs. "would have."*** If the police have probable cause to conduct a search, but do not bother to obtain a warrant, although they had plenty of time to do so, can (should) the inevitable discovery exception be used to avoid the need for a warrant?[a] Consider Bloom, supra, at 95:

"Because the *Nix* decision dealt with a Sixth Amendment violation, the Court probably was not focusing on the effect this exception would have on the Fourth Amendment warrant requirement. To the extent that the *Nix* Court concluded that there would be a limited deterrence effect by utilizing the inevitable discovery exception, its reasoning was flawed with regard to the warrant requirement.

"[The] existence of the inevitable discovery exception *will* provide the police with an incentive to avoid the warrant requirement. The police might seek the most expeditious method of obtaining the evidence without regard to its illegality, knowing that, as long as they could have obtained the evidence legally, their efforts will not result in its suppression. [For] example, if the police can demonstrate that they *could* have gotten a search warrant, what incentive will there be for them to go actively through the procedural hassle of actually obtaining one, since the effects of an illegal warrantless search could be nullified by the application of the inevitable discovery exception?"

See also Easterbrook, J., observing in *United States v. Brown,* 64 F.3d 1083, 1085 (7th Cir.1995), that in a situation where the police have probable cause, but do not, as they should, obtain a warrant, "what makes a discovery 'inevitable' is not probable cause alone [but] probable cause plus a chain of events that would have led to a warrant (or other justification) independent of the search." Otherwise, adds Judge Easterbrook, "the requirement of a warrant for a residential entry will never be enforced by the exclusionary rule."

The "inevitable discovery" exception permits the use of unlawfully obtained evidence if it "ultimately or inevitably *would* have been discovered by lawful means. *Nix v. Williams* (emphasis added). It does not apply simply because the police *could* have or *might* have obtained the evidence lawfully—simply because

a. A similar question may be asked about illegal searches of vehicles which turn up items that would have been discovered through an inventory search. On this issue compare *United States v. Halls,* 40 F.3d 275 (8th Cir.1994) and *United States v. Mancera–Londono,* 912 F.2d 373 (9th Cir.1990) with *United States v. $639,558.00 in United States Currency,* 955 F.2d 712 (D.C.Cir.1992) and *United States v. Infante–Ruiz,* 13 F.3d 498 (1st Cir.1994).

"the police had *the capacity* (which they did not exercise)" to proceed lawfully. CRIMPROC § 9.3 (emphasis added).

Cf. Scalia, J., speaking for the Court in *Kyllo v. United States* (p. 257): "The fact that equivalent information could sometimes by obtained by other means does not make lawful the use of means that violate the Fourth Amendment. The police, might, for example, learn how many people are in a particular house by setting up year-round surveillance; but that does not make breaking and entering to find out the same information lawful."

6. *Inevitable discovery and knock-and-announce requirements.*. In *Wilson v. Arkansas*, the knock-and-announce case discussed at p. 309, the Court declined to reach an argument the state advanced as an alternative ground for affirming the denial of defendant's motion to suppress. Analogizing to the "independent source" doctrine applied in *Segura* and the "inevitable discovery" rule adopted in *Nix v. Williams*, the state argued that "any evidence seized after an unreasonable, unannounced entry is causally disconnected from the constitutional violation and that exclusion goes beyond the goal of precluding any benefit to the government flowing from the constitutional violation." If the state's argument were to prevail, would it completely gut all knock-and-announce requirements? See SEARCHSZR § 11.4.

7. *The cross-fire between "standing" and "inevitable discovery": Can "lack of standing" be a basis for "inevitable discovery"? Must the inevitable discovery be "lawful"?* UNITED STATES v. JOHNSON, 380 F.3d 1013 (7th Cir.2004) raises the question whether the fact that *an illegal search of other people* would have turned up the incriminating evidence *actually seized illegally from the defendant* should allow the prosecution to use that evidence against the defendant. The case arose as follows: Although they lacked any grounds for an arrest, or even a *Terry* stop, the police approached Johnson and two others sitting in his parked car and ordered them to get out. While one of the officers searched under the car seat and found drugs there, another officer searched the two passengers and found drugs and counterfeit money on their persons. The officers then searched the trunk of the car and found more incriminating evidence. The district court admitted the evidence, noting that irrespective of the drugs found under the car seat, once drugs were found on the passengers the police had probable cause to search the entire vehicle. To be sure, the search of the passengers was illegal, but, concluded the district judge, the "injury" to Johnson—the use of the incriminating evidence found in his car trunk to convict him—was not caused by a violation of *his* rights. The Seventh Circuit, per POSNER, J., reversed:

"[All Johnson] is trying to do is to prevent the use of evidence seized from him—from the trunk of *his* car. And so the question is not his 'standing' to challenge the use against him of evidence seized illegally from other people—no such evidence [was] used against him." [To admit the evidence on the ground that *an illegal search of other people would have* produced the evidence illegally seized from defendant] would have the paradoxical effect that two illegal searches would make a legal search—in fact would make two legal searches. For on the government's view, not only could the illegally seized evidence in the trunk be used against the victim of the illegal seizure; equally the evidence illegally seized from the two passengers could be used against the two of them, since once the police officers found the contraband in the trunk they would be entitled to arrest and search the passengers, who could not challenge the seizure from the trunk because it wasn't their car. The upshot is that when the victims of an illegal search are linked in such a way that evidence seized from one will provide grounds for a reasonable belief that the others also have evidence, the government's view would deprive the exclusionary rule of any deterrent effect.

"This is a slight overstatement. The police were gambling when they conducted their illegal searches of the three occupants of Johnson's car. Had there been no contraband on Johnson's person or in the car itself but only in the pockets of the passengers, the evidence seized from them could not have been used against them, though it might on the government's view be usable against Johnson if there were anything to link him to the activities of his two passengers. But in any case in which the police have a strong hunch (though not enough to enable them to obtain a warrant or to search without a warrant) that all the members of a linked group have some contraband, the police could, if the government is right, search all the members of the group without fear that any contraband found on them could not be used in evidence. Individual police officers would still have to worry about being sued for damages; but if damages were considered a completely adequate deterrent to violations of the Fourth Amendment, the exclusionary rule would have been abandoned long ago.

"[If] police conduct an illegal search that does no harm because the same evidence would have been obtained lawfully, there is no need to punish them; but this assumes that the evidence would indeed have been obtained *lawfully*, for only then is there is no harmful illegality. Consistent with this analysis, the canonical statements of the independent-source and ineveitable-discovery doctrines uniformly refer to a 'lawful' independent source and to 'lawful' inevitable discovery. *Murray v. United States*, *Nix v. Williams* * * *.

"These cases are not in conflict with [cases barring] a defendant from challenging evidence seized in violation of someone else's rights. The evidence challenged here *was* seized in violation of the defendant's rights—it was taken from underneath Johnson's seat and from the trunk. The government's argument is that the violation is cancelled by the fact that the evidence would have been discovered as a consequence of the illegal search of the passengers, to which he could not object. The fallacious character of the argument is demonstrated by the fact that if the passengers tried to exclude the evidence in their own cases, they would be met by the identical argument: the evidence would have been discovered in an illegal search (that of Johnson) to which they cannot object. In the ordinary case in which a defendant would like to get mileage from challenging the illegal search of a third party, that party, at least, can challenge the search. But the government's position is that because there were two illegal searches in this case no one can invoke the exclusionary rule against the use of the evidence obtained by the searches. In other words, the more illegal searches there are, the narrower is the scope of application of the exclusionary rule. We cannot see what sense that makes.

"Yet the only similar case that we have found, *United States v. Scott*, 270 F.3d 30 (1st Cir.2001), disagrees that the evidence must be suppressed in such a case. [*Scott*] ruled that the illegality of the independent source should be only a relevant and not a dispositive factor. The ultimate question, the court held, should be whether the application of the independent-source rule in the particular circumstances of the case would give the police an incentive in future such cases to commit similar illegal acts; and the court decided that it would not. The illegal independent source had been a statement given by a suspect who had not been read the *Miranda* warnings, and the court emphasized that the question whether he was entitled to those warnings was close and that the officer was trying to get evidence against the person he was questioning and had no thought that the questioning might provide an independent source of the evidence that had been obtained form the defendant illegally.

"The First Circuit's analysis is * * * inconsistent with the logic of the independent-source/inevitable-discovery doctrine. That doctrine * * * merely recognizes that if there is a lawful basis for the seizure of some evidence, the fact that the seizure was also based on illegal acts need not trigger punishment, because the acts did no harm (no harm so far as obtaining the evidence was concerned—there might be collateral damage, remediable by [civil suits]). There is a need for punishment when the only basis for the seizure of the evidence is a series of illegal acts. The assumption that the independent source must be 'lawful' [is] part of the essential logic of the rule and of its origins in fundamental principles of tort law."[a]

C. Is a Confession Obtained in Violation of the *Miranda* Rules a "Poisonous Tree"?

[See UNITED STATES v. PATANE, p. 703; MISSOURI v. SEIBERT, p. 707; and the Notes and Questions following these cases.]

SECTION 3. USE OF ILLEGALLY OBTAINED EVIDENCE FOR IMPEACHMENT PURPOSES

A. The Expansion of a Once-Narrow Exception

1. In *Walder v. United States,* 347 U.S. 62 (1954), defendant, charged with various illegal narcotics transactions, asserted early on his direct examination that he had never possessed any narcotics or sold or given any narcotics to anyone in his life. The Court held, per Frankfurter, J., that this assertion "opened the door," for purposes of attacking the defendant's credibility, to evidence of heroin seized from the defendant's home, in his presence, in an earlier, unrelated case. "Of his own accord," observed the Court, "the defendant went beyond a mere denial of complicity in the crimes of which he was charged and made the sweeping claim that he had never dealt in or possessed any narcotics. [A defendant] must be free to deny all the elements of the case against him without thereby giving leave to the Government to introduce by way of rebuttal evidence illegally secured by it, and thereby not available for its case in chief. Beyond that, however, there is hardly justification for letting the defendant affirmatively resort to perjurious testimony in reliance on the Government's disability to challenge his credibility."

The instant situation, emphasized the *Walder* Court, is to be "sharply contrasted" with that presented by *Agnello v. United States,* 269 U.S. 20 (1925). There, the government sought to "smuggle in" the tainted evidence on cross-examination by asking the defendant whether he had ever seen narcotics before, and eliciting the expected denial. In *Agnello,* the defendant "did nothing" to waive his constitutional protection or to justify cross-examination with respect to the illegally seized evidence.

2. HARRIS v. NEW YORK, 401 U.S. 222 (1971), often called the first blow the Burger Court struck *Miranda,* arose as follows: Petitioner, charged with selling heroin to an undercover officer, took the stand in his own defense. He admitted knowing the officer, but denied making a sale of heroin. Statements made by petitioner immediately following his arrest which partially contradicted his direct trial testimony were used to impeach his credibility. According to the Court, petitioner made no claim that the statements were coerced or involuntary,[b] but they were preceded by defective *Miranda* warnings, and thus inadmissible to

a. Because the *Johnson* case created an intercircuit conflict, it was circulated to the full court in advance of publication. No judge voted to hear the case en banc.

b. According to Alan Dershowitz & John Hart Ely, *Harris v. New York: Some Anxious Observations on the Candor and Logic of the Emerging Nixon Majority,* 80 Yale L.J. 1198, 1201 (1971), "the record is clear" that he did.

establish the prosecution's case in chief. A 5–4 majority, per BURGER, C.J., held that under the circumstances "petitioner's credibility was appropriately impeached by use of his earlier conflicting statements."

The Court noted that "[s]ome comments in the *Miranda* opinion can indeed be read as indicating a bar to use of [a statement obtained in violation of *Miranda*] for any purpose," but dismissed this discussion as "not at all necessary to the Court's holding" and not "controlling."[c] The Court noted, but also seemed untroubled by the fact, "that Walder was impeached as to collateral matters included in his direct examination, whereas petitioner here was impeached as to testimony bearing more directly on the crimes charged." The Court next observed:

"The impeachment process here undoubtedly provided valuable aid to the jury in assessing petitioner's credibility, and the benefits of this process should not be lost [because] of the speculative possibility that impermissible police conduct will be encouraged thereby. Assuming that the exclusionary rule has a deterrent effect * * * sufficient deterrence flows when the evidence in question is made unavailable to the prosecution in its case in chief.

"[The privilege to testify in one's defense] cannot be construed to include the right to commit perjury. [The] prosecution here did no more than utilize the traditional truth-testing devices of the adversary process. [The] shield provided by *Miranda* cannot be perverted into a license to use perjury by way of a defense, free from the risk of confrontation with prior inconsistent utterances."

Dissenting Justice BRENNAN, joined by Douglas and Marshall, JJ., criticized the majority for disregarding language in *Miranda* and for selectively quoting from *Walder*. The dissent emphasized that "*Walder* was not a case where tainted evidence was used to impeach an accused's direct testimony on matters directly related to the case against him," but only such testimony "on matters *collateral* to the crime charged." Continued the dissent:

"While *Walder* did not identify the constitutional specifics that guarantee 'a defendant the fullest opportunity to meet the accusation against him [and] permit him to be free to deny all the elements of the case against him,' in my view *Miranda* identified the Fifth Amendment's privilege against self-incrimination as one of those specifics. [It] is fulfilled only when an accused is guaranteed the right 'to remain silent unless he chooses to speak in the *unfettered* exercise of his own will' (emphasis added). The choice of whether to testify in one's own defense must therefore be 'unfettered' * * *. [But] the accused is denied an 'unfettered' choice when the decision whether to take the stand is burdened by the risk that an illegally obtained prior statement may be introduced to impeach his direct testimony denying complicity in the crime charged against him."[d]

3. *The Fourth Amendment vs. the Fifth.* Should the Court have considered the significance of *Miranda's* Fifth Amendment underpinning before applying (or extending) the Fourth Amendment *Walder* case to *Harris?* Is impeachment by means of evidence obtained in violation of the Fourth Amendment more defensible than such use of evidence obtained in violation of the Self–Incrimination Clause of the Fifth because the Fourth's "exclusionary rule" is a court-created device designed to deter the police and as the link between police illegality

c. But consider Geoffrey Stone, *The Miranda Doctrine in the Burger Court,* 1977 Sup. Ct.Rev. 99, 107–08: "Rightly or wrongly, *Miranda* was deliberately structured to canvass a wide range of problems, many of which were not directly raised by the cases before the Court. This approach was thought necessary in order to 'give concrete constitutional guidelines for law enforcement agencies and courts to follow.' Thus, a technical reading of *Miranda,* such as that employed in *Harris,* would enable the Court to label many critical aspects of the decision mere dictum and therefore not 'controlling.' "

d. Black, J., also dissented, without opinion.

and subsequent evidence becomes more attenuated it becomes less likely that exclusion would affect future police conduct? On the other hand, is the essence of the constitutional wrong under the Fifth the *use* against him of a defendant's compelled testimony, not the mere act of compelling him to speak (otherwise no immunity statute would be constitutional)? Doesn't the Self–Incrimination Clause by its own terms seem to prohibit the use of statements obtained in violation of its command? See Dershowitz & Ely, fn. a supra, at 1214–15; Stone, fn. b supra, at 110–111.

4. The Court went a step beyond *Harris* in *Oregon v. Hass,* 420 U.S. 714 (1975). In *Hass,* after being advised of his rights, the defendant *asserted* them—he asked for a lawyer. But the police refused to honor his request and continued to question him. A 6–2 majority, per Blackmun, J., ruled that here, too, the resulting statements could be used for impeachment purposes. "One might concede," wrote the Court, "that when proper *Miranda* warnings have been given, and the officer then continues his interrogation after the suspect asks for an attorney, the officer may be said to have little to lose and perhaps something to gain by way of possibly uncovering impeachment material. This speculative possibility, however, is even greater where the warnings are defective and the defect is not known to the officers. In any event, the balance was struck in *Harris,* and we are not disposed to change it now."

But wasn't a *different* balance struck in *Hass?* Dissenting Justice Brennan, joined by Marshall, J., thought so: "Even after *Harris,* police had some incentive for following *Miranda* by warning an accused of his [rights]. If the warnings were given, the accused might still make a statement which could be used in the prosecution's case-in-chief. Under today's holding, however, once the warnings are given, police have almost no incentive for following *Miranda's* requirement that '[i]f the individual states that he wants an attorney, the interrogation must cease until an attorney is present.' If the requirement is followed there will almost surely be no statement since the attorney will advise the accused to remain silent. If, however, the requirement is disobeyed, the police may obtain a statement which can be used for impeachment if the accused has the temerity to testify in his own defense."

5. ***Does the Harris–Hass exception apply even when a police officer deliberately fails to honor a suspect's request for counsel for the very purpose of obtaining evidence for impeachment purposes? Even when an officer fails to honor a suspect's request for counsel pursuant to a police department policy to violate Miranda in order to obtain evidence for impeachment purposes?*** In PEOPLE v. PEEVY, 953 P.2d 1212 (1998), the California Supreme Court, per GEORGE, J., answered the first question in the affirmative. However, it did not reach the second question because the issue had not been timely raised below. As for the first question, the court rejected the defendant's argument that the *Harris-Hass* rule was based upon the assumption that a *purposeful or deliberate* violation of *Miranda* and *Edwards* would not occur:

"Language in *Hass* and subsequent cases [demonstrates the U.S. Supreme Court's belief] that the *Harris* rule sufficiently deters individual police misconduct, *whether the misconduct occurred as the result of negligence or design.* In *Hass,* there is some indication that the violation of the suspect's rights was deliberate. [In] *Michigan v. Harvey* [p. 930], it is even more apparent that the interrogating police officer's failure to honor the defendant's Sixth Amendment right to counsel was deliberate.

"[Moreover,] it would be anomalous to hold that the applicability of the *Harris* rule depends upon the subjective intent of the interrogating police officer, when other applications of the *Miranda* rule generally do not turn upon the individual officer's state of mind, but rather upon the accused's perception of his or her circumstances.[a] [Evidence] of deliberation on the part of the police and—as apparent in this case—of a purpose to violate the suspect's rights in order to secure evidence [may] call into question the accuracy of the high court's conclusion in *Harris* that police misconduct will be deterred adequately by excluding improperly obtained evidence from the prosecution's case-in-chief, but such evidence does not render the *Harris* rule inapplicable."

Although concurring Justice MOSK concurred in the result, he made clear his belief that if a statement secured in violation of a suspect's right to counsel had been obtained by a member of a law enforcement agency pursuant to that agency's policy to violate *Miranda*[b] the statement could not be used for impeachment purposes:

"Any policy of a law enforcement agency to obtain statements from criminal suspects in violation of *Miranda* would strike through the suspect's 'prophylactic' rights towards his substantive Fifth Amendment privilege against self-incrimination itself. [Moreover,] any policy of a law enforcement agency to obtain statements from criminal suspects in violation of *Miranda* would necessarily constitute proof that 'sufficient deterrence' of [police misconduct] does not, in fact, 'flow from exclusion of such statements from the prosecution's case-in-chief' [quoting from *Harris*]. It would rather present itself as an actual fact.

"[It] may indeed be true, as stated in *Michigan v. Tucker*, that '[where] official action [is] pursued in complete good faith [the] deterrence rationale loses much of its force.' But if so, it must also be true that, where official action is pursued in utter bad faith, as in accordance with the type of policy in question, the deterrence rationale retains its force without any diminution whatsoever."[c]

6. In UNITED STATES v. HAVENS, 446 U.S. 620 (1980), what had "started out in *Walder* as a narrow and reasonable exception" to the exclusionary rule took on "awesome proportions," CRIMPROC § 9.6(a). On direct examination, defendant denied being involved with his codefendant in the transportation of cocaine and on cross-examination denied being involved in sewing a pocket (in which drugs were found) into his codefendant's clothing or having in his own suitcase cloth from which the swatch was cut to make the pocket. Defendant's testimony was impeached by admitting the illegally seized cloth, but the Fifth Circuit reversed, maintaining that illegally seized evidence could be used for impeachment only if it contradicts a defendant's direct testimony. A 5–4 majority, per WHITE, J., disagreed:

"[The] policies of the exclusionary rule no more bar impeachment here than they did in *Walder, Harris,* and *Hass.* [The] incremental furthering of [the ends of the exclusionary rules] by forbidding impeachment of the defendant who testifies was deemed insufficient to permit or require that false testimony go unchallenged, with the resulting impairment of the integrity of the fact-finding goals of the criminal trial. We reaffirm this assessment of the competing interests, and hold that a defendant's statements made in response to proper cross-examination reasonably suggested by the defendant's direct examination are subject to other-

a. Compare the dissenting opinion in *Missouri v. Seibert*, p. 707. Consider, too, Note 4 following *Seibert*.

b. Recent litigation has uncovered California training materials teaching police officers that it is permissible to continue to question suspects who have invoked their right to counsel or their right to remain silent in order to obtain statements that may be used for impeachment purposes or to discover other evidence. The police commonly refer to this technique as questioning "outside *Miranda*." See Charles D. Weisselberg, *Saving Miranda*, 84 Cornell L.Rev. 109, 132–62 (1998). For more extensive discussion of questioning "outside *Miranda*," see pp. 934–36.

c. Compare the opinion of the Court and the concurring opinions by Breyer and Kennedy, JJ., in *Missouri v. Seibert*. Consider, too, Note 4 following *Seibert*.

wise proper impeachment by the government, albeit by evidence that has been illegally obtained."

Dissenting Justice BRENNAN, joined by Stewart, Marshall and Stevens, JJ., on this point, protested: "The identical issue was confronted in *Agnello,* which determined—contrary to the instant decision—that it was constitutionally impermissible to admit evidence obtained in violation of the Fourth Amendment to rebut a defendant's response to a matter first raised during the Government's cross-examination. [The] exclusionary rule exception established by *Harris* and *Hass* may be fairly easily cabined by defense counsel's unwillingness to forego certain areas of questioning. But [today's holding] passes control of the exception to the Government, since the prosecutor can lay the predicate for admitting otherwise suppressible evidence with his own questioning."

Justice Brennan (joined only by Marshall, J., on this point) then voiced "a more fundamental difference with the Court's holding here, which culminates the approach taken in *Harris* and *Hass*":

"[T]he Court has undertaken to strike a 'balance' between the 'policies' it finds in the Bill of Rights and the 'competing interest' in accurate trial determinations. This balancing effort is completely freewheeling. Far from applying criteria intrinsic to the Fourth and Fifth Amendments, the Court resolves succeeding cases simply by declaring that so much exclusion is enough to deter police misconduct. That hardly conforms to the disciplined analytical method described as 'legal reasoning,' through which judges endeavor to formulate or derive principles of decision that can be applied consistently and predictably.[a] [More] disturbingly, by treating Fourth and Fifth Amendment privileges as mere incentive schemes, the Court denigrates their unique status as *constitutional* protections."

7. The Court refuses to extend the impeachment exception to defense witnesses other than the defendant. In JAMES v. ILLINOIS, 493 U.S. 307 (1990), the Court halted nearly forty years of the impeachment exception's expansion. A 5–4 majority, per BRENNAN, J., refused to expand the "impeachment exception" to the exclusionary rule to permit the prosecution to impeach the testimony of *all* defense witnesses with illegally obtained evidence. According to the majority, expanding the impeachment exception to such an extent "would not further the truthseeking value with equal force but would appreciably undermine the deterrent effect of the exclusionary rule."

The case arose as follows: A day after a murder occurred, the police took James, a suspect, into custody. He was found at his mother's beauty salon sitting under a hair dryer; when he emerged, his hair was black and curly. When the police questioned James about his prior hair color, he told them it had been reddish-brown, long, and combed straight back. When questioned later at the police station, James stated that he had his hair dyed black and curled at the beauty parlor in order to change his appearance. Because the police lacked probable cause for James' arrest, both statements regarding his hair were suppressed.

At the trial, five eye witnesses testified that the person responsible for the murder had long, "reddish" hair, worn in a slicked-back style and that they had seen James several weeks earlier, at which time he had the aforementioned hair color and style. James did not testify in his own defense. He called as a witness Jewel Henderson, a family friend. She testified that on the day of the shooting James' hair had been black. The state then impeached Henderson's testimony by

a. Support for this criticism may be found in James Kainen, *The Impeachment Exception to the Exclusionary Rules: Policies, Principles and Politics,* 44 Stan.L.Rev. 1301 (1992).

reporting James' prior admissions that he had reddish hair at the time of the shooting and had dyed and curled his hair the next day in order to change his appearance. James ultimately was convicted of murder. The Illinois Supreme Court concluded, that, in order to deter "perjury by proxy," the impeachment exception ought to allow the state to impeach the testimony of defense witnesses other than the defendant himself. The U.S. Supreme Court reversed:

"Expanding the class of impeachable witnesses from the defendant alone to all defense witnesses would create different incentives affecting the behavior of both defendants and law enforcement officers. As a result, this expansion would not promote the truthseeking function to the same extent as did creation of the original exception, and yet it would significantly undermine the deterrent effect of the general exclusionary rule. Hence, we believe that this proposed expansion would frustrate rather than further the purposes underlying the exclusionary rule.

"The previously recognized exception penalizes defendants for committing perjury by allowing the prosecution to expose their perjury through impeachment using illegally obtained evidence. [But] the exception leaves defendants free to testify truthfully on their own behalf; they can offer probative and exculpatory evidence to the jury without opening the door to impeachment by carefully avoiding any statements that directly contradict the suppressed evidence. The exception thus generally discourages perjured testimony without discouraging truthful testimony.

"In contrast, expanding the impeachment exception to encompass the testimony of all defense witnesses would not have the same beneficial effects. First, the mere threat of a subsequent criminal prosecution for perjury is far more likely to deter a witness from intentionally lying on a defendant's behalf than to deter a defendant, already facing conviction for the underlying offense, from lying on his own behalf. Hence the Illinois Supreme Court's underlying premise that a defendant frustrated by our previous impeachment exception can easily find a witness to engage in 'perjury by proxy' is suspect.

"More significantly, expanding the impeachment exception to encompass the testimony of all defense witnesses likely would chill some defendants from presenting their best defense—and sometimes any defense at all—through the testimony of others. Whenever police obtained evidence illegally, defendants would have to assess prior to trial the likelihood that the evidence would be admitted to impeach the otherwise favorable testimony of any witness they call. Defendants might reasonably fear that one or more of their witnesses, in a position to offer truthful and favorable testimony, would also make some statement in sufficient tension with the tainted evidence to allow the prosecutor to introduce that evidence for impeachment. [As] a result, an expanded impeachment exception likely would chill some defendants from calling witnesses who would otherwise offer probative evidence.[6]

"This realization alters the balance of values underlying the current impeachment exception governing defendants' testimony. * * * Given the potential chill created by expanding the impeachment exception, the conceded gains to the truthseeking process from discouraging or disclosing perjured testimony would be offset to some extent by the concomitant loss of probative witness testimony.

6. * * * [The] dissent embraces the Illinois Supreme Court's suggestion that prosecutors could be allowed to impeach witnesses only when their testimony is in "direct conflict" with the illegally seized evidence. [But] the result of [an] inquiry distinguishing between "direct" and "indirect" evidentiary conflicts is far from predictable. [The] uncertainty whether a court might find a witness' testimony to pose a "direct" conflict and therefore trigger the impeachment exception likely will chill defendant's presentation of potential witnesses in many cases.

Thus, the truthseeking rationale supporting the impeachment of defendants in *Walder* and its progeny does not apply to other witnesses with equal force.

"Moreover, the proposed expansion of the current impeachment exception would significantly weaken the exclusionary rule's deterrent effect on police misconduct. This Court has characterized as a mere 'speculative possibility,' *Harris v. New York,* the likelihood that permitting prosecutors to impeach defendants with illegally obtained evidence would encourage police misconduct. Law enforcement officers will think it unlikely that the defendant will first decide to testify at trial and will also open the door inadvertently to admission of any illegally obtained evidence. Hence, the officers' incentive to acquire evidence through illegal means is quite weak.

"In contrast, expanding the impeachment exception to *all* defense witnesses would significantly enhance the expected value to the prosecution of illegally obtained evidence. First, this expansion would vastly increase the number of occasions on which such evidence could be used. Defense witnesses easily outnumber testifying defendants, both because many defendants do not testify themselves and because many if not most defendants call multiple witnesses on their behalf. Moreover, due to the chilling effect identified above, illegally obtained evidence holds even greater value to the prosecution for each individual witness than for each defendant. The prosecutor's access to impeachment evidence would not just deter perjury; it would also deter defendants from calling witnesses in the first place, thereby keeping from the jury much probative exculpatory evidence. For both of these reasons, police officers and their superiors would recognize that obtaining evidence through illegal means stacks the deck heavily in the prosecution's favor. It is thus far more than a 'speculative possibility' that police misconduct will be encouraged by permitting such use of illegally obtained evidence.

"The United States argues that this result is constitutionally acceptable because excluding illegally obtained evidence solely from the prosecution's case in chief would still provide a quantum of deterrence sufficient to protect the privacy interests underlying the exclusionary rule. We disagree. [Much] if not most of the time, police officers confront opportunities to obtain evidence illegally after they have already legally obtained (or know that they have other means of legally obtaining) sufficient evidence to sustain a prima facie case. In these situations, a rule requiring exclusion of illegally obtained evidence from only the government's case in chief would leave officers with little to lose and much to gain by overstepping constitutional limits on evidence gathering. Narrowing the exclusionary rule in this manner, therefore, would significantly undermine the rule's ability 'to compel respect for the constitutional guaranty in the only effectively available way—by removing the incentive to disregard it.' So long as we are committed to protecting the people from the disregard of their constitutional rights during the course of criminal investigations, inadmissibility of illegally obtained evidence must remain the rule, not the exception."[a]

Dissenting Justice KENNEDY, joined by Rehnquist, C.J., and O'Connor and Scalia, JJ., maintained that the majority had given the exclusionary rule excessive protection but had afforded the truth-seeking function of the criminal trial inadequate weight:

"[The] line drawn by today's opinion grants the defense side in a criminal case broad immunity to introduce whatever false testimony it can produce from the mouth of a friendly witness. [A] more cautious course is available, one that retains Fourth Amendment protections and yet safeguards the truth-seeking function of the criminal trial.

a. Stevens, J., who joined the opinion of the Court, also wrote a separate opinion.

"[The] interest in protecting the truth-seeking function of the criminal trial is every bit as strong in this case as in our earlier cases that allowed rebuttal with evidence that was inadmissible as part of the prosecution's case in chief. [To] deprive the jurors of knowledge that statements of the defendant himself revealed the witness' testimony to be false would result in a decision by triers of fact who were not just kept in the dark as to excluded evidence, but positively misled. The potential for harm to the truth-seeking process resulting from the majority's new rule in fact will be greater than if the defendant himself had testified. It is natural for jurors to be skeptical of self-serving testimony by the defendant. Testimony by a witness said to be independent has the greater potential to deceive. And if a defense witness can present false testimony with impunity, the jurors may find the rest of the prosecution's case suspect, for ineffective and artificial cross-examination will be viewed as a real weakness in the State's case. Jurors will assume that if the prosecution had any proof the statement was false, it would make the proof known. The majority does more than deprive the prosecution of evidence. The State must also suffer the introduction of false testimony and appear to bolster the falsehood by its own silence.

"[Where] the jury is misled by false testimony, otherwise subject to flat contradiction by evidence illegally seized, the protection of the exclusionary rule is 'perverted into a license to use perjury by way of a defense, free from the risk of confrontation with prior inconsistent utterances.' *Havens.* The perversion is the same where the perjury is by proxy."

Notes and Questions

(a) *The "Pinocchio defense witness" (a defense witness other than the defendant who lies at trial to benefit the defendant).* Consider Note, 1990 U.Ill.L.F. 375, 473: "Although Pinocchio is deterred from lying by the threat of perjury prosecution, cases abound where defense witnesses nevertheless commit perjury. [Meanwhile, the defendant, Stromboli (in the Pinocchio story the puppeteer who caused Pinocchio to become a liar)], benefits from the lies by receiving an acquittal. To further the truthfinding function of the criminal justice system, the goal of judicial integrity, and the policy against perjury, Stromboli also must be deterred from resorting to Pinocchio's perjurious testimony. [If] perjurious testimony is an affront to the legal system, it does not matter whether the perjury comes from the defendant's own lips or the lips of the Pinocchio defense witness."

(b) *The dissent's selective assumptions.* The *James* dissent, notes James Spira, *James v. Illinois: A Halt to the Expansion of the Impeachment Exception,* 15 So.Ill.U.L.J. 27, 51 (1990), "is willing to assume that a defense witness, unschooled and unfamiliar with the law, will be well versed in the quantum of proof necessary for a perjury conviction, but is unwilling to assume that police, who are in and out of court constantly, will not realize that the discovery of illegally obtained evidence will aid a conviction in light of an expanded impeachment exception."

(c) *Why should the impeachment of defense witnesses be restricted more severely than impeachment of defendants?* Consider James Kainen, *The Impeachment Exception to the Exclusionary Rules: Policies, Principles, and Politics,* 44 Stan.L.Rev. 1301, 1322–23 (1992):

"Although he argued that limitations on the impeachment of defense witnesses were necessary to confine the incentive to gather proof illegally to an acceptable level, Justice Kennedy was unable to explain why identical restrictions should not also be applied to the impeachment of defendants. Alternatively, if the impeachment of defendants should not be restricted, then such restrictions are similarly unnecessary to protect defense witnesses. As a result, Justice Kennedy could not demonstrate that extending the exception as he proposed would effect net gains, just as the majority could not demonstrate that its result would effect net losses when both truth-seeking and deterrence costs were tallied. * * *

"Justice Kennedy's truth-seeking analysis contended that contradiction of defense witness testimony is particularly important because juries are more likely to believe such testimony. [If so,] witness testimony should be more readily impeached than that of defendants."

(d) *Are the impeachment exception cases based on a faulty premise?* Do *James* and other cases dealing with the impeachment exception rest on the premise that it is possible to accommodate both rules of evidence and principles of constitutional criminal procedure within a neutral framework? Is this premise sound? Are the contradictory values reflected in constitutional criminal procedure principles and evidentiary concepts susceptible to neutral accommodation? Should any analysis of the scope of the exclusionary rules be recast exclusively as an issue of constitutional procedure, rather than as a compromise between those rules and the rules of evidence? See Kainen, supra, at 1304–05, 1326–27, 1362–72.

B. What Kinds of Constitutional or Other Violations Are Encompassed Within the Impeachment Exception?

1. *New Jersey v. Portash,* 440 U.S. 450 (1979) held, per Stewart, J. that testimony given by a person in response to a grant of legislative immunity could not be used to impeach him at his subsequent trial for extortion and misconduct in office. "Central to the decisions" in *Harris* and *Hass,* emphasized the Court, was the fact that the defendant made no claim that the statements were coerced. But testimony before a grand jury in response to a grant of use immunity "is the essence of coerced testimony." Balancing of interests was thought to be necessary in *Harris* and *Hass* "when the attempt to deter unlawful police conduct collided with the need to prevent perjury. Here, by contrast, we deal with the constitutional privilege against compulsory self-incrimination in its most pristine form. Balancing, therefore, is not simply unnecessary. It is impermissible."

2. In *Mincey v. Arizona* (1978), p. 557, the Court also distinguished *Harris* and *Hass* and made clear that the use of an "involuntary" or "coerced" statement even for impeachment purposes would constitute "a denial of due process of law." But the Court's discussion seemed to overlook the possibility that an "involuntary" statement may be trustworthy in a particular case.

3. ***Use of statements obtained in violation of the Sixth Amendment Jackson rule.*** In MICHIGAN v. HARVEY, 494 U.S. 344 (1990), a 5–4 majority, per REHNQUIST, C.J., held that statements obtained in violation of the rule established in *Michigan v. Jackson* (p. 658), may be used to impeach a defendant's false or inconsistent testimony:

"*Michigan v. Jackson* is based on the Sixth Amendment, but its roots lie in this Court's decisions in *Miranda* and succeeding cases. [*Edwards*] added a second layer of protection [to] *Miranda,* [establishing a] prophylactic rule designed to prevent police from badgering a defendant into waiving his previously asserted *Miranda* rights.

"*Jackson* simply superimposed the Fifth Amendment analysis of *Edwards* onto the Sixth Amendment. Reasoning that 'the Sixth Amendment right to counsel at a postarraignment interrogation requires at least as much protection as the Fifth Amendment right to counsel at any custodial interrogation,' [the *Jackson* Court] concluded that the *Edwards* protections should apply when a suspect charged with a crime requests counsel outside the context of interrogation. This rule, like *Edwards,* is based on the supposition that suspects who assert their right to counsel are unlikely to waive that right voluntarily in subsequent interrogations.

"We have already decided [that] statements taken in violation [of] the prophylactic *Miranda* rules [are] admissible to impeach conflicting testimony by the defendant. *Harris v. New York*; *Oregon v. Hass.* [There] is no reason for a different result in a *Jackson* case, where the prophylactic rule is designed to ensure voluntary, knowing, and intelligent waivers of the Sixth Amendment right to counsel rather than the Fifth Amendment privilege against self-incrimination or 'right to counsel.' [We] have never prevented use by the prosecution of relevant voluntary statements by a defendant, particularly when the violations alleged by a defendant relate only to procedural safeguards that are 'not themselves rights protected by the Constitution.' [In] such cases, we have decided that the 'search for truth in a criminal case' outweighs the 'speculative possibility' that exclusion of evidence might deter future violations of rules not compelled directly by the Constitution in the first place. *Hass.* [The *Hass* case] was decided 15 years ago, and no new information has come to our attention which should lead us to think otherwise now."

Dissenting Justice STEVENS (author of the Court's opinion in *Jackson*), joined by Brennan, Marshall and Blackmun, JJ., maintained that the Court had made it clear that "the constitutional rule recognized in *Jackson* is based on the Sixth Amendment interest in preserving 'the integrity of an accused's choice to communicate with police only through counsel,' "and that "the Court should acknowledge as much and hold that the Sixth Amendment is violated when the fruits of the State's impermissible encounter with the represented defendant are used for impeachment just as it is when the fruits are used in the prosecutor's case in chief":

"[Unlike the situation when evidence is seized in violation of the Fourth Amendment or a statement is obtained in violation of *Miranda,* the] exclusion of statements made by a represented and indicted defendant outside the presence of counsel follows not as a remedy for a violation that has preceded trial but as a necessary incident of the constitutional right itself.[g] '[T]he Sixth Amendment right to counsel exists, and is needed, in order to protect the fundamental right to a fair trial.' It is not implicated, as a general matter, in the absence of some effect of the challenged conduct on the trial process itself. It is thus the use of the evidence for trial, not the method of its collection prior to trial, that is the gravamen of the Sixth Amendment claim."

4. *Use of statements obtained in violation of the Massiah right to counsel.* In *Harvey* the Court left open the question whether statements obtained in violation of *Massiah*—sometimes called the "core" Sixth Amendment protection, other times called the "pure" right to counsel—may be used to impeach a defendant. When the Court does address the issue, how should it decide it? How significant is it that unlike the *Jackson* rule, which the Court characterized as "prophylactic" in nature because based on *Edwards v. Arizona,* the *Massiah* doctrine is a constitutional rule (or is it)? How significant is it that the great bulk of statements obtained in violation of *Massiah* are voluntary statements? How

g. As Professor Schulhofer has commented: "[T]he *Massiah* 'exclusionary rule' is not merely a prophylactic device; it is not designed to reduce the *risk* of actual constitutional violations and is not intended to deter any pretrial behavior whatsoever. Rather, *Massiah* explicitly permits government efforts to obtain information from an indicted suspect, so long as that information is not used 'as evidence against *him* at his trial.' The failure to exclude evidence, therefore, cannot be considered *collateral* to some more fundamental violation. Instead, it is the admission at trial that in itself denies the constitutional right." Stephen Schulhofer, *Confessions and the Court,* 79 Mich.L.Rev. 865, 889 (1981). * * *

significant is it that in *Patterson v. Illinois* (p. 740), the Court rejected the view that the *Massiah* right is "superior" to or "greater" than the *Miranda* right?

C. Use of Defendant's Prior Silence for Impeachment Purposes

1. After being arrested for selling marijuana to an informant, defendants were given the *Miranda* warnings and chose to remain silent. At trial, each defendant claimed that he had been "framed" by narcotics agents. In an effort to undercut their testimony, the prosecution was allowed to ask each defendant why he had not told this story to the arresting officer. In *Doyle v. Ohio,* 426 U.S. 610 (1976), a 6–3 majority, per Powell, J., held such use of a defendant's post-arrest silence, after receiving the *Miranda* warnings, impermissible. Not only is "every post-arrest silence * * * insolubly ambiguous because of what the State is required to advise the person arrested," but use of the silence to impeach would be "fundamentally unfair" given the fact that the *Miranda* warnings contain the "implicit" "assurance" that "silence will carry no penalty."[a] But *Doyle* has been distinguished in three subsequent impeachment cases.

2. ***Impeachment by prior inconsistent statements after receiving Miranda warnings.*** After being arrested while driving a stolen car and given the *Miranda* warnings, defendant agreed to talk to the police. But he gave a different version of the auto theft than he subsequently did when he testified in his own defense. On cross-examination, he was asked why he gave a different story at the time of his arrest. *Anderson v. Charles,* 447 U.S. 404 (1980) (per curiam), had little difficulty in permitting such cross-examination: "[*Doyle*] does not apply to cross-examination that merely inquires into prior inconsistent statements. Such questioning makes no unfair use of silence, because a defendant who voluntarily speaks after receiving *Miranda* warnings has not been induced to remain silent."

3. ***Use of defendant's prearrest silence for impeachment purposes.*** In *Jenkins v. Anderson,* 447 U.S. 231 (1980), where at his murder trial petitioner claimed self-defense, the prosecutor was allowed to question him about the fact that he had not surrendered to the authorities until two weeks after the killing. In closing argument, the prosecutor again referred to petitioner's prearrest silence, noting that he had "waited" at least two weeks before "reporting" the stabbing to anyone, suggesting that he would have spoken out if he had truly killed in self-defense. The Court, per Powell, J., held (1), relying heavily on *Raffel v. United States,* 271 U.S. 494 (1926), that the Self–Incrimination Clause is not violated by the use of prearrest silence to impeach a defendant's credibility;[a] and (2) *Doyle* presents no obstacle for "no governmental action induced petitioner to remain silent before arrest. The failure to speak occurred before petitioner was taken into custody and given *Miranda* warnings."[b]

a. But cf. *South Dakota v. Neville* (1983) (also discussed at p. 616, fn. a), upholding a statute permitting a person suspected of driving while intoxicated to refuse to submit to a blood-alcohol test, but authorizing revocation of the driver's license of a person so refusing the test and also allowing such refusal to be used against him at trial. Although the defendant in *Neville* had not been told of the latter possibility, the Court thought it "unrealistic to say that the warnings given here implicitly assure a suspect that no consequences other than those mentioned will occur. Importantly, the warning that he could lose his driver's license made it clear that refusing the test was not a 'safe harbor' free of adverse consequences."

a. For strong criticism of this portion of the opinion, see Stephen A. Saltzburg, *Foreword: The Flow and Ebb of Constitutional Criminal Procedure in the Warren and Burger Courts,* 69 Geo. L.J. 151, 204–05 (1980).

b. But see Craig M. Bradley, *Havens, Jenkins, and Salvucci, and the Defendant's "Right" to Testify,* 18 Am.Crim.L.Rev. 419, 434–35 (1981), maintaining that the silence in *Jenkins* was just as equivocal as that in *Doyle* for "an individual's reluctance to hand himself over to the police and admit a stabbing, in self-defense or otherwise," is not probative of guilt.

Dissenting Justice Marshall, joined by Brennan, J., contended that the Court's holding "has three patent—and in my view, fatal—defects": (1) Considering the various possible explanations for silence (e.g., Jenkins' story would have implicated him in the homicide), "the mere fact of prearrest silence is so unlikely to be probative of the falsity of the defendant's trial strategy that its use for impeachment is contrary to [due process]." (2) "[T]he drawing of an adverse inference from the failure to volunteer incriminating statements impermissibly infringes the privilege against self-incrimination." (3) "[T]he availability of the inference for impeachment purposes impermissibly burdens the decision to exercise the constitutional right to testify in one's own defense."

4. *Use of defendant's post-arrest silence for impeachment purposes.* When arrested, Weir, a murder suspect, said nothing, but the "significant difference" between this case and *Doyle* is that Weir did not receive any *Miranda* warnings during the period in which he remained silent immediately after his arrest. When Weir testified at his trial that he had acted in self-defense, the prosecutor cross-examined him as to why, when arrested, he had not offered this exculpatory explanation. *Fletcher v. Weir,* 455 U.S. 603 (1982) (per curiam), held that "in the absence of the sort of affirmative assurances embodied in the *Miranda* warnings" a state may permit cross-examination about post-arrest silence when a defendant chooses to take the stand. The Court rejected the argument that an arrest, by itself, is "governmental action which implicitly induces a defendant to remain silent," deeming such "broadening of *Doyle* * * * unsupported by the reasoning of that case and contrary to our post-*Doyle* decisions."

Notes and Questions

(a) Suppose, when arrested, Weir had said, "I believe I have a perfectly valid defense, but I don't think I should talk to you until I first have a chance to talk to my lawyer." Could that statement and/or the subsequent post-arrest silence be used for impeachment purposes?

(b) Suppose, when being driven to the station house, a suspect asks the arresting officer, "Do I have a right to remain silent?" Or, "Do I have a right to discuss my situation with a lawyer before saying anything about it to a police officer?" How should the officer respond?

(c) Suppose, when being driven to the station house, a suspect asks the arresting officer whether he has a right to remain silent or whether his silence can be used against him at the trial and the officer meets such questions with a stony silence? What result if the suspect then says nothing during the rest of the drive? What result if the suspect then starts talking and makes incriminating statements?

D. Use of Post-Miranda Warnings Silence or Assertion of Rights to Rebut Defense of Insanity

May a defendant's post-Miranda warnings silence or request for counsel be offered not to impeach but as substantive evidence to rebut defendant's defense of insanity at the time of the offense? No, answers *Wainwright v. Greenfield,* 474 U.S. 284 (1986). On three occasions shortly after his arrest in Florida for sexual battery, Greenfield was given the Miranda warnings. Each time he exercised his

"Anyone who believes that volunteering information to police is 'natural' for a resident of Detroit's inner-city has an unusually optimistic view of human nature." See also Note, 94 Harv.L.Rev. 77, 84–85 (1980).

right to remain silent and stated that he wished to speak with an attorney before answering any questions. Greenfield later pled guilty by reason of insanity. At his trial two police officers described the occasions on which Greenfield had exercised his right to remain silent and had expressed a desire to consult with counsel. In his closing argument, the prosecutor reviewed this police testimony and suggested that Greenfield's responses to the warnings demonstrated a degree of comprehension inconsistent with his claim of insanity. Greenfield was convicted and sentenced to life imprisonment. The Court, per Stevens, J., overturned his conviction, holding that Doyle applied to his case:

"The point of [Doyle] is that it is fundamentally unfair to promise an arrested person that his silence will not be used against him and thereafter to breach that promise by using the silence to impeach his trial testimony. It is equally unfair to breach that promise by using silence to overcome a defendant's plea of insanity. In both situations [the State] implicitly promises that any exercise of these rights will not be penalized."[a]

E. How Much Leeway Do the "Impeachment" Cases and "Fruit of the Poisonous Tree" Cases Give A "Bad Man of the Law"?

"Ten years ago, Albert Alschuler hypothesized about the advice that 'Justice Holmes' 'bad man of the law' " might offer in a [police] training manual.[134] Alschuler thought that a bad officer, one who cared only about the material consequences of and not the reason for his conduct, might author a manual advising police to continue to interrogate a suspect who asked for counsel or wished to remain silent. Alschuler's writing proved prescient. In deciding [such cases as *Harris*, *Hass*, *Tucker* and *Elstad*] the Court could not have intended to give police grounds to disobey this portion of *Miranda* deliberately, but this disregard is the natural consequence of these decisions. [These cases] provide an unfortunate opening for the quintessential 'bad man of the law.' "

—Charles D. Weisselberg, *Saving Miranda* 84 Cornell L.Rev. 109, 132 (1998).

Pointing to police training materials uncovered in the course of litigation seeking to stop officers in two California police departments from questioning custodial suspects after they have asserted their *Miranda* rights, Professor Weisselberg, supra, reports that "[in] California and, to a certain extent in other states, police have developed the tactics of questioning 'outside *Miranda*,' meaning questioning over the direct and unambiguous assertion of Fifth Amendment rights." Set forth below are extracts from the remarks of Devallis Rutledge in a California police training videotape. Mr. Rutledge is an Orange County Deputy District Attorney and a member of the California Commission on Peace Officer Standards and Training. The full transcript of the videotape is reprinted in the Appendix to Weisselberg's article.

a. Rehnquist, J., joined by the Chief Justice, concurred in the result because one of the prosecutor's remarks was "an improper comment on respondent's silence." But he maintained that "a request for a lawyer may be highly relevant where the plea is based on insanity"—"there is no 'insoluble ambiguity' in the request; it is a perfectly straightforward statement tending to show that an individual is able to understand his rights and is not incoherent or obviously confused or unbalanced"—and he did not read the warnings "as containing any promise, express or implied, that the words used in responding to notice of the right to a lawyer will not be used by the State to rebut a claim of insanity."

134. Albert W. Alschuler, *Failed Pragmatism: Reflections on the Burger Court*, 100 Harv.L.Rev. 1436, 1442 (1987) (quoting O. W. Holmes, *The Path of the Law*, 10 Harv.L.Rev. 457, 459 (1897)).

CALIFORNIA POLICE TRAINING VIDEOTAPE—QUESTIONING "OUTSIDE *MIRANDA*" (1990)

This has to do with questioning "outside *Miranda*." * * *

What if you've got a guy [in custody] that you've only got one shot at? This is it, it's now or never because you're gonna lose him—he's gonna bail out or a lawyer's on the way down there, or you're gonna have to take him over to some other officials—you're never gonna have another chance at this guy, this is it. And you Mirandize him and he invokes [his rights]. What you can do—legally do—in that instance in go "outside *Miranda*" and continue to talk to him because you've got other legitimate purposes in talking to him other than obtaining an admission of guilt that can be used in his trial. And that's what *Miranda* protects him against—you compelling him to make a statement that is later used in trial to convict him of the charge.

But you may want to go "outside *Miranda*" and get information to help you clear cases. [Or,] maybe it will help you recover a dead body or missing person. * * * You may be able to recover stolen property. He tells you where the property is ditched, his statement will not be admissible against him in trial if you go "outside *Miranda*," but you'll get the property back and the owner will get the property back. That's a legitimate function. Maybe his statement "outside *Miranda*" will reveal methods—his methods of operation. How he was able to obtain these credit cards and how he was able to pull of his scam or whatever. * * *

Or his statements might reveal the existence and the location of physical evidence. You've got him, but you'd kinda like to have the gun that he used or the knife that he used or whatever else it was. But he ditched it somewhere and you can't find it. And so you've arrested him, he's invoked *Miranda* and you say, "Well I'd still like to find the evidence in the case." So you go "outside *Miranda*," and if he talks "outside *Miranda*"—if the only thing that was shutting him up was the chance of it being used against him in court—and then you go "outside *Miranda*" and take a statement and then he tells you where the stuff is, we can go and get all that evidence.

And it forces the defendant to commit to a statement that will prevent him from pulling out some defense and using it at trial—that he's cooked up with some defense lawyer—that wasn't true. So if you get a statement "outside *Miranda*" and he tells you that he did it and how he did it or if he gives you a denial of some sort, he's tied to that, he is married to that, because the U.S. Supreme Court [and] the California Supreme Court [have] told us that we can use statements "outside *Miranda*" to impeach or to rebut. We can't use them for our case-in-chief. The D.A. can't trot them out to the jury before he says, "I rest," but if the defendant then gets up there and gets on the stand and lies and says something different, we can use his "outside *Miranda*" statements to impeach him. We can use it to rebut his case.

* * * The *Miranda* exclusionary rule is limited to the defendant's own statement out of his mouth. That is all that is excluded under *Miranda*. It doesn't have a fruits of the poisonous tree theory attached to it the way constitutional violations do. When you violate *Miranda*, you're not violating the Constitution. *Miranda* is not in the Constitution. It's a court-created decision that affects the admissibility of testimonial evidence and that's all it is. [There's] no law says you can't question people "outside *Miranda*." You don't violate the Constitution. The Constitution doesn't say you have to do that. It's a court decision. So all you're violating is a court decision controlling admissibility of evidence. So you're not

doing anything unlawful, you're not doing anything illegal, you're not violating anybody's civil rights, you're not doing nothing improper. [When we question someone who has invoked his *Miranda* rights] [all] we lose is the statement taken in violation of *Miranda*. We do not lose physical evidence that resulted from that. We do not lose the testimony of other witnesses that we learned about only by violating his *Miranda* invocation.

Professor Weisselberg's warning

Professor Weisselberg (p. 934 supra, at 188) warns: "[If] the Court allows [the tactic of questioning 'outside *Miranda*' to continue], the practice signifies the end of *Miranda*, or at least the original version of *Miranda*. [When] courts are unwilling to act in the face of open and direct defiance of a principle of law, that principle cannot survive."[a]

Do you agree? Does a majority of the Court agree? Reconsider *Hass* (p. 924), *Patane* (p. 703) and *Seibert* (p. 707).

SECTION 4. ALLOCATION OF THE BURDENS OF PROOF

PEOPLE v. BERRIOS

270 N.E.2d 709 (N.Y.1971).

SCILEPPI, Judge.

In each of [these] appeals, the defendants have been charged with possession of heroin and arresting officers have testified that glassine envelopes containing narcotics were dropped on the ground as the defendants were approached by the police.[b] We have been called upon to decide whether, in these "dropsy" cases, or for that matter whenever a warrantless search is presented, it is the People who must bear the burden of proving the legality of the search and seizure. [In each of the cases before the court, an officer testified that as he made a movement toward the defendant—leaving his car in one case, instructing the defendant to stop in another—the defendant dropped a glassine envelope containing narcotics. The officer was undercover in one case and in uniform in another.]

Simply stated, [defendants] have contended that the police testimony in these cases is inherently untrustworthy and the product of fabrication; hence, the

a. See also Charles D. Weisselberg, *In the Stationhouse After Dickerson*, 99 Mich.L.Rev. 1121 (2001).

b. In New York, as in most jurisdictions, challenges to the admissibility of evidence on the ground that it was illegally obtained must be presented by a pretrial motion to suppress. The motion must set forth the objection with sufficient particularity, which usually requires that the defense specify the nature of the alleged illegality in the acquisition of evidence (e.g., that a statement was obtained in violation of *Miranda*, or that the search in question was incident to an arrest not supported by probable cause). See CRIMPROC § 10.1(b). Assuming the form of the motion is correct, the trial judge will then hold a pretrial hearing at which both sides can offer its testimony regarding the acquisition of the evidence and cross-examine the other side's witnesses. Denial of the pretrial motion does not allow an immediate appeal by the defense, but the prosecution often can appeal the granting of the motion. See Ch. 28, § 3.

In those jurisdictions that do not require a pretrial motion, an objection may be made at trial, contemporaneously with the introduction of the evidence. An objection at this point ordinarily requires the trial court to recess the trial in order to conduct a hearing on the suppression objection. Whether a state requires a pretrial motion or a contemporaneous objection, failure to make a timely objection can result in the procedural forfeiture of the objection. See *Wainwright v. Sykes*, p. 1640; and CRIMPROC § 10.2(a).

argument is advanced that we should require that the People bear the burden of proving admissibility and depart from our present rule which places the burden of showing inadmissibility on the defendant. No argument is proffered that this departure is required by either the State or Federal Constitutions; rather, it is asserted that the change in burden of proof is necessary to alleviate the possibility of perjured police testimony. It is noted by this court that the District Attorney of New York County has joined defense counsel in [one] case in suggesting the change in burden of proof. This concession does not, however, relieve us from the performance of our judicial function and does not require us to adopt the proposal urged upon us. [W]e are not persuaded that a change in burden of proof is indicated.

Thus far, we have made it clear that where a defendant challenges the admissibility of physical evidence or makes a motion to suppress, he bears the ultimate burden of proving that the evidence should not be used against him. [Since] such a person makes the claim because he contends that he is aggrieved and requests the court to give redress to an alleged wrong, it is most reasonable to require him to bear the burden of proof of that wrong. The People must, of course, always show that police conduct was reasonable. Thus, though a defendant who challenges the legality of a search and seizure has the burden of proving illegality, the People are nevertheless put to "the burden of *going forward* to show the legality of the police conduct in the first instance". These considerations require that the People show that the search was made pursuant to a valid warrant, consent, incident to a lawful arrest or, in cases such as those here, that no search at all occurred because the evidence was dropped by the defendant in the presence of the police officer.

* * * We have been told that with the advent of *Mapp v. Ohio,* there has been a great incidence of "dropsy" testimony by police officers. Hence, this court has been asked to infer that the police are systematically evading the mandate of *Mapp* by fabricating their testimony. [We] reject this frontal attack on the integrity of our entire law enforcement system. * * * Some police officers, as well as some in other callings may be tempted to tamper with the truth. But there is no valid proof that all members of law enforcement agencies or that all other citizens who testify are perjurers. Therefore, all policemen should not be singled out as suspect as a matter of law.

The fact that some witnesses may lie does not require a change in the burden of proof for it is our view that the proposal made in this appeal is no more effective in preventing perjury than the present burden of proof. Under both the suggested change and the present system, the defendant must still refute the testimony of the police officer. Thus, even where the officer testifies that glassine envelopes were dropped by the defendant or to facts which would sustain a warrantless search, the court would still be faced with the same credibility question. Since a change in the burden of proof would be ineffective to combat the alleged evil about which the defendants herein complain, principles of *stare decisis* do not allow a departure from our present rule of burden of proof.

[There] are more appropriate methods of dealing with the abuses about which the defendants complain. For example, [police departments] can effectively formulate internal procedures and policies within the department to eliminate any such abuses. [The] district attorneys of this State should evaluate the testimony of police officers, as they do the testimony of all witnesses, in determining what proof will be offered in the prosecution of a case. * * *

FULD, Chief Judge (dissenting).

[The] District Attorney of New York County informs us [that]: "For the last ten years participants in the system of justice—judges, prosecutors, defense attorneys and police officials—have privately and publicly expressed the belief that in some substantial but indeterminable percentage of dropsy cases, the testimony [that a defendant dropped narcotics or gambling slips to the ground as a police officer approached him] is tailored to meet the requirements of search-and-seizure rulings" and "it is very difficult in many [such] cases to distinguish between fact and fiction." When so able and dedicated a prosecutor as District Attorney Frank Hogan believes that there is basis for questioning the truthfulness of the testimony in a "substantial * * * percentage of dropsy cases," the conclusion seems to me inescapable [that] the integrity of the judicial process demands that there be a reallocation of the burden of proof. * * *

Underlying the Fourth and Fourteenth Amendments is the basic proposition that "no man is to be convicted on unconstitutional evidence." In light of the situation as it today exists, the present rule—which imposes upon the accused the burden of proving the illegality of a seizure on a motion to suppress—subverts this principle by making it possible for some defendants to be convicted on evidence obtained in violation of constitutional guarantees. This follows from the fact that a trial judge who is unsure whether the prosecution's account of the seizure is credible must, nevertheless, resolve his doubt in favor of the People and admit the evidence. To thus increase the likelihood of a conviction on proof of dubious constitutionality must be stamped as highly unreasonable and unfair. A change in the rule will help assure that a defendant's constitutional rights will not be violated since, by placing the burden on the People, the judge will be permitted to suppress evidence in cases where, for instance, he finds the testimony of each side evenly balanced on the scales of credibility and is unable to make up his mind as to who is telling the truth.

[Those] who recognize the problem and favor a change in the burden of proof rule do not, contrary to the majority's assertion, intend an "attack on the integrity of our entire law enforcement system." Rather, their concern is solely to promote adherence to the principles articulated in *Mapp v. Ohio.*

[Reason] and the imperative of judicial integrity, as well as substantial authority, dictate that the burden of proving the lawfulness of a search or seizure should be cast on the People in all narcotics and gambling cases when the search or seizure has been effected without a warrant. To do less, to shift the burden of proof to the People only in the classic dropsy situation, seems to me, as it does to the New York County District Attorney, "unrealistic." This is so, as he observes, not only because an "untruthful officer fearing rejection of tailored dropsy testimony could easily shift to the other scenarios which are familiar in narcotics and gambling cases in the lower courts" but also because "it is the experience of many prosecutors and judges that the problems of credibility and fact-finding raised [are] not limited to literal dropsy cases [but] appear in all types of possessory narcotics and gambling cases."

BURKE, JASEN and GIBSON, JJ., concur with SCILEPPI, J. FULD, C.J., dissents and votes to reverse in a separate opinion in which BERGAN and BREITEL, JJ., concur.

Notes and Questions

1. ***How common is police "falsification"***? As pointed out in Gabriel J. Chin & Scott C. Wells, *"The Blue Wall of Silence" As Evidence of Bias and Motive to Lie: A New Approach to Police Perjury*, 59 U.Pitt.L.Rev. 233, 234 (1998), in 1994 the Mollen Commission, established to investigate police misconduct in New York, "reported that police 'falsification'—which includes 'testimonial perjury, * * * documentary perjury, [and] falsification of police records'—is one of the

most common forms of police corruption facing the nation's criminal justice system. In fact, the Mollen Commission indicated that in New York, 'the practice of police falsification [is] so common in certain precincts that it has spawned its own word: "testilying." See also Morgan Cloud, *Judges, "Testilying," and the Constitution*, 69 S.Cal.L.Rev. 1341 (1996); Donald A. Dripps, *Police, Plus Perjury, Equals Polygraphy*, 86 J.Crim.L. & C. 693 (1996); Christopher Slobogin, *Testilying: Police Perjury and What to Do About It*, 67 U.Colo.L.Rev. 1037 (1996).

2. ***Was there police perjury in the O.J. Simpson case?*** Detective Mark Fuhrman tried to defend the warrantless search of Simpson's residential property shortly after the murder of his former wife by testifying that at the time of the search the police did not know "if we have a murder-suicide, a kidnapping, another victim" and "we had to find out if there's anybody in the residence that's injured, to save their life, to save other people's lives." Despite the incredulous public response to the claim, two judges denied Simpson's suppression motions. For a discussion of why the police testimony about the purpose of the search of Simpson's residence "raised the specter of perjury designed to shield the fruits of an illegal search," see Morgan Cloud, supra, at 1357–61.

3. ***State variations.*** Aside from the justification of a search on the basis of consent—where the burden universally is placed on the prosecution—states vary considerably in the allocation of both the burden of going forward and the ultimate burden of proof (the burden of persuasion) on Fourth Amendment claims. Ignoring minor variations, the state's position on these burdens usually will fall within one of four general categories:

(a) Under the New York approach, as noted in *Berrios,* the prosecution has the burden of going forward—i.e., introducing evidence that, if accepted, would establish the legality of the search. Thus, in a case involving a search incident to arrest, the prosecution would initially introduce the testimony of an officer showing that probable cause for the arrest existed and that the search was within the scope permitted incident to an arrest. The burden of persuasion would then be on the defendant to rebut this evidence and prove that the search was invalid.

(b) Several states place *both* burdens of proof on the defendant. This position has been justified on several grounds: "(a) the burden should be upon the moving party, (b) there is a presumption of regularity attending the actions of law enforcement officials, (c) relevant evidence is generally admissible and thus exceptions must be justified by those claiming the exception, and (d) [this allocation] will deter spurious allegations wasteful of court time." SEARCHSZR § 11.2(b).

(c) A majority of the states follow the pattern of allocation adopted in the federal courts—if the search was pursuant to a warrant, the defendant has the burden of proof, but if the police acted without a warrant, the burden is on the prosecution. The burden of going forward follows the burden of proof. Where there was a search without a warrant, the defendant must make a prima facie showing of that fact before the prosecution is put to its burdens. Very often, however, the parties will agree as to how the evidence was obtained and an allegation of seizure without a warrant will be sufficient.

As noted in SEARCHSZR § 11.2(b), the federal pattern's "warrant-no-warrant dichotomy is typically explained on the ground that when the police have acted with a warrant 'an independent determination on the issue of probable cause has already been made by a magistrate, thereby giving rise to a presumption of legality,' while when they have acted without a warrant 'the evidence comprising probable cause is particularly within the knowledge and control of the arresting agencies.' Moreover, it is said that '[w]ithout such a rule there would be little reason for law enforcement agencies to bother with the formality of a warrant.' "

(d) In some jurisdictions, the prosecution has both burdens of proof on all Fourth Amendment objections. The reason commonly given as noted in SEARCHSZR § 11.2(b), is that "the state is the party which seeks to use the evidence and thus ought to bear the burden of establishing that it was lawfully come by."

4. *Practical consequences of the allocation.* Of what practical significance is the allocation of the ultimate burden of proof on Fourth Amendment claims? Compare the views of the majority and dissent in *Berrios* on the relation of the burden of proof to judicial treatment of police testimony in "dropsy" cases. Assuming one shared the objective of the dissent, would a better solution have been a direction to the lower courts to subject such testimony to "close scrutiny," in much the same way that a jury is directed that testimony of an accomplice or paid informer should be "scrutinized and received with care"? See Comment, 60 Geo.L.J. 507, 519–20 (1971).

Comments of defense counsel suggest that the allocation of the burden of going forward, and even the specificity required in the motion to suppress, may be more significant than the allocation of the ultimate burden of proof. Thus, Anthony Amsterdam, *Trial Manual for the Defense of Criminal Cases* § 252 (5th ed.1988), notes that a basic tactical objective of the defense is to avoid first disclosing its factual theories, lest the police "conform their testimony" to evade those theories. If defendant is required to go forward with the evidence, he often must, as a practical matter, first take the stand to tell "his side of the story." Although the officers, as prospective witnesses, usually may be excluded from the courtroom while this testimony is given, the defendant still is not in as good a position to rebut their testimony as he would be if he testified last. The defense bearing the burden of production may seek to satisfy it without using the defendant's testimony by calling the officers as its own witnesses. However, this tactic may backfire if the court is unwilling to treat the officers as "adverse" witnesses subject to impeachment. Id. at § 253.

5. *Constitutional requirements.* Why was it that the defendants in *Berrios* failed to argue that the federal constitution required the prosecution to bear the burden of proof? *Bumper v. North Carolina,* p. 453, held, as a matter of constitutional law, that when a prosecutor relies upon consent "he has the burden of proving that the consent was, in fact, freely and voluntarily given." If the Fourth Amendment requires that the prosecution bear the burden on this issue, why not on others? The Supreme Court has stated in various opinions that the Fourth Amendment generally requires a search warrant, and "the burden is on those seeking [an] exemption from [that] requirement to show the need for it." See, e.g., *Chimel v. California,* p. 351. Do such statements imply that, where a search is conducted without a warrant, the prosecution must bear the burden of proving facts that justify the search under one of the recognized exceptions to the warrant requirement, or do the statements refer only to the state's burden in appellate argument of justifying any request that the Supreme Court recognize a new or expanded exception to the warrant requirement? See SEARCHSZR § 11.2(b) (the former interpretation seems closer to the mark).

6. *Confessions*. *Miranda* clearly places the burden on the prosecution to respond to a *Miranda* objection by showing that the "defendant knowingly and intelligently waived his privilege against self-incrimination and his right to retained or appointed counsel" (p. 584). Most jurisdictions also place upon the prosecution the burdens of production and persuasion in responding to a claim that a confession was involuntary. A few states, however, place the burden of proving involuntariness on the defendant. *Lego v. Twomey,* discussed at Note 10, raises serious doubts as to the constitutionality of this practice. Though concerned primarily with the applicable standard of proof, *Lego* indicated that it was the constitutional obligation of the prosecution to meet that standard of proof.

7. ***Identification testimony***. *United States v. Wade,* p. 757, indicates that, once the Sixth Amendment is shown to be applicable, the prosecution carries the burden of establishing that defendant intelligently waived his right to counsel at a lineup. But what is the proper allocation of the burden on an objection that a lineup or other identification procedure was so unfairly conducted as to violate due process? Several courts have assumed, without extensive discussion, that the defendant, as the moving party, bears the burden of establishing the due process violation. CRIMPROC § 10.4(d). But compare *People v. Young,* 176 N.W.2d 420 (Mich.App.1970), holding that the prosecution bears the burdens of production and persuasion whenever the identification procedure was conducted "out of the presence of defendant's attorney." Does *Young* constitute an open invitation to defense "fishing expeditions," that will be "automatically available in all lineup-cases"? See *State v. Bishop,* 183 N.W.2d 536 (Minn.1971).

8. ***Entrapment.*** Reconsider Note 4 at p. 516.

9. ***Exclusionary rule limitations.*** Once a constitutional violation is established, does the burden of proof necessarily lie with the prosecution to establish that its evidence is not the fruit of the poisonous tree? See e.g., *Wade,* p. 757 (as to proof that the in-court identification was not tainted by the unconstitutional lineup); *Nardone,* p. 906 (once illegal wiretap established, government must convince the trial court that its proof had an independent origin). Consider also *Nix v. Williams,* p. 916, as to the government's burden in establishing that the same evidence would have inevitably been discovered by lawful means.

10. ***Standards of proof.*** Assuming that the prosecution bears the burden of persuasion on a particular exclusionary rule objection, what standard of proof should apply? In LEGO v. TWOMEY, 404 U.S. 477 (1972), the Court rejected the contention that the voluntariness of a confession must be established by proof beyond a reasonable doubt and accepted a preponderance of the evidence standard. Justice WHITE's opinion for the Court reasoned that *In re Winship,* 397 U.S. 358 (1970), requiring proof beyond a reasonable doubt at trial, was not controlling: "Since the purpose that a voluntariness hearing is designed to serve has nothing whatever to do with improving the reliability of jury verdicts, we cannot accept the charge that judging the admissibility of a confession by a preponderance of the evidence undermines the mandate of *In re Winship.* * * * *Winship* [only] confirm[ed] the fundamental right that protects 'the accused against conviction except upon proof beyond a reasonable doubt of every fact necessary to constitute the crime with which he is charged.' A high standard of proof is necessary, we said, to ensure against unjust convictions by giving substance to the presumption of innocence. A guilty verdict is not rendered less reliable or less consonant with *Winship* simply because the admissibility of a confession is determined by a less stringent standard."

Lego also rejected the contention that application of a reasonable doubt standard was necessary "to give adequate protection to those values that the exclusionary rules are designed to serve": "Evidence obtained in violation of the Fourth Amendment has been excluded from federal criminal trials for many years. The same is true of coerced confessions offered in either federal or state trials. [But] no substantial evidence has accumulated that federal rights have suffered from determining admissibility by a preponderance of the evidence. Petitioner offers nothing to suggest [otherwise]. Without good cause, we are unwilling to expand currently applicable exclusionary rules by erecting additional barriers to placing truthful and probative evidence before state juries and by revising the standards applicable in collateral proceedings. [The] exclusionary rules are very much aimed at deterring lawless conduct by police and prosecution and it is very doubtful that escalating the prosecution's burden of proof in Fourth and Fifth Amendment suppression hearings would be sufficiently productive in this respect to outweigh the public interest in placing probative evidence before juries for the purpose of arriving at truthful decisions about guilt or innocence."[a]

11. Is *Lego* inconsistent with the philosophy underlying *Chapman v. California* (Ch. 28, § 5)? Cf. Note, 7 Harv.C.R.-C.L.L.Rev. 651 (1972), suggesting that the reasoning that led the *Lego* majority to conclude that implementation of a constitutional right did not require proof beyond a reasonable doubt could just as readily have led the Court in Chapman to conclude that there was no need to require the especially stringent harmless error standard imposed there. The dissent in *Lego* (see fn. a supra) also argued that the majority's position there was inconsistent with "the rule that automatically reverses a conviction when an involuntary confession was admitted at trial." Cf. Stephen A. Saltzburg, *Standards of Proof and Preliminary Questions of Fact*, 27 Stan.L.Rev. 271 (1975), arguing that a reasonable doubt standard should have been required in *Lego* because, inter alia, the test of involuntariness (as opposed to other exclusionary rule standards) is designed to exclude unreliable evidence and the admission of unreliable confessions is especially dangerous because juries give such evidence great weight.

12. The Supreme Court noted in *Lego* that, while due process was satisfied by application of the preponderance standard, the states were always "free, pursuant to their own law, to adopt a higher standard." Several states have done exactly that. See CRIMPROC § 10.4. On the other hand, the states uniformly have held that the standard of proof applicable to Fourth Amendment claims, except on the issue of consent, will be the preponderance standard. Id. In a jurisdiction that has adopted the reasonable doubt standard for the determination of the voluntariness of confession, why shouldn't the same standard apply to search and seizure claims? See Saltzburg, supra.

13. ***Waiver of Miranda rights***. In COLORADO v. CONNELLY (p. 726) the Court held that the state need only prove a waiver of *Miranda* rights by the preponderance of the evidence. The majority, per REHNQUIST, C.J., reasoned:

"[The state supreme court] held that the State must bear its burden of proving waiver [by] 'clear and convincing evidence.' Although we have stated in passing that the State bears a 'heavy' burden in proving waiver Miranda,[b] we have never held that the 'clear and convincing evidence' standard is the appropriate one. [In] *Lego v. Twomey,* [we] upheld a procedure in which the State established the voluntariness of a confession by no more than a preponderance of the evidence [for] two reasons. First, the voluntariness determination has nothing to do with the reliability of jury verdicts; rather, it is designed to determine the

a. Powell and Rehnquist, JJ., did not participate in the *Lego* decision. Dissenting Justice Brennan, joined by Justice Douglas and Marshall, argued that "the preponderance standard does not provide sufficient protection against the danger that involuntary confessions will be employed at trial." The preponderance standard, noted the dissent, was accepted in civil cases on the assumption that it was no more serious an error to have an erroneous decision in favor of one party or another, but the same could not be said for errors relating to the admission of confessions."

b. In dissent, Justice Brennan, joined by Marshall, J. argued that the Court's ruling ignored both "the explicit command of *Miranda*" in describing the state's burden as "heavy" and the implications of *Wade*, which specifically referred to the "clear and convincing" standard in describing the prosecution's burden of establishing that an in-court-identification was not tainted by an unconstitutional identification.

presence of police coercion. [Second,] we rejected Lego's assertion that a high burden of proof was required to serve the values protected by the exclusionary rule. [If,] as we held in *Lego* [a case the Court reaffirmed in *Connelly*], the voluntariness of a confession need be established only by a preponderance of the evidence, then a waiver of the auxiliary protections established in *Miranda* should require no higher burden of proof. * * * "[c]

Does *Connelly* make *Miranda* "a much less prophylactic rule and a substantially more direct application of the fifth amendment compulsion standard"? Does *Connelly* "fuse" the fifth amendment compulsion standard with *Miranda?* See Mark Berger, *Compromise and Continuity: Miranda Waivers, Confession Admissibility, and the Retention of Interrogation Protections,* 49 U.Pitt.L.Rev. 1007, 1040–41 (1988). What follows from the fact that *Miranda* establishes special prophylactic rules governing custodial police interrogation? That special procedural requirements regulating the waiver process are also called for? Or that further protections governing the waiver process are unnecessary and undesirable, because likely to interfere unduly with appropriate police questioning? See id. at 1062.

14. ***The trier of fact.*** The factfinder on the constitutionality of a search has traditionally been the judge, but prior to *Jackson v. Denno,* 378 U.S. 368 (1964), many states followed one of two procedures that gave factfinding responsibility to the jury in judging the voluntariness of a confession. In states following the "Massachusetts rule," the trial court initially ruled on the admissibility of the confession. If the judge found the confession involuntary, that ruling was final. However, if the judge found the confession voluntary, it was then admitted subject to the jury's independent determination of voluntariness. In states following the "New York rule," the determination of voluntariness was left primarily to the jury. The judge would make an initial determination as to whether reasonable persons could differ on the issue of voluntariness and if they could the issue went to the jury. The jury was instructed on the voluntariness standard and told to consider the confession only if it found it to be voluntary.

Jackson held the New York procedure unconstitutional. The crux of *Jackson*'s reasoning was subsequently summarized in *Lego:* "We concluded that the New York procedure was constitutionally defective because at no point along the way did a criminal defendant receive a clear-cut determination that the confession used against him was in fact voluntary. The trial judge was not entitled to exclude a confession merely because he himself would have found it involuntary, and, while we recognized that the jury was empowered to perform that function, we doubted it could do so reliably. Precisely because confessions of guilt, whether coerced or freely given, may be truthful and potent evidence, we did not believe a jury [could] ignore the probative value of a truthful but coerced confession; it was also likely, we thought, that in judging voluntariness itself the jury would be influenced by the reliability of a confession it considered an accurate account of the facts. * * * "

15. As the Court noted in *Lego*, the *Jackson* case "cast no doubt upon" the Massachusetts procedure,[d] and many states continue to use that procedure

c. In dissent, Justice Brennan argued that *Lego* was distinguishable because it involved a situation in which the defendant was not in custody. The special setting of custodial interrogation, because it poses an increased danger of police overriding, justified "plac[ing] a higher burden of proof on the government in establishing a waiver of *Miranda* rights."

d. In distinguishing the Massachusetts procedure, the Court stressed that the judge there "himself resolves evidentiary conflicts and gives his own answer to the coercion issue" (although most follow the "orthodox" procedure of having voluntariness determined initially and finally by the judge). Why should a defendant be given a "second crack" at the voluntariness issue, before the jury, where no such opportunity is given as to Fourth Amendment or other constitutional violations?

Of course, even under the orthodox procedure, the defendant may bring to the jury's attention the circumstances surrounding the confession for the purpose of challenging its credibility. Indeed, in *Crane v. Kentucky,* 476 U.S. 683 (1986), a unanimous Court held that a trial court's foreclosure of a defendant's attempt to introduce testimony about the "physical and psychological environment" in which the confession was obtained deprived defendant of his "fundamental constitutional right to a fair opportunity to present a defense." As the Court there noted, "The [*Jackson*] requirement that the [trial] court make a pretrial *voluntariness* determination does not undercut the defendant's traditional prerogative to challenge the confession's *reliability* during the course of the same trial."

16. Does it follow from *Lego* that it would be improper for a trial court to hear testimony on a constitutional challenge to the admissibility of evidence without first excluding the jury? Consider WATKINS v. SOWDERS, 449 U.S. 341 (1981). *Watkins* involved two state cases in which hearings on the admissibility of identification testimony were held in the presence of the jury. In each case, in challenging an in-court identification, the defense sought to establish that the identification was based on a pretrial identification procedure that was so suggestive as to violate due process. Over defense objection, the challenge was heard in the presence of the jury, and was rejected by the trial judge. The Supreme Court found no constitutional error. It recognized that various lower courts had emphasized the prudence of holding a suppression hearing outside the presence of the jury, but stressed that it was concerned only with whether that practice was constitutionally required. On this issue, STEWART, J., noted for the Court:

"The Court in *Jackson* did reject the usual presumption that a jury can be relied upon to determine issues according to the trial judge's instructions, [but only] because of the peculiar problems the issue of the voluntariness of a confession presents. [Where] identification evidence is at issue, however, no such special considerations [apply]. It is the reliability of identification evidence that primarily determines its admissibility. *Manson v. Brathwaite* [p. 777]. And the proper evaluation of evidence under the instructions of the trial judge is the very task our system must assume juries can perform. * * *"

"A judicial determination outside the presence of the jury of the admissibility of identification evidence may often be advisable. In some circumstances, not presented here, such a determination may be constitutionally necessary. But it does not follow that the Constitution requires a *per se* rule compelling such a procedure in every case."[e]

and the jury therefore only considers those confessions the judge believes to be voluntary. The dissenters responded that the acceptance of the Massachusetts rule revealed the "hollowness" of the Court's holding. They argued that the distinction between the New York and Massachusetts rule was more theoretical than real. They suggested, in particular, that in "cases of doubt," a judge operating under the Massachusetts rule was likely to "resolve the doubt in favor of admissibility, relying on the final determination by the jury."

e. The dissenting justices (Brennan, J., joined by Marshall, J.) argued that "the powerful impact that such eyewitness identification evidence has on juries, regardless of its reliability, virtually mandates that, when such evidence is inadmissible, the jury should know nothing about the evidence."

Index

References are to Pages

References are to Pages

References are to Pages

References are to Pages

References are to Pages

References are to Pages

†